GM
CAVALIER/SKYHAWK/SUNBIRD/SUNFIRE
1982-96 REPAIR MANUAL

CHILTON'S

President, Chilton Enterprises	David S. Loewith
Senior Vice President	Ronald A. Hoxter
Publisher & Editor-In-Chief	Kerry A. Freeman, S.A.E.
Executive Editors	Dean F. Morgantini, S.A.E., W. Calvin Settle, Jr., S.A.E.
Managing Editor	Nick D'Andrea
Special Products Manager	Ken Grabowski, A.S.E., S.A.E.
Senior Editors	Jacques Gordon, Michael L. Grady, Ben Greisler, S.A.E., Debra McCall, Kevin M. G. Maher, Richard J. Rivele, S.A.E., Richard T. Smith, Jim Taylor, Ron Webb
Project Managers	Martin J. Gunther, Will Kessler, A.S.E., Richard Schwartz
Production Manager	Andrea Steiger
Product Systems Manager	Robert Maxey
Director of Manufacturing	Mike D'Imperio
Editor	Christine L. Nuckowski

CHILTON BOOK COMPANY

ONE OF THE **DIVERSIFIED PUBLISHING COMPANIES,**
A PART OF **CAPITAL CITIES/ABC, INC.**

Manufactured in USA
© 1996 Chilton Book Company
Chilton Way, Radnor, PA 19089
ISBN 0-8019-8795-4
Library of Congress Catalog Card No. 96-83967
1234567890 5432109876

D1279174

Contents

1 GENERAL INFORMATION AND MAINTENANCE

1-2 HOW TO USE THIS BOOK
1-3 TOOLS AND EQUIPMENT
1-6 SERVICING YOUR VEHICLE SAFELY
1-15 ROUTINE MAINTENANCE
1-45 FLUIDS AND LUBRICANTS
1-62 JUMP STARTING A DEAD BATTERY

2 ENGINE ELECTRICAL

2-2 HIGH ENERGY IGNITION (HEI) SYSTEM
2-10 DIRECT IGNITION SYSTEMS (DIS)
2-16 FIRING ORDERS
2-17 CHARGING SYSTEM
2-24 STARTING SYSTEM
2-31 SENDING UNITS AND SENSORS

3 ENGINE AND ENGINE OVERHAUL

3-2 ENGINE MECHANICAL
3-4 SPECIFICATIONS CHARTS
3-121 EXHAUST SYSTEM

4 DRIVEABILITY AND EMISSION CONTROLS

4-2 AIR POLLUTION
4-5 EMISSION CONTROLS
4-27 ELECTRONIC ENGINE CONTROLS
4-41 TROUBLE CODES
4-56 COMPONENT LOCATION DIAGRAMS
4-67 VACUUM DIAGRAMS

5 FUEL SYSTEM

5-2 CARBURETED FUEL SYSTEM
5-13 THROTTLE BODY (TBI) INJECTION SYSTEMS
5-25 BOTTOM FEED PORT (BFP) INJECTION SYSTEM
5-29 MULTI-PORT (MFI) & SEQUENTIAL (SFI) FUEL INJECTION SYSTEMS

6 CHASSIS ELECTRICAL

6-2 TROUBLESHOOTING ELECTRICAL SYSTEMS
6-10 SUPPLEMENTAL INFLATABLE RESTRAINT
6-15 HEATER & A/C
6-37 RADIO
6-44 WINDSHIELD WIPERS
6-58 LIGHTING
6-71 WIRING DIAGRAMS

Contents

7-2 MANUAL TRANSAXLE
7-46 CLUTCH
7-58 AUTOMATIC TRANSAXLE

DRIVE TRAIN 7

8-2 WHEELS
8-3 FRONT SUSPENSION
8-19 SPECIFICATIONS CHARTS
8-22 REAR SUSPENSION
8-28 STEERING

SUSPENSION AND STEERING 8

9-2 BRAKE OPERATING SYSTEM
9-12 FRONT DISC BRAKES
9-19 REAR DRUM BRAKES
9-25 PARKING BRAKE
9-32 ANTI-LOCK BRAKE SYSTEM (ABS)
9-60 SPECIFICATIONS CHARTS

BRAKES 9

10-2 EXTERIOR
10-39 INTERIOR

BODY AND TRIM 10

10-72 GLOSSARY

GLOSSARY

10-77 MASTER INDEX

MASTER INDEX

SAFETY NOTICE

Proper service and repair procedures are vital to the safe, reliable operation of all motor vehicles, as well as the personal safety of those performing repairs. This manual outlines procedures for servicing and repairing vehicles using safe, effective methods. The procedures contain many NOTES, CAUTIONS, and WARNINGS which should be followed along with standard procedures to eliminate the possibility of personal injury or improper service which could damage the vehicle or compromise its safety.

It is important to note that the repair procedures and techniques, tools and parts for servicing motor vehicles, as well as the skill and experience of the individual performing the work vary widely. It is not possible to anticipate all of the conceivable ways or conditions under which vehicles may be serviced, or to provide cautions as to all of the possible hazards that may result. Standard and accepted safety precautions and equipment should be used when handling toxic or flammable fluids, and safety goggles or other protection should be used during cutting, grinding, chiseling, prying, or any other process that can cause material removal or projectiles.

Some procedures require the use of tools specially designed for a specific purpose. Before substituting another tool or procedure, you must be completely satisfied that neither your personal safety, nor the performance of the vehicle will be endangered.

Although information in this manual is based on industry sources and is complete as possible at the time of publication, the possibility exists that some car manufacturers made later changes which could not be included here. While striving for total accuracy, Chilton Book Company cannot assume responsibility for any errors, changes or omissions that may occur in the compilation of this data.

PART NUMBERS

Part numbers listed in this reference are not recommendation by Chilton for any product by brand name. They are references that can be used with interchange manuals and aftermarket supplier catalogs to locate each brand supplier's discrete part number.

SPECIAL TOOLS

Special tools are recommended by the vehicle manufacturer to perform their specific job. Use has been kept to a minimum, but where absolutely necessary, they are referred to in the text by the part number of the tool manufacturer. These tools can be purchased, under the appropriate part number, from your local dealer or regional distributor, or an equivalent tool can be purchased locally from a tool supplier or parts outlet. Before substituting any tool for the one recommended, read the SAFETY NOTICE at the top of this page.

ACKNOWLEDGMENTS

Portions of materials contained herein have been reprinted with permission of General Motors Corporation, Service Technology Group.

FLUIDS AND LUBRICANTS
AUTOMATIC TRANSAXLE 1-51
BODY LUBRICATION 1-60
BRAKE MASTER CYLINDER 1-57
CHASSIS GREASING 1-60
CLUTCH MASTER CYLINDER 1-58
COOLING SYSTEM 1-53
ENGINE 1-47
FLUID DISPOSAL 1-45
FUEL AND ENGINE OIL
  RECOMMENDATIONS 1-46
MANUAL TRANSAXLE 1-50
POWER STEERING PUMP 1-58
STEERING GEAR 1-59
WHEEL BEARINGS 1-61
WINDSHIELD WASHER PUMP 1-59
HOW TO USE THIS BOOK 1-2
JACKING 1-63
JUMP STARTING A DEAD BATTERY
JUMP STARTING
  PRECAUTIONS 1-62
JUMP STARTING PROCEDURE 1-62
ROUTINE MAINTENANCE
AIR CLEANER 1-15
AIR CONDITIONING 1-37
BATTERY 1-23
CV-BOOT 1-28
DISTRIBUTOR CAP AND
  ROTOR 1-34
EARLY FUEL EVAPORATION (EFE)
  HEATER 1-25
EVAPORATIVE CANISTER 1-21
FUEL FILTER 1-16
HOSES 1-27
IDLE SPEED AND MIXTURE
  ADJUSTMENTS 1-37
IGNITION TIMING 1-35
PCV VALVE 1-19
SERPENTINE DRIVE BELTS 1-27
SPARK PLUG WIRES 1-33
SPARK PLUGS 1-28
STANDARD DRIVE BELTS 1-26
TIMING BELT 1-27
TIRES AND WHEELS 1-43
WINDSHIELD WIPERS 1-41
SERIAL NUMBER IDENTIFICATION
BODY 1-8
ENGINE 1-8
TRANSAXLE 1-10
VEHICLE 1-8
VEHICLE EMISSION CONTROL
  INFORMATION (VECI) LABEL 1-10
SERVICING YOUR VEHICLE SAFELY
DO'S 1-6
DON'TS 1-7
SPECIFICATIONS CHARTS
CAPACITIES 1-64
ENGINE IDENTIFICATION 1-8
MAINTENANCE INTERVALS 1-64
TUNE-UP SPECIFICATIONS 1-37
VEHICLE IDENTIFICATION 1-8

TOOLS AND EQUIPMENT
SPECIAL TOOLS 1-5
TOWING THE VEHICLE 1-62
TRAILER TOWING
COOLING 1-61
GENERAL RECOMMENDATIONS 1-61
HANDLING A TRAILER 1-62
HITCH WEIGHT 1-61
TRAILER WEIGHT 1-61

1

GENERAL INFORMATION AND MAINTENANCE

FLUIDS AND LUBRICANTS 1-45
HOW TO USE THIS BOOK 1-2
JACKING 1-63
JUMP STARTING A DEAD
BATTERY 1-62
ROUTINE MAINTENANCE 1-15
SERIAL NUMBER IDENTIFICATION 1-8
SERVICING YOUR VEHICLE
SAFELY 1-6
SPECIFICATIONS CHARTS 1-8
TOOLS AND EQUIPMENT 1-3
TOWING THE VEHICLE 1-62
TRAILER TOWING 1-61

HOW TO USE THIS BOOK

Chilton's Total Car Care for the Chevrolet Cavalier, Buick Skyhawk, Cadillac Cimarron, Pontiac 2000, Sunbird and Sunfire, and the Oldsmobile Firenza is intended to help you learn more about the inner workings of your vehicle and save you money on its upkeep and operation.

The first two sections will be the most used, since they contain maintenance and tune-up information and procedures. Studies have shown that a properly tuned and maintained car can get at least 10% better gas mileage than an out-of-tune car. The other sections deal with the more complex systems of your car. Operating systems from engine through brakes are covered to the extent that the do-it-yourselfer becomes mechanically involved. It will give you detailed instructions to help you change your own brake pads and shoes, replace spark plugs, and do many more jobs that will save you money, give you personal satisfaction, and help you avoid expensive problems.

A secondary purpose of this book is a reference for owners who want to understand their car and/or their mechanics better. In this case, no tools at all are required.

Before removing any bolts, read through the entire procedure. This will give you the overall view of what tools and supplies will be required. There is nothing more frustrating than having to walk to the bus stop on Monday morning because you were short one bolt on Sunday afternoon. So read ahead and plan ahead. Each operation should be approached logically and all procedures thoroughly understood before attempting any work.

All sections contain adjustments, maintenance, removal and installation procedures, and repair or overhaul procedures. When repair is not considered practical, we tell you how to remove the part and then how to install the new or rebuilt replacement. In this way, you at least save the labor costs.

Two basic mechanic's rules should be mentioned here. One, whenever the left side of the car or engine is referred to, it is meant to specify the driver's side of the car. Conversely, the right side of the car means the passenger's side. Secondly, most screws and bolts are removed by turning counterclockwise, and tightened by turning clockwise.

Safety is always the most important rule. Constantly be aware of the dangers involved in working on an automobile and take the proper precautions. See the section in Servicing Your Vehicle Safely and the SAFETY NOTICE on the acknowledgment page.

Pay attention to the instructions provided. There are 3 common mistakes in mechanical work:

1. Incorrect order of assembly, disassembly or adjustment. When taking something apart or putting it together, doing things in the wrong order usually just cost you extra time; however, it CAN break something. Read the entire procedure before beginning disassembly. Do everything in the order in which the instructions say you should do it, even if you can't immediately see a reason for it. When you're taking apart something that is very intricate (for example, a carburetor), you might want to draw a picture of how it looks when assembled at one point in order to make sure you get everything back in its proper position. (We will supply exploded view whenever possible). When making adjustments, especially tune-up adjustments, do them in order; often, one adjustment affects another, and you cannot expect even satisfactory results unless each adjustment is made only when it cannot be changed by any order.

2. Overtorquing (or undertorquing). While it is more common for over-torquing to cause damage, undertorquing can cause a fastener to vibrate loose causing serious damage. Especially when dealing with aluminum parts, pay attention to torque specifications and utilize a torque wrench in assembly. If a torque figure is not available, remember that if you are using the right tool to do the job, you will probably not have to strain yourself to get a fastener tight enough. The pitch of most threads is so slight that the tension you put on the wrench will be multiplied many, many times in actual force on what you are tightening. A good example of how critical torque is can be seen in the case of spark plug installation, especially where you are putting the plug into an aluminum cylinder head. Too little torque can fail to crush the gasket, causing leakage of combustion gases and consequent overheating of the plug and engine parts. Too much torque can damage the threads, or distort the plug which changes the s park gap.

➡**There are many commercial products available for ensuring that fasteners won't come loose, even if they are not torqued just right (a very common brand is Loctite®). If you're worried about getting something together tight enough to hold, but loose enough to avoid mechanical damage during assembly, one of these products might offer substantial insurance. Read the label on the package and make sure the products is compatible with the materials, fluids, etc.. involved before choosing one.**

3. Crossthreading. This occurs when a part such as a bolt is screwed into a nut or casting at the wrong angle and forced. Cross threading is more likely to occur if access is difficult. It helps to clean and lubricate fasteners, and to start threading with the part to be installed going straight in. Then, start the bolt, spark plug, etc.. with your fingers. If you encounter resistance, unscrew the part and start over again at a different angle until it can be inserted and turned several turns without much effort. Keep in mind that many parts, especially spark plugs, used tapered threads so that gentle turning will automatically bring the part you're treading to the proper angle if you don't force it or resist a change in angle. Don't put a wrench on the part until its's been turned a couple of turns by hand. If you suddenly encounter resistance, and the part has not seated fully, don't force it. Pull it back out and make sure it's clean and threading properly.

Always take your time and be patient; once you have some experience, working on your car will become an enjoyable hobby.

TOOLS AND EQUIPMENT

▶ **See Figures 1, 2, 3, 4, 5, 6, 7, 8, 9, 10, 11, 12 and 13**

Naturally, without the proper tools and equipment it is impossible to properly service you vehicle. It would be impossible to catalog each tool that you would need to perform each or any operation in this book. It would also be unwise for the amateur to rush out and buy an expensive set of tool on the theory that he may need on or more of them at sometime.

The best approach is to proceed slowly gathering together a good quality set of those tools that are used most frequently. Don't be misled by the low cost of bargain tools. It is far better to spend a little more for better quality. Forged wrenches, 6- or 12-point sockets and fine tooth ratchets are by far preferable to their less expensive counterparts. As any good mechanic can tell you, there are few worse experiences than trying to work on a car with bad tools. Your monetary savings will be far outweighed by frustration and mangled knuckles.

Begin accumulating those tools that are used most frequently; those associated with routine maintenance and tune-up.

In addition to the normal assortment of screwdrivers and pliers you should have the following tools for routine maintenance jobs:

• SAE (or Metric) or SAE/Metric wrenches-sockets and combination open end-box end wrenches in sizes from ⅛ in. (3 mm) to ¾ in. (19 mm) and a spark plug socket (¹³⁄₁₆ in. or ⅝ in. depending on plug type).

➡ **If possible, buy various length socket drive extensions. One break in this department is that the metric sockets available in the U.S. will all fit the ratchet handles and extensions you may already have (¼ in., ⅜ in., and ½ in. drive).**

• Jackstands for support
• Oil filter wrench
• Oil filler spout for pouring oil
• Grease gun for chassis lubrication

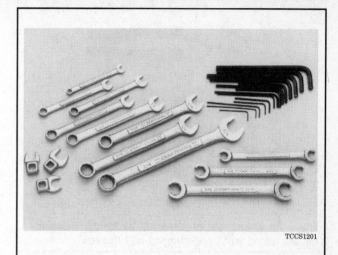

TCCS1201

Fig. 2 In addition to ratchets, a good set of wrenches and hex keys will be necessary

• Hydrometer for checking the battery
• A container for draining oil
• Many rags for wiping up the inevitable mess
• A quality floor jack

In addition to the above items there are several others that are not absolutely necessary, but handy to have around. these include oil-dry (cat box litter works just as well and may be cheaper), a transmission funnel and the usual supply of lubricants, antifreeze and fluids, although these can be purchased as needed. This is a basic list for routine maintenance, but only your personal needs and desire can accurately determine you list of tools.

The second list of tools is required for tune-ups. While the tools involved here are slightly more sophisticated, they need not be outrageously expensive. There are several inexpensive tach/dwell meters on the market that are every bit as good for the average mechanic as an expensive professional model. Just be sure that it goes to a least 1,200-1,500 rpm on the

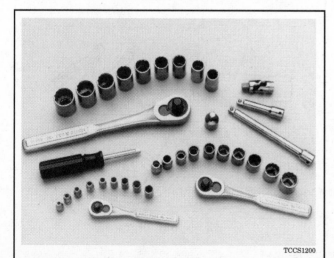

TCCS1200

Fig. 1 All but the most basic procedures will require an assortment of ratchets and sockets

TCCS1202

Fig. 3 A hydraulic floor jack and a set of jackstands are essential for lifting and supporting the vehicle

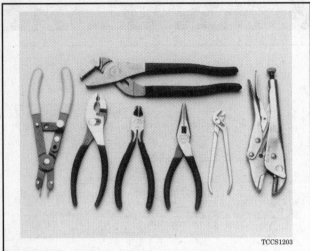

TCCS1203

Fig. 4 An assortment of pliers will be handy, especially for old rusted parts and stripped bolt threads

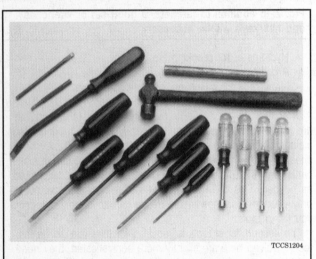

TCCS1204

Fig. 5 You should have various screwdrivers, a hammer, chisels and prybars in your toolbox

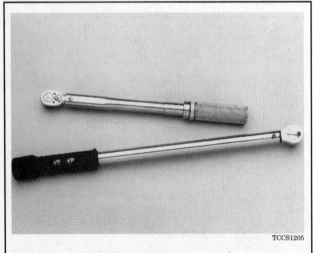

TCCS1205

Fig. 6 Many repairs will require the use of a torque wrench to assure the components are properly fastened

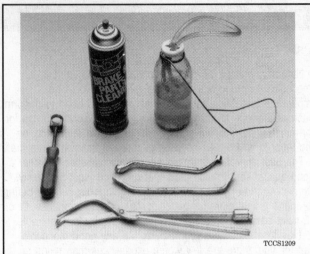

TCCS1209

Fig. 7 Although not always necessary, using specialized brake tools will save time

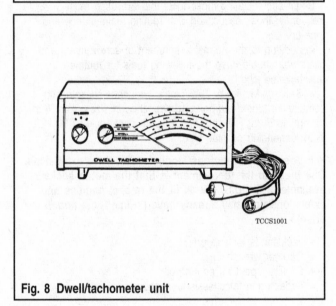

TCCS1001

Fig. 8 Dwell/tachometer unit

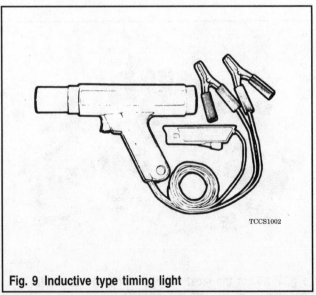

TCCS1002

Fig. 9 Inductive type timing light

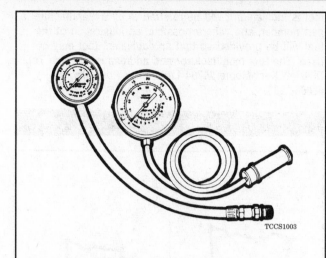

Fig. 10 Compression gauge and a combination vacuum/fuel pressure test gauge

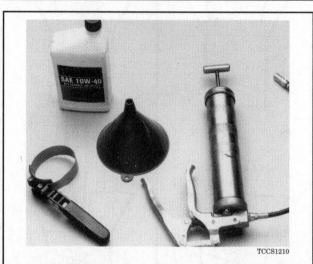

Fig. 11 A few inexpensive lubrication tools will make regular service easier

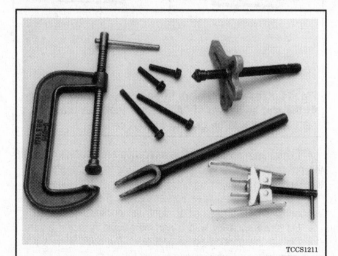

Fig. 12 Various pullers, clamps and separator tools are needed for the repair of many components

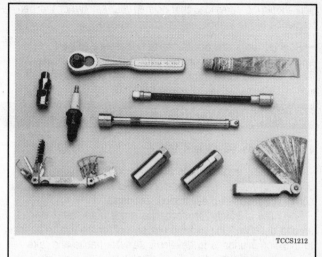

Fig. 13 A variety of tools and gauges are needed for spark plug service

tach scale and that it works on 4, 6 and 8 cylinder engines. A basic list of tune-up equipment could include:

- Tach/dwell meter
- Spark plug wrench
- Timing light (a DC light that works from the car's battery is best, although an AC light that plugs into 110V house current will suffice at some sacrifice in brightness)
- Wire spark plug gauge/adjusting tools
- Set of feeler gauges

In addition to these basic tools, there are several other tools and gauges you may find useful. These include:

- A compression gauge. The screw-in type is slower to use, but eliminates the possibility of a faulty reading due to escaping pressure
- A manifold vacuum gauge
- A test light
- An induction meter. This is used for determining whether or not there is current in a wire. These are handy for use if a wire is broken somewhere in a wiring harness.

As a final note, you will probably find a torque wrench necessary for all but the most basic work. The beam type models are perfectly adequate, although the newer click type are more precise.

Special Tools

Normally, the use of special factory tools is avoided for repair procedures, since these are not readily available for the do-it-yourself mechanic. When it is possible to preform the job with more commonly available tools, it will be pointed out, but occasionally, a special tool was designed to perform a specific function and should be used. Before substituting another tool, you should be convinced that neither your safety nor the performance of the vehicle will be compromised.

➡Special tools are occasionally necessary to perform a specific job or are recommended to make a job easier. Their use has been kept to a minimum. When a special tool is indicated, it will be referred to by a manufacturer's part number. and, where possible, an illustration of the tool will be provided so that an equivalent tool may be used. The tool manufacturer and address is: Service Tool Division Kent-Moore 29784 Little Mack Roseville, MI 48066-2298

SERVICING YOUR VEHICLE SAFELY

▶ See Figures 14, 15 and 16

It is virtually impossible to anticipate all of the hazards involved with automotive maintenance and service, but care and common sense will prevent most accidents.

The rules of safety for mechanics range from "don't smoke around gasoline," to "use the proper tool for the job." The trick to avoiding injuries is to develop safe work habits and take every possible precaution.

Do's

• Do keep a fire extinguisher and first aid kit within easy reach.
• Do wear safety glasses or goggles when cutting, drilling, grinding or prying, even if you have 20-20 vision. If you wear glasses for the sake of vision, wear safety goggles over your regular glasses.
• Do shield your eyes whenever you work around the battery. Batteries contain sulfuric acid. In case of contact with the eyes or skin, flush the area with water or a mixture of water and baking soda and get medical attention immediately.
• Do use safety stands for any under vehicle service. Jacks are for raising vehicles; safety stands are for making sure the vehicle stays raised until you want it to come down. Whenever the car is raised, block the wheels remaining on the ground and set the parking brake.
• Do use adequate ventilation when working with any chemicals or hazardous materials. Like carbon monoxide, the asbestos dust resulting from brake lining wear can be poisonous in sufficient quantities.
• Do disconnect the negative battery cable when working on the electrical system. The secondary ignition system can contain current as high as 40,000 volts.
• Do follow manufacturer's directions whenever working with potentially hazardous materials. Both brake fluid and antifreeze are poisonous if taken internally.
• Do properly maintain your tools. Loose hammerheads, mushroomed punches and chisels, frayed or poorly grounded electrical cords, excessively worn screwdrivers, spread wrenches (open end), cracked sockets, slipping ratchets, or faulty droplight sockets can cause accidents.
• Likewise, keep your tools clean; a greasy wrench can slip off a bolt head, ruining the bolt and often ruining your knuckles in the process.
• Do use the proper size and type of tool for the job being done.
• Do when possible, pull on a wrench handle rather than push on it, and adjust you stance to prevent a fall.

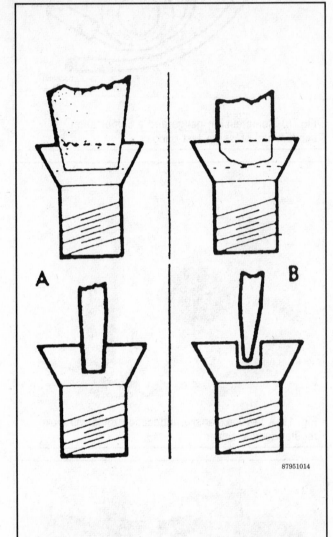

Fig. 14 Keep screwdrivers in good shape. They should fit the slot as shown in "A". If they look like those in "B", they should be ground or replaced

• Do be sure that adjustable wrenches are tightly closed on the nut or bolt and pulled so that the face is on the side of the fixed jaw.
• Do select a wrench or socket that fits the nut or bolt. The wrench or socket should sit straight, not cocked.
• Do strike squarely with a hammer; avoid glancing blows.
• Do set the parking brake and block the drive wheels if the work requires a running engine.

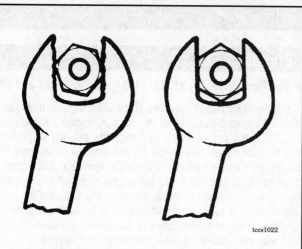

Fig. 15 When using an open end wrench, make sure it is the correct size

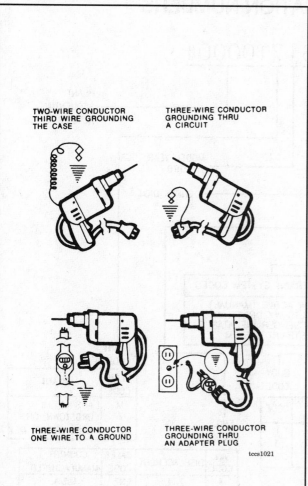

TWO-WIRE CONDUCTOR
THIRD WIRE GROUNDING
THE CASE

THREE-WIRE CONDUCTOR
GROUNDING THRU
A CIRCUIT

THREE-WIRE CONDUCTOR
ONE WIRE TO A GROUND

THREE-WIRE CONDUCTOR
GROUNDING THRU
AN ADAPTER PLUG

tccs1021

Fig. 16 When using electric tools, make sure they are properly grounded

Don'ts

• Don't run the engine in a garage or anywhere else without proper ventilation — EVER! Carbon monoxide is poisonous; it takes a long time to leave the human body and you can build up a deadly supply of it in your system by simply breathing in a little every day. You may not realize you are slowly poisoning yourself. Always use power vents, windows, fans or open the garage doors.

• Don't work around moving parts while wearing a necktie or other loose clothing. Short sleeves are much safer than long, loose sleeves; hard-toed shoes with neoprene soles protect your toes and give a better grip on slippery surfaces. Jewelry such as watches, fancy belt buckles, beads or body adornment of any kind is not safe working around a car. Long hair should be tied back under a hat or cap.

• Don't use pockets for toolboxes. A fall or bump can drive a screwdriver deep into your body. Even a wiping cloth hanging from the back pocket can wrap around a spinning shaft or fan.

• Don't smoke when working around gasoline, cleaning solvent or other flammable material.

• Don't smoke when working around the battery. When the battery is being charged, it gives off explosive hydrogen gas.

• Don't use gasoline to wash your hands; there are excellent soaps available. Gasoline contains compounds which are hazardous to your health. Gasoline also remove all the natural oils from the skin so that bone dry hands will such up oil and grease.

• Don't service the air conditioning system unless you are equipped with the necessary tools and training. The refrigerant, R-12 or R-134a, is extremely cold when compressed, and when released into the air will instantly freeze any surface it contacts, including your eyes. Although the refrigerant is normally non-toxic, R-12 becomes a deadly poisonous gas in the presence of an open flame. One good whiff of the vapors from burning refrigerant can be fatal.

• Don't release refrigerant into the atmosphere. In most states, it is now illegal to discharge refrigerant into the atmosphere due to the harmful effects Freon® (R-12) has on the ozone layer. Check with local authorities about the laws in your state.

• Don't use screwdrivers for anything other than driving screws! A screwdriver used as an prying tool can snap when you least expect it, causing injuries. At the very least, you'll ruin a good screwdriver.

• Don't use a bumper jack (that little ratchet, scissors, or pantograph jack supplied with the car) for anything other than chaining a flat! These jacks are only intended for emergency use out on the road; they are NOT designed as a maintenance tool. If you are serious about maintaining your car yourself, invest in a hydraulic floor jack of a least 1½ ton capacity, and at least two sturdy jackstands.

SERIAL NUMBER IDENTIFICATION

Vehicle

▶ See Figures 17 and 18

The Vehicle Identification Number (VIN) is a seventeen digit sequence stamped on a plate attached to the left front of the instrument panel, visible through the windshield.

Body

The body style identification plate is located on the front bar, just behind the right headlamp.

Engine

▶ See Figures 19, 20, 21, 22, 23, 24, 25, 26, 27, 28 and 29

Engine identification can take place using various methods. The VIN, described earlier in this section, contains a code identifying the engine which was originally installed in the vehicle. In most cases, this should be sufficient for determining the engine with which your car is currently equipped. But, some older vehicles may have had the engine replaced or changed by a previous owner. If this is the case, the first step in identification is to locate an engine serial number and code which is stamped on the block or located on adhesive labels that may be present on valve covers or other engine components.

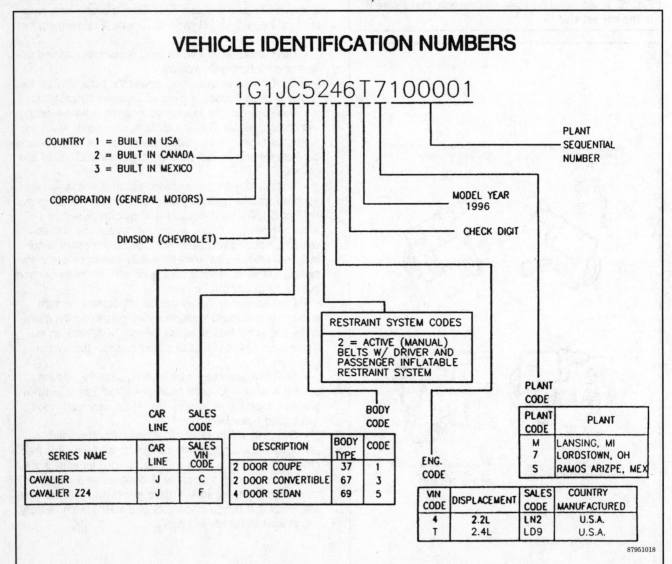

VEHICLE IDENTIFICATION NUMBERS

1G1JC5246T7100001

COUNTRY 1 = BUILT IN USA
2 = BUILT IN CANADA
3 = BUILT IN MEXICO

CORPORATION (GENERAL MOTORS)

DIVISION (CHEVROLET)

PLANT SEQUENTIAL NUMBER

MODEL YEAR 1996

CHECK DIGIT

RESTRAINT SYSTEM CODES

2 = ACTIVE (MANUAL) BELTS W/ DRIVER AND PASSENGER INFLATABLE RESTRAINT SYSTEM

CAR LINE   SALES CODE

BODY CODE

ENG. CODE

PLANT CODE

SERIES NAME	CAR LINE	SALES VIN CODE
CAVALIER	J	C
CAVALIER Z24	J	F

DESCRIPTION	BODY TYPE	CODE
2 DOOR COUPE	37	1
2 DOOR CONVERTIBLE	67	3
4 DOOR SEDAN	69	5

PLANT CODE	PLANT
M	LANSING, MI
7	LORDSTOWN, OH
S	RAMOS ARIZPE, MEX

VIN CODE	DISPLACEMENT	SALES CODE	COUNTRY MANUFACTURED
4	2.2L	LN2	U.S.A.
T	2.4L	LD9	U.S.A.

87951018

Fig. 17 Explanation of a Vehicle Identification Number (VIN) — 1996 Cavalier shown

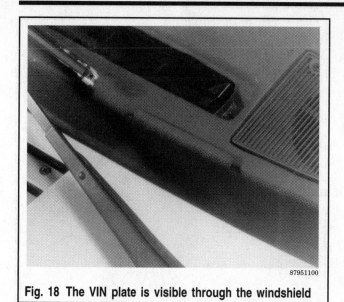

Fig. 18 The VIN plate is visible through the windshield

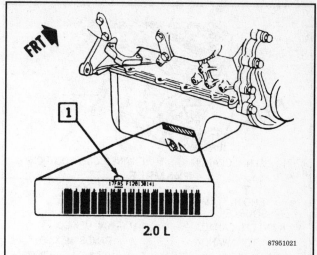

2.0 L

Fig. 21 The engine identification tag is located on the oil pan for the 2.0L (VIN P) engine

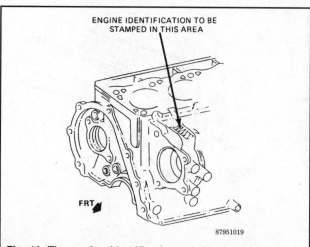

ENGINE IDENTIFICATION TO BE STAMPED IN THIS AREA

FRT

Fig. 19 The engine identification number is stamped on top of the water pump housing for the 1982 1.8L and 2.0L OHV engines

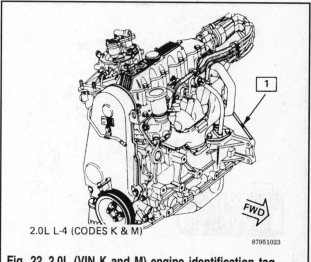

2.0L L-4 (CODES K & M)

Fig. 22 2.0L (VIN K and M) engine identification tag location

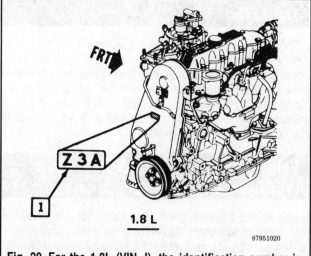

FRT

Z 3 A

1

1.8 L

Fig. 20 For the 1.8L (VIN J), the identification number is stamped on the engine front cover

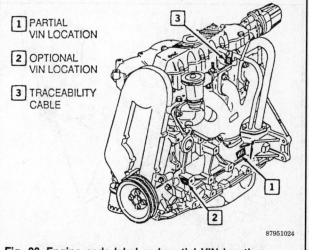

1 PARTIAL VIN LOCATION

2 OPTIONAL VIN LOCATION

3 TRACEABILITY CABLE

Fig. 23 Engine code label and partial VIN location — 2.0L (VIN H) engine

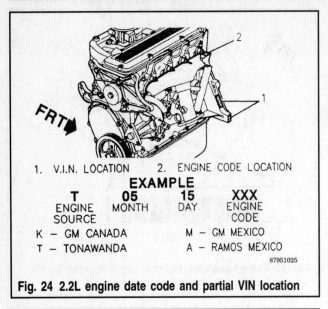

1. V.I.N. LOCATION   2. ENGINE CODE LOCATION

EXAMPLE

T	05	15	XXX
ENGINE SOURCE	MONTH	DAY	ENGINE CODE

K — GM CANADA   M — GM MEXICO
T — TONAWANDA   A — RAMOS MEXICO

87951025

Fig. 24 2.2L engine date code and partial VIN location

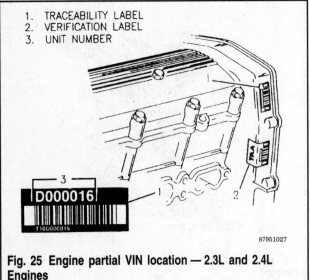

1. TRACEABILITY LABEL
2. VERIFICATION LABEL
3. UNIT NUMBER

D000016

87951027

Fig. 25 Engine partial VIN location — 2.3L and 2.4L Engines

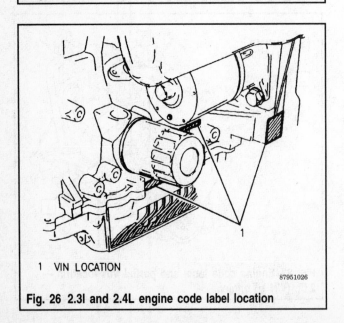

1 VIN LOCATION

87951026

Fig. 26 2.3l and 2.4L engine code label location

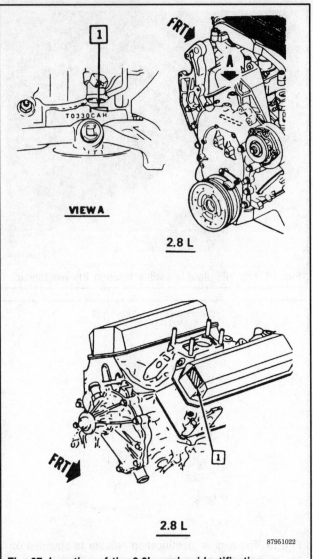

VIEW A

2.8 L

2.8 L

87951022

Fig. 27 Location of the 2.8L engine identification number — 1986 vehicle shown

Transaxle

The manual transaxle identification number is stamped on a pad on the forward side of the transaxle case, between the upper and middle transaxle-to-engine mounting bolts. The automatic transaxle identification number is stamped on the oil flange pad to the right of the oil dipstick, at the rear of the transaxle. The automatic transaxle model code tag is on top of the case, next to the shift lever.

Vehicle Emission Control Information (VECI) Label

The Vehicle Emission Control Information Label is located in the engine compartment, (fan shroud, radiator support, hood underside, etc.) of every vehicle produced by General Motors. The label contains important emission specifications and setting procedures, as well as a vacuum hose schematic with various emissions components identified.

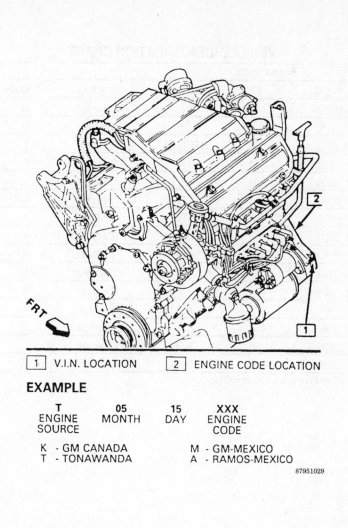

1 V.I.N. LOCATION   2 ENGINE CODE LOCATION

EXAMPLE

T	05	15	XXX
ENGINE SOURCE	MONTH	DAY	ENGINE CODE

K - GM CANADA   M - GM-MEXICO
T - TONAWANDA   A - RAMOS-MEXICO

87951029

Fig. 28 Engine date code and partial VIN location — 3.1L engine

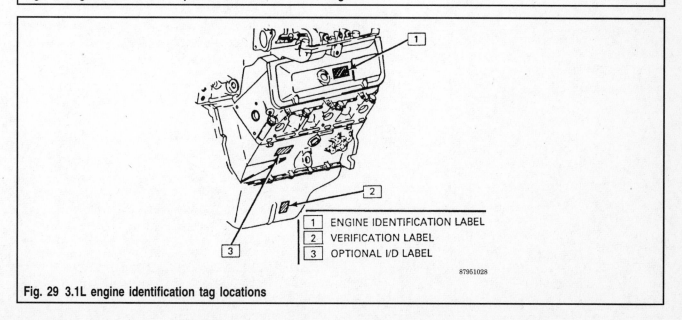

1 ENGINE IDENTIFICATION LABEL
2 VERIFICATION LABEL
3 OPTIONAL I/D LABEL

87951028

Fig. 29 3.1L engine identification tag locations

VEHICLE IDENTIFICATION CHART

Engine Code						Model Year	
Code	Liters	Cu. In. (cc)	Cyl.	Fuel Sys.	Eng. Mfg.	Code	Year
G (1982)	1.8	110 (1819)	4	2bbl	Chevrolet	C	1982
O	1.8	110 (1819)	4	TBI	Pontiac	D	1983
J	1.8	110 (1819)	4	MFI-Turbo	Pontiac	E	1984
B	2.0	121 (2000)	4	①	Chevrolet	F	1985
P	2.0	121 (2000)	4	TBI	Chevrolet	G	1986
1	2.0	121 (2000)	4	TFI	Chevrolet	H	1987
K	2.0	121 (2000)	4	TFI	GM-Brazil	J	1988
M	2.0	121 (2000)	4	MFI-Turbo	GM-Brazil	K	1989
H	2.0	121 (2000)	4	MFI	GM-Brazil	L	1990
G (1990-91)	2.2	134 (2180)	4	TBI	Chevrolet	M	1991
4	2.2	134 (2180)	4	②	Chevrolet	N	1992
D	2.3	138 (2261)	4	MFI	Chev/BOC	P	1993
T (1996)	2.4	146 (2398)	4	SFI	Chev/BOC	R	1994
W	2.8	173 (2835)	6	MFI	Chevrolet	S	1995
T	3.1	192 (3146)	6	MFI	Chevrolet	T	1996

NOTE: Some 1983-85 Canadian models with the 2.0L engine use a 2 bbl carburetor

① 1982: 2 bbl carburetor
   1983 and later: TBI

② 1992-95: TBI
   1996: SFI

2bbl: 2 barrel carburetor
TBI: Throttle Body fuel Injection
MFI: Multi-port Fuel Injection
SFI: Sequential Fuel Injection
BOC: Buick/Oldsmobile/Cadillac

87951500

ENGINE IDENTIFICATION

Year	Model	Engine Displacement Liters (cc)	Engine Series (ID/VIN)	Fuel System	No. of Cylinders	Engine Type
1982	Cavalier	1.8L (1819)	G	2bbl	4	OHV
	2000/Sunbird	1.8L (1819)	G	2bbl	4	SOHC
	2000/Sunbird	1.8L (1819)	O	TBI	4	SOHC
	Skyhawk	1.8L (1819)	G	2bbl	4	SOHC
	Skyhawk	1.8L (1819)	O	TBI	4	SOHC
	Firenza	1.8L (1819)	G	2 bbl	4	OHV
	Firenza	1.8L (1819)	G	2 bbl	4	OHV
	Cimarron	2.0L (1998)	P	TBI	4	OHV
1983	Cavalier	2.0L (1998)	B	2bbl	4	OHV
	Cavalier	2.0L (1998)	P	TBI		OHV
	2000/Sunbird	1.8L (1819)	O	TBI	4	SOHC
	2000/Sunbird	2.0L (1998)	B	2bbl	4	OHV
	2000/Sunbird	2.0L (1998)	P	TBI	4	OHV
	Skyhawk	1.8L (1819)	O	TBI	4	SOHC
	Skyhawk	2.0L (1998)	B	2bbl	4	OHV
	Skyhawk	2.0L (1998)	P	TBI	4	OHV
	Firenza	1.8L (1819)	O	TBI	4	SOHC
	Firenza	2.0L (1998)	B	2bbl	4	OHV
	Firenza	2.0L (1998)	P	TBI	4	OHV
	Cimarron	2.0L (1998)	B	2bbl	4	OHV
	Cimarron	2.0L (1998)	P	TBI	4	OHV
1984	Cavalier	2.0L (1998)	B	2bbl	4	OHV
	Cavalier	2.0L (1998)	P	TBI		OHV
	2000/Sunbird	1.8L (1819)	O	TBI	4	SOHC
	2000/Sunbird	1.8L (1819)	J	MFI-Turbo	4	SOHC
	2000/Sunbird	2.0L (1998)	B	2bbl	4	OHV
	2000/Sunbird	2.0L (1998)	P	TBI	4	OHV
	Skyhawk	1.8L (1819)	O	TBI	4	SOHC
	Skyhawk	1.8L (1819)	J	MFI-Turbo	4	SOHC
	Skyhawk	2.0L (1998)	B	2bbl	4	OHV
	Skyhawk	2.0L (1998)	P	TBI	4	OHV
	Firenza	1.8L (1819)	O	TBI	4	SOHC
	Firenza	2.0L (1998)	B	2bbl	4	OHV
	Firenza	2.0L (1998)	P	TBI	4	OHV
	Cimarron	2.0L (1998)	B	2bbl	4	OHV
	Cimarron	2.0L (1998)	P	TBI	4	OHV
1985	Cavalier	2.0L (2000)	P	TBI	4	OHV
	Cavalier	2.8L (2835)	W	MFI	6	OHV
	Sunbird	1.8L (1819)	O	TBI	4	SOHC
	Sunbird	1.8L (1819)	J	MFI-Turbo	4	SOHC
	Skyhawk	1.8L (1819)	O	TBI	4	SOHC
	Skyhawk	1.8L (1819)	J	MFI-Turbo	4	SOHC
	Skyhawk	2.0L (2000)	P	TBI	4	OHV
	Firenza	1.8L (1819)	O	TBI	4	SOHC
	Firenza	2.0L (2000)	P	TBI	4	OHV
	Firenza	2.8L (2835)	W	MFI	6	OHV
	Cimarron	2.0L (1998)	P	TBI	4	OHV
	Cimarron	2.8L (2875)	W	MFI	6	OHV

ENGINE IDENTIFICATION

Year	Model	Engine Displacement Liters (cc)	Engine Series (ID/VIN)	Fuel System	No. of Cylinders	Engine Type
1986	Cavalier	2.0L (2000)	P	TBI	4	OHV
	Cavalier	2.8L (2835)	W	MFI	6	OHV
	Sunbird	1.8L (1819)	O	TBI	4	SOHC
	Sunbird	1.8L (1819)	J	MFI-Turbo	4	SOHC
	Skyhawk	1.8L (1819)	O	TBI	4	SOHC
	Skyhawk	1.8L (1819)	J	MFI-Turbo	4	SOHC
	Skyhawk	2.0L (2000)	P	TBI	4	OHV
	Firenza	1.8L (1819)	O	TBI	4	SOHC
	Firenza	2.0L (2000)	P	TBI	4	OHV
	Firenza	2.8L (2835)	W	MFI	6	OHV
	Cimarron	2.0L (1998)	P	TBI	4	OHV
	Cimarron	2.8L (2875)	W	MFI	6	OHV
1987	Cavalier	2.0L (2000)	1	TBI	4	OHV
	Cavalier	2.8L (2835)	W	MFI	6	OHV
	Sunbird	2.0L (1998)	K	TBI	4	SOHC
	Sunbird	2.0L (1998)	M	MFI-Turbo	4	SOHC
	Skyhawk	2.0L (1983)	1	TBI	4	OHV
	Skyhawk	2.0L (1983)	K	TBI	4	SOHC
	Skyhawk	2.0L (1983)	M	MFI-Turbo	4	OHV
	Firenza	2.0L (1983)	1	TBI	4	OHV
	Firenza	2.0L (1983)	K	TBI	4	SOHC
	Firenza	2.8L (2835)	W	MFI	6	OHV
	Cimarron	2.8L (2835)	W	MFI	6	OHV
1988	Cavalier	2.0L (2000)	1	TBI	4	OHV
	Cavalier	2.8L (2835)	W	MFI	6	OHV
	Sunbird	2.0L (1998)	M	MFI	4	SOHC
	Skyhawk	2.0L (1983)	K	TBI	4	SOHC
	Firenza	2.0L (1983)	1	TBI	4	OHV
	Firenza	2.0L (1983)	K	TBI	4	SOHC
	Cimarron	2.8L (2835)	W	MFI	6	OHV
1989	Cavalier	2.0L (2000)	1	TBI	4	OHV
	Cavalier	2.8L (2835)	W	MFI	6	OHV
	Sunbird	2.0L (1998)	K	TBI	4	SOHC
	Sunbird	2.0L (1998)	M	MFI-Turbo	4	SOHC
	Skyhawk	2.0L (2000)	1	TBI	4	OHV
1990	Cavalier	2.2L (2180)	G	TBI	4	OHV
	Cavalier	3.1L (3130)	T	MFI	6	OHV
	Sunbird	2.0L (1998)	K	TBI	4	SOHC
	Sunbird	2.0L (1998)	M	MFI	4	SOHC
1991	Cavalier	2.2L (2180)	G	TBI	4	OHV
	Cavalier	3.1L (3130)	T	MFI	6	OHV
	Sunbird	2.0L (1998)	K	TBI	4	SOHC
	Sunbird	3.1L (3136)	T	MFI	6	OHV
1992	Cavalier	2.2L (2180)	4	TBI	4	OHV
	Cavalier	3.1L (3130)	T	MFI	6	OHV
	Sunbird	2.0L (1998)	H	MFI	4	SOHC
	Sunbird	3.1L (3136)	T	MFI	6	OHV

87951502

ENGINE IDENTIFICATION

Year	Model	Engine Displacement Liters (cc)	Engine Series (ID/VIN)	Fuel System	No. of Cylinders	Engine Type
1993	Cavalier	2.2L (2180)	4	TBI	4	OHV
	Cavalier	3.1L (3130)	T	MFI	6	OHV
	Sunbird	2.0L (1998)	H	MFI	4	SOHC
	Sunbird	3.1L (3136)	T	MFI	6	OHV
1994	Cavalier	2.2L (2180)	4	TBI	4	OHV
	Cavalier	3.1L (3130)	T	MFI	6	OHV
	Sunbird	2.0L (1998)	H	MFI	4	SOHC
	Sunbird	3.1L (3136)	T	MFI	6	OHV
1995	Cavalier	2.2L (2195)	4	MFI	4	OHV
	Cavalier	2.3L (2261)	D	MFI	4	DOHC
	Sunfire	2.2L (2195)	4	MFI	4	OHV
	Sunfire	2.3L (2261)	D	MFI	4	DOHC
1996	Cavalier	2.2L (2195)	4	SFI	4	OHV
	Cavalier	2.4L (2398)	T	SFI	4	DOHC
	Sunfire	2.2L (2195)	4	SFI	4	OHV
	Sunfire	2.4L (2398)	T	SFI	4	DOHC

2 bbl: 2 barrel carburetor
TBI: Throttle Body fuel Injection
MFI: Multi-port Fuel Injection
SFI: Sequential Fuel Inection
OHV: Overhead valves
SOHC: Single overhead camshaft
DOHC: Double overhead camshaft

87951503

ROUTINE MAINTENANCE

Routine maintenance is the self-explanatory term used to describe the sort of periodic work necessary to keep a car in safe and reliable working order. A regular program aimed at monitoring essential systems ensures that the car's components are functioning correctly (and will continue to do so until the next inspection, one hopes), and can prevent small problems from developing into major headaches. Routine maintenance also pays off big dividends in keeping major repair costs at a minimum, extending the life of the car, and enhancing resale value, should you ever desire to part with your new J-car.

The J-cars require very little in the way of routine maintenance. However, a very definite maintenance schedule is provided by General Motors, and must be followed not only to keep the new car warranty in effect, but also to keep the car working properly. The Maintenance Intervals chart in this section outlines the routine maintenance which must be performed according to intervals based on either accumulated mileage or time. Your J-car also came with a maintenance schedule provided by GM. Adherence to these schedules will result in a longer life for your car, and will, over the long run, save you money and time.

The checks and adjustments in the following sections generally require only a few minutes of attention every few weeks; the services to be performed can be easily accomplished in a morning. The most important part of any maintenance program is regularity. The few minutes or occasional morning spent on these seemingly trivial tasks will forestall or eliminate major problems later.

Air Cleaner

All the dust present in the air is kept out of the engine by means of the air cleaner filter element. Proper maintenance is vital, as a clogged element not only restricts the air-flow, and thus the power, but may also cause premature engine wear.

The filter element should be checked at least every 15,000 miles (24,000 km) and replaced every 30,000 miles (48,000 km); more often if the car is driven in dry, dusty areas. The condition of the element should be checked periodically; if it appears to be overly dirty or clogged, the element should be replaced.

➡ The paper element should never be cleaned or soaked with gasoline, cleaning solvent or oil.

REMOVAL & INSTALLATION

♦ See Figures 30, 31 and 32

On many early model engines, the air cleaner is located in the center of the engine compartment, directly over the carburetor or throttle body. On some of the 1987 and later engines the air cleaner is more conveniently located toward the front of the engine compartment with an air duct connected to the throttle body. Depending upon the year of the vehicle and which engine it is equipped with, the air cleaner assembly lid may be retained by a wing nut, screws or different types of retaining clamps and/or fasteners.

1. Unscrew the wing nut or retaining screw(s), or unfasten the clamp(s), as applicable, securing the air cleaner lid, then lift off the housing lid.

2. Lift out the filter element and, if necessary, replace with a new one.

3. Before reinstalling the filter element, wipe out the housing with a damp cloth. Check the lid gasket to ensure that it has a tight seal.

To install:

4. Position the filter element in the air cleaner housing, the close the lid and tighten the wing nut, retaining screw(s) or clamps, as applicable.

Fig. 31 Remove the air cleaner housing lid, then . . .

Fig. 32 . . . lift the air cleaner filter element from the housing

Fuel Filter

✳✳CAUTION

Before removing any fuel system component, always relieve pressure from the system. Never smoke when working around gasoline! Avoid all sources of sparks or ignition. Gasoline vapors are EXTREMELY volatile!

FUEL PRESSURE RELEASE

Carbureted Engines

To release the fuel pressure on the carbureted system, remove the fuel filler cap from the fuel tank in order to allow the fuel vapor to escape, the reinstall the cap. A rag should be placed around a fuel fitting before it is disconnected in order to catch any remaining fuel which may escape.

Fig. 30 Unfasten the air cleaner cover wing nuts

Throttle Body Injection (TBI)

1983-91 1.8L AND 2.0L (OHC) ENGINES, 1983-84 2.0L (OHV) AND 1992-94 2.2L (VIN 4) ENGINES

1. Loosen the fuel filler cap to relieve tank pressure.
2. Remove the fuel pump fuse from the fuse block.
3. Start the engine and allow it to run until it stops due to lack of fuel.
4. Engage the starter (turn key to **START**) for 3 seconds to dissipate pressure in the fuel lines.
5. Turn the ignition **OFF** and connect the fuel pump fuse.
6. Disconnect the negative battery cable to avoid possible fuel discharge if an accidental attempt is made to start the engine.

1985-86 2.0L (OHV), 1989 2.0L (OHV) AND 1990-91 2.2L (OHV) ENGINES

The TBI injection systems used on these engines contain a constant bleed feature in the pressure regulator that relieves pressure any time the engine is turned off. Therefore, no special relieve procedure is required, however, a small amount of fuel may be released when the fuel line is disconnected.

✴✴CAUTION

To reduce the chance of personal injury, cover the fuel line with cloth to collect the fuel and then place the cloth in an approved container. Never smoke when working around gasoline! Avoid all sources of sparks or ignition. Gasoline vapors are EXTREMELY volatile!

1987-88 2.0L (OHV)

The TBI Model 700 used on these engines contains no constant bleed feature to relieve pressure as the 1985-86 models therefore, the following procedure must be followed:
1. Place the transmission selector in PARK (automatic transaxles) or NEUTRAL (manual transaxles), then set the parking brake and block the drive wheels.
2. Loosen the fuel filler cap to relieve tank pressure.
3. Detach the fuel pump at the rear body connector.

✴✴CAUTION

A small amount of fuel may be released after the fuel line is disconnected. To reduce the chance of personal injury, cover the fuel line with cloth to collect the fuel and then place the cloth in an approved container. Never smoke when working around gasoline! Avoid all sources of sparks or ignition. Gasoline vapors are EXTREMELY volatile!

4. Start the engine and allow it to run a few seconds until it stops for lack of fuel.
5. Engage the starter for three seconds to dissipate fuel pressure in the lines. The fuel connections are now safe for servicing.
6. When pressure is relieved and servicing is complete, reconnect the fuel pump at the rear body connector.

Multi-port Fuel Injection (MFI)

2.0L (VIN M) OHC, 1995 2.2L (VIN 4) AND 2.3L, 2.8L and 3.IL ENGINES

1. Disconnect the negative battery cable to avoid fuel discharge if an accidental attempt is made to start the engine.
2. Loosen the fuel filler cap to relieve the tank pressure.
3. Connect a J-34730-1 fuel gage or equivalent to the fuel pressure valve. Wrap a shop towel around the fitting while connecting the gage to avoid spillage.
4. Install a bleed hose into an approved container and open the valve to bleed the system pressure.

1992 2.0L (VIN H) OHC ENGINES

1. Loosen fuel filler cap to relieve tank pressure (do not tighten at this time).
2. Remove fuel pump fuse from the fuel block.
3. Start the engine and run until fuel supply remaining in fuel pipes is consumed. Engage starter for 3 seconds to assure relief of any remaining pressure.
4. Install the fuel pump fuse.
5. Disconnect negative battery cable. Perform the necessary service work.

Sequential Fuel Injection (SFI)

1996 2.3L AND 2.4L ENGINES

1. Loosen the fuel filler cap to relieve tank pressure (do not tighten at this time).
2. Raise and safely support the vehicle.
3. Detach the fuel pump electrical connector.
4. Carefully lower the vehicle.
5. Start the engine and run until the fuel supply remaining in the fuel pipes is consumed.
6. Engage the starter (turn key to **START**) for 3 seconds to dissipate pressure in the fuel lines. Turn the ignition **OFF**.
7. Raise and safely support the vehicle.
8. Attach the fuel pump electrical connector, then carefully lower the vehicle.
9. Disconnect the negative battery cable to avoid fuel discharge if an accidental attempt is made to start the engine.

REMOVAL & INSTALLATION

✴✴CAUTION

Filter replacement should not be attempted when the engine is HOT. Additionally, it is a good idea to place some absorbent rags under the fuel fittings to absorb any gasoline which will spill out when the lines are loosened.

Carbureted Engines
▶ See Figure 33

All models have a fuel filter located within the carburetor body. The fuel filter has a check valve to prevent fuel spillage in the event of an accident. When the filter is replaced, make sure the new one is of the same type. All filters are of the paper element type. Replace the filter every 15,000 miles (24,000 km).

1. Remove the air cleaner.

2. Place a few absorbent rags underneath the fuel line where it joins the carburetor.

3. Detach the fuel line connection at the fuel inlet filter nut. A backup wrench should be used to prevent the filter from loosening while trying to remove the line.

4. Carefully unscrew the fuel inlet filter nut from the carburetor. As the nut is removed, the filter will be pushed part way out by spring pressure.

5. Remove the filter and spring.

To install:

6. Install the new spring and filter with the hole in the filter toward the nut.

7. Position a new gasket on the inlet fitting nut, then install the nut into the carburetor. Tighten to 25 ft. lbs. (34 Nm).

8. Connect the fuel line, then tighten the connector to 18 ft. lbs. (24 Nm.) while holding the inlet nut with a backup wrench to prevent the filter nut from turning.

9. Install the air cleaner.

10. Start the engine and check for leaks.

Fuel Injected Engines

▶ **See Figures 34 and 35**

➡Most 1992 and later model vehicles are equipped with "Quick Connect" fuel fittings. For more information regarding these fittings, please refer to Section 5 of this manual.

An inline filter can be found in the fuel feed line attached to the rear crossmember of the vehicle. To locate the filter, follow the fuel line back from the throttle body. Inline filters are often mounted to the frame rail underneath the vehicle. It may be necessary to raise and safely support the vehicle using jackstands in order to access the filter.

✳✳CAUTION

Before disconnecting any component of the fuel system, refer to the fuel pressure release procedures found earlier in this section.

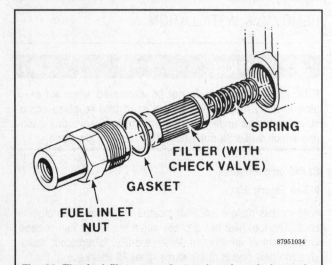

Fig. 33 The fuel filter on carbureted engines is located under the air cleaner, within the carburetor body

SPRING

FILTER (WITH CHECK VALVE)

GASKET

FUEL INLET NUT

87951034

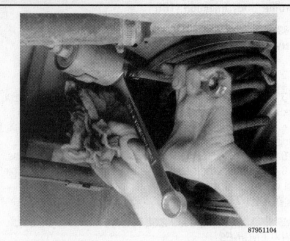

87951104

Fig. 34 Place a rag under the filter to catch any fuel which may spill out, then unfasten the fuel lines, using a back-up wrench

1. Properly relieve the fuel system pressure as outlined earlier in this section.

2. If necessary, raise and safely support the vehicle with jackstands.

➡**Always use a back-up wrench anytime the fuel filter is removed or installed.**

3. Using a backup wrench (where possible) to prevent overtorquing the lines or fittings, loosen and disconnect the fuel lines from the filter. Be sure to position a rag in order to catch any remaining fuel which may escape when the fittings are loosened. Remove and discard any fuel line O-rings.

4. For 1992-96 vehicles, grasp the filter and nylon fuel connection line fitting. Twist the "quick-connect" fitting ¼ or a turn in each direction to loosen any dirt within the fitting. Use compressed air to blow out the dirt from the fittings at the end of the fuel filter.

5. If equipped, detach the quick-connect fitting by pushing inward toward the filter and grasping the plastic tab around the connector and pull apart. If additional assistance is required to disconnect the fitting, tool J 38778 or equivalent can be placed between the filter and the fitting release mechanism to carefully force the two apart. Be careful not to bend the special tool.

6. Remove the fuel filter from the retainer or mounting bolt. For most filters which are retained by band clamps, loosen the fastener(s) and remove the filter. For some filters, it may be necessary to completely remove the clamp and filter assembly.

To install:

7. Before installing a new filter, apply a few drops of clean engine oil to the male tube end of the filter. This will ensure proper attachment and prevent a fuel leak.

8. Position the filter and retaining bracket with the directional arrow facing away from the fuel tank, towards the throttle body.

➡**The filter has an arrow (fuel flow direction) on the side of the case, be sure to install it correctly in the system, the with arrow facing away from the fuel tank.**

9. Install and tighten the filter/bracket retainer(s), as applicable.

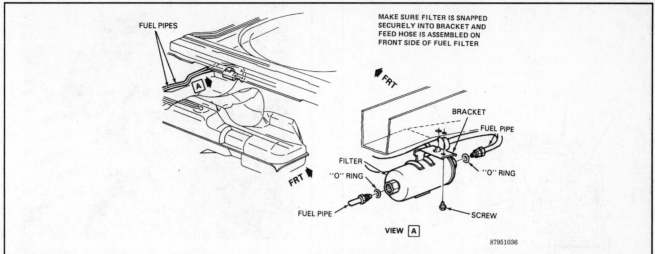

FUEL PIPES

MAKE SURE FILTER IS SNAPPED
SECURELY INTO BRACKET AND
FEED HOSE IS ASSEMBLED ON
FRONT SIDE OF FUEL FILTER

FRT

BRACKET

FUEL PIPE

FILTER

"O" RING

"O" RING

FUEL PIPE

SCREW

VIEW A

FRT

87951036

Fig. 35 Most fuel filters are retained by band clamps; you must loosen the retainers or completely remove the clamp and filter as an assembly

10. If equipped with "quick-connect" fittings, push the connectors together to cause the retaining tabs/fingers to snap into place. Pull on both ends of the connection to be sure they are secure.

11. Using new O-rings, connect the fuel lines to the filter, then tighten, using a backup wrench to prevent damage, to 20-22 ft. lbs. (27-30 Nm).

12. If raised, carefully lower the vehicle.

13. Connect the negative battery cable and tighten the fuel filler cap, then start the engine and check for leaks.

PCV Valve

▶ **See Figures 36 and 37**

All of the vehicles covered by this manual, except the 2.3L (VIN D) and the 2.4L (VIN T), utilize a Positive Crankcase Ventilation (PCV) or Crankcase Ventilation (CV) valve, which regulates crankcase ventilation during various engine running conditions. At high vacuum (idle speed and partial load range) it will open slightly and at low vacuum (full throttle) it will open fully. This causes vapors to be drawn from the crankcase by engine vacuum and then sucked into the combustion chamber where they are dissipated.

The PCV system must be operating properly in order to allow evaporation of fuel vapors and water from the crankcase. This system should be serviced and both the PCV valve or hose and filter (located in the air cleaner) replaced every 30,000 miles (48,000 km). Normal service entails cleaning the passages of the system hoses with solvent, inspecting them for cracks and breaks, then replacing them as necessary. The PCV or CV valve contains a check valve and, when working properly, this valve will make a rattling sound when the outside case is tapped. If it fails to rattle, then it is probably stuck in a closed position and needs to be replaced.

The PCV system is designed to prevent the emission of gases from the crankcase into the atmosphere. It does this by connecting a outlet (usually the valve cover) to the intake with a hose. The crankcase gases travel through the hose to the intake where they are returned to the combustion chamber to be burned. If maintained properly, this system reduces conden-

sation in the crankcase and the resultant formation of harmful acids and oil dilution. A clogged PCV valve will often cause a slow or rough idle due to a richer fuel mixture. A vehicle equipped with a PCV system has air going through a hose to the intake manifold from an outlet at the valve cover. To compensate for this extra air going to the manifold, carburetor specifications require a richer (more gas) mixture at the carburetor. If the PCV valve or hose is clogged, this air doesn't go to the intake manifold and the fuel mixture is too rich. A rough, slow idle results. The valve should be checked before making any carburetor adjustments. Clamp the hose shut. If the engine speed decreases less than 50 rpm, the valve is clogged and should be replaced. If the engine speed decreases much more than 50 rpm, then the valve good. The PCV valve is an inexpensive item and it is suggested that is be replaced, if suspect. If the new valve doesn't noticeably improve engine idle, the problem might be a restriction in the PCV hose.

For the 2.3L and 2.4L engines, blow-by gases are passed through a Crankcase Ventilation (CV) oil/air separator hose into the intake manifold. Incorporated in the CV system is a crankcase ventilation heater assembly, a positive temperature coefficient device, which serves to prevent icing in the CV system.

The PCV valve must be replaced every 30,000 miles (48,000 km). More information regarding the PCV/CV system, including system tests, is located in Section 4 of this manual.

REMOVAL & INSTALLATION

▶ **See Figures 38, 39 and 40**

Valve

The valve is located in a rubber grommet in the valve cover, connected to the air cleaner housing by a large diameter rubber hose. To replace the valve:

1. Pull the valve (with the hose attached) or the hose from the rubber grommet in the valve cover.

2. Remove the valve from the hose.

3. Install a new valve into the hose.

4. Press the valve or hose back into the rubber grommet in the valve cover.

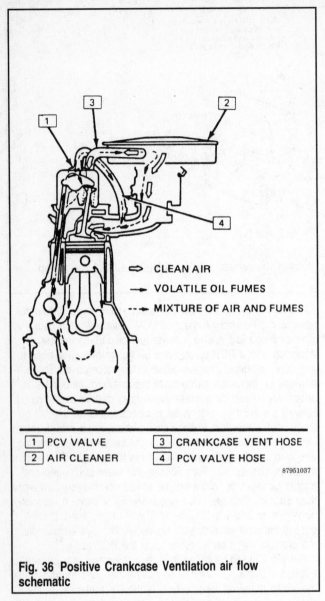

CLEAN AIR

VOLATILE OIL FUMES

MIXTURE OF AIR AND FUMES

| 1 | PCV VALVE | 3 | CRANKCASE VENT HOSE |
| 2 | AIR CLEANER | 4 | PCV VALVE HOSE |

87951037

Fig. 36 Positive Crankcase Ventilation air flow schematic

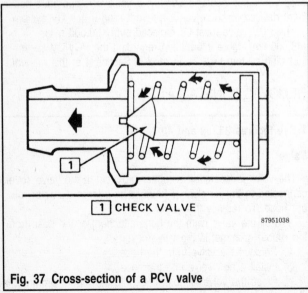

1 CHECK VALVE

87951038

Fig. 37 Cross-section of a PCV valve

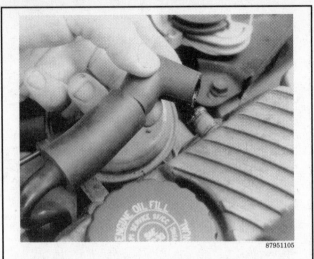

87951105

Fig. 38 Pull the hose from the nipple in the valve or camshaft cover

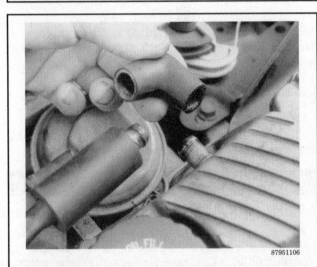

87951106

Fig. 39 Remove the extension from the hose, to access the valve, then . . .

87951107

Fig. 40 . . . remove the PCV valve from the hose

PCV Filter

Some models have a PCV filter, located in the air cleaner housing. This filter must be replaced at every 50,000 miles (80,500 km), or sooner, upon inspection.

1. Remove the air cleaner housing lid.
2. Slide back the filter retaining clip and remove the old filter.
3. Install the new filter, replace the retaining clip and replace the housing lid.

FUNCTIONAL CHECK

If the engine is idling rough, check for a clogged PCV valve, dirty vent filter or air cleaner element, or for a plugged hose. Test the system using the following procedure and replace components as necessary.

1. Remove the PCV valve from the rocker cover.
2. Run the engine at idle and place your thumb over the end of the valve to check for vacuum.
3. If no vacuum exists, check for plugged hoses, manifold port vacuum at the carburetor or TBI unit, or a defective PCV valve.
4. To check the PCV valve, remove the valve from the hose and shake it. If a rattling noise is heard, the valve is good. If no noise was heard, the valve is plugged and replacement is necessary.

Evaporative Canister

♦ See Figures 41, 42 and 43

This system is designed to limit gasoline vapor, which normally escapes from the fuel tank and the intake manifold, from discharging into the atmosphere. Vapor absorption is accomplished through the use of the charcoal canister. The canister absorbs fuel vapors and stores then until they can be remove and burned in the combustion process. Removal of the vapors from the canister to the engine is accomplished through: a canister mounted purge valve, the throttle valve position, a Thermostatic Vacuum Switch (TVS) or a computer controlled canister purge solenoid.

In addition to the canister, the fuel tank requires a non-vented gas cap. This cap does not allow fuel vapor to discharge into the atmosphere. All fuel vapor travels through a vent line (inserted high into the domed fuel tank) directly to the canister.

Check the evaporative emission control system every 15,000 miles (24,000 km). Check the fuel vapor lines and the vacuum hoses for proper connections and correct routing, as well as condition. Replace clogged, damaged or deteriorated parts as necessary.

For more details on the Evaporative Emissions Control (EEC) system, please refer to Section 4.

FUNCTIONAL TEST

1. Apply a short length of hose to the lower tube of the purge valve and attempt to blow through it. Little or no air should pass into the canister.
2. With a hand vacuum pump, apply a vacuum of 15 in. Hg (50 kPa) to the control valve tube (usually the upper tube). If the diaphragm does not hold vacuum for at least 20 seconds, the diaphragm is leaking and the canister must be replaced.
3. If the diaphragm holds vacuum, again try to blow through the hose connected to the lower tube while vacuum is still being applied. An increased flow of air should be observed. If not, the canister must be replaced.

REMOVAL & INSTALLATION

♦ See Figures 44 and 45

1. Disconnect the negative battery cable.
2. If necessary for access, removed the right hand engine splash shield.
3. Tag and disconnect the hoses from the canister.

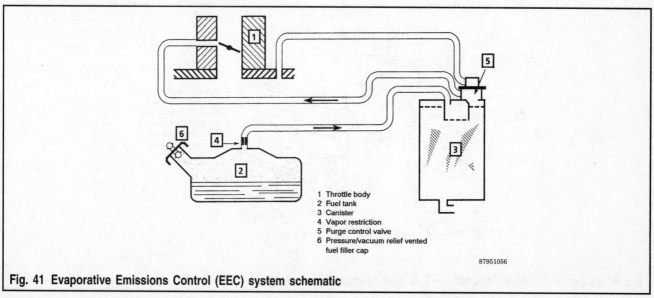

1 Throttle body
2 Fuel tank
3 Canister
4 Vapor restriction
5 Purge control valve
6 Pressure/vacuum relief vented fuel filler cap

87951056

Fig. 41 Evaporative Emissions Control (EEC) system schematic

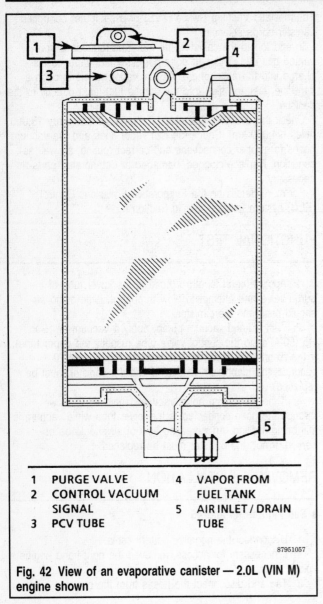

1	PURGE VALVE	4	VAPOR FROM
2	CONTROL VACUUM		FUEL TANK
	SIGNAL	5	AIR INLET / DRAIN
3	PCV TUBE		TUBE

87951057

Fig. 42 View of an evaporative canister — 2.0L (VIN M) engine shown

1 Canister purge
2 Vapor from fuel tank
3 Carbon
4 Air

87951058

Fig. 43 Evaporative canister — 2.2L (VIN 4) shown

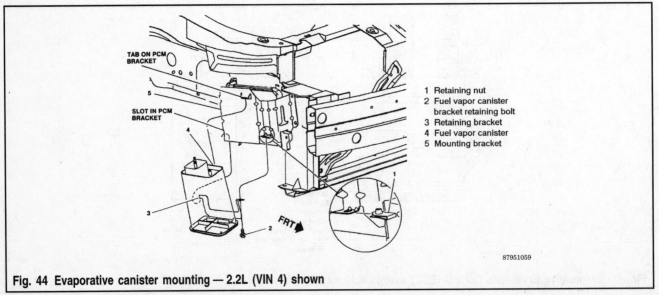

TAB ON PCM BRACKET

SLOT IN PCM BRACKET

FRT

1 Retaining nut
2 Fuel vapor canister bracket retaining bolt
3 Retaining bracket
4 Fuel vapor canister
5 Mounting bracket

87951059

Fig. 44 Evaporative canister mounting — 2.2L (VIN 4) shown

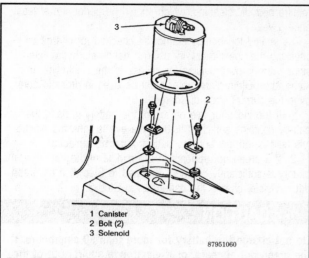

1 Canister
2 Bolt (2)
3 Solenoid

87951060

Fig. 45 There are two bolts retaining the canister on the 2.8L engine

4. For some vehicles such as the 2.0L (VIN M) engine, perform the following:

   a. Raise and safely support the vehicle, then unfasten the four right side air dam bolts.

   b. Unfasten the right side fender filler panel bolts and filler panel.

   c. Disconnect the hose from the bottom of the canister.

➡**If the vehicle is equipped with A/C, it may be necessary to gently hold the refrigerant lines out of the way for removal.**

5. Unfasten the canister retaining bolt(s), then remove the canister and retainer.

6. Remove the retainer from the canister.

7. Installation is the reverse of the removal procedure. The hose connections on the top of the canister should face the front of the vehicle.

Battery

GENERAL MAINTENANCE

▶ **See Figures 46, 47, 48 and 49**

All vehicles were originally equipped with a maintenance free battery as standard equipment, eliminating the need for fluid level checks and the possibility of checking specific gravity using a hand held tester. Nevertheless, the battery does require some attention.

At least once a year, the battery terminals and the cable clamps should be cleaned. Remove the post clamps or side terminal bolts and the cables, negative cable first. Clean the cable clamps and the battery terminals with a wire brush until all corrosion, grease, etc.. is removed and the metal is shiny. It is especially important to clean the inside of the clamp thoroughly. A small deposit of foreign material or oxidation can prevent a sound electrical connection and inhibit either starting or charging. Special tools are available for cleaning the side terminal clamps and terminals.

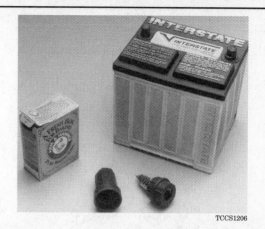

TCCS1206

Fig. 46 Battery maintenance may be accomplished with household items (such as baking soda to neutralize spilled acid) or with special tools such as this post and terminal cleaner

TCCS1207

Fig. 47 The underside of this special battery tool has a wire brush to clean post terminals

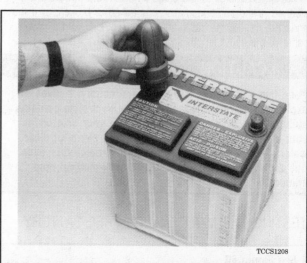

TCCS1208

Fig. 48 Place the tool over the terminals and twist to clean the post

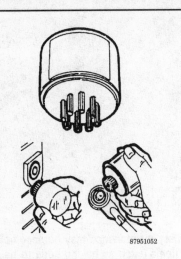

Fig. 49 Special tools are also available for cleaning the posts and clamps of side terminal batteries

Before installing the cables, loosen the battery hold-down clamp, remove the battery, and check the battery tray. Clear it of any debris and check it for soundness. Rust should be wire brushed away, and the metal given a coat of anti-rust paint. Replace the battery and tighten the hold-down clamp securely, but be careful not to overtighten, which will crack the battery case.

➡Surface coatings on battery cases can actually conduct electricity which will cause a slight voltage drain, so make sure the battery case is clean. Batteries can be cleaned using a paste made from a mixture of baking soda and water. Spread the paste on any corrosion, wait a few minutes, and rinse with water. Finish the job by cleaning metal parts with a wire brush.

After the clamps and terminals are clean, reinstall the cables, negative cables last. Give the clamps and terminals a thin external coat of nonmetallic grease after installation, to retard corrosion.

Check the cables at the same time that the terminals are cleaned. If the cable insulation is cracked or broken, or if the ends are frayed, the cable should be replaced with a new cable of the same length and gauge.

❋❋CAUTION

Keep flame or sparks away from the battery. It gives off explosive hydrogen gas. The battery electrolyte contains sulfuric acid. If you should get any on your skin or in your eyes, flush the affected areas with plenty of clear water. Always wear safety glasses to protect your eyes, but should any acid contact them, seek medical help immediately.

TESTING THE MAINTENANCE FREE BATTERY

◗ See Figure 50

Maintenance free batteries do not require normal attention as far as fluid level checks are concerned. However, the terminals require periodic cleaning, which should be performed at least once a year.

The sealed top battery cannot be checked for charge by checking the specific gravity using a hand-held hydrometer since there is no provision for access to the electrolyte. Instead, the built-in hydrometer must be used in order to determine the current state of charge.

1. If the indicator eye on top of the battery is dark, the battery contains sufficient fluid. If the eye is light, the electrolyte fluid is too low and the battery must be replaced.

2. If a green dot appears in the middle of the dark eye, the battery is sufficiently charged. Proceed to Step 4. If no green dot is visible, charge the battery as in Step 3.

❋❋CAUTION

Do not charge the battery for more than 50 amp/hours. If the green dot appears, or if electrolyte squirts out of the vent hole, stop the charge and proceed to Step 4.

3. Charge the battery referring to the proper charging rate (amps) for the necessary time span and rate of charge.
- 75 amps — 4 min
- 50 amps — 1 hr
- 25 amps — 2 hr
- 10 amps — 5 hr

➡It may be necessary to tip the battery from side to side to get the green dot to appear after charging.

❋❋CAUTION

When charging the battery, the electrical system and control unit can be quickly damaged by improper connections, high output battery chargers or incorrect service procedures.

4. Connect a battery load tester and a voltmeter across the battery terminals (the battery cables should be disconnected from the battery). Apply a 300 amp load to the battery for 15 seconds to remove the surface charge. Remove the load.

5. Wait 15 seconds to allow the battery to recover. Apply the appropriate test load, as specified on the battery label, for

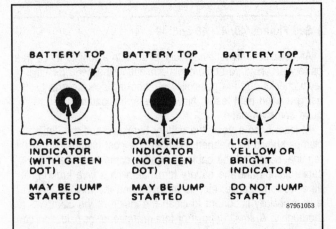

Fig. 50 Maintenance free batteries contain a built-in hydrometer to help determine battery charge

15 seconds while reading the voltage, then disconnect the load. Some appropriate loads on original batteries are:

- 75-60 — 260 amps
- 78A-72 — 300 amps
- 83-50 — 150 amps
- 83-60 — 180 amps
- 85A-60 — 170 amps
- 87A-60 — 230 amps
- 89A-60 — 270 amps
- 1981103 — 200 amps
- 1981104 — 250 amps
- 1981105 — 270 amps
- 1981577 — 260 amps

6. Check the results against the appropriate minimum voltage based on the battery temperature. If the battery voltage at or above the specification for the temperature listed, the battery is good. If the voltage falls below specification, the battery should be replaced.

- 70°F or above — 9.6 volts
- 60°F — 9.5 volts
- 50°F — 9.4 volts
- 40°F — 9.3 volts
- 30°F — 9.1 volts
- 20°F — .9 volts
- 10°F — 8.7 volts
- 0°F — 8.5 volts

REPLACEMENT

▶ See Figure 51

When battery replacement becomes necessary, select a battery with a rating equal to or greater than the one which was originally installed. Deterioration and aging of the battery cables, starter motor, and associated wires makes the battery's job harder in successive years. The slow increase in electrical resistance over time makes it prudent to install a new battery with a greater capacity than the old. Details on the role the battery plays in the vehicle's electrical systems are covered in Section 3 of this manual.

1. Carefully disconnect the negative (ground) cable from the battery terminal.

✳✳CAUTION

Always use caution when working on or near the battery. Never allow a tool to bridge the gap between the negative and positive battery terminals. Also, be careful not to allow a tool to provide a ground between the positive cable and any metal component on the vehicle. Either of these conditions will cause a short leading to sparks and possibly, personal injury.

2. With the negative battery cable disconnected and out of the way, carefully disconnect the positive cable from the battery terminal.

3. Loosen the nut and/or bolt securing the clamp, then remove the battery hold-down clamp.

4. Wearing and old pair of work gloves or using a battery lifting tool to protect you from any remaining battery acid, carefully lift the battery out of the vehicle and place in a safe

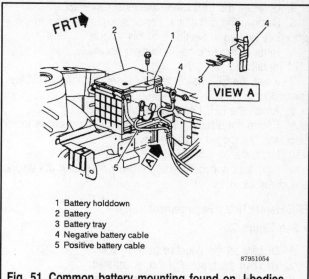

1 Battery holddown
2 Battery
3 Battery tray
4 Negative battery cable
5 Positive battery cable

87951054

Fig. 51 Common battery mounting found on J-bodies

location. Be sure to keep the battery away from open flame and to protect the surrounding areas from acid.

5. Before installing the battery, clean the battery terminals and the cables thoroughly.

6. Check the battery tray to be sure it is clear of any debris. If it is rusty, it should be wire-brushed clean and given a coat of anti-rust paint, or replaced. Inspect the cables for damage and/or corrosion. Replace as necessary.

To install:

7. Carefully lower the battery into position, making sure not to allow the terminals to short on any bare metal. Be sure the battery is centered in the lip of the tray.

8. Install the hold-down clamp. Tighten to 6 ft. lbs. (8 Nm), which is tight enough to hold the battery in place, but loose enough to prevent the case from cracking.

9. Connect the positive, then the negative battery cables. Installation torque for the cables is 9 ft. lbs. (12 Nm). Give the terminals a light external coat of nonmetallic grease after installation to retard corrosion.

➡**Make absolutely sure that the battery is connected properly before you turn on the ignition switch. Reversed polarity can burn out the alternator and regulator in a matter of seconds.**

Early Fuel Evaporation (EFE) Heater

The EFE heating system is used on all carbureted engines. The purpose of the heating unit is to further vaporize the fuel droplets as they enter the intake manifold; vaporization of the air/fuel mixture ensures complete combustion which provides the maximum power and minimum emissions output for the fuel used.

REMOVAL & INSTALLATION

1. Disconnect the negative battery cable.
2. Remove the air cleaner.
3. Tag and detach all electrical, vacuum and fuel connections from the carburetor.

4. Unfasten the EFE heater electrical connector.

5. Remove the carburetor. For details, please refer to the procedure located in Section 5 of this manual.

6. Remove the EFE heater isolator assembly.

To install:

7. Install the EFE heater isolator assembly, then install the carburetor.

8. Attach the EFE heater electrical connection.

9. Fasten the electrical, vacuum and fuel connections to the carburetor, as tagged during removal.

10. Install the air cleaner.

11. Connect the negative battery cable, then start the engine and check for leaks.

EFE Heater Relay Replacement

▶ See Figure 52

1. Disconnect the negative battery cable.
2. Remove the bracket at the fender skirt.
3. Detach the relay electrical connections.
4. Unfasten the retaining bolts, then remove the relay.
5. Installation is the reverse of the removal procedure.

Standard Drive Belts

INSPECTION AND ADJUSTMENT

▶ See Figures 53 and 54

Every 12 months or 15,000 miles (24,000 km), check the water pump, alternator, power steering pump (if so equipped), and air conditioning compressor (if so equipped) drive belts for proper tension. Also look for signs of wear, fraying, separation, glazing and so on, and replace the belts as required.

Belt tension should be checked with a gauge made for the purpose. If a gauge is not available, tension can be checked with moderate thumb pressure applied to the belt at its longest span midway between pulleys. If the belt has a free span less than twelve inches, it should deflect approximately $1/8$-$1/4$ in. (3 — 6mm). If the span is longer than twelve inches, deflection can range between $1/8$-$3/8$ in. (3 — 9mm).

1. Loosen the driven accessory's pivot and adjustment bolts. The pivot bolts are the bolts that enable the accessory to move in the either direction for adjustment. The adjustment bolts are the bolts in the slotted brackets.

2. Move the accessory toward or away from the engine until the tension is correct. You can use a wooden hammer handle or a broomstick as a lever, but do not use anything metallic.

3. Tighten the bolts and recheck the tension. If new belts have been installed, run the engine for a few minutes, then recheck and readjust as necessary.

It is better to have belts too loose than too tight, because overtight belts will lead to bearing failure, particularly in the water pump and alternator. However, loose belts place an extremely high impact load on the driven component due to the whipping action of the belt.

REPLACEMENT

▶ See Figure 55

1. Loosen the accessory-to-mounting bracket bolt(s) and adjusting bolt.
2. Rotate the accessory to relieve belt tension.
3. Slip the drive belt from the accessory pulley and remove it from the engine.

➡If the engine uses more than one belt, it may be necessary to remove belts that are in front of the belt being removed

To install:

4. Place the new belt over the crankshaft or drive pulley and stretch over the driven (accessory) pulley.
5. If removed, install the other belts in the same way.
6. Adjust the belts to the proper tension.
7. Tighten the adjusting and mounting bolts.

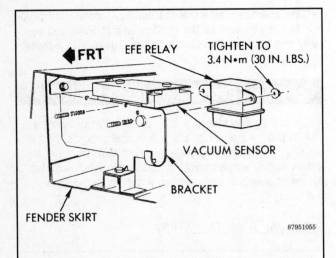

Fig. 52 EFE heater relay replacement — all carbureted engines use an EFE heater

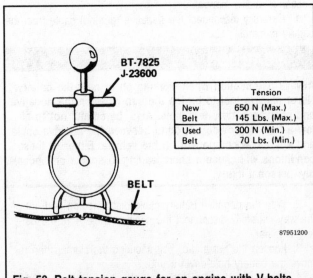

	Tension
New Belt	650 N (Max.) 145 Lbs. (Max.)
Used Belt	300 N (Min.) 70 Lbs. (Min.)

Fig. 53 Belt tension gauge for an engine with V-belts

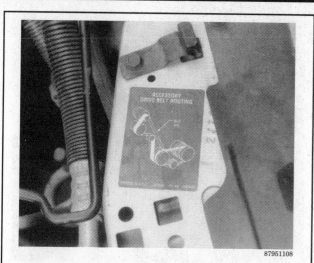

Fig. 54 Many vehicles will have a decal illustrating the correct accessory belt routing

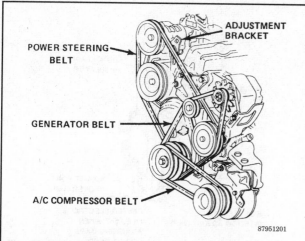

Fig. 55 If the engine uses more than one belt, it may be necessary to remove belts that are in front of the belt being removed

Serpentine Drive Belts

Models equipped with the V6 engine and most 1987 and later engines use a single (serpentine belt) to drive all engine accessories. The serpentine belt driven accessories are rigidly mounted with belt tension maintained by a spring loaded tensioner assembly. The belt tensioner has the ability to control belt tension over a fairly broad range of belt lengths. However, there are limits to the tensioner's ability to compensate for varying lengths of belts. Poor tension control and/or damage to the tensioner could result with the tensioner operating outside of its range.

INSPECTION AND ADJUSTMENT

1. If fraying of the belt is noticed, check to make sure both the belt and the tensioner assembly are properly aligned and

that the belt edges are not in contact with the flanges of the tensioner pulley.

2. If, while adjusting belt tension, tensioner runs out of travel, the belt is stretched beyond adjustment and should be replaced.

3. If a whining is heard around the tensioner or idler assemblies, check for possible bearing failure.

➡️**Routine inspection of the belt may reveal cracks in the belt ribs. These cracks will not impair belt performance and therefore should not be considered a problem requiring belt replacement. However, the belt should be replaced if belt slip occurs or if sections of the belt ribs are missing.**

REPLACEMENT

To replace the belt push (rotate) the the belt tensioner and remove the belt. Use a 15mm socket on the 4-cyl. engines and a ¾ in. open end wrench on the V6 engines.

Timing Belt

INSPECTION

Vehicles equipped with the 1.8L (VIN O and J) and the 2.0L (VIN K and M) engines are the only vehicles covered by this manual which utilize a timing belt. The timing belt should be inspected for cracks, wear or other damage and should be replaced every 60,000 miles (100,000 km).

For the timing belt removal and installation procedure, please refer to Section 3 of this manual.

Hoses

Upper and lower radiator hoses and all heater hoses should be checked for deterioration, leaks and loose hose clamps every 15,000 miles (24,000 km). To remove the hoses:

1. Drain the radiator as detailed later in this section.

2. Loosen the hose clamps at each end of the hose to be removed.

3. Working the hose back and forth, slide it off its connection and then install the new hose.

➡️**If the hose is stuck, use a suitable razor cutting tool or knife, and carefully slit the hose enough to split it open along the connecting neck.**

4. Position the hose clamps at least ¼ in. from the end of the new hose and tighten them.

➡️**Always make sure that the hose clamps are beyond the bead and placed in the center of the clamping surface before tightening them.**

CV-Boot

INSPECTION

▶ See Figures 56 and 57

CV-joint boots should be periodically inspected. It would be a wise idea to examine the boot every time your vehicle is raised and supported. Check the boot for signs of cracks, tears or splits and repair/replace as necessary. For CV-boot and joint repair, as well as overhaul procedures, please refer to Section 7 of this manual.

Spark Plugs

GENERAL INFORMATION

▶ See Figures 58, 59, 60 and 61

A typical spark plug consists of a metal shell surrounding a ceramic insulator. A metal electrode extends downward through the center of the insulator and protrudes a small distance. Located at the end of the plug and attached to the side of the outer metal shell is the side electrode. The side electrode bends in at a 90° angle so that its tip is just past and parallel to the tip of the center electrode. The distance between these two electrodes (measured in thousandths of an inch or hundredths of a millimeter) is called the spark plug gap.

Spark plugs ignite the air and fuel mixture in the cylinder as the piston reaches the top of the compression stroke. The controlled explosion that results forces the piston down, turning the crankshaft and the rest of the drivetrain.

Fig. 57 View of a CV-boot in good condition

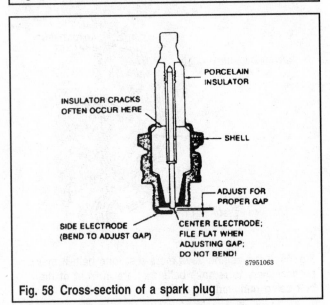

Fig. 58 Cross-section of a spark plug

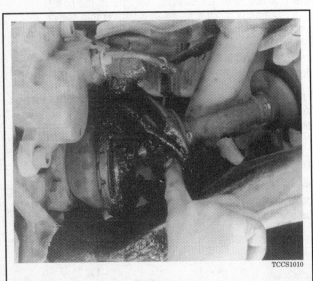

Fig. 56 View of a torn CV-boot

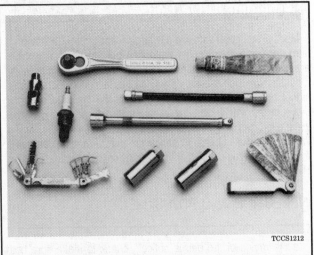

Fig. 59 A variety of tools and gauges are needed for spark plug service

Tracking Arc
High voltage arcs between a fouling deposit on the insulator tip and spark plug shell. This ignites the fuel/air mixture at some point along the insulator tip, retarding the ignition timing which causes a power and fuel loss.

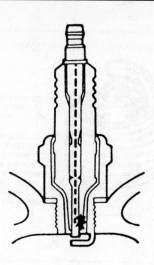

Wide Gap
Spark plug electrodes are worn so that the high voltage charge cannot arc across the electrodes. Improper gapping of electrodes on new or "cleaned" spark plugs could cause a similar condition. Fuel remains unburned and a power loss results.

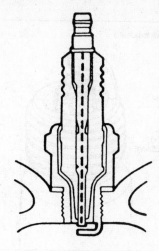

Flashover
A damaged spark plug boot, along with dirt and moisture, could permit the high voltage charge to short over the insulator to the spark plug shell or the engine. AC's buttress insulator design helps prevent high voltage flashover.

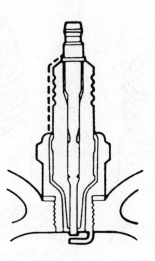

Fouled Spark Plug
Deposits that have formed on the insulator tip may become conductive and provide a "shunt" path to the shell. This prevents the high voltage from arcing between the electrodes. A power and fuel loss is the result.

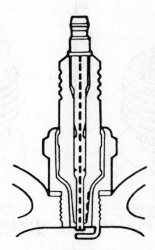

Bridged Electrodes
Fouling deposits between the electrodes "ground out" the high voltage needed to fire the spark plug. The arc between the electrodes does not occur and the fuel air mixture is not ignited. This causes a power loss and exhausting of raw fuel.

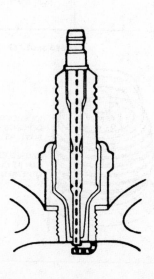

Cracked Insulator
A crack in the spark plug insulator could cause the high voltage charge to "ground out." Here, the spark does not jump the electrode gap and the fuel air mixture is not ignited. This causes a power loss and raw fuel is exhausted.

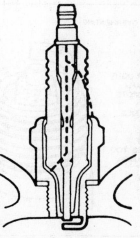

tccs2001

Fig. 60 Used spark plugs which show damage may indicate engine problems

GAP BRIDGED

IDENTIFIED BY DEPOSIT BUILD—UP CLOSING GAP BETWEEN ELECTRODES.

CAUSED BY OIL OR CARBON FOULING. REPLACE PLUG, OR, IF DEPOSITS ARE NOT EXCESSIVE THE PLUG CAN BE CLEANED.

OIL FOULED

IDENTIFIED BY WET BLACK DEPOSITS ON THE INSULATOR SHELL BORE ELECTRODES.

CAUSED BY EXCESSIVE OIL ENTERING COMBUSTION CHAMBER THROUGH WORN RINGS AND PISTONS, EXCESSIVE CLEARANCE BETWEEN VALVE GUIDES AND STEMS, OR WORN OR LOOSE BEARINGS. CORRECT OIL PROBLEM. REPLACE THE PLUG.

CARBON FOULED

IDENTIFIED BY BLACK, DRY FLUFFY CARBON DEPOSITS ON INSULATOR TIPS, EXPOSED SHELL SURFACES AND ELECTRODES.

CAUSED BY TOO COLD A PLUG, WEAK IGNITION, DIRTY AIR CLEANER, DEFECTIVE FUEL PUMP, TOO RICH A FUEL MIXTURE, IMPROPERLY OPERATING HEAT RISER OR EXCESSIVE IDLING. CAN BE CLEANED.

NORMAL

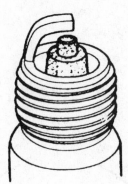

IDENTIFIED BY LIGHT TAN OR GRAY DEPOSITS ON THE FIRING TIP.

PRE-IGNITION

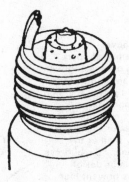

IDENTIFIED BY MELTED ELECTRODES AND POSSIBLY BLISTERED INSULATOR. METALIC DEPOSITS ON INSULATOR INDICATE ENGINE DAMAGE.

CAUSED BY WRONG TYPE OF FUEL, INCORRECT IGNITION TIMING OR ADVANCE, TOO HOT A PLUG, BURNT VALVES OR ENGINE OVERHEATING. REPLACE THE PLUG.

OVERHEATING

IDENTIFIED BY A WHITE OR LIGHT GRAY INSULATOR WITH SMALL BLACK OR GRAY BROWN SPOTS AND WITH BLUISH-BURNT APPEARANCE OF ELECTRODES.

CAUSED BY ENGINE OVER-HEATING, WRONG TYPE OF FUEL, LOOSE SPARK PLUGS, TOO HOT A PLUG, LOW FUEL PUMP PRESSURE OR INCORRECT IGNITION TIMING. REPLACE THE PLUG.

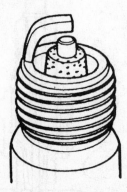

FUSED SPOT DEPOSIT

IDENTIFIED BY MELTED OR SPOTTY DEPOSITS RESEMBLING BUBBLES OR BLISTERS.

CAUSED BY SUDDEN ACCELERATION. CAN BE CLEANED IF NOT EXCESSIVE, OTHERWISE REPLACE PLUG.

tccs2002

Fig. 61 Inspect the spark plug to determine engine running conditions

The average life of a spark plug in your vehicle is 30,000 miles (48,000 km) for vehicles through 1994 and 100,000 miles (161,000 km) for 1995-96 vehicles. Part of the reason for this extraordinarily long life is the exclusive use of unleaded fuel, which reduces the amount of deposits within the combustion chamber and on the spark plug electrodes themselves, compared with the deposits left by the leaded gasoline used in the past. An additional contribution to long life is made by the HEI (High Energy Ignition) System, which fires the spark plugs with over 35,000 volts of electricity. The high voltage serves to keep the electrodes clear, and because it is a cleaner blast of electricity than that produced by conventional breaker-points ignitions, the electrodes suffer less pitting and wear.

Nevertheless, the life of a spark plug is dependent on a number of factors, including the mechanical condition of the engine, driving conditions, and the driver's habits.

When you remove the plugs, check the condition of the electrodes; they are a good indicator of the internal state of the engine. Since the spark plug wires should be checked every 15,000 miles (24,000 km), the spark plugs can be removed and examined at the same time. This will allow you to keep an eye on the mechanical status of the engine.

A small deposit of light tan or rust-red material on a spark plug that has been used for any period of time is to be considered normal. Any other color, or abnormal amounts of wear or deposits, indicates that there is something amiss in the engine.

The gap between the center electrode and the side or ground electrode can be expected to increase not more than 0.001 in. (0.254mm) every 1,000 miles (1,600 km) under normal conditions.

When a spark plug is functioning normally or, more accurately, when the plug is installed in an engine that is functioning properly, the plugs can be taken out, cleaned, regapped, and reinstalled in the engine without doing the engine any harm.

When, and if, a plug fouls and begins to misfire, you will have to investigate, correct the cause of the fouling, and either clean or replace the plug.

➡**There are several reasons why a spark plug will foul and you can often learn what is at fault by just looking at the plug. Refer to the spark plug diagnosis figure in this section for some of the most common reasons for plug fouling.**

Spark Plug Heat Range
◗ **See Figure 62**

Spark plugs suitable for use in your car's engine are offered in a number of different heat ranges. The amount of heat which the plug absorbs is determined by the length of the lower insulator. The longer the insulator, the hotter the plug will operate; the shorter the insulator, the cooler it will operate. A spark plug that absorbs (or retains) little heat and remains too cool will accumulate deposits of oil and carbon, because it is not hot enough to burn them off. This leads to fouling and consequent misfiring. A spark plug that absorbs too much heat will have no deposits, but the electrodes will burn away quickly and, in some cases, pre-ignition may result. Pre-ignition occurs when the spark plug tips get so hot that they ignite the fuel/mixture before the actual spark fires. This premature ignition will usually cause a pinging sound under conditions of low

speed and heavy load. In severe cases, the heat may become high enough to start the fuel/air mixture burning throughout the combustion chamber rather than just to the front of the plug. In this case, the resultant explosion (detonation) will be strong enough to damage pistons, rings, and valves.

In most cases the factory recommended heat range is correct; it is chosen to perform well under a wide range of operating conditions. However, if most of your driving is long distance, high speed travel, you may want to install a spark plug one step colder than standard. If most of your driving is of the short trip variety, when the engine may not always reach operating temperature, a hotter plug may help burn off the deposits normally accumulated under those conditions.

REMOVAL

◗ **See Figures 63, 64 and 65**

When you're removing spark plugs, you should work on one at a time. Don't start by removing the plug wires all at once because unless you number them, they are going to get mixed up. On some models though, it will be more convenient for you to remove all the wires before you start to work on the plugs. If this is necessary, take a minute before you begin and number the wires with tape before disconnecting them. The time you spend doing this will pay off later when it comes time to reconnect the wires to the plugs.

➡**Do not remove spark plugs from a warm engine or damage to the threads may occur. Wait until the engine has sufficiently cooled before attempting to remove the plugs.**

1. Disconnect the negative battery cable.
2. The spark plug boots have large grips to aid in removal. Grasp the wire by the rubber boot and twist the boot ½ turn in either direction to break the tight seal between the boot and the plug. Then twist and pull on the boot to remove the wire from the spark plug. DO NOT pull on the spark plug wire itself or you may separate the plug connector from the end of the wire. When the wire has been removed, take a wire brush and clean the area around the plug. An evaporative spray cleaner such a those designed for brake applications will also work

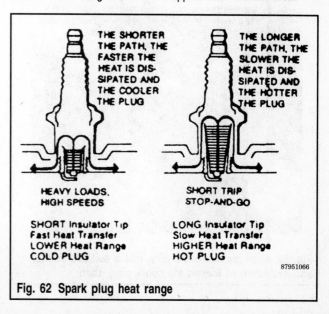

THE SHORTER THE PATH, THE FASTER THE HEAT IS DISSIPATED AND THE COOLER THE PLUG

THE LONGER THE PATH, THE SLOWER THE HEAT IS DISSIPATED AND THE HOTTER THE PLUG

HEAVY LOADS, HIGH SPEEDS

SHORT TRIP STOP-AND-GO

SHORT Insulator Tip
Fast Heat Transfer
LOWER Heat Range
COLD PLUG

LONG Insulator Tip
Slow Heat Transfer
HIGHER Heat Range
HOT PLUG

87951066

Fig. 62 Spark plug heat range

well. Make sure that all the foreign material is removed so that none will enter the cylinder after the plug has been removed.

➡**If you have access to a compressor, use the air hose to blow all material away from the spark plug bores before loosening the plug. Always protect your eyes with safely glasses when using compressed air.**

3. Remove the plug using the proper size socket, extensions, and universals as necessary. Hold the socket or the extension close to the plug with your free hand as this will help lessen the possibility of applying a shear force which might snap the spark plug in half.

4. If removing the plug is difficult, drip some penetrating oil (Liquid Wrench®, WD-40®) on the plug threads, allow it to work, then remove the plug. Also be sure that the socket is straight on the plug, especially on those hard to reach plugs. Again, if the socket is cocked to one side, a shear force may be applied and could snap the plug in half.

5. Remove the plugs by unscrewing them the rest of the way.

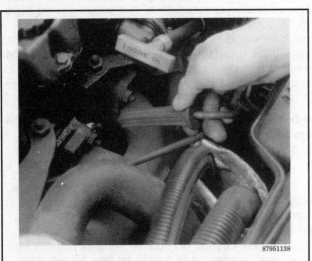

Fig. 63 Always grasp the wire by the rubber boot, NEVER the wire itself

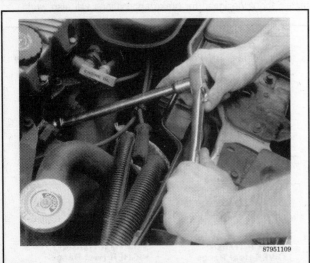

Fig. 64 After removing the wire, use a suitable socket and extension to loosen the spark plug, then . . .

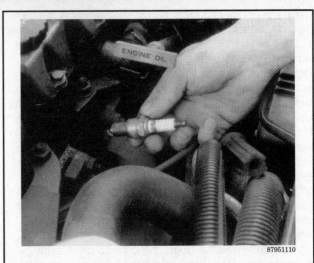

Fig. 65 . . . remove the spark plug from the cylinder head

INSPECTION

➤ **See Figures 66, 67 and 68**

Check the plugs for deposits and wear. If they are not going to be replaced, clean the plugs thoroughly. Remember that any kind of deposit will decrease the efficiency of the plug. Plugs can be cleaned on a spark plug cleaning machine, which can sometimes be found in service stations, or you can do an acceptable job of cleaning with a stiff brush. If the plugs are cleaned, the electrodes must be filed flat. use an ignition points file, not an emery board or the like, which will leave deposits. The electrodes must be filed perfectly flat with sharp edges; rounded edges reduce the spark plug voltage by as much as 50%.

Check and adjust the spark plug gap immediately before installation. The ground electrode (the L-shaped one connected to the body of the plug) must be parallel to the center electrode and the specified size wire gauge (see Tune-Up Specifications) should pass through the gap with a slight drag. Al-

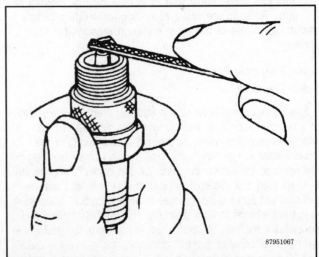

Fig. 66 Spark plugs that are in good condition can be filed and re-used

ways check the gap on new plugs, too; since they are not always set correctly at the factory.

Do not use a flat feeler gauge when measuring the gap, because the reading will be inaccurate. Wire gapping tools usually have a bending tool attached. Use that to adjust the side electrode until the proper distance is obtained. Absolutely never bend the center electrode. Also, be careful not to bend the side electrode too far or too often; it may weaken and break off within the engine, requiring removal of the cylinder head to retrieve it.

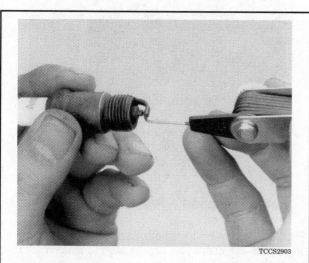

Fig. 67 Always use a wire gauge to check the electrode gap on used plugs

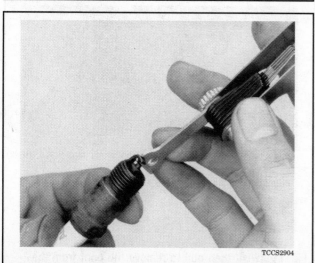

Fig. 68 Adjust the gap by bending the side electrode very slightly towards or away from the center electrode

INSTALLATION

1. Inspect the spark plugs and clean or replace, as necessary. Inspect the spark plug boot for tears or damage. If a damaged boot is found, the spark plug wire must be replaced.

➡**Although an effort has been made to supply you with representative gap specifications, the spark plug gap will vary based on the engine and emission package with which your vehicle is equipped. Refer to the underhood emission control label to determine the proper specification for your vehicle.**

2. Using a feeler gauge, check and adjust the spark plug gap to specification. When using a gauge, the proper size should pass between the electrodes with a slight drag. The next larger size should not be able to pass while the next smaller size should pass freely.

✳✳WARNING

Do not use the spark plug socket to thread the plugs. Always thread the plug by hand to prevent the possibility of cross-threading and damaging the cylinder head bore.

3. Lubricate the spark plug threads with a drop of clean engine oil, then carefully start the spark plugs by hand and tighten a few turns until a socket is needed to continue tightening the plug. Do not apply the same amount of force you would use for a bolt; just snug them in. If a torque wrench is available, tighten the plugs to 11-15 ft. lbs. (15-20 Nm) for plugs with a tapered seat. For plugs without a tapered seat, tighten to 25 ft. lbs. (34 Nm).

➡**While over-tightening the spark plug is to be avoided, under-tightening is just as bad. If combustion gases leak past the threads, the spark plug will overheat and rapid electrode wear will result.**

4. Install the wires on their respective plugs. Make sure the wires are firmly connected. You will be able to feel or hear them click into place.
5. Connect the negative battery cable.

Spark Plug Wires

TESTING

Every 15,000 miles (24,000 km), inspect the spark plug wires for burns, cuts, or breaks in the insulation. Check the boots and the nipples on the distributor cap or ignition coil. Replace any damaged wiring.

Every 45,000 miles (72,000 km) or so, the resistance of the wires should be checked with an ohmmeter. Wires with excessive resistance will cause misfiring, and may make the engine difficult to start in damp weather. Generally, the useful life of the cables is 45,000-60,000 miles (72,000-96,000 km).

To check resistance, remove the distributor cap, leaving the wires in place. Connect one lead of an ohmmeter to an electrode within the cap; connect the other lead to the corresponding spark plug terminal (remove it from the spark plug for this test). Replace any wire which shows a resistance over 30,000 ohms. Generally speaking, it is preferable that resistance be below 25,000 ohms, but 30,000 ohms must be considered the outer limit of acceptability. It should be remembered that resistance is also a function of length; the longer the wire, the greater the resistance. Thus, if the wires on your car are longer than the factory originals, resistance will be higher, quite possible outside these limits.

Wire length can therefore be used to determine appropriate resistance values:

- 0-15 in. (0-38cm) — 3,000-10,000 ohms
- 15-25 in. (38-64cm) — 4,000-15,000 ohms
- 25-35 in. (64-89cm) — 6,000-20,000 ohms
- Wire over 35 in. (89cm) — 25,000 ohms

REMOVAL & INSTALLATION

➡**If all of the wires must be disconnected from the spark plugs or from the distributor at the same time, be sure to tag the wires to assure proper reconnection.**

When installing a new set of spark plug wires, replace the wires one at a time so there will be no mix-up. Start by replacing the longest cable first. Install the boot firmly over the spark plug. Route the wire exactly the same as the original. Insert the nipple firmly onto the tower on the distributor cap, then install the cap cover and latches to secure the wires. Be sure to apply silicone dielectric compound to the spark plug wire boots and tower connectors prior to installation.

Distributor Cap and Rotor

REMOVAL & INSTALLATION

▶ **See Figures 69, 70, 71, 72, 73, 74 and 75**

1. Disconnect the negative battery cable.
2. If necessary, detach the wiring connector from the distributor.
3. Remove the retainer and spark plug wires from the cap. If there is no wire retainer, be sure to tag all of the wires before disconnecting them from the distributor cap. Tagging the wires will help preserve the proper firing order and greatly ease cap installation.
4. If retained by spring loaded locktabs, depress, twist and release the distributor cap-to-housing locktabs, then lift off the cap assembly. Most integral coil distributor caps will be retained by two or four spring loaded locktabs.
5. If retained by mounting screws, loosen the screws, then remove the cap from the distributor assembly.

➡**Although most rotors can only be installed in one direction, it is still wise to note the position of the rotor before remove to assure proper installation and ignition timing.**

6. Note the position of the rotor, unfasten the attaching screws, if applicable, then remove the rotor.

To install:

7. Install the rotor in the position noted earlier, then secure using the retaining screws.

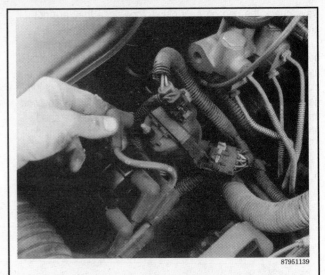
Fig. 69 Detach the coil wire — 1988 2.0L Sunbird shown

Fig. 70 If necessary to remove any of the spark plug wires from the distributor cap, be sure to matchmark or tag them first

Fig. 71 Twist, then pull to remove the boot from the cap

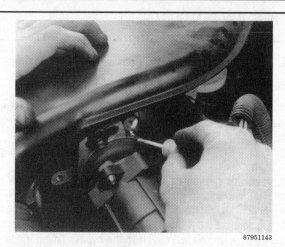

Fig. 72 On some vehicles, it will help to matchmark the position of the distributor to the housing, as on the 1988 Sunbird

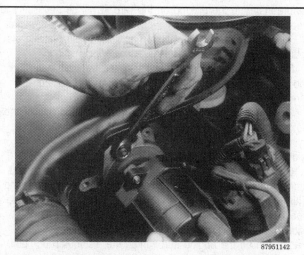

Fig. 73 Unfasten the mounting bolts or screws, then remove the distributor cap

Fig. 74 Matchmark the position of the rotor to ensure correct installation, then . . .

Fig. 75 . . . remove the rotor from the engine

8. Position the distributor cap to the housing, then secure using the housing retainers.

9. Fasten the spark plugs and retainer to the cap. If no wire retainer is used, carefully connect the wires to the cap as tagged during removal.

10. Attach the wiring connector to the distributor, as applicable.

11. Connect the negative battery cable.

Ignition Timing

GENERAL INFORMATION

➡️**Late model vehicles, both 4 cylinder and 6 cylinder engines, have Distributorless Ignition Systems (DIS). Because the reluctor wheel is an integral part of the crankshaft, and the crankshaft sensor is mounted in a fixed position, timing adjustment is not possible.**

Basic ignition timing is critical to the proper operation of the Electronic Spark Control (ESC) system. Always follow the Vehicle Emission Control Information (VECI) label procedures when adjusting ignition timing.

Some engines will incorporate a magnetic timing probe hole for use with special electronic timing equipment. Consult the manufacturer's instructions for the use of this electronic timing equipment.

Ignition timing is the measurement, in degrees of crankshaft rotation, of the point at which the spark plugs fire in each of the cylinders. It is measured in degrees before or after Top Dead Center (TDC) of the compression stroke.

Because it takes a fraction of a second for the spark plug to ignite the mixture in the cylinder, the spark plug must fire a little before the piston reaches TDC. Otherwise, the mixture will not completely ignited as the piston passes TDC and the full power of the explosion will not be used by the engine.

The timing measurement is given in degrees of crankshaft rotation before the piston reaches TDC (BTDC). If the setting for the ignition timing is 5° BTDC, the spark plug must fire 5°

before each piston reaches TDC. This only holds true, however, when the engine is at idle speed.

As the engine speed increases, the pistons go faster. The spark plugs have to ignite the fuel even sooner if it is to be completely ignited when the piston reaches TDC.

If the ignition is set too far advanced (BTDC), the ignition and expansion of the fuel in the cylinder will occur too soon and tend to force the piston down while it is still traveling up. This causes engine ping. If the ignition spark is set too far retarded, after TDC (ATDC), the piston will have already passed TDC and started on its way down when the fuel is ignited. This will cause the piston to be forced down for only a portion of its travel. This will result in poor engine performance and lack of power.

Ignition timing for this engine should be accomplished using the averaging method in which the timing of each cylinder can be brought into closer agreement with the base timing specification.

The averaging method involves the use of a double notched crankshaft pulley. When timing the engine, the coil wire, instead of the Number 1 plug wire, should be used to trigger the timing light. The notch for the No. 1 cylinder is scribed across all three edges of the double sheave pulley. Another notch located 180° away from the No. 1 cylinder notch is scribed only across the center section of the pulley to make it distinguishable from the No. 1 cylinder notch.

Since the trigger signal for the timing light is picked up at the coil wire, each spark firing results in a flash from the timing light. A slight jiggling of the timing notch may be apparent since each cylinder firing is being displayed. Optimum timing of all cylinders is accomplished by centering the total apparent notch width about the correct timing specification.

There are three basic types of timing light available. The first is a simple neon bulb with two wire connections (one for the spark plug and one for the plug wire, connecting the light in series). This type of light is quite dim, and must be held closely to the marks to be seen, but it is quite inexpensive. The second type of light operates from the car's battery. Two alligator clips connect to the battery terminals, while a third wire connects to the spark plug with an adapter. This type of light is more expensive, but the xenon bulb provides a nice bright flash which can even be seen in sunlight. The third type replaces the battery source with 110 volt house current. Some timing lights have other functions built into them, such as dwell meters, tachometers, or remote starting switches. These are convenient, in that they reduce the tangle of wires under the hood, but may duplicate the functions of tools you already have.

Because your car has electronic ignition, you should use a timing light with an inductive pickup. This pickup simply clamps around the Number 1 spark plug wire (in this case, the coil wire), eliminating the adapter. It is not susceptible to crossfiring or false triggering, which may occur with a conventional light due to the greater voltages produced by HEI.

INSPECTION & ADJUSTMENT

1.8L and 2.0L OHV Engines

1982-86 VEHICLES

1. Refer to the instructions on the emission control sticker inside the engine compartment. follow all instructions on the label.

2. Locate the timing marks on the crankshaft pulley and the front of the engine.

3. Clean off the marks so that you can see them. Chalk or white paint will help to make them more visible.

4. Attach a tachometer to the engine as detailed previously.

5. Disconnect the 4-terminal EST connector at the distributor so that the engine will switch to the bypass timing mode (please refer to Section 4 for more information).

6. Attach a timing light as per the manufacturer's instructions. Clamp the inductive pick-up around the HIGH TENSION COIL WIRE (not the No. 1 spark plug wire) at the distributor. Before installing the pick-up on the wire, it will be necessary to peel back the protective plastic cover which encases the wire.

7. Loosen the distributor clamp bolt slightly so that the distributor may be rotated as necessary to adjust timing.

8. Check that all wires are clear of the fan and then start the engine. Allow the engine to reach normal operating temperature.

9. Aim the timing light at the marks. A slight jiggling of the notch on the pulley may appear due to the fact that each cylinder is being displayed as it fires. The apparent notch width cannot be reduced by a timing adjustment.

10. Center the total apparent notch width about the correct timing mark on the indicator by rotating the distributor housing. This will insure that the average cylinder timing is as close to specifications as possible. Once again, the apparent notch width cannot be reduced by timing adjustment.

11. Turn off the engine and tighten the distributor lock bolt. Start the engine and recheck the timing. Sometimes the distributor will move a little during the tightening process. If the ignition timing is within 1° of the correct setting, that is close enough; a tolerance of up to 2° is permitted by the manufacturer.

12. Turn off the engine and disconnect the timing light and the tachometer. Reconnect the 4-terminal EST connector.

2.0L (VIN 1) 2.2L, 2.8L and 3.1L Engines

1987-96 VEHICLES

The ignition timing on engines with distributorless ignitions, is controlled by the Electronic Control Module (ECM) or Powertrain Control Module (PCM), as applicable. No adjustments are possible.

2.0L (VIN K and M) Engines

1. Refer to the underhood emission control label and follow all of the timing instructions if they differ from below.

2. Warm the engine to normal operating temperature.

3. Place the transmission in N or P. Apply the parking brake and block wheels.

4. Air conditioning, cooling fan and choke must be OFF. Do not remove the air cleaner, except as noted.

5. Ground the ALCL connector under the dash by installing a jumper wire between the **A** and **B** terminals. The Check Engine light should begin flashing.

6. Connect an inductive timing light to the No. 1 spark plug wire lead and record timing.

7. Connect an inductive timing light to the No. 4 spark plug wire lead and record timing.

8. Add the 2 timing numbers and divide by 2 to obtain "average timing". For example: No. 1 timing = 4 degrees and No. 4 timing = 8 degrees; $4 + 8 = 12 / 2 = 6$ degrees average timing. If a change is necessary, subtract the average timing from the timing specification to determine the amount of timing change to No. 1 cylinder. For example: if the timing specification is 8 degrees and the average timing is 6 degrees, advance the No. 1 cylinder 2 degrees to set the timing.

9. To correct the timing, loosen the distributor hold-down clamp, adjust the distributor and retighten the hold-down bolt.

10. Once the timing is properly set, remove the jumper wire from the ALCL connector.

11. If necessary to clear the ECM memory, disconnect the ECM harness from the positive battery pigtail for 10 seconds with the key in the **OFF** position.

Idle Speed and Mixture Adjustments

CARBURETED ENGINES

All carbureted vehicles are equipped with an Idle Speed Control (ISC) motor which is in turn controlled by the Electronic Control Module (ECM). All idle speeds are programmed into the ECM's memory and then relayed to the ISC motor as any given situation requires. Curb idle is pre-set at the factory and not routinely adjustable. Although curb idle is not to be adjusted under normal conditions, it can be adjusted, but only upon replacement of the ISC (for further details, refer to Section 5).

The idle mixture screws are concealed under staked-in plugs. Idle mixture is not considered to be a normal tune-up procedure, because of the sensitivity of emission control adjustments. Mixture adjustment requires not only the special tools with which to remove the concealing plugs, but also the addition of an artificial enrichment substance (generally propane) which must be introduced into the carburetor by means of a finely calibrated metering valve. These tools are not generally available and require a certain amount of expertise to use, therefore, mixture adjustments are purposely not covered in this book. If you suspect that your car's carburetor requires a mixture adjustment, we strongly recommend that the job be referred to a qualified service technician.

FUEL INJECTED ENGINES

The fuel injected vehicles are controlled by a computer which supplies the correct amount of fuel during all engine operating conditions; no adjustment is necessary.

Air Conditioning

➡Be sure to consult the laws in your area before servicing the air conditioning system. In most areas, it is illegal to perform repairs involving refrigerant unless the work is done by a certified technician. Also, it is quite likely that you will not be able to purchase refrigerant without proof of certification.

SAFETY PRECAUTIONS

There are two major hazards associated with air conditioning systems and they both relate to the refrigerant gas. First, the refrigerant gas (R-12 or R-134a) is an extremely cold substance. When exposed to air, it will instantly freeze any surface it comes in contact with, including your eyes. The other hazard relates to fire (if your vehicle is equipped with R-12. Although normally non-toxic, the R-12 gas becomes highly poisonous in the presence of an open flame. One good whiff of the vapor formed by burning R-12 can be fatal. Keep all forms of fire (including cigarettes) well clear of the air conditioning system.

Because of the inherent dangers involved with working on air conditioning systems, these safety precautions must be strictly followed.

• Avoid contact with a charged refrigeration system, even when working on another part of the air conditioning system or vehicle. If a heavy tool comes into contact with a section of tubing or a heat exchanger, it can easily cause the relatively soft material to rupture.

• When it is necessary to apply force to a fitting which contains refrigerant, as when checking that all system couplings are securely tightened, use a wrench on both parts of the fitting involved, if possible. This will avoid putting torque on refrigerant tubing. (It is also advisable to use tube or line wrenches when tightening these flare nut fittings.)

➡R-12 refrigerant is a chlorofluorocarbon which, when released into the atmosphere, can contribute to the depletion of the ozone layer in the upper atmosphere. Ozone filters out harmful radiation from the sun.

• Do not attempt to discharge the system without the proper tools. Precise control is possible only when using the service gauges and a proper A/C refrigerant recovery station. Wear protective gloves when connecting or disconnecting service gauge hoses.

• Discharge the system only in a well ventilated area, as high concentrations of the gas which might accidentally escape can exclude oxygen and act as an anesthetic. When leak testing or soldering, this is particularly important, as toxic gas is formed when R-12 contacts any flame.

• Never start a system without first verifying that both service valves are properly installed, and that all fittings throughout the system are snugly connected.

• Avoid applying heat to any refrigerant line or storage vessel. Charging may be aided by using water heated to less than 125°F (50°C) to warm the refrigerant container. Never allow a refrigerant storage container to sit out in the sun, or near any other source of heat, such as a radiator or heater.

GASOLINE ENGINE TUNE-UP SPECIFICATIONS

Year	Engine ID/VIN	Engine Displacement Liters (cc)	Spark Plugs Gap (in.)	Ignition Timing (deg.) MT	AT	Fuel Pump (psi)	Idle Speed (rpm) MT	AT	Valve Clearance In.	Ex.
1982	G	1.8 (1819)	0.045 ①	12B	12B	4.5-6	②	②	HYD	HYD
	O	1.8 (1819)	0.060	8	8B	9-13	②	②	HYD	HYD
	B	2.0 (1998)	②	②	②	4.5-6	②	②	HYD	HYD
1983	O	1.8 (1819)	0.060	8	8B	9-13	②	②	HYD	HYD
	J	1.8 (1819)	0.035	②	②	30-40	②	②	HYD	HYD
	P	2.0 (1998)	0.035	②	②	12	②	②	HYD	HYD
	B	2.0 (1998)	0.035	-	12B	12	②	②	HYD	HYD
1984	O	1.8 (1819)	0.060	8	8B	9-13	②	②	HYD	HYD
	J	1.8 (1819)	0.035	②	②	30-40	②	②	HYD	HYD
	P	2.0 (1998)	0.035	②	②	12	②	②	HYD	HYD
1985	O	1.8 (1819)	0.060	8B	8B	9-13	③	③	HYD	HYD
	J	1.8 (1819)	0.035	②	②	26-32	③	③	HYD	HYD
	P	2.0 (1998)	0.035	NA	NA	12	NA	NA	HYD	HYD
	W	2.8 (2835)	0.045	NA	NA	9-13	NA	NA	HYD	HYD
1986	O	1.8 (1819)	0.060	8B	8B	9-13	③	③	HYD	HYD
	J	1.8 (1819)	0.035	②	②	26-32	③	③	HYD	HYD
	P	2.0 (1998)	0.035	NA	NA	12	NA	NA	HYD	HYD
	W	2.8 (2835)	0.045	NA	NA	9-13	NA	NA	HYD	HYD
1987	K	2.0 (1998)	0.045	8B	8B	9-13	③	③	HYD	HYD
	M	2.0 (1998)	0.035	8B	8B	41-47	③	③	HYD	HYD
	1	2.0 (1998)	0.035	②	②	10-12	③	③	HYD	HYD
	W	2.8 (2835)	0.045	②	②	9-13	③	③	HYD	HYD
1988	K	2.0 (1998)	0.045	8B	8B	9-13	③	③	HYD	HYD
	M	2.0 (1998)	0.035	8B	8B	25-30	③	③	HYD	HYD
	1	2.0 (1998)	0.035	②	②	10-12	③	③	HYD	HYD
	W	2.8 (2835)	0.045	②	②	9-13	③	③	HYD	HYD
1989	K	2.0 (1998)	0.045	8B	8B	9-13	③	③	HYD	HYD
	M	2.0 (1998)	0.035	8B	8B	25-30	③	③	HYD	HYD
	1	2.0 (1998)	0.035	②	②	10-12	③	③	HYD	HYD
	W	2.8 (2835)	0.045	②	②	9-13	③	③	HYD	HYD
1990	K	2.0 (1988)	0.045	8B	8B	9-13	③	③	HYD	HYD
	M	2.0 (1998)	0.035	8B	8B	35-38	③	③	HYD	HYD
	G	2.2 (2180)	0.035	②	②	9-13	③	③	HYD	HYD
	T	3.1 (3130)	0.045	②	②	34-47	③	③	HYD	HYD
1991	K	2.0 (1998)	0.045	②	②	9-13	600	500	HYD	HYD
	G	2.2 (2180)	0.035	②	②	9-13	③	③	HYD	HYD
	T	3.1 (3130)	0.045	②	②	41-47	③	③	HYD	HYD
1992	H	2.0 (1998)	0.045	②	②	41-47	600	600	HYD	HYD
	G	2.2 (2180)	0.035	②	②	9-13	③	③	HYD	HYD
	T	3.1 (3130)	0.045	②	②	41-47	③	③	HYD	HYD
1993	H	2.0 (1998)	0.045	②	②	41-47	③	③	HYD	HYD
	4	2.2 (2180)	0.045	②	②	41-47	③	③	HYD	HYD
	T	3.1 (3136)	0.045	②	②	41-47	675	675	HYD	HYD
1994	H	2.0 (1998)	0.045	②	②	41-47	③	③	HYD	HYD
	4	2.2 (2180)	0.045	②	②	41-47	③	③	HYD	HYD
	T	3.1 (3136)	0.045	②	②	41-47	③	③	HYD	HYD

87951505

GASOLINE ENGINE TUNE-UP SPECIFICATIONS

Year	Engine ID/VIN	Engine Displacement Liters (cc)	Spark Plugs Gap (in.)	Ignition Timing (deg.)		Fuel Pump (psi)	Idle Speed (rpm)		Valve Clearance	
				MT	AT		MT	AT	In.	Ex.
1995	4	2.2 (2195)	0.060	②	②	41-47	③	③	HYD	HYD
	D	2.3 (2262)	0.060	②	②	41-47	③	③	HYD	HYD
1996	4	2.2 (2195)	0.060	②	②	41-47	③	③	HYD	HYD
	T	2.4 (2392)	0.060	②	②	41-47	③	③	HYD	HYD

NOTE: The Vehicle Emission Control Information label often reflects specification changes made during production. The label figures must be used if they differ from those in this chart.

B - Before top dead center

HYD - Hydraulic

NA - Not available

1 Certain models may use 0.035 in. gap. See the underhood specifications sticker to be sure

2 Refer to the Vehicles Emission Control Information label

3 Idle speed is maintained by the computer control module (ECM/PCM). There is no recommended adjustment procedure.

87951506

* Always wear goggles to protect your eyes when working on a system. If refrigerant contacts the eyes, it is advisable in all cases to consult a physician immediately.

* Frostbite from liquid refrigerant should be treated by first gradually warming the area with cool water, and then gently applying petroleum jelly. A physician should be consulted.

* Always keep refrigerant drum fittings capped when not in use. If the container is equipped with a safety cap to protect the valve, make sure the cap is in place when the can is not being used. Avoid sudden shock to the drum, which might occur from dropping it, or from banging a heavy tool against it. Never carry a drum in the passenger compartment of a vehicle.

* Always completely discharge the system into a suitable recovery unit before painting the vehicle (if the paint is to be baked on), or before welding anywhere near refrigerant lines.

* When servicing the system, minimize the time that any refrigerant line or fitting is open to the air in order to prevent moisture or dirt from entering the system. Contaminants such as moisture or dirt can damage internal system components. Always replace O-rings on lines or fittings which are disconnected. Prior to installation coat, but do not soak, replacement O-rings with suitable compressor oil.

GENERAL SERVICING PROCEDURES

➡It is recommended, and possibly required by law, that a qualified technician perform the following services.

❉❉WARNING

Some of the vehicles covered by this manual may be equipped with R-134a refrigerant systems, rather than R-12. Be ABSOLUTELY SURE what type of system you are working on before attempting to add refrigerant. Use of the wrong refrigerant or oil will cause damage to the system.

The most important aspect of air conditioning service is the maintenance of a pure and adequate charge of refrigerant in the system. A refrigeration system cannot function properly if a significant percentage of the charge is lost. Leaks are common because the severe vibration encountered underhood in an automobile can easily cause a sufficient cracking or loosening of the air conditioning fittings; allowing, the extreme operating pressures of the system to force refrigerant out.

The problem can be understood by considering what happens to the system as it is operated with a continuous leak. Because the expansion valve regulates the flow of refrigerant to the evaporator, the level of refrigerant there is fairly constant. The receiver/drier stores any excess refrigerant, and so a loss will first appear there as a reduction in the level of liquid. As this level nears the bottom of the vessel, some refrigerant vapor bubbles will begin to appear in the stream of liquid supplied to the expansion valve. This vapor decreases the capacity of the expansion valve very little as the valve opens to compensate for its presence. As the quantity of liquid in the condenser decreases, the operating pressure will drop there and throughout the high side of the system. As the refrigerant continues to be expelled, the pressure available to force the liquid through the expansion valve will continue to decrease, and, eventually, the valve's orifice will prove to be too much of a restriction for adequate flow even with the needle fully withdrawn.

At this point, low side pressure will start to drop, and a severe reduction in cooling capacity, marked by freeze-up of the evaporator coil, will result. Eventually, the operating pressure of the evaporator will be lower than the pressure of the atmosphere surrounding it, and air will be drawn into the system wherever there are leaks in the low side.

Because all atmospheric air contains at least some moisture, water will enter the system mixing with the refrigerant and oil. Trace amounts of moisture will cause sludging of the oil, and corrosion of the system. Saturation and clogging of the filter/drier, and freezing of the expansion valve orifice will eventually result. As air fills the system to a greater and greater extent, it will interfere more and more with the normal flows of refrigerant and heat.

From this description, it should be obvious that much of the repairman's focus in on detecting leaks, repairing them, and then restoring the purity and quantity of the refrigerant charge.

A list of general rules should be followed in addition to all safety precautions:

• Keep all tools as clean and dry as possible.

• Thoroughly purge the service gauges/hoses of air and moisture before connecting them to the system. Keep them capped when not in use.

• Thoroughly clean any refrigerant fitting before disconnecting it, in order to minimize the entrance of dirt into the system.

• Plan any operation that requires opening the system beforehand, in order to minimize the length of time it will be exposed to open air. Cap or seal the open ends to minimize the entrance of foreign material.

• When adding oil, pour it through an extremely clean and dry tube or funnel. Keep the oil capped whenever possible. Do not use oil that has not been kept tightly sealed.

• Purchase refrigerant intended for use only in automatic air conditioning systems.

• Completely evacuate any system that has been opened for service, or that has leaked sufficiently to draw in moisture and air. This requires evacuating air and moisture with a good vacuum pump for at least one hour. If a system has been open for a considerable length of time it may be advisable to evacuate the system for up to 12 hours (overnight).

• Use a wrench on both halves of a fitting that is to be disconnected, so as to avoid placing torque on any of the refrigerant lines.

• When overhauling a compressor, pour some of the oil into a clean glass and inspect it. If there is evidence of dirt, metal particles, or both, flush all refrigerant components with clean refrigerant before evacuating and recharging the system. In addition, if metal particles are present, the compressor should be replaced.

• Schrader valves may leak only when under full operating pressure. Therefore, if leakage is suspected but cannot be located, operate the system with a full charge of refrigerant and look for leaks from all Schrader valves. Replace any faulty valves.

Additional Preventive Maintenance

USING THE SYSTEM

The easiest and most important preventive maintenance for your A/C system is to be sure that it is used on a regular basis. Running the system for five minutes each month (no matter what the season) will help assure that the seals and all internal components remain lubricated.

ANTIFREEZE

▶ See Figure 76

In order to prevent heater core freeze-up during A/C operation, it is necessary to maintain a proper antifreeze protection. Use a hand-held antifreeze tester (hydrometer) to periodically check the condition of the antifreeze in your engine's cooling system.

➡Antifreeze should not be used longer than the manufacturer specifies.

RADIATOR CAP

For efficient operation of an air conditioned vehicle's cooling system, the radiator cap should have a holding pressure which

Fig. 76 An antifreeze tester can be use to determine the freezing and boiling level of the coolant in your vehicle

meets manufacturer's specifications. A cap which fails to hold these pressures should be replaced.

CONDENSER

Any obstruction of or damage to the condenser configuration will restrict the air flow which is essential to its efficient operation. It is therefore a good rule to keep this unit clean and in proper physical shape.

➡Bug screens which are mounted in front of the condenser (unless they are original equipment) are regarded as obstructions.

CONDENSATION DRAIN TUBE

This single molded drain tube expels the condensation, which accumulates on the bottom of the evaporator housing, into the engine compartment. If this tube is obstructed, the air conditioning performance can be restricted and condensation buildup can spill over onto the vehicle's floor.

SYSTEM INSPECTION

➡R-12 refrigerant is a chlorofluorocarbon which, when released into the atmosphere, can contribute to the depletion of the ozone layer in the upper atmosphere. Ozone filters out harmful radiation from the sun.

The easiest and often most important check for the air conditioning system consists of a visual inspection of the system components. Visually inspect the air conditioning system for refrigerant leaks, damaged compressor clutch, compressor drive belt tension and condition, plugged evaporator drain tube, blocked condenser fins, disconnected or broken wires, blown fuses, corroded connections and poor insulation.

A refrigerant leak will usually appear as an oily residue at the leakage point in the system. The oily residue soon picks up dust or dirt particles from the surrounding air and appears greasy. Through time, this will build up and appear to be a heavy dirt impregnated grease. Most leaks are caused by damaged or missing O-ring seals at the component connections, damaged charging valve cores or missing service gauge port caps.

For a thorough visual and operational inspection, check the following:

1. Check the surface of the radiator and condenser for dirt, leaves or other material which might block air flow.

2. Check for kinks in hoses and lines. Check the system for leaks.

3. Make sure the drive belt is under the proper tension. When the air conditioning is operating, make sure the drive belt is free of noise or slippage.

4. Make sure the blower motor operates at all appropriate positions, then check for distribution of the air from all outlets with the blower on **HIGH**.

➡️**Keep in mind that under conditions of high humidity, air discharged from the A/C vents may not feel as cold as expected, even if the system is working properly. This is because the vaporized moisture in humid air retains heat more effectively than does dry air, making the humid air more difficult to cool.**

5. Make sure the air passage selection lever is operating correctly. Start the engine and warm it to normal operating temperature, then make sure the hot/cold selection lever is operating correctly.

DISCHARGING, EVACUATING AND CHARGING

Discharging, evacuating and charging the air conditioning system must be performed by a properly trained and certified mechanic in a facility equipped with refrigerant recovery/recycling equipment that meets SAE standards for the type of system to be serviced.

If you don't have access to the necessary equipment, we recommend that you take your vehicle to a reputable service station to have the work done. If you still wish to perform repairs on the vehicle, have them discharge the system, then take your vehicle home and perform the necessary work. When you are finished, return the vehicle to the station for evacuation and charging. Just be sure to cap ALL A/C system fittings immediately after opening them and keep them protected until the system is recharged.

Windshield Wipers

For maximum effectiveness and longest element life, the windshield and wiper blades should be kept clean. Dirt, tree sap, road tar and so on will cause streaking, smearing and blade deterioration if left on the glass. It is advisable to wash the windshield carefully with a commercial glass cleaner at least once a month. Wipe off the rubber blades with a wet rag afterwards. Do not attempt to move the wipers back and forth by hand; damage to the motor and drive mechanism will result.

To inspect and/or replace the wiper blades, place the wiper switch in the LOW speed position and the ignition switch on the **ACC** position. When the wiper blades are approximately vertical on the windshield, turn the ignition switch to **OFF**.

Examine the wiper blades. If the blades are found to be cracked, broken or torn, they should be replaced immediately. Replacement intervals will vary with usage, although ozone deterioration usually limits blade life to about one year. If the wiper pattern is smeared or streaked, or if the blade chatters across the glass, the blades should be replaced. It is easiest and most sensible to replace them in pairs.

BLADE REPLACEMENT

▶ **See Figure 77**

Most original wiper blades found on J-body vehicles are easily replaceable. The wiper blade slide from the arm assembly once the catch is released (the arm-to-blade latch pin is depressed). If your vehicle is equipped with after market blades, there are several different types of refills and your car may have any kind. Aftermarket blades and arms rarely use the exact same type blade or refill as the original equipment. Here are some common aftermarket blades, not all may be available for your vehicle.

The Anco® type has two release buttons, approximately 1/3 of the way up from the ends of the blade frame. Pushing the buttons down releases a lock and allows the rubber blade to be removed from the frame. The new refill slides back into the frame and locks in place.

Some Trico® refills are removed by locating where the metal backing strip or the refill is wider. Insert a small screwdriver blade between the frame and metal backing strip. Press down to release the refill from the retaining tab.

Other types is Trico® refills have two metal tabs which are unlocked by squeezing them together. The rubber filler can then be withdrawn from the frame jaws. A new refill is installed by inserting it into the front frame jaws and sliding it rearward to engage the remaining jaws. There are usually four jaws; be certain when installing that the refill is engaged in all of them. At the end of its travel, the tabs will lock into place on the front jaws of the wiper blade frame.

Another type of refill is made from polycarbonate. The refill has a simple locking device at one end which flexes downward out of the groove into which the jaws of the holder fit, allowing easy release. By sliding the new refill through all the jaws and pushing through the slight resistance when it reaches the end of its travel, the refill will lock into position.

To replace the Tridon® refill, it is necessary to remove the wiper arm or blade. This refill has a plastic backing strip with a notch about 1 in. (25mm) from the end. Hold the blade (frame) on a hard surface so the frame is tightly bowed. Grip the tip of the backing strip and pull up while twisting counterclockwise. The backing strip will snap out of the retaining tab. Do this for the remaining tabs until the refill is free of the arm. The length of these refill is molded into the end and they should be replaced with identical types.

Regardless of the type of refill used, make sure that all the frame jaws are engaged as the refill is pushed into place and locked. If the metal blade holder and frame are allowed to touch the glass during wiper operation, the glass will be scratched.

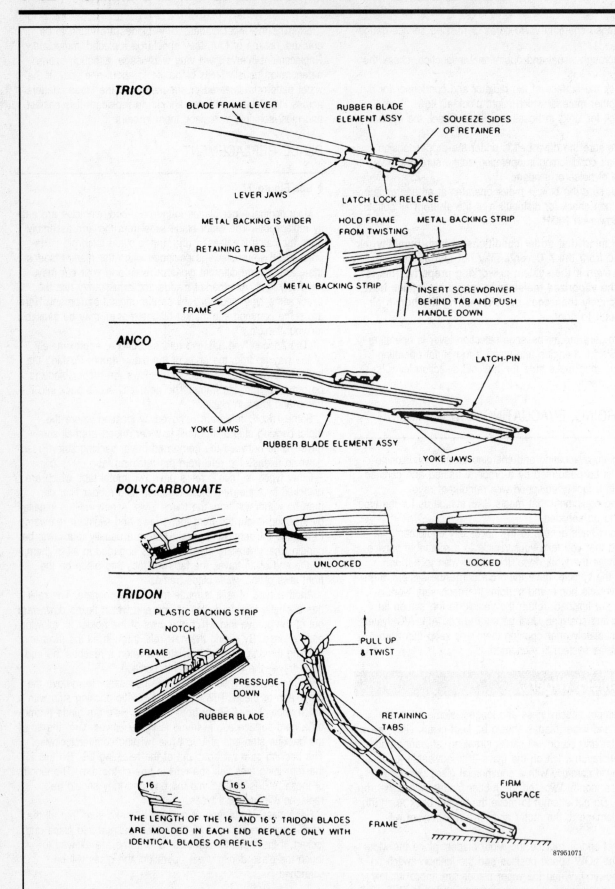

Fig. 77 Your car may be equipped with one of several types of wiper blade inserts

Tires and Wheels

▶ See Figures 78, 79, 80 and 81

Inspect your tires often for signs of improper inflation and uneven wear, which may indicate a need for balancing, rotation or wheel alignment. Check the tires frequently for cuts, stone bruises, abrasions, blister and for objects that may have become embedded in the tread. More frequent inspections are recommended when rapid or extreme temperature changes occur, or where road surfaces are rough and/or occasionally littered with debris. Check the condition of the wheels and replace any that are bent, cracked, severely dented or have excessive run-out.

The tires on your car have built-in wear indicators molded into the bottom of the tread grooves. The indicators will begin to appear as the tire approaches replacement tread depth. Once the indicators are visible across 2 or more adjacent grooves at 3 or more locations, the tires should be replaced.

Wear that occurs only on certain portions of the tires may indicate a particular problem, which when corrected or avoided,

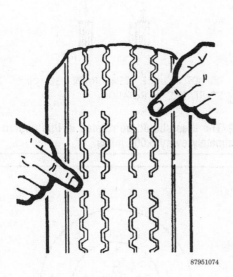

87951074

Fig. 78 If the tires are used beyond the point of tread life, built-in wear indicators will begin to appear as lines across the tread

may significantly extend tire life. Wear that occurs only in the center of the tire indicates either overinflation or heavy acceleration on a drive wheel. Wear occurring at the outer edges of the tire and not at the center may indicate underinflation, excessively hard cornering or a lack of rotation. If wear occurs at only the outer edge of the tire, there may be a problem with the wheel alignment or the tire, when constructed, contained a non-uniformity defect.

TIRE ROTATION

▶ See Figures 82 and 83

✴✴WARNING

Tighten the wheel lug nuts to 100-103 ft. lbs. (136-140 Nm), in the pattern indicated in the accompanying figure. Avoid overtightening the lug nuts to prevent damage to the brake disc or drum. Alloy wheels can also be cracked by overtightening. Use of a torque wrench is a must when tightening the lug nuts.

Tire rotation is recommended approximately every 6,000 miles (9,600 km), to obtain maximum tire wear. The pattern shown does not include the "temporary use only" spare. Due to their design, radial tires tend to wear faster in the shoulder area particularly in front positions. Radial tires in non-drive locations may develop an irregular wear pattern that can increase tire noise if not rotated. This makes regular rotation especially necessary. Snow tires sometimes have directional arrows molded into the side of the carcass; the arrow shows the direction of rotation. They will wear very rapidly if the rotation is reversed. Studded tires will lose their studs if their rotational direction is reversed.

➡ **Mark the wheel position or direction or rotation on radial tires or studded snow tires before removing them.**

TIRE DESIGN

For maximum service life, tires should be used in sets of five, except on vehicles equipped with a space-saver spare tire. Do not mix tires of different designs, such as steel belted radial, fiberglass belted or bias/belted, or tires of different sizes, such as P165SR-14 and P185SR-14.

Conventional bias ply tires are constructed so that the cords run bead-to-bead at an angle (bias). Alternate plies run at an opposite angle. This type of construction gives rigidity to both tread and sidewall. Bias/belted tires are similar in construction to conventional bias ply tires. Belts run at an angel and also at a 90° angle to the bead, as in the radial tire. Tread life in improved considerably over the conventional bias tire. The radial tire differs in construction, but instead of the carcass plies running at an angle of 90° to each other, they run at an angle of 90° to the bead. This gives the tread a great deal of rigidity and the sidewall a great deal of flexibility and accounts for the characteristic bulge associated with radial tires.

All General Motors vehicles are capable of using radial tires which are the recommended type for all years. If radial tires are used, tires sizes and wheel diameters should be selected

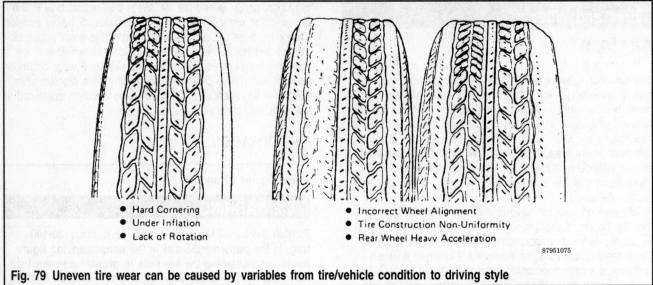

- Hard Cornering
- Under Inflation
- Lack of Rotation

- Incorrect Wheel Alignment
- Tire Construction Non-Uniformity
- Rear Wheel Heavy Acceleration

87951075

Fig. 79 Uneven tire wear can be caused by variables from tire/vehicle condition to driving style

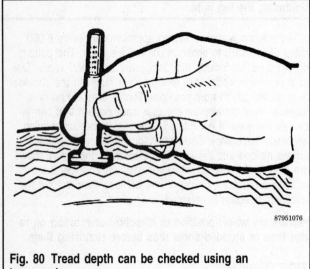

87951076

Fig. 80 Tread depth can be checked using an inexpensive gauge

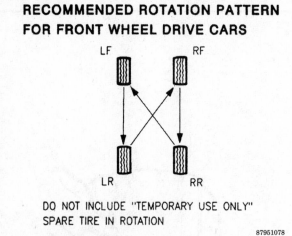

RECOMMENDED ROTATION PATTERN FOR FRONT WHEEL DRIVE CARS

LF   RF

LR   RR

DO NOT INCLUDE "TEMPORARY USE ONLY" SPARE TIRE IN ROTATION

87951078

Fig. 82 The tires should be rotated in this pattern approximately every 6,000 miles

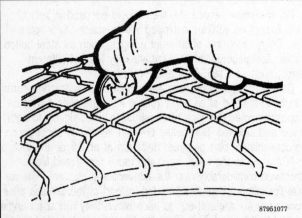

87951077

Fig. 81 If a gauge is not available, a penny may be used to check for tire tread depth; when the top of Lincoln's head is visible, it is probably time for a new tire

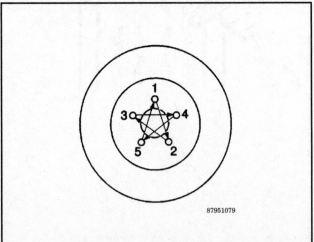

87951079

Fig. 83 This sequence must be used when loosening and tightening the wheel lug nuts

to maintain ground clearance and tire load capacity equivalent to the minimum specified tire. Radial tires should always be used in sets of 5 if the spare is a conventional tire. In an emergency, radial tires can be used with caution on the rear axle only. If this is done, both tires on the rear should be of radial design.

➡**Radial tires should never be used on only the front axle as they can adversely effect steering if tires of different designs are mixed.**

When buying new tires, give some thought to the following points, especially if you are considering a switch to larger tires or a different profile series:

1. All four tires must be of the same construction type. This rule cannot be violated, Radial, bias, and bias-belted tires must not be mixed.

2. The wheels should be the correct width for the tire. Tire dealers have charts of tire and rim compatibility. A mis-match will cause sloppy handling and rapid tire wear. The tread width should match the rim width (inside bead to inside bead) within an inch. For radial tires, the rim should be 80% or less of the tire (not tread) width.

3. The height (mounted diameter) of the new tires can change speedometer accuracy, engine speed at a given road speed, fuel mileage, acceleration, and ground clearance. Tire manufacturers furnish full measurement specifications.

4. The spare tire should be usable, at least for short distance and low speed operation, with the new tires.

5. There shouldn't be any body interference when loaded, on bumps, or in turns.

TIRE STORAGE

Store the tires at the proper inflation pressure if they are mounted on wheels. Keep them in a cool dry place, laid on their sides. If the tires are stored in the garage or basement, DO NOT let them stand on a concrete floor; set them on strips of wood.

TIRE INFLATION

▶ **See Figure 84**

Tire inflation may be the most ignored item of auto maintenance. Gasoline mileage can drop as much as 0.8% for every 1 pound/square inch (psi) of under-inflation. Tires should be checked weekly for proper air pressure. A chart, located either in the glove compartment or on the driver's or passenger's door, gives the recommended inflation pressures. Maximum fuel economy and tire life will result if the pressure is maintained at the highest figure given on the chart. Pressures

should be checked before driving since pressure can increase as much as six pounds per square inch (psi) due to heat buildup. It is a good idea to have you own accurate pressure gauge, because not all gauges on service station air pumps can be trusted. When checking pressures, do not neglect the spare tire. Note that most compact spare tires, require a tire pressure considerably higher than that used in the other tires.

While you are about the task of checking air pressure, inspect the tire treads for cuts, bruises and other damage. Check the air valves to be sure that they are tight. Replace any missing valve caps. Dirt and moisture gathering in the valve stem could lead to an early demise of the stem and a subsequent flat tire.

Check the tires for uneven wear that might indicate the need for front end alignment or tire rotation. Tires should be replaced when a tread wear indicator appears as a solid band across the tread.

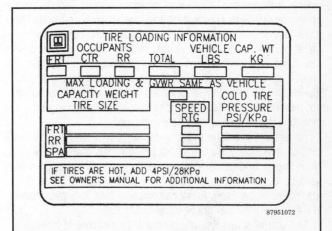

Fig. 84 The tire placard (usually located on the rear face of the driver's door) contains information regarding the tires, including the recommended tire inflation pressure

CARE OF SPECIAL WHEELS

If your car is equipped with aluminum wheels (such as from an aftermarket application), they are normally coated to preserve their appearance. To clean the aluminum wheels, use a mild soap and water solution, then rinse thoroughly with clean water. If you want to use one of the commercially available wheel cleaners, make sure the label indicates that the cleaner is safe for coated wheels. Never use steel wool or any cleaner that contains an abrasive, or use strong detergents that contain high alkaline or caustic agents, as they will damage your wheels.

FLUIDS AND LUBRICANTS

Fluid Disposal

Used fluids such as engine oil, transmission fluid, antifreeze and brake fluid are hazardous waters and must be disposed of properly. Before draining any fluids, consult with your local authorities; in many areas, waste oil, etc.. is being accepted as a part of recycling programs. A number of service stations and auto parts stores are also accepting waste fluids for recycling.

Be sure of the recycling center's policies before draining any fluids, as many will not accept different fluids that have been mixed together, such as oil and antifreeze.

Fuel and Engine Oil Recommendations

FUEL

➡**Some fuel additives contain chemicals that can damage the catalytic converter and/or oxygen sensor. Read all of the labels carefully before using any additive in the engine or fuel system.**

All of the vehicles covered by this manual are designed to run on unleaded fuel. The use of a leaded fuel in a car requiring unleaded fuel will plug the catalytic converter and render it inoperative. It will also increase exhaust backpressure to the point where engine output will be severely reduced. The minimum octane rating of the the unleaded fuel being used must be at least 87, which usually means regular unleaded, but some high performance engines may require higher ratings. Fuel should be selected for the brand and octane which performs best with your engine. Judge a gasoline by its ability to prevent pinging, its engine starting capabilities (cold and hot) and general all weather performance.

As far as the octane rating is concerned, refer to the general engine specifications chart in Section 3 of this manual to find your engine and its compression ratio. If the compression ratio is 9.0:1 or lower, in most cases a regular unleaded grade of gasoline can be used. If the compression ratio is higher than 9.0:1 use a premium grade of unleaded fuel.

The use of a fuel too low in octane (a measure of anti-knock quality) will result in spark knock. Since many factors such as altitude, terrain, air temperature and humidity affect operating efficiency, knocking may result even though the recommended fuel is being used. If persistent knocking occurs, it may be necessary to switch to a higher grade of fuel. Continuous or heavy knocking may result in engine damage.

➡**Your engine's fuel requirement can change with time, mainly due to carbon build-up, which will in turn change the compression ratio. If you engine pings, knocks or diesels (runs with the ignition OFF) switch to a higher grade of fuel. Sometimes, just changing brands will cure the problem. If it becomes necessary to retard the timing from the specifications, don't change it more than a few degrees. Retarded timing will reduce power output and fuel mileage, in addition to making the engine run hotter.**

ENGINE OIL

♦ **See Figure 85**

The SAE (Society of Automotive Engineers) grade number indicates the viscosity of the engine oil, and thus its ability to lubricate at a given temperature. The lower the SAE grade number, the lighter the oil; the lower the viscosity, the easier it is to crank the engine in cold weather. Oil viscosities should be chosen from those oils recommended for the lowest antici-

pated temperatures during the oil change interval. With the proper viscosity, you will be assured of easy cold starting and sufficient engine protection.

Multi-viscosity oils (5W-30, 10W-30, etc..), offer the important advantage of being adaptable to temperature extremes. They allow easy starting at low temperatures, yet they give good protection at high speeds and engine temperatures. This is a decided advantage in changeable climates or in long distance touring.

The American Petroleum Institute (API) designation indicates the classification of engine oil used under certain given operating conditions. Only oils designated for use Service SH, or latest superceding oil grade, should be used. Oils of the SH type perform a variety of functions inside the engine in addition to the basic function as a lubricant. Through a balanced system of metallic detergents and polymeric dispersants, the oil prevents the formation of high and low temperature deposits, and also keeps sludge and dirt particles in suspension. Acids, particularly sulfuric acid, as well as other by products of com-

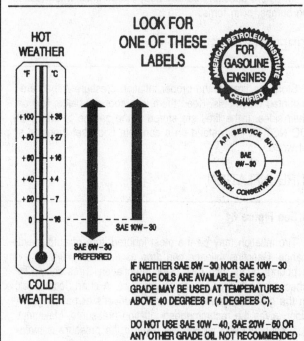

Fig. 85 Recommended SAE engine oil viscosity grades for gasoline engines

bustion, are neutralized. Both the SAE grade number and the API designation can be found on the top of the oil can.

➡ **Non-detergent or straight mineral oils must never be used. Oil viscosities should be chosen from those oils recommended for the lowest anticipated temperatures during the oil change interval.**

Synthetic Oils

There are excellent synthetic and fuel-efficient oils available that, under the right circumstances, can help provide better fuel mileage and better engine protection. However, these advantages come at a price, which can be significantly more than the price per quart of conventional motor oils.

Before pouring any synthetic oils into your car's engine, you should consider the condition of the engine and the type of driving you do. It is also wise to check the vehicle manufacturer's position on synthetic oils.

Generally, it is best to avoid the use of synthetic oil in both brand new and older, high mileage engines. New engines require a proper break-in, and the synthetics are so slippery that they can impede this; most manufacturers recommend that you wait at least 5,000 miles (8,000 km) before switching to a synthetic oil. Conversely, older engines are looser and tend to lose more oil; synthetics will slip past worn parts more readily than regular oil. If your car already leaks oil, (due to worn parts or bad seals/gaskets), it may leak more with a synthetic inside.

Consider your type of driving. If most of your accumulated mileage is on the highway at higher, steadier speed, a synthetic oil will reduce friction and probably help deliver better fuel mileage. Under such ideal highway conditions, the oil change interval can be extended, as long as the oil filter can operated effectively for the extended life of the oil. If the filter can't do its job for this extended period, dirt and sludge will build up in your engine's crankcase, sump, oil pump and lines, no matter what type of oil is used. If using synthetic oil in this manner, your should continue to change the oil filter at the recommended intervals.

Cars used under harder, stop-and-go, short hop circumstances should always be serviced more frequently, and for these cars synthetic oil may not be a wise investment. Because of the necessary shorter change interval needed for this type of driving, you cannot take advantage of the long recommended change interval of most synthetic oils.

Engine

OIL LEVEL CHECK

▶ **See Figures 86, 87 and 88**

➡ **On some of the vehicles covered by this manual, the oil fill cap contains the oil level indicator (dipstick).**

Every time you stop for fuel, check the engine oil making sure the engine has fully warmed and the vehicle is parked on a level surface. Because it takes some time for the oil to drain back to the oil pan, you should wait a few minutes before checking your oil. If you are doing this at a fuel stop, first fill the fuel tank, then open the hood and check the oil, but don't get so carried away as to forget to pay for the fuel. Most station attendants won't believe that you forgot.

1. Make sure the car is parked on level ground.
2. When checking the oil level, it is best for the engine to be at normal operating temperature, although checking the oil immediately after stopping will lead to a false reading. Wait a few minutes after turning off the engine to allow the oil to drain back into the crankcase.
3. Open the hood and locate the dipstick which will be in a guide tube mounted in the upper engine block. Pull the dipstick from its tube, wipe it clean (using a clean, lint free rag) and then reinsert it.
4. Pull the dipstick out again and, holding it horizontally, read the oil level. The oil should be between the FULL and ADD marks on the dipstick. The the oil is below the ADD mark, add oil of the proper viscosity through the capped opening in the top of the cylinder head cover or filler tube, as applicable. see the oil and fuel recommendations listed earlier in this section for the proper viscosity and rating of oil to use.

Fig. 86 Locate the dipstick, remove it from the guide tube, then . . .

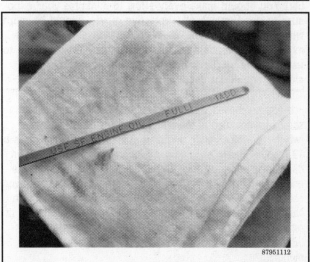

Fig. 87 . . . wipe the dipstick clean and reinsert in the guide tube

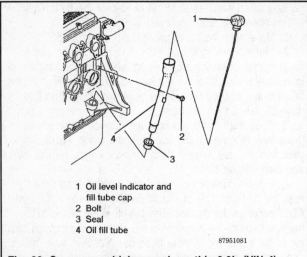

1 Oil level indicator and
  fill tube cap
2 Bolt
3 Seal
4 Oil fill tube

87951081

Fig. 88 On some vehicles, such as this 2.2L (VIN 4) engine, the oil fill cap contains the oil dipstick

5. Insert the dipstick and check the oil level again after adding any oil. Approximately one quart of oil will raise the level from the ADD mark to the FULL mark. Be sure not to overfill the crankcase and waste the oil. Excess oil will generally be consumed at an accelerated rate.

✳✳WARNING

DO NOT overfill the crankcase. It may result in oil-fouled spark plugs, oil leaks cause by oil seal failure or engine damage due to oil foaming.

OIL AND FILTER CHANGE

▶ See Figures 89, 90, 91, 92 and 93

✳✳CAUTION

The EPA warns that prolonged contact with used engine oil may cause a number of skin disorders, including cancer! You should make every effort to minimize your exposure to used engine oil. Protective gloves should be worn when changing the oil. Wash your hands and any other exposed skin areas as soon as possible after exposure to used engine oil. Soap and water, or waterless hand cleaner should be used.

If you purchased your J-car new, the engine oil and filter should be changed at the first 7,500 miles or 12 months (whichever comes first), and then at least every 7,500 miles or 12 months thereafter it the car is operated on a daily or semi-daily basis and most trips are for several miles (allowing the engine to properly warm up). If the car is driven under severe conditions, such as in extremely dusty weather, or when the car is used for trailer towing, prolonged high speed driving, or repeated short trips in freezing weather, it is suggested that the oil and filter be changed every 3,000 miles/4,800 km or 3 months.

Under certain circumstances, General Motors recommends changing both the oil and filter during the first oil change and then only replacing the filter at every other oil change thereaf-

ter. For the small price of an oil filter, it's cheap insurance to replace the filter at every oil change. One of the larger filter manufacturers points out in its advertisements that not changing the filter leaves as much as one quart of dirty oil in the engine. This claim is true and should be kept in mind when changing your oil.

Oil should always be changed after the engine has been running long enough to bring it up to normal operating temperature. Hot oil will flow easier and more contaminants will be removed along with the oil than if it were drained cold. The oil drain plug is located on the bottom of the oil pan (bottom of the engine).

You should have available a container that will hold a minimum of 6 quarts of liquid (to prevent spilling the oil even after it is drained), a wrench to fit the drain plug, a spout for pouring in new oil and a rag or two, which you will always need. If the filter is being replaced, you will also need a band wrench or a filter wrench that fits the end of the filter.

1. Drive the car until the engine is at normal operating temperature. A run to the parts store for oil and a filter should accomplish this. If the engine is not hot when the oil is changed, most of the acids and contaminants will remain inside the engine.

2. Shut the engine **OFF**, make sure the parking brake is firmly set and the drive wheels are blocked.

3. Clearance may be sufficient to access the drain plug without raising the vehicle. If the car must be lifted, be sure to support it safely with jackstands and be sure to position the drain plug at a low point under the vehicle.

4. Slide a drain pan of at least 6 quarts capacity under the oil pan. Wipe the drain plug and surrounding area clean using an old rag.

➡**Six quart plastic drain pan/containers are available, which can be capped, and taken later to a recycling station to dispose of the dirty oil. DO NOT pour the oil on or into the ground.**

5. Using a ratchet, short extension and socket or a box-wrench, loosen the drain plug from the engine oil pan. The drain plug is the bolt inserted at an angle into the lowest point of the oil pan. Turn the plug out by hand, using a rag to shield

87951113

Fig. 89 Using a wrench, loosen the oil panel drain plug, then . . .

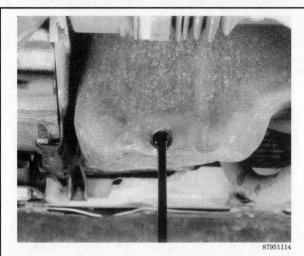

Fig. 90 . . . quickly withdraw the plug and allow it to drain into a pan

Fig. 92 The oil filler cap is usually located on the camshaft carrier or valve cover — 1988 2.0L Sunbird shown

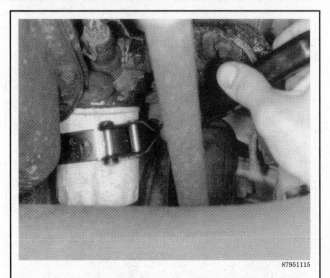

Fig. 91 Use a strap-type wrench to loosen the oil filter

Fig. 93 Fill the crankcase with the proper amount of engine oil, then check the oil level

your fingers. By keeping an inward pressure on the plug as you unscrew it, oil won't escape past the threads and you can remove it without being burned by hot oil.

6. Quickly withdraw the plug and move your hands out of the way, but be careful not to drop the plug into the drain pan, as fishing it out can be an unpleasant mess. Allow the oil to drain completely in the pan, then wipe off the drain plug, removing any traces of metal particles. Pay particular attention to the threads.

7. Install and carefully tighten the drain plug. Be careful not to overtighten the drain plug, otherwise you'll be buying a new pan or a trick replacement plug for stripped threads.

➡Although some manufacturers have at times recommended changing the oil filter every other oil change, we recommend the filter be changed every time you change your oil. The added benefit of clean oil is quickly lost if the oil filter is clogged and the added protection to the heart of your engine far outweighs the few dollars saved by using an old filter.

8. On some vehicles, the oil filter is at the back of the engine. It is impossible to reach from above, and almost as inaccessible from below, because of the location of the fender skirt. It may be easiest to remove the right front wheel and reach through the fender opening to get at the four cylinder oil filter. Use an oil filter strap wrench, or a wrench that fits like a cap over the oil filter, along with a rachet wrench, to loosen the oil filter; these are available at auto parts stores. Cover your hand with a rag and spin the filter off by hand. Keep in mind that it's holding about one quart of dirty, hot oil, so be careful.

9. Clean off the oil filter mounting surface with a clean rag. Be sure that the rag doesn't leave any lint which could clog an oil passage.

10. Apply a thin film of clean engine oil to the filter gasket. Screw the filter on by hand until the gasket makes contact. Then tighten it by hand an additional 1/2-3/4 turn. Do not overtighten. No more, or you'll squash the gasket and the it may leak.

11. Remove the oil filler cap, after wiping the area clean, then refill the engine with the correct amount of fresh oil Please refer to the Capacities chart in this section. If you don't have an oil can spout, you will need a funnel. Be certain you do not overfill the engine, which can cause serious damage. Replace the cap.

12. Check the oil level on the dipstick. It is normal for the level to be a bit above the full mark. Start the engine and allow it to idle for a few minutes.

✳✳WARNING

Do not run the engine above idle speed until it has built up oil pressure, indicated when the oil light goes out.

13. Check around the filter and drain plug for any leaks.

14. Shut off the engine, allow the oil to drain for a minute, and check the oil level.

After completing this job, you will have several quarts of filthy oil to dispose of. The best thing to do with it is to pour it into plastic jugs, such as milk or old antifreeze containers. Then, locate a service station or automotive parts store where you can pour it into their used oil tank for recycling.

✳✳CAUTION

Improperly disposing of used motor oil not only pollutes the environment, it violates Federal law. Dispose of waste oil properly.

Manual Transaxle

FLUID RECOMMENDATIONS

All 4-speed manual transaxles use Dexron® III or IIE (or the latest superceding fluid grade) automatic transmission fluid, which is a thin, reddish fluid. All 5-speeds through 1987 use 5W-30 engine oil. 1988-96 5-speed manual transaxles use Synchromesh® transmission fluid, GM part no. 12345349.

➡**Using the incorrect lubricant in your transaxle can lead to significant transaxle damage and a costly overhaul.**

LEVEL CHECK

▶ **See Figures 94, 95, 96, 97 and 98**

The fluid level in the manual transaxle should be checked every 12 months or 7,500 miles (12,000 km), whichever comes first.

1. Park the car on a level surface. The transaxle should be cool to the touch. If it is hot, check the level later, when it has cooled.

2. Remove the dipstick from the transaxle.

3. Check the level with the marks located on the dipstick.

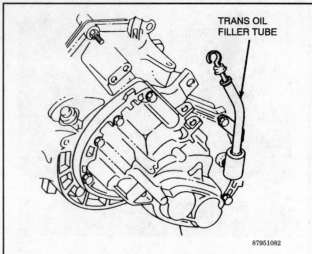

TRANS OIL FILLER TUBE

87951082

Fig. 94 Location of the manual transaxle dipstick and filler tube — 1984 5-speed shown, 4-speed similar

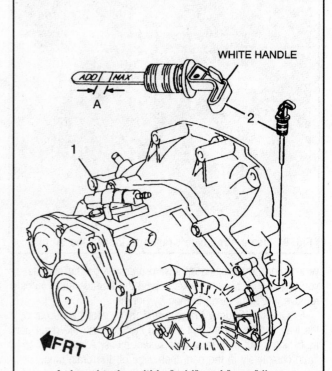

WHITE HANDLE

ADD | MAX

A

FRT

A. Level to be within "add" and "max" lines
1. Transaxle assembly
2. Indicator/fill plug

87951083

Fig. 95 The correct level should be between the "ADD" and "MAX" lines on the indicator — 1995 Isuzu built shown, HM-282 similar

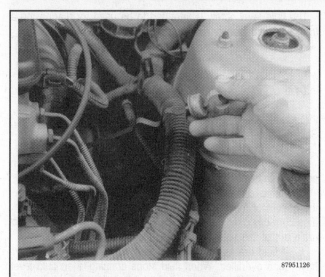

Fig. 96 Remove the dipstick from the transaxle

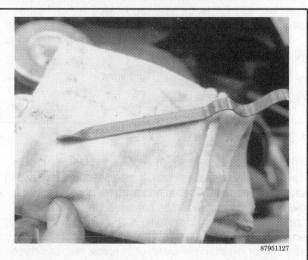

Fig. 97 Check the fluid level of the transaxle with the marks on the dipstick

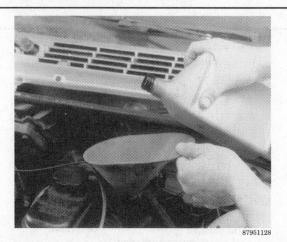

Fig. 98 If the fluid level is low, add it through the filler tube until the level is correct. Make sure not to add too much fluid

4. If lubricant is needed, add it through the filler tube until the level is correct. When the level is correct, reinstall the dipstick firmly.

➡**The dipstick must be fully seated in the filler tube during vehicle operation or leakage will occur at the vent plug.**

DRAIN AND REFILL

Under normal conditions, the manual transaxle fluid does not need to be changed. However, if the car is driven in deep water (as high as the transaxle casing) it is a good idea to replace the fluid. Little harm can come from a fluid change when you have just purchased a used vehicle, especially since the condition of the transaxle is usually not known.

If the fluid is to be drained, it is a good idea to warm the fluid first so it will flow better. This can be accomplished by 15-20 miles (24-32 km) of highway driving. Fluid which is warmed to normal operating temperature will flow faster, drain more completely and remove more contaminants from the housing.

1. Remove the filler plug (or dipstick) from the left side of the transaxle to provide a vent.
2. Raise and support the vehicle safely using jackstands.
3. The drain plug is located on the bottom of the transaxle case. Place a pan under the drain plug and remove it.

❋❋CAUTION

The fluid will be HOT. Push up against the threads as you unscrew the plug to prevent leakage.

4. Allow the fluid to drain completely. Check the condition of the plug gasket and replace it if necessary. Clean off the plug and replace, tightening it until snug.
5. Fill the transaxle with fluid through the fill or dipstick tube. You will need the aid of a long neck funnel or a funnel and a hose to pour through.
6. Use the dipstick to gauge the level of the fluid.
7. Replace the filler plug or dipstick and dispose of the old fluid in the same manner as you would old engine oil.

Take a drive in the car, stop on a level surface, and check the oil level.

Automatic Transaxle

FLUID RECOMMENDATION

When adding to or refilling the automatic transaxle, always use Dexron® III, IIE or latest superceding equivalent transaxle fluid.

LEVEL CHECK

The fluid level in the automatic transaxle should be checked every 12 months or 7,500 miles (12,000 km), whichever comes first. Most of the automatic transaxles have a dipstick for fluid level checks.

Except 4T40E Automatic Transaxle

▶ **See Figure 99**

1. Drive the car until it is at normal operating temperature. The level should not be checked immediately after the car has been driven for a long time at high speed, or in city traffic in hot weather; in those cases, the transaxle should be given a half hour to cool down.

2. Stop the car, apply the parking brake, then shift slowly through all gear positions, ending in Park. Let the engine idle for about five minutes with the selector in Park. The car should be on a level surface.

3. With the engine still running, remove the dipstick, wipe it clean, then reinsert it, pushing it fully home.

4. Wait three seconds, then pull the dipstick out again and, holding it horizontally, read the fluid level. It should be within the cross-hatch area between "ADD" and "FULL".

5. Cautiously feel the end of the dipstick to determine the temperature. Note that on the J-cars the cool and warm level dimples are above the hot level area. If the fluid level is not in the correct area, more will have to be added.

6. Fluid is added through the dipstick tube. You will probably need the aid of a spout or a long-necked funnel. Be sure that whatever you pour through is perfectly clean and dry. Use an automatic transmission fluid marked DEXRON®III, IIE or equivalent. Add fluid slowly, and in small amounts, checking the level frequently between additions. Do not overfill, which will cause foaming, fluid loss, slippage, and possible transaxle damage. It takes only one pint to raise the level from ADD to FULL when the transaxle is hot.

4T40E Automatic Transaxle

▶ **See Figure 100**

✳✳CAUTION

Removal of the fluid level screw when the transaxle fluid is hot may cause injury. Use care to avoid contact of the transaxle fluid to exhaust pipe.

The fluid level screw is intended to be used for diagnosing a transaxle fluid leak or resetting the transaxle fluid level after service that involves a loss of fluid.

1. The fluid level should be checked when the transaxle is near room temperature or at 104°F (40°C). To acquire this, left the car idle for 3-5 minutes with all of the accessories off.

2. Apply the brake, then move the gear shift selector through all gear ranges, pausing three seconds in each range. Shift the lever into "Park".

3. Raise and safely support the vehicle.

4. Place a suitable drain pan under the check plug to catch any fluid that may drip out.

5. Remove the oil check plug. The oil level should be at the bottom of the oil check hole. Because the transaxle operates correctly over a range of fluid levels, fluid may or may not drain out of the screw hole when the screw is removed.

6. If fluid drains through the screw hole, the transaxle may have been overfilled. When fluid stops draining, then fluid level is correct and the check plug may be installed. If fluid does not drain through the screw hole, the transaxle fluid may have been low. Add fluid at the vent cap location in 1 pint increments until the oil level is at the bottom of the oil check hole.

7. Install the oil check plug/fluid level screw and tighten to 10 ft. lbs. (14 Nm).

8. Carefully lower the vehicle.

DRAIN AND REFILL

▶ **See Figure 101**

The fluid should be changed according to the schedule in the Maintenance Intervals chart. If the car is normally used in severe service, such as stop and start driving, trailer towing, or the like, the interval should be halved. If the car is driven under especially nasty conditions, such as in heavy city traffic where the temperature normally reaches 90°F (32°C), or in very hilly or mountainous areas, or in police, taxi, or delivery service, the fluid should be changed every 15,000 miles (24,000 km.).

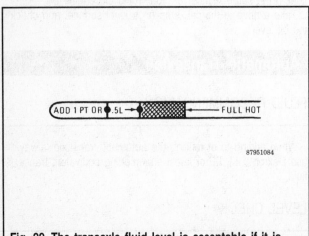

ADD 1 PT OR .5L ▬▬▬ FULL HOT

87951084

Fig. 99 The transaxle fluid level is acceptable if it is anywhere within the crosshatch area on the dipstick. Do NOT add oil unless the fluid level is below the crosshatch area

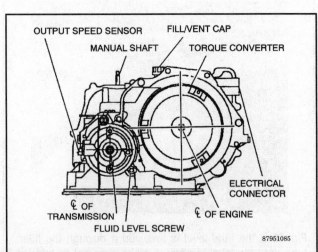

OUTPUT SPEED SENSOR   FILL/VENT CAP
MANUAL SHAFT   TORQUE CONVERTER
ELECTRICAL CONNECTOR
₵ OF TRANSMISSION   ₵ OF ENGINE
FLUID LEVEL SCREW

87951085

Fig. 100 Location of the fluid level screw and the fill/vent cap needed to check the fluid for the 4T40E automatic transaxle.

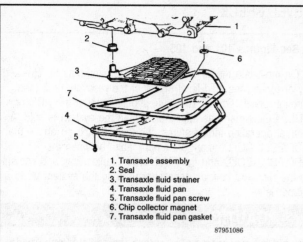

1. Transaxle assembly
2. Seal
3. Transaxle fluid strainer
4. Transaxle fluid pan
5. Transaxle fluid pan screw
6. Chip collector magnet
7. Transaxle fluid pan gasket

87951086

Fig. 101 When removing the transaxle pan and filter, always replace the gasket and O-ring with a new one before installation

The fluid must be hot before it is drained; a 20 minute drive should accomplish this.

1. To drain the automatic transaxle fluid, the fluid pan must be removed. Raise and safely support the vehicle. Place a drain pan underneath the transaxle pan, then remove the pan attaching bolts at the front and sides of the pan.

2. Loosen the rear pan attaching bolts approximately four turns each.

3. Very carefully pry the pan loose. You can use a small prybar for this if you work CAREFULLY. Do not distort the pan flange, or score the mating surface of the transaxle case. You'll be very sorry later if you do. As the pan is pried loose, all of the fluid is going to come pouring out.

4. Remove the remaining bolts and remove the pan and gasket. Throw away the gasket.

5. Clean the pan with solvent and allow it to air dry. If you use a rag to wipe out the pan, you risk leaving bits of lint behind, which will clog the dinky hydraulic passages in the transaxle.

6. Remove and discard the filter and the O-ring seal.

To install:

7. Install a new filter and O-ring, locating the filter against the dipstick stop.

8. Position a new gasket on the pan, then install the pan. Tighten the bolts evenly and in rotation to 8 ft. lbs. (11 Nm.). Do not overtighten.

9. Add approximately 4 qts. (3.8 L) of DEXRON®III or IIE automatic transmission fluid to the transaxle through the dipstick tube. You will need a long necked funnel, or a funnel and tube to do this.

10. With the transaxle in Park, put on the parking brake, block the front wheels, start the engine and let it idle. DO NOT RACE THE ENGINE. DO NOT MOVE THE LEVER THROUGH ITS RANGES.

11. With the lever in Park, check the fluid level. If it's OK, take the car out for a short drive, park on a level surface, and check the level again, as outlined earlier in this section. Add more fluid if necessary. Be careful not to overfill, which will cause foaming and fluid loss.

➡**If the drained fluid is discolored (brown or black), thick, or smells burnt, serious transmission troubles, probably due to overheating, should be suspected. Your car's transaxle should be inspected by a reliable transmission specialist to determine the problem.**

Cooling System

▶ **See Figures 102 and 103**

✳✳CAUTION

Never remove the radiator cap under any conditions while the engine is running! Failure to follow these instructions could result in damage to the cooling system or engine and/or personal injury. To avoid having scalding hot coolant or steam blow out of the radiator, use extreme care when removing the radiator cap from a hot radiator. Wait until the engine has cooled, then wrap a thick cloth around the radiator cap and turn it slowly to the first stop. Step back while the pressure is released from the cooling system. When you are sure the pressure has been released, press down on the radiator cap (still have the cloth in position) turn and remove the radiator cap.

Dealing with the cooling system can be dangerous matter unless the proper precautions are observed. It is best to check the coolant level in the radiator when the engine is cold. The cooling system has, as one of its components, a coolant recovery tank. If the coolant level is at or near the FULL COLD line (engine cold) or the FULL HOT line (engine hot), the level is satisfactory. Always be certain that the filler caps on both the radiator and the recovery tank are closed tightly.

In the event that the coolant level must be checked when the engine is hot and the vehicle is not equipped with a coolant recovery tank, place a thick rag over the radiator cap and slowly turn the cap counterclockwise until it reaches the first detent. Allow all hot steam to escape. This will allow the pressure in the system to drop gradually, preventing an explosion of hot coolant. When the hissing noise stops, remove the cap the rest of the way.

If the coolant level is found to be low, add a 50/50 mixture of antifreeze and clean water. If not equipped with a recovery tank, coolant must be added through the radiator filler neck. On most models, which are equipped with a recovery tank, coolant may be added either through the filler neck on the radiator or directly into the recovery tank.

✳✳CAUTION

Never add coolant to a hot engine unless it is running. If it is not running you run the risk of cracking the engine block.

It is wise to pressure check the cooling system at least once per year. If the coolant level is chronically low or rusty, the system should be thoroughly checked for leaks.

At least once every two years or 30,000 miles (48,000 km), the engine cooling system should be inspected, flushed, and refilled with fresh coolant. If the coolant is left in the system

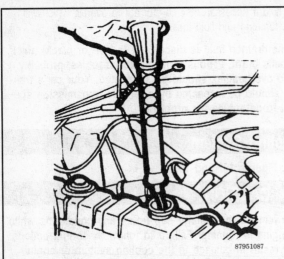

Fig. 102 Coolant protection can easily be checked using a float-type hydrometer tester

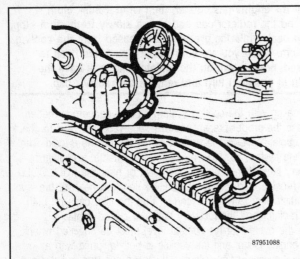

Fig. 103 If possible, a hand-held pressure tester should be used to check system integrity

too long, it loses its ability to prevent rust and corrosion. If the coolant has too much water, it won't protect against freezing.

The pressure cap should be examined for signs of age or deterioration. Fan belt and other drive belts should be inspected and adjusted to the proper tension. (See checking belt tension).

Hose clamps should be tightened, and soft or cracked hoses replaced. Damp spots, or accumulations of rust or dye near hoses, water pump or other areas, indicate possible leakage, which must be corrected before filling the system with fresh coolant.

FLUID RECOMMENDATIONS

Whenever adding or changing fluid, use a good quality ethylene glycol antifreeze) one that will not affect aluminum), mix it with clean water until a 50/50 antifreeze solution is attained.

LEVEL CHECK

▶ **See Figures 104 and 105**

On most late model vehicles, the fluid level may be checked by observing the fluid level marks of the recovery tank (see through plastic bottle). The level should be near the ADD or FULL COLD mark, as applicable, when the system is cold. At normal operating temperatures, the level should be above the ADD/FULL COLD mark or, if applicable, between the ADD/FULL COLD and the FULL HOT marks. Only add coolant to the recovery tank as necessary to bring the system up to a proper level.

✳✳CAUTION

Should it be necessary to remove the radiator cap, made sure that the system has had time to cool, reducing the internal pressure.

On any vehicle that is not equipped with a coolant recovery or overflow tank, the level must be checked by removing the radiator cap. This should only be done when the cooling system has had time to sufficiently cool after the engine has been run. The coolant level should be within 2 in. (51mm) of the base of the radiator filler neck. If necessary, coolant can then be added directly to the radiator.

COOLING SYSTEM INSPECTION

Checking the Radiator Cap Seal
▶ **See Figure 106**

When you are checking the coolant level, check the radiator cap for a worn or cracked gasket. if the cap doesn't seal properly, fluid will be lost and the engine will overheat.

Worn caps should be replaced with a new one.

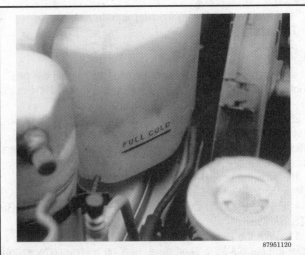

Fig. 104 When the engine is cold, the coolant should be at the "Full Cold" mark on the recovery tank

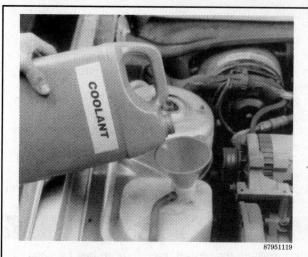

Fig. 105 If necessary, add coolant to the tank until it is at the correct level

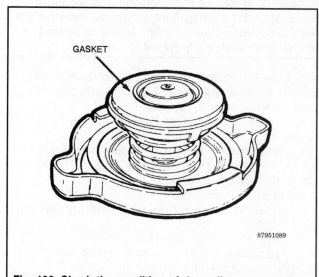

Fig. 106 Check the condition of the radiator cap gasket

Checking the Radiator for Debris
▶ See Figure 107

Periodically clean any debris; leaves, paper, insects, etc.., from the radiator fins. Pick the large pieces off by hand. The smaller pieces can be washed away with water pressure from a hose.

Carefully straighten any bent radiator fins with a pair of needle nose pliers. Be careful, the fins are very soft. Don't wiggle the fins back and forth too much. Straighten them once and try not to move them again.

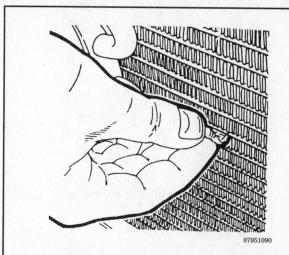

Fig. 107 Clean the front of the radiator of any bugs, leaves or other debris at every yearly coolant change

DRAIN AND REFILL

▶ See Figure 108

✳✳CAUTION

To avoid injuries from scalding fluid and steam, DO NOT remove the radiator cap while the engine and radiator are still HOT.

1. Make sure the engine is cool and the vehicle is parked on a level surface, then remove the radiator neck cap and, if equipped, the recovery tank cap in order to relieve system pressure.

2. Position a large drain pan under the vehicle, then drain the existing coolant by opening the radiator drain valve (petcock). It is sometimes helpful to put a piece of vacuum hose ³⁄₈ inches in diameter and about 12 in. (30 cm) long on the end of the radiator drain cock before opening the drain valve. This will help reduce some of the mess. It is also possible to drain the system by disconnecting the lower radiator hose from the bottom radiator outlet.

✳✳CAUTION

When draining the coolant, keep in mind that cats and dogs are attracted by ethylene glycol antifreeze, and are quite likely to drink any that is left in an uncovered container or in puddles on the ground. This will prove fatal in sufficient quantity. Always drain the coolant into a sealable container. Coolant should be reused unless it is contaminated or several years old.

3. Close the petcock or reconnect the lower hose. If you used it, don't forget to take the piece of vacuum hose off the valve.

4. If necessary, empty the coolant reservoir and flush it. This is most easily done by removing the reservoir tank from the vehicle.

5. Determine the capacity of your coolant system (see capacities specifications). Though the radiator filler neck, add a

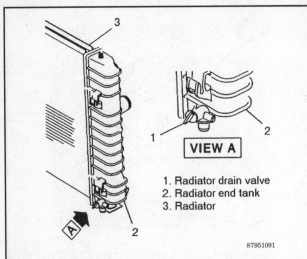

Fig. 108 The radiator drain valve (petcock) is located on the bottom corner of the radiator

1. Radiator drain valve
2. Radiator end tank
3. Radiator

87951091

50/50 mix of quality antifreeze (ethylene glycol) and water to provide the desired protection.

6. Leave the radiator pressure cap off, then start and run the engine until the thermostat heats up and opens, this will allow air to bleed from the system and provide room for additional coolant to be added to the radiator.

7. Add additional coolant to the radiator, as necessary, until the level is within 2 in. (51mm) of the radiator's filler neck base.

8. Stop the engine and check the coolant level.

9. Check the level of protection with an antifreeze tester, then install the radiator pressure cap.

10. If equipped with a coolant recovery/overflow tank, add coolant to the tank, as necessary, to achieve the proper level.

11. Start and run the engine to normal operating temperature, then check the system for leaks.

FLUSHING AND CLEANING THE SYSTEM

The cooling system should be drained, thoroughly flushed and refilled at least every 30,000 miles (48,000 km) or 24 months. These operations should be done with the engine cold, especially if a backpressure flushing kit is being used. Completely draining and refilling the cooling system every two years will remove accumulated rust, scale and other deposits. Coolant in late model cars is a 50/50 mixture of ethylene glycol and water for year round use. Use a good quality antifreeze with water pump lubricants, rust inhibitors and other corrosion inhibitors along with acid neutralizers.

There are many products available for cooling system flushing. If a backpressure flushing kit is used, it is recommended that the thermostat be temporarily removed in order to allow free flow to the system with cold water. Always follow the kit

or cleaner manufacturer's instructions and make sure the product is compatible with your vehicle.

1. Make sure the engine is cool and the vehicle is parked on a level surface, then remove the radiator neck cap and, if equipped, the recovery tank cap in order to relieve system pressure.

2. Position a large drain pan under the vehicle, then drain the existing coolant by opening the radiator drain valve (petcock). It is sometimes helpful to put a piece of vacuum hose $^3/_8$ inches in diameter and about 12 in. (30 cm) long on the end of the radiator drain cock before opening the drain valve. This will help reduce some of the mess. It is also possible to drain the system by disconnecting the lower radiator hose from the bottom radiator outlet.

✳✳CAUTION

When draining the coolant, keep in mind that cats and dogs are attracted by ethylene glycol antifreeze, and are quite likely to drink any that is left in an uncovered container or in puddles on the ground. This will prove fatal in sufficient quantity. Always drain the coolant into a sealable container. Coolant should be reused unless it is contaminated or several years old.

3. Close the radiator/engine drains or reconnect the lower hose, as applicable. If you used it, don't forget to take the piece of vacuum hose off the valve.

4. Fill the system with water, then add a can of quality radiator flush.

5. Idle the engine until the upper radiator hose gets hot and the thermostat has opened. This will allow the solution to fully circulate through the system.

6. Drain the system again.

7. Repeat this process until the drained water is clear and free of scale.

8. Close all drains and connect all the hoses.

9. If equipped with a coolant recovery system, flush the reservoir with water and leave empty.

10. Determine the capacity of your coolant system (see capacities specifications). Add a 50/50 mix of quality antifreeze (ethylene glycol) and water to provide the desired protection.

11. Leave the radiator pressure cap off, then start and run the engine until the thermostat heats up and opens, this will allow air to bleed from the system and provide room for additional coolant to be added to the radiator.

12. Add additional coolant to the radiator, as necessary, until the level is within 2 in. (51mm) of the radiator's filler neck base.

13. Stop the engine and check the coolant level.

14. Check the level of protection with an antifreeze tester, then install the radiator pressure cap.

15. If equipped with a coolant recovery/overflow tank, add coolant to the tank, as necessary, to achieve the proper level.

16. Start and run the engine to normal operating temperature, then check the system for leaks.

Brake Master Cylinder

FLUID RECOMMENDATION

When adding fluid to the brake master cylinder, always use Delco Supreme fluid part no. 1052535 or equivalent DOT-3 brake fluid from a clean, sealed container.

✳✳CAUTION

Brake fluid damages paint. It also absorbs moisture from the air; never leave a container or the master cylinder uncovered longer than necessary. All parts in contact with the brake fluid (master cylinder, hoses, plunger assemblies and etc..) must be kept clean, since any contamination of the brake fluid will adversely affect braking performance.

LEVEL CHECK

▶ See Figures 109, 110, 111 and 112

Once a month, the fluid level in the brake master cylinder should be checked.
  1. Park the car on a level surface.
  2. Clean off the master cylinder cover before removal.
  3. On early models without a filler cap, the cover simply snaps onto the master cylinder body. Use your thumbs to press up on the two tabs on the side of the cover to unsnap it. Later model master cylinders have a fill cap.
  4. Remove the cover or cap, being careful not to drop or tear the rubber diaphragm underneath. Be careful also not to drip any brake fluid on painted surfaces; the stuff eats paint.

➡ **Brake fluid absorbs moisture from the air, which reduces effectiveness, and will corrode brake parts once in the system. Never leave the master cylinder or the brake fluid container uncovered for any longer than necessary.**

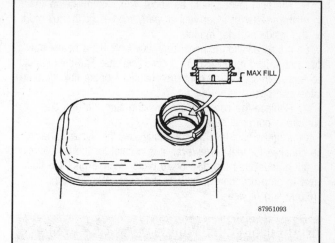

Fig. 110 The fluid level full mark is located on the inside of the reservoir on 1987-96 models

Fig. 111 Clean off the master cylinder cover, then remove the cap

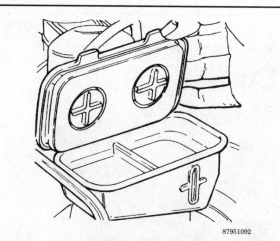

Fig. 109 For vehicles through 1986, the proper brake fluid level is approximately ¼ in. below the lip of the master cylinder

Fig. 112 If necessary, add fluid from a fresh, sealed container

5. The fluid level should be about ¼ in. (6mm) below the lip of the master cylinder well on early models or the full mark on the inside on later models.

6. If fluid addition is necessary, use only extra heavy duty disc brake fluid meeting DOT 3 specifications. The fluid should be from a fresh, sealed container, because brake fluid deteriorates with age.

7. Replace the cover or cap, making sure that the diaphragm is correctly seated.

If the brake fluid level is constantly low, the system should be checked for leaks. However, it is normal for the fluid level to fall gradually as the disc brake pads wear; expect the fluid level to drop not more than ⅛ in. for every 10,000 miles (16,000 km) of wear.

Clutch Master Cylinder

➡The clutch master cylinder is mounted on the firewall next to the brake master cylinder.

FLUID RECOMMENDATIONS

Use only hydraulic clutch fluid part no. 12345347 or equivalent DOT-3 brake fluid.

LEVEL CHECK

▶ **See Figures 113, 114, 115 and 116**

The hydraulic clutch reservoir should be checked at least every 6 months. Fill to the line on the reservoir.

Power Steering Pump

FLUID RECOMMENDATIONS

Use GM Power Steering Fluid no. 1050017 or equivalent.

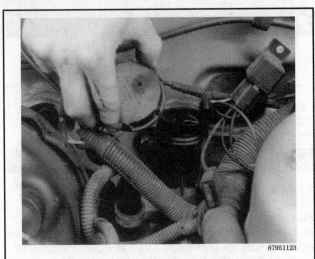

Fig. 114 Remove the clutch master cylinder cap, then . . .

Fig. 115 . . . remove the reservoir diaphragm

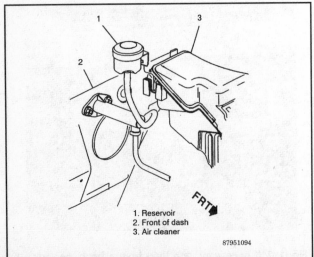

1. Reservoir
2. Front of dash
3. Air cleaner

87951094

Fig. 113 The hydraulic clutch reservoir is mounted on the firewall, next to the brake master cylinder

Fig. 116 If necessary, add fluid to the clutch master cylinder

LEVEL CHECK

♦ **See Figures 117, 118, 119 and 120**

The power steering fluid should be checked at least every 6 months. Power steering fluid level is indicated either by marks on a see-through fluid reservoir or by marks on a fluid level indicator on the reservoir cap. There is a Cold and a Hot mark on the dipstick. To prevent possible overfilling, check the fluid level only when the fluid has warmed to operating temperatures and the engine is shut **OFF**. If necessary, add fluid to the power steering pump reservoir.

Steering Gear

The rack and pinion steering gear used on the J-cars is a sealed unit; no fluid level checks or additions are ever necessary.

Fig. 117 The power steering pump reservoir is usually mounted on the firewall

Fig. 118 Remove the power steering fluid dipstick from the reservoir, then . . .

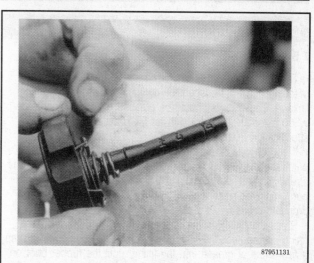

Fig. 119 . . . check the level against the marks on the dipstick

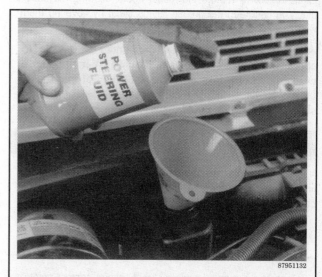

Fig. 120 If the level is low, add fluid to the reservoir

Windshield Washer Pump

FLUID RECOMMENDATIONS AND LEVEL CHECK

The windshield washer pump fluid reservoir is a plastic container usually found on the side of the engine compartment. The reservoir should be filled to the top of the container using a wiper fluid solution which can found at most automotive stores. Do not further dilute the solution (unless it is sold in concentrate, then follow the manufacturer's instructions), as this will adversely affect its ability to keep from freezing at low temperatures. Also, never place another fluid, such a ethylene glycol antifreeze in the reservoir as other fluids could damage pump seals.

Chassis Greasing

▶ See Figure 121

There are only two areas which require regular chassis greasing: the front suspension components and the steering linkage. These parts should be greased every 12 months or 7,500 miles (12,000 km) with an EP grease meeting G.M. specification 6031M.

If you choose to do this job yourself, you will need to purchase a hand operated grease gun, if you do not own one already, and a long flexible extension hose to reach the various grease fittings. You will also need a cartridge of the appropriate grease.

Press the fitting on the grease gun hose onto the grease fitting on the suspension or steering linkage component. Pump a few shots of grease into the fitting, until the rubber boot on the joint begins to expand, indicating that the joint is full. Remove the gun from the fitting. Be careful not to overfill the joints, which will rupture the rubber boots, allowing the entry of dirt. You can keep the grease fittings clean by covering them with a small square of tin foil.

➡This is a good opportunity, while under the vehicle, to check for any tears or holes in the axle CV-joint boots, which may cause loss of or contamination of the axle grease. Damaged boots must be replaced as soon as possible or joint failure could result.

Body Lubrication

Every 12 months or 7,500 miles (12,000 km), the various linkages and hinges on the chassis and body should be lubricated, as follows:

TRANSAXLE SHIFT LINKAGE

Lubricate the manual transaxle shift linkage contact points with the EP grease used for chassis greasing, which should meet G.M. specification 6031M. The automatic transaxle linkage should be lubricated with clean engine oil.

HOOD LATCH AND HINGES

Clean the latch surfaces and apply clean engine oil to the latch pilot bolts and the spring anchor. Use the engine oil to lubricate the hood hinges as well. Use a chassis grease to lubricate all the pivot points in the latch release mechanism.

DOOR HINGES

The gas tank filler door, car door, and rear hatch or trunk lid hinges should be wiped clean and lubricated with clean engine oil. Silicone spray also works well on these parts, but must be applied more often. Use engine oil to lubricate the trunk or hatch lock mechanism and the lock bolt and striker. The door lock cylinders can be lubricated easily with a shot of silicone spray or one of the may dry penetrating lubricants commercially available.

PARKING BRAKE LINKAGE

➡Do NOT lubricate the parking brake cables. Lubrication destroys the plastic coating on the cables.

Use chassis grease on the parking brake cable guides where they contact the links, levers, and pulleys. The grease should be a water resistant one for durability under the car.

ACCELERATOR LINKAGE

Lubricate the carburetor stud, carburetor lever, and the accelerator pedal lever at the support inside the car with clean engine oil.

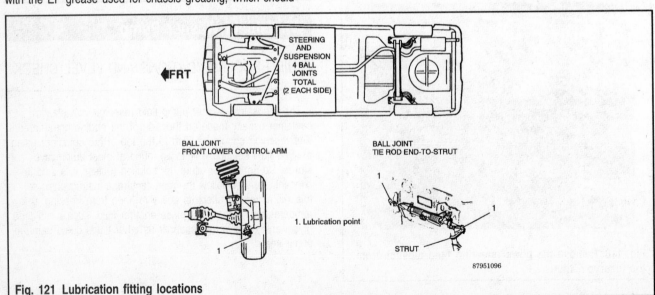

Fig. 121 Lubrication fitting locations

Wheel Bearings

The J-body models are equipped with sealed hub and bearing assemblies. The hub and bearing assemblies are non-serviceable. If the assembly is damaged, the complete unit must be replaced. Refer to Section 8 for the hub and bearing removal and installation procedure.

TRAILER TOWING

General Recommendations

Your car was primarily designed to carry passengers and cargo. It is important to remember that towing a trailer will place additional loads on your vehicle's engine, drivetrain, steering, braking and other systems. However, if you find it necessary to tow a trailer, using the proper equipment is a must.

Local laws may require specific equipment such as trailer brakes or fender mounted mirrors. Check your local laws.

✳✳WARNING

Some early models equipped with the V6 engines were not recommended for trailer towing because of insufficient cooling system capacity. These vehicles could overheat. Check your owners manual or local GM dealer for any trailer towing warnings.

Trailer Weight

The weight of the trailer is the most important factor. A good weight-to-horsepower ratio is about 35:1, 35 lbs. of GCW (Gross Combined Weight) for every horsepower your engine develops. Multiply the engine's rated horsepower by 35 and subtract the weight of the car passengers and luggage. The result is the approximate ideal maximum weight you should tow, although a a numerically higher axle ratio can help compensate for heavier weight.

Hitch Weight

Figure the hitch weight to select a proper hitch. Hitch weight is usually 9-11% of the trailer gross weight and should be measured with the trailer loaded. Hitches fall into three types: those that mount on the frame and rear bumper or the bolt-on or weld-on distribution type used for larger trailers. Axle mounted or clamp-on bumper hitches should never be used.

Check the gross weight rating of your trailer. Tongue weight is usually figured as 10% of gross trailer weight. Therefore, a trailer with a maximum gross weight of 2,000 lb. will have a maximum tongue weight of 200 lb. Class I trailers fall into this category. Class II trailers are those with a gross weight rating of 2,000-3,500 lb., while Class III trailers fall into the 3,500-6,000 lb. category. Class IV trailers are those over 6,000 lb. and are for use with fifth wheel trucks, only.

When you've determined the hitch that you'll need, follow the manufacturer's installation instructions, exactly, especially when it comes to fastener torques. The hitch will subjected to a lot of stress and good hitches come with hardened bolts. Never substitute an inferior bolt for a hardened bolt.

Cooling

ENGINE

One of the most common, if not THE most common, problems associated with trailer towing is engine overheating.

If you have a standard cooling system, without an expansion tank, you'll definitely need to get an aftermarket expansion tank kit, preferably one with at least a 2 quart capacity. These kits are easily installed on the radiator's overflow hose, and come with a pressure cap designed for expansion tanks.

Aftermarket engine oil coolers are helpful for prolonging engine oil life and reducing overall engine temperatures. Both of these factors increase engine life.

While not absolutely necessary in towing Class I and some Class II trailers, they are recommended for heavier Class II and all Class III towing.

Engine oil cooler systems consist of an adapter, screwed on in place of the oil filter, a remote filter mounting and a multi-tube, finned heat exchanger, which is mounted in front of the radiator or air conditioning condenser.

TRANSMISSION

An automatic transmission is usually recommended for trailer towing. Modern automatics have proven reliable and, of course, easy to operate, in trailer towing.

The increased load of a trailer, however, causes an increase in the temperature of the automatic transmission fluid. Heat is the worst enemy of an automatic transmission. As the temperature of the fluid increases, the life of the fluid decreases.

It is essential, therefore, that you install an automatic transmission cooler.

The cooler, which consists of a multi-tube, finned heat exchanger, is usually installed in front of the radiator or air conditioning compressor, and hooked inline with the transmission cooler tank inlet line. Follow the cooler manufacturer's installation instructions.

Select a cooler of at least adequate capacity, based upon the combined gross weights of the car and trailer.

Cooler manufacturers recommend that you use an aftermarket cooler in addition to, and not instead of, the present cooling tank in your radiator. If you do want to use it in place of the radiator cooling tank, get a cooler at least two sizes larger than normally necessary.

➡A transmission cooler can, sometimes, cause slow or harsh shifting in the transmission during cold weather, until the fluid has a chance to come up to normal operating temperature. Some coolers can be purchased with or retrofitted with a temperature bypass valve which will allow fluid flow through the cooler only when the fluid has reached operating temperature, or above.

TOWING THE VEHICLE

The J-cars may not be pushed or towed to start, because doing so may cause the catalytic converter to explode. If the battery is weak, the engine may be jump started, using the procedure outlined in the following section.

Your J-car may be towed on all four wheels at speeds less than 35 mph (60 km/h) for distances up to 50 miles (80 km). The driveline and steering must be normally operable. If either one is damaged, the car may not be flat-towed. If the car is flat-towed (on all four wheels), the steering must be unlocked, the transaxle shifted to Neutral, and the parking brake released. Towing attachment must be made to the main struc-

tural members of the chassis, not to the bumpers or sheetmetal.

The car may be towed on its rear wheels by a wrecker; make sure that safety chains are used. J-cars with manual transaxles may be towed on their front wheels, for short distances and at low speeds. Be sure the transaxle is in Neutral. Cars with automatic transaxles should not be towed on their front wheels; transaxle damage may result. If it is impossible to tow the car on its rear wheels, place the front wheels on a dolly.

JUMP STARTING A DEAD BATTERY

▸ See Figure 122

Whenever a vehicle must be jump started, precautions must be followed in order to prevent the possibility of personal injury. Remember that batteries contain a small amount of explosive hydrogen gas which is a byproduct of battery charging. Sparks should always be avoided when working around batteries, especially when attaching jumper cables. To minimize the possibility of accidental sparks, follow the procedure carefully.

✳✳WARNING

NEVER hook the batteries up in a series circuit or the entire electrical system will go up in smoke, especially the starter!

Jump Starting Precautions

1. Be sure that both batteries are of the same voltage. All vehicles covered by this manual and most vehicles on the road today utilize a 12 volt charging system.
2. Be sure that both batteries are of the same polarity (have the same grounded terminal; in most cases NEGATIVE).
3. Be sure that the vehicles are not touching or a short circuit could occur.
4. On serviceable batteries, be sure the vent cap holes are not obstructed.
5. Do not smoke or allow sparks anywhere near the batteries.
6. In cold weather, make sure the battery electrolyte is not frozen. This can occur more readily in a battery that has been in a state of discharge.
7. Do not allow electrolyte to contact your skin or clothing.

Handling A Trailer

Towing a trailer with ease and safety requires a certain amount of experience. It's a good idea to learn the feel of a trailer by practicing turning, stopping and backing in an open area such as an empty parking lot.

Jump Starting Procedure

1. Make sure that the voltages of the 2 batteries are the same. Most batteries and charging systems are of the 12 volt variety.
2. Pull the jumping vehicle (with the good battery) into a position so the jumper cables can reach the dead battery and that vehicle's engine. Make sure that the vehicles do NOT touch.
3. Place the transmissions of both vehicles in NEUTRAL or PARK, as applicable, then firmly set their parking brakes.

➡If necessary for safety reasons, both vehicle's hazard lights may be operated throughout the entire procedure without significantly increasing the difficulty of jump starting the dead battery.

4. Turn all lights and accessories off on both vehicles. Make sure the ignition switches on both vehicles are turned to the OFF position.
5. Cover the battery cell caps with a rag, but do not cover the terminals.
6. Make sure the terminals on both batteries are clean and free of corrosion or proper electrical connection will be impeded. If necessary, clean the battery terminals before proceeding.
7. Identify the positive (+) and negative (-) terminals on both batteries.
8. Connect the first jumper cable to the positive (+) terminal of the dead battery, then connect the other end of that cable to the positive (+) terminal of the booster (good) battery.
9. Connect one end of the other jumper cable to the negative (-) terminal of the booster battery and the other cable clamp to an engine bolt head, alternator bracket or other solid,

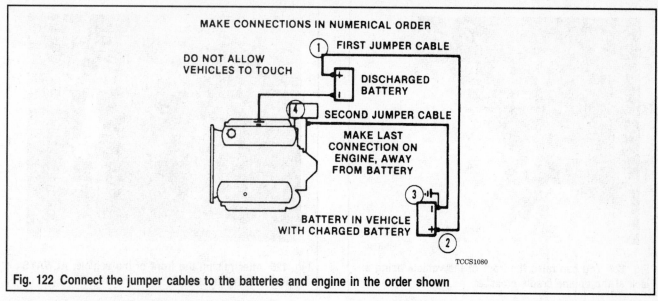

MAKE CONNECTIONS IN NUMERICAL ORDER

① FIRST JUMPER CABLE

DO NOT ALLOW
VEHICLES TO TOUCH

DISCHARGED
BATTERY

SECOND JUMPER CABLE

MAKE LAST
CONNECTION ON
ENGINE, AWAY
FROM BATTERY

③

② BATTERY IN VEHICLE
WITH CHARGED BATTERY

TCCS1080

Fig. 122 Connect the jumper cables to the batteries and engine in the order shown

metallic point on the dead battery's engine. Try to pick a ground on the engine that is positioned away from the battery, in order to minimize the possibility of the 2 clamps touching should one loosen during the procedure. DO NOT connect this clamp to the negative (-) terminal of the bad battery.

✳✳CAUTION

Be very careful to keep the jumper cables away from moving parts (cooling fan, belts, etc..) on both engines.

10. Check to make sure that the cables are routed away from any moving parts, then start the donor vehicle's engine. Run the engine at moderate speed for several minutes to allow the dead battery a chance to receive some initial charge.

11. With the donor vehicle's engine still running slightly above idle, try to start the vehicle with the dead battery. Crank the engine for no more than 10 seconds at a time and let the

starter cool for at least 20 seconds between tries. If the vehicle does not start within 3 tries, it is likely that something else is also wrong.

12. Once the vehicle is started, allow it to run at idle for a few seconds to make sure that it is properly operating.

13. Turn on the headlights, heater blower and, if equipped, the rear defroster of both vehicles in order to reduce the severity of voltage spikes and subsequent risk of damage to the vehicles' electrical systems when the cables are disconnected.

14. Carefully disconnect the cables in the reverse order of connection. Start with the negative cable that is attached to the engine ground, then the negative cable on the donor battery. Disconnect the positive cable from the donor battery, then disconnect the positive cable from the formerly dead battery. Be careful when disconnecting the cables from the positive terminals not to allow the alligator clips to touch any metal on either vehicle or a short circuit and sparks will occur.

JACKING

▶ **See Figures 123, 124, 125, 126 and 127**

The J-cars are supplied with a scissors jack for changing tires. This jack engages in notches behind the front wheel and forward of the rear wheel under the rocker flange. This jack is satisfactory for its intended purpose, changing tires. It should NOT, nor should any jack, be used to support the car while you crawl under it and work. To do so is to recklessly jeopardize your life. Whenever it is necessary to get under a car to perform service operation, always be sure that it is adequately supported using jackstands at the proper points. Always block the wheels when changing tires. Never crawl under the car when it is supported by only the scissors jack.

➡**Once the jackstands are in position and the vehicle's weight has been lowered onto them, shake the car a few times before crawling underneath to make sure the jackstands are securely supporting the weight.**

The car may also be jacked at the rear axle between the spring seats, or at the front end at the engine cradle crossbar

87951133

Fig. 123 A rolling floor jack is probably the easiest type of jack to use

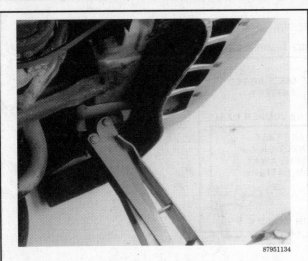

Fig. 124 You can raise the front of the vehicle using a jack at the engine cradle crossbar

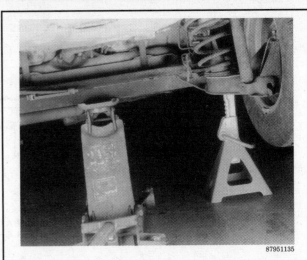

Fig. 125 After raising the front of the vehicle, ALWAYS support it using jackstands

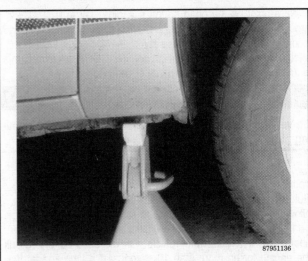

Fig. 126 View of the proper locations for the jackstands on the front of the vehicle

Fig. 127 Proper jackstand location to support the rear end of the vehicle

or lower control arm. The car must never be lifted by the rear lower control arms.

Service operations in this book often require that one end or both ends of the car be raised and safely supported. The ideal method, of course, would be to use a grease pit or hydraulic hoist. Since this is beyond both the resource and requirement of the do-it-yourselfer, a small hydraulic, screw or scissors jack will raise the vehicle sufficiently for almost all procedures in this guide. The rolling floor jack is probably the easiest and most convenient of these to use. But the vehicle must still be supported by at least two sturdy jackstands if you intend to work under the car at any time. An alternate method of raising the car would be drive-on ramps. When using ramps, be sure to block the wheels which remain on the ground. Spend a little extra time to make sure that your car is lifted and supported safely. Remember, the car you are laying under weighs at least 1 ton.

✶✶CAUTION

Concrete blocks are not recommended for supporting a vehicle; they may crumble if the load is not evenly distributed. Boxes and milk crates of any description must not be used.

It is imperative that strict safety precautions be observed both while raising the car and in the subsequent support after the car is raised. If a jack is used to raise the car, the transaxle should be shifted to Park (automatic) or First (manual), the parking brake should be set, and the opposite wheel should be blocked. Jacking should only be attempted on a hard level surface.

MAINTENANCE INTERVALS CHART I of II

Follow Schedule I if the car is mainly operated under one or more of the following conditions:
- When most trips are less than 4 miles (6 kilometers).
- When most trips are less than 10 miles (16 kilometers) and outside temperatures remain below freezing.
- Idling and/or low-speed operation in stop-and-go traffic.
- Towing a trailer
- Operating in dusty areas.

Schedule I should also be followed if the car is used for delivery service, police, taxi or other commercial applications.

The services shown in this schedule up to 48,000 miles (80,000 km) are to be performed after 48,000 miles at the same intervals.

ITEM NO.	TO BE SERVICED	WHEN TO PERFORM Miles (Kilometers) or Months, Whichever Occurs First	3/5	6/10	9/15	12/20	15/25	18/30	21/35	24/40	27/45	30/50	33/55	36/60	39/65	42/70	45/75	48/80
1	Engine Oil & Filter Change*	Every 3,000 (5,000 km) or 3 mos.	•	•	•	•	•	•	•	•	•	•	•	•	•	•	•	•
2	Chassis Lubrication	Every other oil change		•		•		•		•		•		•		•		•
3	Carb. Choke & Hose Insp.* (If Equipped)††	At 6,000 mi. (10,000 km) and then every 30,000 mi. (50,000 km)		•										•				
4	Carb. or Throttle Body Mount Bolt Torque (Some Models)*	At 6,000 mi. (10,000 km) only		•														
5	Eng. Idle Speed Adj. (Some Models)*			•														
6	Tire & Wheel Insp. and Rotation	At 6,000 mi. (10,000 km) and then every 15,000 mi. (25,000 km)		•					•					•				
7	Vac. or Air Pump Drive Belt Insp.*	Every 30,000 mi. (50,000 km) or 24 mos.										•						
8	Cooling System Service*											•						
9	Wheel Brg. Repack (Rear-Wheel-Drive Cars Only)	See explanation for service interval																
10	Transmission/Transaxle Service																	
11	Spark Plug Service*	Every 30,000 mi. (50,000 km)										•						
12	Spark Plug Wire Insp. (Some Models)*											•						
13	PCV Valve Insp. (Some Models)*††											•						
14	EGR System Insp.*††	Every 30,000 mi. (50,000 km) or 36 mos.										•						
15	Air Cleaner & PCV Filter Rep.*											•						
16	Eng. Timing Check (Some Models)*											•						
17	Fuel Tank, Cap & Lines Insp.*††	Every 30,000 (50,000 km)										•						
18	Thermostatically Controlled Air Cleaner Insp. (Some Models)											•						

FOOTNOTES: * An Emission Control Service
†† The U.S. Environmental Protection Agency has determined that the failure to perform this maintenance item will not nullify the emission warranty or limit recall liability prior to the completion of vehicle useful life. General Motors, however, urges that all recommended maintenance services be performed at the indicated intervals and the maintenance be recorded in Section C of the owner's maintenance schedule.

87951510

MAINTENANCE INTERVALS CHART II of II

Follow Schedule II if, as a general rule, the car is driven on a daily basis for several miles (km) and none of the above conditions apply.

The services shown in this schedule up to 45,000 miles (75,000 km) are to be performed after 45,000 miles at the same intervals

ITEM NO.	TO BE SERVICED	WHEN TO PERFORM Miles (Kilometers) or Months, Whichever Occurs First	MILES (000) 7.5 / KILOMETERS (000) 12.5	15 / 25	22.5 / 37.5	30 / 50	37.5 / 62.5	45 / 75
1	Engine Oil & Filter Change*	Every 7,500 mi. (12,500 km) or 12 mos.	•	•	•	•	•	•
	Filter Change*	At first and every other oil change or 12 mos.	•		•		•	
2	Chassis Lubrication	Every 7,500 mi. (12,500 km) or 12 mos.	•	•	•	•	•	•
3	Carb. Choke & Hose Insp.* (If Equipped)††	At 7,500 mi. (12,500 km) and then at each 30,000 mi. (50,000 km) interval	•			•		
4	Carb. or Throttle Body Mount Bolt Torque (Some Models)*	At 7,500 mi. (12,500 km) only	•					
5	Eng. Idle Speed Adj. (Some Models)*		•					
6	Tire & Wheel Insp. and Rotation	At 7,500 mi. (12,500 km) and then every 15,000 mi. (25,000 km)	•		•		•	
7	Vac. or Air Pump Drive Belt Insp.*	Every 30,000 mi. (50,000 km) or 24 mos.				•		
8	Cooling System Service*	Every 30,000 mi. (50,000 km)				•		
9	Wheel Brg. Repack (Rear-Wheel-Drive Cars Only)	Every 30,000 mi. (50,000 km)				•		
10	Transmission/Transaxle Service	See explanation for service interval						
11	Spark Plug Service*					•		
12	Spark Plug Wire Insp. (Some Models)*	Every 30,000 mi. (50,000 km)				•		
13	PCV Valve Insp. (Some Models)*††					•		
14	EGR System Insp.*††	Every 30,000 mi. (50,000 km) or 36 mos.				•		
15	Air Cleaner & PCV Filter Rep.*					•		
16	Eng. Timing Check (Some Models)*					•		
17	Fuel Tank, Cap & Lines Insp.*††	Every 30,000 (50,000 km)				•		
18	Thermostatically Controlled Air Cleaner Insp. (Some Models)*					•		

FOOTNOTES: * An Emission Control Service

†† The U.S. Environmental Protection Agency has determined that the failure to perform this maintenance item will not nullify the emission warranty or limit recall liability prior to the completion of vehicle useful life. General Motors, however, urges that all recommended maintenance services be performed at the indicated intervals and the maintenance be recorded in Section C of the owner's maintenance schedule.

87951511

CAPACITIES

Year	Engine ID/VIN	Engine Displacement Liters (cc)	Engine Oil with Filter (qts.)	Transmission (pts.) 4-Spd	Transmission (pts.) 5-Spd	Transmission (pts.) Auto.	Transfer Case (pts.)	Drive Axle Front (pts.)	Drive Axle Rear (pts.)	Fuel Tank (gal.)	Cooling System (qts.)
1982	G	1.8 (1819)	4.0	5.9	-	10.5	-	-	-	14.0	8.0
	O	1.8 (1819)	①	-	5.0	10.5	-	-	-	14.0	7.9
	B	2.0 (1998)	4.0	5.9	-	10.5	-	-	-	14.0	8.3
1983	O, J	1.8 (1819)	①	-	5.0	10.5	-	-	-	14.0	7.9
	B, P	2.0 (1998)	4.0	5.9	-	10.5	-	-	-	14.0	8.3
1984	O, J	1.8 (1819)	①	-	5.0	10.5	-	-	-	14.0	7.9
	P	2.0 (1998)	4.0	5.9	-	10.5	-	-	-	14.0 ②	8
1985	O	1.8 (1819)	4.5	6.0	4.0	8.0	-	-	-	13.6	③
	J	1.8 (1819)	4.5	6.0	4.0	8.0	-	-	-	13.6	③
	P	2.0 (1998)	4.5	5.9	-	10.5	-	-	-	14.0	8.3
	W	2.8 (2835)	4.0	6.0	-	8.0	-	-	-	14.0 ②	12.4
1986	O	1.8 (1819)	4.5	6.0	4.0	8.0	-	-	-	13.6	③
	J	1.8 (1819)	4.5	6.0	4.0	8.0	-	-	-	13.6	③
	P	2.0 (1998)	4.5	5.9	-	10.5	-	-	-	14.0	8.3
	W	2.8 (2835)	4.0	6.0	-	8.0	-	-	-	14.0	12.4
1987	K	2.0 (1998)	4.5	-	4.0	8.0	-	-	-	13.6	8.5
	M	2.0 (1998)	4.5	-	4.0	8.0	-	-	-	13.6	8.5
	1	2.0 (1998)	4.5	5.9	-	10.5	-	-	-	14.0	8.3
	W	2.8 (2835)	4.0	5.9	-	8.0	-	-	-	14.0 ②	12.4
1988	K	2.0 (1998)	4.0	-	6.0	8.0 ④	-	-	-	13.6	8.0
	M	2.0 (1998)	4.5	-	4.0	8.0 ④	-	-	-	13.6	8.5
	1	2.0 (1998)	4.5	-	4.0	10.5	-	-	-	14.0	8.3
	W	2.8 (2835)	4.0	-	4.0	8.0	-	-	-	14.0	12.4
1989	K	2.0 (1998)	4.5	-	4.0	8.0	-	-	-	13.6	8.5
	M	2.0 (1998)	4.5	-	4.0	8.0	-	-	-	13.6	8.5
	1	2.0 (1998)	4.5	-	4.0	10.5	-	-	-	14.0	8.3
	W	2.8 (2835)	4.0	-	4.0	8.0	-	-	-	14.0	12.4
1990	K	2.0 (1998)	4.5	-	4.0	8.0	-	-	-	13.6	8.5
	M	2.0 (1998)	4.5	-	4.0	8.0	-	-	-	13.6	8.5
	G	2.2 (2180)	4.5	-	4.0	8.0 ⑤	-	-	-	13.6	8.5
	T	3.1 (3130)	4.5	-	4.0	8.0 ⑤	-	-	-	13.6	11.0
1990	K	2.0 (1998)	4.5	-	4.0	8.0	-	-	-	13.6	11.7
	G	2.2 (2180)	4.5	-	4.0	8.0 ⑤	-	-	-	13.6	8.5
	T	3.1 (3130)	4.5	-	4.0	8.0 ⑤	-	-	-	13.6	11.0
1991	H	2.0 (1998)	4.5	-	4.0	8.0	-	-	-	15.2	11.7
	G	2.2 (2180)	4.5	-	4.0	8.0 ⑤	-	-	-	13.6	8.5
	T	3.1 (3130)	4.5	-	4.0	8.0 ⑤	-	-	-	13.6	11.0
1993	H	2.0 (1998)	4.5	-	4.0	8.0	-	-	-	13.6	11.7
	4	2.2 (2180)	4.5	-	4.0	8.0 ⑤	-	-	-	13.6	8.5
	T	3.1 (3130)	4.5	-	4.0	8.0 ⑤	-	-	-	13.6	11.0
1994	H	2.0 (1998)	4.5	-	4.0	8.0	-	-	-	15.2	10.7
	4	2.2 (2180)	4.5	-	4.0	8.0 ⑤	-	-	-	13.6	8.5
	T	3.1 (3136)	4.5	-	4.0	8.0	-	-	-	15.2	13.7

87951508

CAPACITIES

Year	Engine ID/VIN	Engine Displacement Liters (cc)	Engine Oil with Filter (qts.)	Transmission (pts.)			Transfer Case (pts.)	Drive Axle		Fuel Tank (gal.)	Cooling System (qts.)
				4-Spd	5-Spd	Auto.		Front (pts.)	Rear (pts.)		
1995	4	2.2 (2195)	4.5	-	4.0	8.0	-	-	-	15.2	10.7
	D	2.3 (2262)	4.5	-	4.0	22.0	-	-	-	15.2	10.4
1996	4	2.2 (2195)	4.5	-	4.0	8.0	-	-	-	15.2	10.7
	T	2.4 (2392)	4.5	-	4.0	-	-	-	-	15.2	10.4

1 Add 3 quarts as necessary, check oil level at dipstick and add as necessary.
2 Cimarron - 16.0 gallons
3 With Turbo: 7.8 qts.
   Without Turbo: 7.9 qts.
4 With Isuzu transaxle: 3.30 pts.
5 10.0 pts. if equipped with O/D.

87951509

CHARGING SYSTEM
  ALTERNATOR 2-19
  ALTERNATOR PRECAUTIONS 2-19
  BATTERY 2-22
  DESCRIPTION AND
    OPERATION 2-17
  REGULATOR 2-22
**DIRECT IGNITION SYSTEM (DIS) AND
ELECTRONIC IGNITION (EI)
SYSTEMS**
  DIAGNOSIS AND TESTING 2-12
  GENERAL INFORMATION 2-10
  IGNITION COIL ASSEMBLY 2-12
  IGNITION MODULE 2-14
FIRING ORDERS 2-16
**HIGH ENERGY IGNITION (HEI)
SYSTEM**
  DIAGNOSIS & TESTING 2-3
  DISTRIBUTOR 2-8
  GENERAL INFORMATION 2-2
  HALL EFFECT SWITCH 2-8
  IGNITION COIL 2-5
  IGNITION MODULE 2-7
  PICK-UP COIL 2-6
SENDING UNITS AND SENSORS
  COOLANT TEMPERATURE SENDING
    UNIT 2-31
  OIL PRESSURE SWITCH 2-32
  RADIATOR FAN TEMPERATURE
    SWITCH 2-31
SPECIFICATIONS CHARTS
  ALTERNATOR SPECIFICATIONS 2-24
  STARTER SPECIFICATIONS 2-30
STARTING SYSTEM
  DESCRIPTION AND
    OPERATION 2-24
  STARTER 2-25

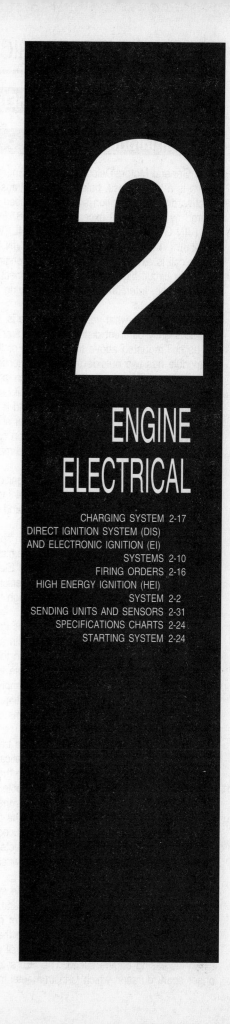

2

ENGINE
ELECTRICAL

CHARGING SYSTEM 2-17
DIRECT IGNITION SYSTEM (DIS)
AND ELECTRONIC IGNITION (EI)
SYSTEMS 2-10
FIRING ORDERS 2-16
HIGH ENERGY IGNITION (HEI)
SYSTEM 2-2
SENDING UNITS AND SENSORS 2-31
SPECIFICATIONS CHARTS 2-24
STARTING SYSTEM 2-24

HIGH ENERGY IGNITION (HEI) SYSTEM

General Information

The General Motors/Delco-Remy High Energy Ignition (HEI) system is a breakerless, pulse-triggered, transistor controlled, inductive discharge ignition system. It is used on all engines covered by this manual except for the 1987-89 2.0L (VIN 1) 2.2L (VIN G and 4), the 2.3L (VIN D), 2.4L (VIN T), 1987 and later 2.8L (VIN W) engines and all 3.1L (VIN T) engines. The ignition coil is externally mounted on the engine, using a secondary circuit high tension wire to connect the coil to the distributor cap. Interconnecting primary wiring as part of the engine harness.

Depending upon what year your vehicle is, it may have one of three slightly different distributors. The first type has the pick-up coil mounted above the module. For the second type, the module has two outside terminal connections for the wiring harness. The third type of distributor which is used with the EST system is a tang driven unit. The unit is mounted horizontally to the valve cover housing and is driven by the camshaft, through a tang on the distributor shaft. All three have separately or remote mounted ignition coils. These distributors operated in basically the same manner but may be tested or removed in different ways.

The distributor contains the electronic ignition module, and the magnetic pick-up assembly which contains a permanent magnet, a pole piece with internal teeth, and a pick-up coil (not to be confused with the ignition coil).

The HEI distributor is equipped to aid in spark timing changes which is necessary to maintain emissions, economy and performance. This is achieved by the Electronic Spark Timing (EST) control system. On these vehicles, timing changes are electronically regulated through the computer control module.

In the HEI system, as in other electronic ignition systems, the breaker points have been replaced with an electronic switch, a transistor, which is located within the ignition module. This switching transistor performs the same function the points did in a conventional ignition system; it simply turns coil primary current on and off at the correct time. Essentially, the electronic and conventional ignition systems operate on the same principal.

The module which houses the switching transistor is controlled (turned on and off) by a magnetically generated impulse induced in the pick-up coil. When the teeth of the rotating timer align with the teeth of the pole piece, the induced voltage in the pick-up coil signals the electronic module to open the coil primary circuit. The primary current then decreases and a high voltage is induced in the ignition coil secondary windings which is then directed through the rotor and high voltage leads (spark plug wires) to fire the spark plugs.

In essence then, the pick-up coil module system simply replaces the conventional breaker points and condenser. The condenser found within the distributor is for radio suppression purposes only and has nothing to do with the ignition process. The module automatically controls the dwell period, increasing it with increasing engine speed. The HEI system features a longer spark duration which is instrumental in firing lean and Exhaust Gas Recirculation (EGR) diluted fuel/air mixtures. Since dwell is automatically controlled, it cannot be adjusted. The module itself is non-adustable and non-repairable and must be replaced if found defective.

All spark timing changes in the HEI (EST) distributors are done electronically by the Electronic Control Module (ECM), which monitors information from the various engine sensors, computes the desired spark timing and signals the distributor to change the timing accordingly. With this distributor, no vacuum or centrifugal advances are used.

A Hall Effect Switch is used on some of the distributors in the EST system. It is mounted above the pick-up coil in the distributor and takes the place of the reference terminal on the distributor module. The Hall Effect Switch provides a voltage signal to the ECM to tell it which cylinder will fire next.

Some of the engines covered by this manual are equipped with Electronic Spark Control (ESC). A knock sensor is mounted in the engine block. It is connected to the ESC module which is mounted to the cowl in the engine compartment. In response to engine knock, the sensor sends a signal to the ESC module. The module will then signal the ECM which will retard the spark timing in the distributor.

HEI SYSTEM PRECAUTIONS

Before proceeding with troubleshooting or HEI system service, please note the following precautions:

Timing Light Use

Inductive pick-up timing lights are the best kind to use with the HEI system. Timing lights which connect between the spark plug and the spark plug wire occasionally (not always) give false readings due to the high voltage of the HEI system which more easily leads to arcing.

Spark Plug Wires

The plug wires used with HEI systems are of a different construction than conventional wires. When replacing them, make sure you get the correct wires, since conventional point system wires won't carry the voltage. Also, handle them carefully to avoid cracking or splitting them and never pierce them.

Tachometer Use

Not all tachometers will operate or indicate correctly when used on a HEI system. While some tachometers may give a reading, this does not necessarily mean the reading is correct. In addition, some tachometers hook up differently from others. If you can't figure out whether or not your tachometer will work on your car, check with the tachometer manufacturer.

HEI System Testers

Instruments designed specifically for testing HEI systems are available from several tool manufacturers. Some of these will even test the module itself. However, most of the tests given in the following require only an ohmmeter and a voltmeter.

Diagnosis & Testing

Diagnosis and testing procedures in this section should be used in conjunction with those in Section 4 (Emission Controls) and Section 5 (Fuel System) of this manual. This will enable you to diagnose problems involving all components controlled by the computer control module.

➡An accurate diagnosis is the first step to problem solution and repair. For several of the following steps, a HEI spark tester, tool ST 125, to ground. Use of this tool is recommended, as there is more control of the high energy spark and less chance of being shocked. If a tachometer is connected to the TACH terminal on the distributor, disconnect it before proceeding with this test.

The symptoms of a defective components within the HEI system are exactly the same as those you would encounter in a conventional system. Some of these symptoms could be:
- Hard or no starting
- Rough idle
- Poor fuel economy
- Engine misses under load or while accelerating

If you suspect a problem in your ignition system, there are certain preliminary checks which you should carry out before you begin to check the electronic portions of the system. First, it is extremely important to make sure the vehicle battery is in a good state of charge. A defective or poorly charged battery will cause the various components of the ignition system to read incorrectly when they are being tested. Second, make sure all wiring connections are clean and tight, not only at the battery, but also at the distributor cap, ignition coil and at the computer control module.

The quickest and easiest test of the ignition system is to check the secondary ignition circuit first (check for spark). If the secondary circuit checks out properly, then the engine condition is probably not the fault of the ignition system. To check the secondary ignition circuit, perform a simple spark test. Remove one of the plug wires and insert a spark tester. If a normal spark occurs, then the problem is most likely not in the ignition system. Check for fuel system problems, or fouled spark plugs.

➡For further diagnosis, please refer to component testing found later in this section.

SECONDARY SPARK

1. Check for spark at the spark plugs by attaching the HEI spark tester, tool ST 125, to one of the plug wires, grounding the HEI spark tester on the engine and cranking the starter.
2. Check fuel system, plug wires, and spark plugs. If spark is present, the HEI system is good.
3. If no spark occurs from EST distributor, disconnect the 4 terminal EST connector and recheck for spark. If spark is present, EST system service check should be performed.

IGNITION COIL

▶ **See Figure 1**

1. Detach the primary wiring connectors and secondary coil wire from the ignition coil.
2. Using an ohmmeter on the high scale, connect one lead to a grounding screw and the second lead to one of the primary coil terminals.
3. The reading should be infinite. If not, replace the ignition coil.
4. Using the low scale, place the ohmmeter leads on both the primary coil terminals.
5. The reading should be very low or zero. If not, replace the ignition coil.
6. Using the high scale, place one ohmmeter lead on the high tension output terminal and the other lead on a primary coil terminal.
7. The reading should NOT be infinite. If it is, replace the ignition coil.

PICK-UP COIL

▶ **See Figure 2**

1. Remove the rotor and pick-up coil leads from the module.
2. Using an ohmmeter, attach one lead to the distributor base and the second lead to one of the pick-up coil terminals of the connector.
3. The reading should be infinite. If not, the pick-up coil is defective.
4. Attach both leads of the ohmmeter to the pick-up terminal ends of the connector.
5. The reading should be a steady value between 500-1500 ohms.
6. If the reading is not within the specifications, the pick-up coil is defective.

➡While testing, flex the leads to determine if wire breaks are present under the wiring insulation.

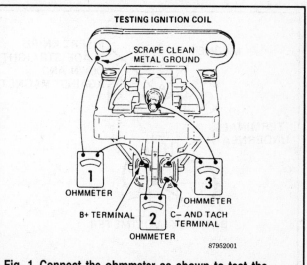

Fig. 1 Connect the ohmmeter as shown to test the ignition coil

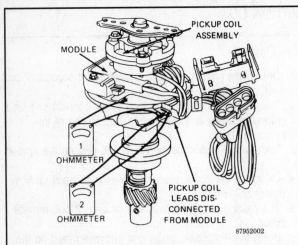

Fig. 2 When testing the pick-up coil, the reading should be a steady value from 500-1500 ohms. If not replace the pick-up coil

IGNITION MODULE

Because of the complexity of the internal circuitry of the HEI/EST module, it is recommended the module be tested with an accurate module tester.

HALL EFFECT SWITCH

◆ **See Figure 3**

1. Remove the switch connectors from the switch.
2. Connect a 12 volt battery and voltmeter to the switch. Note and follow the polarity markings.
3. With a knife blade inserted straight down and against the magnet, the voltmeter should read within 0.5 volts of battery voltage. If not, the switch is defective.
4. Without the knife blade inserted against the magnet, the voltmeter should read less than 0.5 volts. If not, the switch is defective.

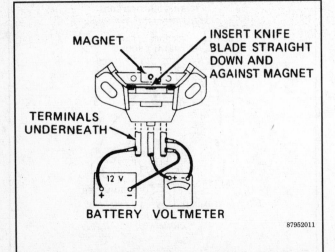

Fig. 3 Testing the Hall Effect Switch; Note that not all distributors are equipped with this switch

ELECTRONIC SPARK TIMING (EST) SYSTEM

The HEI (EST) distributor uses a modified ignition module. This module has seven or eight terminals instead of the four used without EST. Different terminal arrangements are used, depending upon engine application.

To properly control ignition/combustion timing, the ECM (or PCM) needs to know the following information:
- Crankshaft position
- Engine speed (rpm)
- Engine load (manifold pressure or vacuum)
- Atmospheric (barometric) pressure
- Engine temperature
- Transmission gear position (certain models)

The EST system consists of the distributor module, ECM and its connecting wires. The distributor has four wires from the HEI module connected to a four terminal connector, which mates with a four wire connector from the ECM.

These circuits perform the following functions:

1. \Distributor reference at terminal **B**. This provides the ECM with rpm and crankshaft position information.

2. Reference ground at terminal **D**. This wire is grounded in the distributor and makes sure the ground circuit has no voltage drop, which could affect performance. If this circuit is open, it could cause poor performance.

3. Bypass at terminal **C**. At approximately 400 rpm, the ECM applies 5 volts to this circuit to switch the spark timing control from the HEI module to the ECM. An open or grounded bypass circuit will set a Code 42 and the engine will run at base timing, plus a small amount of advance built into the HEI module.

4. EST at terminal **A**. This triggers the HEI module. The ECM does not know what the actual timing is, but it does know when it gets its reference signal. It then advances or retards the spark timing from that point. Therefore, if the base timing is set incorrectly, the entire spark curve will be incorrect.

An open circuit in the EST circuit will set a Code 42 and cause the engine to run on the HEI module timing. This will cause poor performance and poor fuel economy. A ground may set a Code 42, but the engine will not run.

The ECM uses information from the MAP or VAC and coolant sensors, in addition to rpm, in order to calculate spark advance as follows:
- Low MAP output voltage (high VAC sensor output voltage) would require MORE spark advance.
- Cold engine would require MORE spark advance.
- High MAP output voltage (low VAC sensor output voltage) would require LESS spark advance.
- Hot engine would require LESS spark advance.

Detonation could be caused by low MAP output (high VAC sensor output), or high resistance in the coolant sensor circuit.

Poor performance could be caused by high MAP output (low VAC sensor output) or low resistance in the coolant sensor circuit. Refer to the individual component tests in Section 4.

When the systems is operating on the HEI module with no voltage in the bypass line, the HEI module grounds the EST signal. The ECM expects to sense no voltage on the EST line during this condition. If it senses voltage, it sets Code 42 and will not go into the EST mode.

When the rpm for EST is reached (approximately 400 rpm), the ECM applies 5 volts to the bypass line and the EST should no longer be grounded in the HEI module, so the EST voltage should be varying.

If the bypass line is open, the HEI module will not switch to the EST mode, so the EST voltage will be low and Code 42 will be set.

If the EST line is grounded, the HEI module will switch to the EST, but because the line is grounded, there will be no EST signal and the engine will not operate. A Code 42 may or may not be set.

ELECTRONIC SPARK CONTROL (ESC) SYSTEM

The Electronic Spark Control (ESC) operates in conjunction with the Electronic Spark Timing (EST) system and modifies (retards) the spark advance when detonation occurs. The retard mode is held for approximately 20 seconds after which the spark control will again revert to the Electronic Spark Timing (EST) system. There are three basic components of the Electronic Spark Control (ESC) system.

The Electronic Spark Control (ESC) sensor detects the presence (or absence) and intensity of the detonation by the vibration characteristics of the engine. The output is an electrical signal that goes to the controller. A sensor failure would allow no spark retard.

The distributor is an HEI/EST unit with an electronic module, modified so it can respond to the ESC controller signal. This command is delayed when detonation is occurring, thus providing the level of spark retard required. The amount of spark retard is a function of the degree of detonation.

The Electronic Spark Control (ESC) controller processes the sensor signal into a command signal to the distributor, to adjust the spark timing. The process is continuous, so that the presence of detonation is monitored and controlled. The controller is a hard wired signal processor and amplifier which operates from 6–16 volts. Controller failure would be no ignition, no retard or full retard. The controller has no memory storage.

Should a Code 43 be set in the ECM memory, it would indicate that the ESC system retard signal has been sensed by the ECM for too long a period of time. When voltage at terminal **L** of the ECM is low, spark timing is retarded. Normal voltage in the non-retarded mode is approximately 7.5 volts or more.

Ignition Coil

REMOVAL & INSTALLATION

1982-84 Vehicles

1. Disconnect the negative battery cable.
2. Raise and safely support the vehicle.
3. Disconnect the fuel pump outlet pipe from the carburetor, then detach the fuel pump inlet hose.
4. Remove the vacuum pipe bracket retaining nut at the coil, then move the pipe aside for access.
5. Unfasten the two fuel pump retaining nuts, then remove the fuel pump and gasket.
6. Remove the coil mounting bolts and stud.

7. Detach the electrical connectors, then remove the coil.
8. Installation is the reverse of the removal procedure.

1985-86 1.8L (VIN O) Engine

▶ See Figure 4

1. Disconnect the negative battery cable.
2. Remove the air cleaner assembly.
3. Unfasten the ignition coil mounts. There is usually one bolt and one stud.
4. Detach the coil electrical connectors, then remove the coil.

To install:

5. Position the coil, then attach the electrical connectors.
6. Secure the coil using the attaching bolt(s) and stud(s).
7. Install the air cleaner assembly.
8. Connect the negative battery cable.

1985-86 2.0L (VIN P) Engine

EXCEPT FIRENZA

1. Disconnect the negative battery cable.
2. Raise and safely support the vehicle.
3. Label and detach the vacuum pipes from the vacuum pump, then remove the pump.
4. Unfasten the coil mounting bolts.
5. Detach the coil electrical connectors, then remove the ignition coil.
6. Installation is the reverse of the removal procedure.

FIRENZA

1. Disconnect the negative battery cable.
2. Raise and safely support the vehicle.
3. Remove the air cleaner hot air heat tube.
4. Unfasten the retaining bolt(s) and/or stud(s), then detach the electrical connectors and remove the ignition coil from the vehicle.

To install:

5. Position the coil in the vehicle, then attach the electrical connectors and secure using the bolts and nuts.
6. Carefully lower the vehicle.
7. Install the air cleaner hot air tube.

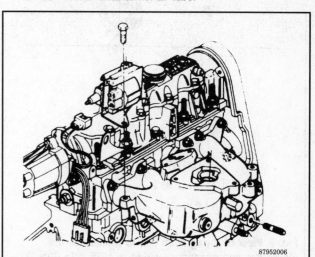

87952006

Fig. 4 Ignition coil location and mounting — 1986 1.8L (VIN O) shown

8. Connect the negative battery cable.

1985-86 2.8L (VIN W) Engine
▶ See Figure 5

1. Disconnect the negative battery cable.
2. Detach the two electrical connectors from the ignition coil.
3. Unfasten the 3 bolts and one screw securing the ignition coil to the bracket.
4. Disconnect the ignition coil lead from the distributor, then remove the coil.
5. Installation is the reverse of the removal procedure.

1987-89 2.0L (VIN K & M) Engine
▶ See Figures 6, 7, 8 and 9

1. Disconnect the negative battery cable.
2. If necessary for access to the coil, remove the air cleaner assembly.
3. Detach the coil wire and electrical connectors.

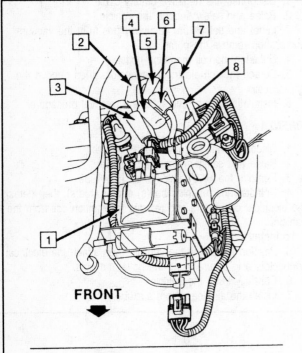

1	COIL
2	CYL. #1
3	CYL. #6
4	CYL. #5
5	CYL. #2
6	DISTRIBUTOR COIL LEAD
7	CYL. #3
8	CYL. #4

87952007

Fig. 5 View of the ignition coil in relation to the distributor and secondary wiring — 1985 2.8L (VIN W) engine shown

87952100

Fig. 6 Disconnect the coil wire, then . . .

87952101

Fig. 7 . . . detach the coil electrical connectors

4. Unfasten the coil mounts, there is usually one bolt and one stud, and remove the coil from the vehicle.
  To install:
5. Position the coil in the vehicle, then attach the electrical connectors.
6. Secure the ignition coil using the retaining bolts and/or nuts.
7. If removed, install the air cleaner assembly.
8. Connect the negative battery cable.

Pick-Up Coil

REMOVAL & INSTALLATION

▶ See Figures 10 and 11

1. Disconnect the negative battery cable.

Fig. 8 Unfasten the ignition coil retaining fasteners, then . . .

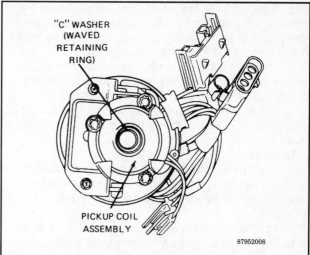

Fig. 10 On the Type I and 3 distributors, you must remove the thin "C" washer to remove the pickup coil

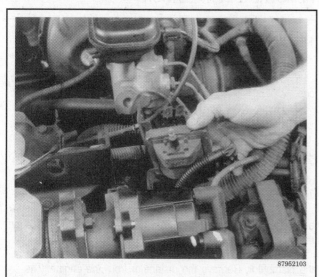

Fig. 9 . . . remove the coil from the vehicle

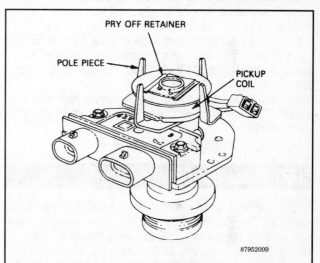

Fig. 11 Carefully pry off the retainer, then remove the pick-up coil on the Type 2 distributors

2. Remove the distributor from the vehicle. For details, please refer to the procedure later in this section. Remove the cap and rotor.

3. If the distributor has a Hall Effect Switch, remove the switch by removing the retaining screws. Matchmark the gear and shaft for installation purposes, then drive the roll pin from the gear and remove the shaft assembly.

4. Remove the thin "C" washer (waved retaining ring) or pry the retainer off (depending upon application), then lift the pick-up coil straight up to remove from the distributor.

To install:

5. Install the pickup coil and the thin "C" washer or retainer.

6. Assemble the shaft, gears parts and roll pin. Use the marks made during removal for alignment purposes.

7. If equipped, install the Hall Effect Switch.

8. Spin the distributor shaft to be sure the teeth do not touch. If the teeth make contact, loosen, then re-tighten the pickup coil teeth and Hall Effect Switch teeth (if used) to eliminate contact.

9. Install the rotor and cap, then install the distributor assembly. For details, please refer to the procedure located later in this section.

10. Connect the negative battery cable.

Ignition Module

REMOVAL & INSTALLATION

▶ See Figure 12

➡It is imperative that silicone lubricant be used under the module when it is installed, to prevent module failure due to overheating.

1. Disconnect the negative battery cable.

2. Remove the distributor from the vehicle. For details, please refer to the procedure later in this section. Remove the cap and rotor.

3. If the distributor has a Hall Effect Switch, remove the switch by unfastening the retaining screws. Matchmark the gear and shaft for installation purposes, then drive the roll pin from the gear and remove the shaft assembly.

4. Remove the thin "C" washer (waved retaining ring) or pry the retainer off (depending upon application), then lift the pick-up coil straight up to remove from the distributor.

5. Detach the wiring connector(s) from the ignition module. Unfasten the two screws, then remove the module and copper shield (if used).

To install:

6. Using a clean, dry rag, wipe the distributor base and module clean, the apply a thin coat of a suitable silicone lubricant between the module and the base for heat dissipation.

7. Position the module and copper shield (if used) to the base, then attach the wiring connectors to the module.

8. Install the pickup coil and the thin "C" washer or retainer.

9. Assemble the shaft, gears parts and roll pin. Use the marks made during removal for alignment purposes.

10. If equipped, install the Hall Effect Switch.

11. Spin the distributor shaft to be sure the teeth do not touch. If the teeth make contact, loosen, then re-tighten the pickup coil teeth and Hall Effect Switch teeth (if used) to eliminate contact.

12. Fasten the rotor and cap, then install the distributor assembly. For details, please refer to the procedure located later in this section.

13. Connect the negative battery cable.

Hall Effect Switch

The Hall Effect Switch, when used, is installed in the HEI distributor. The purpose of the switch is to sense engine speed and send the information to the Electronic Control Module (ECM). To remove the Hall Effect Switch, the distributor shaft must be removed from the distributor.

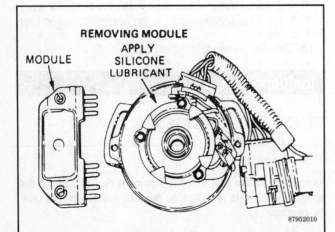

REMOVING MODULE

MODULE

APPLY SILICONE LUBRICANT

87952010

Fig. 12 Before installing the ignition module, apply a suitable silicone lubricant to the module for heat dissipation — type three distributor shown

REMOVAL & INSTALLATION

1. Disconnect the negative battery cable.

2. Remove the distributor from the vehicle. For details, please refer to the procedure later in this section. Remove the cap and rotor.

3. Remove the switch by unfastening the retaining screws.

To install:

4. Position the switch, then securing using the retaining screws.

5. Fasten the rotor and cap, then install the distributor assembly. For details, please refer to the procedure located later in this section.

6. Connect the negative battery cable.

Distributor

REMOVAL & INSTALLATION

1.8L (VIN G) and 2.0L (VIN P) OHV Engines

1. Disconnect the negative battery cable.

2. Tag and disconnect all wires leading from the distributor cap.

3. Remove the air cleaner housing.

4. Remove the distributor cap.

5. Disconnect the AIR pipe-to-exhaust manifold hose at the air management valve.

6. Unscrew the rear engine lift bracket bolt and nut, lift it off the stud and then position the entire assembly out of the way to facilitate better access to the distributor.

7. Mark the position of the distributor, relative to the engine block and then scribe a mark on the distributor body indicating the initial position of the rotor.

8. Remove the hold-down nut and clamp from the base of the distributor. Remove the distributor from the engine. The drive gear on the distributor shaft is helical and the shaft will rotate slightly as the distributor is removed. Note and mark the position of the rotor at this second position. Do not crank the engine while the distributor is removed.

To install:

➡**If the engine position was disturbed while the distributor was removed, refer to the appropriate installation procedure.**

9. To install the distributor, rotate the shaft until the rotor aligns with the second mark you made (when the shaft stopped moving). Lubricate the drive gear with clean engine oil and install the distributor into the engine. As the distributor is installed, the rotor should move to the first mark that you made. This will ensure proper timing. If the marks do not align properly, remove the distributor and try again.

10. Install the clamp and hold-down nut.

➡**You may wish to use a magnet attached to an extension bar to position the clamp on the stud.**

11. Installation of the remaining components is in the reverse order of removal. Check the ignition timing.

1.8L (VIN O & J) and 2.0L (VIN K & M) OHC Engines

▶ See Figures 13, 14 and 15

1. Disconnect the negative battery cable.
2. Tag the spark plug wires, then remove the wires and coil.
3. Matchmark the position of the rotor, distributor body and cylinder head.
4. Detach the coil and EST electrical connectors from the distributor.
5. Unfasten the two distributor hold-down or retaining nuts, then remove the distributor.

➡**If the engine position was disturbed while the distributor was removed, refer to the appropriate installation procedure.**

6. Installation is the reverse of removal. Tighten the hold-down nuts to 13 ft. lbs. (18 Nm). Check the ignition timing.

1985-86 2.8L (VIN W) Engine

1. Disconnect the negative battery cable.
2. Unfasten the two screws securing the distributor cap, then remove the cap.
3. Detach the two electrical connectors from the HEI module.
4. Matchmark the position of the rotor and the distributor in the block, then remove the distributor hold-down screw and clamp.
5. Rotate the distributor to disengage it from the drive gear, then pull it upward to remove it from the engine.

➡**If the engine position was disturbed while the distributor was removed, refer to the appropriate installation procedure.**

6. Installation is the reverse of the removal procedure. Check the ignition timing.

Fig. 14 Remove the distributor from the engine — 1988 2.0L (VIN K) engine shown

Fig. 15 On some vehicles, there is an O-ring on the base of the distributor which can be carefully removed and replaced, if necessary

INSTALLATION IF THE ENGINE WAS DISTURBED

➡**If the engine was cranked while the distributor was removed, you will have to place the engine on TDC of the compression stroke for the No. 1 cylinder to obtain proper ignition timing.**

1. Remove the No. 1 spark plug.
2. Place your thumb over the spark plug hole. Crank the engine slowly until compression is felt. It will be easier if you have someone rotate the engine by hand, using a wrench on the crankshaft pulley.
3. Align the timing mark on the crankshaft pulley with the 0° mark on the timing scale attached to the front of the engine. This places the engine at TDC of the compression stroke.
4. Turn the distributor shaft until the rotor points to the No. 1 spark plug tower on the cap.
5. Install the distributor into the engine. Be sure to align the distributor-to-engine block mark made earlier.

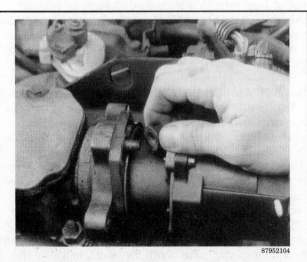

Fig. 13 Unfasten the distributor-to-camshaft carrier retaining nuts — 1988 2.0L (VIN K) Sunbird shown

6. Perform all necessary remaining service steps.

DIRECT IGNITION SYSTEM (DIS) AND ELECTRONIC IGNITION (EI) SYSTEMS

General Information

The Direct Ignition System (DIS) or Electronic Ignition (EI) is used on the 1987-92 2.0L (VIN 1 and H), 2.2L (VIN G and 4), 2.3L (VIN D), 2.4L (VIN T) and all 1987 and later 2.8L (VIN W) and 3.1L (VIN T) engines.

The DIS or EI system does not use the conventional distributor and ignition coil. The system consists of two (4-cylinder) or 3 (6-cylinder) separate ignition coils, an ignition module, DIS ignition module or Ignition Control Module (ICM) as applicable, crankshaft sensor or combination sensor, along with the related connecting wires and Electronic Spark Timing (EST) or Ignition Control (IC) portion of the computer control module (ECM/PCM). The 1996 models also use a Camshaft Position (CMP) sensor.

The distributorless system uses a "waste spark" method of spark distribution. Companion cylinders are paired and the spark occurs simultaneously in the cylinder with the piston coming up on the compression stroke and in the companion cylinder with the piston coming up on the exhaust stroke.

Example of firing order and companion cylinders:

- 1-2-3-4-5-6; 1/4, 2/5, 3/6
- 1-6-5-4-3-2; 1/4, 6/3, 5/2
- 1-3-4-2; 1/4, 2/3

➡Notice the companion cylinders in the V6 engine firing orders remain the same, but the cylinder firing order sequence differs.

The cylinder on the exhaust stroke requires very little of the available voltage to arc, so the remaining high voltage is used by the cylinder in the firing position (TDC compression). This same process is repeated when the companion cylinders reverse roles.

It is possible in an engine no-load condition, for one plug to fire, even though the spark plug lead from the same coil is disconnected from the other spark plug. The disconnected spark plug lead acts as one plate of a capacitor, with the engine being the other plate. These two capacitors plates are charged as a current surge (spark) jumps across the gap of the connected spark plug.

These plates are then discharged as the secondary energy is dissipated in an oscillating current across the gap of the spark plug still connected. Because of the direction of current flow in the primary windings and thus in the secondary windings, one spark plug will fire from the center electrode to the side electrode, while the other will fire from the side electrode to the center electrode.

These systems utilize the EST or IC signal from the computer control module, as do the convention distributor type ignition systems equipped with the EST system to control timing.

In the Direct Ignition or Electronic Ignition system and while under 400 rpm, the DIS ignition module (Ignition Control Module) controls the spark timing through a module timing mode. Over 400 rpm, the ECM/PCM controls the spark timing through

the EST/IC mode. To properly control the ignition timing, the computer control module relies on the following information from the various sensors:

- Engine load (manifold pressure or vacuum)
- Engine coolant temperature
- Atmospheric (barometric) pressure
- Engine temperature
- Manifold/Intake air temperature
- Crankshaft position
- Engine speed (rpm)
- Knock
- TP sensor

SYSTEM COMPONENTS

Crankshaft Position (CKP) Sensor

▶ **See Figure 16**

A magnetic crankshaft sensor (Hall Effect switch) is used which is remotely mounted on the opposite side of the engine from the DIS/IC module. The sensor protrudes in to the engine block, within about 0.050 in. (1.27mm) of the crankshaft reluctor.

The reluctor is a special wheel cast into the crankshaft with seven slots machined into it, six of which are equally spaced 60° apart. A seventh slot is spaced 10° from one of the other slots and serves as a generator of a "sync-pulse". As the reluctor rotates as part of the crankshaft, the slots change the magnetic field of the sensor, creating an induced voltage pulse.

The CKP sensor, ICM or DIS ignition module sends reference signals to the computer control module (ECM/PCM), based on the Crankshaft Position (CKP) sensor pulses, which are used to determine crankshaft position and engine speed. Reference pulses to the computer control module occur at a rate of 1 per each 180° of crankshaft rotation for vehicles through 1993, or 7 per 360° of crankshaft rotation for 1994-96 vehicles. This signal is called the 2X or 7X reference because it occurs 2 or 7 times per crankshaft revolution, depending on the year of your vehicle.

For 1994-96 vehicles, the 7X reference signal is necessary for the PCM to determine when to activate the fuel injectors.

The computer control module (ECM/PCM) activates the fuel injectors, based on the recognition of every other reference pulse, beginning at a crankshaft position 120° after piston Top Dead Center (TDC). By comparing the time between the pulses, the DIS module or Ignition Control Module (ICM) can recognize the pulse representing the seventh slot (sync-pulse) which starts the calculation of ignition coil sequencing. The second crankshaft pulse following the sync-pulse signals the DIS module to fire the No. 2-5 ignition coil, the fourth crankshaft pulse signals the module to fire No. 3-6 ignition coil and the sixth crankshaft pulse signals the module to fire the No. 1-4 ignition coil.

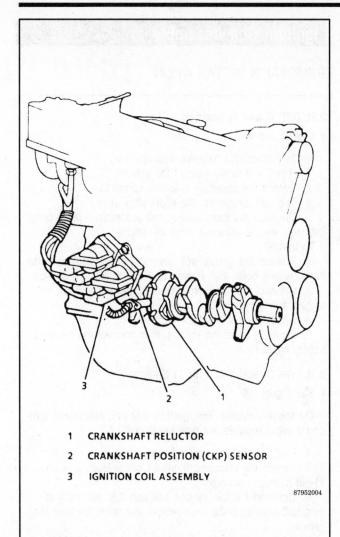

1 CRANKSHAFT RELUCTOR

2 CRANKSHAFT POSITION (CKP) SENSOR

3 IGNITION COIL ASSEMBLY

87952004

Fig. 16 View of the CKP sensor-to-crankshaft reluctor relationship

Ignition Coils

There are two separate coils for the four cylinder engines and three separate coils for the V6 engines, mounted to the coil/module assembly. Spark distribution is synchronized by a signal from the crankshaft sensor which the ignition module uses to trigger each coil at the proper time. Each coil provides the spark for two spark plugs simultaneously (waste spark distribution).

Two types of ignition coil assemblies are used, Type I and Type II. During the diagnosis of the systems, the correct type of ignition coil assembly must be identified and the diagnosis directed to that system.

The 2.0L (VIN H) engine is equipped with the Type 1 module/coil assembly. The Type I assembly has two twin tower ignition coils, combined into a single coil pack unit. This unit is mounted to the DIS module. If any of the coils are faulty, the entire module must replaced. A separate current source through a fused circuit to the module terminal **P** is used to power the ignition coils.

All other engines are equipped with the Type II coil/module assembly. The Type II coil/module assembly has two or three (depending upon engine) separate coils that are mounted to the DIS or IC module. Each coil can be replaced separately. A fused low current source to the module terminal **M**, provides power for the sensors, ignition coils and internal module circuitry.

DIS Module/Ignition Control Module (ICM)

The DIS module or ICM, as it's called in later years, monitors the crankshaft sensor signal, then, based on these signals, sends a reference signal to the computer control module (ECM/PCM) so that correct spark and fuel injector control can be maintained during all driving conditions. During cranking, the module monitors the sync-pulse to begin the ignition firing sequence. Below 400 rpm, the module controls the spark advance by triggering each of the ignition coils at a predetermined interval, based on engine speed only. Above 400 rpm, the ECM controls the spark timing (EST) and compensates for all driving conditions. The module must receive a sync-pulse and then a crank signal, in that order, to enable the engine to start.

The DIS module or Ignition Control Module (ICM) is not repairable. When a module is replaced, the remaining DIS/ICM components must be transferred to the new module.

Direct Ignition Electronic Spark Timing (EST) Circuits

➡**These circuits are applicable for vehicles through 1992 only.**

The EST system is basically the same EST to ECM circuit used on the distributor type ignition systems with EST. This system includes the following circuits:

• DIS Reference (CKT 430) — The crankshaft sensor generates a signal to the ignition module, which results in a reference pulse being sent to the ECM. The ECM uses this signal to calculate crankshaft position and engine speed for injector pulse width.

• Reference Ground (CKT 453) — This wire is grounded through the module and insures that the ground circuit has no voltage drop between the ignition module and the ECM, which can affect performance.

• Bypass signal (CKT 424) — At approximately 400 rpm, the ECM applies 5 volts to this circuit to switch spark timing control from the DIS module to the ECM. An open or grounded by pass circuit will set a code 42 and result in the engine operating in a back-up ignition timing mode (module timing) at a calculated timing value. This may cause poor performance and reduced fuel economy.

• EST circuit (CKT 423) — The DIS module sends a reference signal to the ECM when the engine is cranking. While the engine is under 400 rpm, the DIS module controls the ignition timing. When the engine speed exceeds 400 rpm, the ECM applies 5 volts to the bypass line to switch the timing to the ECM control (EST). An open or ground in the EST circuit will result in the engine continuing to run, but in a back-up ignition timing mode (module timing mode) at a calculated timing value and the SERVICE ENGINE SOON light will not be on. If the EST fault is still present, the next time the engine is restarted, a code 42 will be set and the engine will operate in the module timing mode. This may cause poor performance and reduced fuel economy.

Ignition Control (IC)

➡These circuits are applicable for 1993-96 vehicles only.

This system uses the same circuits between the ICM and the PCM that distributor type systems use. This system includes the following circuits:

• 7X Reference (CKT 483) — The CKP sensor generates a signal to the ICM, resulting in a reference pulse which is sent to the PCM. The PCM uses this signal to determine crankshaft position, engine speed and injector pulse width. The engine will not start or run if this circuit is open or grounded.

• Reference low (CKT 453) — This wire is grounded through the module and insures that the ground circuit has no voltage drop between the ICM and the PCM which may affect engine performance.

• Ignition control 1 & 2 (CKTs 423 & 406) — The PCM sends the Ignition Control (IC) pulses to the ICM on these circuits. These signals are similar to the 7X reference pulse except that the PCM uses sensor inputs to determine the pulse timing to control spark advance. When the PCM receives the 7X signal, it will determine which pair of cylinders will be fired. (1-4 or 2-3). It will tell the ICM which cylinder pair will be fired via CKTs 423 or 406.

Diagnosis And Testing

SYSTEM PERFORMANCE

The computer control module uses information from the MAP and Coolant sensors, in addition to rpm to calculate spark advance as follows;

• Low MAP output voltage = More spark advance.
• Cold engine = More spark advance.
• High MAP output voltage = Less spark advance.
• Hot engine = Less spark advance.

Therefore, detonation could be caused by low MAP output or high resistance in the Engine Coolant Temperature (ECT) sensor circuit. Poor performance could be caused by high MAP output or low resistance in the coolant sensor circuit.

If the engine cranks but will not operate, or starts, then immediately stalls, diagnosis must be accomplished to determine if the failure is in the ignition system or the fuel system. Refer to the individual component tests.

EST PERFORMANCE

The ECM will set timing at a specified value when the diagnostic **TEST** terminal in the ALDL connector is grounded. To check for EST operation, run the engine at 1500 rpm with the terminal ungrounded. Then ground the **TEST** terminal. If the EST is operating, there should be a noticeable engine rpm change. A fault in the EST system will set a trouble code 42.

Ignition Coil Assembly

REMOVAL & INSTALLATION

2.2L (VIN G and 4) Engines

▶ See Figure 17

1. Disconnect the negative battery cable.
2. Raise and safely support the vehicle.
3. Detach the assembly electrical connectors.
4. Tag and disconnect the spark plug wires.
5. Unfasten the three ignition coil assembly-to-block bolts, then remove the assembly from the engine.

To install:

6. Position the ignition coil assembly to the engine. Install the mounting bolts, then tighten to 15-22 ft. lbs. (20-30 Nm).
7. Connect the spark plug wires to the proper coils, as tagged during removal.
8. Attach the coil electrical connectors.
9. Carefully lower the vehicle, then connect the negative battery cable.

2.3L (VIN D) and 2.4L (VIN T) Engines

▶ See Figure 18

➡On these vehicles, the ignition coil and electronic ignition control module are one assembly.

1. Disconnect the negative battery cable.
2. Detach the electronic Ignition Control Module (ICM) 11-pin harness connector.
3. Unfasten the four ignition coil and ICM assembly-to-camshaft housing bolts, then remove the assembly from the vehicle.

If the boots stick to the spark plugs, use tool J 36011 or equivalent, to removed by first twisting, then carefully pulling upward on the retainers. Reinstall the boots and retainers on the ignition coil housing secondary terminals. The boots and retainers must be in place on the ignition coil housing prior to installation or damage to the ignition system could result.

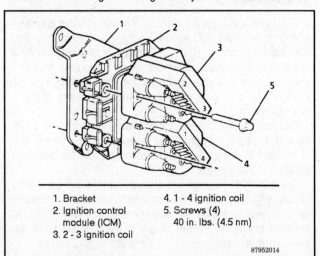

1. Bracket
2. Ignition control module (ICM)
3. 2 - 3 ignition coil
4. 1 - 4 ignition coil
5. Screws (4) 40 in. lbs. (4.5 nm)

87952014

Fig. 17 Exploded view of the ignition coil assembly — 2.2L (VIN 4) engine shown

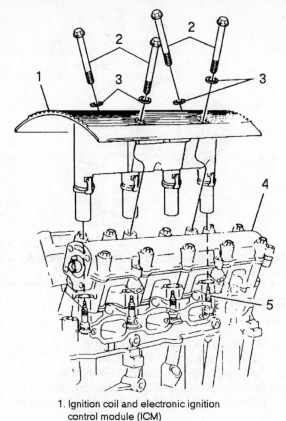

1. Ignition coil and electronic ignition control module (ICM)
2. Ignition coil and electronic ignition control module (ICM) to camshaft housings bolts
3. Isolater washers (4) (with sheet metal surface up)
4. Camshaft housing (intake side) cover
5. Spark plug

87952015

Fig. 18 The ignition coil assembly on the 2.3L and 2.4L engines, is a completely different unit compared to that on the other DIS/EI engines

To install:

4. Fasten the spark plugs and retainers to the housing.

5. While carefully aligning the boots to the spark plug terminals, position the ignition coil and ICM assembly to the engine.

6. Coat the threads of the retaining bolts with 1052080 or equivalent. Install the retaining bolts, then tighten to 16 ft. lbs. (22 Nm).

7. Attach the electronic ICM harness connector.

8. Connect the negative battery cable.

2.0L (VIN 1 and H), 2.8L (VIN W) and 3.1L (VIN T) Engines

▶ See Figures 19 and 20

➡On 3.1L engines, an "Idle Learn" procedure must be performed which requires the use of a scan tool. You may wish to have the coil(s) replaced at a proper service facility.

1. Disconnect the negative battery cable.

2. Detach the electrical wires from the ignition coil assembly.

3. Tag and disconnect the spark plug wires from the assembly.

4. Unfasten the mounting bolts, then remove the assembly from the engine.

➡On the 2.8L and 3.1L engines, with the coil pack removed, each coil can be removed and the ignition module can be removed as well.

To install:

5. Position the ignition coil assembly on the engine. Install the mounting bolts, then tighten to 19 ft. lbs. (25 Nm) for the 2.8L and 3.1L engines. For the 2.0L (VIN 1) engine, tighten to 89 inch lbs. (10 Nm).

6. Attach the plug wires to the proper coils, as tagged during removal.

7. Fasten the ignition coil assembly wiring.

8. Connect the negative battery cable.

➡On the 3.1L engine, this test must be done before the engine is started and requires the use of a Tech 1®, or equivalent, scan tool.

9. If equipped with the 3.1L engine, perform the idle learn procedure to allow the ECM/PCM memory to be updated with the correct IAC valve pintle position and provide for a stable idle speed.

a. Install an appropriate scan tool.

b. Turn the ignition to the **ON** position, engine not running.

c. Select **IAC SYSTEM**, then **IDLE LEARN** in the **MISC TEST** mode.

d. Place the transaxle in park or neutral, as applicable.

e. Proceed with idle learn as directed by the scan tool.

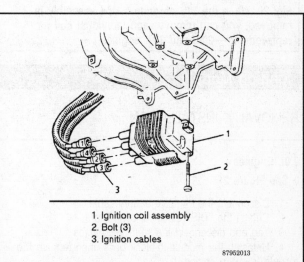

1. Ignition coil assembly
2. Bolt (3)
3. Ignition cables

87952013

Fig. 19 On the 2.0L engine, if any part of the ignition coil is faulty, the entire coil assembly must be replaced

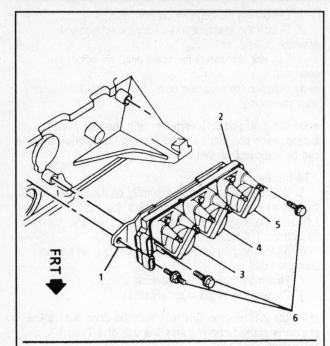

1. Bracket
2. Module
3. 1 - 4 coil
4. 6 - 3 coil
5. 5 - 2 coil
6. Bolts (3) - 19 ft. lbs. (25 m)

87952012

Fig. 20 When the DIS of Ignition Coil assembly is removed, you can remove each individual coil for replacement — 2.8L and 3.1L engines

Ignition Module

REMOVAL & INSTALLATION

2.0L Engines
▶ See Figure 21

1. Disconnect the negative battery cable.
2. Detach the "DIS" electrical connectors.
3. Tag and disconnect the spark plug wires.
4. Unfasten the module-to-block bolts, then remove the module from the engine.
5. Installation is the reverse of the removal procedure.

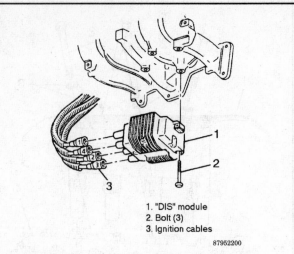

1. "DIS" module
2. Bolt (3)
3. Ignition cables

87952200

Fig. 21 View of the ignition or DIS module location — 2.0L engines

2.2L Engines
▶ See Figure 22

1. Disconnect the negative battery cable.
2. Raise and safely support the vehicle.
3. Remove the ignition coils from the module.
4. Remove the module from the assembly plate.
5. Installation is the reverse of the removal procedure.

2.3L And 2.4L Engines
▶ See Figure 23

1. Disconnect the negative battery cable.
2. Detach the Electronic Ignition Control Module (ICM) electrical connector.
3. Unfasten the coil and module-to-cam housing bolts, then remove the coil and ignition module assembly from the engine.
4. Unfasten the housing-to-cover screws, then pull the housing from the cover.
5. Detach the coil harness connector from the module.

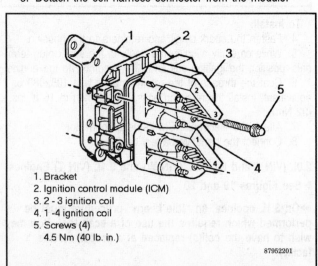

1. Bracket
2. Ignition control module (ICM)
3. 2 - 3 ignition coil
4. 1 - 4 ignition coil
5. Screws (4)
   4.5 Nm (40 lb. in.)

87952201

Fig. 22 The ignition module or (ICM), is located under the coils

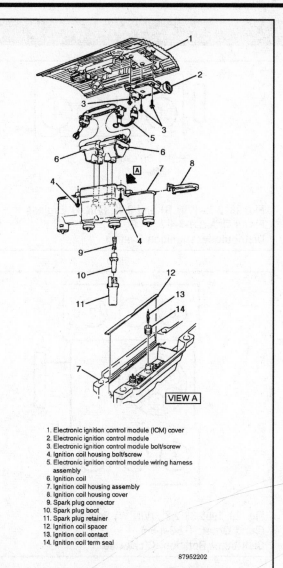

1. Electronic ignition control module (ICM) cover
2. Electronic ignition control module
3. Electronic ignition control module bolt/screw
4. Ignition coil housing bolt/screw
5. Electronic ignition control module wiring harness assembly
6. Ignition coil
7. Ignition coil housing assembly
8. Ignition coil housing cover
9. Spark plug connector
10. Spark plug boot
11. Spark plug retainer
12. Ignition coil spacer
13. Ignition coil contact
14. Ignition coil term seal

87952202

Fig. 23 View of the Ignition Control Module location and related components — 1995 2.3L engine shown

6. Unfasten the module-to-cover screws, then remove the module.

✳✳WARNING

Do NOT wipe the grease from the module or coil if the same module is to be replaced. If a new module is to be installed, a package of silicone grease will be included with it. Spread the grease on the metal face of the module and on the cover where the module seats. This grease is necessary for module cooling.

7. Installation is the reverse of the removal procedure.

2.8L And 3.1L Engines
▶ See Figure 24

➡ On 3.1L engines, an "Idle Learn" procedure must be performed which requires the use of a scan tool. You may wish to have the coil(s) or ignition module replaced at a proper service facility.

1. Disconnect the negative battery cable.
2. Remove the ignition coil assembly from the engine, as outlined earlier in this section.
3. Remove the coils from the assembly.
4. Lift the module from the assembly plate.
To install:
5. Position the ignition module to the assembly plate.
6. Install the coils, then install the coil assembly to the engine.
7. Connect the negative battery cable.
8. If equipped with the 3.1L engine, perform the idle learn procedure to allow the ECM/PCM memory to be updated with the correct IAC valve pintle position and provide for a stable idle speed.
    a. Install an appropriate scan tool.
    b. Turn the ignition to the **ON** position, engine not running.
    c. Select **IAC SYSTEM**, then **IDLE LEARN** in the **MISC TEST** mode.
    d. Place the transaxle in park or neutral, as applicable.
    e. Proceed with idle learn as directed by the scan tool.

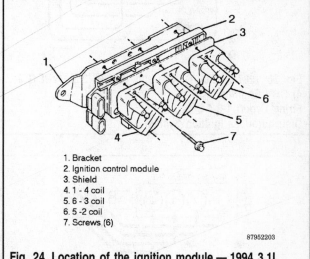

1. Bracket
2. Ignition control module
3. Shield
4. 1 - 4 coil
5. 6 - 3 coil
6. 5 - 2 coil
7. Screws (6)

87952203

Fig. 24 Location of the ignition module — 1994 3.1L engine shown

FIRING ORDERS

◆ See Figures 25, 26, 27, 28, 29 and 30

➡To avoid confusion, label, remove and replace spark plug cables one at a time.

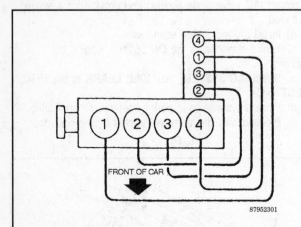

Fig. 25 1982 1.8L (VIN G) and 1983-86 2.0L (VIN B & P) OHV Engines
Firing Order: 1-3-4-2
Distributor Rotation: Clockwise

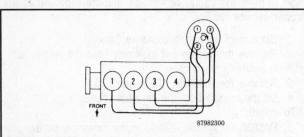

Fig. 26 1987-89 2.0L (VIN 1) and 1990-96 2.2L (VIN G & 4) OHV Engines
Firing Order: 1-3-4-2
Distributorless Ignition System

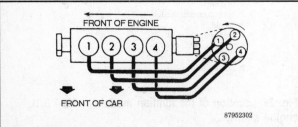

Fig. 27 1983-86 1.8L (VIN O & J) and 1987-91 2.0L (VIN K & M) OHC Engines
Firing Order: 1-3-4-2
Distributor Rotation: Clockwise

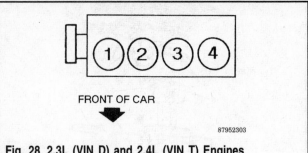

Fig. 28 2.3L (VIN D) and 2.4L (VIN T) Engines
Firing Order: 1-3-4-2
Distributorless Ignition System

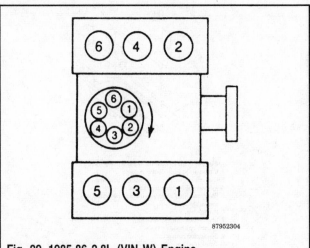

Fig. 29 1985-86 2.8L (VIN W) Engine
Firing Order: 1-2-3-4-5-6
Distributor Rotation: Clockwise

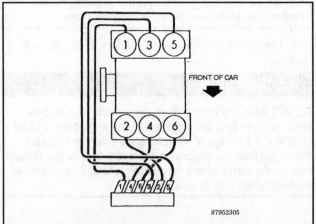

Fig. 30 1987-89 2.8L (VIN W) and 1990-94 3.1L (VIN M) Engines
Firing Order: 1-2-3-4-5-6
Distributorless Ignition System

CHARGING SYSTEM

Description and Operation

▶ See Figures 31, 32, 33 and 34

The automobile charging system provides electrical power for operation of the vehicle's ignition and starting systems and all the electrical accessories. The battery serves as an electrical surge of storage tank, storing (in chemical form) the energy originally produced by the engine driven generator. The system also provides a means of regulating generator output to protect the battery from being overcharged and to avoid excessive voltage to the accessories.

The storage battery is a chemical device incorporating parallel lead plates in a tank containing a sulfuric acid-water solution. Adjacent plates are slightly dissimilar, and the chemical reaction of the two dissimilar plates produces electrical energy when the battery is connected to a load such as the starter motor. The chemical reaction is reversible, so that when the generator is producing a voltage (electrical pressure) greater then that produced by the battery, electricity is forced into the battery, and the battery is returned to its fully charged state.

The vehicle's generator is driven mechanically, through V belts, by the engine crankshaft. It consists of two coils of fine wire, one stationary (the stator), and one movable (the rotor). The rotor may also be known as the armature and consists of fine wire wrapped around an iron core which is mounted on a shaft. The electricity which flows through the two coils of wire (provided initially by the battery in some cases) creates an intense magnetic field around both rotor and stator, and the interaction between the two fields creates voltage, allowing the generator to power the accessories and charge the battery.

Todays automobiles use alternating current generators or alternators because they are more efficient, can be rotated at higher speeds, and have fewer brush problems, In an alternator, the field rotates while all the current produced passes only through the stator windings. The brushes bear against continu-

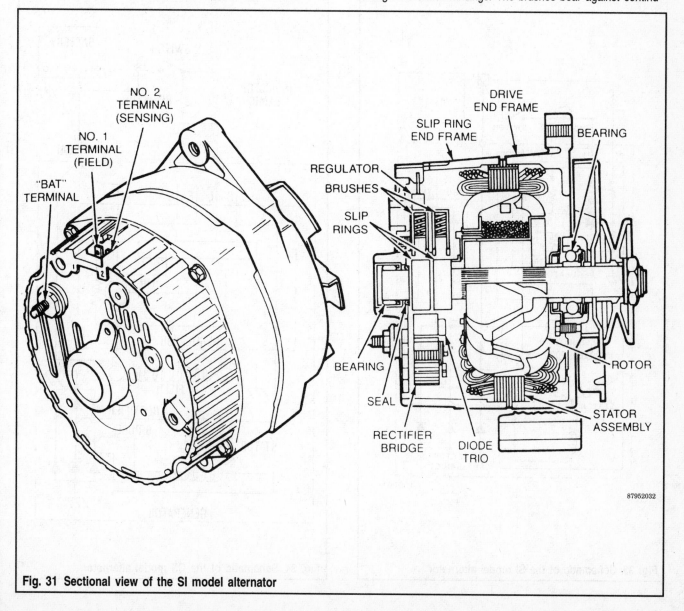

Fig. 31 Sectional view of the SI model alternator

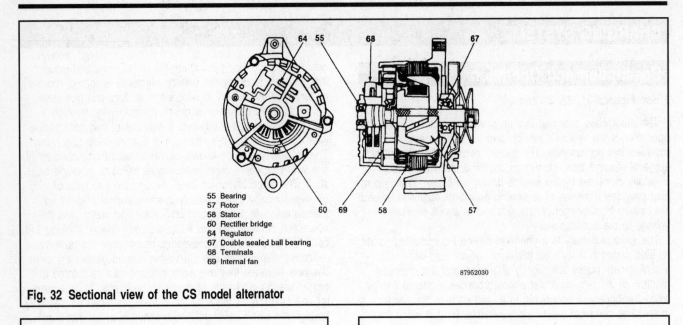

55 Bearing
57 Rotor
58 Stator
60 Rectifier bridge
64 Regulator
67 Double sealed ball bearing
68 Terminals
69 Internal fan

87952030

Fig. 32 Sectional view of the CS model alternator

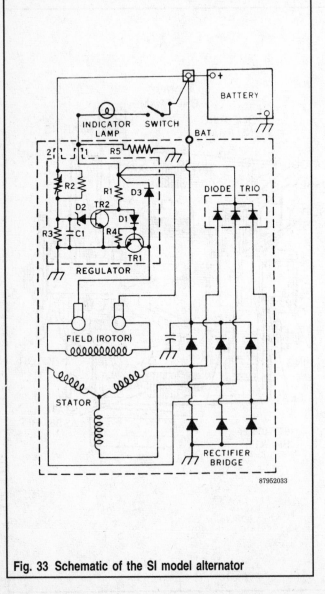

87952033

Fig. 33 Schematic of the SI model alternator

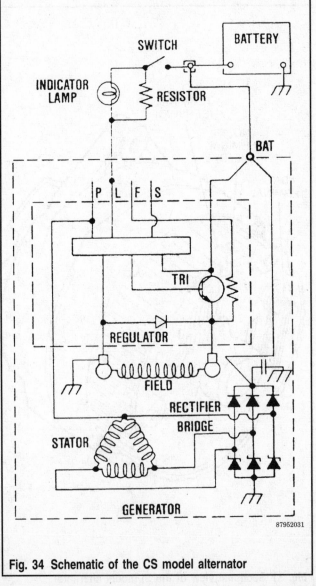

87952031

Fig. 34 Schematic of the CS model alternator

ous slip rings rather than a commutator. This causes the current produced to periodically reverse the direction of its flow. Diodes (electrical one-way switches) block the flow of current from traveling in the wrong direction. A series of diodes is wired together to permit the alternating flow of the stator to be converted to a pulsating, but unidirectional flow of current from traveling in the wrong direction. A series of diodes is wires together to permit the alternating flow of the stator to be converted to a pulsating, but unidirectional flow at the alternator output. The alternator's field is wires in series with the voltage regulator.

The alternating current generator (alternator) supplies a continuous output of electrical energy at all engine speeds. The alternator generates electrical energy for the engine and all electrical components, and recharges the battery by supplying it with current. This unit consists of four main assemblies: two end frame assemblies, a rotor assembly, and a stator assembly. The rotor is supported in the drive end frame by a ball bearing and at the other end by a roller bearing. These bearings are lubricated during manufacture and require no maintenance. There are six diodes in the end frame assembly. Diodes are electrical check valves that change the alternating current supplied from the stator windings to a direct current (DC), delivered to the output (BAT) terminal. Three diodes are negative and are mounted flush with the end frame; the other three are positive and are mounted into a strip called a heat sink. The positive diodes are easily identified as the ones within small cavities or depressions. A capacitor, or condenser, mounted on the end frame protects the rectifier bridge and diode trio from high voltages, and suppresses radio noise. This capacitor requires no maintenance.

Alternator Precautions

To prevent damage to the on-board computer, alternator and regulator, the following precautionary measures must be taken when working with the electrical system.

• Be absolutely sure of the polarity of a booster battery before making connections. Connect the cables positive to positive, and negative to negative. Connect positive cables first and then make the last connection to ground on the body of the booster vehicle so that arcing cannot ignite hydrogen gas that may have accumulated near the battery. Even momentary connection of a booster battery with the polarity reversed will damage alternator diodes.

• Disconnect both vehicle battery cables before attempting to charge a battery.

• Never ground the alternator or generator output or battery terminal. Be cautious when using metal tools around a battery to avoid creating a short circuit between the terminals.

• Never ground the field circuit between the alternator and regulator.

• Never run an alternator or generator without load unless the field circuit is disconnected.

• Never attempt to polarize an alternator.

• Keep the regulator cover in place when taking voltage and current limiter readings.

• Use insulated tools when adjusting the regulator.

• Whenever DC generator-to-regulator wires have been disconnected, the generator must be repolarized. To do this with an externally grounded, light duty generator, momentarily place a jumper wires between the battery terminal and the generator terminal of the regulator. With an internally grounded heavy duty unit, disconnect the wire to the regulator field terminal and touch the regulator battery terminal with it.

• When installing a battery, make sure that the positive and negative cables are not reversed.

• When jump-starting the car, be sure that like terminals are connected. This also applies to using a battery charger. Reversed polarity will burn out the alternator and regulator in a matter of seconds.

• Never operate the alternator with the battery disconnected or on an otherwise uncontrolled open circuit.

• Do not short across or ground any alternator or regulator terminals.

• Do not try to polarize the alternator.

• Do not apply full battery voltage to the field (brown) connector.

• Always disconnect the battery ground cable before disconnecting the alternator lead.

• Always disconnect the battery (negative cable first) when charging it.

• Never subject the alternator to excessive heat or dampness. If you are steam cleaning the engine, cover the alternator.

• Never use arc-welding equipment on the car with the alternator connected.

Alternator

DIAGNOSIS

SI Alternator
▶ See Figure 35

A charge indicator lamp is used in most cars to signal when there is a fault in the charging system. This lamp is located in the gauge package and is used in diagnosis. A voltmeter may be used instead of the charge indicator lamp in diagnosis.

CS-130 & CS-130D Alternator

1. Check the drive belt(s) for wear and tension. Check wiring for obvious damage.
2. Go to Step 7 for vehicles without a charge indicator lamp.
3. With the ignition switch **ON**, and the engine stopped, the lamp should be ON. If not, detach the wiring harness at the alternator and ground the "L" terminal lead.
4. If the lamp illuminates, replace the alternator. If the lamp does not illuminate, locate the open circuit between the grounding lead and the ignition switch. Check the lamp, it may be open.
5. With the ignition switch **ON** and the engine running at moderate speed, the lamp should be OFF. If not, stop the engine, then turn the switch **ON** and detach the wiring harness at the alternator.
6. If the lamp goes out, replace the alternator. If the lamp stays ON, check for a grounded "L" terminal wire in the harness.

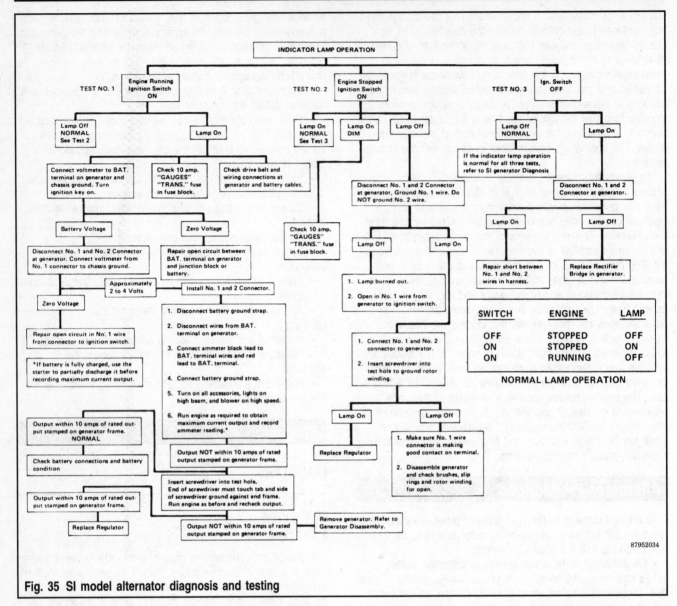

Fig. 35 SI model alternator diagnosis and testing

7. Determine if the battery is undercharged or overcharged.

• An undercharged battery is evidenced by slow cranking or a dark hydrometer.

• An overcharged battery is evidenced by excessive spewing of electrolyte from the vents.

8. Detach the wiring harness connector from the alternator.

9. With the ignition switch **ON**, and the engine not running, connect a voltmeter from ground to the "L" terminal in the wiring harness, and to the "I" terminal, if used.

10. A zero reading indicated an open circuit between the terminal and the battery. Repair the circuit as necessary.

11. Engage the harness connector to the alternator and run the engine at moderate speed with all accessories OFF.

12. Measure the voltage across the battery. If above 16 volts, replace the alternator.

13. Connect an ammeter at the alternator output terminal, run the engine at moderate speed, turn ON all the accessories and load the battery with a carbon pile to obtain maximum amperage. Maintain voltage at 13 volts or above.

14. If the output is within 15 amps of the rated output of the alternator (stamped on the alternator case), the alternator is good. If the output is not within 15 amps, replace the alternator.

REMOVAL & INSTALLATION

Except 2.3L and 2.4L Engines
◗ **See Figures 36, 37, 38, 39, 40, 41 and 42**

1. Disconnect the negative battery cable at the battery.

※※CAUTION

Failure to disconnect the negative cable may result in injury from the positive battery lead at the alternator, and may short the alternator and regulator during the removal process.

2. Disconnect and label the two terminal plug and the battery leads from the rear of the alternator.

Fig. 36 Detach the connector(s) from the rear of the alternator

3. Loosen the alternator mounting bolts. Push the alternator inwards, then slip the drive belt off the pulley.

4. Remove the mounting bolts, then remove the alternator from the vehicle.

To install:

5. Place the alternator in its brackets and install the mounting bolts. Do not tighten them yet.

6. Slip the belt back over the pulley. Pull outwards on the unit and adjust the belt tension (see Section 1). Tighten the mounting and adjusting bolts.

7. Attach the electrical leads to the alternator.

8. Connect the negative battery cable.

2.3L and 2.4L Engines

♦ See Figures 43 and 44

1. Disconnect the negative battery cable.

➡ **To avoid injuring yourself when rotating the serpentine belt tensioner, use a tight fitting 13mm wrench that is at least 24 in. (61cm) long. This can be done using tool J 37059 or equivalent.**

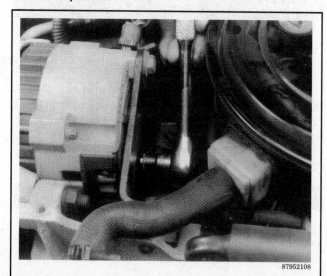

Fig. 37 Unfasten the lower rear mounting bolt

Fig. 38 Loosen the rear upper retainer

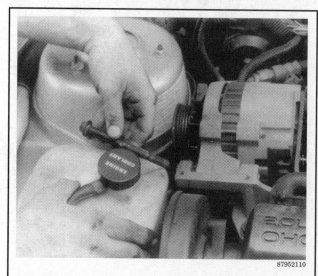

Fig. 39 Unfasten the front mounting bolt, then . . .

Fig. 40 . . . remove the alternator from the vehicle

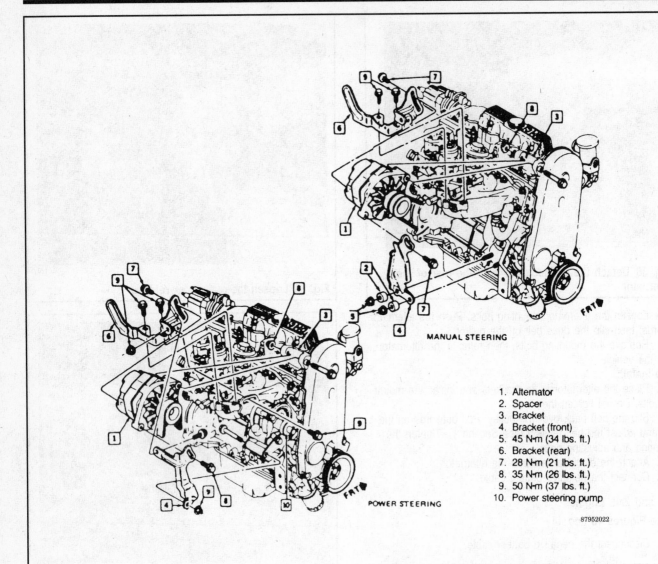

1. Alternator
2. Spacer
3. Bracket
4. Bracket (front)
5. 45 N·m (34 lbs. ft.)
6. Bracket (rear)
7. 28 N·m (21 lbs. ft.)
8. 35 N·m (26 lbs. ft.)
9. 50 N·m (37 lbs. ft.)
10. Power steering pump

MANUAL STEERING

POWER STEERING

87952022

Fig. 41 Removal and installation of the alternator — 1.8L and 2.0L OHC engines, except Turbo

2. Remove the serpentine belt.
3. Raise and safely support the vehicle.
4. Unfasten and remove the lower alternator mounting bolts.
5. Carefully lower the vehicle.
6. Remove the upper alternator bolt, detach the electrical connectors, then remove the alternator from the vehicle.

To install:
7. Position the alternator in the vehicle.
8. Attach the alternator electrical connections. Tighten the "BAT" terminal nut to 65 inch lbs. (7.5 Nm).
9. Install the upper alternator retaining bolt.
10. Raise and safely support the vehicle.
11. Secure the lower alternator mounting bolts, then carefully lower the vehicle.
12. Install the serpentine belt.
13. Connect the negative battery cable.

Regulator

REMOVAL & INSTALLATION

The alternators used in these vehicles have an internal regulator. A solid state regulator is mounted within the alternator. All regulator components are enclosed in a solid mold. The regulator is non-adjustable and requires no maintenance. The alternator is serviced as a complete unit and cannot be overhauled.

Battery

For information regarding battery maintenance and replacement, please refer to Section 1 of this manual.

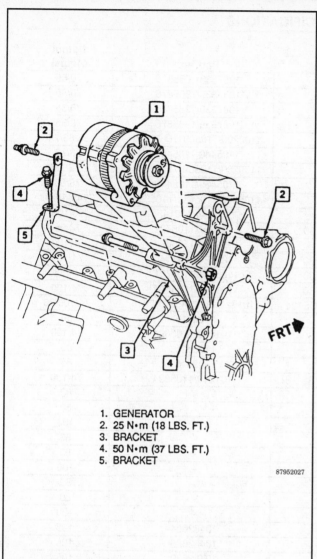

1. GENERATOR
2. 25 N•m (18 LBS. FT.)
3. BRACKET
4. 50 N•m (37 LBS. FT.)
5. BRACKET

87952027

Fig. 42 Alternator mounting for a 1987-89 2.8L and 1990-94 3.1L engine

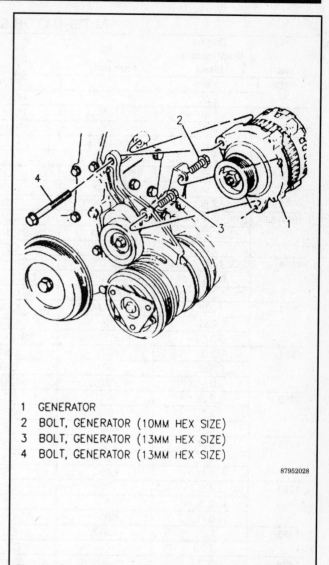

1 GENERATOR
2 BOLT, GENERATOR (10MM HEX SIZE)
3 BOLT, GENERATOR (13MM HEX SIZE)
4 BOLT, GENERATOR (13MM HEX SIZE)

87952028

Fig. 43 On the 2.3L engine, after lowering the vehicle, you can unfasten and remove the upper mounting bolt

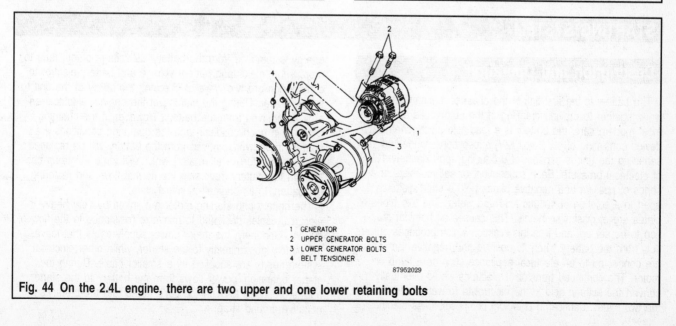

1 GENERATOR
2 UPPER GENERATOR BOLTS
3 LOWER GENERATOR BOLTS
4 BELT TENSIONER

87952029

Fig. 44 On the 2.4L engine, there are two upper and one lower retaining bolts

ALTERNATOR SPECIFICATIONS

Year	Engine Displacement Liters	Alternator	Model	Part No.	Output (Amps)
1982	1.8L	-	10SI/15SI	1987339/1985876	70/85
	2.0L	-	10SI/15SI	1987339/1985876	70/85
1983	1.8L	-	10SI/15SI	1987339/1985876	70/85
	2.0L	-	10SI/15SI	1987339/1985876	70/85
1984	1.8L	C41/C49/K64	12SI	1100290/1105091/1100289	55/63/78
	2.0L	C41/C60	12SI	1105440/1105439	63/78
1985-86	1.8L	K64/K81/K77	12SI	1100289/1105091/1100290	78/66/56
	2.0L	K64/K81	12SI	1105439/1105440	78/68
	2.8L	K22/K81/K77	12SI	1105602/1105611/1105599	94/66/56
1987-88	2.0L (VIN K & M)	K99/K60	CS130	1101144/110145	85/100
	2.0L (VIN 1)	K99/K60	CS121/CS130	1105697/1105701	74/85
	2.8L	K99/K60	CS130	1105698/1105694	85/100
1989	2.0L (VIN K & M)	KG0/K60	CS121/CS130	1101321/1101145	74/100
	2.0L (VIN 1)	KG0/K99	CS121/CS130	1105697/1105701	74/85
	2.8L	KG0/K60	CS121/CS130	1101319/1105694	74/100
1990	2.0L	KG0/K60/K97	CS121/CS130/CS121	1101321/1101145/1102615	74/100/80
	2.2L	K97	CS121	1102615	80
	3.1L	KG0/K60	CS121/CS130	1101319/1105694	74/100
1991	2.0L	K97	CS121	1102615	80
	2.2L	K97	CS121	1102615	80
	3.1L	KG0/K60	CS121/CS130	1101319/1105694	74/100
1992	2.0L	-	CS121	-	80
	2.2L	-	CS121	-	80
	3.1L	K60	CS130	-	100
1993	2.0L	-	CS121	-	80
	2.2L	-	CS121	-	80
	3.1L	K60	CS130	-	100
1994	2.0L	-	CS121	-	80
	2.2L	-	CS121	-	80
	3.1L	K60	CS130	-	100
1995	2.2L	K68	CS130	10463604	105
	2.3L	-	CS130D	10463605	105
1996	2.2L	-	CS130D	10463639	105
	2.4L	-	CS130D	10463638	105

87952500

STARTING SYSTEM

Description and Operation

The battery is the first link in the chain of mechanisms which work together to provide cranking of the automobile engine. In most modern cars, the battery is a lead-acid electrochemical device consisting of six 2 volt (2V) subsections connected in series so the unit is capable of producing approximately 12V of electrical pressure. Each subsection, or sell, consists of a series of positive and negative plates held a short distance apart in a solution of sulfuric acid and water. The two types of plates are of dissimilar metals. This causes a chemical reaction to be set up, and it is this reaction which produces current flow from the battery when its positive and negative terminals are connected to an electrical appliance such as a lamp or motor. The continued transfer of electrons would eventually convert the sulfuric acid in the electrolyte to water, and make the two plates identical in chemical composition. As electrical energy is removed from the battery, its voltage output tend to drop. Thus, measuring battery voltage and battery electrolyte composition are two ways of checking the ability of the unit to supply power. During the starting of the engine, electrical energy is removed from the battery. However, if the charging circuit is in good condition and the operating conditions are normal, the power removed from the battery will be replaced by the generator (or alternator) which will force electrons back through the battery, reversing the normal flow, and restoring the battery to its original chemical state.

The battery and starting motor are linked by very heavy electrical cables designed to minimize resistance to the flow of current. Generally, the major power supply cable that leaves the battery goes directly to the starter, while other electrical system needs are supplied by a smaller cable. During the starter operation, power flows from the battery to the starter and is grounded through the car's frame and the battery's negative ground strap.

The starting motor is a specially designed, direct current electric motor capable of producing a very great amount of power for its size. One thing that allows the motor to produce a great deal of power is its tremendous rotating speed. It drives the engine through a tiny pinion gear (attached to the starter's armature), which drives the very large flywheel ring gear at a greatly reduced speed. Another factor allowing it to produce so much power is that only intermittent operation is required of it. Thus, little allowance for air circulation is required, and the windings can be built into a very small space.

The starter solenoid is a magnetic device which employs the small current supplied by the starting switch circuit of the ignition switch. This magnetic action moves a plunger which mechanically engages the starter and electrically closes the heavy switch which connects it to the battery. The starting switch circuit consists of the starting switch contained within the ignition switch, a transmission neutral safety switch or clutch pedal switch, and the wiring necessary to connect these with the starter solenoid or relay.

A pinion, which is a small gear, is mounted to a one-way drive clutch. this clutch is splined to the starter armature shaft. When the ignition switch is moved to the start position, the solenoid plunger slides the pinion toward the flywheel ring gear via a collar and spring. If the teeth on the pinion and flywheel match properly, the pinion will engage the flywheel immediately. If the gear teeth butt one another, the spring will be compressed and will force the gears to mesh as soon as the starter turns far enough to allow them to do so. As the solenoid plunger reaches the end of its travel, it closes the contacts that connect the battery and starter and then the engine is cranked.

As soon as the engine starts, the flywheel ring gear begins turning fast enough to drive the pinion at an extremely high rate of speed. At this point, the one-way clutch begins allowing the pinion to spin faster that the starter shaft so that the starter will not operate at excessive speed. When the ignition switch is released from the starter position, the solenoid is de-energized, and a spring contained within the solenoid assembly pulls the gear out of mesh and interrupts the current flow to the starter.

Some starters employ a separate relay, mounted away from the starter, to switch the motor and solenoid current on and off. The relay thus replaces the solenoid electrical switch, but does not eliminate the need for a solenoid mounted on the starter used to mechanically engage the starter drive gears. The relay is used to reduce the amount of current the starting switch must carry.

Starter

TESTING

No-Load Test
▶ **See Figure 45**

Make the connections as shown in the illustration. Close the switch and compare the rpm, current and voltage readings with the specifications found in the chart located in this section.

- Current draw and no load speed within specifications indicates normal condition of the starter motor.
- Low free speed and high current draw indicates worn bearings, a bent armature shaft, a shorted armature or grounded armature fields.
- Failure to operate with high current draw indicates a direct ground in the terminal or fields, or frozen bearings.
- Failure to operate with no current draw indicates an open field circuit, open armature coils, broken brush springs, worn brushes or other causes which would prevent good contact between the commutator and the brushes.
- A low no load speed and low current draw indicates high internal resistance due to poor connections, defective leads or a dirty commutator.
- High free speed and current draw usually indicate shorted fields or a shorted armature.

REMOVAL & INSTALLATION

1982-83 1.8L (VIN G & O) and 2.0L (VIN B) Engines
▶ **See Figure 46**

1. Disconnect the negative battery cable at the battery.
2. If necessary for access under the car, raise and safely support the vehicle.
3. From under the vehicle, label and disconnect the solenoid wires and battery cable.
4. Remove the rear motor support bracket.

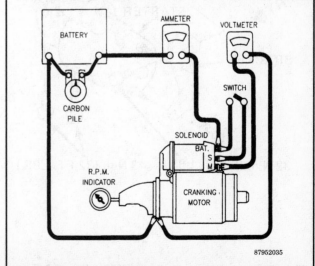

87952035

Fig. 45 Proper connections for the starter no-load test

5. If equipped, remove the A/C compressor support rod.

6. Working under the car, remove the two starter-to-engine bolts, and allow the starter to drop down. Note the location and number of any shims. Remove the starter.

7. Installation is the reverse of the removal procedure. Tighten the mounting bolts to 25-35 ft. lbs. (34-47 Nm). Check the starting system for proper operation.

1984-86 1.8L and 2.0L Engines

EXCEPT 1.8L (VIN O) ENGINE

1. Disconnect the negative battery cable at the battery, then remove the engine harness bracket from the motor mount brace.

2. Remove the upper starter bolt.

3. Raise and safely support the vehicle.

4. Disconnect the fuel lines from the bracket, then loosen the fuel lines at the fuel regulator.

5. Remove the rear starter bracket.

6. Disconnect the cover and wiring to the solenoid and the negative battery cable grounding bolt.

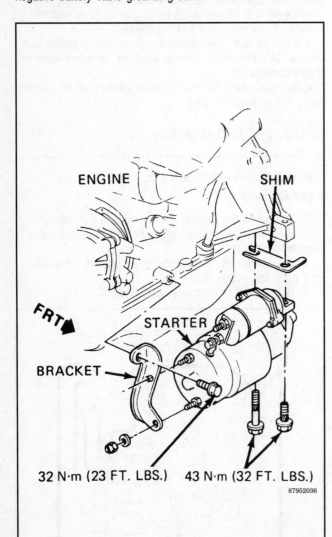

ENGINE   SHIM

FRT

STARTER

BRACKET

32 N·m (23 FT. LBS.)   43 N·m (32 FT. LBS.)

87952036

Fig. 46 Starter motor mounting — 1982 1.8L and 2.0L engines

7. Unfasten the lower starter bolt, then remove the starter from the vehicle.

To install:

8. Position the starter in the vehicle, then install the lower starter bolt.

9. Connect the wiring to the solenoid, then install the cover.

10. Install the rear starter bracket and the bolt for the negative grounding cable.

11. Fasten the fuel line support bracket, then connect the fuel lines.

12. Carefully lower the vehicle.

13. Fasten the upper starter bolt, then fasten the engine harness to the motor mount brace.

14. Connect the negative battery cable.

1.8L (VIN O) ENGINE

1. Disconnect the negative battery cable at the battery.

2. Remove the wiring harness clamp at the motor mount.

3. Unfasten the upper starter-to-engine block bolt.

4. Raise and safely support the vehicle.

5. If equipped with an automatic transaxle, disconnect the speedometer cable, then remove the transaxle rear strut.

6. Remove the throttle cable bracket.

7. Unfasten the rear starter brace bolts, then remove the brace.

8. Remove the lower starter-to-engine block bolt.

9. Detach the starter wiring, then remove the starter by nosing it down between the transaxle and sway bar. It may be necessary to pry the engine forward or detach the sway bar to remove the starter.

To install:

10. Position the starter, then install the lower mounting bolt.

11. Attach the starter wiring.

12. Install the throttle cable bracket.

13. If equipped with an automatic transaxle, install the transaxle rear strut and connect the speedometer cable.

14. Carefully lower the vehicle.

15. Install the upper starter-to-engine block bolt.

16. Fasten the wiring harness clamp at the motor mount, then connect the negative battery cable.

2.0L (VIN K & M) Engines

▶ See Figure 47

MANUAL TRANSAXLE

1. Disconnect the negative battery cable at the battery.

2. Remove the wire loom strap from the upper starter bolt.

3. Disconnect the shift and selector level cables at the external selector lever.

4. Remove the upper and lower transaxle control lever cable bracket and cables.

5. Remove the drive axle support brace.

6. Detach the starter electrical connectors, then remove the starter from the vehicle.

To install:

7. Position the starter in the vehicle, then attach the electrical connectors.

8. Install the drive axle support brace.

9. Install the upper and lower transaxle control lever cables and brackets.

10. Connect the shift and selector lever cable bracket and cable.

11. Fasten the wire loom strap to the upper starter bolt.

12. Connect the negative battery cable.

AUTOMATIC TRANSAXLE

1. Disconnect the negative battery cable at the battery.

2. Remove the blower motor. For details, please refer to the procedure located in Section 6 of this manual.

3. Label and detach the starter electrical connectors.

4. Remove the rear starter brace.

5. Disconnect the wire loom from the upper starter bolt.

6. Unfasten the upper starter bolt, then remove the transaxle strut.

7. Unfasten the lower starter bolt, then remove the starter from the vehicle through the blower motor opening.

To install:

8. Position the starter in the vehicle, then secure with the lower starter bolt.

9. Install the transaxle strut.

10. With the aid of an assistant, secure the upper starter bolt, then connect the wire loom to the upper bolt.

11. Install the rear starter brace.

12. Attach the starter electrical connectors.

13. Install the blower motor, as outlined in Section 6 of this manual.

14. Connect the negative battery cable.

2.0L (VIN H) Engine

▶ See Figure 48

1. Disconnect the negative battery cable at the battery.

2. Remove the upper starter bolt.

3. Raise and safely support the vehicle.

4. For vehicles equipped with an automatic transaxle, detach the starter electrical connectors.

5. Disconnect the engine ground cable at the engine.

6. Remove the rear starter mount.

7. For vehicles equipped with a manual transaxle, detach the starter electrical connectors.

8. If equipped, unfasten the lower starter bolt, then remove the starter from the vehicle.

To install:

9. Position the starter in the vehicle, then secure using the lower retaining bolt.

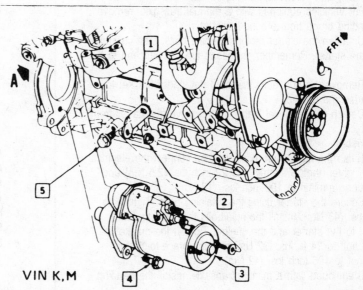

```
1. SUPPORT, STARTER MOTOR
2. NUT — 8 N•m (71 LBS. IN.)
3. STARTER MOTOR
4. BOLT — 43 N•m (32 LBS. IN.)
5. BOLT — 50 N•m (37 LBS. FT.)
```

STARTER NOISE DIAGNOSTIC PROCEDURE

STARTER NOISE DURING CRANKING:
REMOVE 1 – .015'' DOUBLE SHIM OR ADD
SINGLE .015'' SHIM TO OUTER BOLT ONLY.

HIGH PITCHED WHINE AFTER ENGINE
FIRES: ADD .015'' DOUBLE SHIMS UNTIL
NOISE DISAPPEARS (NOT TO EXCEED .045'').

VIEW A

VIN K, M

87952037

Fig. 47 When removing the starter, be sure to note the location of any shims that may have been used — 2.0L (VIN K and M) engines

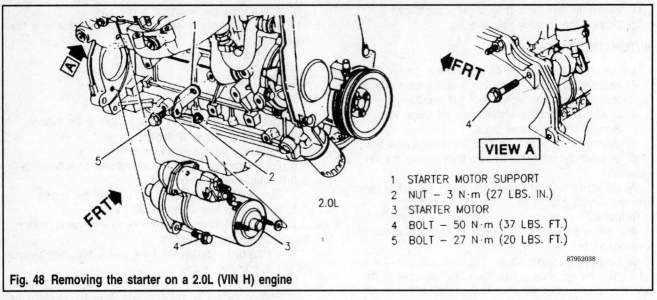

1 STARTER MOTOR SUPPORT
2 NUT – 3 N·m (27 LBS. IN.)
3 STARTER MOTOR
4 BOLT – 50 N·m (37 LBS. FT.)
5 BOLT – 27 N·m (20 LBS. FT.)

87952038

Fig. 48 Removing the starter on a 2.0L (VIN H) engine

10. If equipped with a manual transaxle, attach the starter electrical connectors at this time.

11. Install the rear starter mount.

12. For vehicles with an automatic transaxle, attach the starter electrical connectors at this time.

13. Connect the engine ground cable to the engine.

14. Carefully lower the vehicle.

15. Install the upper starter bolt.

16. Connect the negative battery cable.

2.0L (VIN 1) and 2.2L (VIN 4 & G) Engines

▶ See Figure 49

1. Disconnect the negative battery cable at the battery.

2. Raise and safely support the vehicle.

3. For vehicles equipped with a manual transaxle, remove the bending brace from around the starter.

4. Unfasten the starter motor-to-engine bolts, then carefully lower the starter. Remember, the leads are still attached to the starter.

5. Remove the nuts/bolts that hold the starter bracket to the starter and engine.

6. Detach the electrical leads, then remove the starter from the vehicle.

To install:

7. Raise the starter into position, then connect the electrical leads. Tighten the "S" terminal to 22 inch lbs. (2.5 Nm) and the battery terminal to 106 inch lbs. (12 Nm).

8. Secure the starter using the retaining bolts. Tighten to 32 ft. lbs. (43 Nm). Install the nuts/bolts that hold the start bracket to the starter and the engine. Tighten the bracket-to-engine bolt to 24 ft. lbs. (32 Nm) and the brace-to-starter motor nut to 106 inch lbs. (12 Nm).

9. If equipped with a manual transaxle, install the bending brace.

10. Carefully lower the vehicle, then connect the negative battery cable.

2.3L (VIN D) and 2.4L (VIN T) Engines

▶ See Figure 50

1. Disconnect the negative battery cable at the battery.

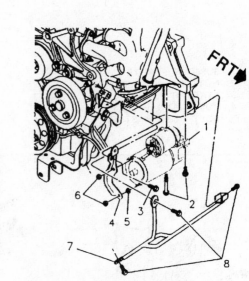

1 STARTER ASSEMBLY
2 BOLT – 43 N·m (32 LBS. FT.)
3 BOLT – 32 N·m (24 LBS. FT.)
4 BRACKET, STARTER MOTOR
5 WASHER
6 NUT – 12 N·m (106 LBS. IN.)
7 BENDING BRACE (MANUAL TRANS ONLY)
8 BOLT – 47 N·m (20 LBS. FT.)

87952039

Fig. 49 Removal and installation of the starter — 2.2L engine shown, 2.0L (VIN 1) similar

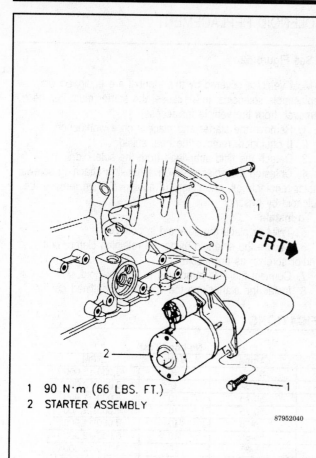

1   90 N·m (66 LBS. FT.)
2   STARTER ASSEMBLY

87952040

Fig. 50 When installing the starter, tighten the mounting bolts to 66 ft. lbs. (90 Nm) on the 2.3L and 2.4L engines

2. Detach the air inlet duct from the throttle body.
3. Remove the top starter bolt.
4. Raise and safely support the vehicle.
5. Remove the lower starter retaining bolt.
6. If necessary, position the engine wiring harness aside.
7. Position the starter to enable access to the solenoid wiring, then detach the wiring.
8. Remove the starter from the vehicle.

To install:
9. Raise the starter to the vehicle, then attach the wiring.
10. Position the starter, then secure using the lower starter bolt. Tighten to 66 ft. lbs. (90 Nm)
11. If moved, reposition the engine wiring harness.
12. Carefully lower the vehicle.
13. Install the top starter bolt, then tighten to 66 ft. lbs. (90 Nm).
14. Fasten the air inlet duct to the throttle body.
15. Connect the negative battery cable.

2.8L (VIN W) and 3.1L (VIN T) Engines
▶ See Figure 51

➡On 3.1L engines, an "Idle Learn" procedure must be performed which requires the use of a scan tool. You may wish to have the starter replaced at a proper service facility.

1. Disconnect the negative battery cable at the battery.
2. Raise and safely support the vehicle.
3. Remove the starter motor-to-engine bolts, then carefully lower the vehicle.
4. Detach the starter electrical leads, then remove the starter from the vehicle.

To install:
5. Position the starter in the vehicle, then connect the electrical leads.
6. Raise and safely support the vehicle, then install the starter-to-engine bolts and tighten to 32 ft. lbs. (43 Nm).
7. Carefully lower the vehicle.

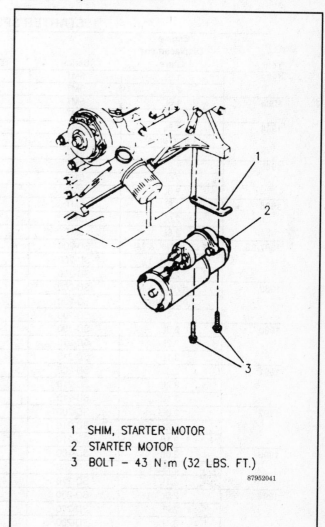

1   SHIM, STARTER MOTOR
2   STARTER MOTOR
3   BOLT – 43 N·m (32 LBS. FT.)

87952041

Fig. 51 Removing the starter — 2.8L and 3.1L engines

8. Connect the negative battery cable. Tighten the cable to 11 ft. lbs. (15 Nm). Be careful not to over-tighten.

➡On 3.1L engines, this test must be done before the engine is started and requires the use of a Tech 1®or equivalent scan tool.

9. If equipped with the 3.1L engine, perform the idle learn procedure to allow the ECM/PCM memory to be updated with the correct IAC valve pintle position and provide for a stable idle speed.

   a. Install a suitable scan tool.
   b. Turn the ignition to the ON position, engine not running.
   c. Select IAC SYSTEM, then IDLE LEARN in the MISC TEST mode.
   d. Place the transaxle in park or neutral, as applicable.
   e. Proceed with idle learn as directed by the scan tool.

SOLENOID REPLACEMENT

◗ See Figure 52

Most vehicles covered by this manual are equipped with replaceable solenoids. In all cases, the starter must first be removed from the vehicle for access.

   1. Remove the starter and place it on a workbench.
   2. If equipped, remove the heat shield.
   3. Detach the field strap/lead from the solenoid.
   4. Unfasten the solenoid-to-drive housing attaching screws, motor terminal bolt, and clamp (if equipped) then remove the solenoid by twisting.
   To install:
   5. Twist or place the solenoid in position.
   6. Secure the solenoid using the retaining clamp, bolt and/or screws, as applicable.
   7. Connect the field strap/lead to the solenoid.
   8. Install the starter into the vehicle, as outlined earlier.

STARTER SPECIFICATIONS

Year	Engine Displacement Liters	Series	Type	No-Load Test		
				Amps	Volts	RPM
1982	1.8L	5MT	-	57-82	9	6,000-12,000
	2.0L	5MT	-	57-82	9	6,000-12,000
1983	1.8L	5MT	-	50-75	10	6,000-11,900
	2.0L	5MT	-	50-75	10	6,000-11,900
1984	1.8L	5MT	-	50-75	10	6,000-11,900
	1.8L (Turbo)	5MT	-	55-85	10	6,000-12,000
	2.0L	5MT	-	55-85	10	6,000-12,000
1985	1.8L	5MT	-	55-85	10	6,000-11,900
	2.0L	5MT	-	50-75	10	6,000-11,900
	2.8L	5MT	-	50-75	10	6,000-11,900
1986	1.8L	5MT	-	55-85	10	6,000-12,000
	2.0L	5MT	-	50-75	10	6,000-12,000
	2.8L	5MT	-	50-75	10	6,000-12,000
1987-88	2.0L (VIN K & M)	SD-200	-	55-85	10	6,000-12,000
	2.0L (VIN 1)	SD-200	-	52-76	10	6,000-12,000
	2.8L	SD-200	-	50-75	10	6,000-11,900
1989	2.0L (VIN K & M)	SD-200	-	55-85	10	6,000-12,000
	2.0L (VIN 1)	SD-200	-	52-76	10	6,000-12,000
	2.8L	SD-200	-	50-75	10	6,000-11,900
1990	2.0L	SD-200	-	55-85	10	6,000-12,000
	2.2L	SD-210	-	52-76	10	6,000-12,000
	3.1L	SD-210	-	50-75	10	6,000-12,000
1991	2.0L	SD-200	-	55-85	10	6,000-12,000
	2.2L	SD-210	-	45-75	10	6,000-11,000
	3.1L	SD-210	-	45-75	10	6,000-11,000
1992	2.0L	SD-200	-	55-85	10	6,000-12,000
	2.2L	SD-210	-	45-75	10	6,000-11,000
	3.1L	SD-210	-	45-75	10	6,000-11,000
1993	2.0L	SD-200	-	55-85	10	6,000-12,000
	2.2L	SD-200	-	52-76	10	6,000-12,000
	3.1L	SD-210	-	45-75	10	6,000-11,000
1994	2.0L	SD-200	-	55-85	10	6,000-12,000
	2.2L	SD-210	-	45-75	10	6,000-11,000
	3.1L	SD-200	-	50-75	10	6,000-12,000
1995	2.2L	SD-210	-	45-75	10	6,000-11,000
	2.3L	SD-200	-	50-75	10	6,000-12,000
1996	2.2L	SD-205	-	50-75	10	6,000-12,000
	2.4L	SD-225	-	50-75	10	6,000-12,000

87952501

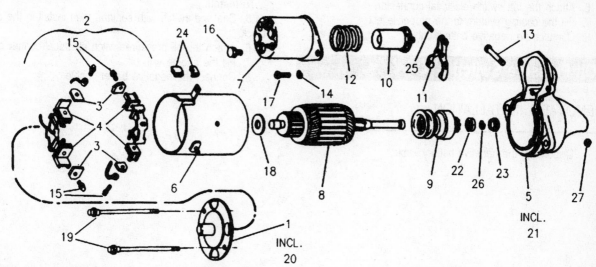

1   FRAME, COMMUTATOR END
2   BRUSH AND HOLDER PKG.
3   BRUSH
4   HOLDER, BRUSH
5   HOUSING, DRIVE END
6   FRAME AND FIELD ASSEMBLY
7   SWITCH, SOLENOID
8   ARMATURE
9   DRIVE ASSEMBLY
10 PLUNGER

11 LEVER, SHIFT
12 SPRING, PLUNGER RETURN
13 SHAFT, SHIFT LEVER
14 WASHER, LOCK
15 SCREW, BRUSH ATTACHING
16 SCREW, FIELD LEAD TO SWITCH
17 SCREW, SWITCH
18 WASHER, BRAKE
19 BOLT, THRU
20 BUSHING, COMMUTATOR END

21 BUSHING, DIVE END
22 COLLAR, PINION STOP
23 COLLAR, THRUST
24 GROMMET
25 PIN, PLUNGER
26 RING, PINION STOP RETAINER
27 RING, LEVER SHAFT RETAINER

87952042

Fig. 52 Exploded view of a late model starter assembly, including the solenoid

SENDING UNITS AND SENSORS

Coolant Temperature Sending Unit

The coolant temperature sending unit is usually located in the thermostat housing. This unit activates the coolant temperature gauge in the instrument cluster.

REMOVAL & INSTALLATION

1. Disconnect the negative battery cable.
2. Properly drain the cooling system to a level below the thermostat housing.
3. Detach the coolant temperature sending unit electrical connector.
4. Remove the sending unit from the thermostat housing.

To install:
5. Coat the sending unit with sealant, then install in the thermostat housing.
6. Attach the sending unit electrical connector.
7. Fill the cooling system to the proper level.
8. Connect the negative battery cable.

Radiator Fan Temperature Switch

REMOVAL & INSTALLATION

1. Disconnect the negative battery cable.
2. Drain the cooling system to a level below the thermostat housing.
3. Detach the fan switch electrical connector.

4. Remove the switch from the thermostat housing.

To install:

5. Coat the switch with sealant, then install in the thermostat housing.

6. Attach the fan switch electrical connector.

7. Fill the cooling system to the proper level.

8. Connect the negative battery cable.

Oil Pressure Switch

REMOVAL & INSTALLATION

1. Disconnect the negative battery cable.

2. Drain the engine oil, as outlined in Section 1 of this manual.

3. Detach the oil pressure switch electrical connector.

4. Remove the switch from the cylinder block.

To install:

5. Coat the switch with sealant, then install in the cylinder block.

6. Attach the oil pressure switch electrical connector.

7. Fill the engine with oil.

8. Connect the negative battery cable.

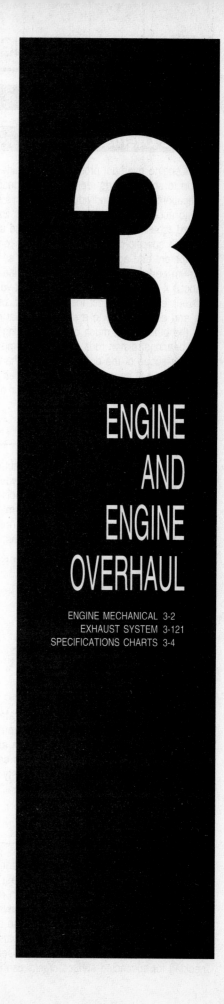

ENGINE MECHANICAL
BLOCK HEATER 3-115
CAMSHAFT 3-103
CAMSHAFT CARRIER COVER 3-32
CAMSHAFT SPROCKET 3-101
CRANKSHAFT AND MAIN
   BEARINGS 3-118
CRANKSHAFT SPROCKET 3-102
CYLINDER HEAD 3-68
ELECTRIC COOLING FAN 3-64
ENGINE 3-19
ENGINE CORE PLUGS (FREEZE
   PLUGS) 3-114
ENGINE OVERHAUL TIPS 3-2
EXHAUST MANIFOLD 3-53
INTAKE MANIFOLD 3-44
OIL PAN 3-83
OIL PUMP 3-87
PISTONS AND CONNECTING
   RODS 3-107
RADIATOR 3-61
REAR MAIN OIL SEAL 3-115
ROCKER ARM (VALVE) COVER 3-29
ROCKER ARMS AND
   PUSHRODS 3-36
THERMOSTAT 3-39
TIMING BELT 3-97
TIMING BELT COVER 3-89
TIMING BELT REAR COVER 3-103
TIMING CHAIN AND
   SPROCKETS 3-93
TIMING CHAIN COVER OIL
   SEAL 3-93
TIMING CHAIN FRONT COVER 3-90
TURBOCHARGER 3-60
VALVE LIFTERS 3-83
VALVE SEATS 3-82
VALVE STEM OIL SEALS 3-82
VALVES AND SPRINGS 3-81
WATER PUMP 3-65
EXHAUST SYSTEM
GENERAL INFORMATION 3-121
SPECIFICATIONS CHARTS
CAMSHAFT SPECIFICATIONS 3-9
CRANKSHAFT AND CONNECTING
   ROD SPECIFICATIONS 3-12
GENERAL ENGINE
   SPECIFICATIONS 3-4
PISTON AND RING
   SPECIFICATIONS 3-15
TORQUE SPECIFICATIONS 3-18
VALVE SPECIFICATIONS 3-6

3

ENGINE
AND
ENGINE
OVERHAUL

ENGINE MECHANICAL 3-2
EXHAUST SYSTEM 3-121
SPECIFICATIONS CHARTS 3-4

ENGINE MECHANICAL

Engine Overhaul Tips

Most engine overhaul procedures are fairly standard. In addition to specific parts replacement procedures and specifications for your individual engine, this section also is a guide to acceptable rebuilding procedures. Examples of standard rebuilding practice are shown and should be used along with specific details concerning your particular engine.

Competent and accurate machine shop services will ensure maximum performance, reliability and engine life. In most instances it is more profitable for the do-it-yourself mechanic to remove, clean and inspect the component, buy the necessary parts and deliver these to a shop for actual machine work.

On the other hand, much of the rebuilding work (crankshaft, block, bearings, piston rods, and other components) is well within the scope of the do-it-yourself mechanic's tools and abilities. You will have to decide for yourself the depth of involvement you desire in an engine repair or rebuild.

TOOLS

The tools required for an engine overhaul or parts replacement will depend on the depth of your involvement. With a few exceptions, they will be the tools found in a mechanic's tool kit (see Section 1 of this manual). More in-depth work will require some or all of the following:
  • a dial indicator (reading in thousandths) mounted on a universal base
  • micrometers and telescope gauges
  • jaw and screw-type pullers
  • scraper
  • valve spring compressor
  • ring groove cleaner
  • piston ring expander and compressor
  • ridge reamer
  • cylinder hone or glaze breaker
  • Plastigage®
  • engine stand

The use of most of these tools is illustrated in this section. Many can be rented for a one-time use from a local parts jobber or tool supply house specializing in automotive work.

Occasionally, the use of special tools is called for. See the information on Special Tools and the Safety Notice in the front of this book before substituting another tool.

INSPECTION TECHNIQUES

Procedures and specifications are given in this chapter for inspecting, cleaning and assessing the wear limits of most major components. Other procedures such as Magnaflux® and Zyglo® can be used to locate material flaws and stress cracks. Magnaflux® is a magnetic process applicable only to ferrous materials. The Zyglo® process coats the material with a fluorescent dye penetrant and can be used on any material. Checking for suspected surface cracks can be more readily made using spot check dye. The dye is sprayed onto the suspected area, wiped off and the area sprayed with a developer. Cracks will show up brightly.

OVERHAUL TIPS

Aluminum has become extremely popular for use in engines, due to its low weight. Observe the following precautions when handling aluminum parts:
  • Never hot tank aluminum parts (the caustic hot tank solution will eat the aluminum.
  • Remove all aluminum parts (identification tag, etc.) from engine parts prior to the tanking.
  • Always coat threads lightly with engine oil or anti-seize compounds before installation, to prevent seizure.
  • Never overtorque bolts or spark plugs especially in aluminum threads.

Stripped threads in any component can be repaired using any of several commercial repair kits (Heli-Coil®, Microdot®, Keenserts®, etc.).

When assembling the engine, any parts that will be exposed to frictional contact, the parts must be prelubed to provide lubrication at initial start-up. Any product specifically formulated for this purpose can be used, but engine oil is not recommended as a prelube in most cases.

REPAIRING DAMAGED THREADS

▶ See Figures 1, 2, 3, 4 and 5

Several methods of repairing damaged threads are available. Heli-Coil® (shown here), Keenserts® and Microdot® are among the most widely used. All involve basically the same principle — drilling out stripped threads, tapping the hole and installing a prewound insert — making welding, plugging and oversize fasteners unnecessary.

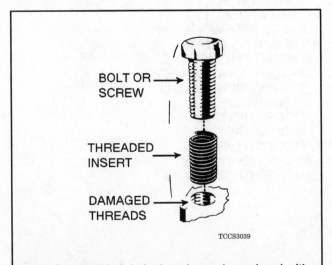

TCCS3039

Fig. 1 Damaged bolt hole threads can be replaced with thread repair inserts

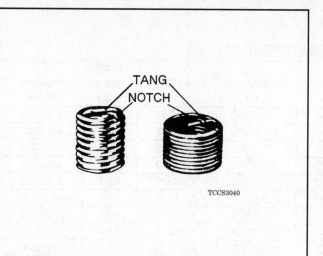

TANG
NOTCH

TCCS3040

Fig. 2 Standard thread repair insert (left), and spark plug thread insert

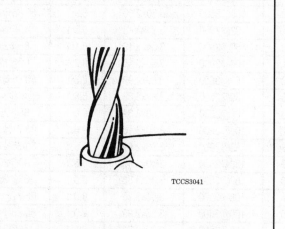

TCCS3041

Fig. 3 Drill out the damaged threads with the specified drill. Be sure to drill completely through the hole or to the bottom of a blind hole

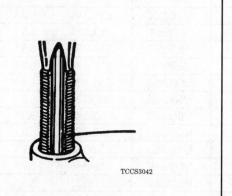

TCCS3042

Fig. 4 Using the kit, tap the hole in order to receive the thread insert. Keep the tap well oiled and back it out frequently to avoid clogging the threads.

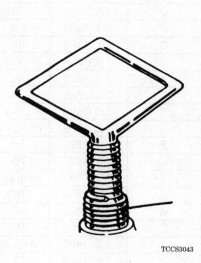

TCCS3043

Fig. 5 Screw the threaded insert onto the installer tool until the tang engages the slot. Thread the insert into the hole until it is ¼ or ½ turn below the top surface, then remove the tool and break off the tang using a punch.

Two types of thread repair inserts are usually supplied: a standard type for most inch coarse, inch fine, metric course and metric fine thread sizes and a spark lug type to fit most spark plug port sizes. Consult the individual manufacturer's catalog to determine exact applications. Typical thread repair kits will contain a selection of prewound threaded inserts, a tap (corresponding to the outside diameter threads of the insert) and an installation tool. Spark plug inserts usually differ because they require a tap equipped with pilot threads and a combined reamer/tap section. Most manufacturers also supply blister-packed thread repair inserts separately in addition to a master kit containing a variety of taps and inserts plus installation tools.

Before attempting to repair a threaded hole, remove any snapped, broken or damaged bolts or studs. Penetrating oil can be used to free frozen threads. The offending item can be removed with locking pliers or using a screw/stud extractor. After the hole is clear, the thread can be repaired, as shown in the series of accompanying illustrations and in the kit manufacturer's instructions.

GENERAL ENGINE SPECIFICATIONS

Year	Engine ID/VIN	Engine Displacement Liters (cc)	Fuel System Type	Net Horsepower @ rpm	Net Torque @ rpm (ft. lbs.)	Bore x Stroke (in.)	Compression Ratio	Oil Pressure @ rpm
1982	G	1.8L (1819)	2bbl	88@5500	100@2800	3.50x2.91	9.0:1	45@2400
	O	1.8L (1819)	TBI	84@5200	102@2800	3.34x3.13	8.8:1	45@2400
	B	2.0L (1998)	2bbl	90@5100	111@2800	3.50x3.15	9.0:1	45@2400
1983	O	1.8L (1819)	TBI	84@5200	102@2800	3.34x3.13	8.8:1	45@2400
	J	1.8L (1819)	MFI-Turbo	150@5600	150@2800	3.34X3.13	8.0:1	65@2500
	P	2.0L (1998)	TBI	86@4900	100@3000	3.50X3.15	9.3:1	68@1200
	B	2.0L (1998)	TBI	90@5100	111@2800	3.50x3.15	9.3:1	45@2400
1984	O	1.8L (1819)	TBI	84@5200	102@2800	3.34x3.13	8.8:1	45@2400
	J	1.8L (1819)	MFI-Turbo	150@5600	150@2800	3.34X3.13	8.0:1	65@2500
	P	2.0L (1998)	TBI	86@4900	100@3000	3.50X3.15	9.3:1	68@1200
1985	O	1.8L (1819)	TBI	84@5200	102@2800	3.34x3.13	8.8:1	45@2400
	J	1.8L (1819)	MFI-Turbo	150@5600	150@2800	3.34x3.13	8.1:1	65@2500
	P	2.0L (1998)	TBI	86@4900	100@3000	3.50x3.15	9.3:1	68@1200
	W	2.8L (2835)	MFI	130@4800	155@3600	3.50x2.99	8.5:1	50-65@1200
1986	O	1.8L (1819)	TBI	84@5200	102@2800	3.34x3.13	8.8:1	45@2400
	J	1.8L (1819)	MFI-Turbo	150@5600	150@2800	3.34x3.13	8.1:1	65@2500
	P	2.0L (1998)	TBI	86@4900	100@3000	3.50x3.15	9.3:1	68@1200
	W	2.8L (2835)	MFI	130@4800	155@3600	3.50x2.99	8.5:1	50-65@1200
1987	K	2.0L (1998)	TBI	102@5200	130@2800	3.39x3.39	8.8:1	45@2400
	M	2.0L (1998)	MFI-Turbo	160@5600	160@2800	3.39x3.39	8.0:1	65@2500
	1	2.0L (1998)	TBI	90@5600	108@3200	3.50x3.15	9.0:1	63-77@1200
	W	2.8L (2835)	MFI	130@4800	155@3600	3.50x2.99	8.5:1	50-65@1200
1988	K	2.0L (1998)	TBI	102@5200	130@2800	3.40x3.40	8.8:1	40@2000
	M	2.0L (1998)	MFI	160@5600	160@2800	3.38x3.38	8.0:1	65@2500
	1	2.0L (1998)	TBI	90@5600	108@3200	3.50x3.15	9.0:1	63-77@1200
	W	2.8L (2835)	MFI	125@4500	160@3600	3.50x2.99	8.9:1	50-65@1200
1989	K	2.0L (1998)	TBI	98@4800	118@3600	3.39x3.39	8.8:1	45@2400
	M	2.0L (1998)	MFI-Turbo	165@5500	165@4000	3.39x3.39	8.0:1	65@2500
	1	2.0L (1998)	TBI	90@5600	108@3200	3.50x3.15	9.0:1	63-77@1200
	W	2.8L (2835)	MFI	120@4800	180@3600	3.50x2.99	8.9:1	50-65@1200
1990	K	2.0L (1998)	TFI	98@4800	118@3600	3.39x3.39	8.8:1	45@2400
	M	2.0L (1998)	MFI-Turbo	165@5500	165@4000	3.39x3.39	8.0:1	65@2500
	G	2.2L (2180)	TBI	95@5200	120@3200	3.50x3.46	9.0:1	63-7&@1200
	T	3.1L (3130)	MFI	140@3600	180@3600	3.50x3.31	8.8:1	55@2000
1991	K	2.0L (1998)	TFI	96@4800	118@3600	3.39x3.39	8.8:1	45@2400
	G	2.2L (2180)	TBI	95@5200	120@3200	3.50x3.46	9.0:1	63-77@1200
	T	3.1L (3130)	MFI	140@4500	180@3600	3.50x3.31	8.5:1	8@600
1992	H	2.0L (1998)	MFI	111@5200	125@3600	3.38x3.38	9.2:1	45@2400
	4	2.2L (2180)	TBI	95@5200	120@3200	3.50x3.46	9.0:1	63-77@1200
	T	3.1L (3130)	MFI	140@4500	180@3600	3.50x3.31	8.5:1	8@600
1993	H	2.0L (1998)	MFI	110@5200	124@3600	3.38x3.38	9.2:1	30@2000
	4	2.2L (2180)	MFI	110@5200	130@3200	3.50x3.46	9.0:1	63-77@1200
	T	3.1L (3130)	MFI	140@4200	185@3200	3.50x3.31	8.5:1	8@600
1994	H	2.0L (1998)	MFI	110@5200	124@3600	3.38x3.38	9.2:1	30@2000
	4	2.2L (2180)	MFI	110@5200	130@3200	3.50x3.46	9.0:1	63-77@1200
	T	3.1L (3130)	MFI	140@4200	185@3200	3.50x3.31	8.5:1	8@600

87953500

GENERAL ENGINE SPECIFICATIONS

Year	Engine ID/VIN	Engine Displacement Liters (cc)	Fuel System Type	Net Horsepower @ rpm	Net Torque @ rpm (ft. lbs.)	Bore x Stroke (in.)	Compression Ratio	Oil Pressure @ rpm
1995	4	2.2L (2180)	MFI	120@5200	130@3200	3.50x3.46	9.0:1	63-77@1200
	D	2.3L (2262)	MFI	150@6100	145@4800	3.63x3.35	9.5:1	30@2000
1996	4	2.2L (2180)	SFI	120@5200	130@4000	3.50x3.46	9.0:1	56@3000
	T	2.4L (2392)	SFI	150@6000	155@4400	3.54x3.70	9.5:1	30@3000

2bbl - 2 barrel carburetor
TBI - Throttle Body fuel Injection
MFI - Multiport Fuel Injection
SFI - Sequential Fuel Injection

87953501

VALVE SPECIFICATIONS

Year	Engine ID/VIN	Engine Displacement Liters (cc)	Seat Angle (deg.)	Face Angle (deg.)	Spring Test Pressure (lbs. @ in.)	Spring Installed Height (in.)	Stem-to-Guide Clearance (in.)		Stem Diameter (in.)	
							Intake	Exhaust	Intake	Exhaust
1982	G	1.8 (1819)	46	45	183 @ 1.33	1.60	0.0011-0.0026	0.0014-0.0031	0.3139-0.3144	0.3129-0.3136
	O	1.8 (1819)	46	46	NA	NA	0.0006-0.0016	0.0012-0.0024	NA	NA
	B	2.0 (1998)	46	45	183 @ 1.33	1.60	0.0011-0.0026	0.0014-0.0031	0.3139-0.3144	0.3129-0.3136
1983	O	1.8 (1819)	46	46	NA	NA	0.0006-0.0016	0.0012-0.0024	NA	NA
	J	1.8 (1819)	46	46	NA	NA	0.0006-0.0016	0.0012-0.0024	NA	NA
	P	2.0 (1998)	46	45	183 @ 1.33	1.60	0.0011-0.0026	0.0014-0.0031	0.3139-0.3144	0.3129-0.3136
	B	2.0 (1998)	46	45	183 @ 1.33	1.60	0.0011-0.0026	0.0014-0.0031	0.3139-0.3144	0.3129-0.3136
1984	O	1.8 (1819)	46	46	NA	NA	0.0006-0.0016	0.0012-0.0024	NA	NA
	J	1.8 (1819)	46	46	NA	NA	0.0006-0.0016	0.0012-0.0024	NA	NA
	P	2.0 (1998)	46	45	183 @ 1.33	1.60	0.0011-0.0026	0.0014-0.0031	0.3139-0.3144	0.3129-0.3136
1985	O	1.8 (1819)	46	45	78-88 @ 1.44	1.440	0.0006-0.0020	0.0010-0.0024	NA	NA
	J	1.8 (1819)	46	45	78-88 @ 1.44	1.440	0.0006-0.0020	0.0010-0.0024	NA	NA
	P	2.0 (1998)	46	45	183 @ 1.33	1.60	0.0011-0.0026	0.0014-0.0031	0.3139-0.3144	0.3129-0.3136
	W	2.8 (2835)	46	45	195 @ 1.18	1.57	0.0010-0.0027	0.0010-0.0027	0.3410-0.3416	0.3410-0.3416
1986	O	1.8 (1819)	46	45	78-88 @ 1.44	1.440	0.0006-0.0020	0.0010-0.0024	NA	NA
	J	1.8 (1819)	46	45	78-88 @ 1.44	1.440	0.0006-0.0020	0.0010-0.0024	NA	NA
	P	2.0 (1998)	46	45	183 @ 1.33	1.60	0.0011-0.0026	0.0014-0.0031	0.3139-0.3144	0.3129-0.3136
	W	2.8 (2835)	46	45	195 @ 1.18	1.57	0.0010-0.0027	0.0010-0.0027	0.3410-0.3416	0.3410-0.3416
1987	K	2.0 (1998)	46	46	63-71 @ 1.48	1.476	0.0006-0.0017	0.0012-0.0024	0.2753-0.2747	0.2760-0.2755
	M	2.0 (1998)	46	46	74-82 @ 1.48	1.476	0.0006-0.0017	0.0012-0.0024	0.2753-0.2747	0.2760-0.2755
	1	2.0 (1998)	45	45	105 ①	1.60	0.0011-0.0023	0.0014-0.0028	NA	NA
	W	2.8 (2835)	46	45	195 @ 1.18	1.57	0.0010-0.0027	0.0010-0.0027	0.3410-0.3416	0.3410-0.3416

87953502

VALVE SPECIFICATIONS

Year	Engine ID/VIN	Engine Displacement Liters (cc)	Seat Angle (deg.)	Face Angle (deg.)	Spring Test Pressure (lbs. @ in.)	Spring Installed Height (in.)	Stem-to-Guide Clearance (in.) Intake	Stem-to-Guide Clearance (in.) Exhaust	Stem Diameter (in.) Intake	Stem Diameter (in.) Exhaust
1988	K	2.0 (1998)	45	46	63-71 @ 1.48	1.476	0.0006-0.0017	0.0012-0.0024	0.2753-0.2747	0.2755-0.2760
	M	2.0 (1998)	45	46	74-82 @ 1.48	1.476	0.0006-0.0017	0.0012-0.0024	0.2753-0.2747	0.2755-0.2760
	1	2.0 (1998)	45	45	105 ①	1.60	0.0011-0.0023	0.0014-0.0028	NA	NA
	W	2.8 (2835)	46	45	195 @ 1.18	1.57	0.0010-0.0027	0.0010-0.0027	0.3410-0.3416	0.3410-0.3416
1989	K	2.0 (1998)	46	45	63-71 @ 1.48	1.476	0.0006-0.0017	0.0012-0.0024	0.2753-0.2747	0.2755-0.2760
	M	2.0 (1998)	45	46	74-82 @ 1.48	1.476	0.0006-0.0017	0.0012-0.0024	0.2753-0.2747	0.2755-0.2760
	1	2.0 (1998)	45	45	105 ①	1.60	0.0011-0.0023	0.0014-0.0028	NA	NA
	W	2.8 (2835)	46	45	195 @ 1.18	1.57	0.0010-0.0027	0.0010-0.0027	0.3410-0.3416	0.3410-0.3416
1990	K	2.0 (1998)	46	45	63-71 @ 1.476	1.476	0.0006-0.0017	0.0012-0.0024	0.2760-0.2753	0.2755-0.2747
	M	2.0 (1998)	46	45	74-82 @ 1.48	1.476	0.0006-0.0017	0.0012-0.0024	0.2760-0.2753	0.2755-0.2747
	G	2.2 (2180)	46	45	208-222 @ ② 1.22	1.61 ③	0.0011-0.0026	0.0014-0.0030	NA	NA
	T	3.1 (3130)	46	45	90 ②	1.60 ③	0.0010-0.0027	0.0010-0.0027	NA	NA
1991	K	2.0 (1998)	45	46	63-71 @ 1.48	1.476	0.0006-0.0017	0.0012-0.0024	0.2760-0.2755	0.2753-0.2747
	G	2.2 (2180)	46	45	208-222 @ ② 1.22	1.61 ③	0.0011-0.0026	0.0014-0.0030	NA	NA
	T	3.1 (3130)	46	45	90 ②	1.60 ③	0.0010-0.0027	0.0010-0.0027	NA	NA
1992	H	2.0 (1998)	45	46	63-71 @ 1.48	1.476	0.0006-0.0017	0.0012-0.0024	0.2760-0.2755	0.2753-0.2747
	4	2.2 (2180)	46	45	208-222 @ ② 1.22	1.61 ③	0.0011-0.0026	0.0014-0.0030	NA	NA
	T	3.1 (3130)	46	45	90 ②	1.60 ③	0.0010-0.0027	0.0010-0.0027	NA	NA
1993	H	2.0 (1998)	46	45	90 @ 1.70	1.693	0.0008-0.0021	0.0014-0.0030	0.2753-0.2747	0.2760-0.2755
	4	2.2 (2180)	46	45	225-233 @ ② 1.25	1.64 ③	0.0011-0.0026	0.0014-0.0031	NA	NA
	T	3.1 (3130)	46	45	90 ②	1.60 ③	0.0010-0.0027	0.0010-0.0027	NA	NA

87953503

VALVE SPECIFICATIONS

Year	Engine ID/VIN	Engine Displacement Liters (cc)	Seat Angle (deg.)	Face Angle (deg.)	Spring Test Pressure (lbs. @ in.)	Spring Installed Height (in.)	Stem-to-Guide Clearance (in.)		Stem Diameter (in.)	
							Intake	Exhaust	Intake	Exhaust
1994	H	2.0 (1998)	45	46	63-71 @ 1.48	1.476	0.0006- 0.0017	0.0012- 0.0024	0.2753- 0.2747	0.2760- 0.2755
	4	2.2 (2180)	46	45	225-233 @ ② 1.25	1.64 ③	0.0011- 0.0026	0.0014- 0.0031	NA	NA
	T	3.1 (3130)	46	45	90 ②	1.60 ③	0.0010- 0.0027	0.0010- 0.0027	NA	NA
1995	4	2.2 (2180)	46	45	225-233 @ ② 1.25	1.64 ③	0.0011- 0.0026	0.0014- 0.0031	NA	NA
	D	2.3 (2262)	45	44	193-207 @ 1.04	1.44 ③	0.0010- 0.0027	0.0015- 0.0032	0.2740- 0.2750	0.2740- 0.2750
1996	4	2.2 (2180)	46	45	220-236 @ ② 1.28		0.0010- 0.0027	0.0014- 0.0031	NA	NA
	T	2.4 (2392)	45	④	122-133 @ ② 1.44	0.978- 1.002	0.0009- 0.0025	0.0016- 0.0032	0.2331- 0.2339	0.2326- 0.2334

NA - Not Available
1 With valve closed
2 With valve open
3 With valve closed
4 Intake: 46 degrees, Exhaust: 45.5 degrees

87953504

CAMSHAFT SPECIFICATIONS
All measurements given in inches.

Year	Engine ID/VIN	Engine Displacement Liters (cc)	Journal Diameter					Elevation		Bearing Clearance	Camshaft End Play
			1	2	3	4	5	In.	Ex.		
1982	G	1.8 (1819)	1.8677-1.8696	1.8677-1.8696	1.8677-1.8696	1.8677-1.8696	1.8677-1.8696	0.2625	0.2625	0.0010-0.0039	NA
	O	1.8 (1819)	1.6714-1.6720	1.6812-1.6816	1.6911-1.6917	1.7009-1.7015	1.7108-1.7114	0.2409	0.2409	NA	0.0160-0.0640
	B	2.0 (1998)	1.8677-1.8696	1.8677-1.8696	1.8677-1.8696	1.8677-1.8696	1.8677-1.8696	0.2600	0.2600	0.0010-0.0039	NA
1983	O	1.8 (1819)	1.6714-1.6720	1.6812-1.6816	1.6911-1.6917	1.7009-1.7015	1.7108-1.7114	0.2409	0.2409	NA	0.0160-0.0640
	J	1.8 (1819)	1.6714-1.6720	1.6812-1.6816	1.6911-1.6917	1.7009-1.7015	1.7108-1.7114	0.2409	0.2409	NA	0.0160-0.0640
	P	2.0 (1998)	1.8677-1.8696	1.8677-1.8696	1.8677-1.8696	1.8677-1.8696	1.8677-1.8696	0.2600	0.2600	0.0010-0.0039	NA
	B	2.0 (1998)	1.8677-1.8696	1.8677-1.8696	1.8677-1.8696	1.8677-1.8696	1.8677-1.8696	0.2600	0.2600	0.0010-0.0039	NA
1984	O	1.8 (1819)	1.6714-1.6720	1.6812-1.6816	1.6911-1.6917	1.7009-1.7015	1.7108-1.7114	0.2409	0.2409	NA	0.0160-0.0640
	J	1.8 (1819)	1.6714-1.6720	1.6812-1.6816	1.6911-1.6917	1.7009-1.7015	1.7108-1.7114	0.2409	0.2409	NA	0.0160-0.0640
	P	2.0 (1998)	1.8677-1.8696	1.8677-1.8696	1.8677-1.8696	1.8677-1.8696	1.8677-1.8696	0.2600	0.2600	0.0010-0.0039	NA
1985	O	1.8 (1819)	1.6714-1.6720	1.6812-1.6816	1.6911-1.6917	1.7009-1.7015	1.7108-1.7114	0.2409	0.2409	0.0010-0.0039	0.0016-0.0063
	J	1.8 (1819)	1.6714-1.6720	1.6812-1.6816	1.6911-1.6917	1.7009-1.7015	1.7108-1.7114	0.2409	0.2409	0.0010-0.0039	0.0016-0.0063
	P	2.0 (2000)	1.8677-1.8696	1.8677-1.8696	1.8677-1.8696	1.8677-1.8696	1.8677-1.8696	0.2625	0.2625	0.0010-0.0039	NA
	W	2.8 (2835)	1.8690	1.8690	1.8690	1.8690	NA	0.2630	0.2730	0.0010-0.0040	NA
1986	O	1.8 (1819)	1.6714-1.6720	1.6812-1.6816	1.6911-1.6917	1.7009-1.7015	1.7108-1.7114	0.2409	0.2409	0.0010-0.0039	0.0016-0.0063
	J	1.8 (1819)	1.6714-1.6720	1.6812-1.6816	1.6911-1.6917	1.7009-1.7015	1.7108-1.7114	0.2409	0.2409	0.0010-0.0039	0.0016-0.0063
	P	2.0 (2000)	1.8677-1.8696	1.8677-1.8696	1.8677-1.8696	1.8677-1.8696	1.8677-1.8696	0.2625	0.2625	0.0010-0.0039	NA
	W	2.8 (2835)	1.8690	1.8690	1.8690	1.8690	NA	0.2630	0.2730	0.0010-0.0040	NA
1987	K	2.0 (1998)	1.6714-1.6720	1.6810-1.6816	1.6911-1.6917	1.7009-1.7015	1.7108-1.7114	0.2409	0.2409	0.0008-0.0032	0.0016-0.0064
	M	2.0 (1998)	1.6714-1.6720	1.6810-1.6816	1.6911-1.6917	1.7009-1.7015	1.7108-1.7114	0.2409	0.2409	0.0008-0.0032	0.0016-0.0064
	1	2.0 (2000)	1.8677-1.8696	1.8677-1.8696	1.8677-1.8696	1.8677-1.8696	1.8677-1.8696	0.2625	0.2625	0.0010-0.0039	NA
	W	2.8 (2835)	1.8690	1.8690	1.8690	1.8690	NA	0.2630	0.2730	0.0010-0.0040	NA

87953505

CAMSHAFT SPECIFICATIONS

All measurements given in inches.

Year	Engine ID/VIN	Engine Displacement Liters (cc)	Journal Diameter					Elevation		Bearing Clearance	Camshaft End Play
			1	2	3	4	5	In.	Ex.		
1988	K	2.0 (1998)	1.6714-1.6720	1.6810-1.6816	1.6911-1.6917	1.7009-1.7015	1.7108-1.7114	0.2409	0.2409	0.0008-0.0032	0.0016-0.0064
	M	2.0 (1998)	1.6714-1.6720	1.6810-1.6816	1.6911-1.6917	1.7009-1.7015	1.7108-1.7114	0.2409	0.2409	0.0008-0.0032	0.0016-0.0064
	1	2.0 (2000)	1.8677-1.8696	1.8677-1.8696	1.8677-1.8696	1.8677-1.8696	1.8677-1.8696	0.2625	0.2625	0.0010-0.0039	NA
	W	2.8 (2835)	1.8670-1.8810	1.8670-1.8810	1.8670-1.8810	1.8670-1.8810	NA 1.8810	0.2630	0.2730	0.0010-0.0040	NA
1989	K	2.0 (1998)	1.6714-1.6720	1.6810-1.6816	1.6911-1.6917	1.7009-1.7015	1.7108-1.7114	0.2409	0.2409	0.0008-0.0032	0.0016-0.0064
	M	2.0 (1998)	1.6714-1.6720	1.6810-1.6816	1.6911-1.6917	1.7009-1.7015	1.7108-1.7114	0.2409	0.2409	0.0008-0.0032	0.0016-0.0064
	1	2.0 (2000)	1.8677-1.8696	1.8677-1.8696	1.8677-1.8696	1.8677-1.8696	1.8677-1.8696	0.2625	0.2625	0.0010-0.0039	NA
	W	2.8 (2835)	1.8670-1.8810	1.8670-1.8810	1.8670-1.8810	1.8670-1.8810	NA	0.2630	0.2730	0.0010-0.0040	NA
1990	K	2.0 (1998)	1.6706-1.6712	1.6812-1.6818	1.6911-1.6917	1.7009-1.7015	1.7100-1.7106	0.2366	0.2515	0.0011-0.0035	0.0016-0.0064
	M	2.0 (1998)	1.6706-1.6712	1.6812-1.6818	1.6911-1.6917	1.7009-1.7015	1.7100-1.7106	0.2366	0.2515	0.0011-0.0035	0.0016-0.0064
	G	2.2 (2180)	1.8670-1.8690	1.8670-1.8690	1.8670-1.8690	1.8670-1.8690	1.8670-1.8690	0.2590	0.2590	0.0010-0.0039	NA
	T	3.1 (3130)	1.8680-1.8810	1.8680-1.8810	1.8680-1.8810	1.8680-1.8810	NA	0.2630	0.2730	0.0010-0.0039	NA
1991	K	2.0 (1998)	1.6706-1.6712	1.6812-1.6818	1.6911-1.6917	1.7009-1.7015	1.7100-1.7106	0.2366	0.2515	0.0011-0.0035	0.0016-0.0064
	G	2.2 (2180)	1.8670-1.8690	1.8670-1.8690	1.8670-1.8690	1.8670-1.8690	1.8670-1.8690	0.2590	0.2590	0.0010-0.0039	NA
	T	3.1 (3130)	1.8680-1.8810	1.8680-1.8810	1.8680-1.8810	1.8680-1.8810	NA	0.2630	0.2730	0.0010-0.0039	NA
1992	H	2.0 (1998)	1.6706-1.6712	1.6812-1.6818	1.6911-1.6917	1.7009-1.7015	1.7100-1.7106	0.2626	0.2626	0.0011-0.0035	0.0016-0.0064
	4	2.2 (2180)	1.8670-1.8690	1.8670-1.8690	1.8670-1.8690	1.8670-1.8690	1.8670-1.8690	0.2590	0.2590	0.0010-0.0039	NA
	T	3.1 (3130)	1.8680-1.8810	1.8680-1.8810	1.8680-1.8810	1.8680-1.8810	NA	0.2630	0.2730	0.0010-0.0039	NA
1993	H	2.0 (1998)	1.6706-1.6712	1.6812-1.6818	1.6911-1.6917	1.7009-1.7015	1.7100-1.7106	0.2626	0.2626	0.0011-0.0035	0.0016-0.0064
	4	2.2 (2180)	1.8670-1.8690	1.8670-1.8690	1.8670-1.8690	1.8670-1.8690	1.8670-1.8690	0.2590	0.2590	0.0010-0.0039	NA
	T	3.1 (3130)	1.8680-1.8810	1.8680-1.8810	1.8680-1.8810	1.8680-1.8810	NA	0.2630	0.2730	0.0010-0.0039	NA

87953506

CAMSHAFT SPECIFICATIONS
All measurements given in inches.

Year	Engine ID/VIN	Engine Displacement Liters (cc)	Journal Diameter					Elevation		Bearing Clearance	Camshaft End Play
			1	2	3	4	5	In.	Ex.		
1994	H	2.0 (1998)	1.6706-1.6712	1.6812-1.6818	1.6911-1.6917	1.7009-1.7015	1.7100-1.7106	0.2626	0.2626	0.0011-0.0035	0.0016-0.0063
	4	2.2 (2180)	1.8670-1.8690	1.8670-1.8690	1.8670-1.8690	1.8670-1.8690	1.8670-1.8690	0.2590	0.2590	0.0010-0.0039	NA
	T	3.1 (3130)	1.8680-1.8810	1.8680-1.8810	1.8680-1.8810	1.8680-1.8810	NA	0.2630	0.2730	0.0010-0.0039	NA
1995	4	2.2 (2180)	1.8670-1.8690	1.8670-1.8690	1.8670-1.8690	1.8670-1.8690	1.8670-1.8690	0.2880	0.2880	0.0010-0.0039	NA
	D	2.3 (2262)	1.5720-1.5730	1.3750-1.3760	1.3750-1.3760	1.3750-1.3760	1.3750-1.3760	0.3750	0.3750	0.0020-0.0040	0.0010-0.0090
1996	4	2.2 (2195)	1.8680-1.8690	1.8680-1.8690	1.8680-1.8690	1.8680-1.8690	1.8680-1.8690	0.2880	0.2880	0.0010-0.0039	NA
	T	2.4 (2392)	1.5720-1.5728	1.3751-1.3760	1.3751-1.3760	1.3751-1.3760	1.3751-1.3760	0.3540	0.3460	0.0019-0.0043	0.0009-0.0088

NA - Not Available

87953507

CRANKSHAFT AND CONNECTING ROD SPECIFICATIONS

All measurements are given in inches.

Year	Engine ID/VIN	Engine Displacement Liters (cc)	Crankshaft Main Brg. Journal Dia.	Crankshaft Main Brg. Oil Clearance	Crankshaft Shaft End-play	Crankshaft Thrust on No.	Connecting Rod Journal Diameter	Connecting Rod Oil Clearance	Connecting Rod Side Clearance
1982	G	1.8 (1819)	2.4944- ① 2.4954	0.0006- ② 0.0018	0.0019- 0.0071	4	1.9983- 1.9993	0.0009- 0.0031	0.0039- 0.0240
	O	1.8 (1819)		0.0006- 0.0016	0.0027- 0.0118	3	1.9278- 1.9286	0.0007- 0.0024	0.0027- 0.0095
	B	2.0 (1998)	2.4944- ① 2.4954	0.0006- ② 0.0018	0.0019- 0.0071	4	1.9983- 1.9993	0.0009- 0.0031	0.0039- 0.0240
1983	O	1.8 (1819)	③	0.0006- 0.0016	0.0027- 0.0118	3	1.9278- 1.9286	0.0007- 0.0024	0.0027- 0.0095
	J	1.8 (1819)		0.0006- 0.0016	0.0027- 0.0118	3	1.9278- 1.9286	0.0007- 0.0024	0.0027- 0.0095
	P	2.0 (1998)	2.4944- ① 2.4954	0.0006- ② 0.0018	0.0019- 0.0071	4	1.9983- 1.9993	0.0009- 0.0031	0.0039- 0.0240
	B	2.0 (1998)	2.4944- ① 2.4954	0.0006- ② 0.0018	0.0019- 0.0071	4	1.9983- 1.9993	0.0009- 0.0031	0.0039- 0.0240
1984	O	1.8 (1819)	③	0.0006- 0.0016	0.0027- 0.0118	3	1.9278- 1.9286	0.0007- 0.0024	0.0027- 0.0095
	J	1.8 (1819)	③	0.0006- 0.0016	0.0027- 0.0118	3	1.9278- 1.9286	0.0007- 0.0024	0.0027- 0.0095
	P	2.0 (1998)	2.4944- ① 2.4954	0.0006- ② 0.0018	0.0019- 0.0071	4	1.9983- 1.9993	0.0009- 0.0031	0.0039- 0.0240
1985	O	1.8 (1819)	③	0.0006- 0.0016	0.0027- 0.0118	3	1.9278- 1.9286	0.0007- 0.0024	0.0027- 0.0095
	J	1.8 (1819)	③	0.0006- 0.0016	0.0027- 0.0118	3	1.9278- 1.9286	0.0007- 0.0024	0.0027- 0.0095
	P	2.0 (2000)	2.4944- 2.4954	0.0006- ② 0.0018	0.0019- 0.0071	4	1.9983- 1.9993	0.0009- 0.0031	0.0039- 0.0240
	W	2.8 (2835)	2.4397- 2.4946	0.0017- 0.0030	0.0020- 0.0067	3	1.9984- 1.9994	0.0014- 0.0036	0.0060- 0.0170
1986	O	1.8 (1819)	③	0.0006- 0.0016	0.0027- 0.0118	3	1.9278- 1.9286	0.0007- 0.0024	0.0027- 0.0095
	J	1.8 (1819)	③	0.0006- 0.0016	0.0027- 0.0118	3	1.9278- 1.9286	0.0007- 0.0024	0.0027- 0.0095
	P	2.0 (2000)	2.4944- ④ 2.4954	0.0006- ② 0.0018	0.0019- 0.0071	4	1.9983- 1.9993	0.0009- 0.0031	0.0039- 0.0240
	W	2.8 (2835)	2.4397- 2.4946	0.0017- 0.0030	0.0020- 0.0067	3	1.9984- 1.9994	0.0014- 0.0036	0.0060- 0.0170
1987	K	2.0 (1998)	⑤	0.0006- 0.0016	0.0003- 0.0012	3	1.9278- 1.9286	0.0007- 0.0024	0.0027- 0.0095
	M	2.0 (1998)	⑤	0.0006- 0.0016	0.0003- 0.0012	3	1.9278- 1.9286	0.0007- 0.0024	0.0027- 0.0095
	1	2.0 (2000)	2.4945- 2.4954	0.0006- 0.0019	0.0020- 0.0080	4	1.9983- 1.9994	0.0010- 0.0031	0.0040- 0.0150
	W	2.8 (2835)	2.4397- 2.4946	0.0017- 0.0030	0.0020- 0.0067	3	1.9984- 1.9994	0.0014- 0.0036	0.0060- 0.0170

87953508

CRANKSHAFT AND CONNECTING ROD SPECIFICATIONS

All measurements are given in inches.

Year	Engine ID/VIN	Engine Displacement Liters (cc)	Crankshaft				Connecting Rod		
			Main Brg. Journal Dia.	Main Brg. Oil Clearance	Shaft End-play	Thrust on No.	Journal Diameter	Oil Clearance	Side Clearance
1988	K	2.0 (1998)	⑤	0.0006-0.0016	0.0003-0.0012	3	1.9278-1.9286	0.0007-0.0024	0.0027-0.0095
	M	2.0 (1998)	⑤	0.0006-0.0016	0.0003-0.0012	3	1.9278-1.9286	0.0007-0.0024	0.0027-0.0095
	1	2.0 (2000)	2.4945-	0.0006-0.0019	0.0020-0.0080	4	1.9983-1.9994	0.0010-0.0031	0.0040-0.0150
	W	2.8 (2835)	2.4397-2.4946	0.0017-0.0030	0.0020-0.0067	3	1.9984-1.9994	0.0014-0.0036	0.0060-0.0170
1989	K	2.0 (1998)	⑤	0.0006-0.0016	0.0003-0.0012	3	1.9279-1.9287	0.0007-0.0024	0.0027-0.0095
	M	2.0 (1998)	⑤	0.0006-0.0016	0.0003-0.0012	3	1.9279-1.9287	0.0007-0.0024	0.0027-0.0095
	1	2.0 (2000)	2.4945-2.4954	0.0006-0.0019	0.0020-0.0080	4	1.9983-1.9994	0.0010-0.0031	0.0040-0.0150
	W	2.8 (2835)	2.4397-2.4946	0.0017-0.0030	0.0020-0.0067	3	1.9984-1.9994	0.0014-0.0036	0.0060-0.0170
1990	K	2.0 (1998)	2.2828-2.2833	0.0006-0.0016	0.0003-0.0012	3	1.9279-1.9287	0.0007-0.0024	0.0027-0.0095
	M	2.0 (1998)	2.2828-2.2833	0.0006-0.0016	0.0003-0.0012	3	1.9279-1.9287	0.0007-0.0024	0.0027-0.0095
	G	2.2 (2180)	2.4945-2.4954	0.0006-0.0019	0.0020-0.0070	4	1.9983-1.9994	0.0010-0.0030	0.0040-0.0150
	T	3.1 (3130)	2.6473-2.6483	0.0012-0.0030	0.0020-0.0080	3	1.9983-1.9994	0.0010-0.0040	0.0140-0.0270
1991	K	2.0 (1998)	2.2828-2.2833	0.0006-0.0016	0.0028-0.0012	3	1.9279-1.9287	0.0007-0.0025	0.0028-0.0095
	G	2.2 (2180)	2.4945-2.4954	0.0006-0.0019	0.0020-0.0070	4	1.9983-1.9994	0.0010-0.0030	0.0040-0.0150
	T	3.1 (3130)	2.6473-2.6483	0.0012-0.0030	0.0020-0.0080	3	1.9983-1.9994	0.0010-0.0040	0.0140-0.0270
1992	H	2.0 (1998)	2.2828-2.2833	0.0006-0.0016	0.0028-0.0118	3	1.9279-1.9287	0.0007-0.0025	0.0028-0.0095
	4	2.2 (2180)	2.4945-2.4954	0.0006-0.0019	0.0020-0.0070	4	1.9983-1.9994	0.0010-0.0030	0.0040-0.0150
	T	3.1 (3130)	2.6473-2.6483	0.0012-0.0030	0.0020-0.0080	3	1.9983-1.9994	0.0010-0.0040	0.0140-0.0270
1993	H	2.0 (1998)	2.2828-2.2833	0.0006-0.0016	0.0028-0.0118	3	1.9279-1.9287	0.0007-0.0025	0.0028-0.0095
	4	2.2 (2180)	2.4945-2.4954	0.0006-0.0019	0.0020-0.0070	4	1.9983-1.9994	0.0010-0.0030	0.0040-0.0150
	T	3.1 (3130)	2.6473-2.6483	0.0012-0.0030	0.0020-0.0080	3	1.9983-1.9994	0.0010-0.0040	0.0140-0.0270

87953509

CRANKSHAFT AND CONNECTING ROD SPECIFICATIONS

All measurements are given in inches.

Year	Engine ID/VIN	Engine Displacement Liters (cc)	Crankshaft				Connecting Rod		
			Main Brg. Journal Dia.	Main Brg. Oil Clearance	Shaft End-play	Thrust on No.	Journal Diameter	Oil Clearance	Side Clearance
1994	H	2.0 (1998)	2.2828-2.2833	0.0006-0.0016	0.0028-0.0118	3	1.9279-1.9287	0.0007-0.0025	0.0028-0.0095
	4	2.2 (2180)	2.4945-2.4954	0.0006-0.0019	0.0020-0.0070	4	1.9983-1.9994	0.0010-0.0030	0.0040-0.0150
	T	3.1 (3130)	2.6473-2.6483	0.0012-0.0030	0.0020-0.0080	3	1.9983-1.9994	0.0010-0.0040	0.0140-0.0270
1995	4	2.2 (2180)	2.4945-2.4954	0.0006-0.0019	0.0020-0.0070	4	1.9983-1.9994	0.0010-0.0030	0.0040-0.0150
	D	2.3 (2262)	2.0470-2.0480	0.0005-0.0023	0.0030-0.0090	3	1.8887-1.8897	0.0005-0.0020	0.0059-0.0177
1996	4	2.2 (2195)	2.4945-2.4954	0.0006-0.0019	0.0020-0.0070	4	1.9983-1.9994	0.0098-0.0031	0.0039-0.0149
	T	2.4 (2392)	2.3626-2.3634	0.0005-0.0030	0.0005-0.0030	3	1.8887-1.8897	0.0005-0.0020	0.0059-0.0177

NA - Not Available
1 No. 5: 2.4936-2.4946
2 No. 5: 0.0014-0.0027
3 Bearings are identified by color:
   Brown: 2.2830-2.2832
   Green:: 2.2827-2.2830
4 No. 5: 2.4936-2.4946
5 Bearings are identified by color:
   Brown: 2.2830-2.2833
   Green:: 2.2827-2.2830

87953510

PISTON AND RING SPECIFICATIONS

All measurements are given in inches.

Year	Engine ID/VIN	Engine Displacement Liters (cc)	Piston Clearance	Ring Gap			Ring Side Clearance		
				Top Compression	Bottom Compression	Oil Control	Top Compression	Bottom Compression	Oil Control
1982	G	1.8 (1819)	0.0008-0.0018	0.0098-0.0197	0.0098-0.0197	Snug	0.0012-0.0027	0.0012-0.0027	0.0078
	O	1.8 (1819)	0.0004-0.0012	0.0010-0.0020	0.0010-0.0020	0.0010-0.0020	0.0020-0.0030	0.0010-0.0024	Snug
	B	2.0 (1998)	0.0008-0.0018	0.0098-0.0197	0.0098-0.0197	Snug	0.0012-0.0027	0.0012-0.0027	0.0078
1983	O	1.8 (1819)	0.0004-0.0012	0.0010-0.0020	0.0010-0.0020	0.0010-0.0020	0.0020-0.0030	0.0010-0.0024	Snug
	J	1.8 (1819)	0.0004-0.0012	0.0010-0.0020	0.0010-0.0020	0.0010-0.0020	0.0020-0.0030	0.0010-0.0024	Snug
	P	2.0 (1998)	0.0008-0.0018	0.0098-0.0197	0.0098-0.0197	Snug	0.0012-0.0027	0.0012-0.0027	0.0078
	B	2.0 (1998)	0.0008-0.0018	0.0098-0.0197	0.0098-0.0197	Snug	0.0012-0.0027	0.0012-0.0027	0.0078
1984	O	1.8 (1819)	0.0004-0.0012	0.0010-0.0020	0.0010-0.0020	0.0010-0.0020	0.0020-0.0030	0.0010-0.0024	Snug
	J	1.8 (1819)	0.0004-0.0012	0.0010-0.0020	0.0010-0.0020	0.0010-0.0020	0.0020-0.0030	0.0010-0.0024	Snug
	P	2.0 (1998)	0.0007-0.0017	0.0098-0.0197	0.0098-0.0197	Snug	0.0012-0.0027	0.0012-0.0027	0.0078
1985	O	1.8 (1819)	0.0008	0.0120-0.0200	0.0120-0.0200	0.0160-0.0550	0.0020-0.0040	0.0010-0.0025	0.0047
	J	1.8 (1819)	0.0008	0.0120-0.0200	0.0120-0.0200	0.0160-0.0550	0.0020-0.0040	0.0010-0.0025	0.0047
	P	2.0 (2000)	0.0007-0.0017	0.010-0.020	0.010-0.020	SNUG	0.0012-0.0027	0.0012-0.0027	0.0078
	W	2.8 (2835)	0.0012-0.0027	0.010-0.020	0.010-0.020	0.020-0.055	0.0012-0.0027	0.0016-0.0037	0.0078 MAX
1986	O	1.8 (1819)	0.0008	0.0120-0.0200	0.0120-0.0200	0.0160-0.0550	0.0020-0.0040	0.0010-0.0025	0.0047
	J	1.8 (1819)	0.0008	0.0120-0.0200	0.0120-0.0200	0.0160-0.0550	0.0020-0.0040	0.0010-0.0025	0.0047
	P	2.0 (2000)	0.0007-0.0017	0.010-0.020	0.010-0.020	SNUG	0.0012-0.0027	0.0012-0.0027	0.0078
	W	2.8 (2835)	0.0012-0.0027	0.010-0.020	0.010-0.020	0.020-0.055	0.0012-0.0027	0.0016-0.0037	0.0078 MAX
1987	K	2.0 (1998)	0.0004-0.0012	0.0098-0.0177	0.0118-0.0197	NA	0.0024-0.0036	0.0019-0.0032	NA
	M	2.0 (1998)	0.0004-	0.0098-0.020	0.0118-0.025	NA 0.055	0.0024-0.0032	0.0019-0.0032	NA 0.0070
	1	2.0 (2000)	0.0010-0.0022	0.010-0.020	0.010-0.020	0.010-0.050	0.0010-0.0030	0.0010-0.0030	0.0080
	W	2.8 (2835)	0.0020-0.0030	0.010-0.020	0.010-0.020	0.020-0.055	0.0010-0.0030	0.0010-0.0030	0.0080

87953511

PISTON AND RING SPECIFICATIONS

All measurements are given in inches.

Year	Engine ID/VIN	Engine Displacement Liters (cc)	Piston Clearance	Ring Gap			Ring Side Clearance		
				Top Compression	Bottom Compression	Oil Control	Top Compression	Bottom Compression	Oil Control
1988	K	2.0 (1998)	0.0004-0.0012	0.0098-0.0177	0.0118-0.0197	NA	0.0024-0.0036	0.0019-0.0032	NA
	M	2.0 (1998)	0.0012-0.0020	0.0098-0.0177	0.0118-0.0197	NA	0.0024-0.0036	0.0019-0.0032	NA
	1	2.0 (2000)	0.0010-0.0022	0.010-0.020	0.010-0.020	0.010-0.050	0.0010-0.0030	0.0010-0.0030	0.0080
	W	2.8 (2835)	0.0020-0.0030	0.010-0.020	0.010-0.020	0.020-0.055	0.0010-0.0030	0.0010-0.0030	0.0080
1989	K	2.0 (1998)	0.0004-0.0012	0.0098-0.0177	0.0118-0.0197	NA	0.0024-0.0036	0.0019-0.0032	NA
	M	2.0 (1998)	0.0012-0.0020	0.0098-0.0177	0.0118-0.0197	NA	0.0024-0.0036	0.0019-0.0032	NA
	1	2.0 (2000)	0.0098-0.0022	0.010-0.020	0.010-0.020	0.010-0.050	0.0010-0.0030	0.0010-0.0030	0.0080
	W	2.8 (2835)	0.0020-0.0030	0.010-0.020	0.010-0.020	0.020-0.055	0.0010-0.0030	0.0010-0.0030	0.0080
1990	K	2.0 (1998)	0.0004-0.0012	0.0098-0.0177	0.0118-0.0197	NA	0.0024-0.0036	0.0019-0.0032	NA
	M	2.0 (1998)	0.0012-0.0020	0.0098-0.0177	0.0118-0.0197	NA	0.0024-0.0036	0.0019-0.0032	NA
	G	2.2 (2180)	0.0007-0.0017	0.010-0.020	0.010-0.020	0.010-0.050	0.0020-0.0030	0.0020-0.0030	0.0020-0.0082
	T	3.1 (3130)	0.0009-0.0022	0.010-0.020	0.020-0.028	0.010-0.030	0.0020-0.0030	0.0020-0.0030	0.0008
1991	K	2.0 (1998)	0.0004-0.0012	0.0098-0.0177	0.0118-0.0197	NA	0.0024-0.0036	0.0019-0.0032	NA
	G	2.2 (2180)	0.0007-0.0017	0.010-0.020	0.010-0.020	0.010-0.050	0.0020-0.0030	0.0020-0.0030	0.0020-0.0082
	T	3.1 (3130)	0.0009-0.0022	0.010-0.020	0.020-0.028	0.010-0.030	0.0020-0.0030	0.0020-0.0030	0.0080
1992	H	2.0 (1998)	0.0004-0.0012	0.0098-0.0177	0.0188-0.0197	NA	0.0024-0.0036	0.0019-0.0032	NA
	4	2.2 (2180)	0.0007-0.0017	0.010-0.020	0.010-0.020	0.010-0.050	0.0020-0.0030	0.0020-0.0030	0.0020-0.0082
	T	3.1 (3130)	0.0009-0.0022	0.010-0.020	0.020-0.028	0.010-0.030	0.0020-0.0030	0.0020-0.0030	0.0080
1993	H	2.0 (1998)	0.0004-0.0012	0.0098-0.0177	0.0118-0.0197	NA	0.0024-0.0036	0.0019-0.0032	NA
	4	2.2 (2180)	0.0007-0.0017	0.010-0.020	0.010-0.020	0.010-0.050	0.0020-0.0030	0.0020-0.0030	0.0020-0.0082
	T	3.1 (3130)	0.0009-0.0022	0.010-0.020	0.020-0.028	0.010-0.030	0.0020-0.0030	0.0020-0.0030	0.0080

87953512

PISTON AND RING SPECIFICATIONS

All measurements are given in inches.

Year	Engine ID/VIN	Engine Displacement Liters (cc)	Piston Clearance	Ring Gap			Ring Side Clearance		
				Top Compression	Bottom Compression	Oil Control	Top Compression	Bottom Compression	Oil Control
1994	H	2.0 (1998)	0.0004-0.0012	0.0098-0.0177	0.0118-0.0197	NA	0.0024-0.0036	0.0019-0.0032	NA
	4	2.2 (2180)	0.0007-0.0017	0.010-0.020	0.010-0.020	0.010-0.050	0.0020-0.0030	0.0020-0.0030	0.0020-0.0082
	T	3.1 (3130)	0.0009-0.0022	0.010-0.020	0.020-0.028	0.010-0.030	0.0020-0.0030	0.0020-0.0030	0.0080
1995	4	2.2 (2180)	0.0007-0.0017	0.010-0.020	0.010-0.020	0.010-0.050	0.0020-0.0030	0.0020-0.0030	0.0020-0.0082
	D	2.3 (2262)	0.0007-0.0020	0.014-0.024	0.016-0.026	0.016-0.055	0.0030-0.0050	0.0020-0.0030	NA
1996	4	2.2 (2195)	0.0007-0.0017	0.0100-0.0200	0.0100-0.0200	0.0100-0.0500	0.0019-0.0027	0.0019-0.0027	0.0019-0.0082
	T	2.4 (2392)	0.0007-0.0020	0.0060-0.0120	0.0119-0.0161	0.0157-0.0551	0.0016-0.0031	0.0012-0.0028	0.0098-0.0256

NA - Not Available

87953513

TORQUE SPECIFICATIONS
All readings in ft. lbs.

Year	Engine ID/VIN	Engine Displacement Liters (cc)	Cylinder Head Bolts	Main Bearing Bolts	Rod Bearing Bolts	Crankshaft Damper Bolts	Flywheel Bolts	Manifold Intake	Manifold Exhaust	Spark Plugs	Lug Nut
1982	G	1.8 (1819)	65-75	63-74	34-40	66-84	45-55	20-25	22-28	15	100
	O	1.8 (1819)	(1)	57	39	20 (2)	45	25	16	15	100
	B	2.0 (1998)	65-75 (1)	63-74	34-43	66-89	45-63 (3)	18-25	20-30	15	100
1983	O	1.8 (1819)	(1)	57	39	20 (2)	45	25	16	15	100
	J	1.8 (1819)	(1)	57	39	20 (2)	45	25	16	15	100
	P	2.0 (1998)	65-75	63-77	34-43	68-89	45-63 (3)	18-25	20-30	15	100
	B	2.0 (1998)	65-75	63-77	34-43	68-89	45-63 (3)	18-25	20-30	15	100
1984	O	1.8 (1819)	(1)	57	39	20 (2)	45	25	16	15	100
	J	1.8 (1819)	(1)	57	39	20 (2)	45	25	16	15	100
	P	2.0 (1998)	65-75	63-77	34-43	68-89	45-63 (3)	18-25	20-30	15	100
1985	O	1.8 (1819)	(1)	57	39	115	45	25	16	15	100
	J	1.8 (1819)		57	39	115	45	25	16	15	100
	P	2.0 (1998)	65-75	63-77	34-43	68-89	(16)	18-25	20-30	15	100
	W	2.8 (2835)	70	68	37	75	45	23	23	15	100
1986	O	2.0 (1998)	(1)	57	39	115	45	25	16	15	100
	J	2.0 (1998)	(1)	57	39	115	45	25	16	15	100
	P	2.0 (1998)	65-75	63-77	34-43	68-89	(16)	18-25	20-30	15	100
	W	2.8 (2835)	70	68	37	75	45	23	23	15	100
1987	K	2.0 (1998)	(1)	(4)	(5)	114	(6)	16	16	15	100
	M	2.0 (1998)	(1)	(4)	(5)	114	(6)	16	16	15	100
	1	2.0 (1998)	(17)	63-77	34-43	66-89	(16)	15-22	6-13	20	80-100
	W	2.8 (2835)	70	68	37	75	45	23	23	15	100
1988	K	2.0 (1998)	(1)	(4)	(5)	114	48 (7)	16	115 (8)	15	100
	M	2.0 (1998)	(1)	(4)	(5)	114	48 (7)	16	115 (8)	15	100
	1	2.0 (1998)	(17)	63-77	34-43	66-89	(16)	15-22	6-13	20	80-100
	W	2.8 (2835)	70	68	37	75	45	23	23	15	100
1989	K	2.0 (1998)	(1)	(4)	(5)	114	48 (7)	16	115 (8)	15	100
	M	2.0 (1998)	(1)	(4)	(5)	114	48 (7)	16	115 (8)	15	100
	1	2.0 (1998)	(17)	63-77	34-43	66-89	(16)	15-22	6-13	20	80-100
	W	2.8 (2835)	70	68	37	75	45	23	23	15	100
1990	K	2.0 (1998)	(1)	(4)	(5)	114	48 (7)	16	115 (8)	15	100
	M	2.0 (1998)	(1)	(4)	(5)	114	48 (7)	16	115 (8)	15	100
	G	2.2 (2180)	(18)	77	38	85 (20)	52-55	18	6-13	20	80-100
	T	3.1 (3130)	(19)	73	49	66-85	45-59	(21)	18	20	100
1991	K	2.0 (1998)	(1)	(4)	(5)	114	48 (7)	16	115	15	100
	G	2.2 (2180)	(18)	77	38	85 (20)	52-55	18	6-13	20	80-100
	T	3.1 (3130)	(19)	73	39	66-85	45-59	(21)	18	20	100
1992	H	2.0 (1998)	(1)	(4)	(5)	114	(6)	16	16	15	100
	4	2.2 (2180)	(18)	77	38	85 (20)	52-55	18	6-13	20	80-100
	T	3.1 (3130)	(19)	73	39	66-85	45-59	(21)	18	20	100
1993	H	2.0 (1998)	(1)	(4)	(5)	114	(6)	16	16	15	100
	4	2.2 (2180)	(18)	77	38	85 (20)	52-55	18	6-13	20	80-100
	T	3.1 (3130)	(19)	73	39	66-85	45-59	(21)	18	20	100
1994	H	2.0 (1998)	(1)	(4)	(5)	114	48	16	16	15	100
	4	2.2 (2180)	(18)	77	38	85 (20)	52-55	18	6-13	20	100
	T	3.1 (3130)	(19)	73	39	66-85	45-59	(21)	18	20	100

87953514

TORQUE SPECIFICATIONS
All readings in ft. lbs.

Year	Engine ID/VIN	Engine Displacement Liters (cc)	Cylinder Head Bolts	Main Bearing Bolts	Rod Bearing Bolts	Crankshaft Damper Bolts	Flywheel Bolts	Manifold		Spark Plugs	Lug Nut
								Intake	Exhaust		
1995	4	2.2 (2180)	①	77	38	77 ②	52-55	24	6-13	20	100
	D	2.3 (2262)	⑩	⑫	⑫	129	⑮	19	31	17	100
1996	4	2.2 (2180)	⑨	70	38	77	55	10	11	11	100
	T	2.4 (2398)	⑩	⑫	⑫	⑭	⑮	31	11	11	100

NA - Not Available

1   Step 1: 18 ft. lbs.
Step 2: Plus three turns of 60 degrees
Step 3: Plus 30-50 degrees after warm-up
2   Crankshaft pulley-to-sprocket bolts
3   Automatic transaxle: 45-59 ft. lbs.
4   Step 1: 44 ft. lbs.
Step 2: Plus 40-50 degrees
5   Step 1: 26 ft. lbs.
Step 2: Plus 40-45 degrees
6   Step 1: 48 ft. lbs.
Step 2: Plus 30 degrees
7   Manual transaxle: Plus 30 degrees
8   Inch lbs.
9   Short bolts: 43 ft. lbs. plug 90 degrees
Long bolts: 46 ft. lbs. plus 90 degrees
10   Bolts 1-8: 30 ft. lbs. plus 90 degrees
Bolts 9-10: 26 ft. lbs. plus 90 degrees
11   Step 1: 40 ft. lbs.
Step 2: Plug 90 degrees
12   Step 1: 15 ft. lbs
Step 2: Plus 90 degrees

13   Step 1: 22 ft. lbs.
Step 2: Plus 45 degrees
14   Step 1: 129 ft. lbs
Step 2: Plus 90 degrees
15   Step 1: 22 ft. lbs.
Step 2: Plus 45 degrees
16   Manual transaxle: 45-63 ft. lbs
Automatic transaxle: 45-59 ft. lbs.
17   Short bolts: 62-70 ft. lbs.
Long bolts: 73-83 ft. lbs.
18   Step 1: 41 ft. lbs.
Step 2: Tighten an additional 45 degrees
Step 3: Repeat step 2
Step 4: Long bolts - 1, 4-5, 8-9 an additional 45 degress
Step 5: Short bolts - 2-3, 6-7, 10 an additional 10 degrees
19   33 ft. lbs. plus 90 degrees
20   Center bolt spec. shown; Pulley-to-hub bolts to 37 ft. lbs.
21   Step 1: 15 ft . lbs.
Step 2: 24 ft. lbs.

87953515

Engine

REMOVAL & INSTALLATION

✳✳CAUTION

When draining the coolant, keep in mind that cats and dogs are attracted by ethylene glycol antifreeze, and are quite likely to drink any that is left in an uncovered container or in puddles on the ground. This will prove fatal in sufficient quantity. Always drain the coolant into a sealable container. Coolant should be reused unless it is contaminated or several years old.

1982-83 1.8L and 2.0L Engines

1. Disconnect the battery cables at the battery, negative cable first.
2. Remove the air cleaner. Drain the cooling system.
3. Remove the power steering pump (if so equipped) and position it out of the way. Leave the lines connected. Remove the windshield washer bottle and lay it aside.
4. If the car is equipped with A/C, remove the relay bracket at the bulkhead connector. Remove the bulkhead connector, then separate the wiring harness connections.
5. If equipped with cruise control, remove the servo bracket and position it out of the way.
6. Tag and disconnect all vacuum hoses and wires.
7. Unfasten the master cylinder attaching nuts at the vacuum booster, then lay it aside.
8. Detach the heater hose at the hot water pipe on the engine.
9. Remove the fan assembly. Remove the horn.
10. Disconnect the carburetor or TBI body linkage.
11. Raise the front of the car and support it with jackstands.
12. Properly relieve the fuel system pressure (see Section 1), then disconnect the fuel line and the heater hose at the intake manifold.
13. If equipped with A/C, remove the air conditioning brace.
14. Remove the exhaust pipe shield.

15. As outlined in Section 2 of this manual, remove the starter.

16. Disconnect the exhaust pipe at the manifold.

17. Remove the front tire and wheel assemblies.

18. Disconnect the stabilizer bar from the lower control arms. Remove the ball joints from the steering knuckle.

19. Remove the drive axles at the transaxle, then remove the transaxle strut.

20. If equipped with A/C, remove the inner fender shield. Remove the drive belt, tag and disconnect the wires, then remove the compressor. Do NOT disconnect any of the refrigerant lines.

21. Remove the rear engine mount, nuts and plate.

22. If equipped with an automatic transaxle, remove the oil filter.

23. Disconnect the speedometer cable.

24. Carefully lower the vehicle.

25. If equipped with an automatic transaxle, disconnect the oil cooler lines at the transaxle.

26. Remove the front engine mount nuts.

27. For vehicles equipped with a manual transaxle, disconnect the clutch cable at the transaxle. For automatic transaxle equipped vehicles, disconnect the detent cable at the transaxle.

28. Remove the transaxle mount.

29. Install a suitable engine lifting device, Lift the engine and transaxle assembly out of the car.

To install:

30. Install the engine mount alignment bolt (M6 x 1 x 65) to ensure proper powertrain alignment.

31. Lower the engine into the car, leaving the lifting device attached.

32. Install the transaxle bracket. Install the mount to the side frame and secure with NEW mount bolts.

33. With the weight not yet on the mounts, tighten the transaxle bolts. Tighten the right front mount nuts.

34. Lower the engine fully onto the mounts, remove the lifting device and then raise the front of the car.

35. Installation of the remaining components is in the reverse order of removal. Check the powertrain alignment bolt; if excessive force is required to remove the bolt, loosen the transaxle adjusting bolts and realign the powertrain. Adjust the drive belts and the clutch cable (if equipped with manual transaxle).

36. Connect the negative battery cable, then start the engine and check for proper operation, fluid levels, and/or leaks.

1984-86 1.8L (OHC) Engines

1. Disconnect the negative, then positive battery cables. Detach the engine ground wire.

2. Properly drain the cooling system into a suitable container.

3. Remove the air cleaner.

4. Disconnect the radiator hoses.

5. Label and detach the following wires:
   - Bulkhead (engine harness)
   - Brake master cylinder
   - A/C relay cluster switches (if equipped)
   - Windshield wiper motor
   - Cooling fan, relay and ground
   - ECM (pull the harness through the bulkhead
   - Temperature switch at the thermostat housing

6. Label and disconnect the fuel injection and MAP sensor and canister vacuum hoses.

7. Disconnect the throttle cable from the bracket and throttle body and the shift cable at the transaxle.

8. Detach the power steering hoses at the cut-off switch and the return hose at the pump.

9. Raise and safely support the vehicle.

10. Remove the speedometer cable and bracket.

11. Disconnect the exhaust pipe at the exhaust manifold and hangers, then position it aside.

12. Disconnect the hoses at the heater core, fuel lines and, if equipped with an automatic transaxle, the oil cooler lines.

13. Remove the front wheel and tire assemblies.

14. Remove the brake calipers. Be sure to support the calipers in the wheel opening with a piece of wire. Do NOT let the calipers hang by the brake line.

15. If equipped, disconnect the wires at the A/C compressor.

16. Using the proper equipment, evacuate the A/C system, then disconnect the lines from the compressor.

17. Remove the suspension supports. Remove the 2 center bolts on each side, then remove the bolt each end and loosen the remaining bolt.

✳✳CAUTION

Be sure to properly support the vehicles, engine and transaxle weight during the following steps.

18. For vehicles equipped with an automatic transaxle, remove the rear transaxle lateral strut.

19. Remove the transaxle strut (front).

20. Support the front of the car with jackstands under the radiator core support.

21. Reposition the jack to the rear of the cowl with a 4 in. x 4 in. x 6 ft. (102mm x 102mm x 1.8m) piece of wood spanning the vehicle's width.

22. Raise the car enough to remove the jackstands. Position a dolly under the engine and transaxle with three 4 in. x 4 in. x 12 in. (102mm x 102mm x 30cm) wood blocks as a support. Carefully, lower the weight of the car onto the dolly.

23. Remove the remaining bolt at each end of the right and left front suspension supports.

24. Unfasten the one long mount-to-bracket bolt, then remove the transaxle mount.

25. Remove the front engine mount. There should be 2 mount-to-bracket retaining bolts.

➡**The lower strut bolt opening is a slot, rather than a round hole. This is to allow for camber adjustment. Be sure to carefully scribe the position of the strut on the hub to preserve camber adjustments.**

26. Unfasten the knuckle-to-strut bolts. There are 2 per side.

27. Raise the car, leaving the engine, transaxle and suspension on the dolly. Separate the engine and transaxle.

To install:

28. With the aid of an assistant, assemble the engine and transaxle, then position in the chassis.

29. Install the transaxle mount, and secure by tightening the long mount-to-bracket bolt.

30. Install the rear engine mount, then secure using the 2 mount-to-bracket-bolts. Install the front engine mount the same way.

31. Loosely bolt each end of the right and left front suspension supports.

32. Making sure to align with the marks made during removal, install the knuckle-to-strut bolts. There are two on each side; tighten to 133 ft. lbs. (180 Nm).

33. Raise the car, then remove the dolly. Using jackstands, remove the 6 ft. (1.8m) piece of wood, then move the hoist to the front of the vehicle.

34. Install the remaining bolts in the right and left front suspension supports, then tighten to 65 ft. lbs. (88 Nm).

35. Install the front and rear transaxle struts.

36. If equipped, connect the wiring at the A/C compressor.

37. Remove the wire supporting the brake calipers, then install the calipers.

38. Install the front wheel and tire assemblies.

39. Connect the following hoses:
- Oil cooler lines (if equipped with an automatic transaxle)
- Fuel lines
- Heater core hoses.

40. Fasten the exhaust pipe to the manifold and hangers.

41. Connect the speedometer cable, then install the bracket.

42. Carefully lower the vehicle.

43. If equipped, connect the power steering return hose at the pump and the cut-off switch.

44. Connect the shift cable at the transaxle and the throttle cable to the bracket and throttle body assembly.

45. Attach the vacuum hoses to the MAP sensor and canister and the throttle body assembly.

46. Connect the following wires, as tagged during removal:
- Temperature switch at the thermostat housing
- ECM wiring (feed the harness through the bulkhead
- A/C relay cluster switches (if equipped)
- Windshield wiper motor
- Cooling fan, relay and ground
- Brake master cylinder
- Bulkhead (engine harness)

47. Connect the radiator hose(s).

48. Fill the cooling system with the proper type and quantity of suitable coolant.

49. If equipped, connect the A/C lines. Using the proper equipment, recharge the A/C system.

50. Connect the positive, then negative battery cables, then attach the engine ground wire.

1984-89 2.0L (OHV) Engines

1. Disconnect the negative, then the positive battery cables.

2. Properly drain the cooling system into a suitable container.

3. Remove the air cleaner assembly.

4. Disconnect the accelerator and T.V. cables at the throttle body.

5. Detach the ECM wiring harness at the throttle body.

6. Tag and disconnect all vacuum hoses, then remove the upper and lower radiator hoses and heater hoses at the engine.

7. Remove the exhaust heat shield.

8. For vehicles equipped with A/C, remove the adjustment bolt at the motor mount.

9. Disconnect the engine wiring harness at the bulkhead.

10. Remove the windshield washer bottle.

11. Remove the serpentine or alternator, power steering and A/C belts, as applicable.

12. If not done already, properly relieve the fuel system pressure. Disconnect the fuel lines.

13. Raise and safely support the vehicle.

14. If equipped with A/C, remove the A/C brace.

15. Remove the inner fender splash shield.

16. If equipped with A/C, remove the compressor, but do NOT disconnect the refrigerant lines.

17. Remove the flywheel splash shield.

18. Disconnect the starter wires.

19. Remove the front starter brace, then remove the starter as outlined in Section 2 of this manual.

20. Unfasten the torque converter bolts.

21. Remove the crankshaft pulley. Using tool J-24420 or equivalent, remove the crankshaft hub.

22. Remove the oil filter.

23. Unfasten and remove the engine-to-transaxle support bracket.

24. Remove the right rear motor mount.

25. Disconnect the exhaust pipe at the exhaust manifold, then disconnect the exhaust pipe at the center hanger and loosen the muffler hanger.

26. Remove the T.V. and shift cable bracket at the intake manifold.

27. Unfasten the 2 lower bellhousing bolts.

28. Carefully lower the vehicle.

29. Unfasten then remove the right front motor mount nuts.

30. Remove the alternator and adjusting brace.

31. Remove the brake master cylinder from the booster, then set aside, making sure it is suitably supported.

32. Install a suitable engine lifting device.

33. Remove the right front motor mount bracket.

34. Unfasten the remaining upper bellhousing bolts.

35. While lifting the engine, remove the power steering pump. Carefully lift the engine from the vehicle.

To install:

36. Position, then partially lower the engine assembly into the vehicle. Install the power steering pump, while lowering the engine.

37. Fasten the upper bellhousing bolts.

38. Install the right front motor mount bracket.

39. Remove the engine lifting device.

40. Fasten the master cylinder to the power brake booster.

41. Install the alternator and adjusting brace.

42. Install the right front motor mount nuts.

43. Raise and safely support the vehicle.

44. Install the remaining lower bellhousing bolts.

45. Install the T.V. and shift cable bracket.

46. Fasten the exhaust pipe at the center hanger, then tighten the muffler hanger. Connect the exhaust pipe at the exhaust manifold.

47. Install the right rear motor mount. If the rear engine mount bracket is removed, it will be necesary to perform the

following steps to ensure proper engine mount bracket locations.

    a. Loosely install the engine mount bracket.

    b. Raise the engine and transaxle.

    c. Tighten the engine mount nuts and bolts.

48. Install the engine-to-support bracket.

49. Install the oil filter.

50. Using the correct tool, install the crankshaft hub and pulley.

51. Install the torque converter retaining bolts.

52. Install the front starter brace, then the starter.

53. Connect the starter wires.

54. Install the flywheel splash shield.

55. If equipped with A/C, install the compressor.

56. Install the inner fender splash shield.

57. If equipped with A/C, install the A/C brace.

58. Carefully lower the vehicle.

59. Connect the fuel lines.

60. Install the serpentine, alternator, power steering and/or A/C belts, as applicable.

61. Install the windshield washer bottle.

62. Connect the engine wiring harness at the bulkhead.

63. For vehicles equipped with A/C, install the adjustment bolt at the motor mount.

64. Install the exhaust heat shield.

65. Connect the vacuum hoses and the upper and lower radiator hoses and heater hoses at the engine.

66. Attach the ECM harness at the engine.

67. Connect the accelerator and T.V. cables at the throttle body.

68. Install the air cleaner assembly.

69. Fill the engine cooling system with the correct amount and type of coolant.

70. Connect the postive, followed by the negative battery cables.

71. Start the engine, then inspect for proper brake system operation, proper fluid levels and/or leakage.

2.0L (OHC) Engines

➡**This procedure requires the use of a special tool.**

1. Remove battery cables.

2. Drain cooling system.

3. Remove air cleaner.

4. Disconnect engine electrical harness at bulkhead.

5. Disconnect electrical connector at brake cylinder.

6. Remove throttle cable from bracket and E.F.I. assembly.

7. Remove vacuum hoses from E.F.I. assembly.

8. Remove power steering high pressure hose at cut-off switch.

9. Remove vacuum hoses at the MAP sensor and canister.

10. Disconnect air conditioning relay cluster switches.

11. Remove power steering return hose at pump.

12. Disconnect ECM wire connections and feed harness through bulkhead and lay harness over engine.

13. Remove upper and lower radiator hoses from engine.

14. Remove electrical connections from temperature switch at thermostat housing.

15. Disconnect transmission shift cable at transmission.

16. Hoist car.

17. Remove speedometer cable at transmission and bracket.

18. Disconnect exhaust pipe at exhaust manifold.

19. Remove exhaust pipe from converter.

20. Remove heater hoses from heater core.

21. Remove fuel lines at flex hoses.

22. Remove transmission cooler lines at flex hoses.

23. Remove left and right front wheels.

24. Remove right hand spoiler section and splash shield.

25. Remove right and left brake calipers and support with wire.

26. Remove right and left tie rod ends.

27. Disconnect electrical connections at air conditioning compressor.

28. Remove air conditioning compressor and mounting brackets, support air conditioning compressor with wire in wheel opening.

29. Remove front suspension support attachment bolts (6 bolts each side).

30. Lower car.

31. Support front of vehicle by placing two short jackstands under core support.

32. Position front post hoist to the rear of cowl.

33. Position a 4 in. (102mm) x 4 in. (102mm) x 6 ft. (2m) timber on front post hoist.

34. Raise vehicle enough to remove jackstands.

35. Position a 4-wheel dolly under engine and transaxle assembly.

36. Position three (3) 4 in. (102mm) x 4 in. (102mm) x 12 in. (305mm) blocks under engine and transaxle assembly only, letting support rails hang free.

37. Lower vehicle onto 4-wheel dolly slightly.

38. Remove rear transaxle mount attachment bolts (2).

39. Remove left front engine mount attachment bolts (3).

40. Remove two (2) engine support to body attachment bolts behind right-hand inner axle U-joint.

41. Remove one (1) attaching bolt and nut from right-hand chassis side rail to engine mount bracket.

42. Remove six (6) strut attachment nuts.

43. Raise vehicle letting engine, transaxle and suspension resting on 4-wheel dolly.

Reverse the removal procedure for engine installation with the following exceptions:

44. With one man's assistance, position engine and transaxle assembly in chassis.

45. Install transaxle and left front mounts to side rail bolts loosely.

46. Install a M6 x 1 x 65 alignment bolt in left front mount to prevent powertrain misalignment.

47. Tighten the transaxle mount bolts to 42 ft. lbs. and left front mount bolts to 18 ft. lbs.

48. Install right rear mount to body bolts and tighten to 38 ft. lbs. (52 Nm).

49. Install right rear mount to chassis side rail bolt and nut, then tighten to 38 ft. lbs. (52 Nm).

50. Place a floor jack under control arms, jack struts into position and install retaining nuts.

51. Raise vehicle.

52. Using a transmission jack or suitable lifting equipment, raise control arms and attach tie rod ends.

2.2L Engines

1990-93 VEHICLES

➡ **The following procedure is for the engine and transaxle assembly.**

1. Disconnect the battery.
2. Drain the cooling system.
3. Relieve the fuel system pressure.
4. Disconnect the hood lamp wiring, if so equipped and remove the hood.
5. Disconnect the throttle body intake duct.
6. Remove the rear sight shields.
7. Disconnect the upper radiator hose.
8. Disconnect the brake booster vacuum hose.
9. Disconnect the alternator top brace and wiring.
10. Disconnect and tag the upper engine harness from the engine.
11. Discharge the A/C system as outlined in Section 1.
12. Disconnect the A/C compressor to condenser and accumulator lines.
13. Raise and support the vehicle safely.
14. Remove the left splash shield.
15. Disconnect the exhaust system.
16. Disconnect and tag the lower engine wiring.
17. Remove the flywheel inspection cover.
18. Remove the front wheels.
19. Disconnect the lower radiator hose.
20. Disconnect the heater hoses from the heater core.
21. Remove the brake calipers from the steering knuckle and wire up out of the way as outlined in Section 9.
22. Disconnect the tie rods from the struts.
23. Lower the vehicle.
24. Remove the clutch slave cylinder.
25. With the fuel system pressure released, place an absorbent shop towel around the connections and disconnect the fuel lines.
26. Disconnect the transaxle linkage at the transaxle.
27. Disconnect the accelerator cables from the TBI unit.
28. Disconnect the cruise control cables from the TBI unit.
29. Disconnect the throttle valve cables from the TBI, on vehicles equipped with an automatic transaxle.
30. Disconnect the automatic transaxle cooling lines.
31. Disconnect the power steering hoses from the power steering pump.
32. Remove the center suspension support bolts.
33. Align Engine/Transaxle Frame Handler tool No. J 36295 or equivalent under the suspension supports, engine and transaxle; lower vehicle to dolly and add support under the engine.
34. Safely support the rear of the vehicle.
35. Disconnect the upper transaxle mount.
36. Remove the upper strut bolts and nuts.
37. Disconnect the front engine mount.
38. Disconnect the rear engine mount.
39. Remove the 4 rear suspension support bolts.
40. Remove the 4 front suspension support bolts and wire the bolt holes together to prevent axle separation.
41. Raise the vehicle and remove the engine and transaxle assembly on tool No. J 36295 or equivalent.

To install:

42. Lower the vehicle and install the engine and transaxle assembly using tool No. J 36295 or equivalent.

43. Install the suspension supports bolts and tighten to 65 ft. lbs. for the front and rear suspension supports and 66 ft. lbs. for the center suspension support.
44. Install the transaxle mount but do not tighten.
45. Install the rear engine mount but do not tighten.
46. Install the front engine mount but do not tighten.
47. Tighten the manual transaxle mounting bolts as follows:
    • Front transaxle strut to body bolts to 40 ft. lbs.
    • Rear transaxle mount to body bolts to 23 ft. lbs.
48. Tighten the automatic transaxle mount bolts to 22 ft. lbs.
49. Tighten the front and rear engine mount bolts, please refer to the engine mount illustration.

➡ **All engine mount bolts that have been removed must be cleaned and a new thread locking compound applied to the threads before reinstallation.**

50. Install the power steering hoses.
51. Connect the accelerator, cruise control and T.V. cables to the TBI.
52. Connect the transaxle cooling lines to the automatic transaxle.
53. Connect the transaxle linkage.
54. Reconnect the fuel lines.
55. Reconnect the clutch slave cylinder.
56. Raise and support the vehicle safely.
57. Install the tie rods.
58. Install the calipers to the steering knuckle.
59. Install the heater hoses to the heater core.
60. Install the lower radiator hose.
61. Install the A/C compressor.
62. Install the flywheel inspection cover.
63. Install the engine splash shield.
64. Install the front wheel and tighten the wheel stud nuts to 100 ft. lbs. (136 Nm).
65. Lower the vehicle.
66. Install the upper engine wiring.
67. Install the compressor to condenser and accumulator lines.
68. Install the brake booster vacuum hose.
69. Install the upper radiator hose.
70. Raise and support the vehicle safely.
71. Install the lower engine wiring.
72. Reconnect the exhaust system.
73. Lower the vehicle.
74. Connect the TBI wiring.
75. Install the air cleaner assembly.
76. Recharge the A/C system.
77. Check and adjust the wheel alignment.
78. Install the hood and connect the battery.

1994-96 VEHICLES

1. Properly relieve the fuel system pressure, then disconnect the negative battery cable.
2. Drain the cooling system into a suitable container.
3. Remove the air cleaner outlet duct.
4. Detach the upper radiator hose at the coolant outlet.
5. Disconnect the brake booster vacuum hose.
6. Tag and detach the following electrical connections:
    • Idle Air Control (IAC)
    • Alternator
    • Throttle Position (TP) sensor
    • Manifold Absolute Pressure (MAP) sensor

- EVAP emission solenoid
- Fuel injector harness
- Exhaust Gas Recirculation (EGR) valve
- Engine Coolant Temperature (ECT) sensor
- Transaxle Converter Clutch (TCC)
- Oxygen (O^2) sensor
- Park/Neutral position switch
- Engine grounds

7. Remove the serpentine drive belt.

8. Disconnect the transaxle shift control cable from the range select lever and bracket.

9. Detach the coolant surge tank hose, then remove the tank.

10. Disconnect the vacuum line near the master cylinder.

11. Install J 28467-A or equivalent engine support fixture.

12. Disconnect the lower radiator hose from the water pump.

13. Raise and safely support the vehicle.

14. Remove both front wheel and tire assemblies, then remove both splash shields.

15. Disconnect the exhaust pipe at the manifold and catalytic converter.

16. Remove the engine mount strut.

17. Disconnect the wheel speed sensor wire harness from the control arms.

18. Separate the ball joints from the steering knuckles. Using tool J 24319-01 or equivalent, separate the tie rod ends from the struts.

19. Detach the brake lines from the suspension supports.

20. If equipped, remove the A/C compressor and support with the lines attached.

21. Tag and detach the following electrical connectors:
- Electronic Ignition Module
- Vehicle Speed Sensors (VSS)
- Cooling Fan
- Starter
- A/C compressor
- Oil pressure and level sensors
- Engine grounds

22. Disconnect the power steering lines from the rack and pinion assembly. Detach the flexible coupling joint at the rack and pinion assembly.

23. Disconnect the accelerator control, cruise control (if equipped) and the T.V. cables from the accelerator control bracket.

24. Remove the suspension support assembly.

25. Disconnect the heater hoses at the front of the dash.

26. Remove both drive axles from the transaxle, then position them aside.

27. Disconnect the fuel lines.

28. Detach the cooler lines from the transaxle, then remove the transaxle mount.

29. Remove the engine mount assembly.

30. Place a suitable support under the vehicle. Carefully lower the vehicle so that it rests lightly on the support.

31. Remove the support fixture from the engine, then raise the vehicle, leaving the engine and transaxle assembly on the table.

32. Unfasten the retaining bolts, then separate the engine from the transaxle.

To install:

33. Position the engine to the transaxle, then install the retaining bolts. Tighten the bolts to 55 ft. lbs. (75 Nm).

34. Lower the vehicle onto the engine and transaxle assembly.

35. Install J 28467-A or equivalent engine support fixture onto the engine.

36. Install the engine mount assembly, then install the transaxle mount.

37. Attach the cooler lines to the transaxle.

38. Connect the fuel lines.

39. Install both drive axles into the transaxle.

40. Connect the heater hoses to the front of the cowl.

41. Install the suspension support assembly.

42. Connect the accelerator, cruise control, and T.V. cables to the accelerator control bracket.

43. Attach the flexible coupling joint to the rack and pinion assembly.

44. Connect the power steering lines to the rack and pinion assembly.

45. Attach the following electrical connectors as tagged during removal:
- Electronic Ignition Module
- Vehicle Speed Sensors (VSS)
- Cooling Fan
- Starter
- A/C compressor
- Oil pressure and level sensors
- Engine grounds

46. Install the A/C compressor, if equipped.

47. Connect the brake lines to the suspension support.

48. Fasten the tie rod ends to the struts, then connect the ball joints to the steering knuckles.

49. Connect the wheel speed sensor wire harness to the control arms.

50. Install the engine mount strut.

51. Fasten the exhaust pipe to the exhaust manifold and catalytic converter.

52. Install the splash shields and the wheel and tire assemblies.

53. Carefully lower the vehicle.

54. Connect the lower radiator hose to the water pump.

55. Remove the engine support fixture.

56. Attach the vacuum line, located near the master cylinder.

57. Install the coolant surge tank, then connect the tank's hose.

58. Connect the transaxle shift control cable.

59. Install the serpentine drive belt.

60. Attach the following electrical connectors, as tagged during removal:
- Idle Air Control (IAC)
- Alternator
- Throttle Position (TP) sensor
- Manifold Absolute Pressure (MAP) sensor
- EVAP emission solenoid
- Fuel injector harness
- Exhaust Gas Recirculation (EGR) valve
- Engine Coolant Temperature (ECT) sensor
- Transaxle Converter Clutch (TCC)
- Oxygen (O^2) sensor
- Park/Neutral position switch
- Engine grounds

61. Connect the brake booster vacuum hose.

62. Attach the upper radiator hose and the air cleaner outlet duct.

63. Fill the cooling system and crankcase with the correct type and amount of fluids.

64. Connect the negative battery cable, then start the engine. Check for proper operation, fluid levels and/or leaks.

2.3L and 2.4L Engines

1. If equipped with A/C, have a repair shop recover the refrigerant using the proper equipment.

2. Disconnect the negative battery.

3. Properly drain the cooling system into an approved container.

4. Relieve the fuel system pressure.

5. Remove the left sound insulator, then disconnect the clutch pushrod form the pedal assembly.

6. Disconnect the heater hose at the thermostat assembly, then detach the radiator inlet (upper) hose.

7. Remove the air cleaner assembly and the coolant fan.

8. If equipped with A/C, disconnect the compressor/condenser hose assembly at the compressor, then discard the O-rings.

9. Disconnect the two vacuum hoses from the front of the engine.

10. Tag and detach the following electrical connectors:
- Alternator
- A/C compressor (if equipped)
- Fuel injector harness
- Idle Air Control (IAC) and TP sensor at the throttle body
- Manifold Absolute Pressure (MAP) sensor
- Intake Air Temperature (IAT) sensor
- EVAP canister purge solenoid
- Starter solenoid
- Ground connections
- Negative battery cable from the transaxle
- Electronic ignition coil and module assembly
- Engine Coolant Temperature (ECT) sensor(s)
- Oil pressure sensor/switch
- Oxygen (O^2) sensor
- Crankshaft Position (CKP) sensor
- Back-up lamp switch, then position the harness aside

11. Disconnect the power brake vacuum hose from the throttle body. Detach the power brake vacuum tube-to-check valve hose from the tube.

12. Remove the throttle cable and bracket.

13. Unfasten the power steering pump rear bracket, then remove the bracket and vacuum tube as an assembly.

14. Unfasten the power steering pivot bolt, then remove the pump and drive belt. Position the pump aside, with the lines still attached.

✳✳CAUTION

After relieving the fuel system pressure, a small amount of fuel may be released when servicing the fuel lines or connections. To prevent personal injury, cover the fuel line fittings with a shop towel before disconnecting to catch any fuel that may leak out. Place the towel in an approved container when the disconnection is completed.

15. Carefully disconnect the fuel lines.

16. Disconnect the shift cables. Detach the clutch actuator line.

17. Remove the exhaust manifold and heat shield.

18. Disconnect the radiator outlet (lower) hose from the radiator.

19. Install J 28467-A or equivalent engine support fixture.

20. Unfasten the bolt attaching the coolant recovery/surge tank, then position the tank aside with the hoses still connected.

21. Remove the engine mount assembly.

22. Raise and safely support the vehicle, then remove the front wheel and tire assemblies. Remove the right splash shield.

23. Remove the radiator air deflector.

24. Tag and detach the following electrical connections:
- Vehicle Speed Sensor (VSS)
- Knock sensor
- Starter solenoid
- If equipped, both front ABS wheel speed sensors

25. Remove the engine mount strut and the transaxle mount.

26. Separate the ball joints from the steering knuckles.

27. Remove the suspension supports, crossmember, and stabilizer shaft as an assembly.

28. Disconnect the heater outlet hose from the radiator outlet pipe.

29. Remove the axle shaft from the transaxle and intermediate shaft, then position aside.

30. If equipped, disconnect the A/C lines from the oil pan.

31. Remove the flywheel housing cover.

32. Position a suitable support below the engine, then carefully lower the car onto the support.

33. Matchmark the threads on the support fixture hooks so that the setting can be duplicated when reinstalling the engine. Remove the engine support fixture J-hooks.

34. Raise the vehicle slowly off the engine and transaxle assembly. If may be necessary to move the engine/transaxle assembly rearward to clear the intake manifold.

35. Noting the position of the bolts, separate the engine from the transaxle.

To install:

✳✳WARNING

Be sure the retaining bolts are in their correct locations. If not, engine damage may occur.

36. Assemble the engine to the transaxle.

37. Position the engine and transaxle assembly under the engine compartment, then slowly lower the vehicle over the assembly until the transaxle mount is indexed, then install the retaining bolt.

38. Install engine support fixture J 28467-A or equivalent, making sure to adjust it to the previous setting.

39. Install the engine mount assembly and transaxle mount.

40. Carefully raise the vehicle off the support.

41. Attach the axle shafts to the transaxle.

42. Connect the heater outlet hose to the radiator outlet pipe.

43. Install the suspension supports, crossmember and stabilizer shaft assembly.

44. Attach the ball joints to the steering knuckles, then secure with the nuts.

45. Install the engine strut mount.

46. If equipped, connect the A/C line to the oil pan.

47. Attach the following electrical connectors, as tagged during removal:
   - Vehicle Speed Sensor (VSS)
   - Knock sensor
   - Starter solenoid
   - If equipped, both front ABS wheel speed sensors
48. Install the flywheel housing cover.
49. Fasten the radiator air deflector.
50. Connect the lower radiator hose.
51. Install the right splash shield, then the front wheel and tire assemblies.
52. Carefully lower the vehicle, then remove the engine support fixture.
53. Install the coolant recovery/surge tank, then secure using the retaining bolt.
54. Attach the following electrical connections, as tagged during removal:
   - Alternator
   - A/C compressor (if equipped)
   - Fuel injector harness
   - Idle Air Control (IAC) and TP sensor at the throttle body
   - Manifold Absolute Pressure (MAP) sensor
   - Intake Air Temperature (IAT) sensor
   - EVAP canister purge solenoid
   - Starter solenoid
   - Ground connections
   - Negative battery cable to the transaxle
   - Electronic ignition coil and module assembly
   - Engine Coolant Temperature (ECT) sensor(s)
   - Oil pressure sensor/switch
   - Oxygen (O^2) sensor
   - Crankshaft Position (CKP) sensor
   - Back-up lamp switch
55. Attach the vacuum hoses.
56. If equipped with A/C, attach the compressor/condenser hose assembly to the compressor.
57. Fasten the clutch actuator line.
58. Install the exhaust manifold and heat shield.
59. Connect the fuel lines.
60. Connect the positive battery cable.
61. Fasten the power steering pump pivot-to-block bolt. Install the power steering pump rear bracket and tension belt.
62. Connect the vacuum hoses to the intake manifold and to the tube from the brake booster.
63. Install the throttle cable and bracket.
64. Install the coolant fan and air cleaner assembly.
65. Attach the radiator outlet (upper) hose. Fill the cooling system with the proper type and quantity of coolant.
66. Connect the clutch pushrod to the pedal assembly, then install the left sound insulator.
67. Attach the heater hose at the thermostat housing.
68. Fill the transaxle with fluid, then fill the crankcase with oil.
69. Connect the negative battery cable.
70. If equipped with A/C, evacuate, charge and leak test the system.
71. Start the engine and check the fluid levels, proper operation of the engine and/or fluid leakage.

2.8L and 3.1L Engines

1985-88 VEHICLES

1. Disconnect the negative battery cable. Drain the cooling system and remove the air cleaner assembly.
2. Remove the air flow sensor. Remove the exhaust crossover heat shield and remove the crossover pipe.
3. Remove the serpentine belt tensioner and belt.
4. Remove the power steering pump mounting bracket. Disconnect the heater pipe at the power steering pump mounting bracket.
5. Disconnect the radiator hoses from the engine.
6. Disconnect the accelerator and throttle valve cable at the throttle valve.
7. Remove the alternator. Tag and disconnect the wiring harness at the engine.
8. Relieve the fuel pressure (see Section 1) and disconnect the fuel hose. Disconnect the coolant bypass and the overflow hoses at the engine.
9. Tag and remove the vacuum hoses to the engine.
10. Raise the vehicle and support it safely.
11. Remove the inner fender splash shield. Remove the harmonic balancer.
12. Remove the flywheel cover. Remove the starter bolts. Tag and disconnect the electrical connections to the starter. Remove the starter.
13. Disconnect the wires at the oil sending unit.
14. Remove the air conditioning compressor and related brackets.
15. Disconnect the exhaust pipe at the rear of the exhaust manifold.
16. Remove the flex plate-to-torque converter bolts.
17. Remove the transaxle-to-engine bolts. Remove the engine-to-rear mount frame nuts.
18. Disconnect the shift cable bracket at the transaxle. Remove the lower bell housing bolts.
19. Lower the vehicle and disconnect the heater hoses at the engine.
20. Install a suitable engine lifting device. While supporting the engine and transaxle, remove the upper bell housing bolts.
21. Remove the front mounting bolts.
22. Remove the master cylinder from the booster.
23. Remove the engine assembly from the vehicle.

To install:
24. Install the engine and remove the engine lifting device.
25. Install the master cylinder to the booster.
26. Install the front mounting bolts.
27. Install the upper bell housing bolts.
28. Connect the heater hoses at the engine.
29. Connect the shift cable bracket at the transaxle. Install the lower bell housing bolts.
30. Install the transaxle-to-engine bolts. Install the engine-to-rear mount frame nuts.
31. Install the flex plate-to-torque converter bolts.
32. Connect the exhaust pipe at the rear of the exhaust manifold.
33. Install the air conditioning compressor and related brackets.
34. Connect the wires at the oil sending unit.
35. Install the flywheel cover. Install the starter bolts. Connect the electrical connections to the starter. Install the starter.

36. Install the inner fender splash shield. Install the harmonic balancer.

37. Lower the vehicle.

38. Install the vacuum hoses to the engine.

39. Connect the fuel hose. Connect the coolant bypass and the overflow hoses at the engine.

40. Install the alternator. Connect the wiring harness at the engine.

41. Connect the accelerator and throttle valve cable at the throttle valve.

42. Connect the radiator hoses to the engine.

43. Install the power steering pump mounting bracket. Connect the heater pipe at the power steering pump mounting bracket.

44. Install the serpentine belt tensioner and belt.

45. Install the air flow sensor. Install the exhaust crossover heat shield and crossover pipe.

46. Connect the negative battery cable. Fill the cooling system and install the air cleaner assembly.

1989-93 VEHICLES

1. Disconnect the negative battery cable. Properly drain the cooling system into a suitable container.

2. Remove the air cleaner and duct assembly.

3. Disconnect the exhaust manifold/crossover assembly.

4. Remove the serpentine belt tensioner and idler, if equipped.

5. Detach the radiator hoses from the engine.

6. Disconnect the cables from the bracket at the plenum.

7. Remove the alternator. Tag and disconnect the wiring harness at the engine.

8. Relieve the fuel pressure (see Section 1) and disconnect the fuel hose.

9. Disconnect the coolant bypass and the overflow hoses at the engine.

10. Support the engine using J 28467-A or equivalent engine support fixture.

11. Raise and safely support the vehicle.

12. Remove the inner fender splash shield.

13. Remove the flywheel cover.

14. Unfasten the starter bolts. Tag and detach the electrical connections to the starter, then remove the starter.

15. Remove the air conditioning compressor and related brackets.

16. Disconnect the exhaust pipe at the rear of the exhaust manifold.

17. Remove the flywheel-to-torque converter bolts.

18. Disconnect the engine mounts.

19. If equipped with a manual transaxle, disconnect the intermediate shaft bracket to the engine.

20. Disconnect the shift cable bracket at the transaxle. Remove the lower bell housing bolts.

21. Carefully lower the vehicle, then disconnect the heater hoses at the engine.

22. Install a suitable engine lifting device. While supporting the engine and transaxle, remove the J 28467-A engine support fixture.

23. Support the transaxle, then remove the transaxle bolts.

24. Remove the engine assembly from the vehicle.

To install:

25. Install J 28467-A engine support fixture, or equivalent.

26. Remove the engine lifting device.

27. Support the transaxle, then install the transaxle bolts.

28. Connect the heater hoses at the engine.

29. Raise and safely support the vehicle.

30. Fasten the lower bell housing bolts.

31. Install the shift cable bracket at the transaxle.

32. If equipped with a manual transaxle, connect the intermediate shaft bracket to the engine.

33. Reconnect the engine mounts, then tighten as follows:
- Front engine mount-to-bracket bolt to 50 ft. lbs. (68 Nm).
- Front engine mount-to-frame bolt (top) to 54 ft. lbs. (73 Nm).
- Front engine mount-to-frame bolt (bottom) to 61 ft. lbs. (83 Nm).
- Engine mount bracket-to-body lower bolt to 47 ft. lbs. (64 Nm).
- Engine mount bracket-to-body upper bolt to 74 ft. lbs. (100 Nm).
- Rear engine mount-to-engine bolt to 40 ft. lbs. (54 Nm).
- Rear engine bracket-to-body bolt to 45 ft. lbs. (61 Nm).

➡**All engine mount bolts that have been removed must be cleaned and a new thread locking compound applied to the threads before reinstallation.**

34. Install the flywheel-to-torque converter bolts.

35. Connect the exhaust pipe at the rear of the exhaust manifold.

36. Install the air conditioning compressor.

37. Install the starter.

38. Fasten the flywheel cover.

39. Install the inner fender splash shield.

40. Carefully lower the vehicle, then remove J 28467-A engine support fixture, or equivalent.

41. Connect the coolant bypass and the overflow hoses at the engine.

42. Reconnect the fuel lines.

43. Attach the wiring harness at the engine.

44. Install the alternator.

45. Connect the cables from the bracket at the plenum.

46. Fasten the radiator hoses.

47. Install the serpentine belt tensioner and idler, if equipped.

48. Refill the cooling system to the correct level with the proper type of coolant.

49. Install the air cleaner and duct assembly.

50. Connect the battery cable(s), then start the engine and check for proper operation and/or leaks.

1994 VEHICLES

➡**On these 3.1L engines, an "Idle Learn" procedure must be performed which requires the use of a scan tool.**

1. Properly relieve the fuel system pressure.

2. Disconnect the negative, then positive battery cables, then remove the battery from the vehicle.

3. Remove the air cleaner assembly.

4. Properly drain the cooling system into an approved container.

5. For vehicles equipped with a manual transaxle, remove the left side sound insulator, then disconnect the push rod from the clutch pedal.

6. Disconnect the exhaust crossover pipe from the exhaust manifolds.

7. Remove the serpentine drive belt.

8. Disconnect the coolant bleed hose from the pipe. Disconnect the radiator hoses from the themostat housing and water pump. Remove the cooling fan assembly.

9. Disconnect the throttle, cruise control and T.V. cables from the throttle body.

10. Detach the power steering line from the bracket behind the alternator.

11. Remove the rear alternator brace, then the alternator.

12. Tag and detach the following electrical connections at the engine:
- Oxygen (O^2) sensor
- Engine Coolant Temperature (ECT) sensor
- EGR valve
- Manifold Absolute Pressure (MAP) sensor
- Idle Air Control (IAC) valve
- Throttle Position (TP) sensor
- Transaxle Converter Clutch (TCC)
- Park/Neutral Position switch (vehicles with an automatic transaxle only)
- Back-up Light switch (vehicles with a manual transaxle only)
- Ground connections

13. Disconnect the fuel lines.

14. Detach the coolant bypass hose at the engine.

15. Tag and disconnect all vacuum hoses from the engine.

16. Detach the power steering pressure and return lines.

17. Unfasten the clutch actuator cylinder quick disconnect fitting.

18. Disconnect the shift cables from the transaxle.

19. Unfasten the nuts from the top of the strut towers to allow tool J 28467-A, or equivalent, to be installed. Support the vehicles using tool J 28467-A or equivalent.

20. Remove the transaxle mount and bracket as an assembly.

21. Loosen the A/C accumulator bracket, then raise the accumulator a few inches to gain access to the upper front engine mount bolts. Remove the upper fasteners from the front engine mount.

22. Raise and safely support the vehicle.

23. Remove the front tire and wheel assemblies.

24. Remove the front air deflector and the right front splash shield.

25. If equipped, detach the front ABS wheel speed sensor connectors and harnesses from the suspension support.

26. Remove both front ball joints. For details, please refer to the procedure located in Section 8 of this manual.

27. Detach the engine mount strut from the transaxle bracket. Remove the front suspension support.

28. Remove the oil pressure switch from the engine.

➡ **Make sure to use rags or shop towels between the A/C compressor and the radiator to prevent damage to the radiator cooling fins.**

29. If equipped, remove the A/C compressor, leaving the lines attached, Support the compressor on the lower radiator tie-bar.

30. Disconnect the exhaust pipe at the rear of the manifold..

31. Detach the drive axles from the transaxles. Remove the strut mount bracket.

32. Tag and detach the following lower electrical connectors:
- Electronic Ignition system module
- Knock sensor
- Vehicle Speed Sensor (VSS)
- Connections at the starter
- Secondary ignition wires from the coils

33. As outlined in Section 2 of this manual, remove the starter.

34. Remove the flywheel housing or transaxle converter cover.

35. For vehicles equipped with a manual transaxle, remove the intermediate shaft bracket from the engine.

36. For vehicles equipped with an automatic transaxle, remove the shift cable bracket at the transaxle (press fit).

37. Disconnect the automatic transaxle cooler lines from the transaxle, if applicable.

38. Unfasten the lower engine mount bolts, then remove the rear engine mount.

39. Disconnect the heater hoses from the front of the dash.

40. Carefully lower the vehicle enough to place an engine/transaxle table under the vehicle.

41. Remove the engine and transaxle assembly from the vehicle.

42. Detach the transaxle selector cable bracket.

43. Unfasten the bolt, the remove the automatic transaxle fluid level indicator and fill tube assembly.

44. Remove the rear engine mount assembly from the engine, then remove the transaxle-to-engine bracket.

45. Unfasten the flywheel-to-torque converter bolts, then separate the engine from the transaxle.

To install:

46. Fasten the engine to the transaxle.

47. Install the flywheel-to-torque converter bolts.

48. Install the transaxle-to-engine bracket, then attach the rear engine mount assembly to the engine.

49. Position the automatic transaxle fluid level indicator and fill tube assembly and secure with the retaining bolt.

50. Install the transaxle selector cable bracket.

51. Carefully lower the vehicle enough to place an engine/transaxle table under the vehicle.

52. Position the engine and transaxle assembly into the vehicle.

53. Install the rear engine mount, then install the lower engine mount bolts.

54. Connect the heater hoses to the front of the dash.

55. Attach the automatic transaxle cooler lines to the transaxle, if applicable.

56. Install the shift cable bracket (press fit) to the automatic transaxle.

57. If equipped with a manual transaxle, fasten the intermediate shaft bracket to the engine.

58. Install the electronic ignition system coil and module assembly.

59. Fasten the flywheel housing or transaxle converter cover.

60. Install the starter, as outlined in Section 2 of this manual.

61. Attach the following electrical connectors, as tagged during removal:
- Electronic Ignition system module
- Knock sensor
- Vehicle Speed Sensor (VSS)
- Electrical connections at the starter
- Secondary ignition (spark plug) wires to the coils

62. Install the strut mount bracket.
63. Fasten the drive axles to the transaxle.
64. Attach the exhaust pipe to the rear of the manifold.
65. Remove the shop towels or rag from the lower radiator tie-bar, then install the A/C compressor.
66. Install the oil pressure switch.
67. Install the front suspension support, then install the engine mount strut-to-transaxle bracket.
68. As outlined in Section 8 of this manual, install both front ball joints.
69. If equipped, attach the front ABS wheel speed sensor connectors and harnesses to the suspension support.
70. Install the right front splash shield and the front air deflector.
71. Install both front tire and wheel assemblies, then carefully lower the vehicle.
72. Attach the upper fasteners to the front engine mount.
73. After carefully pushing the A/C accumulator back into place, tighten the accumulator bracket.
74. Install the transaxle mount and bracket as an assembly.
75. Remove tool J 28467-A or equivalent engine support fixture, then install the retaining nuts to the top of the strut towers.
76. Connect the transaxle shift cables.
77. For vehicles equipped with a manual transaxle, install the clutch actuator cylinder.
78. Connect the power steering pressure and return lines.
79. Attach all vacuum hoses, as tagged during removal.
80. Fasten the coolant bypass hose.
81. Connect the fuel lines.
82. Attach the following electrical connections, as tagged during removal:
- Ground connections
- Back-up Light switch (vehicles with a manual transaxle only)
- Park/Neutral Position switch (vehicles with an automatic transaxle only)
- Transaxle Converter Clutch (TCC)
- Throttle Position (TP) sensor
- Idle Air Control (IAC) valve
- Manifold Absolute Pressure (MAP) sensor
- EGR valve
- Engine Coolant Temperature (ECT) sensor
- Oxygen (O^2) sensor

83. Install the alternator, as outlined in Section 2 of this manual. Install the rear alternator brace.
84. Attach the power steering line.
85. Connect the throttle, cruise control (if equipped) and the T.V. cables to the throttle body.
86. Install the coolant fan assembly.
87. Attach the radiator hoses and the coolant bleed hose.
88. Install the serpentine belt.

89. Fasten the exhaust crossover pipe to the exhaust manifolds.
90. If equipped with a manual transaxle, fasten the push rod and left side sound insulator to the clutch pedal.
91. Install the air cleaner assembly, then install the battery. Connect the positive, then negative battery cables.
92. Fill the coolant, oil, transaxle and power steering fluids to the proper levels.

➡On the 3.1L engine, a Tech 1® scan tool is needed to perform the "Idle Learn" procedure.

93. For the 3.1L engine perform the following "Idle Learn" procedure;
   a. Install a Tech 1® scan tool.
   b. Turn the ignition to the **ON** position, engine not running.
   c. Select **IAC SYSTEM**, then **IDLE LEARN** in the **MISC TEST** mode.
   d. Place the transaxle in park or neutral, as applicable.
   e. Proceed with idle learn as directed by the scan tool.
94. Bleed the power steering system.
95. Start the engine, then check for proper fluid levels and/or leaks.

Rocker Arm (Valve) Cover

REMOVAL & INSTALLATION

1.8L, 2.0L and 2.2L OHV Engines

1982-86 VEHICLES

▶ See Figure 6

1. Disconnect the negative battery cable.
2. Remove the air cleaner.
3. For the 2.0L engine, disconnect the canister purge line and the PCV valve.
4. For the 2.0L engine, tag and disconnect plug wires at the spark plugs, then pull the wires away from the rocker arm cover.
5. For the 1.8L engine, remove the distributor cap with the spark plug wires. Remove the spark plug wire clip from the rocker arm cover and lay the wires and cap aside.
6. For the 1.8L engine, tag and disconnect the vacuum hoses and pipes at the alternator bracket, at the front of the valve cover, at the deceleration valve and at the PCV valve. Detach the wires at the oxygen sensor, carburetor choke (if equipped) and the ground wire at the bracket.
7. Loosen the accelerator linkage bracket.
8. Remove the rocker arm cover bolts.

➡When removing the rocker arm (valve) cover, be sure not to distort the sealing flange.

9. Remove the rocker arm cover. If the cover adheres to the cylinder head, lightly tap the end of the cover with a rubber mallet. If necessary, carefully pry until loose.
10. Clean the sealing surfaces of the cylinder head and the cover.

2. Disconnect the air intake hose at the throttle body and air cleaner.

3. For the 2.0L engine, detach the hose from the intake to the cover.

4. For the 2.2L engine, disconnect the PCV hose(s).

5. Unfasten the rocker arm cover bolts and remove the cover. Remove and discard the gasket.

6. Clean the sealing surfaces of the cylinder head and the cover using a suitable degreaser.

To install:

7. Install a new gasket, then reposition the cover and tighten the bolts evenly to 8 ft. lbs. (10 Nm).

8. For the 2.2L engine, connect the PCV hose(s).

9. For the 2.0L engine, attach the intake-to-cover hose.

10. Attach the air intake hose at the throttle body and air cleaner.

11. Connect the negative battery cable, then start the engine and check for leaks.

1995-96 VEHICLES

1. Disconnect the negative battery cable.

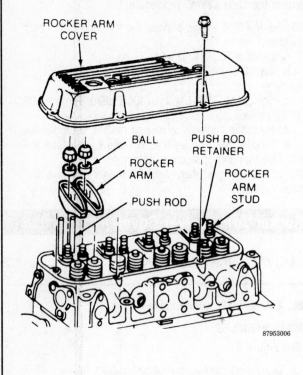

NOTE: AT TIME OF INSTALLATION, FLANGES MUST BE FREE OF OIL. A 2.0-3.0 BEAD OF SEALANT MUST BE APPLIED TO FLANGES AND SEALANT MUST BE WET TO TOUCH WHEN BOLTS ARE TORQUED.

ROCKER ARM COVER

BALL
PUSH ROD RETAINER
ROCKER ARM
ROCKER ARM STUD
PUSH ROD

87953006

Fig. 6 Make sure to tighten the rocker arm cover bolts to specification when the RTV sealant is still wet

To install:

11. Place a ⅛ in. (3mm) wide bead of RTV sealant all around the rocker arm cover sealing surface.

➡ **When going around the attaching bolt holes, always flow the RTV on the inboard side of the bolt holes.**

12. Install the valve cover and tighten the bolts evenly to 8 ft. lbs. (10 Nm) while the sealant is still wet.

➡ **Keep the sealant out of the bolt holes as this could cause a "hydraulic lock" condition which could damage the head casting.**

13. The rest of installation is the reverse of the removal procedure.

14. Connect the negative battery cable, then start the engine and check for leaks.

1987-94 VEHICLES

▶ See Figure 7

1. Disconnect the negative battery cable.

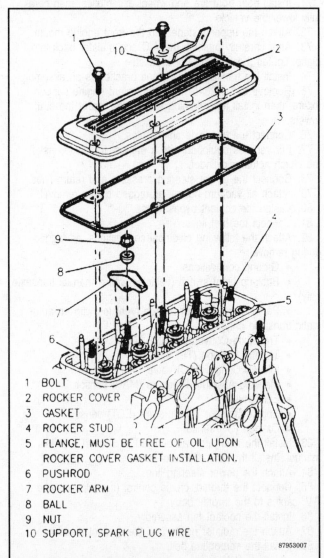

1. BOLT
2. ROCKER COVER
3. GASKET
4. ROCKER STUD
5. FLANGE, MUST BE FREE OF OIL UPON ROCKER COVER GASKET INSTALLATION.
6. PUSHROD
7. ROCKER ARM
8. BALL
9. NUT
10. SUPPORT, SPARK PLUG WIRE

87953007

Fig. 7 Rocker arm (valve) cover removal and installation — 1994 2.2L (VIN 4) engine shown

2. Remove the air cleaner outlet duct.

3. Disconnect the accelerator control, cruise control (if equipped), and T.V. cables at the accelerator control bracket.

4. Remove the accelerator control bracket.

5. Disconnect the crankcase vent valve hose.

6. Unfasten the retaining bolts, then remove the rocker arm (valve) cover from the vehicle. Remove and discard the gasket.

7. Clean off the cylinder head and cover sealing surfaces.

To install:

8. Position a new rocker arm gasket, then install the cover. Tighten the retaining bolt to 89 inch lbs. (10 Nm).

9. Connect the crankcase vent valve hose.

10. Install the accelerator control bracket. Tighten the retaining bolts to 18 ft. lbs. (25 Nm).

11. Attach the accelerator control, cruise control (if equipped) and TV cables at the control bracket.

12. Install the air cleaner outlet duct.

13. Connect the negative battery cable, then start the engine and check for leaks.

2.8L and 3.1L Engines

1985-86 VEHICLES (LEFT SIDE)

▶ See Figure 8

1. Disconnect the negative battery cable.
2. Detach the coil at the bracket.
3. Disconnect the PCV hose.
4. Tag and disconnect the spark plug wires at the plugs, then pull the wires away from the rocker arm cover.
5. If necessary for access, loosen the accelerator linkage bracket.

➠**When removing the rocker arm cover, use extreme care not to distort the sealing flange or leakage will result.**

6. Unfasten the retaining bolts, then remove the rocker arm cover. If the cover adheres to the cylinder head, lightly tap the end of the cover with a rubber mallet. If necessary, carefully pry until loose. Do not distort the sealing flange.

7. Clean the sealing surfaces of the head and the cover.

To install:

8. Place a ⅛ in. (3mm) wide bead of RTV sealant at the intake manifold and the cylinder head split line.

9. Position the valve cover, then evenly tighten the bolts to 90 inch lbs. (10 Nm) while the sealant is still wet.

10. Install the remaining parts, then connect the negative battery cable. Start the engine and check for leaks.

1985-86 VEHICLES (RIGHT SIDE)

1. Disconnect the negative battery cable.
2. Remove the intake runners.

➠**When removing the rocker arm cover, use extreme care not to distort the sealing flange or leakage will result.**

3. Unfasten the rocker arm cover securing bolts, then remove the rocker arm cover. If the cover adheres to the cylinder head, lightly tap the end of the cover with a rubber mallet. If necessary, carefully pry until loose. Do not distort the sealing flange.

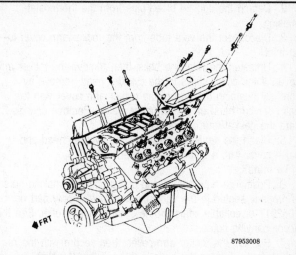

Fig. 8 Removing the rocker arm (valve) cover — 1985 2.8L engine shown

To install:

4. Clean the sealing surfaces of the head, intake manifold and the valve cover.

5. Place a ⅛ in. (3mm) wide bead of RTV sealant at the intake manifold and the cylinder head split line.

6. Position the valve cover, then install the retaining bolts. Tighten bolts evenly to 90 inch lbs. (10 Nm) while the sealant is still wet.

7. Install the remaining parts, then connect the negative battery cable. Start the engine and check for leaks.

1987-90 VEHICLES (LEFT SIDE)

1. Disconnect the negative battery cable.
2. Detach the bracket tube at the cover.
3. Remove the plug wire cover.
4. Disconnect the heater hose at the filler neck.

➠**When removing the rocker arm cover, use extreme care not to distort the sealing flange or leakage will result.**

5. Unfasten the cover retaining bolts, then remove the cover. If the cover adheres to the cylinder head, lightly tap the end of the cover with a soft rubber mallet or palm of the hand. Do not distort or scratch the sealing flange.

6. Remove and discard the gasket.

To install:

7. Clean the sealing surfaces of the head and the cover.

8. Install a new gasket and make sure it is seated properly in the rocker cover groove.

9. Apply a suitable RTV sealant in the notch.

10. Position the rocker arm cover, then install the retaining bolts. Tighten the bolts evenly to 6-9 ft. lbs. (8-12 Nm).

11. Install the remaining parts, then connect the negative battery cable. Start the engine and check for leaks.

1991-94 VEHICLES (LEFT SIDE)

▶ See Figure 9

➠**On 3.1L engines, an "Idle Learn" procedure must be performed which requires the use of a scan tool.**

1. Disconnect the negative battery cable.

2. Detach the coolant bleed pipe from the thermostat housing.

3. Disconnect the vent tube from the rocker arm cover-to-air inlet.

4. Unfasten the retaining bolts, then remove the rocker arm cover. If the cover sticks to the cylinder head, remove by carefully bumping the end of the rocker arm cover with the palm or your hand or a soft rubber mallet. Remove and discard the gasket and bolt grommets.

5. Clean the sealing surfaces of the cylinder head and valve cover with a suitable degreaser.

To install:

6. Position a new gasket and bolt grommets, making sure it is properly seated in the valve cover groove. Apply part no. 1052917 or suitable sealer in the cylinder head notch. See the accompanying figure.

7. Position the rocker arm cover, then secure with the retaining bolts. Tighten the bolts to 89 inch lbs. (10 Nm).

8. Attach the vent tube to the rocket arm cover.

9. Fasten the coolant bleed tube to the thermostat housing.

10. Connect the negative battery cable.

➡️**On the 3.1L engine, a Tech 1® scan tool is needed to perform the "Idle Learn" procedure.**

11. For the 3.1L engine perform the following "Idle Learn" procedure;

    a. Install a Tech 1® scan tool.

    b. Turn the ignition to the **ON** position, engine not running.

    c. Select **IAC SYSTEM**, then **IDLE LEARN** in the **MISC TEST** mode.

    d. Place the transaxle in park or neutral, as applicable.

    e. Proceed with idle learn as directed by the scan tool.

12. Start the engine and check for leaks.

1987-94 VEHICLES (RIGHT SIDE)

◆ See Figure 9

➡️**On 3.1L engines, an "Idle Learn" procedure must be performed which requires the use of a scan tool.**

1. Disconnect the negative battery cable.

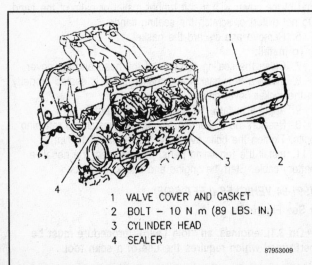

1 VALVE COVER AND GASKET
2 BOLT – 10 N·m (89 LBS. IN.)
3 CYLINDER HEAD
4 SEALER

87953009

Fig. 9 Apply a suitable sealer to the area shown — 1994 3.1L engine shown

2. Unfasten the brake booster vacuum line at the bracket.

3. Disconnect the throttle cable and vacuum line bracket at the plenum.

4. Detach the power steering lines from the alternator bracket stud.

5. Unfasten the rear alternator brace.

6. Remove the serpentine belt.

7. As outlined in Section 2 of this manual, remove the alternator and lay it aside.

8. Tag and disconnect the rear bank spark plug wires from the plugs, then position them aside.

9. Remove the PCV valve.

10. Unfasten the rocker arm cover retaining bolts, then remove the cover. Remove and discard the gasket and bolt grommets.

11. If the cover adheres to the cylinder head, lightly tap the end of the cover with a soft rubber mallet or palm of the hand. Do not distort or scratch the sealing flange.

To install:

12. Clean the sealing surfaces of the head and the cover.

13. Install new bolt grommets, then install a new gasket making sure it is seated properly in the rocker arm cover groove.

14. Apply RTV sealant in the notch.

15. Position the cover, then secure using the retaining bolts. Tighten the bolts evenly to 89 inch lbs. (10 Nm).

16. Install the remaining parts, then connect the negative battery cable.

➡️**On the 3.1L engine, a Tech 1® scan tool is needed to perform the "Idle Learn" procedure.**

17. For the 3.1L engine perform the following "Idle Learn" procedure;

    a. Install a Tech 1® scan tool.

    b. Turn the ignition to the **ON** position, engine not running.

    c. Select **IAC SYSTEM**, then **IDLE LEARN** in the **MISC TEST** mode.

    d. Place the transaxle in park or neutral, as applicable.

    e. Proceed with idle learn as directed by the scan tool.

18. Start the engine and check for leaks.

Camshaft Carrier Cover

REMOVAL & INSTALLATION

1.8L and 2.0L SOHC Engines

◆ See Figures 10, 11, 12, 13 and 14

1. Disconnect the negative battery cable.

2. For non-turbo vehicles, remove the air cleaner.

3. Disconnect the breather hoses.

4. Detach the induction tube on turbo models.

5. Unfasten the retaining bolts, then remove the cover. Remove and discard the gasket.

To install:

6. Clean the sealing surfaces on the camshaft carrier and cover.

7. Reposition the cover with a new gasket and evenly tighten the retainer bolts to 62-84 inch lbs. (7-9.5 Nm).

Fig. 10 Disconnect the PCV hose from the cover — 1988 2.0L Sunbird shown

Fig. 11 Unfasten the camshaft carrier cover retaining bolts, then . . .

Fig. 12 . . . remove the cover

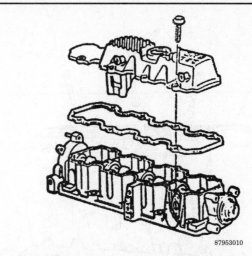

Fig. 13 When installing the camshaft cover, always use a new gasket — 1994 2.0L engine shown

Fig. 14 Use a suitable scraper to CAREFULLY clean the gasket mating surfaces

8. Attach the induction tube, breather hoses, and/or air cleaner as applicable.

9. Connect the negative battery cable, then start the engine and inspect for leaks.

2.3L and 2.4L DOHC Engines

INTAKE CAMSHAFT

▶ See Figures 15, 16, 17, 18 and 19

1. Disconnect the negative battery cable.

2. Detach the ignition coil and module assembly electrical connections.

3. Unfasten the ignition coil and module assembly-to-camshaft housing bolts, then remove the assembly by pulling it straight up.

➡Use tool no. J 36011 to remove any connector that may have stuck to the spark plugs. Use the tool by first twisting, then pulling up on the connector assembly.

4. Remove the power steering pump.

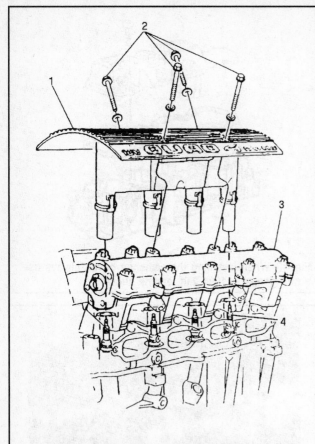

1 IGNITION COIL AND MODULE ASSEMBLY
2 BOLTS – IGNITION COIL AND MODULE ASM. TO
  CRANKSHAFT HOUSING – 22 N•m (16 LB. FT.)
3 COVER – CAMSHAFT HOUSING (INTAKE SHOWN)
4 SPARK PLUG

87953011

Fig. 15 To remove the ignition coil and module assembly, remove the bolts then lift the assembly straight up — DOHC engine shown

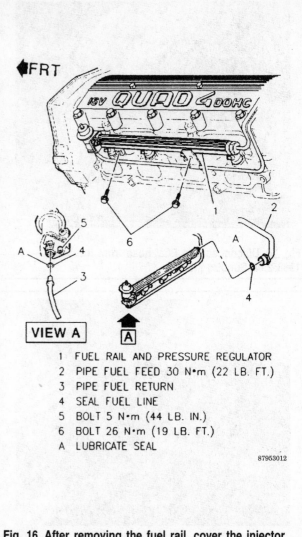

VIEW A

1 FUEL RAIL AND PRESSURE REGULATOR
2 PIPE FUEL FEED 30 N•m (22 LB. FT.)
3 PIPE FUEL RETURN
4 SEAL FUEL LINE
5 BOLT 5 N•m (44 LB. IN.)
6 BOLT 26 N•m (19 LB. FT.)
A LUBRICATE SEAL

87953012

Fig. 16 After removing the fuel rail, cover the injector openings in the cylinder head to prevent any debris from falling in

5. Detach the oil/air separator (crankcase ventilation system). Leave the hoses attached to the separator, disconnect from the oil fill, front cover and intake manifold, then remove as an assembly.

6. Unfasten the vacuum line from the fuel pressure regulator and fuel injector harness connector.

7. Disconnect the fuel line retaining clamp from the bracket on top of the intake cam housing.

8. Unfasten the fuel rail-to-camshaft housing retaining bolts, then remove the fuel rail from the cylinder head. Be sure to cover the injector openings in the cylinder head, cover the injector nozzles and leave the fuel lines attached and position the fuel rail aside (on top of the master cylinder).

9. Disconnect the timing chain housing at the intake camshaft housing but do not remove from the vehicle.

10. Unfasten the cam housing cover-to-housing retaining bolts and the cam housing-to-cylinder head bolts.

11. Use the reverse of the tightening procedure (in the accompanying figure) when loosening the camshaft housing-to-cylinder head bolts.

12. Push the cover off the housing by threading four of the housing-to-head retaining bolts into the tapped holes in the cover. Make sure to tighten the bolts evenly remove the cover from the vehicle.

13. Remove and discard the cover-to-housing seals and clean the mating surfaces.

To install:

14. Position new seals on the camshaft cover. Refer to the accompanying figure.

15. Apply pipe sealant 1052080 or equivalent to the camshaft housing and cover retaining bolt threads. Using J 366660, install the bolts, then tighten in sequence to the specifications in the accompanying figure.

16. Fasten the timing chain housing.

17. Uncover fuel injectors, then lubricate new injector O-ring seals with clean engine oil and install on the injectors.

18. Uncover the injector openings in the cylinder head, then install the fuel rail onto the cylinder head. Install the fuel rail-to-cylinder head retaining bolts and tighten to 19 ft. lbs. (26 Nm).

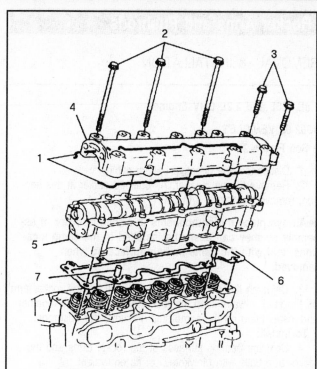

1 SEALS – CAMSHAFT HOUSING TO CAMSHAFT
2 BOLT – CAMSHAFT HOUSING TO CYLINDER
   HEAD – 15 N·m (11 LBS. FT.) PLUS TURN 90°
3 BOLT – CAMSHAFT HOUSING COVER TO
   CAMSHAFT HOUSING – 15 N·m (11 LBS. FT.)
   PLUS TURN 30°
4 COVER – CAMSHAFT
5 CAMSHAFT HOUSING (INTAKE SHOWN)
6 GASKET – CAMSHAFT HOUSING TO CYLINDER
   HEAD
7 DOWEL PIN (2)

87953013

Fig. 17 Exploded view of the cam cover and related components

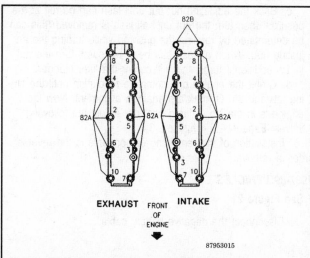

87953015

Fig. 19 Intake and exhaust camshaft bolt tightening sequence

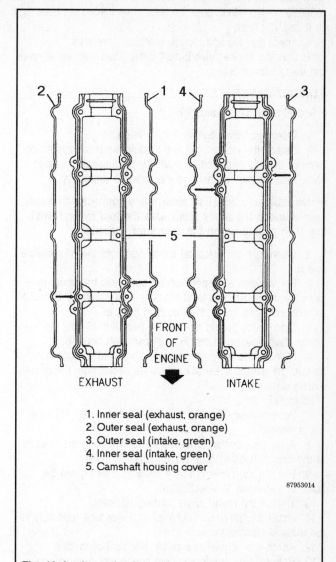

1. Inner seal (exhaust, orange)
2. Outer seal (exhaust, orange)
3. Outer seal (intake, green)
4. Inner seal (intake, green)
5. Camshaft housing cover

87953014

Fig. 18 Intake and exhaust cam housing-to-cover seal locations

19. Install the fuel line retaining clamp and retainer to the bracket on top of the cam housing.

20. Connect the vacuum line to the fuel pressure regulator. Attach the fuel injector harness connector.

21. Install the oil/air separator assembly. You may want to lubricate the hoses to ease installation.

22. Lubricate the inner surface of the camshaft seal with clean engine oil, then install the seal into the camshaft housing using tool J 36015, or equivalent.

23. Using tool J 36015 or equivalent, install the power steering pump drive pulley onto the intake camshaft.

24. Install the power steering pump assembly and the drive belt. Adjust tension to specification.

25. Fasten any spark plug boot connector assembly that stuck to a spark plug back onto the ignition coil and module assembly.

26. Position the coil and module assembly over the spark plugs, then push the assembly straight down. Make sure it is properly seated.

27. Clean off any loose lubricant from the coil and module assembly-to-camshaft housing bolts. Apply pipe sealant

1052080 or equivalent, onto the bolts, then tighten the bolts to 16 ft. lbs. (22 Nm).

28. Attach the coil and module electrical connector.

29. Connect the negative battery cable, then start the engine and inspect for oil leaks.

EXHAUST CAMSHAFT

▶ **See Figures 17, 18 and 19**

1. Disconnect the negative battery cable.

2. Detach the ignition coil and module electrical connection. Remove the coil and module assembly-to-camshaft housing bolts, then remove the assembly by lifting it straight up.

➡**Use tool no. J 36011 to remove any connector that may have stuck to the spark plugs. Use the tool by first twisting, then pulling up on the connector assembly.**

3. Disengage the electrical connection from the oil pressure switch.

4. For vehicles equipped with an automatic transaxle, remove the transaxle fluid level indicator tube assembly from the exhaust camshaft cover, then position it aside.

5. Disconnect, but do not remove from the vehicle, the timing chain housing at the exhaust camshaft housing.

6. Remove the exhaust camshaft cover and gasket, then discard the gasket. Clean all old gasket debris from the cover mating surfaces.

To install:

7. Position new camshaft housing-to-cover seals. No sealant is needed.

8. Apply pipe sealant 1052080 or equivalent to the threads of the camshaft housing and cover retaining bolts.

9. Position the cover onto the housing, then tighten the bolts, in sequence, to specification.

10. Tighten the timing chain housing retainers.

11. Install the transaxle fluid level indicator tube assembly to the exhaust camshaft cover.

12. Attach the oil pressure switch electrical connector.

13. Reinstall any spark plug boot connectors that may have been stuck to a spark plug, back onto the ignition coil and module assembly.

14. Position the coil and module assembly over the spark plugs then push it straight down making sure it is firmly and properly seated.

15. Clean off any lubricant on the coil and module-to-camshaft housing bolts. Apply pipe sealant 1052080 or equivalent to the bolts, then tighten them to 16 ft. lbs. (22 Nm).

16. Attach the ignition coil and module assembly electrical connector.

17. Connect the negative battery cable, then start the engine and inspect for leaks.

Rocker Arms and Pushrods

REMOVAL & INSTALLATION

1.8L, 2.0L and 2.2L OHV Engines

1982-86 VEHICLES

▶ **See Figure 20**

1. Disconnect the negative battery cable.

2. Remove the air cleaner. As outlined earlier in this section, remove the rocker arm cover.

➡**Always place the components in a rack in order of assembly so they can easily be installed in the same locations, and with the same mating surface as when removed.**

3. Unfasten the rocker arm nut and ball. Lift the rocker arm off the stud. Always keep the rocker arm assemblies together and install them on the same stud. Remove the pushrods.

To install:

4. Coat the bearing surfaces of the rocker arms and the rocker arm balls with Molykote® or its equivalent.

5. Install the pushrods making sure that they seat properly in the lifter.

6. Install the rocker arms, balls and nuts. Tighten the rocker arm nuts until all lash is eliminated.

7. Adjust the valves when the lifter is on the base circle of a camshaft lobe:

a. Crank the engine until the mark on the crankshaft pulley lines up with the **O** mark on the timing tab. Make sure that the engine is in the No. 1 firing position. Place your fingers on the No. 1 rocker arms as the mark on the crank pulley comes near the **O** mark. If the valves are not moving, the engine is in the No. 1 firing position. If the valves move, the engine is in the No. 4 firing position; rotate the engine one complete revolution and it will be in the No. 1 position.

b. When the engine is in the No. 1 firing position, adjust the following valves: Exhaust - 1,3 Intake - 1,2

c. Back the adjusting nut out until lash can be felt at the pushrod, then turn the nut until all lash is removed (this can be determined by rotating the pushrod while turning the adjusting nut). When all lash has been removed, turn the nut in 1½ additional turns, this will center the lifter plunger.

d. Crank the engine one complete revolution until the timing tab and the **O** mark are again in alignment. Now the engine is in the No. 4 firing position. Adjust the following valves: Exhaust - 2,4 Intake - 3,4

8. Installation of the remaining components is the reverse order of removal.

1987-89 VEHICLES

▶ **See Figure 21**

1. Disconnect the negative battery cable.

NOTE: AT TIME OF INSTALLATION, FLANGES MUST BE FREE OF OIL. A 2.0-3.0 BEAD OF SEALANT MUST BE APPLIED TO FLANGES AND SEALANT MUST BE WET TO TOUCH WHEN BOLTS ARE TORQUED.

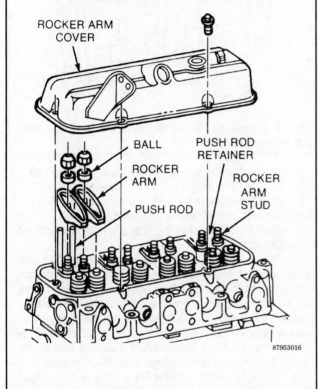

Fig. 20 Removing the rocker arms and pushrods — 1982 1.8L (OHV) engine shown

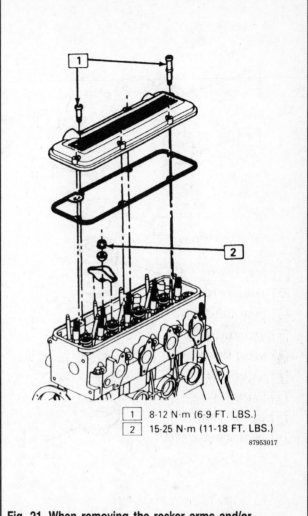

| 1 | 8-12 N·m (6-9 FT. LBS.) |
| 2 | 15-25 N·m (11-18 FT. LBS.) |

87953017

Fig. 21 When removing the rocker arms and/or pushrods, always keep the assemblies together to ensure they are installed in the same locations that they were removed from

2. Remove the air cleaner. Remove the rocker arm cover. For details, please refer to the procedure located earlier in this section.

➡Always place the components in a rack in order of assembly so they can easily be installed in the same locations, and with the same mating surface as when removed.

3. Unfasten the rocker arm nut(s) and ball(s). Lift the rocker arm off the stud. Always keep the rocker arm assemblies together and install them on the same stud. Remove the pushrods.

To install:

4. Coat the bearing surfaces of the rocker arms and the rocker arm balls with Molykote® or its equivalent.

5. Install the pushrods, making sure that they seat properly in the lifters.

6. Install the rocker arms, then secure using the balls and nuts. Tighten the rocker arm nuts to 11-18 ft. lbs. (15-25 Nm).

7. As outlined earlier, install the rocker cover.

8. Connect the negative battery cable.

1.8L and 2.0L SOHC Engines

▶ See Figure 22

➡A special compressing tool is required for this procedure.

1. Disconnect the negative battery cable.

2. As outlined earlier, remove the camshaft carrier cover.

3. Using a valve train compressing fixture, tool J-33302 or equivalent, depress all the lifters at once.

4. Remove the rocker arms, placing them on the workbench in the same order that they were removed. Remove the thrust piece.

5. Remove the hydraulic valve lash compensators, keeping them in the order in which they were removed.

➡The valve lash compensators are not serviceable. If damaged or faulty, they must be replaced.

To install:

6. Compress the valve springs with tool J-33302 or equivalent.

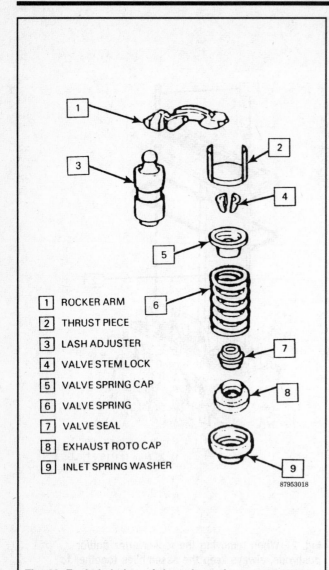

Fig. 22 Exploded view of the valve train components — 1989 2.0L shown

1	ROCKER ARM
2	THRUST PIECE
3	LASH ADJUSTER
4	VALVE STEM LOCK
5	VALVE SPRING CAP
6	VALVE SPRING
7	VALVE SEAL
8	EXHAUST ROTO CAP
9	INLET SPRING WASHER

87953018

7. Install the valve lash compensators into their original positions.

8. Install the thrust piece and rocker arms.

9. As outlined earlier, install the camshaft carrier cover.

10. Connect the negative battery cable.

2.8L and 3.1L Engines

1985-86 VEHICLES

▶ **See Figures 23 and 24**

1. Disconnect the negative battery cable.

2. As outlined earlier, remove the rocker arm (valve) covers.

3. Remove the rocker arm nuts, rocker arm balls, rocker arms and push rods, then place in a rack so that they may be reinstalled in the same location.

To install:

4. Install the pushrods making sure that they seat properly in the lifter.

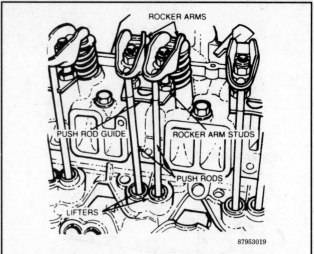

Fig. 23 Assembled view of the valve mechanism — 1986 2.8L engine shown

5. Coat the bearing surfaces of the rocker arms and the rocker arm balls with Molykote® or its equivalent.

6. Install the rocker arms, balls and nuts. Tighten the rocker arm nuts until all lash is eliminated.

7. Adjust the valves when the lifter is on the base circle of a camshaft lobe:

a. Turn the engine until the mark on the crankshaft pulley lines up with the **O** mark on the timing tab. Make sure that the engine is in the No. 1 firing position. Place your fingers on the No. 1 rocker arms as the mark on the crank pulley comes near the **O** mark. If the valves are not moving, the engine is in the No. 1 firing position. If the valves move, the engine is in the No. 4 firing position; rotate the engine one complete revolution and it will be in the No. 1 position.

b. When the engine is in the No. 1 firing position, adjust the following valves: Exhaust - 1,2,3 Intake - 1,5,6

c. Back the adjusting nut out until lash can be felt at the pushrod, then turn the nut until all lash is removed (this can be determined by rotating the pushrod while turning the adjusting nut). When all lash has been removed, turn the nut in 1½ additional turns, this will center the lifter plunger.

d. Turn the engine one complete revolution until the timing tab and the **O** mark are again in alignment. Now the engine is in the No. 4 firing position. Adjust the following valves: Exhaust - 4,5,6 Intake - 2,3,4

8. Install the rocker arm (valve) cover, as outlined earlier.

9. Connect the negative battery cable, then start the engine and check the timing. Adjust if necessary.

1987-94 VEHICLES

➡**On 3.1L engines, an ''Idle Learn'' procedure must be performed which requires the use of a scan tool.**

1. Disconnect the negative battery cable.

2. As outlined earlier, remove the rocker arm covers.

3. Unfasten the rocker arm nuts. When removing the components, make sure to keep them separated so they can be installed in the same location.

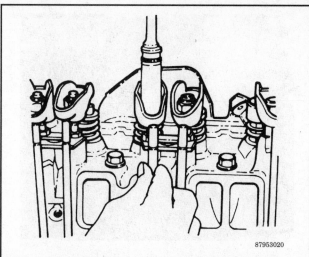

Fig. 24 On 1985-86 2.8L engines, the valves must be adjusted when removing the rocker arm assemblies

4. Remove the rocker arm pivot ball(s), rocker arms, push rod guides and push rods, then place them in a rack so that they may be reinstalled in the same location.

➡Intake pushrods are marked orange and are 6 in. (152.4mm) long. Exhaust pushrods are marked blue and are 6⅜ in. (161.9mm) long.

To install:

5. Install the pushrods (correct length) making sure that they seat properly in the lifter.

6. Coat the bearing surfaces of the rocker arms and the rocker arm balls with Molykote® or its equivalent.

7. Install the pushrod guides, rocker arms, pivot balls and nuts.

8. Tighten the rocker arm nuts to 14-20 ft. lbs. (19-27 Nm).

9. Install the rocker arm covers.

10. Connect the negative battery cable.

➡On the 3.1L engine, a Tech 1® scan tool is needed to perform the "Idle Learn" procedure.

11. For the 3.1L engine perform the following "Idle Learn" procedure;

   a. Install a Tech 1® scan tool.

   b. Turn the ignition to the **ON** position, engine not running.

   c. Select **IAC SYSTEM**, then **IDLE LEARN** in the **MISC TEST** mode.

   d. Place the transaxle in park or neutral, as applicable.

   e. Proceed with idle learn as directed by the scan tool.

Thermostat

REMOVAL & INSTALLATION

Poor heater output and slow warmup is often caused by a thermostat stuck in the open position; occasionally one sticks shut causing immediate overheating. Do not attempt to correct a chronic overheating condition by permanently removing the thermostat. Thermostat flow restriction is designed into the sys-

tem; without it, localized overheating (due to coolant turbulence) may occur, causing expensive troubles.

✳✳CAUTION

When draining the coolant, keep in mind that cats and dogs are attracted by ethylene glycol antifreeze, and are quite likely to drink any that is left in an uncovered container or in puddles on the ground. This will prove fatal in sufficient quantity. Always drain the coolant into a sealable container. Coolant should be reused unless it is contaminated or several years old.

1.8L and 2.0L OHV Engines

1982-86 VEHICLES

▶ See Figure 25

The thermostat is located inside a housing on the back of the cylinder head. It is not necessary to remove the radiator hose from the thermostat housing when removing the thermostat.

1. Disconnect the negative battery cable.

2. Properly drain the cooling system into an approved container.

3. Remove the air cleaner.

4. On some models it may be necessary to disconnect the A.I.R. pipe at the upper check valve and the bracket at the water outlet.

5. Disconnect the electrical lead.

6. Remove the two retaining bolts from the thermostat housing and lift up the housing with the house attached. Lift out the thermostat. Clean the mating surfaces.

To install:

7. Apply a ⅛ in. (3mm) bead of silicone sealer to the housing mating surface.

8. Place the thermostat, with the power element down, in housing, then install the water outlet while the sealer is still wet. Tighten the housing retaining bolts to 6 ft. lbs. (8 Nm).

9. Connect the electrical lead.

10. If applicable, attach the A.I.R. pipe at the check valve and bracket at the water outlet.

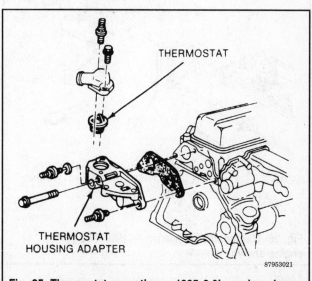

Fig. 25 Thermostat mounting — 1985 2.0L engine shown

11. Install the air cleaner.

12. Fill the cooling system to the proper level, using the correct type of fluid.

13. Connect the negative battery cable, then start the engine and check for coolant leaks.

1987-89 VEHICLES

▶ See Figure 26

1. Disconnect the negative battery cable.

2. Properly drain the coolant until the level is below the thermostat.

3. If necessary for access, remove the air cleaner assembly.

4. Unfasten the coolant outlet-to-inlet manifold attaching bolt and nut.

5. Remove the coolant outlet, then remove the thermostat. Remove and discard the gasket, then clean the inlet manifold mating surfaces.

To install:

6. Position the thermostat in the inlet manifold.

➡ **When installing a thermostat, be sure to use a new gasket.**

7. Attach the coolant outlet to the inlet manifold. Coat the attaching bolt and nut with sealer, then tighten to 90 inch lbs. (10 Nm).

8. If removed, install the air cleaner assembly.

9. Refill the engine cooling system to the proper level.

10. Connect the negative battery cable, then start the engine and check for coolant leaks.

1.8L and 2.0L OHC Engines

▶ See Figures 27, 28, 29, 30 and 31

1. Remove the thermostat housing/radiator cap.

2. Grasp the handle of the thermostat and pull it from the housing.

3. Clean the thermostat housing and gasket. Replace the gasket if damaged.

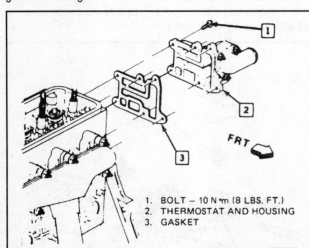

1. BOLT — 10 N·m (8 LBS. FT.)
2. THERMOSTAT AND HOUSING
3. GASKET

87953022

Fig. 26 Thermostat installation — 1989 2.0L (OHV) engine shown

87953205

Fig. 27 Remove the radiator cap for access to the thermostat — 1988 2.0L (VIN K) Sunbird shown

87953206

Fig. 28 Remove the thermostat by pulling it out by the handle

To install:

4. Install the thermostat in the housing, carefully pushing it down as far as it will go to make sure it's properly seated.

5. Install the housing cap on the engine.

2.2L Engines

1987-91 VEHICLES

▶ See Figure 32

1. Disconnect the negative battery cable.

2. Drain the cooling system to a level below the thermostat housing.

3. Detach the upper radiator hose from the thermostat housing.

4. Unfasten the thermostat housing mounting nuts, then remove the housing.

5. Remove the thermostat. Clean all gasket surfaces completely.

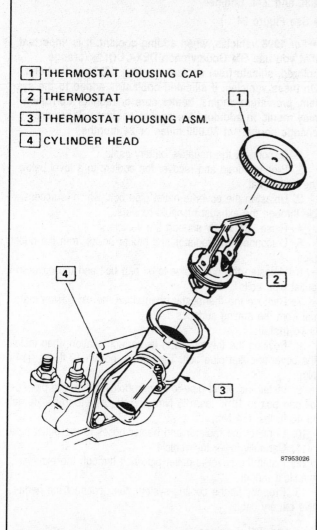

1 THERMOSTAT HOUSING CAP
2 THERMOSTAT
3 THERMOSTAT HOUSING ASM.
4 CYLINDER HEAD

87953026

Fig. 29 Removing the thermostat is simply a matter of removing the housing cap and pulling the thermostat up

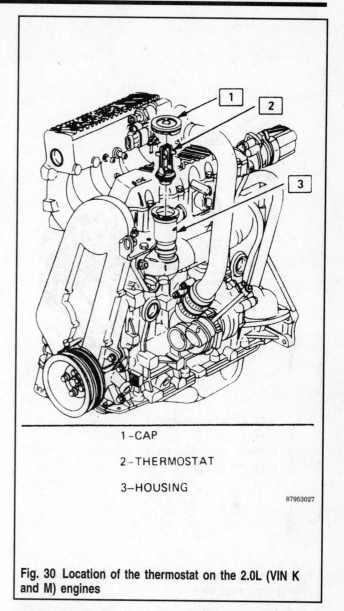

1 – CAP

2 – THERMOSTAT

3 – HOUSING

87953027

Fig. 30 Location of the thermostat on the 2.0L (VIN K and M) engines

To install:

6. Apply a thin bead of sealer around the gasket contact surface of the housing, then install a new gasket.

7. Position the thermostat in the housing.

8. Install the thermostat housing on the engine and tighten the mounting nuts to 89 inch lbs. (10 Nm).

9. Attach the upper radiator hose to the thermostat housing.

10. Refill the cooling system.

11. Connect the negative battery cable, then start the engine and check for leaks.

1992-96 VEHICLES

◗ See Figure 33

➡For 1996 vehicles, when adding coolant, it is important that you use GM Goodwrench DEX-COOL® (orange colored, silicate free) coolant meeting GM specifications. On these vehicles, if silicated coolant is added to the sys-tem, premature engine, heater core or radiator corrosion may result. In addition, the engine coolant will require change sooner; at 30,000 miles or 24 months.

1. Disconnect the negative battery cable.

2. Properly drain and recover the coolant until the level is below the thermostat.

3. Unfasten the coolant outlet-to-inlet manifold attaching bolt and nut, then remove the outlet.

4. Remove the thermostat. Clean the inlet manifold and outlet mating surfaces.

To install:

5. Place the thermostat in the inlet manifold.

6. Attach the coolant outlet to the inlet manifold, using the bolt and nut. Tighten to 89 inch lbs. (10 Nm).

7. Refill the engine cooling system.

8. Connect the negative battery cable, then start the engine and check for coolant leaks.

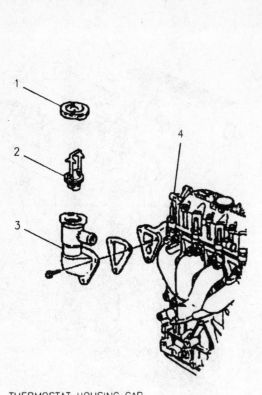

1 THERMOSTAT HOUSING CAP
2 THERMOSTAT
3 THERMOSTAT HOUSING ASM.
4 CYLINDER BLOCK

87953028

Fig. 31 Thermostat and housing mounting — 1994 2.0L (VIN 1) engine shown

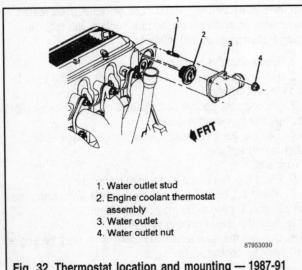

1. Water outlet stud
2. Engine coolant thermostat assembly
3. Water outlet
4. Water outlet nut

87953030

Fig. 32 Thermostat location and mounting — 1987-91 2.2L engines

2.3L and 2.4L Engines

▶ See Figure 34

➡For 1996 vehicles, when adding coolant, it is important that you use GM Goodwrench DEX-COOL® (orange colored, silicate free) coolant meeting GM specifications. On these vehicles, if silicated coolant is added to the system, premature engine, heater core or radiator corrosion may result. In addition, the engine coolant will require change sooner; at 30,000 miles or 24 months.

1. Disconnect the negative battery cable.
2. Properly drain and recover the coolant to a level below the thermostat.
3. Unfasten the cover-to-outlet pipe bolt, which is accessible through the exhaust manifold runners.
4. Raise and safely support the vehicle.
5. Disconnect the radiator and heater hoses from the outlet pipe.
6. Unfasten the outlet pipe-to-oil pan bolt and the cover-to-outlet pipe bolts.
7. Remove the thermostat, then clean the old gasket material from the mating surfaces.
   To install:
8. Position the thermostat in its correct location, then install the cover-to-outlet pipe bolt. Tighten the bolt to 10 ft. lbs. (14 Nm).
9. Install the outlet pipe-to-oil pan bolt. Tighten the pipe-to-oil pan bolt to 19 ft. lbs. (26 Nm) and the pipe-to-transaxle bolt to 40 ft. lbs. (54 Nm).
10. Connect the radiator and heater hoses to the outlet pipe.
11. Carefully lower the vehicle.
12. Install the cover-to-outlet pipe bolt through the exhaust manifold runner.
13. Properly fill the cooling system, then connect the negative battery cable.

2.8L and 3.1L Engines

▶ See Figure 35

1. Disconnect the negative battery cable.
2. Properly drain and recover the cooling system until the level is below the thermostat.
3. For the 3.1L engine, remove the air cleaner assembly.
4. Some models with cruise control have a vacuum modulator attached to the thermostat housing with a bracket. If your vehicle is equipped as such, remove the bracket from the housing.
5. Unfasten the coolant outlet-to-inlet manifold attaching bolt and nut, then remove the outlet and lift the thermostat out of the manifold. Clean the mating surfaces.
   To install:
6. Position the thermostat in the inlet manifold.
7. Attach the coolant outlet to the inlet manifold. Coat the attaching nut and bolt with sealer, then tighten to 18 ft. lbs. (25 Nm).
8. If necessary, install the cruise control vacuum modulator bracket to the housing.
9. For the 3.1L engine, install the air cleaner assembly.
10. Refill the engine cooling system. On the 2.8L engine, use the vent plug on the thermostat housing.
11. Connect the negative battery cable. Start the engine, then check for coolant leaks and correct as required.

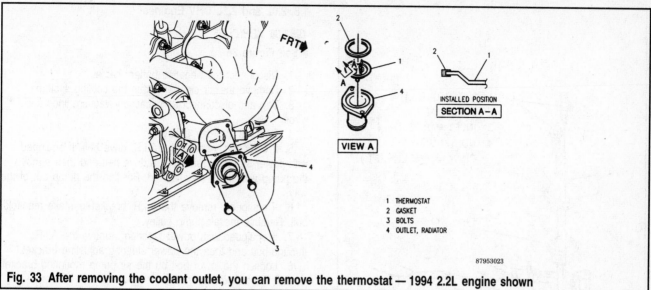

1 THERMOSTAT
2 GASKET
3 BOLTS
4 OUTLET, RADIATOR

87953023

Fig. 33 After removing the coolant outlet, you can remove the thermostat — 1994 2.2L engine shown

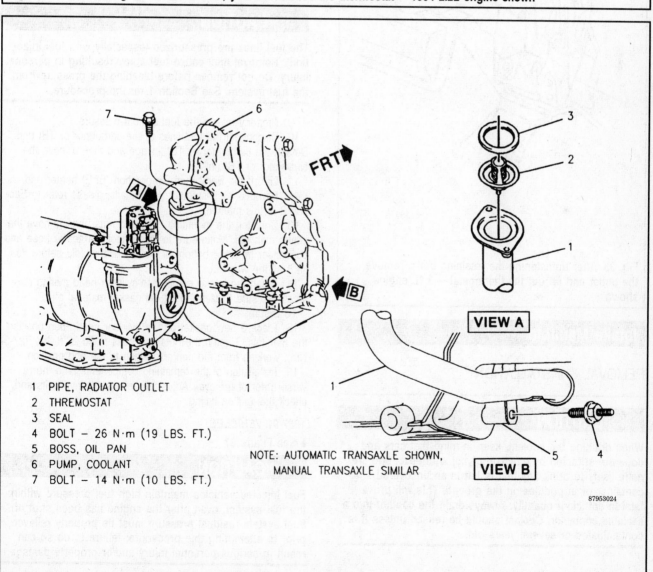

1 PIPE, RADIATOR OUTLET
2 THREMOSTAT
3 SEAL
4 BOLT – 26 N·m (19 LBS. FT.)
5 BOSS, OIL PAN
6 PUMP, COOLANT
7 BOLT – 14 N·m (10 LBS. FT.)

NOTE: AUTOMATIC TRANSAXLE SHOWN,
MANUAL TRANSAXLE SIMILAR

87953024

Fig. 34 Thermostat removal and installation — 2.3L and 2.4L engines

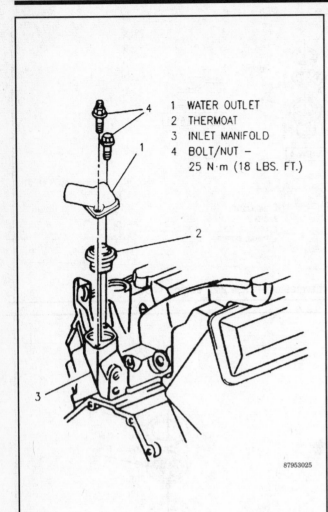

1 WATER OUTLET
2 THERMOAT
3 INLET MANIFOLD
4 BOLT/NUT —
   25 N·m (18 LBS. FT.)

87953025

Fig. 35 After unfastening the retaining bolts, remove the outlet and lift out the thermostat — 3.1L engine shown

Intake Manifold

REMOVAL & INSTALLATION

> **✳✳CAUTION**
>
> When draining the coolant, keep in mind that cats and dogs are attracted by ethylene glycol antifreeze, and are quite likely to drink any that is left in an uncovered container or in puddles on the ground. This will prove fatal in sufficient quantity. Always drain the coolant into a sealable container. Coolant should be reused unless it is contaminated or several years old.

1.8, 2.0L and 2.2L OHV Engines

1982-86 VEHICLES

▶ See Figure 36

1. Disconnect the negative battery cable.
2. Remove the air cleaner. Drain the cooling system.
3. Tag and disconnect all necessary vacuum lines and wires.
4. Remove the idler pulley.
5. If equipped, remove the A.I.R. drive belt. If equipped with power steering, remove the drive belt and then remove the pump with the lines attached. Position the pump out of the way.
6. If equipped, remove the A.I.R. bracket-to-intake manifold bolt. Remove the air pump pulley.
7. If equipped with power steering, remove the A.I.R. through-bolt and then the power steering adjusting bracket.
8. Loosen the lower bolt on the air pump mounting bracket so that the bracket will rotate.

> **✳✳CAUTION**
>
> The fuel lines are pressurized (especially with fuel injection). Removal may cause fuel spray resulting in personal injury. Do not remove before bleeding the pressure from the fuel system. See Section 1 for the procedure.

9. Properly relieve the fuel system pressure.
10. Disconnect the fuel lines at the carburetor or TBI unit. Detach the carburetor or TBI linkage and then remove the carburetor or TBI unit.
11. Lift off the Early Fuel Evaporation (EFE) heater grid.
12. Remove the distributor. For details, please refer to Section 2 of this manual.
13. Unfasten the mounting bolts and nuts, then remove the intake manifold. Make sure to disconnect the heater hose and condenser from the bottom of the intake manifold before you lift it all the way out.
14. Clean the intake manifold-to-cylinder head mating surfaces. Be sure to clean all of old gasket material off.
To install:
15. Place a new gasket on the cylinder head, then position the manifold. Tighten the nuts and bolts to 20-25 ft. lbs. (27-34 Nm), working from the center position to the end position.
16. Installation of the remaining components is in the reverse order of removal. Adjust all necessary drive belts and check the ignition timing.

1987-91 VEHICLES

▶ See Figure 37

> **✳✳CAUTION**
>
> Fuel injected vehicles maintain high fuel pressure within the fuel system, even after the engine has been shut off. Fuel system residual pressure must be properly relieved, prior to attempting this procedure; failure to do so can result in serious personal injury and/or property damage.

1. Disconnect the negative battery cable.
2. Remove the air cleaner. Properly drain the cooling system into an approved container.

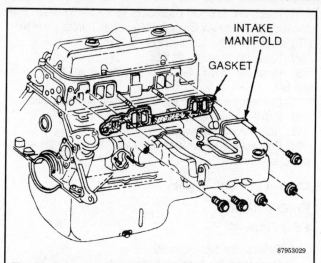

Fig. 36 Removing the intake manifold — 1982-86 OHV engines

3. Tag and disconnect all necessary vacuum lines and wires from the intake manifold and throttle body.

4. Disconnect and cap the fuel lines from the throttle body.

5. Detach the control cables from the throttle body lever.

6. Unfasten the throttle body mounting screws, then remove the throttle body from the intake manifold.

7. Remove the serpentine belt.

8. Unfasten the power steering pump-to-bracket bolts and support the pump out of the way. DO NOT disconnect the power steering hoses from the pump.

9. Raise and safely support the vehicle.

10. Remove the control cable bracket from the intake manifold.

11. Disconnect the heater (coolant) hose from the bottom of the intake manifold.

12. Unfasten the lower intake manifold bolts.

13. Carefully lower the vehicle.

14. Unfasten the intake manifold-to-cylinder head nuts/bolts, then remove the intake manifold.

15. Use a gasket scraper to carefully clean the gasket mating surfaces.

To install:

16. Position a new gasket, then install the intake manifold and tighten the manifold-to-cylinder head nuts/bolts (in the proper sequence) to 18 ft. lbs. (25 Nm).

17. Raise and safely support the vehicle.

18. Connect the heater hose to the underside of the intake manifold.

19. Install the control cable bracket to the intake manifold.

20. Carefully lower the vehicle.

21. Install the power steering pump in the mounting bracket, then tighten the mounting bolts.

22. Position the throttle body assembly on the intake manifold, then tighten the mounting bolts to 17 ft. lbs. (23 Nm).

23. Connect the control cables to the throttle body lever, then attach the fuel lines to the throttle body.

24. Attach the vacuum lines and wires, as tagged during removal.

25. Install the air cleaner assembly.

26. Connect the negative battery cable.

27. Properly fill the cooling system.

28. Pressurize the fuel system before starting the vehicle, and make sure there are no leaks.

29. Start the engine and check for oil and/or coolant leaks.

1992-96 VEHICLES

▶ See Figures 38 and 39

These vehicles use a two-piece intake manifold. The upper half, sometimes called a plenum, contains the throttle body and the control cable connections. The lower half has individual port runner to each intake port on the cylinder head. The lower half of the manifold bolts to the cylinder head and houses the fuel injectors. Note that these pieces are cast aluminum. Care should be exercised when working with any light allow component.

1. Properly relieve the fuel system pressure.

2. Disconnect the negative battery cable.

3. Remove the throttle body air intake duct.

4. Drain the cooling system into an approved container.

5. Identify, tag and disconnect all necessary vacuum lines.

6. Disconnect the control cables from the throttle body lever and remove the control cable bracket form the intake manifold.

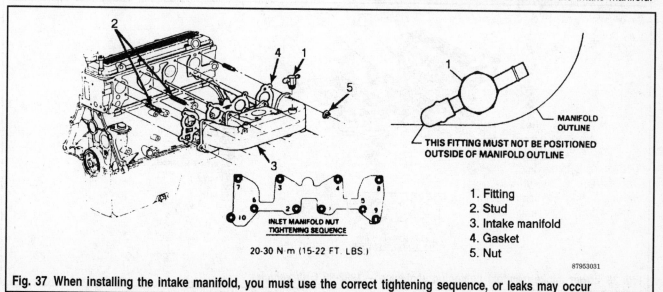

1. Fitting
2. Stud
3. Intake manifold
4. Gasket
5. Nut

INLET MANIFOLD NUT TIGHTENING SEQUENCE

20-30 N·m (15-22 FT. LBS.)

THIS FITTING MUST NOT BE POSITIONED OUTSIDE OF MANIFOLD OUTLINE

Fig. 37 When installing the intake manifold, you must use the correct tightening sequence, or leaks may occur

7. Remove the serpentine belt.

8. Remove the power steering pump and lay it aside with the fluid lines attached.

9. Remove the transaxle fill tube.

10. Tag and disconnect the following electrical wires:
- Idle Air Control (IAC) valve
- Throttle Position (TP) sensor
- Manifold Absolute Pressure (MAP) sensor
- EVAP Emission solenoid
- Fuel injector harness
- Exhaust Gas Recirculation (EGR) valve

11. Remove the MAP sensor.

12. Unfasten the upper intake manifold mounting bolts, then remove the upper intake manifold.

13. Disconnect the fuel lines from the fuel rail.

14. Remove the EGR valve injector, then remove the EGR valve.

15. Remove the fuel injector retainer bracket, regulator and injectors.

16. Unfasten and remove the control cable bracket.

17. If necessary for access, raise and safely support the vehicle.

18. Unfasten the six intake manifold nuts, then remove the manifold.

19. Clean the gasket mounting surfaces.

To install:

20. Install a new gasket, then position the lower intake manifold. Tighten the lower intake manifold nuts in the proper sequence to 24 ft. lbs. (33 Nm).

21. Connect the control cables and cable bracket.

22. Install the EGR valve.

23. Attach the fuel lines to the fuel rail.

24. Install the fuel injectors, regulator and injector retainer bracket, then tighten the retaining bolts to 22 inch lbs. (3.5 Nm).

25. Install the EGR valve injector so that the port is facing directly towards the throttle body.

26. Install the upper intake manifold assembly. Tighten the upper intake manifold nuts in the proper sequence to 22 ft. lbs. (30 Nm).

27. Install the MAP sensor.

28. Attach the electrical connectors to the MAP sensor, EGR solenoid valve, Idle Air Control (IAC) valve, Throttle Position (TP) sensor, and the fuel injectors.

29. Install the transaxle fill tube.

30. Install the power steering pump, then install the serpentine belt.

31. Connect the vacuum lines, as tagged during removal.

32. Install the air intake duct.

33. Refill the coolant system.

34. Connect the negative battery cable, then start the engine and check for leaks.

1.8L and 2.0L OHC Engines

EXCEPT TURBO

▶ See Figure 40

1. Release the fuel pressure.

2. Disconnect the negative battery cable.

3. Properly drain the cooling system into an approved container.

4. Remove the alternator and bracket at the camshaft carrier.

5. Remove the power steering pump, then position it aside with the lines still attached.

6. Remove the ignition coil.

7. Disconnect the throttle cable from the intake manifold bracket.

8. Detach the throttle and TV cables from the throttle body.

9. Disconnect the wiring from the throttle body.

10. Detach the vacuum brake hose at the filter.

11. Disconnect the coolant hoses at the water pump and intake manifold and the inlet tube-to-water pump.

12. For access to the lower retaining nuts, detach the ECM electrical harness.

13. Unfasten the retaining nuts and washers, then remove the intake manifold. Clean the mating surfaces of the cylinder head and intake manifold.

To install:

14. Place a new gasket on the cylinder head, then position the intake manifold. Tighten intake manifold retaining nuts and washers evenly in sequence to 20-25 ft. lbs. (27-34 Nm) for

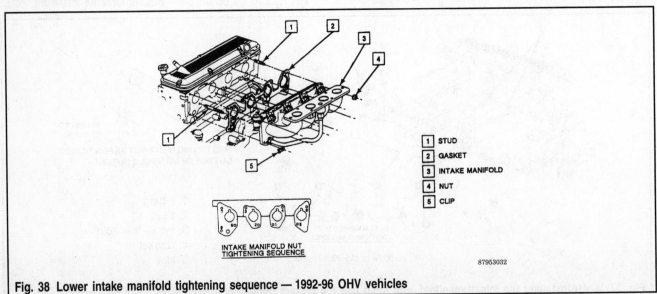

1	STUD
2	GASKET
3	INTAKE MANIFOLD
4	NUT
5	CLIP

INTAKE MANIFOLD NUT
TIGHTENING SEQUENCE

87953032

Fig. 38 Lower intake manifold tightening sequence — 1992-96 OHV vehicles

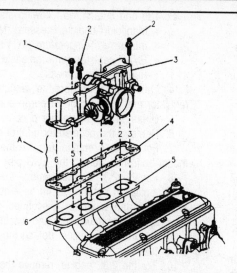

A UPPER INTAKE MANIFOLD
   ASSEMBLY TIGHTENING
   SEQUENCE
1 BOLT
2 STUD
3 UPPER INTAKE MANIFOLD ASSEMBLY
4 GASKET
5 LOWER INTAKE MANIFOLD
6 EGR VALVE INJECTOR

87953033

Fig. 39 The upper manifold bolts to the lower one, but be sure to use the correct sequence when tightening

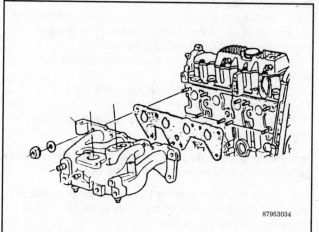

87953034

Fig. 40 Intake manifold mounting — 1.8L and 2.0L OHC engines; EXCEPT turbo

1982-86 and 16 ft. lbs. (22 Nm) for 1987-92. Start with the inner nuts and work outward.

15. Attach the ECM wiring harness.
16. Connect the coolant hoses at the water pump and intake manifold and the inlet tube-to-water pump.
17. Fasten the inlet and return fuel lines.
18. Connect the vacuum brake hose at the filter.
19. Attach the wiring at the throttle body.
20. Connect the throttle and TV cables to the throttle body. Attach the throttle cable to the intake manifold bracket.
21. Install the ignition coil.
22. Attach the power steering bracket to the intake manifold.
23. Install the power steering pump.
24. Attach the alternator and bracket to the camshaft carrier.
25. Fill the engine cooling system.
26. Install the air cleaner.
27. Connect the negative battery cable, then start the engine and check for leaks.

TURBO

▶ **See Figures 41 and 42**

1. Properly relieve the fuel system pressure.
2. Disconnect the negative battery cable.
3. Drain the cooling system into an approved container.
4. Unfasten the induction tube and hoses.
5. Detach the wiring to the throttle body, Manifold Absolute Pressure (MAP) sensor and the wastegate.
6. Disconnect the PCV hose, then detach the vacuum hose from the throttle body.
7. Detach the throttle cable and, if equipped, the cruise control cable.
8. Disconnect the wiring from the ignition coil.
9. Remove the manifold support bracket.
10. Unfasten the bolt attaching the rear alternator bracket to the alternator.
11. Remove the power steering adjusting bracket and the alternator front adjusting bracket.
12. Disconnect the fuel lines from the fuel rail inlet and the regulator outlet.

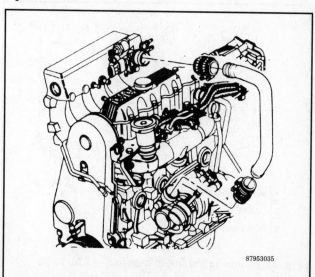

87953035

Fig. 41 Disconnect the turbo injection tube and hoses

13. Unfasten the retaining nuts and washers, then remove the intake manifold and gasket. If installing a new manifold, don't forget to transfer all necessary parts from the old manifold to the new one.

14. Clean the cylinder head and intake manifold mating surfaces so they are clean of old gasket material and other debris.

To install:

15. Place a new gasket on the cylinder head, then position the intake manifold. Tighten the retaining nuts and washers to 18 ft. lbs. (25 Nm).

16. Attach the fuel lines to the regulator outlet and fuel rail inlet.

➡Any time the rear power steering adjusting bracket is loosened or removed, proper adjusting bolt torque is essential for belt and pulley alignment. The rear adjusting bracket must be the last part secured to prevent distorting the accessory drive system to prevent the belt from coming off.

17. Install the power steering and alternator adjusting brackets.

18. Attach the wiring to the fuel injectors and ignition coil.

19. Connect the throttle cable and cruise control cable, if applicable.

20. Attach the vacuum hoses and PCV hose.

21. Connect the wiring to the throttle body, MAP sensor and wastegate.

22. Attach the induction tube and hoses.

23. Fill the engine cooling system.

24. Connect the negative battery cable, then start the engine and check for vacuum and/or fluid leaks and proper engine operation.

2.3L and 2.4L Engines

▶ **See Figures 43, 44, 45, 46, 47 and 48**

1. Properly relieve the fuel system pressure.

2. Disconnect the negative battery cable, then properly drain the cooling system.

3. Tag and detach the following electrical connectors:
- Manifold Absolute Pressure (MAP) sensor
- Intake Air Temperature (IAT) sensor
- EVAP canister purge solenoid
- Fuel injector harness

4. Label and disconnect the vacuum hoses from the fuel regulator and EVAP canister purge solenoid to canister.

5. Unfasten the air cleaner duct.

6. Remove the accelerator control cable bracket.

7. For the 2.4L engine, remove the stud-ended alternator mount bolt, then detach the EGR pipe from the EGR adapter.

8. For the 2.3L engine, remove the oil air separator (crankcase ventilation system) as an assembly. Leave the hoses attached to the separator. Disconnect the hoses from the oil fill, chain cover, intake duct and the intake manifold.

9. For the 2.3L engine, detach the oil/air separator from the oil fill tube.

10. For the 2.3L engine, remove the oil fill cap and oil level indicator assembly.

11. For the 2.3L engine, unfasten the oil fill tube bolt/screw, then pull the tube upward to remove.

12. Remove the fill tube out the top, rotating as necessary to gain clearance for the oil/air separator nipple between the intake tubes and fuel rail electrical harness.

13. For the 2.4L engine, raise and safely support the vehicle.

14. Remove the intake manifold support brace.

15. If raised, carefully lower the vehicle.

16. Unfasten the manifold retaining nuts and bolts, then remove the intake manifold from the engine.

➡If installing a new intake manifold, transfer all necessary parts from the old manifold to the new one.

17. Using a suitable scraping tool, clean the old gasket material from the intake manifold mating surfaces. Do NOT let any debris fall into the engine!

To install:

18. Install the manifold with a new gasket.

➡Make sure that the numbers stamped on the gasket are facing towards the manifold surface.

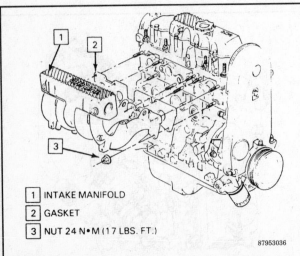

1 INTAKE MANIFOLD
2 GASKET
3 NUT 24 N•M (17 LBS. FT.)

87953036

Fig. 42 Removing the intake manifold — 2.0L turbo engine

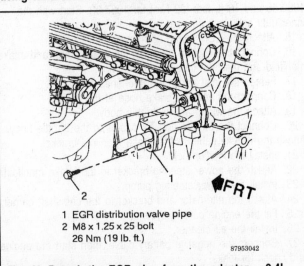

1 EGR distribution valve pipe
2 M8 x 1.25 x 25 bolt
26 Nm (19 lb. ft.)

87953042

Fig. 43 Detach the EGR pipe from the adapter — 2.4L engine only

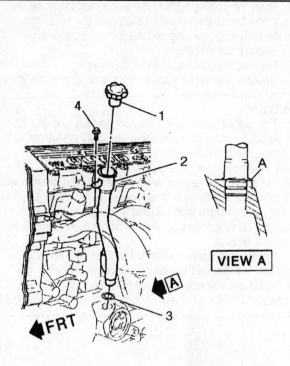

1. Oil fill cap
2. Oil fill tube
3. O-ring - Lubricate O-ring in engine oil before assembling
4. Oil fill tube bolt - (M6 x 1.00 x 16)
   8 Nm (71 lb. in.)
A. Fill tube flange must be seated firmly against block

87953043

Fig. 44 On the 2.3L engine, you must remove the oil fill tube

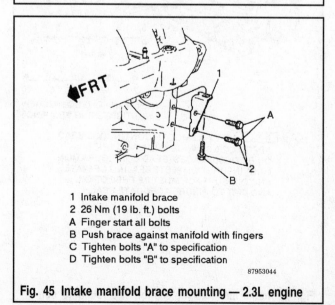

1 Intake manifold brace
2 26 Nm (19 lb. ft.) bolts
A Finger start all bolts
B Push brace against manifold with fingers
C Tighten bolts "A" to specification
D Tighten bolts "B" to specification

87953044

Fig. 45 Intake manifold brace mounting — 2.3L engine

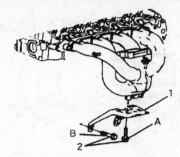

A Finger start all bolts
B Push against manifold with fingers
C Tighten bolts "A" to specification
D Tighten bolts "B" to specification
1 Intake manifold brace
2 Bolt

87953045

Fig. 46 For the 2.4L engine, you must raise the vehicle for access to the manifold brace

19. Follow the tightening sequence in the accompanying figure, then tighten the bolts/nuts to 19 ft. lbs. (26 Nm) for 2.3L engines and to 18 ft. lbs. (24 Nm) for 2.4L engines.

20. For the 2.4L engine, raise and safely support the vehicle.

21. Install the intake manifold brace and retainers.

22. If raised, carefully lower the vehicle.

23. For the 2.3L engine, install the oil/air separator assembly.

24. For the 2.3L engine, lubricate a new oil fill tube O-ring seal with clean engine oil, then install the tube down between intake manifold. Rotate as needed to gain clearance for the oil/air separator nipple on the fill tube.

25. If removed, position the oil fill tube in its cylinder block opening. Align the fill tube so it is in about its proper position. Place the palm of your hand over the oil fill opening and press straight down to seat the fill tube and O-ring into the cylinder block.

26. If necessary, connect the oil/air separator hose to the oil fill tube. You can lubricate the hose as necessary to ease installation. Install the oil fill tube bolt/screw. Fasten the cap.

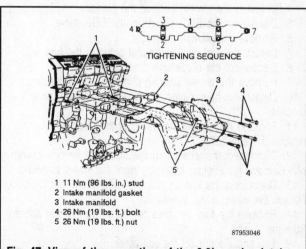

TIGHTENING SEQUENCE

1 11 Nm (96 lbs. in.) stud
2 Intake manifold gasket
3 Intake manifold
4 26 Nm (19 lbs. ft.) bolt
5 26 Nm (19 lbs. ft.) nut

87953046

Fig. 47 View of the mounting of the 2.3L engine intake manifold. When tightening the bolts, be sure to follow the proper tightening sequence

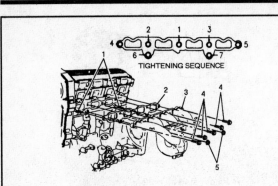

1 12 Nm (100 lb. in.) stud
2 Intake manifold gasket
3 Intake manifold
4 24 Nm (17 lb. ft.) bolt
5 24 Nm (17 lb. ft.) nut

87953047

Fig. 48 On the 2.4L engine, note that the sequence and torque for the intake manifold retaining bolts it different from that of the 2.3L engine

27. For the 2.4L engine, attach the EGR pipe to the adapter; tighten the fasteners to 19 ft. lbs. (26 Nm). Install the stud-ended alternator bolt.

28. Install the accelerator control cable bracket.

29. Connect the vacuum hoses to the fuel regulator and EVAP canister purge solenoid.

30. Attach all electrical connectors, as tagged during removal.

31. Install the air cleaner duct.

32. Refill the coolant to it's proper level.

33. Connect the negative battery cable, then start the engine and inspect for leaks.

2.8L and 3.1L Engines

1985-88 VEHICLES

▶ See Figure 49

1. Properly relieve the fuel system pressure.
2. Disconnect the negative battery cable.
3. Detach the accelerator and TV cable bracket at the plenum.
4. Unfasten the throttle body at the plenum.
5. Disconnect the EGR pipe from the EGR valve.
6. Remove the plenum assembly.
7. Detach the fuel inlet and outlet pipes at the fuel rail.
8. Disconnect the serpentine drive belt.
9. Remove the power steering pump mounting bracket.
10. Detach the heater pipe at the power steering pump bracket.
11. Tag and disconnect the wiring at the alternator, then remove the alternator.
12. Disconnect the wires from the cold start injector assembly. Remove the injector assembly from the intake manifold.
13. Disconnect the idle air vacuum hose at the throttle body. Detach the wires at the injectors.
14. Remove the fuel rail, breather tube and the fuel runners from the engine.
15. Tag and disconnect the coil wires.
16. Remove the rocker arm covers.

17. Drain the cooling system, the disconnect the radiator hose at the thermostat housing. Disconnect the heater hose from the thermostat housing and the thermostat wiring.

18. Remove the distributor.

19. Remove the thermostat assembly housing.

20. Unfasten the intake manifold bolts and remove the intake manifold from the engine.

To install:

21. The gaskets are marked for right and left side installation; do not interchange them. Clean the sealing surfaces of the engine block and intake manifold, and apply a $^3/_{16}$ in. (5mm) wide bead of silicone sealer to each ridge.

22. Place the new gaskets onto the heads. The gaskets will have to be cut slightly to fit past the center pushrods. Do not cut any more material than necessary. Hold the gaskets in place by extending the ridge bead of sealer $^1/_4$ in. (6mm) onto the gasket ends.

23. Position the intake manifold. The area between the ridges and the manifold should be completely sealed.

24. Install the retaining bolts and nuts, and tighten in sequence to 23 ft. lbs. (31 Nm). Do not overtighten; the manifold

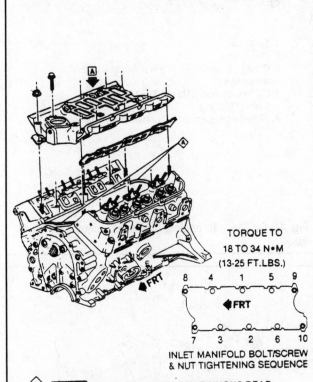

TORQUE TO
18 TO 34 N•M
(13-25 FT.LBS.)

INLET MANIFOLD BOLT/SCREW
& NUT TIGHTENING SEQUENCE

Ⓐ NOTE APPLY A SMOOTH CONTINUOUS BEAD APPROX. 2.0-3.0 WIDE AND 3.0-5.0 THICK ON BOTH SURFACES. BEAD CONFIGURATION MUST INSURE COMPLETE SEALING OF WATER AND OIL. SURFACE MUST BE FREE OF OIL AND DIRT TO INSURE ADEQUATE SEAL.

87953037

Fig. 49 Intake manifold installation and retaining bolt torque sequence — 1985 2.8L engine shown

is made from aluminum, and can be warped or cracked with excessive force.

25. The rest of installation is the reverse of removal. Adjust the ignition timing after installation, and check the coolant level after the engine has warmed up.

1989-93 VEHICLES

▶ See Figure 50

1. Properly relieve the fuel system pressure.
2. Disconnect the negative battery cable.
3. Detach the cables at the plenum.
4. Unfasten the brake vacuum pipe at the plenum.
5. Disconnect the throttle body and the EGR pipe from the EGR valve.
6. Remove the plenum assembly.
7. Disconnect the fuel line along the fuel rail.
8. Remove the serpentine drive belt.
9. Unfasten the alternator, then move it to one side. Loosen the alternator bracket.
10. Remove the power steering pump and move to one side.
11. Disconnect the idle air vacuum hose at the throttle body.
12. Detach the the wires at the fuel injectors.
13. Remove the fuel rail, breather tube and the fuel runners from the engine.
14. Tag and disconnect the plug wires at the manifold.
15. Remove the rocker arm covers; refer to the necessary service procedure located in this section.
16. Drain the cooling system, the disconnect the radiator hose at the thermostat housing. Disconnect the heater hose from the thermostat housing and tag and disconnect the thermostat wiring.
17. Unfasten the intake manifold bolts and remove the intake manifold from the engine.

➡Retain the Belleville washer in the same orientation on the 4 center bolts.

18. Loosen the rocker arms and remove the pushrods.

➡Intake pushrods are marked orange and are 6 in. (152.4mm) long. Exhaust pushrods are marked blue and are 6⅜ in. (161.9mm) long.

19. Remove and discard the intake manifold gasket.
   To install:
20. Clean the gasket material and grease from the mating surfaces.
21. Place a 0.08-0.12 in. (2-3mm) bead of RTV sealant on each ridge where the front and rear of the intake manifold contact the block.
22. Install the new intake manifold gasket.
23. Install the pushrods and make sure they are seated properly in the lifter.

➡Intake pushrods are marked orange and are 6 in. (152.4mm) long. Exhaust pushrods are marked blue and are 6⅜ in. (161.9mm) long.

24. Install the rocker arm nuts and tighten to 18 ft. lbs. (24 Nm).
25. Install the intake manifold and retaining bolts. Tighten the bolts to 15 ft. lbs. (20 Nm) in the proper sequence shown, then retighten in sequence to 24 ft. lbs. (33 Nm).

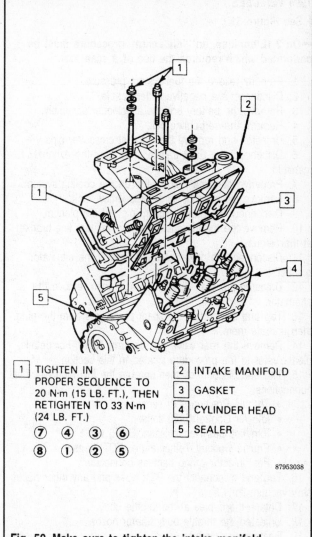

1	TIGHTEN IN PROPER SEQUENCE TO 20 N·m (15 LB. FT.), THEN RETIGHTEN TO 33 N·m (24 LB. FT.)	2	INTAKE MANIFOLD
	⑦ ④ ③ ⑥	3	GASKET
	⑧ ① ② ⑤	4	CYLINDER HEAD
		5	SEALER

87953038

Fig. 50 Make sure to tighten the intake manifold retaining bolts in the proper sequence — 1993 3.1L engine shown

26. Install the heater pipe to the manifold.
27. Connect the coolant sensor and any other necessary wiring.
28. Fasten the upper radiator hose.
29. Install the rocker arm covers.
30. Connect the breather tube.
31. Install the fuel rail and attach the wires to the injectors.
32. Connect the idle air vacuum hose at the throttle body.
33. Install the alternator and bracket.
34. Install the power steering gear and pump.
35. Connect the power steering line at the alternator bracket.
36. Install the serpentine drive belt.
37. Connect the fuel lines to the fuel rail and to the bracket.
38. Install the plenum, plug harness and EGR valve.
39. Install the throttle body.
40. Attach the cables at the plenum.
41. Connect the negative battery cable and fill the cooling system.

1994 VEHICLES

▶ See Figure 51

➥**On 3.1L engines, an "Idle Learn" procedure must be performed which requires the use of a scan tool.**

1. Properly relieve the fuel system pressure.
2. Disconnect the negative battery cable.
3. Remove the battery and the air cleaner assembly.
4. Remove the serpentine belt.
5. Unfasten and remove the exhaust crossover pipe.
6. Disconnect the EGR transfer tube from the exhaust manifold.
7. Properly drain and recover the engine cooling system.
8. Remove the radiator surge or overflow tank.
9. Disconnect the brake vacuum pipe at the plenum.
10. Remove the throttle cable and the vacuum line bracket at the plenum.
11. Disconnect the power steering lines at the alternator bracket.
12. Unfasten the rear alternator brace, then remove the alternator.
13. Tag and disconnect the spark plug wires from the plug, then unroute them.
14. Remove the rear valve (rocker arm) cover. For details, please refer to the procedure located in this section.
15. Tag and disconnect, then unroute the following electrical connections:
   • Throttle Position (TP) sensor
   • Idle Air Control (IAC) sensor
   • Exhaust Gas Recirculation (EGR) valve
   • Engine Coolant Temperature (ECT) sensor
   • Fuel injector wiring harness connector
16. Tag and disconnect the PCV hose and any other necessary vacuum lines.
17. Detach the cables at the throttle body.
18. Unfasten the throttle body heater hoses.
19. Remove the plenum.
20. Disconnect the fuel lines from the fuel rail and the fuel lines at the bracket.
21. Unfasten the power steering pump mounting bolts, then position the pump aside with the lines attached.
22. Disconnect the coolant bleed pipe from the thermostat housing.
23. Detach the heater pipe from the cylinder heads, thermostat housing and the water pump. Disconnect the upper radiator hose at the themostat housing.
24. Remove the thermostat housing.
25. As outlined earlier, remove the front valve (rocker arm) cover.

➥**When removing the manifold, make sure to retain the washers in the same orientation on the 4 center bolts.**

26. Unfasten the retaining bolts and/or nuts, then remove the intake manifold.
27. Loosen the rocker arms, then remove the pushrods.

➥**Intake pushrods are marked orange and are 6 in. (152.4mm) long. Exhaust pushrods are marked blue and are 6⅜ in. (161.9mm) long.**

28. Remove and discard the intake gasket, then clean the mating surfaces free of gasket material and old RTV sealant.

To install:

29. Place a 0.08-0.12 in. (2-3mm) bead of RTV sealant on each ridge where the front and rear of the intake manifold contact the block.

➥**Intake pushrods are marked orange and are 6 in. (152.4mm) long. Exhaust pushrods are marked blue and are 6⅜ in. (161.9mm) long.**

30. Position a new intake manifold gasket, then install the pushrods, making sure they seat in the lifters.
31. Tighten the rocker arm nuts to 18 ft. lbs. (25 Nm).
32. Position the intake manifold, then tighten the retaining bolts, in the proper sequence, in two steps; first to 15 ft. lbs. (20 Nm), then to 24 ft. lbs. (33 Nm).
33. Install the front valve (rocker arm) cover.
34. Attach the heater pipe to the manifold.
35. Install the thermostat housing, then attach the upper radiator hose to the housing.
36. Connect the heater pipe to the cylinder heads, water pump and themostat housing.
37. Attach the coolant bleed pipe to the thermostat housing.

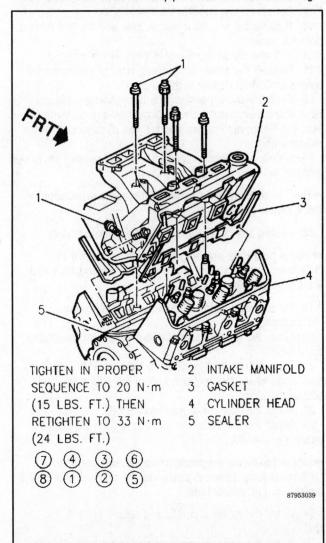

TIGHTEN IN PROPER SEQUENCE TO 20 N·m (15 LBS. FT.) THEN RETIGHTEN TO 33 N·m (24 LBS. FT.)

2 INTAKE MANIFOLD
3 GASKET
4 CYLINDER HEAD
5 SEALER

⑦ ④ ③ ⑥
⑧ ① ② ⑤

87953039

Fig. 51 When removing the intake manifold, be sure to keep the washers in the same orientation on the 4 center bolts

38. Install the power steering pump.

39. Attach the fuel lines to the fuel rail, the fasten fuel lines at the bracket.

40. Install the plenum.

41. Attach the throttle body heater hoses, then connect the cables to the throttle body.

42. Connect the PCV hose, and any other vacuum lines disconnected during removal.

43. Route and attach the following electrical connections, as tagged during removal:
   • TP sensor
   • IAC valve
   • EGR valve
   • ECT sensor
   • Fuel injector wiring harness connector

44. Install the rear valve (rocker arm) cover.

45. Route and connect all spark plug wires, as tagged during removal.

46. Install the alternator and the alternator brace, then attach the power steering line to the brace.

47. Attach the throttle cable and vacuum lines bracket to the plenum.

48. Connect the brake vacuum pipe to the plenum.

49. Install the radiator surge or overflow tank.

50. Attach the EGR transfer tube to the exhaust manifold.

51. Connect the exhaust crossover to the exhaust manifolds.

52. Install the air cleaner assembly and the battery, then connect the negative battery cable.

➡ On the 3.1L engine, a Tech 1® scan tool is needed to perform the "Idle Learn" procedure.

53. For the 3.1L engine perform the following "Idle Learn" procedure;
   a. Install a Tech 1® scan tool.
   b. Turn the ignition to the **ON** position, engine not running.
   c. Select **IAC SYSTEM**, then **IDLE LEARN** in the **MISC TEST** mode.
   d. Place the transaxle in park or neutral, as applicable.
   e. Proceed with idle learn as directed by the scan tool.

54. Fill the cooling system, then start the engine and check for leaks.

Exhaust Manifold

REMOVAL & INSTALLATION

1.8L, 2.0L and 2.2L OHV Engines
▶ See Figures 52 and 53

1. Disconnect the negative battery cable.
2. Detach the oxygen sensor wire.
3. Remove the serpentine belt or alternator drive belt.
4. Remove the alternator-to-bracket bolts, then support the alternator (with the wires attached) out of the way.
5. For 1982-84 vehicles equipped with the A.I.R. or pulse air system, disconnect the pipes and hoses.
6. Raise and support the vehicle safely.

7. Unfasten the exhaust pipe-to-exhaust manifold bolts, then carefully lower the vehicle.

8. If necessary for access to remove the manifold, remove the oil fill tube and disconnect the heater outlet hose assembly nut from the exhaust manifold.

9. Remove the exhaust manifold-to-cylinder head bolts.

10. Detach the exhaust manifold from the exhaust pipe flange.

11. Unfasten the retaining nuts, then remove the exhaust manifold from the vehicle. Remove and discard the gasket(s).

To install:

12. Using a gasket scraper, carefully clean the gasket mounting surfaces.

13. To install, use new gaskets and reverse the removal procedures. Tighten the exhaust manifold-to-cylinder head nuts to 3-12 ft. lbs. (4-16 Nm) and the bolts to 6-13 ft. lbs. (8-18 Nm).

14. Start the engine and check for exhaust leaks.

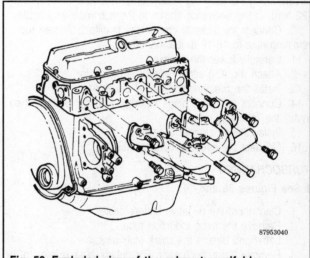

Fig. 52 Exploded view of the exhaust manifold mounting — 1982 OHV 1.8L engine shown

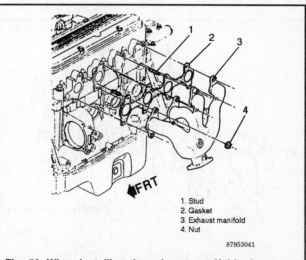

1. Stud
2. Gasket
3. Exhaust manifold
4. Nut

Fig. 53 When installing the exhaust manifold, always use a new gasket — 1995 OHV 2.2L engine shown

1.8L and 2.0L OHC Engines

EXCEPT TURBOCHARGER

▶ **See Figure 54**

1. Disconnect the negative battery cable.
2. Remove the air cleaner assembly.
3. Tag and disconnect the spark plug wires from the spark plugs, then remove the retainers.
4. Remove the oil dipstick tube and the breather.
5. Detach the Oxygen (O_2) sensor electrical connector.
6. Raise and safely support the vehicle.
7. Remove the exhaust pipe from the manifold, then support the pipe.
8. Unfasten the retaining nuts, then remove the exhaust manifold by lowering it from the bottom of the vehicle. Remove and discard the gasket. Clean the exhaust manifold and cylinder head gasket mating surfaces.

   To install:

9. Use a new gasket, position the exhaust manifold, then secure using the retaining nuts. Tighten the nuts to 16 ft. lbs. (22 Nm), in the sequence shown in the accompanying figure.
10. Connect the exhaust pipe to the manifold. Tighten the retaining nuts to 16-19 ft. lbs. (22-26 Nm).
11. Carefully lower the vehicle.
12. Attach the (O_2) sensor electrical connector.
13. Install the breather and the oil dipstick tube.
14. Connect the spark plugs as tagged during remove, then install the retainers.
15. Install the air cleaner assembly.
16. Connect the negative battery cable.

TURBOCHARGER

▶ **See Figures 55 and 56**

1. Disconnect the negative battery cable.
2. Remove the turbo induction tube.
3. Label and detach the spark plug wires.
4. Remove the turbocharger. For details, please refer to the procedure located later in this section.
5. If applicable, detach the wiring from the oxygen sensor.

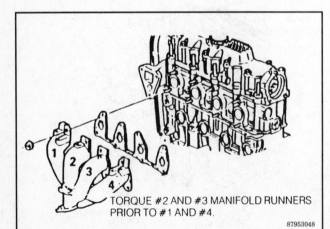

TORQUE #2 AND #3 MANIFOLD RUNNERS PRIOR TO #1 AND #4.

87953048

Fig. 54 When installing the exhaust manifold, tighten runners #2 and #3 before #1 and #4 — except 2.0L Turbo engines

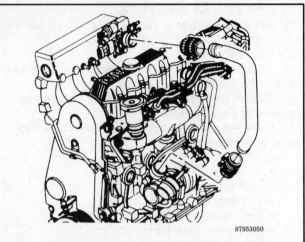

87953050

Fig. 55 Removing the turbo induction tube is simply a matter of unfastening the clamps, then removing the tube from the engine

6. Unfasten the bolts and nuts retaining the exhaust manifold to the block and exhaust pipe, then remove the manifold. Remove and discard the gasket.

   To install:

➡ Before installing a new gasket on the 1.8L MFI Turbo engine (code J), check for the location of the stamped part number on the surface. This gasket should be installed with this number toward the manifold. The gasket appears to be the same in either direction but it is not. Installing the gasket backwards will result in a leak.

7. Install the exhaust manifold with a new gasket. Install the retainers, then tighten (in the sequence shown in the accompanying figure) the studs to 20 ft. lbs. (27 Nm,) and the nuts to 16 ft. lbs. (22 Nm).
8. Connect the exhaust pipe to the exhaust manifold and tighten the nuts to 19 ft. lbs. (25 Nm).
9. Attach the wire to the oxygen sensor, if applicable.
10. Install the turbocharger. For details, please refer to the procedure located later in this section.
11. Connect the spark plug wires as tagged during removal.
12. Install the turbo induction tube.
13. Connect the negative battery cable.

2.3L and 2.4L Engines

▶ **See Figures 57, 58, 59, 60 and 61**

1. Disconnect the negative battery cable
2. Detach the Oxygen (O_2) sensor connector.
3. Raise and safely support the vehicle.
4. Unfasten the exhaust manifold brace-to-manifold bolt and the oil pan nuts, if necessary.
5. Remove the upper heat shield.
6. For the 2.3L engine, remove the manifold-to-exhaust pipe spring loaded nuts.

➡ Do NOT bend the exhaust flex decoupler more than necessary to remove it. Excessive movement will damage the flex decoupler.

7. For the 2.4L engine, remove the manifold-to-exhaust flex decoupler fasteners.

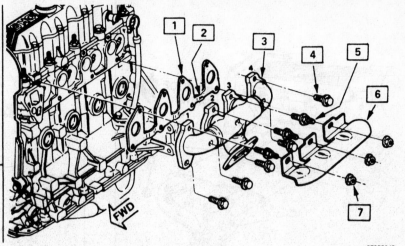

1—GASKET
2—EXPANSION JOINTS
　　FACE OUTWARD
3—MANIFOLD ASM.
4—BOLT & LOCKWASHER ASM.
　　27 N·m (20 LB.FT.)
5—STUD BOLT & LOCKWASHER
　　ASM. 27 N·m (20 LB.FT.)
6—SHIELD
7—NUT 22 N·m (16 LB.FT.)

TORQUE NO. 2 & 3 MANIFOLD
RUNNERS PRIOR TO NO. 1 & 4
RUNNERS

87953049

Fig. 56 Exhaust manifold mounting and retainer tightening sequence — 2.0L engine

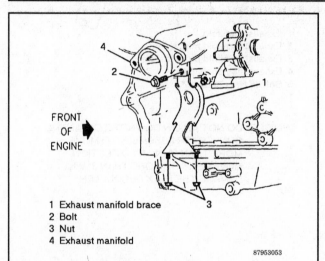

FRONT
OF
ENGINE

1 Exhaust manifold brace
2 Bolt
3 Nut
4 Exhaust manifold

87953053

Fig. 57 On the 2.4L engine, remove the bolt and nuts, then remove the brace

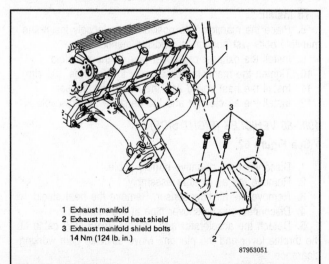

1 Exhaust manifold
2 Exhaust manifold heat shield
3 Exhaust manifold shield bolts
　14 Nm (124 lb. in.)

87953051

Fig. 58 Unfasten the retaining bolts, then remove the heat shield — 2.4L engine shown, 2.3L similar

8. Pull down and back on the exhaust pipe to disengage it from the exhaust manifold bolts.

9. Carefully lower the vehicle.

10. Unfasten the exhaust manifold-to-cylinder head retaining nuts/bolts, then remove the manifold. Remove and discard the gaskets and/or seals. Clean the mating surfaces.

To install:

11. Use gaskets, then position the exhaust manifold. Tighten the retaining nuts to 31 ft. lbs. (42 Nm) for the 2.3L engine or to 110 inch lbs. (12.5 Nm) for the 2.4L engine, in the sequence shown in the accompanying figures.

12. Raise and safely support the vehicle.

13. Install the heat shield. Tighten the bolts to 124 inch lbs. (14 Nm).

14. Fasten the exhaust manifold brace-to-manifold bolt and the oil pan nuts. Tighten the bolts to 41 ft. lbs. (56 Nm) and the nuts to 19 ft. lbs. (26 Nm).

15. For the 2.3L engine, install the manifold-to-exhaust pipe nuts. Be sure to turn both nuts in evenly to avoid cocking the exhaust pipe and binding the nuts.

16. For the 2.4L engine, install the manifold-to-flex decoupler fasteners. Tighten the bolts to 26 ft. lbs. (35 Nm).

17. Carefully lower the vehicle.

18. Attach the O_2 connector. Coat the threads of the sensor with anti-seize compound 5613695 or equivalent.

19. Connect the negative battery cable and check for leaks.

2.8L and 3.1L Engines

1985-86 VEHICLES (LEFT SIDE)

▶ See Figure 62

1. Disconnect the negative battery cable.
2. Remove the air cleaner assembly.
3. Remove the air flow sensor.
4. Unfasten, then remove the engine heat shield.
5. Detach the crossover pipe at the exhaust manifold.
6. Unfasten the exhaust manifold bolts, then remove the manifold.
7. Clean the surfaces of the cylinder head and manifold.

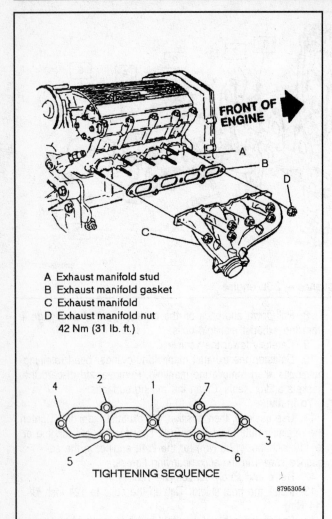

A Exhaust manifold stud
B Exhaust manifold gasket
C Exhaust manifold
D Exhaust manifold nut
   42 Nm (31 lb. ft.)

TIGHTENING SEQUENCE

87953054

Fig. 59 When installing the exhaust manifold, always use a new gasket and tighten the retainers in the correct sequence — 2.3L engine

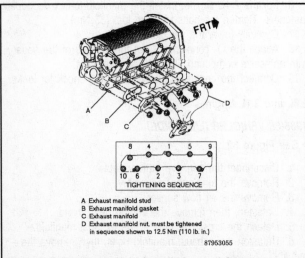

A Exhaust manifold stud
B Exhaust manifold gasket
C Exhaust manifold
D Exhaust manifold nut, must be tightened
   in sequence shown to 12.5 Nm (110 lb. in.)

87953055

Fig. 60 Exhaust manifold installation and fastener tightening sequence — 2.4L engine

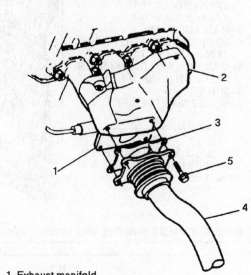

1 Exhaust manifold
2 Exhaust manifold heat shield
3 Exhaust manifold pipe gasket
4 Exhaust flex decoupler
5 Bolt 35 Nm (26 lb. ft.)

NOTICE: DO NOT ALLOW DOWNPIPE CATALYTIC CONVERTER ASSEMBLY TO MOVE MORE THAN 3" IN ANY DIRECTION. MOVEMENT OF MORE THAN 3" WILL DAMAGE THE FLEX DECOUPLER.

87953056

Fig. 61 Installing the exhaust flex decoupler, which is found on the 2.4L engine

To install:

8. Place the manifold into position, then loosely install the manifold bolts just enough to hold the manifold.
9. Install the exhaust crossover pipe to the manifold.
10. Tighten the manifold bolts evenly to 25 ft. lbs. (34 Nm).
11. Install the heat shield and the mass flow sensor.
12. Install the air cleaner and the negative battery cable.

1985-86 VEHICLES (RIGHT SIDE)

▶ **See Figure 62**

1. Disconnect the negative battery cable.
2. Remove the air cleaner assembly.
3. Remove the air flow sensor. Remove the heat shield.
4. Disconnect the crossover pipe at the manifold.
5. Detach the accelerator and Throttle Valve (TV) cable at the throttle lever and the plenum. Move aside to gain working clearance.
6. Disconnect the power steering line at the power steering pump.
7. Remove the EGR valve assembly.
8. Raise and safely support the vehicle.

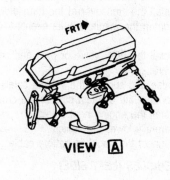

VIEW A

VIEW B

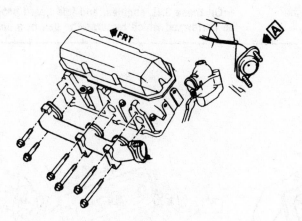

87953057

Fig. 62 Exhaust manifold removal and installation — 1985-86 2.8L engines

9. Disconnect the exhaust pipe at the exhaust manifold.

10. Carefully lower the vehicle.

11. Unfasten the exhaust manifold bolts, then remove the manifold.

12. Clean the surfaces of the cylinder head and manifold.

To install:

13. Place the manifold into position and loosely install the retaining bolts just enough to hold the manifold.

14. Raise and safely support the vehicle.

15. Install the exhaust pipe at the manifold.

16. Carefully lower the vehicle.

17. Tighten the manifold bolts, evenly, to 25 ft. lbs. (34 Nm).

18. Install the EGR valve and related parts.

19. Connect the power steering line at the power steering pump.

20. Attach the accelerator and throttle valve cable at the throttle lever and the plenum.

21. Connect the crossover pipe at the manifold.

22. Install the heat shield and the mass air flow sensor.

23. Install the air cleaner assembly and connect the negative battery cable.

1987-93 VEHICLES (LEFT SIDE)

▶ See Figures 63, 64 and 65

1. Disconnect the negative battery cable.

2. Remove the air cleaner assembly.

3. Remove the air cleaner inlet hose and the mass air flow sensor, on models so equipped.

4. Properly drain the coolant, then remove the coolant by-pass pipe

5. Remove the heat shield.

6. Disconnect the exhaust crossover pipe at the manifold.

7. Unfasten the exhaust manifold bolts and remove the exhaust manifold or manifold/crossover assembly.

To install:

8. Clean the surfaces of the cylinder head and manifold.

9. Using a new gasket, place the manifold into position and loosely install the manifold bolts.

10. Attach the exhaust crossover pipe to the manifold.

11. Tighten the exhaust manifold bolts evenly to 18-21 ft. lbs. (24-28 Nm).

12. Install the heat shield. Tighten the nuts to 89 inch lbs. (10 Nm).

13. Connect the coolant pipe.

14. Install the air cleaner inlet hose and the air cleaner assembly

15. Fill the cooling system.

16. Connect the negative battery cable.

1987-93 VEHICLES (RIGHT SIDE)

▶ See Figures 63, 64 and 65

1. Disconnect the negative battery cable.
2. For 1993 vehicles, remove the air cleaner assembly.
3. Raise and safely support the vehicle.
4. Remove the heat shield.
5. Disconnect the exhaust pipe at the crossover.
6. Carefully lower the vehicle.
7. Remove the EGR valve or pipe.
8. Disconnect the oxygen sensor wire.
9. Unfasten the exhaust manifold bolts, then remove the manifold.

10. Clean the mating surfaces of the cylinder head and manifold. Discard the gasket.

To install:

11. Use a new manifold gasket, place the manifold into position and loosely install the manifold bolts.

12. Install the crossover at the manifold.

13. Tighten the manifold bolts evenly to 21-25 ft. lbs. (28-34 Nm).

14. Install the EGR valve or pipe and connect the oxygen sensor wire.

15. Raise and support the vehicle safely.

16. Connect the exhaust pipe to the crossover.

17. Install the engine heat shield.

18. Carefully lower the vehicle.

19. Connect the negative battery cable.

1994 VEHICLES (LEFT SIDE)

▶ See Figure 66

➡On these 3.1L engines, and Idle Learn procedure must be performed which requires the use of a scan tool.

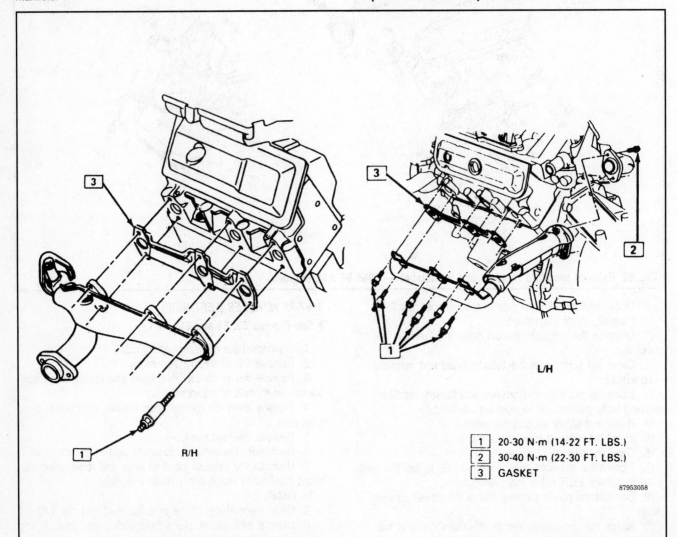

1	20-30 N·m (14-22 FT. LBS.)
2	30-40 N·m (22-30 FT. LBS.)
3	GASKET

87953058

Fig. 63 Exhaust manifold removal and installation — 1987 2.8L engine shown

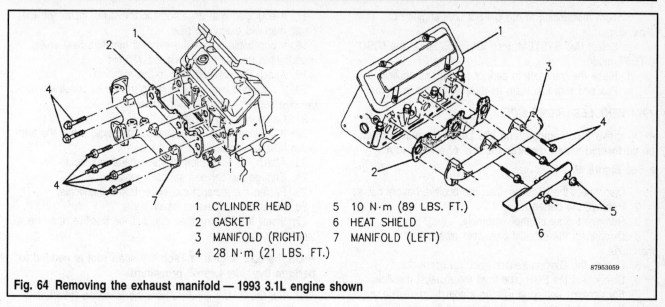

1 CYLINDER HEAD   5 10 N·m (89 LBS. FT.)
2 GASKET   6 HEAT SHIELD
3 MANIFOLD (RIGHT)   7 MANIFOLD (LEFT)
4 28 N·m (21 LBS. FT.)

87953059

Fig. 64 Removing the exhaust manifold — 1993 3.1L engine shown

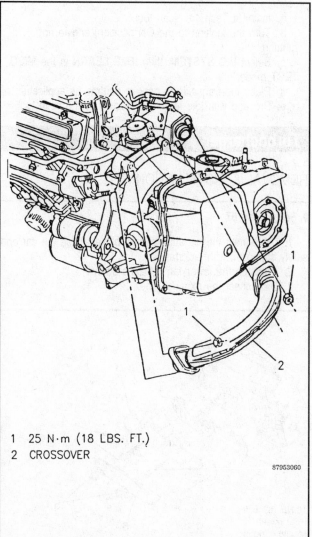

1 25 N·m (18 LBS. FT.)
2 CROSSOVER

87953060

Fig. 65 The exhaust crossover pipe on the 3.1L engines is retained by two nuts

1. Disconnect the negative, then the positive battery cables.
2. Remove the battery.
3. Remove the air cleaner assembly.
4. Raise and safely support the vehicle.
5. Unfasten the lower cooling fan bolt and detach the electrical connector.
6. Carefully lower the vehicle.
7. Remove the cooling fan assembly.
8. Disconnect the exhaust crossover pipe.
9. Tag and disconnect the left side spark plug wires from the spark plugs and position aside.
10. Remove the exhaust manifold heat shield.
11. Unfasten the retaining bolts, then remove the exhaust manifold.
12. Clean the mating surfaces of the cylinder head and manifold. Discard the gasket.

To install:

13. Use a new manifold gasket, place the manifold into position and loosely install the manifold bolts.
14. Tighten the exhaust manifold bolts to 21 ft. lbs. (28 Nm).
15. Install the exhaust manifold heat shield. Tighten the retaining nuts to 89 inch lbs. (10 Nm).
16. Attach the spark plug wires to the plugs, as tagged during removal.
17. Fasten the exhaust crossover pipe to the manifolds.
18. Install the cooling fan, and secure with the upper retaining bolts.
19. Raise and safely support the vehicle.
20. Install the lower cooling fan assembly bolt and attach the electrical connector.
21. Carefully lower the vehicle.
22. Install the air cleaner assembly.
23. Install the battery, then connect the positive, then the negative battery cables.

➡**On the 3.1L engine, a Tech 1® scan tool is needed to perform the "Idle Learn" procedure.**

24. For the 3.1L engine perform the following "Idle Learn" procedure;
   a. Install a Tech 1® scan tool.

b. Turn the ignition to the **ON** position, engine not running.

c. Select **IAC SYSTEM**, then **IDLE LEARN** in the **MISC TEST** mode.

d. Place the transaxle in park or neutral, as applicable.

e. Proceed with idle learn as directed by the scan tool.

1994 VEHICLES (RIGHT SIDE)

➡On these 3.1L engines, and Idle Learn procedure must be performed which requires the use of a scan tool.

▶ **See Figure 66**

1. Disconnect the negative, then the positive battery cables.
2. Remove the battery.
3. Remove the air cleaner assembly.
4. Disconnect the exhaust crossover pipe from the manifolds.
5. Detach the Oxygen sensor electrical connector.
6. Disconnect the EGR pipe from the exhaust manifold.
7. For vehicles equipped with an automatic transaxle, remove the transaxle fluid level indicator and fill tube.
8. Raise and safely support the vehicle.
9. For vehicles equipped with an automatic transaxle, remove the suspension support crossmember brace.
10. For vehicles equipped with a manual transaxle, remove the heat shield. If equipped with an automatic transaxle, remove the nut but do not remove the heat shield from the vehicle at this time.
11. Disconnect the exhaust pipe from the exhaust manifold.
12. If equipped with an automatic transaxle, remove the exhaust manifold extension pipe.
13. Unfasten the retaining bolts, then remove the exhaust manifold from the vehicle. If equipped with an automatic transaxle, remove the heat shield with the exhaust manifold.
14. Clean the mating surfaces of the cylinder head and manifold. Discard the gasket.

To install:

15. Use a new manifold gasket, place the manifold (and heat shield, if automatic) into position and loosely install the manifold bolts.
16. Tighten the exhaust manifold bolts to 21 ft. lbs. (28 Nm).

17. If equipped with an automatic transaxle, install the exhaust manifold extension pipe.
18. If applicable, install the exhaust manifold heat shield, then tighten the nut to 89 inch lbs. (10 Nm).
19. Attach the exhaust pipe to the manifold.
20. If equipped with an automatic transaxle, install the suspension support crossmember brace.
21. Carefully lower the vehicle.
22. If equipped with an automatic transaxle, install the transaxle fluid level indicator and fill tube.
23. Attach the EGR pipe to the exhaust manifold.
24. Engage the Oxygen sensor connector.
25. Fasten the exhaust crossover to the manifolds.
26. Install the air cleaner assembly.
27. Install the battery, then connect the positive, then negative battery cables.

➡On the 3.1L engine, a Tech 1® scan tool is needed to perform the "Idle Learn" procedure.

28. For the 3.1L engine perform the following "Idle Learn" procedure;

a. Install a Tech 1® scan tool.

b. Turn the ignition to the **ON** position, engine not running.

c. Select **IAC SYSTEM**, then **IDLE LEARN** in the **MISC TEST** mode.

d. Place the transaxle in park or neutral, as applicable.

e. Proceed with idle learn as directed by the scan tool.

Turbocharger

REMOVAL & INSTALLATION

▶ **See Figure 67**

1. Disconnect the negative battery cable. Raise the car and safely support it with jackstands.
2. Unfasten the lower fan retaining screw.
3. Disconnect the exhaust pipe.

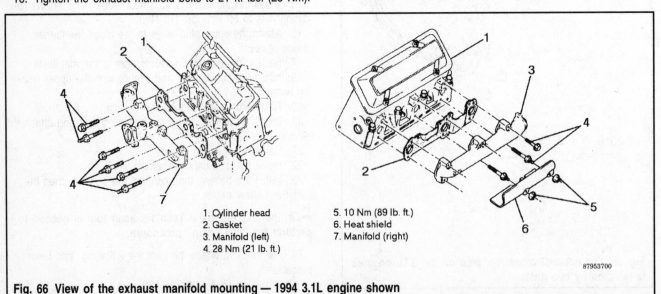

1. Cylinder head
2. Gasket
3. Manifold (left)
4. 28 Nm (21 lb. ft.)
5. 10 Nm (89 lb. ft.)
6. Heat shield
7. Manifold (right)

87953700

Fig. 66 View of the exhaust manifold mounting — 1994 3.1L engine shown

4. Remove the rear air conditioning support bracket and loosen the remaining bolts.

5. Remove the turbo support bracket-to-engine bolt.

6. Disconnect the oil drain hose at the turbocharger.

7. Carefully lower the vehicle.

8. Disconnect the coolant recovery pipe, then move it to one side.

9. Detach the induction tube.

10. Remove the cooling fan.

11. Disconnect, then remove the oxygen sensor.

12. Unfasten the oil feed pipe at the union. Disconnect the water feed pipe.

13. Disconnect the air intake duct and vacuum hose at the actuator.

14. Unfasten the exhaust manifold retaining nuts and remove the exhaust manifold and turbocharger.

To install:

15. Install the exhaust manifold and turbocharger. Tighten the bolts evenly to 16 ft. lbs. (22 Nm).

16. Install the exhaust manifold retaining nuts.

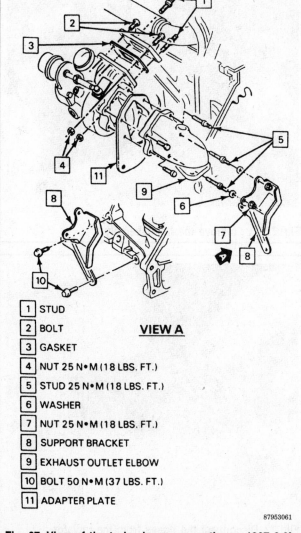

1	STUD
2	BOLT
3	GASKET
4	NUT 25 N•M (18 LBS. FT.)
5	STUD 25 N•M (18 LBS. FT.)
6	WASHER
7	NUT 25 N•M (18 LBS. FT.)
8	SUPPORT BRACKET
9	EXHAUST OUTLET ELBOW
10	BOLT 50 N•M (37 LBS. FT.)
11	ADAPTER PLATE

VIEW A

87953061

Fig. 67 View of the turbocharger mounting — 1987 2.0L MFI-Turbo shown

17. Attach the air intake duct and vacuum hose at the actuator.

18. Connect the oil feed pipe at the union.

19. Attach the oxygen sensor.

20. Install the cooling fan.

21. Connect the induction tube.

22. Position and attach the coolant recovery pipe.

23. Raise and safely support the vehicle.

24. Fasten the rear turbo support bracket bolt to the engine.

25. Install the rear air conditioning support bracket.

26. Connect the oil drain hose at the turbocharger.

27. Fasten the lower fan screw.

28. Attach the exhaust pipe.

29. Connect the negative battery cable, then start the engine and check for intake and/or exhaust leaks.

Radiator

REMOVAL & INSTALLATION

❊❊CAUTION

When draining the coolant, keep in mind that cats and dogs are attracted by ethylene glycol antifreeze, and are quite likely to drink any that is left in an uncovered container or in puddles on the ground. This will prove fatal in sufficient quantity. Always drain the coolant into a sealable container. Coolant should be reused unless it is contaminated or several years old.

1982-94 Vehicles

▶ See Figures 68, 69, 70, 71, 72, 73, 74, 75, 76 and 77

1. Disconnect the negative battery cable.

2. Properly drain and recover the cooling system into an approved container.

3. If necessary for access, remove the air cleaner cover and air cleaner.

4. Remove any necessary upper radiator/air duct shrouding.

5. Detach the forward lamp harness from the frame and unplug the fan connector.

6. Unfasten the fan frame-to-radiator support attaching bolts and then remove the fan assembly.

7. Scribe a line around the hood latch for installation purposes, then remove the latch from the radiator support.

8. If equipped, remove the radiator air inlet ducts.

9. Disconnect the upper and lower radiator hoses and the coolant recovery hose from the radiator.

10. Detach the transmission oil cooler lines from the radiator and wire them out of the way. If equipped with A/C, remove the 4 radiator to condenser bolts and the radiator tank to refrigerant line clamp bolt.

11. Unfasten the radiator-to-radiator support attaching bolts and clamps, then remove the radiator from the vehicle.

To install:

12. Place the radiator in the vehicle so that the bottom is positioned in the lower mounting pads. Tighten the attaching bolts and clamps.

13. If equipped with A/C, tighten the 4 radiator-to-condenser bolts and the condenser bolt-to-refrigerant line clamp bolt.

Fig. 68 Unfasten the upper radiator shrouding/air duct retaining bolts, then . . .

Fig. 69 . . . remove the shrouding to expose the fan assembly

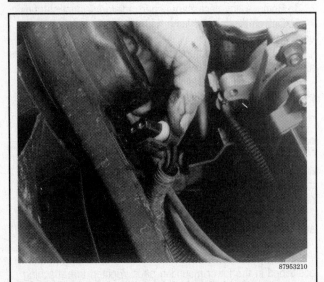

Fig. 70 Detach the radiator fan electrical connector

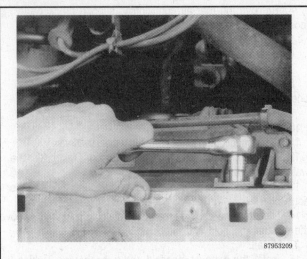

Fig. 71 Unfasten the fan-to-radiator support retaining bolts, then . . .

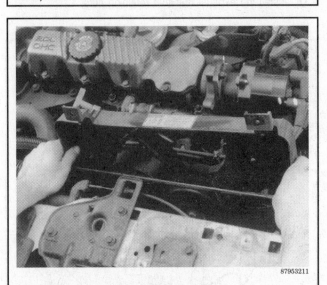

Fig. 72 . . . remove the fan assembly

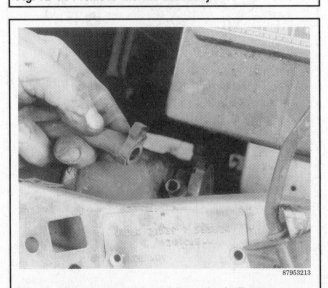

Fig. 73 Disconnect the hoses from the radiator

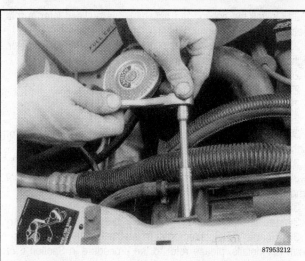

Fig. 74 Unfasten the radiator-to-support retaining bolts, then . . .

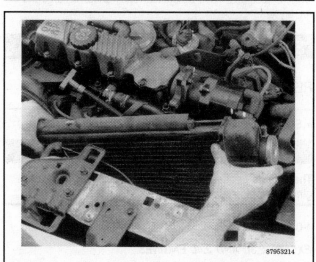

Fig. 75 . . . remove the radiator assembly from the vehicle

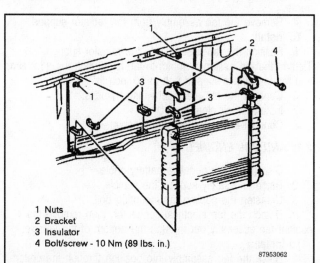

1 Nuts
2 Bracket
3 Insulator
4 Bolt/screw - 10 Nm (89 lbs. in.)

87953062

Fig. 76 The radiator is secured using brackets and retaining bolts and/or screws — 1994 2.2L engine shown

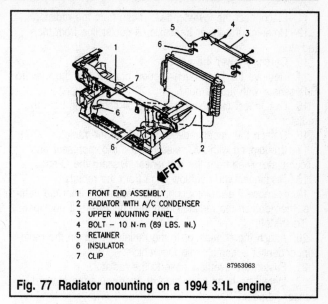

1 FRONT END ASSEMBLY
2 RADIATOR WITH A/C CONDENSER
3 UPPER MOUNTING PANEL
4 BOLT – 10 N·m (89 LBS. IN.)
5 RETAINER
6 INSULATOR
7 CLIP

87953063

Fig. 77 Radiator mounting on a 1994 3.1L engine

14. Connect the transmission oil cooler lines, then tighten the bolts to 20 ft. lbs. (27 Nm).

15. Attach the upper and lower radiator hoses and the coolant recovery hose to the radiator.

16. Install the radiator air inlet ducts.

17. Install the fan, making sure the bottom leg of the frame fits into the rubber grommet (if used) at the lower radiator support. Install the retaining bolts and tighten them to 80 inch lbs. (9 Nm).

18. Fasten the fan connector, then attach the forward lamp harness to the fan frame. If used, be sure to connect the engine ground strap to the strut brace.

19. Install any necessary upper radiator shrouding.

20. Fill the coolant system, connect the negative battery cable, then check for coolant leaks.

1995-96 Vehicles

▶ See Figure 78

➡For 1996 vehicles, when adding coolant, it is very important to use GM Goodwrench DEX-COOL®, which is an orange colored, silicate free coolant. If silicated coolant is used on these vehicles, premature engine, heater core and/or radiator corrosion may result. In addition, the engine coolant will require change sooner, at 30,000 miles (50,000km) or 24 months.

1. If equipped with A/C, have a certified repair shop recover the refrigerant.

2. Disconnect the negative battery cable.

3. Disable the Supplemental Inflatable Restraint (SIR) system. For details, please refer to the procedure located in Section 6 of this manual.

4. Properly drain and recover the coolant in an approved container.

5. Unfasten the hood latch from the mounting plate.

6. Remove the right and left headlamp assemblies.

7. Remove the radiator mounts.

8. Raise and safely support the vehicle.

9. Detach the forward SIR sensor harness.

10. Remove the cooling fan assembly. For details, please refer to the procedure located later in this section.

11. Disconnect the lower radiator hose from the radiator.

12. Unfasten the lower transaxle oil cooler line from the radiator.

13. Carefully lower the vehicle.

14. Remove the hood latch support bracket and the forward SIR sensor with the harness.

15. Disconnect the upper transaxle oil cooler line from the radiator.

16. Detach the upper radiator hose from the radiator.

17. If equipped with A/C, disconnect the compressor and accumulator lines from the condenser. Discard the O-rings.

18. Disconnect the overflow hose from the radiator.

19. Remove the radiator/condenser assembly from the vehicle, then detach the radiator from the condenser, if equipped.

To install:

20. Attach the condenser to the radiator. Position the radiator/condenser assembly into the vehicle.

21. Fasten the overflow hose to the radiator.

22. Install the hood latch bracket, then route the forward sensor harness.

23. Raise and safely support the vehicle.

24. Install the cooling fan assembly, as outlined later in this section.

25. Fasten the lower transaxle oil cooler line to the radiator, tighten to 22 ft. lbs. (30 Nm).

26. Connect the lower radiator hose.

27. Attach the forward SIR sensor connector.

28. Carefully lower the vehicle.

29. Attach the upper radiator hose.

30. Fasten the upper transaxle oil cooler line to the radiator, tighten to 22 ft. lbs. (30 Nm).

31. Install the hood latch support.

32. If equipped, using new O-rings, connect the compressor and accumulator hoses to the condenser.

33. Install the left and right headlamp assemblies.

34. Install the hood latch assembly, then adjust if necessary.

35. Enable the Supplemental Inflatable Restraint (SIR) system. For details, please refer to the procedure in Section 6 of this manual.

36. Connect the negative battery cable.

37. If equipped, have a certified repair shop recharge the A/C system.

Electric Cooling Fan

REMOVAL & INSTALLATION

▶ See Figures 79 and 80

✳✳CAUTION

The electric cooling fan can start whether or not the engine is running.

4-Cylinder Engines

EXCEPT 2.3L AND 2.4L ENGINES

1. Disconnect the negative battery cable.

2. Remove the air cleaner duct.

3. Detach the wiring harness from the motor and the fan frame.

4. Remove the fan assembly from the radiator support.

To install:

5. Position the fan assembly to the radiator support. Tighten the fan assembly motor-to-fan to 29 inch lbs. (3.2 Nm) and fan-to-radiator support bolt to 80 inch lbs. (9 Nm).

6. Connect the fan electrical wiring harness.

7. Install the air cleaner duct.

8. Connect the negative battery cable.

2.3L AND 2.4L ENGINES

1. Disconnect the negative battery cable.

2. Raise and safely support the vehicle.

3. Unfasten the cooling fan mounting bolt.

4. Detach the fan electrical connector, then remove the coolant fan assembly out through the bottom of the vehicle.

To install:

5. Raise the fan assembly into position through the bottom of the vehicle.

6. Attach the fan electrical connector, then install the mounting bolt. Tighten the bolt to 53 inch lbs. (6 Nm).

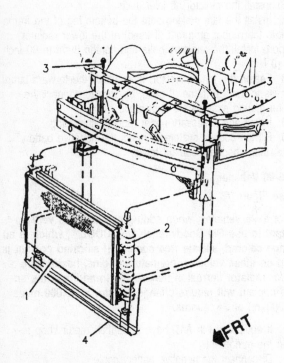

1 Condensor
2 Radiator
3 Upper radiator support bolt
4 Lower tie bar

87953064

Fig. 78 Radiator removal and installation — 1995-96 vehicles

7. Connect the negative battery cable.

6-Cylinder Engines

1. Disconnect the negative battery cable. Drain engine coolant to level below the upper radiator hose.

2. Remove the air cleaner duct and the air cleaner assembly.

3. Scribe a latch position mark for reassembly purposes, then remove the main hood latch assembly.

4. Disconnect the upper radiator hose from the radiator and position aside.

5. On vehicles equipped with an automatic transaxle, disconnect, then position the transaxle cooler lines aside.

6. Detach the electrical wiring harness connector at the coolant fan, then remove the fan assembly from the radiator support.

To install:

7. Position the fan assembly onto the radiator support. Tighten the fan assembly motor-to-fan bolt to 29 inch lbs. (3.2 Nm) and fan-to-radiator support bolt to 80 inch lbs. (9 Nm).

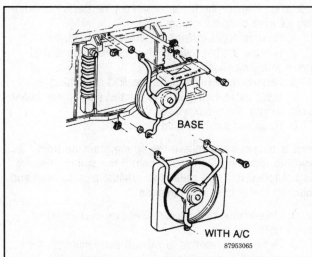

Fig. 79 Early model cooling fans; with and without A/C — 1982 vehicle shown

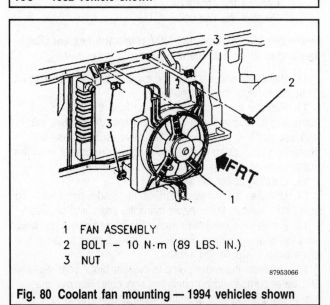

1 FAN ASSEMBLY
2 BOLT – 10 N·m (89 LBS. IN.)
3 NUT

87953066

Fig. 80 Coolant fan mounting — 1994 vehicles shown

8. Attach the fan electrical wiring harness.

9. For automatic transaxle equipped vehicles, connect the transaxle oil cooler lines to to the radiator.

10. Using the marks scribed during removal for alignment, install the main hood latch.

11. Install the air cleaner assembly and duct.

12. Properly refill the engine cooling system, then connect the negative battery cable.

Water Pump

REMOVAL & INSTALLATION

✳✳CAUTION

When draining the coolant, keep in mind that cats and dogs are attracted by ethylene glycol antifreeze, and are quite likely to drink any that is left in an uncovered container or in puddles on the ground. This will prove fatal in sufficient quantity. Always drain the coolant into a sealable container. Coolant should be reused unless it is contaminated or several years old.

1.8L, 2.0L and 2.2L OHV Engines

▶ **See Figures 81 and 82**

1. Disconnect the negative battery cable.

2. Properly drain the cooling system into an approved container.

3. Remove all accessory drive belts or the serpentine belt.

4. Remove the alternator and bracket. For details, please refer to Section 2 of this manual.

5. Unscrew the water pump pulley mounting bolts and then pull off the pulley.

6. Unfasten the mounting bolts, then remove the water pump.

7. Using a putty knife, clean the gasket mounting surfaces.

To install:

8. Place a ⅛ in. (3mm) wide bead of RTV sealant on the water pump sealing surface or install a new gasket, on models so equipped. Install the pump and tighten the retaining bolts to 18 ft. lbs. (25 Nm).

9. Install the water pump pulley, then tighten the mounting bolts to 22 ft. lbs. (30 Nm).

10. As outlined in Section 2, install the alternator and bracket.

11. Install the drive belts or serpentine belt, as applicable.

12. Fill the cooling system to the proper level.

13. Connect the negative battery cable, then start the engine and check for leaks.

1.8L and 2.0L OHC Engines

▶ **See Figure 83**

1. Disconnect the negative battery cable.

2. Properly drain the engine cooling system into an approved container.

3. Remove the timing belt as described later in this section.

4. Remove the timing belt rear protective covers.

5. Disconnect the hose from the water pump.

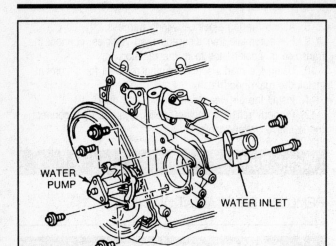

Fig. 81 Water pump mounting — 1982 1.8L OHV engine shown

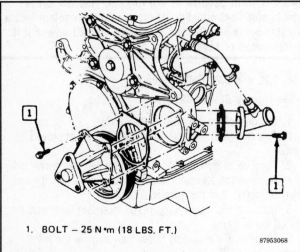

1. BOLT – 25 N•m (18 LBS. FT.)

Fig. 82 Location and mounting of the water pump on the 2.0L and 2.2L OHV engines

6. Unfasten the retaining bolt(s), then remove the water pump and seal ring. Inspect the ring for damage and replace if necessary. Clean the pump mating surfaces.

To install:

7. Install the seal ring and water pump. Do not fully tighten the retaining bolts. They will be tightened to specification during installation of the timing belt.

8. Connect the hose to the water pump.

9. Install the timing belt rear protective covers.

10. Install the timing belt and adjust it to specifications, as outlined later in this section. Tighten the water pump mounting bolts to 18-21 ft. lbs. (21-25 Nm).

11. Fill the engine cooling system to the proper level.

12. Connect the negative battery cable, then start the engine and check for leaks and make sure the coolant level is correct.

2.3L and 2.4L Engines

▶ See Figure 84

1. Disconnect the negative battery cable
2. Detach the oxygen sensor connector.

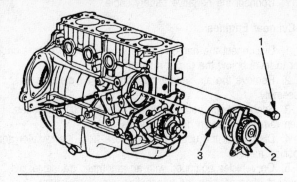

1 28 Nm (21 lb. ft.) bolt
2 Water pump
3 Seal ring

Fig. 83 Water pump location on the 1.8L and 2.0L OHC engines

3. Properly drain the engine coolant into a suitable container. Remove the heater hose from the thermostat housing for more complete coolant drain.

4. Remove upper exhaust manifold heat shield.

5. Remove the bolt that attaches the exhaust manifold brace to the manifold.

6. Remove the lower exhaust manifold heat shield.

7. Break loose the manifold to exhaust pipe spring loaded bolts using a 13mm box wrench.

8. Raise and safely support the vehicle.

➡**It is necessary to relieve the spring pressure from 1 bolt prior to removing the second bolt. If the spring pressure is not relieved, it will cause the exhaust pipe to twist and bind up the bolt as it is removed.**

9. Unfasten the two radiator outlet pipe-to-water pump cover bolts.

10. Remove the manifold to exhaust pipe bolts from the exhaust pipe flange as follows:
    a. Unscrew either bolt clockwise 4 turns.
    b. Remove the other bolt.
    c. Remove the first bolt.

➡**On the 2.4L engines, DO NOT rotate the flex coupling more than 4° or damage may occur.**

11. Pull down and back on the exhaust pipe to disengage it from the exhaust manifold bolts.

12. Remove the radiator outlet pipe from the oil pan and transaxle. If equipped with a manual transaxle, remove the exhaust manifold brace. Leave the lower radiator hose attached and pull down on the outlet pipe to remove it from the water pump. Leave the radiator outlet pipe hang.

13. Carefully lower the vehicle.

14. Unfasten the exhaust manifold-to-cylinder head retaining nuts, then remove the exhaust manifold, seals and gaskets.

15. For the 2.4L engine, remove the front timing chain cover and the chain tensioner. For details, please refer to the procedure located later in this section.

16. Unfasten the water pump-to-cylinder block bolts. Remove the water pump-to-timing chain housing nuts. Remove the water pump and cover mounting bolts and nuts. Remove the

water pump and cover as an assembly, then separate the two pieces.

To install:

17. Thoroughly clean and dry all mounting surfaces, bolts and bolt holes. Using a new gasket, install the water pump to the cover and tighten the bolts finger-tight.

18. Lubricate the splines of the water pump with clean grease and install the assembly to the engine using new gaskets. Install the mounting bolts and nuts finger-tight.

19. Lubricate the radiator outlet pipe O-ring with antifreeze and slid the pipe onto the water pump cover. Instal the bolts finger-tight.

20. With all gaps closed, tighten the bolts, in the following sequence, to the proper values:

    a. Pump assembly-to-chain housing nuts — 19 ft. lbs. (26 Nm).

    b. Pump cover-to-pump assembly — 106 inch lbs. (12 Nm).

    c. Cover-to-block, bottom bolt first — 19 ft. lbs. (26 Nm).

    d. Radiator outlet pipe assembly-to-pump cover — 125 inch lbs. (14 Nm).

21. Using new gaskets, install the exhaust manifold. Make sure to following the tightening sequence and torque specifications given in the exhaust manifold procedure located in this section.

22. Raise and safely support the vehicle.

23. Index the exhaust manifold bolts into the exhaust pipe flange.

24. Connect the exhaust pipe to the manifold. Install the exhaust pipe flange bolts evenly and gradually to avoid binding. Turn the bolts in until fully seated.

25. Connect the radiator outlet pipe to the transaxle and oil pan. Install the exhaust manifold brace, if removed.

26. On the 2.4L engine, install the timing chain tensioner and front cover.

27. Install the lower heat shield.

28. Carefully lower the vehicle.

29. Fasten the bolt that attaches the exhaust manifold brace to the manifold.

30. Tighten the manifold-to-exhaust pipe nuts to specification.

31. Install the upper heat shield.

32. Attach the oxygen sensor connector.

33. Fill the radiator with coolant until it comes out the heater hose outlet at the thermostat housing. Then connect the heater hose. Leave the radiator cap off.

34. Connect the negative battery cable, then start the engine. Run the vehicle until the thermostat opens, fill the radiator and recovery tank to their proper levels, then turn the engine off.

35. Once the vehicle has cooled, recheck the coolant level.

2.8L and 3.1L Engines

▶ See Figure 85

1. Disconnect battery negative cable.

2. Properly drain and recover the cooling system into an approved container.

3. Disconnect the serpentine belt at the water pump pulley.

4. On 1985-86 models, if equipped with A/C, disconnect the wires at the air conditioning pressure cycling switch and remove the cycling switch.

5. Unfasten the water pump pulley retaining bolts, then remove the pulley.

6. Unfasten the pump attaching bolts, then remove the water pump.

To install:

7. Clean the gasket mating surfaces.

8. Using a new gasket, install the water pump, then tighten the pump to block bolts to 18 ft. lbs. (24 Nm) for 2.8L engines and to 89 inch lbs. (10 Nm) for 3.1L engines.

9. Install the water pump pulley. Tighten the mounting bolt to 15 ft. lbs. (20 Nm).

10. On 1985-86 models, if equipped, install the air conditioning pressure cycling switch and connect the wires.

11. Install the serpentine belt.

12. Fill the cooling system to the proper level.

13. Connect the negative battery cable, then start the engine and check for leaks.

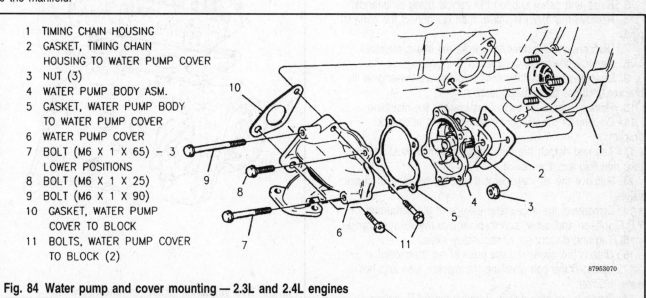

1	TIMING CHAIN HOUSING
2	GASKET, TIMING CHAIN HOUSING TO WATER PUMP COVER
3	NUT (3)
4	WATER PUMP BODY ASM.
5	GASKET, WATER PUMP BODY TO WATER PUMP COVER
6	WATER PUMP COVER
7	BOLT (M6 X 1 X 65) – 3 LOWER POSITIONS
8	BOLT (M6 X 1 X 25)
9	BOLT (M6 X 1 X 90)
10	GASKET, WATER PUMP COVER TO BLOCK
11	BOLTS, WATER PUMP COVER TO BLOCK (2)

87953070

Fig. 84 Water pump and cover mounting — 2.3L and 2.4L engines

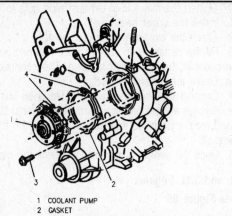

1 COOLANT PUMP
2 GASKET
3 BOLT — 10 N·m (89 LBS. IN.)
4 LOCATOR (MUST BE VERTICAL)

87953071

Fig. 85 Water (coolant) pump mounting — 2.8L and 3.1L engines

Cylinder Head

REMOVAL & INSTALLATION

1.8L, 2.0L and 2.2L OHV Engines

1982-86 VEHICLES

▸ See Figure 86

➡ **The engine should be overnight cold before removing the cylinder head.**

1. Disconnect the negative battery cable.
2. Relieve the fuel system pressure.
3. Drain the cooling system into a clean container; the coolant can be reused if it is still good.
4. Remove the air cleaner assembly.
5. Raise and safely support the vehicle using jackstands.
6. Remove the exhaust shield, then disconnect the exhaust pipe.
7. Disconnect the heater hose from the intake manifold.
8. Carefully lower the vehicle.
9. Unscrew the mounting bolts and remove the engine lift bracket (includes air management).
10. Remove (mark for correct installation) the distributor.
11. Disconnect the vacuum manifold at the alternator bracket.
12. Tag and detach the remaining vacuum lines at the intake manifold and thermostat.
13. Remove the air management pipe at the exhaust check valve.
14. Disconnect the accelerator linkage at the carburetor or T.B.I. unit, as applicable, and then remove the linkage bracket.
15. Tag and disconnect all necessary wires.
16. Detach the upper radiator hose at the thermostat.
17. Unfasten the bolt attaching the dipstick tube and hot water bracket.
18. Remove the idler pulley. Remove the A.I.R. and/or power steering pump drive belts.

19. For early model vehicles, unfasten the A.I.R. bracket-to-intake manifold bolt. If equipped with power steering, remove the air pump pulley, the A.I.R. through-bolt and the power steering adjusting bracket. Loosen the A.I.R. mounting bracket lower bolt so that the bracket will rotate.
20. If equipped with power steering, remove the power steering pump and lay aside with the lines still attached.
21. Disconnect and plug the fuel line(s) at the carburetor or TBI.
22. Remove the alternator with the wires attached and position aside. Remove the alternator brace from the head, then remove the upper mounting bracket.
23. Remove the rocker arm (valve) cover. Remove the rocker arms and pushrods.
24. Remove the cylinder head bolts in the reverse order given in the illustration. Remove the cylinder head with the carburetor or T.B.I. unit, intake and exhaust manifolds still attached.

To install:
25. To install, the gasket surfaces on both the head and the block must be clean of any foreign matter and free of any

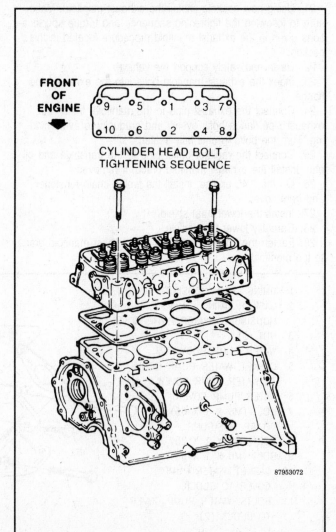

FRONT OF ENGINE

CYLINDER HEAD BOLT TIGHTENING SEQUENCE

87953072

Fig. 86 This sequence MUST be followed when installing the cylinder head bolts — 1982-86 1.8L and 2.0L OHV engines

nicks or heavy scratches. Cylinder bolt threads in the block and the bolt must be clean.

26. Place a new cylinder head gasket in position over the dowel pins on the block. Carefully guide the cylinder head into position.

27. Coat the cylinder bolts with sealing compound and install them finger tight.

28. Using a torque wrench, tighten the cylinder head bolts as follows:

    a. 1982-85 vehicles: gradually tighten the bolts to 65-75 ft. lbs. (88-102 Nm) in the sequence shown in the illustration.

    b. 1986 vehicles: gradually tighten the bolts to 70-73 ft. lbs. (95-95 Nm) in the sequence shown in the illustration.

29. Install the rocker arms and pushrods and adjust the valve lash.

30. Install the cylinder head cover.

31. Install the alternator brace on the head, then fasten the upper mounting bracket.

32. Attach the wires, then install the alternator.

33. Connect the fuel line at the carburetor.

34. Install the A.I.R. bracket-to-intake manifold bolt. If equipped with power steering, install the air pump pulley, the A.I.R. through-bolt and the power steering adjusting bracket.

35. Install the idler pulley. Install the A.I.R. and/or power steering pump drive belts.

36. Install the bolt attaching the dipstick tube and hot water bracket.

37. Connect all wires, as tagged during removal.

38. Install the upper radiator hose at the thermostat.

39. Install the linkage bracket and connect the accelerator linkage at the carburetor or TBI.

40. Install the air management pipe at the exhaust check valve.

41. Connect the remaining vacuum lines at the intake manifold and thermostat.

42. Install the distributor.

43. Connect the vacuum manifold at the alternator bracket.

44. Install the engine lift bracket (includes air management).

45. Install the heater hose at the intake manifold.

46. Connect the exhaust pipe.

47. Install the exhaust shield.

48. Install the air cleaner.

49. Fill the cooling system.

50. Connect the negative battery cable, then start the engine and check for leaks.

1987-91 VEHICLES

▶ See Figures 87 and 88

➡The engine must be cold before removing the cylinder head. Always release the fuel pressure before starting repair.

1. Relieve the fuel system pressure.

2. Disconnect the negative battery cable.

3. Properly drain the cooling system into a suitable container.

4. Remove the TBI cover.

5. Raise and safely support the vehicle.

6. Remove the exhaust shield. Disconnect the exhaust pipe.

7. Detach the heater hose from the intake manifold.

8. Remove the accelerator and TV cable bracket.

9. Carefully lower the vehicle.

10. Tag and disconnect the remaining vacuum lines at the intake manifold.

11. Disconnect the accelerator linkage at the TBI unit.

12. Tag and detach all necessary wires.

13. Unfasten the upper radiator hose at the thermostat.

14. Remove the serpentine belt.

15. Remove the power steering pump and lay aside with the fluid lines attached.

16. Make sure the fuel system pressure is released, then disconnect and plug the fuel lines.

17. Remove the alternator with the wires attached. Remove the rear alternator brace.

18. Remove the rocker arm (valve) cover. Remove the rocker arms and pushrods keeping all parts in order for correct installation.

19. Unfasten the cylinder head bolts. Remove the cylinder head with the TBI unit, intake and exhaust manifolds still attached.

To install:

20. The gasket surfaces on both the head and the block must be clean of any foreign matter and free of any nicks or heavy scratches. Bolt threads in the block and the bolts must be clean.

21. Place a new cylinder head gasket in position over the dowel pins on the block. Carefully guide the cylinder head into position.

22. Coat the cylinder bolts with sealing compound and install them finger tight.

23. For 1987-89 vehicles, tighten the long bolts to 73-83 ft lbs. (99-113 Nm) and the short bolts to 62-70 ft lbs. (85-95 Nm), in the sequence shown in the illustration.

24. For 1990-91 vehicles, tighten the bolts twice, in the sequence shown in the accompanying figure. For the first pass, tighten the long bolts to 23 ft. lbs. (32 Nm) and the short bolts and stud to 22 ft. lbs. (29 Nm). Make a second pass, tightening the long bolts to 78 ft. lbs. (106 Nm) and the short bolts to 66 ft. lbs. (90 Nm).

25. Install the pushrods and rocker arms, then install the rocker arm (valve) cover.

26. Install the alternator brace, connect the wires, then install the alternator.

27. Attach the fuel lines.

28. Install the power steering pump.

29. Install the serpentine belt.

30. Fasten the upper radiator hose at the thermostat.

31. Connect the wires as tagged during removal.

32. Attach the accelerator linkage at the throttle body.

33. Connect the vacuum lines at the intake manifold and thermostat.

34. Raise and safely support the vehicle.

35. Connect the heater hose to the intake manifold.

36. Install the accelerator and T.V. cable bracket.

37. Fasten the exhaust pipe, then carefully lower the vehicle.

38. Install the TBI cover.

39. Properly fill the cooling system, then connect the negative battery cable. Start the engine and check for leaks.

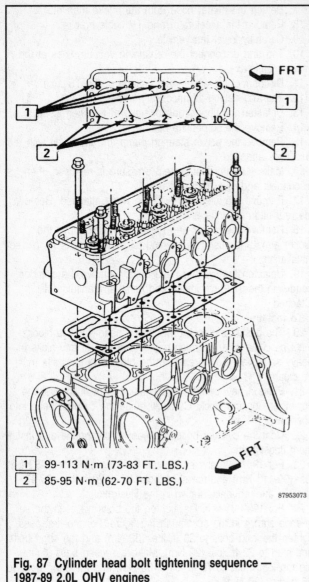

1   99-113 N·m (73-83 FT. LBS.)

2   85-95 N·m (62-70 FT. LBS.)

87953073

**Fig. 87 Cylinder head bolt tightening sequence —
1987-89 2.0L OHV engines**

1992-96 VEHICLES

▶ **See Figure 89**

➡**The engine must be cold before removing the cylinder
head. Always release the fuel pressure before starting
repair.**

1. Properly relieve the fuel system pressure.
2. Disconnect the negative battery cable.
3. Drain the cooling system into an approved container.
4. Label and disconnect the vacuum lines.
5. Tag and detach the following electrical connections:
   - Idle Air Control (IAC) valve
   - Throttle Position (TP) sensor
   - Manifold Absolute Pressure (MAP) sensor
   - EVAP emission solenoid
   - Fuel injector harness
   - Exhaust Gas Recirculation (EGR) valve
6. Disconnect the accelerator linkage, T.V. cable, cruise
control cable (if equipped), and the splash shield at the throttle
body.
7. Remove the coolant reservoir (overflow or surge tank).

8. Remove the serpentine belt.
9. Unfasten the alternator rear brace, then remove the
alternator.
10. Disconnect the power steering lines, then remove the
pump.
11. Remove the serpentine drive belt tensioner.
12. Tag and disconnect the spark plug wires from the plugs.
13. Detach the EVAP canister purge line from beneath the
manifold.
14. Disconnect the upper radiator hose from the thermostat.
15. Unfasten the throttle body cables from the bracket.
16. Remove the transaxle fill tube and level indicator.
17. Disconnect the coolant inlet hose on the cylinder head.
18. Detach and plug the fuel lines.
19. Disconnect the heater hose from the cylinder head.
20. Remove the intake manifold brace (located on the power
steering bracket).
21. Remove the rocker arm (valve) cover. Remove the
rocker arms and pushrods keeping all parts in order for correct
installation.
22. Remove the spark plug wire bracket and the engine lift
bracket.
23. Raise and safely support the vehicle.
24. Disconnect the exhaust pipe from the manifold. You may
have to remove the oil filter to access, so don't forget to drain
the crankcase first!
25. Carefully lower the vehicle.
26. Unfasten the cylinder head bolts, then remove the head.
   To install:
27. The gasket surfaces on both the head and the block
must be clean of any foreign matter and free of any nicks or
heavy scratches. Bolt threads in the block and the bolts must
be clean.
28. Place a new cylinder head gasket in position over the
dowel pins on the block. Carefully guide the cylinder head into
position. Install the cylinder head bolts finger tight.
29. Tighten the bolts, in the sequence shown in the accompanying figure, as follows:
   a. Long bolts: tighten to 46 ft. lbs. (63 Nm).
   b. Short bolts: tighten to 43 ft. lbs. (58 Nm).
   c. Tighten all bolts, in sequence, an additional angle of
   90° using tool J 36660 or equivalent.
30. Install the engine lift bracket and the spark plug wire
bracket.
31. Install the pushrods and rocker arms, then install the
rocker arm (valve) covers.
32. Fasten the intake manifold brace to the power steering
bracket.
33. Unplug, then connect the fuel lines.
34. Connect the coolant inlet hose onto the cylinder head.
35. Attach the upper radiator hose to the thermostat
housing.
36. Connect the EVAP emission canister purge line under
the manifold.
37. Attach the throttle body cables and bracket.
38. Install the transaxle level indicator and fill tube, secure
with the retaining bolt.
39. Connect the spark plug wires, as tagged during removal.
40. Install the serpentine drive belt tensioner.
41. Install the power steering pump, then connect the fluid
lines.
42. Install the alternator and rear brace.

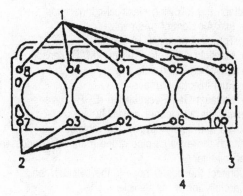

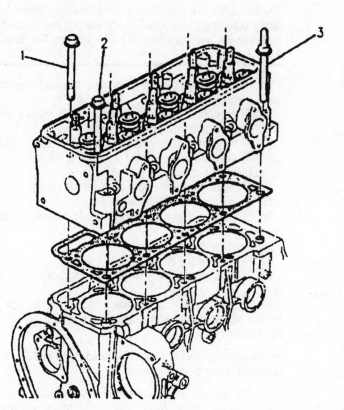

1. Long bolts
2. Short bolts
3. Stud
4. Numbers on gasket indicate torque sequence

87953074

Fig. 88 Cylinder head bolt tightening sequence — 1990-91 2.2L OHV engines

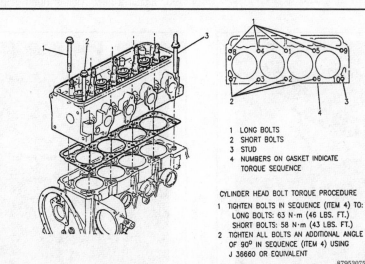

1 LONG BOLTS
2 SHORT BOLTS
3 STUD
4 NUMBERS ON GASKET INDICATE TORQUE SEQUENCE

CYLINDER HEAD BOLT TORQUE PROCEDURE

1 TIGHTEN BOLTS IN SEQUENCE (ITEM 4) TO:
   LONG BOLTS: 63 N·m (46 LBS. FT.)
   SHORT BOLTS: 58 N·m (43 LBS. FT.)
2 TIGHTEN ALL BOLTS AN ADDITIONAL ANGLE
   OF 90° IN SEQUENCE (ITEM 4) USING
   J 36660 OR EQUIVALENT

87953075

Fig. 89 Cylinder head bolt torque sequence for 1992-96 2.2L engines

43. Fasten the serpentine drive belt.

44. Install the coolant recovery reservoir (overflow or surge tank).

45. Route and connect the vacuum lines, as tagged during removal.

46. Attach the following electrical connectors:
   - Idle Air Control (IAC) valve
   - Throttle Position (TP) sensor
   - Manifold Absolute Pressure (MAP) sensor
   - EVAP emission solenoid
   - Fuel injector harness
   - Exhaust Gas Recirculation (EGR) valve

47. Install the air cleaner assembly.

48. Raise and safely support the vehicle.

49. Attach the exhaust pipe at the manifold. If necessary, install an oil filter.

50. Connect the heater hose to the cylinder head.

51. Carefully lower the vehicle.

52. Refill the crankcase and the coolant.

53. Connect the negative battery cable, then bleed the power steering system. For details, please refer to Section 8 of this manual.

54. Start the engine and check for leaks.

1.8L and 2.0L OHC Engines

▶ See Figures 90, 91, 92, 93, 94, 95, 96, 97, 98, 99 and 100

1. Properly relieve the fuel system pressure.

2. Disconnect the negative battery cable.

3. Remove air cleaner or induction tube (turbo engines).

4. Drain cooling system.

5. Remove alternator and pivot bracket at camshaft carrier housing.

6. Remove power steering pump and bracket, then position aside.

7. Detach ignition coil electrical connections and remove coil.

8. Tag and disconnect spark plug wires and distributor cap and remove.

9. Remove throttle cable from bracket at intake manifold.

10. Disconnect throttle cable, downshift cable and T.V. cable from the throttle body assembly.

11. Detach the ECM connectors from throttle body assembly.

12. Remove vacuum brake hose at filter.

13. Disconnect inlet and return fuel lines at flex joints.

❊❊CAUTION

The fuel lines are pressurized. Removal may cause fuel spray resulting in personal injury. Do not remove before bleeding the pressure from the fuel system. See Section 1 for the procedure.

14. Remove water pump bypass hose at intake manifold and water pump.

15. Disconnect ECM harness connectors at intake manifold.

16. Detach the heater hose from intake manifold.

17. Disconnect exhaust pipe at exhaust manifold. On turbo engines, disconnect the exhaust manifold at the turbo connection.

18. Disconnect breather hose at camshaft carrier.

19. Remove upper radiator hose.

20. Disconnect engine electrical harness and wires from thermostat housing.

21. Remove timing cover.

22. Remove timing probe holder.

23. Loosen water pump retaining bolts and remove timing belt.

24. Loosen camshaft carrier and cylinder head attaching bolts a little at a time, in the sequence shown in the accompanying figure.

➡**Camshaft carrier and cylinder head bolts should only be removed when engine is cold.**

25. Remove camshaft carrier assembly.

26. Remove cylinder head, intake manifold and exhaust manifold as an assembly. Remove and discard the gasket.

27. The gasket surfaces on both the head and the block must be clean of any foreign matter and free of any nicks or heavy scratches. Bolt threads in the block and the bolts must be clean.

To install:

28. Install a new cylinder head gasket in position on the block.

Fig. 90 Remove the alternator and bracket from the camshaft carrier housing

Fig. 91 Unfasten the camshaft carrier/cylinder head bolt in sequence

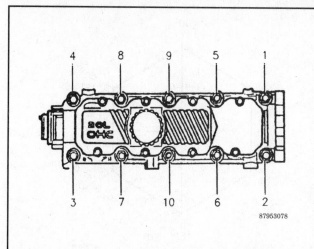

Fig. 92 Camshaft carrier and cylinder head bolt loosening sequence — 1.8L and 2.0L OHC engines

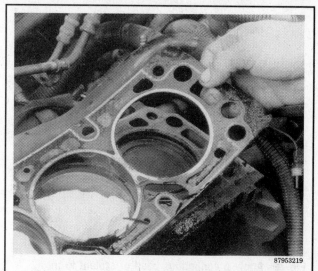

Fig. 95 Remove and discard the cylinder head gasket

Fig. 93 Remove the retaining bolts, then . . .

Fig. 96 Carefully use a suitable scraper to clean the gasket mating surfaces

29. Apply a continuous bead of sealer to the cam carrier.

30. Install the cylinder head, reassembled with the intake and exhaust manifolds, if removed.

31. Position the camshaft carrier on the cylinder head and tighten the bolts, in the sequence in the accompanying figure, to the correct torque.

   a. Tighten all bolts in sequence to 18 ft. lbs. (25 Nm).

   b. Tighten all bolts an additional 180° in 3 steps of 60° each.

32. Install timing belt.

33. Install timing probe holder.

34. Install timing cover.

35. Connect engine electrical harness and wires at thermostat housing.

36. Install upper radiator hose.

37. Connect breather hose at camshaft carrier.

38. Connect exhaust pipe at exhaust manifold. On turbo engines, connect the exhaust manifold at the turbo connection.

39. Connect heater hose at intake manifold.

40. Attach the ECM harness connectors at intake manifold.

Fig. 94 Remove the camshaft carrier/cylinder head, intake manifold and exhaust manifold as an assembly

Fig. 97 Apply a continuous bead of sealant to the camshaft carrier mating surface

Fig. 98 Tighten the cylinder head/camshaft carrier retaining bolts in sequence and to the proper torque specifications to avoid leakage, or other engine damage

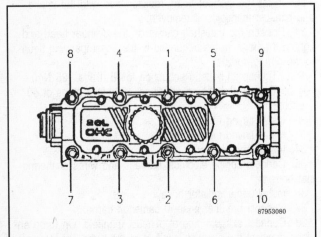

Fig. 99 Camshaft carrier and cylinder head bolts tightening sequence — 1.8L and 2.0L OHC engines

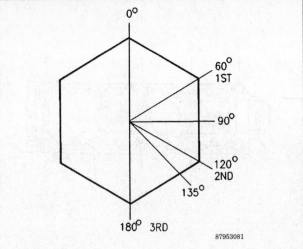

Fig. 100 Tighten all bolts an additional 60°, three times (in sequence)

41. Install water pump bypass hose at intake manifold and water pump.

42. Connect inlet and return fuel lines at flex joints.

43. Install vacuum brake hose at filter.

44. Attach the ECM connectors at throttle body assembly.

45. Connect throttle cable, downshift cable and T.V. cable at throttle body assembly.

46. Install throttle cable at bracket on intake manifold.

47. Connect the spark plug wires as tagged during removal, then install the distributor cap.

48. Attach the ignition coil electrical connections, then install the coil.

49. Install power steering pump and bracket.

50. Install alternator and pivot bracket on camshaft carrier housing.

51. Fill cooling system.

52. Install air cleaner or induction tube (turbo engines).

2.3L Engines

▶ See Figures 101 and 102

1. Properly relieve the fuel system pressure.

2. Disconnect the negative battery cable, then drain cooling system into a suitable container.

3. Detach the heater inlet and throttle body heater hoses from water outlet. If accessible at this time, disconnect the upper radiator hose from the water outlet.

4. Remove the exhaust manifold. For details, please refer to the procedure located in this section.

5. Remove the intake and exhaust camshaft housings.

6. Unfasten the oil fill tube bolt/screw then remove the oil fill cap and level indicator assembly. Pull the oil fill tube upward to unseat from block.

7. Label and disengage the injector harness electrical connector.

8. Detach the throttle body-to-air intake duct.

9. Tag and disconnect the power brake vacuum hose from the throttle body.

10. Remove the throttle cable bracket.

11. Remove the throttle body from the intake manifold with the electrical harness and throttle cable attached and position the assembly aside.

12. Tag and disconnect the MAP sensor vacuum hose from the intake manifold, then remove the intake manifold brace.

13. Detach the electrical connectors from the MAP sensor, IAT sensor and the EVAP canister purge solenoid.

14. If not already done, detach the upper (inlet) radiator hose from the water outlet.

15. Disengage the coolant temperature sensor connector(s).

16. Unfasten the cylinder head bolts in reverse order of the installation sequence shown in the accompanying figures.

17. Lift the cylinder head from the engine block. Remove and discard the gasket. Inspect the oil flow check valve for freedom of movement.

18. Using a suitable solvent, thoroughly clean and dry all bolts, bolt holes and mating surfaces. Inspect the head bolts for any damage and replace, if necessary. If using a scraper to clean the old gasket material from the mating surfaces, use only a plastic or wood one, NOT a metal scraper. Do NOT allow any debris to fall into the engine!

To install:

19. Place a new cylinder head gasket on the cylinder block, then carefully position the cylinder head in place.

20. Sparingly coat the head bolt threads with clean engine oil, then allow the oil to drain off before installing.

21. Tighten the cylinder head bolts to the specifications shown in the accompanying figure.

22. Engage the coolant temperature sensor electrical connector(s).

23. Connect the upper radiator hose to the water outlet.

24. Install the intake manifold bracket.

25. Attach the following electrical connections: MAP sensor, IAT sensor, and the purge solenoid.

26. Using a new gasket, install the throttle body to the intake manifold.

27. Install the accelerator control cable bracket.

28. Connect the throttle body-to-air intake duct.

29. Install the oil fill tube and level indicator.

30. Install the intake and exhaust camshaft housings.

31. Install the exhaust manifold. For details, please refer to the procedure located in this section.

32. Connect the heater inlet and throttle body heater hoses to the water outlet.

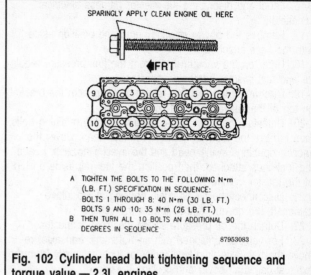

Fig. 102 Cylinder head bolt tightening sequence and torque value — 2.3L engines

33. Fill all fluids to their proper levels.

34. Connect the battery cable, start the engine and check for leaks.

2.4L Engines

▶ See Figure 103

1. Properly relieve the fuel system pressure.

2. Disconnect the negative battery cable, then drain cooling system into a suitable container.

3. Remove the throttle body-to-air cleaner duct.

4. Detach the heater inlet and throttle body heater hoses from water outlet.

5. Tag and disconnect the power brake vacuum hose from the throttle body.

6. Label and detach the electrical connections from the following components:
   - MAP sensor
   - IAT sensor
   - EVAP canister purge solenoid
   - Camshaft Position (CMP) sensor (if accessible at this time)

7. Remove the alternator stud-ended bolt.

8. Detach the intake manifold brace, then remove the intake manifold. For details, please refer to the procedure located in this section.

9. Install the alternator stud-ended bolt.

10. Install engine support fixtures J 28467-400 and J 28367-A to support the engine.

11. Remove the exhaust manifold.

12. Tag and disconnect the ignition coil and module assembly electrical connections.

13. Unfasten the coil and module assembly-to-camshaft housing bolts, then remove the assembly by pulling straight up. Use tool J 36011 or equivalent to remove any connectors that may stick to the spark plugs. Use the tool by first twisting, then pulling up on the connector assembly.

14. If not already done, detach the Camshaft Position (CMP) sensor connector.

15. Unfasten the oil fill tube bolt/screw then remove the oil fill cap and level indicator assembly. Pull the oil fill tube upward to unseat from block.

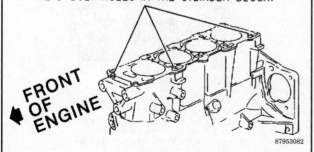

Fig. 101 Make sure to thoroughly clean any oil, coolant or other debris from the bolt holes in the cylinder block

16. Label and disengage the injector harness electrical connector.

17. Remove the power steering pump and position aside with the lines attached.

18. Unfasten the vacuum lines from the fuel pressure regulator and fuel injector harness connector.

19. Disconnect the fuel line retaining clamp from the bracket on top of the intake camshaft housing.

20. Unfasten the fuel rail-to-camshaft housing retaining bolts, then remove the fuel rail from the cylinder head. Cover the injector openings in the head and the injector nozzles. Leave the fuel lines attached, then position the fuel rail aside on top of the master cylinder.

21. Disconnect the timing chain housing at the intake camshaft, but do not remove it from the vehicle.

22. Detach the oil pressure switch electrical connector.

23. For vehicles equipped with an automatic transaxle, remove the transaxle fluid level indicator tube assembly from the exhaust camshaft cover and position it aside.

➡ Any time the camshaft housing-to-cylinder head retaining bolts are loosened or removed, the housing-to-head gasket MUST be replaced.

24. Unfasten the intake camshaft housing-to-cylinder head retaining bolts using the reverse of the tightening sequence found in the accompanying figure.

✳✳WARNING

Turn the camshaft housing upside down as soon as it is removed from the cylinder head. The lifters will fall out of the camshaft housing if it is not turned upside down. The lifters can be damaged if they fall out and hit a hard surface.

25. Remove the intake camshaft housing and gasket.

26. Unfasten the exhaust camshaft housing-to-cylinder head retaining bolts using the reverse of the tightening sequence found in the accompanying figure.

27. Remove the exhaust camshaft housing and gasket.

28. Detach the upper (inlet) radiator hose from the water outlet.

29. Disengage the coolant temperature sensor connector(s).

30. Unfasten the cylinder head bolts in reverse order of the installation sequence shown in the accompanying figures.

31. Lift the cylinder head from the engine block. Remove and discard the gasket. Inspect the oil flow check valve for freedom of movement.

32. Using a suitable solvent, thoroughly clean and dry all bolts, bolt holes and mating surfaces. Inspect the head bolts for any damage and replace, if necessary. If using a scraper to clean the old gasket material from the mating surfaces, use only a razor blade gasket scraper. Be extremely careful not to gouge or scratch the gasket surfaces. Hold the scraper so the blade is as parallel to the surface as possible. Do NOT allow any debris to fall into the engine!

To install:

33. Place a new cylinder head gasket on the cylinder block, then carefully position the cylinder head in place.

34. Sparingly coat the head bolt threads with clean engine oil, then allow the oil to drain off before installing.

35. Tighten the cylinder head bolts to the specifications shown in the accompanying figure.

✳✳WARNING

Roll the camshaft housing right side up as it is installed onto the cylinder head. The lifters can be damaged if they fall out and hit a hard surface.

36. Install the intake and exhaust camshaft housings and gaskets, and secure with the retaining bolts. Apply a suitable pipe sealant to the camshaft housing retaining bolt threads. Use tool J 36660 or equivalent to install and tighten the bolts, in sequence.

37. Install the timing chain and housing.

38. Uncap the fuel injectors, lubricate new O-ring seals with clean engine oil and install them on the injectors. Uncover the injector openings in the head, then install the fuel rail. Tighten the retaining bolts to 19 ft. lbs. (26 Nm).

39. Attach the fuel line retaining clamp and retainer to the bracket on top of the camshaft housing.

40. Connect the vacuum line to the fuel pressure regulator, then attach the fuel injector harness connector.

41. Attach the CMP sensor connector.

42. Install the power steering pump assembly.

43. Attach the oil pressure switch electrical connector.

44. For vehicles with an automatic transaxle, install the transaxle fluid level indicator to the exhaust camshaft cover.

45. Install any spark plug boot connector assembly that stuck to a spark plug back onto the ignition coil and module assembly. Position the assembly over the spark plugs and push straight down.

46. Apply a suitable pipe sealant to the ignition coil and module cover assembly-to-camshaft housing bolts, then install the bolts and tighten to 16 ft. lbs. (22 Nm). Attach the ignition coil and module assembly electrical connector.

47. Remove engine support fixtures J 28467-A and J 28367-400. Remove the stud-ended alternator bolt.

48. Using a new gasket, install the intake manifold. Install the manifold brace.

49. Fasten the stud-ended alternator bolt.

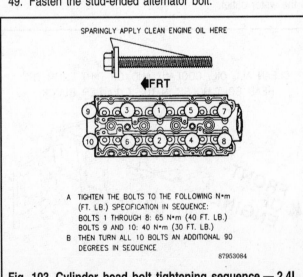

Fig. 103 Cylinder head bolt tightening sequence — 2.4L engines

50. Attach the coolant temperature sensor electrical connector(s).

51. Connect the upper radiator hose to the water outlet.

52. Attach the following electrical connections: MAP sensor, IAT sensor, and the purge solenoid.

53. Using a new gasket, install the exhaust manifold.

54. Connect the throttle body-to-air intake duct.

55. Fill all fluids to their proper levels.

56. Connect the battery cable, start the engine and check for leaks.

2.8L and 3.1L Engines

1985-86 VEHICLES (LEFT SIDE)

▶ See Figure 104

1. Disconnect the negative battery cable.

2. Raise and safely support the vehicle.

3. Properly drain the cooling system, then carefully lower the vehicle.

4. Remove the intake and exhaust manifolds. For details, please refer to the procedures located earlier in this section.

5. Remove the oil level indicator tube.

6. Disconnect the wiring harness at the left head.

7. Remove the alternator bracket.

8. Loosen the rocker arm bolts until you are able to remove the pushrods, then remove the pushrods.

9. Unfasten the cylinder head retaining bolts, then remove the cylinder head.

To install:

10. Clean all gasket surfaces on the cylinder head, block and intake manifold and clean the bolt threads and bolts.

11. Place a new head gasket in position over the dowel pins with the words "This Side Up" facing upward.

12. Coat the cylinder head bolts with sealer and tighten them to 77 ft. lbs. (104 Nm) in the sequence shown in the accompany figure.

13. Install the pushrods, making sure the lower ends are in the lifter seats, and loosely retain with the rocker arms.

14. Install the intake manifold and gaskets.

15. Install the exhaust manifold.

16. Attach the wiring harness.

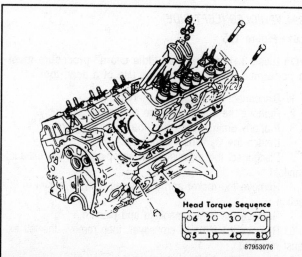

Fig. 104 Cylinder head bolt tightening sequence — 1985-86 2.8L engines

87953076

17. Install the oil level indicator.

18. Install the alternator bracket.

19. Fill the cooling system.

20. Adjust the drive belt and the valve lash.

21. Connect the negative battery cable, then start the engine and check for leaks.

1985-86 VEHICLES (RIGHT SIDE)

▶ See Figure 104

1. Disconnect the negative battery cable.

2. Raise and safely support the vehicle.

3. Drain the cooling system, then lower the vehicle.

4. If equipped, remove the cruise control servo bracket.

5. Remove the intake and exhaust manifolds. For details, please refer to the procedure earlier in this section.

6. Tag and disconnect the spark plug wires, then remove the plugs.

7. Loosen the rocker arm bolts and remove the pushrods.

8. Unfasten the cylinder head bolts, then remove the cylinder head.

To install:

9. Clean all gasket surfaces on the cylinder head, block and intake manifold and clean the bolt threads and bolts.

10. Place a new head gasket in position over the dowel pins with the words "This Side Up" facing upward. Position the cylinder head.

11. Coat the cylinder head bolts with sealer, then tighten to 77 ft. lbs. (104 Nm), in the sequence shown in the accompanying figure.

12. Install the pushrods in the lifter seats and loosely retain with the rocker arms.

13. Install the intake manifold and gaskets.

14. If equipped, install the cruise control servo bracket.

15. Install the spark plugs, then connect the wires as tagged during removal.

16. Install the exhaust manifold.

17. Fill the cooling system.

18. Connect the negative battery cable, then start the vehicle and check for leaks.

1987-93 VEHICLES (LEFT SIDE)

▶ See Figure 105

1. Relieve the fuel system pressure and disconnect the negative battery cable.

2. Properly drain the cooling system.

3. Remove the rocker arm (valve) cover.

4. Remove the intake manifold as outlined earlier in this section.

5. Disconnect the exhaust crossover at the right exhaust manifold.

6. Remove the oil level indicator tube bracket.

7. Loosen the rocker arms nuts enough to remove the pushrods, then remove the pushrods.

8. Starting with the outer bolts, remove the cylinder head bolts. Remove the cylinder head with the exhaust manifold.

9. Clean and inspect the surfaces of the cylinder head, block and intake manifold. Clean the threads in the block and the threads on the bolts.

To install:

10. Align the new gasket over the dowels on the block with the note "This Side Up" facing the cylinder head.

11. Position the cylinder head and exhaust manifold crossover assembly on the engine.

12. Coat the cylinder head bolts with a proper sealer and install the bolts hand tight.

13. Tighten the bolts, in the correct sequence, to 33 ft. lbs. (45 Nm), then rotate an additional 90° (¼ turn).

14. Install the pushrods in the same order they were removed.

➡Intake pushrods are marked orange and are 6 in. (152.4mm) long. Exhaust pushrods are marked blue and are 6⅜ in. (161.9mm) long.

15. Install the rocker arms. The correct rocker arm torque is 14-20 ft. lbs. (19-27 Nm).

16. Install the intake manifold using a new gasket and following the correct sequence, tighten the bolts to the correct specification.

17. The remainder of the installation is the reverse of the removal.

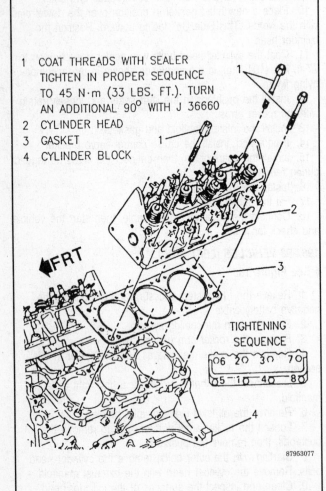

1 COAT THREADS WITH SEALER TIGHTEN IN PROPER SEQUENCE TO 45 N·m (33 LBS. FT.). TURN AN ADDITIONAL 90° WITH J 36660
2 CYLINDER HEAD
3 GASKET
4 CYLINDER BLOCK

◀FRT

TIGHTENING SEQUENCE

06 20 30 70
5 10 40 80

87953077

Fig. 105 Cylinder head bolt tightening sequence — 1987-94 2.8L and 3.1L engines

1987-93 VEHICLES (RIGHT SIDE)

▶ See Figure 105

1. Disconnect the negative battery cable. Drain the cooling system.

2. Raise and safely support the vehicle.

3. Disconnect the exhaust manifold from the exhaust pipe.

4. Carefully lower the vehicle. Disconnect the exhaust manifold from the cylinder head and remove the manifold.

5. Remove the rocker cover, then remove the intake manifold. For details, please refer to the procedure located in this section.

6. Loosen the rocker arms enough so the pushrods can be removed. Note the position of the pushrods for assembly.

7. Starting with the outer bolts, unfasten the cylinder head bolts and remove the cylinder head.

8. Clean and inspect the surfaces of the cylinder head, engine block and intake manifold. Clean the threads in the engine block and the threads on the cylinder head bolts.

To install:

9. Align the new gasket on the dowels on the engine block with the note "This Side Up" facing the cylinder head.

10. Position the cylinder head on the engine. Coat the head bolts with a proper sealer. Install and tighten the bolts hand tight.

11. Tighten the bolts, in sequence, to 33 ft. lbs. (45 Nm), then rotate an additional 90° (¼ turn).

12. Install the pushrods in the same order as they were removed.

➡Intake pushrods are marked orange and are 6 in. (152.4mm) long. Exhaust pushrods are marked blue and are 6⅜ in. (161.9mm) long.

13. Install the rocker arms. The correct rocker arm torque is 14-20 ft. lbs. (1987-88), 18 ft. lbs. (1989-92).

14. Install the intake manifold using a new gasket. Following the correct sequence, torque the bolts to the proper specification.

15. The remainder of the installation is the reverse of the removal.

16. Connect the negative battery cable, then start the engine and check for leaks.

1994 VEHICLES (LEFT SIDE)

▶ See Figure 105

➡On these 3.1L engines, an "Idle Learn" procedure must be performed which requires the use of a scan tool.

1. Disconnect the negative battery cable.

2. Remove the battery and the air cleaner assembly.

3. Properly drain and recover the cooling system.

4. Detach the O_2 sensor connector.

5. Disconnect the exhaust crossover pipe from the exhaust manifold.

6. Remove the rocker arm covers, as outlined earlier in this section.

7. Remove the intake manifold and plenum.

8. Remove the exhaust crossover, then remove the left exhaust manifold.

9. Remove the oil level indicator.

10. Tag and disconnect the spark plug wires at the left cylinder head.

11. Loosen the rocker arms nuts enough to remove the pushrods, then remove the pushrods.

➡️Intake pushrods are marked orange and are 6 in. (152.4mm) long. Exhaust pushrods are marked blue and are 6⅜ in. (161.9mm) long.

12. Starting with the outer bolts, unfasten the cylinder head bolts and remove the cylinder head.

13. Clean and inspect the surfaces of the cylinder head, engine block and intake manifold. Clean the threads in the engine block and the threads on the cylinder head bolts.

To install:

14. Align the new gasket on the dowels on the engine block with the note "This Side Up" facing the cylinder head.

15. Position the cylinder head on the engine. Coat the head bolts with a proper sealer. Install and tighten the bolts hand tight.

16. Tighten the bolts, in sequence, to 33 ft. lbs. (45 Nm), then rotate an additional 90° (¼ turn).

17. Install the pushrods in the same order as they were removed. Make sure they seat properly in the lifters. Tighten the rocker arm nuts.

➡️Intake pushrods are marked orange and are 6 in. (152.4mm) long. Exhaust pushrods are marked blue and are 6⅜ in. (161.9mm) long.

18. Install the intake manifold and plenum.
19. Install the rocker arm covers.
20. Install the oil level indicator.
21. Install the left exhaust manifold.
22. Attach the O_2 sensor connector.
23. Connect the exhaust crossover pipe to the exhaust manifolds.
24. Install the battery and air cleaner assembly.
25. Fill the cooling system, then connect the negative battery cable.

➡️On the 3.1L engine, a Tech 1® scan tool is needed to perform the "Idle Learn" procedure.

26. For the 3.1L engine perform the following "Idle Learn" procedure;

    a. Install a Tech 1® scan tool.

    b. Turn the ignition to the **ON** position, engine not running.

    c. Select **IAC SYSTEM**, then **IDLE LEARN** in the **MISC TEST** mode.

    d. Place the transaxle in park or neutral, as applicable.

    e. Proceed with idle learn as directed by the scan tool.

27. Start the engine and check for leaks.

1994 VEHICLES (RIGHT SIDE)

▶ See Figure 105

➡️On these 3.1L engines, an "Idle Learn" procedure must be performed which requires the use of a scan tool.

1. Disconnect the negative battery cable.
2. Remove the air cleaner assembly.
3. Properly drain and recover the cooling system.
4. Detach the O_2 sensor connector.
5. Disconnect the exhaust crossover pipe from the exhaust manifold.

6. Remove the right exhaust manifold.
7. Remove the rocker arm covers, as outlined earlier in this section.
8. Remove the intake manifold and plenum.
9. Loosen the rocker arms nuts enough to remove the pushrods, then remove the pushrods.

➡️Intake pushrods are marked orange and are 6 in. (152.4mm) long. Exhaust pushrods are marked blue and are 6⅜ in. (161.9mm) long.

10. Starting with the outer bolts, unfasten the cylinder head bolts and remove the cylinder head.

11. Clean and inspect the surfaces of the cylinder head, engine block and intake manifold. Clean the threads in the engine block and the threads on the cylinder head bolts.

To install:

12. Align the new gasket on the dowels on the engine block with the note "This Side Up" facing the cylinder head.

13. Position the cylinder head on the engine. Coat the head bolts with a proper sealer. Install and tighten the bolts hand tight.

14. Tighten the bolts, in sequence, to 33 ft. lbs. (45 Nm), then rotate an additional 90° (¼ turn).

15. Install the pushrods in the same order as they were removed. Make sure they seat properly in the lifters. Tighten the rocker arm nuts.

➡️Intake pushrods are marked orange and are 6 in. (152.4mm) long. Exhaust pushrods are marked blue and are 6⅜ in. (161.9mm) long.

16. Install the intake manifold and plenum.
17. Install the rocker arm covers.
18. Install the right exhaust manifold.
19. Attach the O_2 sensor connector.
20. Connect the exhaust crossover pipe to the exhaust manifolds.
21. Install the air cleaner assembly.
22. Fill the cooling system, then connect the negative battery cable.

➡️On the 3.1L engine, a Tech 1® scan tool is needed to perform the "Idle Learn" procedure.

23. For the 3.1L engine perform the following "Idle Learn" procedure;

    a. Install a Tech 1® scan tool.

    b. Turn the ignition to the **ON** position, engine not running.

    c. Select **IAC SYSTEM**, then **IDLE LEARN** in the **MISC TEST** mode.

    d. Place the transaxle in park or neutral, as applicable.

    e. Proceed with idle learn as directed by the scan tool.

24. Start the engine and check for leaks.

CLEANING & INSPECTION

▶ See Figures 106 and 107

1. With the valves installed to protect the valve seats, remove carbon deposits from the combustion chambers and valve heads with a drill-mounted wire brush. Be careful not to damage the cylinder head gasket surface. If the head is to be

disassembled, proceed to Step 3. If the head is not to be disassembled, proceed to Step 2.

2. Remove all dirt, oil and old gasket material from the cylinder head with solvent. Clean the bolt holes and the oil passage. Be careful not to get solvent on the valve seals as the solvent may damage them. If available, dry the cylinder head with compressed air. Check the head for cracks or other damage, and check the gasket surface for burrs, nicks and flatness. If you are in doubt about the head's serviceability, consult a reputable automotive machine shop.

3. Remove the valves, springs and retainers, then clean the valve guide bores with a valve guide cleaning tool. Remove all dirt, oil and old gasket material from the cylinder head with solvent. Clean the bolt holes and the oil passage.

4. Remove all deposits from the valves with a wire brush or buffing wheel. Inspect the valves as described later in this section.

5. Check the head for cracks using a dye penetrant in the valve seat area and ports, head surface and top. Check the gasket surface for burrs, nicks and flatness. If you are in doubt

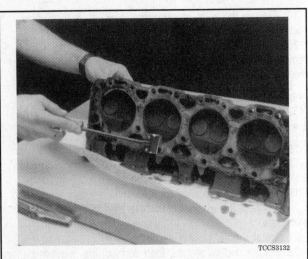

Fig. 106 Use a gasket scraper to remove the bulk of the old head gasket from the mating surface

TCCS3132

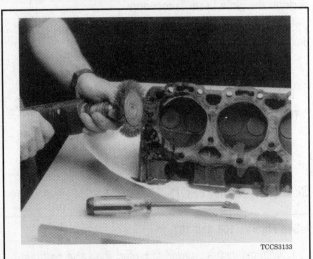

Fig. 107 An electric drill equipped with a wire wheel will expedite complete gasket removal

TCCS3133

about the head's serviceability, consult a reputable automotive machine shop.

➡️If the cylinder head was removed due to an overheating condition and a crack is suspected, do not assume that the head is not cracked because a crack is not visually found. A crack can be so small that it cannot be seen by eye, but can pass coolant when the engine is at operating temperature. Consult an automotive machine shop that has testing equipment to make sure the head is not cracked.

6. Inspect the valves for burned heads, cracked faces or damaged stems.

7. Measure the valve stem clearance as follows:

a. Clamp a dial indicator on one side of the cylinder head. Locate the indicator so that movement of the valve stem from side to side (crosswise to the head) will cause direct movement of the indicator stem. The indicator stem must contact the side of the valve stem just above the guide.

b. Drop the valve head 0.590 in. (1.5mm) off the valve seat.

c. Move the stem of the valve from side to side, using light pressure to obtain a clearance reading. If the clearance exceeds specifications, it will be necessary to ream the valve guides for oversize valves. Service valves are available as follows:

• 1.8L and 2.0L (OHV), 2.8L and 3.1L engines: standard, 0.0035 in. (0.089mm), 0.0155 in. (0.394mm) and 0.0305 in. (0.775mm) O.S. sizes.

• 2.2L (OHV) engine: standard, 0.075mm, 0.150mm and 0.300mm O.S. sizes.

• 1.8L and 2.0L (OHC) engine: standard, 0.075mm, 0.150mm and 0.250mm O.S. sizes.

• 2.3L and 2.4L (OHC) engines: 0.0050 in. (0.127mm) O.S. size.

➡️If valve guides must be reamed this service is available at most machine shops.

8. Check the valve spring tension with tool J-8056, spring tester. Springs should be compressed to the specified height and checked against the specifications chart. Springs should be replaced if not within (10 lbs. of the specified load (without dampers).

9. Inspect the rocker arms studs for wear or damage.

➡️If a dial indicator is not available to you, take your cylinder head to a qualified machine shop for inspection.

RESURFACING

▸ See Figures 108 and 109

Whenever the cylinder head is removed, check the flatness of the cylinder head gasket surface as follows:

1. Make sure all dirt and old gasket material has been cleaned from the cylinder head. Any foreign material left on the head gasket surface can cause a false measurement.

2. Place a straightedge across the gasket surface of the cylinder head. Using feeler gauges, determine the clearance at the center of the straightedge.

Fig. 108 Check the cylinder head for warpage along the center using a straightedge and a feeler gauge

Fig. 109 Be sure to check for warpage across the cylinder head at both diagonals

3. If warpage exceeds 0.003 in. (0.076mm) in a 6 in. (152mm) span, or 0.006 in. (0.152mm) over the total length, the cylinder head must be resurfaced.

4. If necessary to refinish the cylinder head gasket surface, do not plane or grind off more than 0.254mm (0.010 in.) from the original gasket surface.

➡When resurfacing the cylinder head(s) on V6 engines, the intake manifold mounting position is altered, and must be corrected by machining a proportionate amount from the intake manifold flange. Consult an experienced machinist about this service.

Valves and Springs

REMOVAL & INSTALLATION

1. Remove the cylinder head.

2. Block the head on its side, or install a pair of head-holding brackets made especially for valve removal.

3. Use a socket slightly larger than the valve stem and keepers, place the socket over the valve stem and gently hit the socket with a plastic hammer to break loose any varnish buildup.

4. Remove the valve keepers, retainer, spring shield and valve spring using a valve spring compressor (the locking C-clamp type is the easiest kind to use).

5. Put the parts in a separate container numbered for the cylinder being worked on; do not mix them with other parts removed.

6. Remove and discard the valve stem oil seals. A new seal will be used at assembly time.

7. Remove the valves from the cylinder head and place them, in order, through numbered holes punched in a stiff piece of cardboard or wood valve holding stick.

➡The exhaust valve stems on some engines are equipped with small metal caps. Take care not to lose the caps. Make sure to reinstall them at assembly time. Replace any caps that are worn.

8. Use an electric drill and rotary wire brush to clean the intake and exhaust valve ports, combustion chamber and valve seats. In some cases, the carbon will need to be chipped away. Use a blunt pointed drift for carbon chipping. Be careful around the valve seat areas.

9. Use a wire valve guide cleaning brush and safe solvent to clean the valve guides.

10. Clean the valves with a revolving wires brush. Heavy carbon deposits may be removed with the blunt drift.

➡When using a wire brush to clean carbon on the valve ports, valves etc., be sure that the deposits are actually removed, rather than burnished.

11. Wash and clean all valve springs, keepers, retaining caps etc., in safe solvent.

12. Clean the head with a brush and some safe solvent and wipe dry.

13. Check the head for cracks. Cracks in the cylinder head usually start around an exhaust valve seat because it is the hottest part of the combustion chamber. If a crack is suspected but cannot be detected visually have the area checked with dye penetrant or other method by the machine shop.

To install:

14. Install the valves in the cylinder head and metal caps.

15. Install new valve stem oil seals.

16. Install the valve keepers, retainer, spring shield and valve spring using a valve spring compressor (the locking C-clamp type is the easiest kind to use).

17. Check the valve spring installed height, shim or replace as necessary.

INSPECTION

Valves

Reface, or have the valves and valve seats refaced. The valve seats should be a true 46° angle. Remove only enough material to clean up any pits or grooves. Be sure the valve seat is not too wide or narrow. Use a 60° grinding wheel to remove material from the bottom of the seat for raising and a 30° grinding wheel to remove material from the top of the seat to narrow.

After machine work has been performed on the valves, it may be necessary to lap the valve to assure proper contact. For this, you should first contact your machine shop to determine if lapping is necessary. Some machine shops will perform this for you as part of the service, but the precision machining which is available today often makes lapping unnecessary. Additionally, the hardened valves/seats used in modern automobiles may make lapping difficult or impossible. If your machine shop recommends that you lap the valves, proceed as follows:

1. Coat the valve face and seat with a light coat of valve grinding compound. Attach the suction cup end of the valve grinding tool to the head of the valve (it helps to moisten it first).

2. Rotate the tool between the palms, changing position and lifting the tool often the prevent grooving. Lap in the valve until a smooth, evenly polished surface is evident on both the seat and the face.

3. Remove the valve from the cylinder head. Wipe away all traces of grinding compound from the surfaces. Clean out the valve guide with a solvent-soaked rag. Make sure there are NO traces of compound in or on the head.

4. Proceed through the remaining valves, lapping them on at a time to their seats. Clean the are after each valve is done.

5. When all the valves have been lapped, thoroughly clean or wash the head with solvent. There must be NO trace of grinding compound present.

Valves should be refaced to a true angle of 45° (OHV) engines and 46° (OHC) engines. Remove only enough metal to clean up the valve face or to correct runout. If the edge of a valve head, after machining, is $1/32$ in. (0.8mm) or less, replace the valve. The tip of the valve stem should also be dressed on the valve grinding machine, however, do not remove more than 0.010 in. (0.254mm).

Valve Guides

After all cylinder head parts are reasonably clean, check the valve stem-to-guide clearance. If a dial indicator is not on hand, a visual inspection can give you a fairly good idea if the guide, valve stem or both are worn.

Insert the valve into the guide until slight away from the valve seat. Wiggle the valve sideways. A small amount of wobble is normal, excessive wobble means a worn guide or valve stem. If a dial indicator is on hand, mount the indicator so that the stem of the valve is at 90° to the valve stem, as close to the valve guide as possible. Move the valve off the seat, and measure the valve guide-to-stem clearance by rocking the stem back and forth to actuate the dial indicator. Measure the valve stem using a micrometer and compare to specifications to determine whether stem or guide wear is causing excessive clearance.

The valve guide, if worn, must be repaired before the valve seats can be resurfaced. The machine shop will be able to handle the guide reaming for you. In some cases, if the guide is not too badly worn, knurling may be all that is required. Knurling is a process in which metal inside the valve guide bore is displaced and raised, thereby reducing clearance. The possibility of knurling rather than replacing the guides should be discussed with a machinist.

Valve Springs

Place the valve spring on a flat surface next to a carpenter's square. Measure the height of the spring, and rotate the spring against the edge of the square to measure distortion. If the spring height varies (by comparison) by more than $1/16$ in. (1.6mm) or if the distortion exceeds $1/16$ in. (1.6mm), replace the spring.

Have the valve springs tested for spring pressure at the installed and compressed (installed height minus valve lift) height using a valve spring tester. Springs should be within one pound, plus or minus each other. Replace springs as necessary.

VALVE SPRING INSTALLED HEIGHT

After installing the valve spring, measure the distance between the spring mounting pad and the lower edge of the spring retainer. Compare the measurement to specifications. If the installed height is incorrect, add shim washers between the spring mounting pad and the spring. Use only washers designed for valve springs, available at most parts houses.

Check the installed height of the valve springs, using a narrow thin scale. On the OHV 4-cylinder engine, measure from the top of the spring seat to the bottom of the cap.

On the V6 engine measure from the top of the spring damper "feet" to the bottom inside of the oil shedder for exhaust and from the top of the spring shim to the bottom of the valve cap for the intake. If this is found to exceed the specified height, install an additional valve spring seat shim approximately 0.7mm thick.

➡ **At no time should the valve spring be shimmed to give an installed height under the minimum specified.**

Valve Stem Oil Seals

REPLACEMENT

Use the procedure outlined earlier in this section to remove the cylinder head. Remove the camshaft (if OHC engine), rockers, valve keepers, retainer spring shield and valve spring (using a suitable valve spring compressor. Make sure to keep the components in order for installation. Remove the oil seals by lifting them out of the cylinder head with your fingers or a suitable valve seal removal tool. Discard them and replace with new ones during installation. Don't forget that if an oversize valve is used, an oversize valve stem oil seal must be used also.

Valve Seats

REPLACEMENT

If the valve seat is damaged or burnt and cannot be serviced by refacing, it may be possible to have the seat machined and an insert installed. Consult an automotive machine shop for their advice.

Valve Lifters

REMOVAL & INSTALLATION

4-Cylinder Engines

OHV ENGINES

1. Disconnect the negative battery cable.
2. Remove the rocker arm/valve cover.
3. Loosen rocker arm nut and position rocker arm aside. Remove the pushrod; keep all parts in order for correct installation.
4. With a suitable tool remove the lifter assembly from the bore.
5. Installation is the reverse of the removal procedure. Soak engine lifters in clean engine oil before installation.

OHC ENGINES

1. Disconnect the negative battery cable.
2. Remove the camshaft, as outlined in this section.
3. Remove the lifters from their bores.
4. The installation is the reverse of the removal procedure. Soak the lifters in clean engine oil prior to installation.
5. Connect the negative battery cable, then check the lifters for proper operation.

6-Cylinder Engines

1. Disconnect the negative battery cable. Drain the engine coolant.

✳✳CAUTION

When draining the coolant, keep in mind that cats and dogs are attracted by the ethylene glycol antifreeze, and are quite likely to drink any that is left in an uncovered container or in puddles on the ground. This will prove fatal in sufficient quantity. Always drain the coolant into a sealable container. Coolant should be reused unless it is contaminated or several years old.

2. Remove the intake manifold assembly, refer to the necessary service procedures in this section.
3. Remove the rocker arm nut, rocker arm and pushrod. Keep all parts in order for correct installation.
4. With a suitable tool remove the lifter assembly form the bore.
5. Installation is the reverse of the removal procedure. Soak engine lifters in clean engine oil before installation.

Oil Pan

✳✳CAUTION

The EPA warns that prolonged contact with used engine oil may cause a number of skin disorders, including cancer! You should make every effort to minimize your expo-sure to used engine oil. Protective gloves should be worn when changing the oil. Wash your hands and any other exposed skin areas as soon as possible after exposure to used engine oil. Soap and water, or waterless hand cleaner should be used.

REMOVAL & INSTALLATION

1.8L, 2.0L and 2.2L OHV Engines
▶ See Figure 110

1. Disconnect the negative battery cable.
2. Drain the crankcase. Raise and support the front of the vehicle.
3. On 1982-86 models, remove the air conditioning brace at the starter and air conditioning bracket.
4. Unfasten the exhaust shield and disconnect the exhaust pipe at the manifold.
5. Remove the starter motor and position it out of the way.
6. Remove the flywheel cover.
7. On 1982-90 models, remove the 4 right support bolts. Lower the support slightly to gain clearance for oil pan removal.
8. On cars equipped with automatic transmission, remove the oil filter and extension.
9. Unfasten the oil pan bolts and remove the oil pan.
   To install:
10. Prior to oil pan installation, check that the sealing surfaces on the pan, cylinder block and front cover are clean and free of oil. If installing the old pan, be sure that all old RTV has been removed.
11. Apply a 1/8 in. (3mm) bead of RTV sealant to the oil pan sealing surface. Use a new oil pan rear seal and apply a thin coat of RTV sealant to the ends of the gasket down to the ears and install the pan in place.
12. On 1982-86 models, tighten the front bolts to 7-13 ft. lbs., the rear bolts to 11-18 ft. lbs., the stud to 5-7 ft. lbs., and all others to 4-9 ft. lbs. (5-12 Nm). On 1987-92 models tighten the bolts to 77 inch lbs. (8.6 Nm). On 1993-96 vehicles, tighten the bolts to 89 inch lbs. (10 Nm).
13. On cars equipped with an automatic transaxle, replace the oil filter adapter seal and replace the oil filter adapter.
14. Install the remaining components in the reverse order of removal.

1.8L and 2.0L OHC Engines
▶ See Figures 111, 112, 113, 114, 115, 116, 117 and 118

1. Raise and support the car safely.
2. Remove right front wheel and tire assembly.
3. Remove right hand splash shield.
4. Position jackstands at jacking points.
5. Drain engine oil.
6. If necessary on some models, remove lower air conditioning bracket strut rod attachment bolt and swing aside.
7. Remove exhaust pipe-to-manifold attachment bolts. On turbo models, disconnect the exhaust pipe at the wastegate. Position the pipe out of the way.
8. Remove the flywheel dust cover by unfastening the four retaining bolts.

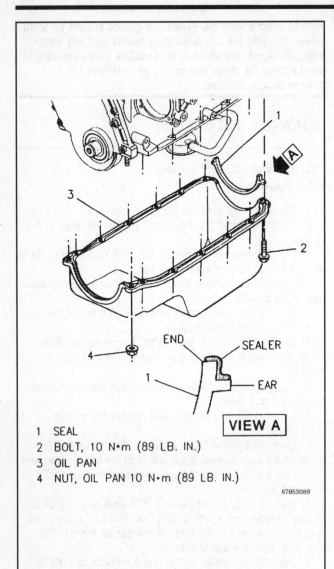

1 SEAL
2 BOLT, 10 N•m (89 LB. IN.)
3 OIL PAN
4 NUT, OIL PAN 10 N•m (89 LB. IN.)

87953089

Fig. 110 Oil pan installation — 1995 2.2L OHV engine shown

87953222

Fig. 111 Unfasten the exhaust pipe-to-manifold retaining bolts, then . . .

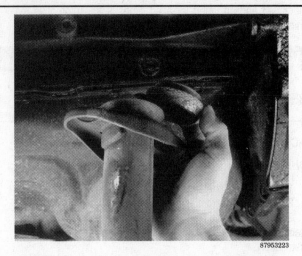

87953223

Fig. 112 Detach the exhaust pipe and position it out of the way

87953224

Fig. 113 Unfasten the flywheel dust cover retaining bolts, then . . .

87953225

Fig. 114 . . . remove the flywheel dust cover

9. Unfasten the oil pan bolts, then remove the pan and scraper.

To install:

10. Clean the sealing surfaces, install the oil pan with a new gasket and apply RTV as shown in the illustration. Install the bolts to the oil pan with Loctite® on the threads. Tighten the pan bolts to 4 ft. lbs. (5 Nm).

11. Installation of the remaining components is the reverse of the removal procedure.

2.3L and 2.4L Engines

♦ See Figures 119 and 120

1. Disconnect the negative battery cable. Raise and safely support the vehicle.

2. Properly drain the engine oil and the cooling system into suitable containers.

3. Remove the flywheel housing or transaxle converter cover, as applicable.

4. Remove the right front wheel and tire assembly, then remove the right splash shield.

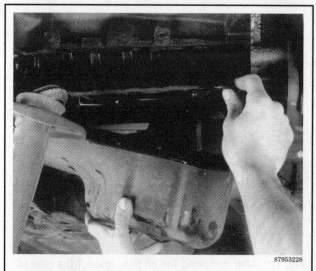
Fig. 117 Remove the oil pan assembly

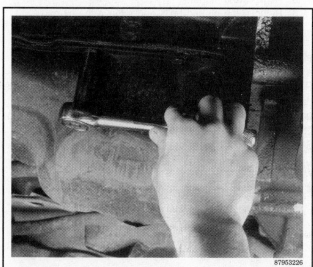
Fig. 115 Unfasten the oil pan retaining bolts

Fig. 118 Clean the oil pan gasket mating surfaces

5. Remove the serpentine drive belt.

6. Unfasten the A/C compressor lower retaining bolts.

7. Remove the transaxle-to-engine brace.

8. Disconnect the engine mount strut bracket.

9. Unfasten the radiator outlet pipe bolts, then remove the pipes from the oil pan.

10. Remove the exhaust manifold brace.

11. Unfasten the oil pan-to-flywheel cover bolt and nut.

12. Remove the flywheel cover stud for clearance.

13. Disconnect the radiator outlet pipe from the lower radiator hose and oil pan.

14. Detach the oil level sensor connector.

15. Unfasten the oil pan retaining bolts, then remove the pan and gasket. Inspect the gasket for damage. If it's O.K. you can reuse it. No sealer is necessary.

To install:

16. Position the gasket, then install the oil pan. Loosely install the retaining bolts.

17. Place the spacer in its approximate installed location by allow clearance to tighten the pan bolt directly above the

Fig. 116 Carefully lower the oil pan

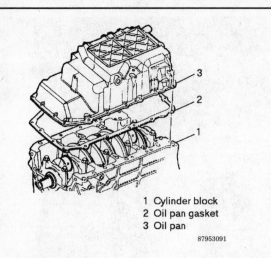

1 Cylinder block
2 Oil pan gasket
3 Oil pan

87953091

Fig. 119 After removing the oil pan, inspect the gasket. If it's not damaged you can reuse it

spacer. Tighten the oil pan bolts to the specifications given in the accompanying figure.

18. Position the spacer into its proper position, then install the stud.

19. Fasten the oil pan-to-transaxle nut.

20. Attach the oil level sensor connector.

21. Connect the radiator outlet pipe to the oil pan and fasten with the retaining bolts.

22. Install the engine mount strut bracket.

23. Fasten the transaxle-to-engine brace. Tighten to 37 ft. lbs. (50 Nm).

24. Secure the A/C compressor bolts.

25. Install the serpentine drive belt.

26. Fasten the right splash shield, then install the wheel and tire assembly.

27. Install the flywheel housing or transaxle converter cover.

28. Fill the cooling system and engine crankcase with the correct type of fluids.

29. Connect the negative battery cable.

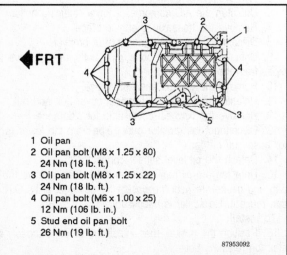

◀**FRT**

1 Oil pan
2 Oil pan bolt (M8 x 1.25 x 80)
   24 Nm (18 lb. ft.)
3 Oil pan bolt (M8 x 1.25 x 22)
   24 Nm (18 lb. ft.)
4 Oil pan bolt (M6 x 1.00 x 25)
   12 Nm (106 lb. in.)
5 Stud end oil pan bolt
   26 Nm (19 lb. ft.)

87953092

Fig. 120 Oil pan tightening specifications — 2.3L and 2.4L engines

2.8L and 3.1L Engines

1985-88 VEHICLES

▶ See Figure 121

1. Disconnect the battery ground.
2. Raise and support the car on jackstands.
3. Drain the oil.

✱✱CAUTION

The EPA warns that prolonged contact with used engine oil may cause a number of skin disorders, including cancer! You should make every effort to minimize your exposure to used engine oil. Protective gloves should be worn when changing the oil. Wash your hands and any other exposed skin areas as soon as possible after exposure to used engine oil. Soap and water, or waterless hand cleaner should be used.

---

4. Remove the bellhousing cover.
5. Remove the starter.
6. Remove the oil pan bolts and remove the oil pan.

To install:

7. Installation is the reverse of removal. On 1985-86 models, the pan is installed using RTV gasket material in place of a gasket. Make sure that the sealing surfaces are free of old RTV material. Use a ⅛ in. (3mm) bead of RTV material on the pan sealing flange. On 1987-88 models the pan is installed using a gasket. Torque the M8 x 1.25 x 14.0 pan bolts to 15-30 ft. lbs. (20-41 Nm) and the M6 x 1 x 16.0 pan bolts to 6-15 ft. lbs. (8-20 Nm).

1989-94 VEHICLES

▶ See Figure 122

1. Disconnect the negative battery cable.
2. Remove the serpentine belt and the tensioner.
3. Support the engine with tool J-28467 or equivalent.
4. Raise and safely support the vehicle. Drain the engine oil.
5. Remove the starter shield and the flywheel cover. Remove the starter.
6. Remove the engine to frame mount retaining nuts.
7. Lower the vehicle.
8. Support the engine using tool J-28467-A or equivalent, then raise and support the vehicle safely.
9. Remove the right tire and wheel assembly. Remove the right inner fender splash shield.
10. Unfasten the oil pan retaining bolts and nuts and remove the oil pan.

To install:

11. Clean the gasket mating surfaces.
12. Install a new gasket on the oil pan. Apply silicon sealer to the portion of the pan that contacts the rear of the block.
13. Install the oil pan retaining nuts. Tighten the nuts to 71-89 inch lbs. (8-10 Nm).
14. Install the oil pan retaining bolts. Tighten the rear bolts to 18 ft. lbs. (25 Nm) and the remaining bolts to 71-89 inch lbs. (8-10 Nm).
15. Install the right inner fender splash shield.
16. Lower the vehicle and remove the engine support tool.
17. Raise and support the vehicle safely.

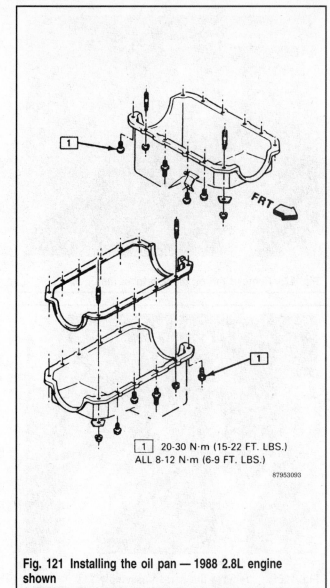

Fig. 121 Installing the oil pan — 1988 2.8L engine shown

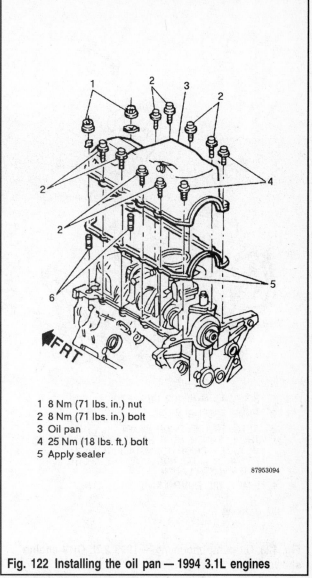

1 8 Nm (71 lbs. in.) nut
2 8 Nm (71 lbs. in.) bolt
3 Oil pan
4 25 Nm (18 lbs. ft.) bolt
5 Apply sealer

87953094

Fig. 122 Installing the oil pan — 1994 3.1L engines

18. Install the engine to frame mounting nuts.
19. Install the starter and splash shield. Install the flywheel shield.
20. Lower the vehicle and fill the crankcase with oil, install the belt tensioner and belt and connect the negative battery cable. Run the engine to normal operating temperature and check for leaks.

Oil Pump

REMOVAL & INSTALLATION

1.8L, 2.0L and 2.2L OHV Engines
▶ See Figure 123

1. Disconnect the negative battery cable.
2. As outlined earlier, remove the engine oil pan.
3. Unfasten the pump to rear bearing cap bolt and remove the pump and extension shaft.

4. Remove the extension shaft and retainer.
To install:
5. Heat the retainer in hot water prior to assembling the extension shaft.
6. Install the extension to the oil pump, being careful not to crack the retainer.
7. Fasten pump to rear bearing cap bolt and torque is 26-38 ft. lbs. (35-51 Nm).
8. Install the oil pan.
9. Connect the negative battery cable.

1.8L and 2.0L OHC Engines
▶ See Figures 124, 125, 126 and 127

1. Remove the crankshaft sprocket.
2. Remove the timing belt rear covers.
3. Disconnect the oil pressure switch wires.
4. Remove the oil pan.
5. Remove the oil filter.
6. Unbolt and remove the oil pick-up tube and screen.
7. Unbolt and remove the oil pump.
8. On the 2.0L engine, pry out the front oil seal.

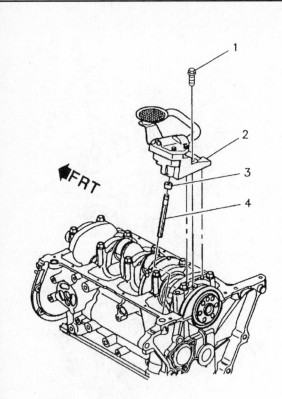

1 BOLT, 43 N•m (32 LBS. FT.)
2 PUMP ASSEMBLY, OIL
3 RETAINER, OIL PUMP SHAFT
   THE RETAINER MUST BE HEATED AND SOAKED
   IN WATER PRIOR TO INSTALLATION. THE
   RETAINER MUST NOT HAVE ANY SPLITS IN IT
   AFTER INSTALLATION.
4 SHAFT, OIL PUMP DRIVE

87953095

Fig. 123 Oil pump mounting — 1995 2.2L OHV engine shown

87953231

Fig. 124 View of the oil pick-up tube and screen, after the pan is removed

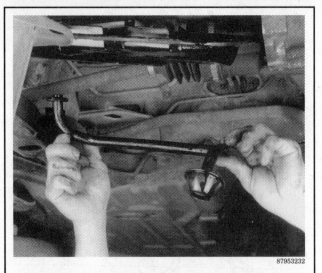

87953232

Fig. 125 Remove the oil pick-up tube, then . . .

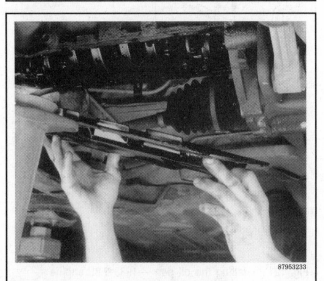

87953233

Fig. 126 . . . remove the screen assembly

To install:

9. Installation is the reverse of removal. Use new gaskets in all instances. On the 2.0L engine, install a new front seal using tool J33083 Seal Installer. Tighten the oil pump bolts to 60 inch lbs. (6.7 Nm). Install the bolts to the oil pan with Loctite® on the threads. Tighten the pan bolts to 48 inch lbs. (5.4 Nm), and the oil pickup tube bolts to 60 inch lbs. (6.7 Nm).

2.3L and 2.4L Engines

▶ See Figure 128

1. Disconnect the negative battery cable.
2. Remove the oil pan.
3. Remove the balance shaft chain cover and chain guide (tensioner).
4. Unfasten the oil pump bolts, then remove the pump cover.
5. Pull the housing to disconnect the gear from the balance shaft. Remove the oil pump housing assembly from the balance shaft assembly.

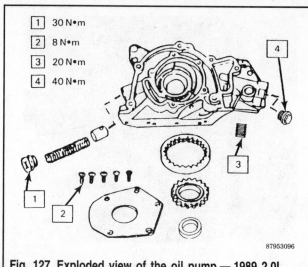

Fig. 127 Exploded view of the oil pump — 1989 2.0L engine shown

To install:

6. Position the oil pump and cover to the balance shaft housing. Tighten the pump-to-block bolts to 40 ft. lbs. (54 Nm).

7. Install the balance shaft chain tensioner. Tighten the bolt to 115 inch lbs. (13 Nm).

8. Install the balance shaft chain cover. Tighten the bolt to 115 inch lbs. (13 Nm).

9. Install the oil pan.

10. Connect the negative battery cable.

2.8L and 3.1L Engines

▶ See Figure 129

1. Disconnect the negative battery cable. Drain the engine oil.

2. Remove the oil pan as described earlier.

3. Unbolt and remove the oil pump and pickup/drive shaft extension.

To install:

4. Position the oil pump and drive shaft extension. Engage the drive shaft extension into the drive gear.

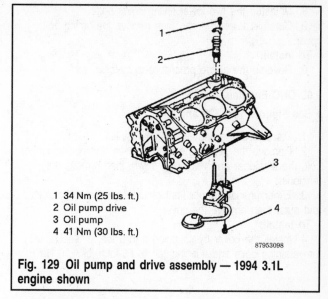

1 34 Nm (25 lbs. ft.)
2 Oil pump drive
3 Oil pump
4 41 Nm (30 lbs. ft.)

Fig. 129 Oil pump and drive assembly — 1994 3.1L engine shown

5. Install the pump-to-rear bearing cap bolt. Tighten to 30 ft. lbs. (41 Nm).

6. Install the oil pan. Fill the crankcase with oil.

7. Connect the negative battery cable.

Timing Belt Cover

REMOVAL & INSTALLATION

1.8L OHC Engines

▶ See Figure 130

1. Disconnect the negative battery cable.
2. Unfasten the alternator pivot bolts.
3. Remove the power steering belt.
4. Unfasten the two upper timing belt cover bolts.
5. Disconnect the canister purge hose.
6. Raise the car and support it safely.
7. Remove the right front wheel and the splash shield.

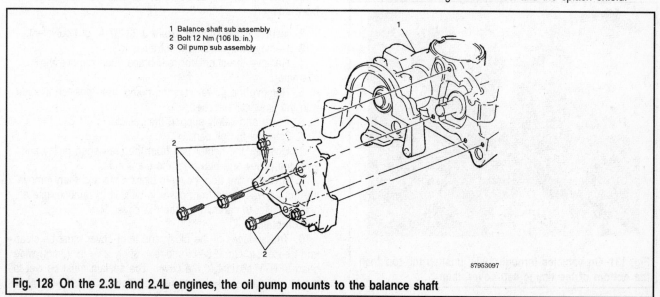

1 Balance shaft sub assembly
2 Bolt 12 Nm (106 lb. in.)
3 Oil pump sub assembly

Fig. 128 On the 2.3L and 2.4L engines, the oil pump mounts to the balance shaft

8. Unfasten the two lower timing cover bolts.

9. Carefully lower the car, then remove the timing belt cover.

To install:

10. Reverse the above procedure to install.

2.0L OHC Engines

▶ See Figures 131, 132 and 133

1. Disconnect the negative battery cable.

2. Remove the serpentine belt. Unfasten the belt tensioner bolt, the tensioner arm will swing down, then remove the tensioner.

3. Either unsnap (upper first) or unfasten the cover bolts and nuts, then remove the cover.

To install:

4. Install the cover by snapping it in place, or secure with the retaining bolts and nut. Tighten to 89 inch lbs. (10 Nm).

Fig. 132 . . . remove the timing belt cover — 1988 2.0L (VIN K) Sunbird shown

5. Place the serpentine belt tensioner into position, then tighten the retaining bolt to 40 ft. lbs. (54 Nm). Install the serpentine belt.

6. Connect the negative battery cable.

Timing Chain Front Cover

REMOVAL & INSTALLATION

1.8L, 2.0L and 2.2L OHV Engines

▶ See Figure 134

➡The following procedure requires the use of a special tool.

1. Remove the engine drive belts (1982-86 vehicles) or the serpentine belt and tensioner (1987-96 vehicles).

➡Although not absolutely necessary, removal of the right front inner fender splash shield will facilitate access to the front cover.

2. Install engine support fixture J 28467-A, or equivalent.

3. Remove the engine mount assembly.

4. Remove the alternator rear brace, then remove the alternator.

5. Remove the power steering pump, then position it aside with the lines still attached.

6. Raise and safely support the vehicle.

7. Remove the oil pan.

8. Unscrew the center bolt from the crankshaft pulley and slide the pulley and hub from the crankshaft.

9. Unfasten the front cover-to-block bolts and then remove the front cover. If the front cover is difficult to remove, use a plastic mallet to carefully loosen the cover.

To install:

10. The surfaces of the block and front cover must be clean and free of oil. On 1982-86 models, apply a ⅛ in. (3mm) wide bead of RTV sealant to the cover. The sealant must be wet to the touch when the bolts are torqued down. On 1987-96 mod-

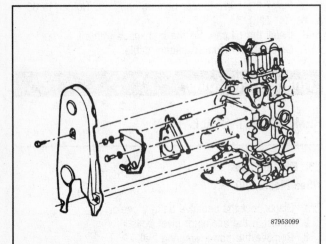

Fig. 130 Timing belt cover mounting — 1.8L OHC engines

Fig. 131 On vehicles through 1988, unsnap the top then the bottom of the timing belt cover, then . . .

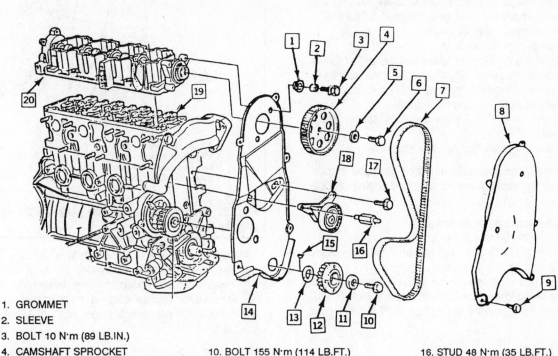

1. GROMMET
2. SLEEVE
3. BOLT 10 N·m (89 LB.IN.)
4. CAMSHAFT SPROCKET
5. WASHER
6. BOLT 45 N·m (33 LB.FT.)
7. TIMING BELT
8. FRONT COVER
9. BOLT 9 N·m (80 LB.IN.)

10. BOLT 155 N·m (114 LB.FT.)
11. WASHER
12. CRANSHAFT SPROCKET
13. WASHER
14. REAR COVER
15. KEYWAY

16. STUD 48 N·m (35 LB.FT.)
17. BOLT 48 N·m (35 LB.FT.)
18. TENSIONER
19. ENGINE
20. CAMSHAFT

87953100

Fig. 133 Exploded view of the timing belt cover and related components — 1989 2.0L OHC engine shown

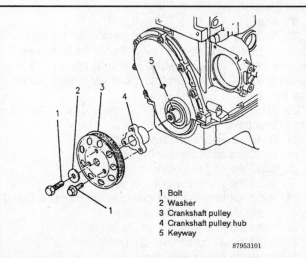

1 Bolt
2 Washer
3 Crankshaft pulley
4 Crankshaft pulley hub
5 Keyway

87953101

Fig. 134 Removing the timing chain front cover — 1995 2.2L engine shown

els a gasket is used. Torque the bolts to 6-9 ft. lbs. (8-12 Nm).

➡**When applying RTV sealant to the front cover, be sure to keep it out of the bolt holes.**

11. Position the front cover on the block using a centering tool (J-23042) and tighten the screws.
12. Installation of the remaining components is in the reverse order of removal.

2.3L and 2.4L Engines

▶ **See Figures 135 and 136**

1. Disconnect the negative battery cable.
2. Remove the coolant recovery reservoir.
3. Remove the serpentine drive belt using a 13mm wrench that is at least 24 in. (61cm) long.
4. For the 2.3L engine, remove the alternator, then position it aside.

5. For the 2.3L engine, install engine support J 28467-A or equivalent. Reinstall the alternator through-bolt, then attach the engine support fixture.

6. For the 2.4L engine, install tool K 28467-400 onto the alternator stud-ended bolt, and engine support fixture.

7. Remove upper cover fasteners.

8. Detach the cover vent hose.

9. Remove the right engine mount and the engine mount bracket or bracket adapter. Whenever the engine mounting bracket adapter is removed, the bolts MUST be replaced.

10. Raise and safely support the vehicle.

11. Remove the right front wheel and tire assembly and the splash shield.

12. Remove the crankshaft balancer assembly.

➡**Do not install an automatic transaxle-equipped engine balancer on a manual-transaxle equipped engine or vice-versa.**

13. Remove lower cover fasteners.

14. Carefully lower the vehicle.

15. Remove the front cover and gasket. Inspect the gasket for damage and replace if necessary.

16. The installation is the reverse of the removal procedure. Tighten the timing chain cover fasteners to 106 inch lbs. (12 Nm). Tighten the balancer attaching bolt to 74 ft. lbs. (100 Nm).

2.8L and 3.1L Engines

▶ **See Figures 137 and 138**

1. Disconnect the battery ground cable.

2. Drain the cooling system.

3. On 1985-86 models, disconnect the MAP sensor and the EGR solenoid.

4. On 1985-86 models, remove the coolant recovery tank.

5. Remove the serpentine belt adjustment pulley.

6. Remove the alternator and disconnect the electrical wires.

7. Remove the power steering pump bracket.

8. Disconnect the heater pipe at the power steering bracket.

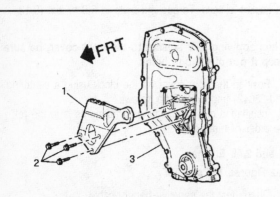

1 Engine mounting bracket adapter
2 Bolt (M12 x 1.75 x 40) 60 Nm (44 lb. ft.)
    NOTE- THESE BOLTS MUST BE REPLACED
    ANYTIME THEY ARE REMOVED
3 Engine front cover

87953102

Fig. 135 Removing the engine mounting bracket adapter

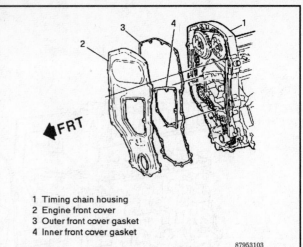

1 Timing chain housing
2 Engine front cover
3 Outer front cover gasket
4 Inner front cover gasket

87953103

Fig. 136 Timing chain cover and gasket — 2.3 and 2.4L engines

9. Jack up the car and support it safely.

10. Remove the inner splash shield.

11. Remove the air conditioning compressor belt.

12. Remove the flywheel cover at the transaxle.

13. Remove the harmonic balancer with tool J-23523-1 or equivalent.

➡**The outer ring (weight) of the harmonic balancer is bonded to the hub with rubber. Breakage may occur if the balancer is hammered back onto the crankshaft. A press or special installation tool is necessary.**

14. Remove the serpentine belt idler pulley.

15. Unfasten the pan-to-front cover bolts and remove the lower cover bolts.

16. Carefully lower the vehicle.

17. Disconnect the radiator hose at the water pump.

18. Remove the heater pipe at the goose neck.

19. Detach the bypass and overflow hoses.

20. Disconnect the canister purge hose.

21. Unfasten the upper front cover bolts and remove the front cover.

To install:

22. Clean all the gasket mounting surfaces on the front cover and block and place a new gasket to the front cover sealing surface. Apply a continuous 1/8 in. (3mm) wide bead of sealer (1052357 or equivalent) to the oil pan sealing surface of the front cover.

23. Place the front cover on the engine and install the upper front cover bolts.

24. Raise the vehicle and support it safely.

25. Install the lower cover bolts.

26. Install the oil pan to cover screws.

27. Install the serpentine belt idler pulley.

28. Install the harmonic balancer. (See the Harmonic Balancer Removal and Installation procedure.)

29. Install the flywheel cover on the transaxle.

30. Install the air conditioning compressor belt.

31. Install the inner splash shield.

32. Lower the vehicle and install the remainder of the parts in the reverse order of removal.

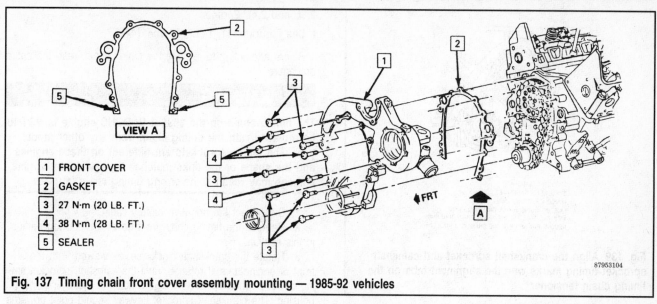

Fig. 137 Timing chain front cover assembly mounting — 1985-92 vehicles

1	FRONT COVER
2	GASKET
3	27 N·m (20 LB. FT.)
4	38 N·m (28 LB. FT.)
5	SEALER

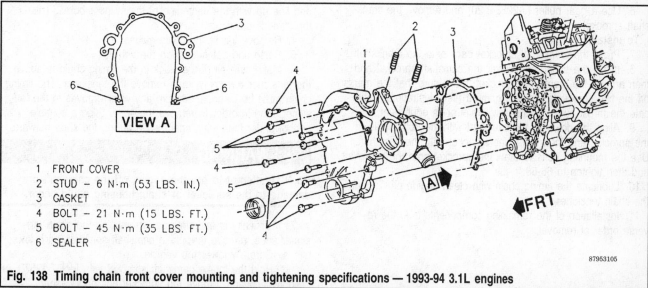

Fig. 138 Timing chain front cover mounting and tightening specifications — 1993-94 3.1L engines

1	FRONT COVER
2	STUD – 6 N·m (53 LBS. IN.)
3	GASKET
4	BOLT – 21 N·m (15 LBS. FT.)
5	BOLT – 45 N·m (35 LBS. FT.)
6	SEALER

Timing Chain Cover Oil Seal

REPLACEMENT

1.8L, 2.0L, 2.8L and 3.1L OHV Engines

The oil seal can be replaced with the cover either on or off the engine. If the cover is on the engine, remove the crankshaft pulley and hub first. Pry out the seal using a suitable prying tool, being careful not to distort the seal mating surface. Install the new seal so that the open side or lip side is towards the engine. Press it into place with a seal driver made for the purpose. General Motors recommends a tool, J-35468 Seal Centering Tool. Install the hub if removed.

Timing Chain and Sprockets

REMOVAL & INSTALLATION

1.8L and 2.0L and 2.2L OHV Engines

▶ See Figures 139 and 140

1. Disconnect the negative battery cable.
2. Remove the front cover as previously detailed.
3. Place the No. 1 piston at TDC of the compression stroke so that the marks on the camshaft and crankshaft sprockets are in alignment (see illustration).
4. Loosen the timing chain tensioner nut as far as possible without actually removing it.
5. Remove the camshaft sprocket bolts and remove the sprocket and chain together. If the sprocket does not slide from the camshaft easily, a light blow with a soft mallet at the lower edge of the sprocket will dislodge it.

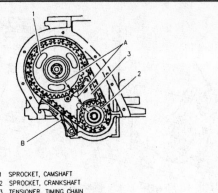

1 SPROCKET, CAMSHAFT
2 SPROCKET, CRANKSHAFT
3 TENSIONER, TIMING CHAIN
A LINE UP TIMING MARKS ON SPROCKETS
   WITH THE TABS ON THE TIMING CHAIN TENSIONER
B REMOVE PIN AFTER TIMING CHAIN IS INSTALLED

87953106

Fig. 139 Align the crankshaft sprocket and camshaft sprocket timing marks with the alignment tabs on the timing chain tensioner

6. Use a gear puller (J-2288-8-20) and remove the crankshaft sprocket.

To install:

7. Press the crankshaft sprocket back onto the crankshaft.

8. Install the timing chain over the camshaft sprocket and then around the crankshaft sprocket. Make sure that the marks on the two sprockets are in alignment (see illustration). Lubricate the thrust surface with Molykote® or its equivalent.

9. Align the dowel in the camshaft with the dowel hole in the sprocket and then install the sprocket onto the camshaft. Use the mounting bolts to draw the sprocket onto the camshaft and then tighten to 66-68 ft. lbs.

10. Lubricate the timing chain with clean engine oil. Tighten the chain tensioner.

11. Installation of the remaining components is in the reverse order of removal.

2.3L and 2.4L Engines

▶ See Figures 141, 142, 143 and 144

Before attempting to remove the timing chain, read the entire procedure.

> ✳✳**WARNING**
>
> The timing chain on the 1996 2.4L DOHC engine is NOT to be replaced with the timing chain from any other model year. The timing sprockets are different on these engines and the shape of the links matches the sprockets. Engine damage may result if the wrong timing chain is used.

1. Disconnect the negative battery cable.

2. Remove the timing chain front cover, as outlined earlier in this section.

3. Rotate the crankshaft clockwise, as viewed from the front of engine/normal rotation, until the camshaft sprocket timing dowel pin holes line up with the holes in the timing chain housing. The crankshaft sprocket keyway should point upwards and line up with the centerline of the cylinder bores. This is the "timed" position.

4. Remove the timing chain guides.

5. Raise and safely support the vehicle.

6. Make sure all of the slack in the timing chain is above the tensioner assembly, then remove the tensioner. The timing chain must be disengaged from any wear grooves in the tensioner shoe in order to remove the shoe. Slide a suitable prytool under the timing chain while pulling the shoe outward.

> ✳✳**WARNING**
>
> Do NOT attempt to pry the socket off the camshaft or damage to the sprocket or chain housing could occur.

7. If difficulty is encountered in removing the chain tensioner shoe, remove the intake camshaft sprocket, as follows;

  a. Carefully lower the vehicle.

  b. Hold the intake camshaft sprocket with tool J 39579, or equivalent, and remove the sprocket bolt and washer.

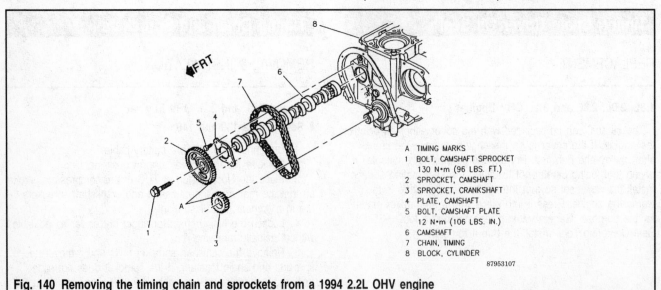

A TIMING MARKS
1 BOLT, CAMSHAFT SPROCKET
   130 N•m (96 LBS. FT.)
2 SPROCKET, CAMSHAFT
3 SPROCKET, CRANKSHAFT
4 PLATE, CAMSHAFT
5 BOLT, CAMSHAFT PLATE
   12 N•m (106 LBS. IN.)
6 CAMSHAFT
7 CHAIN, TIMING
8 BLOCK, CYLINDER

87953107

Fig. 140 Removing the timing chain and sprockets from a 1994 2.2L OHV engine

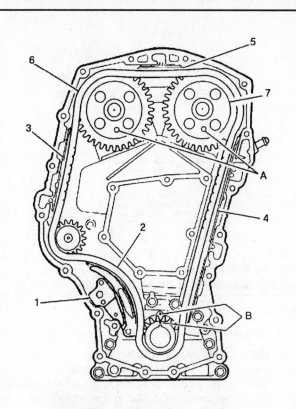

A Camshaft timing alignment pin location
B Crankshaft gear timing mark
1 Shoe assembly timing chain tensioner
2 Timing chain
3 R.H. timing chain guide
4 L.H. timing chain guide
5 Upper timing chain guide
6 Exhaust camshaft sprocket
7 Intake camshaft sprocket

87953108

Fig. 141 The chain must be in the "timed" position — 2.3L and 2.4L engines

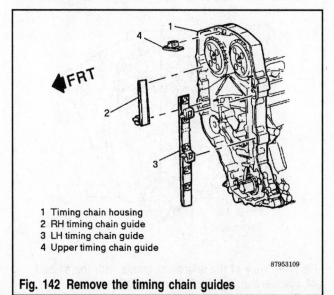

1 Timing chain housing
2 RH timing chain guide
3 LH timing chain guide
4 Upper timing chain guide

87953109

Fig. 142 Remove the timing chain guides

c. Remove the washer from the bolt and rethread the bolt back into the camshaft by hand. The bolt provides a surface to push against.

d. Remove the camshaft sprocket using a three-jaw puller in the three relief holes in the sprocket.

8. Unfasten the tensioner assembly retaining bolts, then remove the tensioner.

➡**The timing chain and crankshaft sprocket MUST be marked before removal. If the chain or sprocket is installed with the wear pattern in the opposite direction, noise and increased wear may occur.**

9. Mark the crankshaft sprocket and timing chain outer surface for reassembly, then remove the chain.

10. Clean the old sealant off the bolt with a wire brush. Clean the threaded hole in the camshaft with a round nylon brush. Inspect the parts for wear and replace as necessary. Note that some scoring of the chain shoe and guides is normal.

To install:

✳✳WARNING

Failure to follow this procedure may result in severe engine damage.

11. Position the intake camshaft sprocket onto the camshaft with the surface marked during removal showing.

12. Install the intake camshaft sprocket retaining bolt and washer, tighten to 52 ft. lbs. (70 Nm) while holding the sprocket with tool J 39579 (if removed). Use sealant 12345493 or equivalent on the camshaft sprocket bolt.

13. Place tool J 36008, or equivalent camshaft aligning pins, through the holes in the camshaft sprockets into the holes in the timing chain housing. This positions the cams for correct timing.

14. If the camshafts are out of position and must be rotated more than 1/8 turn in order to install the alignment dowel pins, proceed as follows:

a. The crankshaft MUST be rotate 90° clockwise off of TDC in order to five the valves adequate clearance to open.

b. Once the camshafts are in position and the dowels installed, rotate the crankshaft counter clockwise back to TDC.

✳✳WARNING

Do not rotate the crankshaft clockwise to TDC; valve or piston damage could result.

➡**The side of the timing chain that was marked during removal must be showing when the chain is installed.**

15. Place the timing chain over the exhaust camshaft sprockets, around the idler sprocket and around the camshaft sprocket.

16. Set the camshafts at the timed position and install the timing chain. Remove the alignment dowel pin from the intake camshaft. Using tool J 39579, rotate the intake camshaft sprocket counter clockwise enough to slide the timing chain over the intake camshaft sprocket. Release the camshaft sprocket wrench (J 39579). The length of the chain between the two camshaft sprockets will tighten. If properly timed, the

intake camshaft alignment dowel pin should slide in easily. If the dowel pin does not fully index, the camshafts are NOT timed correctly and the procedure must be repeated.

17. Leave the alignment dowel pins installed. Raise and safely support the vehicle.

18. With the slack removed from the chain between the intake camshaft sprocket and the crankshaft sprocket, the timing marks on the crankshaft and cylinder block should be aligned. If the marks are not aligned, move the chain one tooth forward or rearward, remove the slack and recheck the marks.

19. Reload the timing chain tensioner assembly to its "zero" position as follows:

   a. Form a keeper from a piece of heavy gauge wire, as shown in the accompanying figure.

   b. Apply slight force on the tensioner blade to compress the plunger.

   c. Insert a small prytool into the reset access hole, and pry the ratchet pawl away from the ratchet teeth while forcing the plunger completely in the hole.

   d. Install the keeper between the access hole and the blade.

20. Install the tensioner assembly to the timing chain housing. Recheck the plunger assembly installation, it is correctly installed when the long end is toward the crankshaft. Install the tensioner retaining bolts; tighten to 89 inch lbs. (10 Nm).

21. Carefully lower the vehicle enough to reach and remove the alignment dowel pins.

✷✷WARNING

Severe engine damage could result if the engine is not properly timed.

22. Rotate the crankshaft clockwise (normal rotation) two full rotations. Align the crankshaft keyway with the mark on the cylinder block and reinstall the alignment dowel pins. The pins will slide in easily if the engine is correctly timed.

23. Install the timing chain guides, then install the front (timing chain) cover.

24. Connect the negative battery cable.

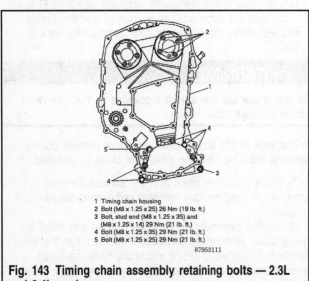

1 Timing chain housing
2 Bolt (M8 x 1.25 x 25) 26 Nm (19 lb. ft.)
3 Bolt, stud end (M8 x 1.25 x 35) and (M8 x 1.25 x 14) 29 Nm (21 lb. ft.)
4 Bolt (M8 x 1.25 x 35) 29 Nm (21 lb. ft.)
5 Bolt (M8 x 1.25 x 25) 29 Nm (21 lb. ft.)

87953111

Fig. 143 Timing chain assembly retaining bolts — 2.3L and 2.4L engines

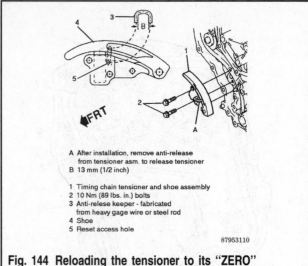

A After installation, remove anti-release from tensioner asm. to release tensioner
B 13 mm (1/2 inch)

1 Timing chain tensioner and shoe assembly
2 10 Nm (89 lbs. in.) bolts
3 Anti-release keeper - fabricated from heavy gage wire or steel rod
4 Shoe
5 Reset access hole

87953110

Fig. 144 Reloading the tensioner to its "ZERO" position, then install to the chain housing

2.8L and 3.1L Engines
▶ See Figures 145 and 146

1. Disconnect the negative battery cable.

2. Remove the front cover, as outlined earlier.

3. Place the No. 1 piston at TDC and the stamped timing marks on both sprockets are closest to one another and in line between the shaft centers (No. 4 firing position).

4. Take out the three bolts that hold the camshaft sprocket to the camshaft. This sprocket is a light press fit on the camshaft and will come off readily. If the sprocket does not come off easily, a light blow on the lower edge of the sprocket with a plastic mallet should dislodge the sprocket. The chain comes off with the camshaft sprocket. A gear puller will be required to remove the crankshaft sprocket.

To install:

5. Without disturbing the position of the engine, mount the new crank sprocket on the shaft, then mount the chain over the camshaft sprocket. Arrange the camshaft sprocket in such a way that the timing marks will line up between the shaft

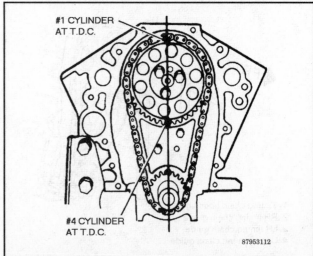

#1 CYLINDER AT T.D.C.

#4 CYLINDER AT T.D.C.

87953112

Fig. 145 View of the alignment marks with the #1 and #4 cylinders at Top Dead Center (TDC)

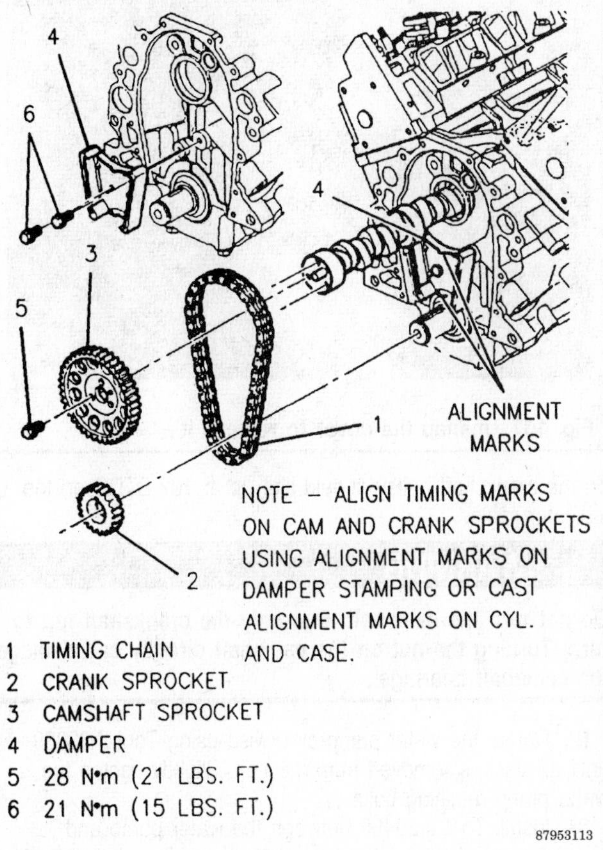

4
6
3
5
1
2

ALIGNMENT
MARKS

NOTE – ALIGN TIMING MARKS
ON CAM AND CRANK SPROCKETS
USING ALIGNMENT MARKS ON
DAMPER STAMPING OR CAST
ALIGNMENT MARKS ON CYL.
AND CASE.

1 TIMING CHAIN
2 CRANK SPROCKET
3 CAMSHAFT SPROCKET
4 DAMPER
5 28 N•m (21 LBS. FT.)
6 21 N•m (15 LBS. FT.)

87953113

Fig. 146 Exploded view of the timing chain and related components — 2.8L and 3.1L engines

centers and the camshaft locating dowel will enter the dowel hole in the cam sprocket.

6. Place the cam sprocket, with its chain mounted over it, in position on the front of the camshaft and pull up with the three bolts that hold it to the camshaft. Torque the bolts to 18 ft. lbs. (25 Nm).

7. Lubricate the timing chain with oil.

8. After the sprockets are in place, turn the engine two full revolutions to make certain that the timing marks are in correct alignment between the shaft centers.

Timing Belt

REMOVAL & INSTALLATION

1.8L and 2.0L OHC Engine

1983-88 VEHICLES

▶ See Figures 147, 148, 149, 150, 151, 152, 153, 154, 155 and 156

➡The following procedure requires the use of a special adjustment tool J33039 and tension gauge J26486-A or their equivalents.

1. Remove the timing belt front cover, as outlined earlier in this section.

2. Raise and support the vehicle safely.

3. Remove the crankshaft pulley as follows:

   a. Remove the inner fender splash shield,

   b. Unfasten the retaining bolts, the remove the crankshaft pulley.

4. Carefully lower the vehicle until it is just above the floor.

5. If equipped, remove the coolant reservoir.

6. If necessary at this time, remove the lower portion of the timing belt cover.

7. Loosen the water pump retaining bolts and rotate the water pump to loosen the timing belt.

8. Remove the timing belt.

To install:

9. Position the timing belt over the sprockets.

10. Install the crankshaft pulley.

11. Check that the mark on the camshaft sprocket lines up with mark on the camshaft carrier, on the 1.8L engine and the mark on the camshaft sprocket must line up with the mark on the rear timing belt cover on the 2.0L engine.The timing mark

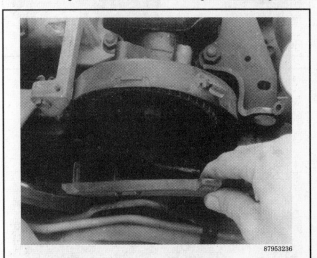

87953236

Fig. 147 Remove the upper part of the timing belt cover by unsnapping it — 1988 2.0L (VIN K) Sunbird shown

Fig. 148 Unfasten the retaining bolts, then . . .

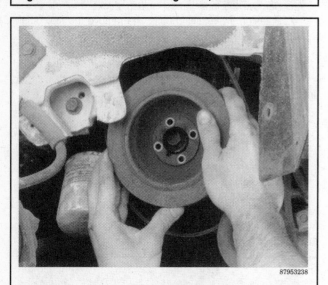

Fig. 149 . . . remove the crankshaft pulley

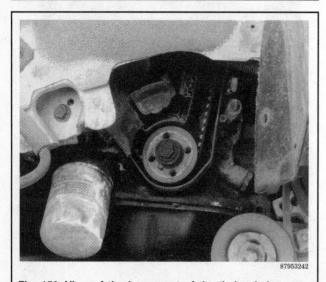

Fig. 150 View of the lower part of the timing belt cover

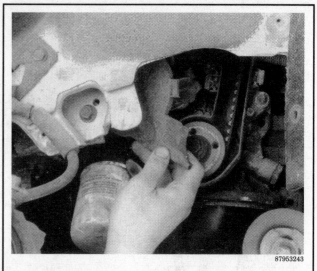

Fig. 151 Unsnap the cover to remove it

on the crankshaft pulley should line up at 10° BTDC on the indicator scale.

✳✳WARNING

Do not turn the camshaft. Use only the crankshaft nut to turn. Turning the nut on the camshaft directly can damage the camshaft bearings.

12. Rotate the water pump clockwise using Tool J-33039 until all slack is removed from the belt. Slightly tighten the water pump retaining bolts.

13. Install Tool J-26486 between the water pump and camshaft sprockets so that the pointer is midway between the sprockets.

14. If the tension is incorrect, loosen the water pump and rotate it using Tool J-33039 until the proper tension is obtained.

15. Fully tighten the water pump retaining bolts to 18 ft. lbs. (24 Nm), taking care not to further rotate the water pump.

16. Install the timing probe holder. Tighten the nuts to 19 ft. lbs. (26 Nm).

17. If removed, install the coolant recovery reservoir.

18. Install the timing belt front cover, snap into place ot tighten the attaching bolts to 5 ft. lbs. (7 Nm), depending upon application.

19. Install and adjust the alternator and power steering belt. Refill the cooling system, if necessary.

1989-92 VEHICLES

▶ See Figure 157

1. Disconnect the negative battery cable.
2. Remove the serpentine belt and timing belt cover.
3. Loosen the water pump bolts and release tension with tool J-33039 or equivalent.
4. Raise and support the vehicle safely.
5. Remove the crankshaft pulley.
6. Carefully lower the vehicle, then remove the timing belt.

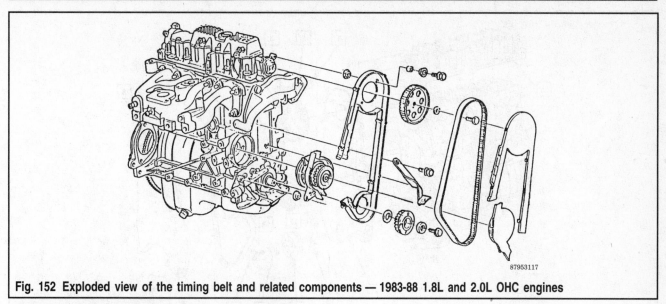

Fig. 152 Exploded view of the timing belt and related components — 1983-88 1.8L and 2.0L OHC engines

Fig. 153 The mark on the camshaft sprocket must line up with the mark on the rear timing belt cover — 1988 2.0L (VIN K) Sunbird shown

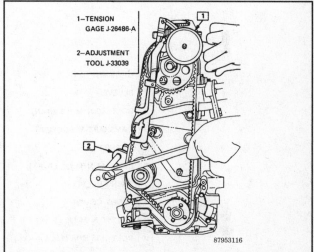

1—TENSION GAGE J-26486-A

2—ADJUSTMENT TOOL J-33039

Fig. 155 Adjusting the timing belt tension — 1983-88 1.8L and 2.0L OHC engines

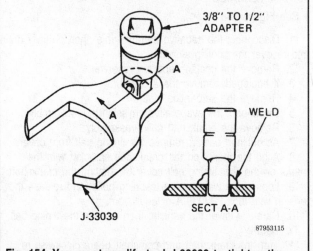

3/8'' TO 1/2'' ADAPTER

WELD

SECT A-A

J-33039

Fig. 154 You must modify tool J-33039 to tighten the timing belt

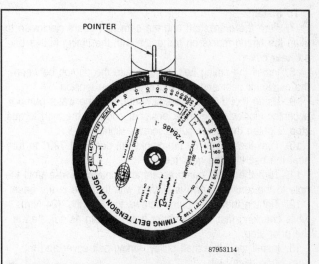

POINTER

Fig. 156 Timing belt adjustment tool J-26486-A, used on the 1983-88 1.8L and 2.0L OHC engines

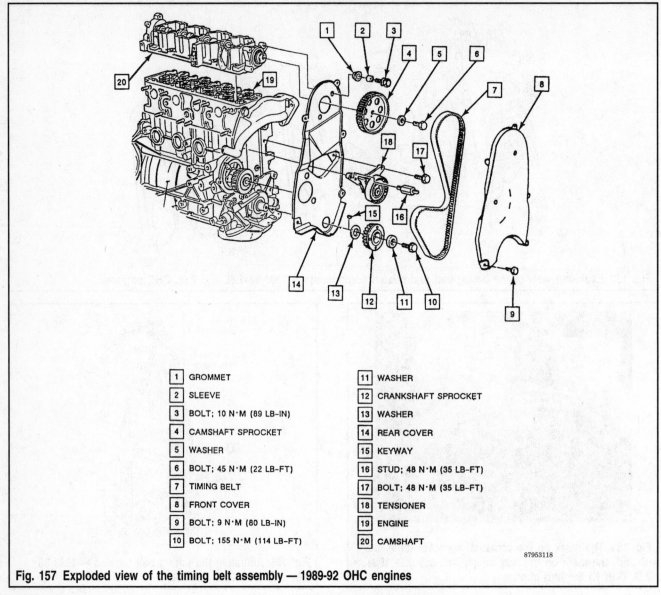

1	GROMMET	11	WASHER
2	SLEEVE	12	CRANKSHAFT SPROCKET
3	BOLT; 10 N·M (89 LB–IN)	13	WASHER
4	CAMSHAFT SPROCKET	14	REAR COVER
5	WASHER	15	KEYWAY
6	BOLT; 45 N·M (22 LB–FT)	16	STUD; 48 N·M (35 LB–FT)
7	TIMING BELT	17	BOLT; 48 N·M (35 LB–FT)
8	FRONT COVER	18	TENSIONER
9	BOLT; 9 N·M (80 LB–IN)	19	ENGINE
10	BOLT; 155 N·M (114 LB–FT)	20	CAMSHAFT

87953118

Fig. 157 Exploded view of the timing belt assembly — 1989-92 OHC engines

To install:

7. Turn the crankshaft and the camshaft gears clockwise to align the timing marks on the gears with the timing marks on the rear cover.

8. Install the timing belt, making sure the portion between the camshaft gear and crankcase gear is in tension.

9. Using tool J-33039 or equivalent, turn the water pump eccentric clockwise until the tensioner contacts the high torque stop. Tighten the water pump screws slightly.

10. Turn the engine by the crankshaft gear bolt 720° to fully seat the belt into the gear teeth.

11. Turn the water pump eccentric counterclockwise until the hole in the tensioner arm is aligned with the hole in the base.

12. Tighten the water pump screws to 18 ft. lbs. (24 Nm), while checking that the tensioner holes remain as adjusted in the prior step.

13. Install the crankshaft pulley, timing belt cover and the serpentine drive belt.

1993-94 VEHICLES
▶ See Figure 158

1. Disconnect the negative battery cable, then partially drain and recover the cooling system.

2. Remove the coolant recovery reservoir.

3. If equipped, remove the A/C belt.

4. Remove the serpentine belt.

5. Disconnect the evaporative emission pipe assembly.

6. Remove the crankshaft pulley assembly.

7. As outlined earlier, remove the timing belt front cover.

8. Align the marks on the crankshaft sprocket with the marks on the rear timing belt cover by rotating the crankshaft.

9. Loosen the water pump retaining bolts, and release the tension with tool J 33039-A or equivalent.

10. Carefully lower the vehicle, then remove the timing belt.

To install:

11. Turn the crankshaft and camshaft gears clockwise to align the timing marks on the gears with the timing marks on the rear cover.

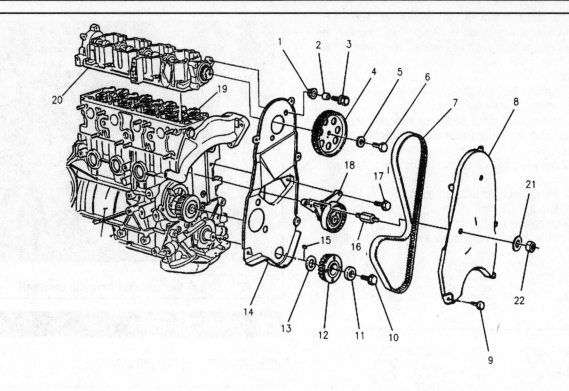

1	GROMMET	12	CRANKSHAFT SPROCKET
2	SLEEVE	13	WASHER
3	BOLT — 10 N·m (89 LBS. IN.)	14	REAR COVER
4	CAMSHAFT SPROCKET	15	KEYWAY
5	WASHER	16	STUD — 25 N·m (18 LBS. FT.)
6	BOLT — 45 N·m (22 LBS. FT.)	17	BOLT — 25 N·m (18 LBS. FT.)
7	TIMING BELT	18	TENSIONER
8	FRONT COVER	19	ENGINE
9	BOLT — 9 N·m (80 MLBS. IN.)	20	CAMSHAFT
10	BOLT — 155 N·m (144 LBS. FT.)	21	WASHER
11	WASHER	22	NUT

87953119

Fig. 158 Timing belt installation and tightening specifications — 1993-94 2.0L OHC engines

12. Install the timing belt, making sure that the portion between the camshaft gear and crankshaft gear is in tension.

13. Using tool J 33039-A, or equivalent adjustment tool, turn the coolant pump eccentric clockwise until the tensioner arm contacts the high torque stop. Tighten the water pump screws slightly.

14. Turn the engine by the crankshaft gear bolt 720° clockwise to fully seat the belt into the gear teeth.

15. Turn the coolant pump eccentric counter clockwise until the hole in the tensioner arm is aligned with the hole in the base. This must be done with the engine at room temperature, approximately 68°F (20°C).

16. Tighten the water pump screws while checking that the tensioner holes remain as adjusted as in step 15.

17. As outlined earlier, install the timing belt cover.

18. Install the crankshaft pulley.

19. Connect the evaporative emission pipe assembly.

20. Install the serpentine drive belt and the A/C belt (if equipped).

21. Install the coolant recovery reservoir.

22. Properly fill the cooling system, then connect the negative battery cable.

Camshaft Sprocket

REMOVAL & INSTALLATION

OHC Engines

▶ See Figures 159, 160 and 161

1. Remove the camshaft carrier cover as previously outlined.

2. Remove the timing belt front cover.

3. Align the mark on camshaft sprocket with mark on or camshaft carrier or rear timing belt cover.

4. If equipped, remove the timing probe holder.

5. Loosen the water pump retaining bolts and remove the timing belt from the camshaft sprocket.

6. Hold the camshaft with an open-end wrench. For this purpose a hexagonal is provided in the camshaft. Unfasten the camshaft sprocket retaining bolt and washer, then remove the sprocket.

To install:

7. Install the camshaft sprocket and align marks on camshaft sprocket and camshaft carrier.

8. Hold the camshaft with a hexagonal open-end wrench. Install the sprocket washer and retaining bolt. Tighten to 34 ft. lbs. (45 Nm).

9. Install the timing belt on sprockets and adjust as previously outlined.

10. Install timing probe holder, if so equipped, and tighten the nuts to 19 ft. lbs. (26 Nm).

11. Install timing belt front cover.

12. Install the camshaft carrier cover as previously outlined.

Fig. 161 . . . pull the sprocket from the camshaft

Crankshaft Sprocket

REMOVAL & INSTALLATION

OHC Engines

◗ See Figure 162

1. Remove the timing belt front cover.

2. As outlined earlier, remove the timing belt.

3. Unfasten the crankshaft sprocket-to-crankshaft attaching bolt and thrust washer, then remove the sprocket.

To install:

4. Position the sprocket over the key on end of crankshaft.

5. Install the thrust washer and the attaching bolt. Tighten to as follows:

- 1982-83 vehicles: 115 ft. lbs. (156 Nm)
- 1984-87 vehicles: 107 ft. lbs. plus a 45° rotation
- 1988 vehicles: 96 ft. lbs. (130 Nm) plus a 45° rotation
- 1989-94 vehicles: 114 ft. lbs. (154 Nm)

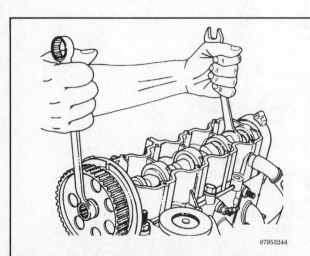

Fig. 159 Hold the camshaft with an open-end wrench and unfasten the camshaft sprocket retaining bolt and washer

Fig. 160 Remove the retaining bolt and washer, then . . .

Fig. 162 Unfasten the bolt and thrust washer, then remove the crankshaft sprocket

6. Install the timing belt and adjust as previously described.

7. Install the timing belt front cover.

Timing Belt Rear Cover

REMOVAL & INSTALLATION

OHC Engines

1. Remove the timing belt from the crankshaft sprocket as outlined in this section.

2. Remove the timing belt rear cover attaching bolts and the rear cover.

3. Install the rear cover and tighten the attaching bolts to 19 ft. lbs. (25 Nm) on the 1.8L engine, 54 inch lbs. (6 Nm) on the 1987-88 2.0L engine and 89 inch lbs. (10 Nm) on the 1989-94 2.0L engine.

4. Install the timing belt and adjust as previously outlined.

Camshaft

REMOVAL & INSTALLATION

1.8L, 2.0L and 2.2L OHV Engines

▶ See Figure 163

1. As outlined earlier, remove the engine and place it on a suitable engine stand.

2. Remove the cylinder head cover, pivot the rocker arms to the sides, and remove the pushrods, keeping them in order. Remove the valve lifters, keeping them in order. There are special tools which make lifter removal easier.

3. Remove the front cover.

4. If necessary, remove the oil pump drive.

5. If equipped, remove the distributor.

6. Remove the fuel pump and its pushrod.

7. Remove the timing chain and sprocket as described earlier in this section.

8. Carefully pull the camshaft from the block, being sure that the camshaft lobes do not contact the bearings.

To install:

9. To install, lubricate the camshaft journals with clean engine oil. Lubricate the lobes with Molykote® or the equivalent.

10. Install the camshaft into the engine, being extremely careful not to contact the bearings with the cam lobes.

11. Install the timing chain and sprocket. Install the fuel pump and pushrod. Install the timing cover. Install the distributor.

12. Install the valve lifters. If a new camshaft has been installed, new lifters should be used to ensure durability of the cam lobes.

13. Install the pushrods and rocker arms and the intake manifold. Adjust the valve lash after installing the engine. Install the cylinder head cover.

1.8L and 2.0L OHC Engines

▶ See Figure 164

➡ The following procedure requires the use of a special tool.

1. Disconnect the negative battery cable.

2. Remove camshaft carrier cover, as outlined earlier in this section.

3. Using valve train compressing Fixture J-33302, which holds the valves in place, compress valve springs and remove rocker arms.

4. As outlined earlier, remove the timing belt front cover and the timing belt.

5. Remove camshaft sprocket as previously outlined.

6. If equipped, remove the distributor.

7. Remove camshaft thrust plate from rear of camshaft carrier.

8. Slide camshaft rearward, then carefully remove it from the carrier.

To install:

9. Install a new camshaft carrier front oil seal using Tool J-33085.

10. Place camshaft in the carrier.

✸✸WARNING

Take care not to damage the carrier front oil seal when installing the camshaft.

11. Install camshaft thrust plate retaining bolts. Tighten the bolts to 70 inch lbs. (7.8 Nm).

12. Check camshaft end play, which should be within 0.0006-0.0025 in. (0.016-0.064mm).

13. Install distributor.

14. Install camshaft sprocket as previously described.

15. Install timing belt as previously described.

16. Install timing belt front cover.

17. Using valve train compressing fixture J-33302, compress valve springs and replace rocker arms.

18. Install camshaft carrier cover as previously described.

2.3L and 2.4L Engines

INTAKE CAMSHAFT

▶ See Figures 165, 166, 167, 168 and 169

➡ Any time the camshaft housing to cylinder head bolts are loosened or removed, the camshaft housing to cylinder head gasket must be replaced.

1. Relieve the fuel system pressure. Disconnect the negative battery cable.

2. Label and detach the ignition coil and module assembly electrical connections.

3. Unfasten the ignition coil and module assembly to camshaft housing bolts, then remove the assembly by pulling straight up. Use a special spark plug boot wire remover tool to remove connector assemblies, if they have stuck to the spark plugs.

4. If equipped, remove the idle speed power steering pressure switch connector.

5. Loosen the three power steering pump pivot bolts and remove drive belt.

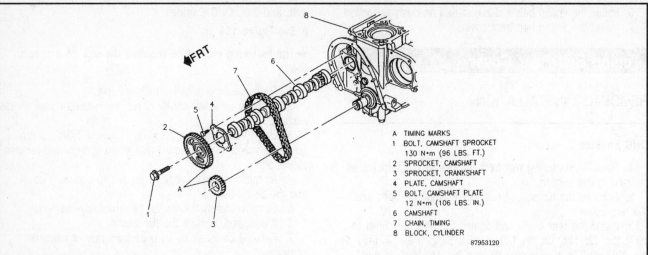

A TIMING MARKS
1 BOLT, CAMSHAFT SPROCKET
  130 N•m (96 LBS. FT.)
2 SPROCKET, CAMSHAFT
3 SPROCKET, CRANKSHAFT
4 PLATE, CAMSHAFT
5 BOLT, CAMSHAFT PLATE
  12 N•m (106 LBS. IN.)
6 CAMSHAFT
7 CHAIN, TIMING
8 BLOCK, CYLINDER

87953120

Fig. 163 After removing the timing chain, you can pull the camshaft from the engine. Be sure the camshaft lobes do NOT contact the bearings

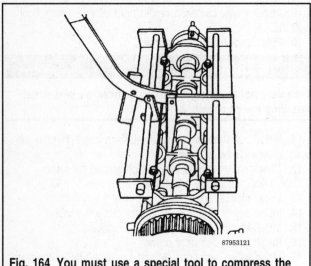

87953121

Fig. 164 You must use a special tool to compress the valve springs

6. Disconnect the two rear power steering pump bracket-to-transaxle bolts.

7. Remove the front power steering pump bracket to cylinder block bolt.

8. Disconnect the power steering pump assembly, then position it aside.

9. Using the special tool, remove the power steering pump drive pulley from the intake camshaft.

10. Remove oil/air separator bolts and hoses. Leave the hoses attached to the separator, disconnect from the oil fill, chain housing and intake manifold. Remove as an assembly.

11. Remove vacuum line from fuel pressure regulator and detach the fuel injector harness connector.

12. Disconnect fuel line attaching clamp from bracket on top of intake camshaft housing.

13. Unfasten the fuel rail-to-camshaft housing attaching bolts, then remove the fuel rail from the cylinder head. Cover or plug injector openings in cylinder head and the injector nozzles. Leave the fuel lines attached, then position fuel rail aside.

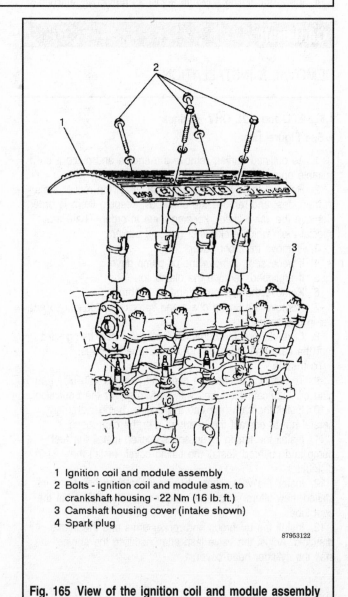

1 Ignition coil and module assembly
2 Bolts - ignition coil and module asm. to
  crankshaft housing - 22 Nm (16 lb. ft.)
3 Camshaft housing cover (intake shown)
4 Spark plug

87953122

Fig. 165 View of the ignition coil and module assembly

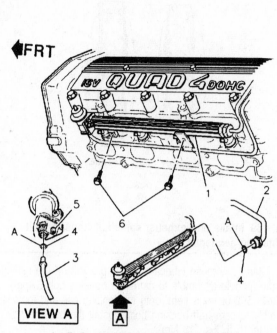

1 FUEL RAIL AND PRESSURE REGULATOR
2 PIPE FUEL FEED 30 N•m (22 LB. FT.)
3 PIPE FUEL RETURN
4 SEAL FUEL LINE
5 BOLT 5 N•m (44 LB. IN.)
6 BOLT 26 N•m (19 LB. FT.)
A LUBRICATE SEAL

87953123

Fig. 166 Fuel injection rail assembly and related components

14. Disconnect the timing chain and housing, but do NOT remove from the engine.

15. Remove the intake camshaft housing cover-to-camshaft housing attaching bolts.

16. Unfasten the intake camshaft housing-to-cylinder head attaching bolts. Use the reverse of the tightening sequence (shown the accompanying figure) when loosening the bolts. Leave two of the bolts loosely in place to hold the camshaft housing while separating the camshaft cover from housing.

17. Push the cover off the housing by threading four of the housing-to-head attaching bolts into the tapped holes in the cam housing cover. Tighten the bolts evenly so the cover does not bind on the dowel pins.

18. Remove the two loosely installed camshaft housing to head bolts and remove the cover. Discard the gaskets.

19. Note the position of the chain sprocket dowel pin for reassembly.

20. Remove intake camshaft oil seal from camshaft and discard seal. This seal must be replaced any time the housing and cover are separated.

21. Remove the camshaft carrier from the cylinder head and remove the gasket. Discard the gasket.

To install:

22. Thoroughly clean the mating surfaces of the camshaft carrier and the cylinder head, bolts and bolt holes. Install a new gasket and place the housing on the head. Install one bolt loosely to hold it in place.

23. Install the lifters into their bores. If the camshaft is being replaced, the lifters must also be replaced. Lubricate camshaft lobes, journals and lifters with camshaft and lifter prelube. The camshaft lobes and journals must be adequately lubricated or engine damage could occur upon start up.

24. Install the camshaft in the same position as when removed. The timing chain sprocket dowel pin should be straight up and align with the centerline of the lifter bores.

25. Install new camshaft housing to camshaft housing cover seals into cover; do not use sealer. Make sure the correct color seal is placed in each groove. Install the cover to the housing.

26. Apply thread locking compound to the camshaft housing and cover attaching bolt threads.

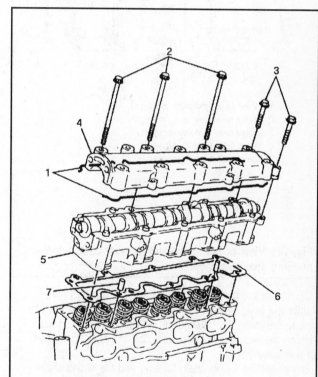

1 Camshaft housing to camshaft seals
2 Camshaft housing to cylinder bolt
   15 Nm (11 lbs. ft.) plus turn 90° head
3 Camshaft housing cover to bolt
   15 Nm (11 lbs. ft.) plus turn 30°
   camshaft housing
4 Camshaft cover
5 Camshaft housing (intake shown)
6 Camshaft housing to cylinder head gasket
7 Dowel pin (2)

87953124

Fig. 167 Exploded view of the camshaft housing, cover and gaskets — 1995 2.3L engine shown

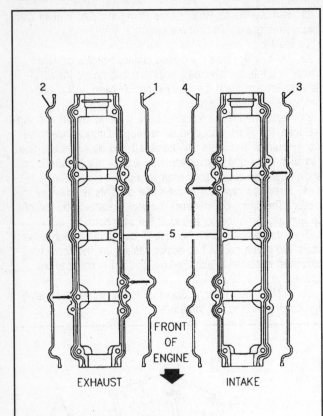

Fig. 168 View of the intake and exhaust camshaft-to-housing seal placement

1 Inner seal (exhaust, orange)
2 Outer seal (exhaust, orange)
3 Outer seal (intake, green)
4 Inner seal (intake, green)
5 Camshaft housing cover

87953125

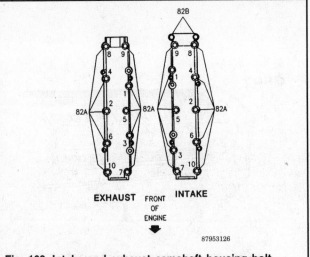

Fig. 169 Intake and exhaust camshaft housing bolt tightening sequence

87953126

27. Install the bolts, then tighten to 11 ft. lbs. (15 Nm). Rotate the bolts (except the two rear bolts that hold the fuel pipe to the camshaft housing) an additional 75°, in sequence. Tighten the two rear bolts to 16 ft. lbs. (15 Nm), then rotate an additional 25°.

28. Install the timing chain housing and the timing chain.

29. Uncover fuel injectors, then install new fuel injector O-ring seals lubricated with oil. Install the fuel rail.

30. Fasten the fuel line attaching clamp and retainer to bracket on top of the intake camshaft housing.

31. Connect the vacuum line to the fuel pressure regulator.

32. Attach the fuel injectors harness connector.

33. Install the oil/air separator assembly.

34. Lubricate the inner sealing surface of the intake camshaft seal with oil and install the seal to the housing.

35. Install the power steering pump pulley onto the intake camshaft.

36. Install the power steering pump assembly and drive belt.

37. Connect the idle speed power steering pressure switch connector.

38. Clean any loose lubricant that is present on the ignition coil and module assembly to camshaft housing bolts. Apply Loctite® 592 or equivalent, onto the ignition coil and module assembly to camshaft housing bolts. Install the bolts and tighten to 13 ft. lbs. (18 Nm).

39. Attach the electrical connectors to ignition coil and module assembly.

40. Connect the negative battery cable, then start the engine and check for leaks.

EXHAUST CAMSHAFT

▶ See Figures 168 and 169

➡Any time the camshaft housing-to-cylinder head bolts are loosened or removed, the camshaft housing to cylinder head gasket must be replaced.

1. Relieve the fuel system pressure. Disconnect the negative battery cable.

2. Label and disconnect the ignition coil and module assembly electrical connections.

3. Unfasten the ignition coil and module assembly-to-camshaft housing bolts, then remove the assembly by pulling straight up. Use a special tool to remove connector assemblies if they have stuck to the spark plugs.

4. If equipped, remove the idle speed power steering pressure switch connector.

5. Remove the transaxle fluid level indicator tube assembly from exhaust camshaft cover and position aside.

6. Remove exhaust camshaft cover and gasket.

7. Disconnect the timing chain and housing but do not remove from the engine.

8. Remove exhaust camshaft housing to cylinder head bolts. Use the reverse of the tightening procedure when loosening camshaft housing while separating camshaft cover from housing.

9. Push the cover off the housing by threading four of the housing to head attaching bolts into the tapped holes in the camshaft cover. When threading the bolt, tighten them evenly so the cover does not bind on the dowel pins.

10. Remove the two loosely installed camshaft housing to cylinder head bolts and remove cover, discard gaskets.

11. Loosely reinstall one camshaft housing to cylinder head bolt to retain the housing during camshaft and lifter removal.

12. Note the position of the chain sprocket dowel pin for reassembly. Remove camshaft being careful not to damage the camshaft or journals.

13. Remove the camshaft carrier from the cylinder head and remove the gasket. Discard the gasket.

To install:

14. Thoroughly clean the mating surfaces of the camshaft carrier and the cylinder head, bolts and bolt holes. Install a new gasket and place the housing on the head. Install 1 bolt loosely to hold in place.

15. Install the lifters into their bores. If the camshaft is being replaced, the lifters must also be replaced. Lubricate camshaft lobes, journals and lifters with camshaft and lifter prelube. The camshaft lobes and journals must be adequately lubricated or engine damage could occur upon start up.

16. Install camshaft in same position as when removed. The timing chain sprocket dowel pin should be straight up and align with the centerline of the lifter bores.

17. Install new camshaft housing-to-camshaft housing cover seals into the cover; do not use sealer. Make sure the correct color seal is placed in each groove. Install the cover to the housing.

18. Apply thread locking compound to the camshaft housing and cover attaching bolt threads.

19. Install bolts, then tighten, in sequence, to 11 ft. lbs. (15 Nm). Then rotate the bolts an additional 75 degrees, in sequence.

20. Install timing chain housing and timing chain.

21. Install the transaxle fluid level indicator tube assembly to the exhaust camshaft cover.

22. Attach the idle speed power steering pressure switch connector.

23. Clean any loose lubricant that is present on the ignition coil and module assembly to camshaft housing bolts. Apply Loctite® 592 or equivalent, onto the ignition coil and module assembly to camshaft housing bolts. Install the bolts and tighten to 13 ft. lbs. (18 Nm).

24. Attach the electrical connectors to ignition coil and module assembly.

25. Connect the negative battery cable, then start the engine and check for leaks.

2.8L and 3.1L Engines

1. Remove the engine assembly as outlined earlier.

2. Remove intake manifold, valve lifters and timing chain cover as described in this section.

3. Remove fuel pump and pump pushrod.

4. Remove camshaft sprocket bolts, sprocket and timing chain. A light blow to the lower edge of a tight sprocket should free it (use a plastic mallet).

5. Remove the timing chain tensioner.

6. If applicable, remove the oil pump drive shaft extension.

7. Install two bolts in cam bolt holes and pull cam from block.

To install:

8. Lubricate the camshaft journals with engine oil and reverse removal procedure aligning the sprocket timing marks.

➡If a new camshaft is being installed, coat the camshaft lobes with GM Engine Oil Supplement (E.O.S.), or equivalent.

BEARING REPLACEMENT

◆ See Figure 170

➡It is recommended that this procedure be performed by a machine shop.

1. Remove the camshaft assembly, for details refer to the necessary service procedure.

2. To remove the camshaft bearings use a special tool (refer to the illustrations) select the proper pilot, nut and thrust washer.

3. Carefully pull out the camshaft bearings.

4. To install the camshaft bearings place the bearing onto the tool and index the oil holes of the bearing with the oil passages in the cylinder block. Pull bearing into proper place.

➡Proper alignment of the oil holes is critical. Restriction of the oil flow will cause severe engine damage.

Pistons and Connecting Rods

◆ See Figures 171, 172, 173, 174 and 175

REMOVAL

1. Disconnect the negative battery cable.

2. Remove the engine assembly from the vehicle and secure on a suitable work stand.

3. Remove the intake manifold and cylinder heads.

4. Remove the oil pan and oil pump.

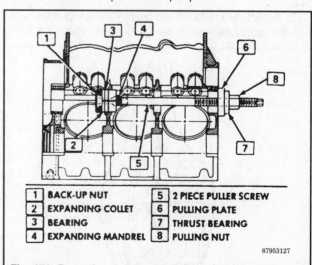

1	BACK-UP NUT	5	2 PIECE PULLER SCREW
2	EXPANDING COLLET	6	PULLING PLATE
3	BEARING	7	THRUST BEARING
4	EXPANDING MANDREL	8	PULLING NUT

87953127

Fig. 170 Removing and installation of the camshaft bearings

5. The position of each piston, connecting rod and connecting rod cap should be noted before any are removed, so they can be reinstalled in the same location.

6. Check the tops of the pistons and the sides of the connecting rods for identifying marks. In some engines, the top of the piston will be numbered to correspond with the cylinder number. The connecting rod and connecting rod cap should have numbers stamped on the machined surfaces next to the rod bolts that correspond with their cylinder number.

7. If no numbers are visible, use a number punch set and stamp the cylinder number on the connecting rod and connecting rod cap.

8. Rotate the crankshaft until the piston to be removed is at the bottom of the cylinder. Examine the cylinder bore above the ring travel. If the bore is worn so that a shoulder or ridge exists at the top of the cylinder, remove the ridge with a ridge reamer to avoid damaging the rings or cracking the ring lands in the piston during removal. Before operating the ridge reamer, place a shop towel on top of the piston to catch the metal shavings.

✳✳WARNING

Be very careful when using a ridge reamer. Only remove the cylinder bore material that is necessary to remove the ridge. If too much cylinder bore material is removed, cylinder overboring and piston replacement may be necessary.

9. Loosen the connecting rod bolt nuts until the nuts are flush with the ends of the bolts. Using a hammer and a brass drift or piece of wood, lightly tap on the nuts/bolts until the connecting rod cap is loosened from the connecting rod. Remove the nuts, rod cap and lower bearing shell.

10. Slip a piece of snug fitting rubber hose over each rod bolt, to prevent the bolt threads from damaging the crankshaft during removal. Using a hammer handle or piece of wood or plastic, push the rod and piston upward in the bore until the connecting rod is clear of the crankshaft journal.

11. Inspect the rod bearings for scoring, chipping or other wear.

12. Inspect the crankshaft rod bearing journal for wear. Measure the journal diameter in several locations around the jour-

TCCS3915

Fig. 172 Remove the ridge from the cylinder bore using a ridge cutter

TCCS3803

Fig. 173 Place lengths of rubber hose over the connecting rod studs in order to protect the crankshaft and cylinders from damage

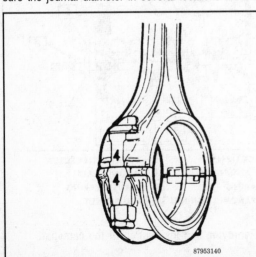

87953140

Fig. 171 Match the connecting rods to their cylinders using a number stamp

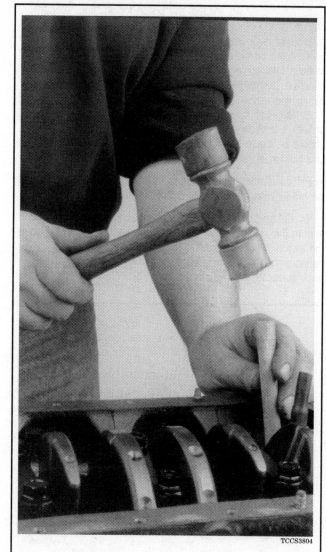

TCCS3804

Fig. 174 Carefully tap the piston out of the bore using a wooden dowel

nal and compare to specification. If the crankshaft journal is scored or has deep ridges, or its diameter is below specification, the crankshaft must be removed from the engine and reground.

13. If the crankshaft journal appears usable, clean it and the rod bearing shells until they are completely free of oil. Blow any oil from the oil hole in the crankshaft.

➡ **The journal surfaces and bearing shells must be completely free of oil to get an accurate reading with Plastigage®.**

14. Pull the connecting rod back onto the crankshaft rod journal and remove the rubber hoses.

15. Place a strip of Plastigage® lengthwise along the bottom center of the lower bearing shell, then install the cap with the shell and torque the connecting rod nuts to specification. Do not turn the crankshaft with the Plastigage® installed in the bearing.

16. Remove the bearing cap with the shell. The flattened Plastigage® will either be sticking to the bearing shell or the crankshaft journal.

17. Using the printed scale on the Plastigage® package, measure the flattened Plastigage® at its widest point. The number on the scale that most closely corresponds to the width of the Plastigage® indicates the bearing clearance in thousandths of an inch or hundredths of a millimeter.

18. Compare the actual bearing clearance with the bearing clearance specification. If the bearing clearance is excessive, the bearing must be replaced or the crankshaft must be ground and the bearing replaced.

➡ **If the crankshaft is still at standard size (has not been ground undersize), bearing shell sets of 0.001, (0.0254mm) 0.002 (0.050mm) and 0.003 in. (0.0762mm) over standard size may be available to correct excessive bearing clearance.**

19. After clearance measuring is completed, be sure to remove the Plastigage® from the crankshaft and/or bearing shell.

20. Again remove the connecting rod cap and install the rubber hose on the rod bolts. Push the rod and piston upward in the bore until the piston rings clear the cylinder block. Remove the piston and connecting rod assembly from the top of the cylinder bore.

CLEANING AND INSPECTION

◆ **See Figures 176, 177, 178, 179, 180 and 181**

1. Remove the piston rings from the piston. The compression rings must be removed using a piston ring expander, to prevent breakage.

2. Clean the ring grooves with a ring groove cleaner, being careful not to cut into the piston metal. Heavy carbon deposits can be cleaned from the top of the piston with a scraper or wire brush, however, do not use a wire wheel on the ring grooves or lands. Clean the oil drain holes in the ring grooves. Clean all remaining dirt, carbon and varnish from the piston with a suitable solvent and a brush; do not use a caustic solution.

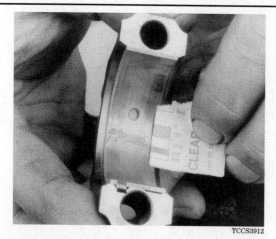

TCCS3912

Fig. 175 Remove the bearing cap and compare the gauging material to the scale provided with the package (check the journal if the material was applied there)

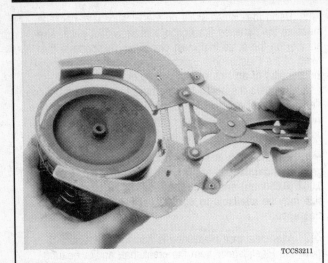

Fig. 176 Use a ring expander tool to remove the piston rings

Fig. 177 Clean the piston grooves using a ring groove cleaner

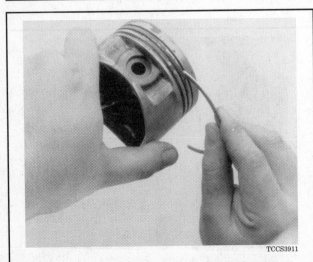

Fig. 178 You can use a piece of an old ring to clean the ring grooves, BUT be careful the ring is sharp

3. After cleaning, inspect the piston for scuffing, scoring, cracks, pitting or excessive ring groove wear. Replace any piston that is obviously worn.

4. If the piston appears okay, measure the piston diameter using a micrometer. Measure the piston diameter in the thrust direction, 90° to the piston pin axis, 3/4 in. (19mm) below the center line of the piston pin bore.

5. Measure the cylinder bore diameter using a bore gauge, or with a telescope gauge and micrometer. The measurement should be made in the piston thrust direction at the top, middle and bottom of the bore.

➡**Piston diameter and cylinder bore measurements should be made with the parts at room temperature, 70°F (21°C).**

6. Subtract the piston diameter measurement made in Step 4 from the cylinder bore measurement made in Step 5. This is the piston-to-bore clearance. If the clearance is within specification, light finish honing is all that is necessary. If the clearance is excessive, the cylinder must be bored and the piston

Fig. 179 Measure the piston's outer diameter using a micrometer

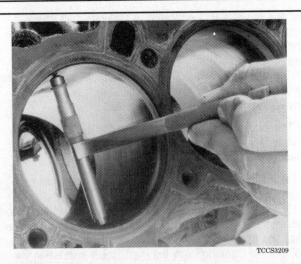

Fig. 180 A telescoping gauge may be used to measure the cylinder bore diameter

replaced. If the pistons are replaced, the piston rings must also be replaced.

7. If the piston-to-bore clearance is okay, check the ring groove clearance. Roll the piston ring around the ring groove in which it is to be installed and check the clearance with a feeler gauge. Compare the measurement with specification. High points in the ring groove that may cause the ring to bind may be cleaned up carefully with a points file. Replace the piston if the ring groove clearance is not within specification.

8. Check the connecting rod for damage or obvious wear. Check for signs of fractures and check the bearing bore for out-of-round and taper.

9. A shiny surface on the pin boss side of the piston usually indicates that the connecting rod is bent or the wrist pin hole is not in proper relation to the piston skirt and ring grooves.

10. Abnormal connecting rod bearing wear can be caused by either a bent connecting rod, an improperly machined journal, or a tapered connecting rod bore.

11. Twisted connecting rods will not create an easily identifiable wear pattern, but badly twisted rods will disturb the action

TCCS3923

Fig. 181 Checking the ring-to-ring groove clearance

of the entire piston, rings, and connecting rod assembly and may be the cause of excessive oil consumption.

12. If the piston must be removed from the connecting rod, mark the side of the connecting rod that corresponds with the side of the piston that faces the front of the engine, so the new piston will be installed facing the same direction. Most pistons have an arrow or notch on the top of the piston, indicating that this side should face the front of the engine. If the original piston is to be reinstalled, use paint or a marker to indicate the cylinder number on the piston, so it can be reinstalled on the same connecting rod.

13. The piston pin is a press fit in the connecting rod. If the piston and/or connecting rod must be replaced, the pin must be pressed into the connecting rod using a fixture that will not damage or distort the piston and/or connecting rod. The piston must move freely on the pin after installation.

HONING

▶ **See Figures 182 and 183**

1. After the piston and connecting rod assembly have been removed, check the clearances as explained in the cleaning and inspection procedure, to determine whether boring and honing or just light honing are required.

2. Honing is best done with the crankshaft removed. This prevents damage to the crankshaft and makes post-honing cleaning easier, as the honing process will scatter metal particles. However, if the crankshaft is in the cylinder block, position the connecting rod journal for the cylinder being honed as far away from the bottom of the cylinder bore as possible, and wrap a shop cloth around the journal.

3. Honing can be done either with a flexible glaze breaker type hone or with a rigid hone that has honing stones and guide shoes. The flexible hone removes the least amount of metal, and is especially recommended if the piston-to-cylinder bore clearance is on the loose side. The flexible hone is useful to provide a finish on which the new piston rings will seat. A rigid hone will remove more material than the flexible hone and requires more operator skill.

4. Regardless of the type of hone used, carefully follow the manufacturers instructions for operation.

5. The hone should be moved up and down the bore at sufficient speed to obtain a uniform finish. A rigid hone will provide a more definite cross-hatch finish; operate the rigid hone at a speed to obtain a 45° included angle in the cross-hatch. The finish marks should be clean but not sharp, free from embedded particles and torn or folded metal.

6. Periodically during the honing procedure, thoroughly clean the cylinder bore and check the piston-to-bore clearance with the piston for that cylinder.

7. After honing is completed, thoroughly wash the cylinder bores and the rest of the engine with hot water and detergent. Scrub the bores well with a stiff bristle brush and rinse thoroughly with hot water. Thorough cleaning is essential, for if any abrasive material is left in the cylinder bore, it will rapidly wear the new rings and the cylinder bore. If any abrasive material is left in the rest of the engine, it will be picked up by the oil and carried throughout the engine, damaging bearings and other parts.

Fig. 182 Using a ball type cylinder hone is an easy way to hone the cylinder bore

Fig. 183 A properly cross-hatched cylinder bore

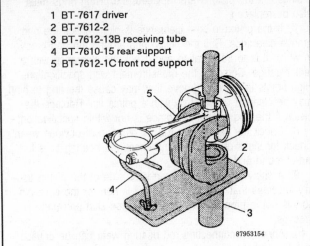
1 BT-7617 driver
2 BT-7612-2
3 BT-7612-13B receiving tube
4 BT-7610-15 rear support
5 BT-7612-1C front rod support

Fig. 184 Removing the piston pin using a suitable tool — 3.1L engine shown

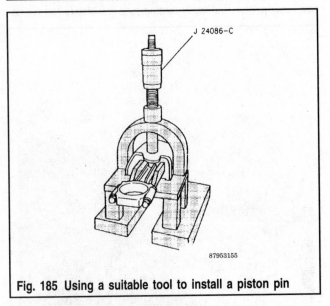
Fig. 185 Using a suitable tool to install a piston pin

8. After the bores are cleaned, wipe them down with a clean cloth coated with light engine oil, to keep them from rusting.

PISTON PIN REPLACEMENT

▶ See Figures 184 and 185

1. Remove the piston rings using a suitable piston ring removal tool.
2. Remove the piston pin lockring, if used.
3. Install the guide bushing of the piston pin removal and installation tool.
4. Install the piston and rod assembly on a support and place the assembly in an arbor press. Press the pin out of the connecting rod using the proper piston pin tool.
5. Assembly is the reverse of the removal procedure.

PISTON RING REPLACEMENT

▶ See Figure 186

1. After the cylinder bores have been finish honed and cleaned, check the piston ring end-gap. Compress the piston rings to be used in the cylinder, one at a time, into that cylinder. Using an inverted piston, push the ring down into the cylinder bore area where normal ring wear is not encountered.
2. Measure the ring end-gap with a feeler gauge and compare to specification. A gap that is too tight is more harmful than one that is too loose (If ring end-gap is excessively loose, the cylinder bore is probably worn beyond specification).
3. If the ring end-gap is too tight, carefully remove the ring and file the ends squarely with a fine file to obtain the proper clearance.
4. Install the rings on the piston, lowest ring first. The lowest (oil) ring is installed by hand; the top 2 (compression) rings must be installed using a piston ring expander tool. There is a

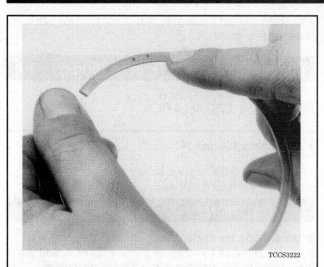

Fig. 186 Most rings are marked to show which side should face upward

high risk of breaking or distorting the compression rings if they are installed by hand.

5. Install the oil ring expander in the bottom ring groove. Make sure the ends butt together and do not overlap. The expander end-gap should be parallel to the piston pin, facing the right cylinder bank.

6. Start the end of an oil ring rail ring into the oil ring groove above the expander. The rail end-gap should be positioned 135° from the expander end-gap. Finish installing the rail ring by spiraling it the remainder of the way on. Repeat the rail installation with the other rail ring. Its gap position must be 135° from the other side of the expander end-gap, 90° from the other rail ring end-gap.

➡**If the instructions on the ring packaging differ from this information regarding ring gap positioning, follow the ring manufacturers instructions.**

7. Install the lower compression ring in the piston ring expander tool with the proper side up (usually the manufacturer's mark faces UP). The piston ring packaging should contain instructions as to the directions the ring sides should face. Spread the ring with the expander tool and install it on the piston. Position the end-gap 180° from the oil ring expander end-gap.

8. Repeat Step 7 to install the top compression ring. Position the end-gap in line with the oil ring expander end-gap. The compression ring end-gaps must not be aligned.

INSTALLATION

▸ **See Figures 187, 188 and 189**

1. Make sure the connecting rod and rod cap bearing saddles are clean and free of nicks or burrs. Install the bearing shells in the connecting rod, making sure the bearing shell tangs are seated in the notches.

➡**Be careful when handling any plain bearings. Hands and working area should be clean. Dirt is easily embedded in the bearing surface and the bearings are easily scratched or damaged.**

2. Make sure the cylinder bore and crankshaft journal are clean.

3. Position the crankshaft journal at its furthest position away from the bottom of the cylinder bore.

4. Coat the cylinder bore with light engine oil.

5. Install the rubber hoses over the connecting rod bolts to protect the crankshaft during installation.

6. Make sure the piston rings are properly installed and the ring end-gaps are correctly positioned. Install a piston ring compressor over the piston and rings and compress the piston rings into their grooves. Follow the ring compressor manufacturers instructions.

7. Place the piston and connecting rod assembly into the cylinder bore. Make sure the assembly is the correct one for that bore and that the piston and connecting rod are facing in the proper direction. Most pistons have an arrow or notch on the top of the piston, indicating that this side should face the front of the engine.

8. Make sure the ring compressor is seated squarely on the block deck surface. If the compressor is not seated squarely, a ring could pop out from beneath the compressor and hang up on the deck surface, as the piston is tapped into the bore, possibly breaking the ring.

9. Make sure that the connecting rod is not hung up on the crankshaft counterweights and is in position to come straight on to the crankshaft.

10. Tap the piston slowly into the bore, making sure the compressor remains squarely against the block deck. When the piston is completely in the bore, remove the ring compressor.

➡**If the connecting rod bearings were replaced, recheck the bearing clearance as described during the removal procedure, before proceeding further.**

11. Coat the crankshaft journal and the bearing shells with engine assembly lube or clean engine oil. Pull the connecting rod onto the crankshaft journal. After the rod is seated, remove the rubber hoses.

12. Install the rod bearing cap, making sure it is the correct one for the connecting rod. Lightly oil the connecting rod bolt

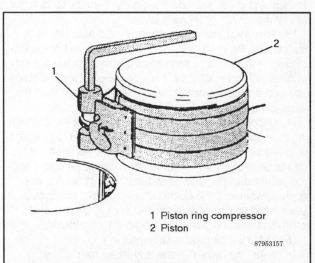

1 Piston ring compressor
2 Piston

Fig. 187 Compress the piston rings into their grooves using a suitable ring compressor

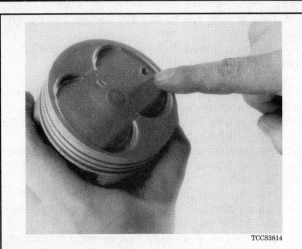

Fig. 188 Most pistons are marked to indicate positioning in the engine (usually a mark means the side facing front)

Fig. 189 Using a wooden hammer handle, carefully tap the piston down through the ring compressor and into the cylinder bore

threads and install the rod nuts. Tighten the nuts to 15 ft. lbs. (20 Nm) plus 75° additional rotation.

13. After each piston and connecting rod assembly is installed, turn the crankshaft over several times and check for binding. If there is a problem and the crankshaft will not turn, or turns with great difficulty, it will be easier to find the problem (rod cap on backwards, broken ring, etc.) than if all the assemblies are installed.

14. Check the clearance between the sides of the connecting rods and the crankshaft using a feeler gauge. Spread the rods slightly with a screwdriver to insert the gauge. If the clearance is below the minimum specification, the connecting rod will have to be removed and machined to provide adequate clearance. If the clearance is excessive, substitute an unworn rod and recheck. If the clearance is still excessive, the crankshaft must be welded and reground, or replaced.

15. Install the oil pump and oil pan.
16. Install the cylinder heads and intake manifold.
17. Install the engine in the vehicle.

18. Start and run the engine, then check for leaks and proper engine operation.

Engine Core Plugs (Freeze Plugs)

REMOVAL & INSTALLATION

▶ See Figures 190 and 191

1. Disconnect the negative battery cable.
2. Drain the cooling system.

✳✳CAUTION

When draining the coolant, keep in mind that cats and dogs are attracted by ethylene glycol antifreeze, and are quite likely to drink any that is left in an uncovered container or in puddles on the ground. This will prove fatal in sufficient quantity. Always drain the coolant into a sealable container. Coolant should be reused unless it is contaminated or several years old.

3. If equipped with drain plugs on the engine remove them. They would be located at the bottom of the block near the oil pan.
4. Remove any components that restrict access to the freeze plugs, like the starter or motor mounts.
5. Wearing proper eye protection, tap the bottom edge of the freeze plug with a punch and hammer. This should tilt the freeze plug, not cut it. Then use pliers to pull or pry the freeze plug from its bore. Another method is to drill the freeze plug and use a slide hammer, but more often there's not enough room to do that.
6. After the plug is removed clean the area completely. Coat the freeze plug and/or bore with gasket sealant.
   To install:
7. Install the freeze plug into the hole, it must do in evenly or it will keep popping back out as you tap on it. Using a plug installer or socket that fits the edge of the plug can help keep it straight as you tap it in place.

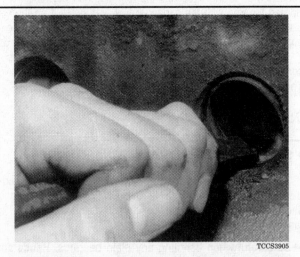

Fig. 190 Using a punch and hammer, the freeze plug can be loosened in the block

Fig. 191 Once the freeze plug has been loosened, it can be removed from the block

8. Fill the engine with coolant, connect the battery cable. Start engine and check for leaks.

Block Heater

REMOVAL & INSTALLATION

Factory block heaters are not installed on these models. If an aftermarket heater has been installed the following procedure will most likely work. There are two basic types, one for the oil and one for the coolant. The oil heater usually just slips into the dipstick tube or replaces the oil drain plug. The following procedure is for the coolant type.

1. Remove the negative battery cable.
2. Drain the cooling system.

✴✴CAUTION

When draining the coolant, keep in mind that cats and dogs are attracted by ethylene glycol antifreeze, and are quite likely to drink any that is left in an uncovered container or in puddles on the ground. This will prove fatal in sufficient quantity. Always drain the coolant into a sealable container. Coolant should be reused unless it is contaminated or several years old.

3. Remove the block heater in the same way as the freeze plugs. Some heater units have a bolt that must be loosened or a V-Clamp that must be removed to remove the heating element.
4. Disconnect the heater connector and remove the heater element.

To install:

5. Coat the new heater with sealant, then install as removed.
6. Fill the engine with coolant, connect the battery cable. Start engine and check for leaks.

Rear Main Oil Seal

REMOVAL & INSTALLATION

1.8L, 2.0L and 2.2L OHV Engines

1982-84 VEHICLES WITH TWO PIECE SEAL

▶ See Figures 192 and 193

1. Remove the oil pan and pump.
2. Remove the rear main bearing cap.
3. Gently pack the upper seal into the groove approximately 1/4 in. (6mm) on each side.
4. Measure the amount the seal was driven in on one side and add 1/16 in. (0.8mm). Cut this length from the old lower cap seal. Be sure to get a sharp cut. Repeat for the other side.
5. Place the piece of cut seal into the groove and pack the seal into the block. Do this for each side.
6. Install a piece of Plastigage® or the equivalent on the bearing journal. Install the rear cap and tighten to 75 ft. lbs. Remove the cap and check the gauge for bearing clearance. If out of specification, the ends of the seal may be frayed or not flush, preventing the cap from proper seating. Correct as required.
7. Clean the journal, and apply a thin film of sealer to the mating surfaces of the cap and tighten to 70 ft. lbs. (95 Nm). Install the pan and pump.

➡Some 1982 1.8L engines (Code G), experience a rear main seal oil leak. To correct this condition a new crankshaft part No. 14086053 and a one piece rear main seal kit part No. 14081761 has been released for service. The one piece seal kit contains an installation tool, rear main seal, and an instruction sheet.

1985-96 VEHICLES WITH ONE PIECE SEAL

▶ See Figures 194 and 195

1. Jack up the engine and support it safely.
2. Remove the transmission as outlined in Section 7.
3. Remove the flywheel.

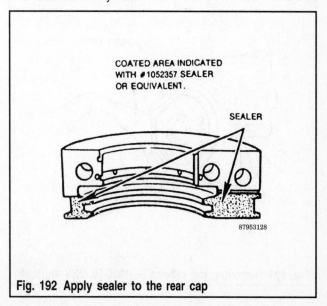

COATED AREA INDICATED WITH #1052357 SEALER OR EQUIVALENT.

SEALER

87953128

Fig. 192 Apply sealer to the rear cap

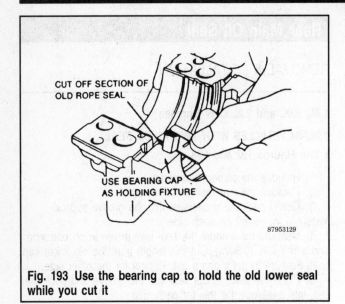

Fig. 193 Use the bearing cap to hold the old lower seal while you cut it

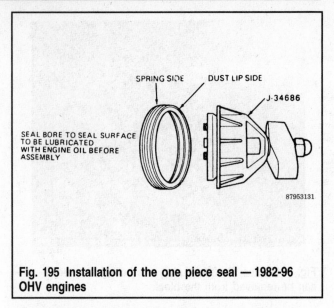

Fig. 195 Installation of the one piece seal — 1982-96 OHV engines

4. Insert a suitable pry tool in through the dust lip and pry out the seal by moving the tool around the seal until it is removed.

➡**Use care not to damage the crankshaft seal surface with a pry tool.**

To install:

5. Before installing, lubricate the seal bore to seal surface with engine oil.

6. Install the new seal using tool J-34686.

7. Slide the new seal over the mandrel until the dust lip bottoms squarely against the tool collar.

8. Align the dowel pin of the tool with the dowel pin hole in the crankshaft and attach the tool to the crankshaft. Tighten the attaching screws to 2-5 ft. lbs. (2.7-6.8 Nm).

9. Tighten the T-handle of the tool to push the seal into the bore. Continue until the tool collar is flush against the block.

10. Loosen the T-handle completely. Remove the attaching screws and the tool.

➡**Check to see that the seal is squarely seated in the bore.**

11. Install the flywheel and transmission.
12. Start the engine and check for leaks.

1.8L and 2.0 OHC Engines

▶ **See Figure 196**

➡**The rear main bearing oil seal is a one piece unit and can be replaced without removing the oil pan or the crankshaft.**

1. Remove the transaxle assembly as outlined in Section 7.
2. Remove the flywheel retaining bolts and remove the flywheel.
3. If equipped with manual transaxle, remove the pressure plate and disc.
4. Pry out the rear main seal.
5. Clean the block and crankcase to seal mating surfaces.

To install:

6. Position the rear main seal to the block and press evenly into place using tool J33084 (1983-86) or tool J-36227 (1987-94 vehicles). Lubricate the outside of the seal to aid assembly.

7. Use new bolts and install the flywheel, then tighten the bolts to 44 ft. lbs. (60 Nm) on 1983-86 vehicles, or 48 ft. lbs. (65 Nm) plus a 30° turn on 1987-94 vehicles.

8. On automatic transaxle models, install the flexplate and tighten to 48 ft. lbs. (65 Nm).

9. Install the pressure plate and disc, if equipped with manual transaxle.

10. Install the transaxle assembly as outlined in Section 7.

2.3L and 2.4L Engines

▶ **See Figure 197**

1. Disconnect the negative battery cable.
2. Remove the transaxle assembly as outlined in Section 7 of this manual.

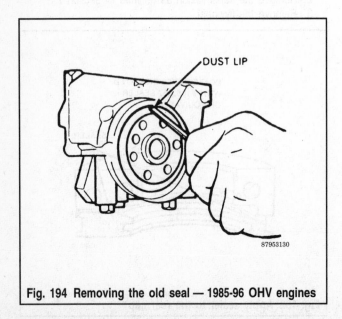

Fig. 194 Removing the old seal — 1985-96 OHV engines

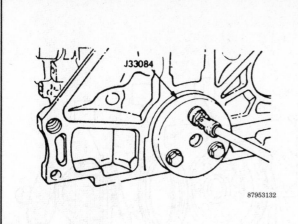

Fig. 196 Installation of the one piece seal — 1983-86 OHC engines

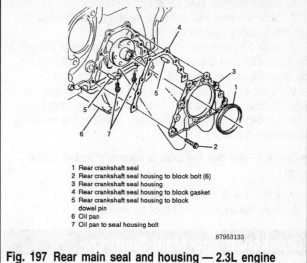

1 Rear crankshaft seal
2 Rear crankshaft seal housing to block bolt (6)
3 Rear crankshaft seal housing
4 Rear crankshaft seal housing to block gasket
5 Rear crankshaft seal housing to block
  dowel pin
6 Oil pan
7 Oil pan to seal housing bolt

Fig. 197 Rear main seal and housing — 2.3L engine shown

3. If equipped with a manual transaxle, remove the pressure plate and clutch disc.

4. Unfasten the flywheel-to-crankshaft bolts, then remove the flywheel.

5. Disconnect the oil pan-to-seal housing bolts

6. Unfasten the seal housing-to-block bolts, then remove the seal housing and gasket.

7. To support the seal housing for seal removal, place two blocks of equal thickness on a flat surface, position the seal housing and blocks so the transaxle side of the seal housing is supported across the dowel pin and center bolt holes on both sides of the seal opening.

➡ **The seal housing could be damaged if not properly supported during seal removal.**

8. Drive the seal evenly out the transaxle side of the seal housing using a small prytool in the relief grooves on the crankshaft side of the seal housing. Discard the seal.

❉❉WARNING

Be careful not to damage the seal housing sealing surface. If damaged, it may result in an oil leak.

To install:

9. Press a new seal into the housing using tool J 36005 or equivalent seal installation tool.

10. Inspect the oil pan gasket inner silicone bead for damage and repair using a silicone sealant, if necessary.

11. Position a new seal housing-to-block gasket over the alignment. The gasket is reversible.

12. Lubricate the lip of the seal with clean engine oil.

13. Install the housing assembly, then tighten the housing-to-block bolts to 106 inch lbs. (12 Nm).

14. Install the oil pan-to-seal housing bolts, then tighten to 106 inch lbs. (12 Nm).

15. Install the flywheel as outlined later in this section.

16. For vehicles equipped with a manual transaxle, install the clutch, pressure plate and clutch cover assembly.

17. Install the transaxle assembly as outlined in Section 7 of this manual.

18. Connect the negative battery cable, then start the engine and check for leaks.

2.8L and 3.1L Engines

▶ **See Figures 198, 199 and 200**

1. Support the engine with J-28467 engine support or equivalent.

2. Remove the transaxle as outlined in Section 7.

3. Remove the flywheel.

4. Insert a suitable pry tool in through the dust lip and pry out the seal by moving the tool around the seal until it is removed.

❉❉WARNING

Use care not to damage the crankshaft seal surface with a pry tool.

To install:

5. Before installing, lubricate the seal bore to seal surface with engine oil.

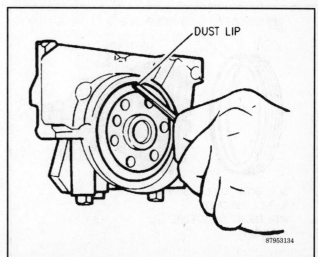

Fig. 198 When removing the rear main seal, be careful not to scratch the bore

6. Install the new seal using tool J-34686.

7. Slide the new seal over the mandrel until the dust lip bottoms squarely against the tool collar.

8. Align the dowel pin of the tool with the dowel pin hole in the crankshaft and attach the tool to the crankshaft. Tighten the attaching screws to 2-5 ft. lbs. (2.7-6.8 Nm).

9. Tighten the T-handle of the tool to push the seal into the bore. Continue until the tool collar is flush against the block.

10. Loosen the T-handle completely. Remove the attaching screws and the tool.

➡ Check to see that the seal is squarely seated in the bore.

11. Install the flywheel and transaxle.

12. Start the engine and check for leaks.

Crankshaft and Main Bearings

REMOVAL & INSTALLATION

▶ See Figure 201

1. Remove the engine assembly as previously outlined.
2. Remove the engine front cover.
3. Remove the timing chain/belt and sprockets.
4. Remove the oil pan.
5. Remove the oil pump.
6. Stamp the cylinder number on the machined surfaces of the bolt bosses of the connecting rods and caps for identification when reinstalling. If the pistons are to be removed from the connecting rod, mark cylinder number on piston with a silver pencil or quick-drying paint for proper cylinder identification and cap to rod location.
7. Remove the connecting rod caps and install thread protectors.
8. Mark the main bearing caps so that they can be installed in their original positions.
9. Remove all the main bearing caps.
10. Note position of keyway in crankshaft so it can be installed in the same position.

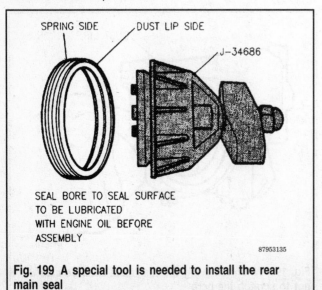

SPRING SIDE   DUST LIP SIDE

J-34686

SEAL BORE TO SEAL SURFACE
TO BE LUBRICATED
WITH ENGINE OIL BEFORE
ASSEMBLY

87953135

Fig. 199 A special tool is needed to install the rear main seal

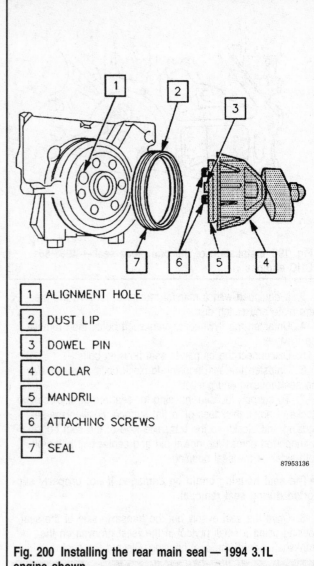

1	ALIGNMENT HOLE
2	DUST LIP
3	DOWEL PIN
4	COLLAR
5	MANDRIL
6	ATTACHING SCREWS
7	SEAL

87953136

Fig. 200 Installing the rear main seal — 1994 3.1L engine shown

11. Lift crankshaft out of block. Rods will pivot to the center of the engine when the crankshaft is removed.

12. Remove both halves of the rear main oil seal.

To install:

13. Measure the crankshaft journals with a micrometer to determine the correct size rod and main bearings to be used. Whenever a new or reconditioned crankshaft is installed, new connecting rod bearings and main bearings should be installed. See Main Bearings and Rod Bearings.

14. Clean all oil passages in the block (and crankshaft if it is being reused).

➡ A new rear main seal should be installed anytime the crankshaft is removed or replaced.

15. Install sufficient oil pan bolts in the block to align with the connecting rod bolts. Use rubber bands between the bolts to position the connecting rods as required. Connecting rod position can be adjusted by increasing the tension on the rubber bands with additional turns around the pan bolts or thread protectors.

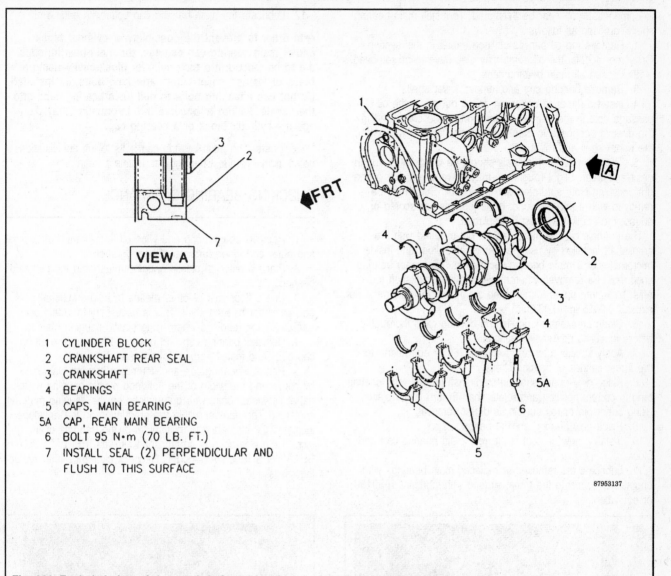

1 CYLINDER BLOCK
2 CRANKSHAFT REAR SEAL
3 CRANKSHAFT
4 BEARINGS
5 CAPS, MAIN BEARING
5A CAP, REAR MAIN BEARING
6 BOLT 95 N•m (70 LB. FT.)
7 INSTALL SEAL (2) PERPENDICULAR AND
   FLUSH TO THIS SURFACE

Fig. 201 Exploded view of the crankshaft and bearings — 1995 2.2L engine shown

16. Position the upper half of main bearings in the block and lubricate with engine oil.

17. Position crankshaft keyway in the same position as removed and lower into block. The connecting rods will follow the crank pins into the correct position as the crankshaft is lowered.

18. Lubricate the thrust flanges with 1050169 Lubricant or equivalent. Install caps with lower half of bearings lubricated with engine oil. Lubricate cap bolts with engine oil and install, but do not tighten.

19. With a block of wood, bump shaft in each direction to align thrust flanges of main bearing. After bumping shaft in each direction, wedge the shaft to the front and hold it while torquing the thrust bearing cap bolts.

❋❋WARNING

In order to prevent the possibility of cylinder block and/or main bearing cap damage, the main bearing caps are to be tapped into their cylinder block cavity using a brass or leather mallet before attaching bolts are installed. Do not use attaching bolts to pull main bearing caps into their seats. Failure to observe this information may damage the cylinder block or a bearing cap.

20. Tighten all main bearing caps to specifications, refer to the Torque Specification Chart.

21. Remove the connecting rod bolt thread protectors and lubricate the connecting rod bearings with engine oil.

22. Install the connecting rod bearing caps in their original position. Tighten the nuts to specification, refer to the Torque Specifications Chart.

23. Complete the installation by reversing the removal steps.

BEARING REPLACEMENT

▶ See Figures 202 and 203

Main bearing clearances must be corrected by the use of selective upper and lower shells. UNDER NO CIRCUMSTANCES should the use of shims behind the shells to compensate for wear be attempted. To install main bearing shells, proceed as follows:

1. Remove the oil pan as outlined earlier in this section. On some models, the oil pump may also have to be removed.

2. Loosen all main bearing caps.

3. Remove bearing cap and remove lower shell.

4. Insert a flattened cotter pin or roll out pin in the oil passage hole in the crankshaft, then rotate the crankshaft in the direction opposite to cranking rotation. The pin will contact the upper shell and roll it out.

5. The main bearing journals should be checked for roughness and wear. Slight roughness may be removed with a fine grit polishing cloth saturated with engine oil. Burrs may be removed with a fine oil stone. If the journals are scored or ridged, the crankshaft must be replaced.

The journals can be measured for out-of-round with the crankshaft installed by using a crankshaft caliper and inside micrometer or a main bearing micrometer. The upper bearing shell must be removed when measuring the crankshaft journals. Maximum out-of-round of the crankshaft journals must not exceed 0.0015 in. (0.037mm).

6. Clean crankshaft journals and bearing caps thoroughly before installing new main bearings.

7. Apply special lubricant, No. 1050169 or equivalent, to the thrust flanges of bearing shells.

8. Place new upper shell on crankshaft journal with locating tang in correct position and rotate shaft to turn it into place using cotter pin or roll out pin as during removal.

9. Place new bearing shell in bearing cap.

10. Install a new oil seal in the rear main bearing cap and block.

11. Lubricate the removed or replaced main bearings with engine oil. Lubricate the thrust surface with lubricant 1050169 or equivalent.

12. Lubricate the main bearing cap bolts with engine oil.

➡In order to prevent the possibility of cylinder block and/or main bearing cap damage, the main bearing caps are to be tapped into their cylinder block cavity using a brass or leather mallet before attaching bolts are installed. Do not use attaching bolts to pull main bearing caps into their seats. Failure to observe this information may damage the cylinder block or a bearing cap.

13. Tighten the main bearing cap bolts to the specifications noted in the Torque Chart located in this section.

CHECKING BEARING CLEARANCE

1. Remove bearing cap and wipe oil from crankshaft journal and outer and inner surfaces of bearing shell.

2. Place a piece of plastic gauging material in the center of bearing.

3. Use a floor jack or other means to hold crankshaft against upper bearing shell. This is necessary to obtain accurate clearance readings when using plastic gauging material.

4. Reinstall bearing cap and bearing. Place engine oil on cap bolts and install Torque bolts to specification.

5. Remove bearing cap and determine bearing clearance by comparing the width of the flattened plastic gauging material at its widest point with graduations on the gauging material container. The number within the graduation on the envelope indicates the clearance in millimeters or thousandths of an inch. If the clearance is greater than allowed, REPLACE BOTH BEARING SHELLS AS A SET. Recheck clearance after replacing shells.

87953249

Fig. 202 Loosening the bearing caps

87953250

Fig. 203 Make sure to tighten the bearing cap bolts to the proper torque specifications

EXHAUST SYSTEM

General Information

▶ See Figures 204 and 205

➡Safety glasses should be worn at all times when working on or near the exhaust system. Older exhaust systems will almost always be covered with loose rust particles which will shower you when disturbed. These particles are more than a nuisance and could injure your eye.

Whenever working on the exhaust system always keep the following in mind:
- Check the complete exhaust system for open seams, holes loose connections, or other deterioration which could permit exhaust fumes to seep into the passenger compartment.
- The exhaust system is usually supported by free-hanging rubber mountings which permit some movement of the exhaust system, but does not permit transfer of noise and vibration into the passenger compartment. Do not replace the rubber mounts with solid ones.
- Before removing any component of the exhaust system, ALWAYS squirt a liquid rust dissolving agent onto the fasteners for ease of removal. A lot of knuckle skin will be saved by following this rule. It may even be wise to spray the fasteners and allow them to sit overnight.
- Annoying rattles and noise vibrations in the exhaust system are usually caused by misalignment of the parts. When aligning the system, leave all bolts and nuts loose until all parts are properly aligned, then tighten, working from front to rear.
- When installing exhaust system parts, make sure there is enough clearance between the hot exhaust parts and pipes and hoses that would be adversely affected by excessive heat. Also make sure there is adequate clearance from the floor pan to avoid possible overheating of the floor.
- Support the car extra securely. Not only will you often be working directly under it, but you'll frequently be using a lot of force, say, heavy hammer blows, to dislodge rusted parts. This can cause a car that's improperly supported to shift and possibly fall.
- If you're using a cutting torch, keep it a great distance from either the fuel tank or lines. Stop what you're doing and feel the temperature of the fuel bearing pipes on the tank frequently. Even slight heat can expand and/or vaporize fuel, resulting in accumulated vapor, or even a liquid leak, near your torch.
- Watch where your hammer blows fall and make sure you hit squarely. You could easily tap a brake or fuel line when you hit an exhaust system part with a glancing blow. Inspect all lines and hoses in the area where you've been working.

❄❄CAUTION

Be very careful when working on or near the catalytic converter. External temperatures can reach 1,500°F (816°C) and more, causing severe burns. Removal or installation should be performed only on a cold exhaust system.

Fig. 204 Under-vehicle view of the exhaust components from the exhaust manifold leading to the catalytic converter

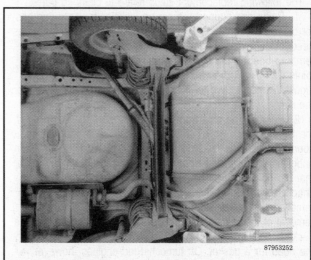

Fig. 205 View of the exhaust pipe running from the catalytic converter to the moffler and tailpipe

SPECIAL TOOLS

A number of special exhaust system tools can be rented from auto supply houses or local stores that rent special equipment. A common one is a tail pipe expander, designed to enable you to join pipes of identical diameter.

It may also be quite helpful to use solvents designed to loosen rusted bolts or flanges. Soaking rusted parts the night before you do the job can speed the work of freeing rusted parts considerably. Remember that these solvents are often flammable. Apply only to parts after they are cool!

COMPONENT REPLACEMENT

▶ **See Figures 206, 207, 208, 209, 210, 211, 212, 213, 214, 215, 216, 217, 218, 219 and 220**

System components may be welded or clamped together. The system consists of a head pipe, catalytic converter, intermediate pipe, muffler and tail pipe, in that order from the engine to the back of the car.

The head pipe is bolted to the exhaust manifold, except on turbocharged engines, in which case it is bolted to the turbocharger outlet elbow. Various hangers suspend the system from the floor pan. When assembling exhaust system parts, the relative clearances around all system parts is extremely critical. Observe all clearances during assembly. In the event that the system is welded, the various parts will have to be cut apart for removal. In these cases, the cut parts may not be reused. To cut the parts, a hacksaw is the best choice. An oxy-acetylene cutting torch may be faster but the sparks are DANGEROUS near the fuel tank, and, at the very least, accidents could happen, resulting in damage to other under-car parts, not to mention yourself!

The following replacement steps relate to clamped parts:

1. Raise and support the car on jackstands. It's much easier on you if you can get the car up on 4 stands. Some pipes need lots of clearance for removal and installation. If the system has been in the car for a long time, spray the clamped joints with a rust dissolving solutions such as WD-40® or Liquid Wrench®, and let it set according to the instructions on the can.

2. Remove the nuts from the U-bolts; don't be surprised if the U-bolts break while removing the nuts. Age and rust account for this. Besides, you shouldn't reuse old U-bolts. When unbolting the headpipe from the exhaust manifold, make sure that the bolts are free before trying to remove them. If you snap a stud in the exhaust manifold, the stud will have to be removed with a bolt extractor, which often necessitates the removal of the manifold itself. On J-cars, the headpipe uses a necked collar for sealing purposes at the manifold, eliminating the need for a gasket. On turbocharged engines, however, a gasket is used at the joint between the headpipe and the turbocharger outlet.

3. After the clamps are removed from the joints, first twist the parts at the joints to break loose rust and scale, then pull the components apart with a twisting motion. If the parts twist freely but won't pull apart, check the joint. The clamp may have been installed so tightly that it has caused a slight crushing of the joint. In this event, the best thing to do is secure a chisel designed for the purpose and, using the chisel and a hammer, peel back the female pipe end until the parts are freed.

4. Once the parts are freed, check the condition of the pipes which you had intended keeping. If their condition is at all in doubt, replace them too. You went to a lot of work to get one or more components out. You don't want to have to go through that again in the near future. If you are retaining a pipe, check the pipe end. If it was crushed by a clamp, it can be restored to its original diameter using a pipe expander,

which can be rented at most good auto parts stores. Check, also, the condition of the exhaust system hangers. If ANY deterioration is noted, replace them. Oh, and one note about parts: use only parts designed for your car. Don't use fits-all parts or flex pipes. The fits-all parts never fit and the flex pipes don't last very long.

5. When installing the new parts, coat the pipe ends with exhaust system lubricant. It makes fitting the parts much easier. It's also a good idea to assemble all the parts in position before clamping them. This will ensure a good fit, detect any problems and allow you to check all clearances between the parts and surrounding frame and floor members.

6. When you are satisfied with all fits and clearances, install the clamps. The headpipe-to-manifold nuts should be torqued to 20 ft. lbs. (27 Nm). If the studs were rusty, wire-brush them clean and spray them with WD-40® or Liquid Wrench®. This will ensure a proper torque reading. Position the clamps on the slip points as illustrated. The slits in the female pipe ends should be under the U-bolts, not under the clamp end. Tighten the U-bolt nuts securely, without crushing the pipe. The pipe fit should be tight, so that you can't swivel the pipe by hand. Don't forget: always use new clamps. When the system is tight, recheck all clearances. Start the engine and check the joints for leaks. A leak can be felt by hand. MAKE CERTAIN THAT THE CAR IS SECURE ON THE JACKSTANDS BEFORE GETTING UNDER IT WITH THE ENGINE RUNNING!! If any leaks are detected, tighten the clamp until the leak stops. If the pipe starts to deform before the leak stops, reposition the clamp and tighten it. If that still doesn't stop the leak, it may be that you don't have enough overlap on the pipe fit. Shut off the engine, let it cool, and try pushing the pipe together further. Be careful, the pipe gets hot quickly.

7. When everything is tight and secure, lower the car and take it for a road test. Make sure there are no unusual sounds or vibration. Most new pipes are coated with a preservative, so the system will be pretty smelly for a day or two while the coating burns off.

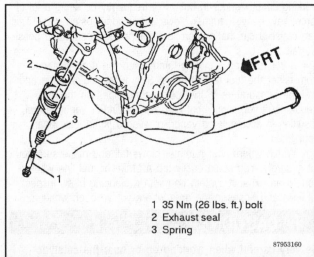

1　35 Nm (26 lbs. ft.) bolt
2　Exhaust seal
3　Spring

87953160

Fig. 206 Manifold attachment — 1995 2.2L with Federal Emissions or manual transaxle

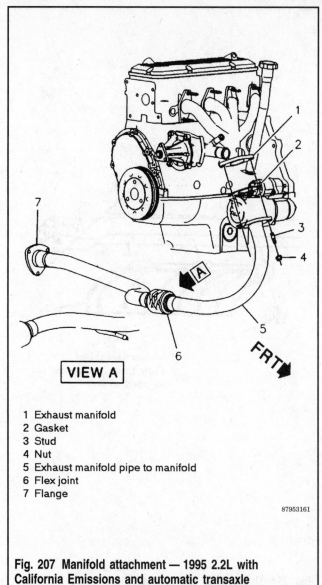

VIEW A

1 Exhaust manifold
2 Gasket
3 Stud
4 Nut
5 Exhaust manifold pipe to manifold
6 Flex joint
7 Flange

87953161

Fig. 207 Manifold attachment — 1995 2.2L with California Emissions and automatic transaxle

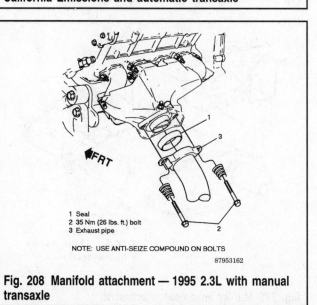

1 Seal
2 35 Nm (26 lbs. ft.) bolt
3 Exhaust pipe

NOTE: USE ANTI-SEIZE COMPOUND ON BOLTS

87953162

Fig. 208 Manifold attachment — 1995 2.3L with manual transaxle

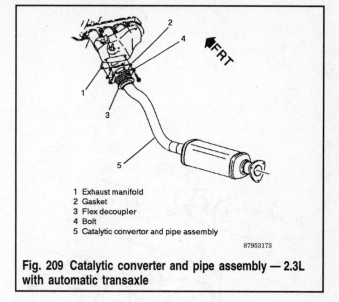

1 Exhaust manifold
2 Gasket
3 Flex decoupler
4 Bolt
5 Catalytic convertor and pipe assembly

87953173

Fig. 209 Catalytic converter and pipe assembly — 2.3L with automatic transaxle

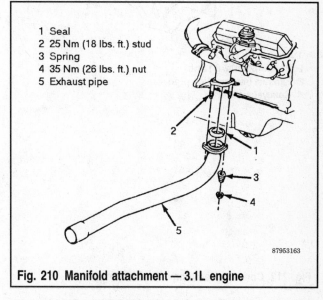

1 Seal
2 25 Nm (18 lbs. ft.) stud
3 Spring
4 35 Nm (26 lbs. ft.) nut
5 Exhaust pipe

87953163

Fig. 210 Manifold attachment — 3.1L engine

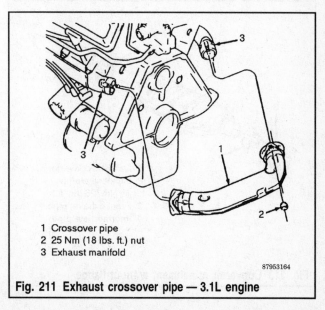

1 Crossover pipe
2 25 Nm (18 lbs. ft.) nut
3 Exhaust manifold

87953164

Fig. 211 Exhaust crossover pipe — 3.1L engine

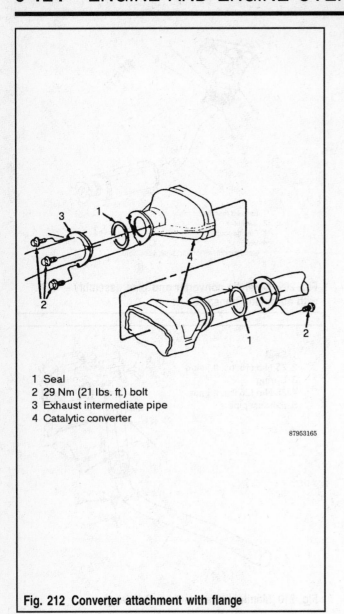

1 Seal
2 29 Nm (21 lbs. ft.) bolt
3 Exhaust intermediate pipe
4 Catalytic converter

87953165

Fig. 212 Converter attachment with flange

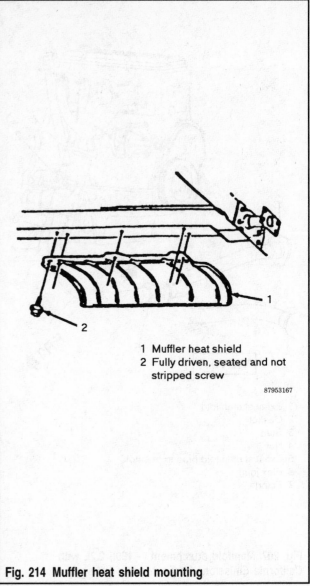

1 Muffler heat shield
2 Fully driven, seated and not stripped screw

87953167

Fig. 214 Muffler heat shield mounting

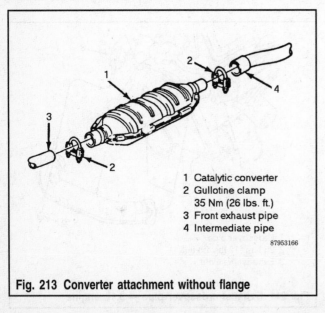

1 Catalytic converter
2 Gullotine clamp
35 Nm (26 lbs. ft.)
3 Front exhaust pipe
4 Intermediate pipe

87953166

Fig. 213 Converter attachment without flange

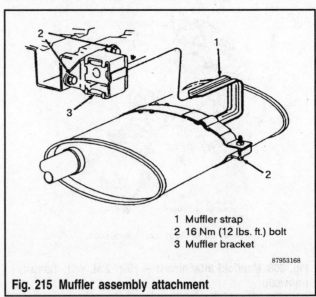

1 Muffler strap
2 16 Nm (12 lbs. ft.) bolt
3 Muffler bracket

87953168

Fig. 215 Muffler assembly attachment

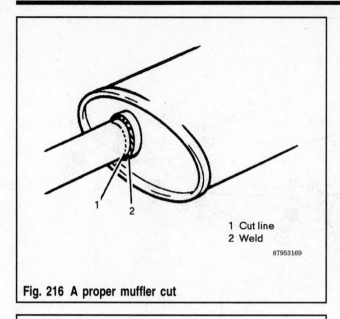

1 Cut line
2 Weld

87953169

Fig. 216 A proper muffler cut

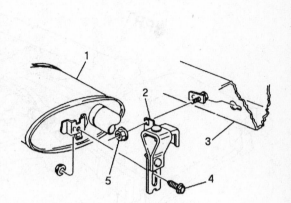

1 Exhaust muffler (right hand)
2 Muffler hanger
3 Frame rail (right side)
4 Hanger to muffler bolt
5 Hanger to frame rail nut

87953171

**Fig. 218 Dual exhaust right-hand muffler hanger —
Pontiac Sunfire 2.3L engine only**

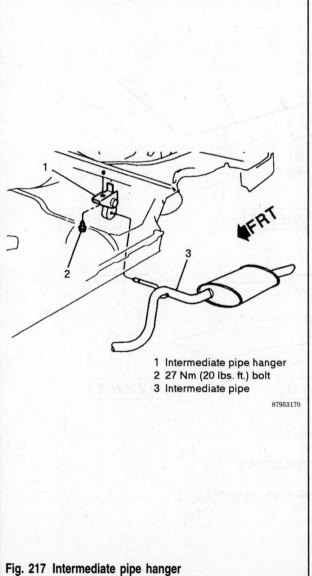

1 Intermediate pipe hanger
2 27 Nm (20 lbs. ft.) bolt
3 Intermediate pipe

87953170

Fig. 217 Intermediate pipe hanger

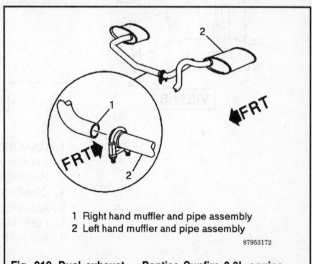

1 Right hand muffler and pipe assembly
2 Left hand muffler and pipe assembly

87953172

**Fig. 219 Dual exhaust — Pontiac Sunfire 2.3L engine
only**

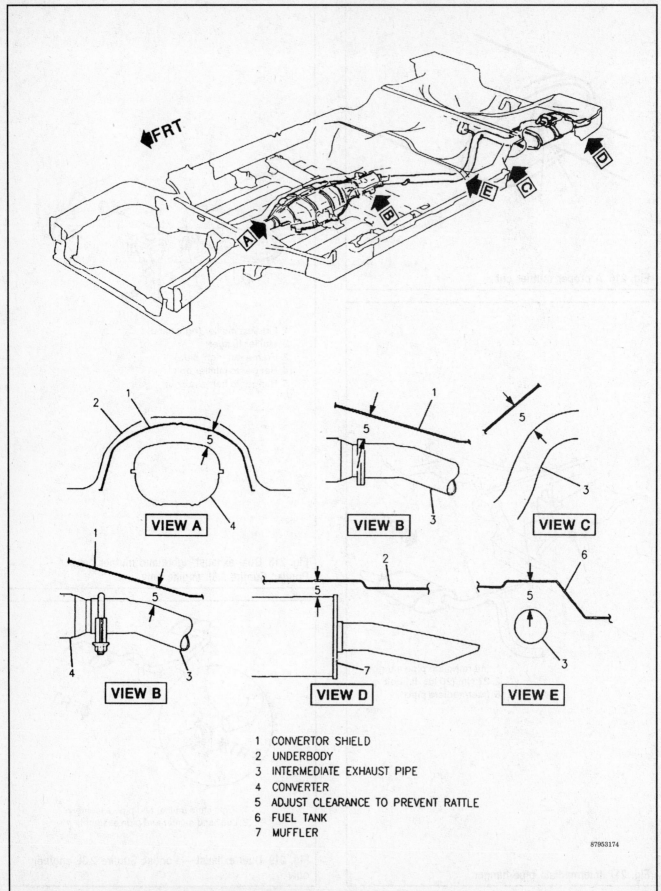

1 CONVERTOR SHIELD
2 UNDERBODY
3 INTERMEDIATE EXHAUST PIPE
4 CONVERTER
5 ADJUST CLEARANCE TO PREVENT RATTLE
6 FUEL TANK
7 MUFFLER

87953174

Fig. 220 Exhaust system to body clearance specifications

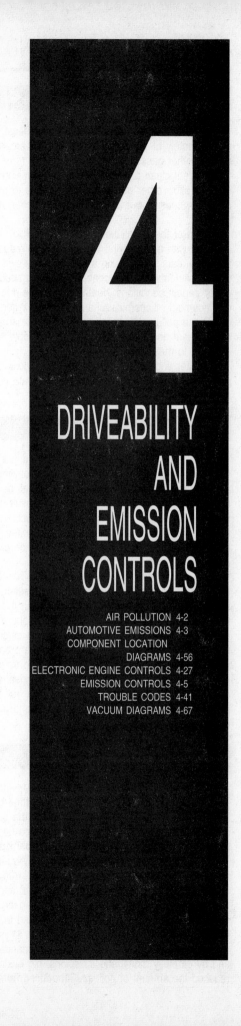

AIR POLLUTION
AUTOMOTIVE POLLUTANTS 4-2
INDUSTRIAL POLLUTANTS 4-2
NATURAL POLLUTANTS 4-2
AUTOMOTIVE EMISSIONS
CRANKCASE EMISSIONS 4-5
EVAPORATIVE EMISSIONS 4-5
EXHAUST GASES 4-3
COMPONENT LOCATION
DIAGRAMS 4-56
ELECTRONIC ENGINE CONTROLS
CAMSHAFT POSITION (CMP)
  SENSOR 4-37
CRANKSHAFT POSITION (CKP)
  SENSOR 4-37
ENGINE COOLANT TEMPERATURE
  (ECT) SENSOR 4-32
ENGINE/POWERTRAIN CONTROL
  MODULE (ECM/PCM) 4-28
GENERAL INFORMATION 4-27
IDLE AIR CONTROL (IAC)
  VALVE 4-31
KNOCK SENSOR (KS) 4-40
MANIFOLD ABSOLUTE PRESSURE
  (MAP) SENSOR 4-35
MANIFOLD AIR TEMPERATURE
  (MAT)/INTAKE AIR TEMPERATURE
  (IAT) SENSOR 4-34
OXYGEN (O_2) SENSOR 4-30
PARK/NEUTRAL SWITCH 4-38
THROTTLE POSITION (TP)
  SENSOR 4-35
VEHICLE SPEED SENSOR
  (VSS) 4-39
EMISSION CONTROLS
AIR INJECTION REACTION (AIR)
  MANAGEMENT SYSTEM 4-23
CATALYTIC CONVERTER 4-20
CRANKCASE VENTILATION
  SYSTEM 4-6
EARLY FUEL EVAPORATION (EFE)
  SYSTEM 4-25
EVAPORATIVE EMISSION CONTROL
  SYSTEM 4-7
EXHAUST GAS RECIRCULATION
  (EGR) SYSTEM 4-9
THERMOSTATIC AIR CLEANER
  (THERMAC) 4-21
TROUBLE CODES
CLEARING CODES 4-43
DIAGNOSIS AND TESTING 4-42
GENERAL INFORMATION 4-41
READING CODES 4-43
TOOLS AND EQUIPMENT 4-41
VACUUM DIAGRAMS 4-67

4

DRIVEABILITY AND EMISSION CONTROLS

AIR POLLUTION 4-2
AUTOMOTIVE EMISSIONS 4-3
COMPONENT LOCATION
  DIAGRAMS 4-56
ELECTRONIC ENGINE CONTROLS 4-27
EMISSION CONTROLS 4-5
TROUBLE CODES 4-41
VACUUM DIAGRAMS 4-67

AIR POLLUTION

The earth's atmosphere, at or near sea level, consists approximately of 78 percent nitrogen, 21 percent oxygen and 1 percent other gases. If it were possible to remain in this state, 100 percent clean air would result. However, many varied sources allow other gases and particulates to mix with the clean air, causing our atmosphere to become unclean or polluted.

Certain of these pollutants are visible while others are invisible, with each having the capability of causing distress to the eyes, ears, throat, skin and respiratory system. Should these pollutants become concentrated in a specific area and under certain conditions, death could result due to the displacement or chemical change of the oxygen content in the air. These pollutants can also cause great damage to the environment and to the many man made objects that are exposed to the elements.

To better understand the causes of air pollution, the pollutants can be categorized into 3 separate types, natural, industrial and automotive.

Natural Pollutants

Natural pollution has been present on earth since before man appeared and continues to be a factor when discussing air pollution, although it causes only a small percentage of the overall pollution problem. It is the direct result of decaying organic matter, wind born smoke and particulates from such natural events as plain and forest fires (ignited by heat or lightning), volcanic ash, sand and dust which can spread over a large area of the countryside.

Such a phenomenon of natural pollution has been seen in the form of volcanic eruptions, with the resulting plume of smoke, steam and volcanic ash blotting out the sun's rays as it spreads and rises higher into the atmosphere. As it travels into the atmosphere the upper air currents catch and carry the smoke and ash, while condensing the steam back into water vapor. As the water vapor, smoke and ash travel on their journey, the smoke dissipates into the atmosphere while the ash and moisture settle back to earth in a trail hundreds of miles long. In some cases, lives are lost and millions of dollars of property damage result.

Industrial Pollutants

Industrial pollution is caused primarily by industrial processes, the burning of coal, oil and natural gas, which in turn produce smoke and fumes. Because the burning fuels contain large amounts of sulfur, the principal ingredients of smoke and fumes are sulfur dioxide and particulate matter. This type of pollutant occurs most severely during still, damp and cool weather, such as at night. Even in its less severe form, this pollutant is not confined to just cities. Because of air movements, the pollutants move for miles over the surrounding countryside, leaving in its path a barren and unhealthy environment for all living things.

Working with Federal, State and Local mandated regulations and by carefully monitoring emissions, big business has greatly reduced the amount of pollutant introduced from its industrial sources, striving to obtain an acceptable level. Because of the mandated industrial emission clean up, many land areas and streams in and around the cities that were formerly barren of vegetation and life, have now begun to move back in the direction of nature's intended balance.

Automotive Pollutants

The third major source of air pollution is automotive emissions. The emissions from the internal combustion engines were not an appreciable problem years ago because of the small number of registered vehicles and the nation's small highway system. However, during the early 1950's, the trend of the American people was to move from the cities to the surrounding suburbs. This caused an immediate problem in transportation because the majority of suburbs were not afforded mass transit conveniences. This lack of transportation created an attractive market for the automobile manufacturers, which resulted in a dramatic increase in the number of vehicles produced and sold, along with a marked increase in highway construction between cities and the suburbs. Multi-vehicle families emerged with a growing emphasis placed on an individual vehicle per family member. As the increase in vehicle ownership and usage occurred, so did pollutant levels in and around the cities, as suburbanites drove daily to their businesses and employment, returning at the end of the day to their homes in the suburbs.

It was noted that a smoke and fog type haze was being formed and at times, remained in suspension over the cities, taking time to dissipate. At first this "smog," derived from the words "smoke" and "fog," was thought to result from industrial pollution but it was determined that automobile emissions shared the blame. It was discovered that when normal automobile emissions were exposed to sunlight for a period of time, complex chemical reactions would take place.

It is now known that smog is a photo chemical layer which develops when certain oxides of nitrogen (NOx) and unburned hydrocarbons (HC) from automobile emissions are exposed to sunlight. Pollution was more severe when smog would become stagnant over an area in which a warm layer of air settled over the top of the cooler air mass, trapping and holding the cooler mass at ground level. The trapped cooler air would keep the emissions from being dispersed and diluted through normal air flows. This type of air stagnation was given the name "Temperature Inversion."

TEMPERATURE INVERSION

In normal weather situations, surface air is warmed by heat radiating from the earth's surface and the sun's rays. This causes it to rise upward, into the atmosphere. Upon rising it will cool through a convection type heat exchange with the cooler upper air. As warm air rises, the surface pollutants are carried upward and dissipated into the atmosphere.

When a temperature inversion occurs, we find the higher air is no longer cooler, but is warmer than the surface air, causing the cooler surface air to become trapped. This warm air blanket can extend from above ground level to a few hundred or even a few thousand feet into the air. As the surface air is trapped, so are the pollutants, causing a severe smog condition. Should this stagnant air mass extend to a few thousand feet high, enough air movement with the inversion takes place to allow the smog layer to rise above ground level but the pollutants still cannot dissipate. This inversion can remain for days over an area, with the smog level only rising or lowering from ground level to a few hundred feet high. Meanwhile, the pollutant levels increase, causing eye irritation, respiratory problems, reduced visibility, plant damage and in some cases, even disease.

This inversion phenomenon was first noted in the Los Angeles, California area. The city lies in terrain resembling a basin and with certain weather conditions, a cold air mass is held in the basin while a warmer air mass covers it like a lid.

Because this type of condition was first documented as prevalent in the Los Angeles area, this type of trapped pollution was named Los Angeles Smog, although it occurs in other areas where a large concentration of automobiles are used and the air remains stagnant for any length of time.

HEAT TRANSFER

Consider the internal combustion engine as a machine in which raw materials must be placed so a finished product comes out. As in any machine operation, a certain amount of wasted material is formed. When we relate this to the internal combustion engine, we find that through the input of air and

fuel, we obtain power during the combustion process to drive the vehicle. The by-product or waste of this power is, in part, heat and exhaust gases with which we must dispose.

The heat from the combustion process can rise to over 4000°F (2204°C). The dissipation of this heat is controlled by a ram air effect, the use of cooling fans to cause air flow and a liquid coolant solution surrounding the combustion area to transfer the heat of combustion through the cylinder walls and into the coolant. The coolant is then directed to a thin-finned, multi-tubed radiator, from which the excess heat is transferred to the atmosphere by 1 of the 3 heat transfer methods, conduction, convection or radiation.

The cooling of the combustion area is an important part in the control of exhaust emissions. To understand the behavior of the combustion and transfer of its heat, consider the air/fuel charge. It is ignited and the flame front burns progressively across the combustion chamber until the burning charge reaches the cylinder walls. Some of the fuel in contact with the walls is not hot enough to burn, thereby snuffing out or quenching the combustion process. This leaves unburned fuel in the combustion chamber. This unburned fuel is then forced out of the cylinder and into the exhaust system, along with the exhaust gases.

Many attempts have been made to minimize the amount of unburned fuel in the combustion chambers due to quenching, by increasing the coolant temperature and lessening the contact area of the coolant around the combustion area. However, design limitations within the combustion chambers prevent the complete burning of the air/fuel charge, so a certain amount of the unburned fuel is still expelled into the exhaust system, regardless of modifications to the engine.

AUTOMOTIVE EMISSIONS

Before emission controls were mandated on internal combustion engines, other sources of engine pollutants were discovered along with the exhaust emissions. It was determined that engine combustion exhaust produced approximately 60 percent of the total emission pollutants, fuel evaporation from the fuel tank and carburetor vents produced 20 percent, with the final 20 percent being produced through the crankcase as a by-product of the combustion process.

Exhaust Gases

The exhaust gases emitted into the atmosphere are a combination of burned and unburned fuel. To understand the exhaust emission and its composition, we must review some basic chemistry.

When the air/fuel mixture is introduced into the engine, we are mixing air, composed of nitrogen (78 percent), oxygen (21 percent) and other gases (1 percent) with the fuel, which is 100 percent hydrocarbons (HC), in a semi-controlled ratio. As the combustion process is accomplished, power is produced to move the vehicle while the heat of combustion is transferred to the cooling system. The exhaust gases are then composed of nitrogen, a diatomic gas (N_2), the same as was introduced in the engine, carbon dioxide (CO_2), the same gas that is used in beverage carbonation, and water vapor (H_2O). The nitrogen (N_2), for the most part, passes through the engine unchanged, while the oxygen (O_2) reacts (burns) with the hydrocarbons

(HC) and produces the carbon dioxide (CO_2) and the water vapors (H_2O). If this chemical process would be the only process to take place, the exhaust emissions would be harmless. However, during the combustion process, other compounds are formed which are considered dangerous. These pollutants are hydrocarbons (HC), carbon monoxide (CO), oxides of nitrogen (NOx) oxides of sulfur (SOx) and engine particulates.

HYDROCARBONS

Hydrocarbons (HC) are essentially fuel which was not burned during the combustion process or which has escaped into the atmosphere through fuel evaporation. The main sources of incomplete combustion are rich air/fuel mixtures, low engine temperatures and improper spark timing. The main sources of hydrocarbon emission through fuel evaporation on most vehicles used to be the vehicle's fuel tank and carburetor float bowl.

To reduce combustion hydrocarbon emission, engine modifications were made to minimize dead space and surface area in the combustion chamber. In addition, the air/fuel mixture was made more lean through the improved control which feedback carburetion and fuel injection offers and by the addition of external controls to aid in further combustion of the hydrocarbons outside the engine. Two such methods were the addition of air injection systems, to inject fresh air into the exhaust manifolds and the installation of catalytic converters, units that are able to burn traces of hydrocarbons without affecting the internal combustion process or fuel economy.

To control hydrocarbon emissions through fuel evaporation, modifications were made to the fuel tank to allow storage of the fuel vapors during periods of engine shut-down. Modifications were also made to the air intake system so that at specific times during engine operation, these vapors may be purged and burned by blending them with the air/fuel mixture.

CARBON MONOXIDE

Carbon monoxide is formed when not enough oxygen is present during the combustion process to convert carbon (C) to carbon dioxide (CO_2). An increase in the carbon monoxide (CO) emission is normally accompanied by an increase in the hydrocarbon (HC) emission because of the lack of oxygen to completely burn all of the fuel mixture.

Carbon monoxide (CO) also increases the rate at which the photo chemical smog is formed by speeding up the conversion of nitric oxide (NO) to nitrogen dioxide (NO_2). To accomplish this, carbon monoxide (CO) combines with oxygen (O_2) and nitric oxide (NO) to produce carbon dioxide (CO_2) and nitrogen dioxide (NO_2). ($CO + O_2 + NO = CO_2 + NO_2$).

The dangers of carbon monoxide, which is an odorless and colorless toxic gas are many. When carbon monoxide is inhaled into the lungs and passed into the blood stream, oxygen is replaced by the carbon monoxide in the red blood cells, causing a reduction in the amount of oxygen supplied to the many parts of the body. This lack of oxygen causes headaches, lack of coordination, reduced mental alertness and, should the carbon monoxide concentration be high enough, death could result.

NITROGEN

Normally, nitrogen is an inert gas. When heated to approximately 2500°F (1371°C) through the combustion process, this gas becomes active and causes an increase in the nitric oxide (NO) emission.

Oxides of nitrogen (NOx) are composed of approximately 97-98 percent nitric oxide (NO). Nitric oxide is a colorless gas but when it is passed into the atmosphere, it combines with oxygen and forms nitrogen dioxide (NO_2). The nitrogen dioxide then combines with chemically active hydrocarbons (HC) and when in the presence of sunlight, causes the formation of photo-chemical smog.

Ozone

To further complicate matters, some of the nitrogen dioxide (NO_2) is broken apart by the sunlight to form nitric oxide and oxygen. ($NO_2 + sunlight = NO + O$). This single atom of oxygen then combines with diatomic (meaning 2 atoms) oxygen (O_2) to form ozone (O_3). Ozone is one of the smells associated with smog. It has a pungent and offensive odor, irritates the eyes and lung tissues, affects the growth of plant life and causes rapid deterioration of rubber products. Ozone

can be formed by sunlight as well as electrical discharge into the air.

The most common discharge area on the automobile engine is the secondary ignition electrical system, especially when inferior quality spark plug cables are used. As the surge of high voltage is routed through the secondary cable, the circuit builds up an electrical field around the wire, which acts upon the oxygen in the surrounding air to form the ozone. The faint glow along the cable with the engine running that may be visible on a dark night, is called the "corona discharge." It is the result of the electrical field passing from a high along the cable, to a low in the surrounding air, which forms the ozone gas. The combination of corona and ozone has been a major cause of cable deterioration. Recently, different and better quality insulating materials have lengthened the life of the electrical cables.

Although ozone at ground level can be harmful, ozone is beneficial to the earth's inhabitants. By having a concentrated ozone layer called the "ozonosphere," between 10 and 20 miles (16-32 km) up in the atmosphere, much of the ultra violet radiation from the sun's rays are absorbed and screened. If this ozone layer were not present, much of the earth's surface would be burned, dried and unfit for human life.

OXIDES OF SULFUR

Oxides of sulfur (SOx) were initially ignored in the exhaust system emissions, since the sulfur content of gasoline as a fuel is less than $\frac{1}{10}$ of 1 percent. Because of this small amount, it was felt that it contributed very little to the overall pollution problem. However, because of the difficulty in solving the sulfur emissions in industrial pollutions and the introduction of catalytic converter to the automobile exhaust systems, a change was mandated. The automobile exhaust system, when equipped with a catalytic converter, changes the sulfur dioxide (SO_2) into the sulfur trioxide (SO_3).

When this combines with water vapors (H_2O), a sulfuric acid mist (H_2SO_4) is formed and is a very difficult pollutant to handle since it is extremely corrosive. This sulfuric acid mist that is formed, is the same mist that rises from the vents of an automobile battery when an active chemical reaction takes place within the battery cells.

When a large concentration of vehicles equipped with catalytic converters are operating in an area, this acid mist may rise and be distributed over a large ground area causing land, plant, crop, paint and building damage.

PARTICULATE MATTER

A certain amount of particulate matter is present in the burning of any fuel, with carbon constituting the largest percentage of the particulates. In gasoline, the remaining particulates are the burned remains of the various other compounds used in its manufacture. When a gasoline engine is in good internal condition, the particulate emissions are low but as the engine wears internally, the particulate emissions increase. By visually inspecting the tail pipe emissions, a determination can be made as to where an engine defect may exist. An engine with light gray or blue smoke emitting from the tail pipe normally indicates an increase in the oil consumption through burning due to internal engine wear. Black smoke would indicate a defective fuel delivery system, causing the engine to operate in a rich mode. Regardless of the color of the smoke, the internal part of the engine or the fuel delivery system should be repaired to prevent excess particulate emissions.

Diesel and turbine engines emit a darkened plume of smoke from the exhaust system because of the type of fuel used. Emission control regulations are mandated for this type of emission and more stringent measures are being used to prevent excess emission of the particulate matter. Electronic components are being introduced to control the injection of the fuel at precisely the proper time of piston travel, to achieve the optimum in fuel ignition and fuel usage. Other particulate after-burning components are being tested to achieve a cleaner emission.

Good grades of engine lubricating oils should be used, which meet the manufacturers specification. Cut-rate oils can contribute to the particulate emission problem because of their low flash or ignition temperature point. Such oils burn prematurely during the combustion process causing emission of particulate matter.

The cooling system is an important factor in the reduction of particulate matter. The optimum combustion will occur, with the cooling system operating at a temperature specified by the manufacturer. The cooling system must be maintained in the same manner as the engine oiling system, as each system is required to perform properly in order for the engine to operate efficiently for a long time.

Crankcase Emissions

Crankcase emissions are made up of water, acids, unburned fuel, oil fumes and particulates. These emissions are classified as hydrocarbons (HC) and are formed by the small amount of unburned, compressed air/fuel mixture entering the crankcase from the combustion area (between the cylinder walls and piston rings) during the compression and power strokes. The head of the compression and combustion help to form the remaining crankcase emissions.

Since the first engines, crankcase emissions were allowed into the atmosphere through a road draft tube, mounted on the lower side of the engine block. Fresh air came in through an open oil filler cap or breather. The air passed through the crankcase mixing with blow-by gases. The motion of the vehicle and the air blowing past the open end of the road draft tube caused a low pressure area (vacuum) at the end of the tube. Crankcase emissions were simply drawn out of the road draft tube into the air.

To control the crankcase emission, the road draft tube was deleted. A hose and/or tubing was routed from the crankcase to the intake manifold so the blow-by emission could be burned with the air/fuel mixture. However, it was found that

intake manifold vacuum, used to draw the crankcase emissions into the manifold, would vary in strength at the wrong time and not allow the proper emission flow. A regulating valve was needed to control the flow of air through the crankcase.

Testing, showed the removal of the blow-by gases from the crankcase as quickly as possible, was most important to the longevity of the engine. Should large accumulations of blow-by gases remain and condense, dilution of the engine oil would occur to form water, soots, resins, acids and lead salts, resulting in the formation of sludge and varnishes. This condensation of the blow-by gases occurs more frequently on vehicles used in numerous starting and stopping conditions, excessive idling and when the engine is not allowed to attain normal operating temperature through short runs.

Evaporative Emissions

Gasoline fuel is a major source of pollution, before and after it is burned in the automobile engine. From the time the fuel is refined, stored, pumped and transported, again stored until it is pumped into the fuel tank of the vehicle, the gasoline gives off unburned hydrocarbons (HC) into the atmosphere. Through the redesign of storage areas and venting systems, the pollution factor was diminished, but not eliminated, from the refinery standpoint. However, the automobile still remained the primary source of vaporized, unburned hydrocarbon (HC) emissions.

Fuel pumped from an underground storage tank is cool but when exposed to a warmer ambient temperature, will expand. Before controls were mandated, an owner might fill the fuel tank with fuel from an underground storage tank and park the vehicle for some time in warm area, such as a parking lot. As the fuel would warm, it would expand and should no provisions or area be provided for the expansion, the fuel would spill out of the filler neck and onto the ground, causing hydrocarbon (HC) pollution and creating a severe fire hazard. To correct this condition, the vehicle manufacturers added overflow plumbing and/or gasoline tanks with built in expansion areas or domes.

However, this did not control the fuel vapor emission from the fuel tank. It was determined that most of the fuel evaporation occurred when the vehicle was stationary and the engine not operating. Most vehicles carry 5-25 gallons (19-95 liters) of gasoline. Should a large concentration of vehicles be parked in one area, such as a large parking lot, excessive fuel vapor emissions would take place, increasing as the temperature increases.

To prevent the vapor emission from escaping into the atmosphere, the fuel systems were designed to trap the vapors while the vehicle is stationary, by sealing the system from the atmosphere. A storage system is used to collect and hold the fuel vapors from the carburetor (if equipped) and the fuel tank when the engine is not operating. When the engine is started, the storage system is then purged of the fuel vapors, which are drawn into the engine and burned with the air/fuel mixture.

EMISSION CONTROLS

There are three sources of automotive pollutants: crankcase fumes, exhaust gases, and gasoline evaporation. The pollutants formed from these substances fall into three categories: unburned hydrocarbons (HC), carbon monoxide

(CO), and oxides of nitrogen (NOx). The equipment that is used to limit these pollutants is commonly called emission control equipment.

Crankcase Ventilation System

OPERATION

▶ See Figures 1, 2 and 3

A crankcase ventilation system is used on all vehicles to evacuate the crankcase vapors. There are 2 types of ventilation systems: Crankcase Ventilation (CV) and Positive Crankcase Ventilation (PCV). Both systems purge crankcase vapors and differ only in the use of fresh air.

The CV system, used on the 2.3L and 2.4L engines, allows crankcase vapors to escape but does not introduce fresh air into the crankcase. However, the CV system on the 3.1L engine, does introduce fresh air into the crankcase.

The PCV system and the CV system on the 3.1L engine, circulates fresh air from the air cleaner or intake duct through the crankcase, where it mixes with blow-by gases and then passes through the Positive Crankcase Ventilation (PCV) valve or constant bleed orifice into the intake manifold.

When manifold vacuum is high, such as at idle, the orifice or valve restricts the flow of blow-by gases into the intake manifold. If abnormal operating conditions occur, the system will allow excessive blow-by gases to back flow through the hose into the air cleaner. These blow-by gases will then be mixed with the intake air in the air cleaner instead of the manifold. The air cleaner has a small filter attached to the inside wall that connects to the breather hose to trap impurities flowing in either direction.

A plugged PCV valve, orifice or hose may cause rough idle, stalling or slow idle speed, oil leaks, oil in the air cleaner or sludge in the engine. A leak could cause rough idle, stalling or high idle speed. The condition of the grommets in the valve cover will also affect system and engine performance.

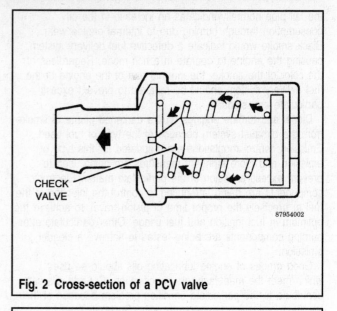

Fig. 2 Cross-section of a PCV valve

CHECK VALVE

87954002

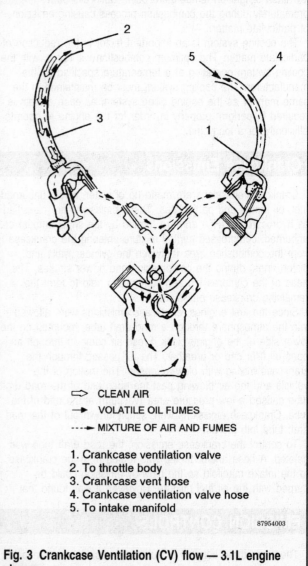

⇨ CLEAN AIR
→ VOLATILE OIL FUMES
---→ MIXTURE OF AIR AND FUMES

1. Crankcase ventilation valve
2. To throttle body
3. Crankcase vent hose
4. Crankcase ventilation valve hose
5. To intake manifold

87954003

Fig. 3 Crankcase Ventilation (CV) flow — 3.1L engine shown

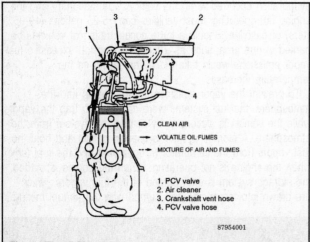

⇨ CLEAN AIR
→ VOLATILE OIL FUMES
---→ MIXTURE OF AIR AND FUMES

1. PCV valve
2. Air cleaner
3. Crankshaft vent hose
4. PCV valve hose

87954001

Fig. 1 The PCV system circulates crankcase vapors into the intake manifold for burning — 1990 2.0L (VIN M) engine shown

TESTING

PCV System

1. Run the engine at idle at normal operating temperature.
2. Remove the PCV valve or orifice from the grommet in the valve cover and place your thumb over the end to check if vacuum is present. If vacuum is not present, check for plugged hoses or manifold port. Repair or replace as necessary.
3. If the engine is equipped with a PCV valve, stop the engine and remove the valve. Shake and listen for the rattle of the check valve needle. If no rattle is heard, replace the valve.

CV System

1. Check the CV system for proper flow by looking for oil sludging or leaks.
2. If noted, check the smaller nipple of the oil/air separator by blowing through it or inserting a 0.06 in. (1.52mm) plug gauge into the orifice inside the nipple.
3. If the orifice is plugged, replace the CV oil/air separator assembly.

REMOVAL & INSTALLATION

Removal and installation of the PCV or CV valve is located in Section 1 of this manual.

Evaporative Emission Control System

OPERATION

▶ **See Figures 4 and 5**

The Evaporative Emission Control System (EECS) is designed to prevent fuel tank vapors from being emitted into the atmosphere. When the engine is not running, gasoline vapors from the tank are stored in in a charcoal canister, mounted under the hood. The charcoal canister absorbs the gasoline vapors and stores them until certain engine conditions are met and the vapors can be purged and burned by the engine. In some vehicles with fuel injection, any liquid fuel entering the canister goes into a reservoir in the bottom of the canister to protect the integrity of the carbon element in the canister above. A few different methods (depending upon application) are used to control the purge cycle of the charcoal canister.

In the first method, the charcoal canister purge cycle is controlled by throttle position without the use of a valve on the canister. A vacuum line connects the canister to a ported vacuum source on the throttle body. When the throttle is at any position above idle, a vacuum is created in the throttle body venturi. That vacuum acts on the canister causing fresh air to be drawn into the bottom of the canister and the fuel vapors to be carried into the throttle body at that vacuum port. The air/vapor flow volume is only what can be drawn through the vacuum port and is fairly constant.

For the second method, the flow volume is modulated with throttle position through a vacuum valve. The ported vacuum

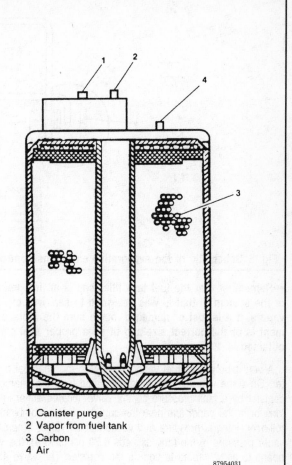

1 Canister purge
2 Vapor from fuel tank
3 Carbon
4 Air

87954031

Fig. 4 Cross-sectional view of an EVAP canister — 1995 vehicle shown

from the throttle body is used to open a diaphragm valve on top of the canister. When the valve is open, air and vapors are drawn into the intake manifold, usually through the same manifold port as the PCV system. With this method, the purge valve cycle is slaved to the throttle opening; more throttle opening, more purge air flow.

And third, the charcoal canister purge valve cycle is controlled by the computer control module through a solenoid valve mounted on or remotely from the canister. When the solenoid is activated, full manifold vacuum is applied to the top of the purge valve diaphragm to open the valve all the way. A high volume of fresh air is drawn into the canister and the gasoline vapors are purged quickly. The ECM activates the solenoid valve when the following conditions are met:

- The engine is at normal operating temperature.
- After the engine has been running for a specified period of time.
- Vehicle speed is above a predetermined speed.
- Throttle opening is above a predetermined value.

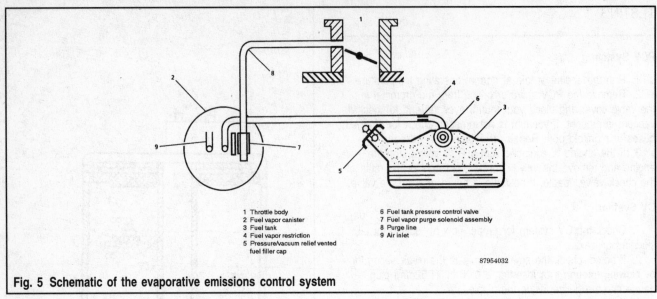

1 Throttle body
2 Fuel vapor canister
3 Fuel tank
4 Fuel vapor restriction
5 Pressure/vacuum relief vented
  fuel filler cap

6 Fuel tank pressure control valve
7 Fuel vapor purge solenoid assembly
8 Purge line
9 Air inlet

87954032

Fig. 5 Schematic of the evaporative emissions control system

➡**Remember that the fuel tank filler cap is an integral part of the system in that is was designed to seal in fuel vapors. If it is lost or damaged, make sure the replacement is or the correct size and fit so a proper seal can be obtained.**

A vent pipe allows fuel vapors to flow to the charcoal canister. On some vehicles, the tank is isolated from the charcoal canister by a tank pressure control valve, located either in the tank or in the vapor line near the canister. It is a combination roll-over, integral pressure and vacuum relief valve. When the vapor pressure in the tank exceeds 0.73 psi (5 kPa), the valve opens to allow vapors to vent to the canister. The valve also provides vacuum relief to protect against vacuum build-up in the fuel tank and roll-over spill protection.

Poor engine idle, stalling and poor driveability can be caused by an inoperative canister purge solenoid, a damaged canister or split, damaged or improperly connected hoses.

The most common symptom of problems in this system is fuel odors coming from under the hood. If there is not liquid fuel leak, check for a cracked or damaged vapor canister, inoperative or always open canister control valve, disconnected, mis-routed, kinked or damaged vapor pipe or canister hoses; or a damaged air cleaner or improperly seated air cleaner gasket.

TESTING

Charcoal Canister

1. Visually check the canister for cracks or damage.
2. If fuel is leaking from the bottom of the canister, replace the canister and check for proper hose routing.
3. Check the filter at the bottom of the canister. If dirty, replace the filter.

Tank Pressure Control Valve

1. Using a hand-held vacuum pump, apply a vacuum of 15 in. Hg (51 kPa) through the control vacuum signal tube to the purge valve diaphragm. If the diaphragm does not hold vac-

uum for at least 20 seconds, the diaphragm is leaking. Replace the control valve.
2. With the vacuum still applied to the control vacuum tube, attach a short piece of hose to the valve's tank tube side and blow into the hose. Air should pass through the valve. If it does not, replace the control valve.

Canister Purge Control Valve

1. Connect a clean length of hose to the fuel tank vapor line connection on the canister and attempt to blow through the purge control valve. It should be difficult or impossible to blow through the purge control valve. If air passes easily, the valve is stuck open and should be replaced.
2. Connect a hand-held vacuum pump to the top vacuum line fitting of the purge control valve. Apply a vacuum of 15 in. Hg (51 kPa) to the purge valve diaphragm. If the diaphragm does not hold vacuum for at least 20 seconds, the diaphragm is leaking. Replace the control valve. If it is impossible to blow through the valve, it is stuck closed and must be replaced.
3. On vehicles with a solenoid activated purge control valve, unplug the connector and use jumper wires to supply 12 volts to the solenoid connections on the valve. With the vacuum still applied to the control vacuum tube, the purge control valve should open and it should be easy to blow through. If not, replace the valve.

REMOVAL & INSTALLATION

Charcoal Canister

➡**On some models it may be necessary to remove the right side fender fascia and filler panels to gain access to the canister.**

1. Disconnect the negative battery cable.
2. Tag and disconnect the hoses from the canister.
3. Unfasten the charcoal canister retaining nuts/bolts and remove any retaining straps that may be securing the canister.
4. If necessary for access, and equipped with air conditioning, loosen the attachments holding the accumulator and pipe assembly.

5. Remove the canister from the vehicle.

➡**Always replace any vapor hose(s) that may be showing signs of wear.**

6. Installation is the reverse of the removal procedure. Refer to the Vehicle Emission Control Information label, located in the engine compartment, for proper routing of the vacuum hoses.

Tank Pressure Control Valve

1. Tag and disconnect the hoses from the control valve.
2. Unfasten the mounting hardware.
3. Remove the control valve from the vehicle.
4. Installation is the reverse of the removal procedure. Refer to the Vehicle Emission Control Information label, located in the engine compartment, for proper routing of the vacuum hoses.

Canister Purge Control Solenoid Valve

1. Disconnect the negative battery cable.
2. Tag and detach the electrical connector(s), hose and line from the solenoid valve.
3. Unfasten the retainer (screw, bolts or locking tab), then remove the valve from the vehicle.
4. Installation is the reverse of the removal procedure.

Filter Replacement

1. Remove the vapor canister, as outlined earlier in this section.
2. Pull the filter out from the bottom of the canister.
3. Install a new filter and then replace the canister.

Exhaust Gas Recirculation (EGR) System

OPERATION

▶ **See Figures 6, 7, 8, 9, 10 and 11**

➡**The 2.3L and 2.4L engines do not use an EGR valve.**

The EGR system is used to reduce oxides of nitrogen (NOx) emission levels caused by high combustion chamber temperatures. This is accomplished by the use of an EGR valve which opens, under specific engine operating conditions, to admit a small amount of exhaust gas into the intake manifold, below the throttle plate. The exhaust gas mixes with the incoming air charge and displaces a portion of the oxygen in the air/fuel mixture entering the combustion chamber. The exhaust gas does not support combustion of the air/fuel mixture but it takes up volume, the net effect of which is to lower the temperature of the combustion process. This lower temperature also helps control detonation.

The EGR valve is mounted on the intake manifold and has an opening into the exhaust manifold. The EGR valve is opened by ported vacuum and allows exhaust gases to flow into the intake manifold. If too much exhaust gas enters, combustion will not occur. Because of this, very little exhaust gas is allowed to pass through the valve. The EGR system will be activated once the engine reaches normal operating tempera-

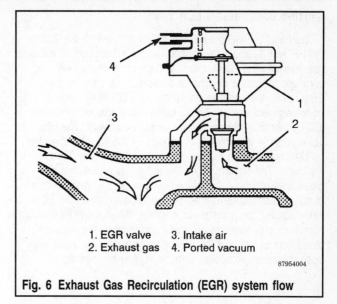

1. EGR valve
2. Exhaust gas
3. Intake air
4. Ported vacuum

Fig. 6 Exhaust Gas Recirculation (EGR) system flow

ture and the EGR valve will open when engine operating conditions are above idle speed and below Wide Open Throttle (WOT). On California vehicles equipped with a Vehicle Speed Sensor (VSS), the EGR valve opens when the VSS signal is greater than 2 mph. The EGR system is deactivated on vehicles equipped with a Transmission Converter Clutch (TCC) when the TCC is engaged.

Too much EGR flow at idle, cruise, or during cold operation may result in the engine stalling after cold start, the engine stalling at idle after deceleration, vehicle surge during cruise and rough idle. If the EGR valve is always open, the vehicle may not idle. Too little or no EGR flow allows combustion temperatures to get too high which could result in spark knock (detonation), engine overheating and/or emission test failure.

There are 5 types of EGR valves used; The negative backpressure EGR valve, positive backpressure EGR valve, Ported EGR valve, Integrated Electronic EGR valve and the Digital EGR valve. The principle of all systems is the same; the only difference is in the method used to control how far the EGR valve opens.

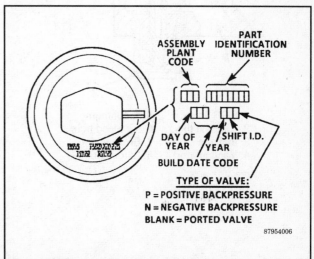

Fig. 7 Ported, negative and positive backpressure EGR valve identification

Negative Backpressure EGR Valve

The negative backpressure EGR valve, used on the 2.0L (VIN P and K) and 2.2L engines, varies the amount of exhaust gas flow into the intake manifold depending on manifold vacuum and variations in exhaust backpressure. Like the ported EGR valve, the negative backpressure EGR valve uses a ported vacuum source. An air bleed valve, located inside the EGR valve assembly acts as a vacuum regulator. The bleed valve controls the amount of vacuum in the vacuum chamber by bleeding vacuum to outside air during the open phase of the cycle. The diaphragm on the valve has an internal air bleed hole which is held closed by a small spring when there is no exhaust backpressure. Engine vacuum opens the EGR valve against the pressure of a spring. When manifold vacuum combines with negative exhaust backpressure, the vacuum bleed hole opens and the EGR valve closes. This valve will open if vacuum is applied with the engine not running.

Positive Backpressure (EGR) Valve

The positive backpressure EGR valve is used on the 1.8L and 2.0L (VIN H) engines. A vacuum bleed valve, located in the EGR valve, acts as a vacuum regulator, controlling vacuum above the EGR valve diaphragm. Exhaust backpressure is passed through the hollow pintle shaft and exerted on the bleed valve. When sufficient backpressure is applied on the bleed valve, the valve will open, allowing vacuum above the diaphragm to vent to the atmosphere. This will result in the EGR valve closing.

Ported EGR Valve

The ported EGR valve, used on the 2.0L (VIN M), takes its name from the fact that it uses a ported vacuum source to open the EGR valve and modulate the EGR flow. The ported vacuum source is a small opening just above the throttle blade in the throttle body. When the throttle begins to open the air passing through the venturi, creates a low pressure which draws on the EGR valve diaphragm causing it to open. As the throttle blade opens further, the ported vacuum increases and opens the valve further.

The ECM controls EGR operation through an EGR control solenoid. Ported vacuum must flow through the EGR control solenoid to open the EGR valve. The ECM uses information received from the Coolant Temperature Sensor (CTS), Throttle Position Sensor (TPS) and the Mass Air Flow (MAF) sensor to determine when to allow EGR operation. When certain parameters are met, such as engine at normal operating temperature and the engine speed is above idle, the ECM signals the solenoid to open, allowing EGR operation.

Integrated Electronic EGR Valve

The integrated electronic EGR valve, used on the 2.8L engines, functions like a ported EGR valve with a remote vacuum regulator, except the regulator and a pintle position sensor are sealed in the back plastic cover. The regulator and position sensor are not serviceable. There is a serviceable filter that provides clean fresh air to the regulator along side the vacuum tube.

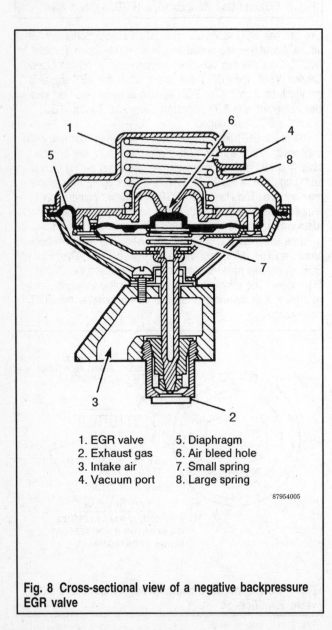

1. EGR valve
2. Exhaust gas
3. Intake air
4. Vacuum port
5. Diaphragm
6. Air bleed hole
7. Small spring
8. Large spring

87954005

Fig. 8 Cross-sectional view of a negative backpressure EGR valve

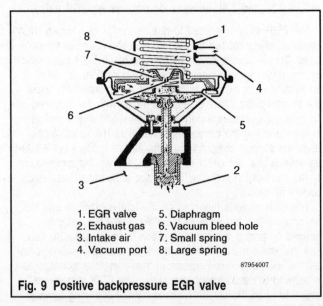

1. EGR valve
2. Exhaust gas
3. Intake air
4. Vacuum port
5. Diaphragm
6. Vacuum bleed hole
7. Small spring
8. Large spring

87954007

Fig. 9 Positive backpressure EGR valve

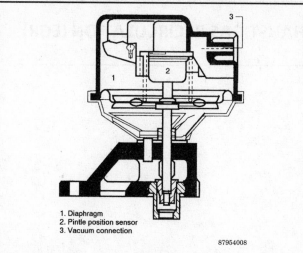

1. Diaphragm
2. Pintle position sensor
3. Vacuum connection

87954008

Fig. 10 The 2.8L engine utilizes a integrated electronic EGR valve

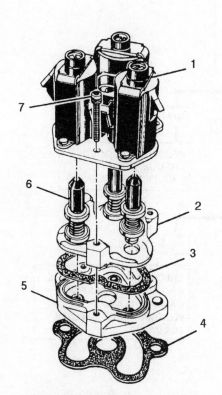

1. Solenoid & mounting plate assembly
2. EGR base plate
3. EGR base gasket
4. Insulator gasket
5. EGR base
6. Armature assembly
7. Screw assembly

87954009

Fig. 11 Exploded view of the digital EGR valve which is used on the 3.1L engine

This valve has a vacuum regulator to which the ECM provides variable current. This variable current produces the desired EGR flow using inputs from the Manifold Absolute Pressure (MAP) sensor, Engine Coolant Temperature (ECT) sensor and engine RPM.

Digital EGR Valve

The digital EGR valve, used on the 3.1L engine, is designed to accurately supply EGR to an engine, independent of intake manifold vacuum. The valve controls EGR flow from the exhaust to the intake manifold through three orifices which increment in size to produce seven combinations. When a solenoid is energized, the armature, with attached shaft and swivel pintle is lifted, opening the orifice. The flow accuracy is dependent on metering orifice size only, which results in improved control.

The swivel pintle feature insures good sealing of exhaust gas, reducing the need of critical assembly alignment. In addition, the effects of EGR leakage on idle quality are reduced because the shaft and seals are exposed to exhaust pressure instead of manifold vacuum. The shafts are sealed from the exhaust chamber by floating seals held in place by the seal spring. These springs also hold the upper seals that seal the armature cavity in the solenoids. The solenoid coils are fastened together to maximize reliability and to seal the coils from the environment. The coils use a common power terminal with individual ground terminals.

The digital EGR valve is opened by the PCM quad-driver, grounding each respective solenoid circuit. This quad-driver activates the solenoid, raises the pintle, and allows exhaust gas flow into the intake manifold. The exhaust gas then moves with the air/fuel mixture into the combustion chamber. If too much exhaust gas enters, combustion will not occur. For this reason, very little exhaust gas is allowed to pass through the valve, with virtually none at idle.

TESTING

◆ **See Figures 12, 13, 14, 15, 16, 17 and 18**

Refer to the appropriate chart the test the EGR system.

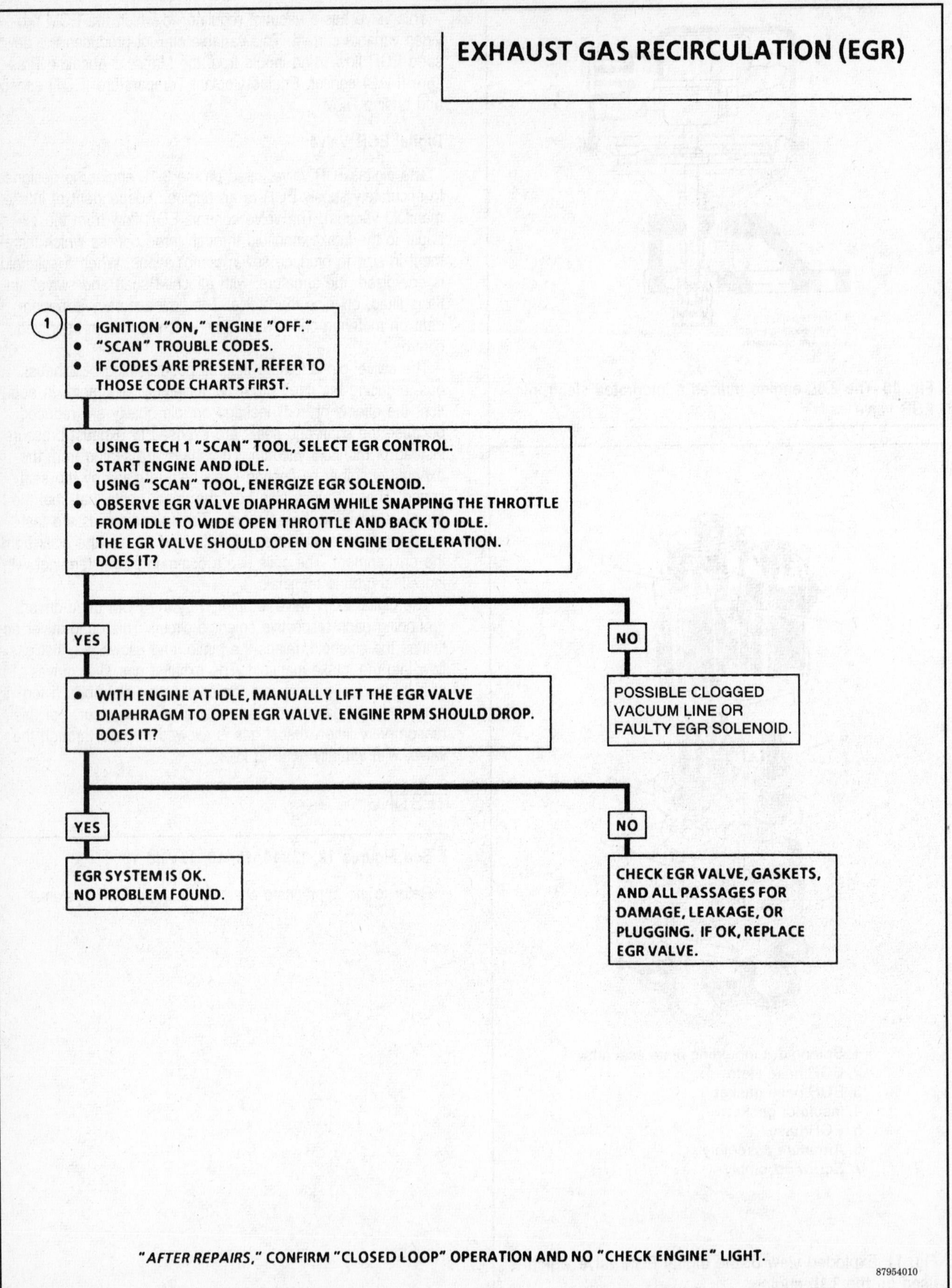

EXHAUST GAS RECIRCULATION (EGR)

1
- IGNITION "ON," ENGINE "OFF."
- "SCAN" TROUBLE CODES.
- IF CODES ARE PRESENT, REFER TO THOSE CODE CHARTS FIRST.

- USING TECH 1 "SCAN" TOOL, SELECT EGR CONTROL.
- START ENGINE AND IDLE.
- USING "SCAN" TOOL, ENERGIZE EGR SOLENOID.
- OBSERVE EGR VALVE DIAPHRAGM WHILE SNAPPING THE THROTTLE FROM IDLE TO WIDE OPEN THROTTLE AND BACK TO IDLE. THE EGR VALVE SHOULD OPEN ON ENGINE DECELERATION. DOES IT?

YES

NO

- WITH ENGINE AT IDLE, MANUALLY LIFT THE EGR VALVE DIAPHRAGM TO OPEN EGR VALVE. ENGINE RPM SHOULD DROP. DOES IT?

POSSIBLE CLOGGED VACUUM LINE OR FAULTY EGR SOLENOID.

YES

NO

EGR SYSTEM IS OK. NO PROBLEM FOUND.

CHECK EGR VALVE, GASKETS, AND ALL PASSAGES FOR DAMAGE, LEAKAGE, OR PLUGGING. IF OK, REPLACE EGR VALVE.

"AFTER REPAIRS," CONFIRM "CLOSED LOOP" OPERATION AND NO "CHECK ENGINE" LIGHT.

87954010

Fig. 12 Positive backpressure EGR system check

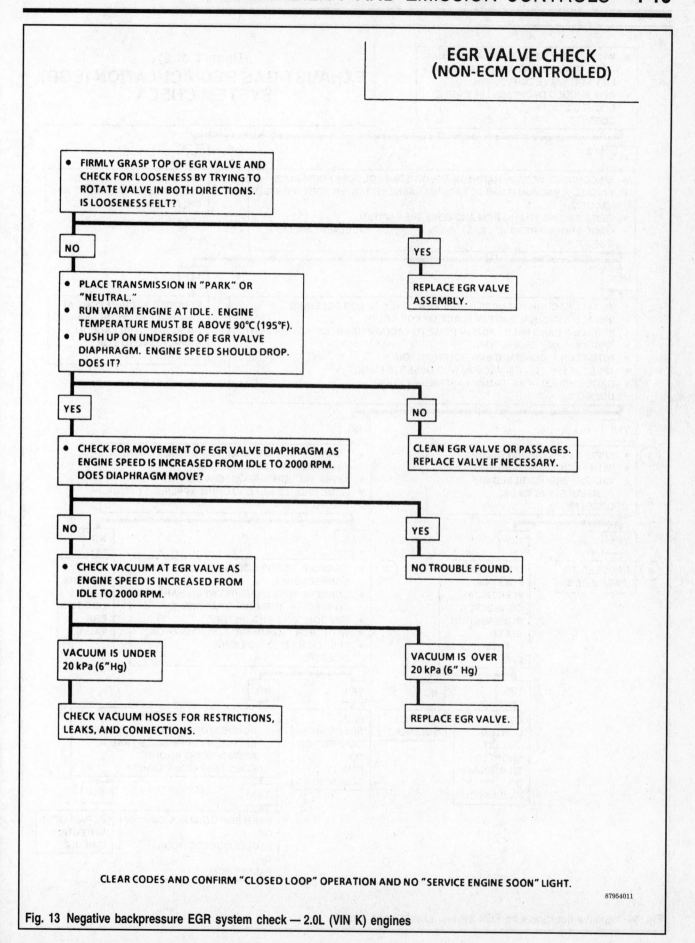

EGR VALVE CHECK
(NON-ECM CONTROLLED)

- FIRMLY GRASP TOP OF EGR VALVE AND CHECK FOR LOOSENESS BY TRYING TO ROTATE VALVE IN BOTH DIRECTIONS. IS LOOSENESS FELT?

NO

YES

- PLACE TRANSMISSION IN "PARK" OR "NEUTRAL."
- RUN WARM ENGINE AT IDLE. ENGINE TEMPERATURE MUST BE ABOVE 90°C (195°F).
- PUSH UP ON UNDERSIDE OF EGR VALVE DIAPHRAGM. ENGINE SPEED SHOULD DROP. DOES IT?

REPLACE EGR VALVE ASSEMBLY.

YES

NO

- CHECK FOR MOVEMENT OF EGR VALVE DIAPHRAGM AS ENGINE SPEED IS INCREASED FROM IDLE TO 2000 RPM. DOES DIAPHRAGM MOVE?

CLEAN EGR VALVE OR PASSAGES. REPLACE VALVE IF NECESSARY.

NO

YES

- CHECK VACUUM AT EGR VALVE AS ENGINE SPEED IS INCREASED FROM IDLE TO 2000 RPM.

NO TROUBLE FOUND.

VACUUM IS UNDER 20 kPa (6" Hg)

VACUUM IS OVER 20 kPa (6" Hg)

CHECK VACUUM HOSES FOR RESTRICTIONS, LEAKS, AND CONNECTIONS.

REPLACE EGR VALVE.

CLEAR CODES AND CONFIRM "CLOSED LOOP" OPERATION AND NO "SERVICE ENGINE SOON" LIGHT.

87954011

Fig. 13 Negative backpressure EGR system check — 2.0L (VIN K) engines

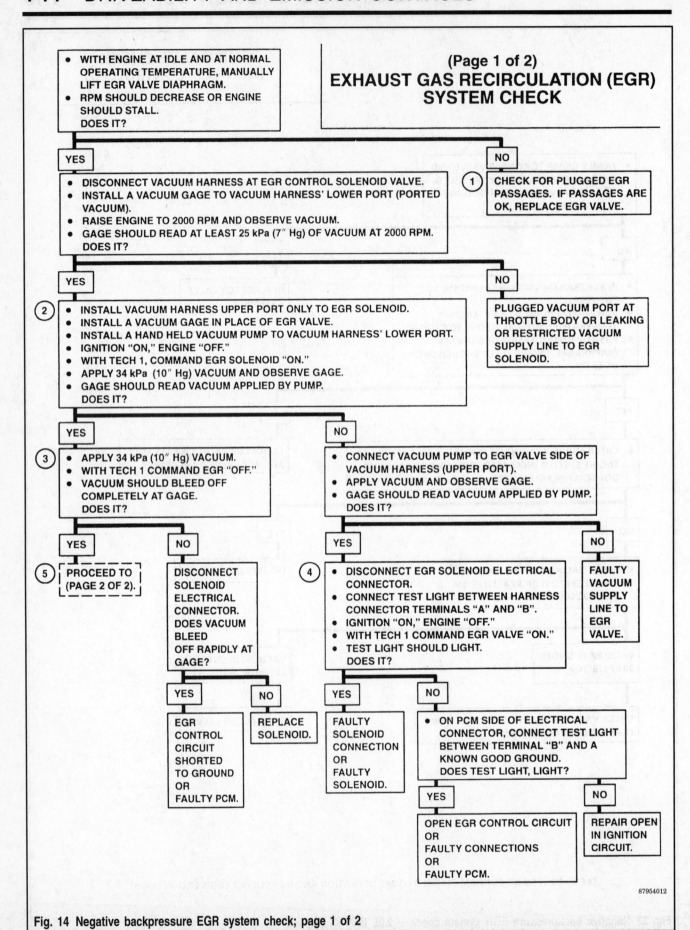

Fig. 14 Negative backpressure EGR system check; page 1 of 2

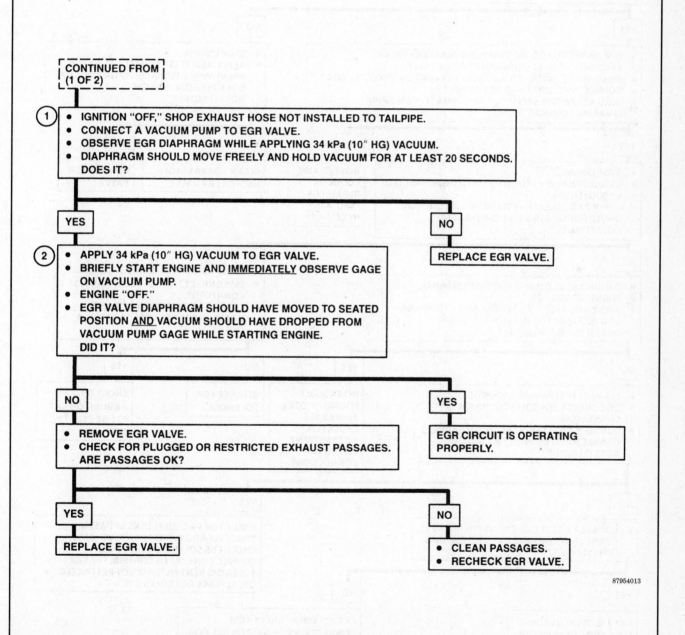

(Page 2 of 2)
EXHAUST GAS RECIRCULATION (EGR) SYSTEM CHECK

CONTINUED FROM
(1 OF 2)

1
- IGNITION "OFF," SHOP EXHAUST HOSE NOT INSTALLED TO TAILPIPE.
- CONNECT A VACUUM PUMP TO EGR VALVE.
- OBSERVE EGR DIAPHRAGM WHILE APPLYING 34 kPa (10″ HG) VACUUM.
- DIAPHRAGM SHOULD MOVE FREELY AND HOLD VACUUM FOR AT LEAST 20 SECONDS. DOES IT?

YES

NO

REPLACE EGR VALVE.

2
- APPLY 34 kPa (10″ HG) VACUUM TO EGR VALVE.
- BRIEFLY START ENGINE AND <u>IMMEDIATELY</u> OBSERVE GAGE ON VACUUM PUMP.
- ENGINE "OFF."
- EGR VALVE DIAPHRAGM SHOULD HAVE MOVED TO SEATED POSITION <u>AND</u> VACUUM SHOULD HAVE DROPPED FROM VACUUM PUMP GAGE WHILE STARTING ENGINE. DID IT?

NO

YES

EGR CIRCUIT IS OPERATING PROPERLY.

- REMOVE EGR VALVE.
- CHECK FOR PLUGGED OR RESTRICTED EXHAUST PASSAGES. ARE PASSAGES OK?

YES

NO

REPLACE EGR VALVE.

- CLEAN PASSAGES.
- RECHECK EGR VALVE.

87954013

Fig. 15 Negative backpressure EGR system check; page 2 of 2

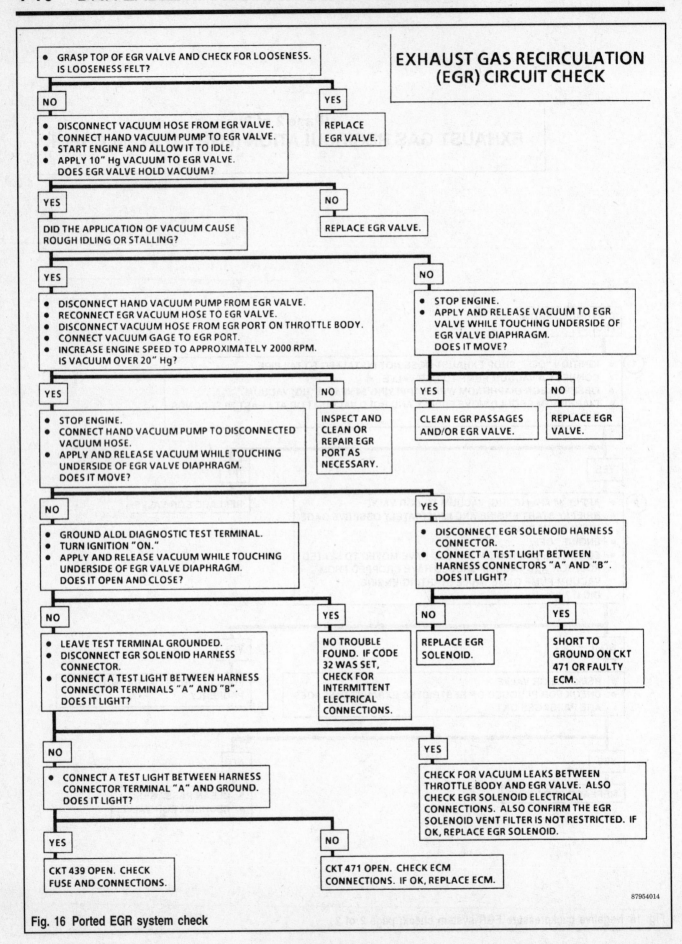

- GRASP TOP OF EGR VALVE AND CHECK FOR LOOSENESS. IS LOOSENESS FELT?

EXHAUST GAS RECIRCULATION (EGR) CIRCUIT CHECK

NO

YES

- DISCONNECT VACUUM HOSE FROM EGR VALVE.
- CONNECT HAND VACUUM PUMP TO EGR VALVE.
- START ENGINE AND ALLOW IT TO IDLE.
- APPLY 10" Hg VACUUM TO EGR VALVE. DOES EGR VALVE HOLD VACUUM?

REPLACE EGR VALVE.

YES

NO

DID THE APPLICATION OF VACUUM CAUSE ROUGH IDLING OR STALLING?

REPLACE EGR VALVE.

YES

NO

- DISCONNECT HAND VACUUM PUMP FROM EGR VALVE.
- RECONNECT EGR VACUUM HOSE TO EGR VALVE.
- DISCONNECT VACUUM HOSE FROM EGR PORT ON THROTTLE BODY.
- CONNECT VACUUM GAGE TO EGR PORT.
- INCREASE ENGINE SPEED TO APPROXIMATELY 2000 RPM. IS VACUUM OVER 20" Hg?

- STOP ENGINE.
- APPLY AND RELEASE VACUUM TO EGR VALVE WHILE TOUCHING UNDERSIDE OF EGR VALVE DIAPHRAGM. DOES IT MOVE?

YES

NO

YES

NO

- STOP ENGINE.
- CONNECT HAND VACUUM PUMP TO DISCONNECTED VACUUM HOSE.
- APPLY AND RELEASE VACUUM WHILE TOUCHING UNDERSIDE OF EGR VALVE DIAPHRAGM. DOES IT MOVE?

INSPECT AND CLEAN OR REPAIR EGR PORT AS NECESSARY.

CLEAN EGR PASSAGES AND/OR EGR VALVE.

REPLACE EGR VALVE.

NO

YES

- GROUND ALDL DIAGNOSTIC TEST TERMINAL.
- TURN IGNITION "ON."
- APPLY AND RELEASE VACUUM WHILE TOUCHING UNDERSIDE OF EGR VALVE DIAPHRAGM. DOES IT OPEN AND CLOSE?

- DISCONNECT EGR SOLENOID HARNESS CONNECTOR.
- CONNECT A TEST LIGHT BETWEEN HARNESS CONNECTORS "A" AND "B". DOES IT LIGHT?

NO

YES

NO

YES

- LEAVE TEST TERMINAL GROUNDED.
- DISCONNECT EGR SOLENOID HARNESS CONNECTOR.
- CONNECT A TEST LIGHT BETWEEN HARNESS CONNECTOR TERMINALS "A" AND "B". DOES IT LIGHT?

NO TROUBLE FOUND. IF CODE 32 WAS SET, CHECK FOR INTERMITTENT ELECTRICAL CONNECTIONS.

REPLACE EGR SOLENOID.

SHORT TO GROUND ON CKT 471 OR FAULTY ECM.

NO

YES

- CONNECT A TEST LIGHT BETWEEN HARNESS CONNECTOR TERMINAL "A" AND GROUND. DOES IT LIGHT?

CHECK FOR VACUUM LEAKS BETWEEN THROTTLE BODY AND EGR VALVE. ALSO CHECK EGR SOLENOID ELECTRICAL CONNECTIONS. ALSO CONFIRM THE EGR SOLENOID VENT FILTER IS NOT RESTRICTED. IF OK, REPLACE EGR SOLENOID.

YES

NO

CKT 439 OPEN. CHECK FUSE AND CONNECTIONS.

CKT 471 OPEN. CHECK ECM CONNECTIONS. IF OK, REPLACE ECM.

87954014

Fig. 16 Ported EGR system check

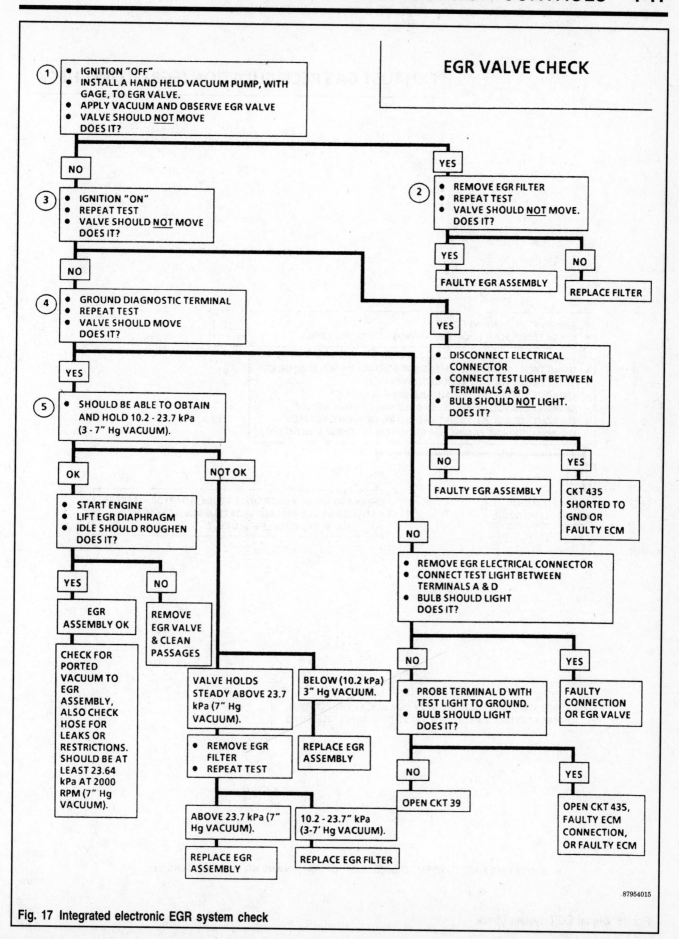

Fig. 17 Integrated electronic EGR system check

87954015

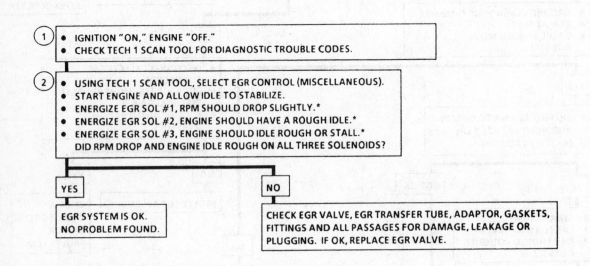

EXHAUST GAS RECIRCULATION (EGR) FLOW CHECK

1
- IGNITION "ON," ENGINE "OFF."
- CHECK TECH 1 SCAN TOOL FOR DIAGNOSTIC TROUBLE CODES.

2
- USING TECH 1 SCAN TOOL, SELECT EGR CONTROL (MISCELLANEOUS).
- START ENGINE AND ALLOW IDLE TO STABILIZE.
- ENERGIZE EGR SOL #1, RPM SHOULD DROP SLIGHTLY.*
- ENERGIZE EGR SOL #2, ENGINE SHOULD HAVE A ROUGH IDLE.*
- ENERGIZE EGR SOL #3, ENGINE SHOULD IDLE ROUGH OR STALL.*
  DID RPM DROP AND ENGINE IDLE ROUGH ON ALL THREE SOLENOIDS?

YES

EGR SYSTEM IS OK.
NO PROBLEM FOUND.

NO

CHECK EGR VALVE, EGR TRANSFER TUBE, ADAPTOR, GASKETS, FITTINGS AND ALL PASSAGES FOR DAMAGE, LEAKAGE OR PLUGGING. IF OK, REPLACE EGR VALVE.

* THESE STEPS MUST BE DONE VERY QUICKLY, AS THE PCM WILL ADJUST THE IDLE AIR CONTROL VALVE TO CORRECT IDLE SPEED.

"AFTER REPAIRS," CONFIRM "CLOSED LOOP" OPERATION AND NO MIL (CHECK ENGINE).

87954016

Fig. 18 Digital EGR system check

REMOVAL & INSTALLATION

EGR Valve

▶ **See Figures 19, 20, 21, 22, 23 and 24**

1. Disconnect the negative battery cable.

2. Remove the air cleaner assembly, as necessary, for access to the EGR valve.

3. Disconnect the EGR vacuum hose or solenoid wire, as required.

4. Unfasten the EGR valve retaining bolts and remove the EGR valve from the manifold. Remove and discard the EGR valve gasket.

To install:

5. If reinstalling the old valve, inspect the EGR valve passages for excessive build-up of deposits, and clean as necessary.

➡**Loose particles should be completely removed to prevent them from being ingested into the engine.**

Fig. 21 After removing the air cleaner assembly, disconnect the vacuum hose from the EGR valve

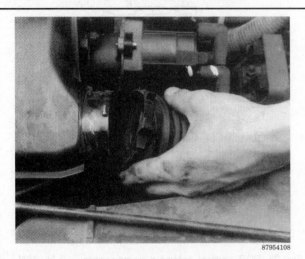

Fig. 19 To remove the air cleaner assembly for access to the EGR valve, detach the ducting, then . . .

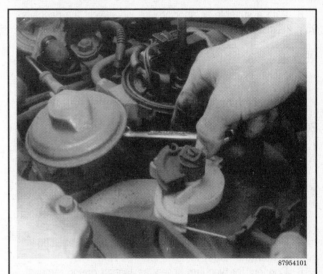

Fig. 22 Unfasten the retaining bolts, then . . .

Fig. 20 . . . remove the air cleaner assembly

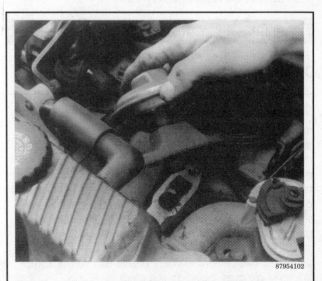

Fig. 23 . . . remove the EGR valve from the vehicle

Fig. 24 Using a suitable tool, carefully clean the gasket mating surfaces

6. With a suitable scraper or wire wheel buff the deposits from the mounting surfaces.

7. Install the EGR valve to the intake manifold using a NEW gasket and tighten the bolts EVENLY.

8. Attach the vacuum hose or solenoid wire connector.

9. Install the air cleaner assembly, if removed.

10. Connect the negative battery cable.

EGR Control Solenoid

▶ **See Figure 25**

1. Disconnect the negative battery cable.

2. Detach the electrical connector at the solenoid.

3. Tag and disconnect the vacuum hose(s).

4. Unfasten the retaining nut(s), then remove the solenoid.

To install:

5. Position the solenoid, then secure with the retaining nuts. Tighten the nut(s) to 17 ft. lbs. (24 Nm).

6. Connect the vacuum hoses, as tagged during removal.

7. Attach the solenoid electrical connector.

8. Connect the negative battery cable.

Catalytic Converter

OPERATION

All engines covered by this manual are equipped with a catalytic converter in order to reduce tail pipe emissions. The catalytic converter is mounted in the engine exhaust stream ahead of the muffler. Its function is to combine carbon monoxide (CO) and hydrocarbons (HC) with oxygen and break down nitrogen oxide (NOx) compounds. These gasses are converted to mostly CO_2 and water. It heats to operating temperature within about 1-2 minutes, depending on ambient temperature and driving conditions and will operate at temperatures up to about 1500°F (816 °C). Inside the converter housing is a single or dual bed ceramic monolith, coated with various combinations of platinum, palladium and rhodium.

The catalytic converter is not serviceable. If tests and visual inspection show the converter to be damaged, it must be re-

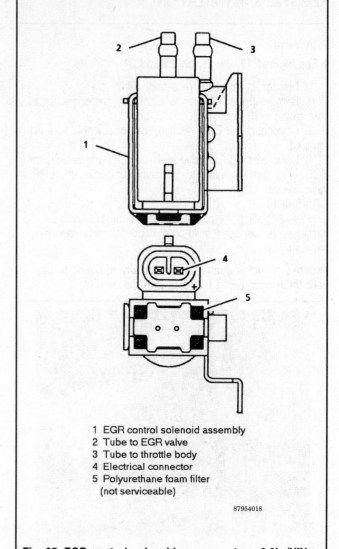

1 EGR control solenoid assembly
2 Tube to EGR valve
3 Tube to throttle body
4 Electrical connector
5 Polyurethane foam filter
  (not serviceable)

Fig. 25 EGR control solenoid components — 2.0L (VIN H) engine shown

placed. There are 2 types of failures: melting or fracturing. The most common failure is melting, resulting from unburned gasoline contacting the monolith, such as when a cylinder does not fire. Usually when the monolith melts, high backpressure results. When it cracks, it begins to break up into small particles that get blown out the tail pipe.

Poor fuel mileage and/or a lack of power can often be traced to a melted or plugged catalytic converter. The damage may be the result of engine malfunction or the use of leaded gasoline in the vehicle. Proper diagnosis for a restricted exhaust system is essential before any components are replaced. The following procedure that can be used to determine if the exhaust system is restricted.

TESTING

Backpressure Diagnosis Test

1. Carefully remove the oxygen sensor.

2. Install an adapter that has the same size threads as the sensor and that will hook up to a pressure gauge. Install in place of the sensor.

3. With engine idling at normal operating temperature, observe the backpressure reading on the gauge. The reading should not exceed 1.25 psi (8.6 kPa).

4. Increase engine speed to 2000 rpm and observe gauge. The reading should not exceed 3 psi (20.7 kPa).

5. If the backpressure at either speed exceeds specification, a restricted exhaust is indicated.

6. Inspect the entire exhaust system for a collapsed pipe, heat distress or possible internal muffler failure.

7. If there are no obvious reasons for the excessive backpressure, the catalytic converter is suspected and should be removed for inspection or replacement.

8. When test is complete, remove the pressure gauge and adapter. Lightly coat the threads of the oxygen sensor with an anti-seize compound. Reinstall the oxygen sensor.

Inspection

1. Raise and safely support the vehicle.
2. Inspect the catalytic converter protector for any damage.

➡ **If any part of the protector is dented to the extent that is contacts the converter, replace the protector.**

3. Check the heat insulator for adequate clearance between the converter and the heat insulator. Repair or replace any damaged components.

4. Unfasten the retaining bolts at the front and the rear, then remove the converter.

5. It should be possible to look into the end of the housing and see light through the other end. If it is melted enough to cause high exhaust backpressure, it will be obvious.

6. Installation is the reverse of the removal procedure. Lower the vehicle, start the engine and check for exhaust leaks.

Thermostatic Air Cleaner (THERMAC)

OPERATION

▶ **See Figures 26 and 27**

Four cylinder engines, through 1986, use the THERMAC system, except those equipped with multi-port fuel injection. This system is designed to warm the air entering the carburetor/throttle body when underhood temperatures are low, and to maintain a controlled air temperature into the carburetor/throttle body at all times. On carbureted engines, by allowing preheated air to enter the carburetor, the amount of time the choke is on is reduced, resulting in better fuel economy and lower emissions. Engine warm-up time is also reduced.

The THERMAC system is composed of the air cleaner body, a filter, sensor unit, vacuum diaphragm, damper door, and associated hoses and connections. Heat radiating from the exhaust manifold is trapped by a heat stove and is ducted to the air cleaner to supply heated air to the carburetor/throttle body. A movable door in the air cleaner case snorkel allows air to

be drawn in from the heat stove (cold operation). The door position is controlled by the vacuum motor, which receives intake manifold vacuum as modulated by the temperature sensor.

TESTING

1. Check the vacuum hoses for leaks, kinks, breaks, or improper connections and correct any defects.

2. With the engine off, check the position of the damper door within the snorkel. A mirror can be used to make this job easier. The damper door should be open to admit outside air.

3. Apply at least 7 in. Hg (24 kPa) of vacuum to the damper diaphragm unit. The door should close. If it doesn't, check the diaphragm linkage for binding and correct hookup.

4. With the vacuum still applied and the door closed, clamp the tube to trap the vacuum. If the door doesn't remain closed, there is a leak in the diaphragm assembly.

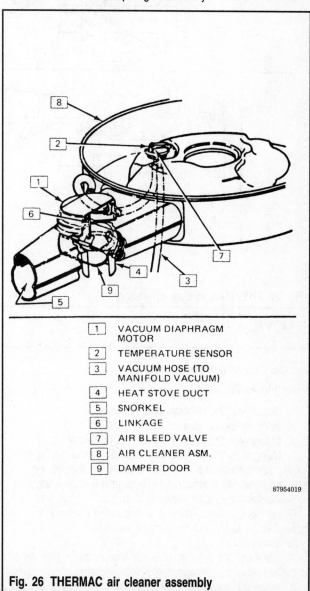

1	VACUUM DIAPHRAGM MOTOR
2	TEMPERATURE SENSOR
3	VACUUM HOSE (TO MANIFOLD VACUUM)
4	HEAT STOVE DUCT
5	SNORKEL
6	LINKAGE
7	AIR BLEED VALVE
8	AIR CLEANER ASM.
9	DAMPER DOOR

87954019

Fig. 26 THERMAC air cleaner assembly

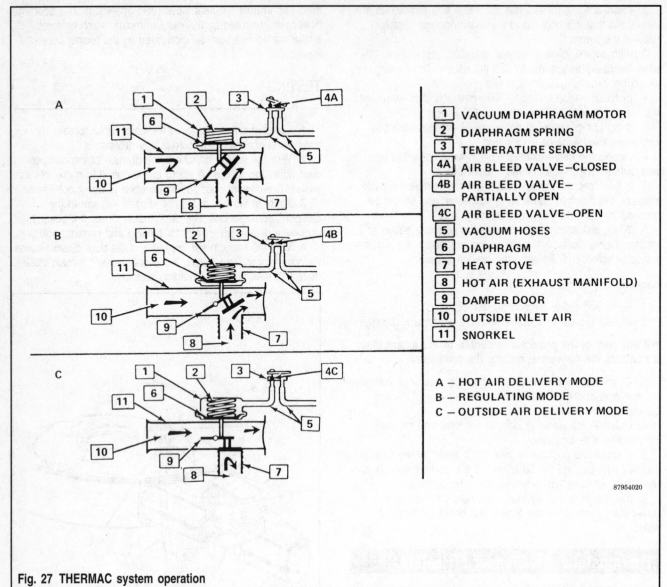

1	VACUUM DIAPHRAGM MOTOR
2	DIAPHRAGM SPRING
3	TEMPERATURE SENSOR
4A	AIR BLEED VALVE—CLOSED
4B	AIR BLEED VALVE—PARTIALLY OPEN
4C	AIR BLEED VALVE—OPEN
5	VACUUM HOSES
6	DIAPHRAGM
7	HEAT STOVE
8	HOT AIR (EXHAUST MANIFOLD)
9	DAMPER DOOR
10	OUTSIDE INLET AIR
11	SNORKEL

A – HOT AIR DELIVERY MODE
B – REGULATING MODE
C – OUTSIDE AIR DELIVERY MODE

87954020

Fig. 27 THERMAC system operation

REMOVAL & INSTALLATION

Vacuum Diaphragm Motor

▶ **See Figure 28**

1. Disconnect the negative battery cable.
2. Remove the air cleaner.
3. Disconnect the vacuum hose from the motor.
4. Using a $\frac{1}{16}$ in. (1.6mm) drill bit, drill out the two spot welds, then enlarge the holes, as required, to remove the retaining strap. Be careful not to damage the snorkel tube.
5. Remove the motor retaining strap.
6. Lift up the motor, tilting it to one side to unhook the motor linkage at the control damper assembly.

To install:

7. Carefully drill a $\frac{7}{64}$ in. (2.8mm) hole in the snorkel tube at the center of the vacuum motor retaining strap.
8. Place the vacuum motor linkage into the control damper assembly.

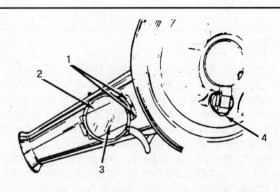

1 Spot welds
2 Motor asm.
3 Retaining strap
4 Install replacement sensor asm. in same position as original asm.

87954021

Fig. 28 Replacing the THERMAC vacuum motor

9. Use the motor retaining strap and sheet metal screw provided in the motor service kit to secure the motor to the snorkel tube. Make sure the screw does not interfere with the operation of the damper assembly. It may be necessary to shorten the screw.

10. Attach the vacuum hose to the motor, then install the air cleaner.

11. Connect the negative battery cable.

Sensor

▶ See Figure 29

1. Disconnect the negative battery cable.
2. Remove the air cleaner.
3. Unfasten the hoses at the sensor.

➡Before sensor removal, make sure to note its position for installation purposes.

4. Carefully pry up the tabs on the sensor retaining clip. Remove the clip and sensor from the air cleaner.

To install:

5. Position the sensor and gasket assembly in its original position.

6. Fasten the retaining clip on the hose connectors.

7. Attach the vacuum hoses to the sensor, then install air cleaner.

8. Connect the negative battery cable.

Air Injection Reaction (AIR) Management System

OPERATION

▶ See Figures 30 and 31

The AIR management system, on 1982-84 vehicles, is used to provide additional oxygen to continue the combustion process after the exhaust gases leave the combustion chamber. Air is injected into either the exhaust port(s), the exhaust manifold(s) or the catalytic converter by an engine driven air pump.

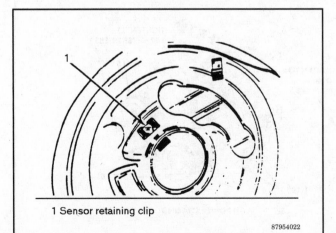

1 Sensor retaining clip

87954022

Fig. 29 You must note the location of the sensor for installation

The system is in operation at all times and will bypass air only momentarily during deceleration and at high speeds. The bypass function is performed by the Air Management Valve, while the check valve protects the air pump by preventing any backflow of exhaust gases.

The AIR management system helps reduce HC and CO content in the exhaust gases by injecting air into the exhaust ports during cold engine operation. This air injection also helps the catalytic converter to reach the proper temperature quicker during warmup. When the engine is warm (Closed Loop), the AIR system injects air into the beds of a three-way converter to lower the HC and the CO content in the exhaust.

The AIR Management system utilizes the following components:

1. An engine driven AIR pump
2. AIR management valves (Air Control, Air Switching)
3. Air flow and control hoses
4. Check valves
5. A dual-bed, three-way catalytic converter

The belt driven, vane-type air pump is located at the front of the engine and supplies clean air to the AIR system for purposes already stated. When the engine is cold, the Electronic Control Module (ECM) energizes an AIR control solenoid. This allows air to flow to the AIR switching valve. The AIR switching valve is then energized to direct air to the exhaust ports.

When the engine is warm, the ECM de-energizes the AIR switching valve, thus directing the air between the beds of the catalytic converter. This provides additional oxygen for the oxidizing catalyst in the second bed to decrease HC and CO, while at the same time keeping oxygen levels low in the first bed, enabling the reducing catalyst to effectively decrease the levels of NOx.

If the AIR control valve detects a rapid increase in manifold vacuum (deceleration), certain operating modes (wide open throttle, etc.) or if the ECM self-diagnostic system detects any problem in the system, air is diverted to the air cleaner or directly into the atmosphere.

The primary purpose of the ECM's divert mode is to prevent backfiring. Throttle closure at the beginning of deceleration will temporarily create air/fuel mixtures which are too rich to burn completely. These mixtures become burnable when they reach the exhaust if combined with the injection air. The next firing of the engine will ignite this mixture causing an exhaust backfire. Momentary diverting of the injection air from the exhaust prevents this.

The AIR management system check valves and hoses should be checked periodically for any leaks, cracks or deterioration.

REMOVAL & INSTALLATION

Air Pump

▶ See Figure 32

1. Disconnect the negative battery cable.
2. Remove the AIR management valves and/or adapter at the pump.
3. Loosen the air pump adjustment bolt, then remove the drive belt.
4. Unfasten the pump mounting bolts, then remove the pump pulley.

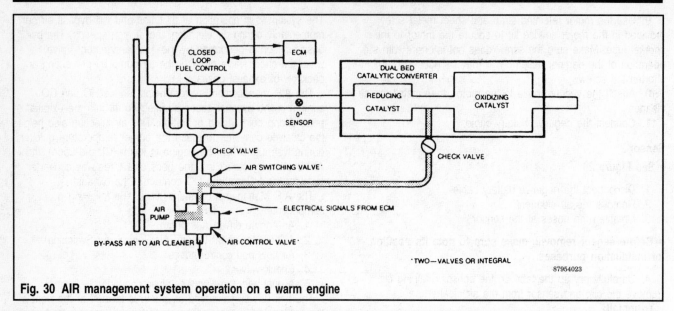

Fig. 30 AIR management system operation on a warm engine

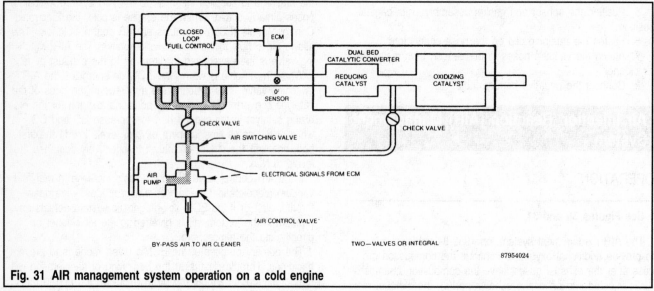

Fig. 31 AIR management system operation on a cold engine

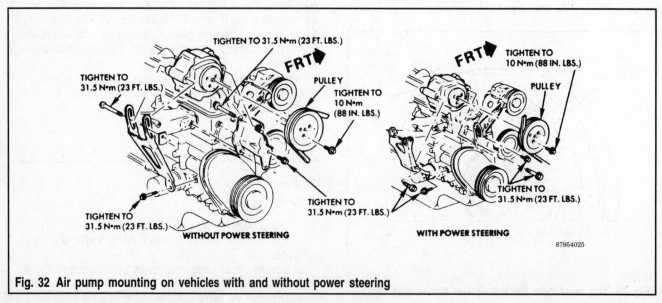

Fig. 32 Air pump mounting on vehicles with and without power steering

5. Unscrew the pump mounting bolts and then remove the pump.

6. Installation is in the reverse order of removal. Be sure to adjust the drive belt tension after installing it.

Check Valve

▶ See Figures 33 and 34

1. Release the clamp, then tag and disconnect the air hoses from the valve.

2. Unscrew the check valve from the air injection pipe.

3. Installation is in the reverse order of removal.

Air Management Valve

1. Disconnect the negative battery cable.
2. Remove the air cleaner.
3. Tag and disconnect the vacuum hose(s) from the valve.
4. Label and detach the air outlet hoses from the valve.

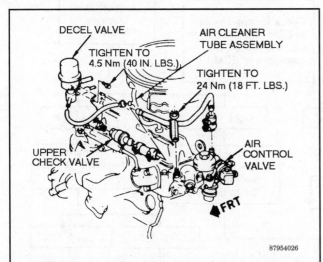

Fig. 33 Location of the upper check valve and related hoses

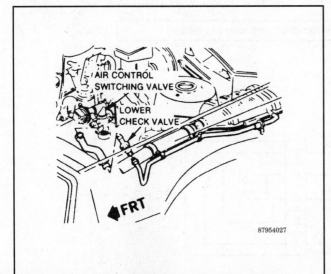

Fig. 34 View of the lower check valve and hoses

5. Bend back the locktabs and then remove the bolts holding the elbow to the valve.

6. Tag and detach any electrical connections at the valve, then remove the valve from the elbow.

7. Installation is in the reverse order of removal.

Early Fuel Evaporation (EFE) System

OPERATION

All carbureted models are equipped with an EFE system to reduce engine warm-up time, improve driveability and reduce emissions. The system is electric and uses a ceramic heater grid located underneath the primary bore of the carburetor as part of the carburetor insulator/gasket. When the ignition switch is turned **ON** and the engine coolant temperature is low, voltage is applied to the EFE relay by the ECM. The EFE relay in turn energizes the heater grid. When the coolant temperature increases, the ECM de-energizes the relay which will then shut off the EFE heater.

TESTING

▶ See Figure 35

If trouble is suspected with the EFE heater grid system, follow the accompanying chart in order to locate the problem. In following this chart you will need some basic electrical test equipped, a volt/ohmmeter and a test light. For more information on electrical system troubleshooting and test equipment, please refer to Section 6 of this manual.

REMOVAL & INSTALLATION

EFE Heater

▶ See Figure 36

1. Disconnect the negative battery cable.
2. Remove the air cleaner.
3. Tag and detach all electrical, vacuum and fuel connections from the carburetor.
4. Disconnect the EFE heater electrical lead.
5. Remove the carburetor, refer to Section 5 for service procedures.
6. Lift off the EFE heater grid assembly.
7. Installation is in the reverse order of removal. Always replace any fuel line clamp or gas hose as necessary.

EFE Heater Relay

▶ See Figure 37

1. Disconnect the negative battery cable.
2. Remove the retaining bracket on the right fender skirt.
3. Tag and detach the relay electrical connections.
4. Unfasten the retaining bolts, then remove the relay.
5. Installation is in the reverse of removal.

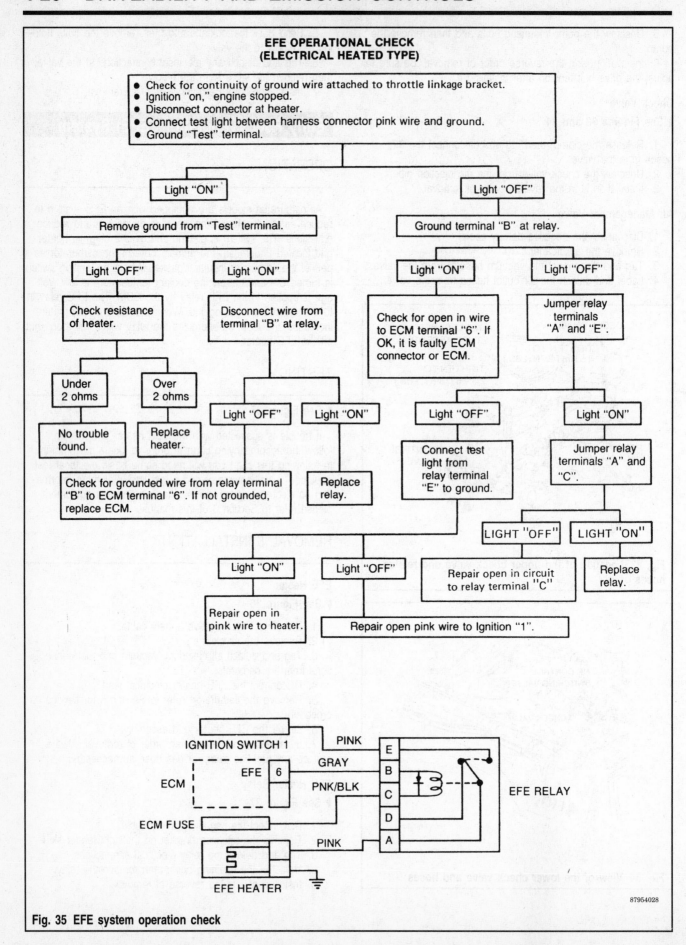

**EFE OPERATIONAL CHECK
(ELECTRICAL HEATED TYPE)**

- Check for continuity of ground wire attached to throttle linkage bracket.
- Ignition "on," engine stopped.
- Disconnect connector at heater.
- Connect test light between harness connector pink wire and ground.
- Ground "Test" terminal.

Light "ON"

Light "OFF"

Remove ground from "Test" terminal.

Ground terminal "B" at relay.

Light "OFF"

Light "ON"

Light "ON"

Light "OFF"

Check resistance of heater.

Disconnect wire from terminal "B" at relay.

Check for open in wire to ECM terminal "6". If OK, it is faulty ECM connector or ECM.

Jumper relay terminals "A" and "E".

Under 2 ohms

Over 2 ohms

Light "OFF"

Light "ON"

Light "OFF"

Light "ON"

No trouble found.

Replace heater.

Replace relay.

Connect test light from relay terminal "E" to ground.

Jumper relay terminals "A" and "C".

Check for grounded wire from relay terminal "B" to ECM terminal "6". If not grounded, replace ECM.

LIGHT "OFF"

LIGHT "ON"

Light "ON"

Light "OFF"

Repair open in circuit to relay terminal "C"

Replace relay.

Repair open in pink wire to heater.

Repair open pink wire to Ignition "1".

IGNITION SWITCH 1 — PINK — E

ECM — EFE — 6 — GRAY — B

PNK/BLK — C

ECM FUSE — D

PINK — A

EFE HEATER

EFE RELAY

87954028

Fig. 35 EFE system operation check

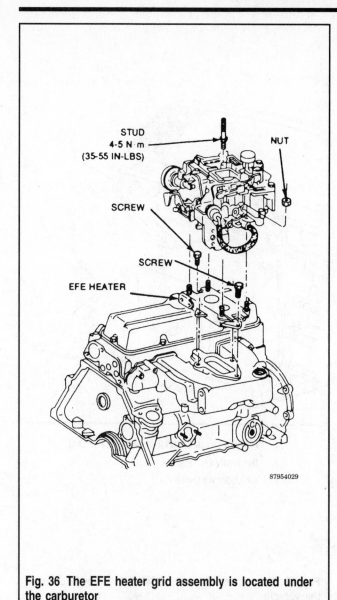

Fig. 36 The EFE heater grid assembly is located under the carburetor

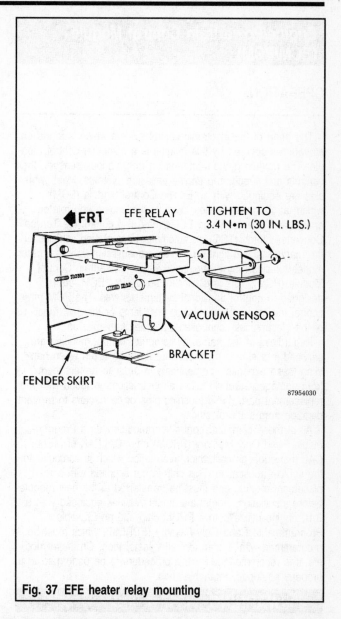

Fig. 37 EFE heater relay mounting

ELECTRONIC ENGINE CONTROLS

General Information

The fuel injection system, described in detail in Section 5 of this manual, is operated along with the ignition system to obtain optimum performance and fuel economy while producing a minimum of exhaust emissions. The various sensors described in this section are used by the computer control module (ECM or PCM depending upon application) for feedback to determine proper engine operating conditions.

➡️Although most diagnosis may be conducted using a Digital Volt/Ohm Meter (DVOM), certain steps or procedures may require use of the TECH 1® diagnostic scan tool (a specialized tester) or an equivalent scan/testing tool. If the proper tester is not available, the vehicle should be taken to a reputable service station which has the appropriate equipment.

When dealing with the electronic engine control system, keep in mind that the system is sensitive to improperly connected electrical and vacuum circuits. The condition and connection of all hoses and wires should always be the first step when attempting to diagnose a driveability problem. Worn or deteriorated hoses and damaged or corroded wires may well make a good component appear faulty.

➡️When troubleshooting the system, always check the electrical and vacuum connectors which may cause the problem before testing or replacing a component.

For more information on troubleshooting the electronic engine control system, please refer to the information on trouble codes later in this section.

Engine/Powertrain Control Module (ECM/PCM)

OPERATION

The heart of the electronic control system which is found on all vehicles covered by this manual is a computer control module. The module gathers information from various sensors, then controls fuel supply and engine emission systems. Most vehicles are equipped with an Engine Control Module (ECM) which, as its name implies, controls the engine and related emissions systems. Some ECMs may also control the Torque Converter Clutch (TCC) on automatic transmission vehicles or the manual upshift light on manual transmission vehicles. Later model vehicles may be equipped with a Powertrain Control Module (PCM). This is similar to the original ECM, but is designed to control additional systems as well. The PCM may control the manual transmission shift lamp or the shift functions of the electronically controlled automatic transmission.

Regardless of the name, all computer control modules are serviced in a similar manner. Care must be taken when handling these expensive components in order to protect them from damage. Carefully follow all instructions included with the replacement part. Avoid touching pins or connectors to prevent damage from static electricity.

All of these computer control modules contain a Programmable Read Only Memory (PROM) chip, CALPAK or MEM-CAL that contains calibration information which is particular to the vehicle application. This chip is not supplied with a replacement module and must be transferred to the new module before installation. Some late model vehicles equipped with a 3.1L engine utilize both a PROM chip and an Erasable Programmable Read Only Memory (EPROM), which must be programmed with a scan tool after installation. On these models, it is recommended for this procedure to be performed at a properly equipped, reputable shop.

✳✳WARNING

To prevent the possibility of permanent control module damage, the ignition switch MUST always be OFF when disconnecting power from or reconnecting power to the module. This includes unplugging the module connector, disconnecting the negative battery cable, removing the module fuse or even attempting to jump your dead battery using jumper cables.

REMOVAL & INSTALLATION

▶ See Figures 38, 39, 40, 41 and 42

1. Turn the ignition switch **OFF**.
2. Disconnect the negative battery cable.
3. For vehicles through 1994, remove the right side hush panel, glove box or interior access panel, as required for access to the control module.
4. For 1995-96 vehicles, remove the right hand engine splash shield. Unfasten the horn attaching bolt, then detach the electrical connector and remove the horn.

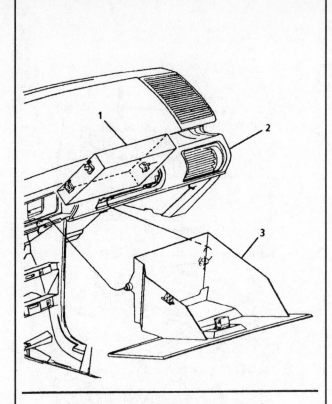

1	POWERTRAIN CONTROL MODULE (PCM)
2	INSTRUMENT PANEL
3	I/P COMPARTMENT

87954035

Fig. 38 On most models, the ECM/PCM is located inside the vehicle

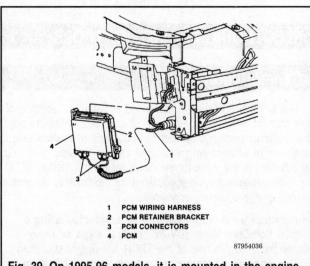

1	PCM WIRING HARNESS
2	PCM RETAINER BRACKET
3	PCM CONNECTORS
4	PCM

87954036

Fig. 39 On 1995-96 models, it is mounted in the engine compartment

5. Detach the electrical harness connectors from the computer control module.

6. Unfasten the module-to-bracket retaining screws, then remove the ECM or PCM as applicable.

7. If replacement of the calibration unit is required, unfasten the access cover retaining screws, then remove the cover from the computer control module. Carefully remove the calibration unit from the ECM/PCM, as follows:

a. If the ECM contains a PROM carrier, use the rocker type PROM removal tool.

b. If the ECM contains a CAL-PAK, grasp the CAL-PAK carrier (at the narrow end only), using the removal tool. Remove the CAL-PAK carrier.

c. If the ECM/PCM contains a MEM-CAL, EPROM or KS Module, push both retaining clips back away from the MEM-CAL/EPROM. At the same time, grasp it at both ends and

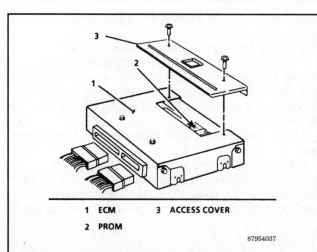

Fig. 40 In order to remove the calibration unit, you must first remove the access cover from the control module — 1992 vehicle shown

| 1 | ECM | 3 | ACCESS COVER |
| 2 | PROM | | |

87954037

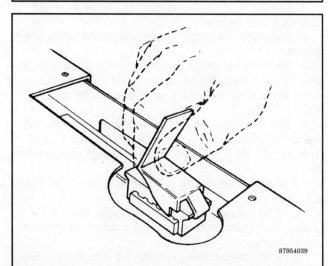

87954039

Fig. 41 Removing the PROM using the special rocker tool

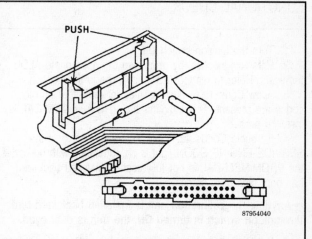

PUSH

87954040

Fig. 42 To remove the EPROM from the PCM, push the retaining clips back away from the unit, grasping both ends, then lift it up out of the socket

lift it up out of the socket. Do not remove the cover of the MEM-CAL/EPROM/KS module.

➡ **Before replacement of a defective computer control module, first check the resistance of each ECM/PCM controlled solenoid. This can be done at the module connector, using an ohmmeter and the ECM or PCM connector wiring diagram. Any computer control module controlled device with low resistance will damage the replacement ECM/PCM due to high current flow through the internal circuits.**

To install:

8. Fit the replacement calibration unit into the socket.

➡ **The small notch of the carrier should be aligned with the small notch in the socket. Press on the ends of the carrier until it is firmly seated in the socket. Do not press on the calibration unit, only the carrier.**

9. Install the access cover, then secure using the retaining screws.

10. Position the computer control module in the vehicle, then install the module-to-bracket retaining screws.

11. Attach the module electrical harness connectors.

12. For vehicles through 1994, install the right side hush panel, glove box or interior access panel as required.

13. For 1995-96 vehicles, install the horn, attach the electrical connector, then fasten with the horn attaching bolt. Tighten the bolt to 6-9 ft. lbs. (8-12 Nm). Install the right hand splash shield.

14. Check that the ignition switch is **OFF**, then connect the negative battery cable.

15. If your vehicle has the 3.1L engine which is equipped with a PCM with EPROM, the EPROM must be reprogrammed using a scan tool and the latest available software. In all likelihood, the vehicle must be towed to a dealer or repair shop containing the suitable equipment for this service.

16. Enter the self-diagnostic system and check for trouble codes to be sure the module and calibration unit are properly installed. For details, refer to the procedure for checking trouble codes, later in this section.

FUNCTIONAL CHECK

1. Turn the ignition switch **ON**.

2. Enter diagnostics, by grounding the appropriate ALDL terminals. Refer to diagnostics procedures in this section.

3. Allow Code 12 to flash 4 times to verify that no other codes are present. This indicates the PROM or MEM-CAL is installed properly.

4. If trouble Codes 42, 43 or 51 are present or if the SERVICE ENGINE SOON light is on constantly with no codes, the PROM/MEM-CAL is not fully seated, installed backward, has bent pins or is defective.

➡**Anytime the calibration unit is installed backward and the ignition switch is turned ON, the unit is destroyed.**

5. If it is not fully seated, press firmly on the ends of the MEM-CAL.

Oxygen (O$_2$) Sensor

OPERATION

▶ **See Figure 43**

The oxygen sensor has the ability to produce a low voltage signal that feeds information on engine exhaust oxygen content to the control module.

The sensor is constructed from a zirconia/platinum electrolytic element. Zirconia is an electrolyte that conducts electricity under certain chemical conditions. The element is made up of a ceramic material which acts as an insulator when cold. At operating temperatures of approximately 600°F (315°C), the element becomes a semiconductor. A platinum coating on the outer surface of the element stimulates further combustion of the exhaust gases right at the surface and this helps to keep the element up to the desired temperature.

The oxygen sensor has an inner cavity which is filled with reference (atmospheric) air. The atmosphere has approximately 21 percent oxygen in it. In the circuit, this inner cavity is the positive terminal, while the outer surface (exposed to the exhaust stream) is the negative or ground terminal.

Due to the element's electrolytic properties, oxygen concentration differences between the reference air and exhaust gases produce small voltages. A rich exhaust (excess fuel) has almost no oxygen. So when there is a large difference in the amount of oxygen touching the inside and outside surfaces, more conduction occurs and the sensor puts out a voltage signal above 0.6 V (600 mV). The signal may vary as high as 0.9 V (999 mV).

With a lean exhaust (excessive oxygen), there is about 2 percent oxygen in the gases. The smaller difference in oxygen content causes less conduction and the sensor produces a smaller voltage somewhere below 0.3 V (300 mV). The signal could drop as low as 0.1 V (100 mV). Commonly, values outside this range will cause a trouble code to set for most

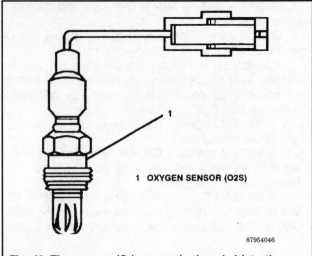

1 OXYGEN SENSOR (O2S)

87954046

Fig. 43 The oxygen (O$_2$) sensor is threaded into the exhaust manifold

control systems. When handling the oxygen sensor, follow these precautions:

• Careful handling of the oxygen sensor is essential.

• The electrical pigtail and connector are permanently attached and should not be removed from the oxygen sensor.

• The in-line electrical connector and louvered end of the oxygen sensor must be kept free of grease, dirt and other contaminants.

• Avoid using cleaning solvents of any type on the oxygen sensor.

• Do not drop or roughly handle the oxygen sensor.

• The oxygen sensor may be difficult to remove if the engine temperature is below 120°F (48°C). Excessive force may damage the threads in the exhaust manifold or exhaust pipe.

TESTING

➡**This test requires the use of a scan tool.**

1. Run the engine at normal operating temperature and connect a scan tool.

2. Disconnect the oxygen sensor. Jumper the purple wire to ground.

3. The scan tool should display O$_2$ voltage below 0.2 volts (200 MV). If it does, then O$_2$ sensor or sensor connection is faulty and must be replaced. If not, proceed to the following step.

4. With the ignition **ON** and the engine off, check the voltage of the tan wire leading to the ECM/PCM using a Digital Voltmeter (DVM). The voltage should be 0.3-0.6 volts (300-600 MV).

a. If the voltage reading is 0.3-0.6 volts, the ECM/PCM is faulty.

b. If the voltage reading is over 0.6 volts, the wire is open, the connection is faulty or the computer control module is faulty.

c. If the voltage reading is under 0.3 volts, the computer control module connections or computer control module is faulty.

REMOVAL & INSTALLATION

▶ **See Figures 44 and 45**

1. Disconnect the negative battery cable.
2. Detach the sensor electrical connector.
3. Carefully remove the Oxygen (O_2) sensor.

To install:

➡**A special anti-seize compound is used on the O_2 sensor threads. This compound is made up of a liquid graphite and glass beads. The graphite will burn away, but the glass beads will remain, making the sensor easier to remove. New or service sensors will already have the compound applied to the threads. If a sensor is removed from the engine, and is to be reinstalled, the threads must have anti-seize compound applied prior to reinstallation.**

4. If reinstalling the old sensor, coat the threads of the sensor with anti-seize compound 5613695 or equivalent.
5. Install the sensor and tighten it to 30 ft. lbs. (41 Nm).

6. Attach the sensor electrical connector.
7. Connect the negative battery cable.

Idle Air Control (IAC) Valve

OPERATION

▶ **See Figure 46**

Engine idle speeds are controlled by the computer control module (ECM/PCM) through the IAC valve mounted on the throttle body. The ECM or PCM sends voltage pulses to the IAC motor windings causing the IAC motor shaft and pintle to move in or out a given distance (number of steps) for each pulse (called counts). The movement of the pintle controls the airflow around the throttle plate, which in turn, controls engine idle speed. Idle air control valve pintle position counts can be observed using a scan tool. Zero (0) counts corresponds to a fully closed passage, while 140 counts or more correspond to full flow.

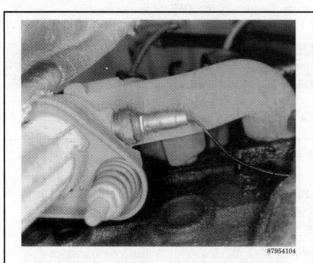

87954104

Fig. 44 The oxygen sensor is usually mounted on the exhaust manifold — 1988 2.0L (VIN K) engine shown

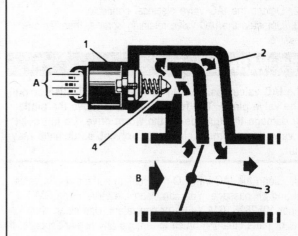

1	VALVE ASSEMBLY - IDLE AIR CONTROL (IAC)
2	BODY ASSEMBLY - THROTTLE
3	VALVE - THROTTLE
4	PINTLE - IAC VALVE
A	ELECTRICAL INPUT SIGNAL
B	AIR INLET

87954044

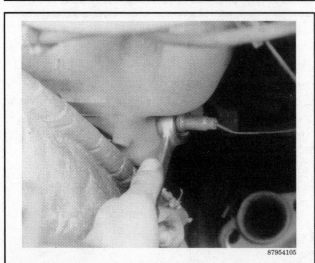

87954105

Fig. 45 A wrench may be used to remove the oxygen sensor

Fig. 46 Schematic of the IAC valve air flow

Idle speed can be categorized in 2 ways: actual (controlled) idle speed and minimum idle speed. Controlled idle speed is obtained by the ECM positioning the IAC valve pintle. Resulting idle speed is determined by total air flow (IAC passage + PCV + throttle valve + calibrated vacuum leaks). Controlled idle speed is specified at normal operating conditions, which consists of engine coolant at normal operating temperature, air conditioning compressor OFF, manual transaxle in neutral or automatic transaxle in D.

Minimum idle air speed is set at the factory with a stop screw. This setting allows enough air flow by the throttle valves to cause the IAC valve pintle to be positioned a calibrated number of steps (counts) from the seat during normal controlled idle operation.

The idle speed is controlled by the computer control module through the IAC valve. No adjustment is required during routine maintenance. Tampering with the minimum idle speed adjustment is highly discouraged and may result in premature failure of the IAC valve.

REMOVAL & INSTALLATION

▶ See Figure 47

1. Disconnect the negative battery cable.
2. Detach the IAC valve electrical connector.
3. Unfasten the IAC valve retaining screws, then remove the valve.

❄❄WARNING

If the IAC valve has been in service, DO NOT push or pull in the valve pintle. The force required to move the pintle may damage the threads on the worm drive. Do not soak the valve in any liquid cleaner or solvent, as damage may result.

4. Clean the IAC valve O-ring sealing surface, pintle valve seat and air passage. You can clean the valve using GM cleaner 1052626, GM X-66A or equivalent. Use clean shop towel or parts cleaning brush to remove any heavy deposits. If the air passage has heavy deposits, remove the throttle body for complete cleaning.

5. Inspect the O-ring for damage and replace, if necessary.
To install:

➡**If you're installing a new IAC valve, you must replace it with an identical part. IAC valve pintle shape and diameter are designed for the specific application.**

6. If you are installing a new IAC valve, measure the distance between the tip of the valve and the mounting flange. If it is greater than 1.10 in. (28mm), use finger pressure to slowly retract the pintle. The force required to retract the pintle of a NEW valve will not cause damage to the valve.

7. Lubricate the O-ring with clean engine oil, then position on the valve.

8. Install the IAC valve assembly, then secure using the attaching screws. Tighten the screws to 27 inch lbs. (30 Nm).

9. Attach the valve electrical connector.
10. Connect the negative battery cable.
11. Reset the IAC valve pintle position, as follows:
    a. Turn the ignition switch to the **ON** position (engine off).
    b. Turn the ignition **OFF** for ten seconds.
    c. Start the engine and check for proper idle operation.

Engine Coolant Temperature (ECT) Sensor

OPERATION

▶ See Figure 48

The Engine Coolant Temperature (ECT) sensor, sometimes referred to as the Coolant Temperature Sensor (CTS), is a thermistor (resistor which changes value based on temperature) mounted in the engine coolant stream. Low coolant temperatures produce a high resistance — 100,000 ohms at -40°F (-40°C), while high temperatures cause low resistance — 70 ohms at 266°F (130°C).

The control module provides a 5 volt reference signal to the sensor through a resistor in the module and measures the

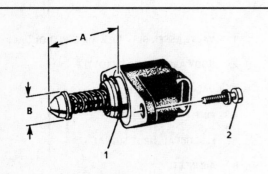

1	IAC VALVE O-RING
2	IAC VALVE ATTACHING SCREW ASSEMBLY
A	DISTANCE OF PINTLE EXTENSION
B	DIAMETER OF PINTLE

87954045

Fig. 47 Idle Air Control (IAC) valve components

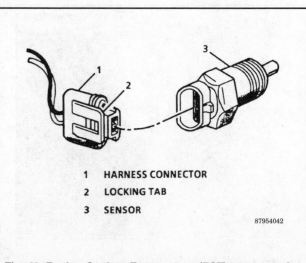

1	HARNESS CONNECTOR
2	LOCKING TAB
3	SENSOR

87954042

Fig. 48 Engine Coolant Temperature (ECT) sensor and connector

voltage. The voltage will be high when the engine is cold and low when the engine is hot. By measuring the voltage, the control module knows the engine coolant temperature. The engine coolant temperature affects most other systems controlled by the module.

TESTING

▶ **See Figure 49**

1. Disconnect the temperature sensor.
2. Connect an ohmmeter between the sensor terminals.
3. Measure the resistance with the engine off and cool. Then measure with the engine running and warmed up. Compare the resistance values obtained with the chart.
4. Replace the sensor if the readings are incorrect.

REMOVAL & INSTALLATION

▶ **See Figure 50**

1. Disconnect the negative battery cable.
2. Properly relieve the cooling system pressure, then drain to a level below the sensor.
3. Detach the ECT sensor electrical connector.
4. Carefully remove the sensor.

To install:

5. Coat the threads of the sensor with a suitable sealant. Install the sensor into the engine, tighten to 19 ft. lbs. (25 Nm).
6. Attach the ECT sensor electrical connector.
7. Refill the cooling system to the proper level.
8. Connect the negative battery cable.

DIAGNOSTIC AID

ENGINE COOLANT TEMPERATURE SENSOR

TEMPERATURE VS. RESISTANCE VALUES (APPROXIMATE)

°C	°F	OHMS
100	212	177
90	194	241
80	176	332
70	158	467
60	140	667
50	122	973
45	113	1188
40	104	1459
35	95	1802
30	86	2238
25	77	2796
20	68	3520
15	59	4450
10	50	5670
5	41	7280
0	32	9420
-5	23	12300
-10	14	16180
-15	5	21450
-20	-4	28680
-30	-22	52700
-40	-40	100700

87954057

Fig. 49 ECT sensor value chart

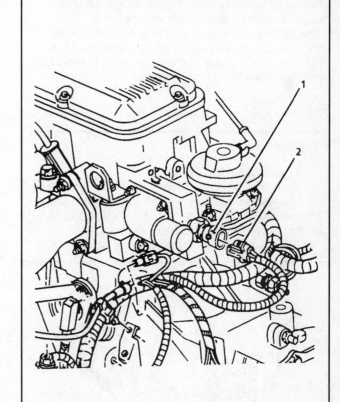

1 **ENGINE COOLANT TEMPERATURE (ECT) SENSOR**

2 **ECT SENSOR ELECTRICAL CONNECTOR**

87954043

Fig. 50 Location of the ECT sensor — 1995 2.2L engine shown

Manifold Air Temperature (MAT)/Intake Air Temperature (IAT) Sensor

OPERATION

▶ See Figure 51

The MAT or IAT sensor (as equipped), is a thermistor (resistor which changes value based on temperature) mounted either in the air intake snorkel or the manifold (depending on the application). Low intake air temperatures produce a high resistance — 100,000 ohms at -40°F (-40°C), while high temperatures cause low resistance — 70 ohms at 266°F (130°C).

The control module provides a 5 volt reference signal to the sensor through a resistor in the module and measures the voltage. The voltage will be high when the air is cold and low when the air is hot. By measuring the voltage, the control module knows the intake/manifold air temperature.

The air temperature signal is used by the control module to delay EGR until the temperature reaches approximately 40°F (5°C). The control module also uses the signal to retard ignition timing during high air temperatures.

TESTING

▶ See Figure 52

1. Disconnect the MAT/IAT sensor.
2. Connect an ohmmeter between the sensor terminals.
3. Measure the resistance with the engine off and cool. Then measure with the engine running and warmed up. Compare the resistance values obtained with the chart.
4. Replace the sensor if the readings are incorrect.

DIAGNOSTIC AID		
MAT SENSOR		
TEMPERATURE TO RESISTANCE VALUES		
(APPROXIMATE)		
°F	°C	OHMS
210	100	185
160	70	450
100	38	1,800
70	20	3,400
40	4	7,500
20	-7	13,500
0	-18	25,000
-40	-40	100,700

87954200

Fig. 52 MAT/IAT sensor value chart

REMOVAL & INSTALLATION

▶ See Figure 53

➡The MAT/IAT sensor is usually located in the air cleaner assembly or in the top of the intake manifold between the runners.

1. Disconnect the negative battery cable.
2. Detach the sensor electrical connector.
3. If necessary, remove the air cleaner assembly cover to gain access to the sensor.
4. Carefully remove the sensor and retainer (if equipped).
5. Installation is the reverse of the removal procedure.

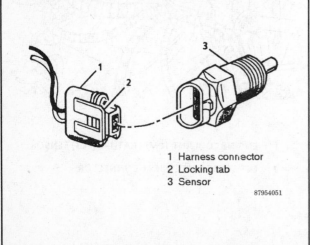

1 Harness connector
2 Locking tab
3 Sensor

87954051

Fig. 51 View of the MAT/IAT sensor and electrical connector — 1995 2.3L shown

87954107

Fig. 53 On the 1988 2.0L (VIN K) engine, the MAT sensor is mounted in the air cleaner assembly

Manifold Absolute Pressure (MAP) Sensor

OPERATION

▶ See Figure 54

The Manifold Absolute Pressure (MAP) sensor measures the changes in intake manifold pressure, which result from engine load and speed changes and converts this information to a voltage output. The MAP sensor reading is the opposite of a vacuum gauge reading: when manifold pressure is high, MAP sensor value is high and vacuum is low. A MAP sensor will produce a low output on engine coastdown with a closed throttle while a wide open throttle will produce a high output. The high output is produced because the pressure inside the manifold is the same as outside the manifold, so 100% of the outside air pressure is measured.

The MAP sensor is also used to measure barometric pressure under certain conditions, which allows the ECM to automatically adjust for different altitudes.

The MAP sensor changes the 5 volt signal supplied by the computer control module (ECM or PCM as applicable), which reads the change and uses the information to control fuel delivery and ignition timing.

TESTING

➡ The test requires the use of a scan tool.

1. If the engine idle is rough, unstable or incorrect, fix before using this test.
2. With the engine idling, hook up a scan tool. If the scan tool does not display a MAP of 4.0 or more volts, the trouble code is intermittent. Check all connections and make sure the sensor is mounted securely.
3. If the MAP is over 4.0 volts, turn the ignition OFF, then detach the MAP sensor connector and turn the ignition to the

ON position. The scan tool should read a voltage of 1 volt or less.

a. If the voltage reading is 1 volt or less, probe CKT 455 with a test light to 12 volts. If the test light lights, the MAP sensor hose is plugged or leaking, or the MAP sensor is faulty. If the test light doesn't light, CKT 455 is open.

b. If the voltage reading is more than 1 volt, CKT 432 is shorted to voltage, shorted to CKT 474 or the ECM/PCM is faulty.

REMOVAL & INSTALLATION

▶ See Figures 55, 56 and 57

1. Disconnect the negative battery cable.
2. If necessary, unfasten the retainer clip from the engine bracket assembly-to-MAP sensor assembly.
3. Disconnect the vacuum line, then detach the electrical connector from the MAP sensor.
4. Remove the MAP sensor from the vehicle.

To install:

5. Attach the vacuum line and the electrical connector to the MAP sensor.
6. Fasten the MAP sensor assembly to the engine bracket.
7. Install the retaining clip.
8. Connect the negative battery cable.

Throttle Position (TP) Sensor

OPERATION

▶ See Figure 58

The TP sensor is mounted to the throttle body, opposite the throttle lever and is connected to the throttle shaft. Its function is to sense the current throttle valve position and relay that information to the ECM. Throttle position information allows the ECM to generate the required injector control signals. The TP sensor consists of a potentiometer which alters the flow of voltage according to the position of a wiper on the variable

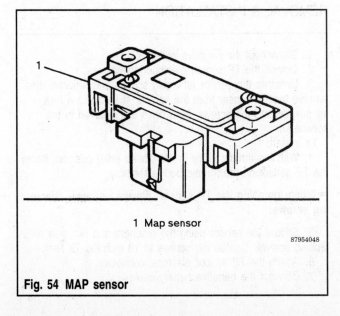

1 Map sensor

87954048

Fig. 54 MAP sensor

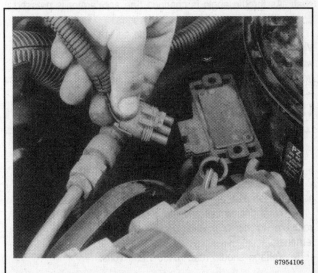

87954106

Fig. 55 Be careful not to break the connector locktab

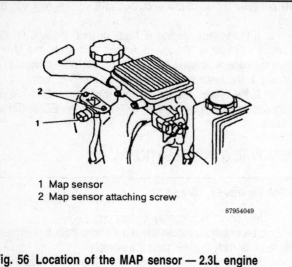

1 Map sensor
2 Map sensor attaching screw

87954049

Fig. 56 Location of the MAP sensor — 2.3L engine shown

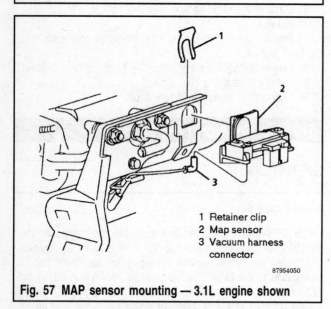

1 Retainer clip
2 Map sensor
3 Vacuum harness connector

87954050

Fig. 57 MAP sensor mounting — 3.1L engine shown

resistor windings, in proportion to the movement of the throttle shaft. As throttle angle is changed (the accelerator is pressed down), the output of the sensor changes.

At closed throttle, the output of the sensor is fairly low (0.5 V). As the throttle opens, the output voltage should rise towards 5 V. By monitoring the sensor output voltage, the control module can determine fuel delivery based on throttle angle.

TESTING

1. Remove air cleaner.
2. Disconnect TP sensor harness from the sensor.
3. Using three jumper wires, connect the TP sensor harness to then sensor.
4. With ignition **ON** and the engine stopped, use a digital voltmeter to measure voltage between the bottom and middle terminals.
5. Voltage should read 0.450-1.250 volts.

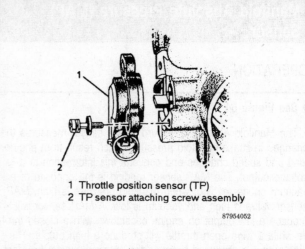

1 Throttle position sensor (TP)
2 TP sensor attaching screw assembly

87954052

Fig. 58 The Throttle Position (TP) sensor is mounted to the throttle body

ADJUSTMENT

➡**The TP sensor is not adjustable on most models. Adjustable TP sensors have elongated mounting holes to allow adjustment.**

1. If necessary, remove the EGR valve and heat shield from engine.
2. Using three 6 in. (152mm) jumpers, connect the TP sensor harness to the TP sensor.
3. With ignition **ON**, engine stopped, use a digital voltmeter to measure voltage between the bottom and middle terminals.
4. Loosen the two TP sensor attaching screws and rotate the sensor to obtain a voltage reading of 0.450-1.250 volts.
5. With the ignition **OFF**, remove the jumpers and reconnect TP sensor harness to TP sensor.
6. Install the EGR valve and heat shield to engine, using new gasket as necessary.
7. Install the air cleaner gasket and air cleaner to throttle body unit.

REMOVAL & INSTALLATION

1. Disconnect the negative battery cable.
2. Detach the TP sensor electrical connector.
3. Unfasten the sensor attaching screws and retainer, then remove the TP sensor from the vehicle. If installing a new sensor, discard the screws. New ones are supplied in the service kit.
   To install:
4. With the throttle valve in the closed (idle) position, install the TP sensor on the throttle body assembly.

➡**When installing the TP sensor, always use new attaching screws.**

5. Secure the sensor using the retainers and two new attaching screws. Tighten the screws to 18 inch lbs. (2 Nm).
6. Attach the TP sensor electrical connector.
7. Connect the negative battery cable.

Camshaft Position (CMP) Sensor

OPERATION

The Camshaft Position (CMP) sensor is used to correlate crankshaft-to-camshaft position so that the PCM can determine which cylinder is ready to be fueled by the injector. The CMP sensor is also used to determine which cylinder is misfiring when when misfire is present. If the computer control module receives an intermittent signal from the CMP, then the "CMP Resync Counter" will increment. When the PCM cannot use the information from the CMP sensor, a Diagnostic Trouble Code (DTC) is set.

REMOVAL & INSTALLATION

1. Disconnect the negative battery cable.
2. Detach the sensor harness connector at the sensor.
3. Unfasten the retaining bolt, then remove the sensor from the camshaft housing. Inspect the sensor O-ring for wear, cracks or leakage and replace if necessary.

To install:

4. Lubricate the O-ring with clean engine oil, then place on the sensor. Install the sensor into the camshaft housing.
5. Install the CMP sensor retaining bolt, then tighten to 88 inch lbs. (10 Nm).
6. Attach the sensor harness connector.
7. Connect the negative battery cable.

Crankshaft Position (CKP) Sensor

OPERATION

The Crankshaft Position (CKP) sensor (formerly named simply crankshaft sensor) is mounted remotely from the ignition module on an aluminum cover plate. Based on CKP sensor pulses, the sensor sends a reference signal to the computer control module, which is used to determine crankshaft position and engine speed.

TESTING

➡This test requires the use of a Tech 1® or equivalent scan tool.

1. Idle the engine for 5 minutes or until the Malfunction Indicator Light (MIL) turns on.
2. Install a scan tool. Does the scan tool display DTC 19 for 1995 and earlier models or DTC P0335 for 1996 vehicles?
3. If the scan tool displays the DTC, proceed as follows:
    a. With the engine running, wiggle the connections of the PCM and CKP sensor and related wires while listening for engine stumble.
    b. If the engine does not stumble, inspect the sensor, sensor wiring and connectors and replace as necessary.

    c. If the engine stumbles, repair the faulty circuit(s) or connector(s) and retest for the DTC.
4. If the scan tool does not display the specified DTC, proceed as follows:
5. Observe the scan tool 7X resync while operating all non-engine components on the vehicle. There should be no 7X resync during the operation of the components.
6. If there is no resync, with the engine running, wiggle the connections of the PCM and CKP sensor and related wires while listening for engine stumble.
    a. If the engine does not stumble, the DTC is intermittent.
    b. If the engine stumbles, repair the faulty circuit(s) or connector(s) and retest for the DTC.
7. If there is resync, repair the circuits of the fault components and retest for the DTC.

REMOVAL & INSTALLATION

Except 2.0L (VIN H) Engine
▶ See Figures 59 and 60

1. Disconnect the negative battery cable.
2. For the 2.2L (VIN G and 4), raise and safely support the vehicle.
3. Disconnect the sensor harness plug/connector.
4. Unfasten the sensor-to-block bolt/nut, then remove the sensor from the engine.
5. Inspect the sensor O-ring for damage and replace, if necessary. Be sure to lubricate the O-ring with clean engine oil prior to installation.

To install:

6. Position the sensor in the block, then install the sensor retaining bolt/nut.
7. Tighten the sensor bolt to 71 inch lbs (8 Nm) for the 2.2L, 2.8L and 3.1L engines. For the 2.3L and 2.4L engines, tighten to 88 inch lbs. (10 Nm).
8. Attach the sensor harness plug/connector.
9. If raised, carefully lower the vehicle.
10. Connect the negative battery cable.

2.0L (VIN H) Engine
▶ See Figure 61

1. Disconnect the negative battery cable.
2. Raise and safely support the vehicle.
3. Remove the two lower power steering bracket nuts.
4. Carefully remove the vehicle, then remove the serpentine belt.
5. Unfasten the four bolts and two nuts, then remove the alternator from its mount, including removing the hinge and crankcase ventilation tube.
6. Remove the upper power steering brace by unfastening the 3 bolts.
7. Unfasten the retaining lower bracket bolts, then set the power steering pump assembly aside.
8. Unfasten the 4 bolts and 1 nut securing the timing belt cover, then remove the cover.
9. Detach the CKP sensor harness behind the engine and cut tie strap.
10. Feed the harness behind the timing plate, then remove the harness and CKP sensor.

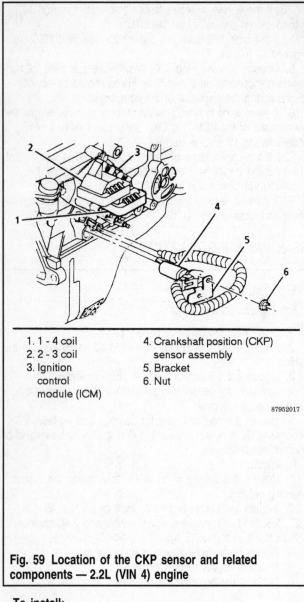

1. 1 - 4 coil
2. 2 - 3 coil
3. Ignition control module (ICM)
4. Crankshaft position (CKP) sensor assembly
5. Bracket
6. Nut

87952017

Fig. 59 Location of the CKP sensor and related components — 2.2L (VIN 4) engine

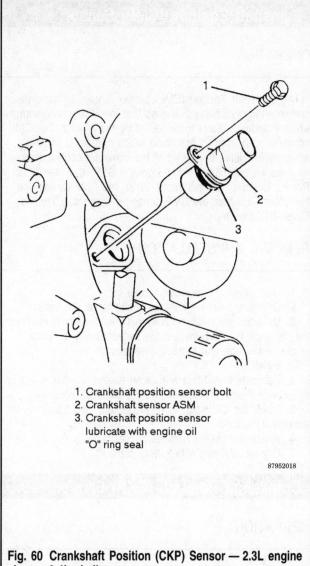

1. Crankshaft position sensor bolt
2. Crankshaft sensor ASM
3. Crankshaft position sensor lubricate with engine oil "O" ring seal

87952018

Fig. 60 Crankshaft Position (CKP) Sensor — 2.3L engine shown, 2.4L similar

To install:
11. Raise and safely support the vehicle.
12. Install the CKP sensor in the engine (1 bolts), then feed the harness through the A/C compressor mount.
13. Carefully lower the vehicle.
14. Feed the sensor wiring harness behind the timing plate.
15. Connect the harness at the rear of the engine, then install the tie strap.
16. Position the timing belt cover, then secure using the retainers.
17. Install the 2 top bolts for the lower power steering bracket.
18. Install the alternator, including the hinge and crankcase ventilation tube.
19. Raise and safely support the vehicle.
20. Secure the two lower power steering bracket nuts.
21. Carefully lower the vehicle.
22. Install the serpentine belt.
23. Attach the sensor-to-engine harness.
24. Connect the negative battery cable.

Park/Neutral Switch

OPERATION

The Park/Neutral (P/N) switch indicates to the computer control module (ECM/PCN) when the transmission is in park or neutral. This information is used for the TCC, and the IAC valve operation.

➡**Vehicle should not be driven with Park/Neutral (P/N) switch disconnected as idle quality will be affected and a possible false Code 24 (VSS) will be set.**

TESTING

➡**This test requires the use of a Tech 1® or equivalent scan tool.**

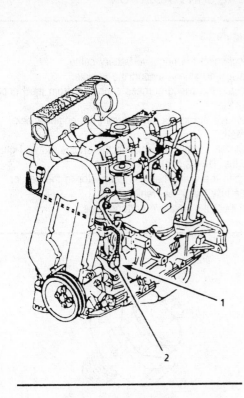

1. Crankshaft position sensor bolt (hidden from view)
2. Crankshaft position sensor

87952016

Fig. 61 The CKP sensor mounting on the 2.0L (VIN H) engine

1. Connect a suitable scan tool as instructed by the manufacturer.
2. With the transaxle in park, the scan tool should indicate Park, or Neutral.
3. If the scan tool indicates park or neutral, shift the transaxle into drive. The scan tool should display a change to indicate drive.
   a. If not, disconnect the switch. This should cause the scan tool to display drive range. If it displays drive range, the switch connection is faulty, or the switch is misadjusted or faulty. If it does not display drive range, CKT 434 is shorted to ground or the computer control module is faulty.
   b. If the scan tool indicates park or neutral, no trouble is found at this time. The code may be intermittent.
4. If the scan tool does not indicate park or neutral proceed as follows:
   a. Detach the switch connector. Jumper the harness connector terminals A and B. The scan tool should indicate park or neutral.
   b. If not, jumper the harness connector (CKT 434) to the engine ground. The scan tool should indicate park or neutral.

If so, there is an open ground circuit. If not CKT 434 is open, the ECM connections are faulty or the ECM is faulty.
5. If the scan tool indicates park or neutral, the switch connection is faulty, or the switch is misadjusted or faulty.

REMOVAL & INSTALLATION

Removal and installation of the switch is located in Section 7 of this manual.

Vehicle Speed Sensor (VSS)

OPERATION

The VSS is located on the transaxle and sends a pulsing voltage signal to the ECM which is converted to miles per hour. This sensor mainly controls the operation of the TCC system, shift light, cruise control and activation of the EGR system.

TESTING

➡**This test requires the use of a Tech 1® or equivalent scan tool.**

1. Raise and safely support the vehicle so the drive wheels are clear of the ground.

✳✳WARNING

Do NOT perform this test without supporting the lower control arms so that the drive axles are in a normal horizontal position. Running the vehicle in gear with the wheels hanging down at full travel may damage the drive axles.

2. With the engine idling in gear, the scan tool should display vehicle speed above zero.
3. If the scan tool displays vehicle speed above zero, the DTC is intermittent. Check the wiring for proper connections and correct harness routing.
4. If the scan tool does not display vehicle speed above zero, check to see if the speedometer works.
5. If the speedometer works, check the PROM for the correct application. If its ok, replace the computer control module.
6. If the speedometer does not work proceed as follows:
   a. Turn the ignition to the **OFF** position.
   b. Disconnect the VSS wiring at the transaxle. Attach signal generator tester J 33431-B, or equivalent, to the VSS harness connector.
   c. Turn the ignition **ON**, then turn the scan tool on and set it to generate a VSS signal.
   d. The scan tool should display vehicle speed above zero. If it doesn't, CKT 400 or 401 is shorted to ground, shorted together, there are faulty connections or faulty computer control module. If it does display vehicle speed above zero, replace the VSS.

REMOVAL & INSTALLATION

1. Disconnect the negative battery cable.
2. Raise and safely support the vehicle.
3. Detach the VSS lead from the transaxle.
4. If necessary, unfasten the governor housing bolts, then remove the housing.
5. Unfasten the bolt or screw and retainer, then remove the VSS assembly from the vehicle. Remove and discard the O-ring.

To install:
6. Lubricate a new O-ring with synchromesh transaxle fluid part no. 12345349 or equivalent, then install on the sensor.
7. Install the VSS assembly, then secure with the retainer and bolt/screw.
8. If removed, install the governor housing and secure with the retaining bolts.
9. Attach the VSS lead to the transaxle.
10. Carefully lower the vehicle.
11. Connect the negative battery cable.

Knock Sensor (KS)

OPERATION

▶ **See Figure 62**

The Knock Sensor (KS) detects abnormal vibration (spark knocking) in the engine. The sensor is mounted in the engine block near the cylinders. The sensor produces an AC output voltage which increases with the severity of the knock. This signal voltage inputs to the ECM/PCM. The computer control module then adjusts the timing to reduce the knock. This allows the engine to use maximum spark advance to improve driveability and fuel economy.

REMOVAL & INSTALLATION

▶ **See Figure 63**

1. Disconnect the negative battery cable.
2. Raise and safely support the vehicle.
3. Detach the wiring harness connector from the Knock Sensor (KS).
4. Remove the knock sensor from the engine block.

To install:
5. Install the knock sensor into the engine block. Tighten to 12-16 ft. lbs. (16-22 Nm).
6. Attach the wiring harness connector to the sensor.
7. Carefully lower the vehicle.
8. Connect the negative battery cable.

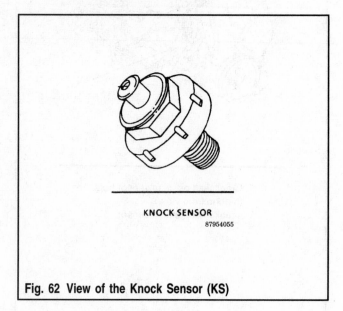

KNOCK SENSOR
87954055

Fig. 62 View of the Knock Sensor (KS)

1 **KNOCK SENSOR**
87954056

Fig. 63 The knock sensor can be found mounted to the engine block — 1992 3.1L engine shown

TROUBLE CODES

General Information

The computer control module (ECM/PCM) is required to maintain the exhaust emissions at acceptable levels. The module is a small, solid state computer which receives signals from many sources and sensors; it uses these data to make judgments about operating conditions and then control output signals to the fuel and emission systems to match the current requirements.

Inputs are received from many sources to form a complete picture of engine operating conditions. Some inputs are simply yes or no messages, such as that from the Park/Neutral switch; the vehicle is either in gear or in Park/Neutral; there are no other choices. Other data is sent in quantitative input, such as engine RPM, coolant temperature and throttle position. The computer control module is pre-programmed to recognize acceptable ranges or combinations of signals and control the outputs to control emissions while providing good driveability and economy. The ECM/PCM also monitors some output circuits, making sure that the components function as commanded. For proper engine operation, it is essential that all input and output components function properly and communicate properly with the computer control module.

Since the control module is programmed to recognize the presence and value of electrical inputs, it will also note the lack of a signal or a radical change in values. It will, for example, react to the loss of signal from the vehicle speed sensor or note that engine coolant temperature has risen beyond acceptable (programmed) limits. Once a fault is recognized, a numeric code is assigned and held in memory. The dashboard warning lamp: CHECK ENGINE or SERVICE ENGINE SOON (SES) will illuminate to advise the operator that the system has detected a fault. This lamp is also known as the Malfunction Indicator Lamp (MIL).

More than one code may be stored. Although not every engine uses every code, possible codes range from 12 to over 100. Additionally, the same code may carry different meanings relative to each engine or engine family.

In the event of an computer control module failure, the system will default to a pre-programmed set of values. These are compromise values which allow the engine to operate, although possibly at reduced efficiency. This is variously known as the default, limp-in or back-up mode. Driveability is almost always affected when the ECM/PCM enters this mode.

LEARNING ABILITY

The computer control module can compensate for minor variations within the fuel system through the block learn and fuel integrator systems. The fuel integrator monitors the oxygen sensor output voltage, adding or subtracting fuel to drive the mixture rich or lean as needed to reach the ideal air fuel ratio of 14.7:1. The integrator values may be read with a scan tool; the display will range from 0-255 and should center on 128 if the oxygen sensor is seeing a 14.7:1 mixture.

The temporary nature of the integrator's control is expanded by the block learn function. The name is derived from the fact that the entire engine operating range (load vs. rpm) is divided into 16 sections or blocks. Within each memory block is stored the correct fuel delivery value for that combination of load and engine speed. Once the operating range enters a certain block, that stored value controls the fuel delivery unless the integrator steps in to change it. If changes are made by the integrator, the new value is memorized and stored within the block. As the block learn makes the correction, the integrator correction will be reduced until the integrator returns to 128; the block learn then controls the fuel delivery with the new value.

The next time the engine operates within the block's range, the new value will be used. The block learn data can also be read by a scan tool; the range is the same as the integrator and should also center on 128. In this way, the systems can compensate for engine wear, small air or vacuum leaks or reduced combustion.

Any time the battery is disconnected, the block learn values are lost and must be relearned by the ECM. This loss of corrected values may be noticed as a significant change in driveability. To reteach the system, make certain the engine is fully warmed up. Drive the vehicle at part throttle using moderate acceleration and idle until normal performance is felt.

DASHBOARD WARNING LAMP

The primary function of the dash warning lamp is to advise the operator and that a fault has been detected, and, in most cases, a code stored. Under normal conditions, the dash warning lamp will illuminate when the ignition is turned **ON**. Once the engine is started and running, the computer control module will perform a system check and extinguish the warning lamp if no fault is found.

Additionally, the dash warning lamp can be used to retrieve stored codes after the system is placed in the Diagnostic Mode. Codes are transmitted as a series of flashes with short or long pauses. When the system is placed in the Field Service Mode, the dash lamp will indicate open loop or closed loop function to the technician.

Tools and Equipment

SCAN TOOLS

Although stored Diagnostic Trouble Codes (DTC's) may be read with only the use of a small jumper wire, the use of a hand-held scan tool such as GM's TECH-1® or equivalent is recommended. There are many manufacturers of these tools; a purchaser must be certain that the tool is proper for the intended use. If you own a scan type tool, it probably came with comprehensive instructions on proper use. Be sure to follow the instructions that came with your unit if they differ from what is given here; this is a general guide with useful information included.

The scan tool allows any stored codes to be read from the ECM or PCM memory. The tool also allows the operator to view the data being sent to the computer control module while the engine is running. This ability has obvious diagnostic advantages; the use of the scan tool is frequently required for component testing. The scan tool makes collecting information easier; the data must be correctly interpreted by an operator familiar with the system.

An example of the usefulness of the scan tool may be seen in the case of a temperature sensor which has changed its electrical characteristics. The ECM is reacting to an apparently warmer engine (causing a driveability problem), but the sensor's voltage has not changed enough to set a fault code. Connecting the scan tool, the voltage signal being sent to the ECM may be viewed; comparison to normal values or a known good vehicle reveals the problem quickly.

The ECM is capable of communicating with a scan tool in 3 modes:

1. Normal or Open Mode. This mode is not applicable to all engines. When engaged, certain engine data can be observed on the scanner without affecting engine operating characteristics. The number of items readable in this mode varies with engine family. Most scan tools are designed to change automatically to the ALDL mode if this mode is not available.

2. ALDL Mode. Also referred to as the 10K or SPECIAL mode, the scanner will present all readable data as available. Certain operating characteristics of the engine are changed or controlled when this mode is engaged. The closed loop timers are bypassed, the spark (EST) is advanced and the PARK/NEUTRAL restriction is bypassed. If applicable, the IAC controls the engine speed to 950-1050 rpm, and, on some engines, the canister purge solenoid is energized.

3. Factory Test. Sometimes referred to as BACK-UP mode, this level of communication is primarily used during vehicle assembly and testing. This mode will confirm that the default or limp-in system is working properly within the computer control module. Other data obtainable in this mode has little use in diagnosis.

➡**A scan tool that is known to display faulty data should not be used for diagnosis. Although the fault may be believed to be in only one area, it can possibly affect many other areas during diagnosis, leading to errors and incorrect repair.**

To properly read system values with a scan tool, the following conditions must be met. All normal values given in the charts will be based on these conditions:
- Engine running at idle, throttle closed
- Engine warm, upper radiator hose hot
- Vehicle in park or neutral
- System operating in closed loop
- All accessories OFF

ELECTRICAL TOOLS

The most commonly required electrical diagnostic tool is the Digital Multimeter, allowing voltage, ohmage (resistance) and amperage to be read by one instrument. The multimeter must be a high-impedance unit, with 10 megohms of impedance in the voltmeter. This type of meter will not place an additional load on the circuit it is testing; this is extremely important in low voltage circuits. The multimeter must be of high quality in

all respects. It should be handled carefully and protected from impact or damage. Replace batteries frequently in the unit.

Other necessary tools include an unpowered test light, a quality tachometer with an inductive (clip-on) pick up, and the proper tools for releasing GM's Metri-Pack, Weather Pack and Micro-Pack terminals as necessary. The Micro-Pack connectors are used at the computer control module electrical connector. A vacuum pump/gauge may also be required for checking sensors, solenoids and valves.

Diagnosis and Testing

TROUBLESHOOTING

Diagnosis of a driveablility and/or emissions problems requires attention to detail and following the diagnostic procedures in the correct order. Resist the temptation to perform any repairs before performing the preliminary diagnostic steps. In many cases this will shorten diagnostic time and often cure the problem without electronic testing.

The proper troubleshooting procedure for these vehicles is as follows:

Visual/Physical Underhood Inspection

This is possibly the most critical step of diagnosis. A detailed examination of connectors, wiring and vacuum hoses can often lead to a repair without further diagnosis. Performance of this step relies on the skill of the technician performing it; a careful inspector will check the undersides of hoses as well as the integrity of hard-to-reach hoses blocked by the air cleaner or other component. Wiring should be checked carefully for any sign of strain, burning, crimping, or terminal pull-out from a connector. Checking connectors at components or in harnesses is required; usually, pushing them together will reveal a loose fit.

Intermittents

If a fault occurs intermittently, such as a loose connector pin breaking contact as the vehicle hits a bump, the computer control module (ECM or PCM depending upon application) will note the fault as it occurs and energize the dash warning lamp. If the problem self-corrects, as with the terminal pin again making contact, the dash lamp will extinguish after 10 seconds but a code will remain stored in the computer control module's memory.

When an unexpected code appears during diagnostics, it may have been set during an intermittent failure that self-corrected; the codes are still useful in diagnosis and should not be discounted.

Circuit/Component Diagnosis and Repair

The fault codes and the scan tool data will lead to diagnosis and checking of a particular circuit. It is important to note that the fault code indicates a fault or loss of signal in an ECM-controlled system, not necessarily in the specific component.

Refer to the appropriate Diagnostic Code chart to determine the codes meaning. The component may then be tested following the appropriate component test procedures found in this section. If the component is OK, check the wiring for shorts or opens. Further diagnoses should be left to an experienced driveability technician.

If a code indicates the ECM to be faulty and the ECM is replaced, but does not correct the problem, one of the following may be the reason:

• There is a problem with the ECM terminal connections: The terminals may have to be removed from the connector in order to check them properly.

• The ECM or PROM is not correct for the application: The incorrect ECM or PROM may cause a malfunction and may or may not set a code.

• The problem is intermittent: This means that the problem is not present at the time the system is being checked. In this case, make a careful physical inspection of all portions of the system involved.

• Shorted solenoid, relay coil or harness: Solenoids and relays are turned "ON" and "OFF" by the ECM using internal electronic switches called "drivers." Each driver is part of a group of four called "Quad-Drivers." A shorted solenoid, relay coil or harness may cause an ECM to fail, and a replacement ECM to fail when it is installed. Use a short tester, J 34696, BT 8405, or equivalent, as a fast, accurate means of checking for a short circuit.

• The Programmable Read Only Memory (PROM) may be faulty: Although the PROM rarely fails, it operates as part of the ECM. Therefore, it could be the cause of the problem. Substitute a known good PROM.

• The replacement ECM may be faulty: After the ECM is replaced, the system should be rechecked for proper operation. If the diagnostic code again indicates the ECM is the problem, substitute a known good ECM. Although this is a rare condition, it could happen.

Reading Codes

Listings of the Diagnostic Trouble Codes (DTC's) for the various engine control system covered in this manual are located in this section. Remember that a code only points to the faulty circuit NOT necessarily to a faulty component. Loose, damaged or corroded connections may contribute to a fault code on a circuit when the sensor or component is operating properly. Be sure that the components are faulty before replacing them, especially the expensive ones.

Keep in mind that most codes are only valid when the trouble is present. If the trouble is intermittent (often caused by loose or corroded terminals on circuit connections), it may lead to a dead end or "Intermittent code" ending in which the exact cause of the fault is still left undetermined. In these cases, check all related vacuum hoses and/or wiring for poor, worn or damaged connections. If bad connections are found, wiggle the connection in attempt to duplicate the fault condition so that troubleshooting may continue. Also, before replacing a computer control module, be ABSOLUTELY certain that the module is at fault. The price of module is usually quite significant and they are almost always NON-RETURNABLE components.

➡**After making repairs, clear the trouble codes and operate the vehicle to see if it will reset, indicating further problems.**

On 1982 models, a 5 terminal connector, located on the right side of the fuse panel, is used to activate the trouble

code system in the ECM. This same connector is used at assembly and known as the Assembly Line Diagnostic Link (ALDL) or Assembly Line Communication Link (ALCL). A trouble code test terminal **D** is located in the 5 terminal connector and a ground terminal **E**, is located next to this terminal. With the ignition **ON**, car not running, jump the test terminal to ground.

On 1983-96 models, the ALDL connector or Data Link Connector (DLC), located under the dash, and sometimes covered with a plastic cover labeled DIAGNOSTIC CONNECTOR, can be activated by grounding test terminal **B**. The terminal is most easily grounded by connecting it to terminal **A** (internal ECM ground), the terminal to the right of terminal **B** on the top row of the ALDL connector. Once terminals **A** and **B** have been connected, the ignition switch must be moved to the **ON** position with the engine not running.

1. Turn the ignition switch **OFF**.

2. The Service Engine Soon or Check Engine light should be flashing. If it isn't, turn the ignition **OFF** and remove the jumper wire. Turn the ignition **ON** and confirm that light is now on. If it is not, replace the bulb and try again. If the bulb still will not light, or if it does not flash with the test terminal grounded, the system should be diagnosed by an experienced driveability technician. If the light is OK, proceed as follows.

3. The code(s) stored in memory may be read either through counting the flashes of the dashboard warning lamp or through the use of a hand-held scan tool. If using the scan tool, connect it correctly to the ALDL.

4. After the terminals are connected, turn the ignition switch to the **ON** position, but DO NOT start the engine. The dash warning lamp should begin to flash Code 12. The code will display as one flash, a pause and two flashes. Code 12 is not a fault code. It is used as a system acknowledgment or handshake code; its presence indicates that the ECM can communicate as requested. Code 12 is used to begin every diagnostic sequence. Some vehicles also use Code 12 after all diagnostic codes have been sent.

5. After Code 12 has been transmitted 3 times, the fault codes, if any, will each be transmitted 3 times. The codes are stored and transmitted in numeric order from lowest to highest.

➡**The order of codes in the memory does not indicate the order of occurrence.**

6. If there are no codes stored, but a driveability or emissions problem is evident, the system should be diagnosed by an experienced driveability technician.

7. If one or more codes are stored, record them. Refer to the applicable Diagnostic Code chart in this section.

8. Switch the ignition **OFF** when finished with code retrieval or scan tool readings.

Clearing Codes

Stored fault codes may be erased from memory at any time by removing power from the ECM for at least 30 seconds. It may be necessary to clear stored codes during diagnosis to check for any recurrence during a test drive, but the stored codes must be written down when retrieved. The codes may still be required for subsequent troubleshooting. Whenever a repair is complete, the stored codes must be erased and the vehicle test driven to confirm correct operation and repair.

✳✳WARNING

The ignition switch must be OFF any time power is disconnected or restored to the ECM. Severe damage may result if this precaution is not observed.

Depending on the electrical distribution of the particular vehicle, power to the ECM may be disconnected by removing the ECM fuse in the fusebox, disconnecting the in-line fuse holder near the positive battery terminal or disconnecting the ECM power lead at the battery terminal. Disconnecting the negative battery cable to clear codes is not recommended as this will also clear other memory data in the vehicle such as radio presets.

DTC	DESCRIPTION
13	Oxygen Sensor Circuit
14	Coolant Sensor
15	Coolant Sensor
21	Throttle Position Sensor
22	Throttle Position Sensor
23	MAT Sensor
24	Vehicle Speed Sensor
25	MAT Sensor
32	EGR System Failure
33	MAF Sensor
34	MAF Sensor
41	Cylinder Select
42	Electronic Spark Timing
44	Lean Exhaust Indication
45	Rich Exhaust Indication
51	PROM
52	CALPAK (Missing)
53	System Over Voltage
54	Fuel Pump Voltage Low
55	ECM

87954070

Fig. 64 Diagnostic Trouble Codes — 1982-86 vehicles

DTC	DESCRIPTION
13	Open Oxygen Sensor Circuit
14	Coolant Sensor Circuit
15	Coolant Sensor Circuit
21	Throttle Position Sensor
22	Throttle Position Sensor
23	MAT Sensor
24	Vehicle Speed Sensor
25	MAT Sensor
33	MAF Sensor
34	MAF Sensor
35	Idle Speed Error
41	Cylinder Select Error (Faulty or Incorrect Mem-Cal)
42	Electronic Spark Timing
43	Electronic Spark Control
44	Lean Exhaust Indication
45	Rich Exhaust Indication
54	Fuel Pump Circuit (Low Voltage)
51	Faulty MEM-CAL
53	System Over Voltage
55	ECM
61	Degraded Oxygen Sensor
63	MAP Sensor
64	MAP Sensor

87954071

Fig. 65 Diagnostic Trouble Codes — 1987 vehicles, except Turbo

DTC	DESCRIPTION
13	Oxygen Sensor Circuit (Open Circuit)
14	Coolant Temperature Sensor Circuit (High Temperature Indicated)
15	Coolant Temperature Sensor Circuit (Low Temperature Indicated)
21	Throttle Position Sensor (TPS) Circuit (Signal Voltage High)
22	Throttle Position Sensor (TPS) Circuit (Signal Voltage Low)
23	Manifold Air Temperature (MAT) Sensor Circuit (Low Temperature Indicated)
24	Vehicle Speed Sensor (VSS) Circuit
25	Manifold Air Temperature (MAT) Sensor Circuit (High Temperature Indicated)
31	Turbo Wastegate Overboost
32	Exhaust Gas Recirculation (EGR) Circuit
33	Manifold Absolute Pressure (MAP) Sensor Circuit (Signal Voltage High)
34	Manifold Absolute Pressure (MAP) Sensor (Signal Voltage Low)
35	Idle Speed Error
42	Electronic Spark Timing (EST) Circuit
43	Electronic Spark Control (ESC) Circuit
44	Oxygen Sensor Circuit (Lean Exhaust Indicated)
45	Oxygen Sensor Circuit (Rich Exhaust Indicated)
51	Mem-Cal Error (Faulty or Incorrect Mem-Cal)

87954072

Fig. 66 Diagnostic Trouble Codes — 1987 Turbo vehicles

DTC	DESCRIPTION
13	Oxygen Sensor Circuit
14	Coolant Temperature Sensor
15	Coolant Temperature Sensor
21	Throttle Position Sensor Circuit
22	Throttle Position Sensor Circuit
23	MAT Sensor Circuit
24	Vehicle Speed Sensor (VSS) Circuit
25	MAT Sensor Circuit
33	MAP Sensor Circuit
34	MAP Sensor Circuit
35	Idle Speed Error
41	Cylinder Select Error (Faulty or Incorrect Mem-Cal)
42	Electronic Spark Timing Circuit
43	Electronic Spark Control Circuit
44	Oxygen Sensor Circuit (Lean)
45	Oxygen Sensor Circuit (Rich)
54	Fuel Pump Circuit
51	Mem-Cal Error
52	Calpak Error
53	System Over Voltage
61	Degraded Oxygen Sensor

87954073

Fig. 67 Diagnostic Trouble Codes — 1988 vehicles, except Turbo

DTC	DESCRIPTION
13	Oxygen Sensor Circuit (Open Circuit)
14	Coolant Temperature Sensor Circuit (High Temperature Indicated)
15	Coolant Temperature Sensor Circuit (Low Temperature Indicated)
21	Throttle Position Sensor (TPS) Circuit (Signal Voltage High)
22	Throttle Position Sensor (TPS) Circuit (Signal Voltage Low)
23	Manifold Air Temperature (MAT) Sensor Circuit (Low Temperature Indicated)
24	Vehicle Speed Sensor (VSS) Circuit
25	Manifold Air Temperature (MAT) Sensor Circuit (High Temperature Indicated)
31	Turbo Wastegate Overboost
32	Exhaust Gas Recirculation (EGR) Circuit
33	Manifold Absolute Pressure (MAP) Sensor Circuit (Signal Voltage High-Low Vacuum)
34	Manifold Absolute Pressure (MAP) Sensor Circuit (Signal Voltage Low-High Vacuum)
35	Idle Speed Error
42	Electronic Spark Timing (EST) Circuit
43	Electronic Spark Control (ESC) Circuit
44	Oxygen Sensor Circuit (Lean Exhaust Indicated)
45	Oxygen Sensor Circuit (Rich Exhaust Indicated)
51	PROM Error (Faulty or Incorrect PROM)

87954074

Fig. 68 Diagnostic Trouble Codes — 1988 Turbo vehicles

DTC	DESCRIPTION
13	Oxygen Sensor Circuit (Open Circuit)
14	Coolant Temperature Sensor Circuit (High Temperature Indicated)
15	Coolant Temperature Sensor Circuit (Low Temperature Indicated)
21	Throttle Position Sensor (TPS) Circuit (Signal Voltage High)
22	Throttle Position Sensor (TPS) Circuit (Signal Voltage Low)
23	Manifold Air Temperature (MAT) Sensor Circuit (Low Temperature Indicated)
24	Vehicle Speed Sensor (VSS) Circuit
25	Manifold Air Temperature (MAT) Sensor Circuit (High Temperature Indicated)
32	Digital EGR Exhaust Gas Recirculation (EGR) Circuit (Electrical Diagnosis)
33	Manifold Absolute Pressure (MAP) Sensor Circuit (Signal Voltage High - Low Vacuum)
34	Manifold Absolute Pressure (MAP) Sensor Circuit (Signal Voltage Low - High Vacuum)
35	Idle Air Control (IAC)
41	Cylinder Select Error (Faulty or Incorrect Mem-Cal)
42	Electronic Spark Timing (EST) Circuit
43	Electronic Spark Control (ESC) Circuit
44	Oxygen Sensor Circuit (Lean Exhaust Indicated)
45	Oxygen Sensor Circuit (Rich Exhaust Indicated)
54	Fuel Pump Circuit (Low Voltage)
51	Mem-Cal Error (Faulty or Incorrect Mem-Cal)
52	Calpak Error (Faulty or Incorrect CalPak)
53	System Over Voltage
61	Degraded Oxygen Sensor
62	Transaxle Gear Switch Signal Circuits (Electrical Diagnosis)
66	A/C Pressure Sensor Circuit

87954075

Fig. 69 Diagnostic Trouble Codes — 1989-90 vehicles, except Turbo

DTC	DESCRIPTION
13	Oxygen Sensor Circuit (Open Circuit)
14	Coolant Temperature Sensor Circuit (High Temperature Indicated)
15	Coolant Temperature Sensor Circuit (Low Temperature Indicated)
21	Throttle Position Sensor (TPS) Circuit (Signal Voltage High)
22	Throttle Position Sensor (TPS) Circuit (Signal Voltage Low)
23	Manifold Air Temperature (MAT) Sensor Circuit (Low Temperature Indicated)
24	Vehicle Speed Sensor (VSS) Circuit
25	Manifold Air Temperature (MAT) Sensor Circuit (High Temperature Indicated)
31	Turbo Wastegate Overboost
32	Exhaust Gas Recirculation (EGR) Circuit
33	Manifold Absolute Pressure (MAP) Sensor Circuit (Signal Voltage High-Low Vacuum)
34	Manifold Absolute Pressure (MAP) Sensor Circuit (Signal Voltage Low-High Vacuum)
35	Idle Speed Error
42	Electronic Spark Timing (EST) Circuit
43	Electronic Spark Control (ESC) Circuit
44	Oxygen Sensor Circuit (Lean Exhaust Indicated)
45	Oxygen Sensor Circuit (Rich Exhaust Indicated)
51	PROM Error (Faulty or Incorrect PROM)

87954076

Fig. 70 Diagnostic Trouble Codes — 1989-90 Turbo vehicles

DTC	DESCRIPTION	ILLUMINATE "SES"
13	Oxygen Sensor (O2S) Circuit - open circuit	YES
14	Engine Coolant Temperature (ECT) Sensor Circuit - high temperature indicated	YES
15	Engine Coolant Temperature (ECT) Sensor Circuit - low temperature indicated	YES
21	Throttle Position (TP) Sensor Circuit - signal voltage high	YES
22	Throttle Position (TP) Sensor Circuit - signal voltage low	YES
23	Intake Air Temperature (IAT) Sensor Circuit - low temperature indicated	YES
24	Vehicle Speed Sensor (VSS) Circuit	YES
25	Intake Air Temperature (IAT) Sensor Circuit - high temperature indicated	YES
32	Exhaust Gas Recirculation (EGR) Circuit Electrical Diagnosis	YES
33	Manifold Absolute Pressure (MAP) Sensor Circuit Signal Voltage high-low vacuum	YES
34	Manifold Absolute Pressure (MAP) Sensor Circuit Signal Voltage low-high vacuum	YES
35	Idle Air Control (IAT) Circuit System Check - Tech 1	YES
41	Cylinder Select Error - faulty or incorrect PROM	YES
42	Ignition Control (IC) Circuit	YES
43	Knock Sensor (KS) Circuit	YES
44	Oxygen Sensor (O2S) Circuit - lean exhaust indicated	YES
45	Oxygen Sensor (O2S) Circuit - rich exhaust indicated	YES
54	Fuel Pump Circuit - low voltage	YES
51	PROM Error - faulty or incorrect MEM-CAL	YES
53	System Over Voltage	YES
61	Degraded Oxygen Sensor	YES
62	Transaxle Gear Switch Signal Circuit	YES
66	A/C Pressure Sensor Circuit	NO

If a DTC not listed above appears on Tech 1, ground DLC diagnostic terminal "B" and observe flashed DTC(s). If DTC does not reappear, Tech 1 data may be faulty. If DTC does reappear, check for incorrect or faulty PROM.

87954077

Fig. 71 Diagnostic Trouble Codes — 1991 2.0L (VIN K), 1991-93 3.1L (VIN T) vehicles

ECM DIAGNOSTIC TROUBLE CODES (DTCs)

DTC	DESCRIPTION	ILLUMINATE MIL (CHECK ENGINE)
13	Oxygen Sensor (O2S) Circuit - open circuit	YES
14	Engine Coolant Temperature (ECT) Sensor Circuit - high/low temperature	YES
19	Crankshaft Position (CKP) Sensor Circuit - incorrect 58X signal - disconnected sensor	YES
21	Throttle Position (TP) Sensor Circuit - signal voltage high/low	YES
23	Intake Air Temperature (IAT) Sensor Circuit - high/low temperature	YES
24	Vehicle Speed Sensor (VSS) Circuit	YES
32	Exhaust Gas Recirculation (EGR) - system failure	YES
33	Manifold Absolute Pressure (MAP) Sensor Circuit - signal voltage high/low - low/high vacuum	YES
44	Oxygen Sensor (O2S) Circuit - lean exhaust indicated	YES
45	Oxygen Sensor (O2S) Circuit - rich exhaust indicated	YES
51	ECM failure (ECM failed or EPROM failure)	YES
66	A/C Refrigerant Pressure Sensor Circuit	NO

If a DTC not listed above appears on Tech 1, ground Data Link Terminal "B" and observe flashed DTCs. If DTC does not reappear, Tech 1 data may be faulty.
If DTC does reappear, check for incorrect or faulty PROM.

87954078

Fig. 72 Diagnostic Trouble Codes — 1992-93 2.0L (VIN H) Sunbird

ECM DIAGNOSTIC TROUBLE CODES		
DTC	DESCRIPTION	ILLUMINATE MIL (CHECK ENGINE)
13	Oxygen Sensor (O2S) Circuit - open circuit	YES
14	Engine Coolant Temperature (ECT) Sensor Circuit - high/low temperature	YES
21	Throttle Position (TP) Sensor Circuit - Signal voltage high/low	YES
23	Intake Air Temperature (IAT) Sensor Circuit - high/low temperature	YES
24	Vehicle Speed Sensor (VSS) Circuit	YES
32	Exhaust Gas Recirculation (EGR) - System failure	YES
33	Manifold Absolute Pressure (MAP) Sensor Circuit - Signal voltage high/low - low/high vacuum	YES
42	Ignition Control (IC) Circuit	YES
44	Oxygen Sensor (O2S) Circuit - lean exhaust indicated	YES
45	Oxygen Sensor (O2S) Circuit - rich exhaust indicated	YES
51	EEPROM or ECM Failure	YES
66	A/C Refrigerant Pressure Sensor Circuit	NO

If a DTC not listed above appears on Tech 1, ground Data Link Terminal "B" and observe flashed DTC(S).
If DTC does not reappear, Tech 1 data may be faulty.
If DTC does reappear, replace ECM and program.

87954079

Fig. 73 Diagnostic Trouble Codes — 1992-93 2.2L (VIN 4) Cavalier

ECM DIAGNOSTIC TROUBLE CODES (DTCs)

DTC	DESCRIPTION	ILLUMINATE MIL (CHECK ENGINE)
13	Oxygen Sensor (O2S) Circuit - open circuit	YES
14	Engine Coolant Temperature (ECT) Sensor Circuit - high/low temperature	YES
19	Crankshaft Position (CKP) Sensor Circuit - incorrect 58X signal - disconnected sensor	YES
21	Throttle Position (TP) Sensor Circuit - signal voltage high/low	YES
23	Intake Air Temperature (IAT) Sensor Circuit - high/low temperature	YES
24	Vehicle Speed Sensor (VSS) Circuit	YES
32	Exhaust Gas Recirculation (EGR) - system failure	YES
33	Manifold Absolute Pressure (MAP) Sensor Circuit - signal voltage high/low - low/high vacuum	YES
44	Oxygen Sensor (O2S) Circuit - lean exhaust indicated	YES
45	Oxygen Sensor (O2S) Circuit - rich exhaust indicated	YES
51	ECM failure (ECM failed or EPROM failure)	YES
66	A/C Refrigerant Pressure Sensor Circuit	NO

If a DTC not listed above appears on Tech 1, ground Data Link Terminal "B" and observe flashed DTCs. If DTC does not reappear, Tech 1 data may be faulty.
If DTC does reappear, check for incorrect or faulty PROM.

87954078

Fig. 74 Diagnostic Trouble Codes — 1992-94 2.0L (VIN H) Sunbird

PCM DIAGNOSTIC TROUBLE CODES

DTC	DESCRIPTION	ILLUMINATE MIL (SERVICE ENGINE SOON)
13	Oxygen Sensor (O2S) Circuit - open circuit	YES
14	Engine Coolant Temperature (ECT) Sensor Circuit - high temperature	YES
15	Engine Coolant Temperature (ECT) Sensor Circuit - low temperature	YES
19	Intermittent 7X Reference Signal	YES
21	Throttle Position (TP) Sensor Circuit - signal voltage high	YES
22	Throttle Position (TP) Sensor Circuit - signal voltage low	YES
23	Intake Air Temperature (IAT) Sensor Circuit - low temperature	YES
24	Vehicle Speed Sensor (VSS) Circuit	YES
25	Intake Air Temperature (IAT) Sensor Circuit - high temperature	YES
26	Quad-Driver Module (QDSM)	NO
27	Quad-Driver Module (QDM1)	YES
28	Quad-Driver Module (QDM2)	NO
32	Exhaust Gas Recirculation (EGR) Valve	YES
33	Manifold Absolute Pressure (MAP) Sensor Circuit - signal voltage high - low vacuum	YES
34	Manifold Absolute Pressure (MAP) Sensor Circuit - signal voltage low - high vacuum	YES
35	Improper Idle Speed (IAC)	YES
43	Electronic Spark Control (ESC) - knock sensor	YES
44	Oxygen Sensor (O2S) Circuit - lean exhaust indicated	YES
45	Oxygen Sensor (O2S) Circuit - rich exhaust indicated	YES
51	EPROM or PCM Failure	YES
53	Improper Ignition Voltage	YES
55	Lean in Power Enrichment	NO
66	A/C Refrigerant Pressure Sensor Circuit	NO

87954081

Fig. 75 Diagnostic Trouble Codes — 1994 2.2L (VIN 4) Cavalier

PCM DIAGNOSTIC TROUBLE CODES

DTC	DESCRIPTION	ILLUMINATE MIL
13	Oxygen Sensor (O2S) Circuit (open circuit)	YES
14	Engine Coolant Temperature (ECT) Sensor (high temperature indicated)	YES
15	Engine Coolant Temperature (ECT) Sensor (low temperature indicated)	YES
21	Throttle Position (TP) Sensor (signal voltage high)	YES
22	Throttle Position (TP) Sensor (signal voltage low)	YES
23	Intake Air Temperature (IAT) Sensor - low temperature indicated	YES
24	Vehicle Speed (VSS) Sensor Circuit (no signal voltage)	YES
25	Intake Air Temperature (IAT) Sensor (high temperature indicated)	YES
32	Exhaust gas recirculation circuit	YES
33	Manifold Absolute Pressure (MAP) Sensor Circuit (signal voltage high - high MAP)	YES
34	Manifold Absolute Pressure (MAP) Sensor Circuit (sensor voltage low - low MAP)	YES
35	Idle Speed Error	YES
41	Cylinder Select Error	YES
42	Knock Sensor (KS) Circuit	YES
43	Ignition Control (IC) Circuit	YES
44	Oxygen Sensor (O2S) Circuit (lean exhaust indicated)	YES
45	Oxygen Sensor (O2S) Circuit (rich exhaust indicated)	YES
53	System Over Voltage	YES
54	Fuel Pump Circuit (low voltage)	YES
51	PROM Error (Faulty or Incorrect EPROM)	YES
55	PCM Error	YES
61	Degraded Oxygen (O2S) Sensor	YES
62	Transaxle Gear Switch Signal Circuit	NO
66	A/C Refrigerant Pressure Sensor Circuit (low pressure)	NO

If a DTC not listed above appears on Tech 1, ground DLC diagnostic terminal "B" and observe flashed DTC(s).
If DTC does not reappear, refer to Tech 1 Operator's Guide.
If DTC does reappear, check for incorrect or faulty EPROM.

87954082

Fig. 76 Diagnostic Trouble Codes — 1994 3.1L (VIN T) Cavalier and Sunbird

PCM DIAGNOSTIC TROUBLE CODES

DTC	DESCRIPTION	ILLUMINATE MIL
13	Oxygen Sensor (O2S) Circuit - open circuit	YES
14	Engine Coolant Temperature (ECT) Sensor Circuit - high temperature	YES
15	Engine Coolant Temperature (ECT) Sensor Circuit - low temperature	YES
19	Intermittent 7X Reference Signal	YES
21	Throttle Position (TP) Sensor Circuit - signal voltage high	YES
22	Throttle Position (TP) Sensor Circuit - signal voltage low	YES
23	Intake Air Temperature (IAT) Sensor Circuit - low temperature	YES
24	Vehicle Speed Sensor (VSS) Circuit	YES
25	Intake Air Temperature (IAT) Sensor Circuit - high temperature	YES
27	Quad-Driver Module (QDM1)	YES
28	Quad- Driver Module (QDM2)	NO
31	PRNDL Error	NO
32	Exhaust Gas Recirculation (EGR) Valve	YES
33	Manifold Absolute Pressure (MAP) Sensor Circuit - signal voltage high - low vacuum	YES
34	Manifold Absolute Pressure (MAP) Sensor Circuit - signal voltage low - high vacuum	YES
35	Idle Speed Error	YES
43	Knock Sensor (KS) Circuit	YES
44	Oxygen Sensor (O2S) Circuit - lean exhaust indicated	YES
45	Oxygen Sensor (O2S) Circuit - rich exhaust indicated	YES
51	EPROM Error	YES
53	Battery Voltage Error	YES
55	Fuel Lean Monitor	NO
66	A/C Refrigerant Pressure Sensor Circuit	NO
72	Loss of Serial Data	NO

87954083

Fig. 77 Diagnostic Trouble Codes — 1995 Cavalier and Sunfire

PCM Diagnostic Trouble Codes

DTC	Description	Illuminate MIL
P0106	Manifold Absolute Pressure (MAP) System Performance	YES
P0107	Manifold Absolute Pressure (MAP) Circuit-Low Voltage	YES
P0108	Manifold Absolute Pressure (MAP) Circuit-High Voltage	YES
P0112	Intake Air Temperature (IAT) Circuit-Low Voltage	YES
P0113	Intake Air Temperature (IAT) Circuit-High Voltage	YES
P0117	Engine Coolant Temperature (ECT) Circuit-Low Voltage	YES
P0118	Engine Coolant Temperature (ECT) Circuit-High Voltage	YES
P0121	Throttle Position (TP) Sensor System Performance	YES
P0122	Throttle Position (TP) Sensor Circuit Low Voltage	YES
P0123	Throttle Position (TP) Sensor Circuit High Voltage	YES
P0125	Engine Coolant Temperature (ECT) Time to "Closed Loop" Fuel Control	YES
P0131	Oxygen Sensor (O2S) Circuit Low Voltage (Sensor 1)	YES
P0132	Oxygen Sensor (O2S) Circuit High Voltage (Sensor 1)	YES
P0133	Oxygen Sensor (O2S) Circuit Slow Response (Sensor 1)	YES
P0134	Oxygen Sensor (O2S) Circuit Insufficient Activity Detected (Sensor 1)	YES
P0137	Heated Oxygen Sensor (HO2S) Circuit Low Voltage (Sensor 2)	YES
P0138	Heated Oxygen Sensor (HO2S) Circuit High Voltage (Sensor 2)	YES
P0140	Heated Oxygen Sensor (HO2S) Insufficient Activity Detected (Sensor 2)	YES
P0141	Heated Oxygen Sensor (HO2S) Heater Circuit (Sensor 2)	YES
P0171	Fuel Trim System Lean	YES
P0172	Fuel Trim System Rich	YES
P0200	Injector Control Circuit	YES
P0300	Engine Misfire Detected	YES
P0301	Cylinder 1 Misfire Detected	YES
P0302	Cylinder 2 Misfire Detected	YES
P0303	Cylinder 3 Misfire Detected	YES
P0304	Cylinder 4 Misfire Detected	YES
P0325	Knock Sensor (KS) Circuit	YES
P0335	Crankshaft Position (CKP) Sensor Circuit	YES
P0341	Camshaft Position (CMP) Sensor Circuit Performance	YES
P0342	Camshaft Position (CMP) Sensor Circuit Low Input	YES
P0401	Exhaust Gas Recirculation (EGR) System Flow Insufficient	YES
P0420	Three Way Catalyst (TWC) System Low Efficiency	YES
P0440	Evaporative Emission (EVAP) Control System	YES
P0442	Evaporative Emission (EVAP) Control System - Small Leak Detected	YES
P0446	Evaporative Emission (EVAP) Control System Vent Control	YES
P0460	Fuel Level Sensor Circuit	NO
P0502	Vehicle Speed Sensor (VSS) Circuit Low Input	YES
P0506	Idle Air Control (IAC) System Low RPM	YES
P0507	Idle Air Control (IAC) System High RPM	YES
P0530	A/C Refrigerant Pressure Sensor Circuit	NO
P0562	System Voltage Low	NO
P0563	System Voltage High	NO
P0600	Loss Of Serial Communication Link	YES
P0601	PCM Memory	YES
P0602	PCM Memory	NO

87954084

Fig. 78 Diagnostic Trouble Codes — 1996 Cavalier and Sunfire

PCM Diagnostic Trouble Codes (continued)

DTC	Description	Illuminate MIL
P0705	Transaxle Range Switch Circuit	NO
P1133	Oxygen Sensor (O2S) Insufficient Switching (Sensor 1)	YES
P1171	Fuel System Lean During Acceleration	NO
P1380	EBCM DTC Detected - Rough Road Data Unusable	NO
P1381	Misfire Detected - No EBCM/PCM Serial Data	NO
P1406	Exhaust Gas Recirculation (EGR) Valve Pintle Position Circuit	YES
P1441	Evaporative Emission (EVAP) Control System Flow During Non-Purge	YES
P1601	Loss of Serial Communication	NO
P1629	Theft Deterrent System - Loss of Cranking Signal	NO

87954085

Fig. 79 Diagnostic Trouble Codes — 1995 Cavalier and Sunfire, continued

COMPONENT LOCATION DIAGRAMS

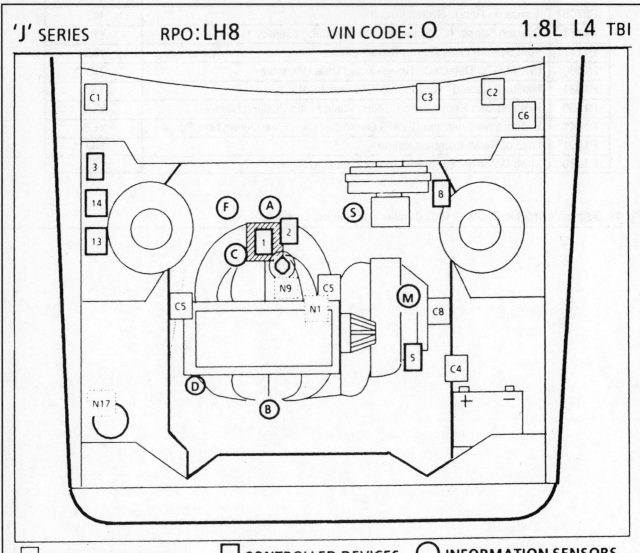

'J' SERIES   RPO: LH8   VIN CODE: O   1.8L L4 TBI

◻ **COMPUTER HARNESS**

C1 Electronic Control Module (ECM)
C2 ALCL diagnostic connector
C3 "SERVICE ENGINE SOON" light
C4 ECM power
C5 ECM harness ground
C6 Fuse panel
C8 Fuel pump test connector

NOT ECM CONNECTED

N1 Crankcase vent valve (PCV)
N9 Exhaust Gas Recirculation valve
N17 Fuel vapor canister

◻ **CONTROLLED DEVICES**

1   Fuel injector solenoid
2   Idle air control valve
3   Fuel pump relay
5   Trans. Conv. Clutch connector
8   Engine fan relay
13 A/C compressor relay
14 A/C fan relay

⬡ Exhaust Gas Recirculation valve

◯ **INFORMATION SENSORS**

A   Manifold pressure (M.A.P.)
B   Exhaust oxygen
C   Throttle position
D   Coolant temperature
F   Vehicle speed
M   P/N switch/neutral start
S   P/S pressure switch

87954058

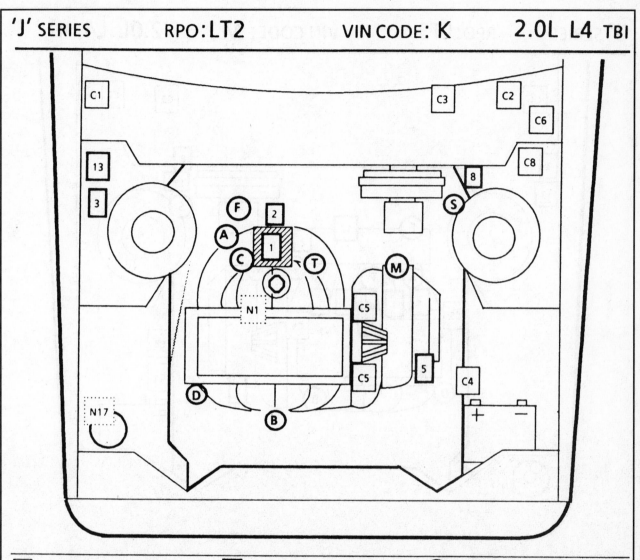

'J' SERIES   RPO: LT2   VIN CODE: K   2.0L L4 TBI

☐ COMPUTER HARNESS

C1   Electronic Control Module (ECM)
C2   ALDL diagnostic connector
C3   "SERVICE ENGINE SOON" light
C4   ECM power
C5   ECM harness grounds
C6   Fuse panel
C8   Fuel pump test connector

⬚ NOT ECM CONNECTED

N1   Crankcase vent valve (PCV)
N17   Fuel vapor canister

⬡ Exhaust Gas Recirculation valve

☐ CONTROLLED DEVICES

1   Fuel injector solenoid
2   Idle air control valve
3   Fuel pump relay
5   Trans. Conv. Clutch connector
8   Engine fan relay
13   A/C compressor relay

◯ INFORMATION SENSORS

A   Manifold pressure (M.A.P.)
    (Mounted On Air Cleaner)
B   Exhaust oxygen
C   Throttle position
D   Coolant temperature
F   Vehicle speed
M   P/N switch/neutral start
S   P/S pressure switch
T   Manifold Air Temperature
    (Mounted On Air Cleaner)

87954059

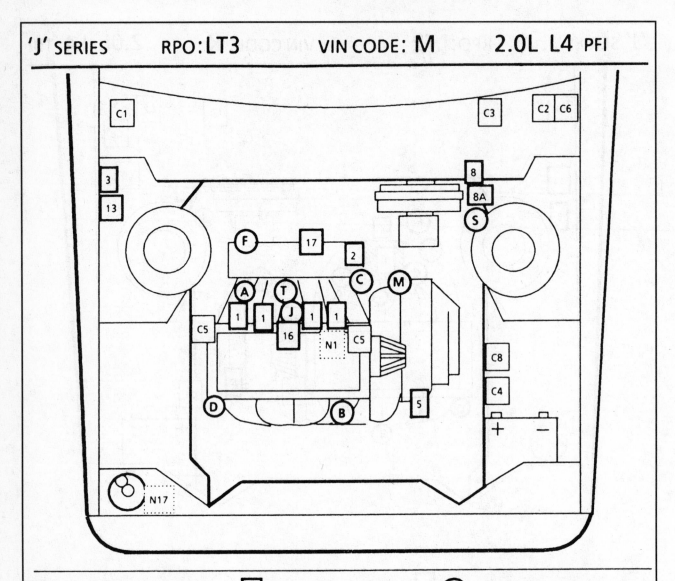

'J' SERIES   RPO: LT3   VIN CODE: M   2.0L L4 PFI

☐ COMPUTER HARNESS

C1 Electronic Control Module (ECM)
C2 ALDL diagnostic connector
C3 "SERVICE ENGINE SOON" light
C4 ECM power (2)
C5 ECM harness grounds
C6 Fuse panel
C8 Fuel pump test connector

NOT ECM CONNECTED

N1 Crankcase vent valve (PCV) (inside PCV hose)
N17 Fuel vapor canister

☐ CONTROLLED DEVICES

1   Fuel injectors
2   Idle air control valve
3   Fuel pump relay
5   Trans. Converter Clutch connector
8   Low speed cooling fan relay
8a High Speed cooling fan relay
13 A/C compressor relay
16 Wastegate solenoid
17 EGR Relay (Below Manifold)

◯ INFORMATION SENSORS

A Manifold pressure (M.A.P.)
B Exhaust oxygen
C Throttle position
D Coolant temperature
F PM Generator
J ESC knock (Below Manifold)
M P/N switch/park neutral
S Power Steering Pressure Switch
T Manifold Air Temperature

87954060

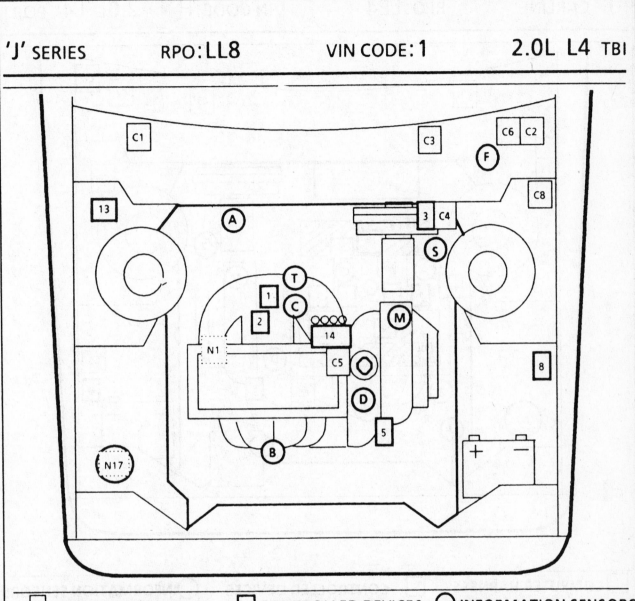

'J' SERIES   RPO: LL8   VIN CODE: 1   2.0L L4 TBI

COMPUTER HARNESS

- C1 Electronic Control Module (ECM)
- C2 ALDL Diagnostic Connector
- C3 "Service Engine Soon" light
- C4 ECM Power Fuse
- C5 ECM Harness Grounds
- C6 Fuse Panel
- C8 Fuel Pump Test Connector

NOT ECM CONNECTED

- N1 Crankcase Vent Valve (PCV)
- N17 Fuel Vapor Canister

Exhaust Gas Recirculation valve

CONTROLLED DEVICES

- 1 Fuel Injector Solenoid
- 2 Idle Air Control Valve
- 3 Fuel Pump Relay
- 5 TCC Solenoid Connector
- 8 Cooling Fan Relay
- 13 A/C Compressor Relay
- 14 Direct Ignition System Assembly

INFORMATION SENSORS

- A Manifold Pressure (MAP)
- B Exhaust Oxygen
- C Throttle Position
- D Coolant Temperature
- F Vehicle Speed
- M P/N Switch
- S P/S Pressure Switch
- T MAT Sensor

87954061

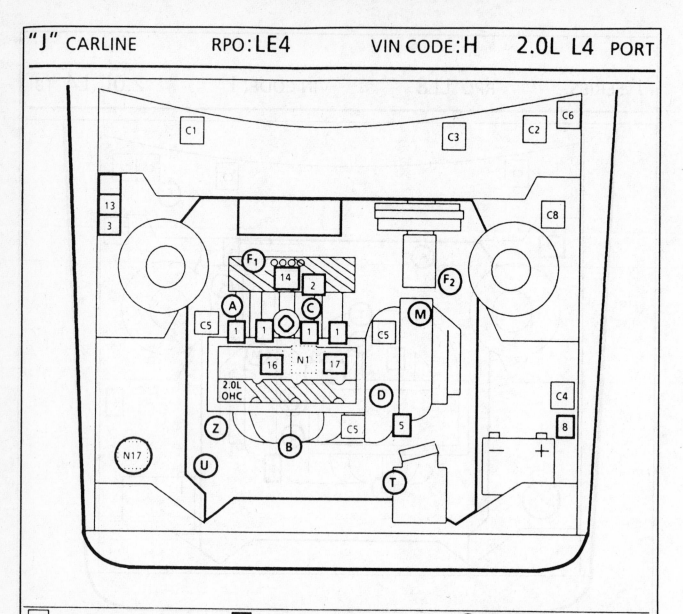

"J" CARLINE   RPO: LE4   VIN CODE: H   2.0L L4 PORT

☐ COMPUTER HARNESS

C1 Electronic Control Module (ECM)
C2 ALDL Diagnostic Connector
C3 "Check Engine" light
C4 Power Feed Connector
C5 ECM Harness Grounds
C6 Fuse Panel
C8 Fuel Pump Test Connector

☐ NOT ECM CONNECTED

N1 Crankcase Vent Valve (PCV)
N17 Fuel Vapor Canister

☐ CONTROLLED DEVICES

1 Fuel Injector
2 Idle Air Control (IAC) Valve
3 Fuel Pump Relay*
5 TCC Solenoid
8 Cooling Fan Relay
13 A/C Compressor Relay*
14 Direct Ignition System (DIS) Coil Assy.
     (Under Intake Plenum)
16 Computer Controlled Purge (CCP) Solenoid
17 Exhaust Gas Recirculation (EGR) Solenoid

⬡ Exhaust Gas Recirculation (EGR) Valve

⭕ INFORMATION SENSORS

A Manifold Absolute Pressure (MAP) Sensor
B Oxygen (O_2) Sensor
C Throttle Position Sensor (TPS)
D Coolant Temperature Sensor (CTS)
F_1 Vehicle Speed (Auto Trans.)
F_2 Vehicle Speed (Manual Trans.)
M Park/Neutral (P/N) Switch
T Intake Air Temperature (IAT) Sensor (In Air Cleaner Assy.)
U A/C Pressure Sensor
Z Crankshaft Position Sensor

* Actual location may vary.

87954062

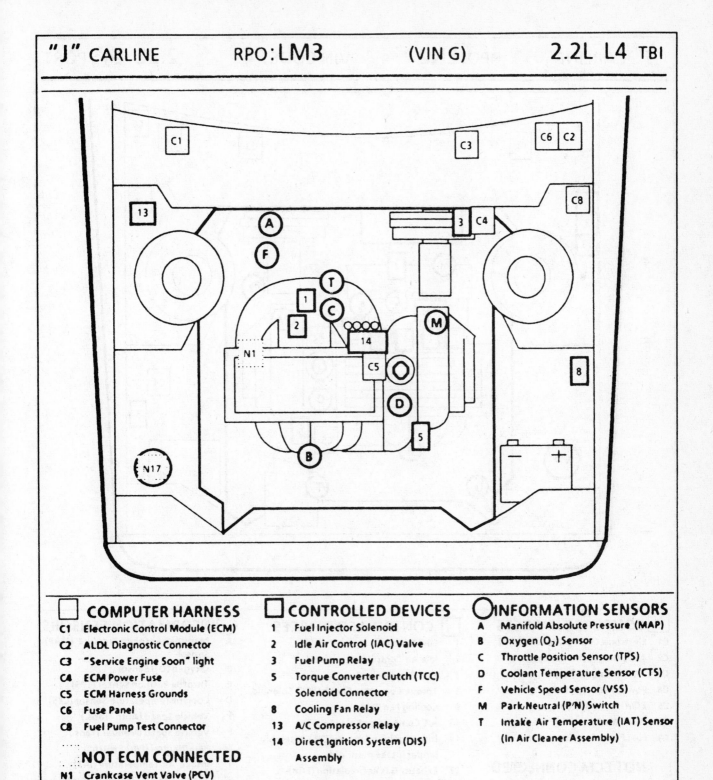

"J" CARLINE **RPO: LM3** **(VIN G)** **2.2L L4 TBI**

COMPUTER HARNESS	CONTROLLED DEVICES	INFORMATION SENSORS
C1 Electronic Control Module (ECM)	**1** Fuel Injector Solenoid	**A** Manifold Absolute Pressure (MAP)
C2 ALDL Diagnostic Connector	**2** Idle Air Control (IAC) Valve	**B** Oxygen (O₂) Sensor
C3 "Service Engine Soon" light	**3** Fuel Pump Relay	**C** Throttle Position Sensor (TPS)
C4 ECM Power Fuse	**5** Torque Converter Clutch (TCC)	**D** Coolant Temperature Sensor (CTS)
C5 ECM Harness Grounds	Solenoid Connector	**F** Vehicle Speed Sensor (VSS)
C6 Fuse Panel	**8** Cooling Fan Relay	**M** Park Neutral (P/N) Switch
C8 Fuel Pump Test Connector	**13** A/C Compressor Relay	**T** Intake Air Temperature (IAT) Sensor
	14 Direct Ignition System (DIS)	(In Air Cleaner Assembly)
	Assembly	

NOT ECM CONNECTED

N1 Crankcase Vent Valve (PCV)
N17 Fuel Vapor Canister

Exhaust Gas Recirculation (EGR) Valve

87954063

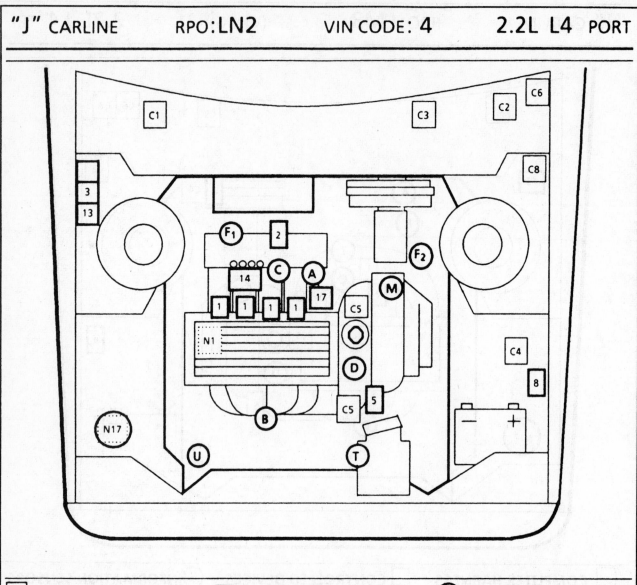

"J" CARLINE   RPO: **LN2**   VIN CODE: **4**   **2.2L L4** PORT

⬜ COMPUTER HARNESS

C1	Electronic Control Module (ECM)
C2	ALDL Diagnostic Connector
C3	"Check Engine" Light
C4	Power Feed Connector
C5	ECM Harness Grounds
C6	Fuse Panel
C8	Fuel Pump Test Connector

⬜ NOT ECM CONNECTED

N1	Crankcase Vent Valve (PCV)
N17	Fuel Vapor Canister

⬜ CONTROLLED DEVICES

1	Fuel Injector
2	Idle Air Control (IAC) Valve
3	Fuel Pump Relay*
5	Torque Converter Clutch (TCC) Solenoid
8	Cooling Fan Relay
13	A/C Compressor Relay*
14	Direct Ignition System (DIS) Assembly (under intake manifold)
17	Exhaust Gas Recirculation (EGR) Solenoid

⬡ Exhaust Gas Recirculation (EGR) Valve

⬭ INFORMATION SENSORS

A	Manifold Absolute Pressure (MAP) Sensor
B	Oxygen (O$_2$) Sensor
C	Throttle Position Sensor (TPS)
D	Coolant Temperature Sensor (CTS)
F$_1$	Vehicle Speed (Auto Trans.)
F$_2$	Vehicle Speed (Manual Trans.)
M	Park/Neutral (P/N) Switch
T	Intake Air Temperature (IAT) Sensor (On Air Cleaner Assembly)
U	A/C Pressure Sensor

*   Actual location may vary

87954064

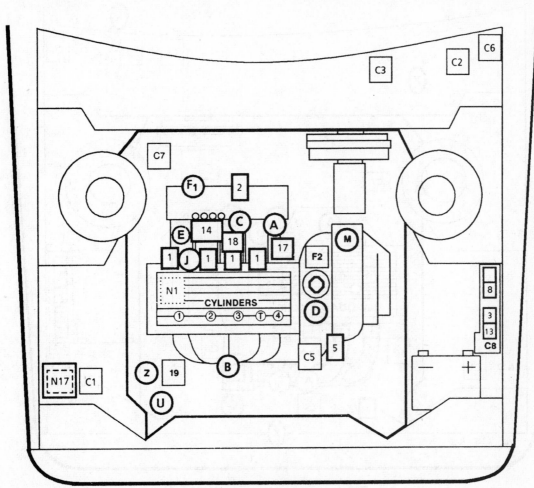

"J" CARLINE   RPO: LN2   VIN CODE: 4   2.2L L4 MFI

FIRING ORDER 1-3-4-2

COMPUTER HARNESS

C1 Powertrain Control Module (PCM)
C2 Data Link Connector (DLC)
C3 Malfunction Indicator Lamp (MIL) "Check Engine"
C4 Power feed connector
C5 PCM harness grounds
C6 Fuse panel
C7 Cruise control module
C8 Fuel pump test connector

NOT PCM CONNECTED

N1 Crankcase vent valve
N17 Evaporative emission canister

CONTROLLED DEVICES

1 Fuel injector
2 Idle Air Control (IAC) valve
3 Fuel pump relay
5 Torque Converter Clutch (TCC) solenoid (backside of Engine block)
8 Cooling fan control relay
13 A/C compressor clutch control relay
14 Electronic ignition assembly (under intake manifold)
17 EGR control solenoid valve (located below MAP sensor)
18 Evaporative canister purge solenoid valve
19 Generator

◯ Exhaust Gas Recirculation (EGR) valve

INFORMATION SENSORS

A Manifold Absolute Pressure (MAP) sensor
B Oxygen Sensor (O2S)
C Throttle Position (TP) sensor
D Engine Coolant Temperature (ECT) sensor
E Crankshaft position sensor
F_1 Vehicle Speed Sensor (VSS) (auto trans.)
F_2 Vehicle Speed Sensor (VSS) (manual trans.)
J Knock Sensor (KS)
M Trans range switch
T Intake Air Temperature (IAT) sensor (on air cleaner assembly)
U A/C refrigerant pressure sensor
W Oil level sensor
Z Coolant level sensor (in oil pan)

87954065

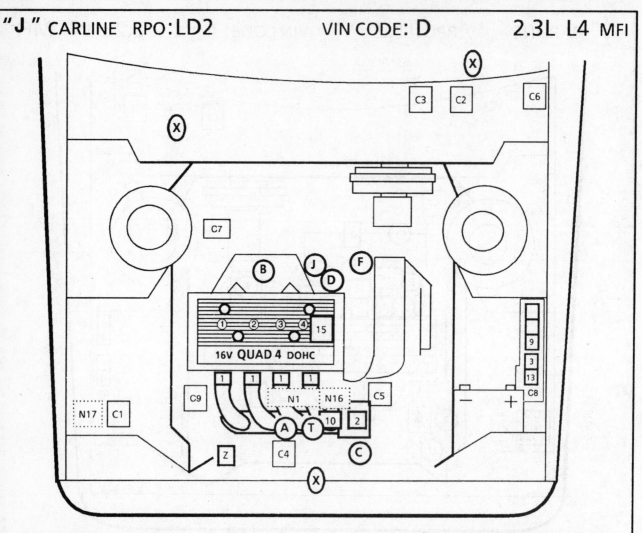

"J" CARLINE RPO: LD2   **VIN CODE: D**   **2.3L L4 MFI**

16V QUAD 4 DOHC

▢ COMPUTER HARNESS

- C1 Powertrain Control Module (PCM)
- C2 Data Link Connector (DLC)
- C3 Malfunction Indicator Lamp (MIL) "Check Engine"
- C4 PCM power
- C5 PCM harness ground
- C6 Fuse panel
- C7 Cruise control module
- C8 Fuel pump test connector
- C9 Alternator

⌐⌐ NOT PCM CONNECTED

- N1 Crankcase vent oil/air separator
- N17 Evaporative Emission (EVAP) canister
- **N16 Crankcase ventilation heater assembly

* Exact placement of relays may vary. Circuit diagrams and wire colors may be used for positive identification.

▢ CONTROLLED DEVICES

- 1 Fuel injector
- 2 Idle Air Control (IAC) valve
- *3 Fuel pump relay
- *9 Engine coolant fan relay
- 10 Evaporative Emission (EVAP) canister purge solenoid valve
- *13 A/C compressor relay
- 15 Electronic Ignition Control Module (ICM) (under ICM cover)
- Ⓧ SIR System Components.

** Used to preheat crankcase ventilation system.

◯ INFORMATION SENSORS

- A Manifold Absolute Pressure (MAP) sensor
- B Oxygen Sensor (O2S)
- C Throttle Position (TP) sensor
- D Engine Coolant Temperature (ECT) sensor
- F Vehicle Speed Sensor (VSS)
- J Knock Sensor (KS) (below manifold)
- T Intake Air Temperature (IAT) sensor
- Z A/C Refrigerant Pressure Sensor.

FIRING ORDER:
1-3-4-2

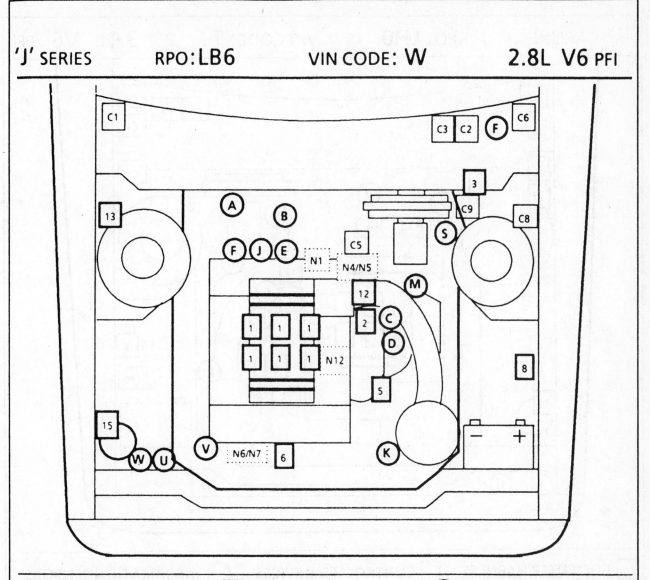

'J' SERIES   RPO: LB6   VIN CODE: W   2.8L V6 PFI

☐ COMPUTER HARNESS

- **C1** Electronic Control Module (ECM)
- **C2** ALDL diagnostic connector
- **C3** "SERVICE ENGINE SOON" light
- **C5** ECM harness ground
- **C6** Fuse panel
- **C8** Fuel pump test connector
- **C9** Fuel pump / ECM fuse

⋯ NOT ECM CONNECTED

- **N1** Crankcase vent valve (PCV)
- **N4** Engine temp. switch (telltale)
- **N5** Engine temp. sensor (gage)
- **N6** Oil press. switch (telltale)
- **N7** Oil press. sensor (gage)
- **N12** Fuel pressure connector

☐ CONTROLLED DEVICES

- **1** Fuel injector
- **2** Idle air control motor
- **3** Fuel pump relay
- **5** Trans. Converter Clutch connector
- **6** Direct Ignition System (DIS)
- **8** Engine fan relay
- **9.** Air Control Solenoid (M/T only)
- **12** Exh. Gas Recirc. valve
- **13** A/C compressor relay
- **15** Fuel vapor canister solenoid

◯ INFORMATION SENSORS

- **A** Manifold Pressure (MAP)
- **B** Exhaust oxygen
- **C** Throttle position
- **D** Coolant temperature
- **E** Crank Shaft Sensor
- **F** Vehicle speed
- **J** Knock (ESC)
- **K** MAT
- **M** P/N switch
- **S** P/S pressure switch
- **U** A/C pressure fan switch
- **V** A/C Low Press. switch (mounted in compressor)
- **W** A/C Hi Press. cut-out sw.

87954068

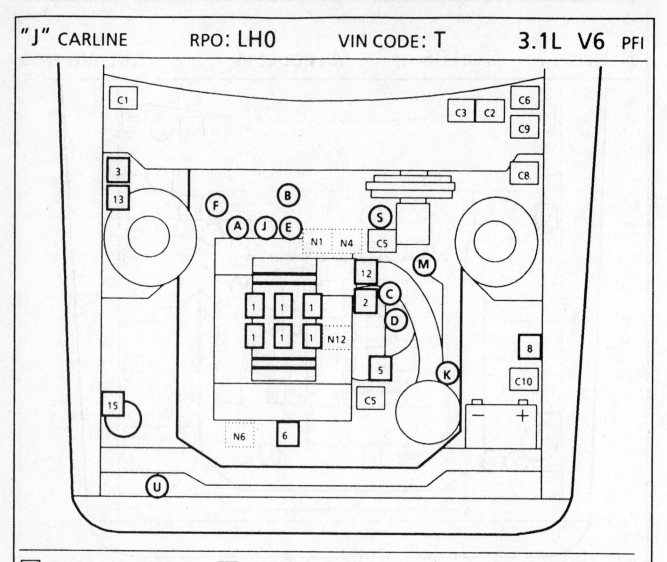

"J" CARLINE   RPO: **LH0**   VIN CODE: **T**   **3.1L V6** PFI

☐ COMPUTER HARNESS

- C1 Electronic Control Module (ECM)
- C2 ALDL diagnostic connector
- C3 "SERVICE ENGINE SOON" light
- C5 ECM harness ground
- C6 Fuse panel
- C8 Fuel pump test connector
- C9 Fuel pump/ECM fuse
- C10 ECM Power Feed

☐ NOT ECM CONNECTED

- N1 Positive Crankcase Ventilation (PCV) valve
- N4 Engine temperature sensor gage and (telltale)
- N6 Fuel pump/oil pressure sensor gage and (telltale)
- N12 Fuel pressure connector

☐ CONTROLLED DEVICES

- 1 Fuel injector
- 2 Idle Air Control (IAC) motor
- 3 Fuel pump relay
- 5 Trans. Converter Clutch connector
- 6 Direct Ignition System (DIS)
- 8 Cooling fan relay
- 12 Exh. Gas Recirc. valve
- 13 A/C compressor relay
- 15 Fuel vapor canister solenoid

◯ INFORMATION SENSORS

- A Manifold Air Pressure (MAP)
- B Exhaust oxygen (O$_2$)
- C Throttle Position Sensor (TPS)
- D Coolant Temperature Sensor (CTS)
- E Crank Shaft Sensor
- F Vehicle Speed Sensor (VSS)
- J Electronic Spark Control (ESC)
- K Intake Air Temperature (IAT)
- M P/N switch
- S P/S pressure switch
- U A/C pressure sensor

87954069

VACUUM DIAGRAMS

Following is a listing of vacuum diagrams for many of the engine and emissions package combinations covered by this manual. Because vacuum circuits will vary based on various engine and vehicle options, always refer first to the vehicle emission control information label. Should the label be missing, or should the vehicle be equipped with a different engine from the original equipment, refer to the diagrams below for the same or similar configuration.

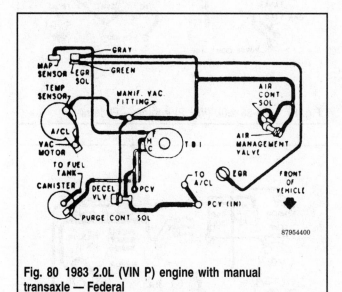

Fig. 80 1983 2.0L (VIN P) engine with manual transaxle — Federal

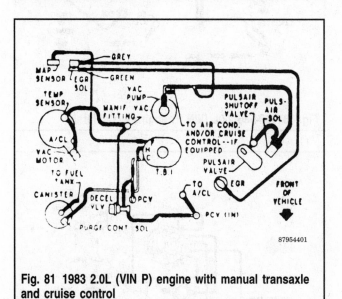

Fig. 81 1983 2.0L (VIN P) engine with manual transaxle and cruise control

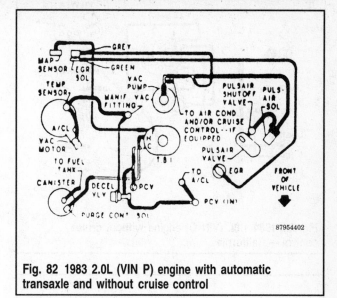

Fig. 82 1983 2.0L (VIN P) engine with automatic transaxle and without cruise control

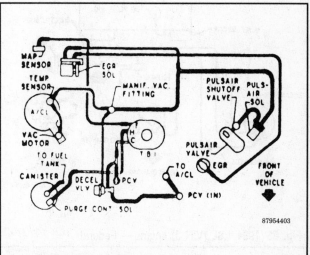

Fig. 83 1983 2.0L (VIN P) engine with manual transaxle and without cruise control

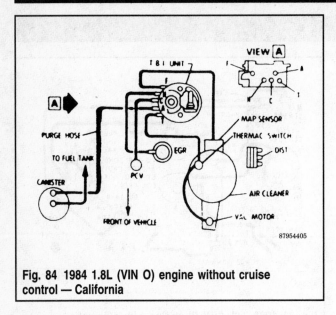

Fig. 84 1984 1.8L (VIN O) engine without cruise control — California

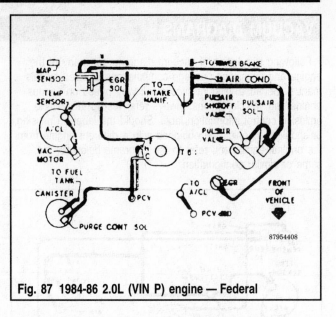

Fig. 87 1984-86 2.0L (VIN P) engine — Federal

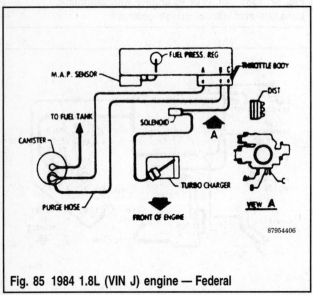

Fig. 85 1984 1.8L (VIN J) engine — Federal

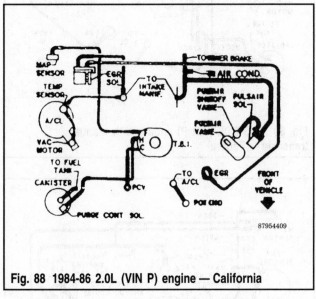

Fig. 88 1984-86 2.0L (VIN P) engine — California

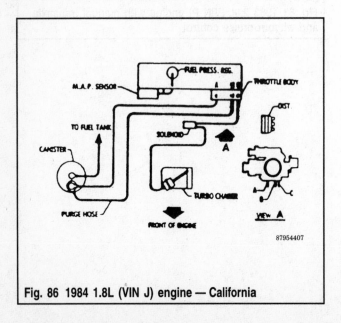

Fig. 86 1984 1.8L (VIN J) engine — California

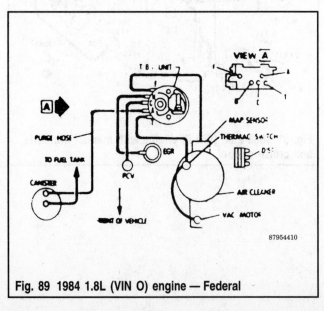

Fig. 89 1984 1.8L (VIN O) engine — Federal

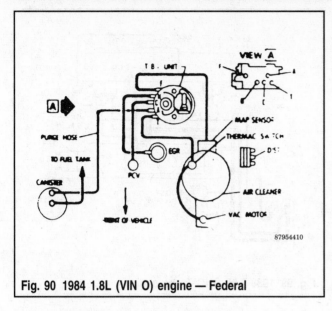

Fig. 90 1984 1.8L (VIN O) engine — Federal

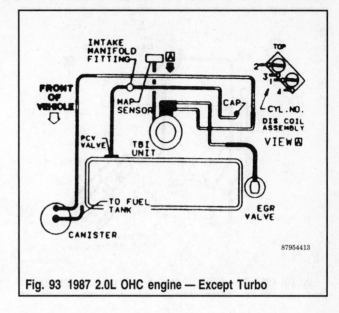

Fig. 93 1987 2.0L OHC engine — Except Turbo

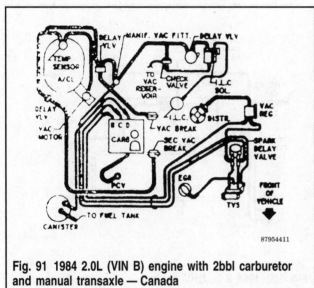

Fig. 91 1984 2.0L (VIN B) engine with 2bbl carburetor and manual transaxle — Canada

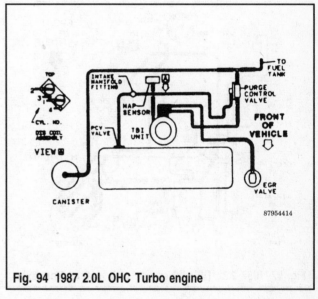

Fig. 94 1987 2.0L OHC Turbo engine

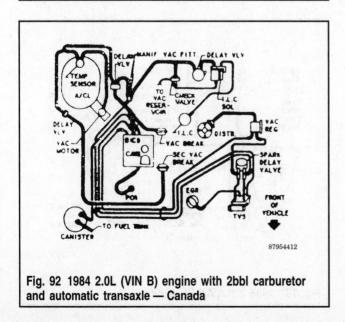

Fig. 92 1984 2.0L (VIN B) engine with 2bbl carburetor and automatic transaxle — Canada

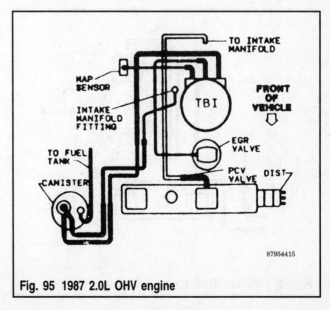

Fig. 95 1987 2.0L OHV engine

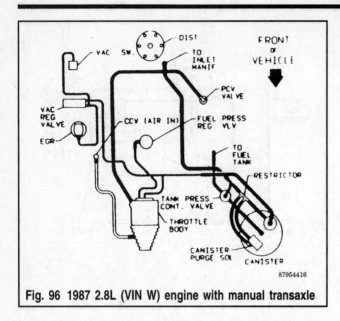

Fig. 96 1987 2.8L (VIN W) engine with manual transaxle

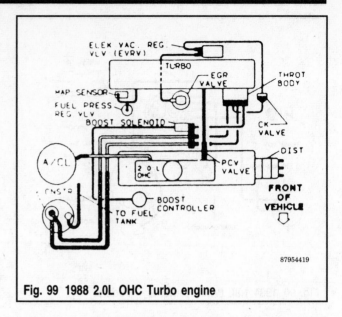

Fig. 99 1988 2.0L OHC Turbo engine

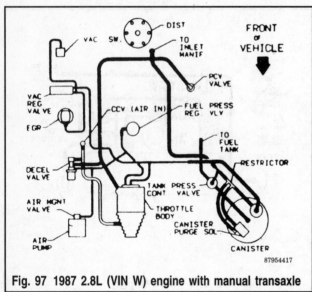

Fig. 97 1987 2.8L (VIN W) engine with manual transaxle

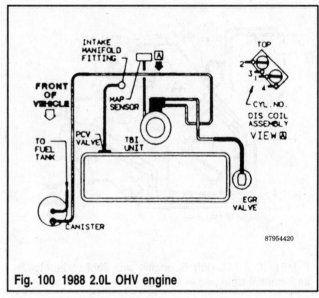

Fig. 100 1988 2.0L OHV engine

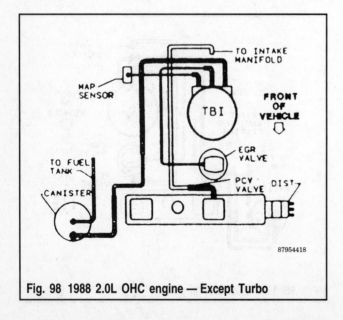

Fig. 98 1988 2.0L OHC engine — Except Turbo

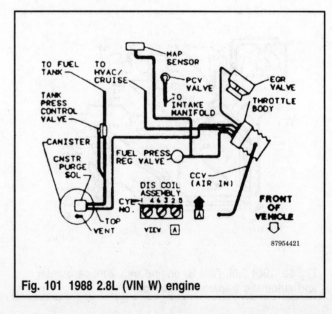

Fig. 101 1988 2.8L (VIN W) engine

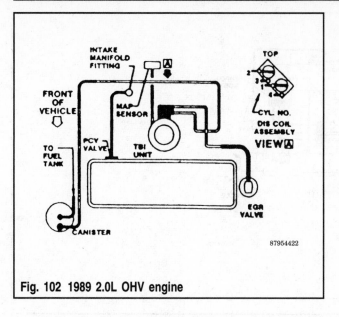

Fig. 102 1989 2.0L OHV engine

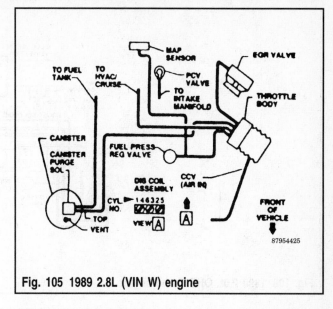

Fig. 105 1989 2.8L (VIN W) engine

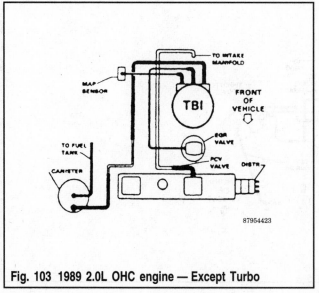

Fig. 103 1989 2.0L OHC engine — Except Turbo

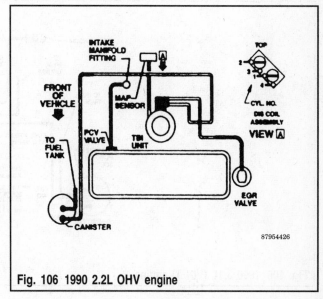

Fig. 106 1990 2.2L OHV engine

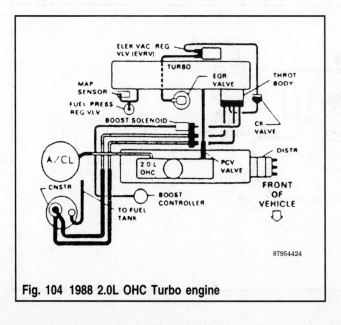

Fig. 104 1988 2.0L OHC Turbo engine

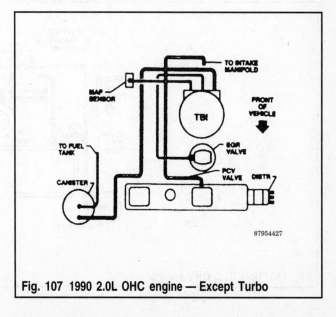

Fig. 107 1990 2.0L OHC engine — Except Turbo

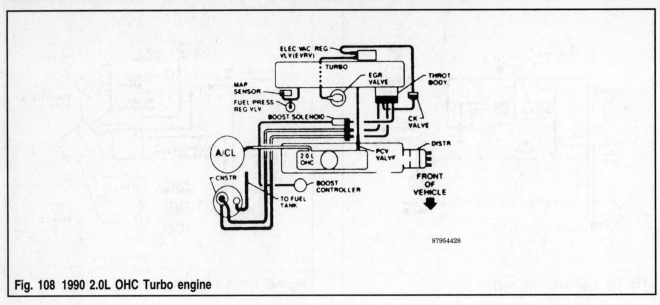

87954428

Fig. 108 1990 2.0L OHC Turbo engine

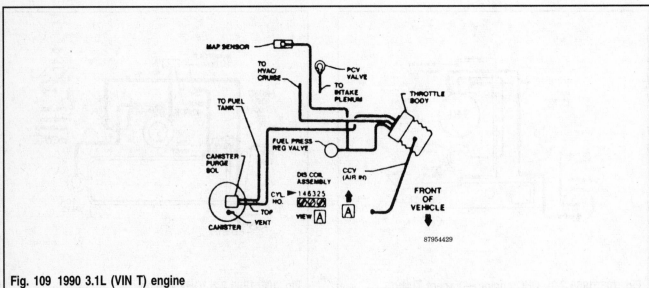

87954429

Fig. 109 1990 3.1L (VIN T) engine

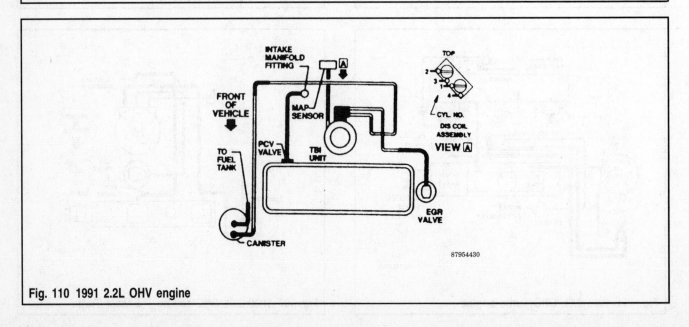

87954430

Fig. 110 1991 2.2L OHV engine

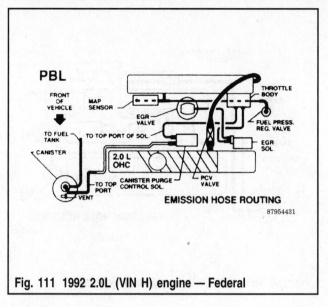

Fig. 111 1992 2.0L (VIN H) engine — Federal

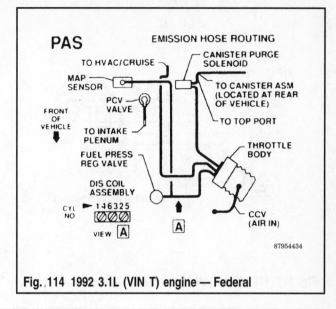

Fig. 114 1992 3.1L (VIN T) engine — Federal

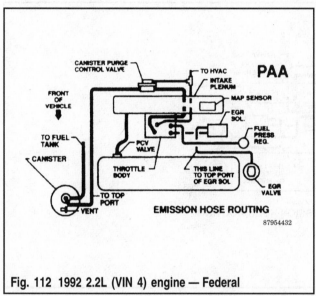

Fig. 112 1992 2.2L (VIN 4) engine — Federal

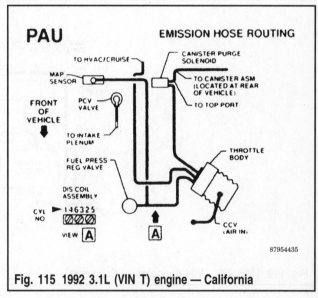

Fig. 115 1992 3.1L (VIN T) engine — California

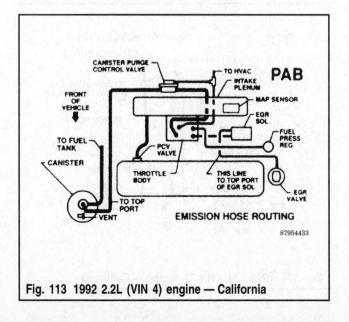

Fig. 113 1992 2.2L (VIN 4) engine — California

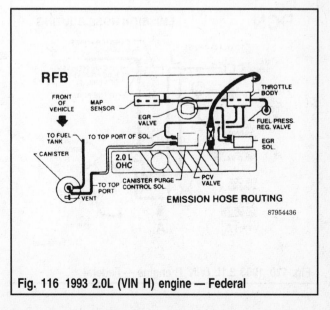

Fig. 116 1993 2.0L (VIN H) engine — Federal

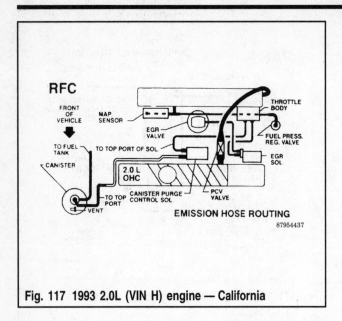

Fig. 117 1993 2.0L (VIN H) engine — California

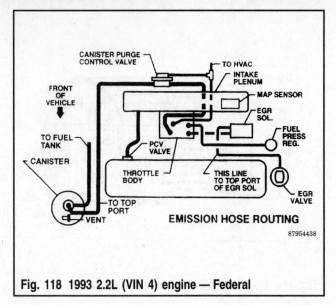

Fig. 118 1993 2.2L (VIN 4) engine — Federal

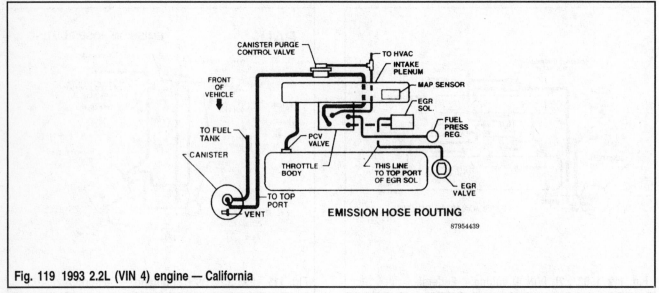

Fig. 119 1993 2.2L (VIN 4) engine — California

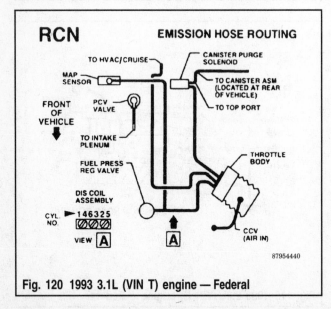

Fig. 120 1993 3.1L (VIN T) engine — Federal

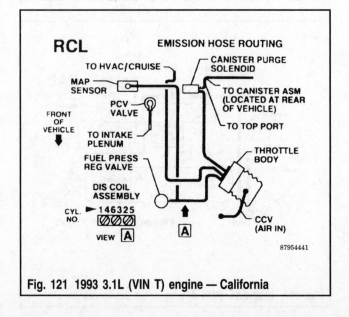

Fig. 121 1993 3.1L (VIN T) engine — California

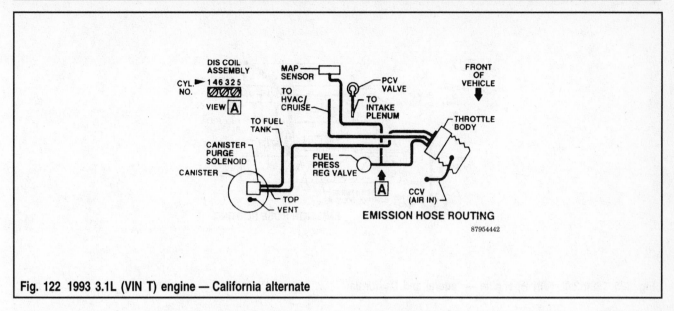

Fig. 122 1993 3.1L (VIN T) engine — California alternate

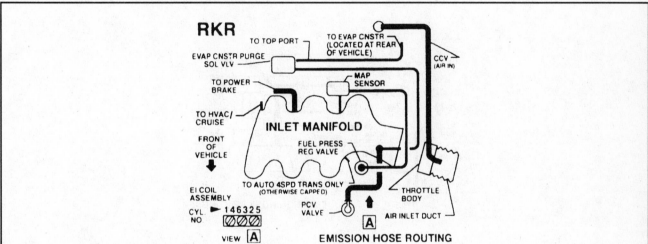

Fig. 123 1993 3.1L (VIN T) engine — Federal alternate

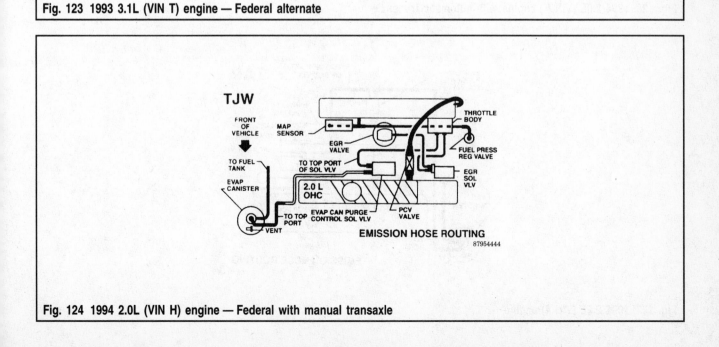

Fig. 124 1994 2.0L (VIN H) engine — Federal with manual transaxle

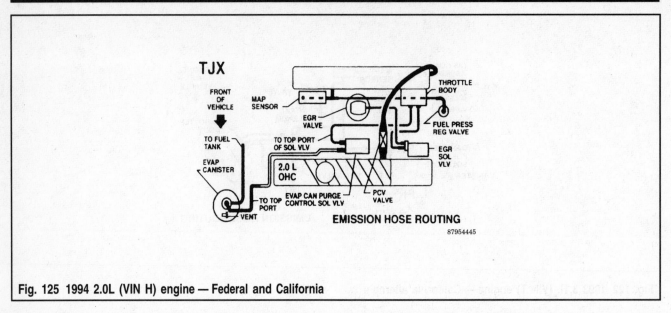

Fig. 125 1994 2.0L (VIN H) engine — Federal and California

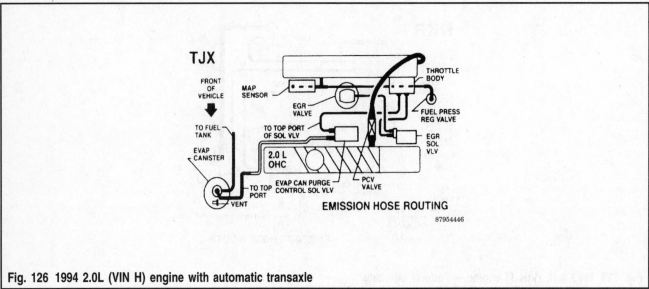

Fig. 126 1994 2.0L (VIN H) engine with automatic transaxle

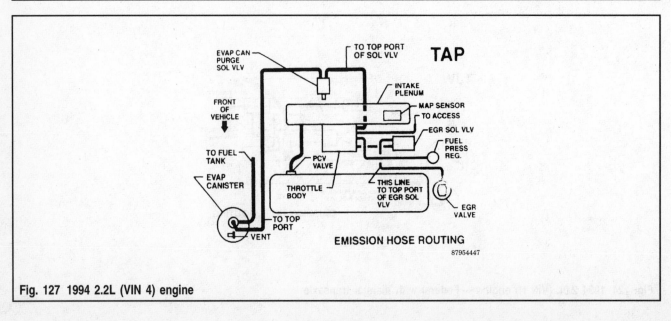

Fig. 127 1994 2.2L (VIN 4) engine

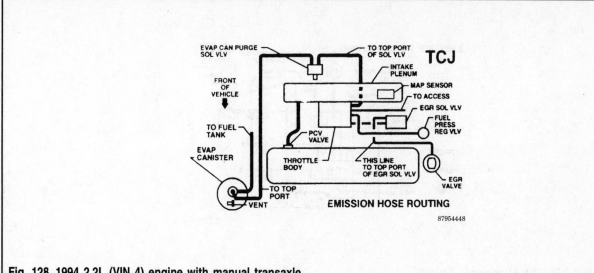

Fig. 128 1994 2.2L (VIN 4) engine with manual transaxle

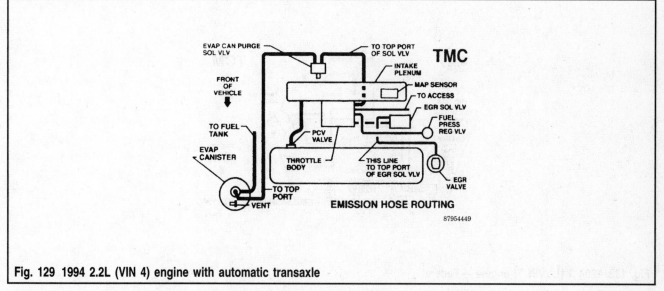

Fig. 129 1994 2.2L (VIN 4) engine with automatic transaxle

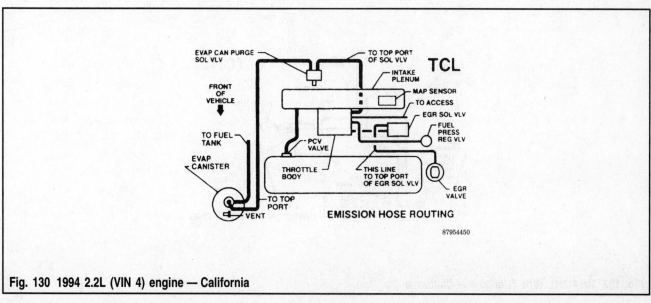

Fig. 130 1994 2.2L (VIN 4) engine — California

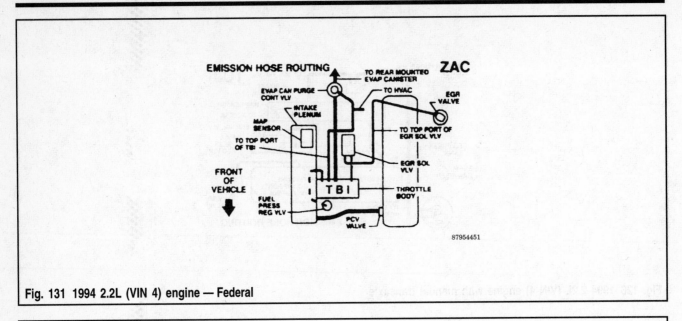

Fig. 131 1994 2.2L (VIN 4) engine — Federal

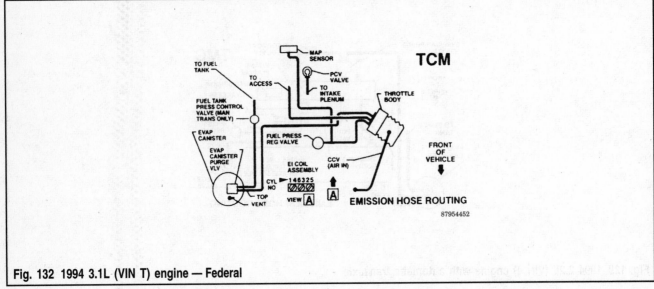

Fig. 132 1994 3.1L (VIN T) engine — Federal

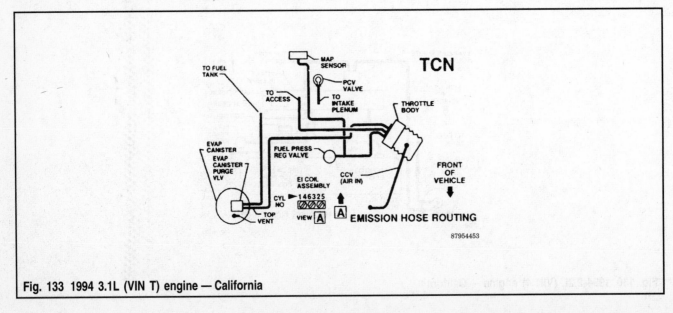

Fig. 133 1994 3.1L (VIN T) engine — California

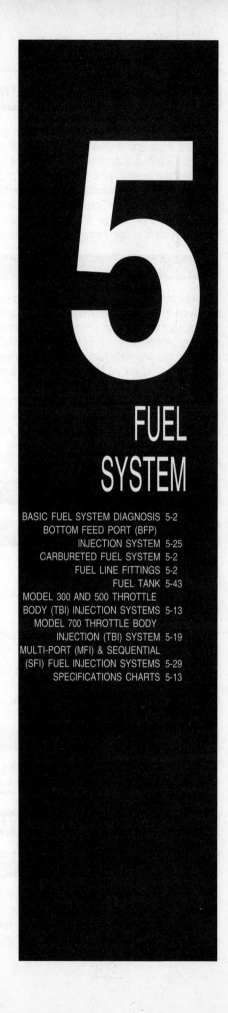

BASIC FUEL SYSTEM DIAGNOSIS
PRECAUTIONS 5-2
BOTTOM FEED PORT (BFP)
INJECTION SYSTEM
BOTTOM FEED PORT FUEL
INJECTORS 5-27
FUEL PRESSURE REGULATOR 5-28
FUEL SYSTEM PRESSURE
RELIEF 5-27
SYSTEM DESCRIPTION 5-25
CARBURETED FUEL SYSTEM
CARBURETOR 5-3
MECHANICAL FUEL PUMP 5-2
FUEL LINE FITTINGS
QUICK-CONNECT FITTINGS 5-2
FUEL TANK
TANK ASSEMBLY 5-43
MODEL 300 AND 500 THROTTLE
BODY (TBI) INJECTION SYSTEMS
FUEL INJECTOR 5-15
FUEL METER BODY 5-18
FUEL METER COVER 5-18
FUEL PRESSURE
REGULATOR/COMPENSATOR 5-17
FUEL PUMP 5-14
RELIEVING FUEL SYSTEM
PRESSURE 5-14
SYSTEM DESCRIPTION 5-13
THROTTLE BODY 5-15
MODEL 700 THROTTLE BODY
INJECTION (TBI) SYSTEM
FUEL INJECTOR 5-23
FUEL PRESSURE REGULATOR 5-24
FUEL PUMP 5-20
FUEL SYSTEM PRESSURE
RELEASE 5-20
SYSTEM DESCRIPTION 5-19
THROTTLE BODY 5-21
TUBE MODULE ASSEMBLY 5-25
MULTI-PORT (MFI) & SEQUENTIAL
(SFI) FUEL INJECTION SYSTEMS
FUEL INJECTORS 5-33
FUEL PRESSURE REGULATOR 5-35
FUEL PUMP 5-30
FUEL RAIL ASSEMBLY 5-37
GENERAL INFORMATION 5-29
RELIEVING FUEL SYSTEM
PRESSURE 5-29
THROTTLE BODY 5-31
SPECIFICATIONS CHARTS
CARBURETOR
SPECIFICATIONS 5-13

5

FUEL SYSTEM

BASIC FUEL SYSTEM DIAGNOSIS 5-2
BOTTOM FEED PORT (BFP)
INJECTION SYSTEM 5-25
CARBURETED FUEL SYSTEM 5-2
FUEL LINE FITTINGS 5-2
FUEL TANK 5-43
MODEL 300 AND 500 THROTTLE
BODY (TBI) INJECTION SYSTEMS 5-13
MODEL 700 THROTTLE BODY
INJECTION (TBI) SYSTEM 5-19
MULTI-PORT (MFI) & SEQUENTIAL
(SFI) FUEL INJECTION SYSTEMS 5-29
SPECIFICATIONS CHARTS 5-13

BASIC FUEL SYSTEM DIAGNOSIS

When there is a problem starting or driving a vehicle, two of the most important checks involve the ignition and the fuel systems. The two questions that mechanics attempt to answer first, "is there spark?" and "is there fuel?" will often lead to solving most basic problems. For ignition system diagnosis and testing, please refer to Section 2 of this manual. If the ignition system checks out (there is spark), then you must determine if the fuel system is operating properly (is there fuel?).

Precautions

Safety is the most important factor when performing not only fuel system maintenance, but any type of maintenance. Failure to conduct maintenance and repairs in a safe manner may result in serious personal injury or death. Maintenance and testing of the vehicle's fuel system components can be accomplished safely and effectively by adhering to the following rules and guidelines:

• To avoid the possibility of fire and personal injury, always disconnect the negative battery cable unless the repair or test procedure requires that battery voltage be applied.

• Always relieve the fuel system pressure prior to disconnecting any fuel system component (injector, fuel rail, pressure regulator, etc.), fitting or fuel line connection. Exercise extreme caution whenever relieving fuel system pressure to avoid exposing skin, face and eyes to fuel spray. Please be advised that fuel under pressure may penetrate the skin or any part of the body that it contacts.

• Always place a shop towel or cloth around the fitting or connection prior to loosening to absorb any excess fuel due to spillage. Ensure that all fuel spillage (should it occur) is quickly removed from engine surfaces. Ensure that all fuel soaked cloths or towels are deposited into a suitable waste container.

• Always keep a dry chemical (Class B) fire extinguisher near the work area.

• Do not allow fuel spray or fuel vapors to come into contact with a spark or open flame.

• Always use a backup wrench when loosening and tightening fuel line connection fittings. This will prevent unnecessary stress and torsion to fuel line piping. Always follow the proper torque specifications.

• Always replace worn fuel fitting O-rings with new ones. Do not substitute fuel hose or equivalent where fuel pipe is installed.

• Due to the possibility of a fire or explosion, never drain or store gasoline in an open container.

FUEL LINE FITTINGS

Quick-Connect Fittings

REMOVAL & INSTALLATION

▶ See Figure 1

➡This procedure requires Tool Set J37088-A fuel line quick-connect separator.

1. Grasp both sides of the fitting. Twist the female connector ¼ turn in each direction to loosen any dirt within the fittings. Using compressed air, blow out the dirt from the quick-connect fittings at the end of the fittings.

❊❊CAUTION

Safety glasses MUST be worn when using compressed air to avoid eye injury due to flying dirt particles!

2. For plastic (hand releasable) fittings, squeeze the plastic retainer release tabs, then pull the connection apart.

3. For metal fittings, choose the correct tool from kit J37088-A for the size of the fitting to be disconnected. Insert the proper tool into the female connector, then push inward to release the locking tabs. Pull the connection apart.

4. If it is necessary to remove rust or burrs from the male tube end of a quick-connect fitting, use emery cloth in a radial motion with the tube end to prevent damage to the O-ring sealing surfaces. Using a clean shop towel, wipe off the male tube ends. Inspect all connectors for dirt and burrs. Clean and/or replace if required.

To install:

5. Apply a few drops of clean engine oil to the male tube end of the fitting.

6. Push the connectors together to cause the retaining tabs/fingers to snap into place.

7. Once installed, pull on both ends of each connection to make sure they are secure.

CARBURETED FUEL SYSTEM

Mechanical Fuel Pump

A mechanical fuel pump is used on the 1982-84 carbureted engines. It is of the diaphragm-type and because of the design is serviced by replacement only. No adjustments or repairs are possible. The pump is operated by an eccentric on the camshaft.

REMOVAL & INSTALLATION

▶ See Figure 2

➡The fuel pump is located at the center rear of the engine.

1. Disconnect the negative cable at the battery. Raise and support the car.

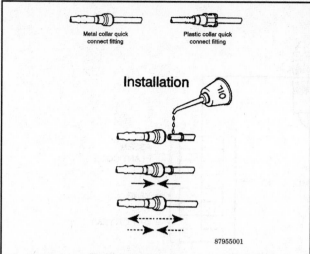

Fig. 1 Make sure you lubricate the male fitting before fastening the quick-connect fittings

2. Disconnect the inlet hose from the pump. Disconnect the vapor return hose, if equipped.

3. Loosen the fuel line at the carburetor, then disconnect the outlet pipe from the pump.

4. Unfasten the two mounting bolts and remove the pump from the engine.

To install:

5. Place a new gasket on the pump, then position the pump on the engine. Tighten the two mounting bolts alternately and evenly. Refer to the illustration for tightening specifications.

6. Install the pump outlet pipe. This is easier if the pipe is disconnected from the carburetor. Tighten the fitting while backing up the pump nut with another wrench. Install the pipe at the carburetor.

7. Install the inlet and vapor hoses. Lower the car, connect the negative battery cable, start the engine, and check for fuel leaks.

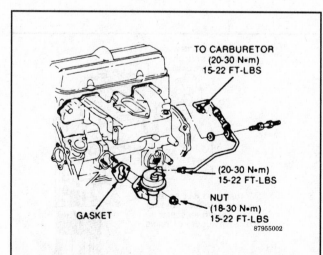

Fig. 2 Removal and installation of the fuel pump on a carbureted engine

TESTING

To determine if the fuel pump is in good condition, tests for both pressure and volume should be performed. The tests are made with the pump installed, and the engine at normal operating temperature and idle speed. Never replace a fuel pump without first performing these simple tests.

Be sure that the fuel filter has been changed at the specified interval, If in doubt, install a new filter then test the system.

Pressure Test

1. Disconnect the fuel line at the carburetor and connect a fuel pump pressure gauge. Fill the carburetor float bowl with gasoline.

2. Start the engine and check the pressure with the engine at idle. If the pump has a vapor return hose, squeeze it off so that an accurate reading can be obtained. Pressure should not be below 4.5 psi (31 kPa).

3. If the pressure is incorrect, replace the pump. If it is ok, go on to the volume test.

Volume Test

1. Disconnect the pressure gauge. Run the fuel line into a graduated container.

2. Run the engine at idle until one pint of gasoline has been pumped. One pint should be delivered in 30 seconds or less. There is normally enough fuel in the carburetor float bowl to perform this test, but refill it if necessary.

3. If the delivery rate is below the minimum, check the lines for restrictions or leaks, then replace the pump.

Carburetor

The Rochester E2SE is used on all models. It is a two barrel, two stage carburetor of downdraft design used in conjunction with the Computer Command Control system of fuel control. The carburetor has special design features for optimum air/fuel mixture control during all ranges of engine operation.

MODEL IDENTIFICATION

▶ **See Figure 3**

General Motors Rochester carburetors are identified by their model code. The first number indicates the number of barrels, while one of the last letters indicates the type of choke used. These are V for the manifold mounted choke coil, C for the choke coil mounted in the carburetor body, and E for electric choke, also mounted on the carburetor. Model codes ending in A indicate an altitude-compensation carburetor.

PRELIMINARY CHECKS

The following should be observed before attempting any adjustments.

1. Thoroughly warm the engine. If the engine is cold, be sure that it reaches operating temperature.

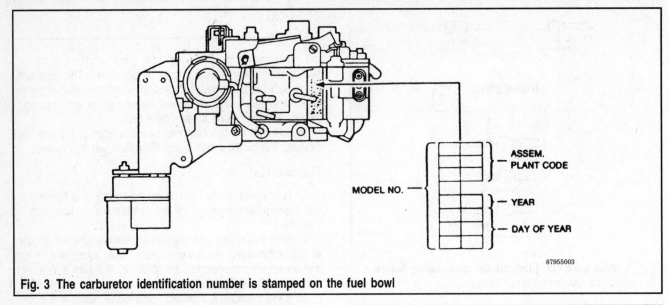

Fig. 3 The carburetor identification number is stamped on the fuel bowl

2. Check the torque of all carburetor mounting nuts and assembly screws. Also check the intake manifold-to-cylinder head bolts. If air is leaking at any of these points, any attempts at adjustment will inevitably lead to frustration.

3. Check the manifold heat control valve (if used) to be sure that it is free.

4. Check and adjust the choke as necessary.

5. Adjust the idle speed and mixture. If the mixture screws are capped, don't adjust them unless all other causes of rough idle have been eliminated. If any adjustments are performed that might possibly change the idle speed or mixture, adjust the idle and mixture again when you are finished.

Before you make any carburetor adjustments make sure that the engine is in tune. Many problems which are thought to be carburetor-related can be traced to an engine which is simply out-of-tune. Any trouble in these areas will have symptoms like those of carburetor problems.

ADJUSTMENTS

Float Adjustment

▶ See Figure 4

1. Remove the air horn from the throttle body.

2. Use your fingers to hold the retainer in place, and to push the float down into light contact with the needle.

3. Measure the distance from the toe of the float (furthest from the hinge) to the top of the carburetor (gasket removed).

4. To adjust, remove the float and gently bend the arm to specification. After adjustment, check the float alignment in the chamber.

Accelerator Pump Adjustment

E2SE carburetors have a non-adjustable pump lever. Adjustment is neither necessary or possible.

Fast Idle Adjustment

▶ See Figure 5

1. Set the ignition timing and curb idle speed, and disconnect and plug hoses as directed on the emission control decal.

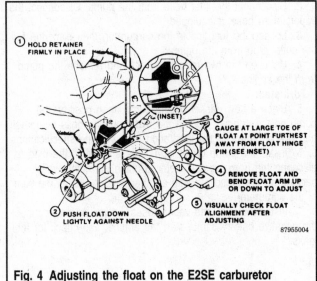

Fig. 4 Adjusting the float on the E2SE carburetor

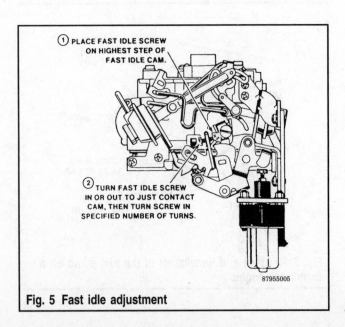

Fig. 5 Fast idle adjustment

2. Place the fast idle screw on the highest step of the cam.

3. Start the engine and adjust the engine speed to specification with the fast idle screw.

Choke Coil Lever Adjustment

▶ See Figure 6

1. Remove the three retaining screws and remove the choke cover and coil. On models with a riveted choke cover, drill out the three rivets and remove the cover and choke coil.

➡A choke stat cover retainer kit is required for reassembly.

2. Place the fast idle screw on the high step of the cam.

3. Close the choke by pushing in on the intermediate choke lever.

4. Insert a drill or gauge of the specified size into the hole in the choke housing. The choke lever in the housing should be up against the side of the gauge.

5. If the lever does not just touch the gauge, bend the intermediate choke rod to adjust.

Fast Idle Cam (Choke Rod) Adjustment

▶ See Figure 7

➡A special angle gauge must be used.

1. Adjust the choke coil lever and fast idle first.

2. Rotate the degree scale until it is zeroed.

3. Close the choke and install the degree scale onto the choke plate. Center the leveling bubble.

4. Rotate the scale so that the specified degree is opposite the scale pointer.

5. Place the fast idle screw on the second step of the cam (against the high step). Close the choke by pushing in the intermediate lever.

6. Bend the fast idle cam rod at the U to adjust the angle to specifications.

Air Valve Rod Adjustment

▶ See Figure 8

1. Seat the vacuum diaphragm with an outside vacuum source. Tape over the purge bleed hole if present.

2. Close the air valve.

3. Insert the specified gauge between the rod and the end of the slot in the plunger.

4. Bend the rod to adjust the clearance.

Primary Side Vacuum Break Adjustment

▶ See Figure 9

1. Follow Steps 1-4 of the Fast Idle Cam Adjustment.

2. Seat the choke vacuum diaphragm with an outside vacuum source.

3. Push in on the intermediate choke lever to close the choke valve, and hold closed during adjustment.

4. Adjust by using a ⅛ in. (3mm) hex wrench to turn the screw in the rear cover until the bubble is centered.

5. After adjusting, apply RTV silicone sealant over the screw to seal the setting.

Secondary Vacuum Break Adjustment

▶ See Figure 10

1. Follow Steps 1-4 of the Fast Idle Cam Adjustment.

2. Seat the choke vacuum diaphragm with an outside vacuum source.

3. Push in on the intermediate choke lever to close the choke valve, and hold closed during adjustment. Make sure the plunger spring is compressed and seated, if present.

4. Adjust by using a ⅛ in. (3mm) hex wrench to turn the screw in the rear cover until the bubble is centered.

5. After adjusting, apply RTV silicone sealant over the screw to seal the setting.

Choke Unloader Adjustment

▶ See Figure 11

1. Follow Steps 1-4 of the Fast Idle Cam Adjustment.

2. Hold the primary throttle wide open.

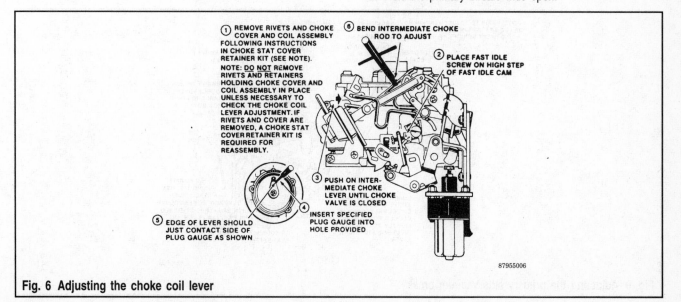

① REMOVE RIVETS AND CHOKE COVER AND COIL ASSEMBLY FOLLOWING INSTRUCTIONS IN CHOKE STAT COVER RETAINER KIT (SEE NOTE).
NOTE: DO NOT REMOVE RIVETS AND RETAINERS HOLDING CHOKE COVER AND COIL ASSEMBLY IN PLACE UNLESS NECESSARY TO CHECK THE CHOKE COIL LEVER ADJUSTMENT. IF RIVETS AND COVER ARE REMOVED, A CHOKE STAT COVER RETAINER KIT IS REQUIRED FOR REASSEMBLY.

⑥ BEND INTERMEDIATE CHOKE ROD TO ADJUST

② PLACE FAST IDLE SCREW ON HIGH STEP OF FAST IDLE CAM

③ PUSH ON INTERMEDIATE CHOKE LEVER UNTIL CHOKE VALVE IS CLOSED

④ INSERT SPECIFIED PLUG GAUGE INTO HOLE PROVIDED

⑤ EDGE OF LEVER SHOULD JUST CONTACT SIDE OF PLUG GAUGE AS SHOWN

87955006

Fig. 6 Adjusting the choke coil lever

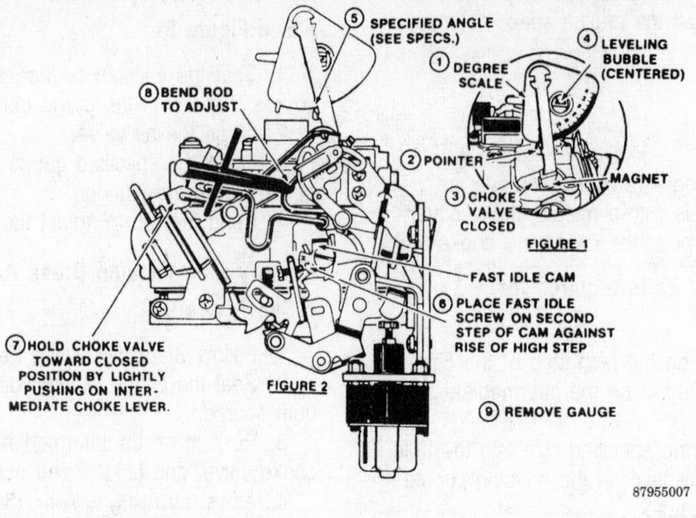

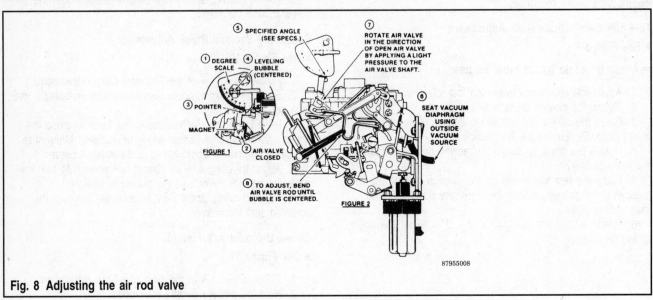

Fig. 7 Fast idle cam (choke rod) adjustment

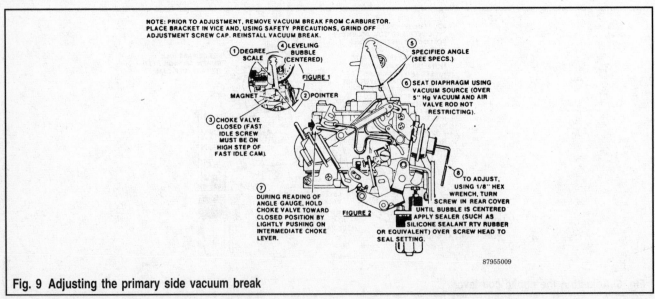

Fig. 8 Adjusting the air rod valve

Fig. 9 Adjusting the primary side vacuum break

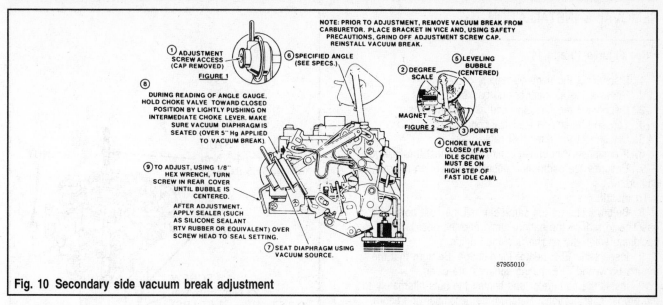

Fig. 10 Secondary side vacuum break adjustment

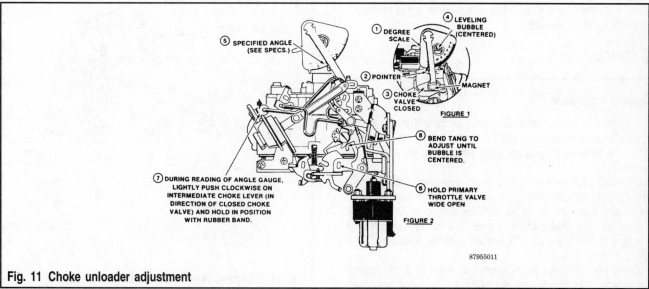

Fig. 11 Choke unloader adjustment

3. If the engine is warm, close the choke valve by pushing in on the intermediate choke lever.

4. Bend the unloader tang until the bubble is centered.

Secondary Lockout Adjustment

▶ See Figure 12

1. Pull the choke wide open by pushing out on the intermediate choke lever.

2. Open the throttle until the end of the secondary actuating lever is opposite the toe of the lockout lever.

3. Gauge clearance between the lockout lever and secondary lever should be as specified.

4. To adjust, bend the lockout lever where it contacts the fast idle cam.

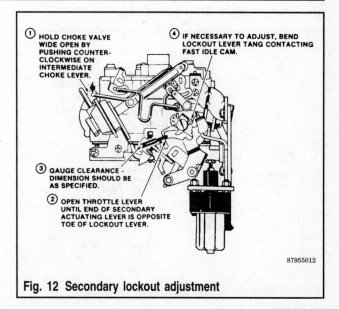

Fig. 12 Secondary lockout adjustment

REMOVAL & INSTALLATION

▶ **See Figures 13 and 14**

1. Disconnect the negative battery cable.
2. Remove the air cleaner and gasket.
3. Disconnect the fuel pipe and all vacuum lines.
4. Tag and detach all electrical connections.
5. Disconnect the downshift cable.
6. If equipped with cruise control, disconnect the linkage.
7. Unscrew the carburetor mounting bolts, then remove the carburetor.

To install:

8. Before installing the carburetor, fill the float bowl with gasoline to reduce the battery strain and the possibility of backfiring when the engine is started again.
9. Inspect the EFE heater for damage. Be sure that the throttle body and EFE mating surfaces are clean.
10. Install the carburetor and tighten the nuts alternately to the proper specifications. Refer to the accompanying figure.
11. Installation of the remaining components is the reverse of the removal procedure.

OVERHAUL

General Information

Efficient carburetion depends greatly on careful cleaning and inspection during overhaul, since dirt, gum, water, or varnish in or on the carburetor parts are often responsible for poor performance.

Overhaul your carburetor in a clean, dust-free area. Carefully disassemble the carburetor, referring often to the exploded views and directions packaged with the rebuilding kit. Keep all similar and look-alike parts segregated during disassembly and cleaning to avoid accidental interchange during assembly. Make a note of all jet sizes.

When the carburetor is disassembled, wash all parts (except diaphragms, electric choke units, pump plunger, and any other plastic, fiber, or rubber parts) in clean carburetor solvent. Do

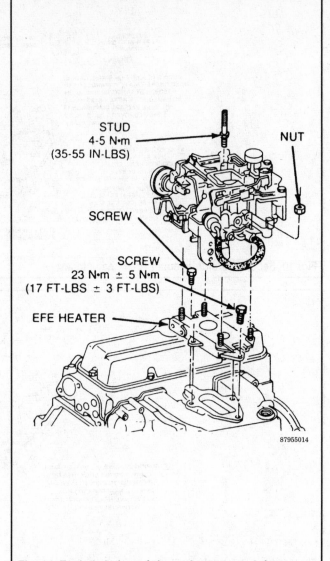

Fig. 14 Exploded view of the carburetor mounting

not leave parts in the solvent any longer than is necessary to sufficiently loosen the deposits. Excessive cleaning may remove the special finish from the float bowl and choke valve bodies, leaving these parts unfit for service. Rinse all parts in clean solvent and blow them dry with compressed air or allow them to air dry. Wipe clean all cork, plastic, and fiber parts with a clean, lint-free cloth.

Blow out all passages and jets with compressed air and be sure that there are no restrictions or blockages. Never use wire or similar tools to clean jets, fuel passages, or air bleeds. Clean all jets and valves separately to avoid accidental interchange.

Check all parts for wear or damage. If wear or damage is found, replace the defective parts. Especially check the following:

1. Check the float needle and seat for wear. If wear is found, replace the complete assembly.
2. Check the float hinge pin for wear and the float(s) for dents or distortion. Replace the float if fuel has leaked into it.
3. Check the throttle and choke shaft bores for wear or an out-of-round condition. Damage or wear to the throttle arm,

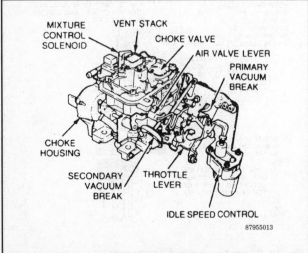

Fig. 13 View of the Rochester E2SE carburetor components

shaft, or shaft bore will often require replacement of the throttle body. These parts require a close tolerance of fit; wear may allow air leakage, which could affect starting and idling.

➡**Throttle shafts and bushings are not included in overhaul kits. They may be purchased separately.**

4. Inspect the idle mixture adjusting needles for burrs or grooves. Any such condition requires replacement of the needle, since you will not be able to obtain a satisfactory idle.

5. Test the accelerator pump check valves. They should pass air one way but not the other. Test for proper seating by blowing and sucking on the valve. Replace the valve check ball and spring as necessary. If the valve is satisfactory, wash the valve parts again to remove breath moisture.

6. Check the bowl cover for warped surfaces with a straightedge.

7. Closely inspect the accelerator pump plunger for wear and damage, replacing as necessary.

8. After the carburetor is assembled, check the choke valve for freedom of operation.

Carburetor overhaul kits are recommended for each overhaul. These kits contain all gaskets and new parts to replace those which deteriorate most rapidly. Failure to replace all parts supplied with the kit (especially gaskets) can result in poor performance later.

Some carburetor manufacturers supply overhaul kits for three basic types: minor repair; major repair; and gasket kits. Basically, they contain the following:

Minor Repair Kits:
- All gaskets
- Float needle valve
- All diagrams
- Spring for the pump diaphragm

Major Repair Kits:
- All jets and gaskets
- All diaphragms
- Float needle valve
- Pump ball valve
- Float
- Complete intermediate rod
- Intermediate pump lever
- Some cover hold-down screws and washers

Gasket Kits:
- All gaskets

After cleaning and checking all components, reassemble the carburetor, using new parts and referring to the exploded view. When reassembling, make sure that all screws and jets are tight in their seats, but do not overtighten as the tips will be distorted. Tighten all screws gradually, in rotation. Do not tighten needle valves into their seats; uneven jetting will result. Always use new gaskets. Be sure to adjust the float level when reassembling.

Disassembly

▶ See Figures 15, 16, 17, 18, 19, 20, 21, 22, 23, 24, 25, 26 and 27

1. Remove the carburetor from the vehicle. Refer to the necessary procedure located earlier in this section.

2. Mount the assembly in a holding fixture (special tool J-9787 or equivalent). Without the use of the holding fixture, it is possible to damage the throttle valves.

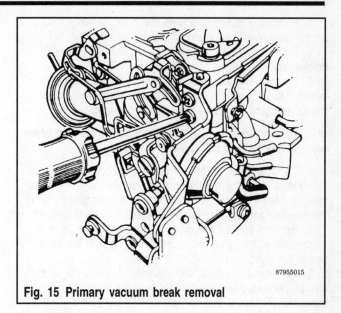
87955015
Fig. 15 Primary vacuum break removal

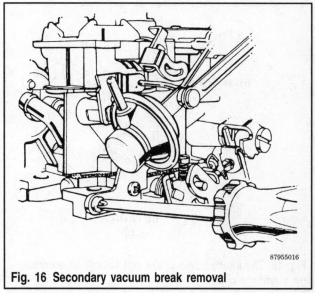
87955016
Fig. 16 Secondary vacuum break removal

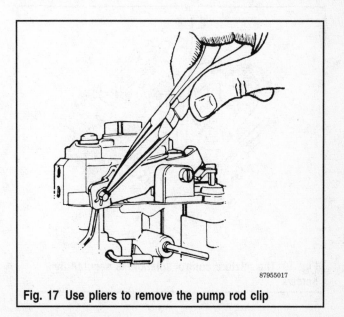
87955017
Fig. 17 Use pliers to remove the pump rod clip

3. Remove 3 attaching screws that hold the idle speed control/primary vacuum break to the carburetor.

4. Remove the idle speed control, vacuum break and bracket as an assembly.

5. Remove the secondary vacuum break and bracket assembly attaching screws from the throttle body. Then rotate the assembly to disengage the vacuum break link.

➡**Do not immerse the idle speed control or vacuum break units in any type of carburetor cleaner.**

6. To remove the air horn assembly, remove the clip from the hole in the pump rod. Remove the choke rod and plastic bushing from the choke lever. Remove the three mixture control solenoid screws, then lift the solenoid out of the air horn.

7. Remove the fast idle cam rod from the choke lever by rotating the rod to align the notch on the rod with the small slot in the lever.

8. To remove the float bowl assembly, remove the air horn gasket. Remove the pump plunger from the pump well. Remove the TP sensor and connector assembly from the float

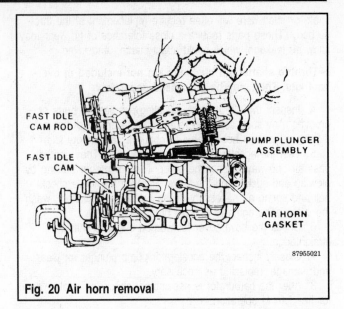

Fig. 20 Air horn removal

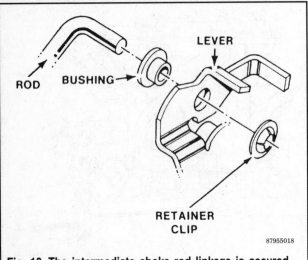

Fig. 18 The intermediate choke rod linkage is secured by a retainer clip

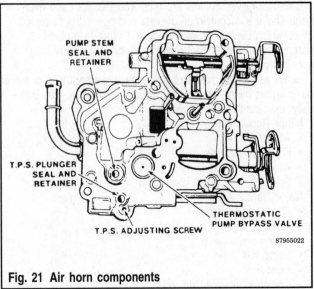

Fig. 21 Air horn components

bowl. Remove the spring from the bottom of the TP sensor well in the bowl.

9. Remove the plastic filler block over the float valve. Remove the float assembly and float valve by pulling up on the hinge pin.

10. Remove the plastic filler block insert from the float bowl cavity.

11. Using a special removal tool or a wide-blade screwdriver that fully fits the slots on the top of the float valve seat and the extended metering jet, remove the float valve seat (with the gasket) and the extended metering jet from the float bowl. Do not remove or change the adjustment of the small calibration screw located deep inside the metering jet.

12. Remove the plastic retainer holding the pump discharge spring and check ball.

13. Remove the fuel inlet nut, gasket, check valve filter assembly and spring.

14. Unfasten the 4 throttle body-to-bowl attaching screws, then remove the throttle body assembly. Remove the throttle body-to-bowl insulator gasket.

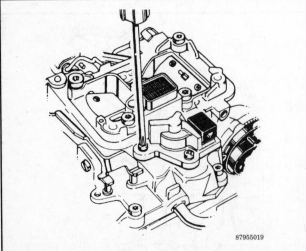

Fig. 19 The mixture control solenoid is secured by screws

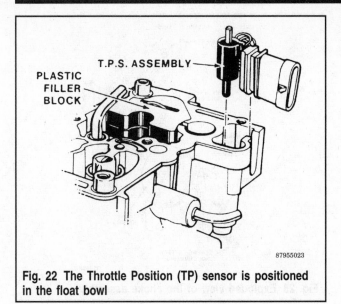

Fig. 22 The Throttle Position (TP) sensor is positioned in the float bowl

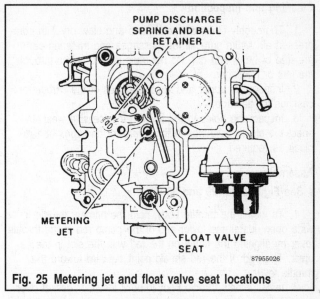

Fig. 25 Metering jet and float valve seat locations

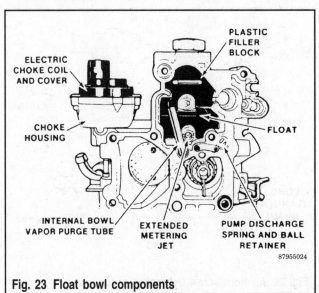

Fig. 23 Float bowl components

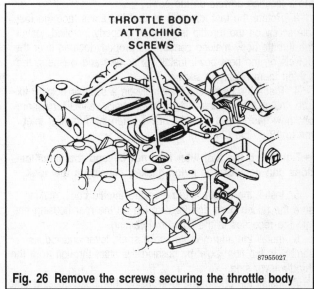

Fig. 26 Remove the screws securing the throttle body

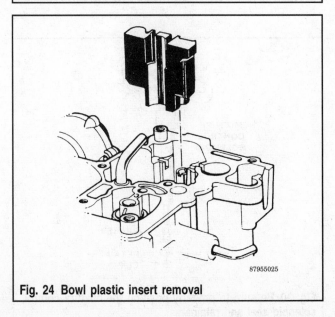

Fig. 24 Bowl plastic insert removal

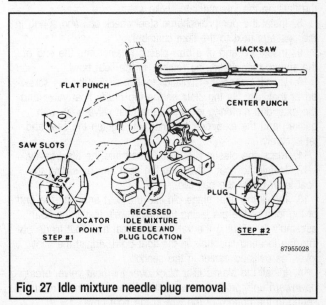

Fig. 27 Idle mixture needle plug removal

Cleaning and Inspection

1. Thoroughly clean all metal parts and blow dry with compressed air. Make sure all fuel passages and metering parts are free of burrs and dirt. Do not pass drills or wires through the jets or passages

2. Inspect the upper and lower surfaces of the carburetor castings for damage.

3. Inspect the holes in the levers for excessive wear. Inspect the plastic bushings in the levers for damage, then replace as required.

Assembly

▶ **See Figures 28, 29 and 30**

1. To install the throttle body, hold the primary throttle lever wide open, install the lower end of the pump rod in the throttle lever by aligning the notch on the rod with the slot in the elver. The end of the rod should point outward toward the throttle lever.

2. Install a new throttle body-to-bowl insulator gasket over the 2 locating dowels on the bowl.

3. Rotate the fast idle cam so that the steps face the fast idle screw on the throttle lever when properly installed, install the throttle body making certain it is properly located over the dowels on the float bowl. Install the screws and washers, then tighten them evenly to secure.

4. Place the carburetor assembly on a suitable holding fixture. Install the fuel inlet filter spring, check valve.filter assembly, new gasket and the inlet nut. Tighten the fuel filter inlet nut to 18 ft. lbs. (24 Nm).

➡**Tightening the fuel filter inlet nut beyond the specifications can damage the nylon gasket, causing a fuel leak.**

5. Install the choke housing on the throttle body, making sure the raised boss and locating lug on the rear housing fit into the recesses in the float bowl casting.

6. Install the intermediate choke shaft, lever and rod assembly in the float bowl by pushing the shaft through from the throttle lever side.

7. Install the choke coil lever inside the choke housing onto the flats on the intermediate choke shaft.

8. Instal the pump discharge steel check ball and spring in the passage next to the float chamber.

9. Insert the end of a new plastic retainer into the end of the spring, then install the retainer in the float bowl.

10. Using a special installation tool or a wide-bladed screwdriver that fully fits the slots on the top of the float valve and the extended metering jet, install the float valve seat (with gasket) and the extended metering jet. Tighten the seat and jet securely.

11. Place the plastic filler block insert into the blow cavity.

12. Install the float valve onto the float arm by sliding the float lever under the pull clip.

13. Install the float hinge pin into the float arm with the end of the loop of the pin facing the pump well. Install the float assembly by aligning the valve in the seat and float hinge pin into the locating channels in the float bowl. Adjust the float lever, as outlined earlier in this section.

14. Install the plastic filler block over the float valve, pressing downward until properly seated. Install the TP sensor return spring in the bottom of the well in the float bowl.

15. Install the TP sensor and electrical connector assembly.

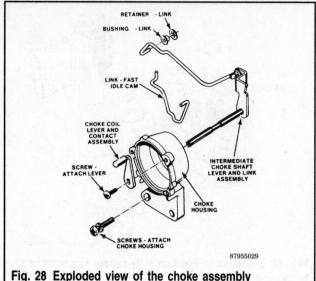

Fig. 28 Exploded view of the choke assembly

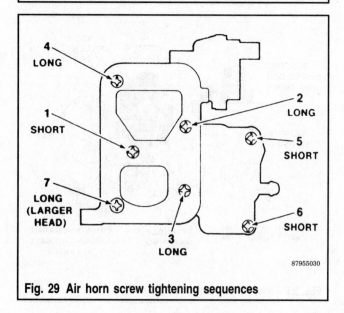

Fig. 29 Air horn screw tightening sequences

Fig. 30 Be sure to properly position the mixture control solenoid seal and retainers

16. Install the air horn gasket on the float bowl, locating gasket over the 2 dowel locating pins on the bowl. Install the pump return spring and plunger assembly in the pump well.

17. Rotate fast idle cam to the full Up position and tilt the air horn assembly to engage the lower end of fast idle cam rod in slot in the fast idle cam and install pump rod end into the pump lever; carefully lower the air horn assembly onto float bowl, guiding pump plunger stem through seal in air horn casting. DO NOT FORCE AIR HORN ASSEMBLY ONTO THE BOWL.

18. Fasten the 7 air horn to bowl attaching screws and lockwashers following proper installation location and tightening sequence. All air horn screws must be tightened EVENLY.

19. Install new retainer clip through hole in end of pump rod extending through pump lever, making sure clip is securely locked in place.

20. Install mixture control solenoid (spacer and rubber seal) on air horn, carefully aligning solenoid stem with recess in bottom of bowl.

21. Secure the plastic bushing in the hole in the choke lever, making sure the small end of the bushing faces the retaining clip when installed. Retain the rod with a new clip.

22. Install secondary side vacuum break assembly.

23. Install primary side vacuum break assembly (with idle speed control and bracket).

24. As outlined earlier in this section, install the carburetor.

E2SE Carburetor Specifications

Carburetor Identification	Float Level (In.)	Fast Idle (rpm)	Choke Coil Lever (In.)	Fast Idle Cam (deg.)	Air Valve Rod (deg.)	Primary Vacuum Break (deg/In.)	Choke Setting (notches)	Secondary Vacuum Break (deg/In.)	Choke Unloader (deg/In.)	Secondary Lockout (In.)
17081600	5/16	①	.085	24	1	20/.110	①	27/.157	35/.220	.012
17081601	5/16	①	.085	24	1	20/.110	①	27/.157	35/.220	.012
17081607	5/16	①	.085	24	1	20/.110	①	27/.157	35/.220	.012
17081700	5/16	①	.085	24	1	20/.110	①	27/.157	35/.220	.012
17081701	5/16 ·	①	.085	24	1	20/.110	①	27/.157	35/.220	.012

① See underhood emissions sticker

87955032

MODEL 300 AND 500 THROTTLE BODY (TBI) INJECTION SYSTEMS

System Description

The single bore, Model 300 throttle body unit used on the 1983-86 1.8L OHC engine and the Model 500 throttle body unit used on the 1982-86 2.0L OHV engine are similar systems.

In these throttle body systems, a single fuel injector mounted at the top of the throttle body sprays fuel down through the throttle valve and into the intake manifold. The throttle body resembles a carburetor in appearance but does away with much of the carburetor's complexity (choke system and linkage, power valves, accelerator pump, jets, fuel circuits, etc.), replacing these with the electrically operated fuel injector.

The injector is actually a solenoid which when activated lifts a pintle valve off its seat, allowing the pressurized (10 psi) fuel behind the valve to spray out. The nozzle of the injector is designed to atomize the fuel for complete air/fuel mixture.

The activating signal for the injector originates with the Electronic Control Module (ECM), which monitors engine temperature, throttle position, vehicle speed and several other engine-related conditions then continuously updates injector opening times in relation to the information given by these sensors.

The throttle body is also equipped with an idle air control valve. When the valve opens it allows air to bypass the throt-tle, which provides the additional air required to idle at elevated speed when the engine is cold. The idle air control motor also compensates for accessory loads and changing engine friction during break-in. The idle speed control valve is controlled by the ECM.

Fuel pressure for the system is provided by an in-tank fuel pump. The pump is a two-stage turbine designed powered by a DC motor. It is designed for smooth, quiet operation, high flow and fast priming. The design of the fuel inlet reduces the possibility of vapor lock under hot fuel conditions. The pump sends fuel forward through the fuel line to a stainless steel high-flow fuel filter mounted on the engine. From the filter the fuel moves to the throttle body. The fuel pump inlet is located in a reservoir in the fuel tank which insures a constant supply of fuel to the pump during hard cornering and on steep inclines. The fuel pump is controlled by a fuel pump relay, which in turn receives its signal from the ECM. A fuel pressure regulator inside the throttle body maintains fuel pressure at 10 psi and routes unused fuel back to the fuel tank through a fuel return line. On the dual throttle body system, a fuel pressure compensator is used on the second throttle body assembly to compensate for a momentary fuel pressure drop between the two units. This constant circulation of fuel through the throttle body prevents component overheating and vapor lock.

The electronic control module (ECM), also called a micro-computer, is the brain of the fuel injection system. After receiving input from various sensing elements in the system the ECM commands the fuel injector, idle air control motor, EST distributor, torque converter clutch and other engine actuators to operate in a pre-programmed manner to improve driveability and fuel economy while controlling emissions. The sensing elements update the computer every tenth of a second for general information and every 12.5 milliseconds for critical emissions and driveability information.

The ECM has limited system diagnostic capability. If certain system malfunctions occur, the diagnostic Check Engine light in the instrument panel will light, alerting the driver to the need for service.

Since both idle speed and mixture are controlled by the ECM on this system, no adjustments are possible or necessary.

Relieving Fuel System Pressure

❄❄CAUTION

To reduce the risk of fire or personal injury, it is necessary to relieve the fuel system pressure before servicing the fuel system.

EXCEPT 1985-86 2.0L (OHV) ENGINES

1. Remove the fuel pump fuse from the fuse block.
2. Crank the engine. The engine will start and run until the fuel supply in the pipes is gone. Crank the engine again for 3 seconds making sure it is out of fuel.
3. Turn the ignition off and replace the fuse.

1985-86 2.0L (OHV)

The TBI injection systems used on the 1985-86 engines contain a constant bleed feature in the pressure regulator that relieves pressure any time the engine is turned off. Therefore, no special relieve procedure is required, however, a small amount of fuel may be released when the fuel line is disconnected.

❄❄CAUTION

To reduce the chance of personal injury, cover the fuel line with cloth to collect the fuel and then place the cloth in an approved container.

Fuel Pump

TESTING

❄❄CAUTION

To reduce the risk of fire and personal injury, it is necessary to relieve the fuel system pressure before servicing fuel system components (Refer to the appropriate procedure).

1.8L and 2.0L OHV Engines

1. Remove the air cleaner. Plug the thermal vacuum port on the throttle body.
2. Remove the fuel line between the throttle body and filter.
3. Install a fuel pressure gauge between the throttle body and fuel filter. The gauge should be able to register at least 15 psi (30 kPa).
4. Start the car. The pressure reading should be 9-13 psi (18-26 kPa).
5. Depressurize the system and remove the gauge.
6. Assemble the system.

1.8L and 2.0L OHC Engines

1. Release the fuel system pressure.

❄❄CAUTION

To reduce the risk of fire or personal injury, it is necessary to relieve the fuel system pressure before servicing the fuel system. Refer to Fuel System Pressure Release in the appropriate fuel injection system in this section.

2. Obtain two sections of ⅜ in. steel tubing. Each should be about 10 in. (254mm) long. Double flare one end of each section.
3. Install a flare nut on each section. Connect each of the above sections of tubing into the flare nut-to-flare nut adapters that are included in J-29658 gauge.
4. Attach the pipe and the adapter assemblies to the J-29658 gauge.
5. Jack up the car and support it safely.
6. Disconnect the front fuel feed hose from the fuel pipe on the body.
7. Install a 10 in. (254mm) length of ⅜ in. fuel hose on the fuel pipe on the body. Attach the other end of the hose onto one of the sections of the pipe mentioned in Step 2. Secure the hose connections with clamps.
8. Start the engine and check for leaks.
9. Observe the fuel pressure reading. It should be 9-13 psi (18-26 kPa).
10. Depressurize the fuel system and remove the gauge with adapters. Reconnect the fuel feed hose to the pipe and torque the clamp to 15 inch lbs. (1.7 Nm).
11. Carefully lower the car, the start the engine and check for fuel leaks.

REMOVAL & INSTALLATION

▶ **See Figure 31**

1. Properly relieve the fuel system pressure, as outlined earlier in this section.
2. Disconnect the negative battery cable.
3. Raise and safely support the vehicle.
4. As outlined later in this section, remove the fuel tank.
5. Remove the fuel lever sending unit and pump assembly by turning the cam lock ring counterclockwise. Lift the assembly from the fuel tank and remove the fuel pump from the fuel level sending unit.
6. Pull the fuel pump up into the attaching hose or pulsator while pulling outward away from the bottom support. After the pump is clear of the bottom support, pull the pump assembly out of the rubber connector or pulsator for removal.

To install:

7. Position and push the pump into the attaching hose.
8. Install the fuel level sending unit and pump assembly into the tank assembly. Use new O-rings during reassembly.

✳✳WARNING

Be careful not to fold over or twist the strainer when installing the sending unit as it will restrict fuel flow. Also, be careful the strainer does not block full travel of the float arm.

9. Install the cam lock over the assembly and lock by turning clockwise.
10. Install the fuel tank.
11. Connect the negative battery cable, then start the engine and check the system for proper operation.

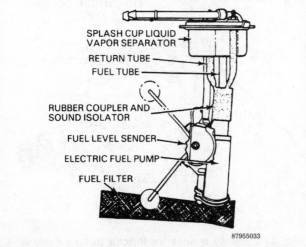

Fig. 31 Vehicles equipped with the 300 and 500 throttle bodies have an in-tank fuel pump

SPLASH CUP LIQUID VAPOR SEPARATOR
RETURN TUBE
FUEL TUBE
RUBBER COUPLER AND SOUND ISOLATOR
FUEL LEVEL SENDER
ELECTRIC FUEL PUMP
FUEL FILTER

87955033

Throttle Body

REMOVAL & INSTALLATION

▶ **See Figures 32 and 33**

1. Disconnect the battery cables at the battery.
2. Remove the air cleaner assembly, noting the connection points of the vacuum lines.
3. Detach the electrical connectors at the injector, idle air control motor, and throttle position sensor.
4. Tag and disconnect the vacuum lines from the TBI unit, noting the connection points. During installation, refer to the underhood emission control information decal for vacuum line routing information.
5. Disconnect the throttle and cruise control (if so equipped) cables at the TBI unit.
6. Unfasten the fuel return line.
7. Disconnect the fuel feed line.
8. Unfasten the retaining bolts, then remove the TBI unit.

To install:

9. Installation is the reverse of removal. Make sure to clean the gasket mating surfaces.
10. Tighten the TBI retaining bolts alternately and evenly to the following specifications:
    - 1983-85 2.0L OHV engine: 26 ft. lbs. (35 Nm).
    - 1986 2.0L OHV engine: 17 ft. lbs. (23 Nm).
    - 1983-86 1.8L OHC engine: 17 ft. lbs. (23 Nm).

Fuel Injector

REMOVAL & INSTALLATION

▶ **See Figures 34 and 35**

1. Relieve the fuel system pressure.
2. Remove the air cleaner.
3. Detach the injector electrical connector by squeezing the two tabs together and pulling straight up.

✳✳WARNING

Use care in removing to prevent damage to the electrical connector pins on top of the injector, injector fuel filter and nozzle. The fuel injector is only serviced as a complete assembly. Do not immerse it in any type of cleaner.

4. Remove the fuel meter cover, as outlined in this section.
5. With the fuel meter cover gasket in place to prevent damage to the throttle body, gently pry up on the injector evenly and carefully remove it, using a suitable prytool.
6. Remove the large O-ring and steel back-up washer from the top of the injector cavity in the fuel meter body, then remove the small O-ring at the bottom of the injector cavity. Discard the gaskets.

To install:

7. Lubricate a new, small O-ring with clean automatic transaxle fluid, then push the O-ring onto the nozzle end of the injector, pressing the ring up against the injector fuel filter.

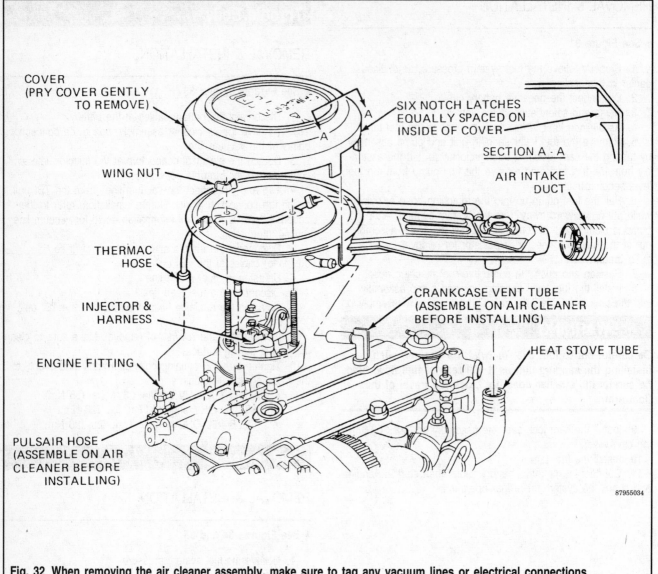

COVER
(PRY COVER GENTLY
TO REMOVE)

SIX NOTCH LATCHES
EQUALLY SPACED ON
INSIDE OF COVER

SECTION A - A

AIR INTAKE
DUCT

WING NUT

THERMAC
HOSE

INJECTOR &
HARNESS

CRANKCASE VENT TUBE
(ASSEMBLE ON AIR CLEANER
BEFORE INSTALLING)

HEAT STOVE TUBE

ENGINE FITTING

PULSAIR HOSE
(ASSEMBLE ON AIR
CLEANER BEFORE
INSTALLING)

87955034

Fig. 32 When removing the air cleaner assembly, make sure to tag any vacuum lines or electrical connections

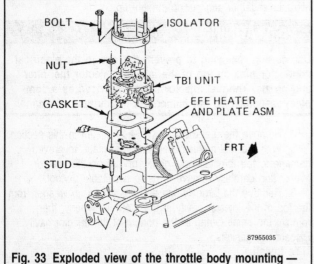

BOLT

ISOLATOR

NUT

TBI UNIT

GASKET

EFE HEATER
AND PLATE ASM

FRT

STUD

87955035

**Fig. 33 Exploded view of the throttle body mounting —
1984 Model 500 throttle body shown**

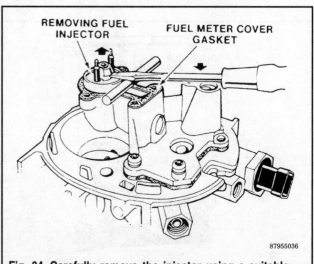

REMOVING FUEL
INJECTOR

FUEL METER COVER
GASKET

87955036

**Fig. 34 Carefully remove the injector using a suitable
prytool**

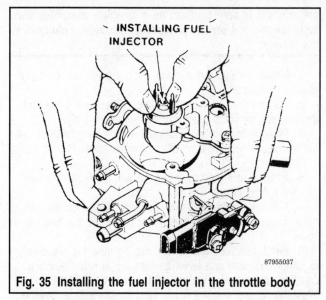

Fig. 35 Installing the fuel injector in the throttle body

8. Place the steel back-up washer in the recess of the fuel meter body. Lubricate a new, large O-ring with clean automatic transaxle fluid, then install the O-ring directly above the back-up washer, pressing the O-ring down into the cavity recess. The O-ring is seated properly when it is flush with the fuel meter body casting surface.

✳✳WARNING

Do not try to reverse this procedure and install backup washer and O-ring after injector is located in the cavity. This will prevent the O-ring from seating in the recess.

9. Install the injector by using a pushing/twisting motion to the center nozzle O-ring in the bottom of the injector cavity and aligning the raised lug on the injector base with the notch case into the fuel meter body. Push down on the injector, making sure it is fully seated in the cavity. The injector installation is correct with the lug seated in the notch and the electrical terminals parallel to the throttle shaft in the throttle body.

10. Install the fuel meter cover, as outlined later in this section.

11. Attach the fuel injector electrical connector.

12. Install the air cleaner assembly.

13. Connect the negative battery cable.

Fuel Pressure Regulator/Compensator

REMOVAL & INSTALLATION

▶ See Figures 36 and 37

1. Properly relieve the fuel system pressure, then disconnect the negative battery cable.

2. Remove air cleaner.

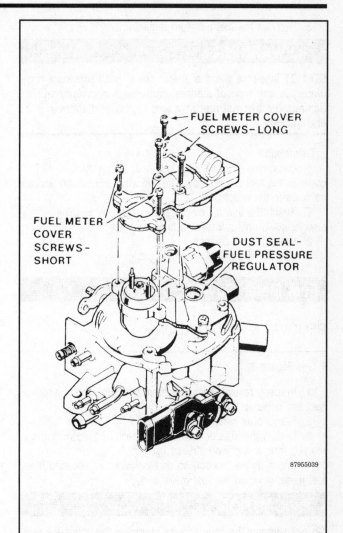

Fig. 36 Note the location of the two short screws on the fuel meter cover/regulator assembly for installation purposes

3. Detach the injector electrical connector by squeezing on the two tabs and pulling straight up.

4. Unfasten the five screws securing fuel meter cover to fuel meter body. Make sure to note the location of the two short screws during removal.

✳✳CAUTION

Do not remove the four screws securing the pressure regulator to the fuel meter cover. The fuel pressure regulator includes a large spring under heavy tension which, if accidentally released, could cause personal injury. The fuel meter cover is only serviced as a complete assembly and includes the fuel pressure regulator preset and plugged at the factory.

5. Remove the fuel pressure regulator.

✳✳WARNING

DO NOT immerse the fuel meter cover (with pressure regulator) in any type of cleaner. Immersion in cleaner will damage the internal fuel pressure regulator diaphragms and gaskets.

To install:

6. Using new gaskets and dust seal, attach the fuel meter cover to the fuel meter body. The two short screws are located adjacent to the injector.

7. Attach the injector electrical connector by pushing straight down until it is seated firmly in place.

8. Install the air cleaner.

9. Connect the negative battery cable.

Fuel Meter Cover

REMOVAL & INSTALLATION

▶ See Figure 36

1. Properly relieve the fuel system pressure, then disconnect the negative battery cable.

2. Remove air cleaner.

3. Detach the injector electrical connector by squeezing on the two tabs and pulling straight up.

4. Unfasten the five screws and lockwashers securing the fuel meter cover to the fuel meter body.

✳✳CAUTION

Do not remove the four screws securing the pressure regulator to the fuel meter cover. The fuel pressure regulator includes a large spring under heavy tension which, if accidentally released, could cause personal injury. The fuel

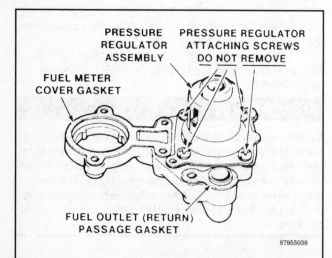

Fig. 37 When removing the fuel pressure regulator, DO NOT remove the four regulator attaching screws

meter cover is only serviced as a complete assembly and includes the fuel pressure regulator preset and plugged at the factory.

5. Lift off the fuel meter cover (including the fuel pressure regulator assembly).

6. Discard the fuel outlet passage gasket. Leave the fuel meter cover gasket in place on the fuel meter body.

7. Remove the sealing ring (dust seal) for the base of the fuel pressure regulator from the fuel meter body.

To install:

8. Install a new dust deal fuel the fuel pressure regulator, into the recess on the fuel meter body.

9. Position a new fuel return passage gasket on the fuel meter cover. Install a new fuel meter gasket on the fuel meter body.

10. Install the fuel meter cover, making sure the pressure regulator dust seal and cover gaskets are in place. Apply a suitable thread locking compound to the threads of the cover attaching screws. Install the attaching screws and lockwasher. The two short screws go next to the fuel injector. Tighten the screws to 28 inch lbs. (3 Nm).

11. Attach the injector electrical connector by pushing straight down until it is seated firmly in place.

12. Install the air cleaner.

13. Connect the negative battery cable.

Fuel Meter Body

REMOVAL & INSTALLATION

▶ See Figure 38

1. Properly relieve the fuel system pressure.

2. Disconnect the negative battery cable.

3. Remove the air cleaner assembly.

4. Remove the fuel inlet and outlet nuts and gaskets from fuel meter body.

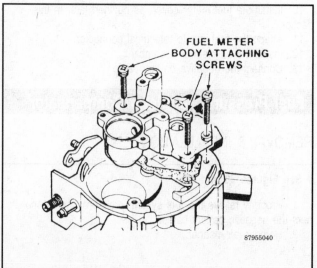

Fig. 38 The fuel meter body is secured by three screws

5. Unfasten three screws and lockwashers, then remove the fuel meter body from the throttle body assembly.

➡**The air cleaner stud must have been removed previously.**

6. Remove and discard the fuel meter body insulator gasket.

To install:

7. Install a new fuel meter body insulator gasket. Place the throttle body assembly in a suitable holding fixture to avoid damaging the throttle valve.

➡**The gasket is installed correctly when the cut-out portions of the gasket match the openings in the throttle body assembly.**

8. Position the fuel meter body on the insulator gasket. Apply the thread locking compound, supplied in the service kit, to the threads on the three fuel meter body attaching screw, following the manufacturers directions.

9. Install the fuel meter body attaching screws and lockwasher, then tighten to 35 inch lbs. (4 Nm).

10. Install the fuel feed and return nut and new gaskets in the fuel meter body. Tighten the nut to 21 ft. lbs. (29 Nm).

11. The remainder of installation is the reverse of the removal procedure.

MODEL 700 THROTTLE BODY INJECTION (TBI) SYSTEM

System Description

▶ See Figures 39 and 40

➡**The Model 700 throttle body system is used on the 1987-91 2.0L OHC (non-turbo) and the 1987-91 2.0L and 2.2L OHV engines.**

The Throttle Body Injection (TBI) system is an electronic fuel metering system in which the amount of fuel delivered by the injector is determined by the Electronic Control Module (ECM). This small, on-board microcomputer monitors various engine and vehicle conditions to calculate the fuel delivery time (pulse width) of the injector. The fuel pulse may be modified by the ECM to account for special operating conditions, such as cranking, cold starting, altitude, acceleration, and deceleration.

The TBI system provides a means of fuel distribution for controlling exhaust emissions within legislated limits. The TBI system, by precisely controlling the air/fuel mixture under all operating conditions, provides as near as possible complete combustion.

In order to regulate the fuel delivery in such an efficient manner, the ECM receives electrical inputs from various sensors about engine operating conditions. An oxygen sensor in the main exhaust stream functions to provide feedback information to the ECM regarding oxygen content in the exhaust. The ECM uses this information from the oxygen sensor, and other sensors, in modifying fuel delivery to achieve, as near as possible, an ideal air/fuel ratio of 14.7:1. This air/fuel ratio allows the 3-way catalytic converter to be more efficient in the conversion process of reducing exhaust emissions while, at the same time, providing acceptable levels of driveability and fuel economy.

The TBI unit is made up of 2 major casting assemblies: (1) a throttle body with a valve to control airflow and (2) a fuel body assembly with an integral pressure regulator and fuel injector to supply the required fuel. A device to control idle speed (IAC) and a device to provide information about throttle valve position (TPS) are included as part of the TBI unit.

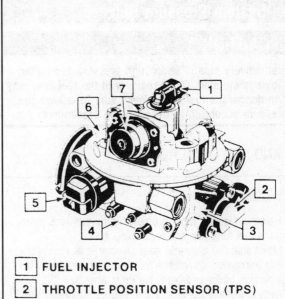

1	FUEL INJECTOR
2	THROTTLE POSITION SENSOR (TPS)
3	THROTTLE BODY ASSEMBLY
4	TUBE MODULE ASSEMBLY
5	IDLE AIR CONTROL (IAC) VALVE
6	FUEL METER ASSEMBLY
7	PRESSURE REGULATOR COVER ASSEMBLY

87955043

Fig. 39 Model 700 TBI unit and integral components

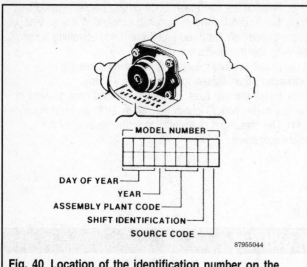

Fig. 40 Location of the identification number on the model 700 TBI units

Fuel System Pressure Release

✳✳CAUTION

The fuel delivery pipe is under high pressure even after the engine is stopped. Direct removal of the fuel line, may result in dangerous fuel spray. Make sure to release the fuel pressure according to the following procedures:

2.0L AND 2.2L OHV ENGINES

1987 Vehicles

1. Release the fuel vapor pressure in the fuel tank by removing the fuel tank cap and reinstalling it.
2. Make sure the transaxle gear selector is in Park, for automatic transaxles, or Neutral, for manual transaxles, then set the parking brake and block the drive wheels.
3. Detach the fuel pump at the rear body connector and wait until the engine stops.
4. Start the engine and allow it to run a few seconds until it runs out of fuel.
5. Once the engine is stopped, crank it for 3 seconds to dissipate the fuel pressure in the lines.

1988-91 Vehicles

1. Disconnect the negative battery cable.
2. Release the fuel vapor pressure in the fuel tank by removing the fuel tank cap and reinstalling it.
3. The internal constant bleed feature of the TBI Models 700 on these vehicles, relieves the fuel pump system pressure when the engine is turned **OFF** and no further pressure relive procedure is required.

2.0L OHC ENGINE

1987-90 Vehicles

1. Release the fuel vapor pressure in the fuel tank by removing the fuel tank cap and reinstalling it.
2. Remove the fuel pump fuse from the fuse block.
3. Start the engine and allow it to run a few seconds until it runs out of fuel.
4. Once the engine is stopped, crank it for about 3 seconds to dissipate the fuel pressure in the lines.
5. If the fuel pressure can't be released in the above manner because the engine failed to run, disconnect the negative battery cable, cover the union bolt of the fuel line with an absorbent rag and loosen the union bolt slowly to release the fuel pressure gradually.
6. When the pressure is relieved and the necessary service is complete, return the fuse to the fuse block.

1991 Vehicles

1. Disconnect the negative battery cable.
2. Release the fuel vapor pressure in the fuel tank by removing the fuel tank cap and reinstalling it.
3. The internal constant bleed feature of this Model 700 TBI unit relieves the fuel pump system pressure when the engine is turned **OFF** and no further pressure relive procedure is required.

Fuel Pump

TESTING

1. Turn the ignition to the **OFF** position.
2. Make sure the fuel tank quantity is sufficient.
3. Install pressure gauge J 29658-B or BT-8205 or equivalent to the fuel line.
4. Apply battery voltage to the fuel pump test connector using a 10 amp fused jumper wire.
5. Note the fuel pressure which should be 9-13 psi. (18-26 kPa).

REMOVAL & INSTALLATION

▶ See Figure 41

1. Properly relieve the fuel system pressure.
2. Disconnect the negative battery cable.
3. Raise and safely support the vehicle.
4. Remove the fuel tank, as outlined later in this section.
5. Remove the fuel tank sending unit and pump assembly by turning the cam lock ring counterclockwise. Lift the assembly from the fuel tank, then remove the fuel pump from the fuel level sending unit.
6. Pull the fuel pump up into the attaching hose or pulsator while pulling outward away from the bottom support. After the pump is clear of the bottom support, pull the pump assembly out of the rubber connector or pulsator for removal.

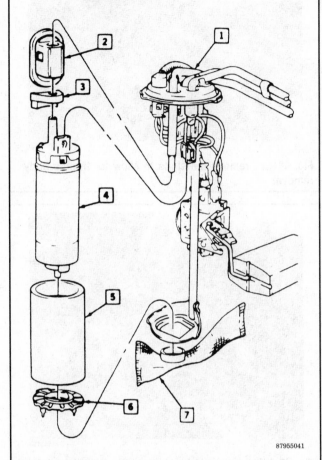

1. FUEL TANK METER ASSY.
2. PULSATOR
3. BUMPER
4. FUEL PUMP
5. SOUND ISOLATOR SLEEVE
6. SOUND INSULATOR
7. FILTER

87955041

Fig. 41 Exploded view of the sending unit and fuel pump assembly

7. Inspect the fuel pump attaching hose for any signs of deterioration, and replace as necessary. Also, make sure to check the rubber sound insulator at the bottom of pump and replace if required.

To install:

8. Position, then push the fuel pump into the attaching hose.

9. Using a new O-ring, install the fuel level sending unit and pump assembly into the tank assembly.

✳✳WARNING

Be careful not to fold over or twist the strainer when installing the sending unit as it will restrict fuel flow. Also, be careful the strainer does not block full travel of the float arm.

10. Position the cam lock over the assembly and lock by turning clockwise. Attach the electrical connector.

11. Install the fuel tank.

12. Connect the negative battery cable, then check the system for proper operation.

Throttle Body

REMOVAL & INSTALLATION

▶ **See Figures 42, 43, 44, 45, 46, 47 and 48**

1. Properly relieve the fuel system pressure.
2. Disconnect the negative battery cable.
3. Remove the air cleaner assembly and gasket.
4. Tag and detach the electrical connectors at the fuel injector, Idle Air Control (IAC) valve, and Throttle Position (TP) sensor.
5. Remove the grommet with the wires from the fuel meter body.
6. Tag and disconnect the vacuum lines at the rear of the throttle body.

87955100

Fig. 42 Be sure to tag the connectors and hoses as you remove them, so they don't get mixed up during installation

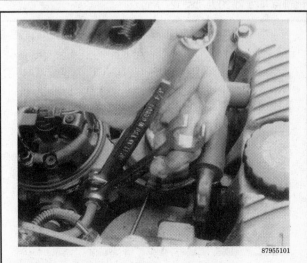

87955101

Fig. 43 Always use a back-up wrench when disconnecting fuel lines to avoid distorting them

Fig. 44 Carefully remove, then discard the fuel line O-rings and replace with new ones for installation

7. Detach the throttle cable, transaxle control cable and cruise control cable (if so equipped) at the TBI unit.

8. Disconnect the fuel feed and return lines. Use tool J 29698-A, or equivalent back-up wrench, on the TBI fuel nuts to prevent them from turning. Remove and discard the fuel line O-rings.

9. Unfasten the retaining bolts and/or studs, then remove the TBI unit. Remove and discard the TBI flange gasket.

➡Stuff a clean rag in the manifold opening to avoid letting any dirt or other debris enter the engine.

10. Clean the gasket mating surfaces on the throttle body and intake manifold.

To install:

11. Position a new flange gasket, then install the TBI unit. Install the attaching bolts/studs and tighten to 12-16 ft. lbs. (17-22 Nm).

12. Place new O-rings on the fuel feed and return lines, then connect the fuel lines. Use tool J 29698-A or equivalent fuel line wrench, to prevent the lines from turning, and tighten the line nuts to 20 ft. lbs. (27 Nm).

Fig. 45 Unfasten the studs securing the throttle body, then . . .

Fig. 46 . . . remove the studs to allow for throttle body removal

Fig. 47 Lift the throttle body assembly from the intake manifold

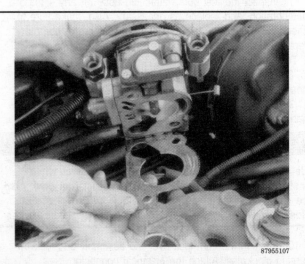

Fig. 48 Remove and discard the throttle body flange gasket

13. Attach the vacuum lines at the rear of the TBI, as tagged during removal.

14. Connect the throttle, transaxle control, and cruise control cables.

15. Attach the electrical connectors, making sure they are fully seated and latched.

16. Tighten the fuel filler cap, if loosened during fuel pressure relief procedure.

17. Connect the negative battery cable, then with the engine **OFF**, check to see that the accelerator pedal is free by depressing, then releasing it. Turn the ignition switch to the **ON** position for 2 seconds, then turn to the **OFF** position for 10 seconds. Again turn the switch to the **ON** position and check for fuel leaks.

18. Install the air cleaner assembly and gasket.

19. Reset the Idle Air Control (IAC) valve pintle position as follows:

   a. Block the drive wheels and apply the parking brake.

   b. Start the engine, and hold the engine speed above 2,000 rpm. Ground the diagnostic test terminal (ALDL) for 10 seconds, then remove the ground.

   c. Turn the ignition **OFF**, then restart the engine and check for proper idle operation.

Fuel Injector

REMOVAL & INSTALLATION

▶ See Figures 49, 50, 51, 52, 53 and 54

❊❊WARNING

When removing the injectors, be careful not to damage the electrical connector pins (on top of the injector), the injector fuel filter and the nozzle. The fuel injector is serviced as a complete assembly ONLY. The injector is an electrical component and should not be immersed in any kind of cleaner.

1. Properly relieve the fuel system pressure, as outlined earlier in this section.

2. Remove the air cleaner.

3. Detach the fuel injector electrical connector.

4. Remove the injector retainer screw and retainer.

5. Using a smooth object such as a fulcrum, place the blade of a suitable prytool under the ridge opposite the connector end and carefully pry the injector out.

6. Remove and discard the upper and lower O-rings from the injector and in the fuel injector cavity.

7. Inspect the filter for evidence of dirt and/or contamination.

To install:

➡Be sure to replace the injector with an identical part. Injectors from other models can fit in the Model 700, but are calibrated for different flow rates. There is a part number located on the top of the injector

8. Lubricate the new upper and lower O-rings with clean engine oil and place them on the injector. Make sure the

Fig. 49 Detach the fuel injector electrical connector

Fig. 50 Unfasten the injector retaining screw

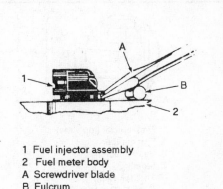

1 Fuel injector assembly
2 Fuel meter body
A Screwdriver blade
B Fulcrum

Fig. 51 Use a fulcrum to aid in prying the fuel injector out

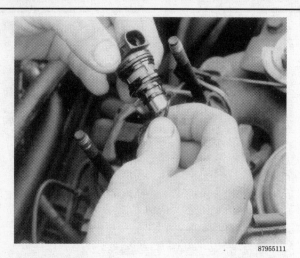

Fig. 52 Remove and discard the injector O-rings and replace with new ones during installation

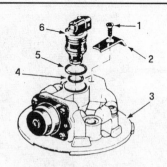

1 Injector retainer screw
2 Injector retainer
3 Fuel meter assembly
4 Fuel injector o-ring (lower)
5 Fuel injector o-ring (upper)
6 Fuel injector assembly

Fig. 53 Always replace the O-rings with new ones

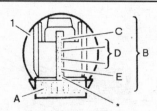

1 Fuel injector (top view)
A Part number
B Build number
C Month
  1-9 (Jan-Sept)
  O, N, D (Oct, Nov, Dec)
D Day
E Year
* Indicates high dynamic range

Fig. 54 To ensure that you are using the correct part, check the fuel injector part number

upper O-ring is in the groove and the lower one is flush up against the filter.

9. Install the fuel injector assembly as follows:
   a. Position the injector in the fuel meter body with the electrical connector facing the cut-out for the wire grommet.
   b. Push the injector down to seat it in the cavity.

➡**Make sure the electrical connector end on the injector is facing in the general direction to the cut-out in the fuel meter body for the wire grommet.**

10. Install the injector retainer, using appropriate thread locking compound on the retainer attaching screw. Tighten to 27 inch lbs. (3 Nm).
11. Tighten the fuel filler cap, if loosened during fuel pressure relief procedure.
12. Connect the negative battery cable, then with the engine **OFF**, check to see that the accelerator pedal is free by depressing, then releasing it. Turn the ignition switch to the **ON** position for 2 seconds, then turn to the **OFF** position for 10 seconds. Again turn the switch to the **ON** position and check for fuel leaks.
13. Install the air cleaner assembly and gasket.

Fuel Pressure Regulator

REMOVAL & INSTALLATION

▶ **See Figure 55**

1. Properly relieve the fuel system pressure.
2. Disconnect the negative battery cable.
3. Remove the air cleaner and gasket, then discard the gasket.
4. While keeping the pressure regulator compressed, unfasten the four pressure regulator attaching screws.

✳✳CAUTION

The pressure regulator contains a large spring under heavy compression. Use care when removing the screws to prevent personal injury.

5. Remove the pressure regulator cover assembly.
6. Remove the spring seat and the pressure regulator diaphragm assembly.

➡**To prevent leaks, the pressure regulator diaphragm assembly must be replaced whenever the cover is removed.**

7. Inspect the pressure regulator valve seat for pitting, nicks or irregularities.
To install:
8. Install the pressure regulator diaphragm assembly, making sure it is seated in the groove in the fuel meter body.
9. Install the regulator spring seat and spring into the cover assembly.
10. Hold the cover in place to prevent the diaphragm from slipping out of the groove, install the cover assembly over the diaphragm.
11. While maintaining pressure on the regulator spring, install the four screw assemblies that have been coated with

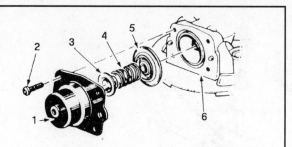

1 Pressure regulator cover assembly
2 Pressure regulator attaching screw
3 Spring seat
4 Pressure regulator spring
5 Diaphragm assembly
6 Fuel meter assembly

87955048

Fig. 55 Exploded view of the pressure regulator assembly

Loctite® 262, or equivalent thread locking compound. Tighten the screws to 21 inch lbs. (2.4 Nm).

12. Tighten the fuel filler cap, if loosened during fuel pressure relief procedure.

13. Connect the negative battery cable, then with the engine **OFF**, check to see that the accelerator pedal is free by depressing, then releasing it. Turn the ignition switch to the **ON** position for 2 seconds, then turn to the **OFF** position for 10 seconds. Again turn the switch to the **ON** position and check for fuel leaks.

14. Install the air cleaner assembly and gasket.

Tube Module Assembly

REMOVAL & INSTALLATION

▶ See Figure 56

1. Disconnect the negative battery cable.
2. Remove the air cleaner assembly.
3. Tag and disconnect the necessary vacuum hoses.
4. Unfasten the tube module attaching screws, then remove the module and gasket. Discard the gasket, then clean off the gasket mating surfaces.
   To install:
5. Position a new tube module gasket, then install the tube module assembly. If there is no threadlocking material remain-

ing on the tube module attaching screws, apply Loctite® 262, or equivalent. Tighten the screws to 27 inch lbs. (3 Nm).

6. Connect the vacuum lines as tagged during removal.
7. Install the air cleaner assembly.
8. Connect the negative battery cable.

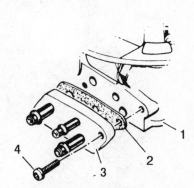

1. Throttle body assembly
2. Tube module assembly gasket
3. Tube module assembly
4. Tube module screw

87955050

Fig. 56 The tube module assembly is mounted to the throttle body

BOTTOM FEED PORT (BFP) INJECTION SYSTEM

System Description

▶ See Figure 57

➡ **The Bottom Feed Port (BFP) injection system is used on the 1992-96 2.2L OHV (VIN 4) engines.**

The function of the fuel metering system is to deliver the correct amount of fuel to the engine under all operating conditions. In this system, fuel is delivered to the engine by individ- ual bottom feed type multi-port fuel injectors mounted in the lower intake manifold near each cylinder.

The computer control module, ECM or PCM depending upon vehicle year, pulses the fuel injectors in pairs. Alternate pairs are pulsed every 180° of crankshaft revolution. This is called Alternating Synchronous Double Fire (ASDF) injection. The ECM or PCM uses two injector driver circuits, each controlling a pair of injectors. The current in each circuit is allowed to climb to a peak of 4 amps and then is reduced to 1 amp to hold the injector open. This happens very quickly.

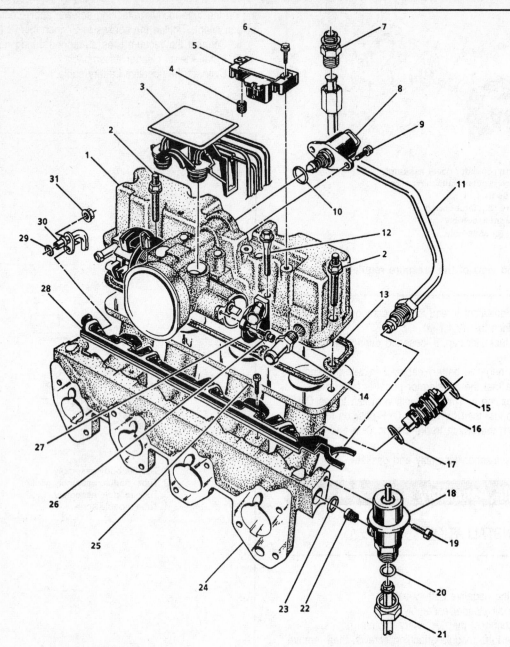

1	MANIFOLD ASM - UPPER	16	INJECTOR ASM - (BOTTOM FEED) MFI FUEL
2	STUD - UPPER INLET MANIFOLD	17	O-RING - LOWER
3	HARNESS ASM - EGR VALVE AND	18	REGULATOR ASM - FUEL PRESSURE
	FUEL PRESSURE REGULATOR VACUUM	19	SCREW - FUEL PRESSURE REGULATOR
4	SEAL - MAP SENSOR		ATTACHING
5	SENSOR - MANIFOLD ABSOLUTE PRESSURE	20	O-RING - FUEL RETURN LINE
	(MAP)	21	PIPE ASM - FUEL INJECTOR FUEL RETURN
6	BOLT - MAP SENSOR ATTACHING	22	SCREEN - FILTER (IF SO EQUIPPED)
7	FITTING AND WASHER ASM	23	O-RING - FUEL INLET FITTING
8	VALVE ASM - IDLE AIR CONTROL (IAC)	24	MANIFOLD ASM - LOWER
9	SCREW - IAC VALVE ATTACHING	25	SCREW - INJECTOR RETAINER ATTACHING
10	O-RING - IAC VALVE	26	SCREW - TP SENSOR ATTACHING
11	TUBE ASM - EGR TRANSPORT	27	SENSOR - THROTTLE POSITION (TP)
12	BOLT - UPPER INLET MANIFOLD	28	RETAINER - INJECTOR
13	GASKET - UPPER INLET MANIFOLD	29	O-RING - FUEL FEED LINE
14	FITTING - POWER BRAKE	30	PIPE ASM - FUEL INJECTION FUEL FEED
15	O-RING- FUEL INJECTOR	31	NUT - FUEL FEED

87955055

Fig. 57 Exploded view of the BFP injection system components

The main control sensor of this system is the Oxygen (O_2) sensor, located in the exhaust manifold. This sensor indicates to the computer control module how much oxygen is in the exhaust gas, and the ECM/PCM changes the air/fuel ratio to the engine by controlling the fuel injectors. The best mixture to keep exhaust emissions to a minimum is 14.7:1 which allows the catalytic converter to operate most efficiently. Because of the constant measuring and adjusting of the air/fuel ratio, the fuel injection system is called a "Closed Loop" system.

Fuel System Pressure Relief

1992 VEHICLES

1. Loosen the full filler cap to relieve the tank vapor pressure. Leave the cap loose at this time.
2. Raise and support the vehicle safely.
3. Detach the fuel pump electrical connector.
4. Carefully lower the vehicle.
5. Start the engine and run until the fuel supply remaining in the fuel pipes is consumed. Engage the starter for 3 seconds to assure relief of any remaining pressure in the lines.
6. Raise and support the vehicle safely.
7. Attach the fuel pump electrical connector.
8. Carefully lower the vehicle.
9. Tighten the fuel filler cap.
10. Disconnect the negative battery cable to avoid possible fuel discharge if an accidental attempt is made to start the engine.

1993-96 VEHICLES

1. Loosen the fuel filler cap to relieve tank pressure (do not tighten at this time).
2. Remove the fuel pump fuse from the fuse block.
3. Start the engine and run until the fuel supply remaining in the fuel pipes is consumed. Engage the starter for 3 seconds to assure relief of any remaining pressure.
4. Replace the fuel pump fuse in the fuse block.
5. Disconnect the negative battery cable to avoid possible fuel discharge if an accidental attempt is made to start the engine.

Bottom Feed Port Fuel Injectors

REMOVAL & INSTALLATION

▶ See Figure 58

❋❋WARNING

Any time the injectors are removed for service, always remove the fuel pressure regulator to drain excess fuel, and prevent fuel from entering the engine cylinders. Flooded cylinders could result in engine damage.

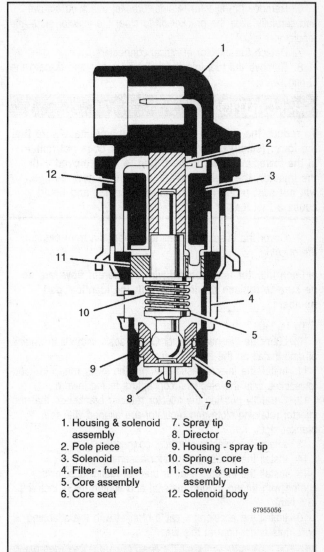

1. Housing & solenoid assembly
2. Pole piece
3. Solenoid
4. Filter - fuel inlet
5. Core assembly
6. Core seat
7. Spray tip
8. Director
9. Housing - spray tip
10. Spring - core
11. Screw & guide assembly
12. Solenoid body

87955056

Fig. 58 Cross-section view of a bottom feed fuel injector

1. Relieve the fuel system pressure as outlined earlier.
2. Disconnect the negative battery cable.
3. Remove the upper manifold assembly.

❋❋CAUTION

To reduce the chance of personal injury, cover the fuel line connections with a shop towel, when disconnecting.

4. Disconnect the fuel return line retaining bracket nut and move the return line away from the regulator.
5. Remove the pressure regulator assembly.

❋❋WARNING

Do not try to remove the injectors by lifting up on the injector retaining bracket while the injectors are still installed in the in the bracket slots or damage to the bracket and/or injectors could result. Do not attempt to remove the bracket without first removing the pressure regulator.

6. Remove the injector retainer bracket attaching screws and carefully slide the bracket off to clear the injector slots and regulator.

7. Detach the injector electrical connectors.

8. Remove the fuel injector(s), then remove and discard the O-ring seals.

✳✳CAUTION

To reduce the risk fire and personal injury, make sure that the lower (small) O-ring of each injector does not remain in the lower manifold. If the O-ring is not removed with the injector, the replacement injector, with new O-rings, will not seat properly in the injector socket and could cause a fuel leak.

9. Cover the injector sockets to prevent dirt from entering the opening.

➡**Each injector is calibrated with a different flow rate so be sure to replace the injector with the identical part numbers.**

To install:

10. Lubricate the new injector O-ring seals with clean engine oil and install on the injector assembly.

11. Install the injector assembly into the lower manifold injector socket, with the electrical connectors facing inward.

12. Carefully position the injector retainer bracket so that the injector retaining slots and regulator are aligned with the bracket slots.

13. Attach the injector electrical connectors.

14. Install the pressure regulator assembly.

15. Install the injector retainer bracket retaining screws, coated with thread locking material and tighten to 31 inch lbs. (3.5 Nm).

16. Install the accelerator cable bracket with the attaching bolts/nuts finger-tight at this time.

✳✳WARNING

The accelerator bracket must be aligned with the accelerator cam to prevent cable wear, which could result in cable breakage.

17. Align the accelerator bracket as follows:

a. Place a steel rule across the bore of the throttle body, with one end in contact with the accelerator bracket.

b. Adjust the accelerator bracket to obtain a $^{25}/_{64}$ in. (9-11mm) gap between the bracket and the throttle body.

c. Tighten the top bolt first and tighten all bolts/nuts to 18 ft. lbs. (25 Nm).

18. Tighten the fuel filer cap.

19. Connect the negative battery cable and turn the ignition **ON** for 2 seconds, **OFF** for 10 seconds, then **ON** and check for fuel leaks.

20. Install the air intake duct.

Fuel Pressure Regulator

REMOVAL & INSTALLATION

▶ **See Figures 57 and 59**

1. Relieve the fuel system pressure as outlined earlier.

2. Disconnect the negative battery cable.

3. Remove the vacuum hose from the regulator.

4. Place a rag under the connection and remove the fuel return pipe clamp.

5. Remove the fuel return pipe and O-ring from the regulator. Discard the O-ring.

6. Unfasten the pressure regulator bracket attaching screw, then remove the pressure regulator assembly and O-ring. Discard the O-ring.

To install:

7. Lubricate a new pressure regulator O-ring with clean engine oil, then install on the pressure regulator.

8. Install the pressure regulator assembly onto the manifold.

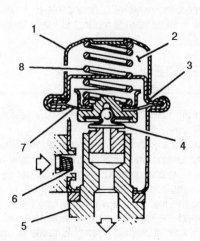

1. Cover
2. Vacuum chamber
   (vacuum source tube not shown)
3. Seal - O-ring
4. Valve - fuel pressure regulator
5. Base assembly
6. Filter - screen (if equipped)
7. Diaphragm
8. Spring

87955057

Fig. 59 Cross-section view of the fuel pressure regulator assembly

9. Install the pressure regulator bracket attaching screw coated with the appropriate thread locking material and tighten to 31 inch lbs. (3.5 Nm).

10. Connect the vacuum hose to the regulator.

11. Lubricate a new fuel return pipe O-ring with clean engine oil, then install on the end of the pipe.

12. Install the fuel return pipe to the pressure regulator and tighten the attaching nut to 22 inch lbs. (30 Nm).

13. Fasten the fuel return pipe clamp attaching nut to the lower manifold assembly.

14. Tighten the fuel filler cap.

15. Connect the negative battery cable and turn the ignition **ON** for 2 seconds, **OFF** for 10 seconds, then **ON** and check for fuel leaks.

MULTI-PORT (MFI) & SEQUENTIAL (SFI) FUEL INJECTION SYSTEMS

General Information

On 1985-94 2.8 and 3.1L and 1995 2.3L engines, the multiport fuel injection (MFI) system is available. The MFI system is controlled by a computer control module (ECM or PCM) which monitors engine operations and generates output signals to provide the correct air/fuel mixture, ignition timing and engine idle speed control. Input to the control unit is provided by an oxygen sensor, coolant temperature sensor, detonation sensor, hot film air mass sensor and throttle position sensor. The ECM/PCM also receives information concerning engine rpm, road speed, transmission gear position, power steering and air conditioning.

On 1.8L and 2.0L OHC, turbocharged models and 1996 2.4L engines, a sequential port fuel injection system (SFI) is used for more precise fuel control. With SFI, metered fuel is timed and injected sequentially through injectors into individual cylinder ports. Each cylinder receives one injection per working cycle (every two revolutions), just prior to the opening of the intake valve. The main difference between the two types of fuel injection systems is the manner in which fuel is injected. In the multiport system, all injectors work simultaneously, injecting half the fuel charge each engine revolution. The control units are different for SFI and MFI systems, but most other components are similar. In addition, the SFI system incorporates a new Computer Controlled Coil Ignition system that uses an electronic coil module that replaces the conventional distributor and coil used on most engines. An electronic spark control (ESC) is used to adjust the spark timing.

Both systems use Bosch injectors, one at each intake port, rather than the single injector found on the earlier throttle body system. The injectors are mounted on a fuel rail and are activated by a signal from the electronic control module. The injector is a solenoid-operated valve which remains open depending on the width of the electronic pulses (length of the signal) from the computer control module (ECM/PCM); the longer the open time, the more fuel is injected. In this manner, the air/fuel mixture can be precisely controlled for maximum performance with minimum emissions.

Fuel is pumped from the tank by a high pressure fuel pump, located inside the fuel tank. It is a positive displacement roller vane pump. The impeller serves as a vapor separator and precharges the high pressure assembly. A pressure regulator maintains 28-36 psi (28-50 psi on turbocharged engines) in the fuel line to the injectors and the excess fuel is fed back to the tank. On MFI systems, a fuel accumulator is used to dampen the hydraulic line hammer in the system created when all injectors open simultaneously.

The Mass Air Flow (MAF) sensor is used to measure the mass of air that is drawn into the engine cylinders. It is located just ahead of the air throttle in the intake system and consists of a heated film which measures the mass of air, rather than just the volume. A resistor is used to measure the temperature of the incoming air and the air mass sensor maintains the temperature of the film at 75° above ambient temperature. As the ambient (outside) air temperature rises, more energy is required to maintain the heated film at the higher temperature and the control unit uses this difference in required energy to calculate the mass of the incoming air. The control unit uses this information to determine the duration of fuel injection pulse, timing and EGR.

The throttle body incorporates an Idle Air Control (IAC) valve that provides for a bypass channel through which air can flow. It consists of an orifice and pintle which is controlled by the ECM through a stepper motor. The IAC provides air flow for idle and allows additional air during cold start until the engine reaches operating temperature. As the engine temperature rises, the opening through which air passes is slowly closed.

The throttle position sensor (TPS) provides the control unit with information on throttle position, in order to determine injector pulse width and hence correct mixture. The TPS is connected to the throttle shaft on the throttle body and consists of a potentiometer with one end connected to a 5 volt source from the ECM and the other to ground. A third wire is connected to the ECM to measure the voltage output from the TPS which changes as the throttle valve angle is changed (accelerator pedal moves). At the closed throttle position, the output is low (approximately 0.4 volts); as the throttle valve opens, the output increases to a maximum 5 volts at wide open throttle (WOT). The TPS can be misadjusted open, shorted, or loose and if it is out of adjustment, the idle quality or WOT performance may be poor. A loose TPS can cause intermittent bursts of fuel from the injectors and an unstable idle because the ECM thinks the throttle is moving. This should cause a trouble code to be set. Once a trouble code is set, the ECM will use a preset value for TPS and some vehicle performance may return. A small amount of engine coolant is routed through the throttle assembly to prevent freezing inside the throttle bore during cold operation.

Relieving Fuel System Pressure

❊❊CAUTION

To reduce the risk of fire or personal injury, it is necessary to relieve the fuel system pressure before servicing the fuel system.

1.8L AND 2.0L OHC ENGINES

1983-84 Vehicles

1. Remove the fuel pump fuse from the fuse block.
2. Crank the engine. The engine will run until it runs out of fuel. Crank the engine again for 3 seconds making sure it is out of fuel.
3. Turn the ignition **OFF** and replace the fuse.

1985-90 Vehicles

1. Disconnect the negative battery cable.
2. Disconnect the fuel filler cap.
3. Connect gauge J-34730-1 or equivalent, to the fuel pressure connection. Wrap a cloth around the fitting to absorb any fuel leakage.
4. Install the bleed hose into an approved container and open the valve to bleed system pressure.

1992 2.0L (VIN H) ENGINES

1. Remove the fuel pump fuse from the fuse block.
2. Crank the engine. The engine will run until it runs out of fuel. Crank the engine again for 3 seconds making sure it is out of fuel.
3. Turn the ignition **OFF** and replace the fuse.

2.3L AND 2.4L ENGINES

1. Loosen the fuel filler cap to relieve tank pressure.
2. Raise and safely support the vehicle.
3. Detach the fuel pump electrical connector.
4. Carefully lower the vehicle.
5. Start the engine and run until the fuel supply in the fuel pipes is consumed. Engage the starter for about 3 seconds to assure relief of the line pressure.
6. Raise and safely support the vehicle, then attach the fuel pump electrical connector.
7. Carefully lower the vehicle, then disconnect the negative battery cable to avoid possible fuel discharge if an accidental attempt is made to start the engine.
8. Tighten the fuel filler cap when service is complete.

2.8L AND 3.1L ENGINES

1. Disconnect the negative battery cable.
2. Loosen the fuel filler cap to relieve tank pressure.
3. Connect gauge J-34730-1, or equivalent, to the fuel pressure connection. Wrap a cloth around the fitting to absorb any fuel leakage.
4. Install the bleed hose into an approved container and open the valve to bleed system pressure.

5. Drain any fuel still in the gauge into an approved container.

Fuel Pump

TESTING

1.8L and 2.0L OHC Engines

1984-85 VEHICLES

1. Connect pressure gauge J-34370-1, or equivalent, to fuel pressure test point on the fuel rail. Wrap a rag around the pressure tap to absorb any leakage that may occur when installing the gauge.
2. Turn the ignition **OFF** for 10 seconds and the A/C **OFF**.
3. Turn the ignition **ON** and the fuel pump should run for about 2 seconds.
4. Note the fuel pressure after the pump stops. The pressure should be 30-40 psi (210-276 kPa) and hold steady.

1986 VEHICLES

1. Connect pressure gauge J-34370-1, or equivalent, to fuel pressure test point on the fuel rail. Wrap a rag around the pressure tap to absorb any leakage that may occur when installing the gauge.
2. Using a fused jumper, run the fuel pump by applying 12 volts to the fuel pump test terminal for several seconds.
3. Note the fuel pressure after the pump stops. The pressure should be 30-40 psi (210-276 kPa) and hold steady.

1987-90 VEHICLES

1. Connect pressure gauge J-34370-1, or equivalent, to fuel pressure test point on the fuel rail. Wrap a rag around the pressure tap to absorb any leakage that may occur when installing the gauge.
2. Disconnect the vacuum hose from the pressure regulator.
3. Turn the ignition **OFF** for 10 seconds and the A/C **OFF**.
4. Turn the ignition **ON** and the fuel pump should run for about 2 seconds.
5. Note the fuel pressure after the pump stops. The pressure should be 35-38 psi (241-262 kPa) and hold steady.

2.8L and 3.1L Engines

1. Connect pressure gauge J-34370-1, or equivalent, to fuel pressure test point on the fuel rail. Wrap a rag around the pressure tap to absorb any leakage that may occur when installing the gauge.
2. Turn the ignition **OFF** for 10 seconds and the A/C **OFF**.
3. Turn the ignition **ON** and the fuel pump should run for about 2 seconds.
4. Note the fuel pressure after the pump stops. The pressure should be 40.5-47 psi (279-324 kPa) and hold steady.

REMOVAL & INSTALLATION

1983-91 Vehicles

▶ See Figure 60

1. Release the fuel system pressure.

✳✳CAUTION

To reduce the risk of fire or personal injury, it is necessary to relieve the fuel system pressure before servicing the fuel system. Refer to Fuel System Pressure Release procedure.

2. Disconnect the negative battery cable.
3. Raise and safely support the vehicle.
4. Drain and remove the fuel tank, as outlined later in this section.
5. Remove the fuel lever sending unit and pump assembly by turning the cam lock ring counterclockwise. Lift the assem-

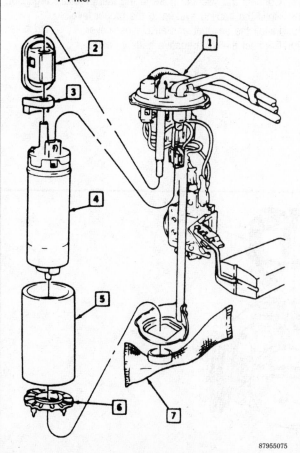

```
1  Fuel tank meter assy.
2  Pulsator
3  Bumper
4  Fuel pump
5  Sound isolator sleeve
6  Sound insulator
7  Filter
```

87955075

Fig. 60 View of the fuel pump and related components — 1983-91 vehicles

bly from the fuel tank and remove the fuel pump from the fuel level sending unit.

6. Pull the fuel pump up into the attaching hose or pulsator while pulling outward away from the bottom support. After the pump is clear of the bottom support, pull the pump assembly out of the rubber connector or pulsator for removal.

To install:

7. Position and push the pump into the attaching hose.
8. Install the fuel level sending unit and pump assembly into the tank assembly. Use new O-ring during reassembly.

✳✳WARNING

Be careful not to fold over or twist the strainer when installing the sending unit as it will restrict fuel flow. Also, be careful the strainer does not block full travel of the float arm.

9. Install the cam lock over the assembly and lock by turning clockwise.
10. Install the fuel tank.
11. Connect the negative battery cable.

1992-96 Vehicles

The electric fuel pumps on these vehicles are located as a part of the module sender assembly. For removal and installation information, please refer to the procedure located later in this section.

Throttle Body

REMOVAL & INSTALLATION

▶ See Figures 61, 62 and 63

➡The TP sensor and IAC valve should NOT come into contact with any type of solvent or cleanser, as this may cause damage.

1. Properly relieve the fuel system pressure.
2. Disconnect the negative battery cable.
3. Remove the air cleaner cover and air duct.
4. Partially drain the coolant to allow the coolant hoses at the throttle body to be removed.
5. Disconnect the vacuum hose from the fuel pressure regulator.
6. Detach the electrical connectors from the TP sensor and IAC valve.
7. Disconnect the throttle, transaxle control and cruise control (if equipped) cables.
8. Unfasten the throttle body attaching bolts, then loosen the throttle body from the intake manifold.
9. Disconnect the coolant hoses from the throttle body.
10. Detach the vacuum hose from the bottom of the throttle body.
11. Remove the throttle body and gasket. Discard the gasket.

To install:

12. Connect the vacuum hose to the bottom of the throttle body.
13. Fasten the coolant hoses to the throttle body.

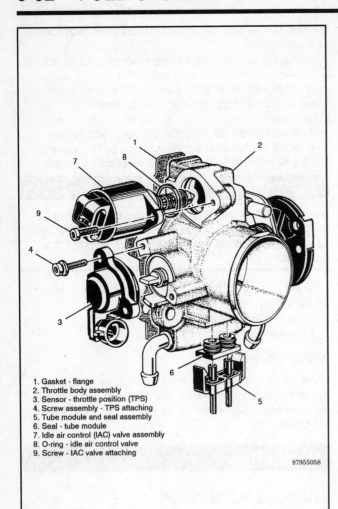

1. Gasket - flange
2. Throttle body assembly
3. Sensor - throttle position (TPS)
4. Screw assembly - TPS attaching
5. Tube module and seal assembly
6. Seal - tube module
7. Idle air control (IAC) valve assembly
8. O-ring - idle air control valve
9. Screw - IAC valve attaching

87955058

Fig. 61 View of the throttle body and integral components — 1992 2.0L (VIN H) engine shown

1 Intake manifold
2 Gasket
3 Throttle body assembly
4 Stud end bolt
5 Bolt

87955060

Fig. 63 Exploded view of the throttle body mounting

14. Position the throttle body, with a new gasket, against the manifold, then secure with the attaching bolts. Tighten the bolts to 11 ft. lbs. (15 Nm).

15. Fasten the throttle, cruise control and transaxle cables to the throttle body.

16. Attach the TP sensor and IAC valve electrical connectors.

17. Connect the vacuum hose to the fuel pressure regulator.

18. Refill the cooling system to the proper level.

19. Install the air duct and air cleaner cover.

20. Connect the the negative battery cable.

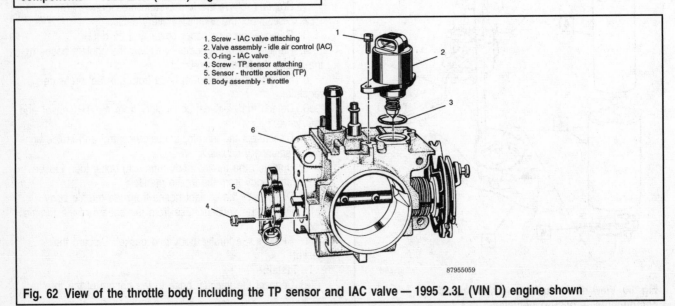

1. Screw - IAC valve attaching
2. Valve assembly - idle air control (IAC)
3. O-ring - IAC valve
4. Screw - TP sensor attaching
5. Sensor - throttle position (TP)
6. Body assembly - throttle

87955059

Fig. 62 View of the throttle body including the TP sensor and IAC valve — 1995 2.3L (VIN D) engine shown

Fuel Injectors

REMOVAL & INSTALLATION

1.8L, 2.0L, 2.3L and 2.4L OHC Engines

▶ See Figures 64, 65 and 66

❊❊WARNING

Use care in removing the fuel injectors to prevent damage to the electrical connector pins on the injector and the nozzle. The fuel injector is serviced as a complete assembly only and should not be immersed in any kind of cleaner.

1. Properly relieve fuel system pressure, as outlined earlier in this section.
2. Disconnect the negative battery cable.
3. Remove the throttle body from the intake manifold.
4. As outlined later in this section, remove the fuel rail.
5. Unfasten and discard the injector retaining clip, then remove the injector assembly. Remove and discard the O-rings from each end of the injector.
   To install:
6. Lubricate new O-rings with clean engine oil, the install on the injector.
7. Position a new injector retaining clip on the injector.
8. Install the injector assembly into the fuel rail injector socket, with the electrical connector facing inward toward the manifold. Push the socket in far enough to engage the retainer clip with the groove on the rail.
9. Install the fuel rail assembly and throttle body.
10. Connect the negative battery cable.

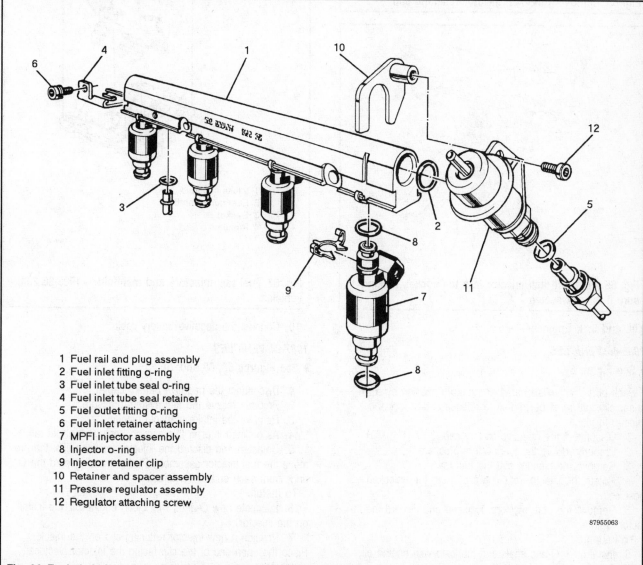

1 Fuel rail and plug assembly
2 Fuel inlet fitting o-ring
3 Fuel inlet tube seal o-ring
4 Fuel inlet tube seal retainer
5 Fuel outlet fitting o-ring
6 Fuel inlet retainer attaching
7 MPFI injector assembly
8 Injector o-ring
9 Injector retainer clip
10 Retainer and spacer assembly
11 Pressure regulator assembly
12 Regulator attaching screw

87955063

Fig. 64 Exploded view of the fuel injector, retaining clip and O-rings

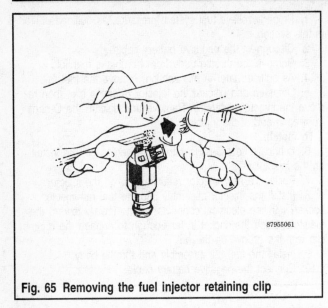

Fig. 65 Removing the fuel injector retaining clip

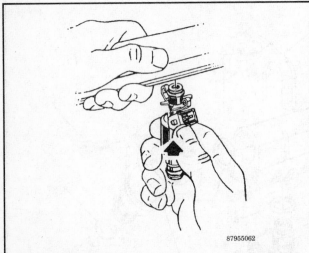

Fig. 66 Push the fuel injector into the socket, making sure it is fully seated

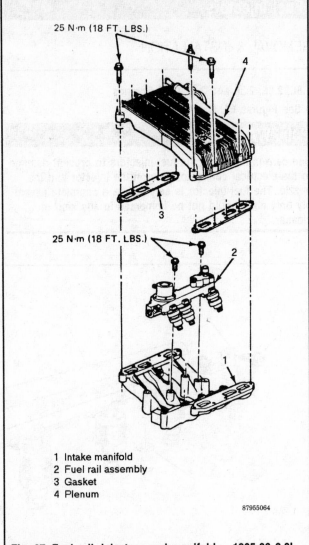

1 Intake manifold
2 Fuel rail assembly
3 Gasket
4 Plenum

Fig. 67 Fuel rail, injectors and manifold — 1985-86 2.8L vehicles

2.8L and 3.1L Engines

1985-86 VEHICLES

▶ See Figure 67

Each port injector is located and held in position by a retainer clip that must be rotated to release and/or lock the injector in place.

1. Disconnect the negative battery cable.
2. Properly relieve the fuel system pressure.
3. Remove the plenum and the fuel rail.
4. Rotate the injector retaining clip(s) the the unlocked position.
5. Remove the port injectors. Remove and discard the injector O-rings.

To install:

6. Install new O-ring seals and lubricate with engine oil.
7. Position the injectors to the fuel rail and pressure regulator assembly.
8. Rotate the injector retaining clips to the locking position.
9. Install the fuel rail and the plenum.

10. Connect the negative battery cable.

1987-94 VEHICLES

▶ See Figures 68, 69 and 70

1. Disconnect the negative battery cable.
2. Properly relieve the fuel system pressure.
3. Remove the intake manifold plenum.
4. As outlined later in this section, remove the fuel rail.
5. Unfasten and discard the injector retaining clip, then remove the fuel injector assembly. Remove and discard the O-rings from each end of the injector.

To install:

6. Lubricate new O-rings with clean engine oil, the install on the injector.
7. Position a new injector retaining clip on the injector. Place the open end of the clip facing the injector electrical connector.
8. Install the injector assembly into the fuel rail injector socket, with the electrical connector facing outward. Push it in far enough to engage the retainer clip with the machined slots on the rail.

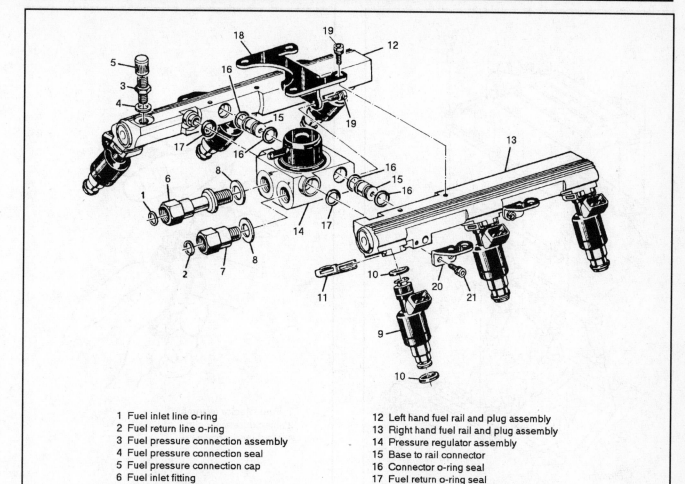

1 Fuel inlet line o-ring	12 Left hand fuel rail and plug assembly
2 Fuel return line o-ring	13 Right hand fuel rail and plug assembly
3 Fuel pressure connection assembly	14 Pressure regulator assembly
4 Fuel pressure connection seal	15 Base to rail connector
5 Fuel pressure connection cap	16 Connector o-ring seal
6 Fuel inlet fitting	17 Fuel return o-ring seal
7 Fuel outlet fitting	18 Pressure regulator mounting bracket
8 Fuel fitting gasket	19 Pressure regulator bracket attaching
9 Fuel injector assembly	screw assembly
10 Injector o-ring seal	20 Rail mounting bracket
11 Injector retainer clip	21 Bracket attaching screw assembly

87955066

Fig. 68 Exploded view of the fuel rail, injectors, retaining clip and O-rings

9. Install the fuel rail assembly and throttle body.
10. Connect the negative battery cable.

➡This test must be done before the engine is started and requires the use of a Tech 1® scan tool.

11. If equipped with the 3.1L engine, perform the idle learn procedure to allow the ECM/PCM memory to be updated with the correct IAC valve pintle position and provide for a stable idle speed.
   a. Install a Tech 1® scan tool.
   b. Turn the ignition to the **ON** position, engine not running.
   c. Select **IAC SYSTEM**, then **IDLE LEARN** in the **MISC TEST** mode.
   d. Place the transaxle in park or neutral, as applicable.
   e. Proceed with idle learn as directed by the scan tool.

Fuel Pressure Regulator

REMOVAL & INSTALLATION

✳✳CAUTION

To reduce the risk of fire or personal injury, it is necessary to relieve the fuel system pressure before servicing the fuel system.

1.8L And 2.0L OHC Engines

EXCEPT 2.0L (VIN H) ENGINES

1. Relieve fuel system pressure.
2. Remove pressure regulator from fuel rail. Place a rag around the base of the regulator to catch any spilled fuel.
3. Installation is the reverse of removal procedure.

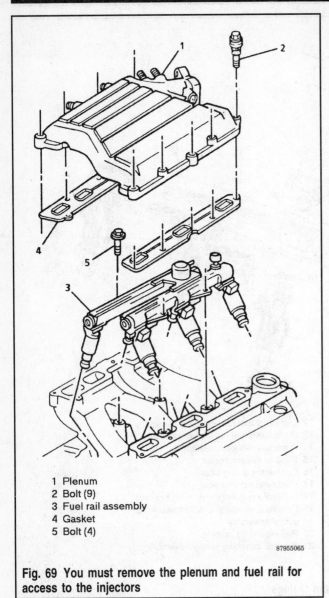

1 Plenum
2 Bolt (9)
3 Fuel rail assembly
4 Gasket
5 Bolt (4)

87955065

Fig. 69 You must remove the plenum and fuel rail for access to the injectors

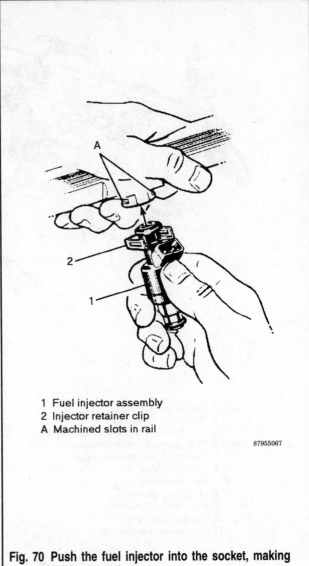

1 Fuel injector assembly
2 Injector retainer clip
A Machined slots in rail

87955067

Fig. 70 Push the fuel injector into the socket, making sure it is fully seated

2.0L (VIN H) ENGINES

▶ See Figure 71

1. Properly relieve the fuel system pressure.
2. Disconnect the negative battery cable.
3. Remove the air duct and air cleaner cover.
4. Disconnect the vacuum hose from the pressure regulator.
5. Using a back-up wrench, remove the fuel return pipe at the pressure regulator.
6. Unfasten the pressure regulator attaching screw, then remove the regulator from the fuel rail, twisting it back and forth while pulling it apart.

To install:

7. If there is not enough thread locking material on the threads of the retaining screw, apply Loctite® 262 or equivalent to the threads.
8. The remainder of installation is the reverse of the removal procedure.

2.3L and 2.4L Engines

▶ See Figure 72

1. Properly relieve the fuel system pressure.
2. Disconnect the negative battery cable.
3. Remove the fuel rail assembly from the vehicle.
4. Unfasten the pressure regulator attaching screw, then remove the regulator, twisting it back and forth while pulling it apart. Remove and discard O-ring.
5. If the regulator is to reinstalled, inspect the filter screen for contamination and discard if necessary.

To install:

6. Lubricate a new rail-to-regulator inlet fitting O-ring seal with clean engine oil, then install in regulator.
7. Install the regulator assembly. Align with the retainer and spacer assembly mounting hole. Coat the retaining screw with Loctite® 262 or equivalent, then tighten to 102 inch lbs. (15 Nm).
8. Install the fuel rail assembly.
9. Connect the negative battery cable.

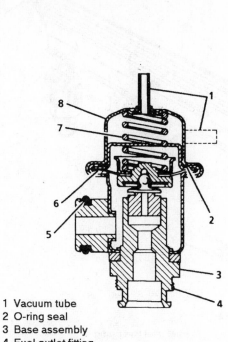

1 Vacuum tube
2 O-ring seal
3 Base assembly
4 Fuel outlet fitting
5 Fuel inlet fitting o-ring
6 Diaphragm
7 Pressure regulator spring
8 Pressure regulator cover

87955068

Fig. 71 Cross-sectional view of the fuel pressure regulator

2.8L and 3.1L Engines

1985-86 VEHICLES

The pressure regulator is factory adjusted and is not serviceable. Do not attempt to remove the regulator from the fuel rail.

1987-94 VEHICLES

▶ See Figure 73

1. Disconnect the negative battery cable.
2. Properly relieve the fuel system pressure.
3. Remove the intake manifold plenum and the fuel rail, as outlined in this section.
4. Unfasten and remove the fuel inlet and outlet fittings and gaskets.
5. Unfasten the pressure regulator bracket attaching screws and mounting bracket.
6. Remove the right and left hand fuel rail assemblies from the pressure regulator assembly.

7. Remove the base-to-rail connectors from the regulator or rails.
8. Disassemble connector O-rings from the base to rail connectors.
9. Remove the fuel return O-ring from the fuel rails. Discard all O-rings.
To install:
10. Lubricate new fuel return O-rings with engine oil and install on the fuel rails.
11. Lubricate new connector O-rings with engine oil and install to the base to rail connectors.
12. Install the base-to-rail connectors in the regulator assembly.
13. Fasten the right and left hand fuel rail assemblies to the pressure regulator assembly.
14. Install the pressure regulator mounting bracket with the attaching screws. Tighten the screws to 28 inch lbs. (3 Nm).
15. Connect new fuel inlet and outlet fitting gaskets and tighten the fittings to 20 inch lbs. (2.2 Nm).
16. Install the fuel rail and intake manifold plenum.
17. Connect the negative battery cable.

➡**This test must be done before the engine is started and requires the use of a Tech 1® scan tool.**

18. If equipped with the 3.1L engine, perform the idle learn procedure to allow the ECM/PCM memory to be updated with the correct IAC valve pintle position and provide for a stable idle speed.
    a. Install a Tech 1® scan tool.
    b. Turn the ignition to the **ON** position, engine not running.
    c. Select **IAC SYSTEM**, then **IDLE LEARN** in the **MISC TEST** mode.
    d. Place the transaxle in park or neutral, as applicable.
    e. Proceed with idle learn as directed by the scan tool.

Fuel Rail Assembly

REMOVAL & INSTALLATION

1.8L And 2.0L OHC Engines

▶ See Figure 74

1. Properly relieve the fuel system pressure.
2. Disconnect the negative battery cable.
3. Remove the throttle body from the intake manifold.
4. Disconnect the PCV and breather hoses from the camshaft cover.
5. Tag and detach the electrical connectors and vacuum hoses from the canister purge solenoid, EGR valve and solenoid and the MAP sensor.
6. Remove the MAP sensor from the bracket.
7. Detach the fuel injector electrical connectors.
8. Unfasten the fuel inlet pipe retainer attaching screw, then remove the retainer and the pump. Remove and discard the O-ring seal located under the seal retainer at the fuel rail.
9. Disconnect the fuel return pipe at the pressure regulator, using a back-up wrench to prevent it from turning.

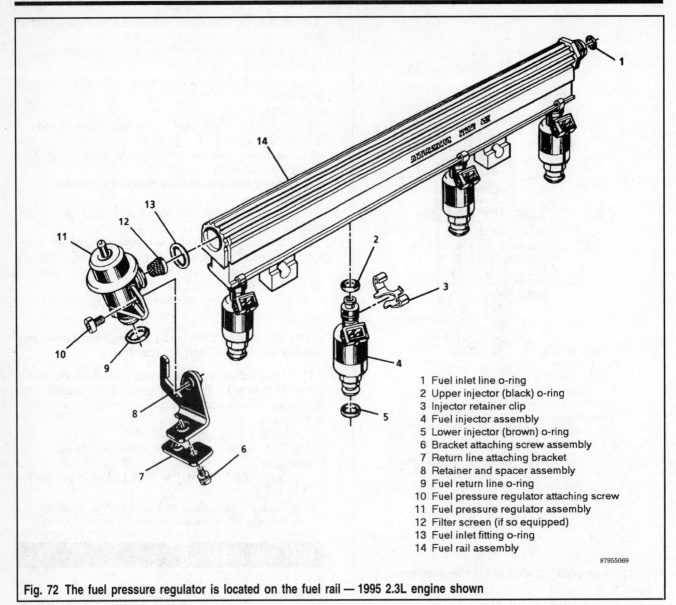

1 Fuel inlet line o-ring
2 Upper injector (black) o-ring
3 Injector retainer clip
4 Fuel injector assembly
5 Lower injector (brown) o-ring
6 Bracket attaching screw assembly
7 Return line attaching bracket
8 Retainer and spacer assembly
9 Fuel return line o-ring
10 Fuel pressure regulator attaching screw
11 Fuel pressure regulator assembly
12 Filter screen (if so equipped)
13 Fuel inlet fitting o-ring
14 Fuel rail assembly

87955069

Fig. 72 The fuel pressure regulator is located on the fuel rail — 1995 2.3L engine shown

10. Unfasten the fuel rail attaching bolts, then remove the fuel rail.

➡**If an injector becomes separated from the rail and remains in the cylinder head, both injector O-ring seals and the retainer clip must be replaced.**

To install:

11. Position the fuel rail assembly, then install the retaining bolts. Tighten the bolts to 19 ft. lbs. (26 Nm).

12. Install a new fuel inlet pipe O-ring seal, coated with clean engine oil, under the seal retainer at the fuel rail. Tighten the retaining screw to 53 inch lbs. (6 Nm).

13. Connect the fuel return pipe. Tighten the fuel return pipe fitting to 14.8 ft. lbs. (20 Nm). Make sure to use a back-up wrench on the pressure regulator fitting to prevent it from turning.

14. Attach the injector electrical connectors.

15. Fasten the MAP sensor to the bracket. Tighten the screws to 27 inch lbs. (3 Nm).

16. Install the canister purge solenoid and bracket and the EGR solenoid and bracket. Tighten the bracket retaining screws to 37 ft. lbs. (50 Nm).

17. Connect the canister purge solenoid and the EGR solenoid and valve vacuum hoses and electrical connectors.

18. Fasten the PCV and breather hoses to the camshaft cover.

19. Install the throttle body, as outlined earlier in this section.

20. Tighten the fuel filler cap.

21. Connect the negative battery cable, then with the engine **OFF**, check to see that the accelerator pedal is free by depressing, then releasing it. Turn the ignition switch to the **ON** position for 2 seconds, then turn to the **OFF** position for 10 seconds. Again turn the switch to the **ON** position and check for fuel leaks.

2.3L and 2.4L Engines

▶ See Figure 75

1. Properly relieve the fuel system pressure.
2. Disconnect the negative battery cable.

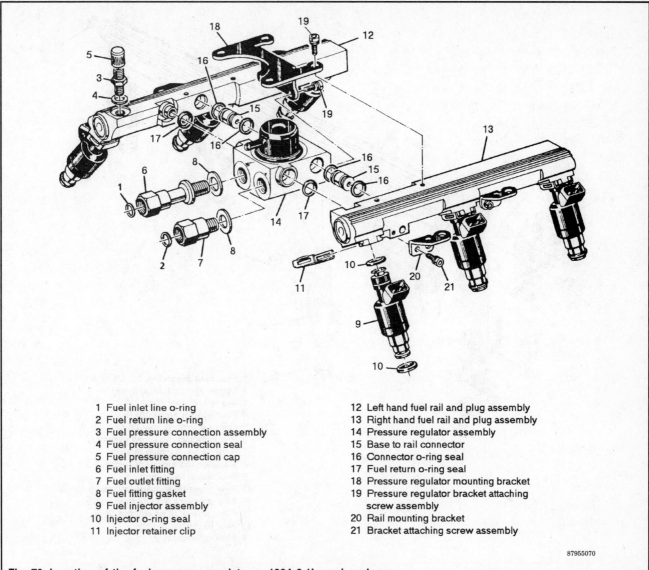

1 Fuel inlet line o-ring
2 Fuel return line o-ring
3 Fuel pressure connection assembly
4 Fuel pressure connection seal
5 Fuel pressure connection cap
6 Fuel inlet fitting
7 Fuel outlet fitting
8 Fuel fitting gasket
9 Fuel injector assembly
10 Injector o-ring seal
11 Injector retainer clip

12 Left hand fuel rail and plug assembly
13 Right hand fuel rail and plug assembly
14 Pressure regulator assembly
15 Base to rail connector
16 Connector o-ring seal
17 Fuel return o-ring seal
18 Pressure regulator mounting bracket
19 Pressure regulator bracket attaching
   screw assembly
20 Rail mounting bracket
21 Bracket attaching screw assembly

87955070

Fig. 73 Location of the fuel pressure regulator — 1994 3.1L engine shown

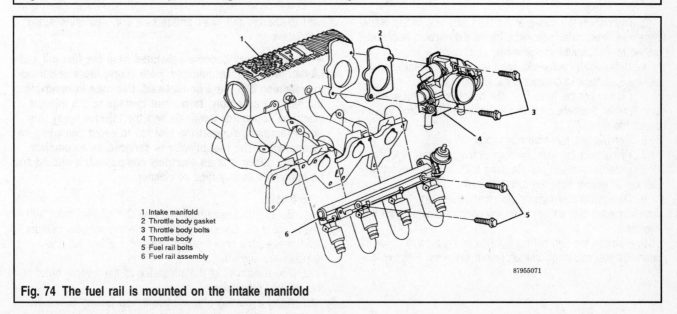

1 Intake manifold
2 Throttle body gasket
3 Throttle body bolts
4 Throttle body
5 Fuel rail bolts
6 Fuel rail assembly

87955071

Fig. 74 The fuel rail is mounted on the intake manifold

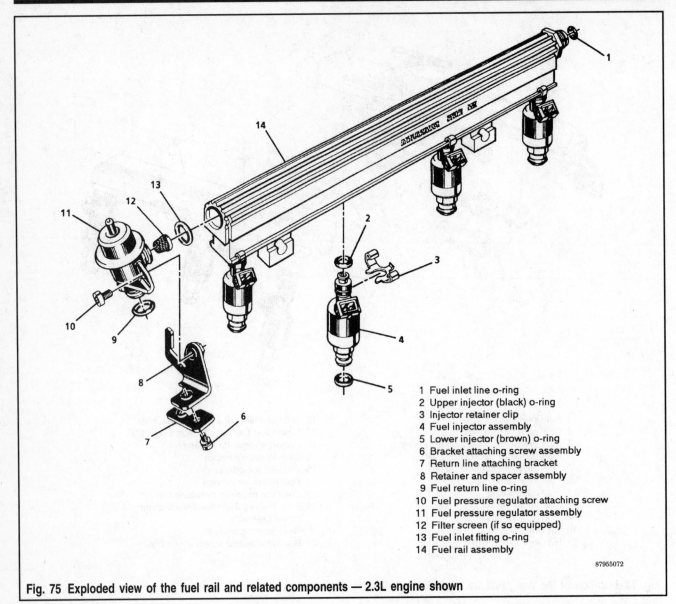

1 Fuel inlet line o-ring
2 Upper injector (black) o-ring
3 Injector retainer clip
4 Fuel injector assembly
5 Lower injector (brown) o-ring
6 Bracket attaching screw assembly
7 Return line attaching bracket
8 Retainer and spacer assembly
9 Fuel return line o-ring
10 Fuel pressure regulator attaching screw
11 Fuel pressure regulator assembly
12 Filter screen (if so equipped)
13 Fuel inlet fitting o-ring
14 Fuel rail assembly

87955072

Fig. 75 Exploded view of the fuel rail and related components — 2.3L engine shown

3. Disconnect the hoses at the front and side of the crank-case ventilation oil/air separator. Leave the vacuum hoses attached to the canister purge valve.

4. Unfasten the bolts securing the crankcase ventilation oil/air separator and canister purge valve.

5. Disconnect the hose from the bottom of the separator, then remove the separator. Position the canister purge valve out of the way.

6. Remove the fuel pipe clamp bolt.

7. Disconnect the vacuum hose at the pressure regulator.

8. Unfasten the fuel rail attaching bolts, then remove the fuel rail assembly from the cylinder head.

9. Detach the fuel injector electrical connectors. Push in the wire connector clip, while pulling the connector away from the injector.

10. Remove the fuel rail assembly, making sure to cover all openings with masking tape to prevent dirt entry. Remove dis-card all O-rings and seals and replace with new ones during installation.

➡️If any injectors become separated from the fuel rail and remain in the intake manifold, both O-ring seals and injector retaining clip must be replaced. Use care in removing the fuel rail assembly, to prevent damage to the injector electrical connector terminals and the injector spray tips. When removed, support the fuel rail to avoid damaging its components. The fuel injector is serviced as a complete unit only. Since it is an electrical component, it should not be immersed in any type of cleaner.

To install:

11. Be sure to lubricate all the new O-rings and seals with clean engine oil. Carefully push the injectors into the cylinder head intake ports until the bolt holes on the fuel rail and manifold are aligned.

12. The remainder of the installation is the reverse order of the removal procedure.

13. Apply a coating of a suitable thread locking compound on the treads of the fittings. Tighten the fuel rail retaining bolts

to 19 ft. lbs. (26 Nm), the fuel feed line nut to 22 ft. lbs. (30 Nm) and the fuel pipe fittings to 20 ft. lbs. (26 Nm).

14. Connect the negative battery cable. Turn the ignition to the **ON** position for two seconds, then turn it to the **OFF** position for ten seconds. Turn again to the **ON** position and check for fuel leaks.

2.8L and 3.1L Engines

1985-86 VEHICLES

▶ **See Figure 76**

1. Disconnect the negative battery cable.
2. Relieve fuel system pressure.
3. Remove the intake manifold plenum, as follows:
   a. Disconnect the vacuum lines.
   b. Remove the EGR-to-plenum nuts.
   c. Unfasten the two throttle body bolts.
   d. Remove the throttle cable to bracket bolts.
   e. Unfasten the plenum bolts and remove the plenum and gasket.
4. Remove the cold start valve and tube assembly.
5. Remove the retaining nut from the stud for the fuel lines at the head.
6. Unfasten the fuel lines at the rail.
7. Disconnect the vacuum line at the regulator.
8. Remove the rail retaining bolts.
9. Disconnect the injector electrical connectors.
10. Remove the fuel rail assembly.

To install:

11. Use new injector O-rings which have been lubricated with engine clean oil.
12. The remainder of installation is the reverse of the removal procedure.
13. Connect the negative battery cable. Turn the ignition to the **ON** position for two seconds, then turn it to the **OFF** position for ten seconds. Turn again to the **ON** position and check for fuel leaks.

1987-94 VEHICLES

▶ **See Figure 77**

1. Disconnect the negative battery cable.
2. Properly relieve fuel system pressure.
3. Remove the intake manifold plenum, as follows:
   a. Disconnect the vacuum lines.
   b. Remove the EGR-to-plenum nuts.
   c. Unfasten the two throttle body bolts.
   d. Remove the throttle cable to bracket bolts.
   e. Unfasten the ignition wire plastic shield bolts.
   f. Remove the plenum bolts and remove the plenum and gasket.

4. Remove the fuel line bracket bolt.
5. Disconnect the fuel lines at the rail.

✳✳CAUTION

Wrap a cloth around the fuel lines to collect fuel, then place the fuel in an approved container.

6. Remove the fuel line O-rings.
7. Disconnect the vacuum line at the pressure regulator.
8. Unfasten the four rail retaining bolts.
9. Detach the injector electrical connectors.
10. Remove the fuel rail assembly.
11. Remove the O-ring seal from each of the spray tip end of the injector.

To install:

12. Lubricate new the O-ring seals, with clean engine oil and install to each of the spray tip ends of the injector.
13. Position the fuel rail assembly in the intake manifold and tilt the rail assembly and install the injectors.
14. Install the fuel rail attaching bolts and tighten to 19 ft. lbs. (26 Nm).
15. Attach the injector electrical connectors.
16. Connect the vacuum line at the pressure regulator.
17. Install new O-rings on the inlet and return fuel lines.
18. Tighten the fuel filler cap.
19. Connect the negative battery cable.
20. Using a back-up wrench, install the fuel inlet and outlet fittings.
21. Connect the negative battery cable. Turn the ignition to the **ON** position for two seconds, then turn it to the **OFF** position for ten seconds. Turn again to the **ON** position and check for fuel leaks.
22. Reversing the removal procedure, install the intake manifold plenum.

➡**This test must be done before the engine is started and requires the use of a Tech 1® scan tool.**

23. If equipped with the 3.1L engine, perform the idle learn procedure to allow the ECM/PCM memory to be updated with the correct IAC valve pintle position and provide for a stable idle speed.
   a. Install a Tech 1® scan tool.
   b. Turn the ignition to the **ON** position, engine not running.
   c. Select **IAC SYSTEM**, then **IDLE LEARN** in the **MISC TEST** mode.
   d. Place the transaxle in park or neutral, as applicable.
   e. Proceed with idle learn as directed by the scan tool.

1 Fuel inlet line o-ring
2 Fuel return line o-ring
3 Fuel rail and pressure regulator assembly
4 Fuel pressure connection assembly
5 Fuel pressure connection assembly seal
6 Fuel pressure connection cap
7 Fuel block
8 Fuel block seal
9 Fuel block attaching screw assembly
10 Port injector
11 O-ring injector seal
12 Injector retainer clip
13 Cold start valve
14 Tube and body assembly
15 Valve o-ring seal
16 Body o-ring seal
17 Tube o-ring seal
18 Cold start fitting

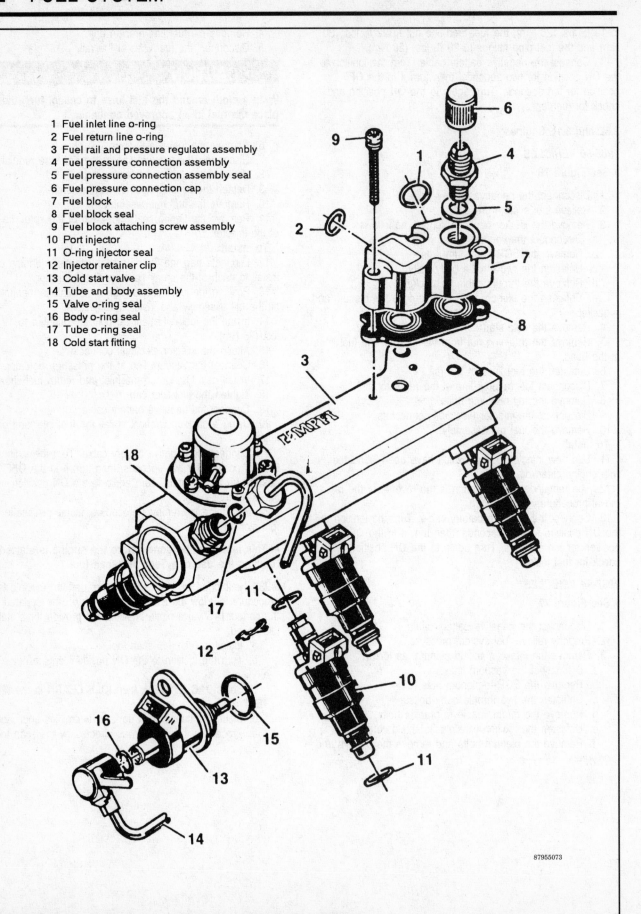

Fig. 76 Exploded view of the fuel rail assembly — 1985-86 2.8L engines

87955073

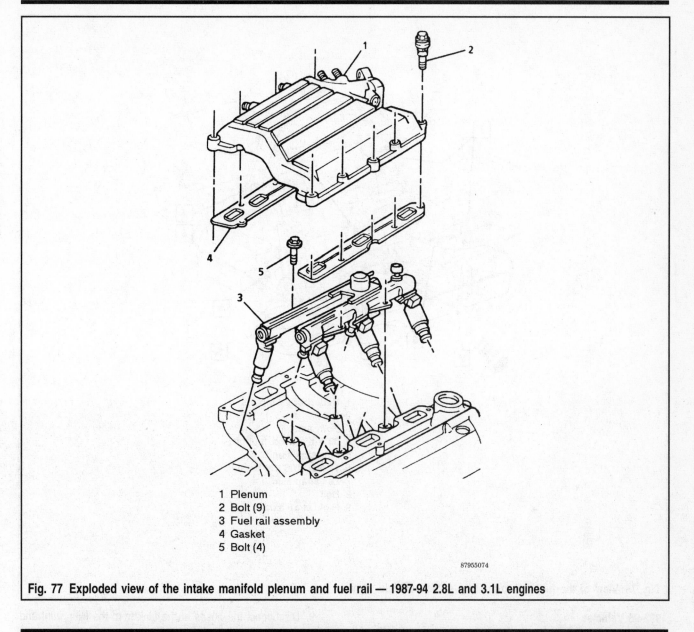

1 Plenum
2 Bolt (9)
3 Fuel rail assembly
4 Gasket
5 Bolt (4)

87955074

Fig. 77 Exploded view of the intake manifold plenum and fuel rail — 1987-94 2.8L and 3.1L engines

FUEL TANK

Tank Assembly

REMOVAL & INSTALLATION

1982-91 Vehicles
▶ See Figure 78

1. Disconnect the negative cable at the battery.
2. Raise and safely support the vehicles.
3. Drain the tank. There is no drain plug, so drain as follows:

   a. If available, use a hand-operated pump device to drain as much fuel through the filler tube as possible.

   b. If a hand-operated pump cannot be used or to complete the draining process, the remaining fuel in the tank must be siphoned through the main (not return) fuel feed line (the line to the fuel pump), because of the restrictor in the filler neck.

4. Detach the tank meter assembly harness connector form the body harness connector.
5. If used, remove the ground wire retaining screw from the underbody.
6. Disconnect the hoses from the tank meter assembly and the hoses at the tank from the filler and vent pipes.
7. If necessary, unplug the level sending unit electrical connector.
8. Support the tank, then unfasten the two tank support straps and lower and remove the tank. Installation is the reverse of removal.
9. Using tool J 24187 or equivalent, remove the fuel tank meter assembly and seal/gasket. Remove the sound insulators.
10. Installation is the reverse of the removal procedure.

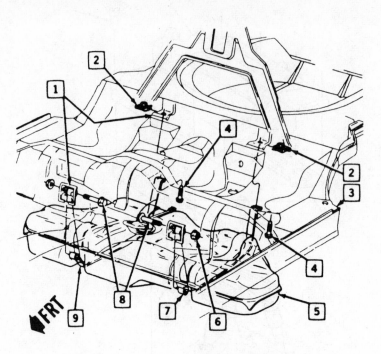

1 Underbody supports
2 Nut
3 Body asm.
4 33 Nm (25 lbs. ft.) bolt
5 Fuel tank asm.
6 12 Nm (106 lbs. in.) nut
7 Left strap asm.
8 Bolt
9 Right strap asm.

87955076

Fig. 78 View of the fuel tank mounting — 1991 vehicle shown

1992-96 Vehicles

▶ **See Figure 79**

1. Disconnect the negative battery cable.
2. Drain the fuel tank by using a hand-operated pump device to drain as much fuel through the filler tube as possible.
3. Raise and safely support the vehicle.
4. Detach the fuel sender electrical connector.
5. Unfasten the muffler hanger bolts.
6. Remove the exhaust rubber hangers, then allow the exhaust system to rest on the rear axle.
7. Disconnect the hoses from the fuel tank sender. Grasp the filter and one nylon fuel connection line fitting. Twist the quick-connect fitting 1/4 turn in each direction to loosen any dirt within the fitting. Repeat for the other fitting. Using compressed air, blow out the dirt from the quick-connect fittings at the end of the fuel filter.
8. Detach the quick-connect fittings by pulling the release tabs back on the fuel line quick connector and pulling apart. If difficulty is encountered, tool J 38778 or equivalent can be used to separate the fitting.

9. Disconnect the hoses at the tank from the filler, vent and vapor pipes.
10. With the help of an assistant, support the fuel tank, then disconnect the two tank retaining straps and lower the tank from the vehicle.
11. Remove the sound insulators.
12. Remove the modular fuel sender, as outlined later in this section.
13. Inspect all connectors for dirt and burrs. Clean or replace, as required. Inspect the fuel line O-rings for cuts, nicks, swelling and/or distortion and replace as necessary.

   To install:
14. Install the fuel sender assembly to the tank, as outlined later in this section.
15. Install the sound insulators.
16. With the help of an assistant, raise the fuel tank to the vehicle, then fasten the retaining straps. Tighten the retaining bolts to 24 ft. lbs. (33 Nm).
17. Connect the hoses to the filler, vent and vapor pipes.

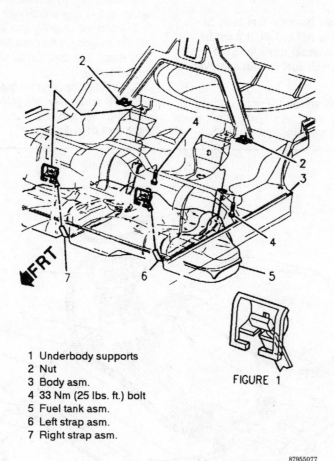

1 Underbody supports
2 Nut
3 Body asm.
4 33 Nm (25 lbs. ft.) bolt
5 Fuel tank asm.
6 Left strap asm.
7 Right strap asm.

FIGURE 1

87955077

Fig. 79 View of fuel tank mounting — 1992-96 vehicles

18. Attach the nylon fuel feed and return connecting line quick-connect fittings to the fuel sender, as follows:

   a. Apply a few drops of clean engine oil to the male connector tube ends.

   b. Push the connectors together to cause the retaining tabs/fingers to snap into place.

   c. Once installed, pull on both ends of each connection to be sure they are secure.

19. Install the exhaust rubber hangers.

20. Install the muffler hanger bolts, then tighten to 11 ft. lbs. (15 Nm).

21. Attach the fuel tank sender electrical connector.

22. Carefully lower the vehicle.

23. Refill the fuel tank, then connect the negative battery cable.

24. Turn the ignition to the **ON** position for two seconds, then turn it to the **OFF** position for ten seconds. Turn again to the **ON** position and check for fuel leaks.

MODULAR FUEL SENDER ASSEMBLY REPLACEMENT

▶ See Figure 80

➡Always replace fuel sender assembly O-ring when reinstalling the fuel sender assembly

1. Properly relieve fuel system pressure.

2. If not done already, disconnect the negative battery cable.

3. Drain fuel from the fuel tank assembly, as outlined in the fuel tank removal procedure.

4. Remove the fuel tank, as outlined earlier in this section.

❋❋CAUTION

The modular fuel sender assembly may spring up from its position.

5. While holding down the modular fuel sender assembly down, remove the snap ring from the designated slots in the retainer.

➡**When removing the fuel sender from the fuel tank, be aware that the reservoir bucket is full of fuel. It must be tipped slightly during removal to avoid damage to the float. Carefully discard the reservoir fuel into an approved container.**

6. Remove and discard the fuel sender O-ring.
To install:
7. Install a new O-ring on fuel sender-to-tank assembly.

8. Align tab on front of sender with the slot on front of the retainer snapring.

9. Slowly apply pressure to the top of the spring loaded sender, until it aligns flush with retainer on tank assembly.

10. Insert the snapring into the designated slots. Be sure that the snapring is fully seated in the retainer.

11. Install fuel tank, the carefully lower the vehicle and refill the gas tank.

12. Connect the negative battery cable, then turn the ignition to the **ON** position for two seconds, then turn it to the **OFF** position for ten seconds. Turn again to the **ON** position and check for fuel leaks.

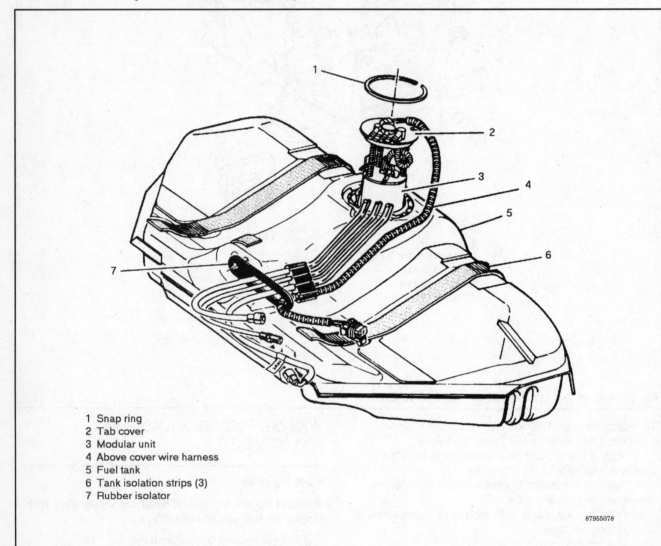

1 Snap ring
2 Tab cover
3 Modular unit
4 Above cover wire harness
5 Fuel tank
6 Tank isolation strips (3)
7 Rubber isolator

87955078

Fig. 80 The module fuel sender assembly is mounted in the fuel tank

AIR CONDITIONER
ACCUMULATOR 6-29
AIR CONDITIONING PRESSURE
SENSOR 6-33
BLOWER SWITCH 6-27
COMPRESSOR 6-22
CONDENSER 6-24
CONTROL PANEL 6-27
CYCLING CLUTCH SWITCH 6-33
EVAPORATOR CORE 6-25
EXPANSION (ORIFICE)
VALVE/TUBE 6-28
REFRIGERANT LINES 6-31
TEMPERATURE CONTROL
CABLE 6-31
CIRCUIT PROTECTION
CIRCUIT BREAKERS 6-69
FLASHERS 6-70
FUSES BLOCK AND FUSES 6-68
FUSIBLE LINKS 6-69
CRUISE CONTROL
CONTROL MODULE 6-34
CONTROL SWITCHES 6-34
SERVO UNIT 6-36
VEHICLE SPEED SENSOR
(VSS) 6-34
ENTERTAINMENT SYSTEMS
RADIO RECEIVER/TAPE PLAYER/CD
PLAYER 6-37
SPEAKERS 6-39
HEATER
BLOWER MOTOR 6-15
BLOWER SWITCH 6-20
CONTROL PANEL 6-20
HEATER CORE 6-16
TEMPERATURE CONTROL
CABLE 6-20
INSTRUMENTS AND SWITCHES
CLOCK 6-58
HEADLIGHT SWITCH 6-57
IGNITION SWITCH 6-58
INSTRUMENT CLUSTER 6-52
SPEEDOMETER CABLE 6-54
SPEEDOMETER, TACHOMETER AND
GAUGES 6-54
WINDSHIELD WIPER SWITCH 6-55
LIGHTING
FOG LAMPS 6-67
HEADLIGHTS 6-58
SIGNAL AND MARKER LIGHTS 6-62
**SUPPLEMENTAL INFLATABLE
RESTRAINT (SIR) SYSTEM**
GENERAL INFORMATION 6-10
TRAILER WIRING 6-68
**UNDERSTANDING AND
TROUBLESHOOTING ELECTRICAL
SYSTEMS**
ADD-ON ELECTRICAL
EQUIPMENT 6-10
ELECTRICAL
TROUBLESHOOTING 6-3

SAFETY PRECAUTIONS 6-2
UNDERSTANDING BASIC
ELECTRICITY 6-2
WIRING HARNESSES 6-8
WINDSHIELD WIPERS AND WASHERS
REAR WINDOW WIPER MOTOR 6-48
WINDSHIELD WASHER FLUID
RESERVOIR & PUMP 6-49
WINDSHIELD WIPER BLADE AND
ARM 6-44
WINDSHIELD WIPER MOTOR 6-45
WIPER LINKAGE 6-49
WIRING DIAGRAMS 6-71

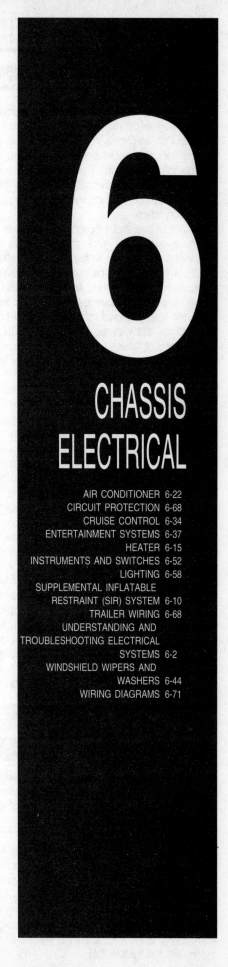

6

CHASSIS ELECTRICAL

AIR CONDITIONER 6-22
CIRCUIT PROTECTION 6-68
CRUISE CONTROL 6-34
ENTERTAINMENT SYSTEMS 6-37
HEATER 6-15
INSTRUMENTS AND SWITCHES 6-52
LIGHTING 6-58
SUPPLEMENTAL INFLATABLE
RESTRAINT (SIR) SYSTEM 6-10
TRAILER WIRING 6-68
UNDERSTANDING AND
TROUBLESHOOTING ELECTRICAL
SYSTEMS 6-2
WINDSHIELD WIPERS AND
WASHERS 6-44
WIRING DIAGRAMS 6-71

UNDERSTANDING AND TROUBLESHOOTING ELECTRICAL SYSTEMS

Over the years import and domestic manufacturers have incorporated electronic control systems into their production lines. In fact, electronic control systems are so prevalent that all new cars and trucks built today are equipped with at least one on-board computer. These electronic components (with no moving parts) should theoretically last the life of the vehicle, provided that nothing external happens to damage the circuits or memory chips.

While it is true that electronic components should never wear out, in the real world malfunctions do occur. It is also true that any computer-based system is extremely sensitive to electrical voltages and cannot tolerate careless or haphazard testing/service procedures. An inexperienced individual can literally cause major damage looking for a minor problem by using the wrong kind of test equipment or connecting test leads/connectors with the ignition switch **ON**. When selecting test equipment, make sure the manufacturer's instructions state that the tester is compatible with whatever type of system is being serviced. Read all instructions carefully and double check all test points before installing probes or making any test connections.

The following section outlines basic diagnosis techniques for dealing with automotive electrical systems. Along with a general explanation of the various types of test equipment available to aid in servicing modern automotive systems, basic repair techniques for wiring harnesses and connectors are also given. Read the basic information before attempting any repairs or testing. This will provide the background of information necessary to avoid the most common and obvious mistakes that can cost both time and money. Although the replacement and testing procedures are simple in themselves, the systems are not, and unless one has a thorough understanding of all components and their function within a particular system, the logical test sequence these systems demand cannot be followed. Minor malfunctions can make a big difference, so it is important to know how each component affects the operation of the overall system in order to find the ultimate cause of a problem without replacing good components unnecessarily. It is not enough to use the correct test equipment; the test equipment must be used correctly.

Safety Precautions

✳✳CAUTION

Whenever working on or around any electrical or electronic systems, always observe these general precautions to prevent the possibility of personal injury or damage to electronic components.

• Never install or remove battery cables with the key **ON** or the engine running. Jumper cables should be connected with the key **OFF** to avoid power surges that can damage electronic control units. Engines equipped with computer controlled systems should avoid both giving and getting jump starts due to the possibility of serious damage to components from arcing in the engine compartment if connections are made with the ignition **ON**.

• Always remove the battery cables before charging the battery. Never use a high output charger on an installed battery or attempt to use any type of "hot shot" (24 volt) starting aid.

• Exercise care when inserting test probes into connectors to insure good contact without damaging the connector or spreading the pins. Always probe connectors from the rear (wire) side, NOT the pin side, to avoid accidental shorting of terminals during test procedures.

• Never remove or attach wiring harness connectors with the ignition switch **ON**, especially to an electronic control unit.

• Do not drop any components during service procedures and never apply 12 volts directly to any component (like a solenoid or relay) unless instructed specifically to do so. Some component electrical windings are designed to safely handle only 4 or 5 volts and can be destroyed in seconds if 12 volts are applied directly to the connector.

• Remove the electronic control unit if the vehicle is to be placed in an environment where temperatures exceed approximately 176°F (80°C), such as a paint spray booth or when arc/gas welding near the control unit location.

Understanding Basic Electricity

Understanding the basic theory of electricity makes electrical troubleshooting much easier. Several gauges are used in electrical troubleshooting to see inside the circuit being tested. Without a basic understanding, it will be difficult to understand testing procedures.

THE WATER ANALOGY

Electricity is the flow of electrons — hypothetical particles thought to constitute the basic stuff of electricity. Many people have been taught electrical theory using an analogy with water. In a comparison with water flowing in a pipe, the electrons would be the water. As the flow of water can be measured, the flow of electricity can be measured. The unit of measurement is amperes, frequently abbreviated amps. An ammeter will measure the actual amount of current flowing in the circuit.

Just as the water pressure is measured in units such as pounds per square inch, electrical pressure is measured in volts. When a voltmeter's two probes are placed on two live portions of an electrical circuit with different electrical pressures, current will flow through the voltmeter and produce a reading which indicates the difference in electrical pressure between the two parts of the circuit.

While increasing the voltage in a circuit will increase the flow of current, the actual flow depends not only on voltage, but on the resistance of the circuit. The standard unit for measuring circuit resistance is an ohm, measured by an ohmmeter. The ohmmeter is somewhat similar to an ammeter, but incorporates its own source of power so that a standard voltage is always present.

CIRCUITS

An actual electric circuit consists of four basic parts. These are: the power source, such as a generator or battery; a hot wire, which conducts the electricity under a relatively high voltage to the component supplied by the circuit; the load, such as a lamp, motor, resistor or relay coil; and the ground wire, which carries the current back to the source under very low voltage. In such a circuit the bulk of the resistance exists between the point where the hot wire is connected to the load, and the point where the load is grounded. In an automobile, the vehicle's frame or body, which is made of steel, is used as a part of the ground circuit for many of the electrical devices.

Remember that, in electrical testing, the voltmeter is connected in parallel with the circuit being tested (without disconnecting any wires) and measures the difference in voltage between the locations of the two probes; that the ammeter is connected in series with the load (the circuit is separated at one point and the ammeter inserted so it becomes a part of the circuit); and the ohmmeter is self-powered, so that all the power in the circuit should be off and the portion of the circuit to be measured contacted at either end by one of the probes of the meter.

For any electrical system to operate, it must make a complete circuit. This simply means that the power flow from the battery must make a complete circle. When an electrical component is operating, power flows from the battery to the component, passes through the component causing it to perform it to function (such as lighting a light bulb) and then returns to the battery through the ground of the circuit. This ground is usually (but not always) the metal part of the vehicle on which the electrical component is mounted.

Perhaps the easiest way to visualize this is to think of connecting a light bulb with two wires attached to it to your vehicle's battery. The battery in your car has two posts (negative and positive). If one of the two wires attached to the light bulb was attached to the negative post of the battery and the other wire was attached to the positive post of the battery, you would have a complete circuit. Current from the battery would flow out one post, through the wire attached to it and then to the light bulb, where it would pass through causing it to light. It would then leave the light bulb, travel through the other wire, and return to the other post of the battery.

AUTOMOTIVE CIRCUITS

The normal automotive circuit differs from this simple example in two ways. First, instead of having a return wire from the bulb to the battery, the light bulb return the current to the battery through the chassis of the vehicle. Since the negative battery cable is attached to the chassis and the chassis is made of electrically conductive metal, the chassis of the vehicle can serve as a ground wire to complete the circuit. Secondly, most automotive circuits contain switches to turn components on and off.

Some electrical components which require a large amount of current to operate also have a relay in their circuit. Since these circuits carry a large amount of current, the thickness of the wire in the circuit (gauge size) is also greater. If this large wire were connected from the component to the control switch on the instrument panel, and then back to the component, a voltage drop would occur in the circuit. To prevent this potential drop in voltage, an electromagnetic switch (relay) is used. The large wires in the circuit are connected from the car battery to one side of the relay, and from the opposite side of the relay to the component. The relay is normally open, preventing current from passing through the circuit. An additional, smaller wire is connected from the relay to the control switch for the circuit. When the control switch is turned on, it grounds the smaller wire from the relay and completes the circuit.

SHORT CIRCUITS

If you were to disconnect the light bulb (from the previous example of a light-bulb being connected to the battery by two wires) from the wires and touch the two wires together (please take our word for this; don't try it), the result will be a shower of sparks. A similar thing happens (on a smaller scale) when the power supply wire to a component or the electrical component itself becomes grounded before the normal ground connection for the circuit. To prevent damage to the system, the fuse for the circuit blows to interrupt the circuit — protecting the components from damage. Because grounding a wire from a power source makes a complete circuit — less the required component to use the power — the phenomenon is called a short circuit. The most common causes of short circuits are: the rubber insulation on a wire breaking or rubbing through to expose the current carrying core of the wire to a metal part of the car, or a shorted switch.

Some electrical systems on the car are protected by a circuit breaker which is, basically, a self-repairing fuse. When either of the described events takes place in a system which is protected by a circuit breaker, the circuit breaker opens the circuit the same way a fuse does. However, when either the short is removed from the circuit or the surge subsides, the circuit breaker resets itself and does not have to be replaced as a fuse does.

Electrical Troubleshooting

When diagnosing a specific problem, organized troubleshooting is a must. The complexity of a modern automobile demands that you approach any problem in a logical, organized manner. There are certain troubleshooting techniques that are standard:

1. Establish when the problem occurs. Does the problem appear only under certain conditions? Were there any noises, odors, or other unusual symptoms?

2. Isolate the problem area. To do this, make some simple tests and observations; then eliminate the systems that are working properly. Check for obvious problems such as broken wires, dirty connections or split/disconnected vacuum hoses. Always check the obvious before assuming something complicated is the cause.

3. Test for problems systematically to determine the cause once the problem area is isolated. Are all the components functioning properly? Is there power going to electrical switches and motors? Is there vacuum at vacuum switches and/or actuators? Is there a mechanical problem such as bent linkage

or loose mounting screws? Performing careful, systematic checks will often turn up most causes on the first inspection without wasting time checking components that have little or no relationship to the problem.

4. Test all repairs after the work is done to make sure that the problem is fixed. Some causes can be traced to more than one component, so a careful verification of repair work is important in order to pick up additional malfunctions that may cause a problem to reappear or a different problem to arise. A blown fuse, for example, is a simple problem that may require more than another fuse to repair. If you don't look for a problem that caused a fuse to blow, a shorted wire (for example) may go undetected.

Experience has shown that most problems tend to be the result of a fairly simple and obvious cause, such as loose or corroded connectors or air leaks in the intake system. This makes careful inspection of components during testing essential to quick and accurate troubleshooting.

BASIC TROUBLESHOOTING THEORY

Electrical problems generally fall into one of three areas:
• The component that is not functioning is not receiving current.
• The component itself is not functioning.
• The component is not properly grounded.

Problems that fall into the first category are by far the most complicated. It is the current supply system to the component which contains all the switches, relay, fuses, etc.

The electrical system can be checked with a test light and a jumper wire. A test light is a device that looks like a pointed screwdriver with a wire attached to it. It has a light bulb in its handle. A jumper wire is a piece of insulated wire with an alligator clip attached to each end.

If a light bulb is not working, you must follow a systematic plan to determine which of the three causes is the villain.

1. Turn on the switch that controls the inoperable bulb.
2. Disconnect the power supply wire from the bulb.
3. Attach the ground wire to the test light to a good metal ground.
4. Touch the probe end of the test light to the end of the power supply wire that was disconnected from the bulb. If the bulb is receiving current, the test light will go on.

➡ **If the bulb is one which works only when the ignition key is turned on (turn signal), make sure the key is turned on.**

If the test light does not go on, then the problem is in the circuit between the battery and the bulb. As mentioned before, this includes all the switches, fuses, and relays in the system. Turn to a wiring diagram and find the bulb on the diagram. Follow the wire that runs back to the battery. The problem is an open circuit between the battery and the bulb. If the fuse is blown and, when replaced, immediately blows again, there is a short circuit in the system which must be located and repaired. If there is a switch in the system, bypass it with a jumper wire. This is done by connecting one end of the jumper wire to the power supply wire into the switch and the other end of the jumper wire to the wire coming out of the switch. If the test

light illuminates with the jumper wire installed, the switch or whatever was bypassed is defective.

➡ **Never substitute the jumper wire for the bulb, as the bulb is the component required to use the power from the power source.**

5. If the bulb in the test light goes on, then the current is getting to the bulb that is not working in the car. This eliminates the first of the three possible causes. Connect the power supply wire and connect a jumper wire from the bulb to a good metal ground. Do this with the switch which controls the bulb works with jumper wire installed, then it has a bad ground. This is usually caused by the metal area on which the bulb mounts to the car being coated with some type of foreign matter.

6. If neither test located the source of the trouble, then the light bulb itself is defective.

The above test procedure can be applied to any of the components of the chassis electrical system by substituting the component that is not working for the light bulb. Remember that for any electrical system to work, all connections must be clean and tight.

TEST EQUIPMENT

➡ **Pinpointing the exact cause of trouble in an electrical system can sometimes only be accomplished by the use of special test equipment. The following describes different types of commonly used test equipment and explains how to use them in diagnosis. In addition to the information covered below, the tool manufacturer's instructions booklet (provided with the tester) should be read and clearly understood before attempting any test procedures.**

Jumper Wires

Jumper wires are simple, yet extremely valuable, pieces of test equipment. They are basically test wires which are used to bypass sections of a circuit. The simplest type of jumper wire is a length of multi-strand wire with an alligator clip at each end. Jumper wires are usually fabricated from lengths of standard automotive wire and whatever type of connector (alligator clip, spade connector or pin connector) that is required for the particular vehicle being tested. The well equipped tool box will have several different styles of jumper wires in several different lengths. Some jumper wires are made with three or more terminals coming from a common splice for special purpose testing. In cramped, hard-to-reach areas it is advisable to have insulated boots over the jumper wire terminals in order to prevent accidental grounding, sparks, and possible fire, especially when testing fuel system components.

Jumper wires are used primarily to locate open electrical circuits, on either the ground (-) side of the circuit or on the hot (+) side. If an electrical component fails to operate, connect the jumper wire between the component and a good ground. If the component operates only with the jumper installed, the ground circuit is open. If the ground circuit is good, but the component does not operate, the circuit between the power feed and component may be open. By moving the jumper wire successively back from the lamp toward the power source, you can isolate the area of the circuit where the open is located. When the component stops functioning, or the power is cut off, the open is in the segment of wire between the jumper and the point previously tested.

You can sometimes connect the jumper wire directly from the battery to the hot terminal of the component, but first make sure the component uses 12 volts in operation. Some electrical components, such as fuel injectors, are designed to operate on about 4 volts and running 12 volts directly to the injector terminals can cause damage.

By inserting an in-line fuse holder between a set of test leads, a fused jumper wire can be used for bypassing open circuits. Use a 5 amp fuse to provide protection against voltage spikes. When in doubt, use a voltmeter to check the voltage input to the component and measure how much voltage is normally being applied.

❋❋CAUTION

Never use jumpers made from wire that is of lighter gauge than that which is used in the circuit under test. If the jumper wire is of too small a gauge, it may overheat and possibly melt. Never use jumpers to bypass high resistance loads in a circuit. Bypassing resistances, in effect, creates a short circuit. This may, in turn, cause damage and fire. Jumper wires should only be used to bypass lengths of wire.

Unpowered Test Lights

The 12 volt test light is used to check circuits and components while electrical current is flowing through them. It is used for voltage and ground tests. Twelve volt test lights come in different styles but all have three main parts; a ground clip, a probe, and a light. The most commonly used 12 volt test lights have pick-type probes. To use a 12 volt test light, connect the ground clip to a good ground and probe wherever necessary with the pick. The pick should be sharp so that it can be probed into tight spaces.

❋❋CAUTION

Do not use a test light to probe electronic ignition spark plug or coil wires. Never use a pick-type test light to probe wiring on computer controlled systems unless specifically instructed to do so. Any wire insulation that is pierced by the test light probe should be taped and sealed with silicone after testing.

Like the jumper wire, the 12 volt test light is used to isolate opens in circuits. But, whereas the jumper wire is used to bypass the open to operate the load, the 12 volt test light is used to locate the presence of voltage in a circuit. If the test light glows, you know that there is power up to that point; if the 12 volt test light does not glow when its probe is inserted into the wire or connector, you know that there is an open circuit (no power). Move the test light in successive steps back toward the power source until the light in the handle does

glow. When it glows, the open is between the probe and point which was probed previously.

➥**The test light does not detect that 12 volts (or any particular amount of voltage) is present; it only detects that some voltage is present. It is advisable before using the test light to touch its terminals across the battery posts to make sure the light is operating properly.**

Self-Powered Test Lights

The self-powered test light usually contains a 1.5 volt penlight battery. One type of self-powered test light is similar in design to the 12 volt unit. This type has both the battery and the light in the handle, along with a pick-type probe tip. The second type has the light toward the open tip, so that the light illuminates the contact point. The self-powered test light is a dual purpose piece of test equipment. It can be used to test for either open or short circuits when power is isolated from the circuit (continuity test). A powered test light should not be used on any computer controlled system or component unless specifically instructed to do so. Many engine sensors can be destroyed by even this small amount of voltage applied directly to the terminals.

Voltmeters

A voltmeter is used to measure voltage at any point in a circuit, or to measure the voltage drop across any part of a circuit. It can also be used to check continuity in a wire or circuit by indicating current flow from one end to the other. Analog voltmeters usually have various scales on the meter dial and a selector switch to allow the selection of different voltages. The voltmeter has a positive and a negative lead. To avoid damage to the meter, always connect the negative lead to the negative (-) side of the circuit (to ground or nearest the ground side of the circuit) and connect the positive lead to the positive (+) side of the circuit (to the power source or the nearest power source). Note that the negative voltmeter lead will always be black and that the positive voltmeter will always be some color other than black (usually red).

Depending on how the voltmeter is connected into the circuit, it has several uses. A voltmeter can be connected either in parallel or in series with a circuit and it has a very high resistance to current flow. When connected in parallel, only a small amount of current will flow through the voltmeter current path; the rest will flow through the normal circuit current path and the circuit will work normally. When the voltmeter is connected in series with a circuit, only a small amount of current can flow through the circuit. The circuit will not work properly, but the voltmeter reading will show if the circuit is complete or not.

Ohmmeters

The ohmmeter is designed to read resistance (which is measured in ohms or Ω) in a circuit or component. Although there are several different styles of ohmmeters, all analog meters will usually have a selector switch which permits the measurement of different ranges of resistance (usually the selector switch allows the multiplication of the meter reading by 10, 100, 1000, and 10,000). A calibration knob allows the meter to be set at zero for accurate measurement. Since all ohmmeters are powered by an internal battery, the ohmmeter can be used as a self-powered test light. When the ohmmeter is connected, current from the ohmmeter flows through the circuit or component being tested. Since the ohmmeter's internal resistance and voltage are known values, the amount of current flow through the meter depends on the resistance of the circuit or component being tested.

The ohmmeter can be used to perform a continuity test for opens or shorts (either by observation of the meter needle or as a self-powered test light), and to read actual resistance in a circuit. It should be noted that the ohmmeter is used to check the resistance of a component or wire while there is no voltage applied to the circuit. Current flow from an outside voltage source (such as the vehicle battery) can damage the ohmmeter, so the circuit or component should be isolated from the vehicle electrical system before any testing is done. Since the ohmmeter uses its own voltage source, either lead can be connected to any test point.

➡When checking diodes or other solid state components, the ohmmeter leads can only be connected one way in order to measure current flow in a single direction. Make sure the positive (+) and negative (-) terminal connections are as described in the test procedures to verify the one-way diode operation.

In using the meter for making continuity checks, do not be concerned with the actual resistance readings. Zero resistance, or any ohm reading, indicates continuity in the circuit. Infinite resistance indicates an open in the circuit. A high resistance reading where there should be none indicates a problem in the circuit. Checks for short circuits are made in the same manner as checks for open circuits except that the circuit must be isolated from both power and normal ground. Infinite resistance indicates no continuity to ground, while zero resistance indicates a dead short to ground.

Ammeters

An ammeter measures the amount of current flowing through a circuit in units called amperes or amps. Amperes are units of electron flow which indicate how fast the electrons are flowing through the circuit. Since Ohms Law dictates that current flow in a circuit is equal to the circuit voltage divided by the total circuit resistance, increasing voltage also increases the current level (amps). Likewise, any decrease in resistance will increase the amount of amps in a circuit. At normal operating voltage, most circuits have a characteristic amount of amperes, called "current draw" which can be measured using an ammeter. By referring to a specified current draw rating, measuring the amperes, and comparing the two values, one can determine what is happening within the circuit to aid in diagnosis. An open circuit, for example, will not allow any current to flow so the ammeter reading will be zero. More current flows through a heavily loaded circuit or when the charging system is operating.

An ammeter is always connected in series with the circuit being tested. All of the current that normally flows through the circuit must also flow through the ammeter; if there is any other path for the current to follow, the ammeter reading will not be accurate. The ammeter itself has very little resistance to current flow and therefore will not affect the circuit, but it will measure current draw only when the circuit is closed and electricity is flowing. Excessive current draw can blow fuses

and drain the battery, while a reduced current draw can cause motors to run slowly, lights to dim and other components to not operate properly. The ammeter can help diagnose these conditions by locating the cause of the high or low reading.

Multimeters

Different combinations of test meters can be built into a single unit designed for specific tests. Some of the more common combination test devices are known as Volt/Amp testers, Tach/Dwell meters, or Digital Multimeters. The Volt/Amp tester is used for charging system, starting system or battery tests and consists of a voltmeter, an ammeter and a variable resistance carbon pile. The voltmeter will usually have at least two ranges for use with 6, 12 and/or 24 volt systems. The ammeter also has more than one range for testing various levels of battery loads and starter current draw. The carbon pile can be adjusted to offer different amounts of resistance. The Volt/Amp tester has heavy leads to carry large amounts of current and many later models have an inductive ammeter pickup that clamps around the wire to simplify test connections. On some models, the ammeter also has a zero-center scale to allow testing of charging and starting systems without switching leads or polarity. A digital multimeter is a voltmeter, ammeter and ohmmeter combined in an instrument which gives a digital readout. These are often used when testing solid state circuits because of their high input impedance (usually 10 megohms or more).

The tach/dwell meter that combines a tachometer and a dwell (cam angle) meter is a specialized kind of voltmeter. The tachometer scale is marked to show engine speed in rpm and the dwell scale is marked to show degrees of distributor shaft rotation. In most electronic ignition systems, dwell is determined by the control unit, but the dwell meter can also be used to check the duty cycle (operation) of some electronic engine control systems. Some tach/dwell meters are powered by an internal battery, while others take their power from the vehicle battery in use. The battery powered testers usually require calibration (much like an ohmmeter) before testing.

TESTING

Open Circuits

To use the self-powered test light or a multimeter to check for open circuits, first isolate the circuit from the vehicle's 12 volt power source by disconnecting the battery or wiring harness connector. Connect the test light or ohmmeter ground clip to a good ground and probe sections of the circuit sequentially with the test light. (start from either end of the circuit). If the light is out/or there is infinite resistance, the open is between the probe and the circuit ground. If the light is on/or the meter shows continuity, the open is between the probe and end of the circuit toward the power source.

Short Circuits

By isolating the circuit both from power and from ground, and using a self-powered test light or multimeter, you can check for shorts to ground in the circuit. Isolate the circuit from power and ground. Connect the test light or ohmmeter ground clip to a good ground and probe any easy-to-reach test point in the circuit. If the light comes on or there is continuity, there is a short somewhere in the circuit. To isolate the short, probe a test point at either end of the isolated circuit (the light should be on/there should be continuity). Leave the test light probe engaged and open connectors, switches, remove parts, etc., sequentially, until the light goes out/continuity is broken. When the light goes out, the short is between the last circuit component opened and the previous circuit opened.

➡**The battery in the test light and does not provide much current. A weak battery may not provide enough power to illuminate the test light even when a complete circuit is made (especially if there are high resistances in the circuit). Always make sure that the test battery is strong. To check the battery, briefly touch the ground clip to the probe; if the light glows brightly the battery is strong enough for testing. Never use a self-powered test light to perform checks for opens or shorts when power is applied to the electrical system under test. The 12 volt vehicle power will quickly burn out the light bulb in the test light.**

Available Voltage Measurement

Set the voltmeter selector switch to the 20V position and connect the meter negative lead to the negative post of the battery. Connect the positive meter lead to the positive post of the battery and turn the ignition switch **ON** to provide a load. Read the voltage on the meter or digital display. A well charged battery should register over 12 volts. If the meter reads below 11.5 volts, the battery power may be insufficient to operate the electrical system properly. This test determines voltage available from the battery and should be the first step in any electrical trouble diagnosis procedure. Many electrical problems, especially on computer controlled systems, can be caused by a low state of charge in the battery. Excessive corrosion at the battery cable terminals can cause a poor contact that will prevent proper charging and full battery current flow.

Normal battery voltage is 12 volts when fully charged. When the battery is supplying current to one or more circuits it is said to be "under load." When everything is off the electrical system is under a "no-load" condition. A fully charged battery may show about 12.5 volts at no load; will drop to 12 volts under medium load; and will drop even lower under heavy load. If the battery is partially discharged the voltage decrease under heavy load may be excessive, even though the battery shows 12 volts or more at no load. When allowed to discharge further, the battery's available voltage under load will decrease more severely. For this reason, it is important that the battery be fully charged during all testing procedures to avoid errors in diagnosis and incorrect test results.

Voltage Drop

When current flows through a resistance, the voltage beyond the resistance is reduced (the larger the current, the greater the reduction in voltage). When no current is flowing, there is no voltage drop because there is no current flow. All points in the circuit which are connected to the power source are at the same voltage as the power source. The total voltage drop always equals the total source voltage. In a long circuit with many connectors, a series of small, unwanted voltage drops

due to corrosion at the connectors can add up to a total loss of voltage which impairs the operation of the normal loads in the circuit. The maximum allowable voltage drop under load is critical, especially if there is more than one high resistance problem in a circuit because all voltage drops are cumulative. A small drop is normal due to the resistance of the conductors.

INDIRECT COMPUTATION OF VOLTAGE DROPS

1. Set the voltmeter selector switch to the 20 volt position.
2. Connect the meter negative lead to a good ground.
3. While operating the circuit, probe all loads in the circuit with the positive meter lead and observe the voltage readings. A drop should be noticed after the first load. But, there should be little or no voltage drop before the first load.

DIRECT MEASUREMENT OF VOLTAGE DROPS

1. Set the voltmeter switch to the 20 volt position.
2. Connect the voltmeter negative lead to the ground side of the load to be measured.
3. Connect the positive lead to the positive side of the resistance or load to be measured.
4. Read the voltage drop directly on the 20 volt scale.

Too high a voltage indicates too high a resistance. If, for example, a blower motor runs too slowly, you can determine if perhaps there is too high a resistance in the resistor pack. By taking voltage drop readings in all parts of the circuit, you can isolate the problem. Too low a voltage drop indicates too low a resistance. Take the blower motor for example again. If a blower motor runs too fast in the MED and/or LOW position, the problem might be isolated in the resistor pack by taking voltage drop readings in all parts of the circuit to locate a possibly shorted resistor.

HIGH RESISTANCE TESTING

1. Set the voltmeter selector switch to the 4 volt position.
2. Connect the voltmeter positive lead to the positive post of the battery.
3. Turn on the headlights and heater blower to provide a load.
4. Probe various points in the circuit with the negative voltmeter lead.
5. Read the voltage drop on the 4 volt scale. Some average maximum allowable voltage drops are:
   - FUSE PANEL: 0.7 volts
   - IGNITION SWITCH: 0.5 volts
   - HEADLIGHT SWITCH: 0.7 volts
   - IGNITION COIL (+): 0.5 volts
   - ANY OTHER LOAD: 1.3 volts

➡**Voltage drops are all measured while a load is operating; without current flow, there will be no voltage drop.**

Resistance Measurement

The batteries in an ohmmeter will weaken with age and temperature, so the ohmmeter must be calibrated or "zeroed" before taking measurements. To zero the meter, place the selector switch in its lowest range and touch the two ohmmeter leads together. Turn the calibration knob until the meter needle is exactly on zero.

➡All analog (needle) type ohmmeters must be zeroed before use, but some digital ohmmeter models are automatically calibrated when the switch is turned on. Self-calibrating digital ohmmeters do not have an adjusting knob, but its a good idea to check for a zero readout before use by touching the leads together. All computer controlled systems require the use of a digital ohmmeter with at least 10 megohms impedance for testing. Before any test procedures are attempted, make sure the ohmmeter used is compatible with the electrical system or damage to the on-board computer could result.

To measure resistance, first isolate the circuit from the vehicle power source by disconnecting the battery cables or the harness connector. Make sure the key is **OFF** when disconnecting any components or the battery. Where necessary, also isolate at least one side of the circuit to be checked in order to avoid reading parallel resistances. Parallel circuit resistances will always give a lower reading than the actual resistance of either of the branches. When measuring the resistance of parallel circuits, the total resistance will always be lower than the smallest resistance in the circuit. Connect the meter leads to both sides of the circuit (wire or component) and read the actual measured ohms on the meter scale. Make sure the selector switch is set to the proper ohm scale for the circuit being tested to avoid misreading the ohmmeter test value.

✳✳WARNING

Never use an ohmmeter with power applied to the circuit. Like the self-powered test light, the ohmmeter is designed to operate on its own power supply. The normal 12 volt automotive electrical system current could damage the meter!

Wiring Harnesses

The average automobile contains about ½ mile of wiring, with hundreds of individual connections. To protect the many wires from damage and to keep them from becoming a confusing tangle, they are organized into bundles, enclosed in plastic or taped together and called wiring harnesses. Different harnesses serve different parts of the vehicle. Individual wires are color coded to help trace them through a harness where sections are hidden from view.

Automotive wiring or circuit conductors can be in any one of three forms:
1. Single strand wire
2. Multi-strand wire
3. Printed circuitry

Single strand wire has a solid metal core and is usually used inside such components as alternators, motors, relays and other devices. Multi-strand wire has a core made of many small strands of wire twisted together into a single conductor. Most of the wiring in an automotive electrical system is made up of multi-strand wire, either as a single conductor or grouped

together in a harness. All wiring is color coded on the insulator, either as a solid color or as a colored wire with an identification stripe. A printed circuit is a thin film of copper or other conductor that is printed on an insulator backing. Occasionally, a printed circuit is sandwiched between two sheets of plastic for more protection and flexibility. A complete printed circuit, consisting of conductors, insulating material and connectors for lamps or other components is called a printed circuit board. Printed circuitry is used in place of individual wires or harnesses in places where space is limited, such as behind instrument panels.

Since automotive electrical systems are very sensitive to changes in resistance, the selection of properly sized wires is critical when systems are repaired. A loose or corroded connection or a replacement wire that is too small for the circuit will add extra resistance and an additional voltage drop to the circuit. A ten percent voltage drop can result in slow or erratic motor operation, for example, even though the circuit is complete. The wire gauge number is an expression of the cross-section area of the conductor. The most common system for expressing wire size is the American Wire Gauge (AWG) system.

Gauge numbers are assigned to conductors of various cross-section areas. As gauge number increases, area decreases and the conductor becomes smaller. A 5 gauge conductor is smaller than a 1 gauge conductor and a 10 gauge is smaller than a 5 gauge. As the cross-section area of a conductor decreases, resistance increases and so does the gauge number. A conductor with a higher gauge number will carry less current than a conductor with a lower gauge number.

➡Gauge wire size refers to the size of the conductor, not the size of the complete wire. It is possible to have two wires of the same gauge with different diameters because one may have thicker insulation than the other.

12 volt automotive electrical systems generally use 10, 12, 14, 16 and 18 gauge wire. Main power distribution circuits and larger accessories usually use 10 and 12 gauge wire. Battery cables are usually 4 or 6 gauge, although 1 and 2 gauge wires are occasionally used. Wire length must also be considered when making repairs to a circuit. As conductor length increases, so does resistance. An 18 gauge wire, for example, can carry a 10 amp load for 10 feet without excessive voltage drop; however if a 15 foot wire is required for the same 10 amp load, it must be a 16 gauge wire.

An electrical schematic shows the electrical current paths when a circuit is operating properly. It is essential to understand how a circuit works before trying to figure out why it doesn't. Schematics break the entire electrical system down into individual circuits and show only one particular circuit. In a schematic, no attempt is made to represent wiring and components as they physically appear on the vehicle; switches and other components are shown as simply as possible. Face views of harness connectors show the cavity or terminal locations in all multi-pin connectors to help locate test points.

If you need to backprobe a connector while it is on the component, the order of the terminals must be mentally reversed. The wire color code can help in this situation, as well as a keyway, lock tab or other reference mark.

WIRING REPAIR

Soldering is a quick, efficient method of joining metals permanently. Everyone who has the occasion to make wiring repairs should know how to solder. Electrical connections that are soldered are far less likely to come apart and will conduct electricity much better than connections that are only "pig-tailed" together. The most popular (and preferred) method of soldering is with an electrical soldering gun. Soldering irons are available in many sizes and wattage ratings. Irons with higher wattage ratings deliver higher temperatures and recover lost heat faster. A small soldering iron rated for no more than 50 watts is recommended, especially on electrical systems where excess heat can damage the components being soldered.

There are three ingredients necessary for successful soldering; proper flux, good solder and sufficient heat. A soldering flux is necessary to clean the metal of tarnish, prepare it for soldering and to enable the solder to spread into tiny crevices. When soldering, always use a rosin core solder which is non-corrosive and will not attract moisture once the job is finished. Other types of flux (acid core) will leave a residue that will attract moisture and cause the wires to corrode. Tin is a unique metal with a low melting point. In a molten state, it dissolves and alloys easily with many metals. Solder is made by mixing tin with lead. The most common proportions are 40/60, 50/50 and 60/40, with the percentage of tin listed first. Low priced solders usually contain less tin, making them very difficult for a beginner to use because more heat is required to melt the solder. A common solder is 40/60 which is well suited for all-around general use, but 60/40 melts easier and is preferred for electrical work.

Soldering Techniques

Successful soldering requires that the metals to be joined be heated to a temperature that will melt the solder, usually 360-460°F (182-238°C). Contrary to popular belief, the purpose of the soldering iron is not to melt the solder itself, but to heat the parts being soldered to a temperature high enough to melt the solder when it is touched to the work. Melting flux-cored solder on the soldering iron will usually destroy the effectiveness of the flux.

➡**Soldering tips are made of copper for good heat conductivity, but must be "tinned" regularly for quick transference of heat to the project and to prevent the solder from sticking to the iron. To "tin" the iron, simply heat it and touch the flux-cored solder to the tip; the solder will flow over the hot tip. Wipe the excess off with a clean rag, but be careful as the iron will be hot.**

After some use, the tip may become pitted. If so, simply dress the tip smooth with a smooth file and "tin" the tip again. Flux-cored solder will remove oxides but rust, bits of insulation and oil or grease must be removed with a wire brush or emery cloth. For maximum strength in soldered parts, the joint must start off clean and tight. Weak joints will result in gaps too wide for the solder to bridge.

If a separate soldering flux is used, it should be brushed or swabbed on only those areas that are to be soldered. Most solders contain a core of flux and separate fluxing is unnecessary. Hold the work to be soldered firmly. It is best to solder on a wooden board, because a metal vise will only rob the piece to be soldered of heat and make it difficult to melt the solder. Hold the soldering tip with the broadest face against the work to be soldered. Apply solder under the tip close to the work, using enough solder to give a heavy film between the iron and the piece being soldered, while moving slowly and making sure the solder melts properly. Keep the work level or the solder will run to the lowest part and favor the thicker parts, because these require more heat to melt the solder. If the soldering tip overheats (the solder coating on the face of the tip burns up), it should be retinned. Once the soldering is completed, let the soldered joint stand until cool. Tape and seal all soldered wire splices after the repair has cooled.

Wire Harness Connectors

Most connectors in the engine compartment or that are otherwise exposed to the elements are protected against moisture and dirt which could create oxidation and deposits on the terminals.

These special connectors are weather-proof. All repairs require the use of a special terminal and the tool required to service it. This tool is used to remove the pin and sleeve terminals. If removal is attempted with an ordinary pick, there is a good chance that the terminal will be bent or deformed. Unlike standard blade type terminals, these weather-proof terminals cannot be straightened once they are bent. Make certain that the connectors are properly seated and all of the sealing rings are in place when connecting leads. On some models, a hinge-type flap provides a backup or secondary locking feature for the terminals. Most secondary locks are used to improve connector reliability by retaining the terminals if the small terminal lock tangs are not positioned properly.

Molded-on connectors require complete replacement of the connection. This means splicing a new connector assembly into the harness. All splices should be soldered to insure proper contact. Use care when probing the connections or replacing terminals in them as it is possible to short between opposite terminals. If this happens to the wrong terminal pair, it is possible to damage certain components. Always use jumper wires between connectors for circuit checking and never probe through weatherproof seals.

Open circuits are often difficult to locate by sight because corrosion or terminal misalignment are hidden by the connectors. Merely wiggling a connector on a sensor or in the wiring harness may correct the open circuit condition. This should always be considered when an open circuit or a failed sensor is indicated. Intermittent problems may also be caused by oxidized or loose connections. When using a circuit tester for diagnosis, always probe connections from the wire side. Be careful not to damage sealed connectors with test probes.

All wiring harnesses should be replaced with identical parts, using the same gauge wire and connectors. When signal wires are spliced into a harness, use wire with high temperature insulation only. It is seldom necessary to replace a complete harness. If replacement is necessary, pay close attention to insure proper harness routing. Secure the harness with suitable plastic wire clamps to prevent vibrations from causing the harness to wear in spots or contact any hot components.

➡**Weatherproof connectors cannot be replaced with standard connectors. Instructions are provided with replacement connector and terminal packages. Some wire harnesses have mounting indicators (usually pieces of colored tape) to mark where the harness is to be secured.**

In making wiring repairs, its important that you always replace damaged wires with wiring of the same gauge as the wire being replaced. The heavier the wire, the smaller the gauge number. Wires are color-coded to aid in identification and whenever possible the same color coded wire should be used for replacement. A wire stripping and crimping tool is necessary to install solderless terminal connectors. Test all crimps by pulling on the wires; it should not be possible to pull the wires out of a good crimp.

Wires which are open, exposed or otherwise damaged are repaired by simple splicing. Where possible, if the wiring harness is accessible and the damaged place in the wire can be located, it is best to open the harness and check for all possible damage. In an inaccessible harness, the wire must be bypassed with a new insert, usually taped to the outside of the old harness.

When replacing fusible links, be sure to use fusible link wire, NOT ordinary automotive wire. Make sure the fusible segment is of the same gauge and construction as the one being replaced and double the stripped end when crimping the terminal connector for a good contact. The melted (open) fusible link segment of the wiring harness should be cut off as close to the harness as possible, then a new segment spliced in as described. In the case of a damaged fusible link that feeds two harness wires, the harness connections should be replaced with two fusible link wires so that each circuit will have its own separate protection.

➡**Most of the problems caused in the wiring harness are due to bad ground connections. Always check all vehicle ground connections for corrosion or looseness before performing any power feed checks to eliminate the chance of a bad ground affecting the circuit.**

Hard-Shell Connectors

Unlike molded connectors, the terminal contacts in hard-shell connectors can be replaced. Weatherproof hard-shell connectors with the leads molded into the shell have non-replaceable terminal ends. Replacement usually involves the use of a special terminal removal tool that depresses the locking tangs (barbs) on the connector terminal and allows the connector to be removed from the rear of the shell. The connector shell should be replaced if it shows any evidence of burning, melting, cracks, or breaks. Replace individual terminals that are burnt, corroded, distorted or loose.

➡**The insulation crimp must be tight to prevent the insulation from sliding back on the wire when the wire is pulled. The insulation must be visibly compressed under the crimp tabs, and the ends of the crimp should be turned in for a firm grip on the insulation.**

The wire crimp must be made with all wire strands inside the crimp. The terminal must be fully compressed on the wire strands with the ends of the crimp tabs turned in to make a firm grip on the wire. Check all connections with an ohmmeter to insure a good contact. There should be no measurable resistance between the wire and the terminal when connected.

Add-On Electrical Equipment

The electrical system in your vehicle is designed to perform under reasonable operating conditions without interference between components. Before any additional electrical equipment is installed, it is recommended that you consult your dealer or a reputable repair facility that is familiar with the vehicle and its systems.

If the vehicle is equipped with mobile radio equipment and/or mobile telephone, it may have an effect upon the operation of the ECM. Radio Frequency Interference (RFI) from the communications system can be picked up by the vehicle's wiring harnesses and conducted into the ECM, giving it the wrong messages at the wrong time. Although well shielded against RFI, the ECM should be further protected by taking the following measures:

• Install the antenna as far as possible from the ECM. For instance, if the ECM is located behind the center console area, then the antenna should be mounted at the rear of the vehicle.

• Keep the antenna wiring a minimum of eight inches away from any wiring running to the ECM and from the ECM itself. NEVER wind the antenna wire around any other wiring.

• Mount the equipment as far from the ECM as possible. Be very careful during installation not to drill through any wires or short a wire harness with a mounting screw.

• Insure that the electrical feed wire(s) to the equipment are properly and tightly connected. Loose connectors can cause interference.

• Make certain that the equipment is properly grounded to the vehicle. Poor grounding can damage expensive equipment.

SUPPLEMENTAL INFLATABLE RESTRAINT (SIR) SYSTEM

General Information

▶ See Figure 1

Beginning in 1995, driver's side and passenger air bags became standard equipment for the Cavalier and Sunfire. The Supplemental Inflatable Restraint (SIR) system offers protection in addition to that provided by the seat belt by deploying an air bag from the center of the steering wheel or dash panel. The air bag deploys when the vehicle is involved in a frontal crash of sufficient force up to 30° off the centerline of the vehicle. To further absorb the crash energy, there is also a knee bolster located beneath the instrument panel in the driver's area and the steering wheel is collapsible.

The system has an energy reserve, which can store a large enough electrical charge to deploy the air bag(s) for up to ten minutes after the battery has been disconnected or damaged. The system **MUST** be disabled before any service is performed on or around SIR components or SIR wiring.

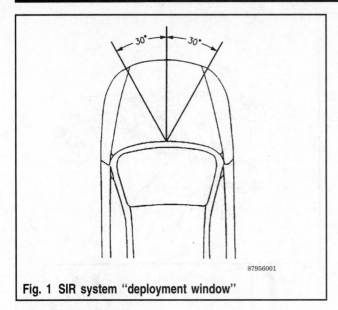

87956001

Fig. 1 SIR system "deployment window"

SYSTEM OPERATION

The SIR system contains a deployment loop for each air bag and a Diagnostic Energy Reserve Module (DERM). The deployment loop supplies current through the inflator module which will cause air bag deployment in the event of a frontal collision of sufficient force. The DERM supplies the necessary power, even if the battery has been damaged.

The deployment loop is made up of the arming sensors, coil assembly, inflator module and the discriminating sensors. The inflator module is only supplied sufficient current when the arming sensor and at least one of the two discriminating sensors close simultaneously. The function of the DERM is to supply the deployment loop a 36 Volt Loop Reserve (36VLR) to assure sufficient voltage to deploy the air bag if ignition voltage is lost in a frontal crash.

The DERM, in conjunction with the sensor resistors, makes it possible to detect circuit and component malfunctions within the deployment loop. If the voltages monitored by the DERM fall outside expected limits, the DERM will indicate a malfunction by storing a diagnostic trouble code and illuminating the AIR BAG lamp.

SYSTEM COMPONENTS

▶ See Figure 2

Diagnostic Energy Reserve Module (DERM)

The DERM is designed to perform five main functions: energy reserve, malfunction detection, malfunction recording, driver notification and frontal crash recording.

The DERM maintains a reserve voltage supply to provide deployment energy for a few seconds when the vehicle voltage is low or lost in a frontal crash. The DERM performs diagnostic monitoring of the SIR system and records malfunctions in the form of diagnostic trouble codes, which can be obtained from a hand scan tool and/or on-board diagnostics. The DERM

warns the driver of SIR system malfunctions by controlling the AIR BAG warning lamp and records SIR system status during a frontal crash.

AIR BAG Warning Lamp

The AIR BAG warning/indicator lamp is used to verify lamp and DERM operation by flashing 7 times when the ignition is first turned **ON**. It is also used to warn the driver of an SIR system malfunction.

Discriminating Sensors

Vehicles equipped with driver's side air bag only, have two discriminating sensors. The forward discriminating sensor is located in front of the radiator. The passenger compartment discriminating sensor is located behind the right side of the instrument panel.

The discriminating sensor consists of a sensing element, diagnostic resistor and normally open switch contacts. The sensing element closes the switch contact when vehicle velocity changes are severe enough to warrant air bag deployment.

Dual Pole Arming Sensor

The dual pole arming sensor is contained in the same housing as the passenger compartment discriminating sensor and is referred to as the dual sensor.

The arming sensor is a switch located in the power side of the deployment loop. It is calibrated to close at low level velocity changes (lower than the discriminating sensors), assuring that the inflator module is connected directly to the 36VLR output of the DERM or Ignition 1 voltage when any discriminating sensor closes.

SIR Coil Assembly

▶ See Figure 3

The SIR coil assembly consists of two current carrying coils. They are attached to the steering column and allow rotation of the steering wheel while maintaining continuous deployment loop contact through the inflator module.

There is a shorting bar on the lower steering column connector that connects the SIR coil to the SIR wiring harness. The shorting bar shorts the circuit when the connector is disengaged. The circuit to the inflator module is shorted in this way to prevent unwanted air bag deployment when servicing the steering column or other SIR components.

Inflator Module

The inflator module consists of an inflatable bag and an inflator (a canister of gas-generating material and an initiating device). When the vehicle is in a frontal crash of sufficient force to close the arming sensor and at least one discriminating sensor simultaneously, current flows through the deployment loop. Current passing through the initiator ignites the material in the inflator module, causing a reaction which produces a gas that rapidly inflates the air bag.

All vehicles are equipped with a driver's side inflator module located in the steering wheel and a passenger side inflator module located in the dash panel.

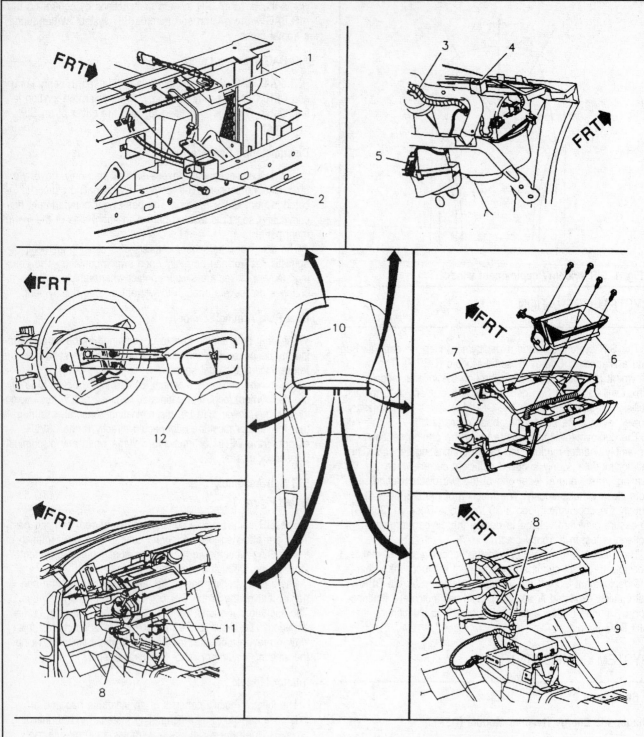

1 HOOD LATCH SUPPORT BRACKET
2 FORWARD DISCRIMINATING SENSOR
3 TIEBAR ASSEMBLY
4 PASSENGER COMPARTMENT
   DISCRIMINATING SENSOR
5 GLOVE BOX LEAD
6 PASSENGER INFLATOR MODULE
7 DASH PANEL ASSEMBLY
8 DASH WIRING HARNESS
9 DERM
10 SIR WIRING HARNESS
11 DUAL POLE ARMING SENSOR
12 DRIVER INFLATOR MODULE

87956002

Fig. 2 SIR system components

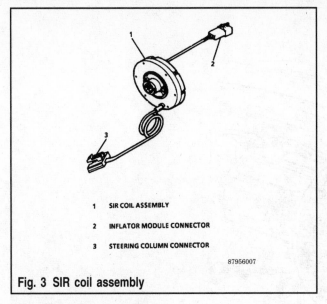

1 SIR COIL ASSEMBLY

2 INFLATOR MODULE CONNECTOR

3 STEERING COLUMN CONNECTOR

87956007

Fig. 3 SIR coil assembly

SERVICE PRECAUTIONS

▶ See Figure 4

• When performing service around the SIR system components or wiring, the SIR system **MUST** be disabled. Failure to do so could result in possible air bag deployment, personal injury or unneeded SIR system repairs.

• When carrying a live inflator module, make sure that the bag and trim cover are pointed away from you. Never carry the inflator module by the wires or connector on the underside of the module. In case of accidental deployment, the bag will then deploy with minimal chance of injury.

• When placing a live inflator module on a bench or other surface, always face the bag and trim cover up, away from the surface.

DISABLING THE SYSTEM

▶ See Figure 5

➡ With the "AIR BAG" fuse removed and the ignition switch ON, the "AIR BAG" warning lamp will be on. The is normal and does not indicate any system malfunction.

1. Turn the steering wheel so that the vehicle's wheels are pointing straight ahead.
2. Turn the ignition switch to **LOCK**, remove the key, then disconnect the negative battery cable.
3. Remove the "AIR BAG" fuse from the fuse block.
4. Remove the steering column filler panel.
5. Disengage the Connector Position Assurance (CPA) and both yellow two way connectors and corresponding CPAs located near the base of the steering column.
6. Connect the negative battery cable.

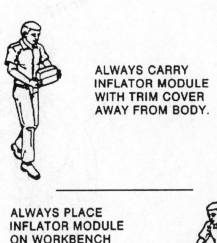

ALWAYS CARRY INFLATOR MODULE WITH TRIM COVER AWAY FROM BODY.

ALWAYS PLACE INFLATOR MODULE ON WORKBENCH WITH TRIM COVER UP, AWAY FROM LOOSE OBJECTS.

87956010

Fig. 4 When carrying a live inflator module, make sure that the bag and trim cover are pointed away from you. Never carry the inflator module by the wires or connector on the underside of the module

ENABLING THE SYSTEM

▶ See Figure 5

1. Disconnect the negative battery cable.
2. Turn the ignition switch to **LOCK**, then remove the key.
3. Engage both yellow SIR connectors and corresponding CPAs located near the base of the steering column.
4. Install the steering column filler panel.
5. Install the "AIR BAG" fuse to the fuse block.
6. Connect the negative battery cable.
7. Turn the ignition switch to **RUN** and make sure that the "AIR BAG" warning lamp flashes seven times and then shuts off. If the warning lamp does not shut off, make sure that the wiring is properly connected. If the light remains on, take the vehicle to a reputable repair facility for service.

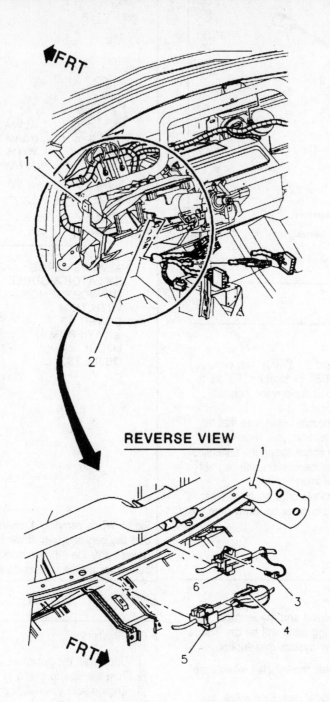

REVERSE VIEW

1 TIEBAR ASSEMBLY
2 STEERING COLUMN BRANCH
3 PASSENGER SIDE CONNECTOR
  POSITION ASSURANCE (CPA)
4 DRIVER SIDE CONNECTOR
  POSITION ASSURANCE (CPA)
5 DRIVER SIDE SIR CONNECTOR
6 PASSENGER SIDE SIR CONNECTOR

87956011

Fig. 5 Location of the driver and passenger side SIR connectors

HEATER

Blower Motor

REMOVAL & INSTALLATION

1982-91 Vehicles

▶ See Figures 6, 7, 8, 9 and 10

1. Disconnect the negative battery cable.
2. Detach the electrical connections at the blower motor and blower resistor.

➡ **On the 3.1L engine remove the tower to tower brace assembly.**

3. On models through 1989, remove the plastic water shield from the right side of the cowl.
4. Unfasten the blower motor retaining screws and then pull the blower motor and cage out.
5. Hold the blower motor cage, then remove the cage retaining nut from the blower motor shaft.
6. Remove the blower motor and cage.

To install:

7. Install the cage on the new motor.
8. Check that the retaining nut is on tight, the motor rotates and the fan cage is not interfering with the motor.
9. Install the motor in the heater assembly (install tower to tower brace assembly if necessary) connect the wiring and check the motor operation in all speeds.

1992-96 Vehicles

▶ See Figure 11

EXCEPT 3.1L ENGINES

1. Disconnect the negative battery cable.
2. For 1995-96 vehicles, remove the right sound insulator.
3. Tag and detach the electrical connector(s) at the blower motor.

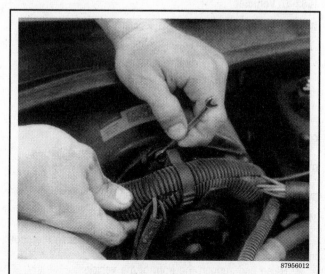

Fig. 6 Unfasten the retaining nuts, then . . .

Fig. 7 . . . pull the motor and cage out

4. For vehicles through 1994, remove the blower motor cooling tube.
5. Unfasten the blower motor retaining screws, then remove the blower motor fan and motor assembly.

➡ **The blower motor and fan are serviced as an assembly.**

To install:

6. Place the blower motor and fan assembly in the correct position.
7. Install and tighten evenly the fan assembly retaining screws.
8. If equipped, connect blower motor cooling tube.
9. Attach the electrical connector(s).
10. For 1995-96 vehicles, install the right sound insulator.
11. Connect the negative battery cable, then check the blower motor operation in all speeds.

3.1L ENGINE

1. Disconnect the negative battery cable.
2. Remove the tower-to-tower brace.
3. Tag and detach the electrical connectors at the blower motor.
4. Disconnect the blower motor cooling tube.
5. Remove the alternator assembly, as outlined in Section 2 of this manual.
6. Unfasten the blower motor retaining screws, then remove the blower motor and fan assembly.

➡ **The blower motor and fan are serviced as an assembly.**

To install:

7. Place the blower motor and fan assembly in the correct position.
8. Install and tighten evenly the fan assembly retaining screws.
9. Install the alternator assembly. Adjust the drive belt.
10. Connect blower motor cooling tube.
11. Attach the electrical connections, then install the tower-to-tower brace.

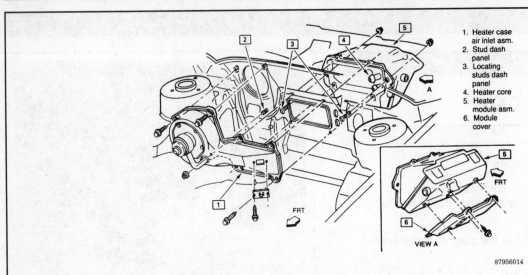

1. Heater case air inlet asm.
2. Stud dash panel
3. Locating studs dash panel
4. Heater core
5. Heater module asm.
6. Module cover

VIEW A

87956014

Fig. 8 Heater module and air inlet assembly — 1982-87 vehicles without A/C

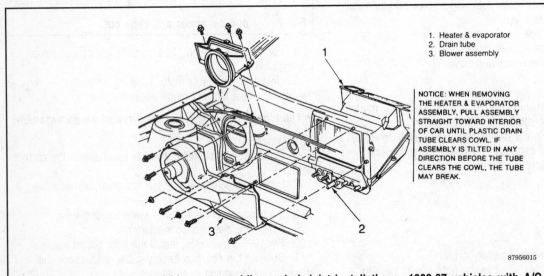

1. Heater & evaporator
2. Drain tube
3. Blower assembly

NOTICE: WHEN REMOVING THE HEATER & EVAPORATOR ASSEMBLY, PULL ASSEMBLY STRAIGHT TOWARD INTERIOR OF CAR UNTIL PLASTIC DRAIN TUBE CLEARS COWL. IF ASSEMBLY IS TILTED IN ANY DIRECTION BEFORE THE TUBE CLEARS THE COWL, THE TUBE MAY BREAK.

87956015

Fig. 9 Heater evaporator and blower assemblies and air inlet installation — 1982-87 vehicles with A/C

12. Connect the negative battery cable and check the blower motor operation in all speeds.

Heater Core

REMOVAL & INSTALLATION

❋❋CAUTION

When draining the coolant, keep in mind that cats and dogs are attracted by ethylene glycol antifreeze, and are quite likely to drink any that is left in an uncovered container or in puddles on the ground. This will prove fatal in sufficient quantity. Always drain the coolant into a sealable container. Coolant should be reused unless it is contaminated or several years old.

1982-87 Vehicles

WITHOUT A/C

1. Disconnect the negative battery cable.
2. Properly drain the cooling system.
3. Disconnect the heater inlet and outlet hoses from the heater core.
4. Remove the heater outlet deflector.
5. Unfasten the retaining screws, then remove the heater core cover.
6. Detach the heater core retaining straps, then then remove the heater core.
7. Installation is the reverse of removal. Refill the cooling system. Check heater system for proper operation.

WITH A/C

1. Disconnect the negative battery cable and drain the cooling system.
2. Raise and support the front of the vehicle.
3. Disconnect the drain tube from the heater case.

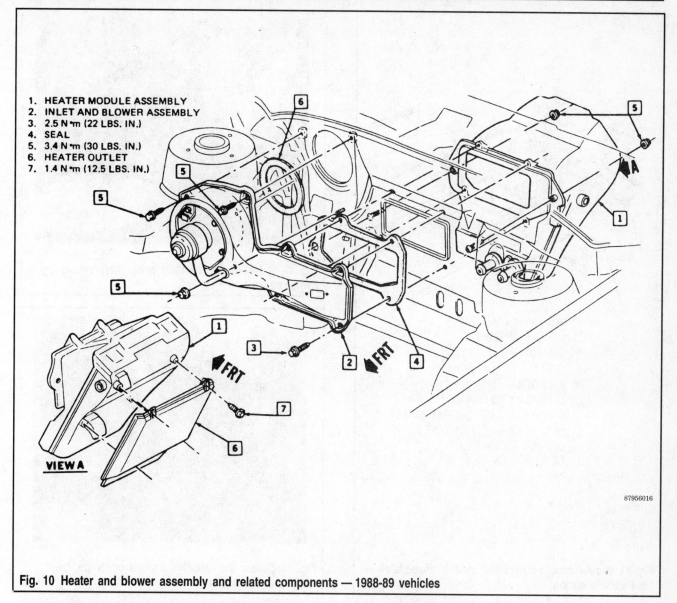

1. HEATER MODULE ASSEMBLY
2. INLET AND BLOWER ASSEMBLY
3. 2.5 N·m (22 LBS. IN.)
4. SEAL
5. 3.4 N·m (30 LBS. IN.)
6. HEATER OUTLET
7. 1.4 N·m (12.5 LBS. IN.)

VIEW A

87956016

Fig. 10 Heater and blower assembly and related components — 1988-89 vehicles

4. Remove the heater hoses from the heater core.
5. Lower the car. Remove the right and left hush panels, the steering column trim cover, the heater outlet duct and the glove box.
6. Remove the heater core cover. Be sure to pull the cover straight to the rear so as not to damage the drain tube.
7. Remove the heater core clamps and then remove the core.
8. Reverse the above procedure to install, and fill the cooling system.

1988-94 Vehicles
▶ See Figures 12, 13 and 14

1. Disconnect the negative battery cable and drain the cooling system.
2. Raise and support the vehicle safely.
3. If equipped, remove the rear lateral transaxle strut mount.
4. Disconnect the drain tube from the heater case.
5. Detach the heater hoses from the heater core.

6. Carefully lower the vehicle.
7. Remove the right and left sound insulators.
8. Unfasten the steering column opening filler. Disconnect the heater outlet deflector (floor air outlet duct).
9. Remove the heater core cover.
10. Detach the heater core retaining straps (clamps), then remove the heater core.
   To install:
11. Install the heater core and retaining straps (clamps).
12. Install the heater core cover.
13. Reconnect the heater outlet deflector (floor air outlet duct).
14. Install the right and left sound insulators. Install the steering column opening filler.
15. Raise and support the vehicle safely.
16. Connect the heater hoses (use new heater hose clamps if necessary) to the heater core.
17. Connect the drain tube to heater case.
18. Connect the rear lateral transaxle strut mount, if equipped.
19. Lower the vehicle.

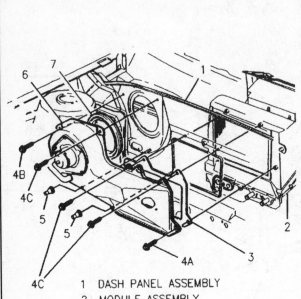

1 DASH PANEL ASSEMBLY
2 MODULE ASSEMBLY
3 GASKET
4 SCREW – 2 N.m (20 LBS. IN.)
  A INSTALL FIRST
  B INSTALL SECOND
  C INSTALL LAST (NO SEQUENCE)
5 NUT – 3 N.m (27 LBS. FT.)
6 BLOWER ASSEMBLY
7 GASKET – AIR INLET

87956017

Fig. 11 Blower case, air inlet and module assemblies — 1994 vehicle shown

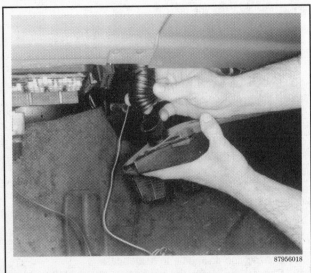

87956018

Fig. 12 Disconnect the floor air outlet duct

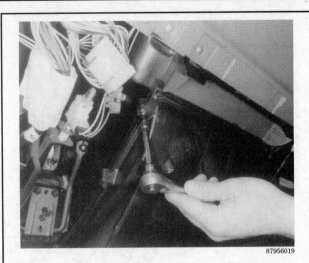

87956019

Fig. 13 Unfasten the retaining bolts, then remove the heater core cover

87956020

Fig. 14 Detach the retaining clamps or straps, then remove the heater core

20. Fill the cooling system and check for leaks. Check heater system for proper operation.

1995-96 Vehicles

▶ **See Figure 15**

1. Disable the SIR system, as outlined in this section.
2. Disconnect the negative battery cable.
3. Properly drain the cooling system.
4. Raise and safely support the vehicle.
5. Detach the heater hoses from the heater core.
6. Carefully lower the vehicle.
7. Remove the instrument panel. For details, please refer to the procedure located in Section 10 of this manual.
8. Remove the DERM with the attaching bracket.
9. Detach the heater core cover.
10. Unfasten the heater core mounting clamps, then remove the heater core.

To install:

11. Position the heater core, then secure with the mounting clamps.

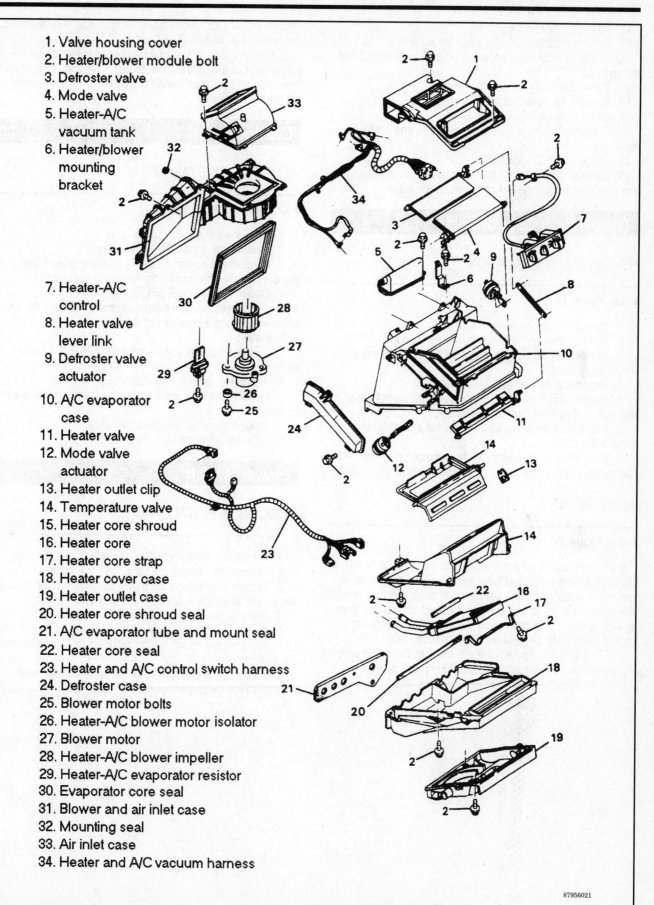

1. Valve housing cover
2. Heater/blower module bolt
3. Defroster valve
4. Mode valve
5. Heater-A/C vacuum tank
6. Heater/blower mounting bracket
7. Heater-A/C control
8. Heater valve lever link
9. Defroster valve actuator
10. A/C evaporator case
11. Heater valve
12. Mode valve actuator
13. Heater outlet clip
14. Temperature valve
15. Heater core shroud
16. Heater core
17. Heater core strap
18. Heater cover case
19. Heater outlet case
20. Heater core shroud seal
21. A/C evaporator tube and mount seal
22. Heater core seal
23. Heater and A/C control switch harness
24. Defroster case
25. Blower motor bolts
26. Heater-A/C blower motor isolator
27. Blower motor
28. Heater-A/C blower impeller
29. Heater-A/C evaporator resistor
30. Evaporator core seal
31. Blower and air inlet case
32. Mounting seal
33. Air inlet case
34. Heater and A/C vacuum harness

87956021

Fig. 15 Exploded view of the heater core and related components — 1996 vehicle shown

12. Attach the heater core cover.

13. Install the DERM with the attaching bracket.

14. Install the instrument panel, as outlined in Section 10 of this manual.

15. Raise and safely support the vehicle.

16. Connect the heater hoses to the core.

17. Carefully lower the vehicle.

18. Properly refill the engine cooling system and check for leaks.

19. Enable the SIR system.

20. Connect the negative battery cable, then start the engine and check for proper system operation and/or leaks.

Temperature Control Cable

REMOVAL & INSTALLATION

▶ See Figure 16

1. Disconnect the negative battery cable.

2. Remove the right side sound insulator panel.

3. If necessary for access, remove the instrument panel (I/P) compartment.

4. Disconnect the cable at the module.

5. Remove the control panel trim plate and control panel assembly, as outlined later in this section.

6. Disconnect the cable from the control assembly, then remove the cable.

7. Installation is the reverse of the removal procedure. Adjust temperature control cable, as outlined later in this section.

ADJUSTMENT

▶ See Figure 17

If the temperature control lever fails to move to full COLD or HOT, or a large amount of lever spring back is noticed when moving to either of the full positions, the cable clip may need adjustment. Failure to grip clip in the correct manner will damage its ability to hold position on the cable. The temperature control cable must be replaced if clip retention fails.

1. To adjust the clip, grip the clip (refer to the accompanying illustration for the correct manner to grip the cable) at module end of cable while pulling temperature control lever to the correct full position (COLD or HOT) and connect.

2. Verify correct adjustment by observing for little or no spring back of the temperature control lever and listening for temperature door "slam" when the control lever is moved to full positions quickly.

Control Panel

REMOVAL & INSTALLATION

▶ See Figures 18, 19 and 20

1. Disconnect the battery ground cable.

2. Remove the instrument panel trim plate.

3. Remove the control assembly retaining screws and pull the control assembly away from the instrument panel.

4. Detach the electrical and vacuum connectors.

5. Disconnect the temperature control cable from the control assembly and remove assembly.

To install:

6. Connect the temperature control cable to the heater control.

7. Attach the vacuum and electrical connectors.

8. Install the control assembly and secure with the retaining screws.

9. Install the instrument panel trim plate.

10. Connect the negative battery cable.

Blower Switch

REMOVAL & INSTALLATION

1. Disconnect the battery ground cable.

2. Remove the instrument panel (I/P) trim plate.

3. Unfasten the control assembly retaining screws, then pull the control assembly away from the instrument panel.

4. Remove the blower switch knob.

5. Detach the electrical connector.

6. Unfasten the blower switch retaining screws and remove the switch.

7. Installation is the reverse of the removal procedure. Check system for proper operation.

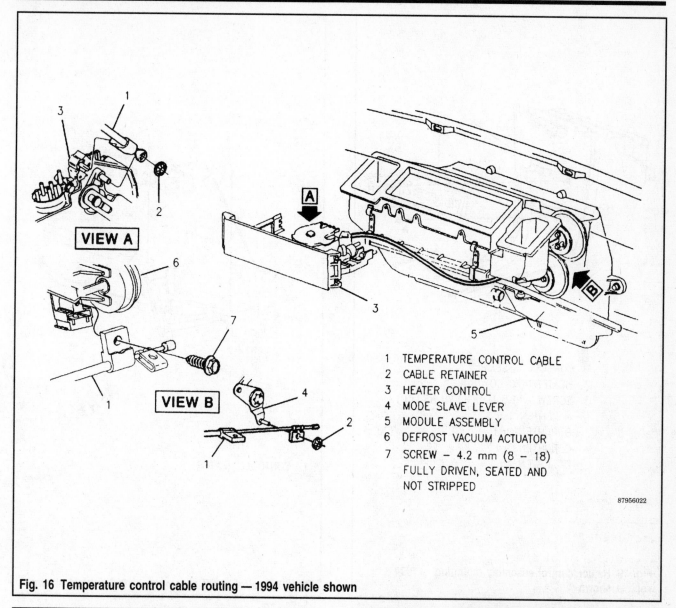

VIEW A

VIEW B

1 TEMPERATURE CONTROL CABLE
2 CABLE RETAINER
3 HEATER CONTROL
4 MODE SLAVE LEVER
5 MODULE ASSEMBLY
6 DEFROST VACUUM ACTUATOR
7 SCREW — 4.2 mm (8 – 18)
   FULLY DRIVEN, SEATED AND
   NOT STRIPPED

87956022

Fig. 16 Temperature control cable routing — 1994 vehicle shown

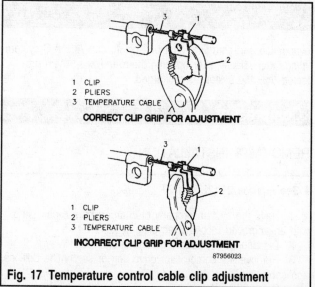

1 CLIP
2 PLIERS
3 TEMPERATURE CABLE

CORRECT CLIP GRIP FOR ADJUSTMENT

1 CLIP
2 PLIERS
3 TEMPERATURE CABLE

INCORRECT CLIP GRIP FOR ADJUSTMENT

87956023

Fig. 17 Temperature control cable clip adjustment

87956024

Fig. 18 Remove the instrument panel trim plate for access to the temperature control panel

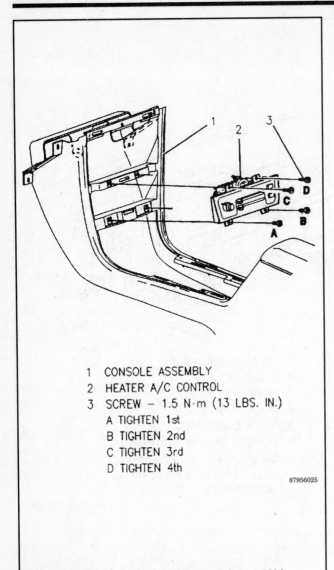

1 CONSOLE ASSEMBLY
2 HEATER A/C CONTROL
3 SCREW – 1.5 N·m (13 LBS. IN.)
  A TIGHTEN 1st
  B TIGHTEN 2nd
  C TIGHTEN 3rd
  D TIGHTEN 4th

87956025

Fig. 19 Heater control assembly mounting — 1994 vehicle shown

1 CONTROL, HEATER

87956026

Fig. 20 Control panel assembly — 1996 vehicle shown

AIR CONDITIONER

➡**Be sure to consult the laws in your area before servicing the air conditioning system. In most areas, it is illegal to perform repairs involving refrigerant unless the work is done by a certified technician. Also, it is quite likely that you will not be able to purchase refrigerant without proof of certification.**

Discharging, evacuating and charging the air conditioning system must be performed by a properly trained and certified mechanic in a facility equipped with refrigerant recovery/recycling equipment that meets SAE standards for the type of system to be serviced.

If you don't have access to the necessary equipment, we recommend that you take your vehicle to a reputable service station to have the work done. If you still wish to perform repairs on the vehicle, have them discharge the system, then take your vehicle home and perform the necessary work. When you are finished, return the vehicle to the station for

evacuation and charging. Just be sure to cap ALL A/C system fittings immediately after opening them and keep them protected until the system is recharged.

Compressor

REMOVAL & INSTALLATION

▶ **See Figures 21, 22 and 23**

1. Have the system properly discharged by a repair shop with an approved recovery/recycling system.
2. Disconnect the battery ground cable.
3. Remove the compressor drive belt or serpentine belt, as applicable.
4. Raise and safely support vehicle on jack stands.
5. Remove the right air deflector and splash shield.

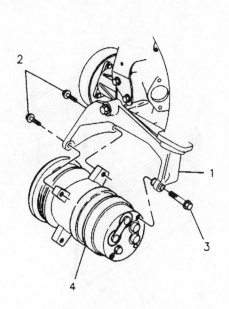

1 BRACKET
2 BOLT, FRONT COMPRESSOR
3 BOLT, REAR COMPRESSOR
4 COMPRESSOR ASSEMBLY

87956027

Fig. 21 View of the compressor mounting — 1996 2.2L engine shown

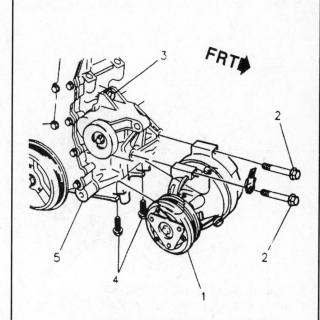

1 COMPRESSOR ASSEMBLY
2 BOLTS, UPPER COMPRESSOR
3 BOLT, COMPRESSOR BRACKET
4 BOLTS, LOWER COMPRESSOR
5 ENGINE ASSEMBLY

87956028

Fig. 22 A/C Compressor mounting — 1996 2.4L engine shown

6. Detach the electrical connectors at the compressor switches.

7. Disconnect the compressor/condenser hose assembly at the rear of the compressor and discard the seals.

8. Unfasten the compressor attaching bolts and remove the compressor.

➡**Drain the compressor oil into a measuring cup this is the amount of new compressor oil to be put into compressor upon installation, unless less then 1 oz. (30 ml) of oil was drained from the compressor. In that case, add 2 oz. (60 ml).**

9. Disconnect the expansion tube. Inspect the tube for contamination or metal cuttings, clean and or replace as necessary.

To install:
10. Ensure that the compressor (new or used) is completely drained of oil. Refill the compressor with new oil the same amount that was drained.

11. Position the compressor and install the attaching bolts.

12. Connect the condenser/compressor hose assembly at the rear of compressor using new sealing washers that don't need to be lubricated.

13. Attach the electrical connectors to the compressor clutch.

14. Install the drive belt and adjust as necessary.

15. Install the right air deflector and splash shield.

16. Carefully lower the vehicle, then connect the negative battery cable.

17. Have a repair shop evacuate, charge and leak test the A/C system, using the correct equipment.

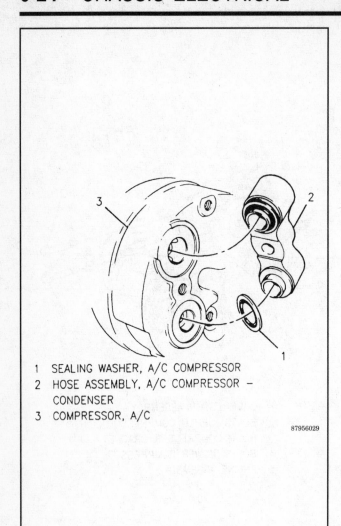

1 SEALING WASHER, A/C COMPRESSOR
2 HOSE ASSEMBLY, A/C COMPRESSOR –
  CONDENSER
3 COMPRESSOR, A/C

87956029

Fig. 23 Install new A/C compressor seals; use the kind which don't need to lubricated

Condenser

REMOVAL & INSTALLATION

▶ See Figure 24

➡**On some vehicles, some steps can be omitted due different body styles and or vehicle options — modify the service procedure steps as necessary. Review the complete service procedure before starting this repair.**

1. Have the system properly discharged by a repair shop with an approved recovery/recycling system.
2. If equipped, disable the SIR system, as outlined in this section.
3. Disconnect the negative battery cable.
4. On models so equipped, manually open headlamp doors (make sure negative battery cable is disconnected) by turning headlamp door actuator knob. Remove the 4 retaining bolts

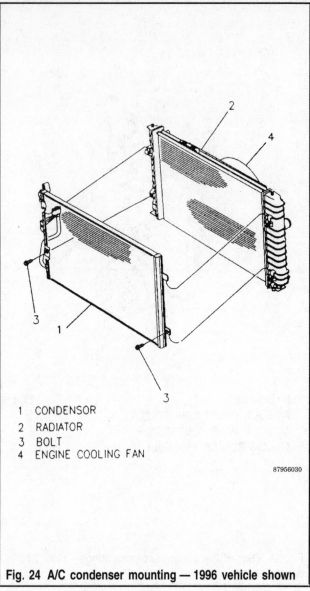

1 CONDENSOR
2 RADIATOR
3 BOLT
4 ENGINE COOLING FAN

87956030

Fig. 24 A/C condenser mounting — 1996 vehicle shown

from the headlamp door actuators and pull actuator assemblies forward as far as possible. Remove the hood latch release cable and front end panel center brace.
5. Remove the right and left headlight trim.
6. Remove the center grille assembly.
7. Remove the right and left headlight housing or headlight assemblies.
8. Remove the hood bracket and latch assembly. If equipped, remove the forward sensor with the harness.
9. Raise and safely support the vehicle.
10. If equipped, disconnect the forward SIR harness, then carefully lower the vehicle.
11. Remove the right radiator support.
12. Disconnect the refrigerant lines from the condenser and discard the O-ring seals.
13. If equipped, remove the condenser air deflector shield.
14. Using a back-up wrench to prevent the block fitting from twisting, unfasten the condenser mounting brackets and remove the condenser. Remove and discard the O-rings.

To install:

15. Position the condenser in vehicle and install the mounting brackets. Use a back-up wrench to prevent the block fitting from twisting.

16. Install the condenser air deflector shield if so equipped.

17. Connect the refrigerant lines to the condenser using new O-ring seals.

➡**If necessary, install headlight actuator assemblies. Install the front end panel center brace and the hood latch release cable.**

18. Install the hood latch and bracket assembly and forward sensor with the harness, if equipped.

19. Install the right radiator mount.

20. Raise and safely support the vehicle.

21. Connect the forward SIR sensor harness, then carefully lower the vehicle.

22. Install the headlight housings, center grille assembly, and headlight trim.

23. If equipped, enable the SIR system.

24. Connect the negative battery cable.

25. Have a repair shop evacuate, charge and leak test the A/C system, using the correct equipment.

Evaporator Core

REMOVAL & INSTALLATION

1982-87 Vehicles

1. Have the system properly discharged by a repair shop with an approved recovery/recycling system.

2. Disconnect the negative battery cable.

3. Raise and safely support the vehicle.

4. On the 1987 Sunbird equipped with an automatic transaxle, remove the bolts to the transaxle support.

5. On the 1987 Firenza, if equipped, disconnect the rear lateral transaxle strut mount.

6. Disconnect the heater hoses and evaporator lines at the heater core and evaporator core.

7. Reattach the drain tube.

8. Remove the right hand and left hand hush panels, steering column trim cover, heater outlet duct and glove box.

9. Remove the heater core cover by pulling straight rearward on the cover to avoid breaking the drain tube.

10. Unfasten the heater core clamps and remove the heater core.

11. Remove the screws holding the defroster vacuum actuator to the module case.

12. Unfasten the evaporator cover and remove the evaporator core.

To install:

13. Reposition the core (if installing a new evaporator core check the refrigerant oil in the system) and install the cover.

14. Install the screws holding the defroster vacuum actuator to the module case.

15. Fasten the heater core clamps and cover.

16. Install the right hand and left hand hush panels, steering column trim cover, heater outlet duct and glove box.

17. Connect the drain tube.

18. Attach the heater hoses and evaporator lines at the heater core and evaporator core.

19. On the 1987 Firenza, connect the rear lateral transaxle strut mount, if equipped.

20. On the 1987 Sunbird, install the bolts to the transaxle support (automatic only).

21. Carefully lower the car.

22. Connect the negative battery cable.

23. Have a repair shop evacuate, charge and leak test the A/C system, using the correct equipment.

1988-96 Vehicles

▶ **See Figures 25 and 26**

1. Have the system properly discharged by a repair shop with an approved recovery/recycling system.

2. If equipped, disable the SIR system.

3. Disconnect the negative battery cable.

4. Drain the cooling system.

5. Raise and support the vehicle safely.

6. If equipped, remove the rear lateral transaxle strut mount.

7. Detach the heater hoses and evaporator lines at the heater core and evaporator core.

8. Disconnect the moisture drain tube from the heater/air conditioning module.

9. Carefully lower the vehicle.

10. For vehicles through 1994, remove the right and left sound insulators, steering column trim cover, the heater outlet duct and the instrument panel compartment.

11. For 1995-96 vehicles, remove the instrument panel.

12. If equipped with air bags, remove the DERM with the attaching bracket.

➡**When removing the heater core, pull straight rearward to avoid breaking the drain tube.**

13. Detach the heater core cover and pull straight rearward.

14. Remove the heater core clamps and remove the core.

15. Unfasten the screws holding the defroster vacuum actuator to the module case.

16. Remove the evaporator cover and the evaporator core.

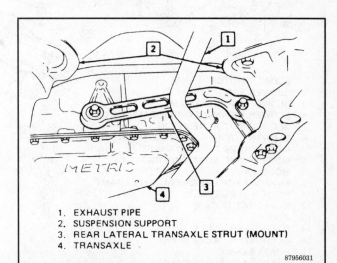

1. EXHAUST PIPE
2. SUSPENSION SUPPORT
3. REAR LATERAL TRANSAXLE STRUT (MOUNT)
4. TRANSAXLE

87956031

Fig. 25 If equipped, such as this 1989 Sunbird, remove the rear lateral transaxle strut

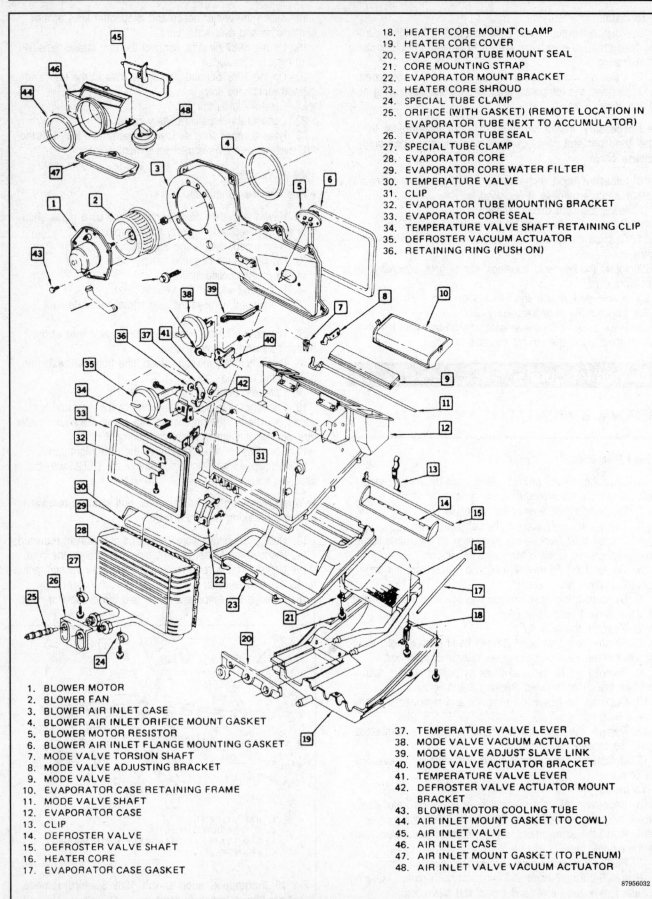

18. HEATER CORE MOUNT CLAMP
19. HEATER CORE COVER
20. EVAPORATOR TUBE MOUNT SEAL
21. CORE MOUNTING STRAP
22. EVAPORATOR MOUNT BRACKET
23. HEATER CORE SHROUD
24. SPECIAL TUBE CLAMP
25. ORIFICE (WITH GASKET) (REMOTE LOCATION IN EVAPORATOR TUBE NEXT TO ACCUMULATOR)
26. EVAPORATOR TUBE SEAL
27. SPECIAL TUBE CLAMP
28. EVAPORATOR CORE
29. EVAPORATOR CORE WATER FILTER
30. TEMPERATURE VALVE
31. CLIP
32. EVAPORATOR TUBE MOUNTING BRACKET
33. EVAPORATOR CORE SEAL
34. TEMPERATURE VALVE SHAFT RETAINING CLIP
35. DEFROSTER VACUUM ACTUATOR
36. RETAINING RING (PUSH ON)

1. BLOWER MOTOR
2. BLOWER FAN
3. BLOWER AIR INLET CASE
4. BLOWER AIR INLET ORIFICE MOUNT GASKET
5. BLOWER MOTOR RESISTOR
6. BLOWER AIR INLET FLANGE MOUNTING GASKET
7. MODE VALVE TORSION SHAFT
8. MODE VALVE ADJUSTING BRACKET
9. MODE VALVE
10. EVAPORATOR CASE RETAINING FRAME
11. MODE VALVE SHAFT
12. EVAPORATOR CASE
13. CLIP
14. DEFROSTER VALVE
15. DEFROSTER VALVE SHAFT
16. HEATER CORE
17. EVAPORATOR CASE GASKET

37. TEMPERATURE VALVE LEVER
38. MODE VALVE VACUUM ACTUATOR
39. MODE VALVE ADJUST SLAVE LINK
40. MODE VALVE ACTUATOR BRACKET
41. TEMPERATURE VALVE LEVER
42. DEFROSTER VALVE ACTUATOR MOUNT BRACKET
43. BLOWER MOTOR COOLING TUBE
44. AIR INLET MOUNT GASKET (TO COWL)
45. AIR INLET VALVE
46. AIR INLET CASE
47. AIR INLET MOUNT GASKET (TO PLENUM)
48. AIR INLET VALVE VACUUM ACTUATOR

87956032

Fig. 26 Exploded view of the A/C components, including the evaporator core

To install:

17. Position the core (if installing a new evaporator core, check the refrigerant oil in system) and install the cover.

18. Fasten the screws holding the defroster vacuum actuator to the module case.

19. Install the heater core clamps and cover.

20. If equipped with air bags, install the DERM with the attaching bracket.

21. For 1995-96 vehicles, install the instrument panel.

22. For vehicles through 1994, install the steering column trim cover, glove box, right hand and left hand sound insulators and the heater outlet duct.

23. Attach the drain tube.

24. Connect the heater hoses and evaporator lines at the heater core and evaporator core, using new O-rings.

25. If equipped, connect the rear lateral transaxle strut mount.

26. Fill the cooling system.

27. If equipped, enable the SIR system.

28. Connect the negative battery cable.

29. Have a repair shop evacuate, charge and leak test the A/C system, using the correct equipment.

Control Panel

REMOVAL & INSTALLATION

1982-94 Vehicles
▶ See Figure 27

1. Disconnect the negative battery cable.
2. Remove the steering column opening filler panel.
3. Remove the cigar lighter and control assembly trim plate.
4. Unfasten the control assembly retaining screws and pull the control assembly rearward.
5. Detach the electrical and vacuum connectors and the temperature control cable from the control assembly, then remove the control assembly.

To install:

6. Attach the electrical and vacuum connectors and the temperature cable to the control assembly.
7. Position the control assembly, then secure with the retaining screws.
8. Install the cigar lighter and the control assembly trim plate.
9. Install the steering column opening filler.
10. Connect the negative battery cable.

1995-96 Vehicles
▶ See Figures 28 and 29

1. Disconnect the negative battery cable.
2. Remove the instrument panel trim and pad.
3. Unfasten the control assembly retaining screws, then pull the control assembly away from the instrument panel.
4. Detach the electrical and vacuum connections.
5. Detach the temperature control cable, then remove the assembly from the vehicle.

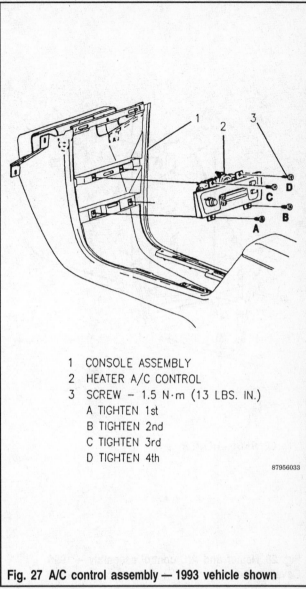

1 CONSOLE ASSEMBLY
2 HEATER A/C CONTROL
3 SCREW – 1.5 N·m (13 LBS. IN.)
A TIGHTEN 1st
B TIGHTEN 2nd
C TIGHTEN 3rd
D TIGHTEN 4th

87956033

Fig. 27 A/C control assembly — 1993 vehicle shown

6. Installation is the reverse of the removal procedure.

Blower Switch

REMOVAL & INSTALLATION

1. Disconnect the negative battery cable.
2. Remove the instrument panel (I/P) trim plate.
3. Unfasten the control assembly retaining screws and pull the control assembly away from the instrument panel.
4. Remove the blower switch knob.
5. Detach the electrical connector.
6. Remove the blower switch retaining screws and remove the switch.
7. Installation is the reverse of the removal procedure. Check system for proper operation.

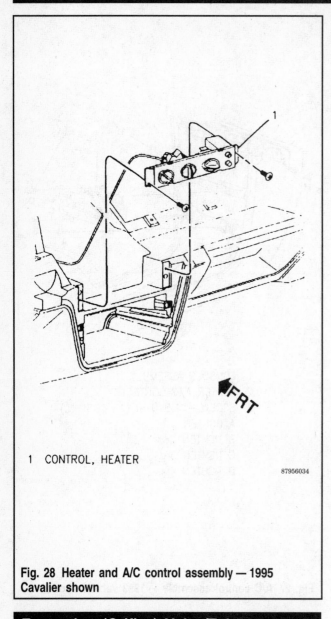

Fig. 28 Heater and A/C control assembly — 1995 Cavalier shown

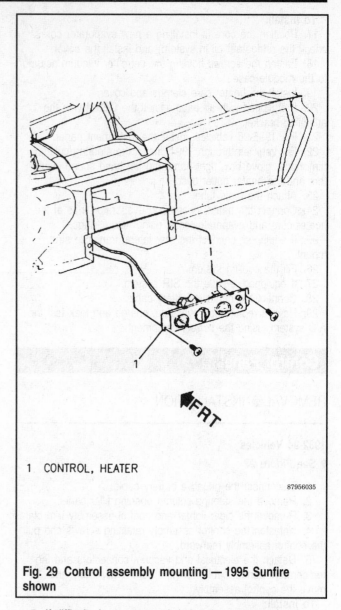

Fig. 29 Control assembly mounting — 1995 Sunfire shown

Expansion (Orifice) Valve/Tube

REMOVAL & INSTALLATION

▶ See Figures 30 and 31

➡**The expansion tube is located at the condenser-to-evaporator tube connection in the evaporator tube.**

1. Have the system properly discharged by a repair shop with an approved recovery/recycling system.
2. Disconnect the negative battery cable.
3. Detach the connection at the condenser and discard the O-ring seals.
4. Loosen the nut and separate the front evaporator tube from the rear evaporator tube to access the expansion tube. Carefully remove the expansion tube with needle-nose pliers or special tools AC-1002 or J-26549-89 expansion tube remover.

5. If difficulty is encountered during the removal of a restricted or plugged expansion tube, the following procedure may be used:
   a. Remove as much of any impacted residue as possible.
   b. Carefully apply heat with a heat gun (hair dryer, epoxy dryer or equivalent) approximately ¼ in. (77mm) away from the dimples on the inlet pipe. Do NOT overheat the pipe.
   c. While applying heat, use expansion tube removal tools AC-1002 or J-26549-89 to grip the expansion tube. Use a turning motion along with a push-pull motion to loosen and remove the expansion tube.

➡**Different designs and colors of orifice tubes may have been used in past vehicles. When replacing an orifice tube, compare its design to the replacement part for correct orifice selection. Different styles of orifice tubes are NOT interchangeable.**

To install:

6. Install the new expansion tube, with the short screen toward the evaporator.

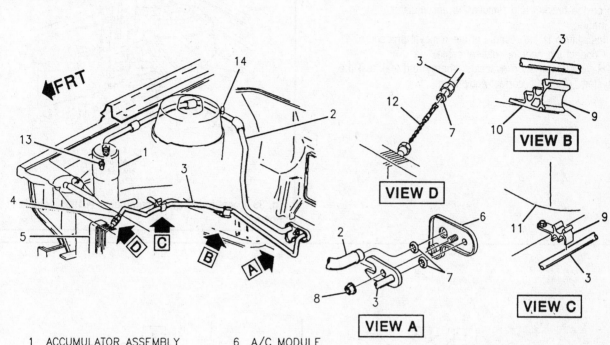

Fig. 30 Location of the expansion (orifice) valve/tube — 1993 vehicle shown

1 ACCUMULATOR ASSEMBLY	6 A/C MODULE	11 ENGINE COOLANT RESERVOIR
2 A/C ACCUMULATOR TUBE	7 "O" RING SEAL	12 EXPANSION TUBE
3 A/C EVAPORATOR TUBE	8 NUT – 16 N·m (12 LBS. FT.)	13 LOW SIDE SERVICE PORT
4 NUT – 25 N·m (19 LBS. FT.)	9 RETAINER, FUEL VAPOR PIPE	14 ASSEMBLY PLANT USE ONLY
5 CONDENSER ASSEMBLY	10 LOWER BODY SIDE RAIL	

87956036

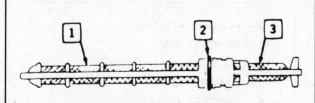

EXPANSION (ORIFICE) TUBE
1.   LONG SCREEN END (INLET)
2.   "O" RING
3.   SHORT SCREEN END (OUTLET)

INSTALL WITH SHORTER SCREEN END TOWARD
EVAPORATOR AND USE NEW "O" RING SEALS

87956037

Fig. 31 Installing the expansion tube

7. Using new O-ring seals, assemble evaporator tube/condenser connection hand-tight.

8. Tighten the liquid line to 17 ft. lbs. (23 Nm).

9. Tighten the brazed nut connection to 12 ft. lbs. (16 Nm).

10. Connect the negative battery cable.

11. Have a repair shop evacuate, charge and leak test the A/C system, using the correct equipment.

Accumulator

REMOVAL & INSTALLATION

▶ See Figures 32 and 33

1. Have the system properly discharged by a repair shop with an approved recovery/recycling system.

2. Disconnect the negative battery cable.

3. Disconnect the refrigerant lines at the accumulator and discard the O-ring seals.

4. If necessary, remove the cruise control stepper motor bracket and position it aside.

5. Either unfasten the screws retaining bracket assembly to vehicle and remove the bracket and accumulator or detach the clamp on the bracket and remove the accumulator.

To install:

6. Installation is the reverse of the removal procedure.

7. Connect the negative battery cable.

8. Have a repair shop evacuate, charge and leak test the A/C system, using the correct equipment.

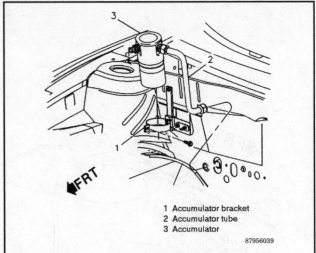

1 Accumulator bracket
2 Accumulator tube
3 Accumulator

87956039

Fig. 33 Location of the accumulator — 1995 vehicle shown

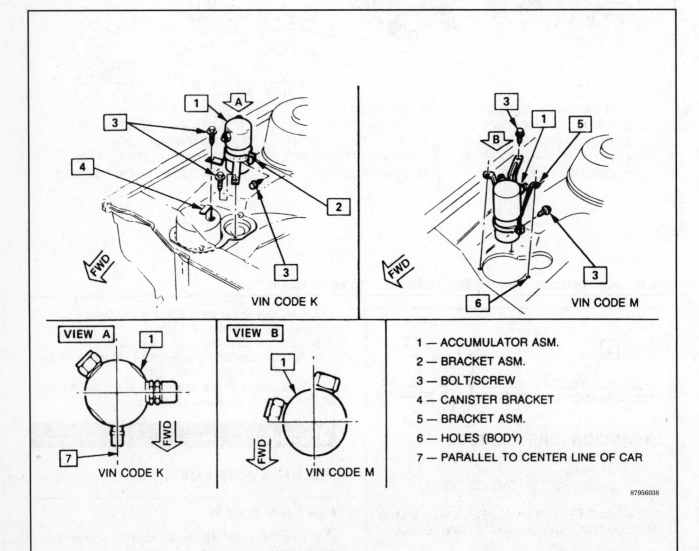

1 — ACCUMULATOR ASM.
2 — BRACKET ASM.
3 — BOLT/SCREW
4 — CANISTER BRACKET
5 — BRACKET ASM.
6 — HOLES (BODY)
7 — PARALLEL TO CENTER LINE OF CAR

87956038

Fig. 32 Accumulator mounting — 1987 vehicle shown

Refrigerant Lines

DISCONNECT & CONNECT

▶ See Figures 34, 35, 36 and 37

Evaporator Line

1. Have the system properly discharged by a repair shop with an approved recovery/recycling system.
2. Disconnect the negative battery cable.
3. Detach the connection from the condenser and discard the O-ring seals.
4. Disconnect the line from the retaining clips on the body side rail.
5. If necessary, disconnect the vacuum hoses from the vapor canister
6. Raise and safely support vehicle on jack stands. Disconnect the block fitting from the evaporator and discard the O-ring seals.
7. Lower the vehicle, then remove the evaporator tube.
To install:
8. Set the evaporator line into position.
9. Raise and safely support vehicle on jack stands. Connect the block fitting to the evaporator using new O-ring seals.
10. Carefully lower the vehicle.
11. If detached, connect the vacuum lines to the vapor canister.
12. Connect the refrigerant line to the retaining clips on the body side rail.
13. Attach the connection at the condenser using new O-ring seals.
14. Connect the negative battery cable.
15. Have a repair shop evacuate, charge and leak test the A/C system, using the correct equipment.

Suction Line (Evaporator to Accumulator)

1. Have the system properly discharged by a repair shop with an approved recovery/recycling system.
2. Disconnect the negative battery cable.
3. Disconnect the line at the accumulator, then remove and discard the O-ring seal.
4. Raise and safely support the vehicle on jackstands.
5. Disconnect the block fitting from the evaporator and discard the O-ring seals.
6. Lower the vehicle, then remove the suction line.
To install:
7. Set the suction line into position.
8. Raise and safely support vehicle on jack stands. Connect the block fitting to the evaporator using new O-ring seals.
9. Carefully lower the vehicle.
10. Attach the line at the accumulator using a new O-ring seal.
11. Connect the negative battery cable.
12. Have a repair shop evacuate, charge and leak test the A/C system, using the correct equipment.

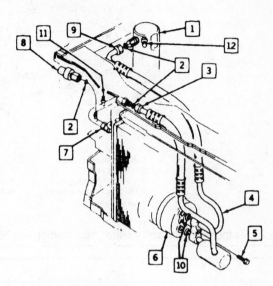

1 Accumulator asm.
2 "O" ring seal
3 16 Nm (12 lbs.ft.) nut
4 A/C compressor/condenser hose asm.
5 32 Nm (24 lbs.ft.) bolt
6 A/C compressor
7 Condenser asm.
8 A/C pressue sensor 5 Nm (44 lbs.in.)
9 41 Nm (30 lbs.ft.) nut
10 Sealing washer
11 High side service port
12 Low side service port

87956040

Fig. 34 Refrigerant lines — 2.0L engine shown

Temperature Control Cable

REMOVAL & INSTALLATION

1. Disconnect the negative battery cable.
2. Remove the right side sound insulator panel.
3. If necessary for access, remove the instrument panel (I/P) compartment.
4. Disconnect the cable at the module.
5. Remove the control panel trim plate and control panel assembly, as outlined in this section.
6. Disconnect the cable from the control assembly, then remove the cable.
7. Installation is the reverse of the removal procedure. Adjust temperature control cable, as outlined later in this section.

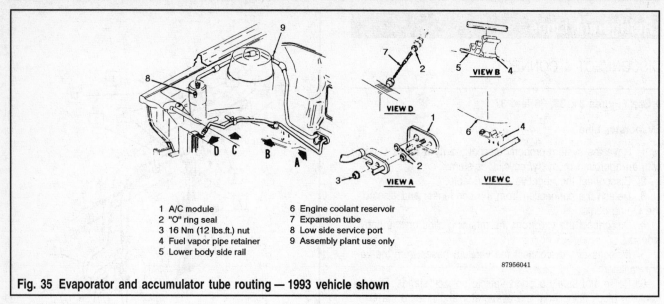

1 A/C module
2 "O" ring seal
3 16 Nm (12 lbs.ft.) nut
4 Fuel vapor pipe retainer
5 Lower body side rail
6 Engine coolant reservoir
7 Expansion tube
8 Low side service port
9 Assembly plant use only

87956041

Fig. 35 Evaporator and accumulator tube routing — 1993 vehicle shown

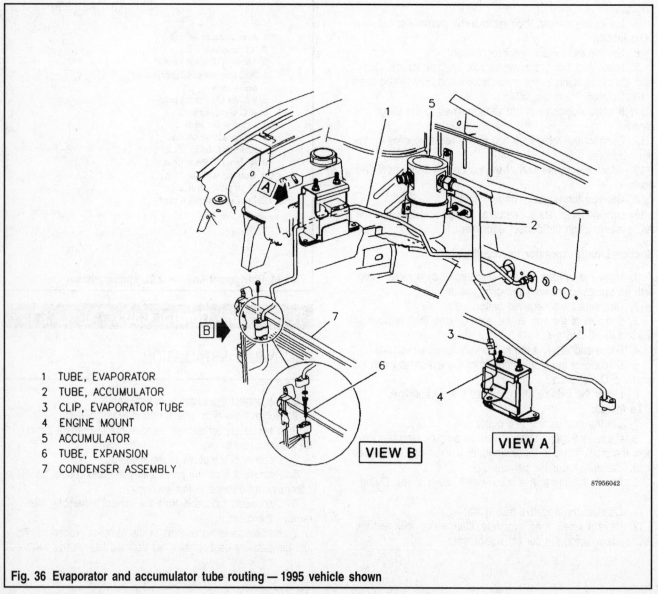

1 TUBE, EVAPORATOR
2 TUBE, ACCUMULATOR
3 CLIP, EVAPORATOR TUBE
4 ENGINE MOUNT
5 ACCUMULATOR
6 TUBE, EXPANSION
7 CONDENSER ASSEMBLY

87956042

Fig. 36 Evaporator and accumulator tube routing — 1995 vehicle shown

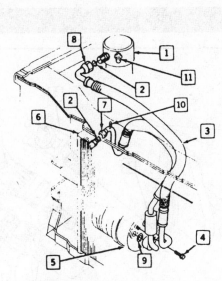

1 A/C accumulator asm.
2 "O" ring seal
3 A/C compressor/condenser
   hose asm.
4 32 Nm (24 lbs.ft.) bolt
5 A/C compressor
6 Condenser asm.
7 25 Nm (18 lbs.ft.) nut
8 42 Nm (31 lbs.ft.) nut
9 Sealing washer
10 High side service port
11 Low side service port

87956043

Fig. 37 Refrigerant line routing — 3.1L engine shown

ADJUSTMENT

▶ **See Figure 38**

If the temperature control lever fails to move to full COLD or HOT, or a large amount of lever spring back is noticed when moving to either of the full positions, the cable clip may need adjustment. Failure to grip clip in the correct manner will damage its ability to hold position on the cable. The temperature control cable must be replaced if clip retention fails.

1. To adjust the clip, grip the clip (refer to the accompanying illustration for the correct manner to grip the cable) at module end of cable while pulling temperature control lever to the correct full position (COLD or HOT) and connect.

2. Verify correct adjustment by observing for little or no spring back of the temperature control lever and listening for temperature door "slam" when the control lever is moved to full positions quickly.

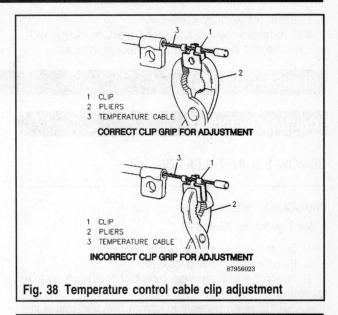

1 CLIP
2 PLIERS
3 TEMPERATURE CABLE

CORRECT CLIP GRIP FOR ADJUSTMENT

1 CLIP
2 PLIERS
3 TEMPERATURE CABLE

INCORRECT CLIP GRIP FOR ADJUSTMENT

87956023

Fig. 38 Temperature control cable clip adjustment

Cycling Clutch Switch

REMOVAL & INSTALLATION

1. Have the system properly discharged by a repair shop with an approved recovery/recycling system.

2. Disconnect the negative battery cable.

3. Detach the electrical connector from the switch in the rear head of the compressor.

4. Remove the switch retaining ring using internal snapring pliers.

5. Remove the switch from the compressor. Remove the O-ring seal from the switch cavity.

6. Installation is the reverse of the removal procedure, using new O-ring seals.

7. Connect the negative battery cable.

8. Have a repair shop evacuate, charge and leak test the A/C system, using the correct equipment.

Air Conditioning Pressure Sensor

REMOVAL & INSTALLATION

1. Have the system properly discharged by a repair shop with an approved recovery/recycling system, only if other work or service to the A/C system is necessary. The sensor is mounted on a Schrader-type valve; do not discharge the system if only the sensor is going to be replaced.

2. Disconnect the negative battery cable.

3. Detach the electrical connector at the sensor.

4. Remove the pressure sensor and discard the O-ring seal.

To install:

5. Place a new O-ring seal lubricated in clean refrigerant on the sensor.

6. Install the pressure sensor. Tighten the sensor to 44 in. lbs. (5 Nm).

7. Attach the electrical connection.

8. If necessary, have a repair shop evacuate, charge and leak test the A/C system, using the correct equipment.

9. Connect the negative battery cable, then check the A/C system for proper operation.

CRUISE CONTROL

Control Switches

REMOVAL & INSTALLATION

Brake/Clutch Pedal Switches

▶ **See Figures 39, 40 and 41**

1. Disconnect the negative battery cable.
2. Remove the left sound insulator.
3. Detach the wiring harness connector or vacuum hose, as applicable.
4. Pull the switch rearward to remove from the retainer in bracket.

To install:

5. With brake or clutch pedal depressed, insert switch into retainer until switch seats on retainer. Audible "clicks" can be heard as the switch is pushed forward through retainer.
6. Pull brake or clutch pedal fully rearward against pedal stop until "clicks" can not be heard. Switch will be moved in retainer.
7. Release brake or clutch pedal and repeat Step 6 to assure that the switch is properly adjusted.
8. Attach wiring harness connector or vacuum hose.
9. Install the sound insulator.
10. Connect the negative battery cable.

Engagement Switch

The cruise control engagement switch is part of the turn signal lever assembly and is not serviceable by itself. The turn signal lever and cruise control switch must be replaced as an assembly. Refer to the necessary service procedures in Section 8.

Vehicle Speed Sensor (VSS)

REMOVAL & INSTALLATION

▶ **See Figure 42**

1. Disconnect the negative battery cable.
2. Raise and safely support the vehicle.
3. Detach the VSS electrical lead from the transaxle.
4. Unfasten the retaining bolts, then remove the sensor from the housing. Remove and discard the sensor O-ring.
5. Installation is the reverse of the removal procedure.

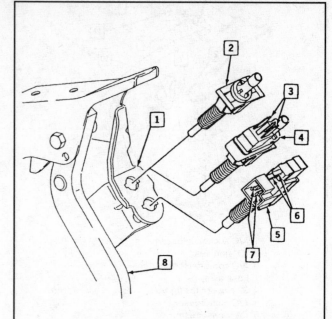

1	BRAKE PEDAL MOUNTING BRACKET
2	CRUISE CONTROL RELEASE VALVE (VACUUM) (MANUAL TRANSAXLE ONLY)
3	TORQUE CONVERTER CLUTCH TERMINALS
4	TCC AND CRUISE CONTROL RELEASE SWITCH/ VALVE (AUTOMATIC TRANSAXLE ONLY)
5	STOPLAMP SWITCH
6	CRUISE CONTROL RELEASE SWITCH TERMINALS
7	STOP LAMP SWITCH TERMINALS
8	BRAKE PEDAL ASM

87956046

Fig. 39 View of the brake pedal switches — 1992 vehicle shown

Control Module

REMOVAL & INSTALLATION

➡The cruise control module location may be located in different areas on some models and engines. The module is usually mounted in the lower left front area near the kickpanel left of the steering wheel, under the steering wheel on the filler panel or above the glove box area to the right side of the vehicle.

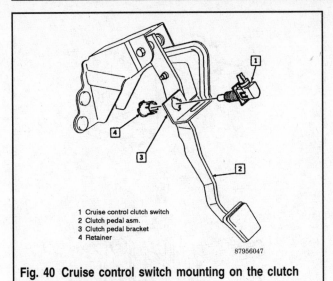

1 Cruise control clutch switch
2 Clutch pedal asm.
3 Clutch pedal bracket
4 Retainer

87956047

Fig. 40 Cruise control switch mounting on the clutch pedal — 1992 vehicle shown

1 Vehicle speed sensor
2 Seal
3 Retainer
4 Bolt

87956045

Fig. 42 View of the VSS mounting — 1996 vehicle with a manual transaxle shown

1982-94 Vehicles

▶ See Figure 43

1. Disconnect the negative battery cable.
2. Unfasten the four screws from steering column opening filler panel, remove the left instrument panel trim plate, or remove the module from the mounting bracket.
3. Detach the control module wiring connector.
4. Remove the control module.
5. Installation is the reverse of the removal procedure.

1995-96 Vehicles

▶ See Figures 44 and 45

1. Disconnect the negative battery cable.
2. Detach the cruise control cable at the engine bracket and TBI cam.
3. Disconnect the cruise control cable from the module assembly.
4. Detach the electrical connector from the module assembly.
5. For the 2.2L and 2.3L engines, unfasten the two nuts from the mounting studs.
6. For the 2.4L engine, slide the module from the mounting bracket.
7. For the 2.2L and 2.3L engines, remove the module assembly from the right strut tower.
8. For the 2.4L engine, remove the module from the firewall.
9. For the 2.2L and 2.3L engines, remove the module assembly from the mounting bracket.

To install:

❊❊WARNING

Do not pre-tap the screws to the module without the bracket in between the module and the screw. The added length of the screw may damage the cruise control module.

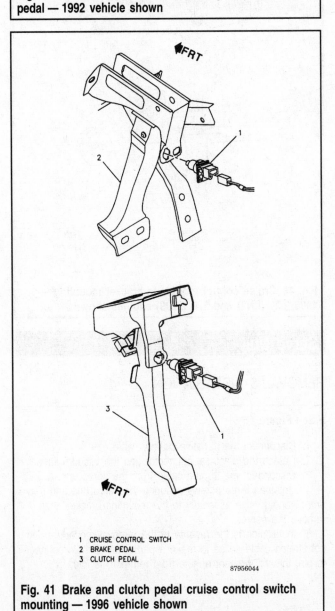

1 CRUISE CONTROL SWITCH
2 BRAKE PEDAL
3 CLUTCH PEDAL

87956044

Fig. 41 Brake and clutch pedal cruise control switch mounting — 1996 vehicle shown

10. For the 2.2L and 2.3L engines, fasten the module to the mounting bracket. Tighten the nuts to 106 inch lbs. (12 Nm).

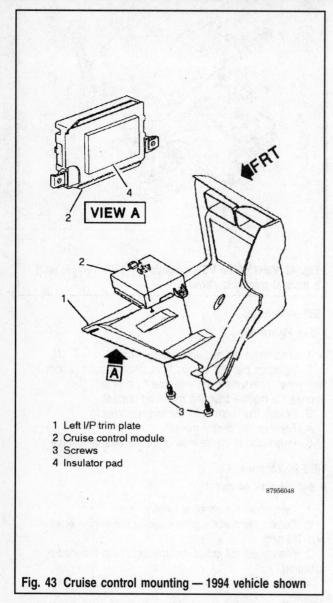

1 Left I/P trim plate
2 Cruise control module
3 Screws
4 Insulator pad

87956048

Fig. 43 Cruise control mounting — 1994 vehicle shown

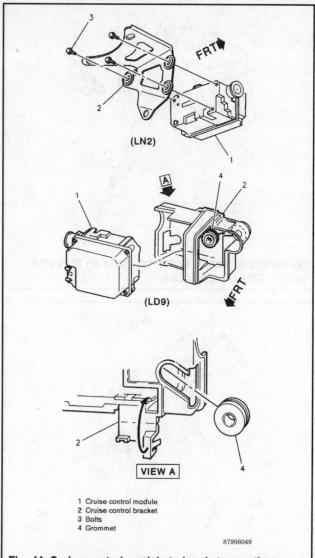

1 Cruise control module
2 Cruise control bracket
3 Bolts
4 Grommet

87956049

Fig. 44 Cruise control module-to-bracket mounting — 1996 2.2L (LN2) and 2.4L (LD9) engines shown

11. For the 2.2L and 2.3L engines, fasten the module to the strut tower. Tighten the nuts to 18 ft. lbs. (25 Nm).

12. For the 2.4L engine, install the module to the firewall.

13. Attach the electrical connector to the module.

14. Connect the cruise control cable to the module assembly.

15. Attach the cruise control cable to the engine bracket and TBI cam.

16. Connect the negative battery cable.

Servo Unit

REMOVAL & INSTALLATION

▶ See Figure 46

1. Disconnect the negative battery cable.
2. Detach the electrical connector and the vacuum lines.
3. Disconnect the throttle cable from the servo unit.
4. Unfasten three screws securing the servo unit and servo unit solenoid valve assembly to the mounting bracket, then remove the servo.
5. Installation is the reverse of the removal procedure. Do not stretch cable so as to make a particular tab hole connect to pin, this will prevent engine from returning to idle.

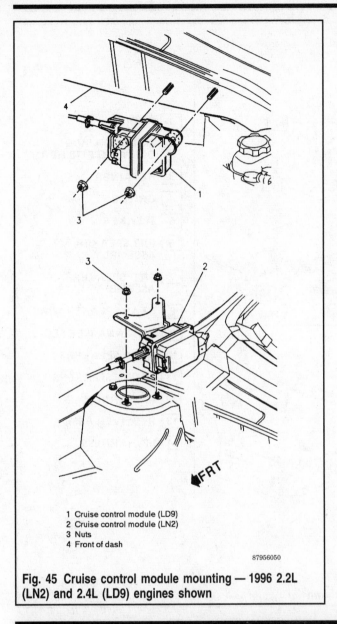

1 Cruise control module (LD9)
2 Cruise control module (LN2)
3 Nuts
4 Front of dash

87956050

Fig. 45 Cruise control module mounting — 1996 2.2L (LN2) and 2.4L (LD9) engines shown

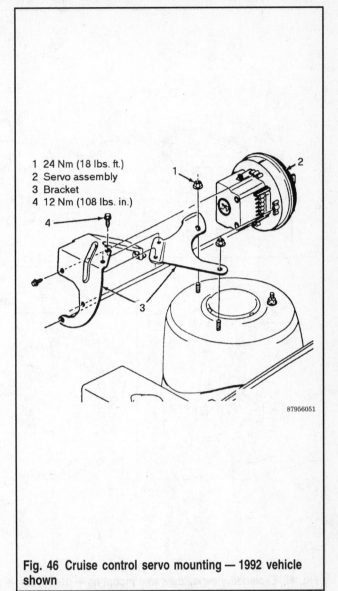

1 24 Nm (18 lbs. ft.)
2 Servo assembly
3 Bracket
4 12 Nm (108 lbs. in.)

87956051

Fig. 46 Cruise control servo mounting — 1992 vehicle shown

ENTERTAINMENT SYSTEMS

Radio Receiver/Tape Player/CD Player

REMOVAL & INSTALLATION

1982-87 Vehicles
▶ See Figure 47

✳✳WARNING

Do not operate the radio with the speaker leads disconnected. Operating the radio without an electrical load will damage the output transistors.

1. Disconnect the negative battery cable.
2. Remove the instrument panel trim plate.

3. Check the right side of the radio to determine whether a nut or a stud is used for side retention.

4. If a nut is used, remove the hush panel and then loosen the nut from below on cars without air conditioning. On cars with air conditioning, remove the hush panel, the A/C duct and the A/C control head for access to the nut. Do not remove the nut; loosen it just enough to pull the radio out. If a rubber stud is used, go on to Step 5.

5. Unfasten the two radio bracket-to-instrument panel attaching screws. Pull the radio forward far enough to disconnect the wiring and antenna and then remove the radio.

6. Installation is the reverse of removal.

1988-94 Vehicles, Except Sunbird
▶ See Figure 48

1. Disconnect the negative battery cable.

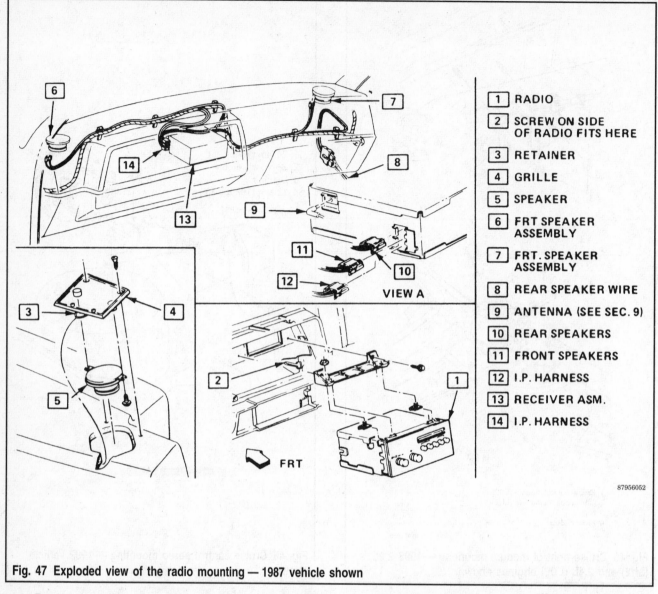

1	RADIO
2	SCREW ON SIDE OF RADIO FITS HERE
3	RETAINER
4	GRILLE
5	SPEAKER
6	FRT SPEAKER ASSEMBLY
7	FRT. SPEAKER ASSEMBLY
8	REAR SPEAKER WIRE
9	ANTENNA (SEE SEC. 9)
10	REAR SPEAKERS
11	FRONT SPEAKERS
12	I.P. HARNESS
13	RECEIVER ASM.
14	I.P. HARNESS

VIEW A

FRT

87956052

Fig. 47 Exploded view of the radio mounting — 1987 vehicle shown

2. Remove the instrument panel cluster or console trim plate.

3. Unfasten the radio-to-instrument panel attaching screws or nuts located at either the top of bottom of the radio.

4. Pull the radio out far enough to disconnect the wiring harness and antenna and remove the radio.

To install:

5. Reposition the radio and connect the wiring harness and antenna.

6. Fasten the radio retaining screws or nuts.

7. Install the instrument panel cluster or console trim plate.

8. Connect the negative battery cable.

1993-94 Sunbird

RADIO CONTROL ASSEMBLY

▶ See Figure 49

1. Disconnect the negative battery cable.

2. Detach the steering column opening filler panel.

3. Remove the instrument panel cluster or console trim plate.

4. Unfasten the radio-to-instrument panel attaching screws or nuts located at the top of the radio control assembly.

5. Pull the radio out far enough to disconnect the wiring harness and antenna and remove the radio.

To install:

6. Reposition the radio and connect the wiring harness and antenna.

7. Fasten the radio retaining screws or nuts.

8. Install the instrument panel cluster or console trim plate.

9. Fasten the steering column opening filler panel.

10. Connect the negative battery cable.

RADIO RECEIVER

▶ See Figure 50

1. Disconnect the negative battery cable.

2. Remove the right sound insulator.

3. Unfasten the nut from the bottom of the receiver securing the receiver to the HVAC duct.

4. Detach the electrical connector, then remove the receiver.

5. Installation is the reverse of the removal procedure.

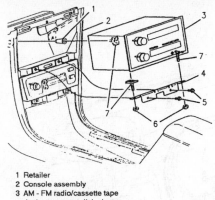

1 Retailer
2 Console assembly
3 AM - FM radio/cassette tape deck or compact disk player
4 Radio to console bracket
5 1.4 Nm (12 lbs.in.) screw
6 3 Nm (27 lbs.in.) nut
7 On stud threaded clip

87956053

Fig. 48 Radio assembly removal — 1993 Cavalier shown

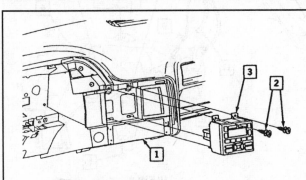

1 INSTRUMENT PANEL ASM.

2 BOLT/SCREW — FULLY DRIVEN, SEATED AND NOT STRIPPED

3 RADIO CONTROL ASM.

87956054

Fig. 49 On the Sunbird, the retaining screws are located at the top of the radio assembly

TAPE OR CD PLAYER

▶ See Figure 51

1. Disconnect the negative battery cable.
2. Remove the accessory trim plate.
3. Detach the two console housing side trim plates.
4. Unfasten the two nuts on the side of the deck, then pull the deck out, detach the electrical connectors and antenna lead and remove the deck.

To install:

5. Position the deck, attach the electrical connectors and antenna lead, then secure with the two retaining screws.
6. Attach the two console housing side trim plates.
7. Install the accessory trim plate.
8. Connect the negative battery cable.

1995-96 Vehicles

▶ See Figures 52 and 53

1. Disable the SIR system, as outlined earlier in this section.

2. If not done already, disconnect the negative battery cable.
3. For the Cavalier, remove the instrument panel cluster trim plate.
4. For the Sunfire, remove the accessory trim plate.
5. Unfasten the retaining screws, then pull the radio assembly forward. Detach the electrical and antenna lead connections, then remove the assembly from the vehicle.

To install:

6. Attach the electrical and antenna lead connections to the radio assembly.
7. Position the assembly, then secure with the retaining screws.
8. For the Cavalier, install the instrument panel cluster trim plate.
9. For the Sunfire, install the accessory trim plate.
10. Connect the negative battery cable,
11. Enable the SIR system, as outlined earlier in this section.

Speakers

REMOVAL & INSTALLATION

Front Dash Mounted

▶ See Figures 54 and 55

1. Disconnect the negative battery cable.
2. Carefully pry gently upwards on the speaker grille with a suitable prytool and remove the grille.
3. Unfasten the two screws retaining the speaker to instrument panel and pull the speaker partially out, to access the wiring.
4. Detach the wiring connector, then remove the speaker from the vehicle.
5. Installation is the reverse of the removal procedure, ensuring that the speaker grille cover snaps snugly into place.

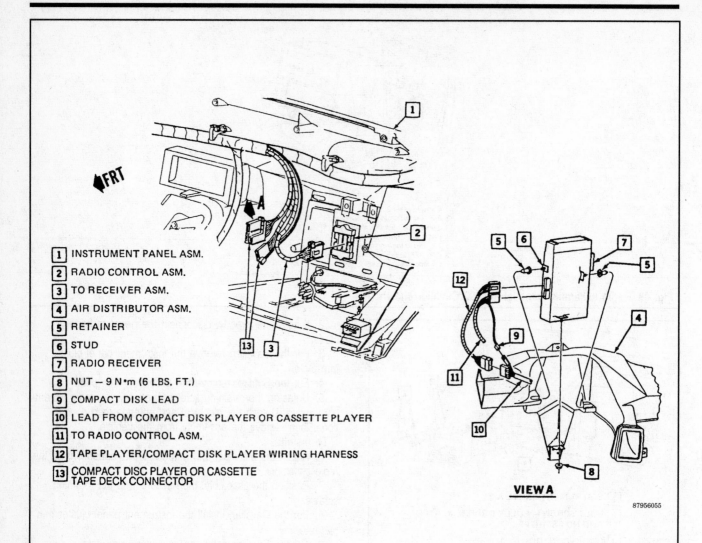

1. INSTRUMENT PANEL ASM.
2. RADIO CONTROL ASM.
3. TO RECEIVER ASM.
4. AIR DISTRIBUTOR ASM.
5. RETAINER
6. STUD
7. RADIO RECEIVER
8. NUT — 9 N•m (6 LBS. FT.)
9. COMPACT DISK LEAD
10. LEAD FROM COMPACT DISK PLAYER OR CASSETTE PLAYER
11. TO RADIO CONTROL ASM.
12. TAPE PLAYER/COMPACT DISK PLAYER WIRING HARNESS
13. COMPACT DISC PLAYER OR CASSETTE TAPE DECK CONNECTOR

VIEW A

Fig. 50 Radio receiver mounting — 1988-92 Sunbird

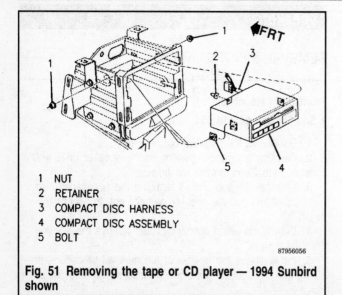

1 NUT
2 RETAINER
3 COMPACT DISC HARNESS
4 COMPACT DISC ASSEMBLY
5 BOLT

Fig. 51 Removing the tape or CD player — 1994 Sunbird shown

1 Instrument panel
2 Radio
3 Screws

Fig. 52 Radio assembly mounting — 1995 Cavalier shown

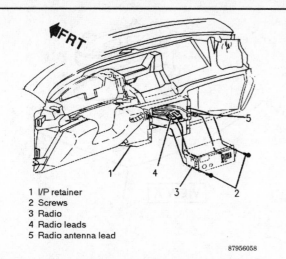

1 I/P retainer
2 Screws
3 Radio
4 Radio leads
5 Radio antenna lead

87956058

Fig. 53 View of the radio mounting — 1995 Sunfire shown

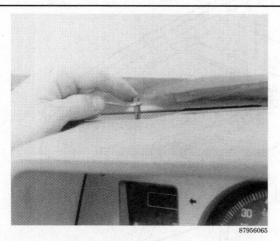

87956065

Fig. 54 A tool like this can be very help for removing the speaker retaining screws when space is too cramped for a screwdriver

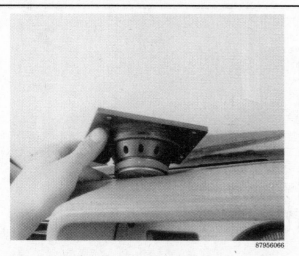

87956066

Fig. 55 Lift the speaker, detach the connector and remove the speaker from the vehicle

Front Door Mounted

1. Disconnect the negative battery cable.
2. Remove the door trim panel for access to the speaker.
3. Unfasten the retaining screws, then pull speaker out, detach the connector and remove the speaker from the vehicle.
4. Installation is the reverse of the removal procedure.

Rear Mounted 2 and 4-Door Models

1982-94 VEHICLES

▶ See Figure 56

1. Disconnect the negative battery cable.
2. Open the deck (trunk) lid.
3. Unfasten the speaker cover retaining screws and remove the cover.
4. Detach the wiring harness connector.
5. Unfasten the spring hook from the spring retainer.
6. Disconnect the speaker retaining tabs from the retaining slots, then remove the speaker.
7. Installation is the reverse of the removal procedure.

1995-96 VEHICLES

▶ See Figures 57 and 58

1. Disconnect the negative battery cable.
2. Remove the rear window panel trim, as outlined in Section 10 of this manual.
3. Press the tab on the front of the rear speaker spacer and lift the spacer.
4. Pull forward on the rear speaker spacer.
5. Detach the speaker wire harness connector.
6. Remove the speaker spacer and speaker.
7. Unfasten the retaining bolts, then remove the speaker from the spacer.

To install:

8. Position the speaker to the spacer, and secure using the retaining bolts. Tighten the bolts to 13 inch lbs (1.5 Nm).
9. Attach the rear speaker wire harness connector.

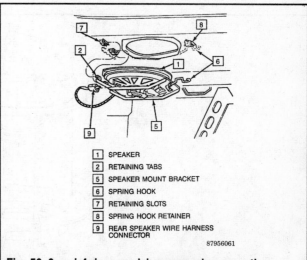

1 SPEAKER
2 RETAINING TABS
5 SPEAKER MOUNT BRACKET
6 SPRING HOOK
7 RETAINING SLOTS
8 SPRING HOOK RETAINER
9 REAR SPEAKER WIRE HARNESS CONNECTOR

87956061

Fig. 56 2 and 4-door model rear speaker mounting — 1994 vehicle shown

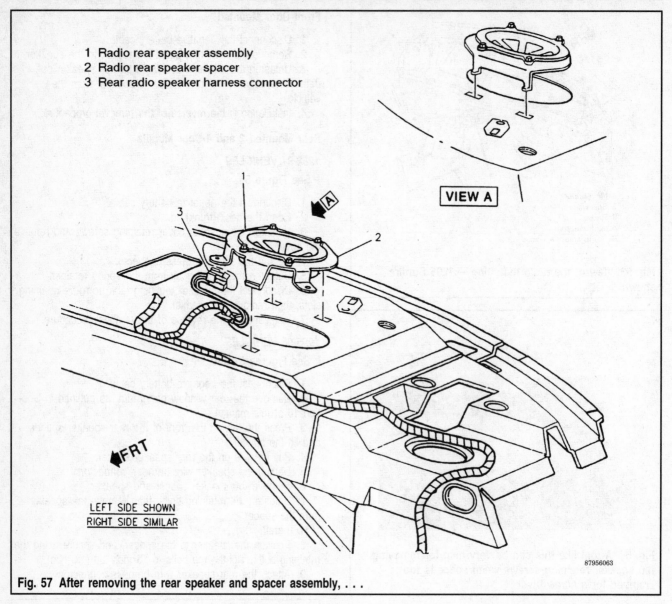

1 Radio rear speaker assembly
2 Radio rear speaker spacer
3 Rear radio speaker harness connector

VIEW A

FRT

LEFT SIDE SHOWN
RIGHT SIDE SIMILAR

87956063

Fig. 57 After removing the rear speaker and spacer assembly, . . .

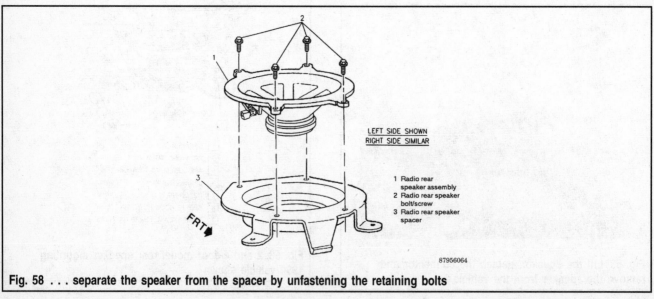

LEFT SIDE SHOWN
RIGHT SIDE SIMILAR

1 Radio rear
   speaker assembly
2 Radio rear speaker
   bolt/screw
3 Radio rear speaker
   spacer

FRT

87956064

Fig. 58 . . . separate the speaker from the spacer by unfastening the retaining bolts

10. Install the spacer by inserting the tabs into the slot at the rear window shelf and press down at the front of the spacer to snap it into place.

11. Install the rear window panel trim.

12. Connect the negative battery cable.

Rear Mounted Station Wagon

▶ See Figure 59

1. Disconnect the negative battery cable.
2. Remove the lift gate trim finishing panel.
3. Unfasten the speaker retaining screws.
4. Detach the wiring harness connector, then remove the speakers.
5. Installation is the reverse of the removal procedure.

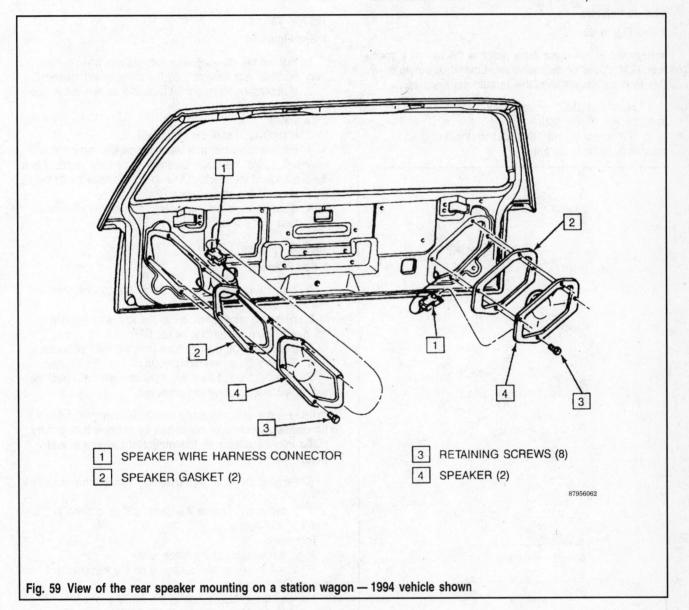

| 1 | SPEAKER WIRE HARNESS CONNECTOR |
| 2 | SPEAKER GASKET (2) |

| 3 | RETAINING SCREWS (8) |
| 4 | SPEAKER (2) |

87956062

Fig. 59 View of the rear speaker mounting on a station wagon — 1994 vehicle shown

WINDSHIELD WIPERS AND WASHERS

Windshield Wiper Blade and Arm

REMOVAL & INSTALLATION

1982-92 Vehicles

▶ See Figure 60

➡Removal of the wiper arms requires the use of a special tool, G.M. J8966 or its equivalent. Equivalent versions of this tool are usually available in auto parts stores.

1. Insert tool J8966, or equivalent, under the wiper arm and lever the arm off the shaft.
2. Disconnect the washer hose from the arm (if so equipped). Remove the arm.

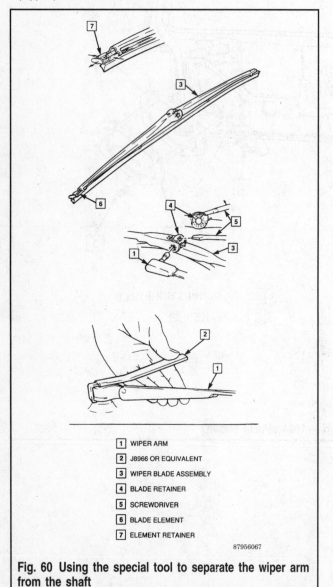

1	WIPER ARM
2	J8966 OR EQUIVALENT
3	WIPER BLADE ASSEMBLY
4	BLADE RETAINER
5	SCREWDRIVER
6	BLADE ELEMENT
7	ELEMENT RETAINER

87956067

Fig. 60 Using the special tool to separate the wiper arm from the shaft

3. If necessary, replace the blade refill as outlined in Section 1 of this manual.
4. Installation is the reverse of removal.

The proper park position is at the top of the blackout line on the glass. If the wiper arms and blades were in the proper position prior to removal, adjustment should not be required.

1993-94 Vehicles

▶ See Figure 61

1. Pull out the retaining latch with suitable prytool, then work the wiper arm assembly off the transmission driveshaft.
2. If necessary, replace the blade refill as outlined in Section 1 of this manual.

To install:

3. If removed, install the blade refill.
4. Position the wiper arm assembly on the transmission driveshaft so that the blade assembly is as near as possible to the top edge of the blackout line on the windshield with the wiper motor in the park position.
5. Seat the wiper arm assembly firmly on the driveshaft, then press in the retaining latch.

1995-96 Vehicles

▶ See Figure 62

1. Turn the ignition switch to the **ACCY** position, then set the wiper switch to the PULSE position.
2. When the wiper arms are at the innerwipe position and not moving, turn the ignition switch **OFF**.
3. Disconnect the washer hose from the washer nozzle.
4. Remove the cover from the nut.
5. Unfasten the nut from the wiper arm assembly and the wiper transmission assembly driveshaft.

➡If the wiper arm assembly cannot be removed from the transmission assembly driveshaft by rocking it, a battery puller may be used with the windshield wipers in mid-wipe.

6. Remove the wiper arm assembly from the transmission driveshaft by rocking.
7. If necessary, replace the blade refill as outlined in Section 1 of this manual.

To install:

8. If removed, install the blade refill.
9. Install the wiper arm assembly on the transmission driveshaft.
   a. Put the ignition switch in the **ACCY** position.
   b. Set the wiper switch to the PULSE position. The windshield wiper system should be operating.
   c. Turn the ignition switch **OFF** when wipers are in this innerwipe position and not moving.
   d. Install the wiper arm assembly on the transmission drive shaft while maintaining a distance of 3.46 in. (87.8mm) for the left hand side or 3.83 in. (97.5mm) for the right hand side between the wiper blade assembly and the bottom of the windshield (see accompanying figure for details).

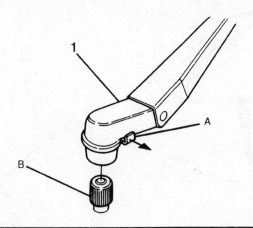

A Arm retaining latch
B Transmission drive shaft
C Blade retaining latch
D Claw set (6)
E Element vertebra
1 Wiper arm assembly
2 Wiper blade assembly
3 Blade superstructure
4 Blade element

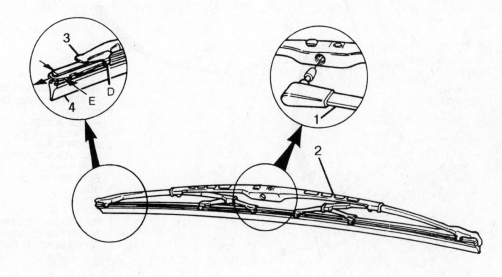

87956071

Fig. 61 Wiper arm, blade and element components

10. Install the retaining nut on the wiper transmission driveshaft and wiper arm assembly. Tighten the nut to 20 ft. lbs. (27 Nm), then install the cover on the nut.

➡**Lubricate the washer hose with windshield washer solvent to ease installation on the nozzle.**

11. Attach the washer hose to the washer nozzle.
12. Operate the wipers and check for proper operation.

ADJUSTMENT

The only adjustment for the wiper arms is to remove an arm from the transmission shaft, rotate the arm the required distance and direction and then install the arm back in position so it is in line with the blackout line on the glass. The wiper motor must be in the park position.

The correct blade-out wipe position on the driver's side is $9/16$-$1\ 3/4$ in. (15-45mm) from the tip of the blade to the left windshield pillar molding (driver's side). The correct blade-down

wipe position on the passenger side of the car is in line with the blackout line at the bottom of the glass.

Windshield Wiper Motor

REMOVAL & INSTALLATION

1982-94 Vehicles
▶ **See Figures 63 and 64**

1. Remove the wiper arm and blade assemblies.
2. Disconnect the negative battery cable.
3. Remove the shroud top vent grille.
4. For vehicles through 1991, loosen (but do not remove) the drive link-to-crank arm attaching nuts and detach the drive link from the motor crank arm.
5. Tag and disconnect all electrical leads from the wiper motor.

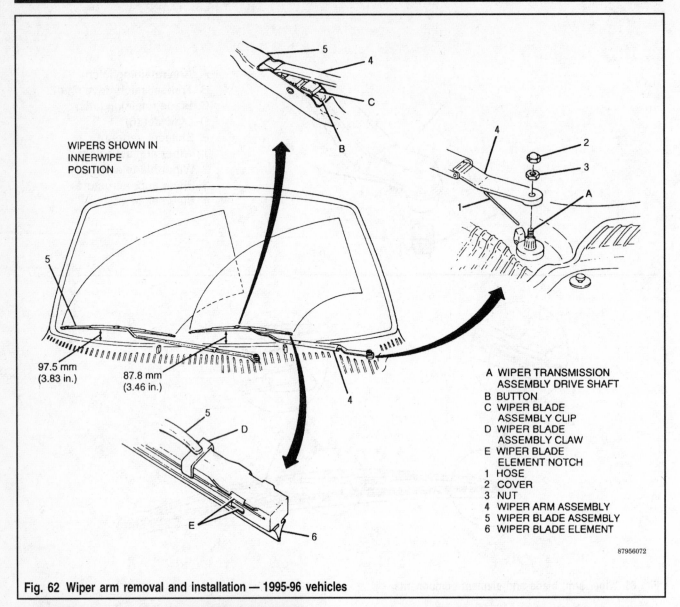

Fig. 62 Wiper arm removal and installation — 1995-96 vehicles

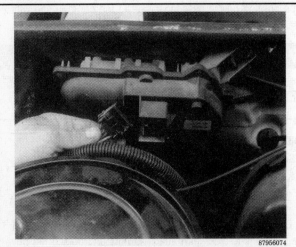

Fig. 63 Detach the electrical connector from the wiper motor — 1988 Sunbird shown

6. Using tool J 39232 or equivalent, remove the transmission drive link from the wiper motor crank arm.

7. For vehicles through 1991, unscrew the mounting bolts, rotate the motor up and outward and remove it.

8. For 1992 vehicles, unfasten the three screws, then remove the wiper motor assembly, guiding the crank arm through the hole.

To install:

9. Guide the crank arm through the opening in the body and then tighten the mounting bolts to 4-6 ft. lbs. (5-8 Nm) and the screws to 80 inch lbs. (9 Nm).

10. Install the drive link to the crank arm with the motor in the park position.

11. Installation of the remaining components is the reverse of removal.

1995-96 Vehicles

▶ See Figures 65, 66, 67, 68, 69 and 70

1. Detach the wiper arm assemblies from the wiper transmission assembly driveshaft.

Fig. 64 Unfasten the mounting bolts, then rotate the motor up and out to remove it — 1988 Sunbird shown

2. Unfasten the four screws, five retainer and the air inlet screen assembly from the vehicle.

3. Detach the electrical connector from the wiper motor assembly.

4. Unfasten the three screws, and remove the wiper drive system module from the vehicle.

5. Using tool J 39232 or equivalent, disconnect the wiper transmission assembly from the wiper motor crank arm assembly.

6. Remove the wiper motor crank arm assembly from the wiper motor assembly, as follows:

a. Loosen the screw.

b. Tap on the screw with a soft-faced mallet while holding up on the wiper motor crank arm assembly, until the crank arm is loose on the wiper motor.

c. Remove the screw and crank arm from the wiper motor.

7. Unfasten the three screws, then remove the wiper from the tube frame.

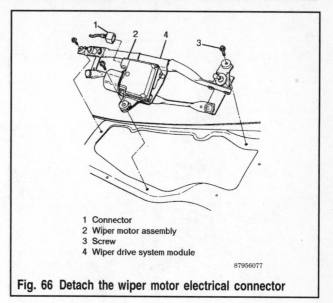

1 Connector
2 Wiper motor assembly
3 Screw
4 Wiper drive system module

Fig. 66 Detach the wiper motor electrical connector

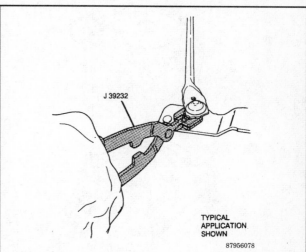

J 39232

TYPICAL APPLICATION SHOWN

Fig. 67 Use the special tool to remove the transmission assembly from the crank arm

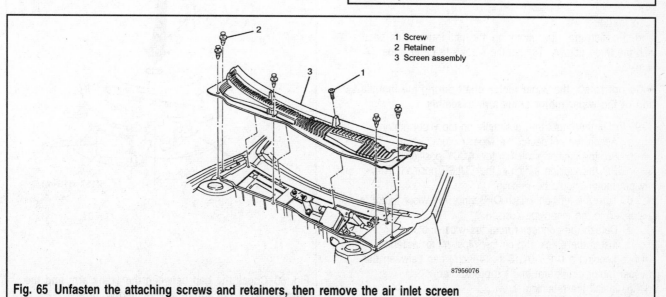

1 Screw
2 Retainer
3 Screen assembly

Fig. 65 Unfasten the attaching screws and retainers, then remove the air inlet screen

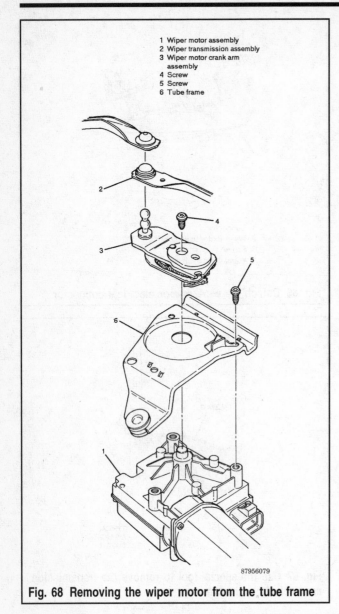

1 Wiper motor assembly
2 Wiper transmission assembly
3 Wiper motor crank arm
  assembly
4 Screw
5 Screw
6 Tube frame

87956079

Fig. 68 Removing the wiper motor from the tube frame

To install:

8. Position the wiper motor on the tube frame, then secure with the three screws. Tighten the screws to 62 inch lbs. (7 Nm).

➡**Do not rotate the wiper motor shaft during the installation of the wiper motor crank arm assembly**

9. Install the crank arm assembly on the wiper motor.

  a. Attach the connector the wiper motor.

  b. Put the ignition switch in the **ACCY** position.

  c. Put the ignition switch in the PULSE position. The wiper motor should be working.

  d. Turn the ignition switch **OFF** while the wiper motor is stopped in the innerwipe position.

  e. Detach the connector from the wiper motor.

  f. Install the crank arm on the wiper motor assembly while keeping a 0.157-0.315 in. (4-8mm) gap between the wiper motor crank arm and the bracket tab.

  g. Install the retaining screw.

  h. Check the gap between the wiper motor crank arm assembly and the bracket tab. If the gap is not 0.157-0.315

in. (4-8mm), remove the crank arm and repeat step 9. Tighten the screw to 12 ft. lbs. (16 Nm).

10. Using tool J 39529, or equivalent, install the wiper transmission on the crank arm.

11. Install the wiper drive system module, then secure with the three retaining screws. Tighten to 88 inch lbs (10 Nm).

12. Attach the electrical connector on the wiper motor.

13. Install the screen assembly using the four screws and five retainers.

14. Connect the wiper arms to the wiper transmission driveshaft.

15. Check the wiper system for proper operation.

Rear Window Wiper Motor

REMOVAL & INSTALLATION

1. Turn the ignition switch **OFF**.

2. Pull the wiper arm from the pivot shaft.

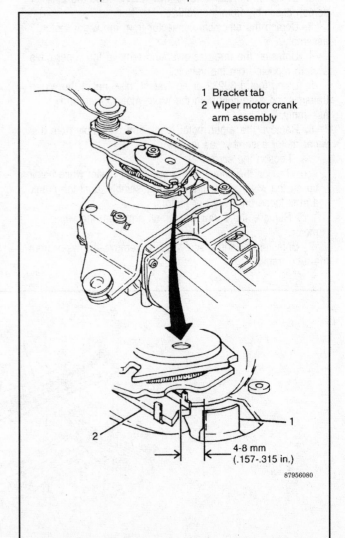

1 Bracket tab
2 Wiper motor crank
  arm assembly

4-8 mm
(.157-.315 in.)

87956080

Fig. 69 Check the gap between the crank arm and the bracket tab. If not within specifications, repeat installation of the crank arm

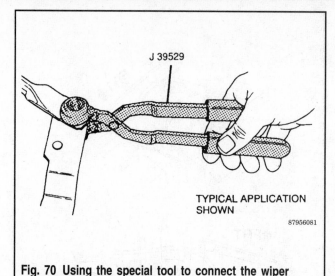

Fig. 70 Using the special tool to connect the wiper transmission to the crank arm

3. Remove the pivot shaft nut and spacers.
4. Open the tailgate and remove the inner trim panel.
5. Remove the license plate housing.
6. Detach the license plate light wiring.
7. Disconnect the wiper motor wiring.
8. Remove the linkage arm locking clip, pry off the arm and remove the linkage.
9. Unfasten the motor and bracket attaching screws and remove the motor.
10. Installation is the reverse of removal.

Wiper Linkage

REMOVAL & INSTALLATION

▶ See Figure 71

1. Remove the wiper arms.
2. Remove the shroud top vent grille.
3. Loosen (but do not remove) the drive link-to-crank arm attaching nuts.
4. Unscrew the linkage-to-cowl panel retaining screws and remove the linkage.
5. Installation is the reverse of removal. Tighten the attaching screws and nuts to 64 inch lbs. (7 Nm).

Windshield Washer Fluid Reservoir & Pump

REMOVAL & INSTALLATION

1982-92 Vehicles
▶ See Figures 72, 73 and 74

1. Disconnect the negative battery cable.
2. Drain washer fluid from the washer reservoir.
3. Detach the electrical connection and washer hoses.

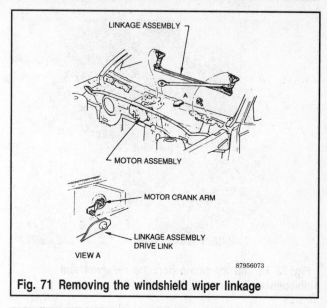

Fig. 71 Removing the windshield wiper linkage

4. Remove the washer reservoir by unfastening the retainers and lifting the reservoir out of the vehicle.
5. Remove the washer pump from the washer reservoir.
6. Installation is the reverse of removal. Make sure washer pump is pushed all the way into the washer reservoir gasket.

1993-94 Vehicles
▶ See Figure 75

1. Disconnect the negative battery cable.
2. Drain the washer fluid from the reservoir.
3. Detach the washer hose and the electrical connector from the washer pump.
4. Unfasten the screw from the mounting tab at the neck of the reservoir.
5. Remove the screw from the tab at the bottom of the container.
6. Extend the outer retaining clip of the mounting bracket outward and pull the container downward out of the mounting bracket.
7. Remove the pump from the reservoir.

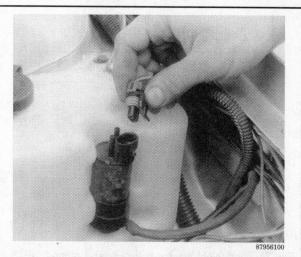

Fig. 72 Detach the windshield washer pump electrical connector, then . . .

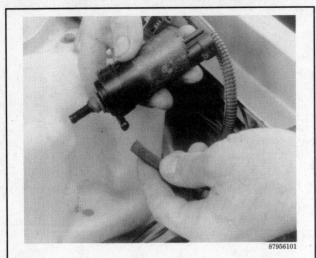

Fig. 73 . . . lift the pump from the reservoir and disconnect the hose

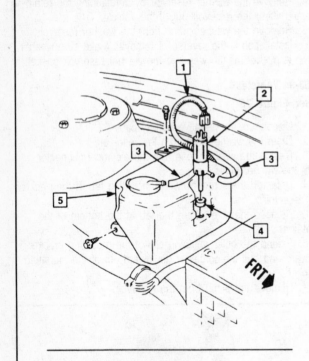

1 WIRING HARNESS

2 WASHER PUMP

3 WASHER HOSES

4 GASKET

5 WASHER RESERVOIR

87956082

Fig. 74 Windshield washer reservoir and pump assembly — 1992 vehicle shown

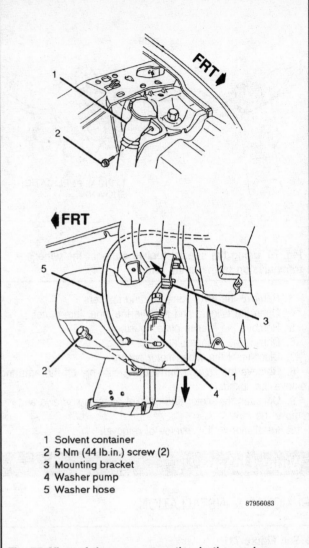

1 Solvent container
2 5 Nm (44 lb.in.) screw (2)
3 Mounting bracket
4 Washer pump
5 Washer hose

87956083

Fig. 75 View of the pump mounting in the washer reservoir — 1994 vehicle shown

To install:

8. Position the washer pump in the reservoir container. Make sure the pump is pushed all the way into the container seal.

9. Insert the neck of the container into the engine compartment., then extend the outer retaining clip of the mounting bracket outward and push the container upward into engagement with both bracket retaining clips.

10. Fasten the two screws in the lower and upper container mounting tabs. Tighten the screws to 44 inch lbs. (5 Nm).

11. Attach the washer hose and the electrical connector.

12. Fill the reservoir with windshield washer solvent, then connect the negative battery cable.

1995-96 Vehicles

▶ See Figures 76 and 77

1. Disconnect the negative battery cable.

2. Detach the connector and the hose from the washer pump.

3. Unfasten the two lower screws and the upper screw, then remove the reservoir from the vehicle.

4. Remove the air induction assembly and two retainers from the reservoir container.

5. Remove the pump as follows:

a. Pull the top of the washer pump out from the side of the reservoir.

b. Pull the washer pump up out of the reservoir.

To install:

6. Install the pump in the reservoir as follows:

a. Push the pump down into the reservoir completely.

b. Push the top of the pump into the side of the reservoir container.

7. Fasten the air induction assembly on the reservoir and secure with the two retainers.

8. Install the reservoir into the vehicle and secure with the three screws. Tighten the screws to 88 inch lbs. (10 Nm).

9. Attach the hose and the electrical connector to the washer pump.

10. Attach the negative battery cable.

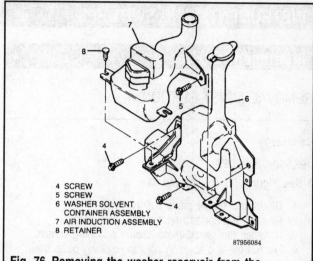

4 SCREW
5 SCREW
6 WASHER SOLVENT
  CONTAINER ASSEMBLY
7 AIR INDUCTION ASSEMBLY
8 RETAINER

87956084

Fig. 76 Removing the washer reservoir from the vehicle — 1996 vehicle shown

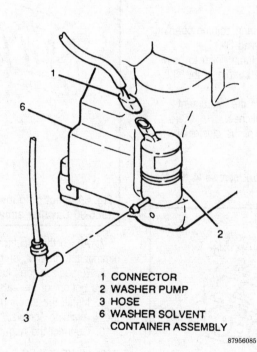

1 CONNECTOR
2 WASHER PUMP
3 HOSE
6 WASHER SOLVENT
  CONTAINER ASSEMBLY

87956085

Fig. 77 Windshield washer pump mounting — 1996 vehicle shown

INSTRUMENTS AND SWITCHES

Instrument Cluster

REMOVAL & INSTALLATION

Cavalier

1982-90 VEHICLES

▶ **See Figures 78, 79, 80 and 81**

1. Disconnect the negative battery cable.
2. Remove the speedometer cluster trim plate.
3. Unfasten the speedometer cluster attaching screws.
4. Loosen the two steering column retaining bolts, then lower the steering column. Pull the cluster away from the instrument panel and disconnect the speedometer cable.
5. Disconnect the vehicle speed sensor connector from the cluster. Tag and detach all other electrical connectors as required.
6. Remove the cluster housing from the vehicle.
7. Installation is the reverse of the removal procedure.

1991-94 VEHICLES

▶ **See Figure 82**

1. Disconnect the negative battery cable.
2. Unfasten the 4 screws from the steering column opening filler and remove the steering column opening filler.
3. Pull down slightly on the steering column collar to gain access and remove the 2 screws from the bottom of the cluster extension and remove the extension.
4. Detach the electrical connectors from the instrument panel dimmer and interior lamp control switches.
5. Unfasten the 2 screws from the top of the cluster and pull the cluster rearward to remove.

To install:

6. Reposition the cluster and install the 2 screws to the top of the cluster.

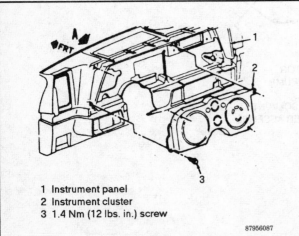

1 Instrument panel
2 Instrument cluster
3 1.4 Nm (12 lbs. in.) screw

87956087

Fig. 78 Base instrument panel cluster installation — 1982-90 Cavalier

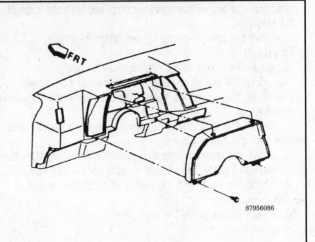

87956086

Fig. 79 Instrument cluster mounting — 1990 Cavalier Z24 shown

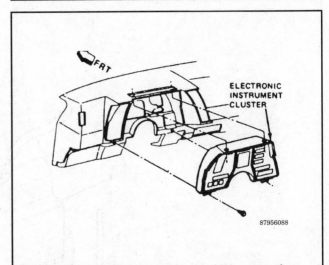

ELECTRONIC INSTRUMENT CLUSTER

87956088

Fig. 80 Electronic instrument panel cluster mounting — 1985-90 Cavalier shown

7. Attach the electrical connectors to the instrument panel dimmer and interior lamp control switches.
8. Reposition the cluster extension and install the 2 screws to the bottom of the cluster extension.
9. Install the steering column opening filler and secure with the 4 retaining screws.
10. Connect the negative battery cable.

1995-96 VEHICLES

▶ **See Figure 83**

1. Disconnect the negative battery cable.
2. Disable the SIR system, as outlined earlier in this section.
3. Remove the instrument panel cluster trim plate.
4. Unfasten the screws from the top of the cluster, then pull the cluster rearward to remove.

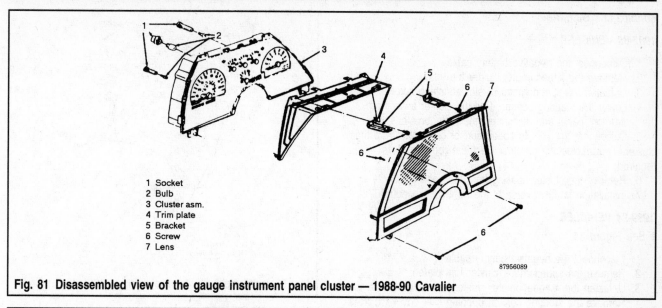

1 Socket
2 Bulb
3 Cluster asm.
4 Trim plate
5 Bracket
6 Screw
7 Lens

87956089

Fig. 81 Disassembled view of the gauge instrument panel cluster — 1988-90 Cavalier

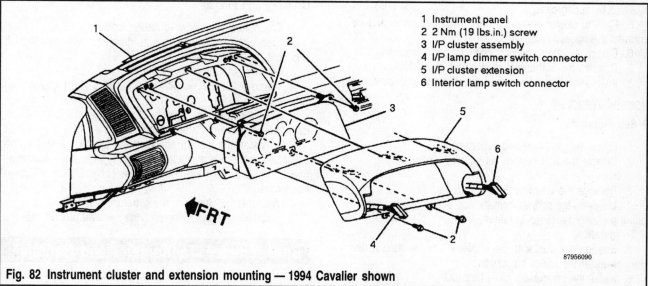

1 Instrument panel
2 2 Nm (19 lbs.in.) screw
3 I/P cluster assembly
4 I/P lamp dimmer switch connector
5 I/P cluster extension
6 Interior lamp switch connector

87956090

Fig. 82 Instrument cluster and extension mounting — 1994 Cavalier shown

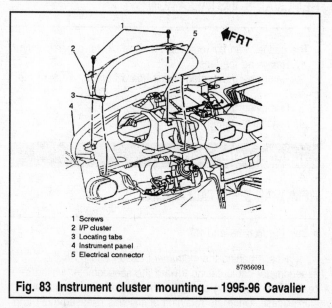

1 Screws
2 I/P cluster
3 Locating tabs
4 Instrument panel
5 Electrical connector

87956091

Fig. 83 Instrument cluster mounting — 1995-96 Cavalier

To install:

5. Position the cluster to the instrument panel, then fasten the screws at the top of the cluster.
6. Install the instrument panel trim plate.
7. Connect the negative battery cable.
8. Enable the SIR system.

Cimarron

1. Disconnect the negative battery cable.
2. Remove the speedometer cluster trim plate.
3. Unfasten the speedometer cluster attaching screws.
4. Lower the steering column. Pull the cluster away from the instrument panel and disconnect the speedometer cable.
5. Disconnect the vehicle speed sensor connector from the cluster. Detach all other electrical connectors as required.
6. Remove the cluster housing from the vehicle.
7. Installation is the reverse of the removal procedure.

Sunbird and Sunfire

1982-88 VEHICLES

1. Disconnect the negative battery cable.
2. Remove the speedometer cluster trim plate.
3. Unfasten the speedometer cluster attaching screws.
4. Lower the steering column. Pull the cluster away from the instrument panel and disconnect the speedometer cable.
5. Disconnect the vehicle speed sensor connector from the cluster. Tag and detach all other electrical connectors as required.
6. Remove the cluster housing from the vehicle.
7. Installation is the reverse of the removal procedure.

1989-94 VEHICLES

▶ See Figure 84

1. Disconnect the negative battery cable.
2. Remove the speedometer cluster trim plate.
3. Unfasten the 4 speedometer cluster attaching screws.
4. Remove the steering column opening filler cover which is retained by spring clips.
5. Pull the cluster away from the instrument panel and disconnect the speedometer cable.
6. Detach all other electrical connectors as required.
7. Remove the instrument cluster from the vehicle.
8. Installation is the reverse of the removal procedure.

1995-96 VEHICLES

▶ See Figure 85

1. Disconnect the negative battery cable.
2. Disable the SIR system, as outlined earlier in this section.
3. Remove the instrument panel trim pad.
4. Unfasten the screws from the top of the cluster, then pull the cluster rearward to remove.

To install:

5. Position the cluster to the instrument panel, then fasten the screws at the top of the cluster.
6. Install the instrument panel trim pad.
7. Connect the negative battery cable.
8. Enable the SIR system.

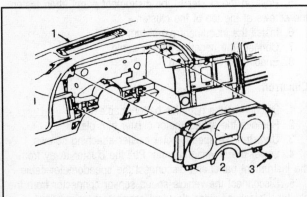

1 Instrument panel asm.
2 I/P cluster asm.
3 1.4 Nm (12 lbs.in.) screw

87956093

Fig. 84 Instrument panel cluster installation — 1989-94 Sunbird

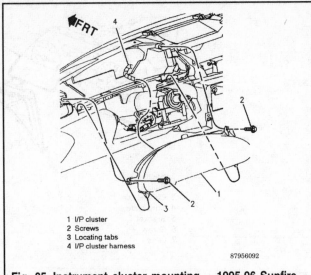

1 I/P cluster
2 Screws
3 Locating tabs
4 I/P cluster harness

87956092

Fig. 85 Instrument cluster mounting — 1995-96 Sunfire

Skyhawk and Firenza

1. Disconnect the negative battery cable.
2. Remove the steering column trim cover. Remove the left and right hand trim cover.
3. Remove the cluster trim cover.
4. Remove the screws attaching the lens and bezel to the cluster carrier.
5. Lower the steering wheel column by removing the 2 upper steering column attaching bolts.
6. Unfasten the screws attaching the cluster housing to the cluster carrier. Pull the cluster out slightly from the instrument panel and disconnect the speedometer cable. Detach all other connectors.
7. Remove the cluster housing from the vehicle.
8. Installation is the reverse of the removal procedure.

Speedometer, Tachometer and Gauges

REMOVAL & INSTALLATION

The gauges can be removed from the cluster assembly by:
1. Removing the lens.
2. Removing the printed circuit board from the back of the cluster.
3. Removing the gauge attaching screws.
4. Installation is the reverse of removal.

Speedometer Cable

REMOVAL & INSTALLATION

▶ See Figures 86 and 87

1. Reach behind the instrument cluster and push the speedometer cable casing toward the speedometer while depressing the retaining spring on the back of the instrument cluster case. Once the retaining spring has released, hold it in

while pulling outward on the casing to disconnect the casing from the speedometer.

➡**Removal of the steering column trim plate and/or the speedometer cluster may provide better access to the cable.**

2. Remove the cable casing sealing plug from the dash panel. Then, pull the casing down from behind the dash and remove the cable.

3. If the cable is broken and cannot be entirely removed from the top, support the car securely, and then unscrew the cable casing connector at the transaxle. Pull the bottom part of the cable out, and then screw the connector back onto the transaxle.

4. Lubricate the new cable. Insert it into the casing until it bottoms. Push inward while rotating it until the square portion at the bottom engages with the coupling in the transaxle, permitting the cable to move in another inch or so. Then, reconnect the cable casing to the speedometer and install the sealing plug into the dash panel.

Windshield Wiper Switch

REMOVAL & INSTALLATION

Except 1989-94 Sunbird And Dash Mounted Type Switches

The wiper switch is located inside the steering column cover. To gain access to the switch the steering wheel, turn signal switch and ignition lock will have to be removed. Refer to Section 8 for these procedures.

1989-94 Sunbird
▶ **See Figure 88**

1. Disconnect the negative battery cable.
2. Remove the right side trim plate from the the instrument panel.
3. Unfasten the wiper switch housing attaching screw.

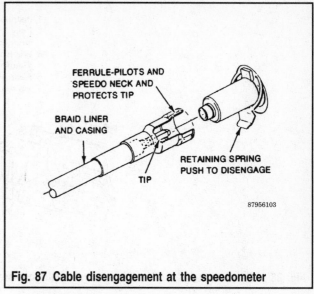

Fig. 87 Cable disengagement at the speedometer

4. Unplug the wiring and remove the switch.
To install:
5. Attach the switch wiring harness connector.
6. Reposition the switch to the to the instrument panel and secure with the attaching screw.
7. Install the right side trim plate to the instrument panel.
8. Connect the negative battery cable.

Dash Mounted Type Switch
▶ **See Figure 89**

1. Disconnect the negative battery cable.
2. Pull out the right pad trim plate.
3. Unfasten the 2 screws securing the switch to the trim plate.
4. Unplug the electrical connection and remove the switch.
To install:
5. Connect the switch electrical connector.
6. Install the 2 screws securing the switch to the trim plate.
7. Install the right pad trim plate.
8. Connect the negative battery cable.

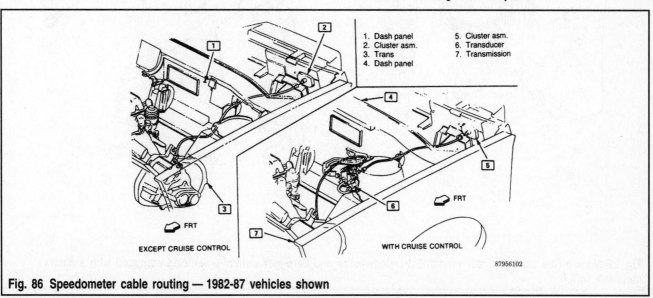

1. Dash panel
2. Cluster asm.
3. Trans
4. Dash panel
5. Cluster asm.
6. Transducer
7. Transmission

EXCEPT CRUISE CONTROL

WITH CRUISE CONTROL

Fig. 86 Speedometer cable routing — 1982-87 vehicles shown

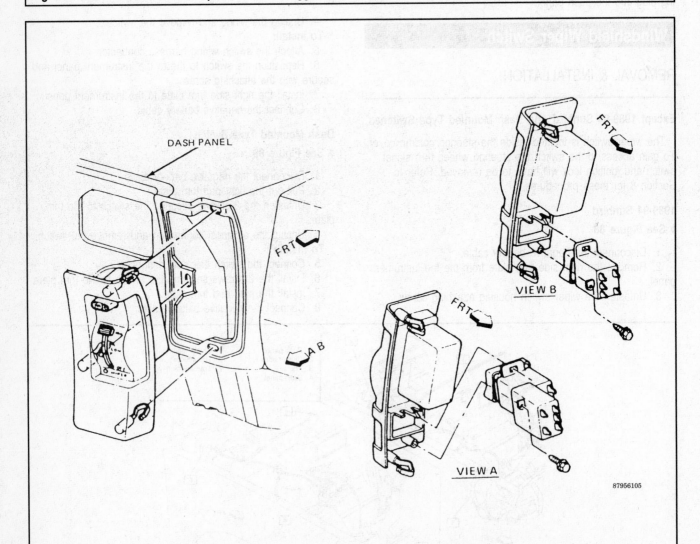

1 Instrument panel assembly
2 Fully driven, seated and not stripped screw
3 Windshield wiper switch
4 Windshield wiper switch housing
5 Rear window defogger/convertible top switch

87956104

Fig. 88 View of the windshield wiper and rear defogger switch removal — 1989-94 Sunbird

DASH PANEL

FRT

FRT

FRT

VIEW B

A B

VIEW A

87956105

Fig. 89 View of the front and rear windshield wiper/washer and defogger switch — vehicles equipped with a dash mounted switch

Headlight Switch

REMOVAL & INSTALLATION

1982-90 All Cavalier

EXCEPT 1985-87 CAVALIER TYPE 10, 1988 RS/ Z24, 1989-90 Z24

▶ See Figure 90

1. Disconnect the negative battery cable.
2. Pull the knob out fully, remove the knob from the rod by depressing the retaining clip from the underside the knob.
3. Remove the trimplate.
4. Remove the switch by removing the nut, rotating the switch 180°, then tilting forward and and pulling out. Disconnect the wire harness.
5. Installation is the reverse of the removal procedure.

1985-87 CAVALIER TYPE 10, 1988 RS/Z24 AND 1989-90 Z24

▶ See Figure 91

1. Disconnect the negative battery cable.
2. Pull out the left pad trim plate.
3. Unfasten the 2 screws securing the switch to the trim plate.
4. Detach the headlight switch electrical connection and remove the switch.
   To install:
5. Attach the switch electrical connector.
6. Fasten the 2 screws securing the switch to the trim plate.

7. Install the left pad trim plate.
8. Connect the negative battery cable.

1991-96 Cavalier

On these models the headlamp/parking lamp switch is a rotating switch, located on the left steering column lever, or multi-function lever, along with the cruise control and turn signal switch. Please refer to the Turn Signal Switch removal procedure in Section 8.

1982-88 J2000, 2000 and Sunbird and Cimarron

1. Disconnect the negative battery cable.
2. Pull the knob out fully, remove the knob from the rod by depressing the retaining clip from the underside the knob.
3. Remove the trimplate.
4. Remove the switch by removing the nut, rotating the switch 180°, then tilting forward and and pulling out. Disconnect the wire harness.
5. Installation is the reverse of the removal procedure.

Firenza, Skyhawk and 1989-94 Sunbird

▶ See Figures 92, 93 and 94

1. Disconnect the negative battery cable.
2. Pull out the left pad trim plate.
3. Unfasten the screws securing the switch to the trim plate.
4. Detach the switch electrical connection and remove the switch.
   To install:
5. Attach the switch electrical connector.
6. Fasten the screws securing the switch to the trim plate.
7. Install the left pad trim plate.
8. Connect the negative battery cable.

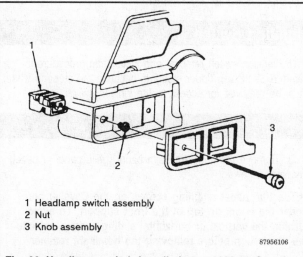

1 Headlamp switch assembly
2 Nut
3 Knob assembly

87956106

Fig. 90 Headlamp switch installation — 1982-90 Cavalier with base instrument panel

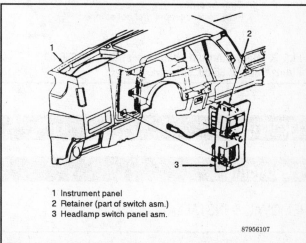

1 Instrument panel
2 Retainer (part of switch asm.)
3 Headlamp switch panel asm.

87956107

Fig. 91 Headlamp switch removal and installation — 1985-87 Cavalier Type 10, 1988 RS and Z24 and 1989-90 Z24

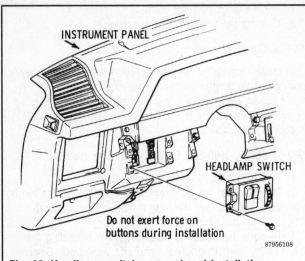

Fig. 92 Headlamp switch removal and installation —
1982-85 Firenza and Skyhawk

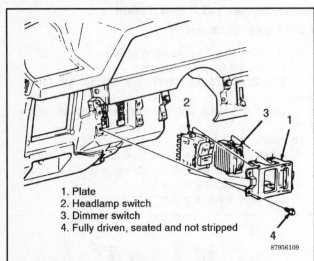

1. Plate
2. Headlamp switch
3. Dimmer switch
4. Fully driven, seated and not stripped

Fig. 93 Removing the headlamp switch — 1986-88
Firenza and 1986-89 Skyhawk

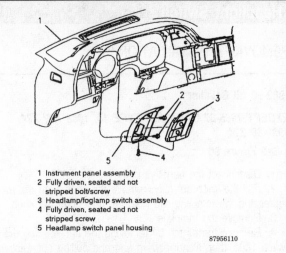

1 Instrument panel assembly
2 Fully driven, seated and not
  stripped bolt/screw
3 Headlamp/foglamp switch assembly
4 Fully driven, seated and not
  stripped screw
5 Headlamp switch panel housing

Fig. 94 Exploded view of the headlamp switch
assembly — 1989-94 Sunbird shown

1995-96 Sunfire

On these vehicles, the headlamp switch is part of the multi-function/turn signal lever. Please refer to Section 8 of this manual for removal and installation of the switch.

Clock

REMOVAL & INSTALLATION

The clock is part of the radio. If the clock is found to be defective the radio will have to be removed and sent to an authorized facility for clock repair.

Ignition Switch

The ignition switch removal and installation procedure is given in Section 8, under steering, because the steering wheel must be removed for access to the ignition switch.

LIGHTING

Headlights

REMOVAL & INSTALLATION

Sealed Beam
▶ See Figures 95, 96, 97, 98, 99, 100, 101, 102 and 103

1. Disconnect the negative battery cable.
2. If equipped with retractable headlights, raise the headlamp door using the manual knob.

3. Remove the headlamp trim panel (grille panel or bezel) attaching screws.

➡The trim panel retaining screws on the Cavalier are under the hood, on top of the front support. To avoid turning the vertical or horizontal aiming screws, refer to the illustration before removing the headlight retainer.

4. Unfasten the four headlamp retaining screws. These are the screws which hold the retaining ring for the bulb to the front of the car. Do not touch the two headlamp aiming screws, at the top and side of the retaining ring, or the headlamp aim will have to be readjusted.
5. Pull the bulb and ring forward and separate them. Unplug the electrical connector from the rear of the bulb.
   To install:
6. Plug the new bulb into the electrical connector.

Fig. 95 Raise the headlamp door using the manual knob

Fig. 96 Unfasten the bezel retaining screws, then . . .

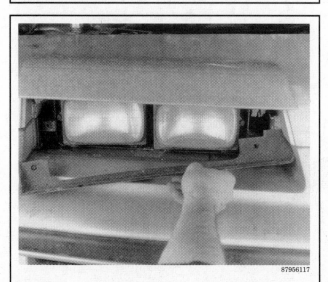

Fig. 97 . . . remove the bezel from the headlamps

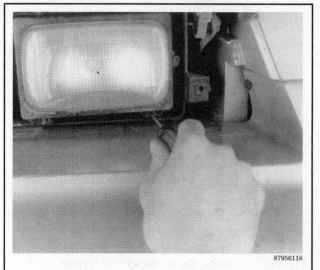

Fig. 98 Unfasten the headlamp retaining ring screws

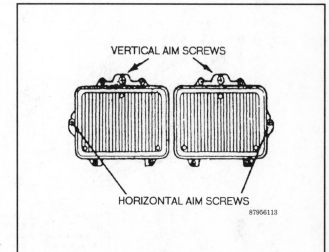

Fig. 99 Do not confuse the headlight aiming screws with the retainer attaching screws

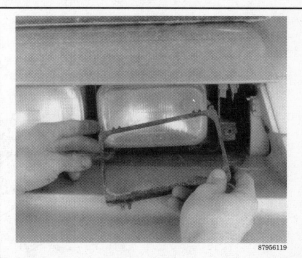

Fig. 100 Pull the retaining ring then the bulb forward, then . . .

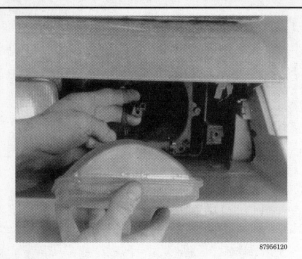

Fig. 101 . . . unplug the connector and remove the headlamp

7. Install the bulb into the retaining ring and install the ring and bulb.

8. If equipped, install the headlamp door.

9. Install the trim panel (grill trim or bezel).

10. Connect the negative battery cable.

Composite

Most of the later model vehicles covered by this manual are equipped with composite headlight assemblies. Due to space constraints, no access may be provided to withdraw the bulbs, so the replacement usually requires removal of the composite assembly.

➡**The composite headlight assemblies use Halogen bulbs which contain a gas under pressure. Improper handling of the bulb could cause it to shatter into flying glass fragments. To help avoid personal injury, follow the precautions closely.**

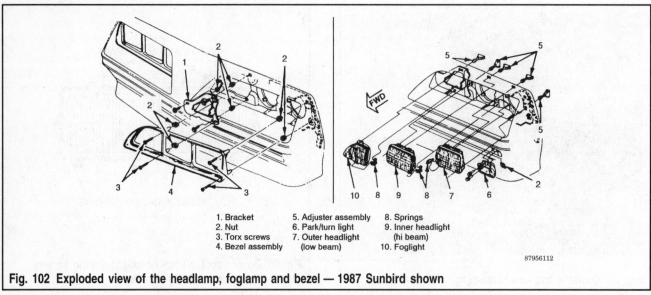

1. Bracket	5. Adjuster assembly	8. Springs
2. Nut	6. Park/turn light	9. Inner headlight
3. Torx screws	7. Outer headlight	(hi beam)
4. Bezel assembly	(low beam)	10. Foglight

Fig. 102 Exploded view of the headlamp, foglamp and bezel — 1987 Sunbird shown

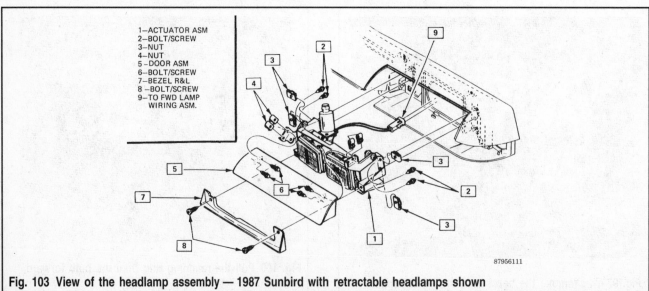

1—ACTUATOR ASM
2—BOLT/SCREW
3—NUT
4—NUT
5—DOOR ASM
6—BOLT/SCREW
7—BEZEL R&L
8—BOLT/SCREW
9—TO FWD LAMP
WIRING ASM.

Fig. 103 View of the headlamp assembly — 1987 Sunbird with retractable headlamps shown

Whenever handling a Halogen bulb, ALWAYS follow these precautions:

• Turn the headlight switch OFF and allow the bulb to cool before changing it. Leave the switch OFF until the change is complete.

• ALWAYS wear eye protection when changing a halogen bulb.

• Handle the bulb only by its base. Avoid touching the glass.

• DO NOT drop or scratch the bulb.

• Keep dirt and moisture off the bulb.

• Place the used bulb in the new bulb's carton and dispose of it properly.

1. Raise the hood and locate the bulb mounting location at the rear of the composite headlamp body.

2. Disconnect the negative battery cable.

3. If necessary for access, remove the splash shield or side marker lamp(s).

4. If there is enough room to access the plastic base, press in and turn the base 1/4 turn counterclockwise and remove from the metal retaining ring by gently pulling back and away from the headlight. Remove the electrical connector from the bulb by raising the locktab and pulling the connector down and away from the bulb's plastic base.

5. If you can't access the bulb from the engine compartment, unfasten the thumb screws, and/or other retainers, then pull the composite headlight assembly forward slightly and disengage the wiring connector. Press in and turn the base 1/4 turn counterclockwise and remove the bulb from the metal retaining ring by gently pulling back and away from the headlight.

To install:

6. Attach the electrical connector on the new bulb's plastic base making sure that the locktab is in place.

7. Install the bulb by inserting the smallest tab located on top of the plastic base into the corresponding notch in the metal retaining ring. Turn clockwise 1/4 turn until it stops. The small plastic tab should be at the top of the metal ring.

8. Install the composite headlight assembly, then secure with the retainers.

9. Connect the negative battery cable, then check for proper headlight operation.

HEADLIGHT AIMING

▶ **See Figure 104**

The headlights must be properly aimed to provide the best, safest road illumination. The lights should be checked for proper aim and adjusted as necessary. Certain state and local authorities have requirements for headlight aiming; these should be checked before adjustment is made.

Headlight adjustment may be temporarily made using a wall, as described below, or on the rear of another vehicle. When adjusted, the lights should not glare in oncoming car or truck windshields, nor should they illuminate the passenger compartment of vehicles driving in front of you. These adjustments are rough and should always be fine-tuned by a repair shop which is equipped with headlight aiming tools. Improper adjustments may be both dangerous and illegal.

For most of the vehicles covered by this manual, horizontal and vertical aiming of each sealed beam unit is provided by two adjusting screws which move the retaining ring and adjusting plate against the tension of a coil spring. There is no adjustment for focus; this is done during headlight manufacturing.

➡ **Because the composite headlight assembly is bolted into position, no adjustment should be necessary or possible. Some applications, however, may be bolted to an adjuster plate or may be retained used adjusting screws. If so, follow this procedure when adjusting the lights, BUT always have the adjustment checked by a reputable shop.**

Before removing the headlight bulb or disturbing the headlamp in any way, note the current settings in order to ease headlight adjustment upon reassembly. If the high or low beam setting of the old lamp still works, this can be done using the wall of a garage or a building:

1. Park the car on a level surface, with the fuel tank about 1/2 full and with the vehicle empty of all extra cargo (unless normally carried). The vehicle should be facing a wall which is no less than 6 feet (1.8m) high and 12 feet (3.7m) wide. The front of the vehicle should be about 25 feet from the wall.

➡ **The car's fuel tank should be about half full when adjusting the headlights. Tires should be properly inflated, and if a heavy load is normally carried in the vehicle, it should remain there.**

2. If aiming is to be performed outdoors, it is advisable to wait until dusk in order to properly see the headlight beams on the wall. If done in a garage, darken the area around the wall as much as possible by closing shades or hanging cloth over the windows.

3. Turn the headlights **ON** and mark the wall at the center of each light's low beam, then switch on the brights and mark the center of each light's high beam. A short length of masking tape which is visible from the front of the truck may be used. Although marking all four positions is advisable, marking one position from each light should be sufficient.

4. If neither beam on one side of the vehicle is working, and if another like-sized car is available, park the second car

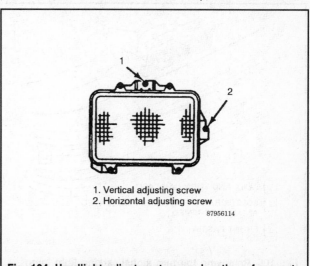

1. Vertical adjusting screw
2. Horizontal adjusting screw

87956114

Fig. 104 Headlight adjustment screw locations for most sealed beam headlight adjusting plates

in the exact spot where the vehicle was and mark the beams using the same-side light on that truck. Then switch the cars so the one to be aimed is back in the original spot. The car must be parked no closer to or farther away from the wall than the second vehicle.

5. Perform any necessary repairs, but make sure the car is not moved, or is returned to the exact spot from which the lights were marked. Turn the headlights **ON** and adjust the beams to match the marks on the wall.

6. Have the headlight adjustment checked as soon as possible by a reputable repair shop.

Signal and Marker Lights

REMOVAL & INSTALLATION

Front Turn Signal and Parking Lights

▶ See Figures 105 and 106

Bulbs at the front of the car can normally be replaced from beneath the car or from under the hood. Some bulbs may require removal of the outer lens. Remove the socket from the lamp housing by twisting, then replace the bulb and reinstall the socket.

1. Disconnect the negative battery cable.

2. On early model vehicles, unfasten the retaining screws, then remove the bezel and light housing from the front fascia of the vehicle. Remove the bulb.

3. On later model vehicles, remove the lamp assembly, unfasten the socket from the lamp housing by turning it counterclockwise, then remove the lamp from the socket by pressing in and turning counterclockwise.

To install:

4. Install the replacement lamp into the socket, matching the directional alignment pins on the base of the bulb with the complementary slots in the socket. This will assure that the proper filament is energized at the right time; i.e.: the turn signal filament and not the parking lamp filament is energized when the turn signal is turned on.

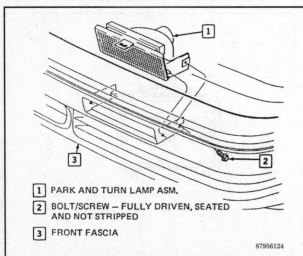

1 PARK AND TURN LAMP ASM.

2 BOLT/SCREW — FULLY DRIVEN, SEATED AND NOT STRIPPED

3 FRONT FASCIA

87956124

Fig. 105 Removing the turn signal/parking light lamp assembly — 1992 Sunbird shown

5. If you can get to the bulb from the engine compartment, push the lamp into the socket and turn clockwise. Install the socket to the lamp housing by turning clockwise.

6. If the bulb can't be accessed from the engine compartment, after the bulb is installed, fasten the housing and bezel to the front fascia of the vehicle.

7. Connect the negative battery cable.

8. Check operation of the parking lamp and turn signal.

Front Side Marker Lights

▶ See Figure 107

1. Disconnect the negative battery cable.

2. If equipped, manually crank up the head lamp door with the hood open.

3. If necessary, remove the headlamp assembly for access to the side marker light retaining screws.

4. Unfasten the side marker housing attaching screws.

5. Lower the housing far enough to remove the socket from the housing by turning 45° counterclockwise.

6. Remove the bulb and socket assembly from the housing, then detach the bulb from the socket.

To install:

7. Position the bulb into the socket making sure it is secure.

8. Install the socket to the lamp housing.

9. Secure the socket to the lamp housing by turning 45° clockwise.

10. Install the side marker housing, then fasten using the attaching screws.

11. If necessary, install the headlight assembly.

12. Connect the negative battery cable.

13. If equipped, lower the headlamp door by turning the head lamps on and off.

Rear Stop And Turn Signal Lamps

▶ See Figures 108 and 109

Various methods are employed to remove and install the components of the tail lamp assemblies. Tail lamp bulbs can be replaced by removing the screws which retain the lamp assemblies to the rear end panel and then removing the lamp assemblies. On some models it will be necessary to remove the wing nut inside the rear compartment which retains the tail lamp to the body.

1. Disconnect the negative battery cable.

2. Open the trunk.

3. Remove the nuts or other retainers from the rear trim, then remove the trim.

4. From inside the trunk, unfasten the wing nuts or other retainers securing the tail lamp housing, then pull the tail lamp assembly out so the bulb sockets can be accessed.

5. Depending upon vehicle application, remove the lamp socket either by rotating it counterclockwise (approximately ¼ turn) until the plastic tabs disengage, or by squeezing the metal tangs while pulling the socket from the light assembly.

6. Remove the bulb from the socket using the appropriate method. Bulbs with blade-type bases pull straight out, while those with round bases and protruding pins (bayonet-type bulbs) must be depressed, then rotated counterclockwise (approximately ⅛ turn) before pulling out.

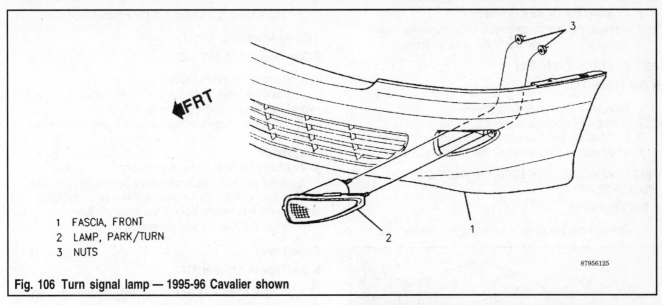

1 FASCIA, FRONT
2 LAMP, PARK/TURN
3 NUTS

87956125

Fig. 106 Turn signal lamp — 1995-96 Cavalier shown

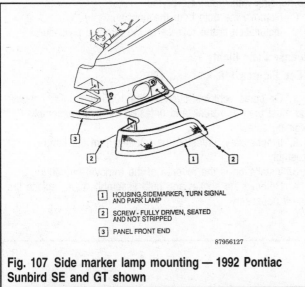

1 HOUSING,SIDEMARKER, TURN SIGNAL AND PARK LAMP
2 SCREW - FULLY DRIVEN, SEATED AND NOT STRIPPED
3 PANEL FRONT END

87956127

Fig. 107 Side marker lamp mounting — 1992 Pontiac Sunbird SE and GT shown

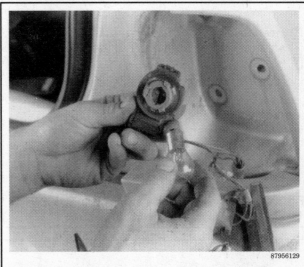

87956129

Fig. 109 . . . then remove the bulb from the socket

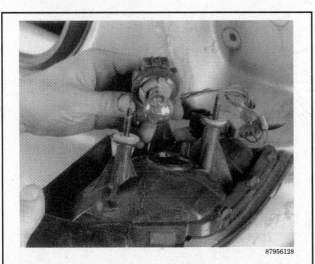

87956128

Fig. 108 After removing the retainers, pull the tail lamp assembly down . . .

To install:

7. Secure the bulb in the socket using the appropriate method. Bulbs with blade-type bases push straight in, while those with round bases and protruding pins (bayonet-type bulbs) must be inserted, then depressed and rotated clockwise (approximately $\frac{1}{8}$ turn).

8. Install the lamp socket using the appropriate method. Depending on the type of socket, either engage the plastic tabs, and rotate the socket clockwise (approximately $\frac{1}{4}$ turn), or push on the socket until the metal tangs engage.

9. Install the housing cover nuts/retainers.
10. Install the rear trim.
11. Connect the negative battery cable, then check the operation of the rear lights.

High-mount Stop Light

1982-94 VEHICLES WITHOUT LUGGAGE RACK

▶ See Figures 110 and 111

1. Remove the two mounting screws.

2. Unfasten the electrical connector.
3. Remove the two cover screws and remove the bulb.
4. Installation is the reverse of the removal procedure.

1982-94 STATION WAGONS
▶ See Figure 112

1. Remove the four mounting screws.
2. Detach the electrical connector.
3. Remove the two cover screws and remove the bulb.
4. Installation is the reverse of the removal procedure.

1982-94 VEHICLES WITH LUGGAGE RACK OR WING/SPOILER
▶ See Figure 113

1. Remove the two cover screws and remove the bulb.

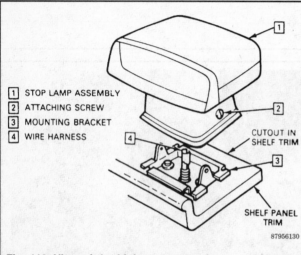

1. STOP LAMP ASSEMBLY
2. ATTACHING SCREW
3. MOUNTING BRACKET
4. WIRE HARNESS

CUTOUT IN SHELF TRIM

SHELF PANEL TRIM

87956130

Fig. 110 View of the high-mount stop lamp — 1982-94 4-door vehicle (without luggage rack)

2. Installation is the reverse of the removal procedure.

1995-96 VEHICLES
▶ See Figures 114 and 115

1. Remove the rear window panel trim.
2. From the trunk, push up on the high-mount stop lamp ratchet mechanism and slide the lamp forward.
3. Detach the lamp harness connector, then remove the lamp.
To install:
4. Attach the lamp harness connector.
5. Install the high-mount stop lamp by inserting the tabs into the slots at the rear window shelf and push the lamp forward until it is secure against the back window.
6. Install the rear window panel trim.

Dome Light
▶ See Figures 116 and 117

1. Pull the dome light lens or carefully pry the lens from the housing with a suitable prytool.
2. Remove the bulb from the housing.
3. Installation is the reverse of the removal procedure.

License Plate Lights
▶ See Figures 118, 119 and 120

1. On some vehicles, such as the 1995-96 Sunfire coupes, you must open the trunk and unfasten the lamp assembly retaining screw.
2. If necessary, unfasten the retainer from the lamp assembly.
3. Installation is the reverse of the removal procedure.
4. Remove the socket and bulb assembly, then replace the bulb if necessary.

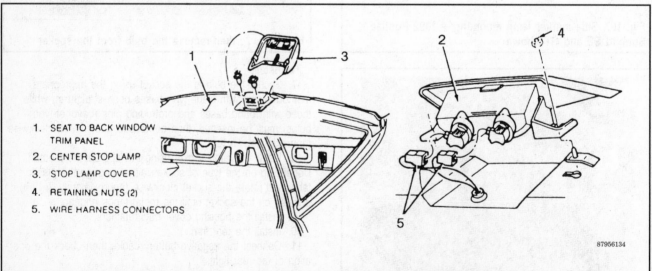

1. SEAT TO BACK WINDOW TRIM PANEL
2. CENTER STOP LAMP
3. STOP LAMP COVER
4. RETAINING NUTS (2)
5. WIRE HARNESS CONNECTORS

87956134

Fig. 111 View of the high-mount stop lamp — 1982-94 2-door vehicle (without luggage rack)

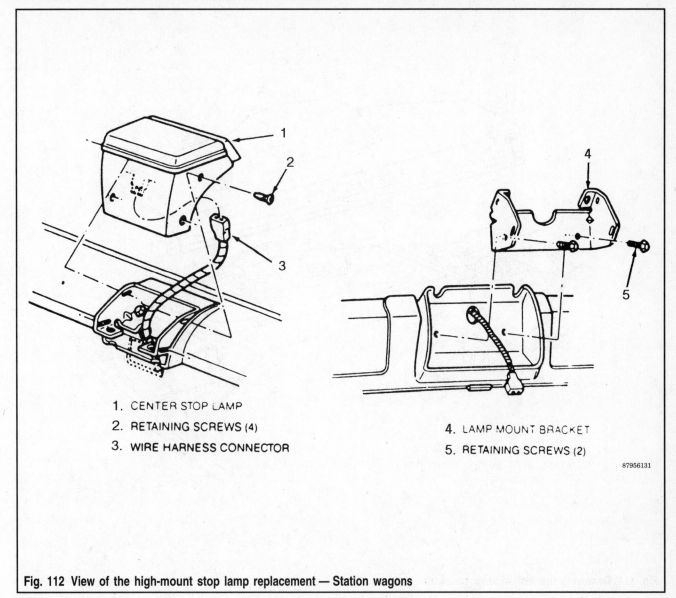

1. CENTER STOP LAMP
2. RETAINING SCREWS (4)
3. WIRE HARNESS CONNECTOR

4. LAMP MOUNT BRACKET
5. RETAINING SCREWS (2)

87956131

Fig. 112 View of the high-mount stop lamp replacement — Station wagons

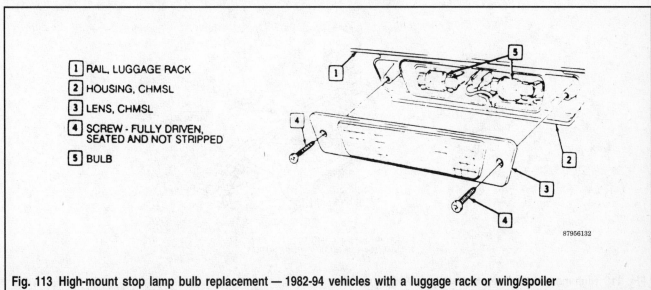

1 RAIL, LUGGAGE RACK
2 HOUSING, CHMSL
3 LENS, CHMSL
4 SCREW - FULLY DRIVEN, SEATED AND NOT STRIPPED
5 BULB

87956132

Fig. 113 High-mount stop lamp bulb replacement — 1982-94 vehicles with a luggage rack or wing/spoiler

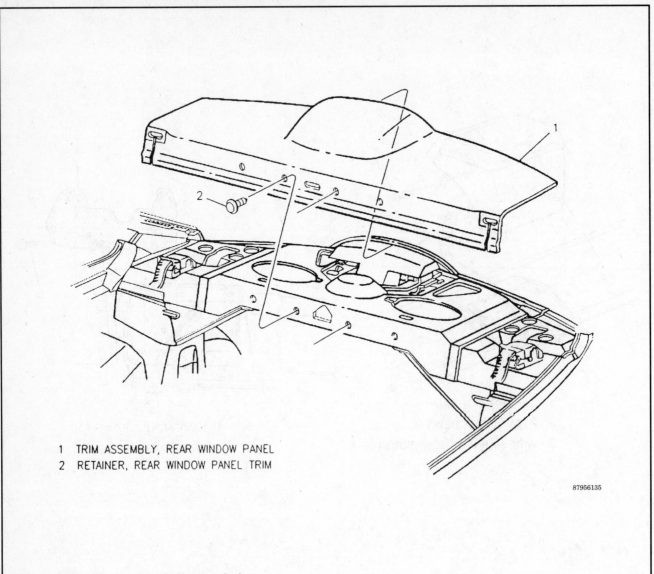

1 TRIM ASSEMBLY, REAR WINDOW PANEL
2 RETAINER, REAR WINDOW PANEL TRIM

87956135

Fig. 114 Removing the rear window panel trim

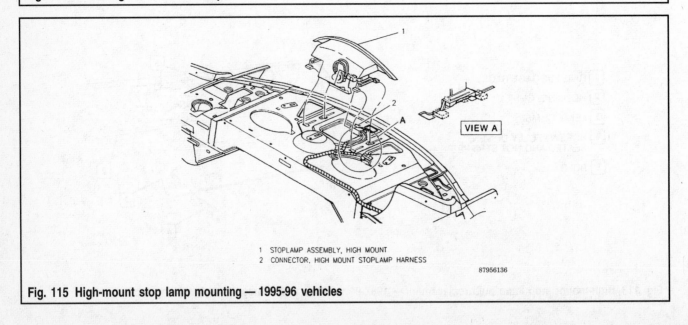

1 STOPLAMP ASSEMBLY, HIGH MOUNT
2 CONNECTOR, HIGH MOUNT STOPLAMP HARNESS

87956136

Fig. 115 High-mount stop lamp mounting — 1995-96 vehicles

Fig. 116 Pull the dome light lens from the housing . . .

Fig. 117 . . . then remove the bulb from the housing

Fig. 118 On this 1988 Sunbird you must unfasten the retainer from the license plate lamp assembly

Fig. 119 Once it is unbolted, remove the light bulb and socket assembly, then . . .

Fig. 120 . . . pull the bulb from the socket

Fog Lamps

REMOVAL & INSTALLATION

1. Unfasten the two screws from the lens retainers.
2. Remove the two lens retainers.
3. Remove the lens/bulb housing.
4. Disconnect the bulb retainer clip.
5. Detach the electrical connector and remove the bulb.
6. Installation is the reverse of the removal procedure.

TRAILER WIRING

Wiring the car for towing is fairly easy. There are a number of good wiring kits available and these should be used, rather than trying to design your own. All trailers will need brake lights and turn signals as well as tail lights and side marker lights. Most states require extra marker lights for overly wide trailers. Also, most states have recently required back-up lights for trailers, and most trailer manufacturers have been building trailers with back-up lights for several years.

Additionally, some Class I, most Class II and just about all Class III trailers will have electric brakes.

Add to this number an accessories wire, to operate trailer internal equipment or to charge the trailer's battery, and you can have as many as seven wires in the harness.

Determine the equipment on your trailer and buy the wiring kit necessary. The kit will contain all the wires needed, plus a plug adapter set which included the female plug, mounted on the bumper or hitch, and the male plug, wired into, or plugged into the trailer harness.

When installing the kit, follow the manufacturer's instructions. The color coding of the wires is standard throughout the industry.

One point to note, some domestic vehicles, and most imported vehicles, have separate turn signals. On most domestic vehicles, the brake lights and rear turn signals operate with the same bulb. For those vehicles with separate turn signals, you can purchase an isolation unit so that the brake lights won't blink whenever the turn signals are operated, or, you can go to your local electronics supply house and buy four diodes to wire in series with the brake and turn signal bulbs. Diodes will isolate the brake and turn signals. The choice is yours. The isolation units are simple and quick to install, but far more expensive than the diodes. The diodes, however, require more work to install properly, since they require the cutting of each bulb's wire and soldering in place of the diode.

One final point, the best kits are those with a spring loaded cover on the vehicle mounted socket. This cover prevents dirt and moisture from corroding the terminals. Never let the vehicle socket hang loosely. Always mount it securely to the bumper or hitch.

➡ **For more information on towing a trailer please refer to Section 1.**

CIRCUIT PROTECTION

Fuses Block and Fuses

Fuses protect all the major electrical systems in the car. In case of an electrical overload, the fuse melts, breaking the circuit and stopping the flow of electricity.

The fuse block on most models covered by this manual is located under the instrument panel to the left of the steering column. The fuse block should be visible from underneath the steering column, near the pedal bracket. If the panel is not visible, check for a removable compartment door or trim panel which may used on later models to hide the block.

If a fuse blows, the cause should be investigated and corrected before the installation of a new fuse. This, however, is easier to say than to do. Because each fuse protects a limited number of components, your job is narrowed down somewhat. Begin your investigation by looking for obvious fraying, loose connections, breaks in insulation, etc. Use the techniques outlined at the beginning of this section. Electrical problems are almost always a real headache to solve, but if you are patient and persistent, and approach the problem logically (that is, don't start replacing electrical components randomly), you will eventually find the solution.

Each fuse block uses miniature fuses (normally plug-in blade terminal-type for these vehicles) which are designed for increased circuit protection and greater reliability. The compact plug-in or blade terminal design allows for fingertip removal and replacement.

Although most fuses are interchangeable in size, the amperage values are not. Should you install a fuse with too high a value, damaging current could be allowed to destroy the component you were attempting to protect by using a fuse in the first place. The plug-in type fuses have a volt number molded on them and are color coded for easy identification. Be sure to only replace a fuse with the proper amperage rated substitute.

A blown fuse can easily be checked by visual inspection or by continuity checking.

REPLACEMENT

◆ **See Figures 121 and 122**

1. Locate the fuse for the circuit in question.

➡ **When replacing the fuse, DO NOT use one with a higher amperage rating.**

2. Check the fuse by pulling it from the fuse block and observing the element. If it is broken, install a replacement fuse the same amperage rating. If the fuse blows again, check

87956142

Fig. 121 The fuse block on most models is located under the instrument panel to the left of the steering column

the circuit for a short to ground or faulty device in the circuit protected by the fuse.

3. Continuity can also be checked with the fuse installed in the fuse block with the use of a test light connected across the 2 test points on the end of the fuse. If the test light lights, replace the fuse. Check the circuit for a short to ground or faulty device in the circuit protected by the fuse.

Fusible Links

A fusible link is a protective device used in an electrical circuit. When the current increases beyond a certain amperage, the fusible metal of the wire link melts, thus breaking the electrical circuit and preventing further damage to other components and wiring. Whenever a fusible link is melted because of a short circuit, correct the cause before installing a new one. There are four different gauge sizes commonly used and they are usually color coded so that they may be easily installed in their original positions.

REPLACEMENT

▶ See Figure 123

1. Disconnect the negative battery cable, followed by the positive cable.
2. Locate the burned out link.
3. If both ends of the link are ring terminal connectors which are easily accessed:
    a. Measure the installed length necessary for the new link.
    b. Unbolt and remove the link and connector pieces.
    c. Obtain a suitable length of link, then strip the insulation off the harness wire back ½ in. (12.7mm) to allow soldering of the new connectors.
    d. Position the new connector around the new link and crimp it securely. Then, solder the connection, using rosin

core solder and sufficient heat to guarantee a good connection. Repeat for the remaining connection.

➡**Whenever splicing a new wire, always bond the splice with rosin core solder, then cover with electrical tape. Use acid core solder may cause corrosion.**

4. If the ends of the connector are not easily access, repair the length in the vehicle:
    a. Strip away the melted insulation and cut the burned link ends from the wire.
    b. Strip the wire back ½ in. (12.7mm) to allow soldering of the new link.
    c. Using a new fusible link of appropriate gauge and length, solder it into the circuit.
5. Tape all exposed wiring with electrical tape and seal with silicone or use a heat shrink tube, if available, to weatherproof the repair.
6. If removed from the vehicle, install the link and secure the connectors.
7. Reconnect the positive, followed by the negative battery cables.

Circuit Breakers

REPLACEMENT

Circuit breakers differ from fuses in that they are reusable. Circuit breakers open when the flow of current exceeds specified value and will close after a few seconds when current flow returns to normal. Some of the circuits protected by circuit breakers include electric windows and power accessories. Circuits breakers are used in these applications due to the fact that they must operated at times under prolonged high current flow due to demand even though there is not malfunction in the circuit.

There are 2 types of circuit breakers. The first type opens when high current flow is detected. A few seconds after the excessive current flow has been removed, the circuit breaker

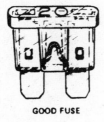

GOOD FUSE   BLOWN FUSE

87956094

Fig. 122 Visual examination will reveal a blown fuse, but it should not be replaced until repairs are made

will close. If the high current flow is experienced again, the circuit will open again.

The second type is referred to as the Positive Temperature Coefficient (PTC) circuit breaker. When excessive current flow passes through the PTC circuit breaker, the circuit is not opened but its resistance increases. As the device heats ups with the increase in current flow, the resistance increases to the point where the circuit is effectively open. Unlike other circuit breakers, the PTC circuit breaker will not reset until the circuit is opened, removing voltage from the terminals. Once the voltage is removed, the circuit breaker will re-close within a few seconds.

Replace the circuit breaker by unplugging the old one and plugging in the new one. Confirm proper circuit operation.

Flashers

REPLACEMENT

The hazard flasher is located forward of the console on all J-Body vehicles. The turn signal flasher is located behind the instrument panel, on the left side of the steering column bracket. Replace the flasher by unplugging the old one and plugging in the new one. Confirm proper flasher operation.

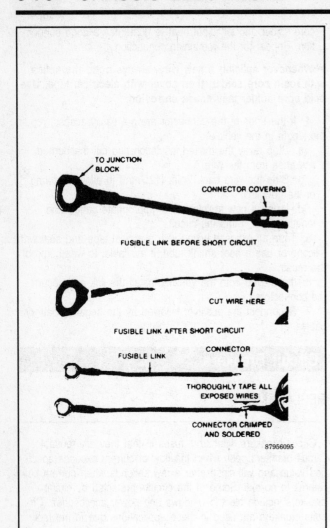

TO JUNCTION BLOCK

CONNECTOR COVERING

FUSIBLE LINK BEFORE SHORT CIRCUIT

CUT WIRE HERE

FUSIBLE LINK AFTER SHORT CIRCUIT

FUSIBLE LINK

CONNECTOR

THOROUGHLY TAPE ALL EXPOSED WIRES

CONNECTOR CRIMPED AND SOLDERED

87956095

Fig. 123 Fusible links may be repaired by soldering a new link into the wire

WIRING DIAGRAMS

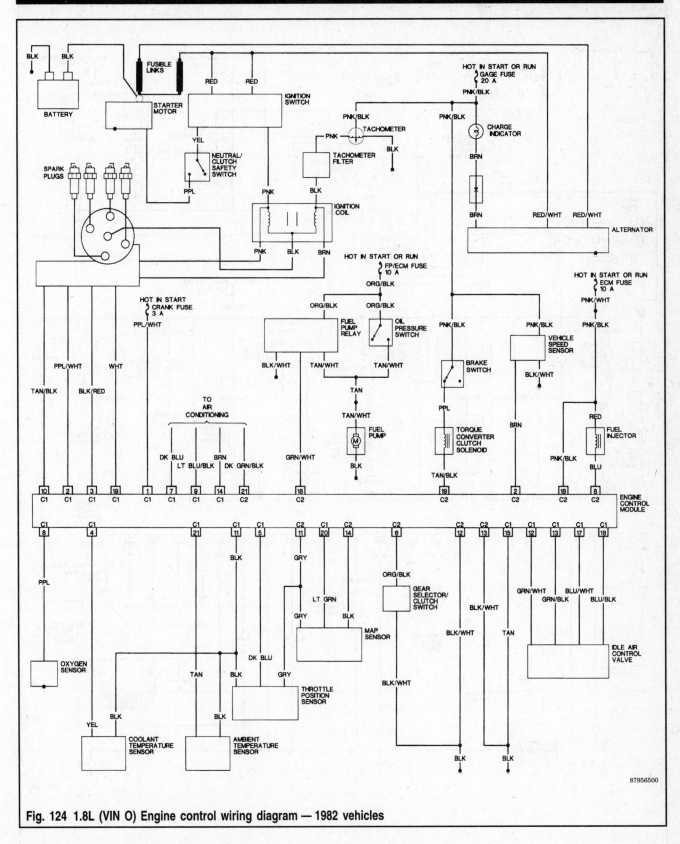

Fig. 124 1.8L (VIN O) Engine control wiring diagram — 1982 vehicles

87956500

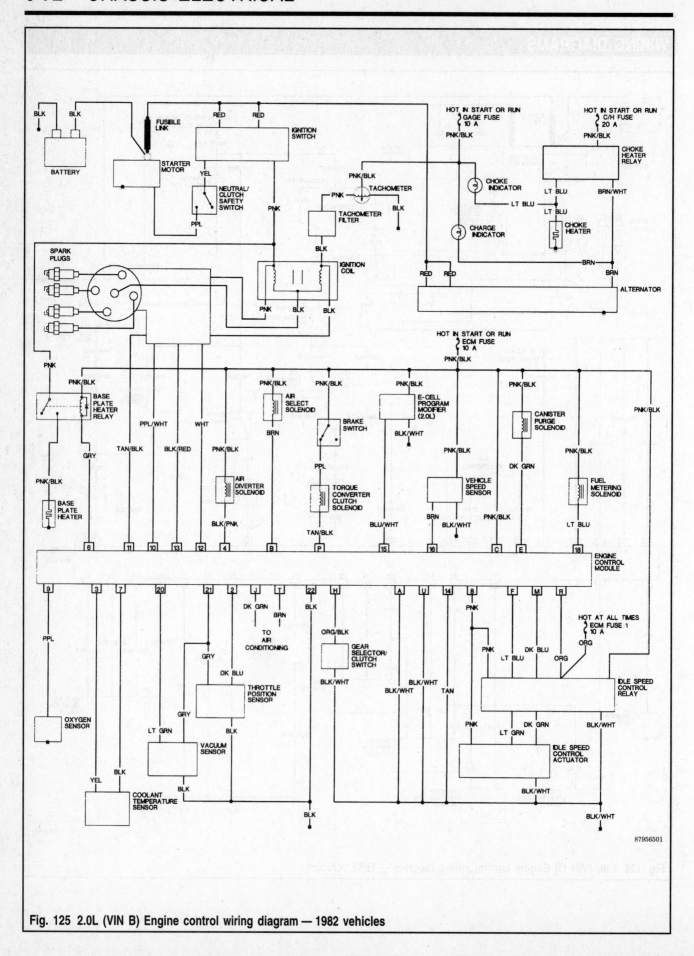

Fig. 125 2.0L (VIN B) Engine control wiring diagram — 1982 vehicles

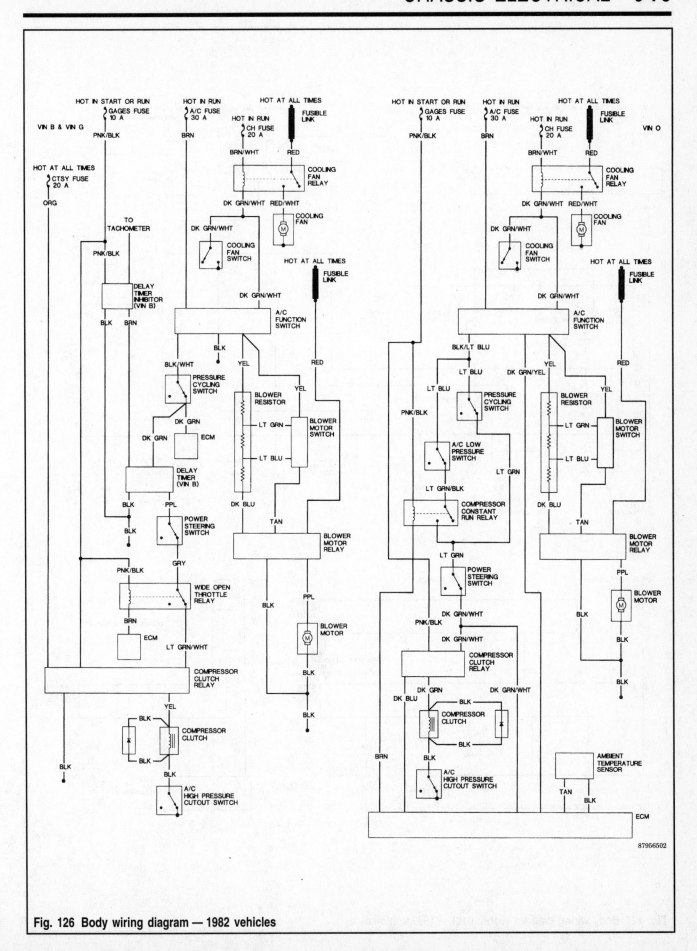

Fig. 126 Body wiring diagram — 1982 vehicles

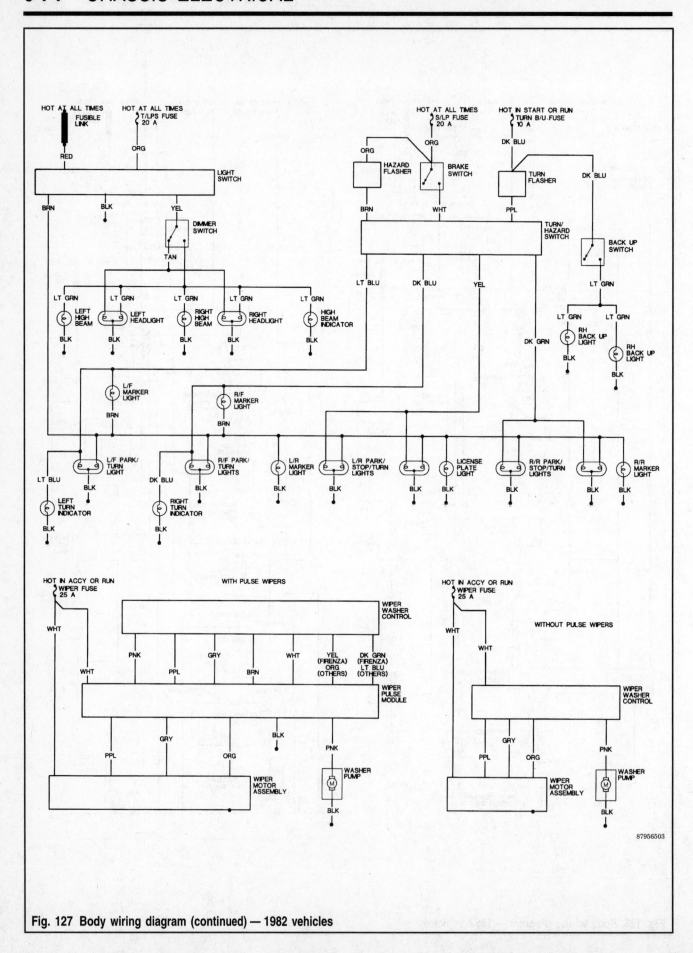

Fig. 127 Body wiring diagram (continued) — 1982 vehicles

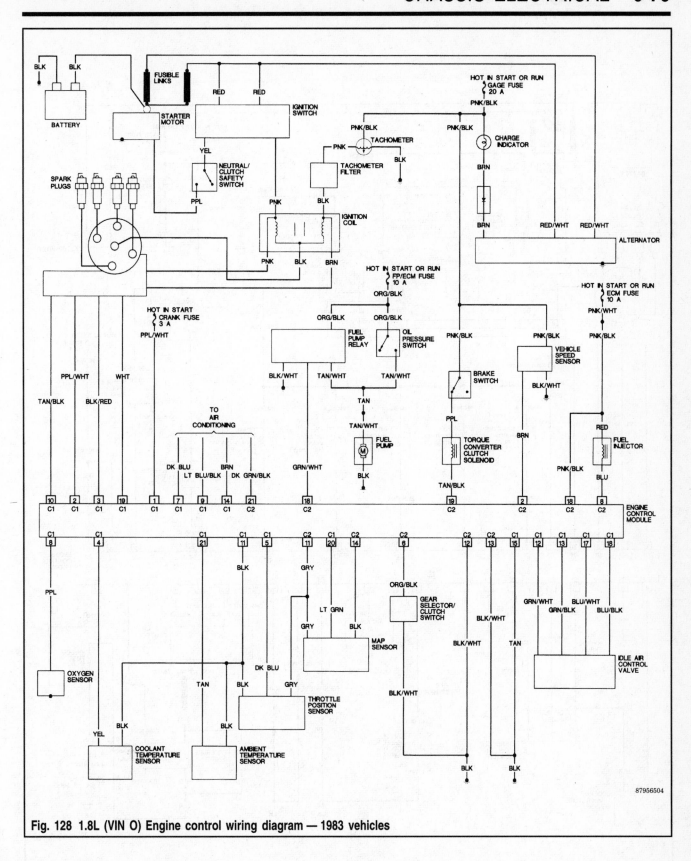

Fig. 128 1.8L (VIN O) Engine control wiring diagram — 1983 vehicles

87956504

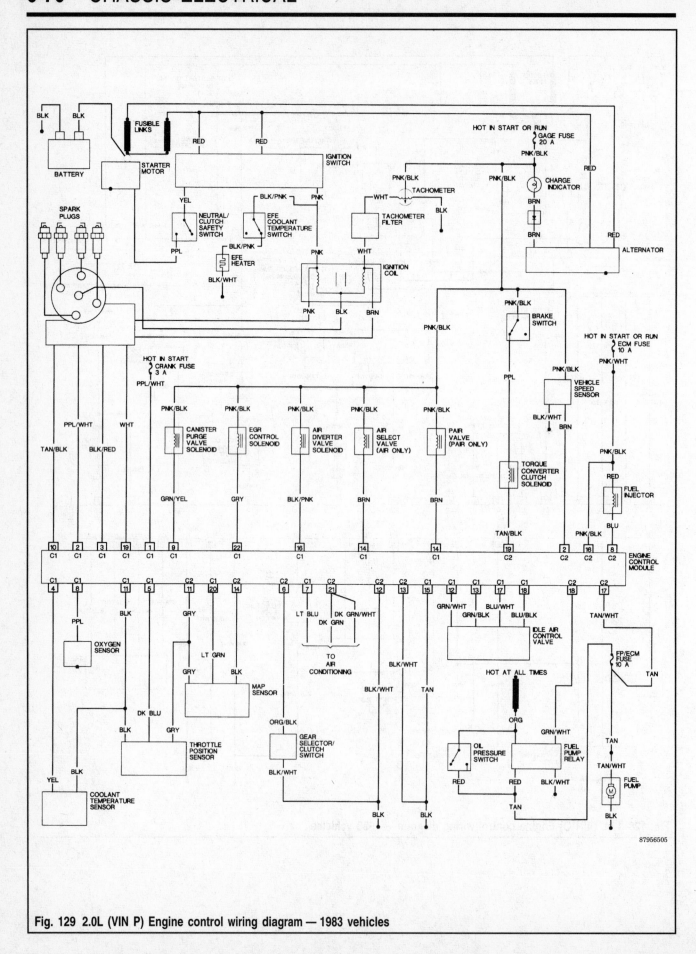

Fig. 129 2.0L (VIN P) Engine control wiring diagram — 1983 vehicles

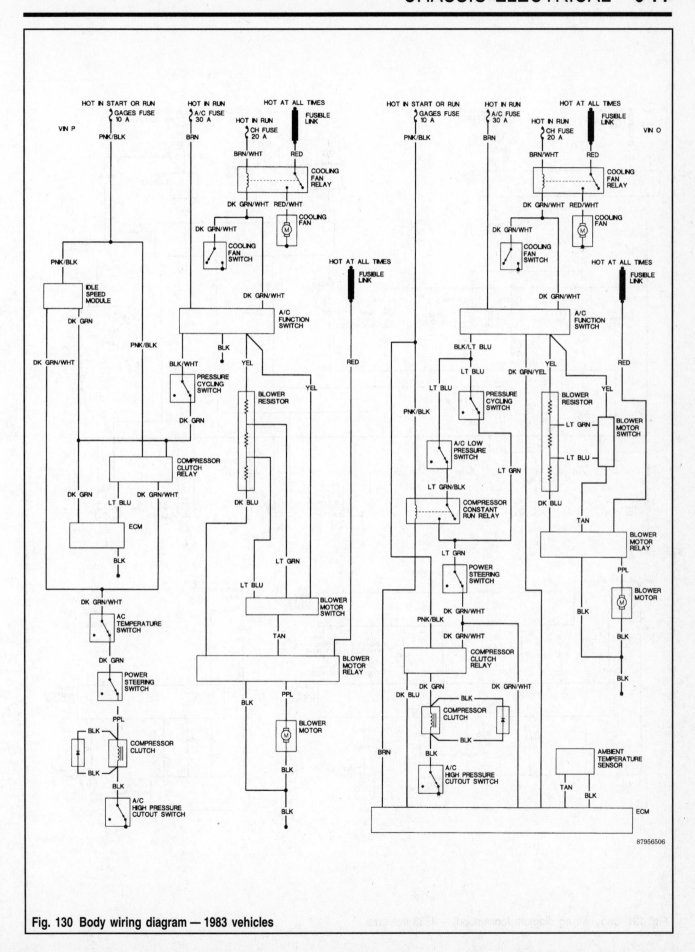

Fig. 130 Body wiring diagram — 1983 vehicles

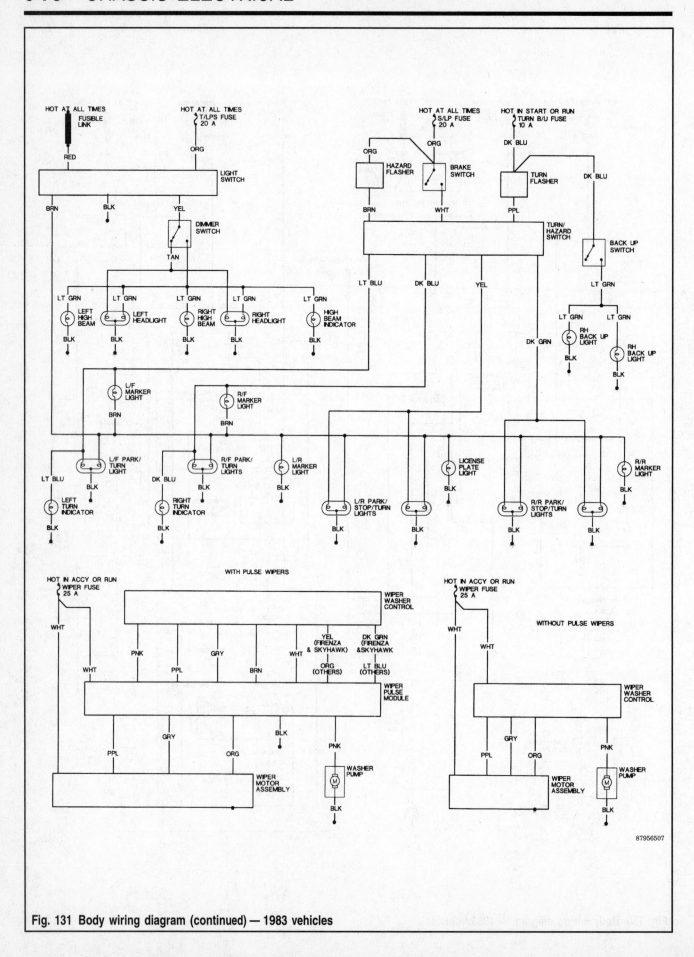

Fig. 131 Body wiring diagram (continued) — 1983 vehicles

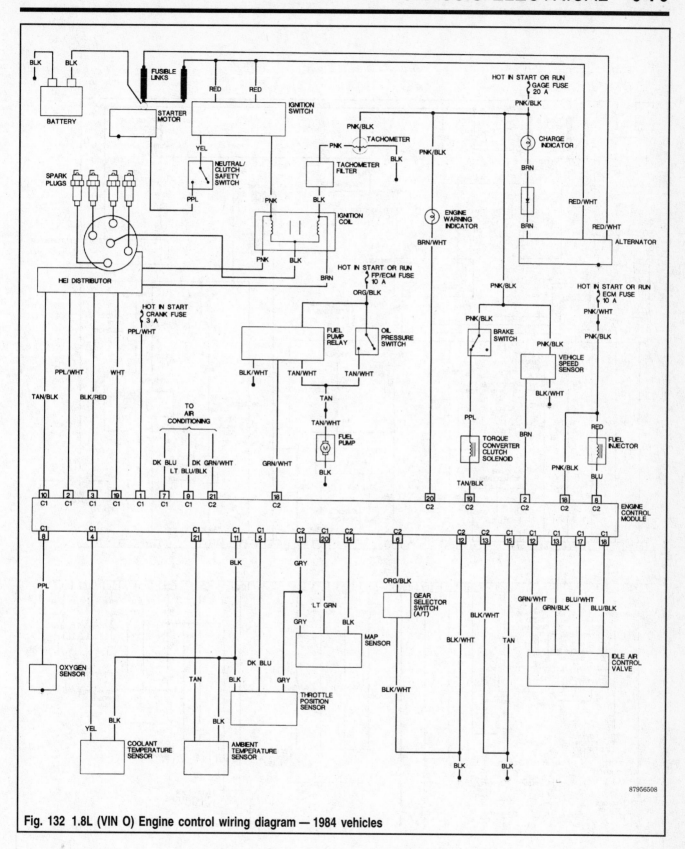

Fig. 132 1.8L (VIN O) Engine control wiring diagram — 1984 vehicles

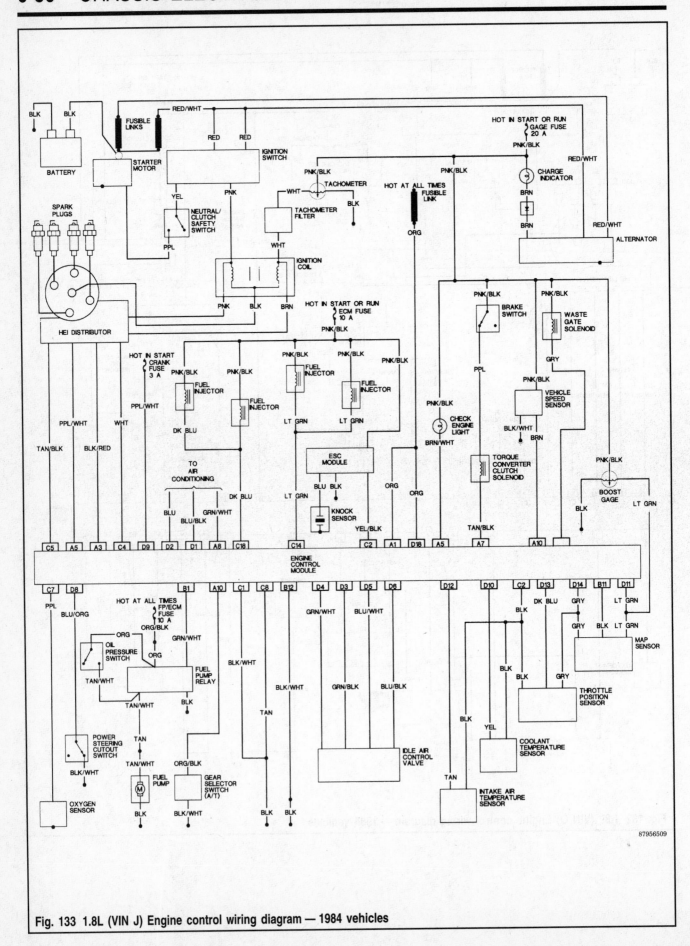

Fig. 133 1.8L (VIN J) Engine control wiring diagram — 1984 vehicles

87956509

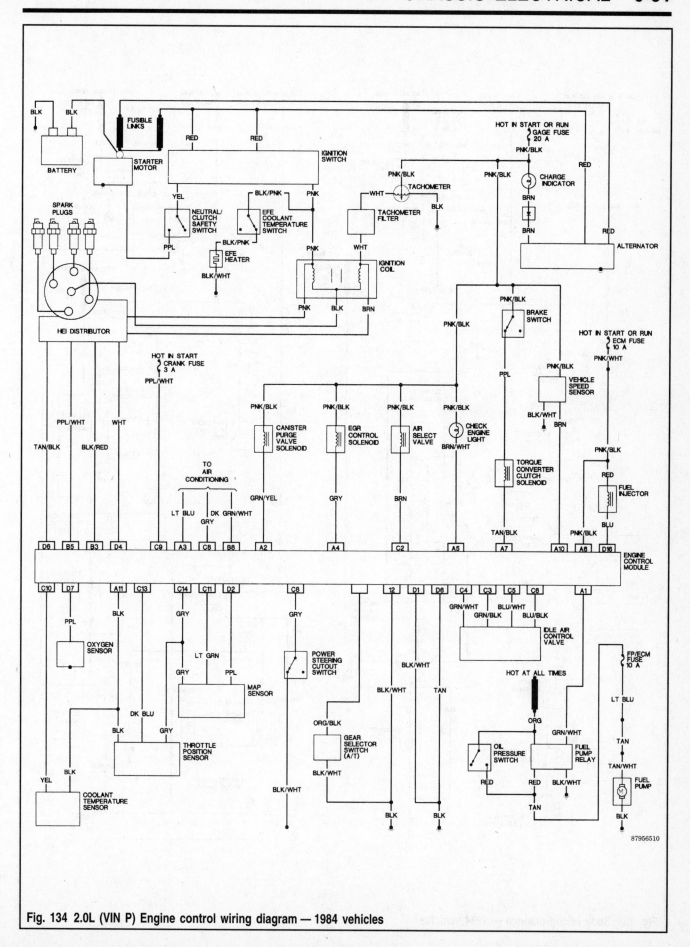

Fig. 134 2.0L (VIN P) Engine control wiring diagram — 1984 vehicles

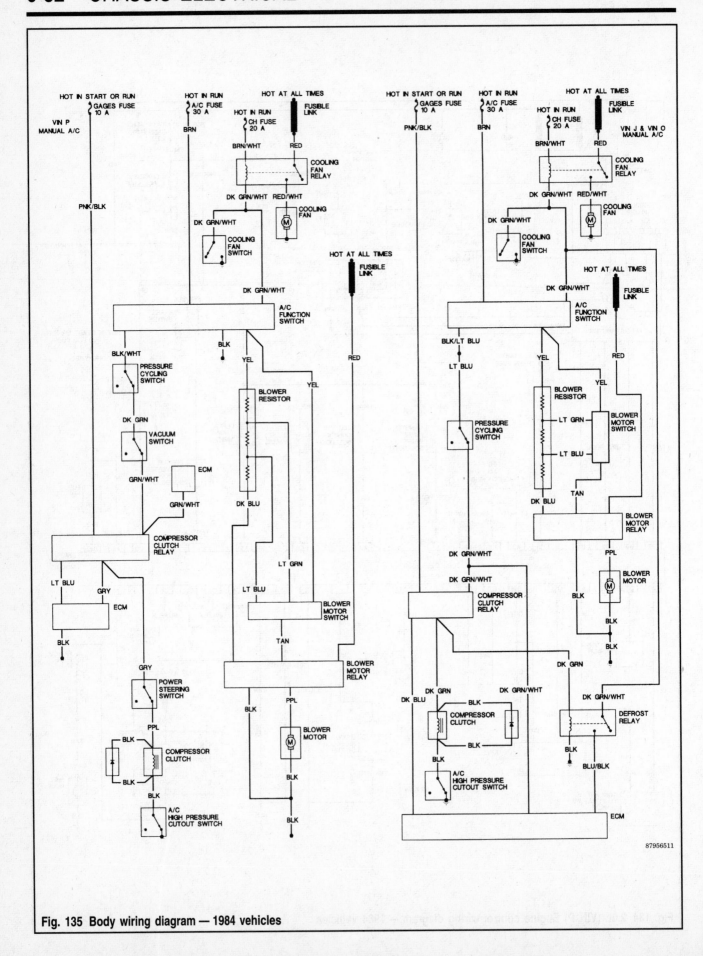

Fig. 135 Body wiring diagram — 1984 vehicles

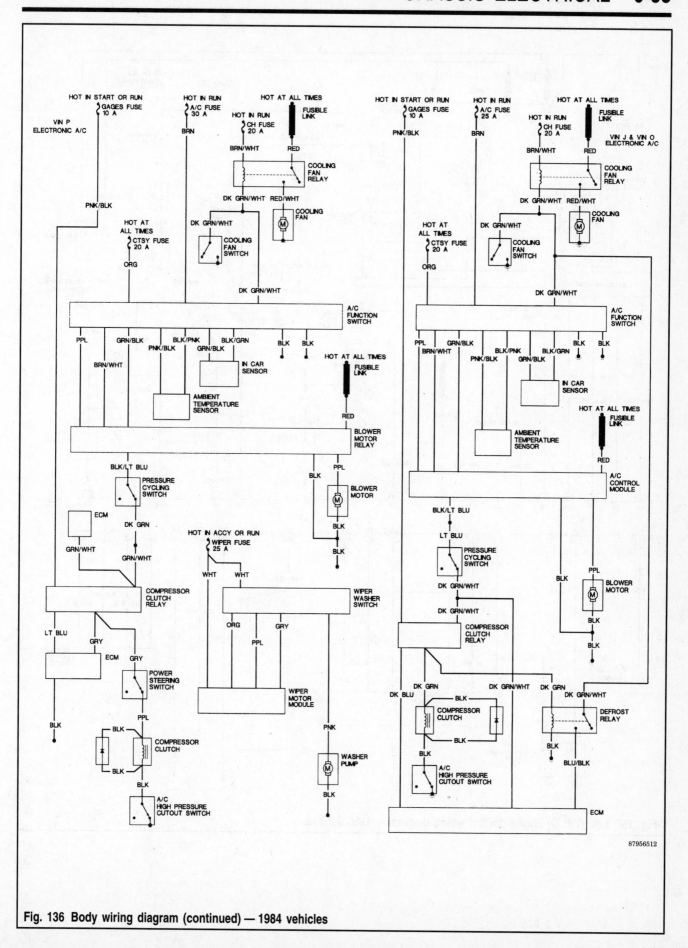

Fig. 136 Body wiring diagram (continued) — 1984 vehicles

87956512

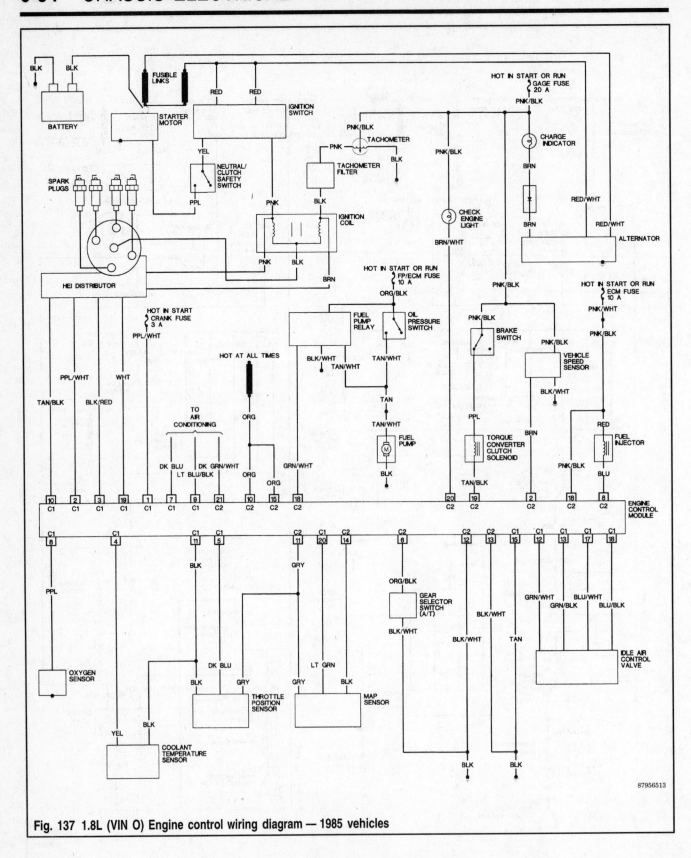

Fig. 137 1.8L (VIN O) Engine control wiring diagram — 1985 vehicles

87956513

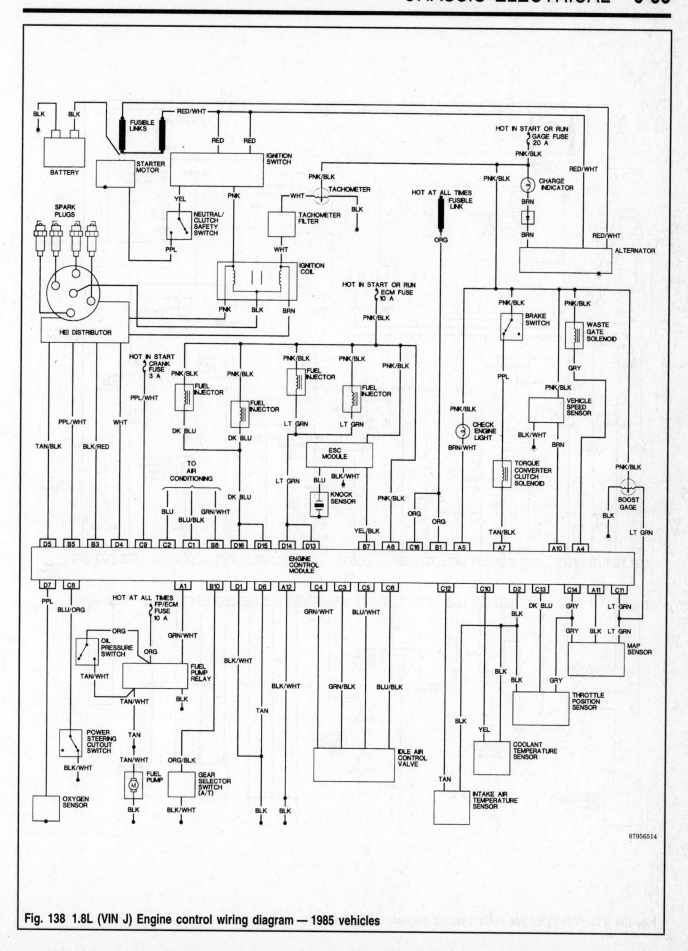

Fig. 138 1.8L (VIN J) Engine control wiring diagram — 1985 vehicles

87956514

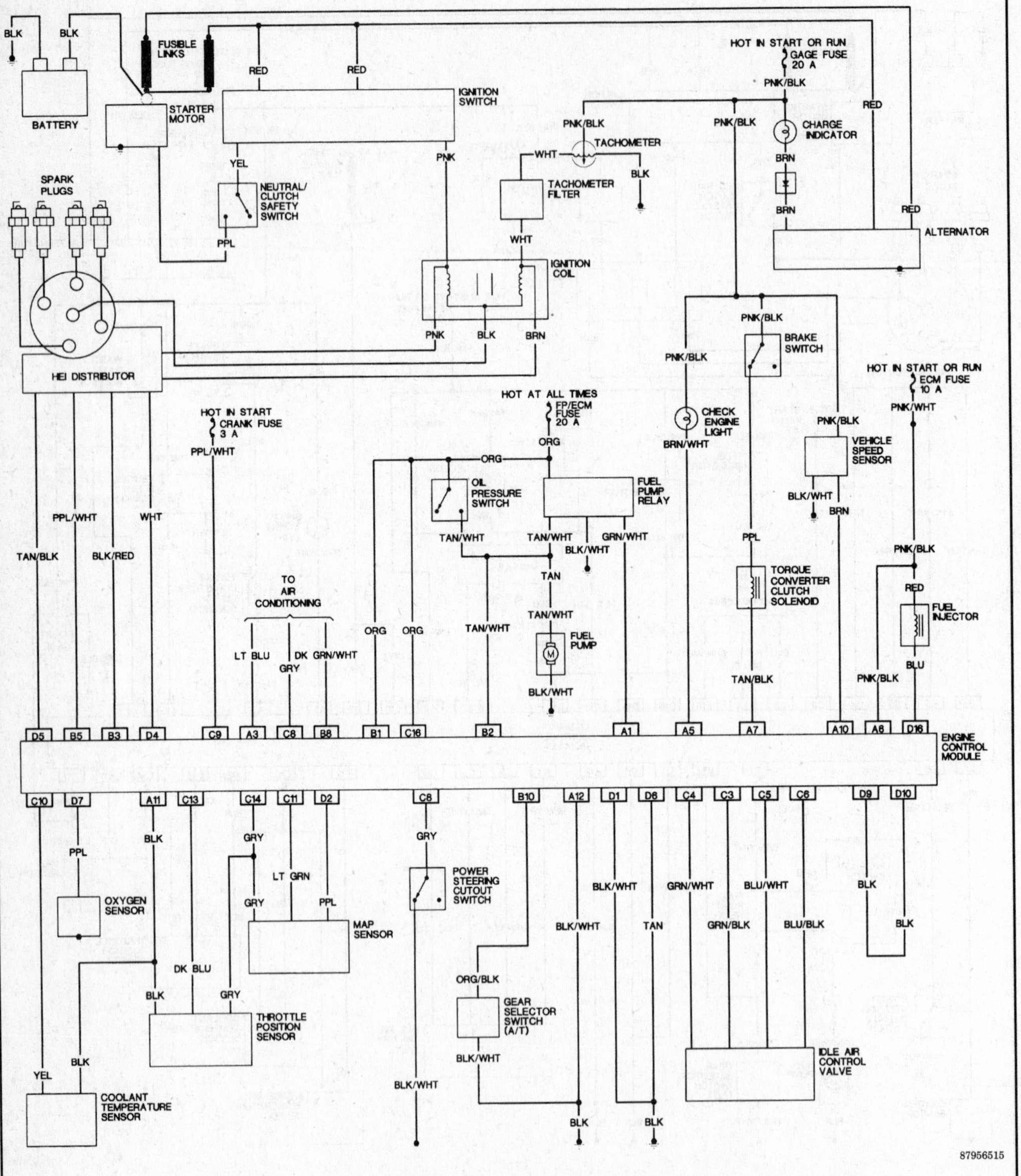

Fig. 139 2.0L (VIN P) Engine control wiring diagram — 1985 vehicles

87956515

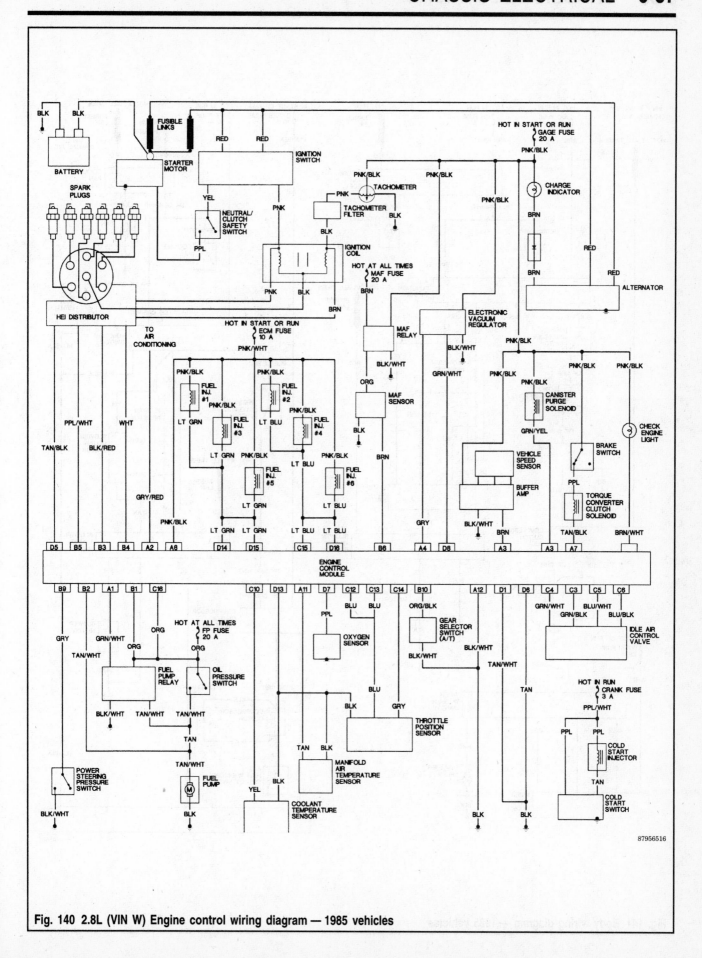

Fig. 140 2.8L (VIN W) Engine control wiring diagram — 1985 vehicles

87956516

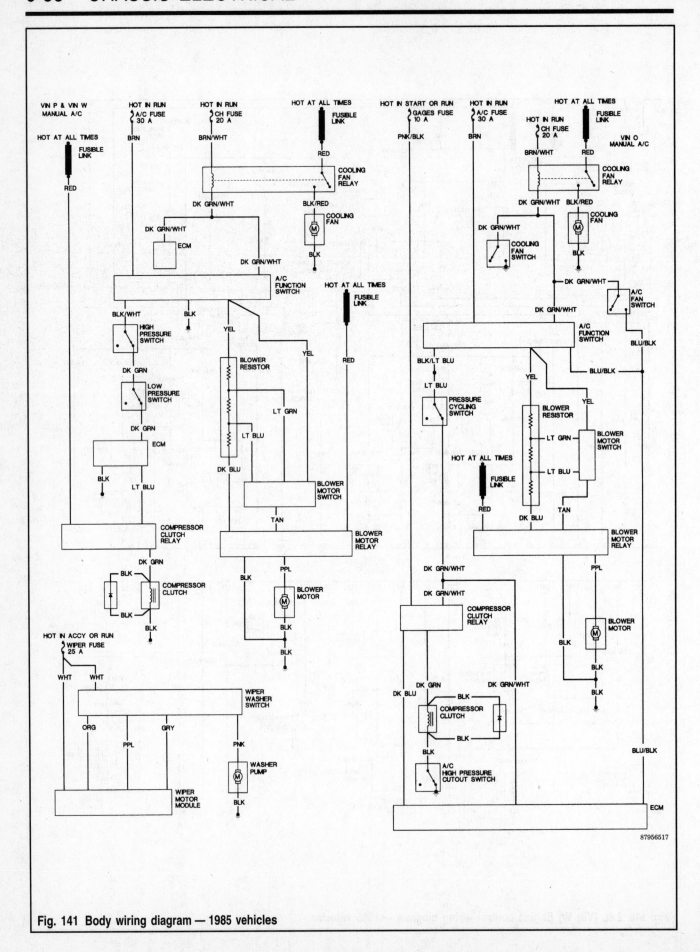

Fig. 141 Body wiring diagram — 1985 vehicles

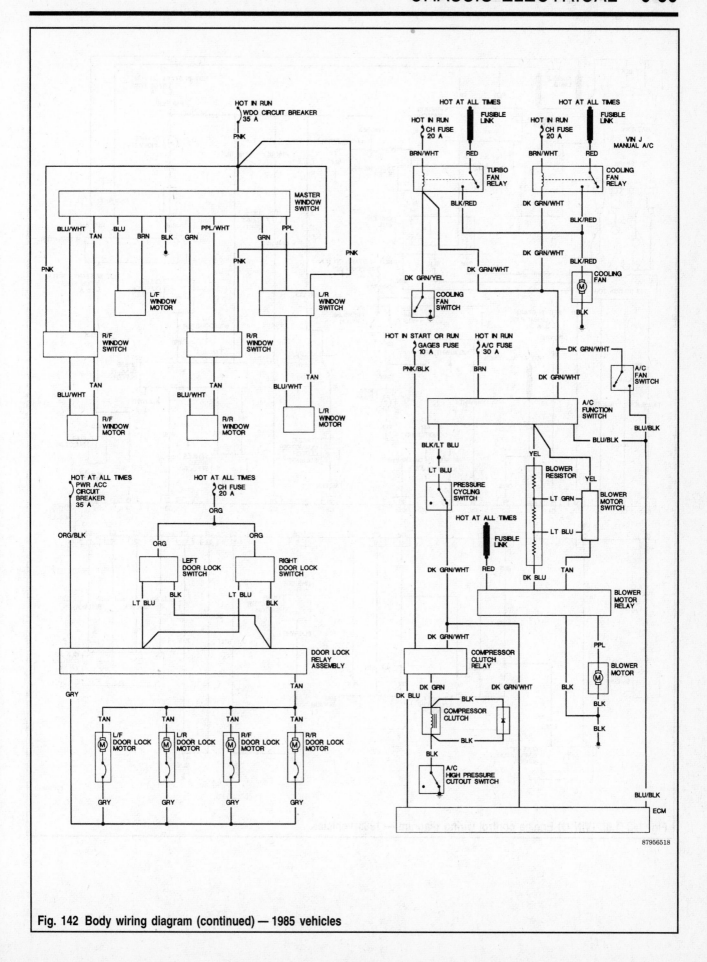

Fig. 142 Body wiring diagram (continued) — 1985 vehicles

87956518

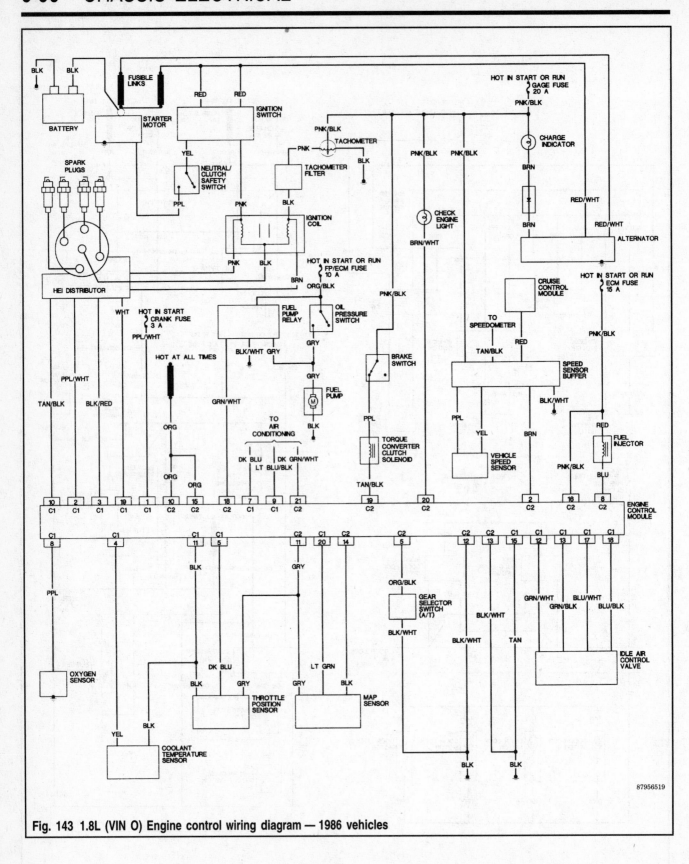

Fig. 143 1.8L (VIN O) Engine control wiring diagram — 1986 vehicles

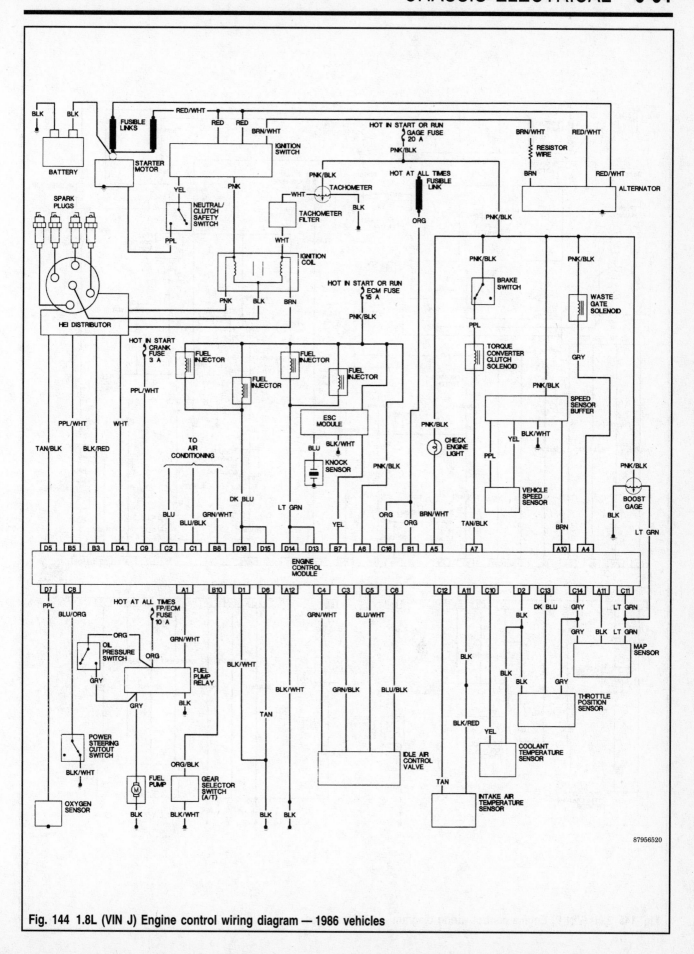

Fig. 144 1.8L (VIN J) Engine control wiring diagram — 1986 vehicles

87956520

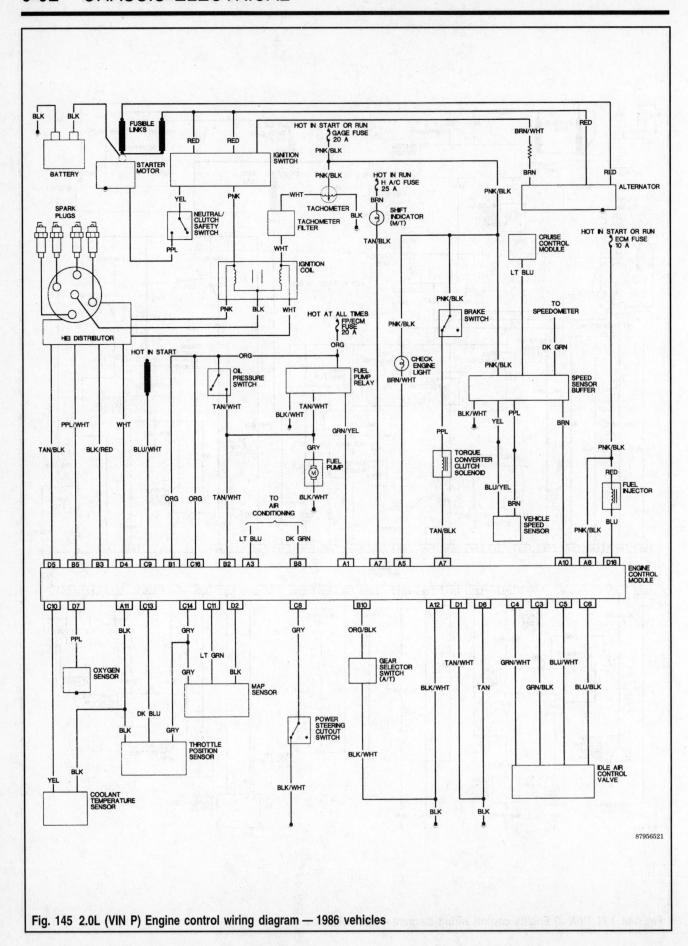

Fig. 145 2.0L (VIN P) Engine control wiring diagram — 1986 vehicles

87956521

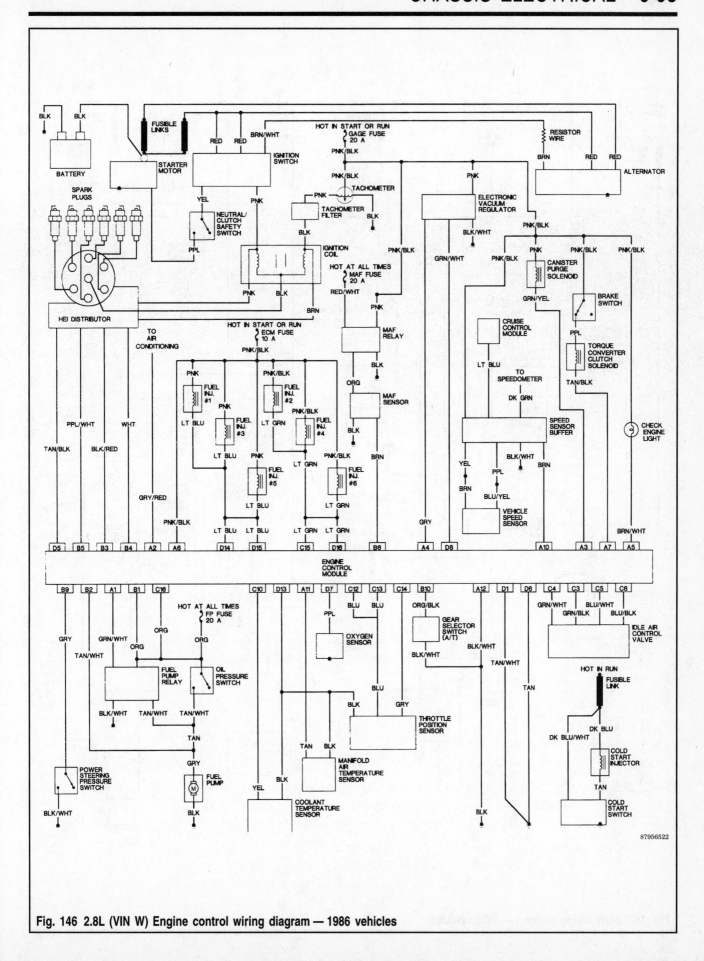

Fig. 146 2.8L (VIN W) Engine control wiring diagram — 1986 vehicles

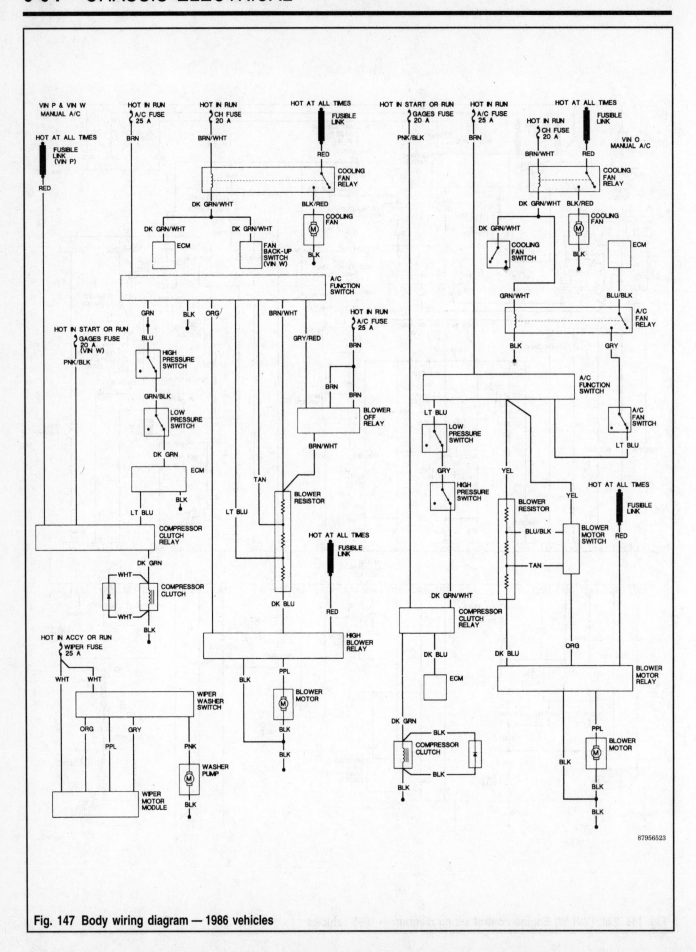

Fig. 147 Body wiring diagram — 1986 vehicles

87956523

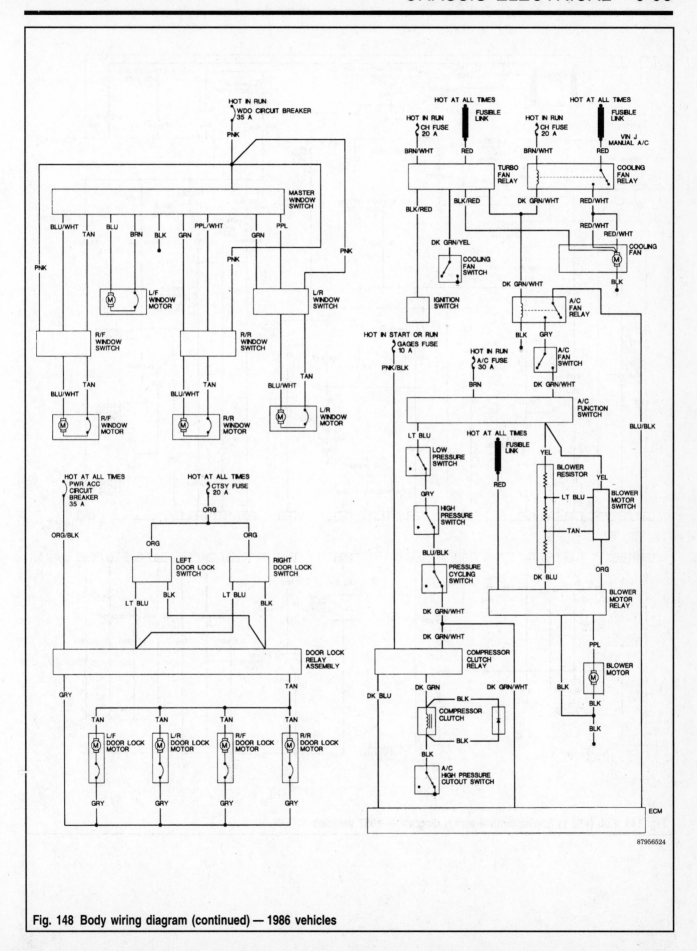

Fig. 148 Body wiring diagram (continued) — 1986 vehicles

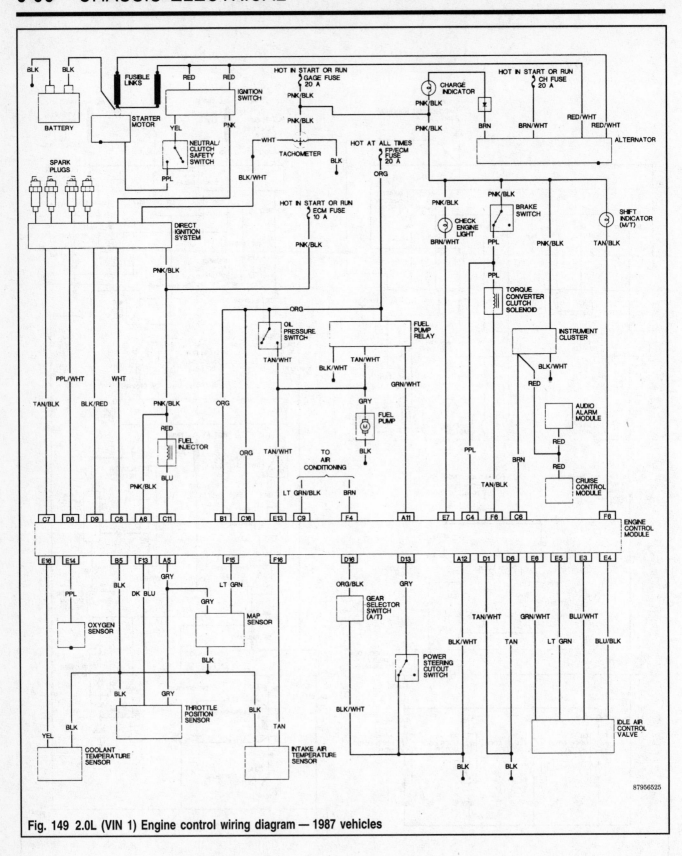

Fig. 149 2.0L (VIN 1) Engine control wiring diagram — 1987 vehicles

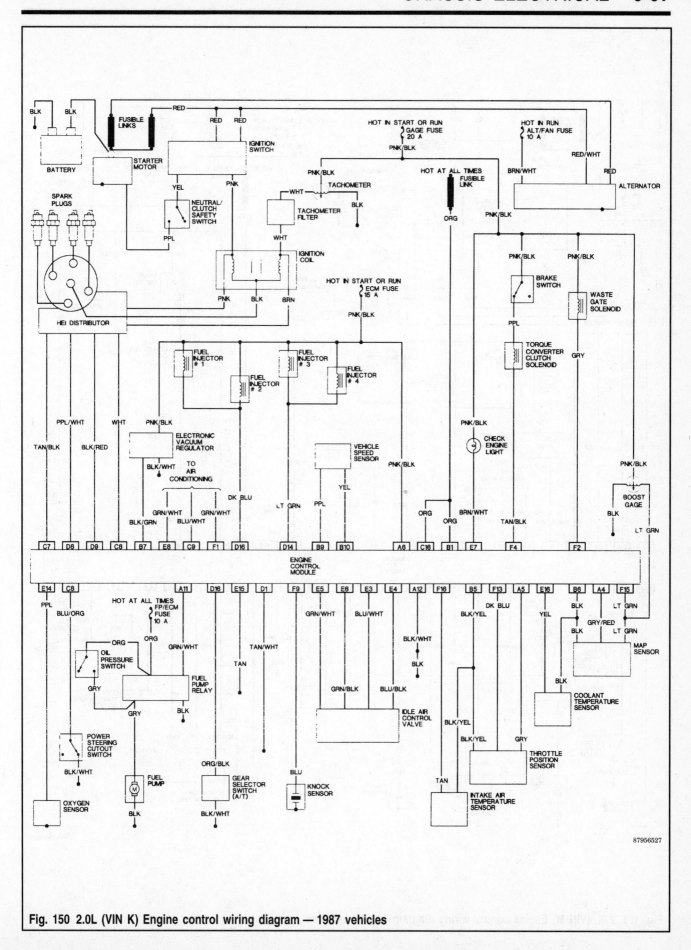

Fig. 150 2.0L (VIN K) Engine control wiring diagram — 1987 vehicles

87956527

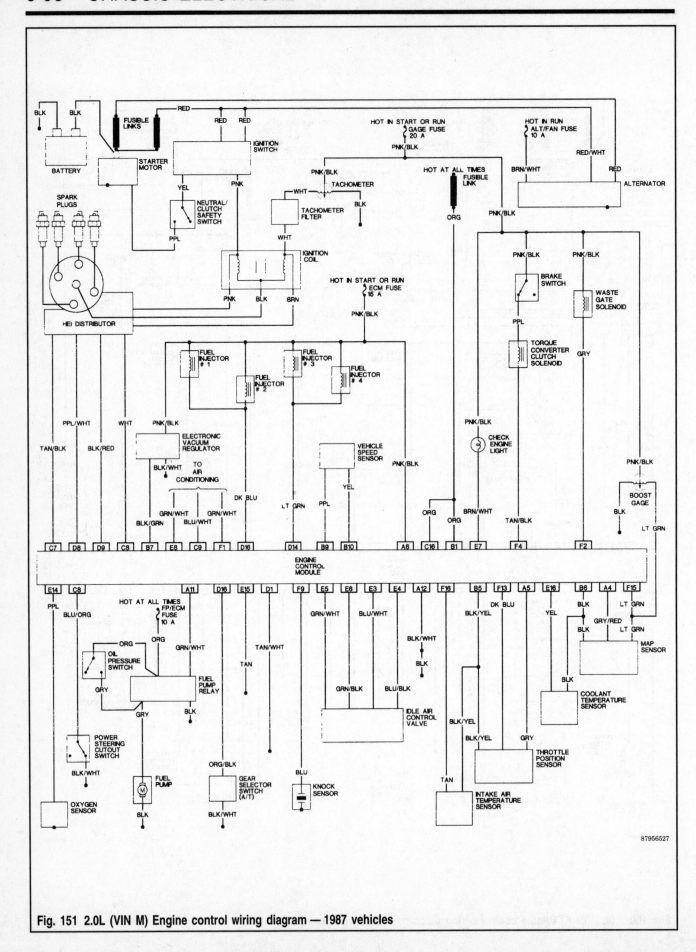

Fig. 151 2.0L (VIN M) Engine control wiring diagram — 1987 vehicles

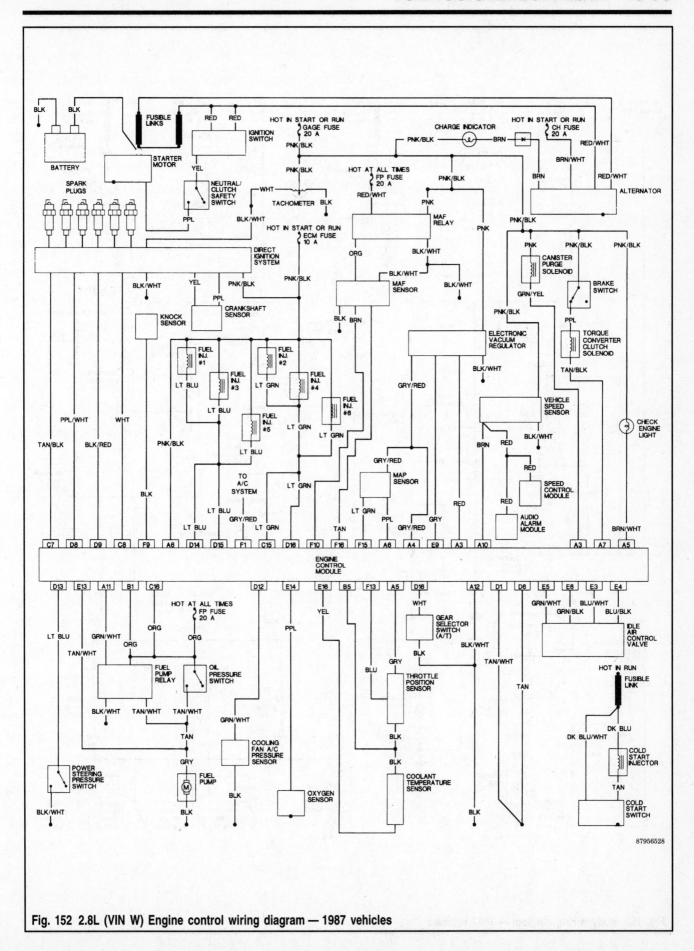

Fig. 152 2.8L (VIN W) Engine control wiring diagram — 1987 vehicles

87956528

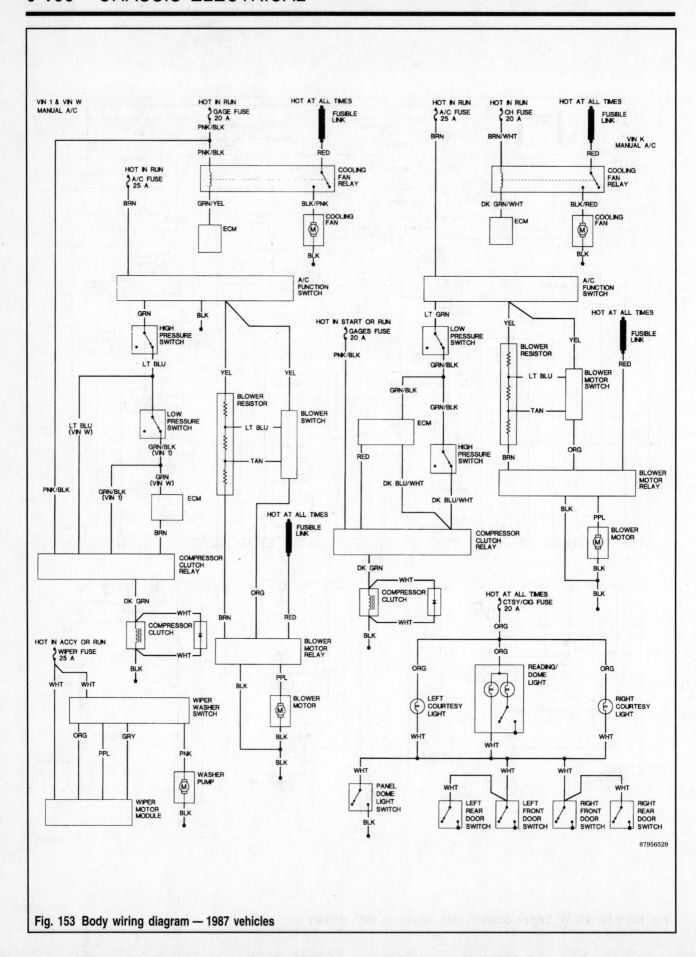

Fig. 153 Body wiring diagram — 1987 vehicles

87956529

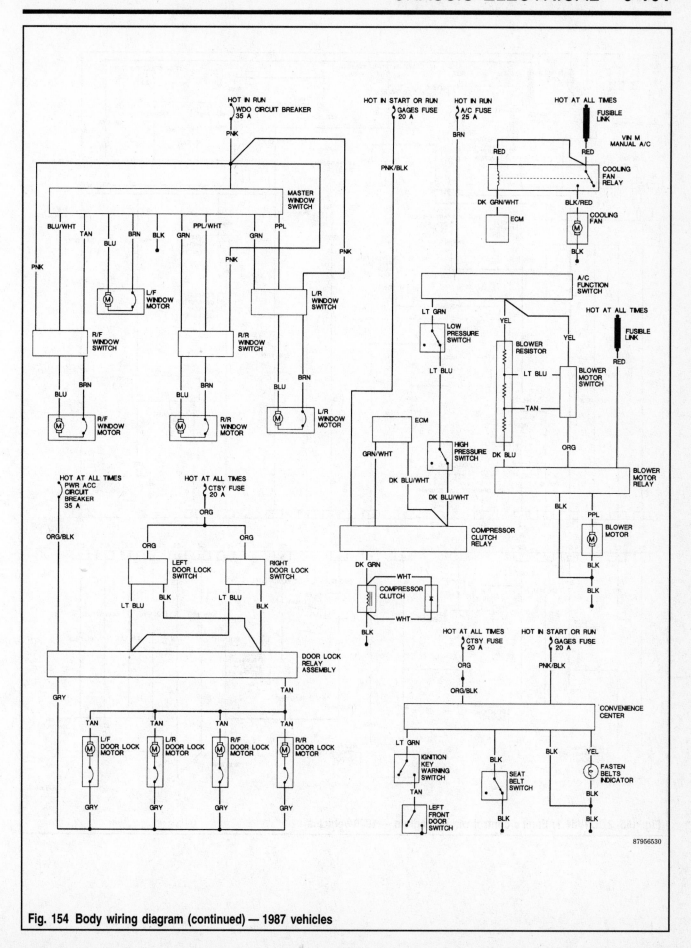

Fig. 154 Body wiring diagram (continued) — 1987 vehicles

87956530

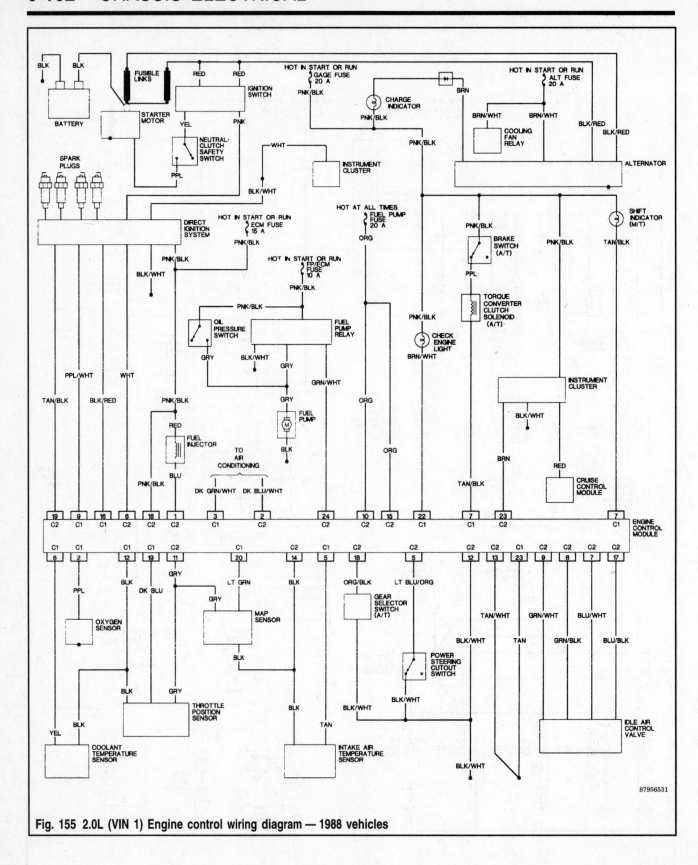

Fig. 155 2.0L (VIN 1) Engine control wiring diagram — 1988 vehicles

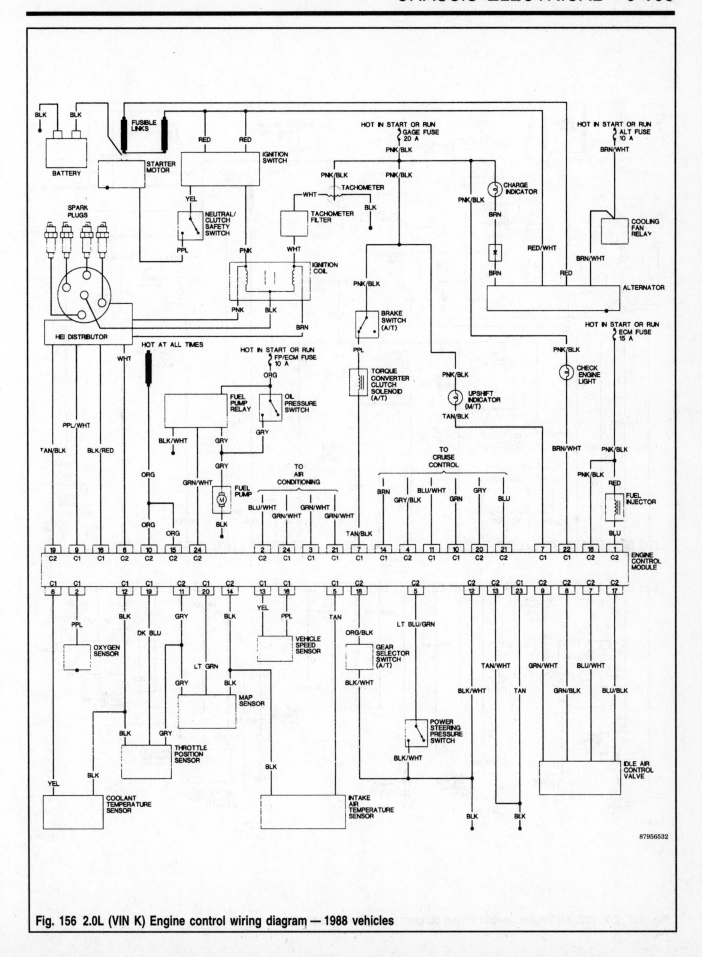

Fig. 156 2.0L (VIN K) Engine control wiring diagram — 1988 vehicles

87956532

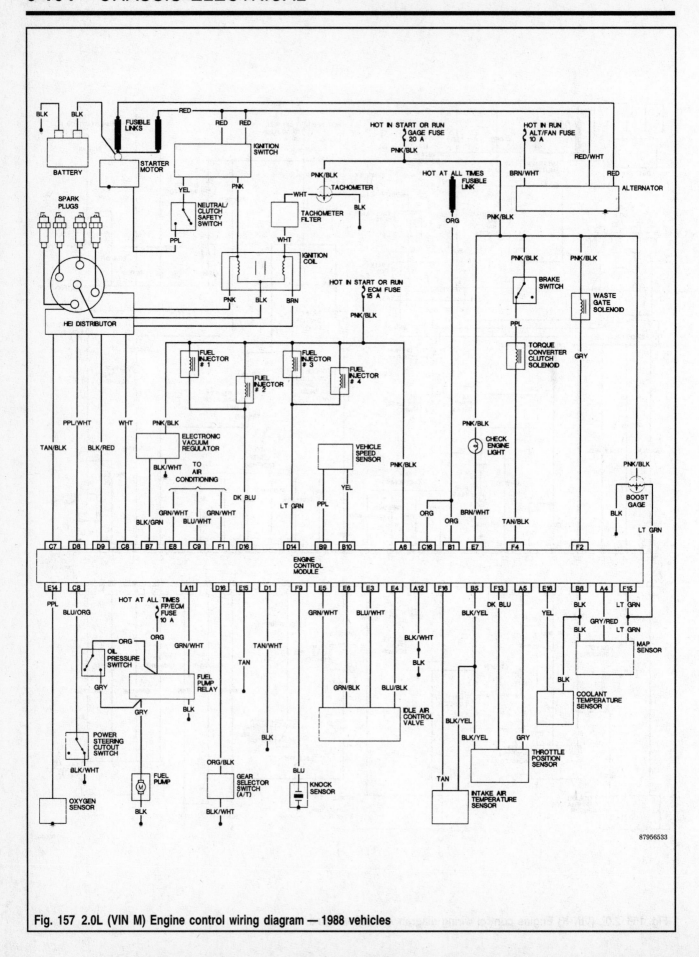

Fig. 157 2.0L (VIN M) Engine control wiring diagram — 1988 vehicles

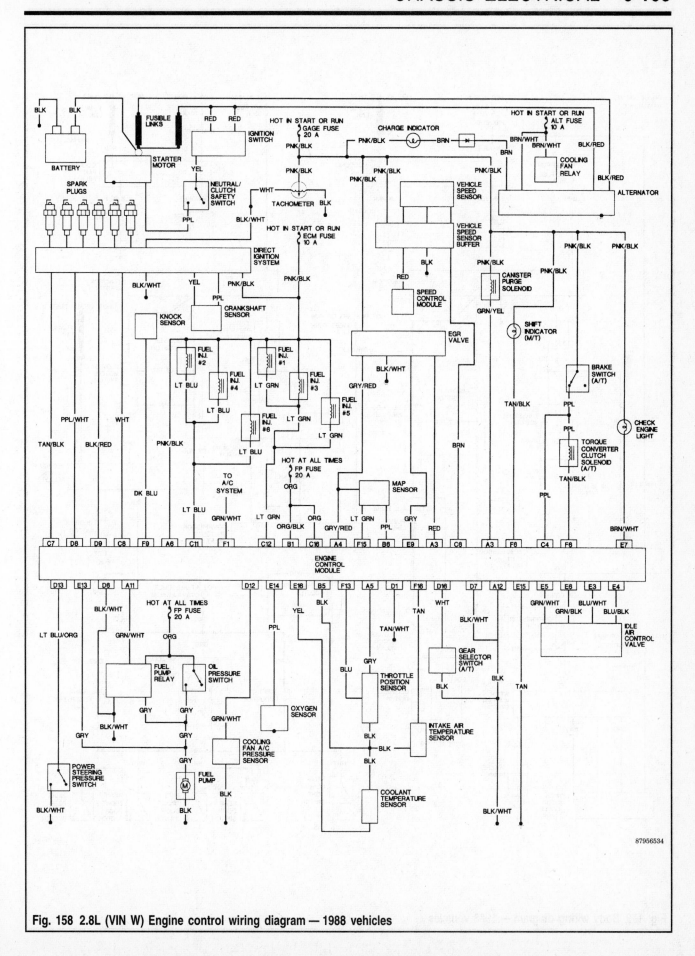

Fig. 158 2.8L (VIN W) Engine control wiring diagram — 1988 vehicles

87956534

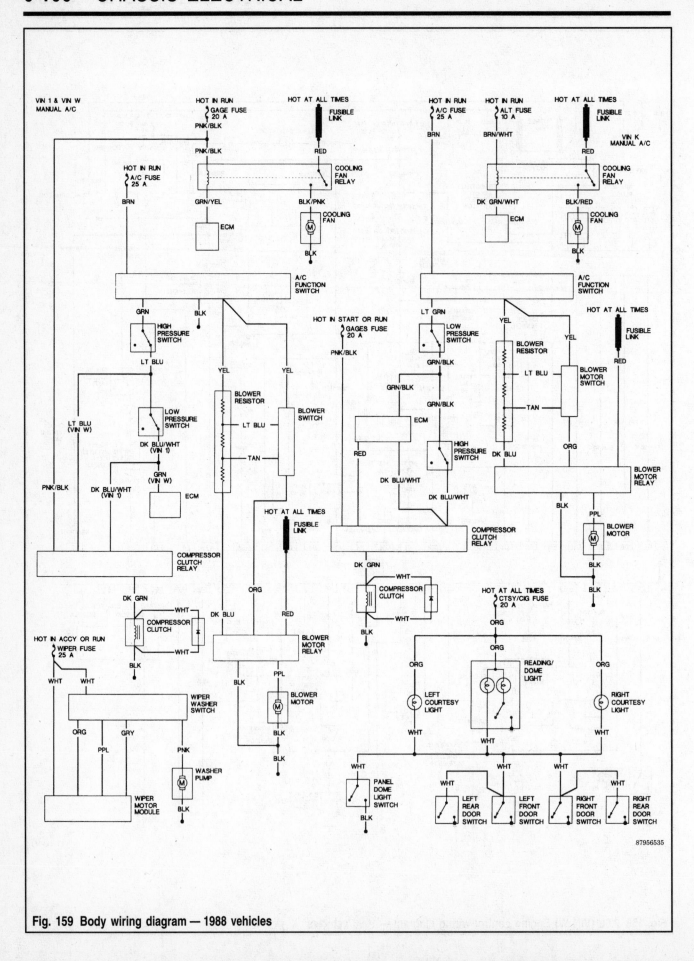

Fig. 159 Body wiring diagram — 1988 vehicles

87956535

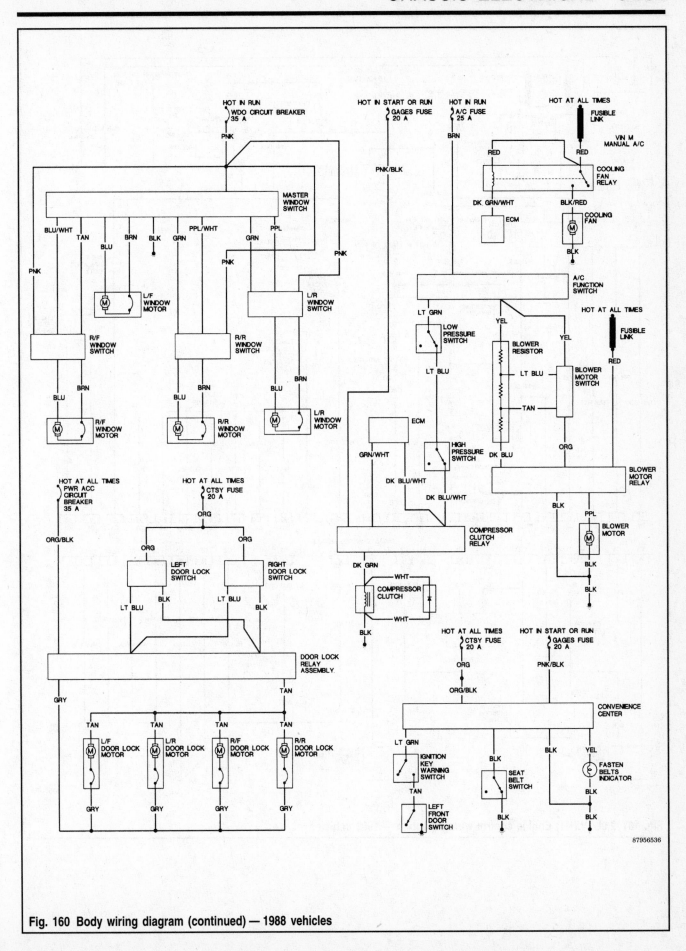

Fig. 160 Body wiring diagram (continued) — 1988 vehicles

87956536

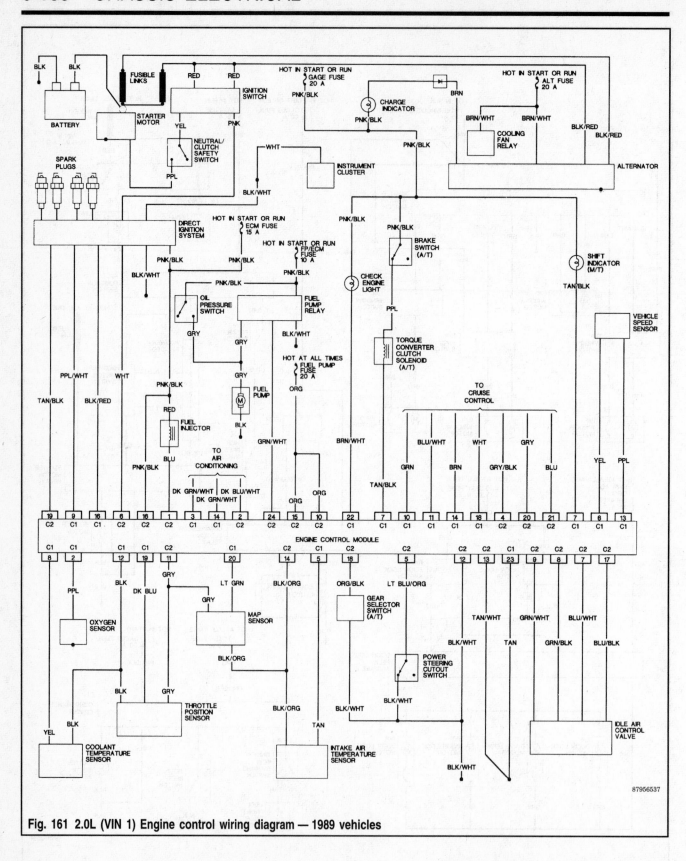

Fig. 161 2.0L (VIN 1) Engine control wiring diagram — 1989 vehicles

87956537

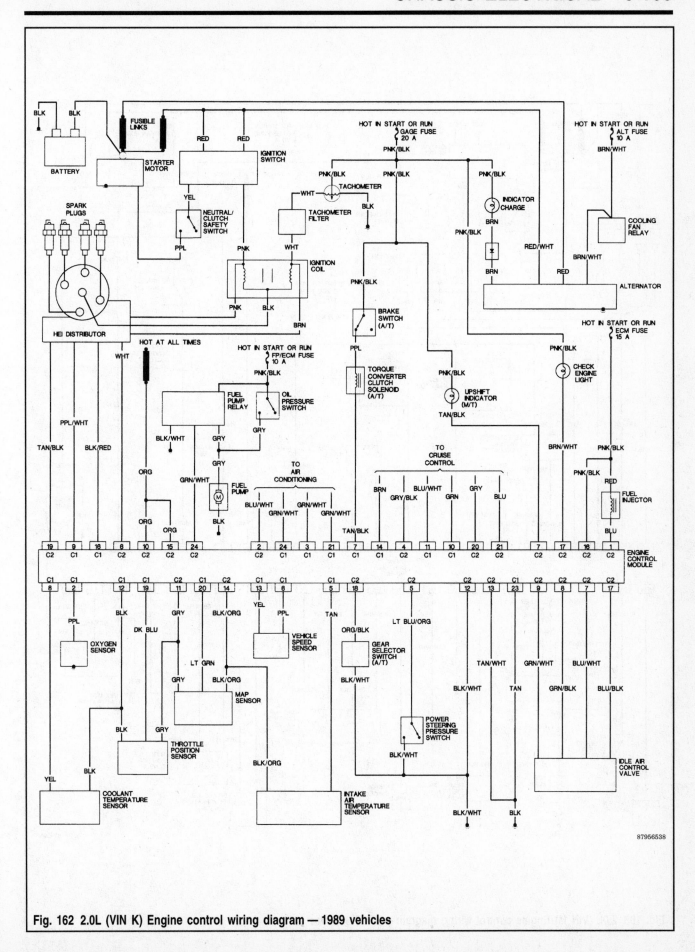

Fig. 162 2.0L (VIN K) Engine control wiring diagram — 1989 vehicles

87956538

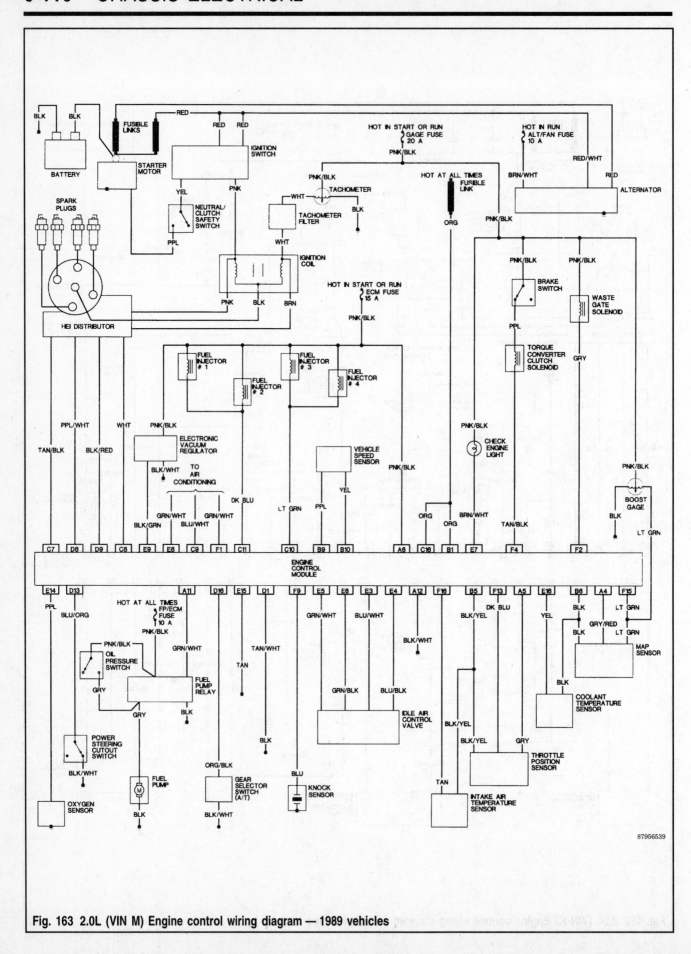

Fig. 163 2.0L (VIN M) Engine control wiring diagram — 1989 vehicles

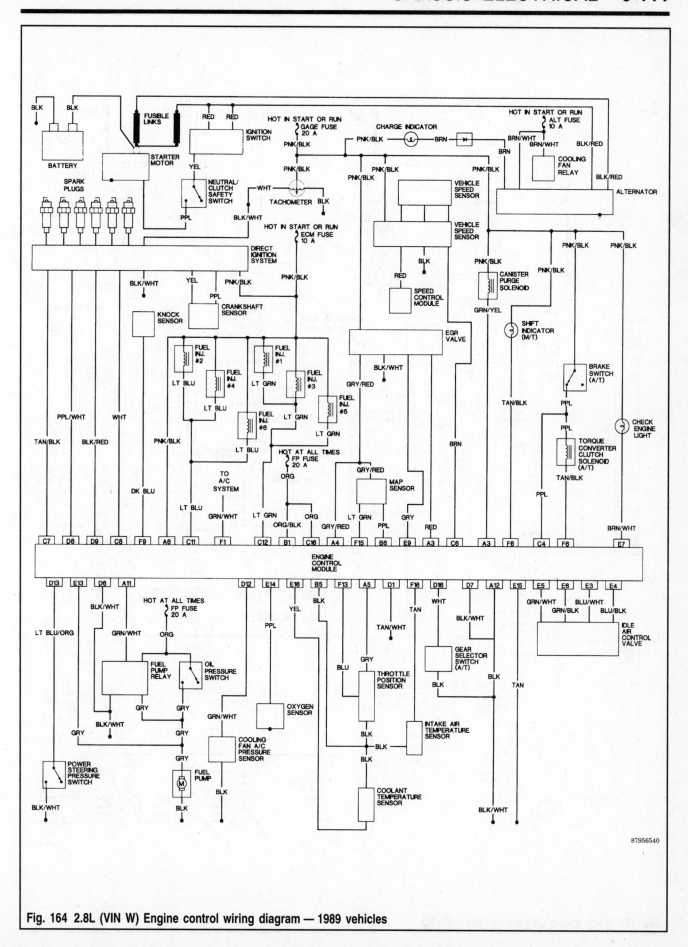

Fig. 164 2.8L (VIN W) Engine control wiring diagram — 1989 vehicles

87956540

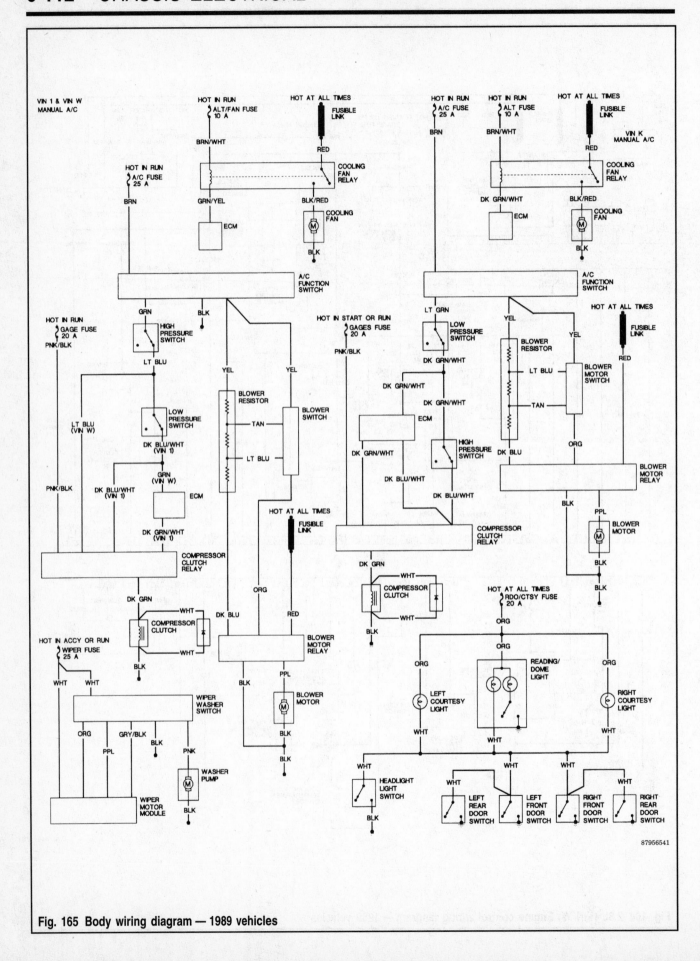

Fig. 165 Body wiring diagram — 1989 vehicles

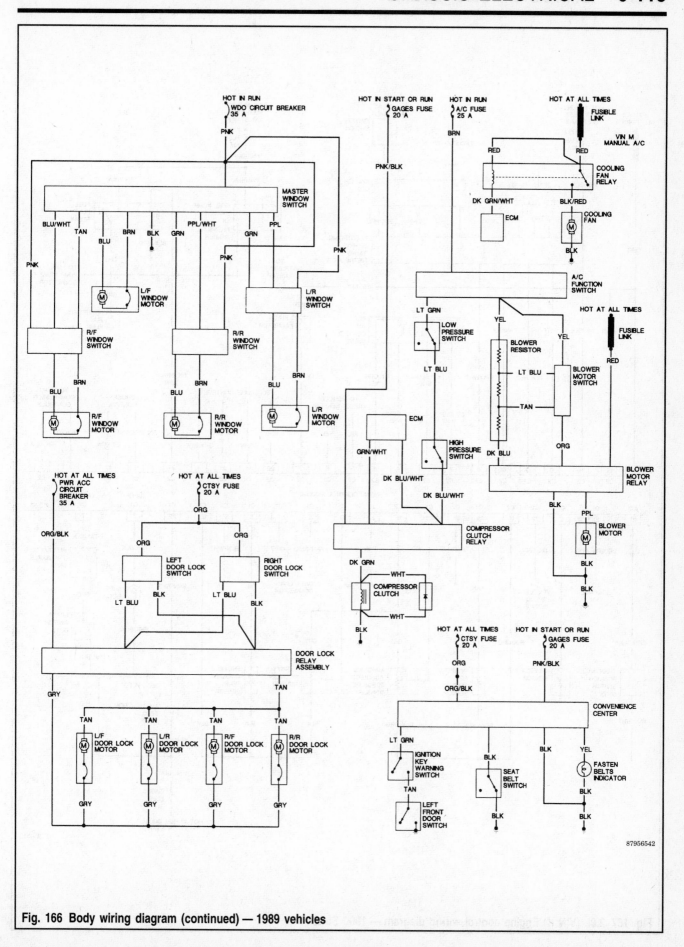

Fig. 166 Body wiring diagram (continued) — 1989 vehicles

87956542

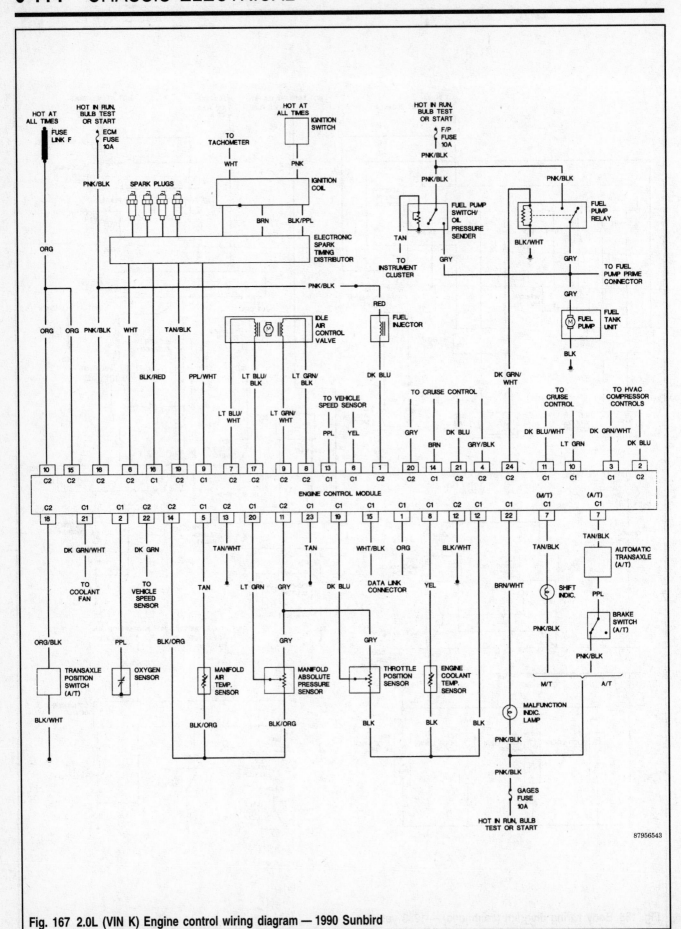

Fig. 167 2.0L (VIN K) Engine control wiring diagram — 1990 Sunbird

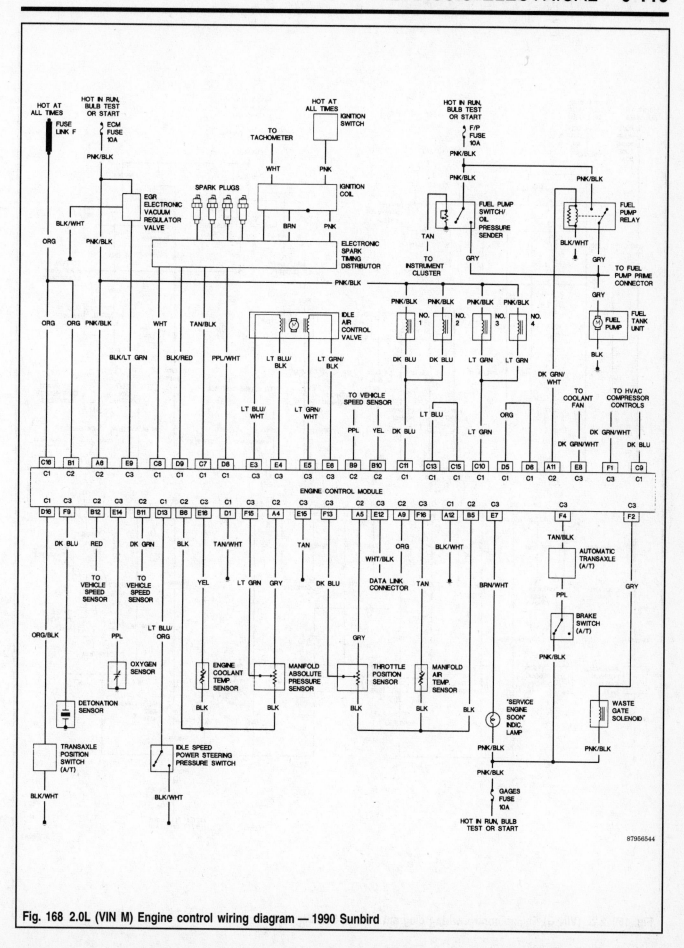

Fig. 168 2.0L (VIN M) Engine control wiring diagram — 1990 Sunbird

87956544

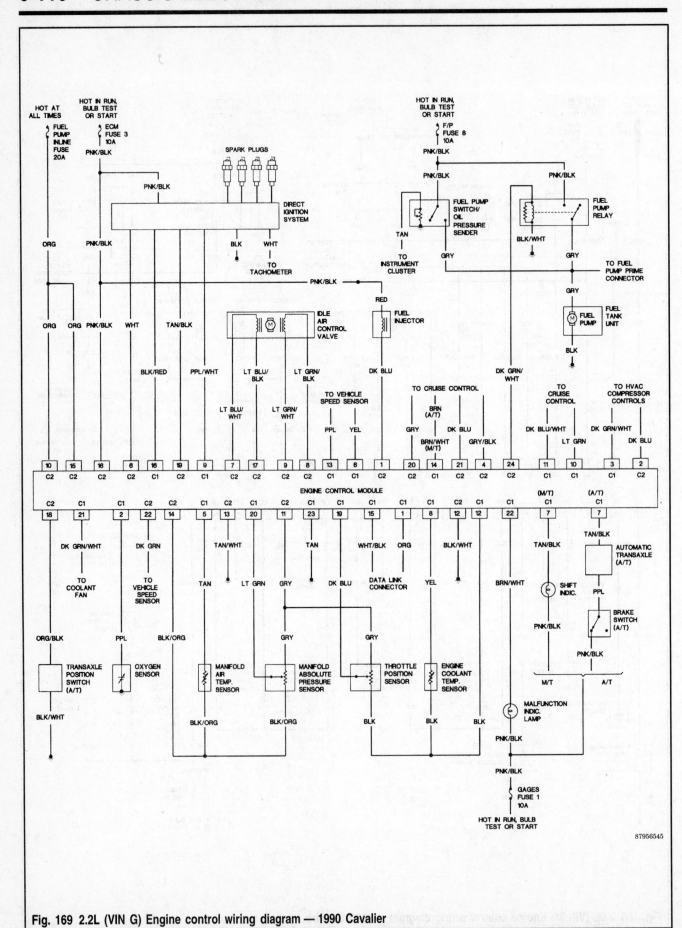

Fig. 169 2.2L (VIN G) Engine control wiring diagram — 1990 Cavalier

87956545

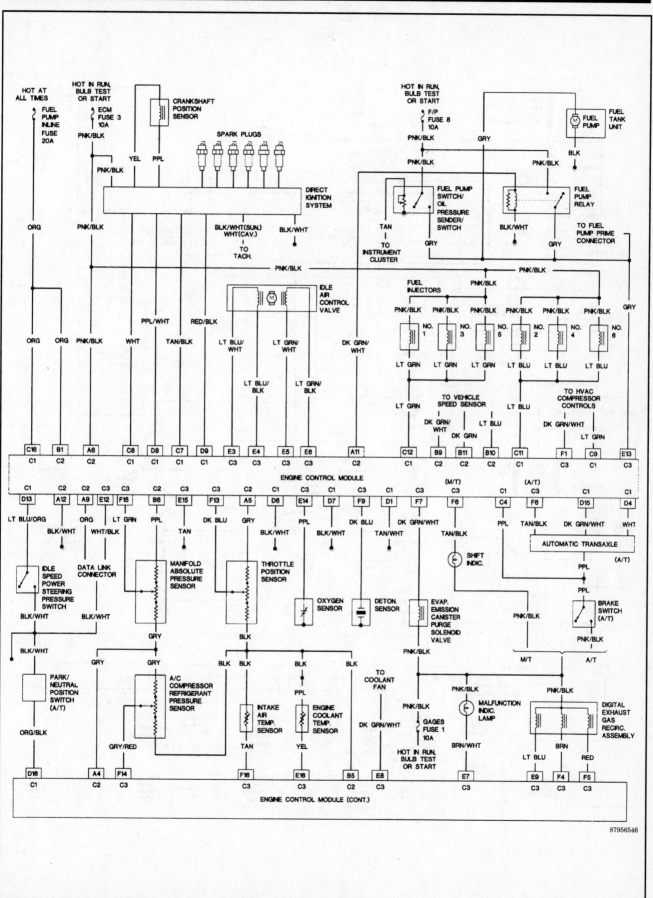

Fig. 170 3.1L (VIN T) Engine control wiring diagram — 1990 vehicles

87956546

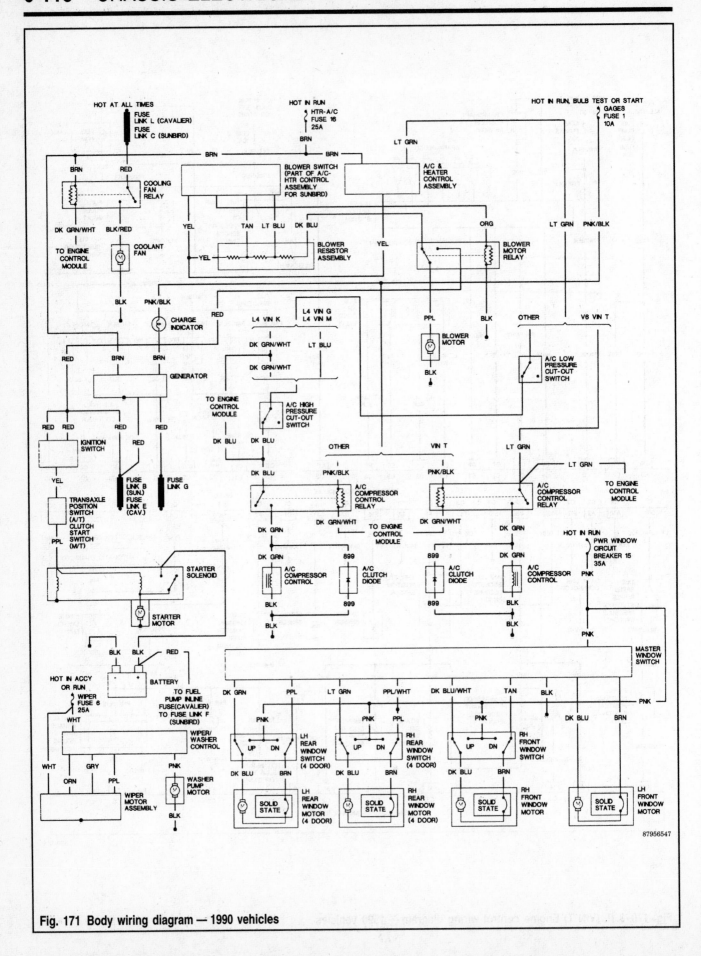

Fig. 171 Body wiring diagram — 1990 vehicles

87956547

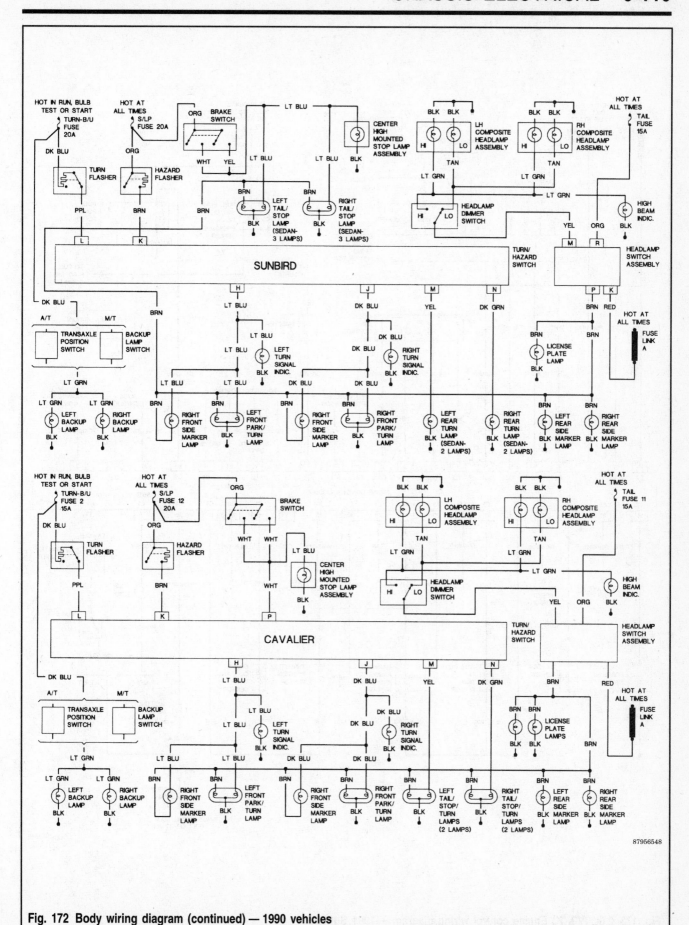

Fig. 172 Body wiring diagram (continued) — 1990 vehicles

87956548

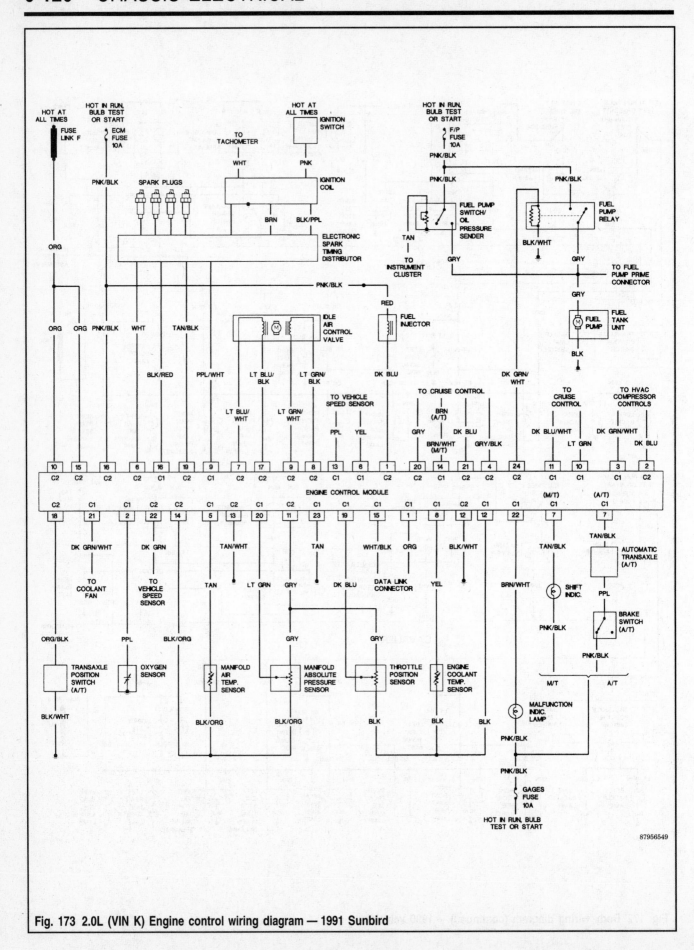

Fig. 173 2.0L (VIN K) Engine control wiring diagram — 1991 Sunbird

87956549

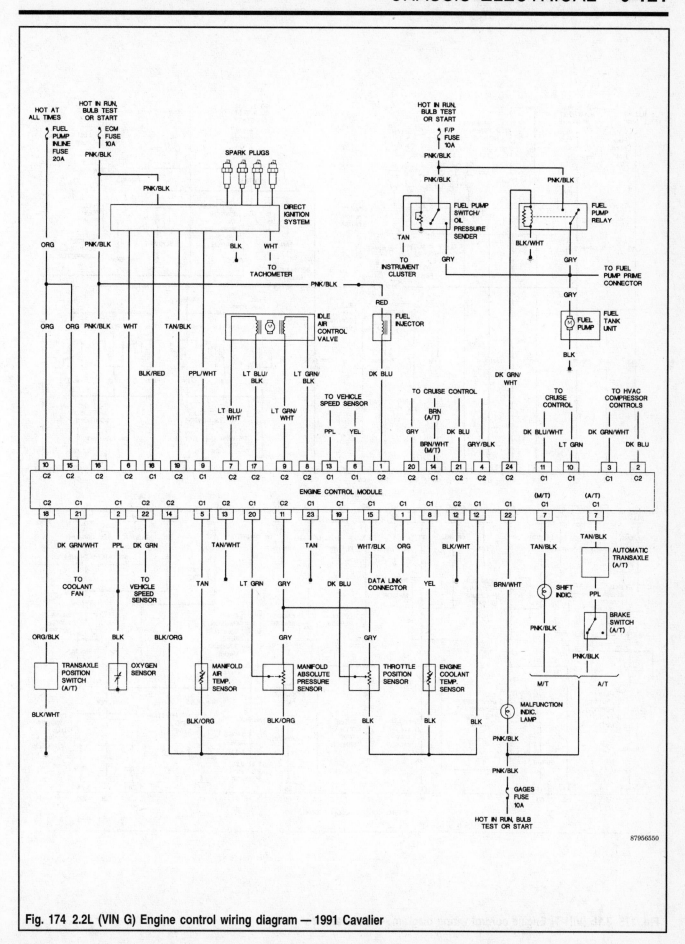

Fig. 174 2.2L (VIN G) Engine control wiring diagram — 1991 Cavalier

87956550

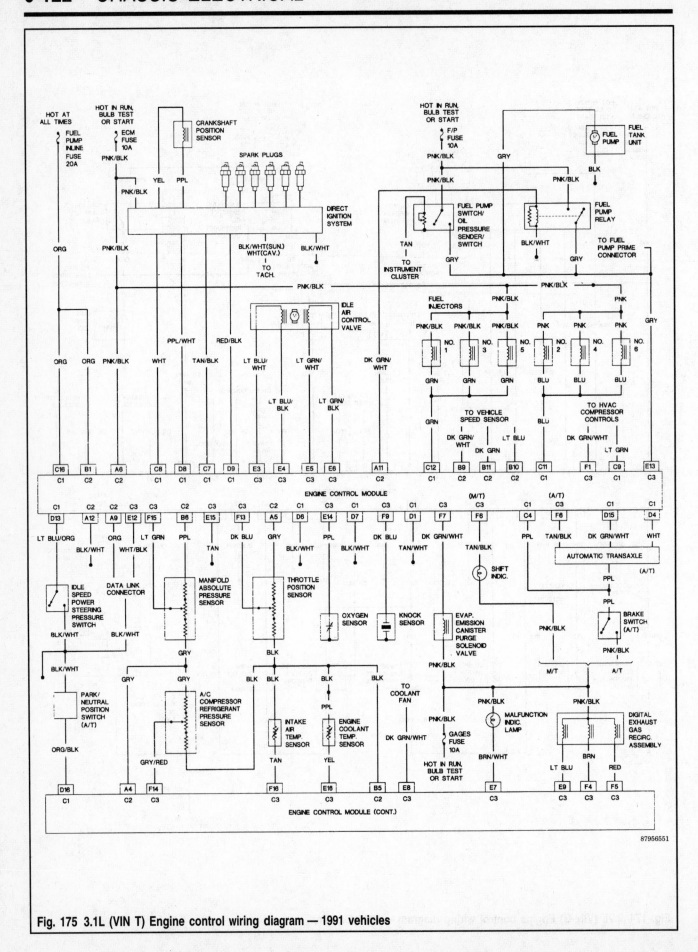

Fig. 175 3.1L (VIN T) Engine control wiring diagram — 1991 vehicles

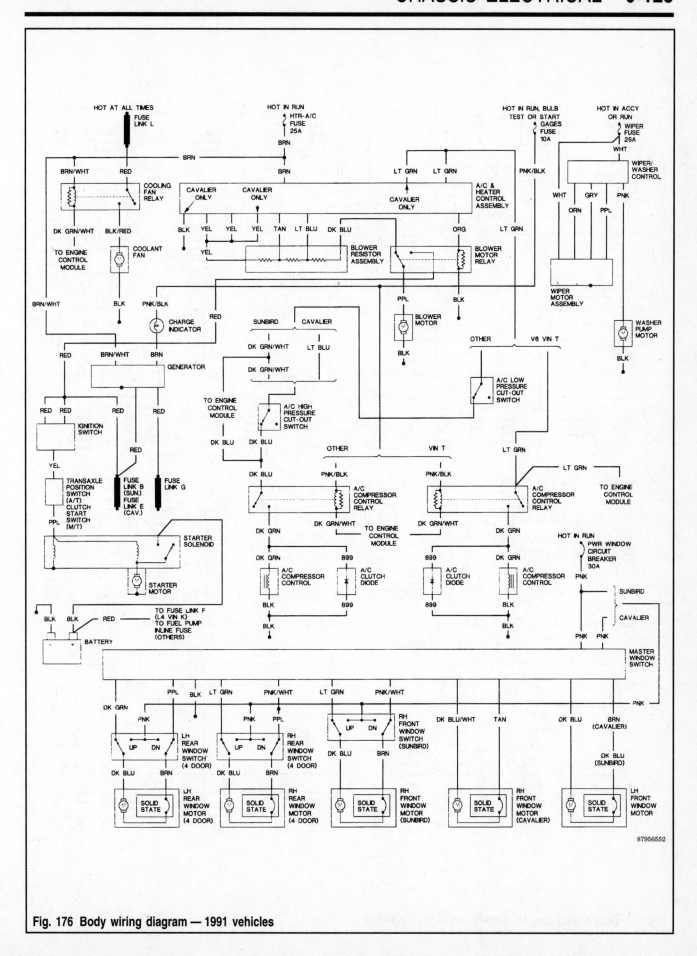

Fig. 176 Body wiring diagram — 1991 vehicles

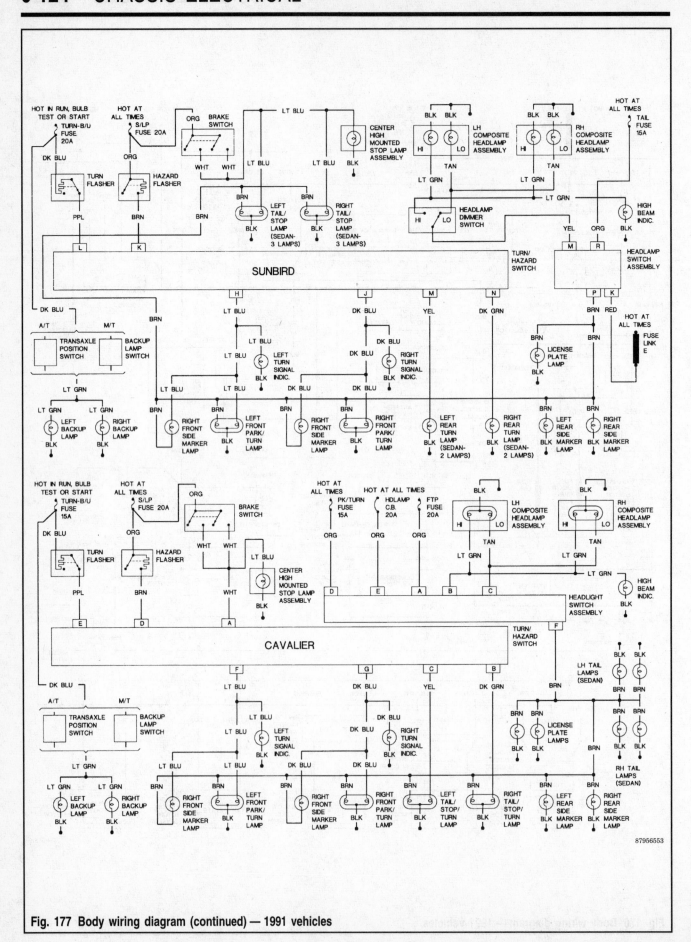

Fig. 177 Body wiring diagram (continued) — 1991 vehicles

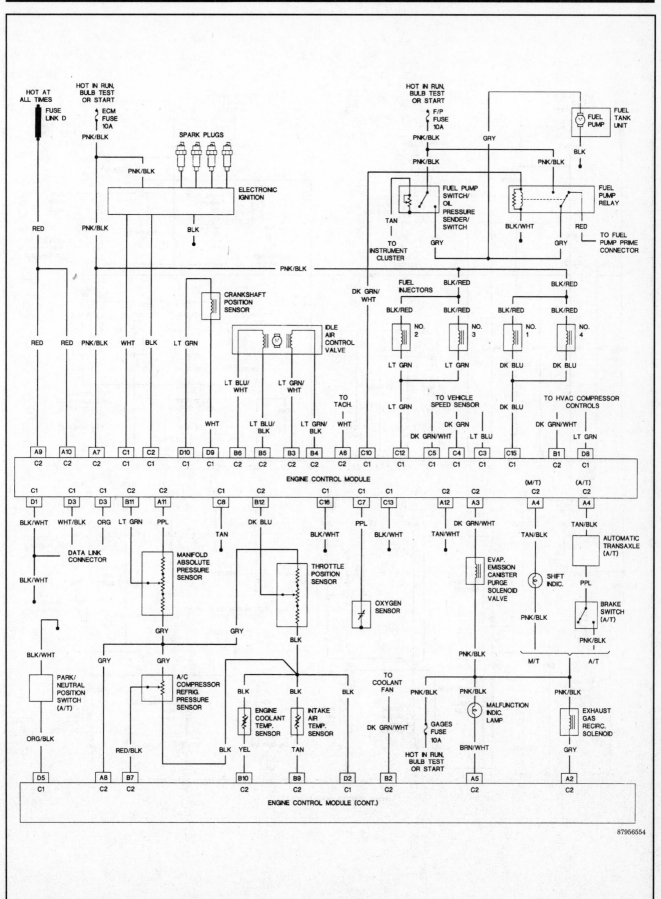

Fig. 178 2.0L (VIN H) Engine control wiring diagram — 1992 Sunbird

87956554

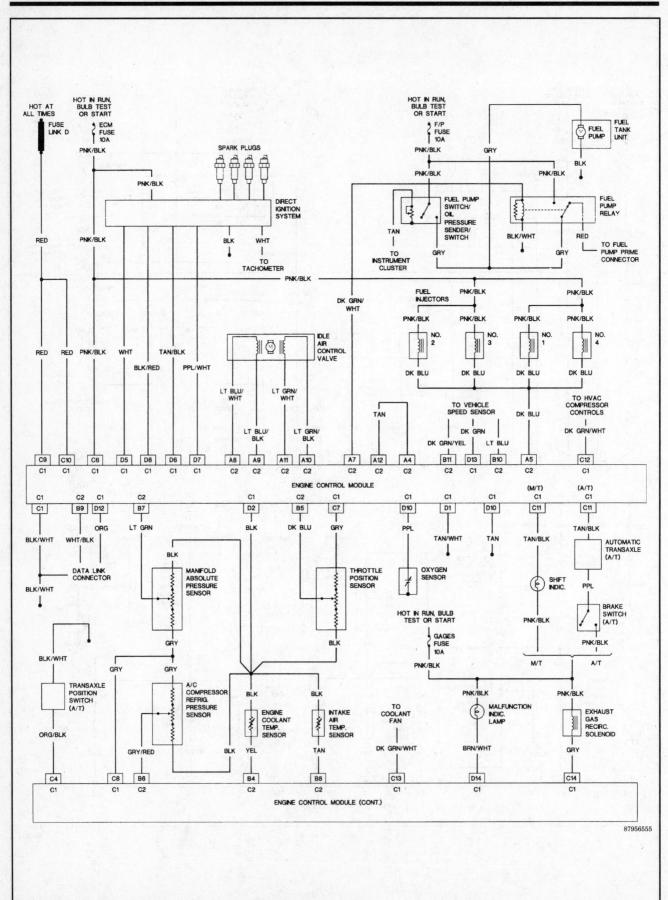

Fig. 179 2.2L (VIN 4) Engine control wiring diagram — 1992 Cavalier

87956555

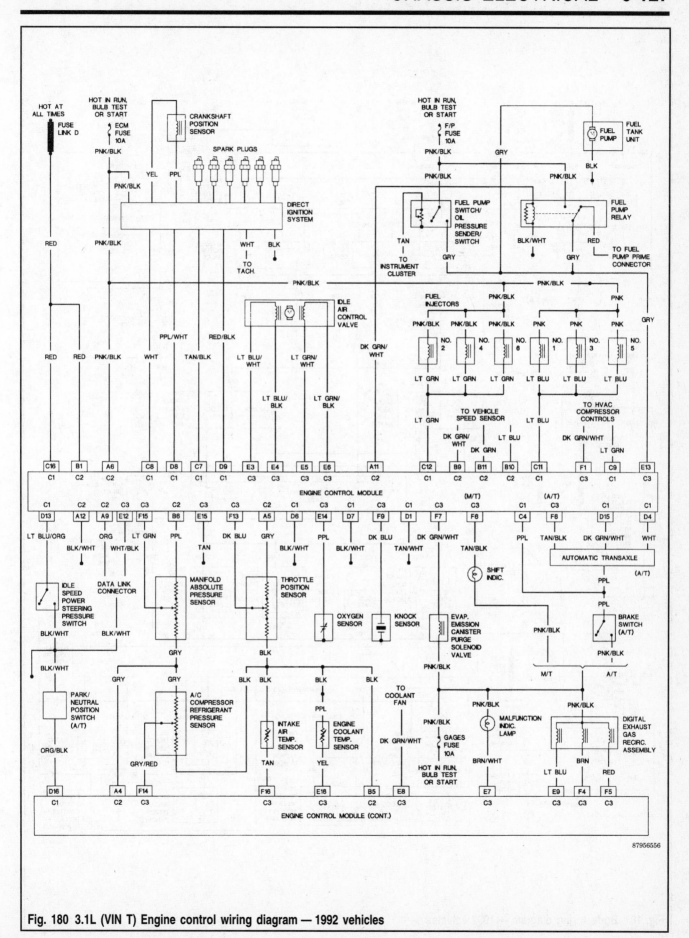

Fig. 180 3.1L (VIN T) Engine control wiring diagram — 1992 vehicles

87956556

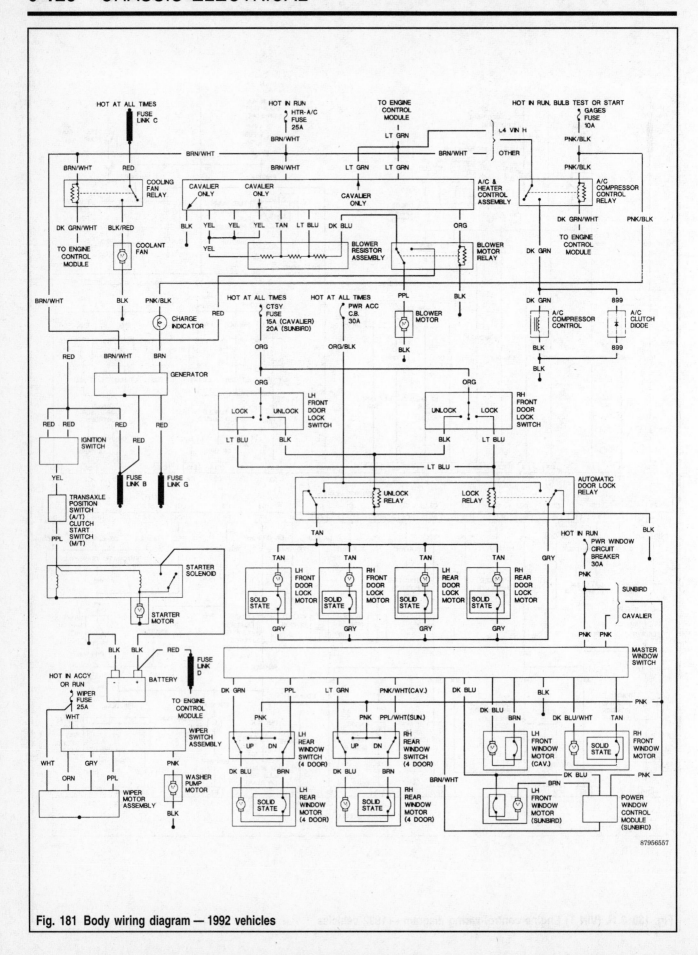

Fig. 181 Body wiring diagram — 1992 vehicles

87956557

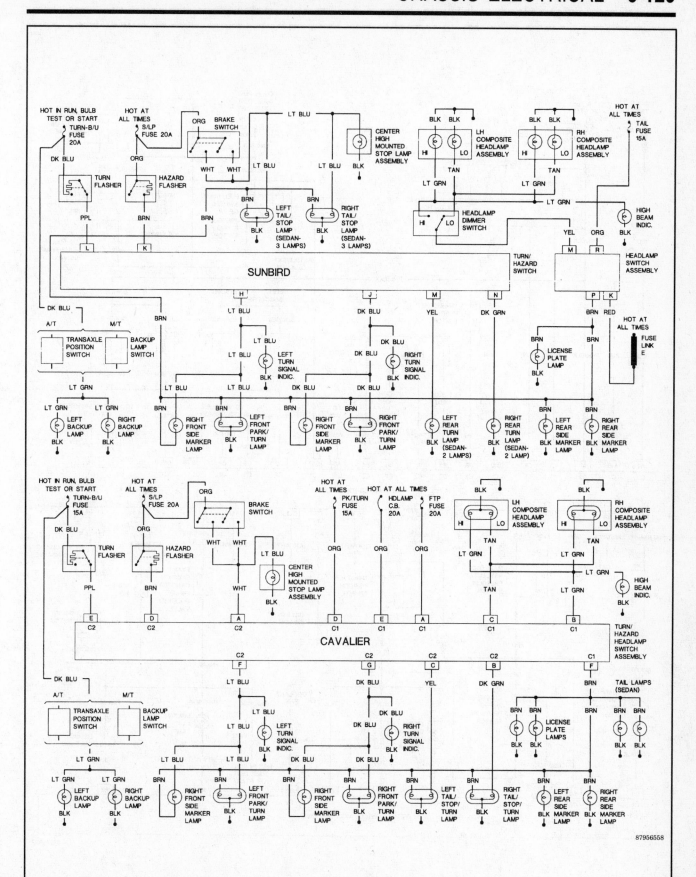

Fig. 182 Body wiring diagram (continued) — 1992 vehicles

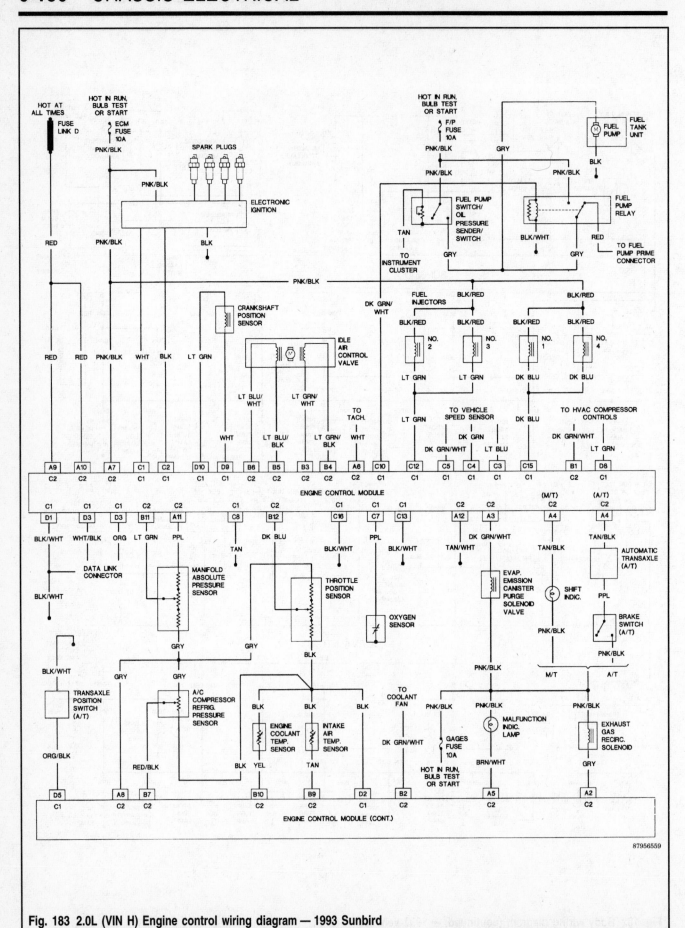

Fig. 183 2.0L (VIN H) Engine control wiring diagram — 1993 Sunbird

87956559

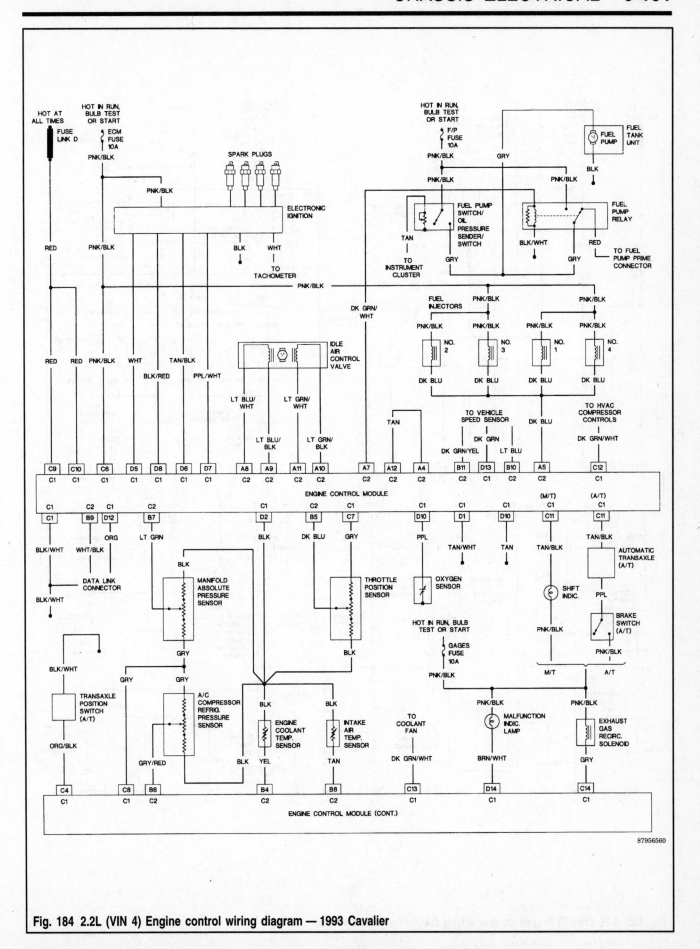

Fig. 184 2.2L (VIN 4) Engine control wiring diagram — 1993 Cavalier

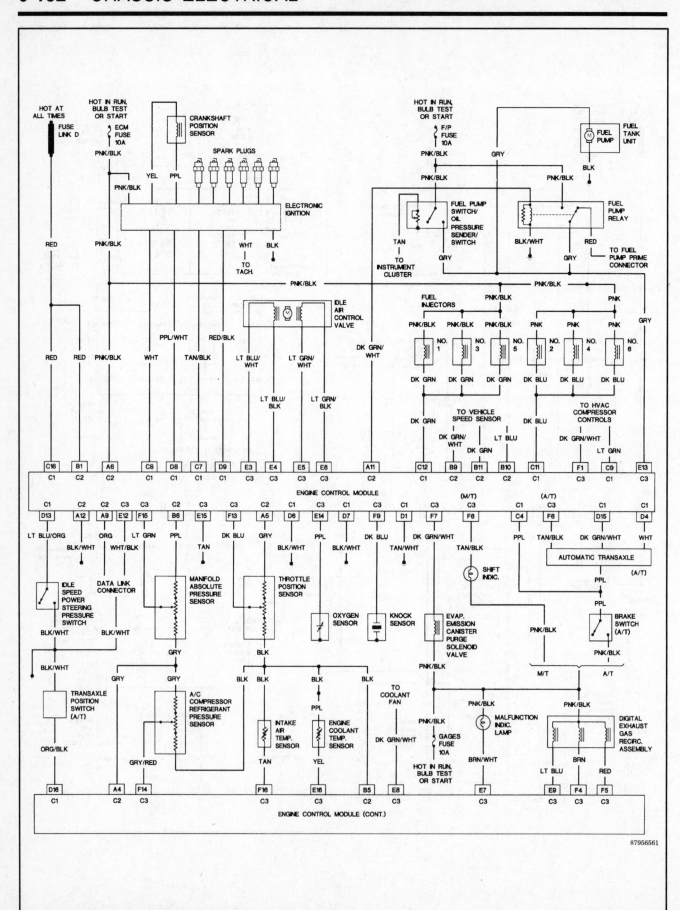

Fig. 185 3.1L (VIN T) Engine control wiring diagram — 1993 vehicles

87956561

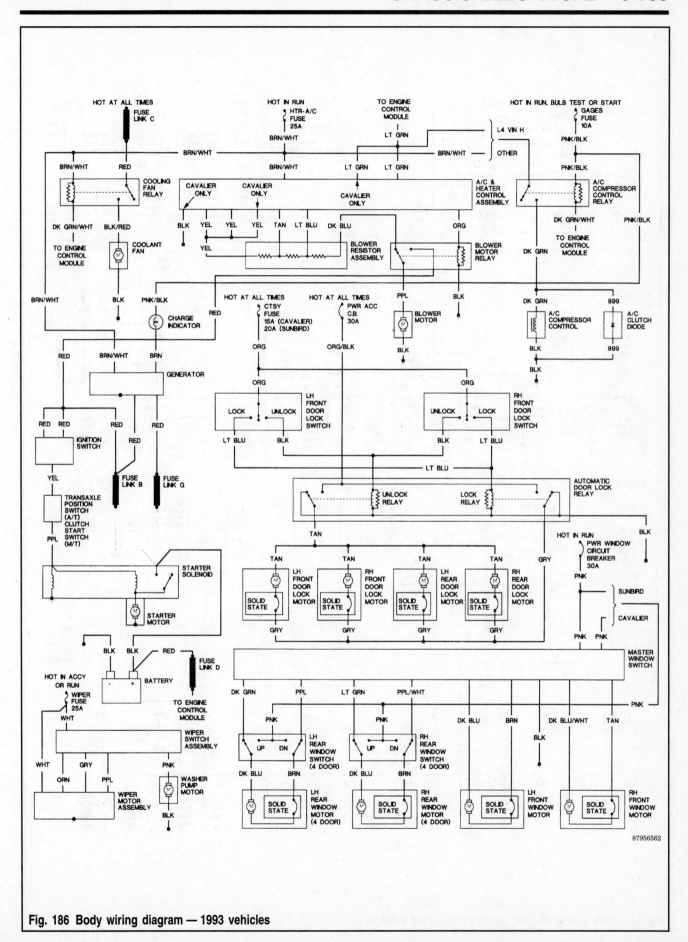

Fig. 186 Body wiring diagram — 1993 vehicles

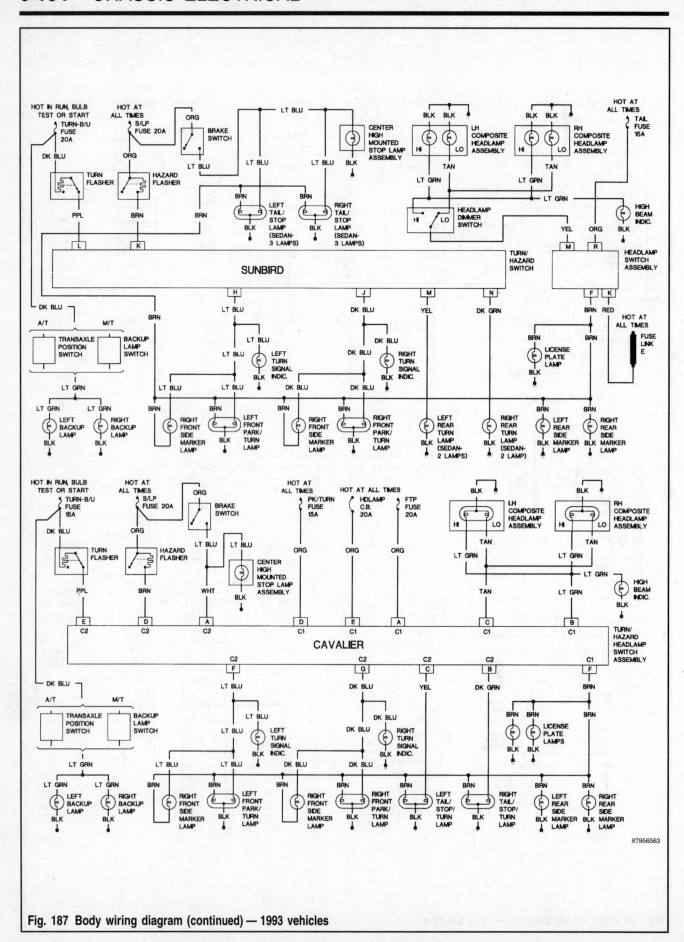

Fig. 187 Body wiring diagram (continued) — 1993 vehicles

87956563

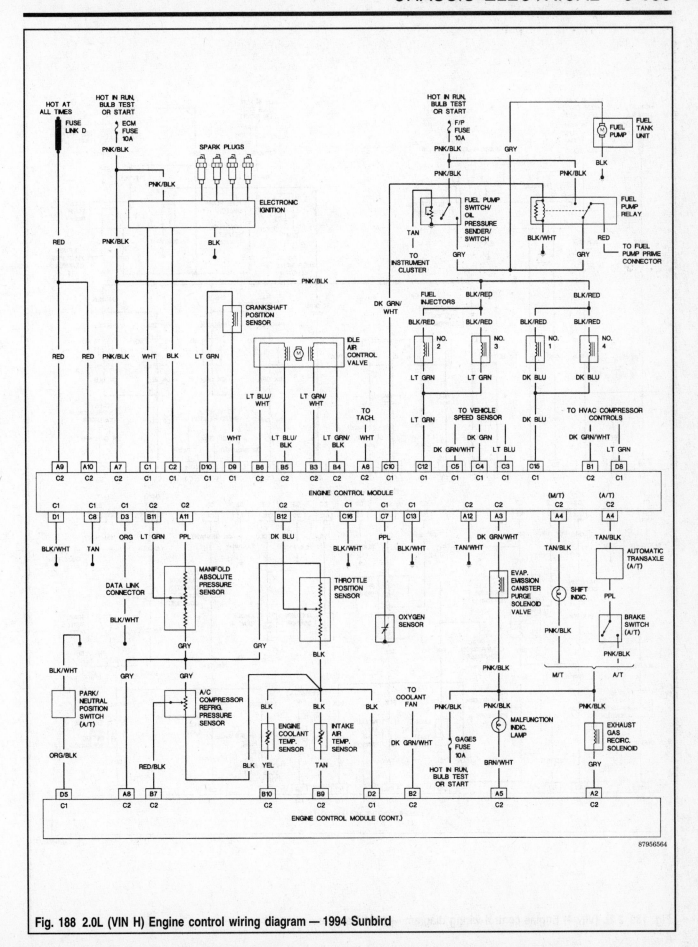

Fig. 188 2.0L (VIN H) Engine control wiring diagram — 1994 Sunbird

87956564

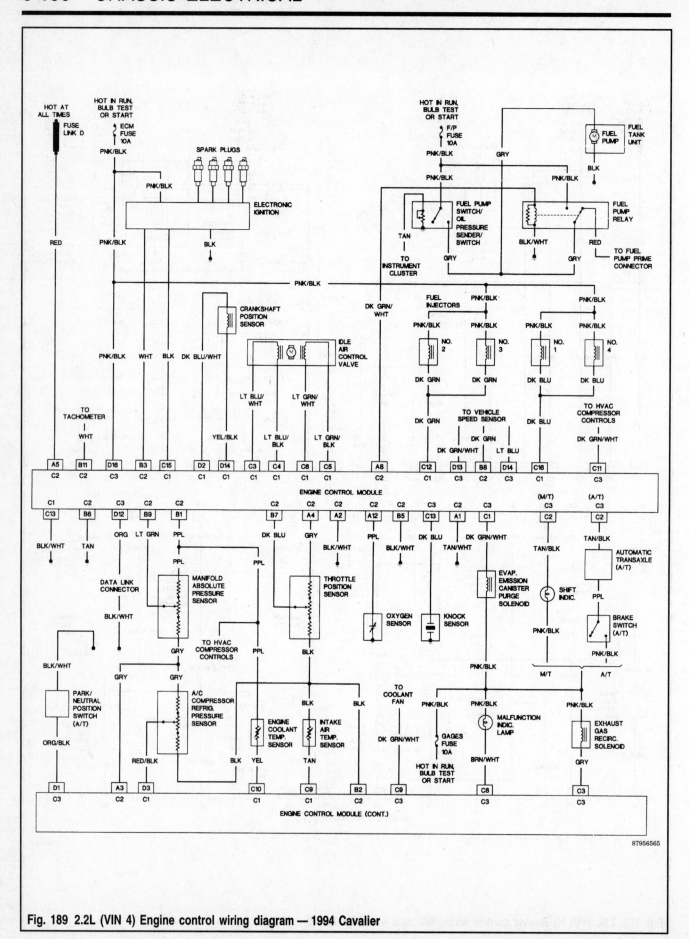

Fig. 189 2.2L (VIN 4) Engine control wiring diagram — 1994 Cavalier

87956565

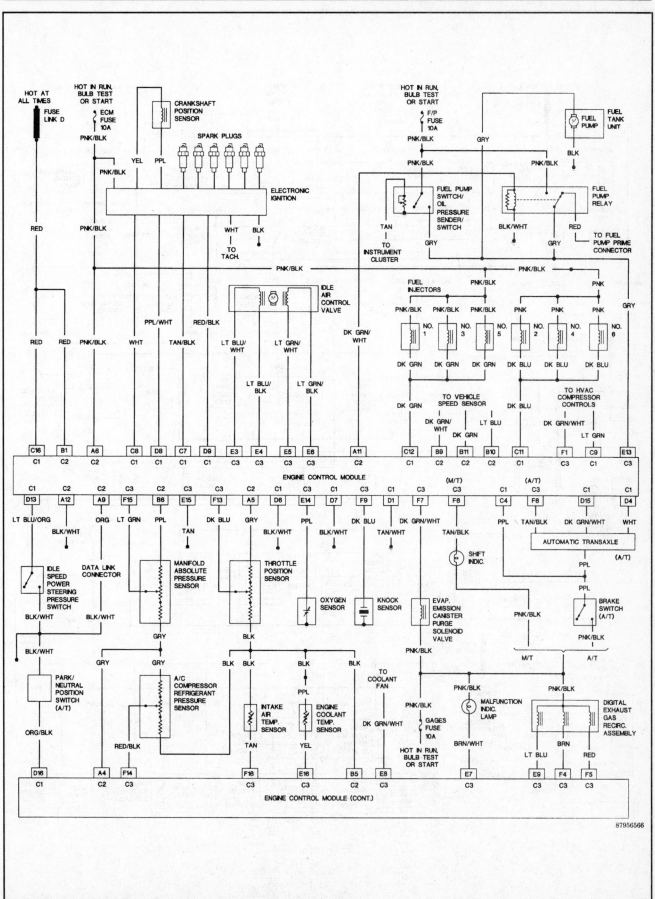

Fig. 190 3.1L (VIN T) Engine control wiring diagram — 1994 vehicles

87956566

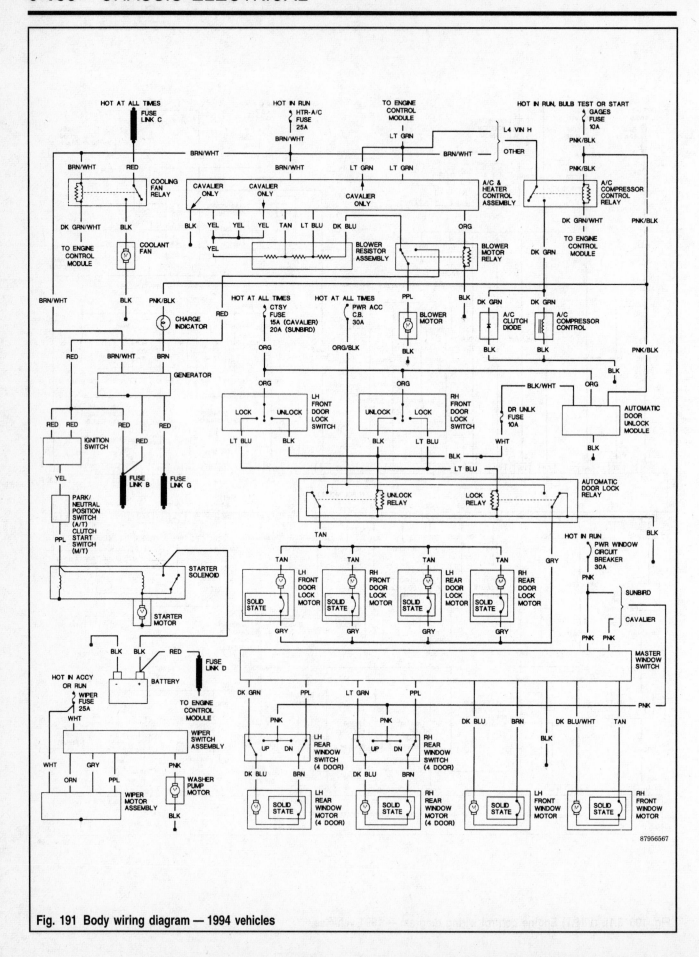

Fig. 191 Body wiring diagram — 1994 vehicles

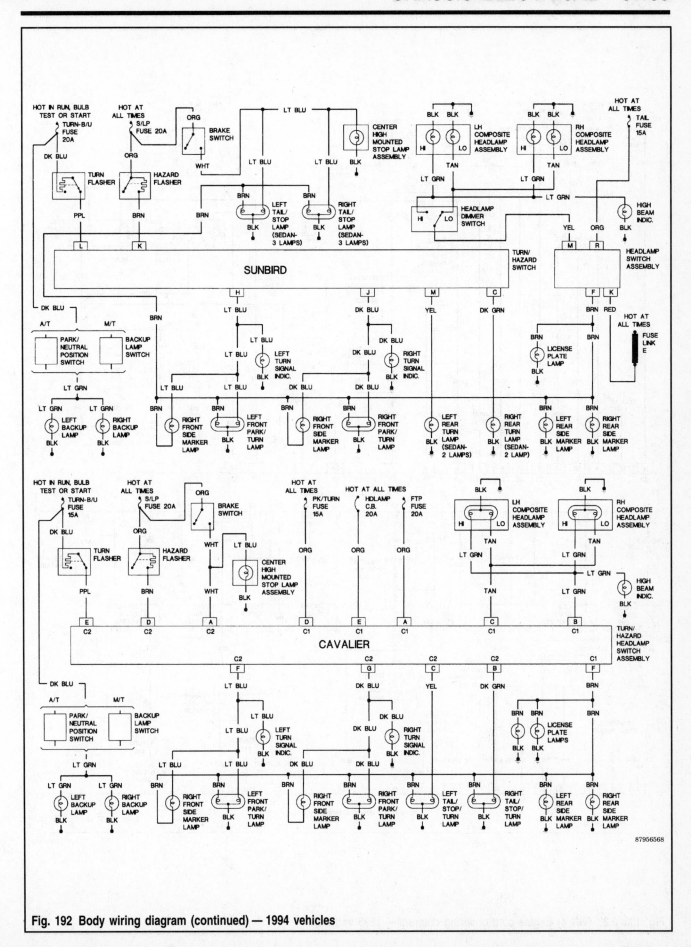

Fig. 192 Body wiring diagram (continued) — 1994 vehicles

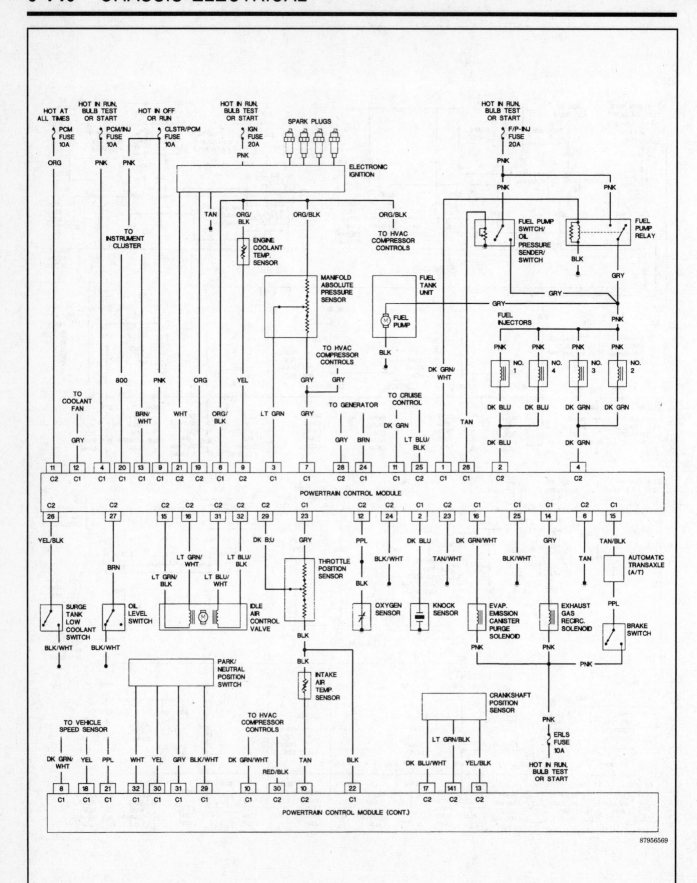

Fig. 193 2.2L (VIN 4) Engine control wiring diagram — 1995 vehicles

87956569

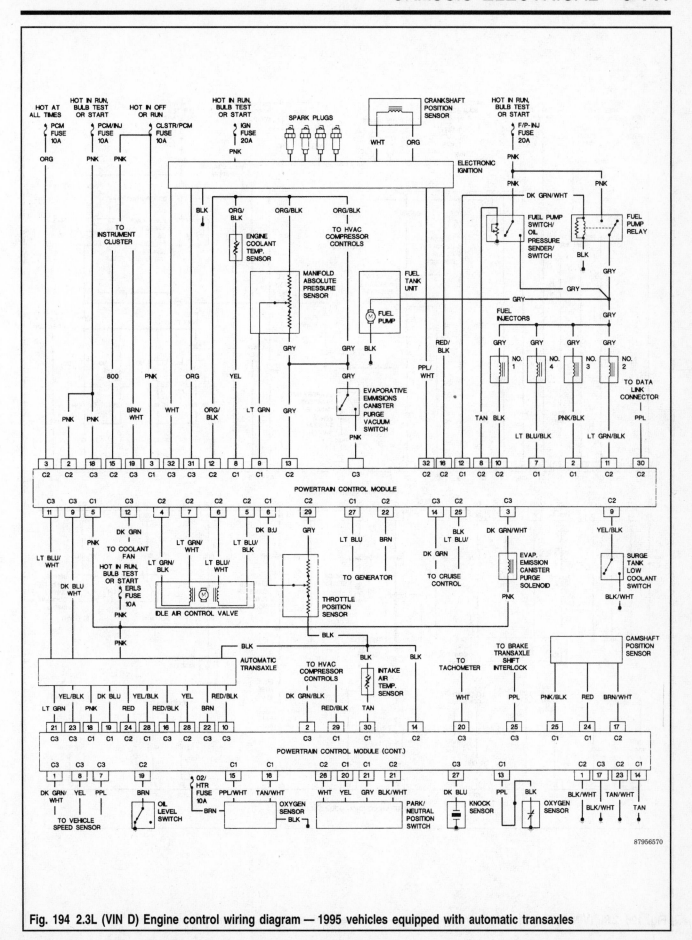

Fig. 194 2.3L (VIN D) Engine control wiring diagram — 1995 vehicles equipped with automatic transaxles

87956570

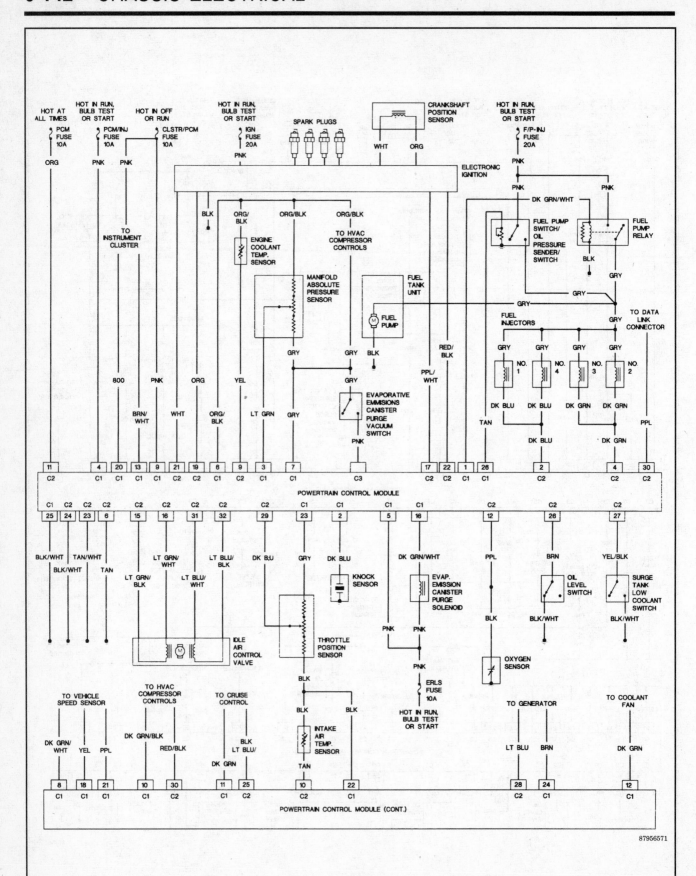

Fig. 195 2.3L (VIN D) Engine control wiring diagram — 1995 vehicles equipped with manual transaxles

87956571

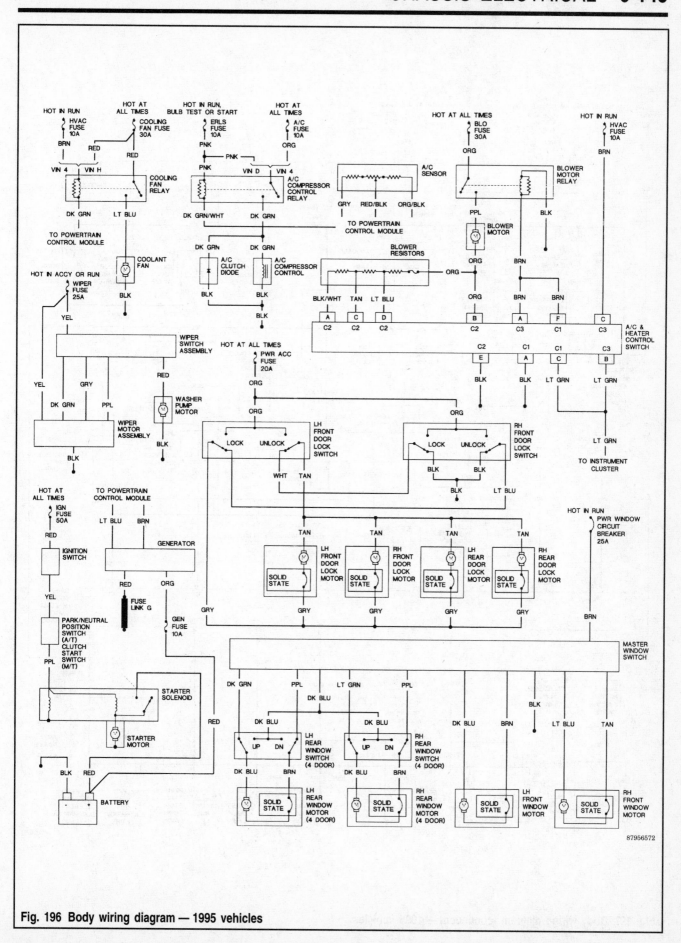

Fig. 196 Body wiring diagram — 1995 vehicles

87956572

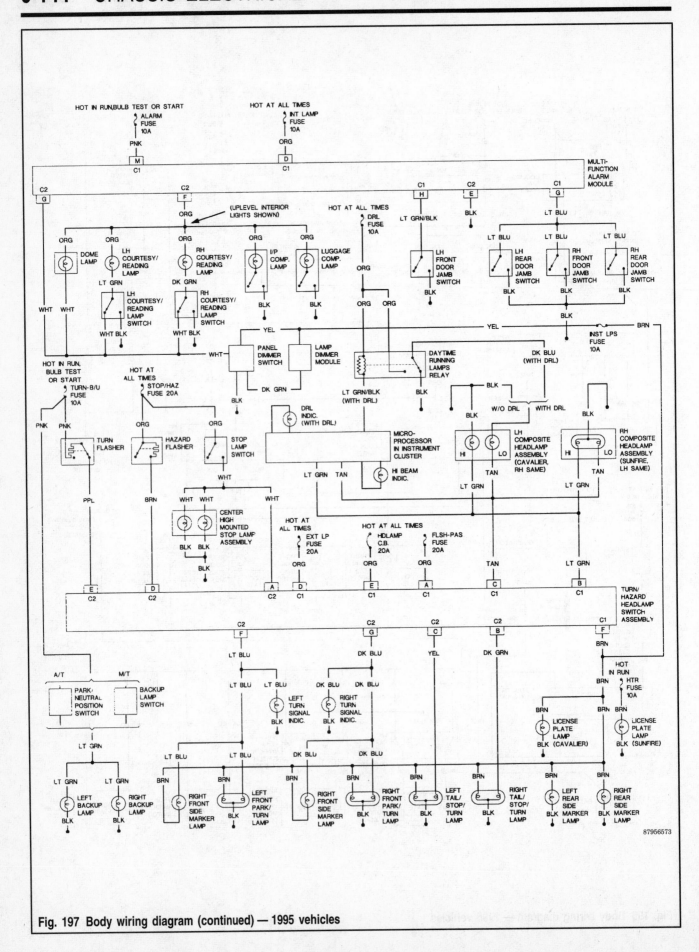

Fig. 197 Body wiring diagram (continued) — 1995 vehicles

87956573

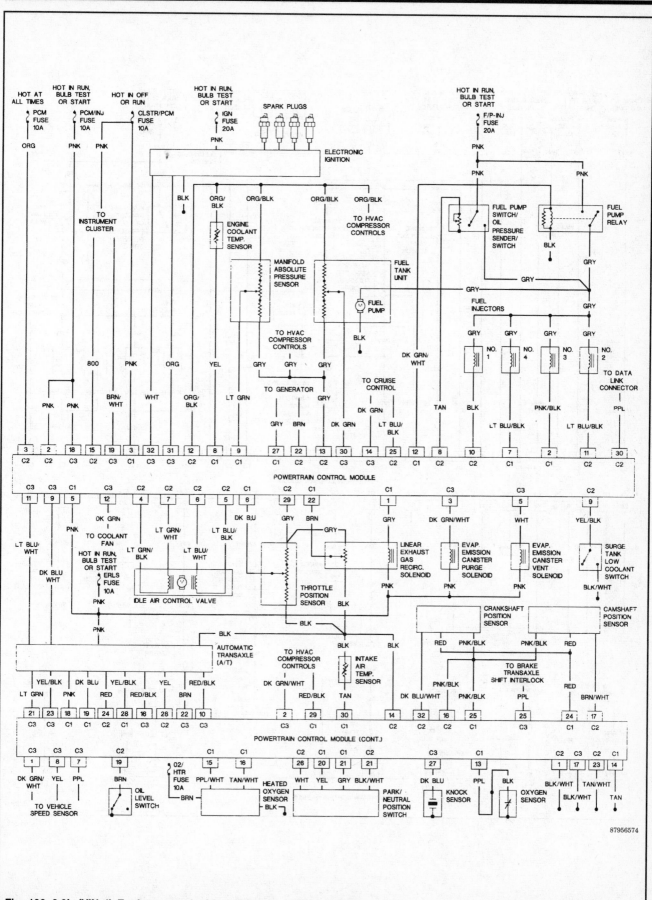

Fig. 198 2.2L (VIN 4) Engine control wiring diagram — 1996 vehicles

87956574

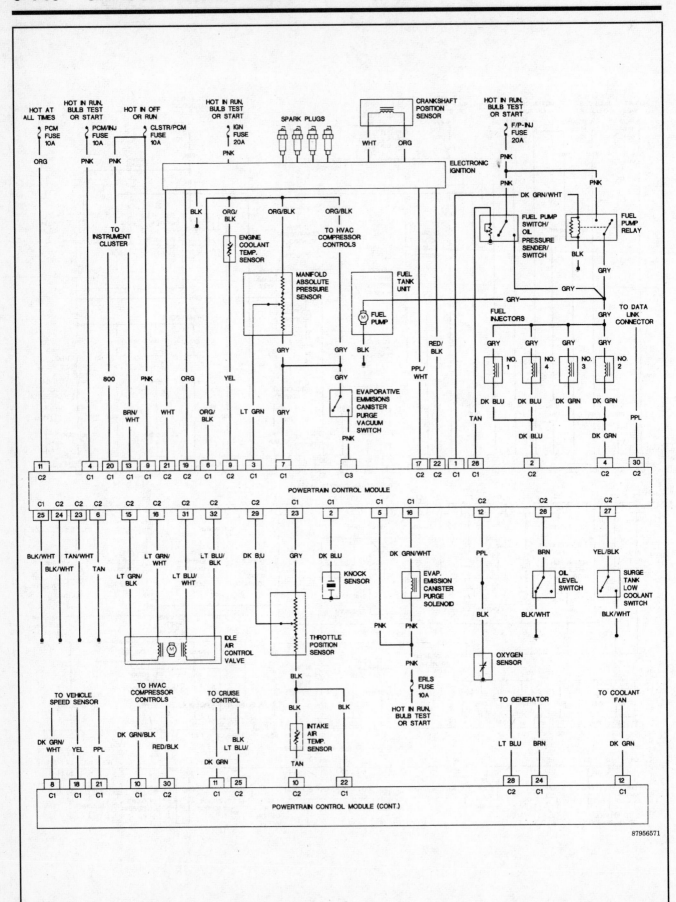

Fig. 199 2.4L (VIN T) Engine control wiring diagram — 1996 vehicles

87956571

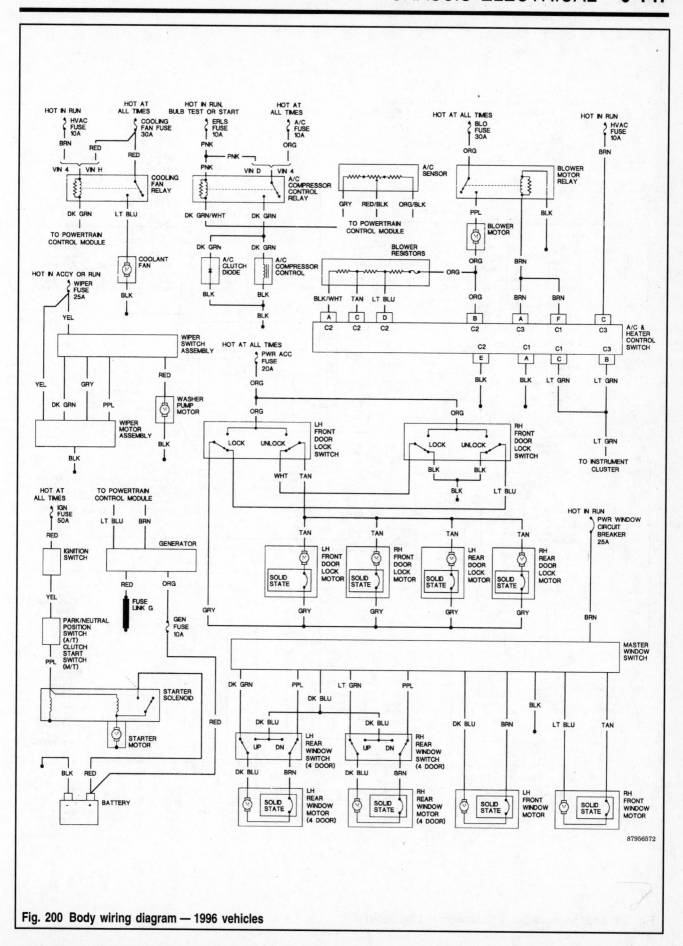

Fig. 200 Body wiring diagram — 1996 vehicles

87956572

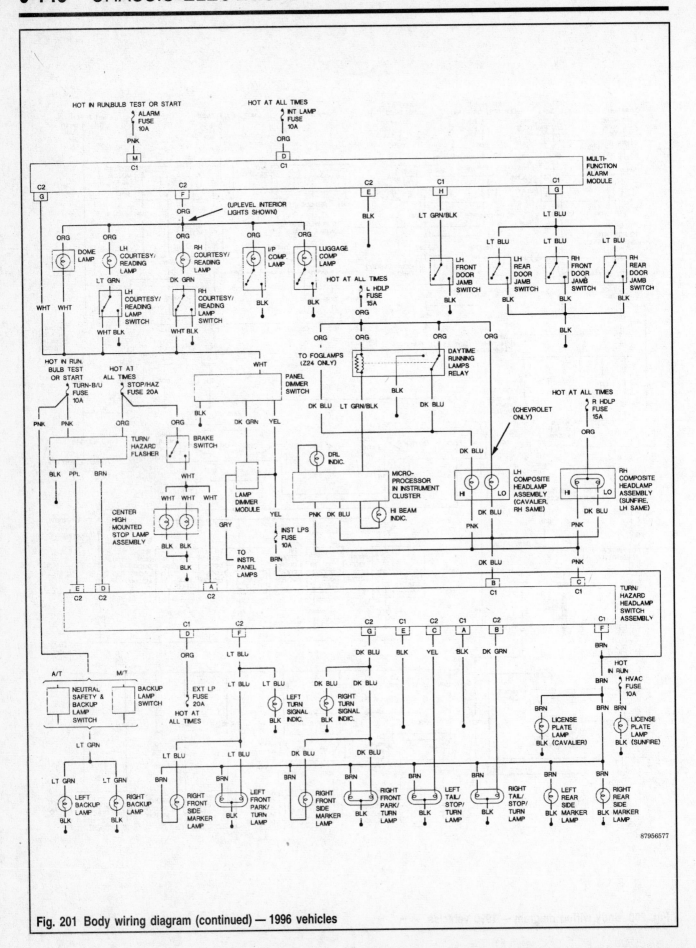

Fig. 201 Body wiring diagram (continued) — 1996 vehicles

87956577

AUTOMATIC TRANSAXLE
ADJUSTMENTS 7-60
FLUID PAN AND FILTER 7-60
HALFSHAFTS 7-68
IDENTIFICATION 7-60
NEUTRAL START/BACK-UP LIGHT
  SWITCH 7-60
TRANSAXLE 7-61
UNDERSTANDING AUTOMATIC
  TRANSAXLES 7-58
CLUTCH
ACTUATOR (SLAVE) CYLINDER 7-56
ADJUSTMENT 7-47
CLUTCH CABLE 7-48
CLUTCH HYDRAULIC SYSTEM 7-51
CLUTCH MASTER CYLINDER 7-56
CLUTCH PEDAL 7-47
DRIVEN DISC AND PRESSURE
  PLATE/CLUTCH COVER AND
  DISC 7-49
UNDERSTANDING THE CLUTCH 7-46
MANUAL TRANSAXLE
ADJUSTMENTS 7-2
BACK-UP LIGHT SWITCH 7-4
CLUTCH SWITCH 7-3
DRIVE AXLES (HALFSHAFTS) 7-17
IDENTIFICATION 7-2
INTERMEDIATE SHAFT 7-13
TRANSAXLE 7-4
UNDERSTANDING THE
  TRANSAXLE 7-2

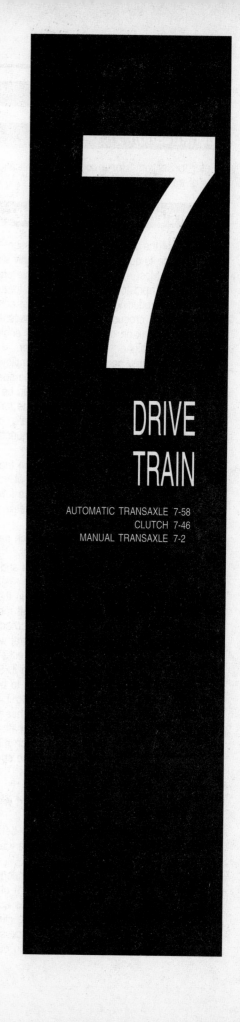

7

DRIVE
TRAIN

AUTOMATIC TRANSAXLE 7-58
CLUTCH 7-46
MANUAL TRANSAXLE 7-2

MANUAL TRANSAXLE

Identification

Refer to Section 1 for a complete identification of all the types of transaxles used.

Understanding the Transaxle

Because of the way an internal combustion engine breathes, it can produce torque, or twisting force, only within a narrow speed range. Most modern, overhead valve engines must turn at about 2,500 rpm to produce their peak torque. By 4,500 rpm they are producing so little torque that continued increases in engine speed produce no power increases.

The torque peak on overhead camshaft engines is, generally, much higher, but much narrower.

The manual transaxle and clutch are employed to vary the relationship between engine speed and the speed of the wheels so that adequate engine power can be produced under all circumstances. The clutch allows engine torque to be applied to the transaxle input shaft gradually, due to mechanical slippage. The car can, consequently, be started smoothly from a full stop.

The transaxle changes the ratio between the rotating speeds of the engine and the wheels by the use of gears. 4-speed or 5-speed transaxles are most common. The lower gears allow full engine power to be applied to the wheels during acceleration at low speeds.

The transaxle contains a mainshaft which passes all the way through the transaxle, from the clutch to the halfshafts. This shaft is separated at 1 point, so that front and rear portions can turn at different speeds.

Power is transmitted by a countershaft in the lower gears and reverse. The gears of the countershaft mesh with gears on the mainshaft, allowing power to be carried from one to the other. All the countershaft gears are integral with that shaft, while several of the mainshaft gears can either rotate independently of the shaft or be locked to it. Shifting from one gear to the next causes one of the gears to be freed from rotating with the shaft and locks another to it. Gears are locked and unlocked by internal dog clutches which slide between the center of the gear and the shaft. The forward gears usually employ synchronizers; friction members which smoothly bring gear and shaft to the same speed before the toothed dog clutches are engaged.

The clutch is operating properly if:

1. It will stall the engine when released with the vehicle held stationary.
2. The shift lever can be moved freely between 1st and reverse gears when the vehicle is stationary and the clutch disengaged.

A clutch pedal free-play adjustment is incorporated in the linkage. If there is about 1-2 in. (25-50mm) of motion before the pedal begins to release the clutch, it is adjusted properly. Inadequate free-play wears all parts of the clutch releasing mechanisms and may cause slippage. Excessive free-play may cause inadequate release and hard shifting of gears.

Some clutches use a hydraulic system in place of mechanical linkage. If the clutch fails to release, fill the clutch master cylinder with fluid to the proper level and pump the clutch pedal to fill the system with fluid. Bleed the system in the same way as a brake system. If leaks are located, tighten loose connections or overhaul the master or slave cylinder as necessary.

Front wheel drive cars do not have conventional rear axles or driveshafts. Instead, power is transmitted from the engine to a transaxle, or a combination of transmission and drive axle, in one unit. Both the transmission and drive axle accomplish the same function as their counterparts in a front engine/rear drive axle design. The difference is in the location of the components.

In place of a conventional driveshaft, a front wheel drive design uses 2 driveshafts, sometimes called halfshafts, which couple the drive axle portion of the transaxle to the wheels. Universal joints or constant velocity joints are used just as they would in a rear wheel drive design.

Adjustments

LINKAGE

No adjustments are possible on the 1988-96 manual transaxle shifting cables or linkage. If the transaxle is not engaging completely, check for stretched cables, broken shifter components or a faulty transaxle.

4-Speed

1982-87 VEHICLES

▶ See Figure 1

1. Disconnect the negative battery cable.
2. Place the transaxle in 1st gear, then loosen the shift cable attaching nuts **E** at the transaxle lever **D** and **F**.
3. Remove the console trim plate and remove the shifter boot and retainer.
4. With the shift lever in the 1st gear position (pulled to the left and held against the stop) insert a yoke clip to hold the lever hard against the reverse lockout stop as shown in view **D**. Install a No. 22 ($^5/_{32}$ in.) drill bit into the alignment hole at the side of the shifter assembly as shown in view **C**.
5. Remove the lash from the transaxle by rotating the upright select lever (lever D) while tightening the cable attaching pin nut **E**.
6. Tighten nut **E** on letter **F**.
7. Remove the drill bit and yoke at the shifter assembly, install the shifter boot and retainer and connect the negative battery cable.
8. Connect the negative battery cable.
9. Install the shifter boot and trim plate.
10. Road test the vehicle to check for good gate feel during shifting. Fine tune the adjustment as necessary.

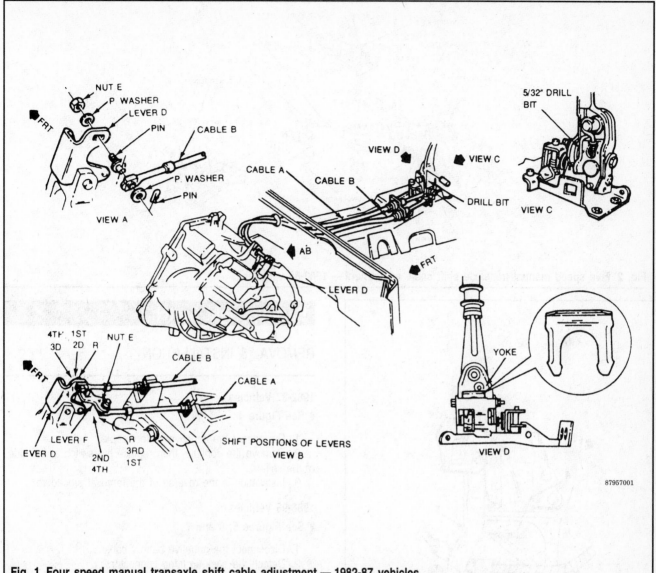

Fig. 1 Four speed manual transaxle shift cable adjustment — 1982-87 vehicles

5-Speed

1983-85 VEHICLES

▶ See Figure 2

1. Disconnect the negative battery cable.
2. Place the transaxle in 3rd gear. Remove the lock pin **H** and reinstall with the tapered end down. This will lock the transaxle in 3rd gear.
3. Loosen the shift cable attaching nuts **E** at the transaxle lever **G** and **F**.
4. Remove the console trim plate and remove the shifter boot. Remove the console.
5. Install a No. 22 (5/32 in.) drill bit into the alignment hole at the side of the shifter assembly as shown in view **A**.
6. Align the hole in select lever (view **B**) with the slot in the shifter plate and install a 9/16 in. drill bit.
7. Tighten nut **E** at levers **G** and **F**.
8. Remove the drill bits from the alignment holes at the shifter. Remove lockpin **H**.

9. Install the console, shifter boot and retainer and connect the negative battery cable.
10. Road test the vehicle to check for good gate feel during shifting. Fine tune the adjustment as necessary.

Clutch Switch

REMOVAL & INSTALLATION

▶ See Figure 3

1. Disconnect the negative battery cable.
2. Detach the instrument panel harness connector from the switch.
3. Unfasten the nuts retaining the switch to the harness bracket, then remove the switch.
4. Installation is the reverse of the removal. Verify proper operation of the switch.

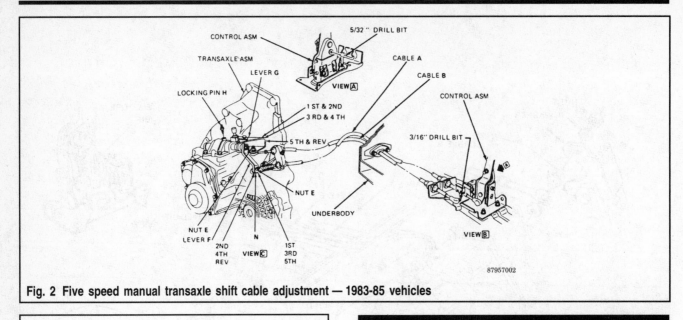

Fig. 2 Five speed manual transaxle shift cable adjustment — 1983-85 vehicles

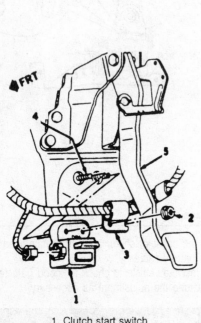

1. Clutch start switch
2. Nut
3. Retaining bracket
4. Mounting stud
5. Clutch pedal
assembly

87957003

Fig. 3 View of the clutch switch installation

Back-up Light Switch

REMOVAL & INSTALLATION

1982-87 Vehicles
▶ See Figure 4

1. Disconnect the negative battery cable.
2. Remove the console, then replace the switch at the side of the shifter.
3. Installation is the reverse of the removal procedure.

1988-96 Vehicles
▶ See Figures 5, 6 and 7

1. Disconnect the negative battery cable.
2. Detach the back-up lamp connector.
3. Unscrew then remove the back-up lamp switch assembly.
   To install:
4. Install the switch with pipe sealant and tighten to 80-84 inch lbs. (9-9.4 Nm).
5. Attach the switch electrical connector.
6. Connect the negative battery cable.

Transaxle

REMOVAL & INSTALLATION

1982-88 Vehicles
▶ See Figures 8, 9, 10 and 11

➡On 1982-84 models, whenever the transaxle mount is removed, the alignment bolt M6 x 1 x 65 must be installed in the right front engine mount to prevent powertrain misalignment

1. Disconnect the negative battery cable.

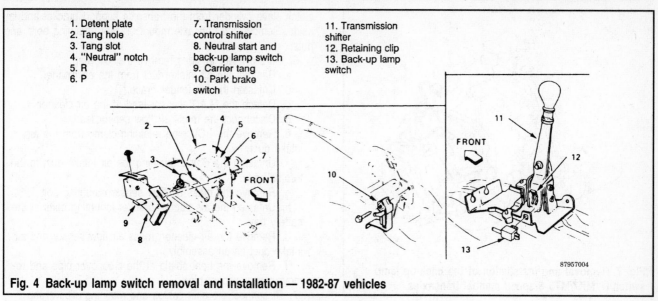

1. Detent plate
2. Tang hole
3. Tang slot
4. "Neutral" notch
5. R
6. P
7. Transmission control shifter
8. Neutral start and back-up lamp switch
9. Carrier tang
10. Park brake switch
11. Transmission shifter
12. Retaining clip
13. Back-up lamp switch

87957004

Fig. 4 Back-up lamp switch removal and installation — 1982-87 vehicles

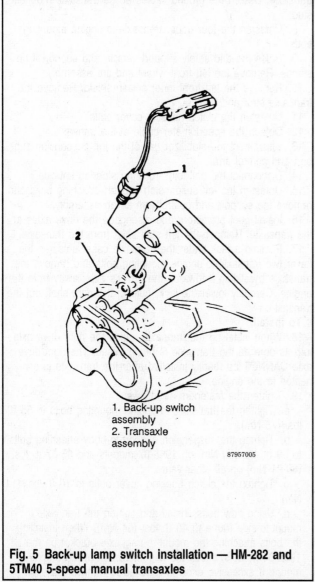
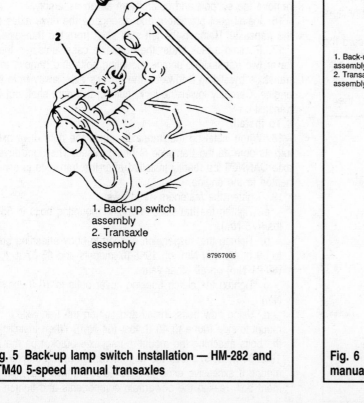

1. Back-up switch assembly
2. Transaxle assembly

87957005

Fig. 5 Back-up lamp switch installation — HM-282 and 5TM40 5-speed manual transaxles

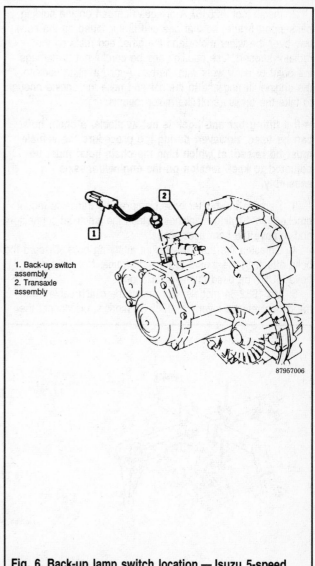

1. Back-up switch assembly
2. Transaxle assembly

87957006

Fig. 6 Back-up lamp switch location — Isuzu 5-speed manual transaxle

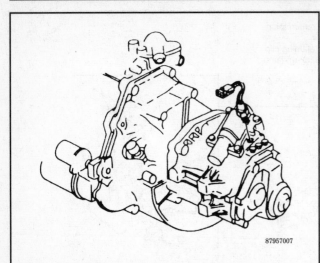

87957007

Fig. 7 Removal and installation of the back-up lamp switch — MK7/MT5 5-speed manual transaxles

2. Install tool J-28467-A or equivalent, an engine holding bar/support fixture, so that one end is supported on the cowl tray over the wiper motor and the other end rests on the radiator support. Use padding and be careful not to damage the paint or body work with the bar. Attach a lifting hook to the engine lift ring and to the bar and raise the engine enough to take the pressure off the motor mounts.

➡️If a lifting bar and hook is not available, a chain hoist can be used, however, during the procedure the vehicle must be raised, at which time the chain hoist must be adjusted to keep tension on the engine/transaxle assembly.

3. Remove the heater hose clamp at the transaxle mount bracket. On 4-cylinder engines, detach the electrical connector and remove the horn assembly.

4. Unfasten the transaxle mount attaching bolts. Discard the bolts attaching the mount to the side frame. Note that new bolts MUST be used during installation.

5. On 1982-84 models, disconnect the clutch cable from the clutch release lever. On 1985-87 models, disconnect the

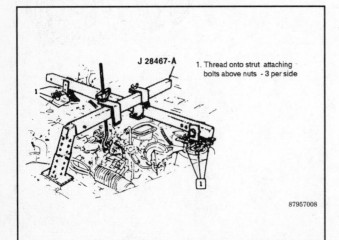

J 28467-A

1. Thread onto strut attaching bolts above nuts - 3 per side

87957008

Fig. 8 Install a suitable engine support tool to take the pressure off the motor mounts

clutch slave cylinder from the transaxle support bracket and lay aside. Remove the transaxle mount bracket attaching bolts and nuts.

6. On 6-cylinder engines remove the following:
   a. Remove the air intake duct from the air cleaner.
   b. Unfasten the left fender brace.
   c. Detach the M.A.T. sensor lead at the air cleaner.
   d. Disconnect the mass air flow sensor lead.
   e. Remove the PCV pipe retaining clamp from the air intake duct.
   f. Unfasten the clamp retaining the air intake duct to the throttle body.
   g. Remove the mass air flow sensor mounting bolt.
   h. Unfasten the air cleaner bracket mounting bolts at the battery tray.
   i. Remove the air cleaner, mass air flow sensor and air intake duct as an assembly.
   j. Remove the heat shield at the crossover pipe and re-move the crossover pipe.

7. Disconnect the shift cables and retaining clips at the transaxle. Detach the ground cables at the transaxle mounting stud.

8. Unfasten the four upper transaxle-to-engine mounting bolts.

9. Raise the and safely support vehicle and support it on stands. Remove the left front wheel and tire assembly.

10. Remove the left front inner splash shield. Remove the transaxle strut and bracket.

11. Unfasten the clutch housing cover bolts.

12. Detach the speedometer cable at the transaxle.

13. Disconnect the stabilizer bar at the left suspension support and control arm.

14. Disconnect the ball joint from the steering knuckle.

15. Unfasten the left suspension support attaching bolts and remove the support and control arm as an assembly.

16. Install boot protectors and disengage the drive axles at the transaxle. Remove the left side shaft from the transaxle.

17. Position a jack under the transaxle case, unfasten the lower two transaxle-to-engine mounting bolts and remove the transaxle by sliding it towards the driver's side, away from the engine. Carefully lower the jack, guiding the right shaft out the transaxle.

To install:

18. When installing the transaxle, guide the right drive axle into its bore as the transaxle is being raised. The right drive axle CANNOT be readily installed after the transaxle is connected to the engine.

19. Tighten the fasteners as follows:
   a. Tighten the transaxle-to-engine mounting bolts to 55 ft. lbs. (75 Nm).
   b. Tighten the suspension support-to-body attaching bolts to 59 ft. lbs. (80 Nm) on 1985-87 models and 65-67 ft. lbs. (88-91 Nm) on all other years.
   c. Tighten the clutch housing cover bolts to 10 ft. lbs. (14 Nm).
   d. Using new bolts, install and tighten the transaxle mount-to-side frame to 40 ft. lbs. (54 Nm). When installing the bolts attaching the mount-to-transaxle bracket on the 1982-84 models, check the alignment bolt at the engine mount. If excessive effort is required to remove the alignment bolt, realign the powertrain components and tighten the

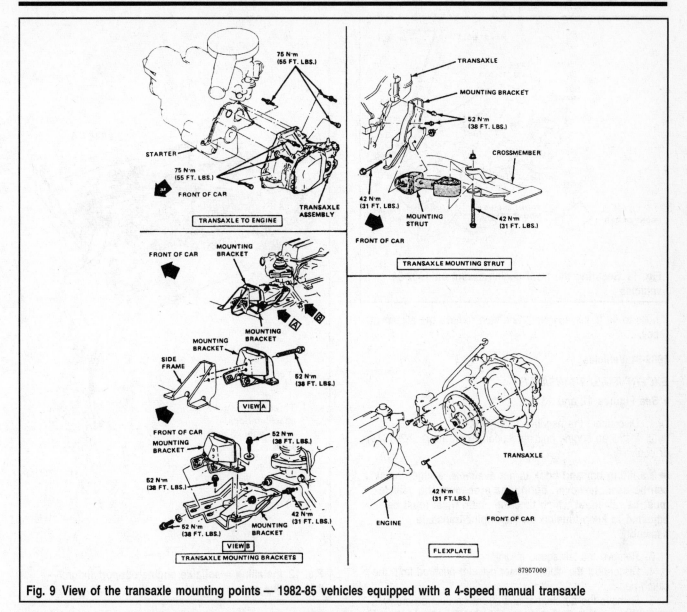

Fig. 9 View of the transaxle mounting points — 1982-85 vehicles equipped with a 4-speed manual transaxle

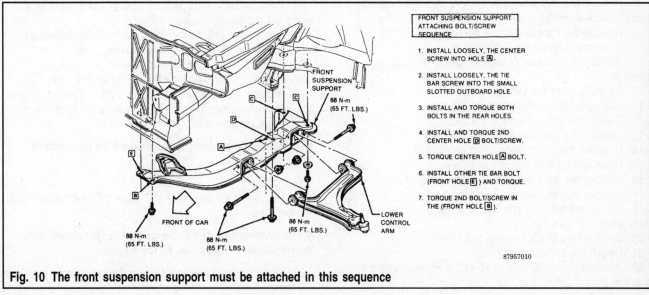

FRONT SUSPENSION SUPPORT ATTACHING BOLT/SCREW SEQUENCE

1. INSTALL LOOSELY, THE CENTER SCREW INTO HOLE A.

2. INSTALL LOOSELY, THE TIE BAR SCREW INTO THE SMALL SLOTTED OUTBOARD HOLE.

3. INSTALL AND TORQUE BOTH BOLTS IN THE REAR HOLES.

4. INSTALL AND TORQUE 2ND CENTER HOLE D BOLT/SCREW.

5. TORQUE CENTER HOLE A BOLT.

6. INSTALL OTHER TIE BAR BOLT (FRONT HOLE E) AND TORQUE.

7. TORQUE 2ND BOLT/SCREW IN THE (FRONT HOLE B).

Fig. 10 The front suspension support must be attached in this sequence

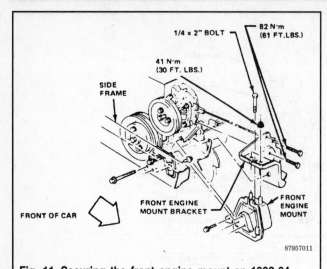

Fig. 11 Securing the front engine mount on 1982-84 vehicles

bolts to 40 ft. lbs. (54 Nm), and then remove the alignment bolt.

1989-91 Vehicles

EXCEPT ISUZU TRANSAXLE

▶ **See Figures 12 and 13**

1. Disconnect the negative battery cable.
2. Install an engine holding support fixture (bar), J-28467-A or equivalent.

➡**If a lifting bar and hook is not available, a chain hoist can be used, however, during the procedure the vehicle must be raised, at which time the chain hoist must be adjusted to keep tension on the engine/transaxle assembly.**

3. Remove the left sound insulator.
4. Disconnect the clutch master cylinder pushrod from the clutch pedal.
5. Remove the air cleaner and air intake duct assembly.
6. Remove the clutch actuator cylinder from the transaxle support bracket and lay it aside.
7. Remove the transaxle mount through-bolt.
8. Raise and support the vehicle safely.
9. Remove the exhaust crossover bolts at the right hand manifold.
10. Carefully lower the vehicle.
11. Disconnect the transaxle mount bracket.
12. Detach the shift cables and linkage.
13. Remove the transaxle vent tube.
14. Unfasten the upper transaxle to engine bolts.
15. Raise and support the vehicle safely.
16. Remove the left front tire and wheel assembly.
17. Remove the left front inner splash shield.
18. Disconnect the transaxle strut and bracket.
19. Drain the transaxle.
20. Unfasten the clutch housing cover bolts.
21. Detach the speedometer cable.
22. Disconnect the stabilizer shaft at the left suspension support and control arm.

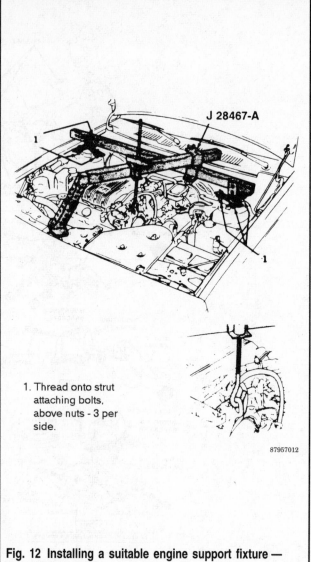

1. Thread onto strut attaching bolts, above nuts - 3 per side.

Fig. 12 Installing a suitable engine support fixture — 3.1L engine shown

23. Remove the left suspension support attaching bolts and swing the suspension support aside.
24. Install drive axle boot protector J-34754 or equivalent and remove the left drive axle from the transaxle.
25. Attach the transaxle case to a jack.
26. Unfasten the remaining transaxle to engine bolts.
27. Remove the transaxle by sliding it away from the engine and carefully lowering the jack while guiding the intermediate shaft out of the transaxle.

➡**The engine may need to be lowered for transaxle-to-body clearance.**

To install:
28. Reposition the transaxle and guide the intermediate shaft into the transaxle.

➡**The intermediate shaft cannot be easily installed after the transaxle is connected to the engine.**

29. Install the transaxle to engine mounting bolts to 55 ft. lbs (75 Nm).

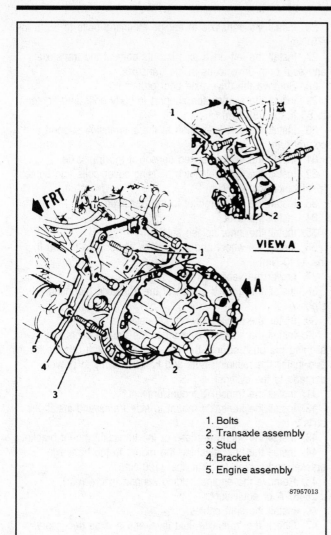

1. Bolts
2. Transaxle assembly
3. Stud
4. Bracket
5. Engine assembly

87957013

Fig. 13 View of the engine-to-transaxle mounting — 5TM40 manual transaxle shown

30. Install the left drive axle into its bore at the transaxle and seat the driveaxle at the transaxle.
31. Remove the drive axle boot protector.
32. Fasten the suspension support to body bolts and tighten to 65 ft. lbs. (88 Nm).
33. Install the stabilizer shaft at the left suspension support and control arm.
34. Attach the speedometer cable.
35. Install the clutch/flywheel housing cover bolts and tighten to 115 inch lbs. (13 Nm).
36. Fasten the strut bracket to the transaxle.
37. Install the strut.
38. Attach the inner splash shield.
39. Install the wheel and tire assembly and tighten the wheel nuts to 100 ft. lbs. (136 Nm).
40. Carefully lower the vehicle.
41. Install the upper engine to transaxle bolts and tighten to 55 ft. lbs. (75 Nm).
42. Install the transaxle vent tube.
43. Attach the shift cables.
44. Install the transaxle mount bracket.

45. Fasten the left exhaust crossover bolts.
46. Raise and support the vehicle safely.
47. Install the exhaust crossover bolts at the right hand manifold.
48. Carefully lower the vehicle.
49. Install the transaxle mount through-bolt.
50. Install the clutch actuator cylinder to the transaxle support bracket.
51. Install the air cleaner and air intake duct assembly.
52. Remove the engine holding support fixture (bar), J-28467-A or equivalent.
53. Connect the clutch master cylinder pushrod to the clutch pedal.
54. Install the left sound insulator.
55. Check the transaxle fluid level and add as necessary.
56. Connect the negative battery cable.

ISUZU TRANSAXLE

▶ **See Figures 14 and 15**

1. Disconnect the negative battery cable.
2. Install an engine holding support fixture (bar), J-28467-A or equivalent and raise the engine enough to take the pressure off the motor mounts.
3. Remove the left sound insulator.
4. Disconnect the clutch master cylinder pushrod from the clutch pedal.
5. Remove the clutch actuator cylinder from the transaxle support bracket and lay it aside.
6. Disconnect the wire harness at the mount bracket.
7. Unfasten the transaxle mount attaching bolts.
8. Remove the transaxle mount bracket attaching bolts and nuts.
9. Remove the shift cables and retaining clamp at the transaxle.
10. Detach the ground cables at the transaxle mounting studs.
11. Detach the back-up switch connector.
12. Raise and support the vehicle safely.
13. Drain the transaxle.
14. Remove the left front wheel assembly.
15. Detach the left front inner splash shield.

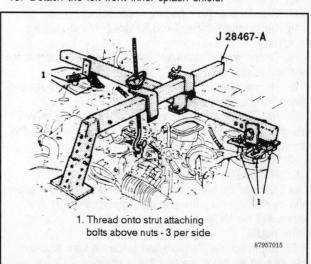

1. Thread onto strut attaching bolts above nuts - 3 per side

87957015

Fig. 14 Installing the engine support tool on the 1991 2.0L (VIN K) engine

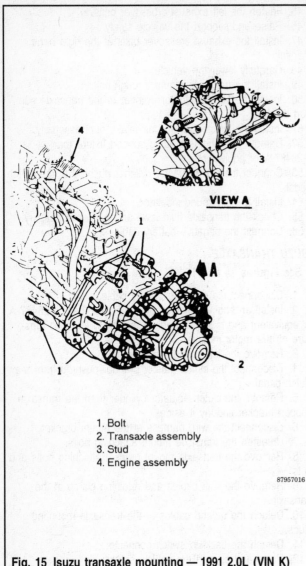

1. Bolt
2. Transaxle assembly
3. Stud
4. Engine assembly

87957016

Fig. 15 Isuzu transaxle mounting — 1991 2.0L (VIN K) engine shown

16. Disconnect the transaxle strut and bracket.
17. Remove the clutch housing cover bolts.
18. Detach the Vehicle Speed Sensor (VSS) at the transaxle.
19. Disconnect the stabilizer shaft at the left suspension support and control arm.
20. Remove the left suspension support attaching bolts and swing the suspension support aside.
21. Install drive axle boot protector J-34754 or equivalent, disconnect the drive axles and remove the left shaft from the transaxle.
22. Attach the transaxle case to a jack.
23. Remove the transaxle to engine bolts.
24. Remove the transaxle by sliding it away from the engine and carefully lowering the jack while guiding the right drive axle out of the transaxle.
   To install:
25. Reposition the transaxle and guide the right drive axle into its bore as the transaxle is being raised.

➡**The right drive axle cannot be easily installed after the transaxle is connected to the engine.**

26. Install the transaxle to engine mounting bolts to 55 ft. lbs (75 Nm).
27. Install the left drive axle into its bore at the transaxle and seat both drive axles at the transaxle.
28. Remove the drive axle boot protector.
29. Install the suspension support to body bolts and tighten to 65 ft. lbs. (88 Nm).
30. Install the stabilizer shaft at the suspension support and control arm.
31. Install the vehicle speed sensor at the transaxle.
32. Install the flywheel/clutch housing cover bolts and tighten to 115 inch lbs. (13 Nm).
33. Install the strut bracket to the transaxle.
34. Install the strut.
35. Install the inner splash shield.
36. Install the wheel and tighten the wheel nuts to 100 ft. lbs. (140 Nm).
37. Lower the vehicle.
38. Install the ground cables at the transaxle mounting studs.
39. Install the back-up switch connector.
40. Install the actuator cylinder to the transaxle bracket aligning the pushrod into the pocket of the clutch release lever and install the retaining nuts and tighten evenly to prevent damage to the cylinder.
41. Install the transaxle mount bracket.
42. Install the transaxle mount to side frame and install the bolts.
43. Install the wiring harness at the transaxle mount bracket.
44. Install the bolt attaching the mount to the transaxle bracket and tighten to 88 ft. lbs. (120 Nm).
45. Remove the engine holding support fixture (bar), J-28467-A or equivalent.
46. Install the shift cables.
47. Check the transaxle fluid level and add as necessary.
48. Connect the negative battery cable.

1992-96 Vehicles

NVG-T550 TRANSAXLES

▶ **See Figures 16 and 17**

1. Disconnect the negative battery cable.
2. Remove the left sound insulator.
3. Disconnect the clutch master cylinder pushrod from the clutch pedal.
4. Remove the air cleaner assembly and the bracket.
5. Unfasten the exhaust crossover pipe.
6. Disconnect the hydraulic line from the clutch slave cylinder.
7. Remove the transaxle shift cables by snapping them off.
8. Remove the shift cable mount bracket.
9. Detach the back-up light switch connector.
10. Disconnect the transaxle vent tube from the transaxle.
11. Unfasten the top two transaxle-to-engine bolts.
12. Install engine support fixture J 28467-A, or equivalent, and raise the engine enough to remove the weight from the engine mounts.
13. Raise and support the vehicle safely, then drain the transaxle fluid.
14. Remove the front tire and wheel assemblies.
15. Remove the left side splash shield.
16. Unfasten the front air deflector.

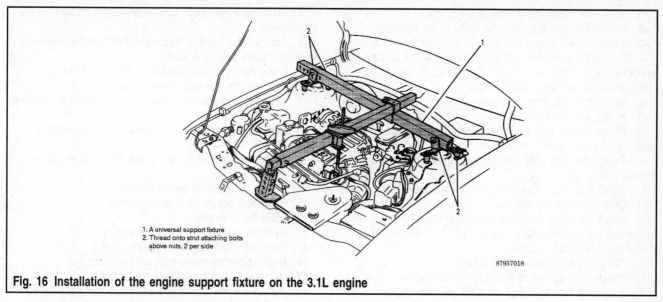

1. A universal support fixture
2. Thread onto strut attaching bolts above nuts, 2 per side

87957018

Fig. 16 Installation of the engine support fixture on the 3.1L engine

17. Remove the right side splash shield.
18. Detach the ABS Wheel Speed Sensor (WSS) connectors from the WSS and harness from the left side suspension support.
19. Remove the left and right ball joint nuts.
20. Unfasten the left stabilizer link.
21. Remove the transaxle strut bracket from the transaxle bolts.
22. Remove the stabilizer bat and left side U-bolt.
23. Unfasten the left suspension support attaching bolts.
24. Remove the intermediate shaft and housing.
25. Remove the left and drive drive axles (halfshafts), as outlined later in this section.
26. Unfasten the rear engine mount through-bolts.
27. Remove the rear engine mount bracket.
28. Detach the following electrical connectors:
    • Vehicle Speed Sensor (VSS)
    • Back-up light switch
29. Remove the starter motor.
30. Unfasten and remove the flywheel cover.
31. Lower the engine with engine support fixture J-28476-A, or equivalent, to ease removal of the transaxle, but be sure to count the number of turns for installation.
32. Detach the ground wires from the lower engine-to-transaxle bolts.
33. Install a transaxle jack, then unfasten the lower engine-to-transaxle bolts. Remove the transaxle.
   To install:
34. Reposition the transaxle and install the lower transaxle bolts. tighten the bolts to 55 ft. lbs. (75 Nm).
35. Attach the ground wires to the lower engine-to-transaxle bolts.
36. Install the flywheel cover, then tighten the retaining bolts to 89 inch lbs. (10 Nm).
37. Install the starter motor.
38. Raise the engine with the support fixture to install the powertrain mounts.
39. Install the rear engine mount bracket, then install the rear engine mount and through-bolts.
40. Attach the VSS and back-up light switch electrical connectors.

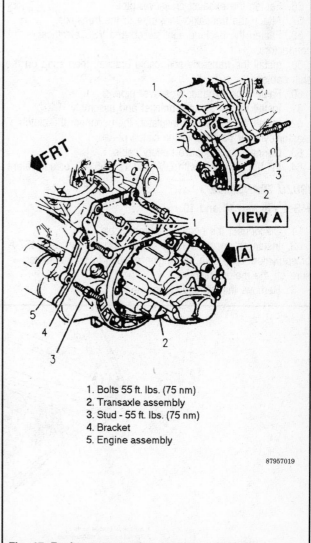

1. Bolts 55 ft. lbs. (75 nm)
2. Transaxle assembly
3. Stud - 55 ft. lbs. (75 nm)
4. Bracket
5. Engine assembly

87957019

Fig. 17 Engine-to-transaxle mounting — NVG-550 manual transaxle shown

41. Install the intermediate shaft and housing.
42. Fasten the right and left drive axles to the transaxle.
43. Install the left suspension support and attaching bolts.
44. Fasten the transaxle strut bracket and the bolt to the transaxle. Tighten the strut bracket bolts to 40 ft. lbs. (54 Nm).
45. Install the left side stabilizer U-bolt.
46. Install both ball joints and cotter pins.
47. Fasten the stabilizer link.
48. Attach the left side ABS WSS harness and attach both ABS wheel speed sensor connectors.
49. Fasten the right side splash shield, front air deflector and the left side splash shield.
50. Install both front wheel and tire assemblies.
51. Carefully lower the vehicle.
52. Install the upper transaxle mount and bracket, as an assembly. Tighten the mount nuts to 23 ft. lbs. (31 Nm) and the bolts to 38 ft. lbs. (52 Nm).
53. Remove the engine support fixture.
54. Attach the fluid line to the clutch slave cylinder.
55. Install the top two upper transaxle bolt, then tighten to 55 ft. lbs. (75 Nm).
56. Fasten the exhaust crossover pipe.
57. Attach the transaxle vent tube to the transaxle.
58. Fasten the back-up light switch and VSS electrical connectors.
59. Install the transaxle shift cable bracket, then snap on the shift cables.
60. Fasten the exhaust crossover pipe.
61. Install the air cleaner bracket and assembly.
62. Install the left sound insulator, then connect the clutch master cylinder pushrod to the clutch pedal.
63. Connect the negative battery cable.
64. Fill the transaxle with GM fluid 123455349, or equivalent.

ISUZU TRANSAXLE

▶ See Figures 18 and 19

1. Disconnect the negative battery cable.
2. Install an engine holding support fixture (bar), J-28467-A or equivalent and raise the engine enough to take the pressure off the motor mounts.
3. Remove the left sound insulator.

4. Disconnect the clutch master cylinder pushrod from the clutch pedal.
5. Remove the clutch actuator cylinder from the transaxle support bracket and lay it aside.
6. Disconnect the wire harness at the mount bracket.
7. Unfasten the transaxle mount attaching bolts.
8. Remove the transaxle mount bracket attaching bolts and nuts.
9. Remove the shift cables and retaining clamp at the transaxle.
10. Detach the ground cables at the transaxle mounting studs.
11. Detach the back-up switch connector.
12. Raise and support the vehicle safely.
13. Drain the transaxle.
14. Remove the left front wheel assembly.
15. Detach the left front inner splash shield.
16. Remove the transaxle front strut and bracket.
17. Unfasten the clutch housing cover bolts.
18. Detach the Vehicle Speed Sensor (VSS) electrical connector at the transaxle.
19. Unfasten the left and right drive axle nuts and the left and right ball joint nuts.
20. Unfasten the left and right stabilizer links.
21. Remove the drive axles (halfshafts).
22. Unfasten the left side U-bolt and remove it from the stabilizer bar.
23. Remove the left suspension support attaching bolts and swing the suspension support aside.
24. Attach the transaxle case to a suitable jack.
25. Unfasten the transaxle-to-engine bolts.
26. Remove the transaxle by sliding it away from the engine and carefully lowering the jack.

To install:
27. Reposition the transaxle, then install the transaxle to engine mounting bolts and tighten to 55 ft. lbs (75 Nm).
28. Install the flywheel housing cover, then tighten the retaining bolts to 89 inch lbs. (10 Nm).
29. Install the left suspension support and secure with the attaching bolts.
30. Fasten the left U-bolt to the stabilizer bar.

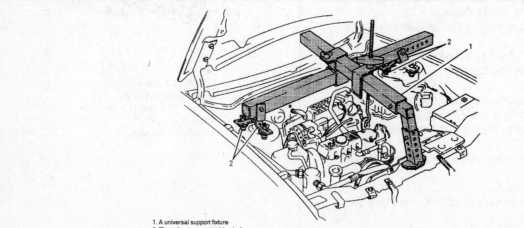

1. A universal support fixture
2. Thread onto strut attaching bolts above nuts, 2 per side

87957021

Fig. 18 Installation of the engine support fixture — 1994 2.0L engine shown

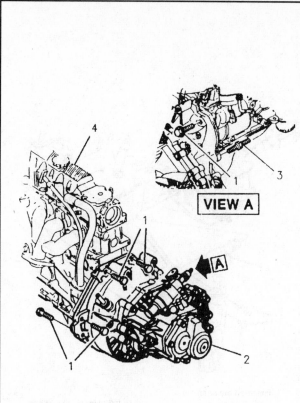

1. Bolt
2. Transaxle assembly
3. Stud
4. Engine assembly

87957023

Fig. 19 Isuzu transaxle mounting — 1994 2.0L engine shown

31. Install the left and right drive axles (halfshafts). Fasten the left and right drive axle, ball joint and stabilizer link nuts.
32. Attach the vehicle speed sensor connector at the transaxle.
33. Instal the front strut bracket to the transaxle. Tighten the bracket bolts to 38 ft. lbs. (52 Nm). Install the front strut. Tighten the mounting bolt and nut to 38 ft. lbs. (52 Nm).
34. Install the inner splash shield.
35. Install the wheel and tire assembly, then tighten the wheel nuts to 100 ft. lbs. (136 Nm).
36. Carefully lower the vehicle.
37. Fasten the ground cables at the transaxle mounting studs.
38. Attach the back-up switch connector.
39. Install the actuator cylinder to the transaxle bracket aligning the pushrod into the pocket of the clutch release lever and install the retaining nuts and tighten evenly to prevent damage to the cylinder.

40. Fasten the transaxle mount bracket. Tighten the bracket-to-transaxle mounting bolts to 55 ft. lbs. (75 Nm). Tighten the bracket-to-clutch cylinder support bolts to 38 ft. lbs. (52 Nm).
41. Install the transaxle mount-to-side frame and install the bolts. Tighten the mount nuts to 23 ft. lbs. (31 Nm) and the bolt to 38 ft. lbs. (52 Nm).
42. Attach the wiring harness at the transaxle mount bracket.
43. Install the bolt attaching the mount to the transaxle bracket and tighten to 83 ft. lbs. (113 Nm).
44. Remove the engine holding support fixture (bar), J-28467-A or equivalent.
45. Install the shift cables, clamp and nut. Tighten the nut to 89 inch lbs. (10 Nm).
46. Attach the clutch pushrod to the clutch pedal.
47. Install the left sound insulator.
48. Connect the negative battery cable.
49. Fill the transaxle with GM fluid 123455349, or equivalent.

Intermediate shaft

REMOVAL & INSTALLATION

2.8L and 3.1L Engines

1987 VEHICLES
▶ See Figure 20

1. Install engine support bar J-28467.
2. Raise and safely support the vehicle.
3. Remove the wheel and tire assembly.
4. Drain the transaxle.
5. Install the modified outer seal protector J-34754 or equivalent.
6. Remove the stabilizer shaft from the right control arm.
7. Separate the right ball joint from the steering knuckle.
8. Disconnect the drive axle (halfshaft) from the intermediate axle shaft.
9. Unfasten the two housing-to-bracket bolts.
10. Remove the bottom bracket-to-engine bolt and loosen the top bolt, then rotate the bracket out of the way.
11. Unfasten the 3 bolts holding the housing to transaxle.
12. Carefully disengage the intermediate axle shaft from the transaxle, then remove the intermediate shaft assembly.
To install:
13. Place the intermediate shaft into position and lock the intermediate axle shaft into the transaxle.
14. Install the 3 bolts holding the housing to the transaxle and tighten to 18 ft. lbs. (24 Nm).
15. Rotate the bracket into position and install the bottom bolt, then tighten both bolts to 37 ft. lbs. (50 Nm).
16. Install the two housing to bracket bolts and tighten to 37 ft. lbs. (50 Nm).
17. Coat the splines with chassis grease.
18. Connect the drive axle to the intermediate axle shaft.
19. Fasten the right ball joint to the knuckle.
20. Install the stabilizer shaft to the right control arm.
21. Install the wheel and tire assembly.
22. Carefully the car, then fill the transaxle with the proper fluid.

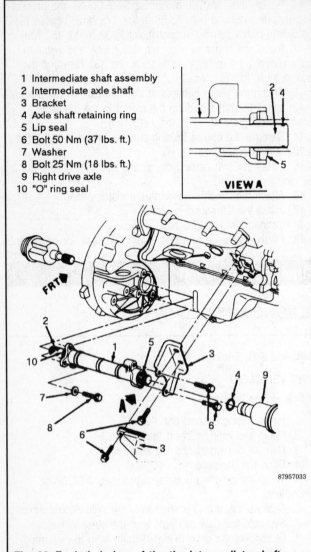

1 Intermediate shaft assembly
2 Intermediate axle shaft
3 Bracket
4 Axle shaft retaining ring
5 Lip seal
6 Bolt 50 Nm (37 lbs. ft.)
7 Washer
8 Bolt 25 Nm (18 lbs. ft.)
9 Right drive axle
10 "O" ring seal

VIEW A

87957033

Fig. 20 Exploded view of the the intermediate shaft removal — 1987 2.8L engine shown

1988-94 VEHICLES

◆ **See Figures 21, 22 and 23**

1. Install engine support bar J-28467 or equivalent.
2. Raise and safely support the vehicle.
3. Remove the right wheel and tire assembly.
4. Install the modified outer seal protector J-34754 or place shop towels underneath the outer joint to protect it from any sharp edges.
5. Remove the stabilizer shaft from the right control arm.
6. Remove the right ball joint from the knuckle.
7. For 1992-94 vehicles, remove the rear engine mount through-bolt.
8. Disconnect the drive axle from the intermediate axle shaft.
9. For 1988-91 vehicles, remove the rear engine mount.
10. Remove the bolt(s) retaining the intermediate shaft to the engine.
11. Carefully disengage the intermediate axle shaft from the transaxle and remove the intermediate shaft assembly.

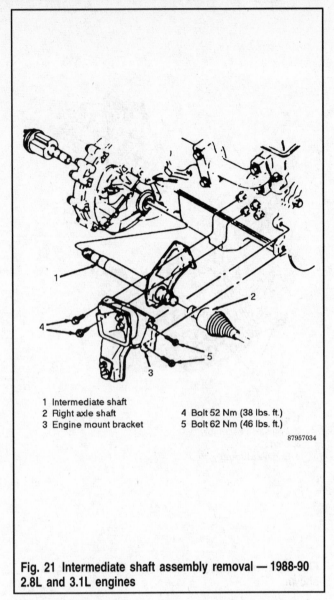

1 Intermediate shaft
2 Right axle shaft
3 Engine mount bracket
4 Bolt 52 Nm (38 lbs. ft.)
5 Bolt 62 Nm (46 lbs. ft.)

87957034

Fig. 21 Intermediate shaft assembly removal — 1988-90 2.8L and 3.1L engines

To install:

12. Place the intermediate shaft assembly into position and lock the intermediate axle shaft into the transaxle.
13. Install the bolt retaining the intermediate shaft to the engine and tighten to 38 ft. lbs. (52 Nm).
14. For 1988-91 vehicles, install the rear engine mount.
15. Coat the intermediate axle shaft with chassis grease and install the intermediate axle shaft to the drive axle.
16. For 1992-94 vehicles, install the rear engine mount through-bolt.
17. Fasten the right ball joint to the knuckle.
18. Install the stabilizer shaft to the right control arm.
19. Remove the seal protector tool or shop towels, as applicable.
20. Install the wheel and tire assembly, then carefully lower the vehicle.
21. Remove the engine support bar holding fixture.
22. Fill the transaxle with the proper fluid.

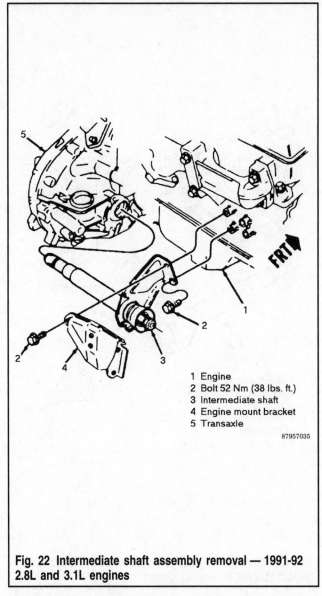

1 Engine
2 Bolt 52 Nm (38 lbs. ft.)
3 Intermediate shaft
4 Engine mount bracket
5 Transaxle

87957035

Fig. 22 Intermediate shaft assembly removal — 1991-92 2.8L and 3.1L engines

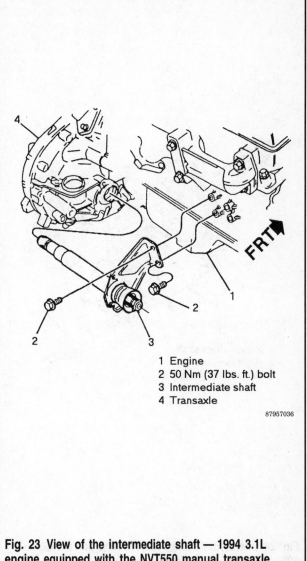

1 Engine
2 50 Nm (37 lbs. ft.) bolt
3 Intermediate shaft
4 Transaxle

87957036

Fig. 23 View of the intermediate shaft — 1994 3.1L engine equipped with the NVT550 manual transaxle

2.0L (VIN M and H), 2.3L (VIN D) and 2.4L (VIN T) Engines

1987 VEHICLES

▶ **See Figure 24**

1. Raise and safely support the vehicle.
2. Remove the wheel and tire assembly.
3. Remove the stabilizer shaft from the right control arm.
4. Using tool J 29330, or equivalent, separate the right ball joint from the knuckle.
5. Disconnect the drive axle from the intermediate axle shaft.
6. Detach the detonation sensor and connection.
7. Remove the power steering pump brace.
8. Unfasten the 3 intermediate shaft bracket bolts, then remove the intermediate shaft from the vehicle.

To install:

9. Install intermediate shaft, secure using the 3 bolts, then tighten the bolts to 35 ft. lbs. (47 Nm).
10. Install the power steering pump brace.
11. Install the detonation sensor.

12. Coat the splines of the intermediate shaft with chassis grease.
13. Attach the drive axle to the intermediate axle shaft.
14. Connect the right ball joint to the knuckle. Tighten to 45 ft. lbs. (60 Nm) and install a new cotter pin.
15. Install the stabilizer shaft to the right control arm.
16. Install the wheel and tire assembly.
17. Carefully lower the vehicles.

1988-90 VEHICLES

▶ **See Figure 25**

1. Raise and safely support the vehicle.
2. Remove the right wheel and tire assembly.
3. Drain the transaxle.
4. Install the modified outer seal protector J-34754.
5. Remove the stabilizer shaft from the right control arm.
6. Separate the right ball joint from the knuckle.
7. Disconnect the drive axle from the intermediate axle shaft.

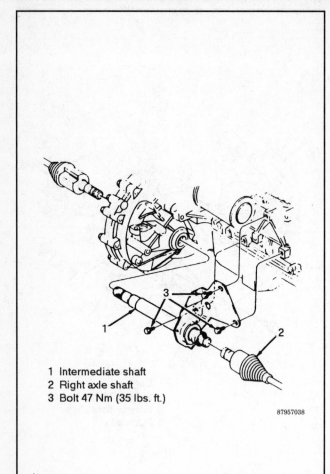

1 Intermediate shaft
2 Right axle shaft
3 Bolt 47 Nm (35 lbs. ft.)

87957038

**Fig. 24 Intermediate shaft removal and installation —
1987 2.0L (VIN M) engine shown**

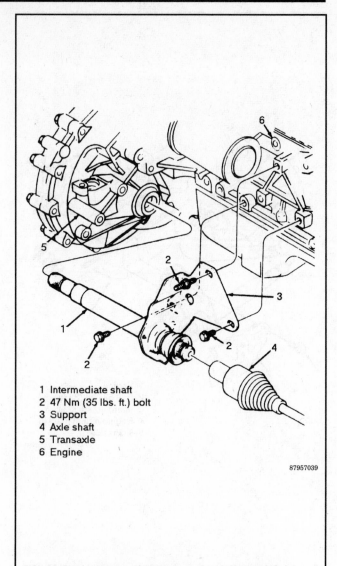

1 Intermediate shaft
2 47 Nm (35 lbs. ft.) bolt
3 Support
4 Axle shaft
5 Transaxle
6 Engine

87957039

**Fig. 25 Intermediate shaft removal and installation —
1990 2.0L (VIN M) engine shown**

8. Unfasten the bracket-to-engine bolts and the stud, then carefully disengage the intermediate axle shaft from the transaxle and remove the assembly.

To install:

9. Place the intermediate shaft into position and lock the intermediate axle shaft into the transaxle.

10. Install the bracket to engine bolts and one stud and tighten to 35 ft. lbs. (47 Nm).

11. Coat the splines of the intermediate shaft with chassis grease.

12. Attach the drive axle to the intermediate axle shaft.

13. Fasten the right ball joint to the knuckle.

14. Install the stabilizer shaft to the right control arm.

15. Install the wheel and tire assembly.

16. Carefully lower the car and fill the transaxle with the proper fluid.

1991-96 VEHICLES

▶ **See Figure 26**

1. Install engine support bar J-28467 or equivalent.
2. Raise and safely support the vehicle.

3. Remove the right wheel and tire assembly.

4. Install the modified outer seal protector J-34754 or place shop towels underneath the outer joint to protect it from any sharp edges.

5. Remove the stabilizer shaft from the right control arm.

6. Remove the right ball joint from the knuckle.

7. Remove the rear engine mount through-bolt.

8. Disconnect the drive axle from the intermediate axle shaft.

9. Remove the bolt(s) retaining the intermediate shaft to the engine.

10. Carefully disengage the intermediate axle shaft from the transaxle and remove the intermediate shaft assembly.

To install:

11. Place the intermediate shaft assembly into position and lock the intermediate axle shaft into the transaxle.

12. Install the bolt retaining the intermediate shaft to the engine and tighten to 38 ft. lbs. (52 Nm).

13. Coat the intermediate axle shaft with chassis grease and install the intermediate axle shaft to the drive axle.

14. Install the rear engine mount through-bolt.

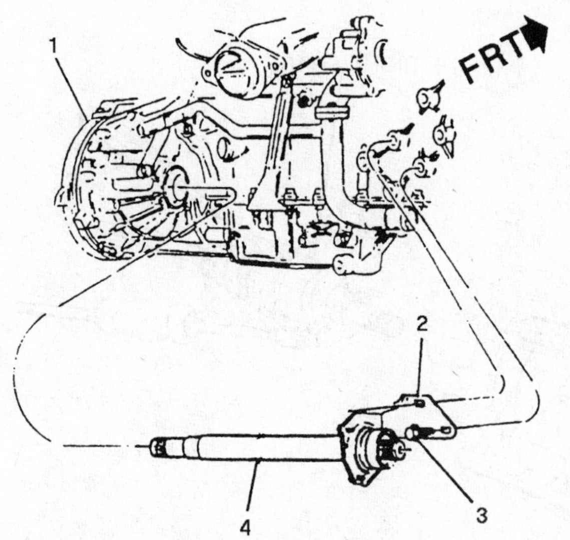

Fig. 26 View of the intermediate shaft — 1994 2.0L engine equipped with the Isuzu manual transaxle

1 Transaxle
2 Intermediate shaft support bracket
3 Bolt
4 Intermediate shaft

87957037

15. Fasten the right ball joint to the knuckle.

16. Install the stabilizer shaft to the right control arm.

17. Remove the seal protector tool or shop towels, as applicable.

18. Install the wheel and tire assembly, then carefully lower the vehicle.

19. Remove the engine support bar holding fixture.

20. Fill the transaxle with the proper fluid.

Drive Axles (Halfshafts)

Halfshafts are flexible assemblies consisting of an inner and outer Constant Velocity (CV) joint connected by an axle shaft.

These vehicles use unequal-length halfshafts. All halfshafts incorporate a male spline; the shafts interlock with the transaxle gears through the use of barrel-type snaprings. Four constant velocity joints are used, two on each shaft. The inner joints are of the double offset design; the outer joints are Rzeppa-type.

REMOVAL & INSTALLATION

1982-86 Vehicles
▶ See Figure 27

1. Remove the hub nut.

2. Raise and safely support the front of the car. Remove the wheel and tire assemblies.

3. Install an axle shaft boot seal protector, G.M. special tool No. J-28712 or the equivalent, onto the outer seal and install J-33162, or equivalent, on the inner seal.

4. Disconnect the brake hose clip from the MacPherson strut, but do not disconnect the hose from the caliper. Remove the brake caliper from the spindle, and hang the caliper out of the way by a length of wire. Do not allow the caliper to hang by the brake hose.

5. Mark the camber alignment cam bolt for reassembly. Remove the cam bolt and the upper attaching bolt from the strut and spindle.

6. Pull the steering knuckle assembly from the strut bracket.

7. Using G.M. special tool J-28468 or the equivalent, remove the axle shaft from the transaxle.

8. Using G.M. special tool J-28733 or the equivalent spindle remover, remove the axle shaft from the hub and bearing assembly.

9. If a new drive axle is to be installed, a new knuckle seal should be installed first.

To install:

10. Loosely install the drive axle into the transaxle and steering knuckle.

11. Loosely attach the steering knuckle to the suspension strut.

12. Install the brake caliper. Tighten the bolts to 30 ft. lbs. (40 Nm).

13. The drive axle is an interference fit in the steering knuckle. Press the axle into place, then install the hub nut. When the shaft begins to turn with the hub, insert a drift through the caliper into one of the cooling slots in the rotor to keep it from turning. Tighten the hub nut to 70 ft. lbs. (100 Nm). to completely seat the shaft.

14. Load the hub assembly by lowering it onto a jackstand. Align the camber cam bolt marks made during removal, install the bolt and tighten to 140 ft. lbs. (190 Nm). Tighten the upper nut to the same value.

15. Install the axle shaft all the way into the transaxle using a screwdriver inserted into the groove provided on the inner retainer. Tap the screwdriver until the shaft seats in the transaxle.

16. Connect the brake hose clip to the strut.

17. Install the tire and wheel, the carefully lower the car and tighten the hub nut to 185 ft. lbs. (260 Nm).

1987-88 Vehicles
▶ See Figures 28 and 29

1. Raise and safely support the vehicle.

2. If necessary, remove the hub cap, then remove the tire and wheel assembly.

3. Insert a drift into the into the caliper and rotor to prevent the rotor from turning, then unfasten the shaft nut and washer.

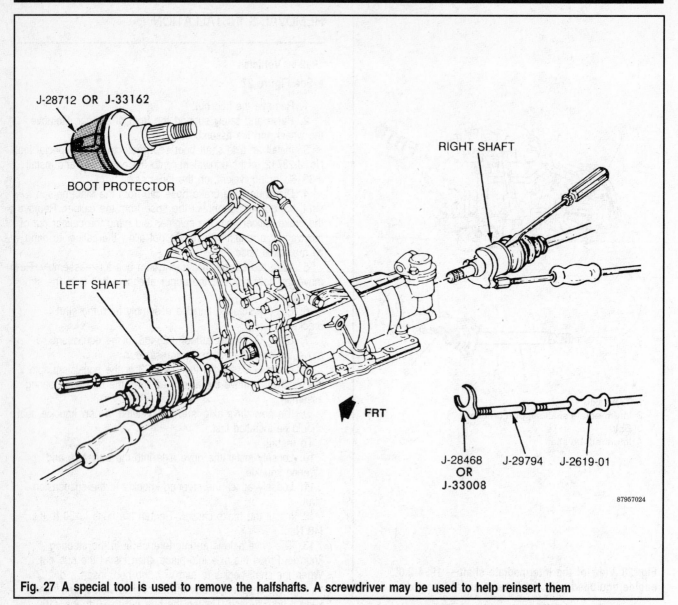

J-28712 OR J-33162

BOOT PROTECTOR

LEFT SHAFT

RIGHT SHAFT

FRT

J-28468
OR
J-33008

J-29794

J-2619-01

87957024

Fig. 27 A special tool is used to remove the halfshafts. A screwdriver may be used to help reinsert them

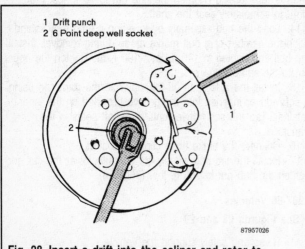

1 Drift punch
2 6 Point deep well socket

2

1

87957026

Fig. 28 Insert a drift into the caliper and rotor to prevent the rotor from turning while removing the shaft nut and washer

4. Remove the caliper from the steering knuckle and suspend the caliper assembly with a wire.

5. Remove the rotor from the hub and bearing assembly.

6. Disconnect the stabilizer shaft from the control arm.

7. Remove the ball joint from the steering knuckle.

8. Remove the drive axle from the transaxle.

9. Remove the drive axle from the hub and bearing assembly using tool J-28733 or equivalent.

To install:

10. Install the drive axle into the hub and bearing assembly and the transaxle.

11. Install the lower ball joint to the steering knuckle.

12. Install the stabilizer shaft to the control arm.

13. Install the rotor to the hub and bearing assembly.

14. Install the caliper to the steering knuckle.

15. Install a washer and a new shaft nut.

16. Insert a drift into the into the caliper and rotor to prevent the rotor from turning and torque drive axle nut to 185 ft. lbs. (260 Nm).

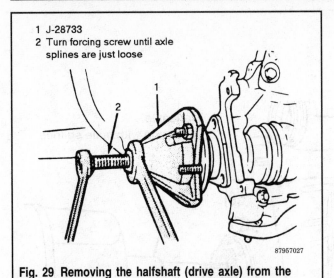

1 J-28733
2 Turn forcing screw until axle splines are just loose

87957027

Fig. 29 Removing the halfshaft (drive axle) from the hub and bearing requires the use of a special tool

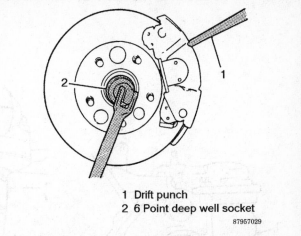

1 Drift punch
2 6 Point deep well socket

87957029

Fig. 30 Before removing the shaft nut and washer, insert a drift into the caliper and rotor to prevent the rotor from turning

17. Seat the drive axle into the transaxle by placing a screwdriver into the groove on the joint housing and tapping until seated.

18. Verify that the drive axle is seated into the transaxle by grasping on the housing and pulling outward.

19. Install the wheel assembly.

20. Lower the car.

1989-96 Vehicles

▶ See Figures 30, 31 and 32

1. Disconnect the negative battery cable.
2. Raise and safely support the vehicle.
3. Remove the tire and wheel assembly.
4. Install drive seal protector J-34754 on the outer joint, or place shop towels underneath the outer joint to protect from any sharp edges.
5. Insert a drift into the into the caliper and rotor to prevent the rotor from turning, then unfasten the shaft nut and washer.

➡Use only the recommended tools for separating the ball joint from the steering knuckle or damage to the ball joint and seal may occur.

6. Remove the lower ball joint cotter pin and nut and loosen the joint using tool J-38892, or equivalent. If removing the right axle, turn the wheel to the left, if removing the left axle, turn the wheel to the right.

7. If equipped with ABS, detach the ABS sensor wire.

8. For vehicles through 1994, separate the joint, with a pry bar between the suspension support.

9. For 1995-96 vehicles, disconnect the stabilizer link, then separate the joint using tool J 38892 or equivalent.

10. Disengage the axle from the hub and bearing using J 28733-A or equivalent.

11. Separate the hub and bearing assembly from the drive axle and move the strut and knuckle assembly rearward.

12. Disconnect the inner joint from the transaxle using tool J-28468 or J-33008 attached to J-29794 and J-2619-01 or from the intermediate shaft (V6 and Turbo engines), if equipped.

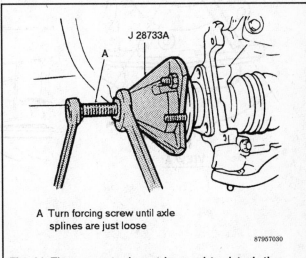

J 28733A

A Turn forcing screw until axle splines are just loose

87957030

Fig. 31 The proper tool must be used to detach the axle from the hub and bearing

To install:

➡Before installing the halfshaft (drive axle) assembly, cover all sharp edges in the area of the halfshaft with shop towels so the seal is not damaged during installation.

13. Install axle seal protector J-37292-A into the transaxle.

14. Insert the drive axle into the transaxle or intermediate shaft (V6 and Turbo engines), if equipped, by placing a suitable tool into the groove on the joint housing and tapping until seated.

✳✳WARNING

Be careful not to damage the axle seal or dislodge the transaxle seal garter spring when installing the axle.

15. Verify that the drive axle is seated into the transaxle by grasping on the housing and pulling outward.

16. Install the drive axle into the hub and bearing assembly.

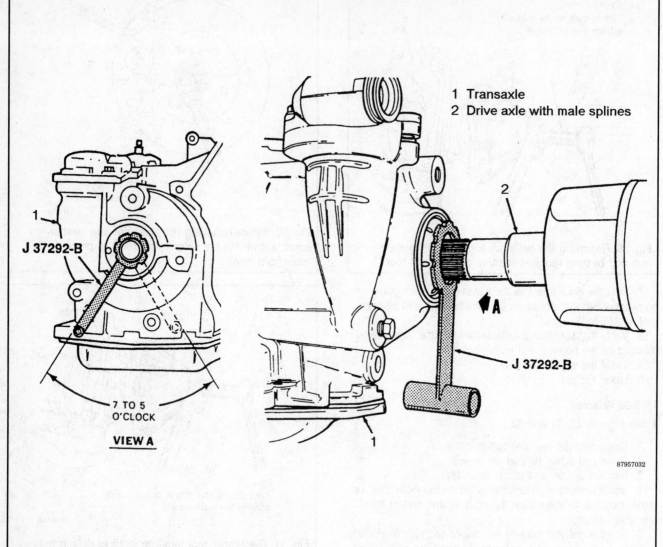

1 Transaxle
2 Drive axle with male splines

J 37292-B

7 TO 5 O'CLOCK

VIEW A

J 37292-B

87957032

Fig. 32 Correct installation of the transaxle seal protector

17. Fasten the lower ball joint to the knuckle. Tighten the ball joint-to-steering knuckle nut to 41-50 ft. lbs. (55-65 Nm) and install a new cotter pin.

18. Install the washer and new drive shaft nut.

19. Insert a drift into the caliper and rotor to prevent the rotor from turning and tighten the drive shaft to 185 ft. lbs. (260 Nm).

20. Remove both J-37292-B and J-34754 seal protectors.

21. Install the tire and wheel assembly.

22. Carefully lower the vehicle and connect the negative battery cable.

CV-JOINT OVERHAUL

1982-85 Double Off-Set and 1982-90 Tri-Pot Design
▶ **See Figures 33, 34, 35, 36, 37, 38, 39, 40, 41, 42, 43, 44, 45, 46, 47, 48, 49, 50, 51, 52, 53 and 54**

For all overhaul procedures for the 1982-85 Double Off-Set type and 1982-90 Tri-Pot type drive axles, please refer to the accompanying figures.

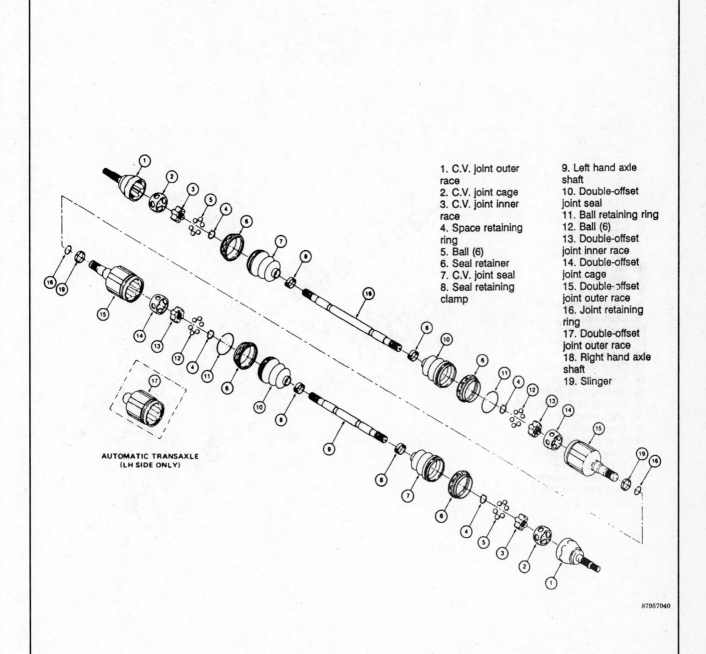

1. C.V. joint outer race
2. C.V. joint cage
3. C.V. joint inner race
4. Space retaining ring
5. Ball (6)
6. Seal retainer
7. C.V. joint seal
8. Seal retaining clamp
9. Left hand axle shaft
10. Double-offset joint seal
11. Ball retaining ring
12. Ball (6)
13. Double-offset joint inner race
14. Double-offset joint cage
15. Double-offset joint outer race
16. Joint retaining ring
17. Double-offset joint outer race
18. Right hand axle shaft
19. Slinger

AUTOMATIC TRANSAXLE
(LH SIDE ONLY)

87957040

Fig. 33 Exploded view of the Double Off-Set design drive axle (halfshaft) — 1982-84 Vehicles

1. Race, c.v. joint outer
2. Cage, c.v. joint
3. Race, c.v. joint inner
4. Ring, shaft retaining
5. Ball (6)
6. Retainer, seal
7. Seal, c.v. joint
8. Clamp, seal retaining
9. Shaft, axle (LH)
10. Seal, tri-pot joint
11. Spider, tri-pot joint
12. Roller, needle
13. Ball, tri-pot joint (3)
14. This no. not used
15. Housing assy, tri-pot (LH)
16. Housing assy, tri-pot (RH)
17. Shaft, axle (RH)
18. Ring, spacer
19. Ring, race retaining
20. Clamp, seal retaining
21. Retainer, needle
22. Ring, needle retainer
23. Ring, joint retaining

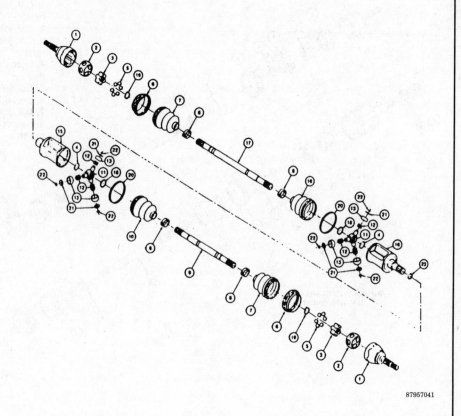

87957041

Fig. 34 Exploded view of the Tri-Pot design drive axle (halfshaft) — 1982-84 Vehicles

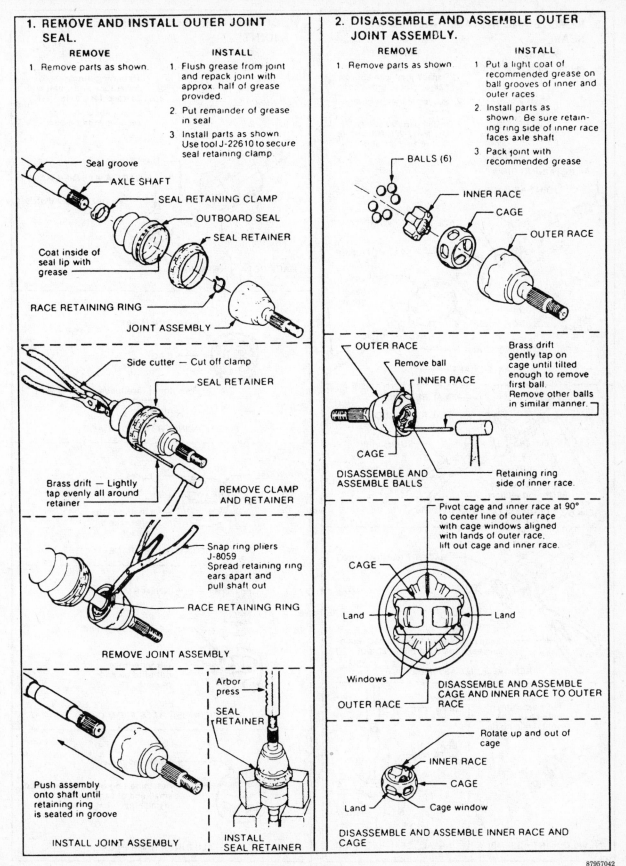

1. REMOVE AND INSTALL OUTER JOINT SEAL.

REMOVE	INSTALL
1. Remove parts as shown.	1. Flush grease from joint and repack joint with approx. half of grease provided.
	2. Put remainder of grease in seal
	3. Install parts as shown. Use tool J-22610 to secure seal retaining clamp.

Seal groove

AXLE SHAFT

SEAL RETAINING CLAMP

OUTBOARD SEAL

SEAL RETAINER

Coat inside of seal lip with grease

RACE RETAINING RING

JOINT ASSEMBLY

Side cutter — Cut off clamp

SEAL RETAINER

Brass drift — Lightly tap evenly all around retainer

REMOVE CLAMP AND RETAINER

Snap ring pliers J-8059 Spread retaining ring ears apart and pull shaft out

RACE RETAINING RING

REMOVE JOINT ASSEMBLY

Push assembly onto shaft until retaining ring is seated in groove

INSTALL JOINT ASSEMBLY

Arbor press

SEAL RETAINER

INSTALL SEAL RETAINER

2. DISASSEMBLE AND ASSEMBLE OUTER JOINT ASSEMBLY.

REMOVE	INSTALL
1. Remove parts as shown.	1. Put a light coat of recommended grease on ball grooves of inner and outer races.
	2. Install parts as shown. Be sure retaining ring side of inner race faces axle shaft.
	3. Pack joint with recommended grease

BALLS (6)

INNER RACE

CAGE

OUTER RACE

OUTER RACE

Remove ball

INNER RACE

Brass drift gently tap on cage until tilted enough to remove first ball. Remove other balls in similar manner.

CAGE

Retaining ring side of inner race.

DISASSEMBLE AND ASSEMBLE BALLS

Pivot cage and inner race at 90° to center line of outer race with cage windows aligned with lands of outer race. lift out cage and inner race.

CAGE

Land

Land

Windows

OUTER RACE

DISASSEMBLE AND ASSEMBLE CAGE AND INNER RACE TO OUTER RACE

Rotate up and out of cage

INNER RACE

CAGE

Land

Cage window

DISASSEMBLE AND ASSEMBLE INNER RACE AND CAGE

87957042

Fig. 35 Double Off-Set CV-joint overhaul (part 1 of 2) — 1982-84 Vehicles

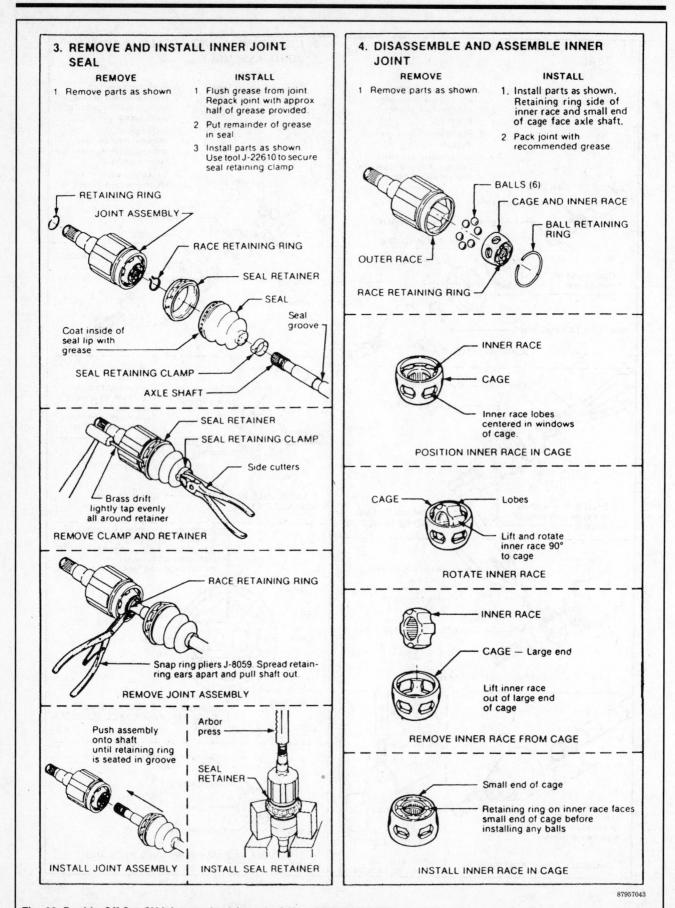

3. REMOVE AND INSTALL INNER JOINT SEAL

REMOVE

1. Remove parts as shown

INSTALL

1. Flush grease from joint. Repack joint with approx half of grease provided.
2. Put remainder of grease in seal.
3. Install parts as shown. Use tool J-22610 to secure seal retaining clamp

RETAINING RING
JOINT ASSEMBLY
RACE RETAINING RING
SEAL RETAINER
SEAL
Seal groove
Coat inside of seal lip with grease
SEAL RETAINING CLAMP
AXLE SHAFT

SEAL RETAINER
SEAL RETAINING CLAMP
Side cutters
Brass drift lightly tap evenly all around retainer

REMOVE CLAMP AND RETAINER

RACE RETAINING RING
Snap ring pliers J-8059. Spread retaining-ring ears apart and pull shaft out.

REMOVE JOINT ASSEMBLY

Push assembly onto shaft until retaining ring is seated in groove

Arbor press
SEAL RETAINER

INSTALL JOINT ASSEMBLY | **INSTALL SEAL RETAINER**

4. DISASSEMBLE AND ASSEMBLE INNER JOINT

REMOVE

1. Remove parts as shown.

INSTALL

1. Install parts as shown. Retaining ring side of inner race and small end of cage face axle shaft.
2. Pack joint with recommended grease.

BALLS (6)
CAGE AND INNER RACE
BALL RETAINING RING
OUTER RACE
RACE RETAINING RING

INNER RACE
CAGE
Inner race lobes centered in windows of cage.

POSITION INNER RACE IN CAGE

CAGE
Lobes
Lift and rotate inner race 90° to cage

ROTATE INNER RACE

INNER RACE
CAGE — Large end
Lift inner race out of large end of cage

REMOVE INNER RACE FROM CAGE

Small end of cage
Retaining ring on inner race faces small end of cage before installing any balls

INSTALL INNER RACE IN CAGE

87957043

Fig. 36 Double Off-Set CV-joint overhaul (part 2 of 2) — 1982-84 Vehicles

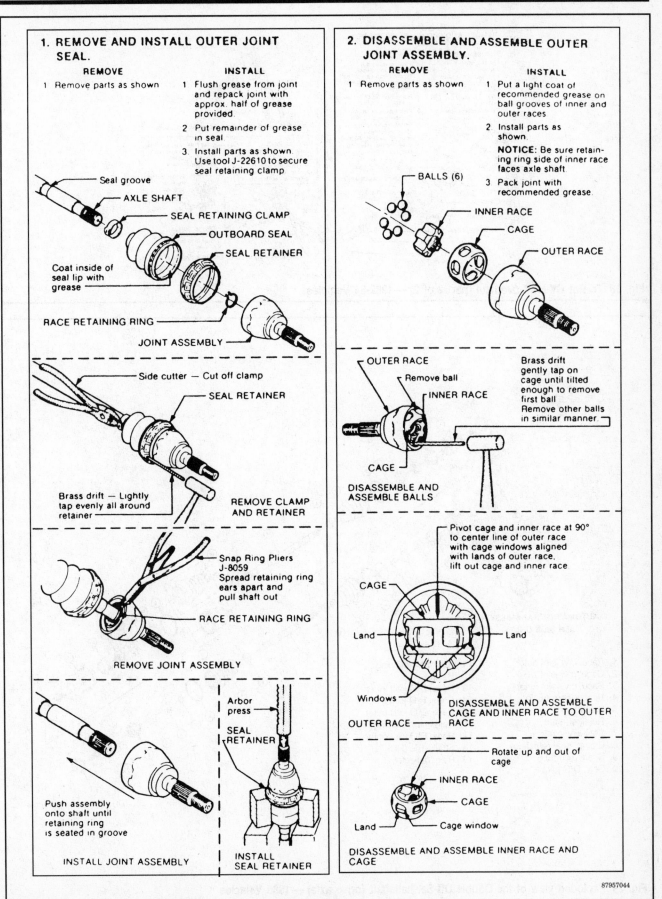

1. REMOVE AND INSTALL OUTER JOINT SEAL.

REMOVE

1 Remove parts as shown

INSTALL

1 Flush grease from joint and repack joint with approx. half of grease provided.

2 Put remainder of grease in seal

3 Install parts as shown. Use tool J-22610 to secure seal retaining clamp.

Seal groove

AXLE SHAFT

SEAL RETAINING CLAMP

OUTBOARD SEAL

SEAL RETAINER

Coat inside of seal lip with grease

RACE RETAINING RING

JOINT ASSEMBLY

Side cutter — Cut off clamp

SEAL RETAINER

Brass drift — Lightly tap evenly all around retainer

REMOVE CLAMP AND RETAINER

Snap Ring Pliers J-8059 Spread retaining ring ears apart and pull shaft out

RACE RETAINING RING

REMOVE JOINT ASSEMBLY

Push assembly onto shaft until retaining ring is seated in groove

INSTALL JOINT ASSEMBLY

Arbor press

SEAL RETAINER

INSTALL SEAL RETAINER

2. DISASSEMBLE AND ASSEMBLE OUTER JOINT ASSEMBLY.

REMOVE

1 Remove parts as shown

INSTALL

1 Put a light coat of recommended grease on ball grooves of inner and outer races

2 Install parts as shown.

NOTICE: Be sure retaining ring side of inner race faces axle shaft.

3 Pack joint with recommended grease.

BALLS (6)

INNER RACE

CAGE

OUTER RACE

OUTER RACE

Remove ball

INNER RACE

CAGE

Brass drift gently tap on cage until tilted enough to remove first ball Remove other balls in similar manner.

DISASSEMBLE AND ASSEMBLE BALLS

Pivot cage and inner race at 90° to center line of outer race with cage windows aligned with lands of outer race, lift out cage and inner race

CAGE

Land

Land

Windows

OUTER RACE

DISASSEMBLE AND ASSEMBLE CAGE AND INNER RACE TO OUTER RACE

Rotate up and out of cage

INNER RACE

CAGE

Land

Cage window

DISASSEMBLE AND ASSEMBLE INNER RACE AND CAGE

87957044

Fig. 37 Tri-Pot CV-joint overhaul (part 1 of 2) — 1982-84 Vehicles

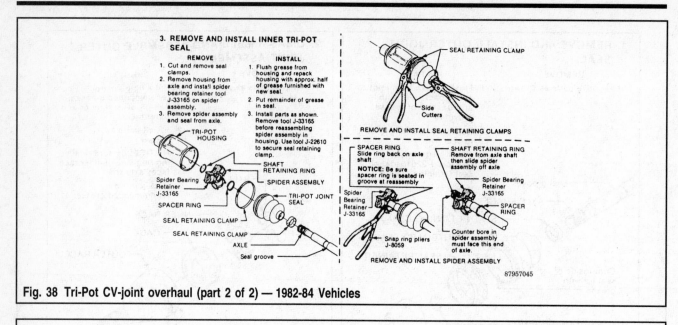

Fig. 38 Tri-Pot CV-joint overhaul (part 2 of 2) — 1982-84 Vehicles

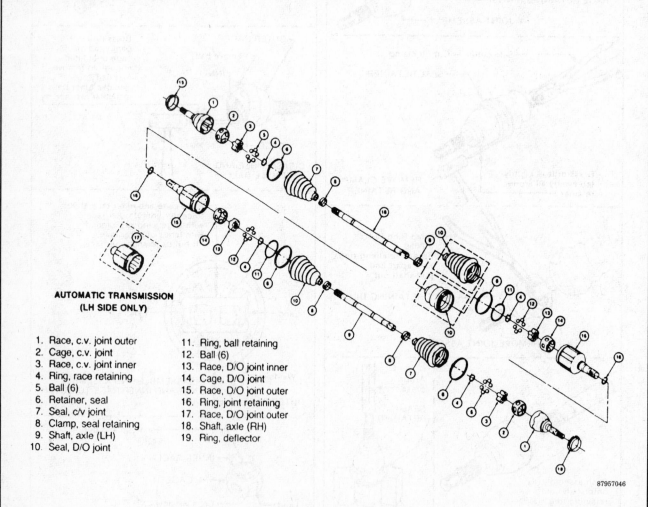

AUTOMATIC TRANSMISSION (LH SIDE ONLY)

1. Race, c.v. joint outer
2. Cage, c.v. joint
3. Race, c.v. joint inner
4. Ring, race retaining
5. Ball (6)
6. Retainer, seal
7. Seal, c/v joint
8. Clamp, seal retaining
9. Shaft, axle (LH)
10. Seal, D/O joint
11. Ring, ball retaining
12. Ball (6)
13. Race, D/O joint inner
14. Cage, D/O joint
15. Race, D/O joint outer
16. Ring, joint retaining
17. Race, D/O joint outer
18. Shaft, axle (RH)
19. Ring, deflector

Fig. 39 Exploded view of the Double Off-Set halfshaft (drive axle) — 1985 Vehicles

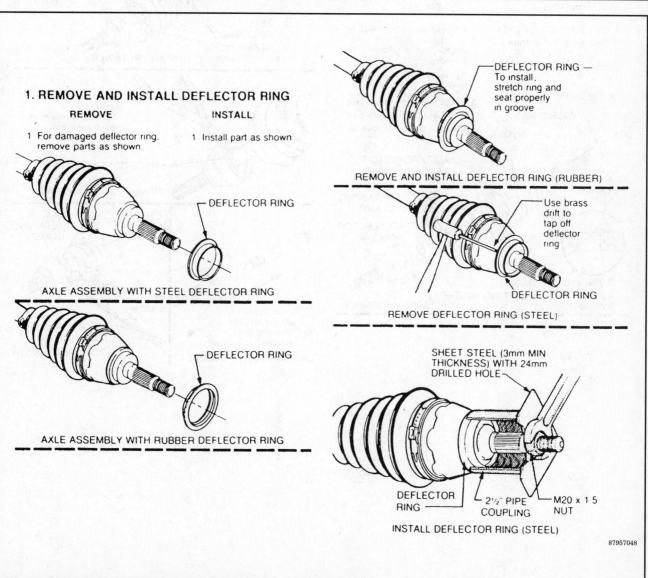

1. REMOVE AND INSTALL DEFLECTOR RING

REMOVE

1. Use brass drift to remove damaged deflector ring.

INSTALL

1. Install deflector ring as shown below.

SHEET STEEL (3mm MIN THICKNESS) WITH 24mm DRILLED HOLE

DEFLECTOR RING

2½" PIPE COUPLING

M20 x 1.5 NUT

DEFLECTOR RING

Install deflector ring

87957047

Fig. 40 Double Off-Set CV-joint overhaul (part 1 of 5) — 1985 Vehicles

1. REMOVE AND INSTALL DEFLECTOR RING

REMOVE

1 For damaged deflector ring, remove parts as shown.

INSTALL

1. Install part as shown

DEFLECTOR RING

AXLE ASSEMBLY WITH STEEL DEFLECTOR RING

DEFLECTOR RING

AXLE ASSEMBLY WITH RUBBER DEFLECTOR RING

DEFLECTOR RING — To install, stretch ring and seat properly in groove

REMOVE AND INSTALL DEFLECTOR RING (RUBBER)

Use brass drift to tap off deflector ring

DEFLECTOR RING

REMOVE DEFLECTOR RING (STEEL)

SHEET STEEL (3mm MIN THICKNESS) WITH 24mm DRILLED HOLE

DEFLECTOR RING

2½" PIPE COUPLING

M20 x 1.5 NUT

INSTALL DEFLECTOR RING (STEEL)

87957048

Fig. 41 Double Off-Set CV-joint overhaul (part 2 of 5) — 1985 Vehicles

2. REMOVE AND INSTALL OUTER JOINT SEAL

REMOVE

1. Cut seal retaining clamps.
2. Remove parts as shown.

INSTALL

1. Flush grease from joint and repack joint with approx. half of grease provided.
2. Put remainder of grease in seal.
3. Install parts as shown. Use tool J-34773 to secure seal retaining clamp. Torque to specifications.

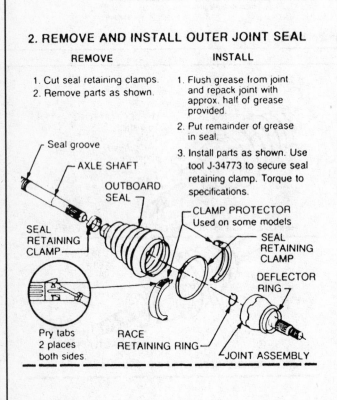

- Seal groove
- AXLE SHAFT
- OUTBOARD SEAL
- SEAL RETAINING CLAMP
- CLAMP PROTECTOR Used on some models
- SEAL RETAINING CLAMP
- DEFLECTOR RING
- RACE RETAINING RING
- JOINT ASSEMBLY

Pry tabs 2 places both sides.

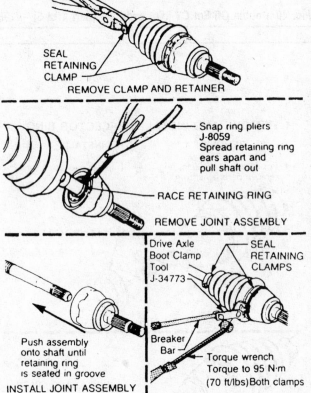

- Side cutter — Cut off clamp
- SEAL RETAINING CLAMP

REMOVE CLAMP AND RETAINER

- Snap ring pliers J-8059 Spread retaining ring ears apart and pull shaft out
- SEAL RETAINING CLAMP
- RACE RETAINING RING

REMOVE JOINT ASSEMBLY

Push assembly onto shaft until retaining ring is seated in groove

INSTALL JOINT ASSEMBLY

- Drive Axle Boot Clamp Tool J-34773
- SEAL RETAINING CLAMPS
- Breaker Bar
- Torque wrench Torque to 95 N·m (70 ft/lbs) Both clamps

87957049

Fig. 42 Double Off-Set CV-joint overhaul (part 3 of 5) — 1985 Vehicles

4. REMOVE AND INSTALL INNER JOINT SEAL

REMOVE

1. Cut seal retaining clamps
2. Remove parts as shown.

INSTALL

1. Flush grease from joint. Repack joint with approx. half of grease provided.

2. Put remainder of grease in seal.

3. Install parts as shown. Use tool J-34773 to secure seal retaining clamp. Torque to specifications.

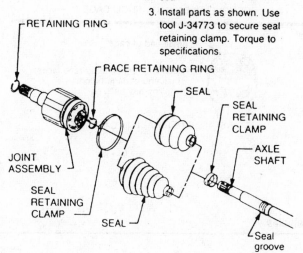

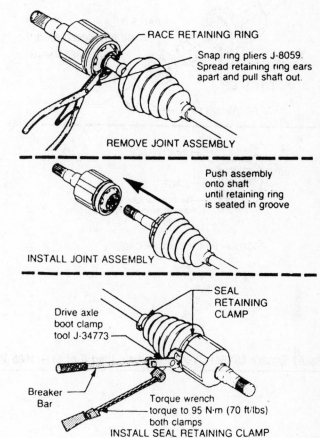

RACE RETAINING RING

Snap ring pliers J-8059. Spread retaining ring ears apart and pull shaft out.

REMOVE JOINT ASSEMBLY

Push assembly onto shaft until retaining ring is seated in groove

INSTALL JOINT ASSEMBLY

SEAL RETAINING CLAMP

Drive axle boot clamp tool J-34773

Breaker Bar

Torque wrench torque to 95 N·m (70 ft/lbs) both clamps

INSTALL SEAL RETAINING CLAMP

87957050

Fig. 43 Double Off-Set CV-joint overhaul (part 4 of 5) — 1985 Vehicles

5. DISASSEMBLE AND ASSEMBLE INNER JOINT

REMOVE

1. Remove parts as shown.

INSTALL

1. Install parts as shown.

   NOTICE: Retaining ring side of inner race and small end of cage face axle shaft.

2. Pack joint with recommended grease.

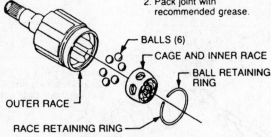

BALLS (6)

CAGE AND INNER RACE

BALL RETAINING RING

OUTER RACE

RACE RETAINING RING

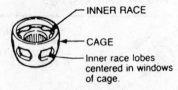

INNER RACE

CAGE

Inner race lobes centered in windows of cage.

POSITION INNER RACE IN CAGE

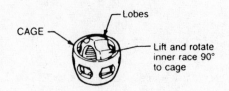

CAGE

Lobes

Lift and rotate inner race 90° to cage

ROTATE INNER RACE

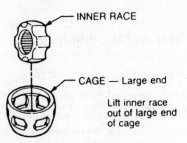

INNER RACE

CAGE — Large end

Lift inner race out of large end of cage

REMOVE INNER RACE FROM CAGE

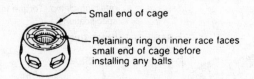

Small end of cage

Retaining ring on inner race faces small end of cage before installing any balls

INSTALL INNER RACE IN CAGE

87957051

Fig. 44 Double Off-Set CV-joint overhaul (part 5 of 5) — 1985 Vehicles

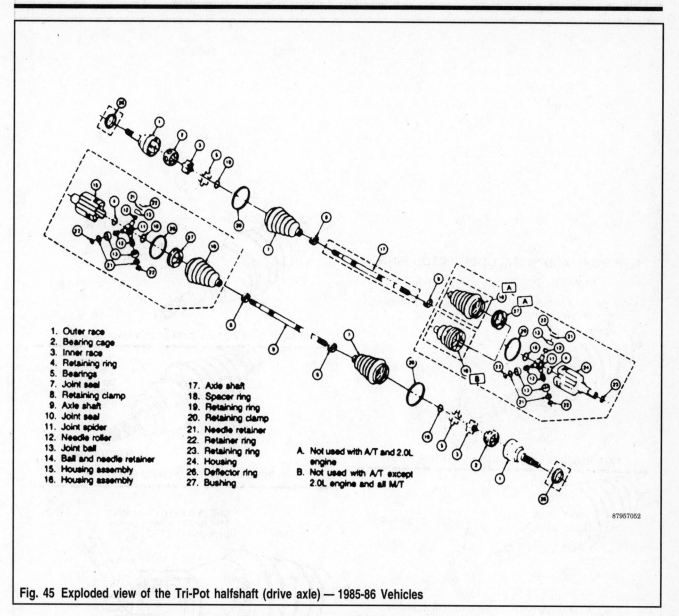

1. Outer race
2. Bearing cage
3. Inner race
4. Retaining ring
5. Bearings
7. Joint seal
8. Retaining clamp
9. Axle shaft
10. Joint seal
11. Joint spider
12. Needle roller
13. Joint ball
14. Ball and needle retainer
15. Housing assembly
16. Housing assembly
17. Axle shaft
18. Spacer ring
19. Retaining ring
20. Retaining clamp
21. Needle retainer
22. Retainer ring
23. Retaining ring
24. Housing
26. Deflector ring
27. Bushing

A. Not used with A/T and 2.0L engine
B. Not used with A/T except 2.0L engine and all M/T

87957052

Fig. 45 Exploded view of the Tri-Pot halfshaft (drive axle) — 1985-86 Vehicles

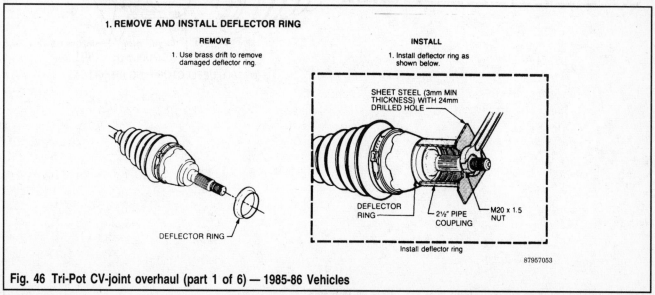

1. REMOVE AND INSTALL DEFLECTOR RING

REMOVE

1. Use brass drift to remove damaged deflector ring.

INSTALL

1. Install deflector ring as shown below.

SHEET STEEL (3mm MIN THICKNESS) WITH 24mm DRILLED HOLE

DEFLECTOR RING

2½" PIPE COUPLING

M20 x 1.5 NUT

Install deflector ring

DEFLECTOR RING

87957053

Fig. 46 Tri-Pot CV-joint overhaul (part 1 of 6) — 1985-86 Vehicles

1. REMOVE AND INSTALL DEFLECTOR RING

REMOVE

INSTALL

1. For damaged deflector ring, remove parts as shown.

1. Install part as shown.

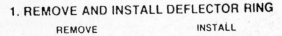

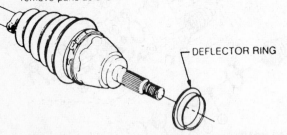

DEFLECTOR RING

AXLE ASSEMBLY WITH STEEL DEFLECTOR RING

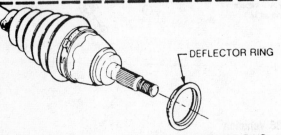

DEFLECTOR RING

AXLE ASSEMBLY WITH RUBBER DEFLECTOR RING

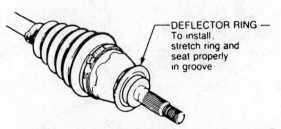

DEFLECTOR RING —
To install, stretch ring and seat properly in groove

REMOVE AND INSTALL DEFLECTOR RING (RUBBER)

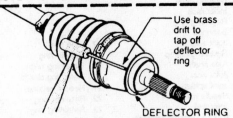

Use brass drift to tap off deflector ring

DEFLECTOR RING

REMOVE DEFLECTOR RING (STEEL)

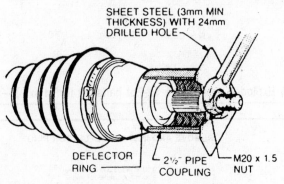

SHEET STEEL (3mm MIN THICKNESS) WITH 24mm DRILLED HOLE

DEFLECTOR RING

2½" PIPE COUPLING

M20 x 1.5 NUT

INSTALL DEFLECTOR RING (STEEL)

87957054

Fig. 47 Tri-Pot CV-joint overhaul (part 2 of 6) — 1985-86 Vehicles

2. REMOVE AND INSTALL OUTER JOINT SEAL

REMOVE

1. Cut seal retaining clamps.
2. Remove parts as shown.

INSTALL

1. Flush grease from joint and repack joint with approx. half of grease provided.
2. Put remainder of grease in seal.
3. Install parts as shown. Use tool J-34773 to secure seal retaining clamp. Torque to specifications.

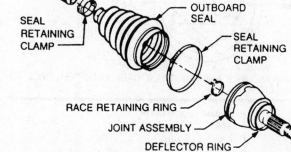

— Seal groove

— AXLE SHAFT

SEAL RETAINING CLAMP

— OUTBOARD SEAL

SEAL RETAINING CLAMP

RACE RETAINING RING —

JOINT ASSEMBLY —

DEFLECTOR RING —

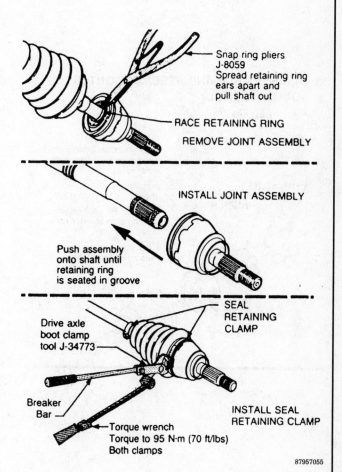

Snap ring pliers J-8059 Spread retaining ring ears apart and pull shaft out

— RACE RETAINING RING

REMOVE JOINT ASSEMBLY

INSTALL JOINT ASSEMBLY

Push assembly onto shaft until retaining ring is seated in groove

Drive axle boot clamp tool J-34773

SEAL RETAINING CLAMP

Breaker Bar

Torque wrench Torque to 95 N·m (70 ft/lbs) Both clamps

INSTALL SEAL RETAINING CLAMP

87957055

Fig. 48 Tri-Pot CV-joint overhaul (part 3 of 6) — 1985-86 Vehicles

3. DISASSEMBLE AND ASSEMBLE OUTER JOINT ASSEMBLY

REMOVE

1. Remove parts as shown.

INSTALL

1. Put a light coat of recommended grease on ball grooves of inner and outer races.

2. Install parts as shown.

   NOTICE: Be sure retaining ring side of inner race faces axle shaft.

3. Pack joint with recommended grease.

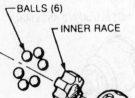

— BALLS (6)

— INNER RACE

CAGE

— OUTER RACE

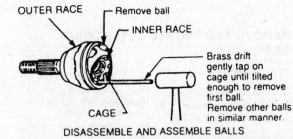

OUTER RACE — Remove ball

— INNER RACE

Brass drift gently tap on cage until tilted enough to remove first ball. Remove other balls in similar manner.

CAGE

DISASSEMBLE AND ASSEMBLE BALLS

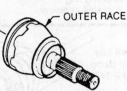

CAGE

Pivot cage and inner race at 90° to center line of outer race with cage windows aligned with lands of outer race, lift out cage and inner race.

Land

Land

Windows

OUTER RACE

DISASSEMBLE AND ASSEMBLE CAGE AND INNER RACE TO OUTER RACE

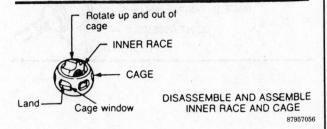

Rotate up and out of cage

— INNER RACE

— CAGE

Land —

Cage window

DISASSEMBLE AND ASSEMBLE INNER RACE AND CAGE

87957056

Fig. 49 Tri-Pot CV-joint overhaul (part 4 of 6) — 1985-86 Vehicles

4. REMOVE AND INSTALL INNER TRI-POT SEAL

REMOVE
1. Cut seal retaining clamps.
2. Remove parts as shown.

INSTALL
1. Flush grease from housing and repack housing with approx. half of grease furnished with new seal.
2. Put remainder of grease in seal.
3. Install parts as shown. Use tool J-34773 to secure seal retaining clamp. Torque to specifications.

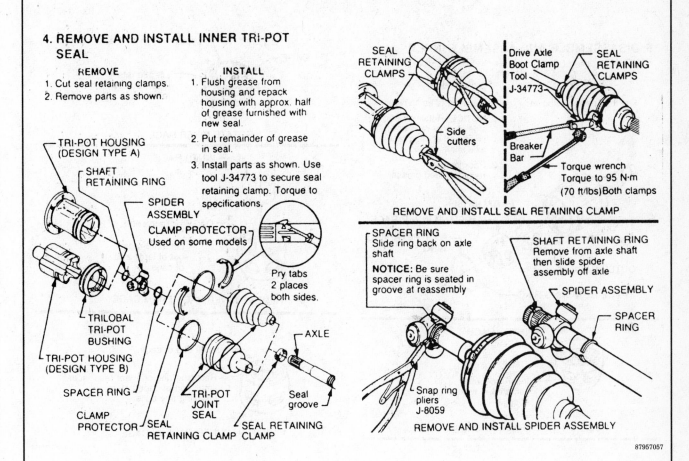

TRI-POT HOUSING (DESIGN TYPE A)

SHAFT RETAINING RING

SPIDER ASSEMBLY

CLAMP PROTECTOR — Used on some models

Pry tabs 2 places both sides.

TRILOBAL TRI-POT BUSHING

TRI-POT HOUSING (DESIGN TYPE B)

SPACER RING

CLAMP PROTECTOR

SEAL RETAINING CLAMP

TRI-POT JOINT SEAL

SEAL RETAINING CLAMP

AXLE

Seal groove

SEAL RETAINING CLAMPS

Side cutters

Drive Axle Boot Clamp Tool J-34773

SEAL RETAINING CLAMPS

Breaker Bar

Torque wrench Torque to 95 N·m (70 ft/lbs) Both clamps

REMOVE AND INSTALL SEAL RETAINING CLAMP

SPACER RING
Slide ring back on axle shaft

NOTICE: Be sure spacer ring is seated in groove at reassembly

Snap ring pliers J-8059

SHAFT RETAINING RING
Remove from axle shaft then slide spider assembly off axle

SPIDER ASSEMBLY

SPACER RING

REMOVE AND INSTALL SPIDER ASSEMBLY

87957057

Fig. 50 Tri-Pot CV-joint overhaul (part 5 of 6) — 1985-86 Vehicles

5. DISASSEMBLE AND ASSEMBLE INNER JOINT

REMOVE

1. Remove parts as shown.

INSTALL

1. Install parts as shown.

NOTICE: Retaining ring side of inner race and small end of cage face axle shaft.

2. Pack joint with recommended grease.

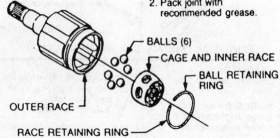

BALLS (6)
CAGE AND INNER RACE
BALL RETAINING RING
OUTER RACE
RACE RETAINING RING

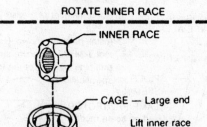

CAGE
Lobes
Lift and rotate inner race 90° to cage

ROTATE INNER RACE

INNER RACE
CAGE — Large end
Lift inner race out of large end of cage

REMOVE INNER RACE FROM CAGE

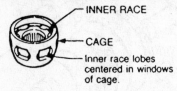

INNER RACE
CAGE
Inner race lobes centered in windows of cage.

POSITION INNER RACE IN CAGE

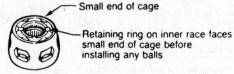

Small end of cage
Retaining ring on inner race faces small end of cage before installing any balls

INSTALL INNER RACE IN CAGE

87957058

Fig. 51 Tri-Pot CV-joint overhaul (part 6 of 6) — 1985-86 Vehicles

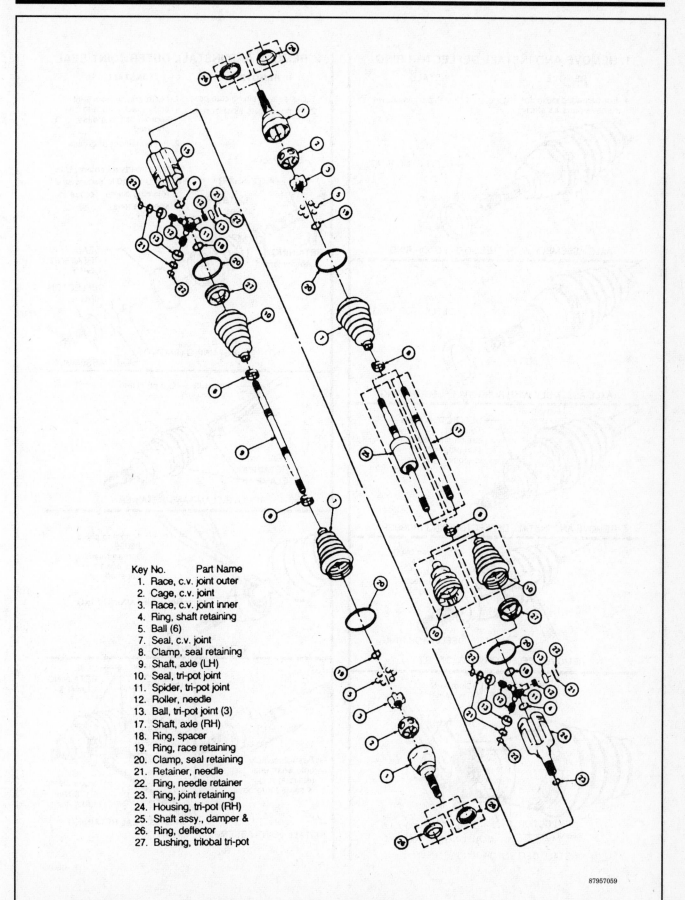

Key No.   Part Name
1. Race, c.v. joint outer
2. Cage, c.v. joint
3. Race, c.v. joint inner
4. Ring, shaft retaining
5. Ball (6)
7. Seal, c.v. joint
8. Clamp, seal retaining
9. Shaft, axle (LH)
10. Seal, tri-pot joint
11. Spider, tri-pot joint
12. Roller, needle
13. Ball, tri-pot joint (3)
17. Shaft, axle (RH)
18. Ring, spacer
19. Ring, race retaining
20. Clamp, seal retaining
21. Retainer, needle
22. Ring, needle retainer
23. Ring, joint retaining
24. Housing, tri-pot (RH)
25. Shaft assy., damper &
26. Ring, deflector
27. Bushing, trilobal tri-pot

87957059

Fig. 52 Exploded view of the Tri-Pot halfshaft (drive axle) — 1987-90 Vehicles

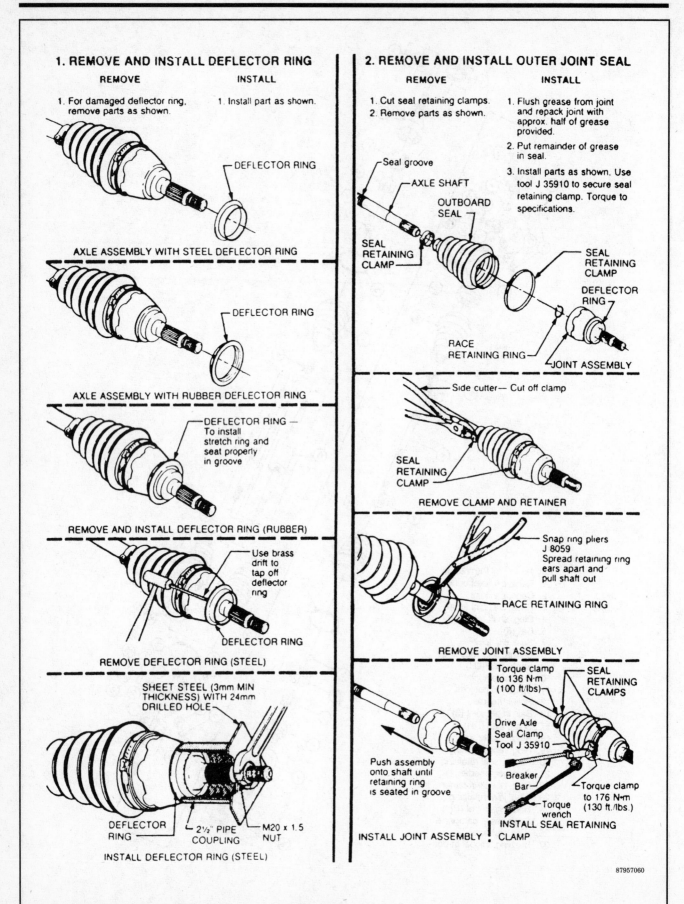

1. REMOVE AND INSTALL DEFLECTOR RING

REMOVE

1. For damaged deflector ring, remove parts as shown.

INSTALL

1. Install part as shown.

— DEFLECTOR RING

AXLE ASSEMBLY WITH STEEL DEFLECTOR RING

— DEFLECTOR RING

AXLE ASSEMBLY WITH RUBBER DEFLECTOR RING

— DEFLECTOR RING —
To install stretch ring and seat properly in groove

REMOVE AND INSTALL DEFLECTOR RING (RUBBER)

Use brass drift to tap off deflector ring

DEFLECTOR RING

REMOVE DEFLECTOR RING (STEEL)

SHEET STEEL (3mm MIN THICKNESS) WITH 24mm DRILLED HOLE

DEFLECTOR RING

2½" PIPE COUPLING

M20 x 1.5 NUT

INSTALL DEFLECTOR RING (STEEL)

2. REMOVE AND INSTALL OUTER JOINT SEAL

REMOVE

1. Cut seal retaining clamps.
2. Remove parts as shown.

INSTALL

1. Flush grease from joint and repack joint with approx. half of grease provided.

2. Put remainder of grease in seal.

3. Install parts as shown. Use tool J 35910 to secure seal retaining clamp. Torque to specifications.

Seal groove

AXLE SHAFT

OUTBOARD SEAL

SEAL RETAINING CLAMP

SEAL RETAINING CLAMP

DEFLECTOR RING

RACE RETAINING RING

JOINT ASSEMBLY

Side cutter — Cut off clamp

SEAL RETAINING CLAMP

REMOVE CLAMP AND RETAINER

Snap ring pliers J 8059 Spread retaining ring ears apart and pull shaft out

RACE RETAINING RING

REMOVE JOINT ASSEMBLY

Push assembly onto shaft until retaining ring is seated in groove

INSTALL JOINT ASSEMBLY

Torque clamp to 136 N·m (100 ft/lbs)

SEAL RETAINING CLAMPS

Drive Axle Seal Clamp Tool J 35910

Breaker Bar

Torque wrench

Torque clamp to 176 N·m (130 ft./lbs.)

INSTALL SEAL RETAINING CLAMP

87957060

Fig. 53 Tri-Pot CV-joint overhaul (part 1 of 2) — 1987-90 Vehicles

3. DISASSEMBLE AND ASSEMBLE OUTER JOINT ASSEMBLY

REMOVE

1. Remove parts as shown.

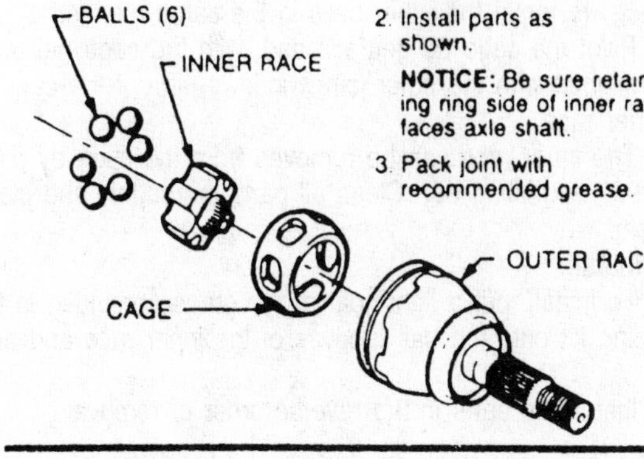

- BALLS (6)
- INNER RACE
- CAGE
- OUTER RACE

INSTALL

1. Put a light coat of recommended grease on ball grooves of inner and outer races.
2. Install parts as shown.
   NOTICE: Be sure retaining ring side of inner race faces axle shaft.
3. Pack joint with recommended grease.

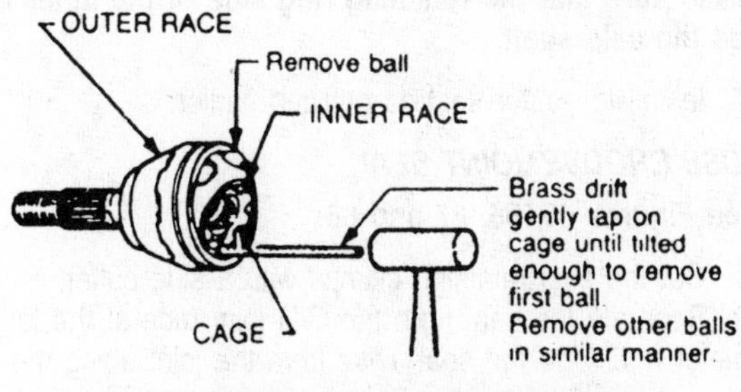

- OUTER RACE
- Remove ball
- INNER RACE
- CAGE

Brass drift gently tap on cage until tilted enough to remove first ball. Remove other balls in similar manner.

DISASSEMBLE AND ASSEMBLE BALLS

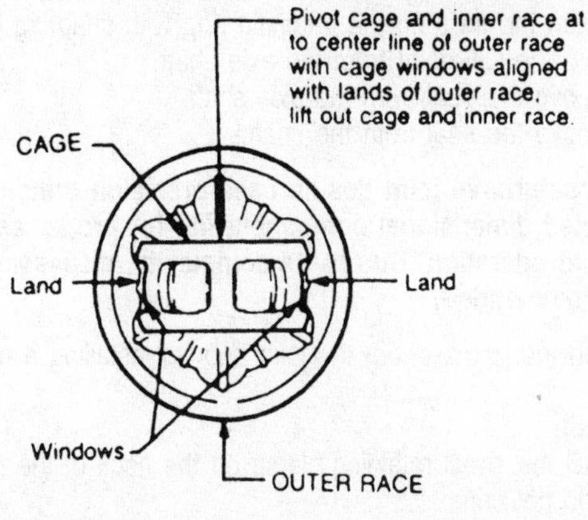

Pivot cage and inner race at 90° to center line of outer race with cage windows aligned with lands of outer race, lift out cage and inner race.

- CAGE
- Land
- Land
- Windows
- OUTER RACE

DISASSEMBLE AND ASSEMBLE CAGE AND INNER RACE TO OUTER RACE

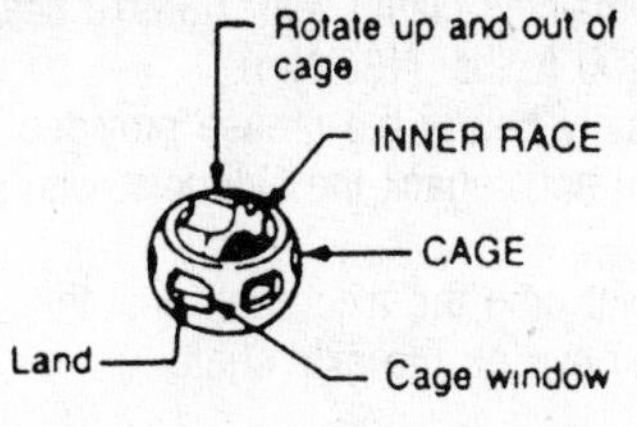

- Rotate up and out of cage
- INNER RACE
- CAGE
- Land
- Cage window

DISASSEMBLE AND ASSEMBLE INNER RACE AND CAGE

4. REMOVE AND INSTALL INNER TRI-POT SEAL

REMOVE

1. Cut seal retaining clamps with side cutters.
2. Remove parts as shown.

- SHAFT RETAINING RING
- SPIDER ASSEMBLY
- TRILOBAL TRI-POT BUSHING
- TRI-POT HOUSING
- SPACER RING
- AXLE
- Seal groove
- SEAL RETAINING CLAMP
- TRI-POT JOINT SEAL
- SEAL RETAINING CLAMP

INSTALL

1. Flush grease from housing and repack housing with approx. half of grease furnished with new seal.
2. Put remainder of grease in seal.
3. Refer to manufacturer's seal installation dimension prior to crimping clamps. Use tool J 35910 or J 35566 to secure seal retaining clamps.

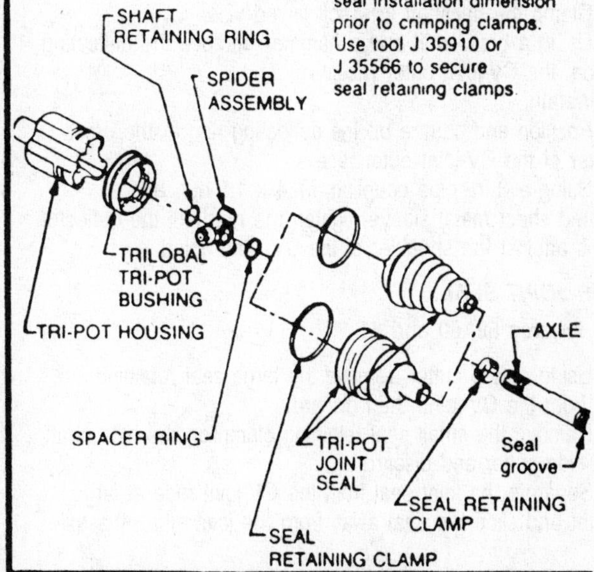

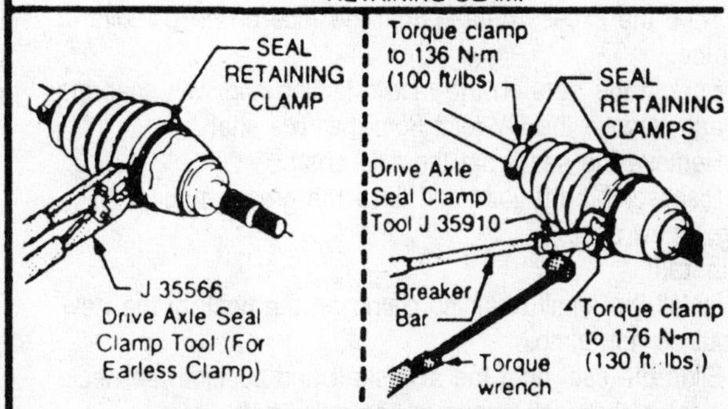

- SEAL RETAINING CLAMP
- J 35566 Drive Axle Seal Clamp Tool (For Earless Clamp)

- Torque clamp to 136 N·m (100 ft/lbs)
- SEAL RETAINING CLAMPS
- Drive Axle Seal Clamp Tool J 35910
- Breaker Bar
- Torque clamp to 176 N·m (130 ft. lbs.)
- Torque wrench

INSTALL SEAL RETAINING CLAMP

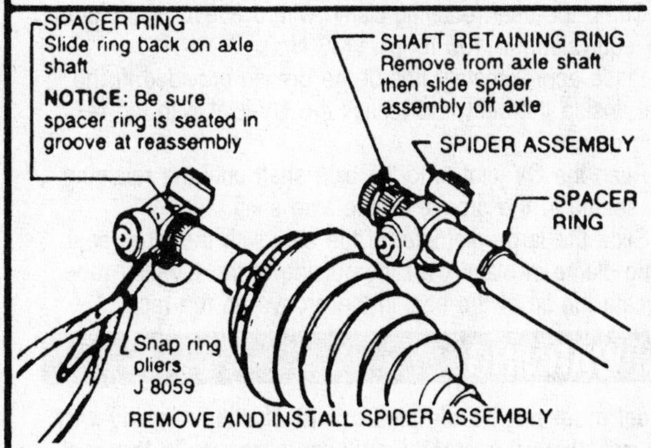

- SPACER RING
  Slide ring back on axle shaft
  NOTICE: Be sure spacer ring is seated in groove at reassembly
- Snap ring pliers J 8059

- SHAFT RETAINING RING
  Remove from axle shaft then slide spider assembly off axle
- SPIDER ASSEMBLY
- SPACER RING

REMOVE AND INSTALL SPIDER ASSEMBLY

87957061

Fig. 54 Tri-Pot CV-joint overhaul (part 2 of 2) — 1987-90 Vehicles

1990-95 Cross-Groove and 1991-96 Tri-Pot Design

▶ **See Figures 55 and 56**

All 1990-95 models equipped with the Hydra-Matic® 5TM40 or NVT550 5-speed manual transaxles use the Cross-Groove type drive axle. All other models use the Tri-Pot type drive axle. The following overhaul procedures incorporate both designs, unless otherwise noted.

OUTER DEFLECTOR RING

▶ **See Figures 57 and 58**

1. Remove the halfshaft (drive axle).
2. Clamp the halfshaft in a soft jawed vise.
3. Using a brass drift and a hammer, remove the deflecting ring from the CV-joint outer race.

To install:

4. Position and square up the deflecting ring at the press diameter of the CV-joint outer race.
5. Using a 3 in. pipe coupling, M24 x 1.5 nut, and a fabricated sheet metal sleeve, tighten the nut until the deflector bottoms against the shoulder of the CV outer joint.

OUTER JOINT SEAL

▶ **See Figures 59, 60 and 61**

1. Using a side cutter, remove the large seal retaining clamp from the CV-joint, then discard.
2. Remove the small seal retaining clamp on the axle shaft with a side cutter and discard.
3. Separate the joint seal from the CV-joint race at large diameter and slide the seal away from the joint along the axle shaft.
4. Wipe the excess grease from the face of the CV-joint inner race.
5. Spread the ears on the race retaining ring with snapring pliers and remove the CV-joint from the axle shaft.
6. Remove the seal from the axle shaft.
7. Disassemble the joint and flush the grease prior to installing a new seal.

To install:

8. Install the small retaining clamp on the neck of the new seal, but do not crimp.
9. Slide the seal onto the axle shaft and position the neck of the seal in the seal groove on the axle shaft.
10. Crimp the seal retaining clamp with J 35910 seal clamp tool or equivalent, to 100 ft. lbs. (136 Nm).
11. Place approximately half of the grease provided in the seal kit, inside the seal and repack the CV-joint with the remaining grease.
12. Push the CV-joint onto the axle shaft until the retaining ring is seated in the groove on the axle shaft.
13. Slide the large diameter of the seal with the large seal retaining clamp in place over the outside of the CV-joint race and locate the lip of the seal in the groove on the race.

❋❋WARNING

The seal must not be dimpled or out of shape in any way. If it is not shaped correctly, equalize pressure in the seal and reshape properly by hand.

14. Crimp the seal retaining clamp with J 35910 seal clamp tool or equivalent, to 130 ft. lbs. (176 Nm).

OUTER JOINT ASSEMBLY

▶ **See Figures 62, 63 and 64**

1. Remove the outer joint seal as outlined earlier.
2. Using a brass drift and a hammer, lightly tap on the inner race cage until it has tilted sufficiently to remove one of the balls. Remove the other balls in the same manner.
3. Pivot the cage 90 degrees and, with the cage ball windows aligned with the outer joint windows, lift out the cage and the inner race.
4. The inner race can be removed from the cage by pivoting it 90° and lifting out. Clean all parts thoroughly and inspect for wear.

To install:

5. To install, put a light coat of the grease provided in the rebuilding kit onto the ball grooves of the inner race and outer joint.
6. Install the parts in the reverse order of removal.

➡**Make sure that the retaining ring side of the inner race faces the axle shaft.**

7. Install the outer seal as outlined earlier.

CROSS-GROOVE JOINT SEAL

▶ **See Figures 65, 66, 67 and 68**

1. Cut the seal retaining clamps with a side cutter.
2. Separate the seal from the C/G joint race at the large diameter and slide the seal away from the joint along the axle shaft.
3. Wipe the excess grease from the C/G joint inner race.
4. Spread the ears on the retaining ring with snapring pliers and remove the C/G joint from the axle shaft.
5. Remove the seal from the axle shaft.
6. Remove the seal from the shaft.

➡**The cross-groove joint design uses precision grinding and selected dimensional component fits for proper assembly and operation. Due to its complexity, disassembly is not recommended.**

7. Flush the grease from the joint prior to installing a new seal.

To install:

8. Install the small retaining clamp on the neck of the new seal, but do not crimp.
9. Slide the seal onto the axle shaft and position the neck of the seal in the seal groove on the axle shaft.
10. Crimp the seal retaining clamp with J 35910 seal clamp tool or equivalent, to 100 ft. lbs. (136 Nm).
11. Place approximately half of the grease provided in the seal kit, inside the seal and repack the C/G joint with the remaining grease.
12. Push the C/G joint onto the axle shaft until the retaining ring is seated in the groove on the axle shaft.

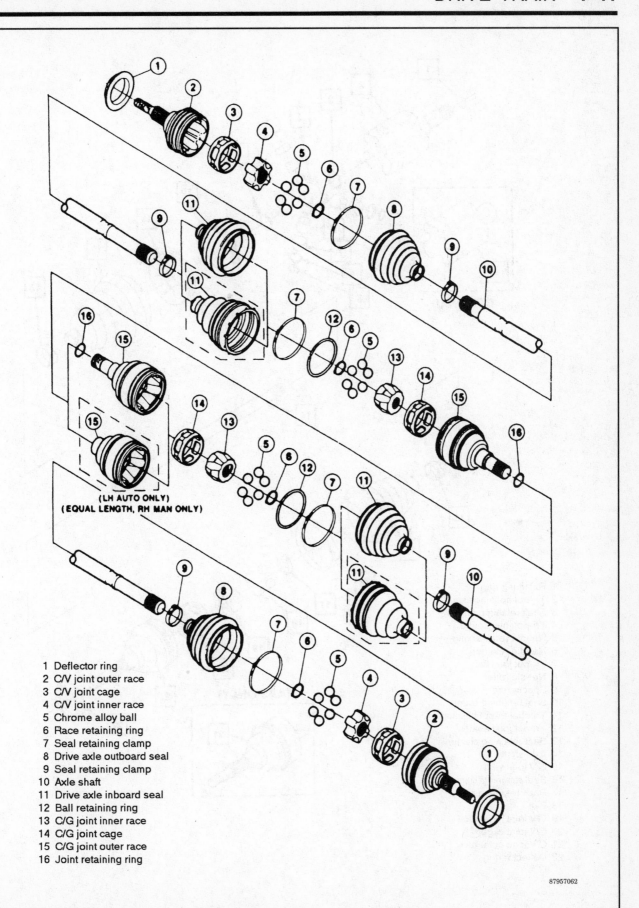

1 Deflector ring
2 C/V joint outer race
3 C/V joint cage
4 C/V joint inner race
5 Chrome alloy ball
6 Race retaining ring
7 Seal retaining clamp
8 Drive axle outboard seal
9 Seal retaining clamp
10 Axle shaft
11 Drive axle inboard seal
12 Ball retaining ring
13 C/G joint inner race
14 C/G joint cage
15 C/G joint outer race
16 Joint retaining ring

(LH AUTO ONLY)
(EQUAL LENGTH, RH MAN ONLY)

87957062

Fig. 55 Exploded view of the Cross-Groove halfshaft (drive axle) — 1990-95 Vehicles

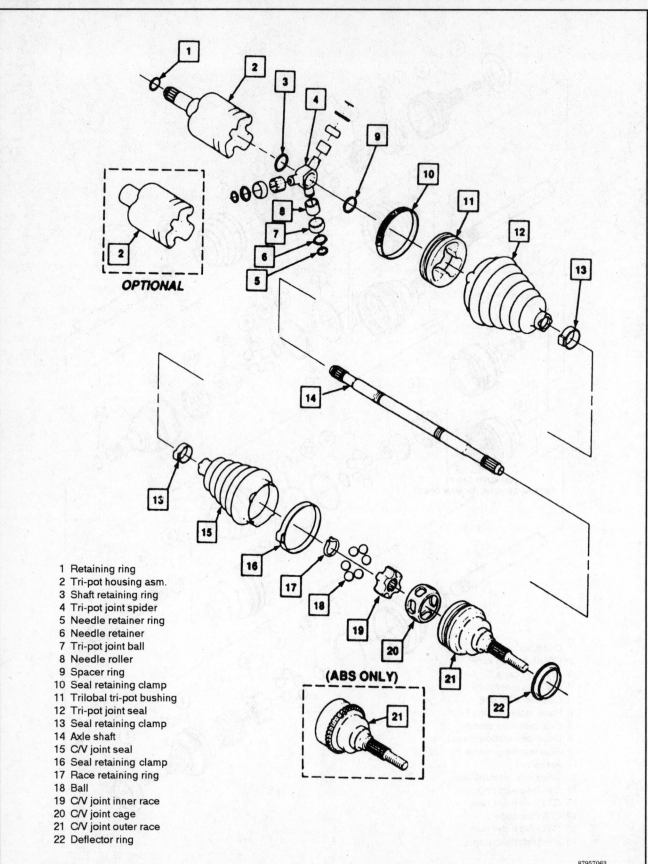

1   Retaining ring
2   Tri-pot housing asm.
3   Shaft retaining ring
4   Tri-pot joint spider
5   Needle retainer ring
6   Needle retainer
7   Tri-pot joint ball
8   Needle roller
9   Spacer ring
10 Seal retaining clamp
11 Trilobal tri-pot bushing
12 Tri-pot joint seal
13 Seal retaining clamp
14 Axle shaft
15 C/V joint seal
16 Seal retaining clamp
17 Race retaining ring
18 Ball
19 C/V joint inner race
20 C/V joint cage
21 C/V joint outer race
22 Deflector ring

OPTIONAL

(ABS ONLY)

87957063

Fig. 56 Exploded view of the Tri-Pot halfshaft (drive axle) — 1991-96 Vehicles

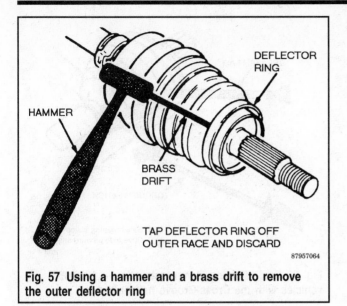

HAMMER

DEFLECTOR
RING

BRASS
DRIFT

TAP DEFLECTOR RING OFF
OUTER RACE AND DISCARD

87957064

**Fig. 57 Using a hammer and a brass drift to remove
the outer deflector ring**

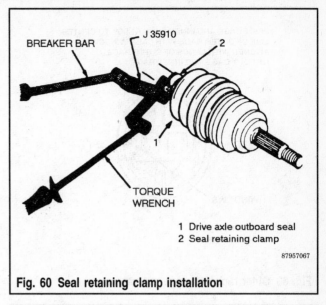

BREAKER BAR

J 35910

2

1

TORQUE
WRENCH

1 Drive axle outboard seal
2 Seal retaining clamp

87957067

Fig. 60 Seal retaining clamp installation

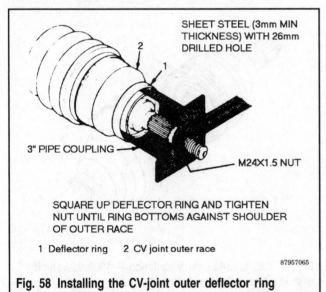

SHEET STEEL (3mm MIN
THICKNESS) WITH 26mm
DRILLED HOLE

2

1

3" PIPE COUPLING

M24X1.5 NUT

SQUARE UP DEFLECTOR RING AND TIGHTEN
NUT UNTIL RING BOTTOMS AGAINST SHOULDER
OF OUTER RACE

1 Deflector ring   2 CV joint outer race

87957065

Fig. 58 Installing the CV-joint outer deflector ring

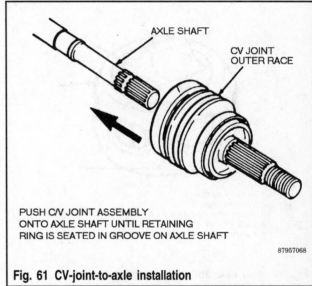

AXLE SHAFT

CV JOINT
OUTER RACE

PUSH C/V JOINT ASSEMBLY
ONTO AXLE SHAFT UNTIL RETAINING
RING IS SEATED IN GROOVE ON AXLE SHAFT

87957068

Fig. 61 CV-joint-to-axle installation

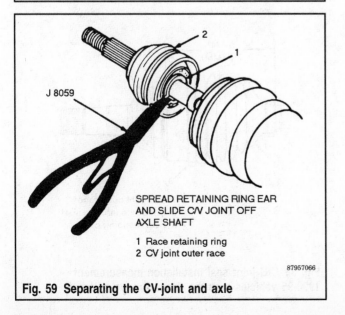

2

1

J 8059

SPREAD RETAINING RING EAR
AND SLIDE C/V JOINT OFF
AXLE SHAFT

1 Race retaining ring
2 CV joint outer race

87957066

Fig. 59 Separating the CV-joint and axle

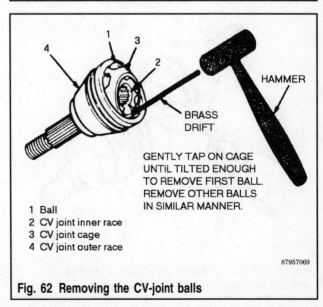

4

1

3

2

BRASS
DRIFT

HAMMER

GENTLY TAP ON CAGE
UNTIL TILTED ENOUGH
TO REMOVE FIRST BALL.
REMOVE OTHER BALLS
IN SIMILAR MANNER.

1 Ball
2 CV joint inner race
3 CV joint cage
4 CV joint outer race

87957069

Fig. 62 Removing the CV-joint balls

PIVOT CAGE AND INNER RACE AT 90° TO CENTER
LINE OF OUTER RACE WITH CAGE WINDOWS
ALIGNED WITH LANDS OF OUTER RACE.
LIFT OUT CAGE AND INNER RACE.

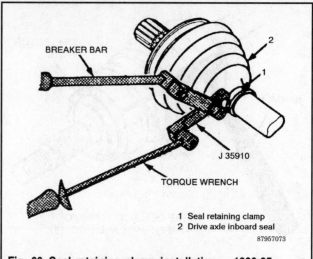

LAND   LAND

WINDOWS

1 CV joint cage
2 CV joint outer race

87957070

Fig. 63 Outer race and cage separation

BREAKER BAR

J 35910

TORQUE WRENCH

1 Seal retaining clamp
2 Drive axle inboard seal

87957073

Fig. 66 Seal retaining clamp installation — 1990-95 vehicles with the Cross-Groove halfshaft

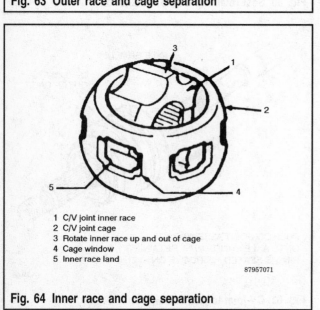

1 C/V joint inner race
2 C/V joint cage
3 Rotate inner race up and out of cage
4 Cage window
5 Inner race land

87957071

Fig. 64 Inner race and cage separation

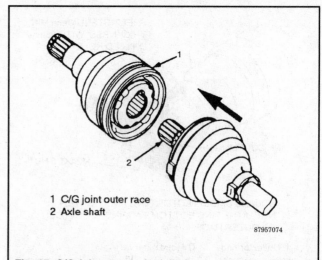

1 C/G joint outer race
2 Axle shaft

87957074

Fig. 67 C/G joint-to-axle installation — 1990-95 vehicles with the Cross-Groove halfshaft

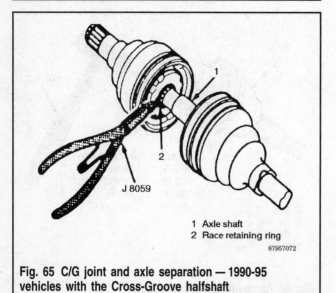

J 8059

1 Axle shaft
2 Race retaining ring

87957072

Fig. 65 C/G joint and axle separation — 1990-95 vehicles with the Cross-Groove halfshaft

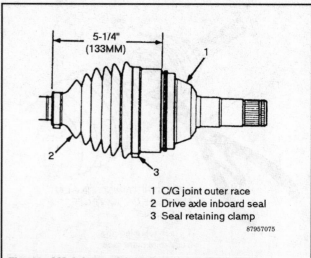

5-1/4"
(133MM)

1 C/G joint outer race
2 Drive axle inboard seal
3 Seal retaining clamp

87957075

Fig. 68 C/G joint seal installation measurement — 1990-95 vehicles with the Cross-Groove halfshaft

13. Slide the large diameter of the seal over the outside of the C/G joint and locate the lip of the seal in the groove on ball retainer.

❋❋WARNING

The seal must not be dimpled or out of shape in any way. If it is not shaped correctly, equalize pressure in the seal and reshape properly by hand.

14. Crimp the seal retaining clamp with J 35910 seal clamp tool or equivalent, to 130 ft. lbs. (176 Nm).

INNER TRI-POT SEAL

▶ **See Figures 69, 70, 71, 72, 73 and 74**

1. Remove the larger seal retaining clamp from the tri-pot joint with a side cutter and discard.

❋❋WARNING

Do not cut through the seal and damage the sealing surface of the tri-pot outer housing and triobal bushing.

2. Remove the small seal retaining clamp from the axle shaft with a side cutter and discard.
3. Separate the seal from the trilobal tri-pot bushing at the large diameter and slide the seal away from the joint along the axle shaft.
4. Remove the tri-pot housing from the spider and shaft.
5. Spread the spacer ring with snapring pliers and slide the spacer ring and tri-pot spider back on the axle shaft.
6. Remove the shaft retaining ring from the groove on the axle shaft and slide the spider assembly off of the shaft.
7. Check the tri-pot balls and needle rollers for damage or wear.

➥Use care when handling the spider assembly as the tri-pot balls and rollers may separate from the spider trunnions.

8. Remove the trilobal tri-pot bushing from the tri-pot housing.
9. Remove the spacer ring and seal from the axle shaft.

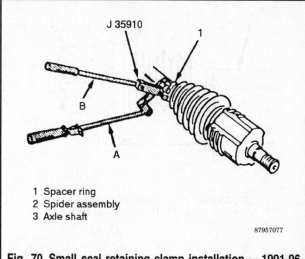

1 Spacer ring
2 Spider assembly
3 Axle shaft

87957077

Fig. 70 Small seal retaining clamp installation — 1991-96 Tri-Pot type axle

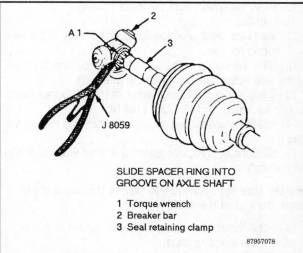

SLIDE SPACER RING INTO GROOVE ON AXLE SHAFT

1 Torque wrench
2 Breaker bar
3 Seal retaining clamp

87957078

Fig. 71 Spider assembly installation — 1991-96 Tri-Pot type axle

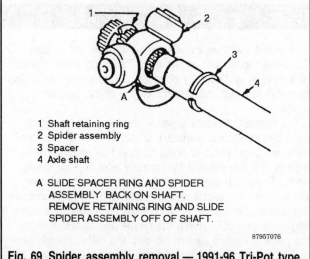

1 Shaft retaining ring
2 Spider assembly
3 Spacer
4 Axle shaft

A SLIDE SPACER RING AND SPIDER ASSEMBLY BACK ON SHAFT. REMOVE RETAINING RING AND SLIDE SPIDER ASSEMBLY OFF OF SHAFT.

87957076

Fig. 69 Spider assembly removal — 1991-96 Tri-Pot type axle

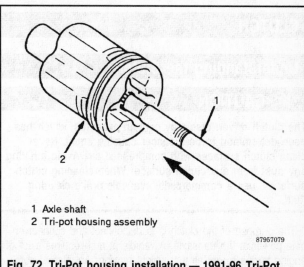

1 Axle shaft
2 Tri-pot housing assembly

87957079

Fig. 72 Tri-Pot housing installation — 1991-96 Tri-Pot type axle

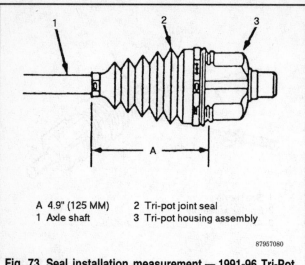

A 4.9" (125 MM)   2 Tri-pot joint seal
1 Axle shaft   3 Tri-pot housing assembly

87957080

Fig. 73 Seal installation measurement — 1991-96 Tri-Pot type axle

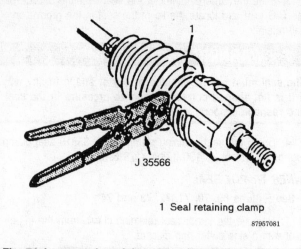

J 35566

1 Seal retaining clamp

87957081

Fig. 74 Large seal retaining clamp installation — 1991-96 Tri-Pot type axle

10. Flush the grease from the tri-pot housing.

To install:

11. Install the small retaining clamp on the neck of the new seal, but do not crimp.

12. Slide the seal onto the axle shaft and position the neck of the seal in the seal groove on the axle shaft.

13. Crimp the seal retaining clamp with J 35910 seal clamp tool or equivalent, to 100 ft. lbs. (136 Nm).

14. Install the spacer ring on the axle shaft and beyond the 2nd groove.

15. Slide the tri-pot spider assembly against the spacer ring on the shaft.

➡**Make sure the counterbored face of the tri-pot spider faces the end of the shaft.**

16. Install the shaft retaining ring in the groove of the axle shaft with the snapring pliers.

17. Slide the tri-pot spider towards the end of the shaft and reseat the spacer ring in the groove on the shaft.

18. Place approximately half of the grease provided in the seal kit, inside the seal and repack the tri-pot housing with the remaining grease.

19. Install the trilobal tri-pot bushing to the tri-pot housing.

20. Position the larger clamp on the seal.

21. Slide the tri-pot housing over the tri-pot spider.

22. Slide the large diameter of the seal, with the larger clamp in place, over the outside of the trilobal bushing and locate the lip of the seal in the bushing groove.

23. Position the tri-pot assembly at the proper vehicle dimension as shown.

❊❊**WARNING**

The seal must not be dimpled or out of shape in any way. If it is not shaped correctly, equalize pressure by carefully inserting a thin flat blunt tool (with no sharp edges) between the large seal opening and the bushing and reshape properly by hand.

24. Crimp the seal retaining clamp with J 35566 seal clamp tool or equivalent.

CLUTCH

Understanding the Clutch

❊❊**CAUTION**

The clutch driven disc may contain asbestos, which has been determined to be a cancer causing agent. Never clean clutch surfaces with compressed air! Avoid inhaling any dust from any clutch surface! When cleaning clutch surfaces, use a commercially available brake cleaning fluid.

The purpose of the clutch is to disconnect and connect engine power at the transaxle. A vehicle at rest requires a lot of engine torque to get all that weight moving. An internal combustion engine does not develop a high starting torque (unlike steam engines), so it must be allowed to operate without any load until it builds up enough torque to move the vehicle. Torque increases with engine rpm. The clutch allows the engine to build up torque by physically disconnecting the engine from the transaxle, relieving the engine of any load or resistance.

The transfer of engine power to the transaxle (the load) must be smooth and gradual; if it weren't, drive line components would wear out or break quickly. This gradual power transfer is made possible by gradually releasing the clutch pedal. The clutch disc and pressure plate are the connecting link between the engine and transaxle. When the clutch pedal is released, the disc and plate contact each other (the clutch is engaged), physically joining the engine and transaxle. When the pedal is pushed inward, the disc and plate separate (the clutch is disengaged), disconnecting the engine from the transaxle.

Most clutches utilize a single plate, dry friction disc with a diaphragm-style spring pressure plate. The clutch disc has a splined hub which attaches the disc to the input shaft. The disc has friction material where it contacts the flywheel and pressure plate. Torsion springs on the disc help absorb engine torque pulses. The pressure plate applies pressure to the clutch disc, holding it tight against the surface of the flywheel. The clutch operating mechanism consists of a release bearing, fork and cylinder assembly.

The release fork and actuating linkage transfer pedal motion to the release bearing. In the engaged position (pedal released), the diaphragm spring holds the pressure plate against the clutch disc, so engine torque is transmitted to the input shaft. When the clutch pedal is depressed, the release bearing pushes the diaphragm spring center toward the flywheel. The diaphragm spring pivots the fulcrum, relieving the load on the pressure plate. Steel spring straps riveted to the clutch cover lift the pressure plate from the clutch disc, disengaging the engine drive from the transaxle and enabling the gears to be changed.

The clutch is operating properly if:

1. It will stall the engine when released with the vehicle held stationary.

2. The shift lever can be moved freely between 1st and reverse gears when the vehicle is stationary and the clutch disengaged.

Adjustment

All 1982-84 models have a self-adjusting clutch mechanism located on the clutch pedal, eliminating the need for periodic free play adjustments. The self-adjusting mechanism should be inspected periodically as follows:

1. Depress the clutch pedal and look for the pawl on the self-adjusting mechanism to firmly engage the teeth on the ratchet.

2. Release the clutch. The pawl should be lifted off of the teeth by the metal stop on the bracket.

On 1985 and later models, the hydraulic clutch system provides automatic clutch adjustment. No adjustment of clutch linkage or pedal position is required.

Clutch Pedal

REMOVAL & INSTALLATION

Cable Clutch
▶ See Figure 75

1. Support the clutch pedal upward against the bumper stop to release the pawl from the detent. Disconnect the clutch cable from the clutch release lever at the transaxle assembly. Be careful to prevent the cable from snapping rapidly toward the rear of the car. The detent in the adjustable mechanism can be damaged by allowing the cable to snap back.

2. Remove the hush panel from inside the car and disconnect the neutral start switch from the pedal and from the bracket.

3. Disconnect the clutch cable from the detent tangs. Lift the locking pawl away from the detent, then slide the cable between the detent and the locking pawl.

4. Unfasten the clutch pedal pivot bolt, then remove the clutch pedal assembly from the bracket.

5. Remove the locking pawl, pivot bolt, spring, pawl and spacer from the pedal assembly.

6. Remove the detent spacer, bushings, spring and the detent from the pedal assembly.

7. Inspect, clean the replace parts as required. If there is tooth damage on the pawl or detent, replace both components.

To install:

8. Assemble the adjusting mechanism to the pedal as follows:

a. Position the detent spring in the side of the detent. Install the detent into the opening of the clutch pedal and hook the detent spring onto the side of the pedal.

b. Install the bushings onto the pedal assembly.

c. Align the detent with the clutch pedal mounting hole and install the spacer.

d. Install the locking pawl, spring, spacer and pivot mounting bolt. The pawl will not operate freely if over-tightened. Tighten to 44 inch lbs. (5 Nm).

9. Attach the clutch pedal to the mounting bracket by installing the pivot bolt and nut. Both pivot bolts (pedal and pawl) must be installed as shown in the accompanying figure.

10. Check the operation of the pawl and detent, making sure that the pawl disengages from the detent when the pedal is pulled to its upper position, and that the detent rotates freely in both directions.

11. Attach the end of the cable to the detent, being sure to route the cable underneath the pawl and into the detent cable groove.

12. Connect the neutral start switch to the pedal and install the mounting screw. Tighten the screw to 26 inch lbs. (3 Nm).

13. Support the clutch pedal upward against the bumper stop to release the pawl from the detent. Attach the other end of the cable to the clutch release lever.

14. Check the clutch operation and adjust by lifting the clutch pedal up to allow the mechanism to adjust the cable length. Depress the pedal slowly several times to set the pawl into mesh with detent teeth.

15. Install the hush panel.

Hydraulic Clutch
▶ See Figure 76

➡ The clutch pedal and bracket are serviced as an assembly.

1. Disconnect the battery ground cable.

2. Remove the sound insulator from inside the vehicle.

3. Disconnect the master cylinder pushrod from the clutch pedal.

4. Unfasten the clutch pedal and bracket mounting nuts, then remove the clutch pedal and bracket assembly.

To install:

5. Position the clutch pedal and bracket assembly into vehicle.

6. Install the retaining nuts. Starting with the lower nuts, tighten the nuts to 17 ft. lbs. (23 Nm).

7. Lubricate and install the master cylinder pushrod bushing onto the clutch pedal.

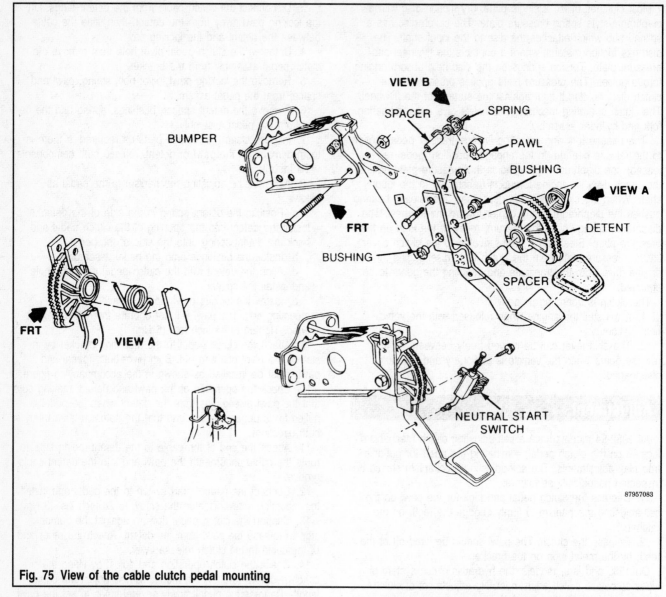

Fig. 75 View of the cable clutch pedal mounting

8. Connect the clutch master cylinder pushrod to the clutch pedal. If equipped with cruise control check the switch adjustment at the clutch pedal bracket.

9. Install the sound insulator.

10. Connect the battery ground cable.

Clutch Cable

REMOVAL & INSTALLATION

▶ See Figure 77

1. Press the clutch pedal up against the bumper stop so as to release the pawl from the detent. Disconnect the clutch cable from the release lever at the transaxle assembly. Be careful that the cable does not snap back toward the rear of the car as this could damage the detent in the adjusting mechanism.

2. Remove the hush panel from inside the car.

3. Disconnect the clutch cable from the detent end tangs. Lift the locking pawl away from the detent and then pull the cable forward between the detent and the pawl.

4. Remove the windshield washer bottle.

5. From the engine side of the cowl, pull the clutch cable out to disengage it from the clutch pedal mounting bracket. The insulators, dampener and washers may separate from the cable in the process.

6. Disconnect the cable from the transaxle mounting bracket, then remove it from the vehicle.

To install:

7. Install the cable into both insulators, damper and washer. Lubricate the rear insulator with tire mounting lube, or equivalent, to ease installation into the pedal mounting bracket.

8. From inside the car, attach the end of the cable to the detent. Be sure to route the cable underneath the pawl and into the detent cable groove.

9. Press the clutch pedal up against the bumper stop to release the pawl from the detent. Install the other end of the cable at the release lever and the transaxle mount bracket.

10. Install the hush panel and the windshield washer bottle.

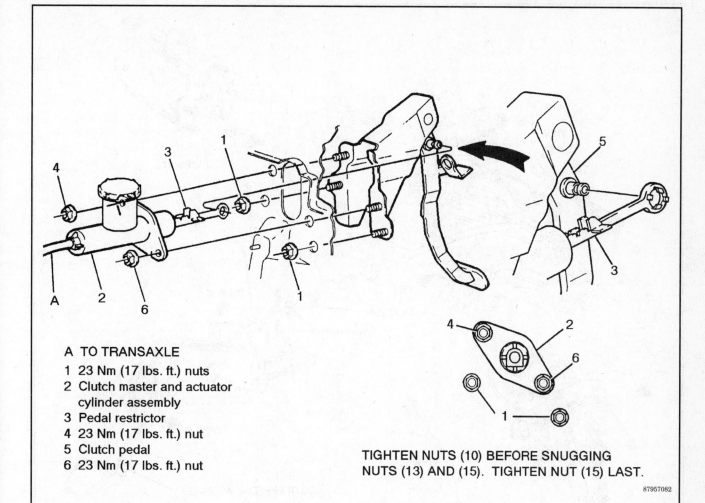

A TO TRANSAXLE
1 23 Nm (17 lbs. ft.) nuts
2 Clutch master and actuator
  cylinder assembly
3 Pedal restrictor
4 23 Nm (17 lbs. ft.) nut
5 Clutch pedal
6 23 Nm (17 lbs. ft.) nut

TIGHTEN NUTS (10) BEFORE SNUGGING
NUTS (13) AND (15). TIGHTEN NUT (15) LAST.

87957082

Fig. 76 View of the clutch pedal assembly mounting — 1992 vehicle equipped with a hydraulic clutch shown

11. Check the clutch operation and adjust as detailed earlier in this sction.

Driven Disc and Pressure Plate/Clutch Cover and Disc

REMOVAL & INSTALLATION

▶ **See Figures 78, 79, 80 and 81**

1. Disconnect the negative battery cable.
2. If equipped with a cable clutch (1982-84 vehicles), disconnect the cable at the clutch release lever and transaxle, as outlined earlier in this section.
3. For 1985-94 vehicles remove the sound insulator from inside the vehicle. Disconnect the clutch master cylinder pushrod from the clutch pedal.

4. For 1995-96 vehicles, disconnect the clutch master cylinder assembly from the clutch actuator (slave) cylinder assembly.
5. Remove the transaxle, as outlined earlier in this section.
6. Mark the pressure plate assembly and the flywheel so that they can be assembled in the same position. They were balanced as an assembly at the factory.
7. Loosen the attaching bolts one turn at a time until spring tension is relieved.
8. Support the pressure plate and remove the bolts. Remove the pressure plate and clutch disc. Do not disassemble the pressure plate assembly; replace it if defective.
9. Inspect the flywheel, clutch disc, pressure plate, throwout bearing and the clutch fork and pivot shaft assembly for wear. Replace the parts as required. If the flywheel shows any signs of overheating, or if it is badly grooved or scored, it should be refaced or replaced.
   To install:
10. Clean the pressure plate and flywheel mating surfaces thoroughly.

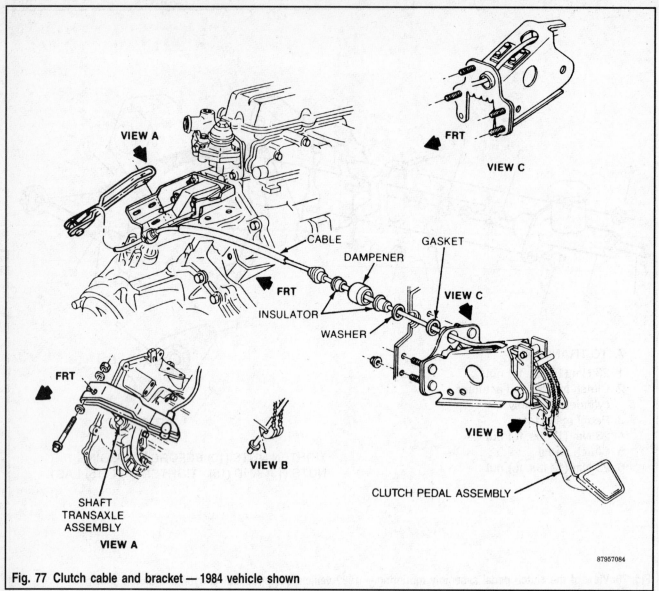

Fig. 77 Clutch cable and bracket — 1984 vehicle shown

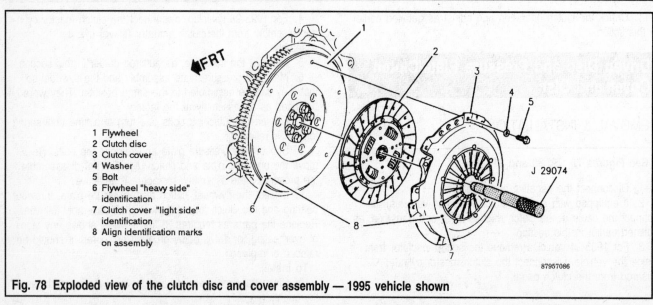

1 Flywheel
2 Clutch disc
3 Clutch cover
4 Washer
5 Bolt
6 Flywheel "heavy side" identification
7 Clutch cover "light side" identification
8 Align identification marks on assembly

Fig. 78 Exploded view of the clutch disc and cover assembly — 1995 vehicle shown

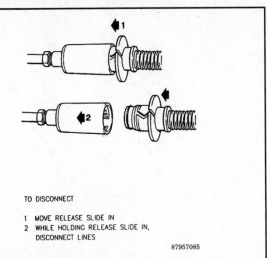

Fig. 79 Disconnect the clutch actuator (slave) cylinder line — 1995-96 vehicles

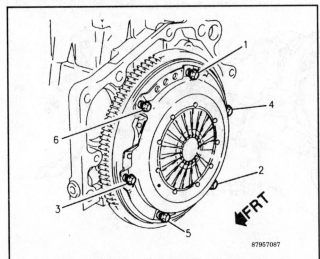

Fig. 80 You must follow the specified sequence when tightening the pressure plate retaining bolts

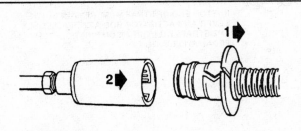

TO CONNECT

1 MOVE RELEASE SLIDE TO OUT
   POSITION (AS SHOWN)
2 WHILE HOLDING RELEASE SLIDE IN OUT POSITION,
   CONNECT LINES (CLICK SHOULD BE HEARD)

87957088

Fig. 81 Connecting the clutch actuator (slave) cylinder line — 1995-96 vehicles

11. Position the clutch disc and pressure plate into the installed position, and support with a dummy shaft or clutch aligning tool, tool J 29074 or equivalent. The clutch plate is assembled with the damper springs offset toward the transaxle. One side of the factory supplied clutch disc is stamped "Flywheel Side".

12. Install the pressure plate-to-flywheel bolts. Tighten them in the sequence shown in the accompanying figure, as follows:

   a. Tighten bolts 1,2,3, then 4,5,6 in the sequence shown to 12 ft. lbs. (16 Nm).

   b. Tighten bolts 1,2,3, then 4,5,6 in the sequence shown to 15-22 ft. lbs. (22-30 Nm) plus an additional 30° turn.

   c. Remove the clutch alignment tool.

13. Lubricate the outside groove and the inside recess of the release bearing with high temperature grease. Wipe off any excess. Install the release bearing.

14. Install the transaxle, as outlined earlier in this section.

15. For 1995-96 vehicles, connect the clutch master cylinder assembly to the clutch actuator (slave) cylinder assembly.

❊❊WARNING

When adjusting the cruise control switch, do NOT exert an upward force on the clutch pedal pad of more than 20 lbs. (89 N) or damage to the master cylinder pushrod retaining ring may result.

16. For 1985-94 vehicles, attach the clutch master cylinder pushrod to the clutch pedal and secure with the retaining clip. If equipped with cruise control, check the switch adjustment at the clutch pedal bracket. Install the sound insulator.

17. For 1995-96 vehicles, properly bleed the hydraulic system, as outlined later in this section.

18. If equipped with a cable clutch, attach the clutch cable at the transaxle and clutch release lever. Check the clutch operation by lifting the clutch pedal up to allow the mechanism to adjust the cable length. Depress the pedal slowly a few times to set the pawl into mesh with the quadrant teeth.

Clutch Hydraulic System

REMOVAL & INSTALLATION

▶ **See Figures 82, 83 and 84**

➡The clutch hydraulic system used on 1985-94 models is serviced as a complete unit (except 1994 3.1L). It has been bled of air and filled with fluid. Individual components of the system are not available separately.

1.8L, 2.0L and 2.2L Engines

1. Disconnect the negative battery cable.
2. Remove the hush panel from inside the vehicle.
3. Disconnect the clutch master cylinder pushrod from the clutch pedal.
4. Unfasten the clutch master cylinder retaining nuts at the front of the dash.
5. Remove the slave cylinder or actuator retaining nuts at the transaxle.
6. Remove the hydraulic system as a unit from the vehicle.

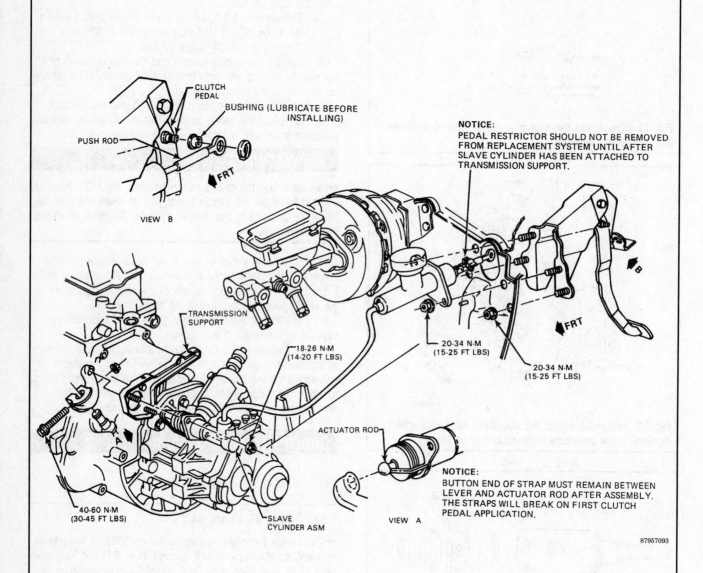

CLUTCH PEDAL

BUSHING (LUBRICATE BEFORE INSTALLING)

PUSH ROD

FRT

VIEW B

NOTICE:
PEDAL RESTRICTOR SHOULD NOT BE REMOVED FROM REPLACEMENT SYSTEM UNTIL AFTER SLAVE CYLINDER HAS BEEN ATTACHED TO TRANSMISSION SUPPORT.

B

FRT

TRANSMISSION SUPPORT

18-26 N·M (14-20 FT LBS)

20-34 N·M (15-25 FT LBS)

20-34 N·M (15-25 FT LBS)

ACTUATOR ROD

40-60 N·M (30-45 FT LBS)

SLAVE CYLINDER ASM

VIEW A

NOTICE:
BUTTON END OF STRAP MUST REMAIN BETWEEN LEVER AND ACTUATOR ROD AFTER ASSEMBLY. THE STRAPS WILL BREAK ON FIRST CLUTCH PEDAL APPLICATION.

87957093

Fig. 82 View of the clutch hydraulic system — 1985-87 vehicles

1. BOLT – 50 N·m (36 LBS. FT.)
2. LEVER
3. TRANSAXLE SUPPORT
4. CLUTCH MASTER AND ACTUATOR CYLINDER ASSEMBLY
5. NUT – 27 N·m (20 LBS. FT.)
6. ACTUATOR ROD
7. BUTTON
   BUTTON END OF STRAP MUST REMAIN BETWEEN LEVER AND ACTUATOR ROD AFTER ASSEMBLY. THE STRAPS WILL BREAK ON FIRST CLUTCH PEDAL APPLICATION.

8. RESTRICTOR
   PEDAL RESTRICTOR SHOULD NOT BE REMOVED FROM REPLACEMENT SYSTEM UNTIL AFTER ACTUATOR CYLINDER HAS BEEN ATTACHED TO TRANSAXLE SUPPORT.
9. NUT – 22 N·m (16 LBS. FT.)
10. CLUTCH PEDAL
11. MASTER CYLINDER PUSHROD – LUBRICATE BEFORE INSTALLING
12. NUT
13. BRACKET

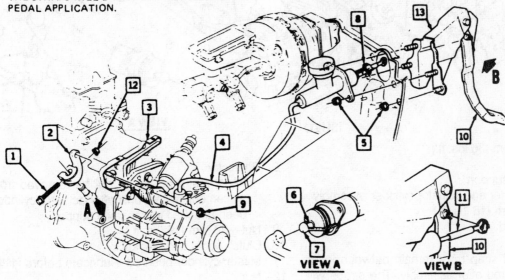

87957094

Fig. 83 Clutch hydraulic system — 1988-89 vehicles

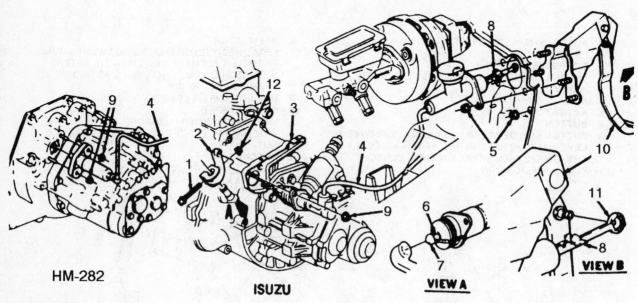

HM-282

ISUZU

VIEW A

VIEW B

1. Bolt—50 N·m (36 lbs. ft.)
2. Lever
3. Transaxle support
4. Clutch master and actuator cylinder assembly
5. Nut—22 N·m (16 lbs. ft.)
6. Actuator rod
7. Button
Button end of strap must remain between lever and actuator rod after assembly. The straps will break on first clutch pedal application.

8. Restrictor
   Pedal restrictor should not be removed from replacement system until after actuator cylinder has been attached to transaxle support.
9. Nut—22 N·m (16 lbs. ft.).
10. Clutch pedal and bracket
11. Master cylinder pushrod—lubricate before installing
12. Nut

87957095

Fig. 84 Location of the clutch hydraulic system components — 1990 vehicles

To install:

7. Install the new slave cylinder or actuator to the transaxle support bracket aligning the pushrod into the pocket on the clutch fork outer lever. Tighten the retaining nuts evenly to prevent damage to the slave cylinder. Tighten to 14-20 ft. lbs. (19-27 Nm).

➡️**Do not remove the plastic pushrod retainer from the slave or actuator cylinder. The straps will break on the first clutch pedal application.**

8. Position the clutch master cylinder to the front of the dash. Install the retaining nuts and tighten the nuts evenly to prevent damage to the master cylinder. Tighten to 15-25 ft. lbs. (20-34 Nm).

9. Remove the pedal restrictor from the pushrod. Lube the pushrod bushing on the clutch pedal. Connect the pushrod to the clutch pedal and install the retaining clip.

10. If equipped with cruise control, check the switch adjustment at the pedal bracket.

✳✳WARNING

When adjusting the cruise control switch, do not exert an upward force on the clutch pedal pad of more than 20 lbs. (89 N) or damage to the master cylinder pushrod retaining ring can result.

11. Install the hush panel.
12. Press the clutch pedal down several times. This will break the plastic retaining straps on the slave or actuator cylinder pushrod. Do not remove the plastic button on the end of the pushrod.
13. Connect the negative battery cable.

2.8L and 3.1L Engines

1. Remove the air intake duct from the air cleaner.
2. Disconnect the negative, then the positive battery cables.
3. Remove the left fender brace, then unfasten the battery hold-down clamp bolt and remove the battery.
4. Detach the MAT or IAT sensor lead from the air cleaner.
5. Unfasten the PCV pipe retaining clamp from the air intake duct.
6. Remove the clamp fastening the air intake duct to the throttle body.
7. Unfasten the MAF sensor mounting bolts, then unfasten the air cleaner bracket mounting bolts at the battery tray.
8. Remove the air cleaner, mass air flow sensor and the air intake duct as an assembly.
9. Detach the electrical lead at the washer bottle. Unfasten the attaching bolts, then remove the washer bottle from the vehicle.
10. If equipped with cruise control, remove the mounting bracket retaining nuts from the strut tower.
11. Remove the hush panel/sound insulator from inside the vehicle.
12. Disconnect the clutch master cylinder pushrod from the clutch pedal.
13. Unfasten the clutch master cylinder retaining nuts at the front of the dash, then remove the master cylinder.

14. For 1993 vehicles, unfasten the clutch actuator cylinder quick disconnect fitting from the master cylinder line.
15. For 1993, vehicles, remove the transaxle, as outlined earlier in this section, then remove the clutch actuator cylinder from the transaxle.
16. For vehicles through 1992, remove the slave or actuator cylinder retaining nuts at the transaxle, then remove the hydraulic system as a unit from the vehicle.

To install:

17. For vehicles through 1992, install the new slave or actuator cylinder to the transaxle support bracket aligning the pushrod into the pocket on the clutch fork outer lever. Tighten the retaining nuts evenly to prevent damage to the slave cylinder. Tighten to 14-20 ft. lbs. (19-27 Nm).

➡️**Do not remove the plastic pushrod retainer from the slave or actuator cylinder. The straps will break on the first clutch pedal application.**

18. For 1993 vehicles, install the clutch actuator cylinder to the transaxle, then install the transaxle assembly. Attach the quick connect fitting to the master cylinder line.
19. Position the clutch master cylinder to the front of the dash. Install the retaining nuts and tighten the nuts evenly to prevent damage to the master cylinder. Tighten to 15-25 ft. lbs. (20-34 Nm).
20. Remove the pedal restrictor from the pushrod. Lube the pushrod bushing on the clutch pedal. Connect the pushrod to the clutch pedal and install the retaining clip.
21. If equipped with cruise control, check the switch adjustment at the pedal bracket.

✳✳WARNING

When adjusting the cruise control switch, do not exert an upward force on the clutch pedal pad of more than 20 lbs. (89 N) or damage to the master cylinder pushrod retaining ring can result.

22. Install the hush panel/sound insulator.
23. For 1993 vehicles, bleed the hydraulic system, as outlined later in this section.
24. For vehicles through 1992, press the clutch pedal down several times. This will break the plastic retaining straps on the slave or actuator cylinder pushrod. Do not remove the plastic button on the end of the pushrod.
25. Install the washer bottle, then attach the electrical connection.
26. Install the air cleaner, mass air flow sensor and the air intake duct as an assembly.
27. Fasten the air cleaner bracket mounting bolts, and the MAF sensor mounting bolt.
28. Install the clamp retaining the air intake duct to the throttle body.
29. Fasten the PCV pipe retaining clamp to the air intake duct.
30. Attach the MAF sensor lead, then connect the MAT or IAT sensor lead at the air cleaner.
31. Install the battery and the left fender brace.
32. Connect the positive, then the negative battery cables.
33. Attach the air intake duct to the air cleaner.

Clutch Master Cylinder

REMOVAL & INSTALLATION

▶ See Figures 85, 86 and 87

➡For 1994 3.1L and all 1995-96 vehicles, the clutch master cylinder can be replaced as a separate assembly.

1. Disconnect the negative battery cable.
2. Remove the sound insulator from inside the vehicle.
3. Disconnect the clutch master cylinder pushrod from the clutch pedal.
4. Unfasten the clutch master cylinder retaining nuts at the front of the cowl, then remove the remote reservoir.
5. Detach the master cylinder assembly from the actuator cylinder by disconnecting the hydraulic line, then remove the master cylinder from the vehicle.

To install:

6. Attach the master cylinder to the actuator cylinder by fastening the hydraulic line.
7. Install the remote fluid reservoir, then secure with the retaining nuts. Tighten the nuts evenly to 18 ft. lbs. (25 Nm).
8. Connect the pushrod to the clutch pedal. If equipped, adjust the cruise control switch, as outlined in Section 6 of this manual.
9. Install the sound insulator.
10. Bleed the hydraulic system, as outlined later in this section.
11. Connect the negative battery cable.

Actuator (Slave) Cylinder

REMOVAL & INSTALLATION

▶ See Figures 85, 87 and 88

➡For 1994 3.1L and all 1995-96 vehicles, the clutch actuator cylinder can be replaced as a separate assembly.

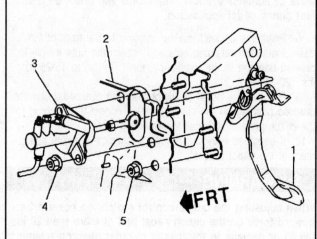

1 Clutch pedal
2 Panel assembly   4 27 Nm (20 lbs. ft.) nut
3 Master cylinder   5 27 Nm (20 lbs. ft.) nut

87957103

Fig. 86 Clutch master cylinder mounting — 1995 vehicle shown

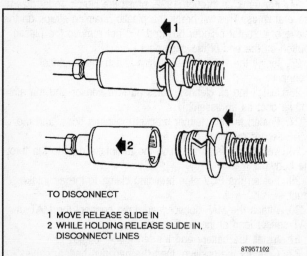

TO DISCONNECT

1 MOVE RELEASE SLIDE IN
2 WHILE HOLDING RELEASE SLIDE IN, DISCONNECT LINES

87957102

Fig. 85 Disconnecting the master cylinder-to-actuator cylinder hydraulic line

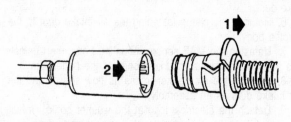

TO CONNECT

1 MOVE RELEASE SLIDE TO OUT POSITION (AS SHOWN)
2 WHILE HOLDING RELEASE SLIDE IN OUT POSITION, CONNECT LINES (CLICK SHOULD BE HEARD)

87957104

Fig. 87 Connecting the master cylinder-to-actuator cylinder hydraulic line

1. For the 3.1L engine, remove the air intake duct from the air cleaner.

2. Disconnect the negative battery cable.

3. Detach the master cylinder assembly from the actuator cylinder by disconnecting the hydraulic line.

4. Remove the transaxle assembly, as outlined earlier in this section.

5. Remove the clutch actuator cylinder from the transaxle.

To install:

6. Lubricate the inside diameter of the bearing with clutch bearing lubricant GM part no. 12345777 or equivalent.

7. Install the actuator cylinder in the transaxle, then install the transaxle assembly.

8. Connect the master cylinder-to-actuator hydraulic line.

9. Bleed the hydraulic system, as outlined later in this section.

10. If removed, install the air intake duct.

11. Connect the negative battery cable.

HYDRAULIC SYSTEM BLEEDING

1988-89 Vehicles

1. Remove any dirt or grease around the clutch master cylinder reservoir cap so that dirt cannot enter the system, then remove the cap and diaphragm.

2. Fill the reservoir to the top step with with Delco Supreme II® GM part no. 1052535, or equivalent approved DOT 3 brake fluid.

3. Fully loosen, but do not remove, the bleeder screw which is located on the slave (actuator) cylinder, next to the inlet connection.

4. Fluid will now flow from the master cylinder to the slave cylinder.

➡It is important that the reservoir remain filled throughout the procedure.

5. Air bubbles should now appear at the bleeder screw.

6. Continue this procedure until a steady stream of fluid without any air bubbles is present, then tighten the bleeder screw to 17 inch lbs. (2 Nm).

7. Check the fluid level in the reservoir and refill to the proper mark.

8. Fasten the master cylinder reservoir cap.

9. The system is now fully bled. Check the clutch operation by starting the engine, pushing the clutch pedal to the floor, then wait ten seconds and place transaxle in reverse.

10. If any grinding of the gears is noted, air may still be present in the system. The entire bleeding procedure must be repeated.

➡Never under any circumstances reuse fluid that has been in the system. The fluid may be contaminated with dirt and moisture.

1990-94 Vehicles

WITH BLEED SCREW

1. Remove any dirt or grease around the clutch master cylinder reservoir cap so that dirt cannot enter the system, then remove the cap and diaphragm.

2. Fill the reservoir to the top step with with Delco Supreme II® GM part no. 1052535, Hydraulic Clutch fluid GM part no. 12345347, or equivalent approved DOT 3 brake fluid.

3. Fully loosen, but do not remove, the bleeder screw on the slave cylinder next to the inlet connection.

4. Fluid will now flow from the master cylinder to the slave cylinder.

➡For efficient gravity fill, keep the reservoir filled throughout the procedure.

5. When a steady stream of fluid without any air bubbles is present, tighten the bleeder screw to 17 inch lbs. (2 Nm).

6. Check the fluid level in the reservoir and refill to the proper mark, then install the master cylinder reservoir diaphragm and cap.

7. The system is now fully bled. Check the clutch operation by starting the engine, pushing the clutch pedal to the floor, then wait ten seconds and place transaxle in reverse.

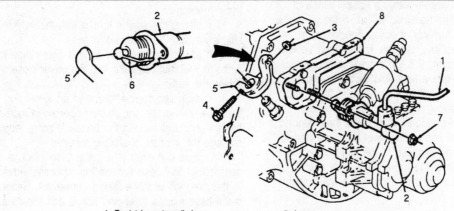

1. To clutch master cylinder
2. Clutch master and actuator cylinder assembly
3. Nut
4. Bolt—50 N·m (36 lbs. ft.)
5. Lever
6. Pushrod retainer (do not remove)
7. Nut
8. Transaxle support

87957097

Fig. 88 Clutch actuator cylinder mounting — Isuzu transaxle shown

8. If any grinding of the gears is noted, air may still be present in the system. The entire bleeding procedure must be repeated.

➡**Never under any circumstances reuse fluid that has been in the system. The fluid may be contaminated with dirt and moisture.**

WITHOUT BLEED SCREW

1. Remove the actuator (slave) cylinder from the transaxle, as outlined earlier in this section.

2. Loosen the master cylinder mounting attaching nuts to the end of the studs, but do not remove the master cylinder.

3. Remove any dirt or grease around the reservoir cap so dirt cannot enter the system, then remove the cap and diaphragm. Fill the reservoir with an approved DOT 3 brake fluid.

4. Depress the hydraulic actuator cylinder pushrod about 0.787 in. (20.0mm) into the slave cylinder bore and hold.

5. Install the diaphragm and cap on the reservoir while holding the slave cylinder pushrod in as described in the previous step.

6. Release the slave cylinder pushrod.

➡**The slave cylinder should be lower than the master cylinder.**

7. Hold the slave cylinder vertically with the pushrod end facing the ground.

8. Press the pushrod into the slave cylinder bore with short 0.390 in. (10.0mm) strokes.

9. Observe the reservoir for air bubbles. Continue until air bubbles no longer enter the reservoir.

10. Install the actuator (slave) cylinder to the transaxle.

11. Tighten the master cylinder attaching nuts to 15 ft. lbs. (20 Nm).

12. Check the fluid reservoir in the clutch master cylinder and add, if necessary. Install the diaphragm and cap to the reservoir.

13. To test the system, start the engine and push the clutch pedal to the floor. Wait 10 seconds and select reverse gear. There should be no gear clash. If clash is present, air may still be present in the system. Repeat bleeding procedure.

1995-96 Vehicles

➡**Do NOT use fluid which has been bled from a system to fill the reservoir, as it may be aerated, have too much moisture or possibly be contaminated.**

1. Remove any dirt or grease around the reservoir cap so dirt cannot enter the system, then remove the cap and diaphragm. Fill the reservoir to the top step with Hydraulic Clutch Fluid GM part. no 12345347 or equivalent approved DOT 3 fluid.

2. Attach a hose to the bleeder screw on the clutch actuator assembly and submerge the other end of the hose in a container of hydraulic clutch fluid.

3. Have an assistant depress the clutch pedal slowly, then hold it down.

4. Loosen the bleeder screw to purge air. Tighten the bleeder screw to 18 inch lbs. (2 Nm).

5. Repeat Step 4 until all air is purged from the system.

6. Fill the reservoir to the top step with Hydraulic Clutch Fluid GM part. no 12345347 or equivalent approved DOT 3 fluid. Install the fluid reservoir cap.

7. Start the engine and push the clutch pedal to the floor. Wait 10 seconds and select reverse gear. There should be no gear clash. If clash is present, air may still be present in the system. The bleeding procedure must be repeated.

AUTOMATIC TRANSAXLE

Understanding Automatic Transaxles

The automatic transaxle allows engine torque and power to be transmitted to the drive wheels within a narrow range of engine operating speeds. The transaxle will allow the engine to turn fast enough to produce plenty of power and torque at very low speeds, while keeping it at a sensible rpm at high vehicle speeds. The transaxle performs this job entirely without driver assistance. The transaxle uses a light fluid as the medium for the transmission of power. This fluid also works in the operation of various hydraulic control circuits and as a lubricant. Because the transaxle fluid performs all of these three functions, trouble within the unit can easily travel from one part to another. For this reason, and because of the complexity and unusual operating principles of the transaxle, a very sound understanding of the basic principles of operation will simplify troubleshooting.

THE TORQUE CONVERTER

The torque converter replaces the conventional clutch. It has three functions:

1. It allows the engine to idle with the vehicle at a standstill, even with the transaxle in gear.

2. It allows the transaxle to shift from range to range smoothly, without requiring that the driver close the throttle during the shift.

3. It multiplies engine torque to an increasing extent as vehicle speed drops and throttle opening is increased. This has the effect of making the transaxle more responsive and reduces the amount of shifting required.

The torque converter is a metal case which is shaped like a sphere that has been flattened on opposite sides. It is bolted to the rear end of the engine's crankshaft. Generally, the entire metal case rotates at engine speed and serves as the engine's flywheel.

The case contains three sets of blades. One set is attached directly to the case. This set forms the torus or pump. Another set is directly connected to the output shaft, and forms the turbine. The third set is mounted on a hub which, in turn, is mounted on a stationary shaft through a one-way clutch. This third set is known as the stator.

A pump, which is driven by the converter hub at engine speed, keeps the torque converter full of transaxle fluid at all times. Fluid flows continuously through the unit to provide cooling.

Under low speed acceleration, the torque converter functions as follows:

The torus is turning faster than the turbine. It picks up fluid at the center of the converter and, through centrifugal force, slings it outward. Since the outer edge of the converter moves faster than the portions at the center, the fluid picks up speed.

The fluid then enters the outer edge of the turbine blades. It then travels back toward the center of the converter case along the turbine blades. In impinging upon the turbine blades, the fluid loses the energy picked up in the torus.

If the fluid were now to immediately be returned directly into the torus, both halves of the converter would have to turn at approximately the same speed at all times, and torque input and output would both be the same.

In flowing through the torus and turbine, the fluid picks up 2 types of flow, or flow in 2 separate directions. It flows through the turbine blades, and it spins with the engine. The stator, whose blades are stationary when the vehicle is being accelerated at low speeds, converts one type of flow into another. Instead of allowing the fluid to flow straight back into the torus, the stator's curved blades turn the fluid almost 90° toward the direction of rotation of the engine. Thus the fluid does not flow as fast toward the torus, but is already spinning when the torus picks it up. This has the effect of allowing the torus to turn much faster than the turbine. This difference in speed may be compared to the difference in speed between the smaller and larger gears in any gear train. The result is that engine power output is higher, and engine torque is multiplied.

As the speed of the turbine increases, the fluid spins faster and faster in the direction of engine rotation. As a result, the ability of the stator to redirect the fluid flow is reduced. Under cruising conditions, the stator is eventually forced to rotate on its one-way clutch in the direction of engine rotation. Under these conditions, the torque converter begins to behave almost like a solid shaft, with the torus and turbine speeds being almost equal.

THE PLANETARY GEARBOX

The ability of the torque converter to multiply engine torque is limited. Also, the unit tends to be more efficient when the turbine is rotating at relatively high speeds. Therefore, a planetary gearbox is used to carry the power output of the turbine to the halfshafts.

Planetary gears function very similarly to conventional transaxle gears. However, their construction is different in that three elements make up one gear system, and, in that all three elements are different from one another. The three elements are: an outer gear that is shaped like a hoop, with teeth cut into the inner surface; a sun gear, mounted on a shaft and located at the very center of the outer gear; and a set of three planet gears, held by pins in a ring-like planet carrier, meshing with both the sun gear and the outer gear. Either the outer

gear or the sun gear may be held stationary, providing more than one possible torque multiplication factor for each set of gears. Also, if all three gears are forced to rotate at the same speed, the gearset forms, in effect, a solid shaft.

Most modern automatics use the planetary gears to provide either a single reduction ratio of about 1.8:1, or 2 reduction gears: a low of about 2.5:1, and an intermediate of about 1.5:1. Bands and clutches are used to hold various portions of the gearsets to the transaxle case or to the shaft on which they are mounted. Shifting is accomplished, then, by changing the portion of each planetary gearset which is held to the transaxle case or to the shaft.

THE SERVOS AND ACCUMULATORS

The servos are hydraulic pistons and cylinders. They resemble the hydraulic actuators used on many familiar machines, such as bulldozers. Hydraulic fluid enters the cylinder, under pressure, and forces the piston to move to engage the band or clutches.

The accumulators are used to cushion the engagement of the servos. The transaxle fluid must pass through the accumulator on the way to the servo. The accumulator housing contains a thin piston which is sprung away from the discharge passage of the accumulator. When fluid passes through the accumulator on the way to the servo, it must move the piston against spring pressure, and this action smooths out the action of the servo.

THE HYDRAULIC CONTROL SYSTEM

The hydraulic pressure used to operate the servos comes from the main transaxle oil pump. This fluid is channeled to the various servos through the shift valves. There is generally a manual shift valve which is operated by the transaxle selector lever and an automatic shift valve for each automatic upshift the transaxle provides: i.e., 2-speed automatics have a low/high shift valve, while 3-speeds have a 1-2 valve, and a 2-3 valve.

There are 2 pressures which effect the operation of these valves. One is the governor pressure which is affected by vehicle speed. The other is the modulator pressure which is affected by intake manifold vacuum or throttle position. Governor pressure rises with an increase in vehicle speed, and modulator pressure rises as the throttle is opened wider. By responding to these 2 pressures, the shift valves cause the upshift points to be delayed with increased throttle opening to make the best use of the engine's power output.

Most transaxles also make use of an auxiliary circuit for downshifting. This circuit may be actuated by the throttle linkage or the vacuum line which actuates the modulator, or by a cable or solenoid. It applies pressure to a special downshift surface on the shift valve or valves.

The transaxle modulator also governs the line pressure, used to actuate the servos. In this way, the clutches and bands will be actuated with a force matching the torque output of the engine.

Identification

All of the J-cars use the Turbo Hydra-Matic 125C automatic transaxle as optional equipment. This is a fully automatic unit of conventional design, incorporating a four element hydraulic torque converter, a compound planetary gear set, and a dual sprocket and drive link assembly. The sprockets and drive link (Hy-Vo chain) connect the torque converter assembly to the transaxle gears. The transaxle also incorporates the differential assembly, which is of conventional design. Power is transmitted from the transaxle to the final drive and differential assembly through helical cut gears.

No overhaul procedures are given in this book because of the complexity of the transaxle. Transaxle removal and installation, adjustment, and halfshaft removal, installation, and overhaul procedures are covered.

By September 1, 1991, Hydra-Matic will have changed the name designation of the THM 125C automatic transaxle. The new name designation for this transaxle will be Hydra-Matic 3T40. Transaxles built between 1989 and 1990 will serve as transitional years in which a dual system, made up of the old designation and the new designation will be in effect. In 1995-96, the Hydra-Matic 4T40-E became available as an optional equipment on some models.

Fluid Pan and Filter

Pan removal, fluid and filter changes are covered in Section 1 of this manual.

Adjustments

SHIFT CONTROL CABLE ADJUSTMENT

1. Place the shift lever in the **N**.

➡**Neutral can be found by rotating the transaxle selector shaft clockwise from P through R to N.**

2. Loosely attach the cable to the transaxle shift lever with a nut. Assemble the cable to the cable bracket and to the shift lever. Tighten the cable to transaxle shift lever nut.

➡**The lever must be held out of P when torquing the nut.**

THROTTLE VALVE (TV) CABLE ADJUSTMENT

Setting of the TV cable must be done by rotating the throttle lever at the carburetor or throttle body. Do not use the accelerator pedal to rotate the throttle lever.

1. With the engine off, depress and hold the reset tab at the engine end of the TV cable.
2. Move the slider until it stops against the fitting.
3. Release the rest tab.
4. Rotate the throttle lever to its full travel.
5. The slider must move (ratchet) toward the lever when the lever is rotated to its full travel position.
6. Recheck after the engine is hot and road test the vehicle.

Neutral Start/Back-up Light Switch

The automatic transaxle utilizes the neutral safety switch and back-up light switch as a combined unit. This switch is located under the console, next to the shifter on 1982-84 models and on top of the of the transaxle on 1985-96 models.

REMOVAL & INSTALLATION

1982-84 Vehicles
▶ **See Figure 89**

1. Disconnect the negative battery cable.
2. Remove the console assembly.
3. Detach the electrical connector.
4. Unfasten the retaining bolt/screw, then remove the switch from the side of the shifter.
5. Installation is the reverse of the removal procedure.

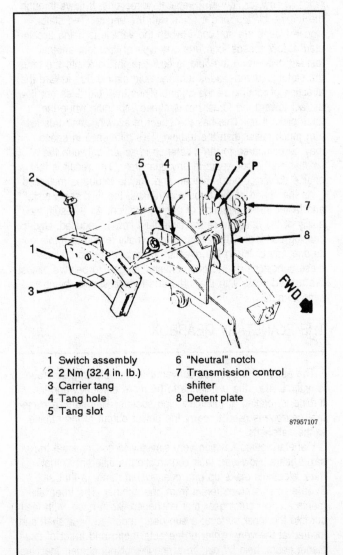

1 Switch assembly	6 "Neutral" notch
2 2 Nm (32.4 in. lb.)	7 Transmission control
3 Carrier tang	shifter
4 Tang hole	8 Detent plate
5 Tang slot	

87957107

Fig. 89 Neutral safety/back-up switch on 1982-84 vehicles is located under the console next to the shifter

1987-96 Vehicles
♦ See Figure 90

1. Disconnect the negative battery cable.
2. Remove the shift linkage.
3. Detach the electrical connector from the switch.
4. Unfasten the switch-to-transaxle screws/bolts, then remove the switch.

To install:

➡ **After switch adjustment, make sure that the engine will only start in "Park" or "Neutral". If the engine will start in any other gear, re-adjust the switch.**

5. If installing the old switch, proceed as follows:
   a. Place the shift shaft/control lever in "Neutral".
   b. Align the flats of the shift shaft with the switch, then loosely install the mounting bolts.

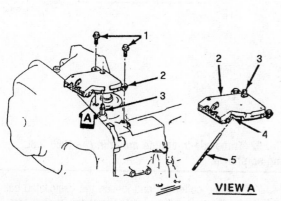

1 24 Nm (18 lbs. ft.) bolt
2 Switch asm.
3 Trans. shaft
4 Service adjustment hole
5 3/32 inch drill bit or 2.34 dia. gage pin

87957109

Fig. 90 View of the neutral safety/back-up light switch — 1992 vehicle shown

c. Insert a gauge pin in the service adjustment hole and rotate the switch until the pin drops to a depth of $^9/_{64}$ in. (9mm).
   d. Tighten the bolts to 18 ft. lbs. (24 Nm), then remove the gauge pin.
6. If installing a new switch, proceed as follows:
   a. Place the shift shaft/control lever in "Neutral".
   b. Align the flats of the shift shaft to the flats in the switch, then install the switch assembly. Tighten the bolts to 18 ft. lbs. (24 Nm).
   c. If the bolt holes do not align with the mounting boss on the transaxle, verify the transaxle is in the "Neutral" position, do not rotate the switch.
   d. If the shift has been rotated and the pin broken, the switch can be adjusted by following the procedure in Step 5.
7. Attach the electrical connector to the switch.
8. Install the shift linkage.
9. Connect the negative battery cable.
10. Start the engine and check the switch operation.

Transaxle

REMOVAL & INSTALLATION

1982-86 Vehicles
♦ See Figures 91 and 92

1. Disconnect the negative battery cable at the battery and where it attaches to the transaxle.
2. On the 1982-84 models, insert a ¼ in. x 2 in. bolt into the hole in the right front motor mount to prevent any mislocation during the transaxle removal.
3. On 4-cylinder engines, remove the air cleaner.
4. On V6 engines remove the following:
   a. Remove the air intake duct from the air cleaner.
   b. Remove the left fender brace.
   c. Disconnect the MAT sensor lead at the air cleaner.
   d. Disconnect the mass air flow sensor lead.
   e. Remove the PCV pipe retaining clamp from the air intake duct.
   f. Remove the clamp retaining the air intake duct to the throttle body.
   g. Remove the mass air flow sensor mounting bolt. Remove the air cleaner bracket mounting bolts at the battery tray.
   h. Remove the air cleaner, mass air flow sensor and air intake duct as an assembly.
   i. Remove the heat shield at the crossover pipe and remove the crossover pipe.
5. Disconnect the T.V. cable at the throttle body.
6. Unscrew the bolt securing the T.V. cable to the transaxle. Pull up on the cable cover at the transaxle until the cable can be seen. Disconnect the cable from the transaxle rod.
7. Remove the wiring harness retaining bolt at the top of the transaxle.
8. Disconnect the hose from the air management valve and then pull the wiring harness up and out of the way.

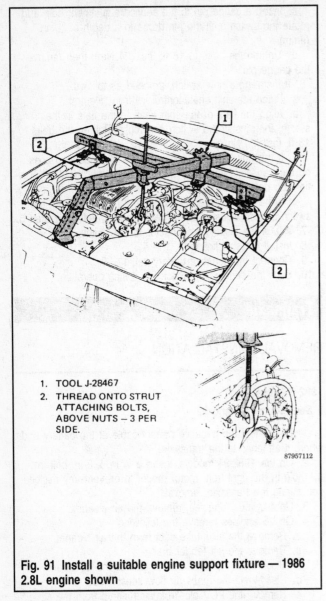

1. TOOL J-28467
2. THREAD ONTO STRUT ATTACHING BOLTS, ABOVE NUTS – 3 PER SIDE.

87957112

Fig. 91 Install a suitable engine support fixture — 1986 2.8L engine shown

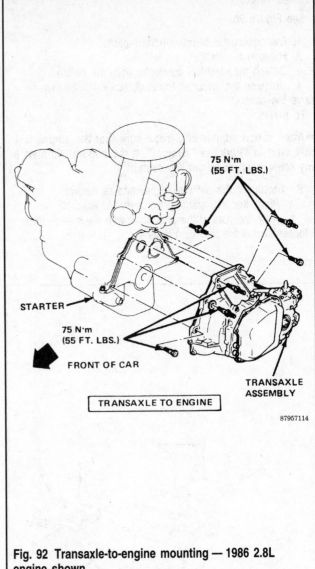

Fig. 92 Transaxle-to-engine mounting — 1986 2.8L engine shown

9. Install an engine support bar as shown in the illustration. Raise the engine just enough to take the pressure off the motor mounts.

✳✳CAUTION

The engine support bar must be located in the center of the cowl and the bolts must be tightened before attempting to support the engine.

10. Remove the transaxle mount and bracket assembly. It may be necessary to raise the engine slightly to aid in removal.
11. Disconnect the shift control linkage from the transaxle.
12. Unfasten and remove the top transaxle-to-engine mounting bolts. Loosen, but do not remove, the transaxle-to-engine bolt nearest to the starter.
13. Unlock the steering column. Raise and support the front of the car. Remove the front wheels.

14. Pull out the cotter pin and loosen the castellated ball joint nut until the ball joint separates from the control arm. Repeat on the other side of the car.
15. Disconnect the stabilizer bar from the left lower control arm.
16. Remove the six bolts that secure the left front suspension support assembly.
17. Install drive axle seal protectors and connect an axle shaft removal tool (J-28468) to a slide hammer (J-23907).
18. Position the tool behind the axle shaft cones and then pull the cones out and away from the transaxle. Remove the axle shafts and plug the transaxle bores to reduce fluid leakage.
19. Remove the nut that secures the transaxle control cable bracket to the transaxle, then remove the engine-to-transaxle stud.
20. Detach the speedometer cable at the transaxle.
21. Disconnect the transaxle strut (stabilizer) at the transaxle.
22. Unfasten the four retaining screws and remove the torque converter shield.

23. Scribe a mark for on the flywheel for reassembly and remove the three bolts securing the torque converter to the flex plate.

24. Disconnect and plug the oil cooler lines at the transaxle. Remove the starter.

25. Unfasten the screws that hold the brake and fuel line brackets to the left side of the underbody. This will allow the lines to be moved slightly for clearance during transaxle removal.

26. Remove the bolt that was loosened in Step 12.

27. Remove the transaxle from the vehicle.

To install:

28. Position the transaxle in the car.

29. Place a small amount of light grease on the torque converter pilot hub.

30. Make sure to properly seat the torque convertor in the oil pump.

31. Guide the right drive axle shaft into its bore as the transaxle is being raised. The right drive axle cannot be installed AFTER the transaxle is connected to the engine.

32. Lower the transaxle to the engine bolts and remove the transaxle jack.

33. Install the transaxle to engine support bracket.

34. Install the transaxle cooler lines.

35. Position the LH axle into the transaxle.

36. Install the torque converter-to-flywheel bolts and tighten to 46 ft. lbs. (62 Nm). Re-torque the first bolt after all three have been tightened.

37. Install the transaxle converter shield.

38. The remainder of the installation is the reverse of removal with the following precautions.

   a. Check the suspension alignment.
   b. Check the transaxle fluid level.

1987-94 Vehicles

▶ **See Figures 93, 94, 95 and 96**

1. Disconnect the negative battery cable.

2. For 1989-93 vehicles, drain the cooling system, then disconnect the heater core hoses.

3. Remove the air intake duct or air cleaner assembly.

4. For 6-cylinder engines only, disconnect the exhaust crossover pipe from the manifolds.

5. Disconnect the TV cable from the throttle lever and the transaxle and unroute.

6. Remove the fluid level indicator and the filler tube.

7. For 1987-88 vehicles, insert a a ¼ in. x 2 in. bolt into the hole in the right front motor mount to maintain drive line alignment.

8. Install J 28467-A or equivalent engine support fixture.

9. Unfasten the nut securing the wiring harness to the transaxle.

10. Remove the wiring harness-to-transaxle nut.

11. Label and detach the wires at the TCC connector and the neutral safety/back up light switch.

✳✳WARNING

When servicing requires that the "T" latch type wiring connector be detached from the switch, be sure to reassemble the "T" latch and the connector. Failure to do so may result in intermittent loss of switch functions.

12. Disconnect the shift linkage from the transaxle.

13. Unfasten the top two transaxle-to-engine bolts.

14. Remove the left upper transaxle mount and bracket assembly.

15. Disconnect the rubber hose from the transaxle-to-vent pipe.

16. Unfasten the remaining upper engine-to-transaxle bolts.

17. Raise and safely support the vehicle.

18. Remove the front wheel and tire assemblies.

19. If equipped, remove both front ABS wheel speed sensors and the harness from the left suspension support.

20. Separate both ball joints from the control arms.

21. Remove the engine-to-transaxle brace.

22. Unfasten the left stabilizer link pin bolt and frame bushing clamp nuts.

23. Remove the left suspension support assembly and cross bar. Remove both drive axles (halfshafts) from the transaxle, then support them.

24. On the 2.0L (VIN H) engine, disconnect the exhaust pipe from the manifold.

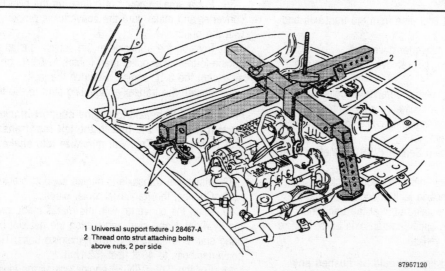

1 Universal support fixture J 28467-A
2 Thread onto strut attaching bolts above nuts, 2 per side

87957120

Fig. 93 View of the correct installation of the engine support fixture on the 2.0L (VIN H) engine

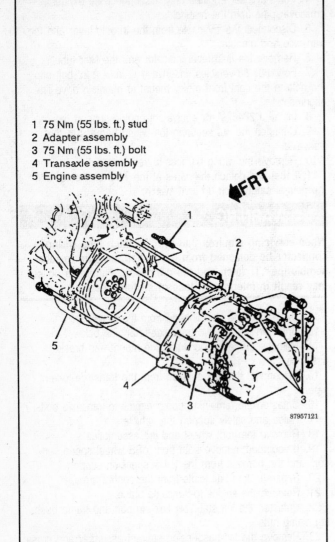

1 75 Nm (55 lbs. ft.) stud
2 Adapter assembly
3 75 Nm (55 lbs. ft.) bolt
4 Transaxle assembly
5 Engine assembly

FRT

87957121

Fig. 94 Engine-to-transaxle mounting — 1994 2.0L (VIN H) engine shown

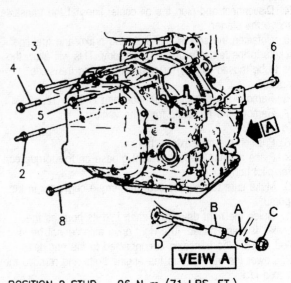

VEIW A

POSITION 2 STUD — 96 N·m (71 LBS. FT.)
POSITION 3 STUD — 96 N·m (71 LBS. FT.)
POSITION 4 AND 6 — 96 N·m (71 LBS. FT.)
POSITION 5 BOLT — 96 N·m (71 LBS. FT.)
POSITION 8 BOLT — 56 N·m (41 LBS. FT.)

A Oil pan
B Spacer
C 56 Nm (41 lbs. ft.) nut
D 13 Nm (115 lbs. in.) stud

87957122

Fig. 95 View of the engine to transaxle mounting and torque specifications — 1994 3.1L engine shown

25. Remove the starter motor, as outlined in Section 2 of this manual.
26. Disconnect the coolant inlet pipe from the transaxle and manifold.
27. Remove the transaxle converter cover.
28. On the 2.0L (VIN H) engine, remove the lower intake manifold brace.
29. Unfasten the torque converter-to-transaxle bolts, then matchmark the converter to the flywheel for assembly.
30. Disconnect and plug the transaxle cooler pipes. Remove the transaxle cable selector bracket.
31. Detach the Vehicle Speed Sensor (VSS) connector from the sensor.
32. Remove the transaxle-to-engine support bracket.
33. Position a suitable transaxle jack under the transaxle, then remove the transaxle mounting strut at the transaxle.
34. Unfasten the remaining engine-to-transaxle bolts, then remove the transaxle from the vehicle.

➡The transaxle cooler and lines should be flushed any time the transaxle is removed for overhaul or to replace the pump, case or converter.

To install:
35. Put a small amount of grease on the pilot hub of the converter and make sure the converter is properly engaged with the pump.
36. Position the transaxle in the vehicle. Install the lower engine-to-transaxle bolts, then tighten to 55 ft. lbs. (75 Nm) for all except the 3.1L engine. Remove the jack.
37. Fasten the transaxle mounting strut to the transaxle.

➡Install the transaxle-to-engine support bracket. It is important to center the bolt in the left rear transaxle mount slot to the body. This will minimize idle shake and harsh engagement.

38. Install the transaxle-to-engine support bracket.
39. Connect the transaxle cooler pipes.
40. Align the converter with the marks made previously on the flywheel. Hand start and tighten the net slot bolt first, then hand start and tighten the two remaining bolts. Tighten the converter bolts to 46 ft. lbs. (62 Nm).
41. For the 2.0L (VIN H) engine, install the lower intake manifold brace.

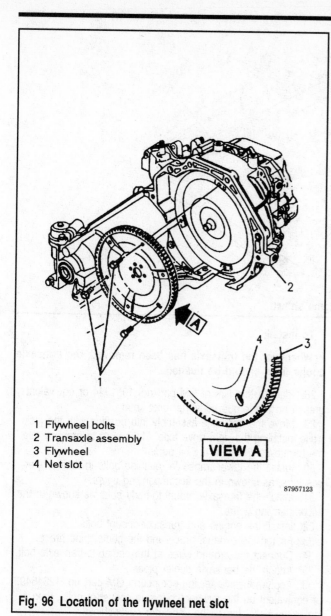

1 Flywheel bolts
2 Transaxle assembly
3 Flywheel
4 Net slot

VIEW A

87957123

Fig. 96 Location of the flywheel net slot

42. Fasten the transaxle selector bracket.
43. Connect the coolant inlet pipe to the transaxle and exhaust manifold studs.
44. Install the transaxle converter cover.
45. Install the starter assembly.
46. For the 2.0L (VIN H) engine, connect the exhaust pipe to the manifold.
47. Install the drive axles (halfshafts) to the transaxle.
48. Fasten the left suspension support assembly and the cross bar.
49. Install the left stabilizer shaft frame bushing clamp nuts and link pin bolt.
50. Install the engine-to-transaxle brace.
51. Fasten the right and left ball joints to the control arms.
52. Attach the VSS connector to the transaxle.
53. Connect the left side ABS harness and the WSS connector to the sensor.
54. Install the wheel and tire assemblies.
55. Carefully lower the vehicle.

56. Install the upper transaxle mount bolts, tighten to 55 ft. lbs. (75 Nm), except for the 3.1L engine. For the 3.1L engine, tighten to the specifications shown in the accompanying figure.
57. Fasten the left side transaxle mount.
58. Attach the shift linkage to the transaxle.
59. Fasten the wiring connectors at the TCC converter and the park/neutral switch.
60. Install the wiring harness and secure to the transaxle with the retaining nut.
61. For 1987-88 vehicles, remove the alignment bolt.
62. Remove the engine support fixture.
63. On the 3.1L engine, install the crossover pipe to the exhaust manifold.
64. Install the oil level indicator and fill tube.
65. Connect the TV cable at the transaxle and throttle lever.
66. Attach the rubber hose to the transaxle vent pipe.
67. Install the air inlet duct or air cleaner assembly.
68. Connect the negative battery cable, then check the transaxle fluid level and add if necessary.

1995-96 Vehicles

3T40 AUTOMATIC TRANSAXLE

▶ **See Figures 97, 98 and 99**

1. Disconnect the negative battery cable.
2. Properly drain the transaxle.
3. Remove the air intake duct.
4. Disconnect the TV cable. Remove the shift cable and bracket.
5. Tag and detach all necessary vacuum lines and electrical connections.
6. Remove the power steering pump and set aside.
7. Remove the transaxle filler tube.
8. Install engine support fixture J 28467-A or equivalent.
9. Remove the top engine-to-transaxle bolts.
10. Raise and safely support the vehicle.
11. Remove both front tire and wheel assemblies. Remove the left splash shield.
12. Remove both front ABS wheel speed sensors and the harness from the left suspension support.
13. As outlined in Section 8 of this manual, remove both lower ball joints.
14. Disconnect the stabilizer shaft links.
15. Remove the front air deflector.
16. Remove the left suspension support and both drive axles.
17. Disconnect the engine-to-transaxle brace, then remove the transaxle converter cover.
18. Remove the starter, as outlined in Section 2 of this manual.
19. Unfasten the flywheel-to-torque converter bolts.
20. Disconnect the transaxle cooler pipes.
21. Detach the ground wires from the engine-to-transaxle bolt.
22. Remove the cooler pipe brace and the exhaust brace.
23. Remove the bolts from the engine and transaxle mount.
24. Support the transaxle with a suitable jack.
25. Unfasten the transaxle mount-to-body bolts.
26. Remove the heater core hose pipe brace-to-transaxle nut and bolt.
27. Unfasten the remaining engine-to-transaxle bolts, then remove the transaxle assembly from the vehicle.

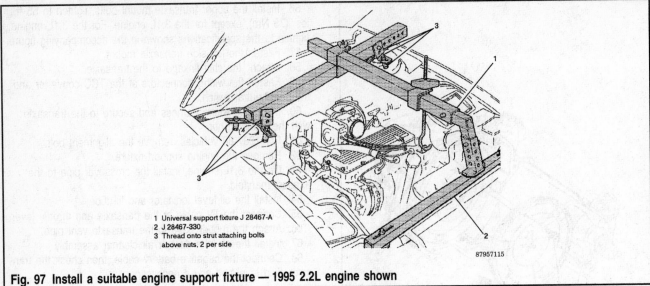

1 Universal support fixture J 28467-A
2 J 28467-330
3 Thread onto strut attaching bolts
   above nuts, 2 per side

87957115

Fig. 97 Install a suitable engine support fixture — 1995 2.2L engine shown

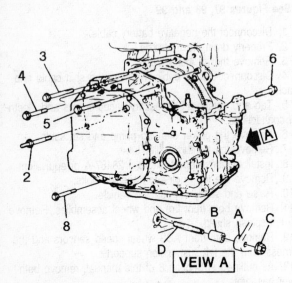

POSITION 2 STUD - 96 Nm (71 LBS. FT.)
POSITION 3 STUD - 96 Nm (71 LBS. FT.)
POSITION 4 AND 6 - 96 Nm (71 LBS. FT.)
POSITION 5 BOLT - 96 Nm (71 LBS. FT.)
POSITION 8 BOLT - 56 Nm (41 LBS. FT.)

A Oil pan
B Spacer
C 56 Nm (41 lbs. ft.) nut
D 13 Nm (115 lbs. in.) stud

87957117

Fig. 98 Transaxle-to-engine bolt positions — 3T40 transaxle shown

To install:

➡ Whenever the transaxle has been removed, the transaxle cooler lines should be flushed.

28. Place a thin film of GM part no. 1051344 or equivalent grease on the torque converter pilot knob.

29. Move the transaxle assembly into position with the jack while installing the right drive axle. Make sure to properly seat the torque converter in the oil pump.

30. Install the lower transaxle retaining bolts in their proper positions, as shown in the accompanying figure.

31. Install the transaxle mount-to-body bolts as shown in the accompanying figure.

32. Install the engine and transaxle mount bolts.

33. Fasten the exhaust brace and the cooler pipe brace.

34. Connect the ground wires at the engine-to-transaxle bolt.

35. Attach the transaxle cooler pipes.

36. Apply adhesive/sealing compound GM part no. 12345493 or equivalent on the flywheel-to-torque converter bolts, then install the bolts. Install the converter cover/shield.

37. Install the starter.

38. Fasten the engine-to-transaxle brace.

39. Install the drive axles and the left suspension support.

40. Fasten the front air deflector.

41. Connect the stabilizer shaft links and the lower ball joints.

42. Install both ABS wheel speed sensors.

43. Fasten the left splash shield, then install the heater core pipe brace nut and bolt.

44. Install the front wheel and tire assemblies, then carefully lower the vehicle.

45. Install the top engine-to-transaxle bolts.

46. Remove the engine support fixture.

47. Install the filler tube.

48. Install the power steering pump assembly, then adjust the belt.

49. Attach the electrical connections and vacuum lines, as tagged during removal.

50. Install the shift cable and bracket. Connect the TV cable.

51. Fasten the air intake duct.

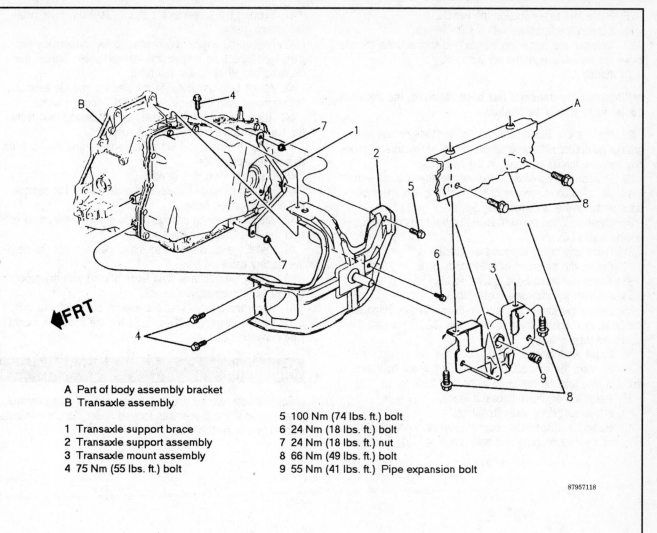

A Part of body assembly bracket
B Transaxle assembly

1 Transaxle support brace
2 Transaxle support assembly
3 Transaxle mount assembly
4 75 Nm (55 lbs. ft.) bolt

5 100 Nm (74 lbs. ft.) bolt
6 24 Nm (18 lbs. ft.) bolt
7 24 Nm (18 lbs. ft.) nut
8 66 Nm (49 lbs. ft.) bolt
9 55 Nm (41 lbs. ft.) Pipe expansion bolt

87957118

Fig. 99 View of the transaxle mount, bracket and bracket — 1995 3T40 transaxle shown

52. Connect the negative battery cable, then fill the transaxle to the proper level.

4T40E TRANSAXLES

1. Disconnect the negative battery cable.
2. Remove the air cleaner assembly.
3. Disconnect the shift linkage from the transaxle.
4. Detach the wiring connections from the transaxle.
5. Install J 28467-A or equivalent engine support fixture.
6. Unfasten the upper engine-to-transaxle bolts.
7. Raise and safely support the vehicle.
8. Remove both front tire and wheel assemblies. Remove the left and right splash shields.
9. Remove both front ABS wheel speed sensors and the harness from the left suspension support.
10. Using tool J 24319-B or equivalent, remove both outer tie rods from the steering knuckle.
11. Separate both ball joints from the steering knuckle using tool J 38892 or equivalent.
12. Remove the front suspension support brace, then re-move the engine mount strut from the strut mount bracket.

13. Support the suspension support assembly, then remove the bolts. Loosen the suspension support assembly enough to disconnect the steering coupling and both power steering fluid lines.
14. Remove both drive axles (halfshafts) from the transaxle, then support them.
15. Unfasten the engine-to-transaxle brace.
16. Remove the shift cable bracket.
17. As outlined in Section 2 of this manual, remove the starter.
18. Unfasten the retaining bolts, then remove the transaxle converter cover/shield.
19. Matchmark the flywheel-to-torque converter for reas-sembly, then unfasten the torque converter-to-flywheel bolts.
20. Disconnect the transaxle cooler pipes. Remove the brake hose bracket-to-body.
21. Unfasten the transaxle mount pipe expansion bolt.
22. Unfasten the transaxle mount-to-body bolts.
23. Carefully lower the vehicle.
24. Lower the transaxle with the engine support fixture enough to remove the transaxle.

25. Raise and safely support the vehicle.
26. Support the transaxle with a suitable jack.
27. Unfasten the remaining transaxle-to-engine bolts, then remove the transaxle from the vehicle.

To install:

➡**Whenever the transaxle has been removed, the transaxle cooler lines should be flushed.**

28. Place a thin film of GM part no. 1051344 or equivalent grease on the torque converter pilot knob. Make sure to properly seat the torque converter in the oil pump.
29. Position the transaxle in the vehicle, then secure with the lower transaxle-to-engine bolts. Tighten to the specifications shown in the accompanying figure.
30. Carefully lower the vehicle. Raise the transaxle with the engine support fixture.
31. Raise and safely support the vehicle.
32. Fasten the transaxle mount-to-body bolts.
33. Attach the brake hose bracket to body.
34. Connect the transaxle cooler pipes.
35. Fasten the torque converter-to-flywheel bolts. Hand start the bolts, then tighten them to 46 ft. lbs. (62 Nm). Install the converter cover/shield.
36. Install the starter.
37. Connect the shift cable bracket. Tighten the bolt to 18 ft. lbs. (25 Nm) and the nut to 37 ft. lbs. (50 Nm).
38. Install the engine-to-transaxle brace.
39. Install both drive axles (halfshafts).
40. Raise the suspension support assembly enough to connect the steering coupling and both power steering fluid lines.

41. Support the suspension support assembly, then install the retaining bolts.
42. Fasten the engine mount strut to the suspension support. Install the front suspension support brace. Tighten the retaining bolt to 49 ft. lbs. (66 Nm).
43. Attach both ball joints to the steering knuckle assembly, then connect both outer tie rods to the steering knuckle.
44. Attach both front ABS wheel speed sensors and fasten the harness to the left suspension support.
45. Install the right and left splash shields and the front tire and wheel assemblies.
46. Carefully lower the vehicle.
47. Install the upper transaxle-to-engine bolts, the remove the engine support fixture.
48. Attach the wiring connections to the transaxle, then connect the shift linkage to the transaxle.
49. Install the air cleaner assembly, then connect the negative battery cable.
50. Check the transaxle fluid lever, and fill with the proper type of oil, if necessary.
51. Apply the brakes, start the engine, then shift the transaxle from "Reverse" to "Drive". Fasten the transaxle mount pipe expansion bolt.

Halfshafts

For halfshaft remove and installation and CV-joint overhaul, please refer to the procedures located under manual transaxle located in this section.

FRONT SUSPENSION
  CONTROL ARM/SUSPENSION
    SUPPORT 8-12
  FRONT END ALIGNMENT 8-18
  FRONT HUB AND BEARING 8-16
  LOWER BALL JOINT 8-8
  MACPHERSON STRUTS 8-4
  STABILIZER SHAFT (SWAY
    BAR) 8-12
  STEERING KNUCKLE 8-16
  STRUT CARTRIDGE 8-8
REAR SUSPENSION
  COIL SPRINGS 8-22
  COIL-OVER SHOCK ABSORBER 8-25
  REAR AXLE/CONTROL ARM 8-25
  REAR END ALIGNMENT 8-26
  REAR HUB AND BEARING 8-26
  SHOCK ABSORBERS 8-22
  STABILIZER BAR 8-26
SPECIFICATIONS CHARTS
  WHEEL ALIGNMENT
    SPECIFICATIONS 8-19
STEERING
  IGNITION LOCK CYLINDER 8-35
  IGNITION SWITCH 8-31
  POWER STEERING PUMP 8-41
  RACK AND PINION UNIT 8-40
  STEERING COLUMN 8-37
  STEERING COLUMN HOUSING
    STEERING SHAFT AND IGNITION
    SWITCH HOUSING JACKET
    BUSHING 8-36
  STEERING LINKAGE 8-39
  STEERING WHEEL 8-28
  TURN SIGNAL (COMBINATION)
    SWITCH 8-29
  WINDSHIELD WIPER SWITCH 8-35
WHEELS
  FRONT AND REAR WHEELS 8-2
  WHEEL LUG STUDS 8-2

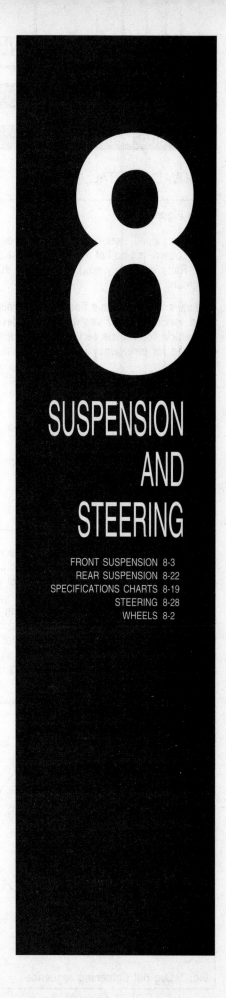

8

SUSPENSION
AND
STEERING

FRONT SUSPENSION 8-3
REAR SUSPENSION 8-22
SPECIFICATIONS CHARTS 8-19
STEERING 8-28
WHEELS 8-2

WHEELS

Front and Rear Wheels

REMOVAL & INSTALLATION

▶ See Figure 1

1. If equipped, remove the hub cap/wheel cover.
2. Loosen, but do not remove the lug nuts.
3. Raise and safely support vehicle so the tire is clear of the ground.

➡ **Always use a suitable floor jack for raising the vehicle to be serviced. Never use the jacking device supplied with the vehicle for vehicle service. That jacking device is designed for emergency use only to change a flat tire.**

4. Remove the lug nuts, then remove the wheel from the vehicle.
   To install:
5. Install the wheel.
6. Install the lug nuts, then hand-tighten in a star pattern.
7. Carefully lower the vehicle.
8. Final tighten the lug nuts, in a star pattern, to 100 ft. lbs. (140 Nm).

INSPECTION

Inspect the tread for abnormal wear, check for nails or other foreign material embedded into the tire. To check for leaks, submerse the wheel assembly into a tub of water and watch for air bubbles.

Wheels must be replaced if they are bent, dented, leak air through welds, have enlongated bolt holes, if wheel nuts won't stay tight, or if the wheels are heavily rusted. Replacement wheels must be equivalent to the original equipment wheels in load capacity, diameter, rim width, offset, and mounting configuration.

A wheel of improper size may affect wheel bearing life, brake cooling, speedometer/odometer calibration, vehicle ground clearance and tire clearance to the body and/or chassis.

➡ **Replacement with used wheels is not recommended as their service history may have included severe treatment or very high mileage and they could fail without warning.**

Wheel Lug Studs

All models use metric wheel nuts and studs. The nut will have the word "metric" stamped on the face and the stud will have the letter "M" into the threaded end.

The thread size of the metric wheel nuts and wheel studs are M12 X 1.5, this signifies:
- M = Metric
- 12 = Diameter in millimeters
- 1.5 = Millimeters per thread

REPLACEMENT

➡ **Never try to reuse a wheel stud. Once a wheel stud has been removed, discard it and replace it with a new one.**

Front Wheels
▶ See Figures 2 and 3

1. Remove the tire and wheel assembly.
2. As described later in this section, remove the hub and bearing assembly.
3. Using tool J 6627-A or equivalent wheel stud remover tool, remove and discard the wheel stud(s).
   To install:
4. Insert the new stud from the rear of the hub.
5. Install flat washers and nut (flat side down), onto the wheel stud, then tighten until the wheel stud is fully seated.
6. Remove the nut and washers.

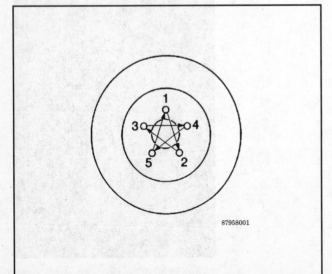

Fig. 1 Lug nut tightening sequence

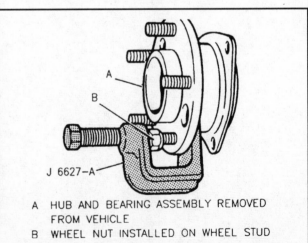

A   HUB AND BEARING ASSEMBLY REMOVED
     FROM VEHICLE
B   WHEEL NUT INSTALLED ON WHEEL STUD

Fig. 2 Once the hub and bearing is removed from the vehicle, use the proper tool to remove the wheel stud(s)

7. Install the hub and bearing assembly as outlined later in this section.

8. Install the tire and wheel assembly.

Rear Wheels

1. Remove the tire and wheel assembly.

2. Remove the brake drum, then remove the hub and bearing assembly. For details, please refer to the procedure located later in this section.

3. Unfasten and remove the wheel stud(s) using tool J 6627-A or an equivalent wheel stud removal tool. Discard the removed stud(s).

To install:

4. Insert the new stud from the rear of the hub.

5. Install 4 flat washers onto the stud.

6. Install the wheel nut with the flat side toward the washers.

7. Tighten the nut until the stud head is properly seated in the hub flange.

8. Remove the nut and washers.

9. Install the hub and bearing assembly and the brake drum.

10. Install the tire and wheel assembly.

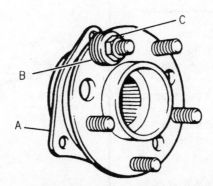

A HUB AND BEARING ASSEMBLY REMOVED
   FROM VEHICLE
B INSERT WASHER OVER WHEEL STUD
C TIGHTEN NUT TO DRAW WHEEL STUD
   INTO CORRECT POSITION

87958003

Fig. 3 Install washers and a nut on the wheel stud, then tighten until the stud is properly seated

FRONT SUSPENSION

The J-cars use MacPherson strut front suspension designs. A MacPherson strut combines the functions of a shock absorber and an upper suspension member (upper arm) into one unit. The strut is surrounded by a coil spring, which provides normal front suspension functions.

The strut bolts to the body shell at its upper end, and to the steering knuckle at the lower end. The strut pivots with the steering knuckle by means of a sealed mounting assembly at the upper end which contains a preloaded, non-adjustable bearing.

The steering knuckle is connected to the chassis at the lower end by a conventional lower control arm, and pivots in the arm in a preloaded ball joint of standard design. The knuckle is fastened to the ball joint stud by means of a castellated nut and cotter pin.

Advantages of the MacPherson strut design, aside from its relative simplicity, include reduced weight and friction, minimal intrusion into the engine and passenger compartments, and ease of service.

MacPherson Struts

The struts retain the springs under tremendous pressure even when removed from the car. For these reasons, several expensive special tools and substantial specialized knowledge are required to safely and effectively work on these parts. We recommend that if spring or shock absorber repair work is required, you remove the strut or struts involved and take them to a repair facility which is fully equipped and familiar with the car.

REMOVAL & INSTALLATION

▶ **See Figures 4, 5, 6, 7, 8, 9 and 10**

1. From inside the engine compartment, pry off the cover on the strut tower, if equipped, then unfasten the upper strut-to-body nuts and/or bolts.

2. Loosen the wheel lug nuts, then raise and safely support the vehicle.

3. Place jackstands under the front crossmember. Lower the vehicle slightly so the weight of the car rests on the jackstands and NOT the control arms.

4. Remove the wheel and tire assembly.

5. Before removing front suspension components, their positions should be marked so they may assemble correctly. Refer to the illustration.

✳✳WARNING

Whenever working near the drive axles, use care to prevent damage from over extension of the drive shaft joints. When either end of the shaft is disconnected, over extension of the joint could result in separation of the internal components and possible joint failure.

6. Install a drive axle joint protective cover (modified), such as J-34754 or equivalent.

7. If necessary, remove the brake line bracket.

8. Remove the cotter pin and nut, then press the tie rod out of the strut bracket using J 24319-01 or equivalent two-armed puller. Discard the cotter pin.

9. Unfasten and remove the strut-to-steering knuckle bolts and carefully lift out the strut.

➡**The steering knuckle MUST be supported to prevent axle joint overextension.**

10. Remove the strut assembly from the vehicle. Be careful to avoid chipping or cracking the spring coating when handling the front suspension coil spring assembly.

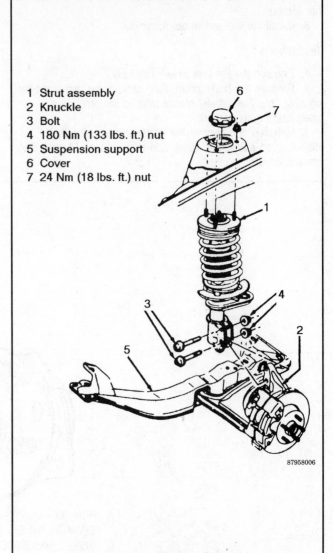

1 Strut assembly
2 Knuckle
3 Bolt
4 180 Nm (133 lbs. ft.) nut
5 Suspension support
6 Cover
7 24 Nm (18 lbs. ft.) nut

87958006

Fig. 4 Exploded view of the strut assembly

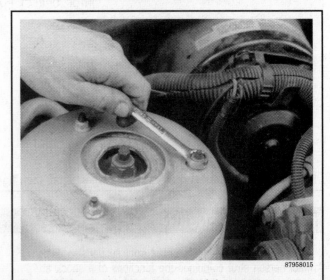

87958015

Fig. 5 Unfasten the strut tower retaining nuts

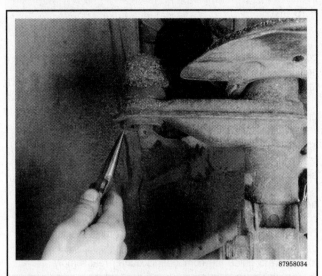

87958034

Fig. 6 Remove and discard the tie rod end cotter pin

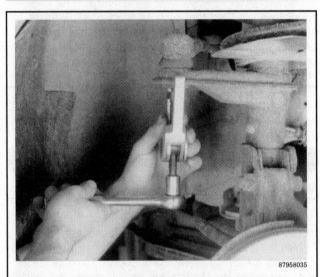

87958035

Fig. 7 Use a suitable tie rod end puller, then . . .

87958036

Fig. 8 . . . separate the tie rod end from the strut bracket

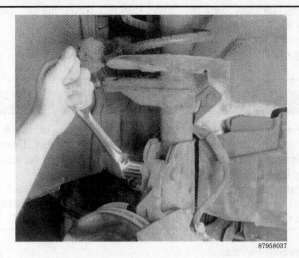

87958037

Fig. 9 Unfasten the strut-to-steering knuckle bolts, then carefully remove the strut assembly

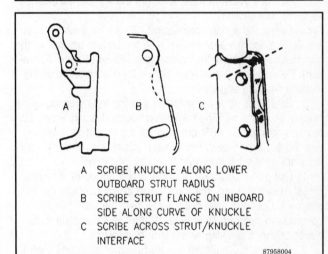

A   SCRIBE KNUCKLE ALONG LOWER
    OUTBOARD STRUT RADIUS
B   SCRIBE STRUT FLANGE ON INBOARD
    SIDE ALONG CURVE OF KNUCKLE
C   SCRIBE ACROSS STRUT/KNUCKLE
    INTERFACE

87958004

Fig. 10 Scribe a matchmark as illustrated, for alignment purposes during installation

To install:

11. Move the strut into position, then install the nuts and/or bolts connecting the strut assembly to the body.

➡**On 1982-87 vehicles, make sure that the flat sides of the strut-to-knuckle bolt heads are horizontal, as shown in the accompanying figure, before tightening.**

12. Align the steering knuckle with the strut flange scribe mark made during removal, then install the bolts and nuts. For 1982 vehicles, tighten to 140 ft. lbs. (190 Nm). For 1983-96 vehicles, tighten to 133 ft. lbs. (180 Nm).

13. Position the tie rod end into the strut assembly, then secure with the tie rod end bolt and new cotter pin. Tighten the tie rod end bolt to 44 ft. lbs. (60 Nm).

14. Tighten the nuts and/or bolts attaching the top of the strut to the body to 18-20 ft. lbs. (25-27 Nm).

15. Install the brake line bracket.

16. Slightly raise the vehicle, then remove the jackstands from under the suspension supports.

17. Install the tire and wheel assembly.

18. Carefully lower the vehicle, then final tighten the lug nuts to 100 ft. lbs. (140 Nm).

OVERHAUL

✲✲CAUTION

The coil springs are retained under considerable pressure. They can exert enough force to cause serious injury. Exercise extreme caution when disassembling the strut for coil spring removal. This procedure requires the use of a spring compressor and several other special tools. It cannot be performed without them. If you do not have access to these tools, DO NOT attempt to disassemble the strut!

1982-84 Vehicles
▶ See Figure 11

1. Remove the strut assembly from the vehicle, as outlined earlier in this section.

2. Clamp the spring compressor J 26584, or equivalent, in a vise. Position the strut assembly in the bottom adapter of the compressor and install the special tool J26584-86 (see illustration). Be sure that the adapter captures the strut and that the locating pins are engaged.

3. Rotate the strut assembly so that the top mounting assembly lip aligns with the compressor support notch. Insert two top adapters (J26584-88) between the top mounting assembly and the top spring seat. Position the adapters so that the split lines are in the 3 o'clock and 9 o'clock positions.

4. Using a 1 in. socket, turn the screw on top of the compressor clockwise until the top support flange contacts the adapters. Continue turning the screw until the coil spring is compressed approximately ½ in. (13mm) or 4 complete turns. Never bottom the spring or the strut damper rod.

5. Unscrew the nut from the strut damper shaft and then lift off the top mounting assembly.

6. Turn the compressor adjusting screw counterclockwise until the spring tension has been relieved. Remove the adapters and then remove the coil spring.

To install:

7. Clamp the strut compressor body J 26584 in a vise.

8. Position the strut assembly in the bottom adapter of the compressor and install the special tool J26584-86 (see illustration). Be sure that the adapter captures the strut and that the locating pins are engaged.

9. Position the spring on the strut. Make sure the spring is properly seated on the bottom of the spring plate.

10. Install the spring strut seat assembly on top of the spring.

11. Place BOTH J 26584-88 top adapters over the spring seat assemblies.

12. Turn the compressor forcing the screw until the compressor top support just contacts the top adapters (do not compress the spring at this time).

13. Install long extension with a socket to fit the hex on the damper shaft through the top of the spring seat. Use the extension to guide the components during reassembly.

✲✲WARNING

NEVER place a hard tool such as pliers or screwdriver against the polished surface of the damper shaft. The shaft can be held up with your fingers or an extension in order to prevent it from receding into the strut assembly while the spring is being compressed.

14. Compress the screw by turning the screw clockwise until approximately 1½ in. (38mm) of damper shaft extends through the top spring plate.

✲✲WARNING

Do not compress the spring until it bottoms.

15. Remove the extension and socket, position the top mounting assembly over the damper shaft and install the nut. Tighten to 68 ft. lbs. (92 Nm).

16. Turn the forcing screw counterclockwise to back off support, remove the top adapters and bottom adapter and remove the strut assembly from the compressor.

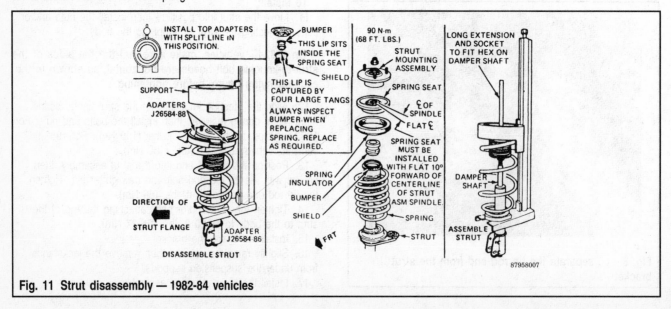

Fig. 11 Strut disassembly — 1982-84 vehicles

87958007

17. Install the strut assembly in the vehicle, as outlined earlier in this section.

1985-96 Vehicles

▶ See Figures 12, 13, 14 and 15

1. Remove the strut assembly from the vehicle, as outlined earlier in this section.

2. Mount the strut compressor J-34013 in holding fixture J-3289-20.

3. Mount the strut assembly into the compressor. Note that the strut compressor has strut mounting holes drilled for specific car lines.

4. Compress the strut approximately ½ its height after initial contact with the top cap.

❋❋WARNING

Never bottom the spring or dampener rod!

5. Remove the nut from the strut dampener shaft and place alignment/guiding rod J-34013-27 on top of the dampener

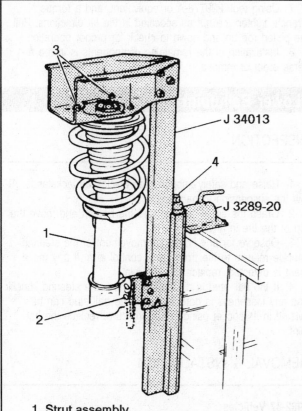

1 Strut assembly
2 Install locking pins through
  strut assembly
3 Tighten nuts until flush with
  strut compressor
4 Compressor forcing screw

87958008

Fig. 12 View of the strut assembly mounted in a compressor

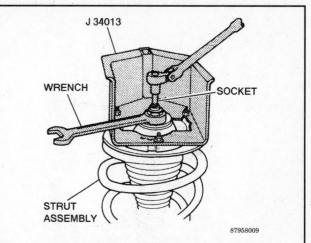

87958009

Fig. 13 Use a socket and a wrench to remove the dampener shaft nut spring cap while compressing the spring

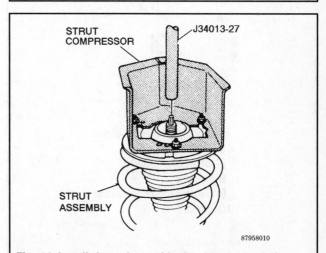

87958010

Fig. 14 Install the rod to guide the dampener shaft straight down through the spring cap while compressing the spring

shaft. Use the rod to guide the dampener shaft straight down through the spring cap while compressing the spring. Remove the components.

➥Be careful to avoid chipping or cracking the spring coating when handling the front suspension coil spring assembly.

To install:

6. Install the bearing cap into the strut compressor if previously removed.

7. Mount the strut assembly in strut compressor, using bottom locking pin only. Extend the dampener shaft and install clamp J-34013-20 on the dampener shaft.

8. Install the spring over the dampener and swing the assembly up so the upper locking pin can be installed.

9. Install all shields, bumpers and insulators on the spring seat. Install the spring seat on top of the spring. Be sure the flat on the upper spring seat is facing in the proper direction. The spring seat flat should be facing the same direction as the centerline of the strut assembly spindle.

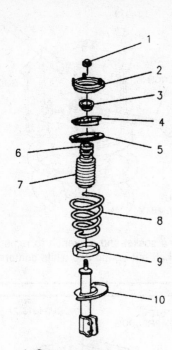

1 Strut mount nut
2 Strut mount
3 Rate washer
4 Spring seat
5 Spring upper insulator
6 Jounce bumper
7 Strut dust shield
8 Spring
9 Spring lower insulator
10 Strut

87958011

Fig. 15 Exploded view of the disassembled strut components

10. Install the guiding rod and turn the forcing screw while the guiding rod centers the assembly. When the threads on the dampener shaft are visible, remove the guiding rod and install the nut. For vehicles through 1994, tighten the nut to 65 ft. lbs. (85 Nm). For 1995-96 vehicles, tighten the nut to 52 ft. lbs. (70 Nm). Use a crowsfoot line wrench while holding the dampener shaft with a socket.

11. Remove the clamp.

Strut Cartridge

REMOVAL & INSTALLATION

▶ See Figure 16

→On 1982-87 models only, the internal piston rod, cylinder assembly and fluid can be replaced utilizing a service cartridge and nut. Internal threads are located inside the tube immediately below a cut line groove.

1. Remove the strut and the coil springs. Clamp the strut in a vise. Do not overtighten it as this will cause damage to the strut tube.

2. Locate the cut line groove just below the top edge of the strut tube. It is imperative that the groove be accurately located as any mislocation will cause inner thread damage. Using pipe cutters, cut around the groove until the tube is completely cut through.

3. Remove and discard the end cap, the cylinder and the piston rod assembly. Remove the strut assembly from the vise and pour out the old fluid.

4. Reclamp the strut in the vise. A flaring cup tool is included in the replacement cartridge kit to flare and deburr the edge that was cut on the strut tube. Place the flaring cup on the open edge of the tube and strike it with a mallet until its flat outer surface rests on the top edge of the tube. Remove the cup and discard it.

5. Try the new nut to make sure that it threads properly. If not, use the flaring cup again until it does.

6. Place the new strut cartridge into the tube. Turn the cartridge until it settles into the indentations at the base of the tube. Place the nut over the cartridge.

7. Using tool J-29778-A or equivalent, and a torque wrench, tighten the nut as specified in the kit directions. Pull the piston rod up and down to check for proper operation.

8. Installation of the remaining components is in the reverse order of removal.

Lower Ball Joint

INSPECTION

1. Raise and safely support the vehicles on jackstands. Allow the suspension to hang free.

2. Grasp the tire at the top and the bottom and move the top of the tire in and out.

3. Observe for any horizontal movement of the steering knuckle relative to the front lower control arm. If any movement is detected, replace the ball joint.

4. If the ball stud is disconnected from the steering knuckle and any looseness is detected, or if the ball stud can be twisted in its socket using finger pressure, replace the ball joint.

REMOVAL & INSTALLATION

1982-87 Vehicles
▶ See Figure 17

1. Loosen the wheel nuts, raise the car, and remove the wheel.

2. Use a ⅛ in. (3mm) drill bit to drill a hole through the center of each of the three ball joint rivets.

3. Use a ½ in. (13mm) drill bit to drill completely through the rivet.

4. Use a hammer and punch to remove the rivets. Drive them out from the bottom.

5. Use the special tool J29330 or a ball joint removal tool to separate the ball joint from the steering knuckle, as shown

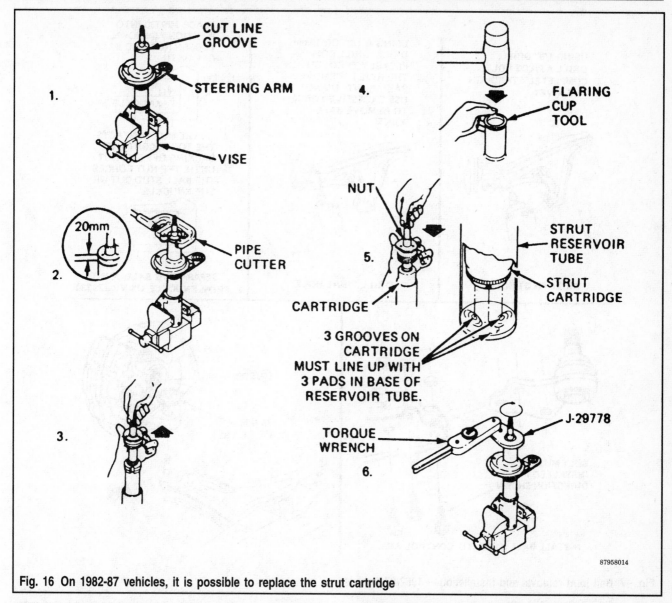

Fig. 16 On 1982-87 vehicles, it is possible to replace the strut cartridge

in the accompanying figure. Don't forget to remove and discard the cotter pin.

6. Disconnect the stabilizer bar from the lower control arm, then remove the ball joint.

To install:

7. Install the new ball joint into the control arm with the three bolts supplied as shown and tighten to 50 ft. lbs. (68 Nm).

8. Installation of the remaining components is in the reverse order of removal.

9. Tighten the castellated nut on the ball joint to 55 ft. lbs. (75 Nm) and use a new cotter pin.

10. Have a reputable repair shop check the toe setting and adjust, if necessary.

1988-96 Vehicles

▶ **See Figures 18, 19, 20, 21 and 22**

1. Raise and support the vehicle safely.
2. Place jack stands under the suspension support.
3. Lower the car slightly so the weight of the car rests on the suspension supports and not the control arms.

4. Remove the tire and wheel assembly.

✳✳WARNING

Use care to prevent damage from over extension of the drive shaft joints. When either end of the shaft is disconnected, over extension of the joint could result in separation of the internal components and possible joint failure. The steering knuckle should be supported and drive axle joint protectors should be used.

5. Install a drive axle joint protective cover (modified), such as J-34754 or equivalent.

6. Remove the cotter pin from the ball joint castellated nut. Discard the pin.

7. Remove the castellated nut and disconnect the ball joint from the steering knuckle using ball joint separator J-34505, J-29330, or equivalent.

➡**Be sure to use on the recommended tool for separating the ball joint from the knuckle. Failure to use the proper tool may cause damage to the ball joint and seal.**

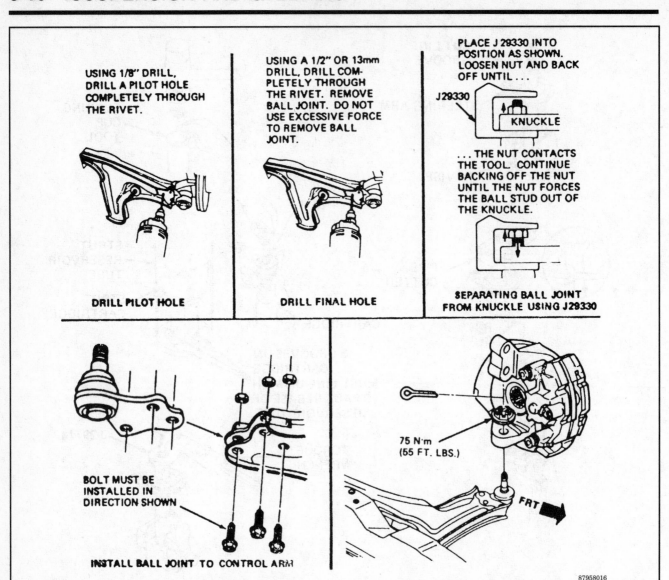

USING 1/8" DRILL, DRILL A PILOT HOLE COMPLETELY THROUGH THE RIVET.

DRILL PILOT HOLE

USING A 1/2" OR 13mm DRILL, DRILL COMPLETELY THROUGH THE RIVET. REMOVE BALL JOINT. DO NOT USE EXCESSIVE FORCE TO REMOVE BALL JOINT.

DRILL FINAL HOLE

PLACE J 29330 INTO POSITION AS SHOWN. LOOSEN NUT AND BACK OFF UNTIL . . .

J29330   KNUCKLE

. . . THE NUT CONTACTS THE TOOL. CONTINUE BACKING OFF THE NUT UNTIL THE NUT FORCES THE BALL STUD OUT OF THE KNUCKLE.

SEPARATING BALL JOINT FROM KNUCKLE USING J29330

BOLT MUST BE INSTALLED IN DIRECTION SHOWN

INSTALL BALL JOINT TO CONTROL ARM

75 N·m (55 FT. LBS.)

FRT

87958016

Fig. 17 Ball joint removal and installation — 1982-87 vehicles

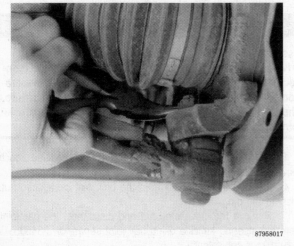

87958017

Fig. 18 Remove and discard the cotter pin from the ball joint

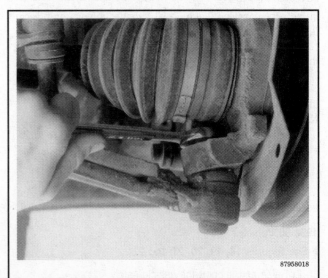

87958018

Fig. 19 Unfasten the ball joint retaining nut

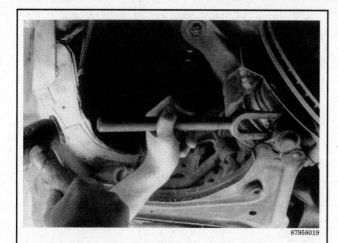

Fig. 20 The recommended procedure for disconnecting the ball joint from the steering knuckle is to use a suitable ball joint separator

8. Drill out the three rivets retaining the ball joint to the lower control arm. Use a ⅛ in. (3mm) drill bit to make a pilot hole through the rivets. Finish drilling the rivets with a ½ in. (13mm) drill bit.

➡**Be careful not to damage the drive axle boot when drilling out the ball joint rivets.**

9. Loosen the stabilizer shaft bushing assembly nut.
10. Remove the ball joint from the steering knuckle and control arm.

To install:

11. Piston the ball joint in the control arm.
12. Install the three ball joint bolts and nuts as shown on the instructions sheet in the ball joint kit, then tighten the bolts to specifications.
13. Position the ball joint stud through the steering knuckle.
14. Install the ball joint nut. Tighten the stabilizer shaft bushing clamp nuts to 15-22 ft. lbs. (20-30 Nm).
15. Fasten the ball joint-to-steering knuckle nut to 55 ft. lbs. (75 Nm), plus a 60° rotation. Do NOT loosen the nut at any time during installation.
16. Install a new cotter pin to the ball joint castellated nut.
17. If installed, remove the boot protector.
18. Fasten the nut attaching the stabilizer link to the stabilizer shaft. Tighten to 22 ft. lbs. (30 Nm), then slightly raise the vehicle and remove the jackstands from under the suspension.
19. Install the front tire and wheel assembly and hand-tighten the lug nuts.
20. Carefully lower the vehicle, then tighten the wheel lug nuts to 103 ft. lbs. (140 Nm).

➡**The front end alignment should be checked and adjusted.**

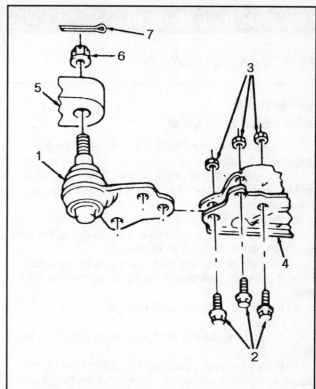

1 Service ball joint
2 Ball joint mounting bolts
3 Nut
4 Control arm
5 Steering knuckle
6 Nut - 50 Nm (37 lbs. ft.) minimum torque 75 Nm (55 lbs. ft.) maximum torque to install pin
7 Pin

Fig. 21 Attach a new ball joint using the three bolts and nuts

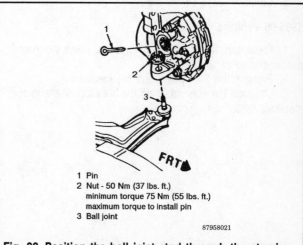

1 Pin
2 Nut - 50 Nm (37 lbs. ft.) minimum torque 75 Nm (55 lbs. ft.) maximum torque to install pin
3 Ball joint

Fig. 22 Position the ball joint stud through the steering knuckle, then fasten the retaining nut and install a new cotter pin

Stabilizer Shaft (Sway Bar)

REMOVAL & INSTALLATION

1982-94 Vehicles

▶ See Figures 23, 24 and 25

1. Raise and safely support the vehicle. Allow the front suspension to hang free.
2. For vehicles through 1991, remove the left front wheel and tire. For 1992-94 vehicles, remove both front wheel and tire assemblies.
3. Detach the stabilizer shaft from the control arms.
4. Unfasten the retaining clamps, then disconnect the stabilizer shaft from the support assemblies.
5. Remove the rear and center bolts from the suspension support assembly, then loosen, but do not remove, the front bolts.
6. Remove the stabilizer shaft with the insulators.
   To install:
7. Position the stabilizer shaft with the insulators, into the vehicle.
8. Fasten the clamps attaching the stabilizer shaft to the suspension support assemblies and hand-tighten the retainers.
9. Move the suspension support assemblies into position and hand-tighten the bolts.
10. Install the nut attaching the stabilizer shaft to the stabilizer links.
11. Tighten the suspension support bolts, in sequence, as follows:
    - Center bolts first, to 66 ft. lbs. (90 Nm)
    - Front bolts second, to 65 ft. lbs. (88 Nm)
    - Rear bolts third, to 65 ft. lbs. (88 Nm)
12. Tighten the stabilizer shaft-to-support assembly nuts to 16-22 ft. lbs. (22-30 Nm) and the stabilizer shaft to control arm nuts to 13-22 ft. lbs. (17-30 Nm).
13. Tighten the clamp nuts to 17 ft. lbs. (23 Nm).
14. Install the wheel and tire assemblies.
15. Carefully lower the vehicle.

1995-96 Vehicles

1. Raise and safely support the vehicle. Allow the front suspension to hang free.
2. Remove the front wheel and tire assemblies.
3. Unfasten the nuts attaching the stabilizer shafts to the stabilizer links.

4. Remove the clamps attaching the stabilizer shaft to the crossmember.
5. Support the rear of the crossmember with suitable adjustable jacks.
6. Remove the rear and center bolts from the crossmember assemblies, as loosen, but do not remove, the front bolts.
7. Lower the crossmember 3 inches (7.6 cm) by adjusting the jacks down.
8. Remove the stabilizer shaft and insulators.
   To install:
9. Position the stabilizer shaft into the vehicle with the insulators and hand-tighten.
10. Install the clamps attaching the stabilizer shaft to the crossmember and hand-tighten.
11. Place the crossmember assemblies into position, then hand-tighten.
12. Tighten the crossmember bolts, in sequence, as follows:
    - Left rear outboard first, to 96 ft. lbs. (130 Nm)
    - Right rear outboard second, to 96 ft. lbs. (130 Nm)
    - Front upper bolts third, to 96 ft. lbs. (130 Nm)
    - Rear inboard bolt last, to 96 ft. lbs. (130 Nm)
13. Tighten the stabilizer shaft-to-support assembly bolts to 49 ft. lbs. (66 Nm).
14. Fasten the stabilizer shaft links-to-control arm nuts and tighten to 13 ft. lbs. (17 Nm).
15. Install the front wheel and tire assemblies, then carefully lower the vehicle.
16. Tighten the wheel lug nuts to 100 ft. lbs. (140 Nm).
17. Have the front end alignment checked by a properly equipped repair shop.

Control Arm/Suspension Support

REMOVAL & INSTALLATION

▶ See Figures 26 and 27

1. Raise and safely support the vehicle. Place jackstands under the suspension supports, then lower the vehicle slightly so the weight of the vehicle rests on the suspension supports, and not on the control arms.
2. Remove the tire and wheel assembly.
3. Unfasten the nut attaching the stabilizer link to the stabilizer shaft, then unfasten the nuts attaching the stabilizer shaft clamps to the suspension support. Detach the stabilizer shaft from the control arm and/or support assembly.

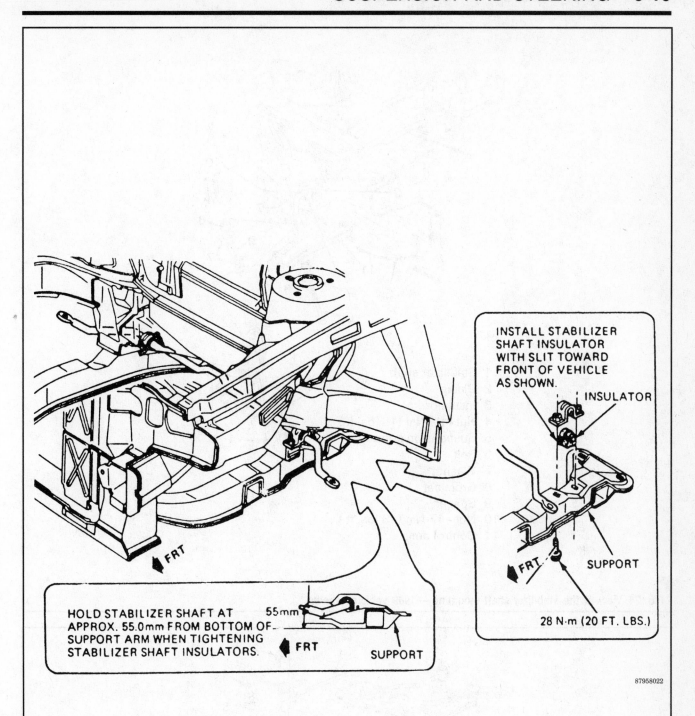

INSTALL STABILIZER SHAFT INSULATOR WITH SLIT TOWARD FRONT OF VEHICLE AS SHOWN.

INSULATOR

FRT

SUPPORT

28 N·m (20 FT. LBS.)

HOLD STABILIZER SHAFT AT APPROX. 55.0mm FROM BOTTOM OF SUPPORT ARM WHEN TIGHTENING STABILIZER SHAFT INSULATORS.

55mm

FRT

SUPPORT

87958022

Fig. 23 Stabilizer shaft removal and installation — 1982-87 vehicles

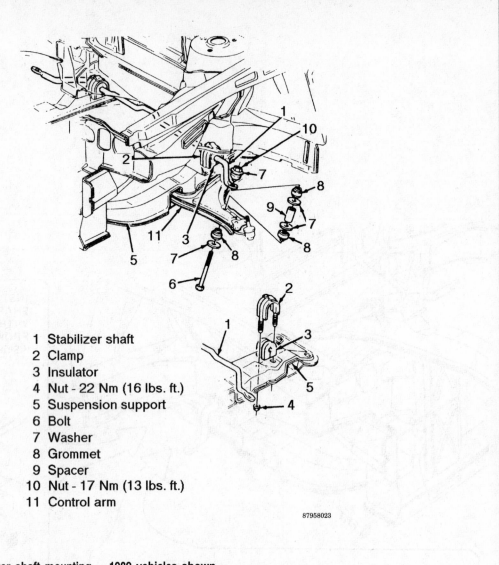

1 Stabilizer shaft
2 Clamp
3 Insulator
4 Nut - 22 Nm (16 lbs. ft.)
5 Suspension support
6 Bolt
7 Washer
8 Grommet
9 Spacer
10 Nut - 17 Nm (13 lbs. ft.)
11 Control arm

87958023

Fig. 24 View of the stabilizer shaft mounting — 1989 vehicles shown

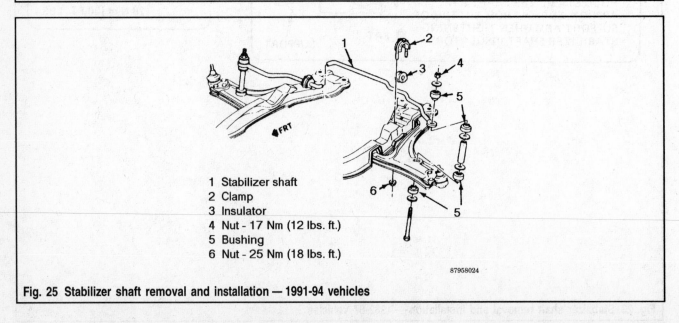

1 Stabilizer shaft
2 Clamp
3 Insulator
4 Nut - 17 Nm (12 lbs. ft.)
5 Bushing
6 Nut - 25 Nm (18 lbs. ft.)

87958024

Fig. 25 Stabilizer shaft removal and installation — 1991-94 vehicles

✳✳WARNING

Be careful to avoid over-extending the axle shaft joints. When either end of the shaft is disconnected, over-extension of the joint could result in separation of internal components and possible joint failure. Failure to observe this can result in interior joint or boot damage and possible joint failure.

4. Disconnect the ball joint from the steering knuckle using separator tool J-29330 or equivalent. For details, see the ball joint removal and installation procedure located in this section.

5. To remove the support assembly with the control arm attached, remove the bolts mounting the support assembly to the car. To remove the control arm only, remove the control arm to support assembly bolts.

To install:

6. Move the control arm into position, then loosely install the bolts attaching the control arm to the suspension support.

7. Place the suspension support into position, guiding the ball joint into the steering knuckle, then loosely install the retaining bolts.

8. Fasten the nuts attaching the stabilizer shaft clamps to the suspension support. Tighten to 22 ft. lbs. (30 Nm).

9. Install the nuts attaching the ball joint to the steering knuckle. Tighten to the specifications located in the ball joint removal and installation procedure, then install a new cotter pin.

10. Install the stabilizer link-to-shaft nut, then tighten to 22 ft. lbs. (30 Nm).

11. Slightly raise the vehicle, then remove the jackstands from the under the suspension supports.

12. Install the tire and wheel assembly.

13. With the vehicle at ground height, tighten the suspension support bolts, as follows:

   a. For 1982-94 vehicles:
   - Center bolts first, to 66 ft. lbs. (90 Nm)
   - Front bolts second, to 65 ft. lbs. (88 Nm)
   - Rear bolts third, to 65 ft. lbs. (88 Nm)

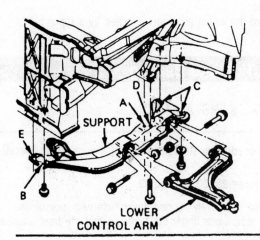

FRONT SUSP SUPPORT ASM ATTACHING BOLT/SCREW SEQUENCE

1. LOOSELY INSTALL CENTER BOLT INTO HOLE (A).
2. LOOSELY INSTALL TIE BAR BOLT INTO OUTBOARD HOLE (B).
3. INSTALL BOTH REAR BOLTS INTO HOLES (C) TORQUE REAR BOLTS.
4. INSTALL BOLT INTO CENTER HOLE(D), THEN TORQUE.
5. TORQUE BOLT IN HOLE (A).
6. INSTALL BOLT INTO FRONT HOLE (E), THEN TORQUE.
7. TORQUE BOLT IN HOLE (B).

SUPPORT-TO-BODY BOLTS . . . . . . .90 N·m (63 FT. LBS.)
LCA PIVOT BOLTS . . . . .95 N·m (67 FT. LBS.)

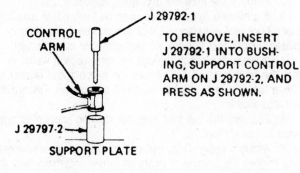

TO REMOVE, INSERT J 29792-1 INTO BUSHING, SUPPORT CONTROL ARM ON J 29792-2, AND PRESS AS SHOWN.

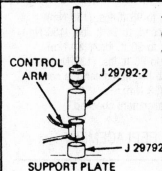

TO INSTALL, SUPPORT CONTROL ARM ON J 29792-3, PLACE BUSHING INTO J 29792-2, AND PRESS BUSING INTO CONTROL ARM USING J 29792-1. LUBRICATE BUSHING.

Fig. 26 Control arm, suspension support and related components — 1982-89 vehicles

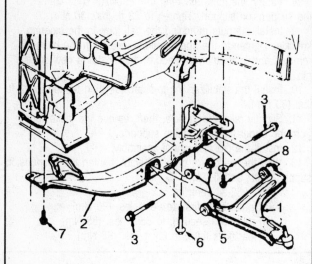

1 Control arm
2 Suspension support
3 Bolt - 83 Nm (61 lbs. ft.)
4 Washer
5 Nut
6 Bolt - 90 Nm (66 lbs. ft.) tighten first
7 Bolt - 88 Nm (65 lbs. ft.) tighten second
8 Bolt - 88 Nm (65 lbs. ft.) tighten third

87958026

Fig. 27 Control arm and suspension support mounting — 1988-86 vehicles

b. For 1995-96 vehicles:
 • Left rear outboard first, to 96 ft. lbs. (130 Nm)
 • Right rear outboard second, to 96 ft. lbs. (130 Nm)
 • Front upper bolts third, to 96 ft. lbs. (130 Nm)
 • Rear inboard bolt last, to 96 ft. lbs. (130 Nm)
14. With the vehicle still at curb height, tighten the control arm retaining bolts to 61 ft. lbs. (83 Nm).
15. Have the front end wheel alignment checked.

CONTROL ARM BUSHING REPLACEMENT

▶ **See Figure 28**

1. Remove the lower control arm as outlined earlier in this section.
2. Install bushing removal tools J 29792 or equivalent.
3. Coat the threads of the tool with extreme pressure lubricant.
4. Remove the lower control arm bushings.
To install:
5. Install the bushing installation tools.

6. Coat the outer case of the bushing with a light coating of a suitable lubricant, then install the lower control arm bushings.
7. As outlined earlier, install the lower control arm.

Steering Knuckle

REMOVAL & INSTALLATION

1. Raise and safely support the vehicle with jackstands. Place the jackstands under the frame so that the front suspension hangs freely.
2. Remove the front tire and wheel assembly.
3. Remove the hub and bearing assembly, as outlined in this section.
4. Unfasten the bolts attaching the knuckle to the strut, then remove the steering knuckle.
To install:
5. Position the steering knuckle into the strut, then install the retaining bolts. Tighten the bolts to 133 ft. lbs. (180 Nm).
6. Install the hub and bearing assembly, as outlined in this section.
7. Install the wheel and tire assembly, then carefully lower the vehicle.
8. Have the wheel alignment checked by a reputable facility.

Front Hub and Bearing

REMOVAL & INSTALLATION

➡**This procedure requires the use of a number of special tools.**

▶ **See Figures 29, 30, 31 and 32**

1. Raise and safely support the vehicle with jackstands. Place the jackstands under the frame so that the front suspension hangs freely.
2. Remove the front tire and wheel assembly.
3. If a silicone (gray) boot is used on the inboard axle joint, place boot seal protector J-33162 or equivalent. If a thermoplastic (black) boot is used, no seal protector is necessary.
4. Insert a drift punch through the rotor cooling vanes to lock the rotor in place and remove the hub nut and washer. Clean the drive axle threads of all dirt and grease. Discard the nut and washer.
5. Separate the ball joint from the steering knuckle as outlined in this section.
6. Attach a puller, G.M. part no. J-28733 or the equivalent, and remove the bearing. If corrosion is present, make sure the bearing is loose in the knuckle before using the puller.
7. Move the axle shaft inward and support at an angle near the normal drive angle.
8. Remove the brake caliper and rotor, as follows:
 a. Remove the caliper mounting bolts.
 b. Remove the caliper from the knuckle and suspend from a length of wire. Do not allow the caliper to hang from the brake hose. Pull the rotor from the knuckle.

FRONT LOWER CONTROL ARM BUSHING

REMOVE   INSTALL

REAR LOWER CONTROL ARM BUSHING

REMOVE   INSTALL

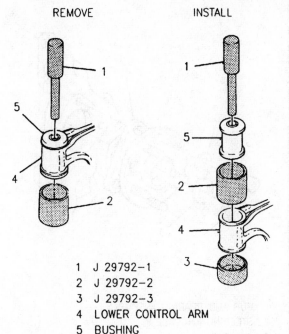

1 J 29792-1
2 J 29792-2
3 J 29792-3
4 LOWER CONTROL ARM
5 BUSHING

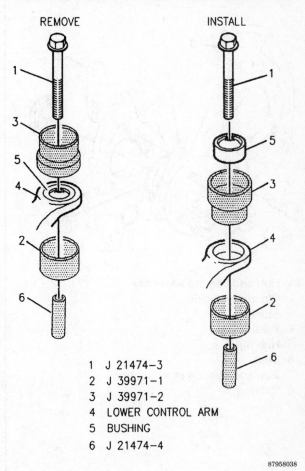

1 J 21474-3
2 J 39971-1
3 J 39971-2
4 LOWER CONTROL ARM
5 BUSHING
6 J 21474-4

87958038

Fig. 28 View of the front and rear lower control arm bushings

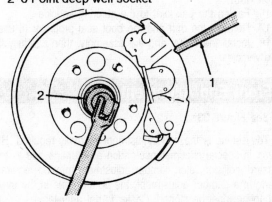

1 Drift punch
2 6 Point deep well socket

87958027

Fig. 29 Insert a drift into the rotor when removing the hub nut

9. Unfasten the three hub and bearing attaching bolts. If the old bearing is to be reused, match mark the bolts and holes for installation. If equipped, the brake rotor splash shield will have to come off, too.

10. Clean the mating surfaces of all dirt and corrosion. Check the knuckle bore and knuckle seal for damage. If a new bearing is to be installed, remove and discard the old knuckle seal and replace with a new one during installation.

To install:

11. Position the hub and bearing assembly and splash shield (if equipped) on the steering knuckle and install the retaining bolts. Tighten the bolts to 70 ft. lbs. (95 Nm).

12. Grease the lips of the new seal before installation; install with a seal driver made for the purpose, G.M. tool no. J-28671 or the equivalent.

13. Install the rotor and caliper. Be sure that the caliper hose isn't twisted. Install the caliper bolts and tighten to 21-38 ft. lbs. (28-51 Nm).

14. Position the axle shaft into the hub and bearing assembly.

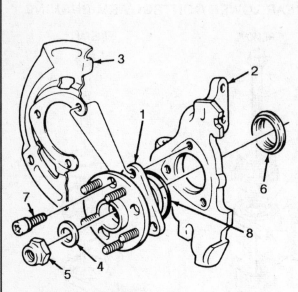

1 Hub and bearing assembly
2 Steering knuckle
3 Shield
4 Washer
5 Hub nut
6 Seal
7 Hub and bearing retaining bolt
8 "O" ring

87958030

Fig. 30 Exploded view of the hub and bearing assembly and related components — 1989 vehicle shown

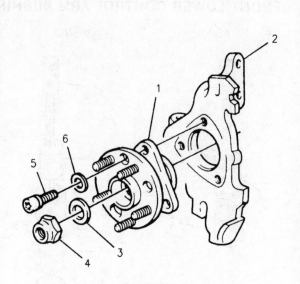

1 HUB AND BEARING ASSEMBLY
2 STEERING KNUCKLE
3 WASHER
4 DRIVE AXLE NUT – 260 N·m (192 LBS. FT.)
5 HUB AND BEARING RETAINING BOLT
6 WASHER

87958032

Fig. 31 Hub and bearing mounting — 1995 vehicle shown

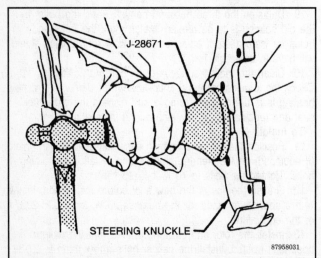

87958031

Fig. 32 Use a seal driver when installing the new seal into the steering knuckle

15. Insert a drift in the rotor, then install a new hub nut and washer. Use a torque wrench to tighten the nut to 185 ft. lbs. (260 Nm).

16. Fasten the ball joint to the steering knuckle.

17. Remove the drift and the boot seal protector (if used).

18. Install the wheel and tire assembly, then carefully lower the vehicles.

Front End Alignment

▶ See Figure 33

Toe setting is the only adjustment normally required. However, in special circumstances such as damage due to road hazard, collision, etc., camber adjustment may be required. To perform a camber adjustment, the bottom hole in the strut mounting must be slotted. Caster is not adjustable.

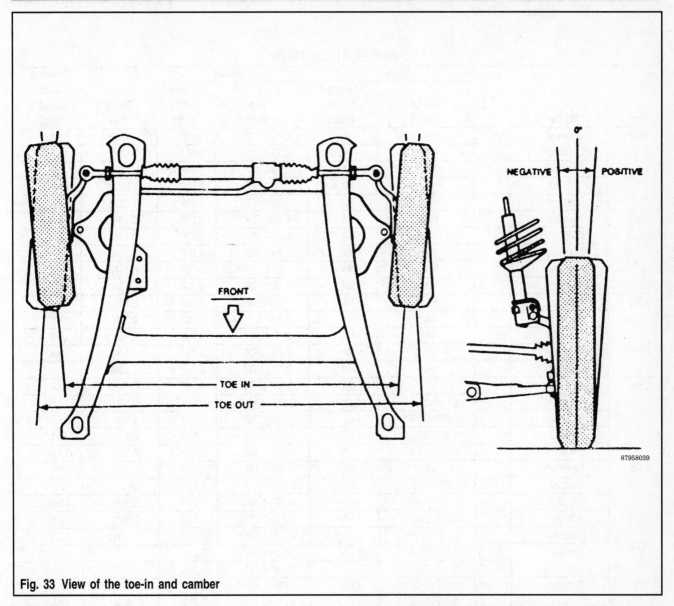

Fig. 33 View of the toe-in and camber

CAMBER

Camber is the tilting of the front wheels from the vertical when viewed from the front of the car. When the wheels tilt outward at the top, the camber is said to be positive (+); when the wheels tilt inward at the top, the camber is said to be negative (-). The amount of tilt is measured in degrees from the vertical and this measurement is called camber angle. Proper camber is critical to assure even tire wear.

TOE-IN

Toe-in is the turning in of the front wheels. The actual amount of toe-in is normally only a fraction of one degree. The purpose of the toe-in specification is to insure parallel rolling of the front wheels. Excessive toe-in or toe-out may increase tire wear. Toe-in also serves to offset the small deflections of the wheel support system which occur when the car is rolling forward. In other words, even when the wheels are set to toe-in slightly when the car is standing still, they tend to roll parallel on the road when the car is moving.

CASTER

Caster is a measurement of the angle between the steering axis and vertical, as viewed from the side of the vehicle when the wheels are in the straight ahead position. Stated another way, it is the tilting of the front steering axis either forward or backward from the vertical. A backward tilt is said to be positive (+) and a forward tilt is said to be negative (-).

WHEEL ALIGNMENT

Year	Model		Caster Range (deg.)	Caster Preferred Setting (deg.)	Camber Range (deg.)	Camber Preferred Setting (deg.)	Toe-in (in.)	Steering Axis Inclination (deg.)
1982	Cavalier		NA	NA	0.10-1.10P	0.60P	0.125P	NA
	2000/Sunbird		NA	NA	0.10-1.10P	0.60P	0.125P	NA
	Skyhawk		NA	NA	0.10-1.10P	0.60P	0.125P	NA
	Firenza		NA	NA	0.10-1.10P	0.60P	0.125P	NA
	Cimarron		NA	NA	0.10-1.10P	0.60P	0.125P	NA
1983	Cavalier		NA	NA	0.20-1.20P	0.70P	0.13N	NA
	2000/Sunbird		NA	NA	0.20-1.20P	0.70P	0.13N	NA
	Skyhawk		NA	NA	0.20-1.20P	0.70P	0.13N	NA
	Firenza		NA	NA	0.20-1.20P	0.70P	0.13N	NA
	Cimarron		NA	NA	0.20-1.20P	0.70P	0.13N	NA
1984	Cavalier		NA	NA	0.20-1.20P	0.70P	0.13N	NA
	2000/Sunbird		NA	NA	0.20-1.20P	0.70P	0.13N	NA
	Skyhawk		NA	NA	0.20-1.20P	0.70P	0.13N	NA
	Firenza		NA	NA	0.20-1.20P	0.70P	0.13N	NA
	Cimarron		NA	NA	0.20-1.20P	0.70P	0.13N	NA
1985	Cavalier		NA	NA	0.19P-3.19P	0.69P	0.25N-0	NA
	Sunbird		0.69P-2.69P	1.69P	0.21P-1.41P	0.81P	0.63N	13.50
	Skyhawk		0.69P-2.69P	1.69P	0.22P-1.50P	0.84P	0.06N	13.50
	Firenza		0.69P-2.69P	1.69P	0.22P-0.41P	0.81P	0.13N	.13.50
	Cimarron		0.72P-2.72P	1.72P	0.22P-1.50P	0.84P	0.63N	13.50
1986	Cavalier		NA	NA	0.19P-3.19P	0.69P	0.13P	NA
	Sunbird		0.69P-2.69P	1.69P	0.21P-1.41P	0.81P	0.63N	13.50
	Skyhawk		0.69P-2.69P	1.69P	0.22P-1.41P	0.81P	0.06N	13.50
	Firenza		0.69P-2.69P	1.69P	0.22P-1.41P	0.81P	0.06N	13.50
	Cimarron		0.72P-2.72P	1.72P	0.22P-1.50P	0.84P	0.62N	13.50
1987	Cavalier	F	0.72P-2.72P	1.72P	0.22P-1.22P	0.81P	①	13.50
		R	-	-	0.34N-0.19P	0.25N	0.13P	-
	Sunbird		0.69P-2.69P	1.69P	0.21P-1.41P	0.81P	0	13.50
	⑤		0.69P-2.69P	1.69P	0.21P-1.41P	0.81P	0.63N	13.50
	Skyhawk		0.72P-2.72P	1.72P	0.25P-1.44P	0.84P	0	13.50
	Firenza ⑧		0.69P-2.69P	1.69P	0.22P-1.41P	0.81P	0	13.50
	⑨		0.69P-2.69P	1.69P	0.22P-1.41P	0.81P	0.06N	13.50
	Cimarron		0.80N-4.20P	1.70P	0.20N-1.80P	0.80P	0	NA
1988	Cavalier	F	0.81P-4.19P	1 2/3	②	③	0	13.50
		R			0.34N-0.19N	0.25N	0.13P	-
	Sunbird		0.81N-4.19P	1.69P	0.19P-1.81P	0.81P	0	13.50
	Skyhawk		0.81P-4.81P	1 2/3	0.19P-1.81P	0.81P	0	13.50
	Firenza		0.81N-4.19P	1.69P	0.19P-1.81P	0.81P	0	13.50
	Cimarron		0.80N-4.20P	1.70P	0.20N-1.80P	0.80P	0	NA
1989	Cavalier	F	0.69P-2.69P	1.69P	④	③	0	13.50
		R	-	-	0.34N-0.19N	0.25N	0.13P	-
	Sunbird	F	0.69P-2.69P	1.69P	0.13N-1.50P	0.81P	0	13.50
		R	-	-	0.75N-0.25P	0.25N	0.13P	-
	Skyhawk	F	0.69P-2.69P	1.69P	0.13-1.50P	0.81P	0	13.50
		R	-	-	0.75N-0.50P	0.25N	0.13P	-

WHEEL ALIGNMENT

Year	Model		Caster Range (deg.)	Caster Preferred Setting (deg.)	Camber Range (deg.)	Camber Preferred Setting (deg.)	Toe-in (in.)	Steering Axis Inclination (deg.)
1990	Cavalier	F	0.69P-2.69P	1.69P	④	③	0	13.50
		R	-	-	0.34N-0.19N	0.25N	0.13P	
	Sunbird	F	0.69P-2.69P	1.69P	0.75N-0.25P	0.25N	0	13.50
	⑥	F	0.69P-2.69P	1.69P	0.69N-0.69P	0	0	13.50
		R	-	-	0.75N-0.25P	0.25N	0.13P	-
1991	Cavalier	F	0.69P-2.69P	1.69P	11/16N-11/16P	0	0	13.50
		R	-	-	13/16N-5/16P	1/4N	1/4P	-
	Sunbird	F	0.69P-2.69P	1.69P	0.69N-0.69P	0	0	13.50
		R	-	-	0.69N-0.31P	0	0	-
1992	Cavalier	F	0.69P-2.69P	1.69P	0.69N-0.69P	0	0	13.50
		R	-	-	13/16N-5/16P	0.25N	0.25P	-
	Sunbird	F	0.69P-2.69P	1.69P	0.69N-0.69P	0	0	13.50
		R	-	-	0.69N-0.31P	0.25N	0.13P	-
1993	Cavalier	F	0.31P-2.31P	1.31P	7/8N-9/16P	0.16N	0	13.50
		R	-	-	0.69N-0.31P	0.25N	0.13P	-
	Sunbird	F	0.31P-2.31P	1.31P	0.88N-0.56P	0.16N	0	13.50
		R	-	-	0.69N-0.31P	0.25N	0.13P	-
1994	Cavalier	F	0.31P-2.31P	1.31P	0.88N-0.56P	5/32N	0	13.50
		R	-	-	0.69N-0.31P	0.25N	0.13P	-
	Sunbird	F	0.31P-2.31P	1.31P	0.88N-0.56P	0.16N	0	13.50
		R	-	-	0.69N-0.31P	0.25N	0.13P	-
1995	Cavalier	F	NA	4.30P ⑦	0.88N-0.56P	0.16N	0	13.50
		R	-	-	0.69N-0.31P	0.25N	0.13P	-
	Sunfire	F	NA	4.30P ⑦	0.88N-0.56P	0.16N	0	13.50
		R	-	-	0.69N-0.31P	0.25N	0.13P	-
1996	Cavalier	F	3.30P-5.30P	4.30P ⑦	0.88N-0.56P	0.02N	0	13.50
		R	-	-	0.69N-0.31P	0.25N	0	-
	Sunfire	F	3.30P-5.30P	4.30P ⑦	0.88N-0.56P	0.02N	0	13.50
		R	-	-	0.69N-0.31P	0.25N	0	-

NA - Not Available
F - Front
R - Rear

1 All except 215-60R 14 tires: 0
   215-60R 14 tires: 1/8P
2 All except Z24: 3/16N-1 13/16P
   Z24: 1N-1P
3 All except Z24: 13/16P
   Z24: 0
4 All except Z24: 1/8P-1 1/2P
   Z24: 1N-1P
5 With P215/60R14 tires
6 With 16" wheels
7 Non-adjustable
8 Except P215-60-R14 tire
9 With P215-60-R14 tire

87958101

REAR SUSPENSION

The J-cars have a semi-independent rear suspension system which consists of an axle with trailing arms and two coil springs, shock absorbers, upper spring insulators and spring compression bumpers. The axle assembly attaches to the body through a rubber bushing located at the front of each control arm. The brackets are integral with the underbody side rails. A stabilizer bar is available as an option.

Two coil springs are used, each being retained between a seat in the underbody and one on the control arm. A rubber cushion is used to isolate the coil spring upper end from the underbody seat, while the lower end sits on a combination bumper and spring insulator.

The double acting shock absorbers are filled with a calibrated amount of fluid and sealed during production. They are non-adjustable, non-refillable and cannot be disassembled.

A single unit hub and bearing assembly is bolted to both ends of the rear axle assembly; it is a sealed unit and must be replaced as one if found to be defective.

Coil Springs

REMOVAL & INSTALLATION

✳✳CAUTION

The coil springs are under a considerable amount of tension. Be very careful when removing or installing them; they can exert enough force to cause very serious injuries. Make sure vehicle is safely supported on the proper type equipment.

▶ See Figures 34 and 35

1. Raise and safely support the vehicle. Remove the rear wheel and tire assemblies.
2. Using the proper equipment, support the weight of the rear axle. Unfasten the right and left brake line bracket attaching screws, then allow the brake line to hang free.

✳✳WARNING

Do NOT suspend the rear axle by the brake hoses or damage to the hoses may result.

3. Unfasten both shock absorber lower attaching bolts from the axle.
4. Carefully lower the axle, then remove the coil spring(s) and/or insulator(s).
To install:
5. Position the spring(s) and insulator(s) in the seats, and raise the axle. The ends of the upper coil in the spring must be positioned in the spring seat and within $9/16$ in. (15mm) of the spring stop.

➡Before installing the springs, it may be necessary to install the upper insulators to the body with adhesive to keep them in position while raising the axle assembly.

6. Install the shock absorber bolts. Tighten to 41 ft. lbs. (55 Nm). Install the brake line brackets. Tighten to 8 ft. lbs. (11 Nm).

Shock Absorbers

REMOVAL & INSTALLATION

▶ See Figures 34 and 36

➡For 1995-96 models, refer to the Coil-Over Shock Absorber procedures.

1. Open the hatch or trunk lid, remove the upper shock absorber cover, then unfasten the upper shock absorber nut.
2. Raise and safely support the vehicle. Support the rear axle with adjustable jackstands.
3. Remove the lower attaching bolt and remove the shock.

➡If both shock absorbers are being replaced, remove the shocks one at a time as suspending rear axle at full length could result in damage to the brake lines/hoses.

To install:
4. If new shock absorbers are being installed, repeatedly compress them while inverted and extend them in their normal upright position. This will purge them of air.
5. Connect the shock absorbers at the lower attachment and install the attaching bolt and nut hand-tight.
6. Lower the vehicle enough to guide the shock absorber upper stud through the body opening, then fasten the upper shock absorber attaching nut loosely. Tighten the lower shock absorber mounting bolt to 35 ft. lbs. (47 Nm).
7. Remove the axle support, then carefully lower the vehicle. Tighten the shock absorber upper nut to 21 ft. lbs. (29 Nm).
8. If equipped, install the retaining nut cover, then install the rear trim cover. Close the trunk or hatch lid.

TESTING

Visually inspect the shock absorber. If there is evidence of leakage and the shock absorber is covered with oil, the shock is defective and should be replaced.

If there is no sign of excessive leakage (a small amount of weeping is normal) bounce the car at one corner by pressing down on the fender or bumper and releasing. When you have the car bouncing as much as you can, release the fender or bumper. The car should stop bouncing after the first rebound. If the bouncing continues past the center point of the bounce more than once, the shock absorbers are worn and should be replaced.

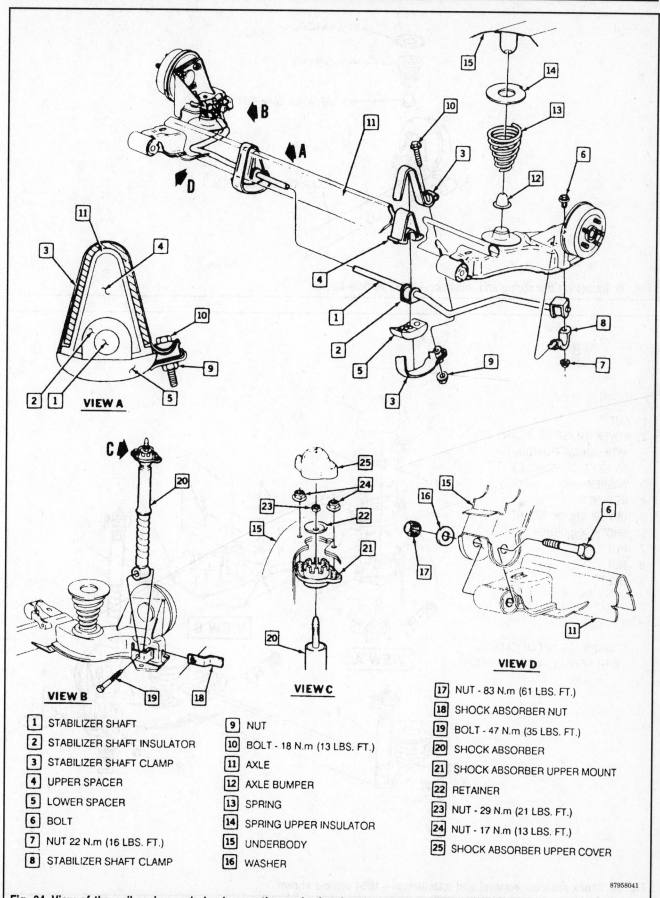

Fig. 34 View of the coil spring and shock mounting and related components — 1991 vehicle shown

VIEW A

VIEW B

VIEW C

VIEW D

1 STABILIZER SHAFT	9 NUT
2 STABILIZER SHAFT INSULATOR	10 BOLT - 18 N.m (13 LBS. FT.)
3 STABILIZER SHAFT CLAMP	11 AXLE
4 UPPER SPACER	12 AXLE BUMPER
5 LOWER SPACER	13 SPRING
6 BOLT	14 SPRING UPPER INSULATOR
7 NUT 22 N.m (16 LBS. FT.)	15 UNDERBODY
8 STABILIZER SHAFT CLAMP	16 WASHER

17 NUT - 83 N.m (61 LBS. FT.)
18 SHOCK ABSORBER NUT
19 BOLT - 47 N.m (35 LBS. FT.)
20 SHOCK ABSORBER
21 SHOCK ABSORBER UPPER MOUNT
22 RETAINER
23 NUT - 29 N.m (21 LBS. FT.)
24 NUT - 17 N.m (13 LBS. FT.)
25 SHOCK ABSORBER UPPER COVER

87958041

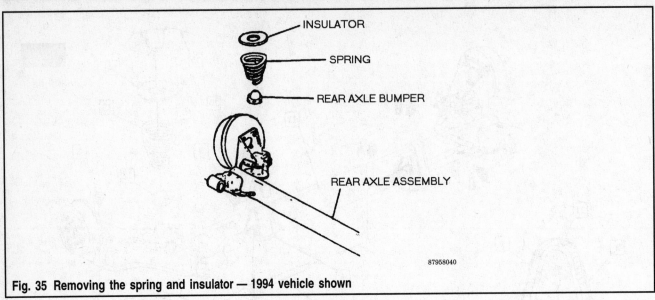

Fig. 35 Removing the spring and insulator — 1994 vehicle shown

1 NUT *
2 COVER (MUST BE INSTALLED WITH ARROW POINTING TO LEFT OF VEHICLE)
3 WASHER
4 RETAINER
5 UPPER SHOCK MOUNT
6 SHOCK ABSORBER
7 NUT *
8 NUT
9 BOLT *

* TORQUE TO SPECIFICATIONS WITH VEHCILE AT CURB HEIGHT

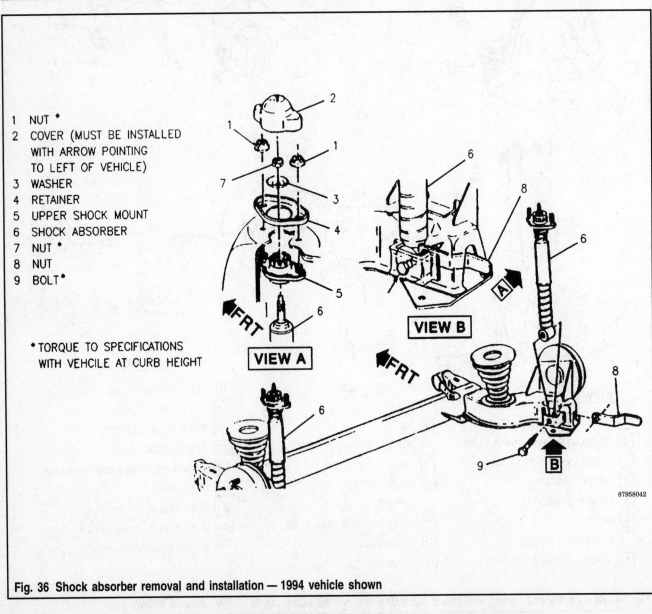

Fig. 36 Shock absorber removal and installation — 1994 vehicle shown

Coil-Over Shock Absorber

REMOVAL & INSTALLATION

▶ **See Figure 37**

➡1995-96 vehicles utilize a shock absorber in which the coil spring is mounted on the shock absorber. It is serviced as a single unit.

1. Open the trunk lid, then unfasten the upper coil-over shock absorber retaining nut. When both shocks are being replaced, remove one shock at a time.
2. Raise and safely support the vehicle, then support the rear axle using adjustable jackstands.
3. Unfasten the bolt from the coil-over shock upper mount.

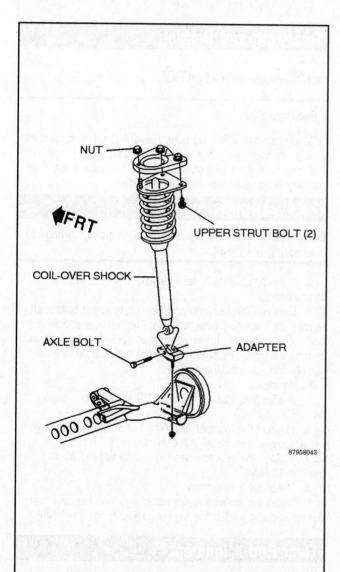

Fig. 37 Exploded view of the coil-over shock absorber assembly which is used on 1995-96 vehicles only

4. Remove the coil-over shock mounting bolt, then remove the assembly from the vehicle.

✳✳WARNING

Do NOT remove both shock absorbers at one time as suspending the rear axle at full length could result in damage to the brake pipes and hoses.

To install:

5. Position the coil-over shock absorber at the lower attachment, then install the retaining bolt hand-tight.
6. Install the upper coil-over shock absorber mounting bolts, hand-tighten the retaining bolt, then carefully lower the vehicle.
7. Fasten the coil-over shock assembly upper mount attaching nut hand-tight.
8. Tighten the lower mounting bolts to 125 ft. lbs. (170 Nm) and the upper mounting bolts and nut to 21 ft. lbs. (28 Nm).
9. Remove the axle support, then lower the vehicle all of the way and tighten the upper shock absorber nut to 21 ft. lbs. (28 Nm).

Rear Axle/Control Arm

The control arms and axle are are one unit. The axle structure itself maintains the geometrical relationship of the wheels relative to the body. The axle assembly attaches to the underbody through a rubber bushing located at the front of each control arm. Each control arm bolts to underbody brackets.

REMOVAL & INSTALLATION

1982-91 Vehicles

1. Raise and safely support the vehicle. Support the vehicle with jackstands under the axle.
2. Remove the stabilizer shaft from the axle assembly.
3. Remove the wheel and tire assembly, then remove the brake drum.

✳✳WARNING

Do not hammer on the brake drum as damage to the bearing could result!

4. Unfasten the shock absorber lower attaching bolts and paddle nuts at the axle, then disconnect the shocks from the control arm/axle.
5. Disconnect the parking brake cable and the rear ABS wiring connector and clip, if equipped, from the axle assembly.
6. Disconnect the brake line at the brackets from the axle assembly. This will ensure that the axle assembly is not suspended by the brake lines.
7. Lower the rear axle, then remove the coil springs and insulators.
8. Unfasten the control arm bolts from the underbody bracket and lower the axle from the underbody.
9. Remove the hub attaching bolts, then and remove the hub, bearing and backing plate assembly from the axle.

To install:

10. Install the hub, bearing and backing plate assembly. Hold the nuts and tighten the attaching bolts to 39 ft. lbs. (53 Nm).

11. Install the stabilizer shaft.

12. Place the axle assembly on a transmission jack and raise into position. Attach the control arm/axle to the underbody bracket with bolts and nuts. Tighten the retainers to 61 ft. lbs. (83 Nm) with the weight of the vehicle on the axle.

13. Install the brake line connections to the axle assembly. Tighten the brake line-to-axle screw to 11 ft. lbs. (15 Nm).

14. Attach the brake cable and the rear ABS wiring connector and clip, if equipped, to the rear axle assembly.

15. Position the coil springs and insulators in seats and raise the rear axle.

16. The end of the upper coil on the springs must be parallel to the axle assembly and seated in the pocket.

17. Install the shock absorber lower attachment bolts and paddle nuts to the rear axle and tighten the bolts to 41 ft. lbs. (56 Nm).

18. Install the parking brake cable to the guide hook and adjust as necessary.

19. Install the brake drums and the wheel and tire assemblies.

20. Bleed the brake system, as outlined in Section 9, then carefully lower the car.

1992-96 Vehicles

▶ **See Figure 38**

1. Raise and safely support the vehicle. Support the rear axle with jackstands.

2. Remove the rear tire and wheel assembly.

3. Disconnect the brake line at the brackets from the axle assembly. This will ensure that the axle assembly is not suspended by the brake lines.

4. Unfasten the lower shock mount bolt.

5. Lower the rear axle.

6. Disconnect the parking brake cable at the equalizer unit right wheel assembly.

7. If equipped, detach the rear ABS wiring connector and mount clip located near the fuel tank.

8. Disconnect the right and left brake lines.

9. Unfasten the control arm bolts and nuts, then remove the axle assembly.

To install:

10. Position the rear axle assembly and loosely install the attaching bolts.

11. Connect the right and left brake lines.

12. Attach the ABS wiring connector and mount clip.

13. Fasten the parking brake cable at the right rear wheel cable connector and cable equalizer.

14. Install the lower mount bolt. Tighten the control arm nuts to 44 ft. lbs. (80 Nm) plus a 120° rotation. Tighten the shock absorber lower attaching bolt and nut to 125 ft. lbs. (170 Nm).

15. Fasten the left and right side brake line bracket mount bolts to the body. Tighten the screws to 97 inch lbs. (11 Nm).

16. Install the tire and wheel assembly, then remove the jackstands from under the vehicle.

17. Carefully lower the vehicle, then bleed the brake system, as outlined in Section 9 of this manual.

Stabilizer Bar

REMOVAL & INSTALLATION

1. Raise the vehicle and support the body with jackstands.

2. Unfasten the nuts and bolts at both the axle and control arm attachments and remove the control arm and remove the bracket, insulator and stabilizer bar.

To install:

3. Install the U-bolts, upper clamp, spacer and insulators in the trailing axle. Position the stabilizer bar in the insulators and loosely install the lower clamp and nuts.

4. Attach the end of the stabilizer bar to the control arms, then tighten all nuts to 13 ft. lbs. (18 Nm).

5. Tighten the axle attaching nut to 10 ft. lbs. (14 Nm).

6. Carefully lower the vehicle.

Rear Hub and Bearing

REMOVAL & INSTALLATION

▶ **See Figure 39**

1. Loosen the wheel lug nuts. Raise and safely support the vehicle, then remove the wheel and tire assembly.

2. Remove the brake drum. Removal procedures are covered in Section 9 of this manual, if needed.

✳✳WARNING

Do not hammer on the brake drum to remove; damage to the bearing will result.

3. If equipped, detach the rear ABS wheel speed sensor wire connector.

4. Unfasten the four hub and bearing retaining bolts and remove the assembly from the axle. The top rear attaching bolt will not clear the brake shoe when removing the hub and bearing assembly. Partially remove the hub and bearing assembly prior to removing this bolt.

To install:

5. If equipped, attach the rear ABS wheel speed sensor wire.

6. Position the top rear attaching bolt in the hub and bearing assembly, then install the assembly.

7. Tighten the hub and bearing-to-axle bolts to 39-44 ft. lbs. (52-60 Nm).

8. Install the brake drum.

9. Install the wheel and tire assembly, then carefully lower the vehicle and tighten the lug nut to 100 ft. lbs. (140 Nm).

Rear End Alignment

The rear end alignment is not adjustable. If the rear wheels appear to be out of alignment, inspect the underbody and rear suspension for damaged and or broken parts.

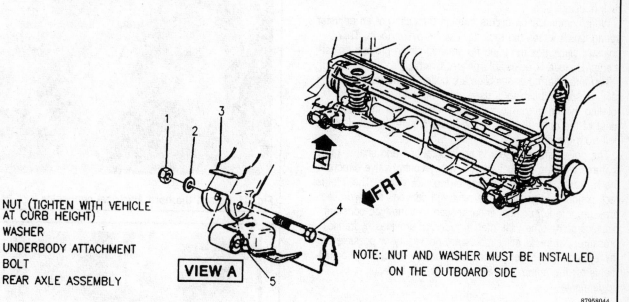

1 NUT (TIGHTEN WITH VEHICLE AT CURB HEIGHT)
2 WASHER
3 UNDERBODY ATTACHMENT
4 BOLT
5 REAR AXLE ASSEMBLY

VIEW A

NOTE: NUT AND WASHER MUST BE INSTALLED ON THE OUTBOARD SIDE

87958044

Fig. 38 Rear axle assembly components — 1995 vehicle shown

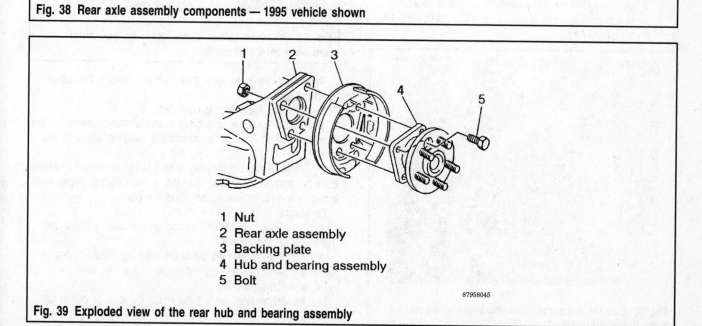

1 Nut
2 Rear axle assembly
3 Backing plate
4 Hub and bearing assembly
5 Bolt

87958045

Fig. 39 Exploded view of the rear hub and bearing assembly

STEERING

Most J-cars are equipped with, as standard equipment, (except Cimarron), a Saginaw manual rack and pinion steering gear. The pinion is supported by and turns in a sealed ball bearing at the top and a pressed-in roller bearing at the bottom. The rack moves in bushings pressed into each end of the rack housing.

Wear compensation occurs through the action of an adjuster spring which forces the rack against the pinion teeth. This adjuster eliminates the need for periodic pinion preload adjustments. Preload is adjustable only at overhaul.

The inner tie rod assemblies are bolted to the front of the rack. A special bushing is used, allowing both rocking and rotating motion of the tie rods. Any service other than replacement of the outer tie rods or the boots requires removal of the unit from the car.

The power steering gear is an integral unit and shares most features with the manual gear. A rotary control valve directs the hydraulic fluid to either side of the rack piston. The integral rack piston is attached to the rack and converts the hydraulic pressure into left or right linear motion. A vane-type constant displacement pump with integral reservoir provides hydraulic pressure. No in-car adjustments are necessary or possible on the system, except for periodic belt tension checks and adjustments for the pump. See Section 1 for belt tension adjustments.

Steering Wheel

REMOVAL & INSTALLATION

▶ **See Figures 40, 41, 42, 43, 44, 45 and 46**

1. If equipped, disable the SIR system. For details, please refer to the procedure located in Section 6 of this manual.
2. If not done already, disconnect the negative cable.
3. Unfasten the retaining screws or pull the pad/center cap from the steering wheel.

Fig. 41 Detach the horn electrical connector

Fig. 42 On some earlier model vehicles, you must remove a retaining circlip

4. Detach the horn lead, then remove remove the retainer (if so equipped).
5. Unfasten the steering shaft nut.
6. There should be alignment marks already present on the wheel and shaft. If not, matchmark the steering wheel to the shaft.
7. Using a suitable steering wheel puller, remove the wheel from the vehicle. On some vehicles, a horn spring, eyelet and insulator are underneath; don't lose the parts.

To install:

8. If equipped, install the spring, eyelet and insulator into the tower on the column.
9. Install the wheel on the shaft, aligning the matchmarks. Install the shaft nut and tighten to 30 ft. lbs. (41 Nm).
10. Install the retainer.
11. Attach the horn lead, then install the pad or center cap.

Fig. 40 Pull the horn pad from the steering wheel — 1988 Sunbird shown

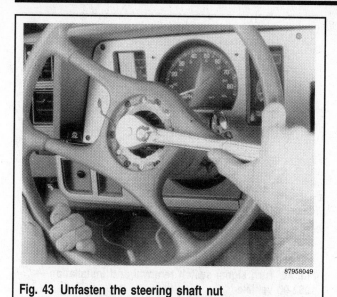

Fig. 43 Unfasten the steering shaft nut

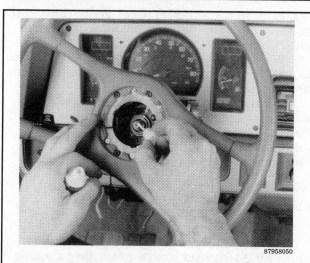

Fig. 44 If there are no factory alignment marks, matchmark the steering wheel to the shaft

Fig. 45 Use a suitable puller to remove the steering wheel from the vehicle

Fig. 46 When installing the steering wheel, make sure the align the matchmarks made during removal

12. If equipped, make sure to enable the SIR system as outlined in Section 6 of this manual.

13. Connect the negative battery cable.

Turn Signal (Combination) Switch

REMOVAL & INSTALLATION

1982-90 Vehicles

▶ See Figures 47, 48 and 49

1. Disconnect the negative battery cable.
2. Remove the steering wheel and the trim cover.
3. Pry the cover from the steering column.
4. Position a U-shaped lockplate compressing tool on the end of the steering shaft and compress the lock plate by turning the shaft nut clockwise. Pry the wire snapring out of the shaft groove.
5. Remove the tool and lift the lockplate off the shaft.

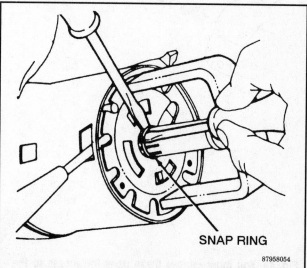

SNAP RING

Fig. 47 Depress the lock plate and remove the snapring

6. Slip the cancelling cam, upper bearing preload spring, and thrust washer off the shaft.

7. Remove the turn signal lever. Remove the hazard flasher button retaining screw and remove the button, spring and knob.

8. Pull the switch connector out of the mast jacket and tape the upper part to facilitate switch removal. Attach a long piece of wire to the turn signal switch connector. When installing the turn signal switch, feed this wire through the column first, and then use this wire to pull the switch connector into position. On tilt wheels, place the turn signal and shifter housing in low position and remove the harness cover.

9. Unfasten the three switch mounting screws. Remove the switch by pulling it straight up while guiding the wiring harness cover through the column.

To install:

10. Install the replacement switch by working the connector and cover down through the housing and under the bracket. On tilt models, the connector is worked down through the housing, under the bracket, and then the cover is installed on the harness.

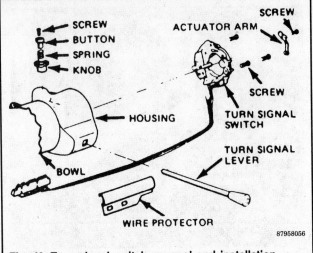

Fig. 49 Turn signal switch removal and installation — 1982-90 vehicles

11. Install the switch mounting screws and the connector on the mast jacket bracket. Install the column-to-dash trim plate.

12. Install the flasher knob and the turn signal lever.

13. With the turn signal lever in neutral and the flasher knob out, slide the thrust washer, upper bearing preload spring, and cancelling cam onto the shaft.

14. Position the lock plate on the shaft and press it down until a new snapring can be inserted in the shaft groove. Always use a new snapring when assembling.

15. Install the cover and the steering wheel.

16. Connect the negative battery cable.

1991-94 Sunbird

▶ See Figure 50

1. Disconnect the negative battery cable.

2. Remove the pad and horn lead, retainer and nut and remove the steering wheel from the column, using a suitable puller.

3. Unfasten the 2 lower column cover retaining screws.

4. Remove the 3 bottom retaining screws from lower column cover.

5. Separate the rose bud fastener (integral to wire harness) from the jacket assembly.

6. Remove the turn signal switch retaining screws.

7. Compress the locking tab and remove the 2 wire harness connector from the switch.

8. Depress the locking tab and remove the cruise connector from the wire harness, if so equipped.

To install:

9. Installation is the reverse of the removal procedure.

10. Tighten the cover and switch retaining screws to 49 inch lbs. (5.5 Nm) and the steering wheel retaining nut to 30 ft. lbs. (41 Nm).

11. Connect the negative battery cable.

1991-94 Cavalier and All 1995-96 Vehicles

▶ See Figure 51

➡This procedure covers removal and installation of the headlamp, headlamp dimmer switch, turn signal and hazard switches, as well as the cruise control switch.

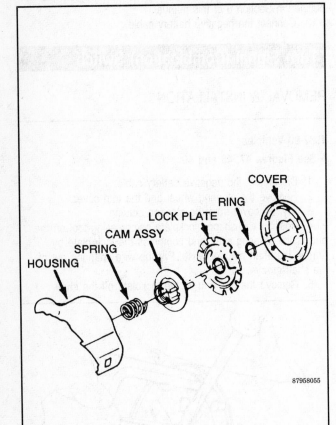

Fig. 48 You must remove these parts for access to the turn signal switch

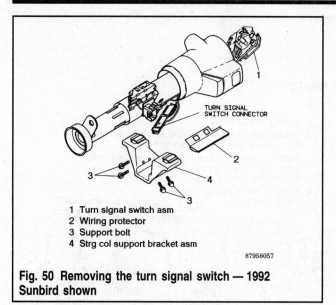

1 Turn signal switch asm
2 Wiring protector
3 Support bolt
4 Strg col support bracket asm

87958057

Fig. 50 Removing the turn signal switch — 1992 Sunbird shown

1. If equipped, disable the SIR system. For details, please refer to the procedure located in Section 6 of this manual.

2. If not already done, disconnect the negative battery cable.

3. Unfasten the horn pad, then remove the steering wheel. For details, please refer to the procedure earlier in this section.

➡️**If necessary, using locking pliers with a piece of rubber (such as a spark plug boot) between the jaws to help prevent damage to the tilt lever during removal.**

4. If equipped, remove the tilt lever from the steering column by grasping the lever firmly and twisting counterclockwise, while pulling it from the column.

5. Remove the upper and lower steering column covers.

6. Remove the dampener assembly, then unfasten and remove the switch assembly from the vehicle.

To install:

7. Position and secure the switch assembly.

8. Install the dampener and the upper and lower steering column covers.

9. If equipped, attach the tilt lever to the column.

10. Install the steering wheel, then fasten the horn pad.

11. If equipped, enable the SIR system, as outlined in Section 6 of this manual.

12. Connect the negative battery cable.

Ignition Switch

REMOVAL & INSTALLATION

1982-91 Vehicles

▶ **See Figures 52, 53 and 54**

The switch is located on the steering column and is completely inaccessible without first lowering the steering column. The switch is actuated by a rod and rack assembly. A gear on

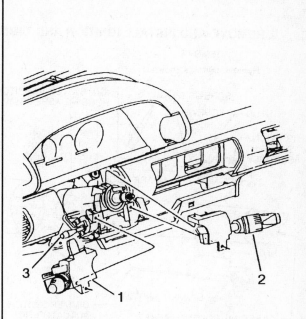

1 Headlamp/Turn signal/Cruise control Hazard switch
2 Windshield wiper/Washer switch
3 Tilt lever (if equipped)

87958058

Fig. 51 View of the steering column showing the turn signal switch location — 1995 vehicle shown

the end of the lock cylinder engages the toothed upper end of the rod.

1. Lower the steering column; be sure to properly support it.

2. Put the switch in the **OFF-UNLOCKED** position. With the cylinder removed, the rod is in **OFF-UNLOCKED** position when it is in the next to the uppermost detent.

3. Unfasten the two switch screws and remove the switch assembly.

To install:

4. Before installing, move the new switch slider (standard columns with automatic transaxle) to the extreme left position. Move the switch slider (standard columns with manual transaxle) to the extreme left position. Move the slider (adjustable columns with automatic transaxle) to the extreme right position and then move the slider one detent to the left (off lock). Move the slider (adjustable columns with manual transaxle) to the extreme right position.

5. Install the activating rod into the switch and assemble the switch on the column. Tighten the mounting screws. Use

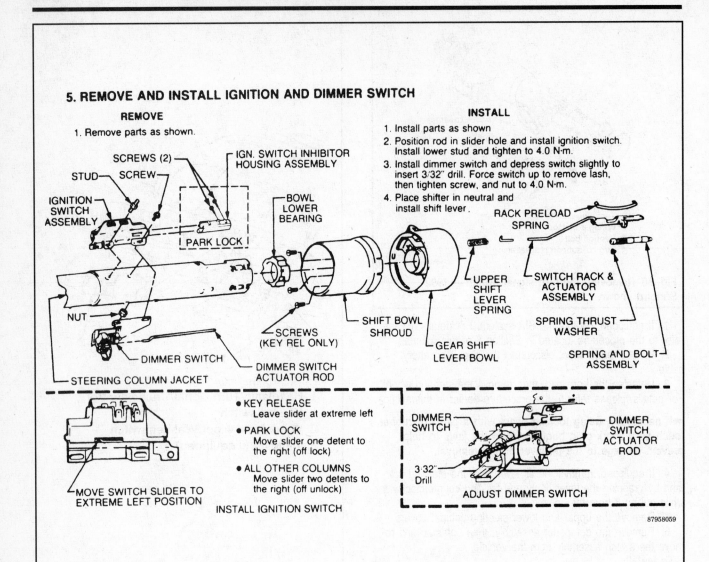

Fig. 52 Removal and installation of the ignition switch and related steering column components — 1990 vehicle shown

only the specified screws, since overlength screws could impair the collapsibility of the column.

6. Reinstall the steering column.

1992-94 Sunbird

▶ **See Figure 55**

1. Disconnect the negative battery cable.
2. Remove the pad and horn lead, retainer and nut and remove the steering wheel from the column, using a suitable puller.
3. Remove the tilt lever, if so equipped.
4. Unfasten the 2 lower column cover retaining screws.
5. Remove the 3 bottom retaining screws from lower column cover.
6. Unfasten the washer head screw and hex nut.
7. Remove the dimmer switch assembly from the rod. Remove the dimmer switch and ignition switch mounting stud.
8. Disconnect the ignition switch from the actuator assembly, by unfastening the two cross recess screws. Detach the electrical connector, then remove the switch.

To install:

➡ **Install the ignition switch to the jacket with the switch in the "OFF-LOCK" position. A new swtich will be pinned in the "OFF-LOCK" position. Don't forget to remove the plastic pin after the switch is attached to the column**

9. Connect the ignition switch to the ignition switch actuator assembly and adjust as follows:
   a. Move the switch slider to the extreme left position.
   b. Move the switch slider one detent to the right **"OFF-LOCK"** position.
10. Install the ignition switch assembly and stud. Tighten the retaining screws to 30 inch lbs. (3.4 Nm).
11. Fasten the dimmer switch assembly to the rod.
12. Install the hex nut and washer head screw and tighten finger-tight.
13. Adjust the dimer switch as follows:
    a. Place a $^3/_{32}$ in. (2.4mm) drill bit in the hole in the switch to limit travel.
    b. Position the switch on the column and push against the dimmer switch rod to remove all lash.

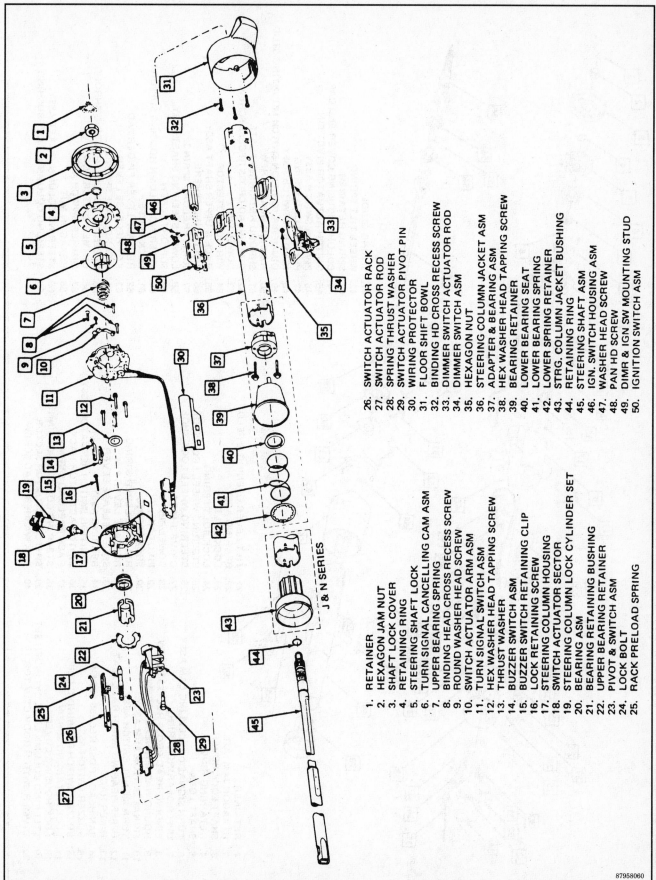

1. RETAINER
2. HEXAGON JAM NUT
3. SHAFT LOCK COVER
4. RETAINING RING
5. STEERING SHAFT LOCK
6. TURN SIGNAL CANCELLING CAM ASM
7. UPPER BEARING SPRING
8. BINDING HEAD CROSS RECESS SCREW
9. ROUND WASHER HEAD SCREW
10. SWITCH ACTUATOR ARM ASM
11. TURN SIGNAL SWITCH ASM
12. HEX WASHER HEAD TAPPING SCREW
13. THRUST WASHER
14. BUZZER SWITCH ASM
15. BUZZER SWITCH RETAINING CLIP
16. LOCK RETAINING SCREW
17. STEERING COLUMN HOUSING
18. SWITCH ACTUATOR SECTOR
19. STEERING COLUMN LOCK CYLINDER SET
20. BEARING ASM
21. BEARING RETAINING BUSHING
22. UPPER BEARING RETAINER
23. PIVOT & SWITCH ASM
24. LOCK BOLT
25. RACK PRELOAD SPRING

26. SWITCH ACTUATOR RACK
27. SWITCH ACTUATOR ROD
28. SPRING THRUST WASHER
29. SWITCH ACTUATOR PIVOT PIN
30. WIRING PROTECTOR
31. FLOOR SHIFT BOWL
32. BINDING HD CROSS RECESS SCREW
33. DIMMER SWITCH ACTUATOR ROD
34. DIMMER SWITCH ASM
35. HEXAGON NUT
36. STEERING COLUMN JACKET ASM
37. ADAPTER & BEARING ASM
38. HEX WASHER HEAD TAPPING SCREW
39. BEARING RETAINER
40. LOWER BEARING SEAT
41. LOWER BEARING SPRING
42. LOWER SPRING RETAINER
43. STRG. COLUMN JACKET BUSHING
44. RETAINING RING
45. STEERING SHAFT ASM
46. IGN. SWITCH HOUSING ASM
47. WASHER HEAD SCREW
48. PAN HD SCREW
49. DIMR & IGN SW MOUNTING STUD
50. IGNITION SWITCH ASM

J & N SERIES

Fig. 53 Exploded view of a steering column including the ignition switch — 1990 vehicle with standard column shown

87958060

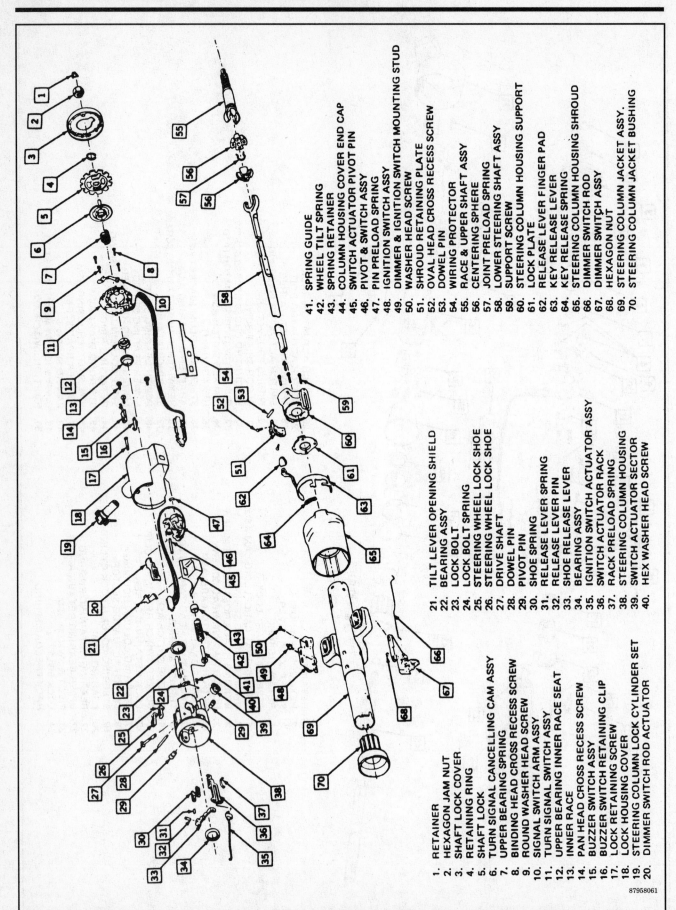

1. RETAINER
2. HEXAGON JAM NUT
3. SHAFT LOCK COVER
4. RETAINING RING
5. SHAFT LOCK
6. TURN SIGNAL CANCELLING CAM ASSY
7. UPPER BEARING SPRING
8. BINDING HEAD CROSS RECESS SCREW
9. ROUND WASHER HEAD SCREW
10. SIGNAL SWITCH ARM ASSY
11. TURN SIGNAL SWITCH ASSY
12. UPPER BEARING INNER RACE SEAT
13. INNER RACE
14. PAN HEAD CROSS RECESS SCREW
15. BUZZER SWITCH ASSY
16. BUZZER SWITCH RETAINING CLIP
17. LOCK RETAINING SCREW
18. LOCK HOUSING COVER
19. STEERING COLUMN LOCK CYLINDER SET
20. DIMMER SWITCH ROD ACTUATOR

21. TILT LEVER OPENING SHIELD
22. BEARING ASSY
23. LOCK BOLT
24. LOCK BOLT SPRING
25. STEERING WHEEL LOCK SHOE
26. STEERING WHEEL LOCK SHOE
27. DOWEL PIN
28. DRIVE SHAFT
29. PIVOT PIN
30. SHOE SPRING
31. RELEASE LEVER SPRING
32. RELEASE LEVER PIN
33. SHOE RELEASE LEVER
34. BEARING ASSY
35. IGNITION SWITCH ACTUATOR ASSY
36. SWITCH ACTUATOR RACK
37. RACK PRELOAD SPRING
38. STEERING COLUMN HOUSING
39. SWITCH ACTUATOR SECTOR
40. HEX WASHER HEAD SCREW

41. SPRING GUIDE
42. WHEEL TILT SPRING
43. SPRING RETAINER
44. COLUMN HOUSING COVER END CAP
45. SWITCH ACTUATOR PIVOT PIN
46. PIVOT & SWITCH ASSY
47. PIN PRELOAD SPRING
48. IGNITION SWITCH ASSY
49. DIMMER & IGNITION SWITCH MOUNTING STUD
50. WASHER HEAD SCREW
51. SHROUD RETAINING PLATE
52. OVAL HEAD CROSS RECESS SCREW
53. DOWEL PIN
54. WIRING PROTECTOR
55. RACE & UPPER SHAFT ASSY
56. CENTERING SPHERE
57. JOINT PRELOAD SPRING
58. LOWER STEERING SHAFT ASSY
59. SUPPORT SCREW
60. STEERING COLUMN HOUSING SUPPORT
61. LOCK PLATE
62. RELEASE LEVER FINGER PAD
63. KEY RELEASE LEVER
64. KEY RELEASE SPRING
65. STEERING COLUMN HOUSING SHROUD
66. DIMMER SWITCH ROD
67. DIMMER SWITCH ASSY
68. HEXAGON NUT
69. STEERING COLUMN JACKET ASSY.
70. STEERING COLUMN JACKET BUSHING

87958061

Fig. 54 Exploded view of the steering column including the ignition switch — 1990 vehicle with tilt column shown

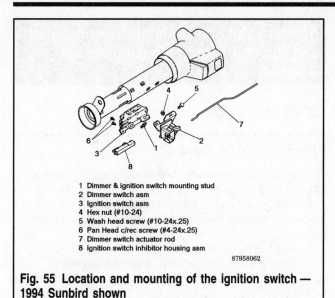

1 Dimmer & ignition switch mounting stud
2 Dimmer switch asm
3 Ignition switch asm
4 Hex nut (#10-24)
5 Wash head screw (#10-24x.25)
6 Pan Head c/rec screw (#4-24x.25)
7 Dimmer switch actuator rod
8 Ignition switch inhibitor housing asm

87958062

Fig. 55 Location and mounting of the ignition switch — 1994 Sunbird shown

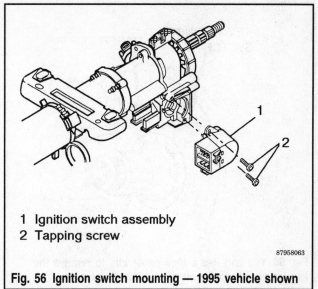

1 Ignition switch assembly
2 Tapping screw

87958063

Fig. 56 Ignition switch mounting — 1995 vehicle shown

c. Remove the drill bit.
14. Attach the switch electrical connector.
15. Install the steering column, as outlined in this section.
16. Connect the negative battery cable.

1992-94 Cavalier and 1995-96 Vehicles
▶ See Figure 56

1. Disconnect the negative battery cable.
2. If equipped, disable the SIR system. For details, please refer to the procedure located in Section 6 of this manual.
3. Remove the steering column as outlined later in this section.
4. Disconnect the wire harness from the ignition switch.
5. Unfasten the retaining screws, then remove the switch.
To install:
6. Installation is the reverse of the removal procedure.
7. If equipped, enable the SIR system as outlined in Section 6 of this manual.

Windshield Wiper Switch

REMOVAL & INSTALLATION

1991-94 Cavalier and 1995-96 Vehicles
▶ See Figure 57

1. If equipped, disable the SIR system. For details, please refer to the procedure located in Section 6 of this manual.
2. Disconnect the negative battery cable.
3. Remove the pad and horn lead, retainer and nut and remove the steering wheel from the column, using a suitable puller.
4. If equipped, remove the tilt lever from the steering column.
5. Remove the upper and lower steering column covers.
6. Remove the dampener assembly.

7. Remove the headlight switch assembly, then remove the windshield wiper switch assembly.
8. Installation is the reverse of the removal procedure.

Ignition Lock Cylinder

REMOVAL & INSTALLATION

1982-90 Vehicles
▶ See Figures 58 and 59

1. Remove the steering wheel.
2. Turn the lock to the **RUN** position.
3. Remove the lock plate, turn signal switch or combination switch, and the key warning buzzer switch. The warning buzzer switch can be fished out with a bent paper clip.

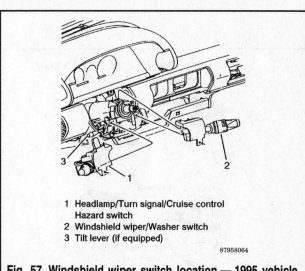

1 Headlamp/Turn signal/Cruise control Hazard switch
2 Windshield wiper/Washer switch
3 Tilt lever (if equipped)

87958064

Fig. 57 Windshield wiper switch location — 1995 vehicle shown

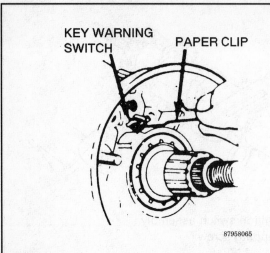

Fig. 58 You can use a bent paper clip to remove the key warning buzzer switch on 1982-90 vehicles

4. Remove the lock cylinder retaining screw and lock cylinder.

✳✳WARNING

If the screw is dropped on removal, it could fall into the column, requiring complete disassembly to retrieve the screw.

To install:

5. Rotate the cylinder clockwise to align the cylinder key with the keyway in the housing.
6. Push the lock all the way in.
7. Install the screw, then tighten it (1.7 Nm) to 15 inch lbs.
8. The rest of installation is the reverse of removal. Turn the lock to **RUN** to install the key warning buzzer switch, which is simply pushed down into place.

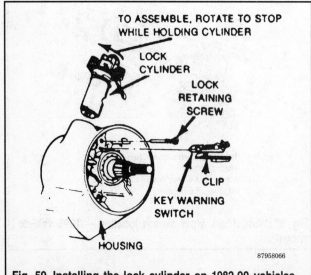

Fig. 59 Installing the lock cylinder on 1982-90 vehicles

Steering Column Housing Steering Shaft and Ignition Switch Housing Jacket Bushing

DISASSEMBLY

▶ See Figures 60, 61 and 62

1. Disconnect the negative battery cable and disable the SIR system, if equipped.
2. Remove the pad and horn lead, retainer and nut and remove the steering wheel from the column, using a suitable puller.
3. Remove the tilt lever, if so equipped.
4. Remove the 2 lower column cover retaining screws.
5. Remove the 3 bottom retaining screws from lower column cover.
6. Disconnect the park lock cable from the ignition switch and lock cylinder assembly by depressing the locking tab with a small screwdriver.
7. Disconnect the wire harness at the bulkhead.
8. Remove the steering column from the vehicle as outlined in this section.
9. Remove the steering column jacket bushing from from the lower end of the jacket assembly.
10. Separate the rose bud fastener (integral to wire harness) from the jacket assembly.
11. Remove the turn signal switch retaining screws.
12. Depress the locking tab and remove the 2 wire harness connector from the switch.
13. Depress the locking tab and remove the cruise connector from the wire harness, if so equipped.
14. Depress the locking tab and remove the harness connector from the wipe/wash switch.
15. Depress the locking tabs and remove the 2 wire harness connectors from the ignition switch.
16. Remove the ignition switch screws and remove the ignition switch from the housing.

➡The turn signal switch must be removed before compressing the cam plate and shaft spring to prevent damage to the switch.

17. Compress the cam plate and shaft spring with tools J 23653-91 and J 23653-C or equivalent, and remove the retaining ring, orientation cam plate, cancelling cam assembly, upper steering shaft spring and thrust washer.
18. Place the lock cylinder in the **RUN** position.
19. Remove the steering shaft assembly from the lower end of the jacket assembly.
20. Remove the shear bolts, shear bolt washers and ignition switch housing as follows:
    a. Drill of the head of the shear bolts with a ¼ in. (6mm) drill bit.
    b. Separate the washers and switch housing from the column housing.
    c. Remove the threaded ends of the shear bolts from the ignition switch housing with pliers.
    d. Clean all metal shavings from the housing.
21. Remove the 4 hex head screws from the housing.

22. Separate the column housing from the jacket assembly.
To install:

➡Firmly seat all the fasteners in the following steps before tightening them to the specified torque.

23. Install the column housing to the jacket assembly and torque to 47 inch lbs. (5.3 Nm).

24. Install the ignition switch housing to the column housing with shear bolt washers and shear bolts. Tighten the shear bolts until the bolt head separates from the body, approximately 8 ft. lbs. (11 Nm).

25. Place the lock cylinder in the **RUN** position.

26. Install the steering shaft assembly into the lower end of the jacket assembly until bottomed.

27. Place the lock cylinder in the **OFF** position and remove the key.

28. Rotate the steering shaft until the lock bolt engages and locks the steering shaft into position.

29. Install the thrust washer and upper steering shaft spring on the steering shaft.

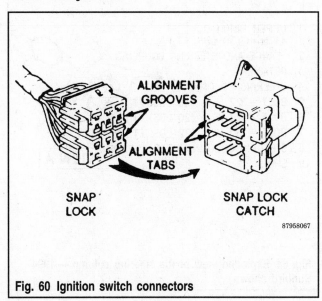

Fig. 60 Ignition switch connectors

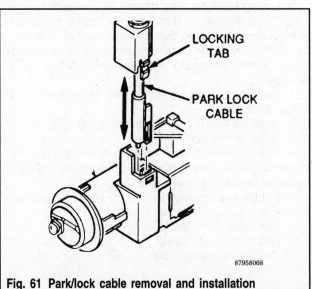

Fig. 61 Park/lock cable removal and installation

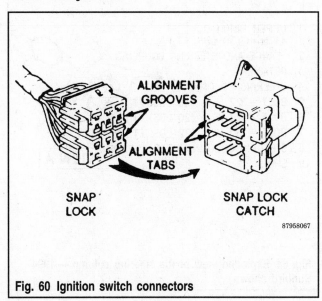

1 Shear bolt
2 Steering column housing
3 Ignition switch housing asm

Fig. 62 Shear bolt removal using a proper sized drill bit

30. Fasten the cancelling cam and orientation cam plate.

31. Install the retaining ring into the groove on the shaft.

32. Place the jacket bushing over the lower end of the steering shaft, into the lower end of the jacket assembly and snap into position.

33. Attach the 2 wire harness connectors to the ignition switch.

34. Fasten the wiper/wash switch retaining screws and tighten to 49 inch lbs. (5.5 Nm).

35. Install the turn signal switch retaining screws and tighten to 49 inch lbs. (5.5 Nm).

36. Install the steering column in the vehicle as outlined later in this section.

37. Connect the wire harness at the bulkhead.

38. Connect the park lock cable to the ignition switch and lock cylinder assembly.

39. Install the rose bud fastener (integral to wiring harness) to the jacket assembly.

40. Tighten the upper and lower cover screws to 49 inch lbs. (5.5 Nm) and the steering wheel retaining nut to 30 ft. lbs. (41 Nm).

Steering Column

REMOVAL & INSTALLATION

❊❊WARNING

The wheels of the car must in the straight ahead position and the key must be in the LOCK position. Once the steering column is removed from the car, the column is extremely susceptible to damage. Dropping the column assembly on its end could collapse the steering shaft or loosen the plastic injections which maintain column rigidity. Leaning on the column assembly could cause the jacket to bend or deform. Under no conditions should the end of the shaft be hammered upon. Any of the above damage could impair the column's collapsible design.

1982-94 Vehicles

EXCEPT 1992-94 CAVALIER

♦ **See Figures 63 and 64**

1. Disconnect the battery ground cable.
2. Remove the left instrument panel sound insulator.
3. Detach the left instrument panel trim pad and steering column trim collar.
4. If the column is to be disassembled, remove the horn contact pad and the steering wheel.
5. Detach the steering shaft to intermediate shaft connection.
6. Unfasten the column bracket support bolts and column bracket support nut.
7. Detach any electrical connections, then remove the steering column from the vehicle.

To install:

8. Insert the steering shaft into the flexible coupling and raise the coupling into position.

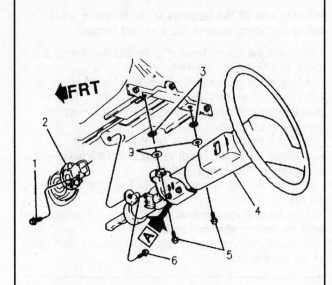

1 UPPER PINCH BOLT —
  41 N·m (30 LBS. FT.)
2 FLANGE AND STEERING COUPLING
3 RETAINERS
4 STEERING COLUMN
5 BOLT — 27 N·m (20 LBS. FT.)
6 BOLT — 27 N·m (20 LBS. FT.)
7 BOLT — 30 N·m (22 LBS. FT.)
8 STEERING COLUMN UPPER SUPPORT
9 SHIMS

Fig. 64 Exploded view of the steering column — 1994 Sunbird shown

9. Loosely install the three steering column attaching bolts.
10. Center the steering shaft within the steering column jacket bushing and tighten the lower attaching bolt. This can be done by moving the steering column jacket jacket assembly up and down or side to side until the steering shaft is centered.
11. Install the two upper attaching bolts and tighten to 20-22 ft. lbs. (27-30 Nm).
12. Install the flexible coupling pinch bolt and tighten to 30-34 ft. lbs. (41-46 Nm).
13. Turn the steering wheel from stop to stop and observe if the steering shaft binds or rubs against the column bushing. Re-center the steering shaft if necessary.
14. Pull the seal assembly up over the end of the column bushing until the seal locks into place.
15. If removed, install the steering wheel.
16. Install the sound insulator.
17. Connect the battery cable.

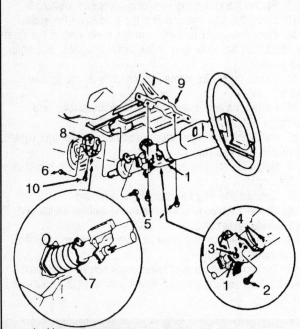

1. Upper support
2. Bolt—install first—27 N·m (20 lbs. ft.)
3. Bolt—install second—27 N·m (20 lbs. ft.)
4. Bolt—install these bolts last—27 N·m (20 lbs. ft.)
5. Bolt—27 N·m (20 lbs. ft.)
6. Upper pinch bolt—46 N·m (34 lbs. ft.)
7. Seal
8. Coupling
9. Instrument panel bracket
10. Lower pinch bolt—40 N·m (29 lbs. ft.)

Fig. 63 Steering column mounting — 1982-90 vehicles

1992-94 Cavalier and 1995-96 Vehicles

▶ See Figure 65

1. If equipped, disable the SIR system. For details, please refer to Section 6 of this manual.

2. If not done already, disconnect the negative battery cable.

3. Snap off the side instrument panel covers.

4. Remove the instrument panel pad. Unfasten the defroster vent screw, the screw under the defroster vent, one screw on each side panel, 2 glove compartment screws (toward the left rear), and the three screws along the top of the glove box. Remove the pad by popping loose or away from the retainers.

5. If equipped, remove the tilt lever.

6. Unfasten the retaining screws, then remove the upper and lower steering column cover and snap apart.

7. Detach the following electrical connections: headlamp switch, windshield wiper switch, cruise control, ignition switch and the headlight switch electrical connection (you can reach the snap from underneath).

8. For vehicles equipped with an automatic transaxle, disconnect the park-lock/brake transmission shift interlock cable from the lock cylinder housing.

9. Unfasten the upper flexible joint pinch bolt.

10. Detach the lower left side wire harness retaining clip.

11. Loosen the lower column bracket support bolts, then remove the upper column bolts.

12. Carefully spread the lower column flexible joint apart using a suitable prytool, then remove the steering column.

To install:

13. Position the steering column in the vehicle.

14. Fasten the lower left side wire harness retaining clip.

15. Install the upper column bolts most of the way in, but not snug.

16. Install the lower column bracket support bolts.

17. Tighten the upper column support bolts to 20 ft. lbs. (27 Nm).

18. Install the upper flexible joint pinch bolt to 30 ft. lbs. (41 Nm).

19. If equipped with an automatic transaxle, attach the park-lock/brake transmission shift interlock cable to the lock cylinder housing.

20. Attach the following electrical connections: headlight switch (must reach from underneath), ignition switch, cruise control, headlamp and wiper switches.

21. Install the upper and lower steering column covers.

22. If equipped, install the tilt lever.

23. Install the instrument panel pad.

24. Snap on the side instrument panel covers (one on each side).

25. If equipped, enable the SIR system as outlined in Section 6 of this manual.

26. Connect the negative battery cable.

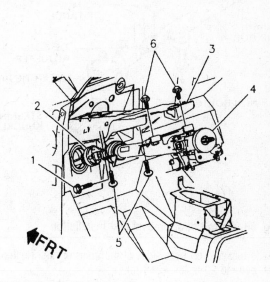

1 UPPER PINCH BOLT
2 FLANGE AND STEERING
   COUPLING
3 UPPER COLUMN
   SUPPORT
4 STEERING COLUMN
5 UPPER COLUMN BOLT
6 LOWER COLUMN BOLT

87958072

Fig. 65 Steering column removal and installation — 1995 vehicle shown

Steering Linkage

REMOVAL & INSTALLATION

Tie Rod Ends

▶ See Figure 66

1. Loosen both pinch bolts at the outer tie rod.

2. Remove the tie rod end from the strut assembly using a suitable removal tool.

3. Unscrew the outer tie rod end from the tie rod adjuster, counting the number of revolutions required before they are disconnected.

To install:

4. Install the new tie rod end, screwing it on the same number of revolutions as counted in Step 3. When the tie rod end is installed, the tie rod adjuster must be centered between the tie rod and the tie rod end, with an equal number of

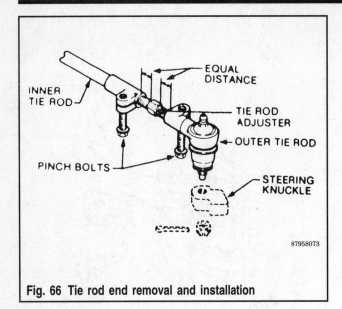

Fig. 66 Tie rod end removal and installation

threads exposed on both sides of the adjuster nut. Tighten the pinch bolts to 20 ft. lbs. (27 Nm).

5. Install the tie rod end to the strut assembly and tighten to 50 ft. lbs. If the cotter pin cannot be installed, tighten the nut up to 1/6 or a turn further. Never back off the nut to align the holes for the cotter pin.

6. Have the front end alignment checked or adjusted.

Rack and Pinion Unit

REMOVAL & INSTALLATION

▶ **See Figures 67 and 68**

1. Disconnect the negative battery cable and disable the SIR system, if equipped.

2. From the driver's side, remove the sound insulator.

3. From under the instrument panel, pull the seal assembly down from the steering column and remove the upper pinch bolt from the flexible coupling.

4. Remove the air cleaner and the windshield washer fluid reservoir, if necessary for easier access.

5. On power steering models: disconnect the pressure line from the steering gear and remove the screw securing the pressure line bracket to the cowl. Move the pressure line aside.

6. Raise and support the car on jackstands.

7. Remove both front wheel and tire assemblies.

8. Disconnect both tie rods from the struts.

9. Carefully lower the car.

10. Remove the right side rack mounting clamp.

11. Remove the left side rack mounting clamp.

12. Move the gear forward slightly. On power steering models, disconnect the fluid return pipe from the gear.

13. Remove the lower pinch bolt from the flexible coupling and separate the rack from the coupling.

14. Remove the dash seal from the rack assembly.

15. Raise and support the car on jackstands.

16. On some models it may be necessary to remove the splash shield from the inner, left fender.

17. Turn the left knuckle and hub assembly to the full left turn position and remove the rack and pinion assembly through the access hole on the left fender.

To install:

18. Installation is the reverse of removal while noting the following points:

a. If the mounting studs backed out during removal, it will be necessary to re-position them prior to rack installation. Double-nut the stud so that it can be torqued to 15 ft. lbs. (20 Nm).

b. It will be helpful to have an assistant inside the car to guide the flexible coupling onto the stub shaft and onto the steering column.

c. Observe the following torques:

- Coupling-to-stub shaft: 1982-86 vehicles: 37 ft. lbs. (50 Nm), 1987-96 vehicles: 29-30 ft. lbs. (39-41 Nm)
- Coupling-to-column: 30 ft. lbs. (41 Nm)
- Mounting clamps: 1982-86 vehicles: 28 ft. lb. (38 Nm), 1987-96 vehicles: 22 ft. lbs. (30 Nm)
- Tie rod nuts: 35-37 ft. lbs. (47-50 Nm)

1. Steering gear asm.
2. L.H. clamp (dark)
3. R.H. clamp (light)
4. Nut—30 N·m (22 lbs. ft.)—hand start all nuts, tighten left side clamp nuts first, then tighten right side nuts.
5. Stud—20 N·m (15 lbs. ft.) after second reuse of stud, thread locking kit no 1052624 must be used.
6. Nut 50 N·m (35 lbs. ft.)
   75 N·m (50 lbs. ft.) maximum to install cotter pin
7. Cotter pin

Fig. 67 Manual rack and pinion assembly

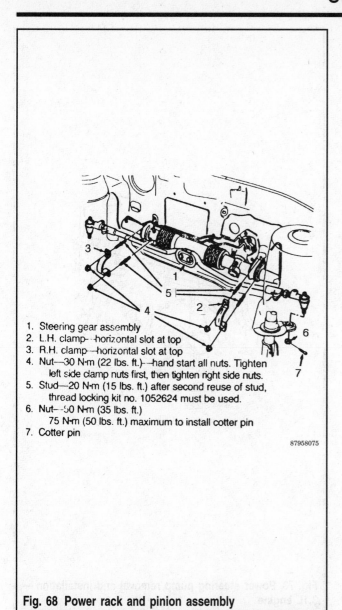

1. Steering gear assembly
2. L.H. clamp—horizontal slot at top
3. R.H. clamp—horizontal slot at top
4. Nut—30 N·m (22 lbs. ft.)—hand start all nuts. Tighten left side clamp nuts first, then tighten right side nuts.
5. Stud—20 N·m (15 lbs. ft.) after second reuse of stud, thread locking kit no. 1052624 must be used.
6. Nut—50 N·m (35 lbs. ft.) 75 N·m (50 lbs. ft.) maximum to install cotter pin
7. Cotter pin

87958075

Fig. 68 Power rack and pinion assembly

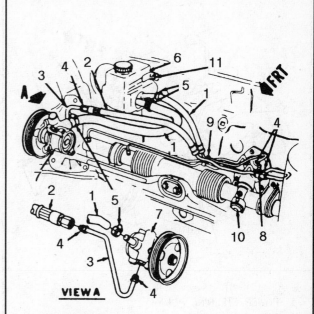

VIEW A

1. OUTLET HOSE
2. INLET HOSE
3. INLET PIPE
4. 27 N·m (20 LBS. FT.)
5. CLAMP 1.7 N·m (15 LBS. IN.)
6. RESERVOIR
7. POWER STEERING PUMP
8. IDLE SPEED POWER STEERING PRESSURE SWITCH
9. RETAINER
10. STEERING GEAR
11. SCREW – 8 N·m (71 LBS. IN.)

87958076

Fig. 69 Power steering fluid line routing — 1.8L and 2.0L engines

Power Steering Pump

REMOVAL & INSTALLATION

▶ **See Figures 69, 70, 71, 72 and 73**

1. Disconnect the negative battery cable.
2. Detach the vent hole at the carburetor if so equipped.
3. Loosen the adjusting bolt and pivot bolt on the pump or release tension on drive belt tensioner assembly, then remove the pump's drive belt.
4. Unfasten the pump-to-bracket or mounting bolts (through the access hole in the pulley as necessary) and remove the adjusting bolt if so equipped.
5. Remove the high pressure fitting from the pump.
6. Disconnect the reservoir-to-pump hose from the pump.
7. Remove the power steering pump from the vehicle. If installing a new pump, transfer the pulley to the new pump.
8. Installation is in the reverse order of removal. Adjust the belt tension and bleed the system, as outlined in this section.

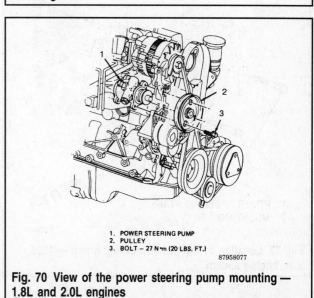

1. POWER STEERING PUMP
2. PULLEY
3. BOLT – 27 N·m (20 LBS. FT.)

87958077

Fig. 70 View of the power steering pump mounting — 1.8L and 2.0L engines

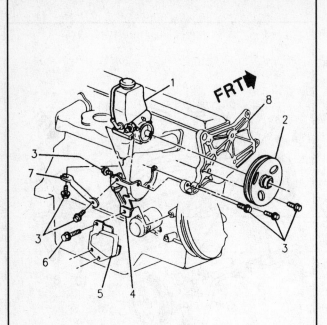

1 POWER STEERING PUMP
2 PULLEY
3 BOLTS – 34 N·m (25 LBS. FT.)
4 POWER STEERING PUMP BRACKET
5 ENGINE MOUNT BRACKET
6 BOLTS – 52 N·m (38 LBS. FT.)
7 BRACE
8 TENSIONER

87958078

Fig. 71 Power steering pump mounting — 1995 2.2L engine shown

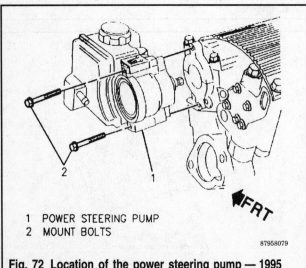

1 POWER STEERING PUMP
2 MOUNT BOLTS

87958079

Fig. 72 Location of the power steering pump — 1995 2.3L engine shown

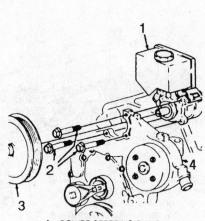

1 POWER STEERING PUMP
2 BOLTS - 25 N.m (18 LBS. FT.)
3 PULLEY
4 FRONT COVER ASSEMBLY

87958080

Fig. 73 Power steering pump removal and installation — 3.1L engine

SYSTEM BLEEDING

1. Raise the front of the vehicle and support safely. This will minimize steering effort. Fill the power steering pump reservoir with the appropriate type of power steering fluid.

2. With the engine off, keep the reservoir full as an assistant turns the steering wheel from lock-to-lock several times. Stop with the steering system at one lock.

3. Start the engine and allow it to idle. Turn the wheel from lock-to-lock several times. Note the amount of air bubbles in the fluid. Repeat the procedure until no more air bubbles appear.

ANTI-LOCK BRAKE SYSTEM (ABS)
ABS CONTROL MODULE 9-54
ABS HYDRAULIC MODULATOR
  ASSEMBLY BLEEDER VALVES 9-50
ABS HYDRAULIC MODULATOR
  SOLENOID 9-56
ABS HYDRAULIC
  MODULATOR/MASTER CYLINDER
  ASSEMBLY 9-52
ABS LAMP DRIVER MODULE 9-50
ABS SERVICE 9-50
DESCRIPTION AND
  OPERATION 9-32
DIAGNOSTIC PROCEDURES 9-33
ELECTRICAL CONNECTORS 9-50
ENABLE RELAY 9-50
FILLING AND BLEEDING 9-56
FLUID LEVEL SENSOR 9-50
SPEED SENSORS 9-54
BRAKE OPERATING SYSTEM
ADJUSTMENT 9-2
BLEEDING THE BRAKE
  SYSTEM 9-10
BRAKE HOSES AND PIPES 9-8
BRAKE LIGHT SWITCH 9-3
BRAKE PEDAL 9-4
CONDITIONS THAT AFFECT BRAKE
  PERFORMANCE 9-2
MASTER CYLINDER 9-4
POWER BRAKE/VACUUM
  BOOSTER 9-4
PROPORTIONING VALVES AND
  FAILURE WARNING SWITCH 9-6
FRONT DISC BRAKES
BRAKE CALIPER 9-15
BRAKE DISC (ROTOR) 9-18
BRAKE PADS 9-12
PARKING BRAKE
CABLES 9-25
PARKING BRAKE LEVER 9-31
REAR DRUM BRAKES
BRAKE BACKING PLATE 9-24
BRAKE DRUMS 9-19
BRAKE SHOES 9-19
WHEEL CYLINDERS 9-23
SPECIFICATIONS CHARTS
BRAKE SPECIFICATIONS 9-60

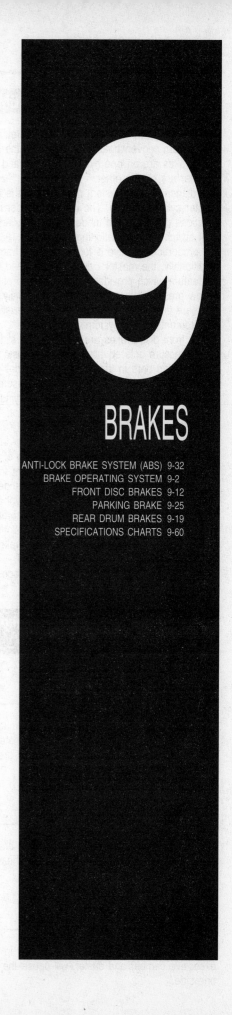

9

BRAKES

ANTI-LOCK BRAKE SYSTEM (ABS) 9-32
BRAKE OPERATING SYSTEM 9-2
FRONT DISC BRAKES 9-12
PARKING BRAKE 9-25
REAR DRUM BRAKES 9-19
SPECIFICATIONS CHARTS 9-60

BRAKE OPERATING SYSTEM

These cars have a diagonally split hydraulic system. This differs from conventional practice in that the left front and right rear brakes are on one hydraulic circuit, and the right front and left rear are on the other.

A diagonally split system necessitates the use of a special master cylinder design. The master cylinder incorporates the functions of a standard tandem master cylinder, plus a warning light switch and proportioning valves. On 1985-86 V6 models the proportioning valve is located on the frame rail. Additionally, the master cylinder is designed with a quick take-up feature which provides a large volume of fluid to the brakes at low pressure when the brakes are initially applied. The low pressure fluid acts to quickly fill the large displacement requirements of the system.

The front disc brakes are single piston sliding caliper units. Fluid pressure acts equally against the piston and the bottom of the piston bore in the caliper. This forces the piston outward until the pad contacts the rotor. The pressure on the caliper bore forces the caliper to slide over, carrying the other pad into contact with the other side of the rotor. The disc brakes are self-adjusting.

Rear drum brakes are conventional duo-servo units. A dual piston wheel cylinder, mounted to the top of the backing plate, actuates both brake shoes. Wheel cylinder force to the shoes is supplemented by the tendency of the shoes to wrap into the drum (servo action). An actuating link, pivot and lever serve to automatically engage the adjuster as the brakes are applied when the car is moving in reverse. Provisions for manual adjustment are also provided. The rear brakes also serve as the parking brakes; linkage is mechanical.

Vacuum boost is a standard unit. The booster is a conventional tandem vacuum unit.

Conditions That Affect Brake Performance

TIRES

Tires with uneven contact and grip on road will cause unequal braking. Tires must be evenly inflated, identical in size and the tread pattern of the right and left tires must be approximately the same.

VEHICLE LOADING

A heavily loaded vehicle requires more braking effort. When a vehicle has unequal loading, the most heavily loaded wheels require more braking power than others.

WHEEL ALIGNMENT

Misalignment of the wheels, particularly in regard to excessive camber and caster, will cause the brakes to pull to one side.

TRAILER TOWING

Towing a trailer requires longer braking distances and tends to overheat the brakes sooner.

Adjustment

DISC BRAKES

The front disc brakes are inherently self-adjusting. No adjustments are either necessary or possible.

DRUM BRAKES

The drum brakes are designed to self-adjust when applied with the car moving in reverse. However, they can also be adjusted manually. This manual adjustment should also be performed whenever the linings are replaced.

1982-86 Vehicles
▶ See Figure 1

1. Raise and safely support the vehicle.
2. Remove the tire and wheel assembly.
3. Remove the drum, then measure the inside diameter of the brake drum with a drum-to-brake shoe gauge, J 21177-A or equivalent.
4. Position the tool on the brake linings, as shown in the accompanying figure, with the setting obtained in Step 3 and adjust the brake shoes so that the lining contacts the inside part of the tool.
5. Use a punch to knock out the stamped area on the brake drum. If this is done with the drum installed on the car, the drum must then be removed to clean out all metal pieces. After adjustments are complete, obtain a hole cover from your dealer (Part no. 4874119 or the equivalent) to prevent entry of dirt and water into the brakes.
6. Use an awl or an adjusting tool especially made for the purpose to turn the brake adjusting screw star wheel. Expand the shoes until the drum can just barely be turned by hand.
7. Back off the adjusting screw 12 notches. If the shoes still are dragging lightly, back off the adjusting screw one or two additional notches. If the brakes still drag, the parking brake adjustment is incorrect or the parking brake is applied. Fix and start over.
8. Install the hole cover into the drum.
9. Check the parking brake adjustment.

➡ On some models, no marked area or stamped area is present on the drum. In this case, a hole must be drilled in the backing plate:

10. All backing plates have two round flat areas in the lower half through which the parking brake cable is installed. Drill a ½ in. (13mm) hole into the round flat area on the backing

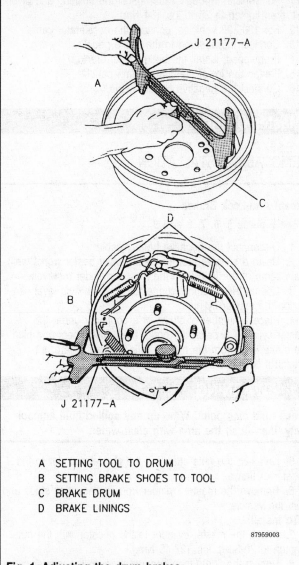

A SETTING TOOL TO DRUM
B SETTING BRAKE SHOES TO TOOL
C BRAKE DRUM
D BRAKE LININGS

87959003

Fig. 1 Adjusting the drum brakes

plate opposite the parking brake cable. This will allow access to the star wheel.

11. After drilling the hole, remove the drum and remove all metal particles. Install a hole plug (Part no. 4874119 or the equivalent) to prevent the entry of water or dirt.

12. Install the brake drum and the wheel and tire assembly, then carefully lower the vehicle.

1987-96 Vehicles

▶ See Figure 1

1. Raise and support the vehicle safely.
2. Matchmark the relationship between the wheel to the axle flange to insure proper balance upon reassembly, then remove the tire and wheel assembly.
3. Matchmark the relationship of the drum to the axle flange, then remove the brake drum.
4. Measure the drum inside diameter using brake shoe gauge J 12177-A, or equivalent.

5. Turning the star wheel, adjust the shoe and lining diameter to be:
   • 0.050 in. (1.27mm) less than the inside drum diameter for each wheel for 1987-90 vehicles.
   • 0.030 in. (0.76mm) less than the inside drum diameter for each wheel for 1991-96 vehicles.
6. Install the drums and wheels, aligning the previous marks.
7. Carefully lower the vehicle.
8. Tighten the wheel nuts to 100 ft. lbs. (136 Nm).
9. Make several alternate forward and reserve stops applying firm force to the brake pedal until ample pedal reserve is built up.

Brake Light Switch

REMOVAL & INSTALLATION

▶ See Figure 2

1. Disconnect the negative battery cable.
2. Remove the drivers side hush panel/sound insulator.
3. Detach the switch electrical connector.
4. If equipped, unfasten the retaining nut from switch.
5. Remove the switch from the retainer by grasping it and pulling it toward the rear of the car.

To install:

6. Insert the brake light switch into the retainer until the switch body seats on the retainer or install the retaining nut.
7. Adjust the brake light switch, as follows:
   a. Pull the brake pedal upward against the internal pedal stop. The switch will be moved in the retainer providing proper adjustment.

➡**Proper switch adjustment is achieved when no clicks are heard as the pedal is pulled upward and when the brake lights do not stay on without brake application.**

8. Attach the switch electrical connector.
9. Install the hush panel/sound insulator.
10. Connect the negative battery cable.

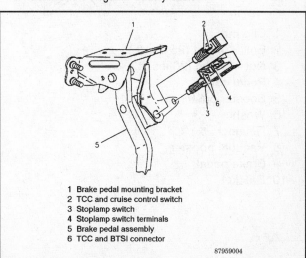

1 Brake pedal mounting bracket
2 TCC and cruise control switch
3 Stoplamp switch
4 Stoplamp switch terminals
5 Brake pedal assembly
6 TCC and BTSI connector

87959004

Fig. 2 The brake light switch is mounted on the brake pedal

Brake Pedal

REMOVAL & INSTALLATION

▶ **See Figures 3 and 4**

1. Disconnect the battery ground cable.
2. Remove the lower steering column panel/sound insulator.
3. For vehicles through 1994, remove the brake pedal bracket.
4. Disconnect the pushrod from the brake pedal.
5. For 1995-96 vehicles, disconnect the accelerator cable.
6. Remove the pivot bolt and bushing.
7. Remove the brake pedal.
8. If necessary, detach any necessary electrical connections from the brake pedal.

To install:

9. If equipped, attach the electrical connections to the brake pedal.
10. Position the brake pedal.

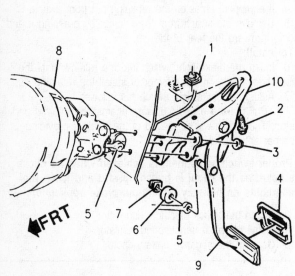

1 Clip nut
2 Bolt - 34 Nm (25 lbs. ft.)
3 Nut - 27 Nm (20 lbs. ft.)
4 Pedal cover
5 Booster push rod
6 Washer
7 Retainer
8 Vacuum booster
9 Brake pedal
10 Bracket

87959006

Fig. 3 Brake pedal assembly and related components — 1993 vehicle shown

11. For vehicles through 1994, install the bushing and pivot bolt, then tighten to 25 ft. lbs. (34 Nm).
12. For 1995-96 vehicles, connect the accelerator cable.
13. Connect the pushrod to the brake pedal.
14. If equipped, install the brake pedal bracket.
15. Fasten the lower steering column panel.
16. Connect the negative battery cable.

Master Cylinder

REMOVAL & INSTALLATION

Except Anti-Lock Brakes
▶ **See Figures 5, 6, 7, 8 and 9**

1. Disconnect the negative battery cable.
2. Using a suitable tool, (a clean turkey baster works well) drain some of the fluid from the master cylinder reservoir.
3. Unplug the electrical connector from the fluid level sensor on the master cylinder.
4. Place a number of cloths or a container under the master cylinder to catch the brake fluid. Disconnect and plug the brake lines from the master cylinder; use a flare nut wrench if one is available.

✳✳WARNING

Brake fluid eats paint. Wipe up any spilled fluid immediately, then flush the area with clear water.

5. Unfasten the nuts attaching the master cylinder to the booster or firewall.
6. Remove the master cylinder from its mounting studs and from the vehicle.

To install:

7. Attach the master cylinder to the booster with the nuts. Tighten to 20-30 ft. lbs. (27-45 Nm.).
8. Unplug the lines, then connect them to the master cylinder. Tighten to 10-15 ft. lbs. (13-20 Nm).
9. Attach the fluid level sensor electrical lead.
10. Bleed the brakes, as outlined in this section.
11. Connect the negative battery cable.

Power Brake/Vacuum Booster

REMOVAL & INSTALLATION

▶ **See Figure 10**

➡It is not necessary to remove or disconnect the master cylinder from the vehicle in order to remove the vacuum booster. However, if both the vacuum booster and master cylinder are to be removed, remove the master cylinder first.

1. Disconnect the negative battery cable.
2. For 1995-96 vehicles, disconnect the positive battery cable, then remove the battery. Remove the air cleaner assembly.
3. Unfasten the master cylinder-to-booster retaining nuts.

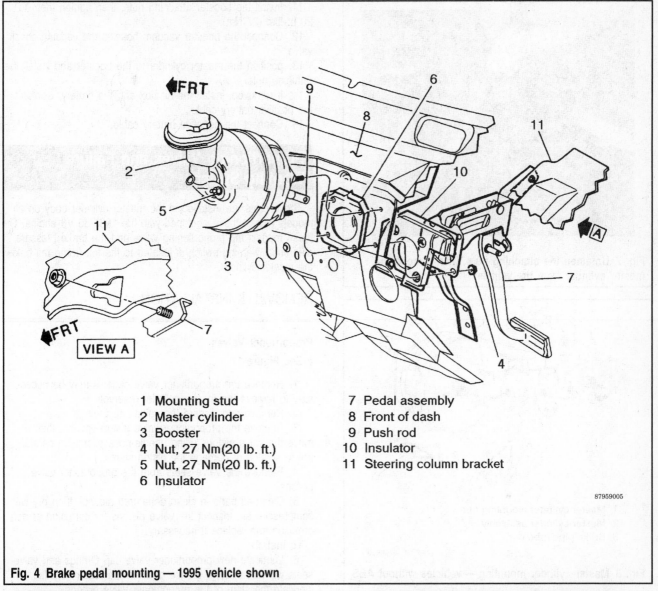

Fig. 4 Brake pedal mounting — 1995 vehicle shown

1 Mounting stud
2 Master cylinder
3 Booster
4 Nut, 27 Nm(20 lb. ft.)
5 Nut, 27 Nm(20 lb. ft.)
6 Insulator
7 Pedal assembly
8 Front of dash
9 Push rod
10 Insulator
11 Steering column bracket

87959005

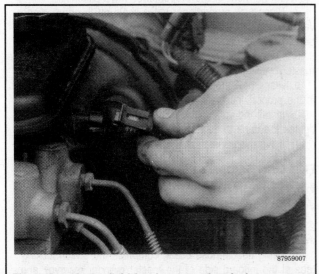

Fig. 5 Detach the fluid level sensor electrical connector

87959007

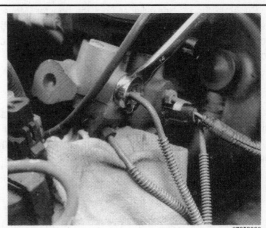

Fig. 6 Placing rags under the brake lines will catch any brake fluid that spills out when the lines are disconnected

87959008

Fig. 7 Unfasten the attaching nuts, then remove the master cylinder from the vehicle

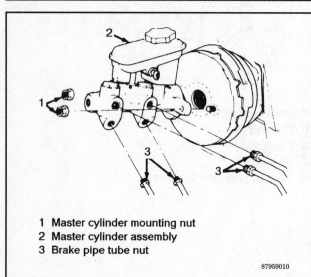

1 Master cylinder mounting nut
2 Master cylinder assembly
3 Brake pipe tube nut

87959010

Fig. 8 Master cylinder mounting — vehicles without ABS

4. Separate the master cylinder from the booster. Move the master cylinder forward just enough to clear the studs on the vacuum booster. This will flex the brake pipes slightly; be careful not to bend or distort the pipes.

5. Disconnect the vacuum hose from the vacuum check valve.

6. Unfasten the booster retaining nuts.

7. Disconnect the vacuum booster pushrod from the brake pedal inside the car. Tilt the entire vacuum booster slightly to work booster pushrod off the pedal clevis pin without putting undue side pressure on the pushrod.

8. Remove the booster from the vehicle.

To install:

9. Position the booster in the vehicle.

10. Connect the booster pushrod to the brake pedal. Tilt the entire booster slightly to work the booster pushrod onto the pedal clevis pin without putting undue pressure on the pushrod. Use your left hand to align the pushrod with the pedal and push together.

11. Install the booster attaching nuts, then tighten them to 20 ft. lbs. (27 Nm).

12. Connect the booster vacuum hose to the vacuum check valve.

13. position the master cylinder to the booster and install the retaining nuts.

14. If removed, install the air box and the battery. Connect the positive battery cable

15. Connect the negative battery cable.

Proportioning Valves and Failure Warning Switch

These parts are installed in the master cylinder body on all models except those equipped with the 1985-86 V6 engine. On these models the proportioning valve and the brake pressure differential warning switch is located to the left frame rail below the master cylinder.

REMOVAL & INSTALLATION

Proportioner Valves

▶ See Figure 11

1. Remove the proportioner valve caps. It may be necessary to remove the master cylinder reservoir.

2. Remove and discard the valve cap O-rings.

3. Remove the proportioner valve piston springs, then remove the valve pistons using needle-nose pliers. Be careful not to scratch or damage the piston stems.

4. Remove the valve seals from the proportioner valve pistons.

5. Clean all parts in clean denatured alcohol, then dry with compressed air. Inspect the valve pistons for corrosion or deformation and replace if necessary.

To install:

6. Lubricate new proportioner valve cap O-rings and valve seals with the silicone grease given in the repair kit. Also, lubricate the stem of the proportioner valve pistons.

7. Place new proportioner valve seals on the proportioner valve pistons with the seal lips facing upward toward the proportioner valve cap.

8. Position the proportioner valve pistons and seals into the master cylinder body.

9. Place new proportioner valve cap O-rings in the grooves in the proportioner valve caps.

10. Install the valve caps in the master cylinder body, then tighten the caps to 20 ft. lbs. (27 Nm).

11. If removed, install the master cylinder reservoir.

Fluid Level Switch

▶ See Figures 12 and 13

1. Disconnect the negative battery cable.

2. Detach the electrical connector from the fluid level switch.

3. Using needle-nose pliers, compress the switch locking tabs at the inboard side of the master cylinder reservoir and remove the switch.

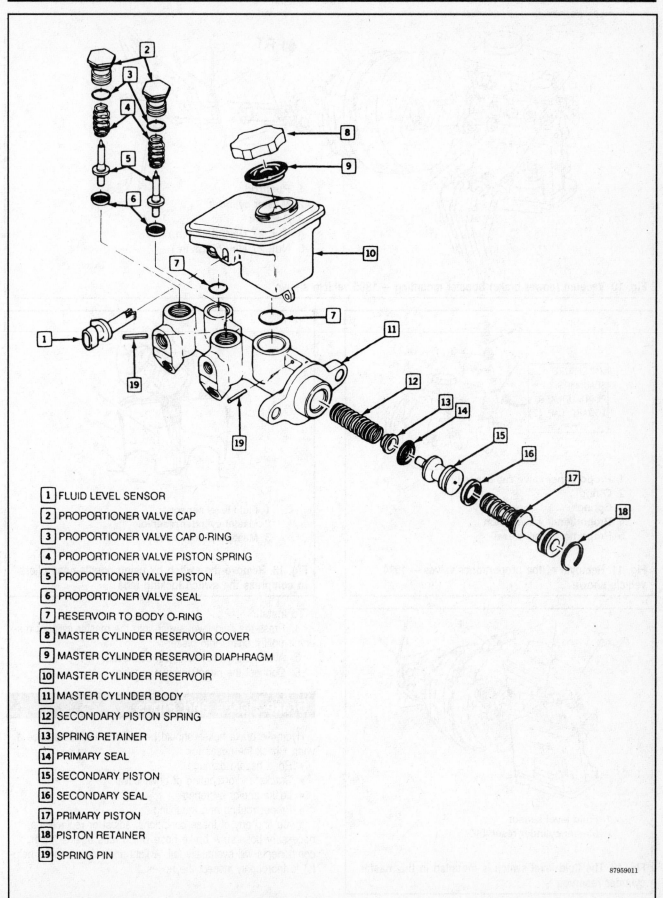

1 FLUID LEVEL SENSOR
2 PROPORTIONER VALVE CAP
3 PROPORTIONER VALVE CAP O-RING
4 PROPORTIONER VALVE PISTON SPRING
5 PROPORTIONER VALVE PISTON
6 PROPORTIONER VALVE SEAL
7 RESERVOIR TO BODY O-RING
8 MASTER CYLINDER RESERVOIR COVER
9 MASTER CYLINDER RESERVOIR DIAPHRAGM
10 MASTER CYLINDER RESERVOIR
11 MASTER CYLINDER BODY
12 SECONDARY PISTON SPRING
13 SPRING RETAINER
14 PRIMARY SEAL
15 SECONDARY PISTON
16 SECONDARY SEAL
17 PRIMARY PISTON
18 PISTON RETAINER
19 SPRING PIN

87959011

Fig. 9 Exploded view of a master cylinder assembly

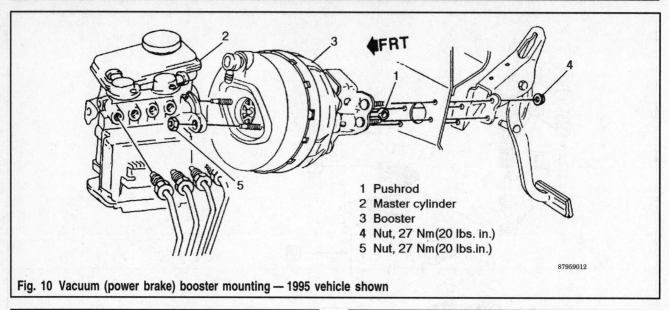

1 Pushrod
2 Master cylinder
3 Booster
4 Nut, 27 Nm(20 lbs. in.)
5 Nut, 27 Nm(20 lbs.in.)

87959012

Fig. 10 Vacuum (power brake) booster mounting — 1995 vehicle shown

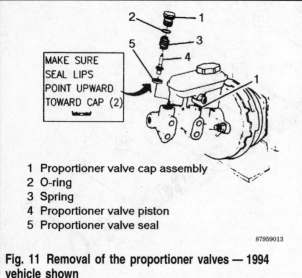

MAKE SURE
SEAL LIPS
POINT UPWARD
TOWARD CAP (2)

1 Proportioner valve cap assembly
2 O-ring
3 Spring
4 Proportioner valve piston
5 Proportioner valve seal

87959013

Fig. 11 Removal of the proportioner valves — 1994 vehicle shown

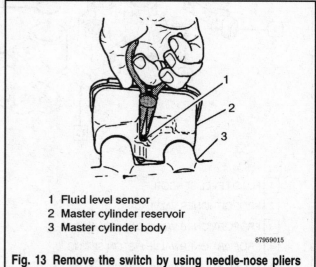

1 Fluid level sensor
2 Master cylinder reservoir
3 Master cylinder body

87959015

Fig. 13 Remove the switch by using needle-nose pliers to compress the switch locking tabs

To install:
4. Press the fluid level switch into the master cylinder reservoir until it snaps into place.
5. Attach the switch electrical connector.
6. Connect the negative battery cable.

Brake Hoses and Pipes

Hydraulic brake hoses should be inspected at least twice a year. Check the hoses for:
- Road hazard damage
- Cracks and/or chafing of outer cover
- Leaks and/or blistering
- Proper routing and mounting

If you find any of these conditions, adjust or replace the necessary hose(s). A brake hose which rubs against other components will eventually fail. A light and mirror can be helpful to thoroughly inspect the hoses.

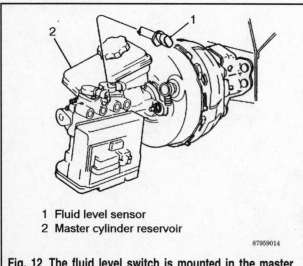

1 Fluid level sensor
2 Master cylinder reservoir

87959014

Fig. 12 The fluid level switch is mounted in the master cylinder reservoir

REMOVAL & INSTALLATION

1. If brake line fittings are corroded, apply a coating of penetrating oil and allow to stand before disconnecting the brake lines.
2. Use a brake line wrench to loosen the brake hose or pipe.
3. Remove the support brackets.
4. Note the location of the brake pipe before removal.
5. Remove the brake pipe or hose.

To install:

6. Install the new hose or pipe, observing the location of original installation.
7. Install the support brackets.
8. Ensure the pipes or hoses are clear of rotating parts and will not chafe on suspension parts.
9. Tighten the brake hose or pipe using a brake line wrench. Do not overtighten.
10. Properly bleed the brake hydraulic system.
11. Test drive the vehicle.

BRAKE PIPE FLARING

▶ **See Figures 14, 15 and 16**

When replacing the steel brake pipes, always use double walled steer piping which is designed to withstand high pressure and resist corrosion. Also, it is important to make sure that the pipe is of the same size to assure both a proper fit and proper brake operation.

✳✳CAUTION

Never use copper tubing. It is subject to fatigue, cracking and/or corrosion, which can result in brake line failure.

Whenever possible, try to work with brake lines that are already cut to the length needed. These lines are available at most auto parts stores and have machine made flares, the quality of which is hard to duplicate with most of the available inexpensive flaring kits.

When the brake are applied, there is a great deal of pressure developed in the hydraulic system. An improperly formed flare can leak with a resultant loss of stopping power. If you have never formed a double-flare, take time to familiarize yourself with the flaring kit; practice forming double-flares on scrap tubing until you are satisfied with the results.

Precautions:

- Always use double walled steel brake pipe.
- Carefully route and retain replacement pipes.
- Always use the correct fasteners and mount in the original location.
- Use only double lap flaring tools. The use of single lap flaring tools produces a flare which may not withstand system pressure.

Flaring Procedure

1. Obtain the recommended pipe and steel fitting nut of the correct size. Use the outside diameter of the pipe to specify size.
2. Cut the pipe to the appropriate length with a pipe cutter. Do not force the cutter. Correct length of pipe is determined by measuring the old pipe using a string and adding approximately ⅛ in. (3mm) for each flare.
3. Make sure the fittings are installed before starting the flare.
4. Chamfer the inside and outside diameter of the pipe with the de-burring tool.
5. Remove all traces of lubricant from the brake pipe and flaring tool.
6. Clamp the flaring tool body in a vise.
7. Select the correct size collet and forming mandrel for the pipe size used.
8. Insert the proper forming mandrel into the tool body. While holding the forming mandrel in place with your finger, thread in the forcing screw until it makes contact and begins to move the forming mandrel. When contact is made, turn the forcing screw back 1 complete turn.
9. Slide the clamping nut over the brake pipe and insert the prepared brake pipe into the correct collet. Leave approximately 0.750 in. (19mm) of tubing extending out of the collet. Insert the assembly into the tool body. The brake pipe end must contact the face of the forming mandrel.
10. Tighten the clamping nut into the tool body very tight or the pipe may push out.
11. Wrench tighten the forcing screw in until it bottoms. Do not overtighten the forcing screw or the flare may become oversized.
12. Back the clamping nut out of the tool body and disassemble the clamping the clamping nut and collet assembly. The flare is now ready for use.
13. Bend the pipe assembly to match the old pipe. Clearance of 0.750 in. (19mm) must be maintained to all moving or vibrating parts.

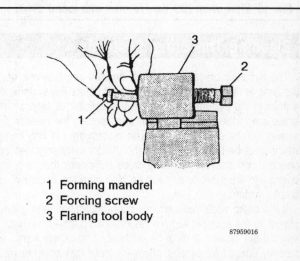

1 Forming mandrel
2 Forcing screw
3 Flaring tool body

87959016

Fig. 14 Insert and hold the forming mandrel in the flaring tool body

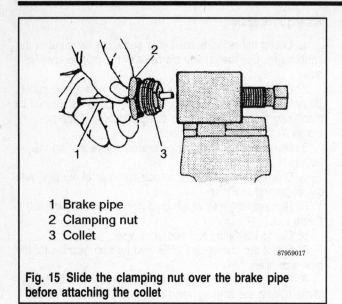

1 Brake pipe
2 Clamping nut
3 Collet

87959017

Fig. 15 Slide the clamping nut over the brake pipe before attaching the collet

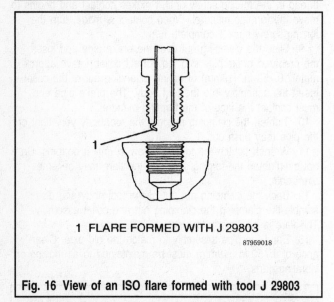

1 FLARE FORMED WITH J 29803

87959018

Fig. 16 View of an ISO flare formed with tool J 29803

Bleeding The Brake System

The hydraulic brake system must be bled any time one of the lines is disconnected or any time air enters the system. If a point in the system, such as a wheel cylinder or caliper brake line is the only point which was opened, the bleeder screws downstream in the hydraulic system are the only ones which must be bled. If however, the master cylinder fittings are opened, or if the reservoir level drops sufficiently that air is drawn into the system, air must be bled from the entire hydraulic system.

If the brake pedal feels spongy upon application, and goes almost to the floor but regains height when pumped, air has entered the system. It must be bled out. If no fittings were recently opened for service, check for leaks that would have allowed the entry of air and repair them before attempting to bleed the system.

As a general rule, once the master cylinder (and the brake pressure modulator valve or combination valve on ABS systems) is bled, the remainder of the hydraulic system should be bled starting at the furthest wheel from the master cylinder and working towards the nearest wheel. Therefore, the correct bleeding sequence for 1982-91 vehicles is:

master cylinder
modulator or combination valve (ABS vehicles only)
right rear wheel cylinder
left front caliper
left rear wheel cylinder
right front caliper

The correct bleeding sequence for 1992-96 vehicles is:
master cylinder
modulator or combination valve (ABS vehicles only)
right rear wheel cylinder
left rear wheel cylinder
right front caliper
left front caliper

Most master cylinder assemblies on these vehicles are NOT equipped with bleeder valves, therefore air must be bled from the cylinders using the front brake pipe connections.

✳✳CAUTION

If the vehicle has anti-lock braking, do not use this procedure without first reading the information on ABS system bleeding found later in this section. Improper service procedures on Anti-Lock Braking Systems (ABS) can cause serious personal injury. Refer to the ABS service procedures.

MANUAL BLEEDING

▶ See Figures 17 and 18

For those of us who are not fortunate enough to have access to a power bleeding tool, the manual brake bleeding procedure will quite adequately remove air from the hydraulic system. The major difference between the pressure and manual bleeding procedures is that the manual method takes more time and will require help from an assistant. One person must depress the brake pedal, while another opens and closes the bleeder screws.

➡**In addition to a length of clear neoprene bleeder hose, bleeder wrenches and a clear bleeder bottle (old plastic jar or drink bottle will suffice), bleeding late-model ABS systems may also require the use of one or more relatively inexpensive combination valve pressure bleeding tools (which are used to depress one or more valves in order to allow component/system bleeding). To fully bleed the late model ABS systems, a scan tool should also be used to run the system through functional tests.**

1. Deplete the vacuum reserve by applying the brakes several times with the ignition **OFF**.
2. Clean the top of the master cylinder, remove the cover and fill the reservoirs with clean fluid. To prevent squirting fluid, and possibly damaging painted surfaces, install the cover

during the procedure, but be sure to frequently check and top off the reservoirs with fresh fluid.

✳✳WARNING

Never reuse brake fluid which has been bled from the system because the old fluid may be contaminated with moisture and/or debris

3. The master cylinder must be bled first if it is suspected to contain air. If the master cylinder was removed and bench bled before installation it must still be bled, but it should take less time and effort. Bleed the master cylinder as follows:

    a. Position a container under the master cylinder to catch the brake fluid.

✳✳WARNING

Do not allow brake fluid to spill on or come in contact with the vehicle's finish as it will remove the paint. In case of a spill, immediately flush the area with water.

    b. Loosen the front brake line at the master cylinder and allow the fluid to flow from the front port.

    c. Have a friend depress the brake pedal slowly and hold (air and/or fluid should be expelled from the loose fitting). Tighten the line, then release the brake pedal and wait 15 seconds. Loosen the fitting and repeat until all air is removed from the master cylinder bore.

    d. When finished, tighten the line fitting to 20 ft. lbs. (27 Nm).

    e. Repeat the sequence at the master cylinder rear pipe fitting.

➡**During the bleeding procedure, make sure your assistant does NOT release the brake pedal while a fitting is loosened or while a bleeder screw is opened. Otherwise, air will be drawn back into the system.**

4. Check and refill the master cylinder reservoir.

➡**Remember, if the reservoir is allowed to empty of fluid during the procedure, air will be drawn into the system and the bleeding procedure must be restarted at the master cylinder assembly.**

5. On late model ABS equipped vehicles, perform the special ABS procedures as described later in this section. On 4 wheel ABS systems the Brake Pressure Modulator Valve (BPMV) must be bled (if it has been replaced or if it is suspected to contain air) and on most Rear Wheel Anti-Lock (RWAL) systems the combination valve must be held open. In both cases, special combination valve depressor tools should be used during bleeding and a scan tool must be used for ABS function tests.

6. If a single line or fitting was the only hydraulic line disconnected, then only the caliper(s) or wheel cylinder(s) affected by that line must be bled. If the master cylinder required bleeding, then all calipers and wheel cylinders must be bled in the proper sequence.

7. The proper sequence for 1982-91 vehicles is:
    a. Right rear

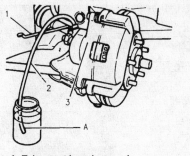

A Tube must be submerged
   in brake fluid
1 Bleeder wrench
2 Tube
3 Caliper

87959019

Fig. 17 Attach a clear plastic hose to the screw and submerge the other end in a transparent container of clean brake fluid

    b. Left front
    c. Left rear
    d. Right front

8. The proper sequence for 1992-96 vehicles is:
    a. Right rear
    b. Left rear
    c. Right front
    d. Left front

9. Bleed the individual calipers or wheel cylinders as follows:

    a. Place a suitable wrench over the bleeder screw and attach a clear plastic hose over the screw end. Be sure the hose is seated snugly on the screw or you may be squirted with brake fluid.

➡**Be very careful when bleeding wheel cylinders and brake calipers. The bleeder screws often rust in position and may easily break off if forced. Installing a new bleeder screw will often require removal of the component and may include overhaul or replacement of the wheel cylinder/caliper. To help prevent the possibility of breaking a bleeder screw, spray it with some penetrating oil before attempting to loosen it.**

    b. Submerge the other end of the tube in a transparent container of clean brake fluid.

    c. Loosen the bleed screw, then have a friend apply the brake pedal slowly and hold. Tighten the bleed screw to 62 inch lbs. (7 Nm), release the brake pedal and wait 15 seconds. Repeat the sequence (including the 15 second pause) until all air is expelled from the caliper or cylinder.

    d. Tighten the bleeder screw to 62 inch lbs. (7 Nm) when finished.

10. Check the pedal for a hard feeling with the engine not running. If the pedal is soft, repeat the bleeding procedure until a firm pedal is obtained.

11. If the brake warning light is on, depress the brake pedal firmly. If there is no air in the system, the light will go out.

12. After bleeding, make sure that a firm pedal is achieved before attempting to move the vehicle.

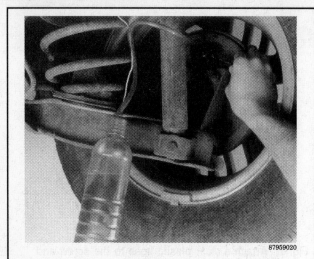

Fig. 18 It's often helpful to attach the bleeder bottle to the frame using an old coat hanger

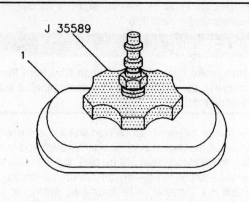

1 Master cylinder reservoir

Fig. 19 View of the pressure bleeder adapter cap installed on the master cylinder

PRESSURE BLEEDING

▶ See Figure 19

For the lucky ones with access to a pressure bleeding tool, this procedure may be used to quickly and efficiently remove air from the brake system. This procedure may be used as a guide, but be careful to follow the tool manufacturer's directions closely. Any pressure bleeding tool MUST be of the diaphragm-type. A proper pressure bleeder tool will utilize a rubber diaphragm between the air source and brake fluid in order to prevent air, moisture oil and other contaminants from entering the hydraulic system.

1. Install Pressure Bleeder Adapter Cap J 35589 or equivalent, to the master cylinder.
2. Charge Diaphragm Type Brake Bleeder J 29532 or equivalent, to 20-25 psi (140-172 kPa).
3. Connect the line to the pressure bleeder adapter cap, then open the line valve.
4. Raise and safely support the vehicle.
5. If it is necessary to bleed all of the calipers/cylinders, the following sequence should be used for 1982-91 vehicles:
   - Right rear
   - Left front
   - Left rear
   - Right front

6. The following sequence should be used for 1992-96 vehicles:
   - Right rear
   - Left rear
   - Right front
   - Left front
7. Place a proper size box end wrench (or tool J 21472) over the caliper/cylinder bleeder valve.
8. Attach a clear tube over the bleeder screw, then submerge the other end of the tube in a clear container partially filled with clean brake fluid.
9. Open the bleeder screw at least ¾ of a turn and allow flow to continue until no air is seen in the fluid.
10. Close the bleeder screw. Tighten the rear bleeder screws to 62 inch lbs. (7 Nm) and the front bleeder screws to 115 inch lbs. (13 Nm).
11. Repeat Steps 6-9 until all of the calipers and/or cylinders have been bled.
12. Carefully lower the vehicle.
13. Check the brake pedal for sponginess. If the condition is found, the entire bleeding procedure must be repeated.
14. Remove tools J 35589 and J 29532.
15. Refill the master cylinder to the proper level with brake fluid.
16. DO NOT attempt to move the vehicle unless a firm brake pedal is obtained.

FRONT DISC BRAKES

▶ See Figure 20

✳✳CAUTION

Brake pads may contain asbestos, which has been determined to be a cancer causing agent. Avoid inhaling any dust from any brake surface. Never clean the brake surfaces with compressed air! When cleaning brake surfaces, use a commercially available brake cleaning fluid.

Brake Pads

REMOVAL & INSTALLATION

▶ See Figures 21, 22, 23, 24, 25, 26 and 27

1. Using a clean turkey baster or equivalent, siphon ⅔ of the brake fluid from the master cylinder reservoir.
2. Loosen the wheel lug nuts, then raise and safely support the vehicle.

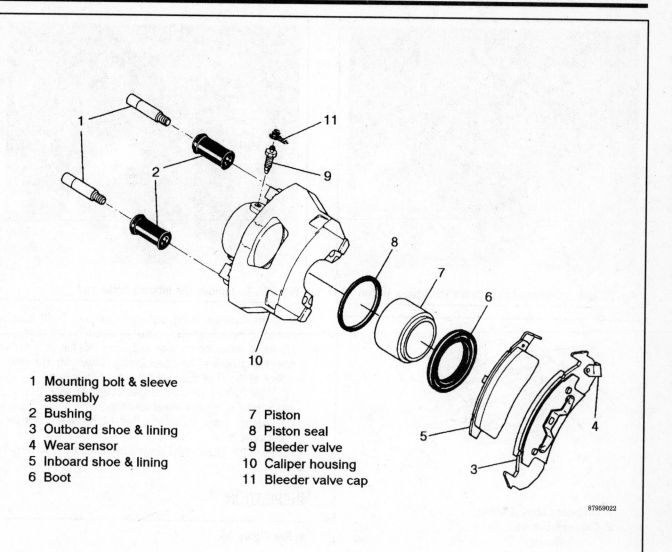

1 Mounting bolt & sleeve
    assembly
2 Bushing
3 Outboard shoe & lining
4 Wear sensor
5 Inboard shoe & lining
6 Boot
7 Piston
8 Piston seal
9 Bleeder valve
10 Caliper housing
11 Bleeder valve cap

87959022

Fig. 20 Exploded view of the front disc brake assembly components — 1996 vehicle shown

3. Remove the tire and wheel assembly.
4. Using a C-clamp, bottom the piston in its bore for clearance to remove it from the rotor.
5. Remove the caliper, as described later in this section.
6. Use a suitable prytool to disengage the buttons on the shoe from the holes in the caliper housing, then remove the outboard shoe and lining.
7. Remove the inboard shoe and lining.
8. Prior to installing new shoes and linings, wipe the outside surface of the boot clean with denatured alcohol.
To install:
9. Use a large C-clamp to compress the piston back into the caliper bore. Be careful not to damage the piston or boot with the C-clamp.
10. After bottoming the piston, lift the inner edge of the boot next to the piston and press out any trapped air. The boot must lie flat.
11. Install the inboard shoe and lining by snapping the shoe retaining spring into the piston inside diameter. The shoe retainer spring is already staked to the inboard shoe. After in-

87959023

Fig. 21 Front disc brake components after removing the wheel and tire assembly

Fig. 22 Use a C-clamp to compress the caliper piston

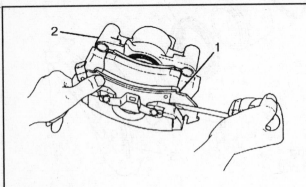

1 Outboard shoe & lining
2 Caliper housing

Fig. 23 Disengage the buttons on the shoe from the holes in the caliper housing to remove the outboard shoe and lining

Fig. 24 Remove the outboard brake pad from the caliper, then . . .

Fig. 25 . . . remove the inboard brake pad

stalling the shoe and lining, make sure the boot is not touching the shoe. If there is contact, reseat or reposition the boot.

12. Install the outboard shoe and lining with the wear sensor at the trailing edge of the shoe. During forward wheel rotation, the back of the shoe must lay flat against the caliper.

13. Install caliper, as outlined later in this section.

14. Install the tire and wheel assembly.

15. Carefully lower the vehicle, then fill the master cylinder to the proper level.

16. Push the brake pedal down firmly three times to seat the linings.

INSPECTION

▶ See Figure 28

➡ Always replace all pads on both front wheels at the same time. Failure to do so will result in uneven braking action and premature wear.

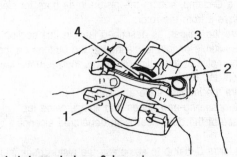

1 Inboard shoe & housing
2 Piston
3 Caliper housing
4 Shoe retainer spring

Fig. 26 Install the inboard shoe and lining, then . . .

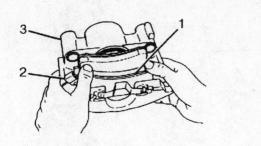

1 Outboard shoe & lining
2 Wear sensor
3 Caliper housing

87959029

Fig. 27 . . . install the outboard shoe and lining

1. Inspect the brake linings approximately every 6,000 miles (9,000 km) or whenever the wheels are removed.
2. Check both ends of the pad and the lining thickness on the inner shoe to make sure it is wearing evenly.

➡**Some inboard shoes have a thermal lining against the shoe, molded integrally with the lining. Do not confuse this lining with uneven inboard-outboard lining wear.**

3. Whenever the thickness of the lining is worn to the wear indicator, replace the pads on both sides.

Brake Caliper

▶ **See Figures 29, 30, 31, 32, 33, 34 and 35**

➡**Always replace the brake calipers on both front wheels at the same time. Failure to do so will result in uneven braking action and premature wear.**

REMOVAL & INSTALLATION

1. Using a clean turkey baster or equivalent, remove about ⅔ of the brake fluid from the master cylinder.
2. Loosen the wheel lug nuts, then raise and safely support the vehicle.
3. Remove the tire and wheel assembly.
4. Sometimes it is helpful to reinstall two of the lug nuts to hold the rotor to the hub and bearing assembly.
5. Push the piston into the caliper bore to provide clearance between the brake pads and the rotor as follows:
   a. Install a large C-clamp over the top of the caliper housing and against the back of the outboard shoe.
   b. Slowly tighten the clamp until the piston is pushed into the caliper bore enough slide the caliper off of the rotor.
6. If the caliper assembly is being removed from the vehicle for overhaul, unfasten the bolt attaching the inlet fitting, then plug the exposed fitting to prevent contamination. If just the pads are being replaced, there is no need to disconnect the inlet fitting.
7. Unfasten the caliper mounting bolt and sleeve assemblies. Some vehicles have a rubber cap over the retaining bolt which must be removed first.
8. Lift the caliper off of the rotor. If the caliper is not being removed for overhaul, suspend it from the strut with a wire hook.
9. Inspect the mounting bolts, sleeves and bushings for damage and replace as necessary.

To install:
10. Liberally coat the inside of the bushings with silicone grease.
11. Position the caliper over the rotor into the knuckle, then fasten the mounting bolt and sleeve assemblies. Tighten to 38 ft. lbs. (51 Nm).
12. If removed, connect the inlet fitting. Tighten to 32 ft. lbs. (44 Nm).
13. Remove the two nuts retaining the rotor to the hub, then install the wheel and tire assembly. Only hand-tighten the lug nuts at this time.

87959030

Fig. 28 Measuring the brake pad thickness to see if the pads need to be replaced

87959024

Fig. 29 Use a C-clamp to carefully bottom out the piston to provide clearance for removal

Fig. 30 If the caliper is being removed for overhaul, unfasten the bolt attaching the fluid line, then plug the line

Fig. 31 Some vehicles have a cap over the retaining bolt which must be removed to access the bolt

Fig. 32 Unfasten, then remove the caliper mounting bolts and sleeves

Fig. 33 Lift the caliper off of the rotor

Fig. 34 If the caliper is not being removed for overhaul, suspend it with a retaining strap or piece of wire from the strut

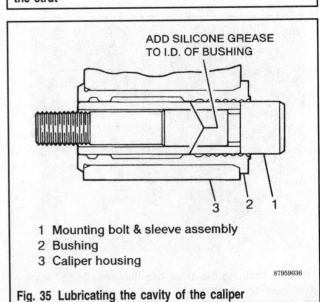

ADD SILICONE GREASE TO I.D. OF BUSHING

1 Mounting bolt & sleeve assembly
2 Bushing
3 Caliper housing

Fig. 35 Lubricating the cavity of the caliper

14. Carefully lower the vehicle, then tighten the lug nuts to 103 ft. lbs (140 Nm).

15. Fill the master cylinder to the proper level, and bleed the brakes if the inlet fitting was removed. Recheck the fluid level.

OVERHAUL

▶ See Figures 36, 37, 38 and 39

1. Remove the caliper from the vehicle. Place the caliper on a workbench.

2. Remove the bushings. Inspect for cuts and nicks. Replace as necessary.

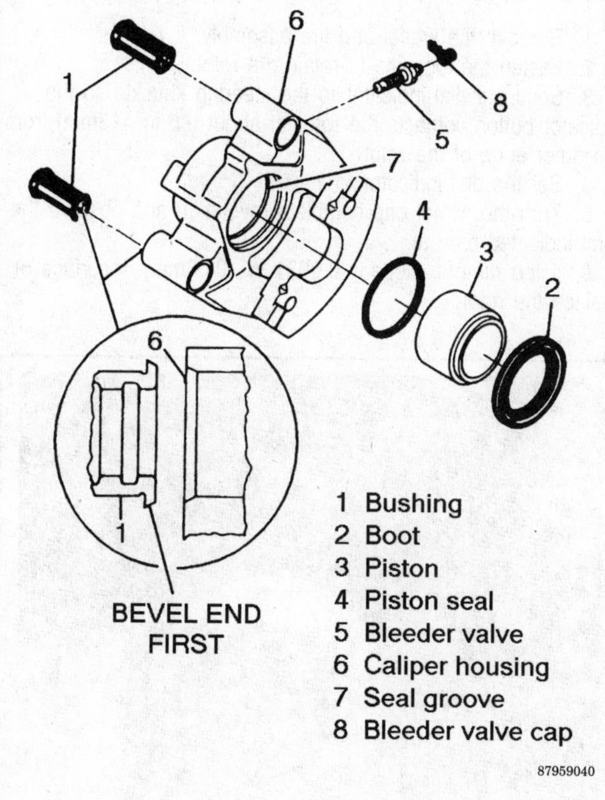

3. Stuff a shop towel or a block of wood into the caliper to catch the piston and apply compressed air to the inlet hole.

❊❊CAUTION

DO NOT apply too much air pressure to the bore, for the piston may jump out, causing damage to the piston and/or the operator. Be absolutely sure to keep your fingers away from the piston while air is being applied.

4. Remove and discard the piston boot and seal. Be careful not to scratch the bore. Use of a metal tool is NOT recommended when removing the boot and the seal because of the possibility of scoring and damaging the bore.

5. Inspect the piston for scoring, nicks, corrosion and worn chrome plating. Replace as necessary.

6. Remove the boot from the caliper housing bolt.

7. Remove the bleeder screw and its rubber cap.

8. Inspect the housing bore and seal groove for scoring, nicks, corrosion and wear. Crocus cloth can be used to polish out light corrosion.

BEVEL END
FIRST

1 Bushing
2 Boot
3 Piston
4 Piston seal
5 Bleeder valve
6 Caliper housing
7 Seal groove
8 Bleeder valve cap

87959040

Fig. 36 Exploded view of the caliper components removed for overhaul

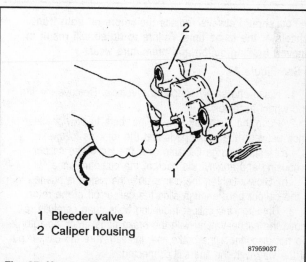

1 Bleeder valve
2 Caliper housing

87959037

Fig. 37 Use compressed air to drive the piston out of the caliper, but make sure to keep your fingers clear!

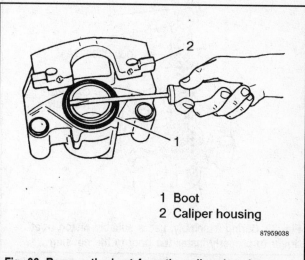

1 Boot
2 Caliper housing

87959038

Fig. 38 Remove the boot from the caliper housing, taking care not to score or damage the bore

9. Remove the bleeder valve and bleeder valve cap.

To install:

10. Install the bleeder valve and bleeder valve cap into the caliper.

11. Lubricate the piston, caliper and seal with clean brake fluid.

12. Install the piston seal into the caliper seal groove. Make sure it is not twisted in the caliper bore groove.

13. Bottom the piston into the bore, then secure the boot using J 29077 or an equivalent piston seal installer tool.

14. Lubricate the bevelled end of the bushings with silicone grease. Pinch the bushing and install the bevelled end first. Push the bushing through the housing mounting bore.

15. Install the caliper assembly, then properly bleed the hydraulic brake system.

Brake Disc (Rotor)

REMOVAL & INSTALLATION

➡**You should always replace the rotors on both front wheels at the same time. Failure to do so will result in uneven braking action and premature wear.**

▶ **See Figure 40**

1. Raise and safely support the vehicle. Remove the tire and wheel assembly.

2. Push the piston into the caliper bore to provide clearance between the brake pads and the rotor as follows:

   a. Install a large C-clamp over the top of the caliper housing and against the back of the outboard shoe.

   b. Slowly tighten the clamp until the piston is pushed into the caliper bore enough slide the caliper off of the rotor.

3. Unfasten the caliper mounting bolts, then carefully remove the caliper (along with the brake pads) from the rotor. Do not disconnect the brake line; instead, wire the caliper out of the way with the line still connected.

4. Remove the rotor by simply pulling it off of the hub and bearing assembly.

5. The installation is the reverse of the removal procedure.

INSPECTION

Check the disc brake rotor for scoring, cracks or other damage. Rotor run-out should be measured while the rotor is installed, while rotor thickness/thickness variation may be checked with the rotor installed or removed. Use a dial gauge to check rotor run-out. Check the rotor thickness to make sure it is greater than minimum thickness and check for thickness variations using a caliper micrometer.

Thickness Variation

1. Measure the thickness at four or more points on the rotor. Make all measure measurements at the same distance in from the edge of the rotor. Use a micrometer calibrated in ten-thousandths of an inch.

2. A rotor that varies in thickness by more than 0.0005 in. (0.013mm) can cause pedal pulsation and/or front end vibration during brake applications. A rotor that does not meet these specifications should be resurfaced to specifications or replaced.

Lateral Run-out

1. Remove the wheel and tire assembly.

2. Fasten the lug nuts to retain the rotor.

3. Secure a dial indicator to the steering knuckle so the indicator button contacts the rotor at about 0.5 in. (13mm) from the outer edge of the rotor.

4. Set the dial indicator to zero.

5. Turn the wheel one complete revolution and observe the total indicated run-out.

6. If the run-out exceeds 0.0031 in. (0.08mm), resurface or replace the rotor.

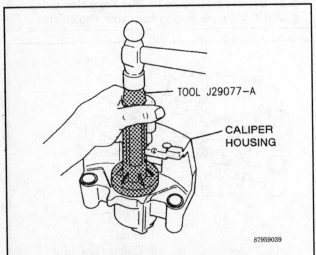

TOOL J29077–A

CALIPER HOUSING

87959039

Fig. 39 During assembly, use a suitable piston boot driver to properly install the boot to the housing

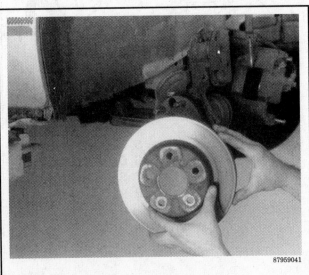

87959041

Fig. 40 Removing the rotor from the hub

REAR DRUM BRAKES

♦ See Figures 41 and 42

❋❋CAUTION

Brake shoes may contain asbestos, which has been determined to be a cancer causing agent. Never clean the brake surfaces with compressed air! Avoid inhaling any dust from any brake surface! When cleaning brake surfaces, use a commercially available brake cleaning fluid.

Brake Drums

REMOVAL & INSTALLATION

♦ See Figure 43

1. Raise and safely support the vehicle.

➡Matchmark the relationship of the wheel to the axle flange and the brake drum to the axle flange to insure proper wheel balance during installation.

2. Remove the wheel and tire assembly.
3. Remove the drum.
4. If the drum is difficult to remove, make sure the parking brake is released, then back off the parking brake cable adjustment. If necessary, use a rubber mallet to tap GENTLY around the inner drum diameter of the spindle. Be careful not to deform the drum by tapping too hard.
5. Inspect the drum for scoring, cracking or grooving. Replace if necessary.

To install:

6. Install the drum aligning the marks made during removal.
7. Using the marks previously made, install the tire and wheel assembly.
8. Carefully lower the vehicle, then tighten the lug nuts to 103 ft. lbs. (140 Nm).

INSPECTION

1. Inspect the brake drum for scoring, cracking or grooving. Light scoring of the drum not exceeding 0.020 in. (0.51mm) in depth will not affect brake operation.
2. Inspect the brake drum for excessive taper and out-of-round. When measuring a drum for out-of-round, taper and wear, take measurements at the open and closed edges of the machined surface and at right angles to each other.

Brake Shoes

❋❋CAUTION

Brake shoes may contain asbestos, which has been determined to be a cancer causing agent. Never clean the brake surfaces with compressed air! Avoid inhaling any dust from any brake surface! When cleaning brake surfaces, use a commercially available brake cleaning fluid.

INSPECTION

1. Remove the wheel and drum.
2. Inspect the shoes for proper thickness. The lining should be at least $1/32$ in. (0.8mm) above the rivet head for riveted brakes and $1/16$ in. (1.6mm) above the mounting surface for bonded brake linings.
3. Inspect the linings for even wear, cracking and scoring. Replace as necessary.

REMOVAL & INSTALLATION

♦ See Figures 44, 45, 46, 47, 48, 49, 50, 51, 52, 53 and 54

➡The brake shoes should be replaced in axle pairs. Failure to replace the component in pairs may cause unequal braking action and premature wear.

1. Raise and safely support the vehicle.
2. Remove the tire and wheel assemblies, then remove the brake drum.

➡If unsure of spring positioning, finish one side before starting the other and use the untouched side as a guide.

3. Using tool J 8049, J 29840 or equivalent brake spring remover and installer, unfasten the primary and secondary shoe return springs from the anchor pin, but leave them installed in the shoes.
4. Remove the hold-down springs, and pins using suitable pliers or brake tool.
5. While lifting up on the actuator lever, remove the actuator link.
6. Remove the actuator lever, lever return spring and the bearing sleeve.
7. Remove the parking brake strut and spring.
8. Remove the brake shoes, which are held together by the lower spring, after disconnecting the parking brake cable from the backing plate.
9. Disconnect the adjusting screw assembly and adjusting screw spring from the brake shoes.
10. Remove the retaining ring, pin and parking brake lever from the secondary brake shoe.
11. Lift the wheel cylinder dust boots and inspect for fluid leakage.
12. Thoroughly clean and dry the backing plate.

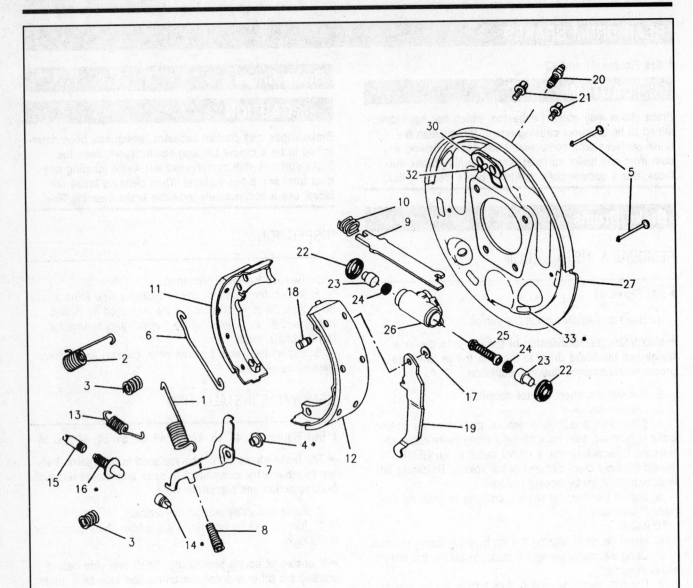

1	RETURN SPRING	11	PRIMARY SHOE AND LINING	21	BOLT
2	RETURN SPRING	12	SECONDARY SHOE AND LINING	22	BOOT
3	HOLD DOWN SPRING	13	ADJUSTING SCREW SPRING	23	PISTON
4	BEARING SLEEVE	14	SOCKET	24	SEAL
5	HOLD-DOWN PIN	15	PIVOT NUT	25	SPRING ASSEMBLY
6	ACTUATOR LINK	16	ADJUSTING SCREW	26	WHEEL CYLINDER
7	ACTUATOR LEVER	17	RETAINING RING	27	BACKING PLATE
8	LEVER RETURN SPRING	18	PIN	30	SHOE RETAINER
9	PARKING BRAKE STRUT	19	PARKING BRAKE LEVER	32	ANCHOR PIN
10	STRUT SPRING	20	BLEEDER VALVE	33	SHOE PADS (6 PLACES)

•LUBRICATE WITH THIN COATING
OF 1052196 LUBRICANT OR EQUIVALENT

87959042

Fig. 41 Exploded view of the rear drum brake system components (drum removed)

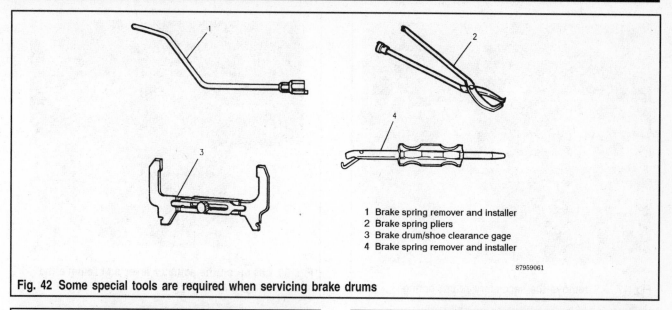

1 Brake spring remover and installer
2 Brake spring pliers
3 Brake drum/shoe clearance gage
4 Brake spring remover and installer

87959061

Fig. 42 Some special tools are required when servicing brake drums

Fig. 43 Remove the brake drum by simply pulling it off

Fig. 45 Use a suitable tool to remove the return springs

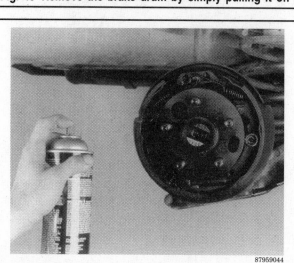

Fig. 44 Use a commercially available spray cleaner to remove brake dust from the components

Fig. 46 Unfasten the primary return spring, then . . .

Fig. 47 . . . remove the secondary return spring

Fig. 48 Use the brake tool to compress the hold-down spring and twist the plate to free the pin

Fig. 49 Once the pin and slot on top of the spring plate are aligned, separate the hold-down spring and pin

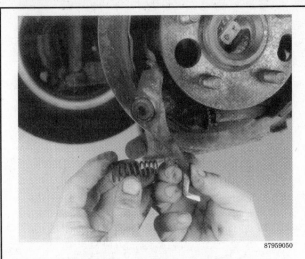

Fig. 50 Lift up on the actuator lever and remove the return spring, then . . .

Fig. 51 . . . remove the actuator link

Fig. 52 Remove the brake shoe assembly which is held together by the lower spring

To install:

13. Remove, clean and dry all parts still on the old shoes with denatured alcohol. Lubricate the star wheel shaft threads and transfer all the parts to the new shoes in their proper locations.

14. To prepare the backing plate, lubricate the bosses, anchor pin and parking brake actuating lever pivot surface lightly with brake lubricant GM part no. 1052916, or equivalent.

15. Install the parking brake lever on the secondary shoe with the pin and retaining ring.

16. Install the adjusting screw assembly and adjusting screw spring on the shoe and lining assembly.

17. Position the shoe and lining assemblies after attaching the parking brake cable.

18. Spread the shoes apart, install the parking brake strut and strut spring. The end without the strut spring should engage the parking brake lever and secondary shoe and lining. The end with the strut spring should engage the primary shoe and lining.

➡In the next step, the bearing sleeve must be installed between the secondary and lining and the actuator lever. Refer to the accompanying figure.

19. Install the bearing sleeve, actuator lever and lever return spring.

20. Install the hold-down pins and springs.

21. Fasten the actuator link on the anchor pin. While holding up the lever, fasten the actuator link into the lever.

22. Secure the shoe return springs, using tool J 8057 or equivalent pliers.

23. Adjust the brakes using the procedure located in this section.

24. Aligning the marks made during removal, install the brake drum.

25. Install the tire and wheel assembly.

26. Carefully lower the vehicle, then tighten the lug nuts to 103 ft. lbs. (140 Nm).

27. Adjust the parking brake, as outlined later in this section.

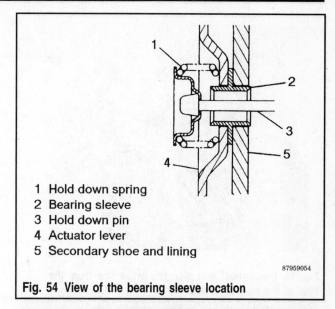

1 Hold down spring
2 Bearing sleeve
3 Hold down pin
4 Actuator lever
5 Secondary shoe and lining

Fig. 54 View of the bearing sleeve location

Wheel Cylinders

REMOVAL & INSTALLATION

▶ **See Figures 55, 56, 57, 58 and 59**

1. Raise and safely support the vehicle.
2. Remove the tire and wheel assembly.
3. Following the procedures located in this section, remove the brake drum and brake shoes (if necessary for access).
4. Unfasten the inlet brake fluid line, then cap the line to prevent contamination from entering.
5. If necessary for access to the cylinder, remove the hub and bearing assembly. On some vehicles, you must loosen the hub assembly bolts and slide the hub forward for additional clearance to remove the wheel cylinder.
6. Clean any dirt from around the wheel cylinder.

➡**On some vehicles, you will need a #6 Torx® driver to remove the wheel cylinder bolts.**

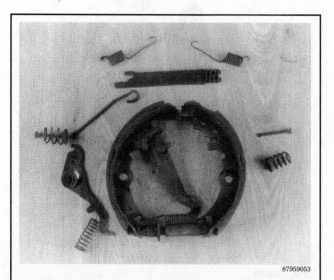

Fig. 53 Exploded view of the drum brake components

Fig. 55 Remove the brake drum, then remove the brake shoes if necessary for access to the wheel cylinder

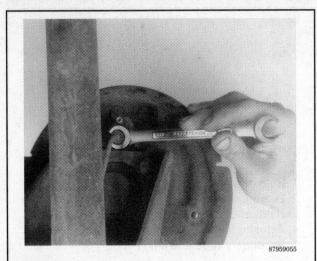

Fig. 56 Disconnect and plug the brake line from the rear of the backing plate

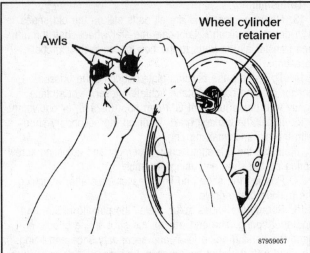

Fig. 57 Two awls may be used to bend the retainer stubs, releasing the wheel cylinder

7. To remove the round retainer type cylinders, insert two awls or pins into the access slots between the wheel cylinder pilot and the retainer locking tabs. Bend both tabs away simultaneously. The wheel cylinder can be removed, as the retainer is released.

8. To remove the bolted wheel cylinders, unfasten the wheel cylinder bolts, then remove the cylinder from the backing plate.

To install:

9. Apply a very thin coating of silicone sealer to the cylinder mounting surface.

10. For round retainer type wheel cylinders, position the cylinder and hold it in place with a wooden block between the cylinder and the axle flange. Carefully seat the new retainer clip, using a 1⅛ in. 12-point socket and socket extension (to help preserve your fingers). The socket is used to assure that the retainer seats evenly.

11. For bolt type wheel cylinders, position, install the cylinder to the backing plate and fasten the attaching bolts. Tighten to 15 ft. lbs. (20 Nm).

12. Uncap, then connect the brake line to the wheel cylinder. Tighten the inlet tube nut to 17 ft. lbs. (23 Nm).

13. If removed, install the hub and bearing assembly. Tighten to 43 ft. lbs. (58 Nm).

14. Install the brake shoes, if removed, and the brake drum.

15. Install the tire and wheel assembly.

16. Carefully lower the vehicle, then tighten the lug nuts to 103 ft. lbs. (140 Nm).

17. Properly bleed the hydraulic brake system.

Brake Backing Plate

REMOVAL & INSTALLATION

▶ See Figures 41 and 60

1. Raise and safely support the vehicle. Remove the rear wheel(s).

2. Remove the brake components, as described earlier in this section.

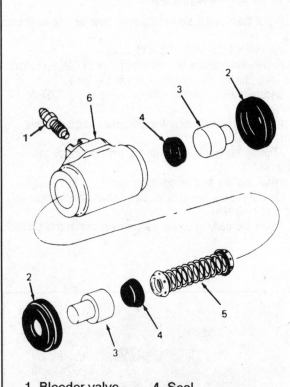

1	Bleeder valve	4	Seal
2	Boot	5	Spring assembly
3	Piston	6	Wheel cylinder body

Fig. 58 Exploded view of the wheel cylinder components

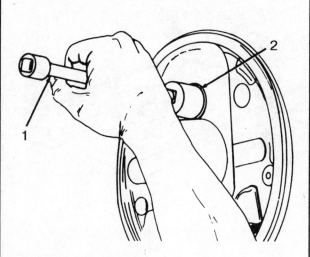

1 Socket extension
2 1-1/8 in., 12 pt. socket

87959059

Fig. 59 If equipped with a round retainer type wheel cylinder, use a socket extension to seat the retainer

3. Remove the wheel cylinder as outlined in this section.

4. Disconnect the parking brake cable from the backing plate.

5. If not removed already, unfasten the retaining bolts, then remove the hub and bearing assembly. For details, please refer to the procedure in Section 8 of this manual.

6. Remove the backing plate from the vehicle.

To install:

7. Install the backing plate to the axle assembly.

8. Position the wheel cylinder to the backing plate and secure with the retainers.

87959060

Fig. 60 Use a box end wrench to release the parking brake cable from the backing plate

9. Install the hub and bearing, then secure using the assembly bolts.

10. Connect the parking brake cable to the backing plate.

11. Uncap and attach the inlet tube and nut to the wheel cylinder. Tight to 17 ft. lbs. (23 Nm).

12. Install the brake system components. Check the brake adjustment.

13. Bleed the brake system.

14. Install the rear wheel(s).

15. Carefully lower the vehicle, then tighten the lug nuts to 103 ft. lbs. (140 Nm).

16. Adjust the parking brake.

PARKING BRAKE

Cables

▶ **See Figures 61, 62, 63 and 64**

REMOVAL & INSTALLATION

Front Cable

1982-94 VEHICLES

1. For vehicles through 1988, block the drive wheels and place the gear selector in **Neutral**.

2. Remove the center console as detailed in Section 10.

3. Disconnect the parking brake cable from the lever.

4. Remove the cable retaining nut and the bracket securing the front cable to the floor panel.

5. Raise the car and loosen the equalizer/adjustment nut.

6. Loosen the catalytic converter shield, then remove the parking brake cable from the body.

7. Disconnect the cable from the equalizer, then remove the cable from the guide and the underbody clips.

To install:

8. Position the cable to the equalizer, guide and underbody clips.

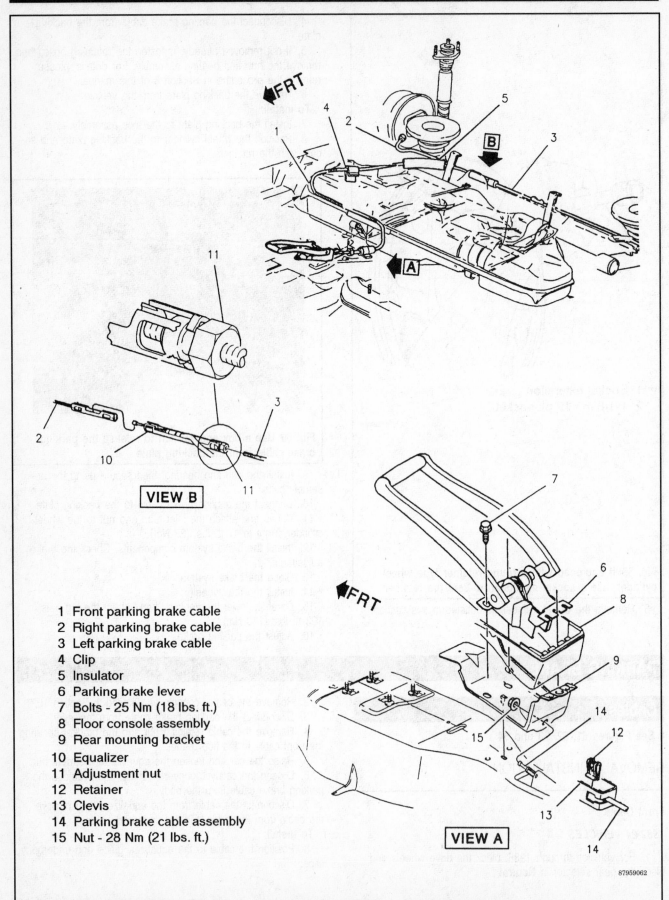

1 Front parking brake cable
2 Right parking brake cable
3 Left parking brake cable
4 Clip
5 Insulator
6 Parking brake lever
7 Bolts - 25 Nm (18 lbs. ft.)
8 Floor console assembly
9 Rear mounting bracket
10 Equalizer
11 Adjustment nut
12 Retainer
13 Clevis
14 Parking brake cable assembly
15 Nut - 28 Nm (21 lbs. ft.)

VIEW B

VIEW A

87959062

Fig. 61 Parking brake cable routing and lever removal and installation — 1993 Sunbird shown

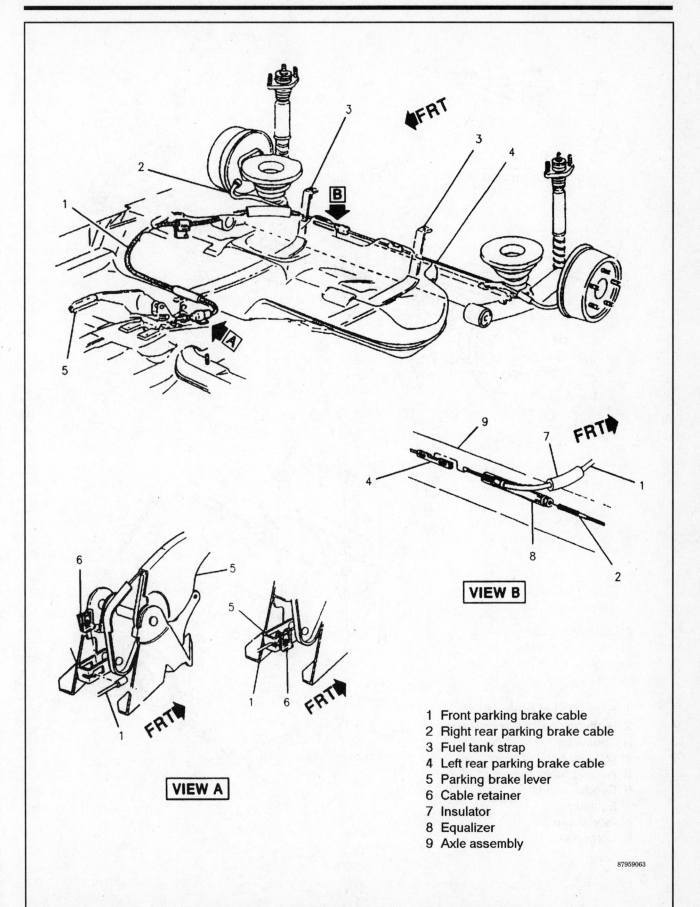

1 Front parking brake cable
2 Right rear parking brake cable
3 Fuel tank strap
4 Left rear parking brake cable
5 Parking brake lever
6 Cable retainer
7 Insulator
8 Equalizer
9 Axle assembly

VIEW A

VIEW B

87959063

Fig. 62 Parking brake cable routing and lever removal and installation — 1994 Cavalier shown

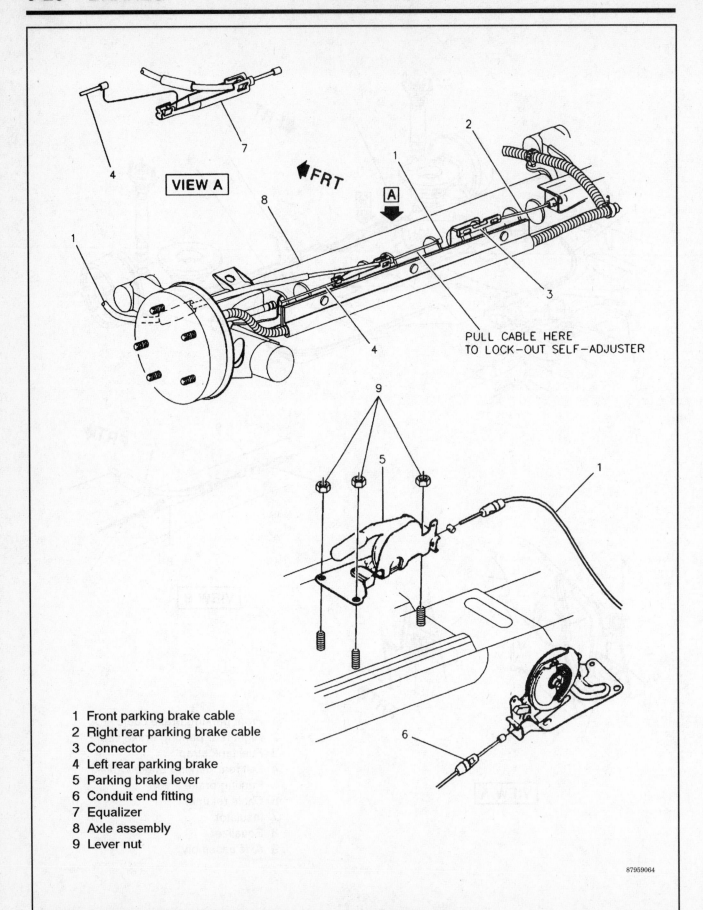

VIEW A

FRT

A

PULL CABLE HERE
TO LOCK-OUT SELF-ADJUSTER

1 Front parking brake cable
2 Right rear parking brake cable
3 Connector
4 Left rear parking brake
5 Parking brake lever
6 Conduit end fitting
7 Equalizer
8 Axle assembly
9 Lever nut

87959064

Fig. 63 View of the parking brake cables and lever mounting — 1995-96 vehicles

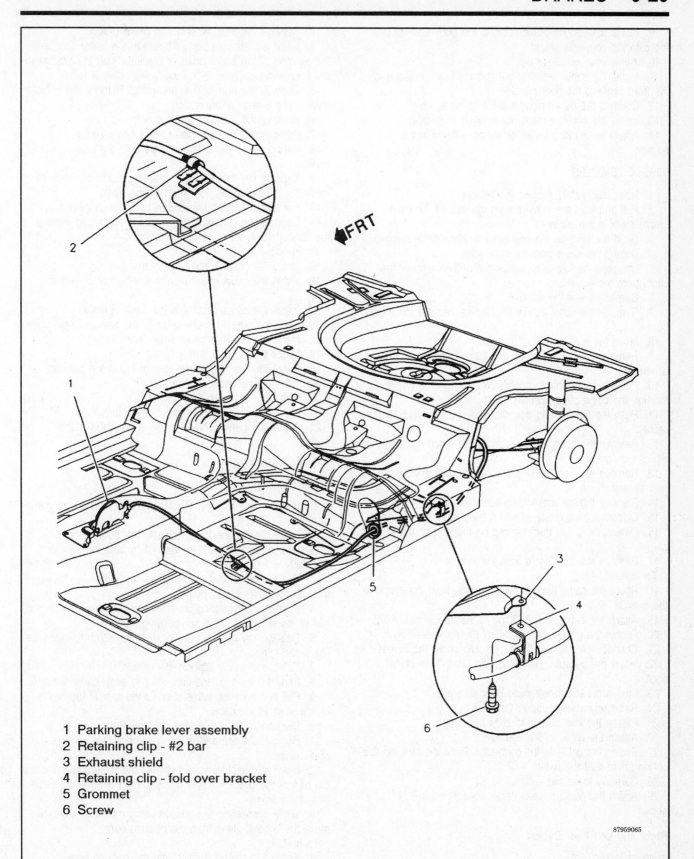

1 Parking brake lever assembly
2 Retaining clip - #2 bar
3 Exhaust shield
4 Retaining clip - fold over bracket
5 Grommet
6 Screw

87959065

Fig. 64 Parking brake cable routing — 1995-96 vehicles

9. Install the parking brake cable to the body and tighten the catalytic converter shield.

10. Tighten the equalizer nut.

11. Install the cable retaining nut and the bracket securing the front cable to the floor panel.

12. Connect the parking brake cable to the lever.

13. Install the center console as detailed in Section 6.

14. Adjust the parking brake cable, as outlined in this section.

1995-96 VEHICLES

1. Raise and safely support the vehicle.

2. Pull and hold the cable toward the rear of the car to create slack in the cable.

3. Bend the tang on the connector to allow cable removal.

4. Detach the cable from the connector.

5. Unfasten the fold over retaining clip, then remove the cable from the equalizer.

6. Carefully lower the vehicle.

7. Remove the console. For the Sunfire, remove the shifter boot.

8. Move the lever to the off position.

9. Remove the cable conduit end fitting from the handle assembly.

10. Pull the cable until the notch on the rachet is visible through the cover plate opening.

11. Push the pawl spring downward toward the notch in the rachet.

12. Release the cable slowly to allow the notch to catch the leg of the spring.

13. Remove the front parking brake cable button from the reel assembly.

14. Remove the left rocker panel/door sill plate.

15. Disconnect the grommet and retainer from the floor pan.

16. Detach the cable from the clip on the #2 bar, under the carpet.

17. Remove the front cable from the vehicle.

To install:

18. Route the cable through the floor pan, from the inside to the outside.

19. Attach the cable conduit fitting to the handle assembly.

20. Fasten the front cable bottom of the reel assembly.

21. Connect the cable to the #2 bar clip under the carpet.

22. Install the console. For the Sunfire, install the shifter boot.

23. Fasten the left rocker panel/door sill plate.

24. Raise and safely support the vehicle.

25. Fasten the fold over bracket to the body.

26. Attach the cable to the equalizer.

27. Fasten the cable to the connector. Bend the tang on the connector to hold the cable.

28. Carefully lower the vehicle.

29. Adjust the parking brake cable, as outlined in this section.

Right and Left Rear Cables

1982-94 VEHICLES

1. Raise and safely support the vehicle.

2. Back off the equalizer/adjustment nut (must be separated from the threaded rod if removing the right cable) until the cable tension is eliminated.

3. Remove the tires, wheels and brake drums.

4. Insert a a suitable prytool between the brake shoe and the top part of the brake adjuster bracket. Push the bracket to the front and then release the top brake adjuster rod.

5. Remove the rear hold-down spring. Remove the actuator lever and the lever return spring.

6. Remove the adjuster screw spring.

7. Remove the top rear brake shoe return spring.

8. Unhook the parking brake cable from the parking brake lever.

9. Depress the conduit fitting retaining tangs and then remove the conduit fitting from the backing plate.

10. Remove the cable end button from the connector.

11. Depress the conduit fitting retaining tangs and remove the conduit fitting from the axle bracket.

To install:

12. Install the conduit fitting to the axle bracket.

13. Install the cable end button to the connector (left side only).

14. Install the conduit fitting to the backing plate.

15. Hook the parking brake cable to the parking brake lever.

16. Install the top rear brake shoe return spring.

17. Install the adjuster screw spring.

18. Install the rear hold-down spring. Install the actuator lever and the lever return spring.

19. Install the top brake adjuster rod.

20. Install the tires, wheels and brake drums.

21. Adjust the parking brake cable, as outlined in this section.

1995-96 VEHICLES

▶ **See Figure 65**

1. Remove the console. For the Sunfire, remove the shifter boot also.

2. Move the parking brake lever to the off position.

3. Disconnect the cable conduit fitting from the handle assembly.

4. Pull the cable until the notch on the rachet is visible through the cover plate opening.

5. Push the pawl spring downward toward the notch in the rachet, as shown in the accompanying figure.

6. Release the cable slowly to allow the notch to catch the leg of the spring.

7. Raise and safely support the vehicle.

8. Bend the tang on the connector to allow cable removal.

9. Pull and hold the cable towards the rear of the car to create slack in the cable.

10. Disconnect the cable from the equalizer.

11. Remove the tire and wheel assembly, then remove the brake drum.

12. Insert a suitable prytool between the brake shoe and the top part of the brake adjuster bracket, then remove the cable from the bracket.

13. While depressing the conduit fitting retaining tangs, remove the conduit fitting from the backing plate.

To install:

14. Position the conduit fitting into the backing plate.

15. Fasten the parking brake cable to the parking brake lever in the drum assembly.

16. Install the brake drum, then install the tire and wheel assembly.

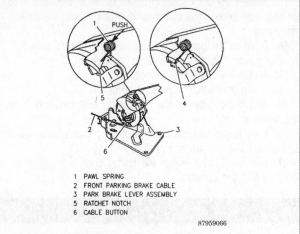

1 PAWL SPRING
2 FRONT PARKING BRAKE CABLE
3 PARK BRAKE LEVER ASSEMBLY
4 RATCHET NOTCH
5 RATCHET NOTCH
6 CABLE BUTTON

87959066

Fig. 65 Pull the cable until the notch on the rachet is visible through the cover plate opening, then push the pawl spring down toward the notch in the rachet

17. Fasten the conduit fitting retaining tangs, and position the conduit fitting into the axle bracket.
18. Attach the cable to the equalizer.
19. Fasten the cable to the connector, then carefully lower the vehicle.
20. For the Sunfire install the shifter boot.
21. Install the console.
22. Adjust the parking brake. Check the brake tension. It may be necessary to adjust the rear brake to obtain proper tension.

ADJUSTMENT

1982-94 Vehicles

▶ See Figure 66

1. Adjust the rear brakes, as outlined in this section.
2. Slowly pull the parking brake lever upward until 5 rachet clicks are heard.
3. Raise and safely support the vehicle.

➡**To prevent damage to the threaded parking brake adjusting rod when servicing the parking brake, clean and lubricate the exposed threaded on each side of the nut.**

4. Tighten the adjusting nut until the left rear wheel can just be turned backward using two hands, but is locked in forward rotation.
5. Release the parking brake.
6. Rotate the rear wheels, they should turn freely in either direction with no drag.
7. Carefully lower the vehicle.

1995-96 Vehicles

The parking brake on these vehicles are basically self-adjusting. Fully apply and release the hand parking brake lever 4-6 times to self-adjust.

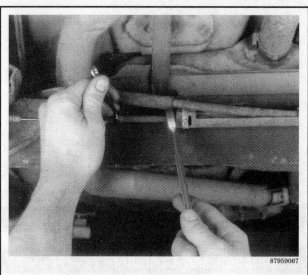

Fig. 66 Parking brake cable adjustment

Parking Brake Lever

REMOVAL & INSTALLATION

1982-94 Vehicles

1. For vehicles through 1988, block the drive wheels and place the gear selector in neutral.
2. Loosen the cable adjustment to allow the cable to be disconnected from the lever.
3. Remove the console, as outlined in Section 10 of this manual.
4. Disconnect the parking brake cable from the lever assembly.
5. If applicable, detach the electrical connector.
6. Unfasten the lever-to-floor pan retaining bolts, then remove the lever from the vehicle.
7. Installation is the reverse of the removal procedure.

1995-96 Vehicles

1. Raise and safely support the vehicle.
2. Pull and hold the cable towards the rear of the car to create slack in the cable.
3. Bend the tank on the connector to allow cable removal, then detach the cable from the connector.
4. Carefully lower the vehicle.
5. Remove the console. For the Sunfire, remove the shifter boot also.
6. Move the lever to the off position.
7. Remove the cable conduit end fitting from the handle assembly.
8. Pull the cable until the notch on the rachet is visible through the cover plate opening.
9. Push the pawl spring downward toward the notch in the rachet.
10. Release the cable slowly to allow the notch to catch the leg of the spring.
11. Remove the front parking brake cable button from the reel assembly.

12. Detach the electrical connector.

13. Unfasten the retaining nuts, then remove the parking brake lever from the vehicle.

To install:

14. Make sure the pawl spring is engaged, as follows:

    a. Pull the cable until the notch on the rachet is visible through the cover plate opening.

    b. Push the pawl spring downward toward the notch in the rachet.

    c. Release the cable slowly to allow the notch to catch the leg of the spring.

15. Fasten the front parking brake cable to the handle assembly and secure the cable conduit fittings into the lever assembly.

16. Position the parking brake lever and secure with the retaining nuts. Tighten the nuts to 18 ft. lbs. (25 Nm).

17. Attach the electrical connector.

18. Raise and safely support the vehicle.

19. Attach the cable to the connector, then carefully lower the vehicle.

20. Fully apply and release the parking brake lever 4-6 times to activate the self-adjust system.

21. For the Sunfire, install the shifter boot.

22. Install the console.

ANTI-LOCK BRAKE SYSTEM (ABS)

Description and Operation

The Anti-lock Braking System (ABS) was first introduced on J-body cars in 1992. ABS provides the driver with 3 important benefits over standard braking systems: increased vehicle stability, improved vehicle steerability, and potentially reduced stopping distances during braking. It should be noted that although the ABS-VI system offers definite advantages, the system cannot increase brake pressure above master cylinder pressure applied by the driver and cannot apply the brakes itself.

The ABS-VI Anti-lock Braking System consists of a conventional braking system with vacuum power booster, compact master cylinder, front disc brakes, rear drum brakes and interconnecting hydraulic brake lines augmented with the ABS components. The ABS-VI system includes a hydraulic modulator assembly, Electronic Control Unit (ECU), Electronic Brake Control Module (EBCM) or Electronic Brake and Traction Control Module (EBTCM) (these are all different "Computer Control Modules" which differ depending upon vehicle year and application), a system relay, 4 wheel speed sensors, interconnecting wiring and an amber ABS warning light.

The ECU/EBCM/EBTCM monitors inputs from the individual wheel speed sensors and determines when a wheel or wheels is/are about to lock up. The ECU/EBCM/EBTCM controls the motors on the hydraulic modulator assembly to reduce brake pressure to the wheel about to lock up. When the wheel regains traction, the brake pressure is increased until the wheel again approaches lock-up. The cycle repeats until either the vehicle comes to a stop, the brake pedal is released, or no wheels are about to lock up. The ECU/EBCM/EBTCM also has the ability to monitor itself and can store diagnostic codes in a non-volatile (will not be erased if the battery is disconnected) memory. The ECU/EBCM/EBTCM is serviced as an assembly.

The ABS-VI braking system employs 2 modes: base (conventional) braking and anti-lock braking. Under normal braking, the conventional part of the system stops the vehicle. When in the ABS mode, the Electromagnetic Brakes (EMB) action of the ABS system controls the two front wheels individually and the rear wheels together. If the one rear wheel is about to lock up, the hydraulic pressure to both wheels is reduced, controlling both wheels together.

BASIC KNOWLEDGE REQUIRED

Before using this section, it is important that you have a basic knowledge of the following items. Without this basic knowledge, it will be difficult to use the diagnostic procedures contained in this section.

Basic Electrical Circuits — You should understand the basic theory of electricity and know the meaning of voltage, current (amps) and resistance (ohms). You should understand what happens in a circuit with an open or shorted wire. You should be able to read and understand a wiring diagram.

Use Of Circuit Testing Tools — You should know how to use a test light and how to use jumper wires to bypass components to test circuits. You should be familiar with the High Impedance Multimeter (DVM) such as J 34029-A. You should be able to measure voltage, resistance and current and be familiar with the meter controls and how to use them correctly.

ONBOARD DIAGNOSTICS

The ABS-VI contains sophisticated onboard diagnostics that, when accessed with a bidirectional scan tool, are designed to identify the source of any system fault as specifically as possible, including whether or not the fault is intermittent. There are 58 diagnostic fault codes to assist the service technician with diagnosis.

The last diagnostic fault code to occur is identified, specific ABS data is stored at the time of this fault, and the first five codes set are stored. Additionally, using a bidirectional scan tool, each input and output can be monitored, thus enabling fault confirmation and repair verification. Manual control of components and automated functional tests are also available when using a GM approved "Scan" tool. Details of many of these functions are contained in the following sections.

ENHANCED DIAGNOSTICS

Enhanced Diagnostic Information, found in the CODE HISTORY function of the bidirectional scan tool, is designed to provide the service technician with specific fault occurrence information. For each of the first five (5) and the very last diagnostic fault codes stored, data is stored to identify the specific fault code number, the number of failure occurrences, and the number of drive cycles since the failure first and last occurred (a drive cycle occurs when the ignition is turned **ON** and the vehicle is driven faster than 10 mph). However, if a fault is present, the drive cycle counter will increment by turning the ignition **ON** and **OFF**. These first five (5) diagnostic fault codes are also stored in the order of occurrence. The order in which the first 5 faults occurred can be useful in determining if a previous fault is linked to the most recent faults, such as an intermittent wheel speed sensor which later becomes completely open.

During difficult diagnosis situations, this information can be used to identify fault occurrence trends. Does the fault occur more frequently now than it did during the last time when it only failed 1 out of 35 drive cycles? Did the fault only occur once over a large number of drive cycles, indication an unusual condition present when the fault occurred? Does the fault occur infrequently over a large number of drive cycles, indication special diagnosis techniques may be required to identify the source of the fault?

If a fault occurred 1 out of 20 drive cycles, the fault is intermittent and has not reoccurred for 19 drive cycles. This fault may be difficult or impossible to duplicate and may have been caused by a severe vehicle impact (large pot hole, speed bump at high speed, etc.) that momentarily opened an electrical connector or caused unusual vehicle suspension movement. Problem resolution is unlikely, and the problem may never reoccur (check diagnostic aids proved for that code). If the fault occurred 3 out of 15 drive cycles, the odds of finding the cause are still not good, but you know how often it occurs and you can determine whether or not the fault is becoming more frequent based on an additional or past occurrences visit if the source of the problem can not or could not be found. If the fault occurred 10 out of 20 drive cycles, the odds of finding the cause are very good, as the fault may be easily reproduced.

By using the additional fault data, you can also determine if a failure is randomly intermittent or if it has not reoccurred for long periods of time due to weather changes or a repair prior to this visit. Say a diagnostic fault code occurred 10 of 20 drive cycles but has not reoccurred for 10 drive cycles. This means the failure occurred 10 of 10 drive cycles but has not reoccurred since. A significant environmental change or a repair occurred 10 drive cycles ago. A repair may not be necessary if a recent repair can be confirmed. If no repair was made, the service can focus on diagnosis techniques used to locate difficult to recreate problems.

Diagnostic Procedures

▶ **See Figures 67, 68, 69, 70, 71, 72, 73, 74 and 75**

When servicing the ABS-VI, the following steps should be followed in order. Failure to follow these steps may result in the loss of important diagnostic data and may lead to difficult and time consuming diagnosis procedures.

1. Connect a bidirectional scan tool, as instructed by the tool manufacturer, then read all current and historical diagnostic codes. Be certain to note which codes are current diagnostic code failures. DO NOT CLEAR CODES unless directed to do so.

2. Using a bidirectional scan tool, read the CODE HISTORY data. Note the diagnostic fault codes stored and their frequency of failure. Specifically note the last failure that occurred and the conditions present when this failure occurred. This last failure should be the starting point for diagnosis and repair.

3. Perform a vehicle preliminary diagnosis inspection. This should include:

a. Inspection of the compact master cylinder for proper brake fluid level.

b. Inspection of the ABS hydraulic modulator for any leaks or wiring damage.

c. Inspection of brake components at all four (4) wheels. Verify no drag exists. Also verify proper brake apply operation.

d. Inspection for worn or damaged wheel bearings that allow a wheel to wobble.

e. Inspection of the wheel speed sensors and their wiring. Verify correct air gap range, solid sensor attachment, undamaged sensor toothed ring, and undamaged wiring, especially at vehicle attachment points.

f. Verify proper outer CV-joint alignment and operation.

g. Verify tires meet legal tread depth requirements.

4. If no codes are present, or mechanical component failure codes are present, perform the automated modulator test using the Tech 1® or T-100® to isolate the cause of the problem. If the failure is intermittent and not reproducible, test drive the vehicle while using the automatic snapshot feature of the bidirectional scan tool.

Perform normal acceleration, stopping, and turning maneuvers. If this does not reproduce the failure, perform an ABS stop, on a low coefficient surface such as gravel, from approximately 30-50 mph (48-80 km/h) while triggering any ABS code. If the failure is still not reproducible, use the enhanced diagnostic information found in CODE HISTORY to determine whether or not this failure should be further diagnosed.

5. Once all system failures have been corrected, clear the ABS codes. The Tech 1® and T-100®, when plugged into the ALDL connector, becomes part of the vehicle's electronic system. The Tech 1® and T-100® can also perform the following functions on components linked by the Serial Data Link (SDL):

- Display ABS data
- Display and clear ABS trouble codes
- Control ABS components
- Perform extensive ABS diagnosis
- Provide diagnostic testing for intermittent ABS conditions

Each test mode has specific diagnosis capabilities which depend upon various keystrokes. In general, five (5) keys control sequencing: "YES," "NO," "EXIT," "UP" arrow and "DOWN" arrow. The FO through F9 keys select operating modes, perform functions within an operating mode, or enter trouble code or model year designations.

In general, the Tech 1® has five (5) test modes for diagnosing the antilock brake system. The five (5) test modes are as follows:

MODE FO: DATA LIST — In this test mode, the Tech 1® continuously monitors wheel speed data, brake switch status and other inputs and outputs.

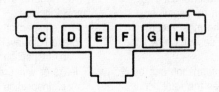

6 WAY EBCM HARNESS CONNECTOR

PIN	CIRCUIT NO.	COLOR	CIRCUIT
C	1284	DK GRN	REAR MOTOR HIGH
D	1285	ORN	REAR MOTOR LOW
E	1281	PNK	L/F MOTOR LOW
F	1280	BLK	L/F MOTOR HIGH
G	1283	BLK	R/F MOTOR LOW
H	1282	PPL	R/F MOTOR HIGH

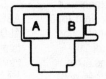

2 WAY EBCM HARNESS CONNECTOR

PIN	CIRCUIT NO.	COLOR	CIRCUIT
A	1633	RED	SWITCHED BATTERY INPUT
B	251	BLK/WHT	GROUND

87959068

Fig. 67 EBCM 6 and 2-way connectors — vehicles through 1995 with and without the Enhanced Traction System (ETS)

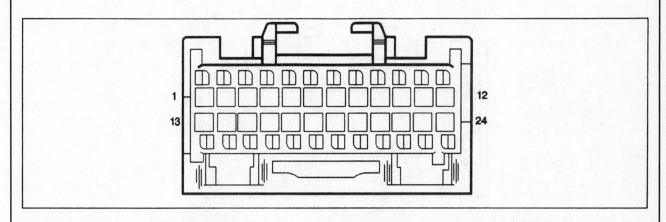

PIN	CIRCUIT NO.	COLOR	CIRCUIT
1	OPEN		NOT USED
2	800	TAN	SERIAL DATA LINK
3	OPEN		NOT USED
4	1289	LT BLU	R/F ABS SOLENOID
5	830	LT BLU	L/F WHEEL SIGNAL HIGH
6	873	YEL	L/F WHEEL SIGNAL LOW
7	882	BRN	R/R WHEEL SIGNAL HIGH
8	883	WHT	R/R WHEEL SIGNAL LOW
9	872	DK GRN	R/F WHEEL SIGNAL HIGH
10	833	TAN	R/F WHEEL SIGNAL LOW
11	885	RED	L/R WHEEL SIGNAL LOW
12	884	BLK	L/R WHEEL SIGNAL HIGH
13	17	WHT	BRAKE SWITCH INPUT
14	41	BRN	SWITCH IGNITION
15	1440	ORN	B+ FEED
16	OPEN		NOT USED
17	OPEN		NOT USED
18	OPEN		NOT USED
19	1286	LT GRN	L/F EMB
20	1287	GRY	R/F EMB
21	849	PNK	BRAKE FLUID LEVEL SWITCH INPUT
22	1632	PNK	ENABLE RELAY CONTROL
23	OPEN		NOT USED
24	1288	DK GRN	L/F ABS SOLENOID

87959069

Fig. 68 EBCM 24-way electrical connector — vehicles through 1995 without the Enhanced Traction System (ETS)

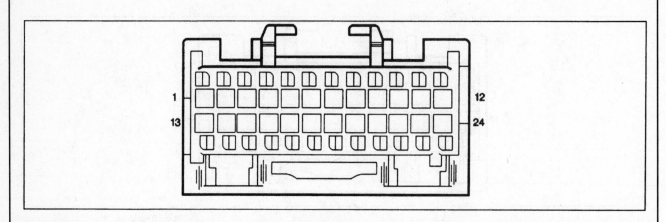

PIN	CIRCUIT NO.	COLOR	CIRCUIT
1	800	TAN	SERIAL DATA
2	1289	LT BLU	R/F ABS SOLENOID CONTROL
3	830	LT BLU	L/F WHEEL SIGNAL HIGH
4	873	YEL	L/F WHEEL SIGNAL LOW
5	882	BRN	R/R WHEEL SIGNAL HIGH
6	883	WHT	R/R WHEEL SIGNAL LOW
7	872	DK GRN	R/F WHEEL SIGNAL HIGH
8	833	TAN	R/F WHEEL SIGNAL LOW
9	884	BLK	L/R WHEEL SIGNAL HIGH
10	885	RED	L/R WHEEL SIGNAL LOW
11	OPEN		NOT USED
12	OPEN		NOT USED
13	17	WHT	BRAKE SWITCH INPUT
14	41	BRN	SWITCHED IGNITION
15	1440	ORN	BATTERY FEED
16	OPEN		NOT USED
17	1286	LT GRN	L/F EMB CONTROL
18	1287	GRY	R/F EMB CONTROL
19	849	PNK	BRAKE FLUID LEVEL SWITCH INPUT
20	1632	PNK	ENABLE RELAY CONTROL
21	OPEN		NOT USED
22	1288	DK GRN	L/F ABS SOLENOID CONTROL
23	OPEN		NOT USED
24	OPEN		NOT USED

87959070

Fig. 69 EBTCM 24-way electrical connector — vehicles through 1995 with the Enhanced Traction System (ETS)

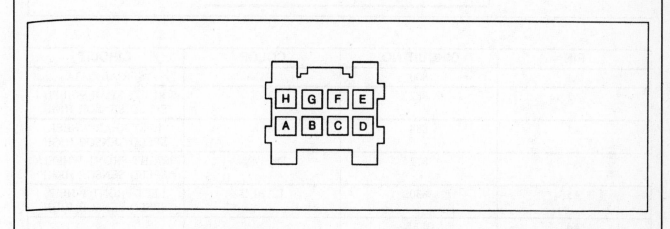

PIN	CIRCUIT NO.	COLOR	CIRCUIT
A	1282	PPL	RIGHT FRONT MOTOR HIGH .
B	1283	BLK	RIGHT FRONT MOTOR LOW
C	1633	RED	SWITCHED BATTERY INPUT
D	251	BLK	GROUND
E	1285	ORN	REAR MOTOR LOW
F	1284	DK GRN	REAR MOTOR HIGH
G	1280	BLK	LEFT FRONT MOTOR HIGH
H	1281	PNK	LEFT FRONT MOTOR LOW

87959071

Fig. 70 EBCM/EBTCM 8-way electrical connector — 1996 vehicles

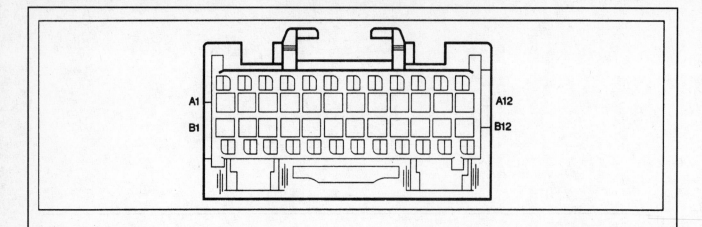

PIN	CIRCUIT NO.	COLOR	CIRCUIT
A1	800	TAN	SERIAL DATA
A2	882	BRN	RIGHT REAR WHEEL SPEED SENSOR HIGH
A3	884	BLK	LEFT REAR WHEEL SPEED SENSOR HIGH
A4	872	DK GRN	RIGHT FRONT WHEEL SPEED SENSOR HIGH
A5	830	LT BLU	LEFT FRONT WHEEL SPEED SENSOR HIGH
A6	OPEN		
A7	OPEN		
A8	OPEN		
A9	439	PNK	SWITCHED IGNITION
A10	1288	DK GRN	LEFT FRONT SOLENOID CONTROL
A11	1632	PNK	ABS RELAY CONTROL
A12	OPEN		
B1	883	WHT	RIGHT REAR WHEEL SPEED SENSOR LOW
B2	885	RED	LEFT REAR WHEEL SPEED SENSOR LOW
B3	833	TAN	RIGHT FRONT WHEEL SPEED SENSOR LOW
B4	873	YEL	LEFT FRONT WHEEL SPEED SENSOR LOW
B5	849	PNK	BRAKE FLUID LEVEL SWITCH INPUT
B6	1289	LT BLU	RIGHT FRONT SOLENOID CONTROL
B7	OPEN		
B8	OPEN		
B9	17	WHT	BRAKE SWITCH INPUT
B10	OPEN		
B11	OPEN		
B12	1440	ORN	BATTERY FEED

87959072

Fig. 71 EBCM/EBTCM 24-way electrical connector — 1996 vehicles

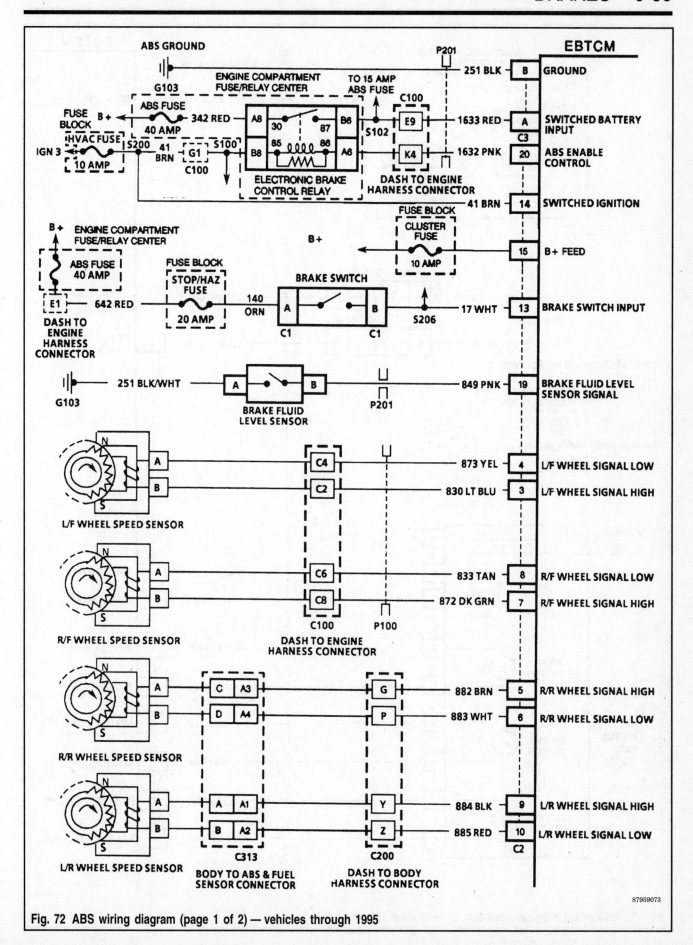

Fig. 72 ABS wiring diagram (page 1 of 2) — vehicles through 1995

87959073

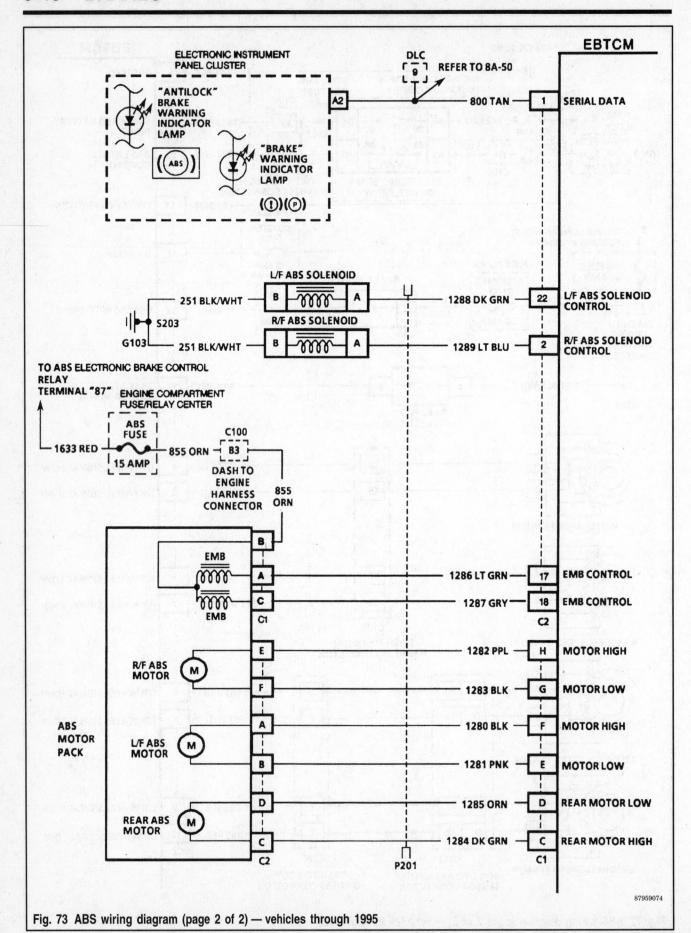

Fig. 73 ABS wiring diagram (page 2 of 2) — vehicles through 1995

87959074

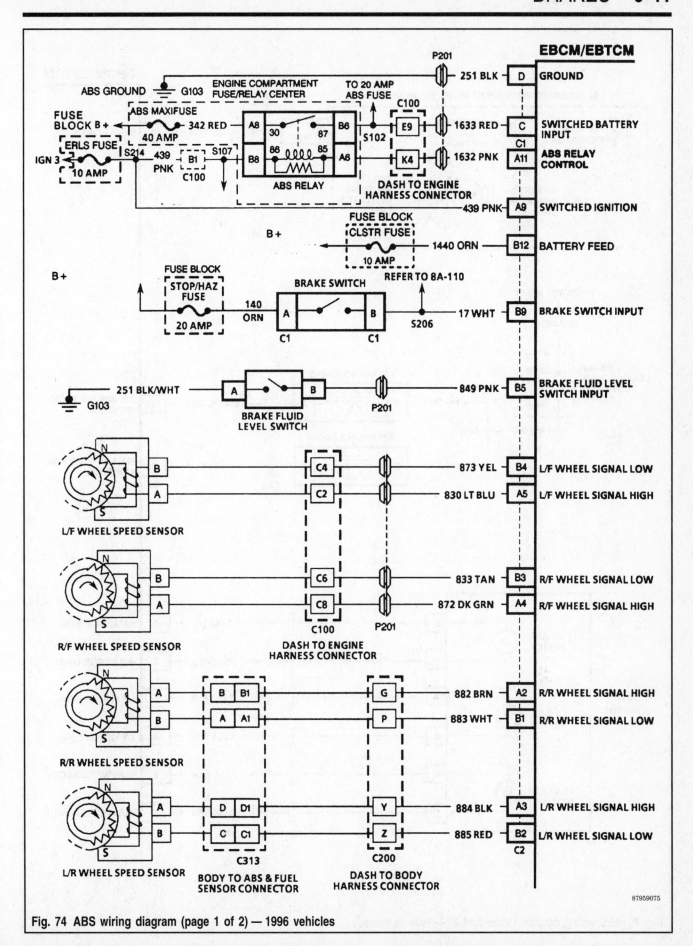

Fig. 74 ABS wiring diagram (page 1 of 2) — 1996 vehicles

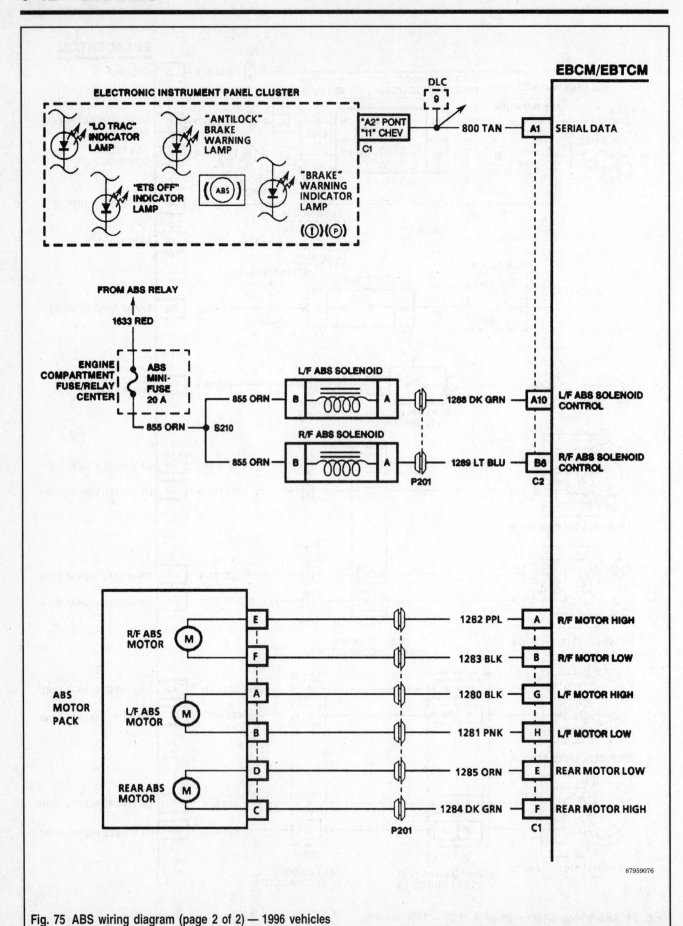

Fig. 75 ABS wiring diagram (page 2 of 2) — 1996 vehicles

MODE F1: CODE HISTORY — In this mode, fault code history data is displayed. This data includes how many ignition cycles since the fault code occurred, along with other ABS information. The first five (5) and last fault codes set are included in the ABS history data.

MODE F2: TROUBLE CODES — In this test mode, trouble codes stored by the EBCM, both current ignition cycle and history, may be displayed or cleared.

MODE F3: ABS SNAPSHOT — In this test mode, the Tech 1® captures ABS data before and after a fault occurrence or a forced manual trigger.

MODE F4: ABS TESTS — In this test mode, the Tech 1® performs hydraulic modulator functional tests to assist in problem isolation during troubleshooting. Included here is manual control of the motors which is used prior to bleeding the brake system.

Press F7 to covert from English to metric.

DISPLAYING CODES

▶ **See Figures 76, 77, 78, 79, 80 and 81**

Diagnostic fault codes can only be read through the use of a bidirectional scan tool. There are no provisions for "Flash Code" diagnostics.

CLEARING CODES

The trouble codes in EBCM memory are erased in one of two ways:
1. Tech 1® "Clear Codes" selection.
2. Ignition cycle default.

These two methods are detailed below. Be sure to verify proper system operation and absence of codes when clearing procedure is completed.The EBCM will not permit code clearing until all of the codes have been displayed. Also, codes cannot be cleared by unplugging the EBCM, disconnecting the battery cables, or turning the ignition **OFF** (except on an ignition cycle default).

Tech 1® "Clear Codes" Method

Select F2 for trouble codes. After codes have been viewed completely, Tech 1® will ask, "CLEAR ABS CODES"; ANSWER "YES." Tech 1® will then read, "DISPLAY CODE HIST. DATA?" "LOST" if the codes have been cleared or "NO" to clear the codes. Answer "NO" and codes will be cleared.

Ignition Cycle Default

If no diagnostic fault code occurs for 100 drive cycles (a drive cycle occurs when the ignition is turned **ON** and the vehicle is driven faster than 10 mph or 16 km/h), any existing fault codes are cleared from the EBCM memory.

INTERMITTENT FAILURES

As with most electronic systems, intermittent failures may be difficult to accurately diagnose. The following is a method to try to isolate an intermittent failure especially wheel speed circuitry failures.

If an ABS fault occurs, the ABS warning light indicator will be on during the ignition cycle in which the fault was detected. If it is an intermittent problem which seems to have corrected itself (ABS warning light off), a history trouble code will be stored. Also stored will be the history data of the code at the time the fault occurred. The Tech 1® must be used to read ABS history data.

INTERMITTENTS AND POOR CONNECTIONS

Most intermittents are caused by faulty electrical connections or wiring, although occasionally a sticking relay or solenoid can be a problem. Some items to check are:

1. Poor mating of connector halves, or terminals not fully seated in the connector body (backed out).
2. Dirt or corrosion on the terminals. The terminals must be clean and free of any foreign material which could impede proper terminal contact.
3. Damaged connector body, exposing the terminals to moisture and dirt, as well as not maintaining proper terminal orientation with the component or mating connector.
4. Improperly formed or damaged terminals. All connector terminals in problem circuits should be checked carefully to ensure good contact tension. Use a corresponding mating terminal to check for proper tension. Refer to "Checking Terminal Contact" later in this section for the specific procedure.
5. The J 35616-A Connector Test Adapter Kit must be used whenever a diagnostic procedure requests checking or probing a terminal. Using the adapter will ensure that no damage to the terminal will occur, as well as giving an idea of whether contact tension is sufficient. If contact tension seems incorrect, refer to "Checking Terminal Contact" later in this section for specifics.
6. Poor terminal-to-wire connection. Checking this requires removing the terminal from the connector body. Some conditions which fall under this description are poor crimps, poor solder joints, crimping over wire insulation rather than the wire itself, corrosion in the wire-to-terminal contact area, etc.
7. Wire insulation which is rubbed through, causing an intermittent short as the bare area touches other wiring or parts of the vehicle.
8. Wiring broken inside the insulation. This condition could cause a continuity check to show a good circuit, but if only 1 or 2 strands of a multi-strand type wire are intact, resistance could be far too high.

Checking Terminal Contact

When diagnosing an electrical system that uses Metri-Pack 150/280/480/630 series terminals (refer to Terminal Repair Kit J 38125-A for terminal identification), it is important to check terminal contact between a connector and component, or between inline connectors, before replacing a suspect component.

Frequently, a diagnostic chart leads to a step that reads "Check for poor connection." Mating terminals must be inspected to ensure good terminal contact. A poor connection between the male and female terminal at a connector may be the result of contamination or deformation.

DTC	DESCRIPTION
14	Electronic Brake Control Relay Contacts Circuit Open
15	Electronic Brake Control Relay Contacts Circuit Shorted to Battery
16	Electronic Brake Control Relay Coil Circuit Open
17	Electronic Brake Control Relay Coil Circuit Shorted to Ground
18	Electronic Brake Control Relay Coil Circuit Shorted to Battery or Coil Shorted
21	Left Front Wheel Speed = 0 or Unreasonable
22	Right Front Wheel Speed = 0 or Unreasonable
23	Left Rear Wheel Speed = 0 or Unreasonable
24	Right Rear Wheel Speed = 0 or Unreasonable
25	Left Front Excessive Wheel Speed Variation
26	Right Front Excessive Wheel Speed Variation
27	Left Rear Excessive Wheel Speed Variation
28	Right Rear Excessive Wheel Speed Variation
36	Low System Voltage
37	High System Voltage
38	Left Front EMB Will Not Hold Motor
41	Right Front EMB Will Not Hold Motor
42	Rear ESB Will Not Hold Motor
44	Left Front Channel Will Not Move
45	Right Front Channel Will Not Move
46	Rear Axle Channel Will Not Move
47	Left Front Motor Free Spins
48	Right Front Motor Free Spins
51	Rear Motor Free Spins
52	Left Front Channel in Release Too Long
53	Right Front Channel in Release Too Long
54	Rear Channel in Release Too Long
55	EBCM Malfunction
56	Left Front Motor Circuit Open
57	Left Front Motor Circuit Shorted to Ground
58	Left Front Motor Circuit Shorted to Battery or Motor Shorted
61	Right Front Motor Circuit Open
62	Right Front Motor Circuit Shorted to Ground
63	Right Front Motor Circuit Shorted to Battery or Motor Shorted
64	Rear Motor Circuit Open
65	Rear Motor Circuit Shorted to Ground
66	Rear Motor Circuit Shorted to Battery or Motor Shorted
67	Left Front EMB Circuit Open or Shorted to Ground
68	Left Front EMB Circuit Shorted to Battery or Driver Open
71	Right Front EMB Circuit Open or Shorted to Ground

87959077

Fig. 76 List of ABS Diagnostic Trouble Codes (DTCs) — vehicles through 1995 without ETS

DIAGNOSTIC TROUBLE CODE AND SYMPTOM TABLE	
72	Right Front EMB Circuit Shorted to Battery or Driver Open
75	Serial Communication Malfunction
76	Left Front Solenoid Circuit Open or Shorted to Battery
77	Left Front Solenoid Circuit Shorted to Ground or Driver Open
78	Right Front Solenoid Circuit Open or Shorted to Battery
81	Right Front Solenoid Circuit Shorted to Ground or Driver Open
82	Calibration Malfunction
86	EBCM Turned "ON" the Red Brake Warning Lamp
91	Open Brake Switch During Deceleration
92	Open Brake Switch When ABS Was Required
93	DTCs 91 or 92 Set in Current or Previous Ignition Cycle
94	Brake Switch Contacts Always Closed
95	Brake Switch Circuit Open
96	Rear Brake Lamp Circuit Open

87959078

Fig. 77 List of ABS Diagnostic Trouble Codes (DTCs) — vehicles through 1995 without ETS, continued

DIAGNOSTIC TROUBLE CODE	DESCRIPTION
14	Electronic Brake Control Relay Contacts Circuit Open
15	Electronic Brake Control Relay Contacts Circuit Shorted to Battery
16	Electronic Brake Control Relay Coil Circuit Open
17	Electronic Brake Control Relay Coil Circuit Shorted to Ground
18	Electronic Brake Control Relay Coil Circuit Shorted to Battery or Coil Shorted
21	Left Front Wheel Speed = 0
22	Right Front Wheel Speed = 0
23	Left Rear Wheel Speed = 0
24	Right Rear Wheel Speed = 0
25	Left Front Excessive Wheel Speed Variation
26	Right Front Excessive Wheel Speed Variation
27	Left Rear Excessive Wheel Speed Variation
28	Right Rear Excessive Wheel Speed Variation
32	Left Front Wheel Speed Sensor Circuit Open or Shorted to Battery/Ground
33	Right Front Wheel Speed Sensor Circuit Open or Shorted to Battery/Ground
34	Left Rear Wheel Speed Sensor Circuit Open or Shorted to Battery/Ground
35	Right Rear Wheel Speed Sensor Circuit Open or Shorted to Battery/Ground
36	Low System Voltage
37	High System Voltage
38	Left Front EMB Will Not Hold Motor
41	Right Front EMB Will Not Hold Motor
42	Rear ESB Will Not Hold Motor
44	Left Front Channel Will Not Move
45	Right Front Channel Will Not Move
46	Rear Axle Channel Will Not Move
47	Left Front Motor Free Spins
48	Right Front Motor Free Spins
51	Rear Motor Free Spins
52	Left Front Channel in Release Too Long
53	Right Front Channel in Release Too Long
54	Rear Channel in Release Too Long
55	EBTCM Malfunction
56	Left Front Motor Circuit Open
57	Left Front Motor Circuit Shorted to Ground
58	Left Front Motor Circuit Shorted to Battery or Motor Shorted
61	Right Front Motor Circuit Open
62	Right Front Motor Circuit Shorted to Ground
63	Right Front Motor Circuit Shorted to Battery or Motor Shorted
64	Rear Motor Circuit Open

87959079

Fig. 78 List of ABS Diagnostic Trouble Codes (DTCs) — vehicles through 1995 with ETS

DIAGNOSTIC TROUBLE CODE AND SYMPTOM TABLE	
CHART	SYMPTOM
65	Rear Motor Circuit Shorted to Ground
66	Rear Motor Circuit Shorted to Battery or Motor Shorted
67	Left Front EMB Circuit Open or Shorted to Ground
68	Left Front EMB Circuit Shorted to Battery or Driver Open
71	Right Front EMB Circuit Open or Shorted to Ground
72	Right Front EMB Circuit Shorted to Battery or Driver Open
75	Serial Communication Malfunction
76	Left Front Solenoid Circuit Open or Shorted to Battery
77	Left Front Solenoid Circuit Shorted to Ground or Driver Open
78	Right Front Solenoid Circuit Open or Shorted to Battery
81	Right Front Solenoid Circuit Shorted to Ground or Driver Open
82	Calibration Malfunction
86	EBTCM Turned "ON" the Red "BRAKE" Warning Lamp
91	Open Brake Switch During Deceleration
92	Open Brake Switch When ABS Was Required
93	DTCs 91 or 92 Set in Current or Previous Ignition Cycle
94	Brake Switch Contacts Always Closed
95	Brake Switch Circuit Open
96	Rear Brake Lamp Circuit Open

87959080

Fig. 79 List of ABS Diagnostic Trouble Codes (DTCs) — vehicles through 1995 with ETS, continued

DIAGNOSTIC TROUBLE CODE	DESCRIPTION
14	ABS Relay Contacts Circuit Open
15	ABS Relay Contacts Circuit Shorted to Battery or Always Closed
16	ABS Relay Coil Circuit Open
17	ABS Relay Coil Circuit Shorted to Ground
18	ABS Relay Coil Circuit Shorted to Battery or Coil Shorted
21	Left Front Wheel Speed = 0
22	Right Front Wheel Speed = 0
23	Left Rear Wheel Speed = 0
24	Right Rear Wheel Speed = 0
25	Left Front Excessive Wheel Speed Variation
26	Right Front Excessive Wheel Speed Variation
27	Left Rear Excessive Wheel Speed Variation
28	Right Rear Excessive Wheel Speed Variation
32	Left Front Wheel Speed Sensor Circuit Open or Shorted to Ground /Battery
33	Right Front Wheel Speed Sensor Circuit Open or Shorted to Ground /Battery
34	Left Rear Wheel Speed Sensor Circuit Open or Shorted to Ground /Battery
35	Right Rear Wheel Speed Sensor Circuit Open or Shorted to Ground /Battery
36	Low System Voltage
37	High System Voltage
38	Left Front ESB Will Not Hold Motor
41	Right Front ESB Will Not Hold Motor
42	Rear ESB Will Not Hold Motor
44	Left Front Channel Will Not Move
45	Right Front Channel Will Not Move
46	Rear Channel Will Not Move
47	Left Front Motor Free Spins
48	Right Front Motor Free Spins
51	Rear Motor Free Spins
52	Left Front Channel in Release Too Long
53	Right Front Channel in Release Too Long
54	Rear Channel in Release Too Long
55	EBCM/EBTCM Malfunction
56	Left Front Motor Circuit Open
57	Left Front Motor Circuit Shorted to Ground
58	Left Front Motor Circuit Shorted to Battery or Motor Shorted
61	Right Front Motor Circuit Open
62	Right Front Motor Circuit Shorted to Ground

87959081

Fig. 80 List of ABS Diagnostic Trouble Codes (DTCs) — 1996 vehicles

DIAGNOSTIC TROUBLE CODE	DESCRIPTION
63	Right Front Motor Circuit Shorted to Battery or Motor Shorted
64	Rear Motor Circuit Open
65	Rear Motor Circuit Shorted to Ground
66	Rear Motor Circuit Shorted to Battery or Motor Shorted
75	Serial Communication Failure
76	Left Front Solenoid Circuit Open or Shorted to Ground
77	Left Front Solenoid Circuit Shorted to Battery
78	Right Front Solenoid Circuit Open or Shorted to Ground
81	Right Front Solenoid Circuit Shorted to Battery
82	Calibration Malfunction
86	EBCM/EBTCM Turned "ON" the Red "BRAKE" Warning Lamp
91	Open Brake Switch Contacts During Deceleration
92	Open Brake Switch Contacts When ABS Was Required
93	DTCs 91 or 92 Set in Current or Previous Ignition Cycle
94	Brake Switch Contacts Always Closed
95	Brake Switch Circuit Open

87959082

Fig. 81 List of ABS Diagnostic Trouble Codes (DTCs) — 1996 vehicles, continued

Contamination is caused by the connector halves being improperly connected, a missing or damaged connector seal, or damage to the connector itself, exposing the terminals to moisture and dirt. Contamination, usually in underhood or underbody connectors, leads to terminal corrosion, causing an open circuit or an intermittently open circuit.

Deformation is caused by probing the mating side of a connector terminal without the proper adapter, improperly joining the connector halves or repeatedly separating and joining the connector halves. Deformation, usually to the female terminal contact tang, can result in poor terminal contact causing an open or intermittently open circuit.

Follow the procedure below to check terminal contact.

1. Separate the connector halves. Refer to Terminal Repair Kit J 38125-A, if available.

2. Inspect the connector halves for contamination. Contamination will result in a white or green buildup within the connector body or between terminals, causing high terminal resistance, intermittent contact or an open circuit. An underhood or underbody connector that shows signs of contamination should be replaced in its entirety: terminals, seals, and connector body.

3. Using an equivalent male terminal from the Terminal Repair Kit J 38125-A, check the retention force of the female terminal in question by inserting and removing the male terminal to the female terminal in the connector body. Good terminal contact will require a certain amount of force to separate the terminals.

4. Using an equivalent female terminal from the Terminal Repair Kit J 38125-A, compare the retention force of this terminal to the female terminal in question by joining and separating the male terminal to the female terminal in question. If the retention force is significantly different between the two female terminals, replace the female terminal in question, using a terminal from Terminal Repair Kit J 38125-A.

ABS Service

PRECAUTIONS

Failure to observe the following precautions may result in system damage.
- Performing diagnostic work on the ABS-VI requires the use of a Tech 1® Scan diagnostic tool or equivalent. If unavailable, please refer diagnostic work to a qualified technician.
- Before performing electric arc welding on the vehicle, disconnect the Electronic Brake Control Module (EBCM) and the hydraulic modulator connectors.
- When performing painting work on the vehicle, do not expose the Electronic Brake Control Module (EBCM) to temperatures in excess of 185°F (85°C) for longer than 2 hours. The system may be exposed to temperatures up to 200°F (95°C) for less than 15 minutes.
- Never disconnect or connect the Electronic Brake Control Module (EBCM) or hydraulic modulator connectors with the ignition switch **ON** or damage to the system will occur.
- Never disassemble any component of the Anti-Lock Brake System (ABS) which is designated non-serviceable; the component must be replaced as an assembly.
- When filling the master cylinder, always use Delco Supreme 11 brake fluid or equivalent, which meets DOT-3 specifications; petroleum-base fluid will destroy the rubber parts.

Electrical Connectors

▶ **See Figure 82**

Some ABS-VI components are equipped with electrical connectors using a Connector Position Assurance (CPA) lock.
1. Remove the lock before separating the electrical connectors.
2. Be careful not to damage the locking pin during removal.
3. Make sure that the rubber connector seal is in place on the connector before and after connection.
4. Always install the lock after the connection is made.

ABS Hydraulic Modulator Assembly Bleeder Valves

REMOVAL & INSTALLATION

▶ **See Figure 83**

1. Remove the bleeder valve or valves.
2. Install the bleeder valve, then tighten to 65 inch lbs. (7 Nm).

Fluid Level Sensor

REMOVAL & INSTALLATION

▶ **See Figure 84**

1. Disconnect the negative battery cable.
2. Detach the electrical connection from the fluid level sensor.
3. Remove the fluid level sensor, using needle-nose pliers to compress the switch locking tabs at the inboard side of the master cylinder.
   To install:
4. Insert the fluid level sensor unit until the locking tabs snap in place.
5. Attach the sensor electrical connector.
6. Connect the negative battery cable.

Enable Relay

REMOVAL & INSTALLATION

▶ **See Figure 85**

1. Disconnect the negative battery cable.
2. Detach the electrical connection.
3. Unfasten the retainer on the bracket, then slide the relay off the bracket.
   To install:
4. Slide the relay onto the bracket and make sure the retainer locks the relay to the bracket. Fasten the retainer.
5. Attach the electrical connection.
6. Connect the negative battery cable.

ABS Lamp Driver Module

REMOVAL & INSTALLATION

1. Disconnect the negative battery cable.
2. Remove the right side lower sound insulator panel.
3. Slide the glove box all the way out or remove it completely.
4. The lamp driver module is above the cruise control module taped to the instrument panel harness and is light green in color.
5. Open the connector and slide the circuit board out of the connector.
   To install:
6. Install the circuit board to the connector.
7. Reposition the connector to the instrument panel harness and make sure it is retaped in place.
8. Slide the glove box back into the dash or reinstall the screws, if removed.
9. Install the right side lower sound insulator panel.
10. Connect the negative battery cable.

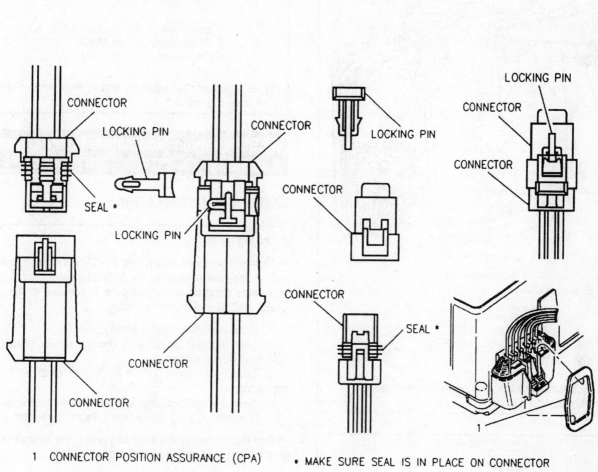

1 CONNECTOR POSITION ASSURANCE (CPA)   * MAKE SURE SEAL IS IN PLACE ON CONNECTOR

87959084

Fig. 82 View of ABS electrical connectors with a CPA lock

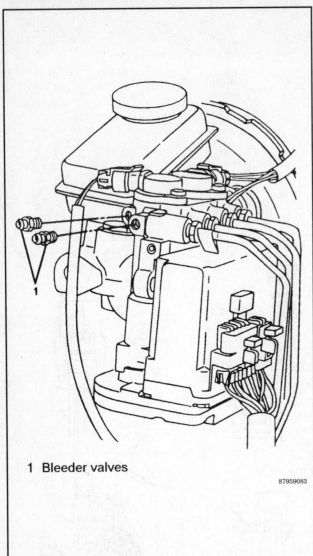

1 Bleeder valves

87959083

Fig. 83 Location of the ABS hydraulic modulator assembly bleeder valves

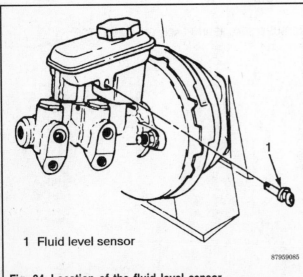

1 Fluid level sensor

87959085

Fig. 84 Location of the fluid level sensor

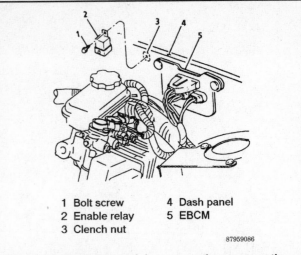

1 Bolt screw	4 Dash panel
2 Enable relay	5 EBCM
3 Clench nut	

87959086

Fig. 85 Unfasten the retaining screw, then remove the relay from the bracket

ABS Hydraulic Modulator/Master Cylinder Assembly

REMOVAL & INSTALLATION

♦ See Figure 86

➡To avoid personal injury, use the Tech 1® scan tool to relieve the gear tension in the hydraulic modulator. This procedure must be performed prior to removal of the brake control and motor assembly.

1. Disconnect the negative battery cable.
2. Disengage the two solenoid electrical connectors and the fluid level sensor connector.
3. Detach the 6-pin and 3-pin motor pack electrical connectors.
4. Wrap a shop towel around the hydraulic brake lines, then disconnect the four brake lines from the modulator.

➡Cap the disconnected lines to prevent the loss of fluid and the entry of moisture and contaminants.

5. Unfasten the 2 nuts attaching the ABS hydraulic modulator/master cylinder assembly to the vacuum booster.
6. Remove the ABS hydraulic modulator assembly from the vehicle.
   To install:
7. Install the ABS hydraulic modulator assembly to the vehicle. Secure using the two attaching nuts and tighten to 20 ft. lbs. (27 Nm).
8. Uncap and connect the 4 brake pipes to the modulator assembly. Tighten to 13 ft. lbs. (17 Nm).
9. Attach the 6-pin and 3-pin electrical connectors.
10. Engage the fluid level sensor connector and the two solenoid electrical connections.
11. Properly bleed the system, as outlined later in this section.
12. Connect the negative battery cable.

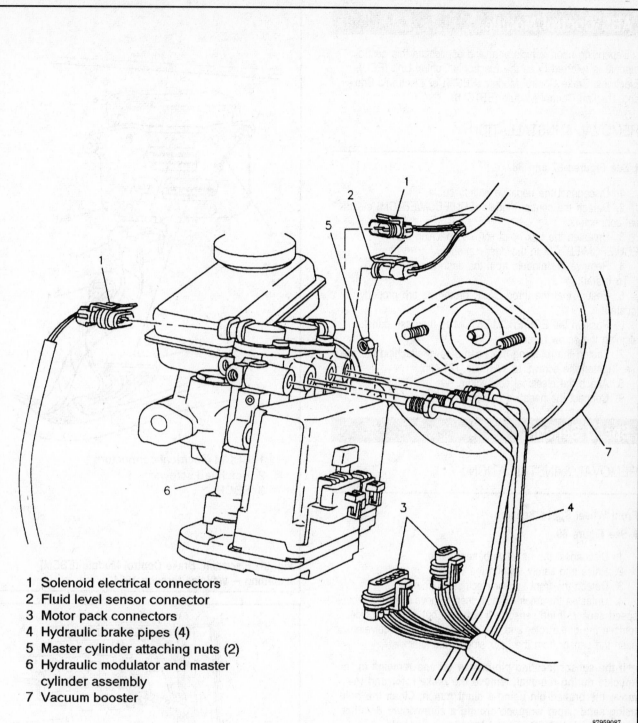

1 Solenoid electrical connectors
2 Fluid level sensor connector
3 Motor pack connectors
4 Hydraulic brake pipes (4)
5 Master cylinder attaching nuts (2)
6 Hydraulic modulator and master
  cylinder assembly
7 Vacuum booster

87959087

Fig. 86 View of the ABS hydraulic modulator/master cylinder assembly — 1995 vehicle shown

ABS Control Module

Depending upon vehicle year and application this control module is referred to as the Electronic Control Unit (ECU), Electronic Brake Control Module (EBCM) or Electronic Brake and Traction Control Module (EBTCM).

REMOVAL & INSTALLATION

▶ **See Figures 87 and 88**

1. Disconnect the negative battery cable.
2. Detach the control module (ECU/EBCM/EBTCM) electrical connectors.
3. Unfasten the hex head screws attaching the ECU/EBCM/EBTCM to the dash panel.
4. Remove the module from the dash panel.

To install:

5. Ensure that the three plastic grommets are properly located.
6. Position the ECU/EBCM/EBTCM to the dash panel, aligning the screw holes.
7. Fasten the retaining hex head screws attaching the module. Tighten the screws to 17 ft. lbs. (21 Nm).
8. Attach the electrical connectors.
9. Connect the negative battery cable.

Speed Sensors

REMOVAL & INSTALLATION

Front Wheel Speed Sensors

▶ **See Figure 89**

1. Disconnect the negative battery cable.
2. Raise and safely support the vehicle.
3. Detach the front sensor electrical connector.
4. Unfasten the retaining bolt, then remove the front wheel speed sensor. If the sensor will not slide out of the knuckle, remove the brake rotor and use a blunt punch or equivalent to push the sensor from the back side of the knuckle.

➡**If the sensor locating pin breaks off and remains in the knuckle during removal, remove the brake rotor and remove the broken pin using a blunt punch. Clean the hole using sand paper wrapped around a screwdriver or other suitable tool. NEVER attempt to enlarge the hole.**

To install:

5. Position the front wheel speed sensor on the mounting bracket.

➡**Make sure the front wheel speed sensor is properly aligned and lays flat against the bracket bosses.**

6. Install the retaining bolts. Tighten to 107 inch lbs. (12 Nm).
7. Attach the front sensor electrical connector.
8. Lower the vehicle.
9. Connect the negative battery cable.

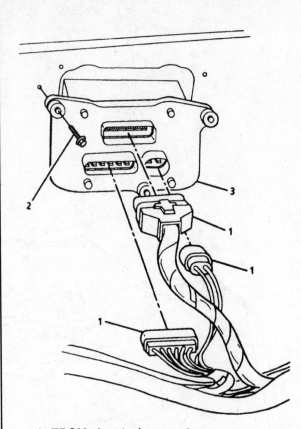

1 EBCM electrical connectors
2 Hex head screws
3 EBCM

87959088

Fig. 87 Electronic Brake Control Module (EBCM) mounting — vehicles through 1994

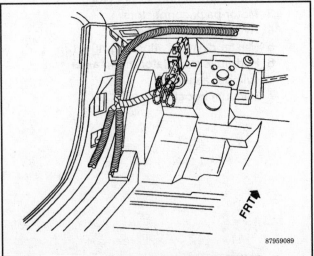

87959089

Fig. 88 Electronic Brake Control Module (EBCM) mounting — 1995 vehicle shown

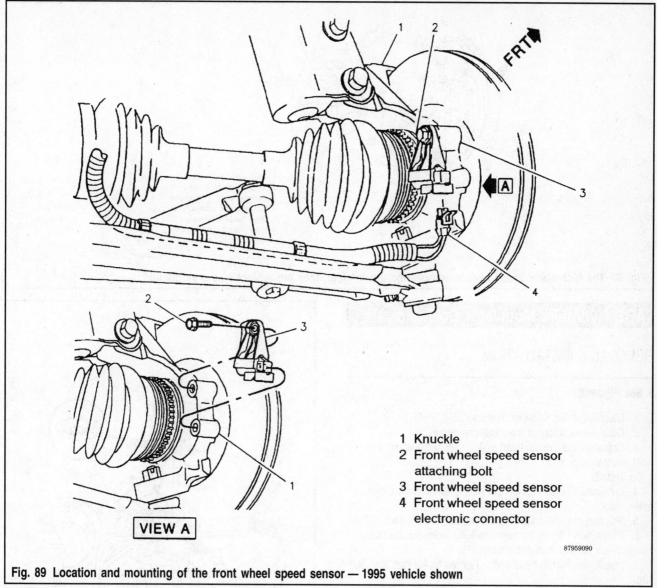

1 Knuckle
2 Front wheel speed sensor attaching bolt
3 Front wheel speed sensor
4 Front wheel speed sensor electronic connector

VIEW A

87959090

Fig. 89 Location and mounting of the front wheel speed sensor — 1995 vehicle shown

Rear Wheel Bearing and Speed Sensor Assembly

▶ See Figure 90

➡The rear integral wheel bearing and sensor assembly must be replaced as a unit.

1. Disconnect the negative battery cable.
2. Raise and safely support the vehicle.
3. Remove the rear wheel and tire assembly.
4. Remove the brake drum.
5. Detach the rear sensor electrical connector.
6. Unfasten the bolts and nuts attaching the rear wheel bearing and speed sensor assembly to the backing plate. Rotate the axle flange to align the large hole with each bolt. Remove the bolt while holding the nut.

➡With the rear wheel bearing and speed sensor attaching bolts/nuts removed, the drum brake assembly is supported only by the brake line connection. To avoid bending or damage to the brake line, do not bump or exert force on the assembly.

7. Remove the rear wheel bearing and speed sensor assembly.

To install:

8. Install the rear wheel bearing and speed sensor assembly by aligning the bolt holes in the wheel bearing and speed sensor assembly, drum brake assembly and rear suspension bracket.

9. Fasten the attaching bolts and nuts. Rotate the axle flange to align the large hole with each bolt location. Install the bolt while holding the nut. Tighten to 37 ft. lbs. (50 Nm).

10. Attach the rear speed sensor electrical connector.

11. Install the brake drum and the rear wheel and tire assembly.

12. Carefully lower the vehicle.

13. Connect the negative battery cable.

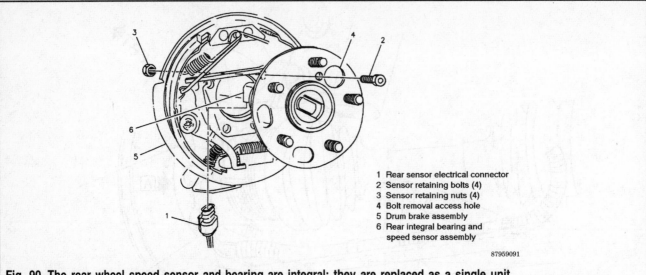

1 Rear sensor electrical connector
2 Sensor retaining bolts (4)
3 Sensor retaining nuts (4)
4 Bolt removal access hole
5 Drum brake assembly
6 Rear integral bearing and
  speed sensor assembly

87959091

Fig. 90 The rear wheel speed sensor and bearing are integral; they are replaced as a single unit

ABS Hydraulic Modulator Solenoid

REMOVAL & INSTALLATION

▶ See Figure 91

1. Disconnect the negative battery cable.
2. Detach the solenoid electrical connector.
3. Unfasten the Torx® head bolts, then remove the solenoid assembly.

To install:

4. Lubricate the O-rings on the new solenoid with clean brake fluid.
5. Position the solenoid so the connectors face each other.
6. Press down firmly by hand until the solenoid assembly flange seats on the modulator assembly.
7. Install the Torx® head bolts. Tighten to 40 inch lbs. (4.5 Nm).
8. Attach the solenoid electrical connector. Make sure the connectors are installed on the correct solenoids.
9. Properly bleed the brake system.
10. Connect the negative battery cable.

Filling and Bleeding

✳✳WARNING

Do NOT allow brake fluid to spill on or come in contact with the vehicle's finish as it will remove the paint. In case of a spill, immediately flush the area with water.

SYSTEM FILLING

The master cylinder reservoirs must be kept properly filled to prevent air from entering the system. No special filling procedures are required because of the anti-lock system.

When adding fluid, use only DOT 3 fluid; the use of DOT 5 or silicone fluids is specifically prohibited. Use of improper or

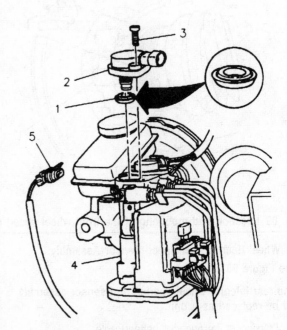

1 Solenoid lip seal
2 Solenoid assembly
3 TORX® head bolt
4 Hydraulic modulator
5 Solenoid electrical connector

87959092

Fig. 91 ABS modulator solenoid mounting — 1995 vehicle shown

contaminated fluid may cause the fluid to boil or cause the rubber components in the system to deteriorate. Never use any fluid with a petroleum base or any fluid which has been exposed to water or moisture.

BLEEDING THE ABS HYDRAULIC SYSTEM

Before bleeding the ABS brake system, the front and rear displacement cylinder pistons must be returned to the topmost position. The preferred method uses a Tech 1® or T-100® scan tool to perform the rehoming procedure. If a Tech 1® is not available, the second procedure may be used, but it must be followed EXACTLY.

Rehome Procedure

WITH TECH 1® OR T-100® (PREFERRED METHOD)

1. Using a Tech 1® or T-100® (CAMS), select "F5: Motor Rehome." The motor rehome function cannot be performed if current DTC's are present. If DTC's are present, the vehicle must be repaired and the codes cleared before performing the motor rehome function.
2. The entire brake system should now be bled using the pressure or manual bleeding procedures outlined later in this section.

WITHOUT TECH 1® OR T-100®

➡ Do not place your foot on the brake pedal through this entire procedure unless specifically instructed to do so.

This method can only be used if the ABS warning lamp is not illuminated and not DTC's are present.
1. Remove your foot from the brake pedal.
2. Start the engine and allow it to run for at least 10 seconds while observing the ABS warning lamp.
3. If the ABS warning lamp turned "ON" and stayed "ON" after about 10 seconds, the bleeding procedure must be stopped and a Tech 1® must be used to diagnose the ABS function.
4. If the ABS warning lamp turned "ON" for about 3 seconds, then turned "OFF" and stayed "OFF," turn the ignition **OFF**.
5. Repeat Steps 1-4 one more time.
6. The entire brake system should now be bled by following the manual or pressure bleeding procedure.

Pressure Bleeding
▶ See Figures 92 and 93

➡ The pressure bleeding equipment must be of the diaphragm type. It must have a rubber diaphragm between the air supply and the brake fluid to prevent air, moisture and other contaminants from entering the hydraulic system.

1. Clean the master cylinder fluid reservoir cover and surrounding area, then remove the cover.
2. Add fluid, if necessary to obtain a proper fluid level.
3. Connect bleeder adapter J 35589, or equivalent, to the brake fluid reservoir, then connect the bleeder adapter to the pressure bleeding equipment.

4. Adjust the pressure bleed equipment t o 5-10 psi (35-70 kPa) and wait about 30 seconds to be sure there is no leakage.
5. Adjust the pressure bleed equipment to 30-35 psi (205-240 kPa).

❋❋WARNING

Use a shop rag to catch the escaping brake fluid. Be careful not to let any fluid run down the motor pack base or into the electrical connector.

6. With the pressure bleeding equipment connected and pressurized, proceed as follows:
   a. Attach a clear plastic bleeder hose to the rearward bleeder valve on the hydraulic modulator.
   b. Slowly open the bleeder valve and allow fluid to flow until no air is seen in the fluid.
   c. Close the valve when fluid flows out without any air bubbles.
   d. Repeat Steps 6b and 6c until no air bubbles are present.
   e. Relocate the bleeder hose on the forward hydraulic modulator bleed valve and repeat Steps 6a through 6d.
7. Tighten the bleeder valve to 80 inch lbs. (9 Nm).
8. Proceed to bleed the hydraulic modulator brake pipe connections as follows with the pressure bleeding equipment connected and pressurized:
   a. Slowly open the forward brake pipe tube nut on the hydraulic modulator and check for air in the escaping fluid.
   b. When the air flow ceases, immediately tighten the tube nut. Tighten the tube nut to 18 ft. lbs. (24 Nm).
9. Repeat Steps 8a and 8b for the remaining three brake pipe connections moving from the front to the rear.
10. Raise and safely support the vehicle.
11. Proceed, as outlined in the following steps, to bleed the wheel brakes in the following sequence: right rear, left rear, right front, then left front.
   a. Attach a clear plastic bleeder hose to the bleeder valve at the wheel, then submerge the opposite hose end in a clean container partially filled with clean brake fluid.
   b. Slowly open the bleeder valve and allow the fluid to flow.
   c. Close the valve when fluid begins to flow without any air bubbles. Tap lightly on the caliper or backing plate to dislodge any trapped air bubbles.
12. Repeat Step 11 on the other brakes using the earlier sequence.
13. Remove the pressure bleeding equipment, including bleeder adapter J 35589.
14. Carefully lower the vehicle, then check the brake fluid and add if necessary. Don't forget to put the reservoir cap back on.
15. With the ignition turned to the **RUN** position, apply the brake pedal with moderate force and hold it. Note the pedal travel and feel. If the pedal feels firm and constant and the pedal travel is not excessive, start the engine. With the engine running, recheck the pedal travel. If it's still firm and constant and pedal travel is not excessive, go to Step 17.

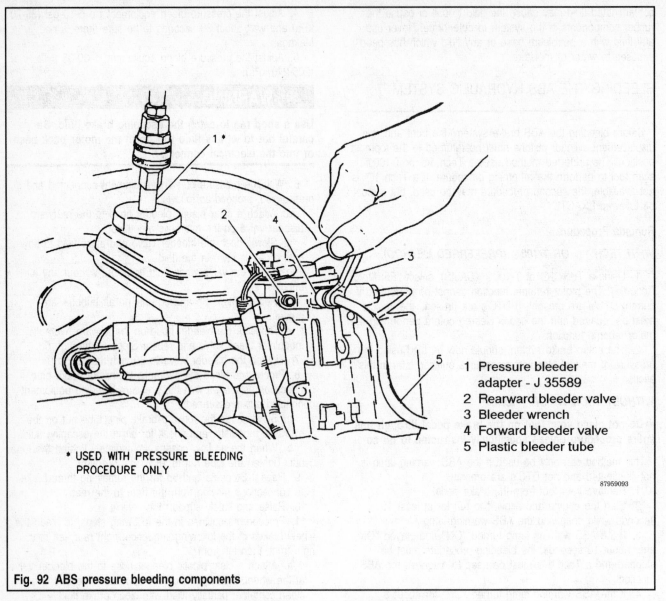

* USED WITH PRESSURE BLEEDING
PROCEDURE ONLY

1 Pressure bleeder
adapter - J 35589
2 Rearward bleeder valve
3 Bleeder wrench
4 Forward bleeder valve
5 Plastic bleeder tube

87959093

Fig. 92 ABS pressure bleeding components

16. If the pedal feels soft or has excessive travel either initially or after the engine is started, the following procedure may be used:

　a. With the Tech 1® scan tool, "release" then "apply" each motor 2-3 times and cycle each solenoid 5-10 times. When finished, be sure to "apply" the front and rear motors to ensure the pistons are in the upmost position. DO NOT DRIVE THE VEHICLE.

　b. If a Tech 1® is not available, remove your foot from the brake pedal, start the engine and allow it run for at least 10 seconds to initialize the ABS. DO NOT DRIVE THE VEHICLE. After 10 seconds, turn the ignition **OFF**. The initialization procedure most be repeated 5 times to ensure any trapped air has been dislodged.

　c. Repeat the bleeding procedure, starting with Step 1.

17. Road test the vehicle, and make sure the brakes are operating properly.

Manual Bleeding

▶ See Figure 94

1. Clean the master cylinder fluid reservoir cover and surrounding area, then remove the cover.

2. Add fluid, if necessary to obtain a proper fluid level, then put the reservoir cover back on.

3. Prime the ABS hydraulic modulator/master cylinder assembly as follows:

　a. Attach a bleeder hose to the rearward bleeder valve, then submerge the opposite hose end in a clean container partially filled with clean brake fluid.

　b. Slowly open the rearward bleeder valve.

　c. Depress and hold the brake pedal until the fluid begins to flow.

　d. Close the valve, then release the brake pedal.

　e. Repeat Steps 3b-3d until no air bubbles are present.

　f. Relocate the bleeder hose to the forward hydraulic modulator bleeder valve, then repeat Steps 3a-3e.

4. Once the fluid is seen to flow from both modulator bleeder valves, the ABS modulator/master cylinder assembly is

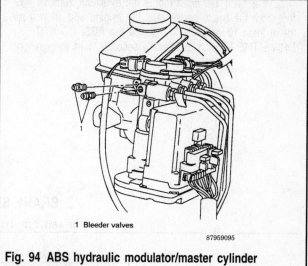

1 Bleeder valves

87959095

Fig. 94 ABS hydraulic modulator/master cylinder bleeder locations

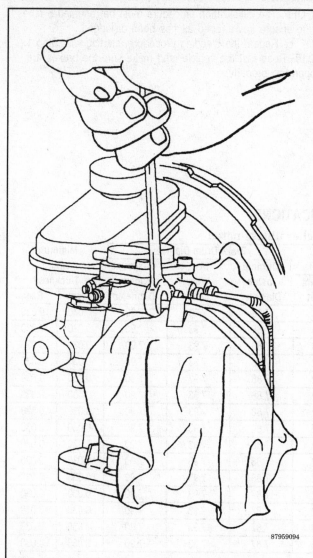

87959094

Fig. 93 Position a shop rag to catch escaping brake fluid

sufficiently full of fluid. However, it may not be completely purged of air. At this point, move to the wheel brakes and bleed them. This ensures that the lowest points in the system are completely free of air and then the assembly can purged of any remaining air.

5. Remove the fluid reservoir cover. Fill to the correct level, if necessary, then fasten the cover.

6. Raise and safely support the vehicle.

7. Proceed, as outlined in the following steps, to bleed the wheel brakes in the following sequence: right rear, left rear, right front, then left front.

   a. Attach a clear plastic bleeder hose to the bleeder valve at the wheel, then submerge the opposite hose end in a clean container partially filled with clean brake fluid.

   b. Open the bleeder valve.

   c. Have an assistant slowly depress the brake pedal.

   d. Close the valve and slowly release the release the brake pedal.

   e. Wait 5 seconds.

   f. Repeat Steps 7a-7e until the brake pedal feels firm at half travel and no air bubbles are observed in the bleeder

hose. To assist in freeing the entrapped air, tap lightly on the caliper or braking plate to dislodge any trapped air bubbles.

8. Repeat Step 7 for the remaining brakes in the sequence given earlier.

9. Carefully lower the vehicle.

10. Remove the reservoir cover, then fill to the correct level with brake fluid and replace the cap.

11. Bleed the ABS hydraulic modulator/master cylinder assembly as follows:

   a. Attach a clear plastic bleeder hose to the rearward bleeder valve on the modulator, then submerge the opposite hose end in a clean container partially filled with clean brake fluid.

   b. Have an assistant depress the brake pedal with moderate force.

   c. Slowly open the rearward bleeder valve and allow the fluid to flow.

   d. Close the valve, then release the brake pedal.

   e. Wait 5 seconds.

   f. Repeat Steps 11a-11e until no air bubbles are present.

   g. Relocate the bleeder hose to the forward hydraulic modulator bleeder valve, then repeat Steps 11a-11f.

12. Carefully lower the vehicle, then check the brake fluid and add if necessary. Don't forget to put the reservoir cap back on.

13. With the ignition turned to the **RUN** position, apply the brake pedal with moderate force and hold it. Note the pedal travel and feel. If the pedal feels firm and constant and the pedal travel is not excessive, start the engine. With the engine running, recheck the pedal travel. If it's still firm and constant and pedal travel is not excessive, road test the vehicle and make sure the brakes are operating properly.

14. If the pedal feels soft or has excessive travel either initially or after the engine is started, the following procedure may be used:

   a. With the Tech 1® scan tool, "Release" then "Apply" each motor 2-3 times and cycle each solenoid 5-10 times. When finished, be sure to "Apply" the front and rear motors to ensure the pistons are in the upmost position. DO NOT DRIVE THE VEHICLE.

b. If a Tech 1® scan tool is not available, remove your foot from the brake pedal, start the engine and allow it run for at least 10 seconds to initialize the ABS. DO NOT DRIVE THE VEHICLE. After 10 seconds, turn the ignition **OFF**. The initialization procedure most be repeated 5 times to ensure any trapped air has been dislodged.

c. Repeat the bleeding procedure, starting with Step 1.

15. Road test the vehicle, and make sure the brakes are operating properly.

BRAKE SPECIFICATIONS

All measurements in inches unless noted

Year	Model	Master Cylinder Bore	Brake Disc			Brake Drum Diameter			Minimum Lining Thickness	
			Original Thickness	Minimum Thickness	Maximum Runout	Original Inside Diameter	Max. Wear Limit	Maximum Machine Diameter	Front	Rear
1982	All	0.940	0.885	0.830	0.004	7.88	7.93	7.90	0.030	0.030
1983	All	0.940	0.885	0.830	0.004	7.88	7.93	7.90	0.030	0.030
1984	All	0.940	0.885	0.830	0.004	7.88	7.93	7.90	0.030	0.030
1985	All	0.874	0.885	0.815	0.002	7.88	7.93	7.90	0.030	0.030
1986	All	0.874	0.885	0.815	0.002	7.88	7.93	7.90	0.030	0.030
1987	All	0.874	0.885	0.815	0.002	7.88	7.93	7.90	0.030	0.030
1988	All	0.874	0.885	0.815	0.002	7.88	7.93	7.90	0.030	0.030
1989	All	0.874	0.885	0.815	0.002	7.88	7.93	7.90	0.030	0.030
1990	All	0.874	0.885	0.815	0.002	7.88	7.93	7.90	0.030	0.030
1991	All	0.874	0.806	0.736	0.002	7.88	7.93	7.90	0.030	0.030
1992	All	0.874	0.806	0.736	0.002	7.88	7.93	7.90	0.030	0.030
1993	All	0.874	0.806	0.736	0.002	7.87	7.93	7.90	0.030	0.030
1994	All	0.874	0.806	0.736	0.002	7.87	7.93	7.90	0.030	0.030
1995	All	0.874	0.786	0.736	0.003	7.87	7.93	7.90	0.030	0.030
1996	All	0.874	0.786	0.736	0.003	7.87	7.93	7.90	0.030	0.030

87959100

EXTERIOR
ANTENNA 10-28
CONVERTIBLE TOP 10-31
DOORS 10-2
FENDERS 10-28
FRONT BUMPERS 10-7
GRILLE 10-21
HATCHBACK ASSEMBLY 10-5
HOOD 10-4
LIFT GATE (STATION WAGON) 10-6
MOLDING, EMBLEM AND NAME
 PLATE 10-3
OUTSIDE MIRRORS 10-28
REAR BUMPERS 10-20
SUNROOF 10-38
TRUNK LID 10-5
INTERIOR
CONSOLE 10-44
DOOR LOCKS 10-49
DOOR PANEL 10-47
FRONT DOOR GLASS 10-53
FRONT SEAT 10-59
FRONT WINDOW REGULATOR AND
 MOTOR 10-53
INSIDE REARVIEW MIRROR 10-59
INSTRUMENT PANEL 10-39
POWER SEAT MOTORS 10-65
REAR DOOR GLASS 10-53
REAR SEAT CUSHION 10-64
REAR WINDOW REGULATOR 10-57
SEAT BELT SYSTEM 10-64
WINDSHIELD GLASS 10-59

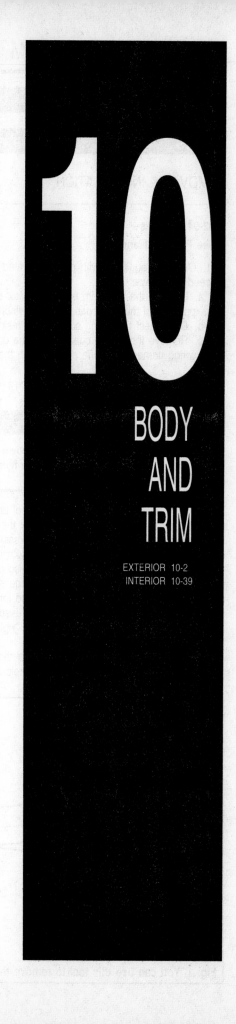

10

BODY AND TRIM

EXTERIOR 10-2
INTERIOR 10-39

EXTERIOR

Doors

REMOVAL & INSTALLATION

1982-94 Vehicles

▶ **See Figures 1 and 2**

1. On doors equipped with power operated components proceed as follows:

a. Remove the door trim panel, insulator pad (if so equipped), and the inner panel water deflector.

b. Disconnect the wiring components inside the door.

c. Remove the rubber conduit from the door, then remove the wiring harness from the door through the conduit access hole.

2. Tape the area (on the door pillar and body pillar) above the lower hinge with fabric tape.

✳✳CAUTION

Before performing the following step, cover the spring with a towel to prevent the spring from flying out and possibly causing personal injury!

3. Insert a suitable, long, flat bladed tool under the pivot point of the hold-open link and over top of the spring. The tool should be positioned so as not to apply pressure to the hold-open link. Cover the spring with a shop cloth and lift the tool to disengage the spring. The spring can also be removed by using tool J-28625, or equivalent, door hinge spring compressor tool. The tool is stamped right side and left side. For all the J-cars the tool stamped, "left side" is used to service the right side hinge spring. The tool stamped, "right side" is used to service the left hand hinge spring.

a. Install the two jaws of the tool over the spring. The jaw with the slots slides over spring at the hold-open link. The

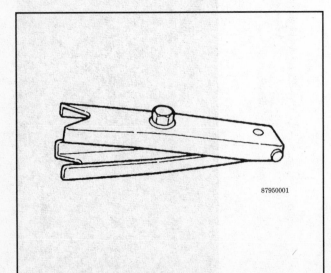

Fig. 1 You can use this tool to remove the spring

jaw with the hole fits over the spring at the bubble on the door hinge pillar.

b. Install the bolt to the jaws of the tool and tighten to compress the spring.

c. Remove the tool and spring from the door hinge assembly. Do not remove the spring from the tool.

4. When removing the hinge pin, save the "barrel" clips as follows:

a. Using two, suitable, flat bladed tools, spread the clip enough to move the clip above the recess toward the pointed end of the pin.

b. As the pin is removed, the clip will ride the shank of the pin and fall free.

c. Reinstall the clips onto the pins before installing the door.

5. With the aid of a helper to support the door, remove the lower hinge pin, using a soft headed hammer and locking type pliers. The helper can aid in removing the hinge pin by raising and lowering the rear of the door.

6. Insert the bolt into the hole of the lower hinge to maintain door attachment during upper hinge pin removal.

7. Remove the upper hinge pin in the same manner as the lower. Remove the bolt from the lower hinge and remove the door from the body.

To install:

➡**Before installing the door, replace the hinge pin clips or reuse the old clips as explained in the removal procedure.**

8. With the aid of a helper, position the door and insert a bolt in the lower hinge hole.

9. The upper hinge pin is inserted with the pointed end up. The lower hinge pin is inserted with the pointed end down. With the door in the full open position, install the upper hinge pin using locking-type pliers and a soft headed hammer. Use a drift punch and hammer to complete pin installation.

10. Remove the screw from the lower hinge and install the lower hinge pin. The use of the special tool J-28625 or equivalent is the recommended method for installing the hinge spring.

✳✳WARNING

If the spring is installed before installing the upper hinge pin, damage to the hinge bushings may result!

11. If the spring was removed using a long, flat bladed tool, install the spring as follows:

a. Place the spring in tool J-28625 or equivalent.

b. Place the tool and spring in a bench vise.

c. Compress the tool in a vise and install the bolt until the spring is fully compressed.

d. Remove the tool with the compressed spring from the vise and install in the proper position in the door lower hinge. The slot in the jaw of the tool fits over the hold-open link. The hole in the other jaw fits over the bubble.

e. Remove the bolt from the tool to install the spring.

f. Remove the tool from the door hinge. (The tool will fall out in three pieces). Cycle the door to check spring operation.

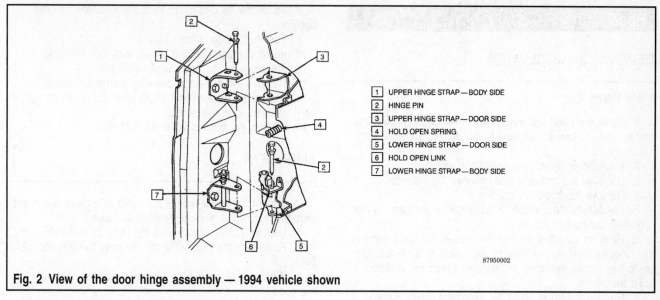

1	UPPER HINGE STRAP—BODY SIDE
2	HINGE PIN
3	UPPER HINGE STRAP—DOOR SIDE
4	HOLD OPEN SPRING
5	LOWER HINGE STRAP—DOOR SIDE
6	HOLD OPEN LINK
7	LOWER HINGE STRAP—BODY SIDE

87950002

Fig. 2 View of the door hinge assembly — 1994 vehicle shown

12. If tool J-28625 or equivalent was used to remove the spring, follow Steps d, e, and f above to install the spring.

13. Remove the tape from the door and body pillars.

14. On the doors with power operated components, install all previously removed parts.

1995-96 Vehicles

1. If equipped with power door components, disconnect the negative battery cable.

2. Make sure the window is raised up to its fully closed position.

3. Remove the inner door trim panel, as outlined later in this section.

4. If equipped with power door components, move the water deflector enough to access the door wiring harness, then detach the electrical connectors and remove the harness.

5. Remove the rubber conduit from the door.

6. Unfasten the door hold-open bolt.

7. Have an assistant support the door.

8. Matchmark the position of the door hinge to the hinge pillar. Unfasten the lower and upper hinge bolts from the pillar.

9. With an assistant's help, detach the door from the body.

10. Matchmark the position of the door hinge to the door, then unfasten the upper and lower hinge retaining bolts. Carefully remove the door from the vehicle.

To install:

11. Snug the upper and lower hinge-to-door bolts so the door can be moved.

12. With the aid of an assistant, position the door to the body.

13. Snug the upper and lower hinge-to-pillar bolts and nuts so that the door can be moved.

14. Carefully close the door. Adjust the door for proper alignment.

15. Slowly open the door.

16. Tighten the upper and lower hinge-to-pillar bolts and nuts to 16 ft. lbs. (22 Nm).

17. Tighten the upper and lower hinge-to-door bolts to 16 ft. lbs. (22 Nm).

18. Check the door for proper alignment. If the door does not align properly, readjust.

19. Install the door detent-to-hinge pillar bolt, then tighten to 80 inch lbs. (9 Nm).

20. If so equipped, install the electrical harness through the conduit access hole and connect the electrical connectors to the power door components.

21. Fasten the rubber conduit to the door.

22. Reposition and secure the door water deflector.

23. Install the inner door trim panel, as outlined later in this section.

24. Connect the negative battery cable.

ADJUSTMENTS

1. Adjust the door so that the door-to-body and lock-to-striker align properly.

2. The hinge-to-door bolts may need to be loosened to adjust the alignment properly.

Molding, Emblem and Name Plate

REPLACEMENT

1. Wash affected panel area with soap and water and wipe dry. Remove all traces of adhesive from the body panel and back of molding using 3M General Purpose Adhesive Cleaner (part number 08984). Do not use this cleaner on air dry enamel.

2. Mark proper position of molding with a length of masking tape. Use adjacent moldings as a guide if necessary.

3. If the body panel is below 70° degrees, warm body panel with heat lamp or heat gun before going to the next service step.

4. Apply a double-coated acrylic foam tape such as 3M Super Automotive Attachment Tape to the molding.

5. Align molding to tape guideline and press firmly in place.

Hood

REMOVAL & INSTALLATION

▶ **See Figure 3**

1. Raise the hood and install protective coverings over the fender areas to prevent damage to the painted surfaces and mouldings.
2. If equipped, detach the underhood wire.
3. Unfasten the retainers, then remove the insulator.
4. Remove the hood latch striker.
5. Matchmark the position of the hinge on the hood to aid alignment during installation.
6. Have an assistant support the front of the hood, remove the hinge-to-hood screws/bolts on each side of the hood, then grasp the rear of the hood and remove it from the vehicle.

To install:

7. Position the hood, using the alignment marks made when removed.

8. Install the hood-to-hinge bolts snug, but do not fully tighten.
9. Fasten the hood latch striker.
10. Install the insulator and secure with the retainers.
11. If equipped, attach the underhood wire.
12. Remove the protective covering from the fenders.
13. Inspect for proper hood alignments and adjust as necessary, as outlined in this section.
14. Tighten the bolts to 20 ft. lbs. (27 Nm).

ALIGNMENT

To raise or lower the rear of the hood to achieve alignment with the rear of the fenders, proceed as follows:

1. Loosen, but do not remove the bolts on one side.
2. Reposition the hood. Tighten the bolts to 20 ft. lbs. (27 Nm).
3. If necessary, repeat the procedure on the other side of the hood.

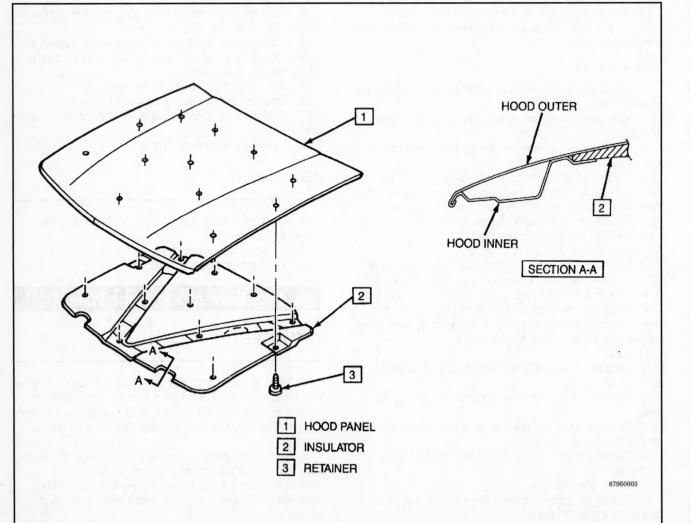

1 HOOD PANEL
2 INSULATOR
3 RETAINER

Fig. 3 Unfasten the retainers, then remove the hood insulator

To raise or lower the front of the hood to achieve alignment with the front of the fenders, proceed as follows:

4. Close the hood securely.
5. Determine the amount of adjustment necessary.
6. Open and support the hood.
7. Adjust the front bumpers by:
   • Turning clockwise to lower the bumper
   • Turning counterclockwise to raise the bumper

Trunk Lid

REMOVAL & INSTALLATION

2 and 4-Door Sedans
▶ **See Figure 4**

The trunk lid hinge is welded to the body and bolts to the lid.

1. Prop the trunk lid open and place protective coverings over the rear compartment to protect the paint from damage.
2. Matchmark the location of the hinge-to-trunk lid bolts, then detach the electrical connections and wiring from the lid (if equipped).
3. Using an assistant (to support the lid), unfasten the hinge-to-lid bolts, then remove the lid from the vehicle.
4. To install, reverse the removal procedures. Adjust the position of the trunk lid to the body.

ADJUSTMENTS

Fore and aft adjustment of the lid assembly is controlled by the hinge-to-lid attaching bolts. To adjust the lid, loosen the hinge-to-lid attaching bolts and shift the lid to the desired position, then tighten the bolts. To increase opening assist, use tool J-211412-1 or equivalent and move the torque rods one step toward the rear of the vehicle. To decrease opening assist, move the torque rods one step toward the front of the vehicle.

Hatchback Assembly

REMOVAL & INSTALLATION

▶ **See Figure 5**

1. Prop open the lid and place protective coverings along the edges of the lift window opening (to protect the paint from damage).
2. Where necessary, disconnect the wire harness from the lift window.
3. While a helper supports the lid, use an awl or flat bladed tool to remove the clips on the gas supports and pull the supports off the retainer studs.
4. Close the lift window assembly.
5. Remove the rear upper garnish moulding at the rear of the headlining.

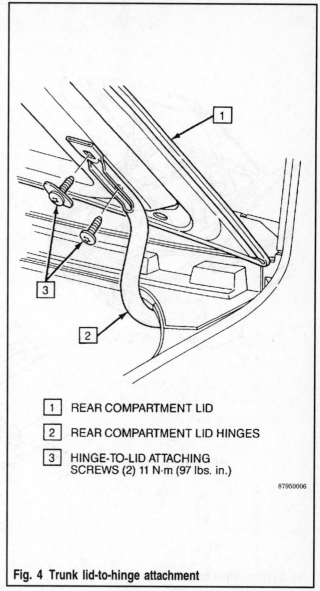

1	REAR COMPARTMENT LID
2	REAR COMPARTMENT LID HINGES
3	HINGE-TO-LID ATTACHING SCREWS (2) 11 N·m (97 lbs. in.)

87950006

Fig. 4 Trunk lid-to-hinge attachment

6. Remove the nuts retaining the lift window/hatchback to the body.
7. With the aid of a helper, remove the lift window assembly from the body.
8. Installation is the reverse of removal.

➡**The gas support assemblies are attached to the lid and the body and are secured by retaining clips and/or bolts.**

ADJUSTMENTS

The rear compartment lift window assembly (hatchback) height, fore and aft and side adjustments are controlled at the hinge to body location. This area of the body has oversize hinge attaching holes in addition to the hinge to body shims. Adjustment at the hinge location must be made at the lower panel by adjusting the rubber bumpers. The retaining bolts holding the hinge to body should be tightened to 15-20 ft. lbs. (20-27 Nm).

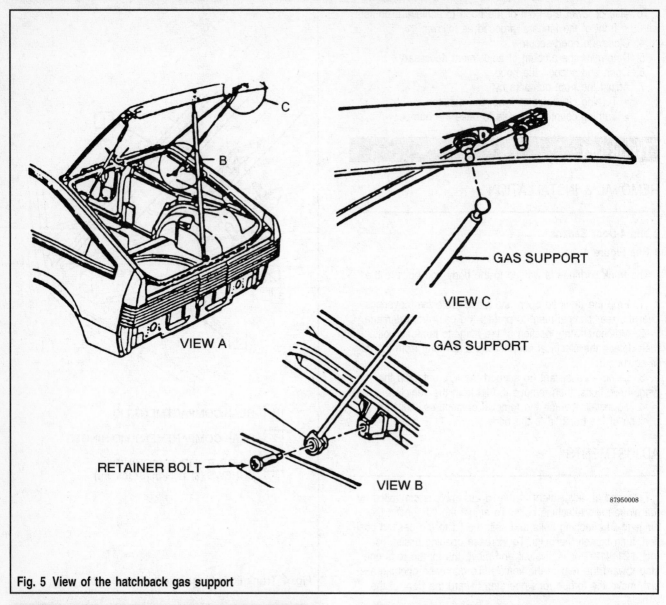

VIEW A

GAS SUPPORT

VIEW C

GAS SUPPORT

RETAINER BOLT

VIEW B

87950008

Fig. 5 View of the hatchback gas support

Lift Gate (Station Wagon)

REMOVAL & INSTALLATION

▶ See Figures 6 and 7

1. Prop open the lift gate and place protective coverings along the edges of the lift gate opening (to protect the paint from damage).
2. Where necessary, disconnect the wire harness from the lift gate.

3. While a helper supports the lid, use an awl or flat bladed tool to remove the clips on the gas supports and pull the supports off the retainer studs.
4. Use a $\frac{3}{16}$ in. (5mm) diameter rod to remove the hinge pins from the hinges. Place the end of the rod against the pointed end of the hinge pin; then strike the rod firmly to shear the retaining clip tabs and drive the pin through the hinge. Repeat the same thing on the opposite side hinge and with the aid of a helper remove the lift gate from the body.
5. To install, reverse the removal procedure. Prior to installing the hinge pins, install new retaining clips in the notches provide in the hinge pins. Position the retaining clips so that the tabs point toward the head of the pin.

➥The gas support assemblies are attached to the lid and the body and are secured by retaining clips and/or bolts.

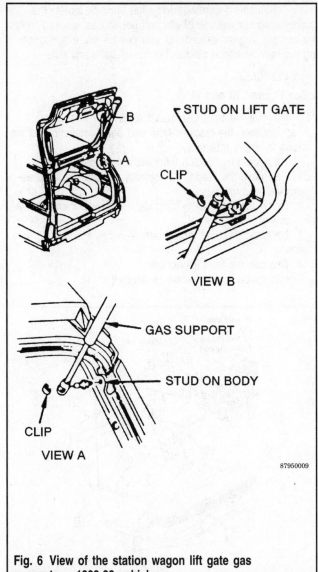

Fig. 6 View of the station wagon lift gate gas supports — 1982-88 vehicles

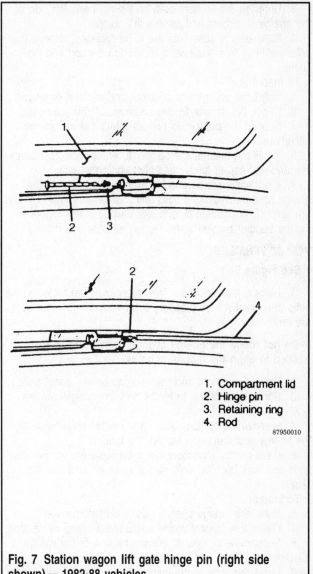

1. Compartment lid
2. Hinge pin
3. Retaining ring
4. Rod

Fig. 7 Station wagon lift gate hinge pin (right side shown) — 1982-88 vehicles

Front Bumpers

REMOVAL & INSTALLATION

Cavalier

1982-83 VEHICLES

▶ See Figure 8

1. Place a jack under the front bumper before removing the bolts to prevent it from dropping down when the bumper bolts are removed.

➡ Do not rotate the energy absorber any more than needed to align the mounting holes.

2. Remove the bolt end cap-to-header panel right and left side. Remove the 2 end cap-to-fender nuts on the right and left side. Push the end cap off the bumper (plastic protrusions through holes in bumper bar).

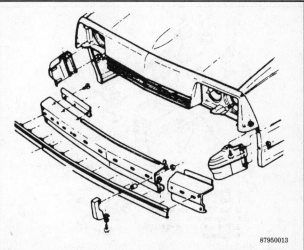

Fig. 8 Front bumper mounting and rub strips — 1982-83 Cavalier

3. Unfasten the bumper bolts on the right and left side at the energy absorbers and remove the bumper.

4. If the energy absorbers are to be replaced, remove the bolts and nuts from the unit, then remove the unit and the shims.

To install:

5. Install the energy and absorber and shims if removed.

6. Check the dimension and add/subtract shims as needed.

7. Support the bumper to prevent rotation of the energy absorbers.

8. Install the bolts at the bumper to energy absorber brackets, and end cap to fender and front end panel nuts.

9. If adjustment is required to align bumper, loosen the energy absorber mounting bolts and position as required (holes are slotted). Adjustment side to side can be made by loosening the bumper bracket bolts. Tighten all bolts and nuts.

1984-87 VEHICLES

▶ **See Figure 9**

1. Place a jack under the front bumper before removing the bolts to prevent it from dropping down when the bumper bolts are removed.

➡**Do not rotate the energy absorber any more than needed to align the mounting holes.**

2. Remove the right and left fascia to header panel bolts.

3. Remove the fascia to fender nuts in the right and left side.

4. Remove the bumper bolts on the right and left side at the energy absorbers and remove the bumper.

5. If the energy absorbers are to be replaced, remove the bolts and nuts from the unit, then remove the unit and the shims.

To install:

6. Install the energy absorber and shims if removed.

7. Check the dimension and add/subtract shims as needed.

8. Support the bumper to prevent rotation of the energy absorbers.

9. Install the bolts at the bumper to energy absorber brackets, and fascia to fender nuts, and fascia to fender panel bolts.

10. If adjustment is required to align bumper, loosen the energy absorber mounting bolts and position as required (holes are slotted). Adjustment side to side can be made by loosening the bumper bracket bolts. Tighten all bolts and nuts.

1988 VEHICLES

▶ **See Figures 10 and 11**

1. Remove the front fascia as follows:

a. Unfasten the fascia-to-front end panel retainers and the fascia-to-fender retainers.

b. If necessary, detach the electrical connectors.

c. Remove the fascia. If necessary remove the lamp assemblies and molding.

2. Remove the fascia molding clips and nuts, then remove the molding.

3. Unfasten the front impact bar-to-energy absorber retainers.

4. Remove the front impact bar.

5. Installation is the reverse of removal.

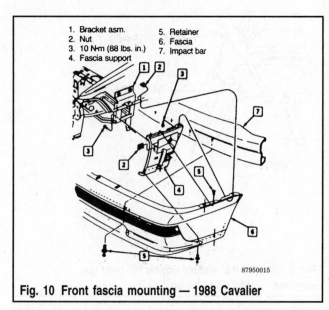

1. Bracket asm.
2. Nut
3. 10 N·m (88 lbs. in.)
4. Fascia support
5. Retainer
6. Fascia
7. Impact bar

87950015

Fig. 10 Front fascia mounting — 1988 Cavalier

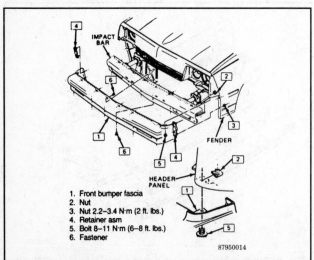

1. Front bumper fascia
2. Nut
3. Nut 2.2–3.4 N·m (2 ft. lbs.)
4. Retainer asm
5. Bolt 8–11 N·m (6–8 ft. lbs.)
6. Fastener

87950014

Fig. 9 Exploded view of the front bumper mounting — 1984-87 Cavalier

1. Shim (as required)
2. Energy absorber
3. 35 N·m (28 lbs. ft.)
4. Impact bar
5. Plate
6. Retainer
7. 27 N·m (20 lbs. ft.)

87950016

Fig. 11 Exploded view of the front impact bar and energy absorber — 1988 Cavalier

1989-94 VEHICLES
▶ See Figures 12 and 13

1. Remove the front end panel/fascia as follows:
   a. Remove the air deflector.
   b. Unfasten the screws, then remove the wheelhouse panel extensions.
   c. Remove the retaining screws, then remove the grille panel.
   d. Unfasten the push-in retainers, then detach the fascia from the impact bar.
   e. Use a drill to remove rivets.
   f. Remove the air deflector from the fascia.
2. Remove front bumper impact bar, as follows:
   a. If equipped, remove the radiator air deflector flap from the inside of the impact bar.
   b. Unfasten the retaining nuts and bolts, then remove the impact bar from the vehicle.
3. Remove the bumper bar/energy absorber assembly from the body.
4. If the energy absorber must be replaced, drill out the pop rivets and replace.
5. Installation is the reverse of the removal procedure.

1995-96 VEHICLES
▶ See Figure 14

1. Remove the front fascia, as follows:
   a. Remove the right and left splash shields.
   b. Unfasten the fender-to-fascia retaining bolts.
   c. Remove the retainers from the top of the fascia.
   d. Separate the fascia from the impact bar.
   e. Detach the connectors from the park and turn signal lamps.
2. Remove the energy absorber and the impact bar from the vehicle.
3. Installation is the reverse of the removal procedure.

2000 and Sunbird

1982-89 VEHICLES
▶ See Figures 15 and 16

1. Remove the front end panel/fascia, as follows:
   a. Unfasten the fascia-to-front end panel retainers.
   b. Remove the fascia-to-fender retainers.
   c. Detach the electrical connections, then remove the fascia.
   d. If necessary, remove the lamp assemblies and molding.
2. Remove the front fascia molding.
3. Unfasten the front impact bar-to-energy absorber retainers, then remove the impact bar.
4. Remove the bumper bar/energy absorber assembly from the body.
5. If the energy absorber must be replaced, drill out the pop rivets and install a new absorber with nuts, bolts and locking washers.
6. Installation is the reverse of the removal procedure.

1990-94 VEHICLES
▶ See Figures 17 and 18

1. Remove the front fascia as follows:
   a. Remove the front end panel.

b. Remove the push-in retainers.
c. Remove the air baffle.
d. Unfasten the bolts.
e. For SE and GT models, remove the retainers and bracket.
f. Unfasten the retaining bolts. Remove the parking lamps sockets.
g. Remove the fascia with the upper outer bracket from the vehicle.
h. Unfasten the retainers, then remove the upper outer bracket from the vehicle.
i. Remove the parking lamp assemblies.
2. Use a suitable prytool to carefully pry the molding from the fascia.
3. Unfasten the retaining nuts and bolts and remove the impact bar from the vehicle.
4. Remove the rivets, then remove the energy absorber from the vehicle.
5. Installation is the reverse of the removal procedure.

Skyhawk and Firenza
▶ See Figure 19

1. Remove the front end panel (fascia).
2. Remove the bumper bar/energy absorber assembly from the body.
3. If the energy absorber must be replaced, drill out the pop rivets and install a new absorber with nuts, bolts and locking washers.

Cimarron
▶ See Figure 20

1. Place a jack under the front bumper before removing the bolts to prevent it from dropping down when the bumper bolts are removed.

➡ Do not rotate the energy absorber any more than needed to align the mounting holes.

2. Remove the bumper extensions.
3. Unfasten the four nuts each side securing the bumper to the energy absorber unit, then remove the bumper from the vehicle.
4. Installation is the reverse of the removal procedure.

Sunfire
▶ See Figure 21

1. Remove the front fascia, as follows:
   a. Remove the right and left splash shields.
   b. Unfasten the fender-to-fascia retaining bolts.
   c. Remove the retainers from the top of the fascia.
   d. Separate the fascia from the impact bar.
   e. Detach the connectors from the park and turn signal lamps.
2. Unfasten the grille retaining screw, then remove the grille from the front fascia.
3. Remove the energy absorber and the impact bar from the vehicle.
4. Installation is the reverse of the removal procedure.

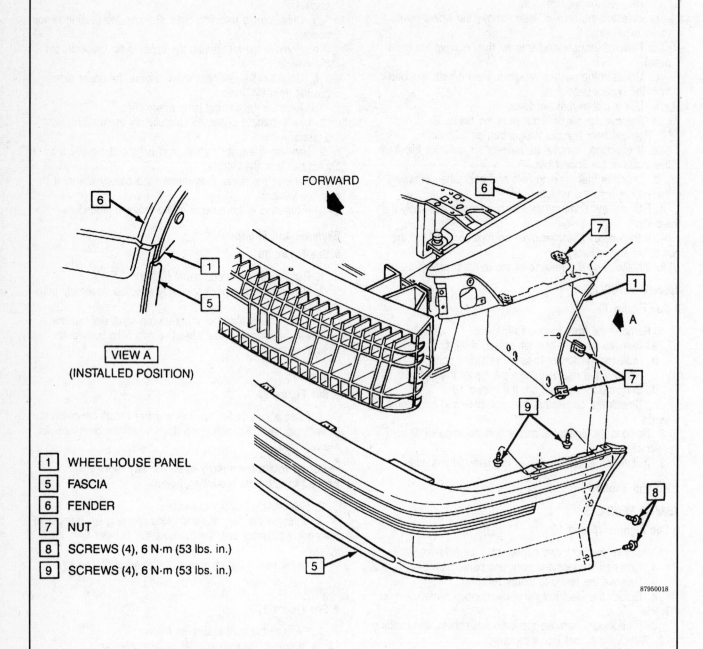

FORWARD

VIEW A
(INSTALLED POSITION)

1	WHEELHOUSE PANEL
5	FASCIA
6	FENDER
7	NUT
8	SCREWS (4), 6 N·m (53 lbs. in.)
9	SCREWS (4), 6 N·m (53 lbs. in.)

87950018

Fig. 12 Front bumper fascia mounting — 1989-94 vehicles

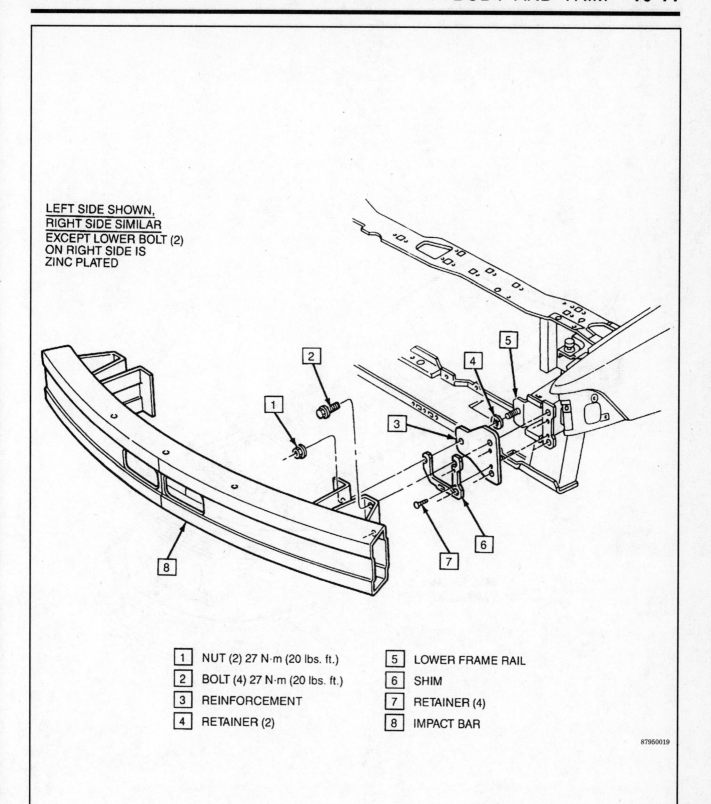

LEFT SIDE SHOWN,
<u>RIGHT SIDE SIMILAR</u>
EXCEPT LOWER BOLT (2)
ON RIGHT SIDE IS
ZINC PLATED

1	NUT (2) 27 N·m (20 lbs. ft.)	5	LOWER FRAME RAIL
2	BOLT (4) 27 N·m (20 lbs. ft.)	6	SHIM
3	REINFORCEMENT	7	RETAINER (4)
4	RETAINER (2)	8	IMPACT BAR

87950019

Fig. 13 Front impact bar mounting — 1994 Cavalier shown

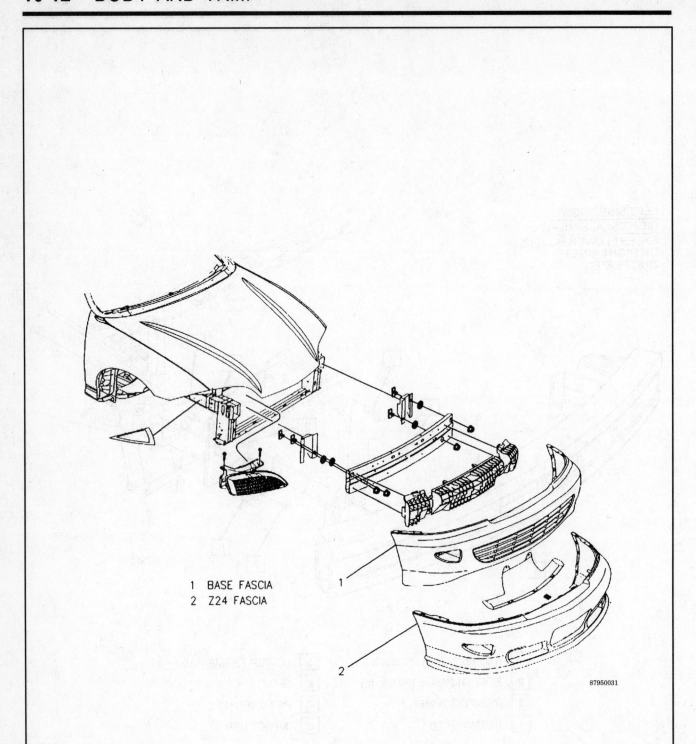

1 BASE FASCIA
2 Z24 FASCIA

87950031

Fig. 14 Exploded view of the front bumper components — 1995-96 Cavalier

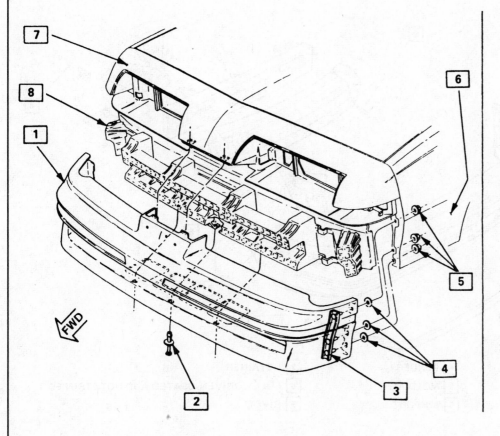

1—FASCIA

2—RETAINER (3)

3—RETAINER

4—RETAINER (PUSH-ON)

5—NUT

6—FENDER ASSEMBLY

7—PANEL ASSEMBLY

8—ABSORBER

87950021

Fig. 15 Front fascia mounting — 1989 Pontiac GT and SE shown

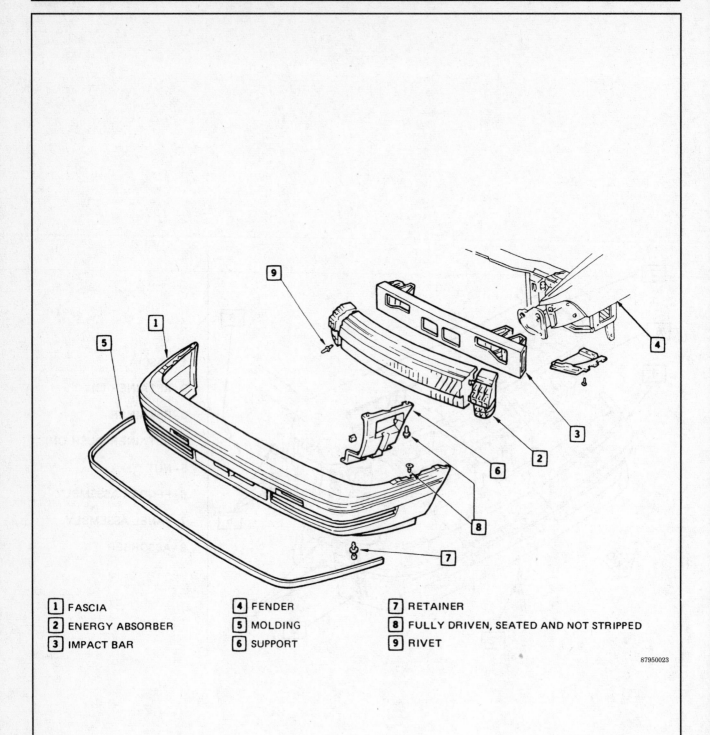

1 FASCIA
2 ENERGY ABSORBER
3 IMPACT BAR

4 FENDER
5 MOLDING
6 SUPPORT

7 RETAINER
8 FULLY DRIVEN, SEATED AND NOT STRIPPED
9 RIVET

87950023

Fig. 16 Exploded view of the front bumper mounting — 1989 Sunbird shown

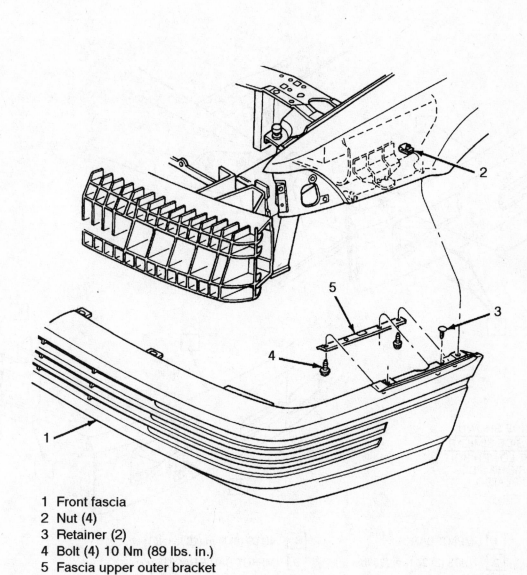

1 Front fascia
2 Nut (4)
3 Retainer (2)
4 Bolt (4) 10 Nm (89 lbs. in.)
5 Fascia upper outer bracket

87950024

Fig. 17 View of the fascia and bracket mounting — 1994 Sunbird shown

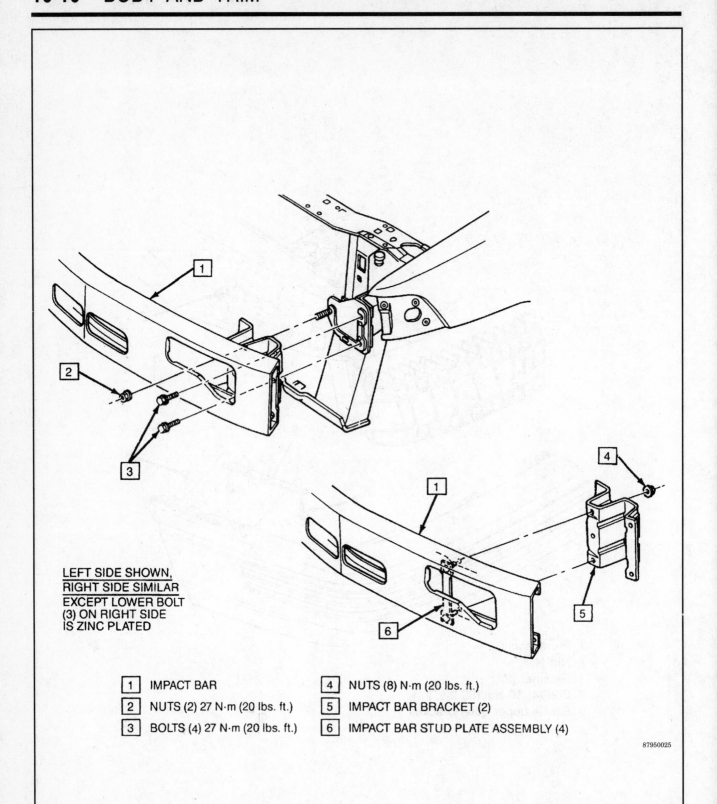

LEFT SIDE SHOWN,
RIGHT SIDE SIMILAR
EXCEPT LOWER BOLT
(3) ON RIGHT SIDE
IS ZINC PLATED

1	IMPACT BAR	4	NUTS (8) N·m (20 lbs. ft.)
2	NUTS (2) 27 N·m (20 lbs. ft.)	5	IMPACT BAR BRACKET (2)
3	BOLTS (4) 27 N·m (20 lbs. ft.)	6	IMPACT BAR STUD PLATE ASSEMBLY (4)

87950025

Fig. 18 Removing the impact bar — 1994 Sunbird shown

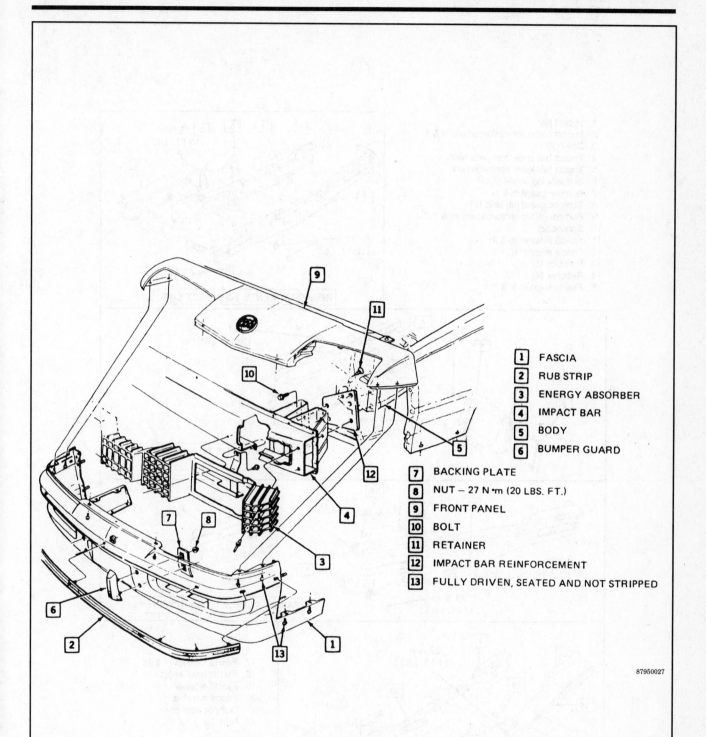

1 FASCIA
2 RUB STRIP
3 ENERGY ABSORBER
4 IMPACT BAR
5 BODY
6 BUMPER GUARD
7 BACKING PLATE
8 NUT — 27 N·m (20 LBS. FT.)
9 FRONT PANEL
10 BOLT
11 RETAINER
12 IMPACT BAR REINFORCEMENT
13 FULLY DRIVEN, SEATED AND NOT STRIPPED

87950027

Fig. 19 Exploded view of the front bumper assembly — 1989 Skyhawk shown

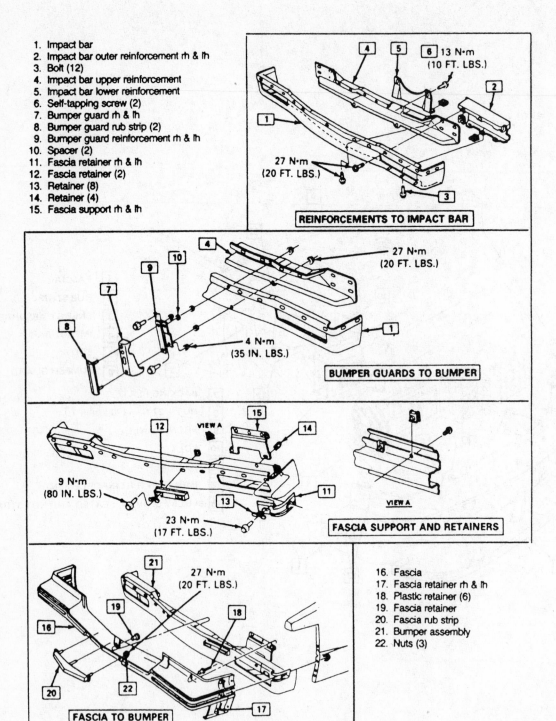

1. Impact bar
2. Impact bar outer reinforcement rh & lh
3. Bolt (12)
4. Impact bar upper reinforcement
5. Impact bar lower reinforcement
6. Self-tapping screw (2)
7. Bumper guard rh & lh
8. Bumper guard rub strip (2)
9. Bumper guard reinforcement rh & lh
10. Spacer (2)
11. Fascia retainer rh & lh
12. Fascia retainer (2)
13. Retainer (8)
14. Retainer (4)
15. Fascia support rh & lh

13 N·m
(10 FT. LBS.)

27 N·m
(20 FT. LBS.)

REINFORCEMENTS TO IMPACT BAR

27 N·m
(20 FT. LBS.)

4 N·m
(35 IN. LBS.)

BUMPER GUARDS TO BUMPER

VIEW A

9 N·m
(80 IN. LBS.)

23 N·m
(17 FT. LBS.)

VIEW A

FASCIA SUPPORT AND RETAINERS

16. Fascia
17. Fascia retainer rh & lh
18. Plastic retainer (6)
19. Fascia retainer
20. Fascia rub strip
21. Bumper assembly
22. Nuts (3)

27 N·m
(20 FT. LBS.)

FASCIA TO BUMPER

87950029

Fig. 20 Exploded view of the front bumper assembly — Cimarron shown

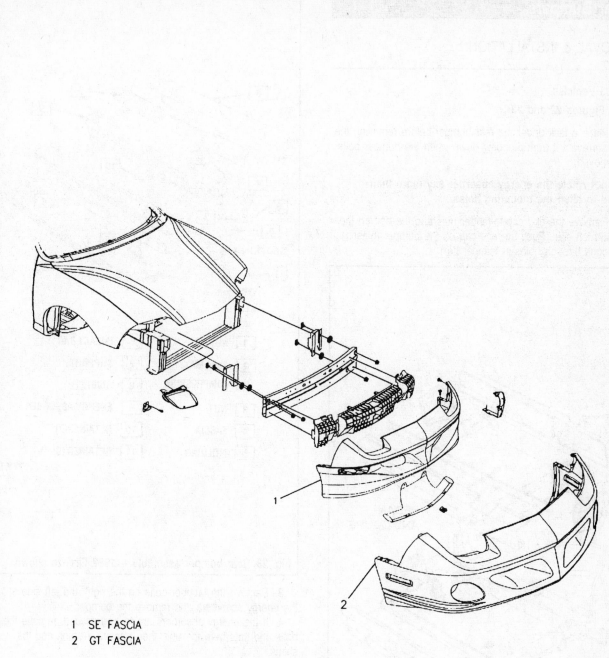

1   SE FASCIA
2   GT FASCIA

87950032

Fig. 21 Exploded view of the Sunfire front bumper components

Rear Bumpers

REMOVAL & INSTALLATION

1982-83 Vehicles

◆ **See Figures 22 and 23**

1. Place a jack under the rear bumper before removing the bolts to prevent it from dropping down when the bumper bolts are removed.

➡**Do not rotate the energy absorber any more than needed to align the mounting holes.**

2. Remove the end cap-to-fender nuts and the bolt on the right and left side. Push the end cap off the bumper (plastic protrusions through holes in bumper bar).

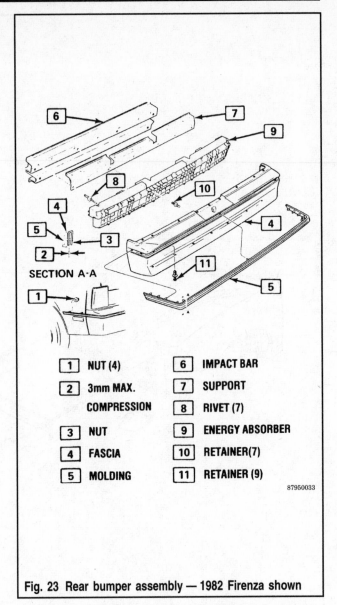

1 NUT (4)		**6** IMPACT BAR
2 3mm MAX. COMPRESSION		**7** SUPPORT
3 NUT		**8** RIVET (7)
4 FASCIA		**9** ENERGY ABSORBER
5 MOLDING		**10** RETAINER(7)
		11 RETAINER (9)

87950033

Fig. 23 Rear bumper assembly — 1982 Firenza shown

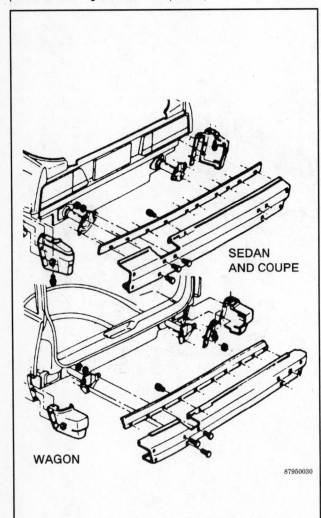

SEDAN AND COUPE

WAGON

87950030

Fig. 22 Exploded view of the rear bumper assembly — 1982-87 Cavalier shown

3. Remove the bumper bolts on the right and left side at the energy absorbers and remove the bumper.

4. If the energy absorbers are to be replaced, remove the bolts and nuts from the unit, then remove the unit and the shims.

To install:

5. Install the energy and absorber and shims if removed.

6. Check the dimension and add/subtract shims as needed.

7. Support the bumper to prevent rotation of the energy absorbers.

8. Install the bolts at the bumper to energy absorber brackets, and end cap to fender nuts and bolts.

9. If adjustment is required to align bumper, loosen the energy absorber mounting bolts and position as required (holes are slotted). Adjustment side-to-side can be made by loosening the bumper bracket bolts. Tighten all bolts and nuts.

1984-87 Vehicles

▶ **See Figure 24**

1. Place a jack under the rear bumper before removing the bolts to prevent it from dropping down when the bumper bolts are removed.

➡**Do not rotate the energy absorber any more than needed to align the mounting holes.**

2. Remove the bumper fascia.
3. Remove the bumper bolts on the right and left side and remove the bumper.
4. If the energy absorbers are to be replaced, remove the bolts and nuts, then remove the unit and the shims.

To install:

5. Install the energy absorber and shims if removed.
6. Check the dimension and add/subtract shims as needed.
7. Support the bumper to prevent rotation of the energy absorbers.
8. Install the bolts at the bumper to energy absorber brackets, and end cap to fender nuts and bolts.

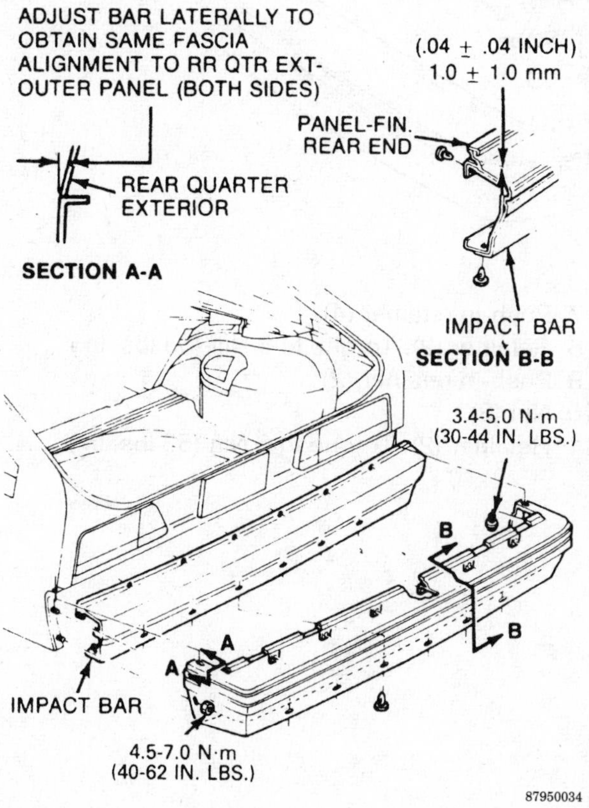

ADJUST BAR LATERALLY TO OBTAIN SAME FASCIA ALIGNMENT TO RR QTR EXT-OUTER PANEL (BOTH SIDES)

(.04 + .04 INCH)
1.0 + 1.0 mm

PANEL-FIN. REAR END

REAR QUARTER EXTERIOR

SECTION A-A

IMPACT BAR
SECTION B-B

3.4-5.0 N·m
(30-44 IN. LBS.)

B

B
B
A
A
A

IMPACT BAR

4.5-7.0 N·m
(40-62 IN. LBS.)

87950034

Fig. 24 View of the rear bumper fascia — 1987 Cavalier shown

9. If adjustment is required to align bumper, loosen the energy absorber mounting bolts and position as required (holes are slotted). Adjustment side-to-side can be made by loosening the bumper bracket bolts. Torque all bolts and nuts.

1988-94 Vehicles

▶ **See Figure 25**

1. Remove side marker lamp assemblies.
2. Unfasten the lower and upper push-in retainers.
3. For 2-door vehicles, remove the fascia seal.
4. Remove the retainers and fascia with supports from vehicle.
5. Remove fascia support from impact bar.
6. If equipped, use a suitable prytool to remove the rear fascia molding from the fascia.
7. Unfasten impact bar retaining nuts and remove the impact bar from energy absorbers.
8. Remove the energy absorber retaining nuts and remove the energy absorber.
9. Installation is the reverse of the removal procedure. Transfer all supports, shims, brackets, retainers and moldings as necessary if replacing with new parts.

1995-96 Vehicles

▶ **See Figures 26 and 27**

1. Remove the rear fascia as follows:
   a. Remove the upper storage net retainers inside the trunk for access to the fascia retaining screws.
   b. Unfasten the two retaining screws from inside the trunk.
   c. Unfasten the four fascia retaining screws located in the rear wheel housing.
   d. Remove the push-in retainers from the lower fascia, then remove the fascia from the impact bar.
2. Remove the energy absorber by removing the rivets. Depending upon application, they may be regular or push-in type rivets.
3. Unfasten the impact bar-to-rear end panel retaining nuts and remove the impact bar from the vehicle.
4. Installation is the reverse of the removal procedure.

Grille

REMOVAL & INSTALLATION

➡**The following procedure includes removal of the front end panel.**

Cavalier

1982-87 MODELS

1. Open the hood.
2. Remove the headlamp bezel screws (there are usually 2 each).
3. Remove the bolt at each fender-to-front end panel at the upper corner near the headlamp.
4. Disconnect the turn signal lamp socket and head lamp wiring.

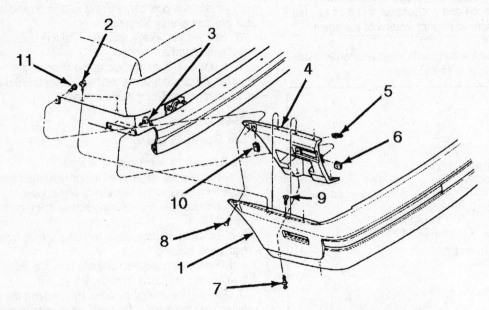

1 Fascia
2 Retainer (4). Torque to 6 Nm (53 lbs. in.)
3 Retainer (4). Torque to 6 Nm (53 lbs. in.)
4 Support (2)
5 Nut (4)
6 Nut (4)

7 Push-in retainer (4)
8 Retainer (2). Torque to 6 Nm (53 lbs. in.)
9 Push-in retainer (2)
10 Nut (2)
11 Retainer (2). Torque to 6 Nm (53 lbs. in.)

87950037

Fig. 25 View of the rear fascia supports — 1994 Sunbird shown

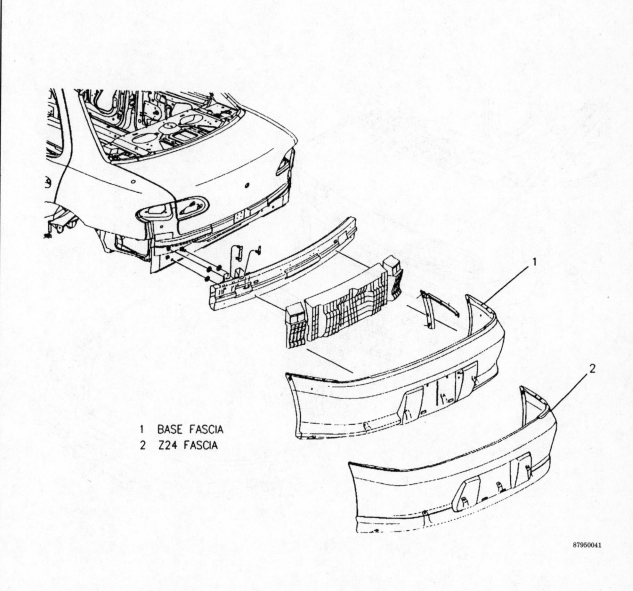

1 BASE FASCIA
2 Z24 FASCIA

87950041

Fig. 26 Exploded view of the rear bumper components — Cavalier shown

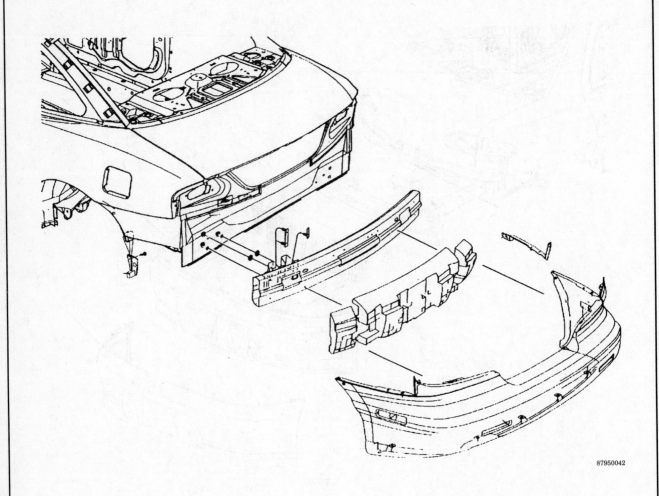

87950042

Fig. 27 Exploded view of the rear bumper components — Sunfire shown

5. Unfasten the screw at each turn signal housing, then remove the housings.

6. Remove the bolt from the panel-to-radiator support located below the turn signal housing area.

7. Unfasten the nut at the panel to the inner fender.

8. Remove the two nuts attaching the bumper end cap to the panel at each side.

9. Remove the three bolts at the baffles located at the radiator support.

10. Transfer the headlamps and grille.

11. Installation is the reverse of the removal procedure.

1988-90 MODELS

▶ See Figure 28

1. Remove the grille push-in retainers, then remove the grille panel from the vehicle.

To install:

2. Position the grille panel to the headlamp and grille mounting panel.

3. Install the push-in retainers in the following sequence:
   a. Top center retainer
   b. Both upper outer retainers
   c. Both bottom retainers

1991-94 MODELS

1. Unfasten the grille retaining screws.

2. Remove the grille panel.

To install:

3. Position the grille panel to the headlamp module assembly.

4. Install the retaining screws and tighten to 13 inch lbs. (2 Nm).

Sunbird, Cimarron, Skyhawk, Firenza

▶ See Figures 29, 30, 31 and 32

On these models please refer to the illustrations. Beginning in 1990, the Sunbird has a separate grille similar to that of the Cavalier, refer to those procedures for removal and installation.

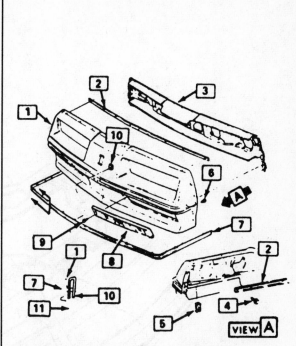

1. Front end panel (fascia)
2. Retainer
3. Reinforcement assembly
4. Screw (9)
5. Nut (16)
6. Screw (6)
7. Moulding
8. Grille (l.h. shown)
9. Screw (16)
10. Nut (15)
11. 3mm max compression

87950045

Fig. 29 Front end panel and grille assembly — Firenza

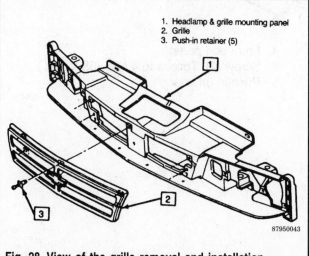

1. Headlamp & grille mounting panel
2. Grille
3. Push-in retainer (5)

87950043

Fig. 28 View of the grille removal and installation — 1988-90 Cavalier

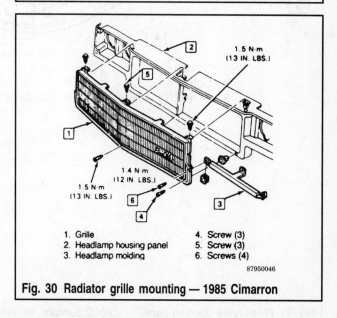

1. Grille
2. Headlamp housing panel
3. Headlamp molding
4. Screw (3)
5. Screw (3)
6. Screws (4)

87950046

Fig. 30 Radiator grille mounting — 1985 Cimarron

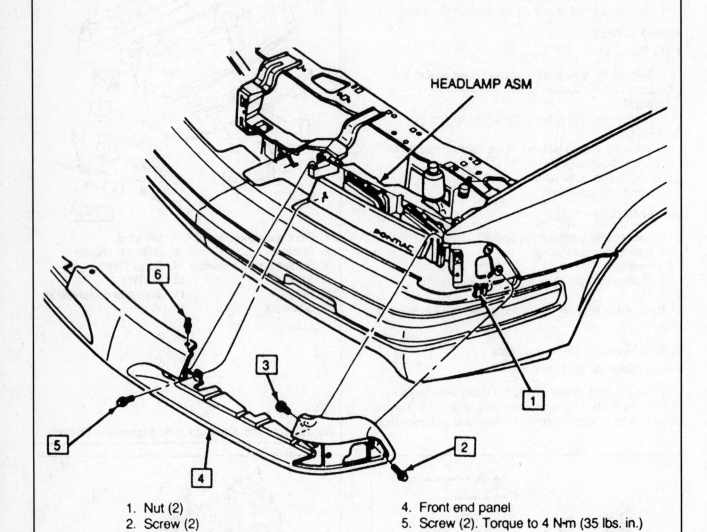

HEADLAMP ASM

1. Nut (2)
2. Screw (2)
3. Screw (2). Torque to 4 N·m (35 lbs. in.)
4. Front end panel
5. Screw (2). Torque to 4 N·m (35 lbs. in.)
6. Push-in retainer

87950048

Fig. 31 Front grille opening panel — 1990-92 Sunbird, except LE

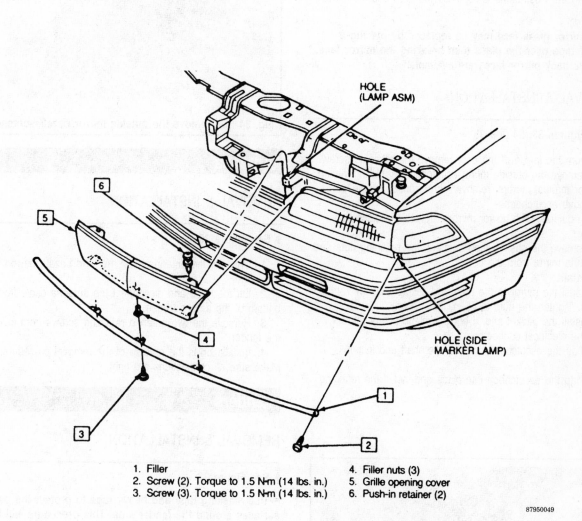

HOLE
(LAMP ASM)

HOLE (SIDE
MARKER LAMP)

1. Filler
2. Screw (2). Torque to 1.5 N·m (14 lbs. in.)
3. Screw (3). Torque to 1.5 N·m (14 lbs. in.)
4. Filler nuts (3)
5. Grille opening cover
6. Push-in retainer (2)

87950049

Fig. 32 Front end panel — 1990 Sunbird LE

Outside Mirrors

With the remote control door outside mirror, the remote control mirror cable must be disengaged from the door trim assembly on the standard trim styles to permit trim panel removal.

On custom trim styles the remote control mirror cable must be disengaged from the upper trim panel and the upper trim panel must be removed to permit lower trim panel removal.

Refer to the illustrations for both custom trim and standard trim.

➡**The mirror glass face may be replaced by placing a piece of tape over the glass then breaking the mirror face. Adhesive back mirror faces are available.**

REMOVAL & INSTALLATION

▶ **See Figures 33, 34 and 35**

1. From the inside of the door remove the retaining screw.
2. Remove the outside mirror escutcheon by pulling inward.
3. For manual mirrors, remove mirror control handle/knob and remove escutcheon.
4. If equipped with power mirrors, detach the electrical connector.
5. Remove the gasket, then unfasten the retaining nuts and remove the mirror from the door.

To install:

6. Install the mirror to the door and secure with the retaining nuts. Tighten the nuts to 45 in. lbs. (5 Nm).
7. Install the gasket and, if equipped with power mirrors, attach the electrical connector.
8. Slide the escutcheon onto handle shaft and install handle.
9. Snap the escutcheon into place and install the retaining screw.

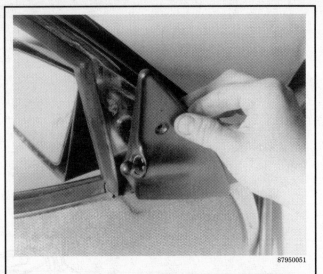

Fig. 34 . . . remove the outside mirror bezel/escutcheon

Antenna

REMOVAL & INSTALLATION

▶ **See Figure 36**

1. Unscrew the antenna mast, nut and bezel from on top of the fender.
2. Lift the hood and disconnect the antenna cable from the bottom of the antenna base.
3. Remove the two antenna retaining screws from inside the fender.
4. Installation is the reverse of the removal procedure. Make sure all connections are tight.

Fenders

REMOVAL & INSTALLATION

▶ **See Figure 37**

➡**Use masking tape and heavy rags to protect the painted surfaces around the fender area. This procedure will help avoid expensive paint damage during fender removal and installation.**

1982-88 Vehicles

1. Remove the lower air deflector.
2. Unfasten the three front end attaching screws. The grille must be removed for access to the top screw.
3. Remove the rocker panel molding if equipped, then unfasten the lower rear attaching screw. Note the number and location of shims for installation.
4. Remove the wiper arms and cowl vent assembly. The two screws at the inside edge of hinge at the cowl are hidden.
5. If removing the fender that has the antenna, remove the antenna mast, nut and two retaining screws from fender. Allow the antenna housing to fall, the antenna will stay in the car.

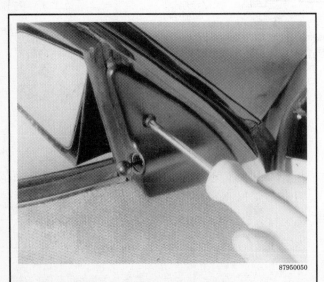

Fig. 33 Unfasten the retaining screw, then . . .

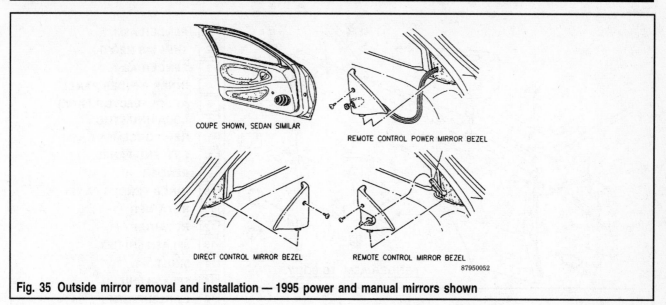

COUPE SHOWN, SEDAN SIMILAR

REMOTE CONTROL POWER MIRROR BEZEL

DIRECT CONTROL MIRROR BEZEL

REMOTE CONTROL MIRROR BEZEL

87950052

Fig. 35 Outside mirror removal and installation — 1995 power and manual mirrors shown

6. Unfasten the top fender attaching screws, then remove the fender assembly. Remove the inner fender panel and all attached parts and transfer onto new fender.

7. Installation is the reverse of the removal procedure.

1989-94 Vehicles

1. Remove the wiper arm assemblies, the shroud panel retaining screws, the washer nozzle hose, then remove the shroud panel.

2. Remove the side marker lamp.

3. Remove the front end panel.

4. If equipped, remove the rocker panel molding.

5. Raise and safely support vehicle on jack stands.

6. Remove the tire and wheel assembly, unfasten the attaching bolts and/or retaining clips from inner wheel housing, then remove the wheel housing.

7. Noting the number and location of any shims, remove the upper and lower fender attaching bolts and shims.

8. Remove the fender and transfer remaining parts onto the new fender.

9. Installation is the reverse of the removal procedure.

1995-96 Vehicles

1. Have an assistant support the hood, then unfasten the hood hinge pivot bolts and remove the hood from the vehicle.

2. Raise and safely support the vehicle, then remove the tire and wheel assembly.

3. Remove the splash shield and wheel housing.

4. Unfasten the fender lower bracket retaining bolts, then remove the bracket.

5. For the Cavalier, remove the front side marker lamp.

6. Detach the front fascia from the fender.

7. Unfasten the fender insulator retainers, then remove the insulator.

8. Remove the fender center bracket retaining bolts, then remove the bracket.

9. Unfasten the lower hood hinge bolts, then remove the hinge.

10. Remove the fender retaining bolts, then remove the fender from the vehicle.

11. Installation is the reverse of the removal procedure.

1 BRACKET ASSEMBLY
2 BEZEL
3 LEAD, ANTENNA
4 SCREWS
5 MAST, FINGERTIGHT, THEN
  TIGHTEN 1/4 TURN

87950053

Fig. 36 View of the antenna mounting — 1995 vehicle shown

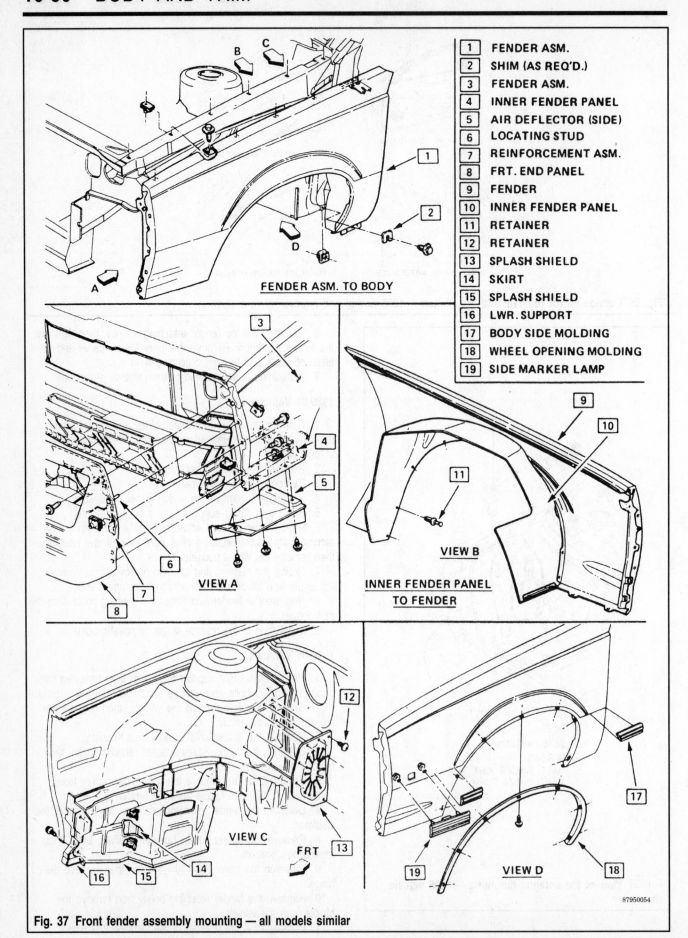

1	FENDER ASM.
2	SHIM (AS REQ'D.)
3	FENDER ASM.
4	INNER FENDER PANEL
5	AIR DEFLECTOR (SIDE)
6	LOCATING STUD
7	REINFORCEMENT ASM.
8	FRT. END PANEL
9	FENDER
10	INNER FENDER PANEL
11	RETAINER
12	RETAINER
13	SPLASH SHIELD
14	SKIRT
15	SPLASH SHIELD
16	LWR. SUPPORT
17	BODY SIDE MOLDING
18	WHEEL OPENING MOLDING
19	SIDE MARKER LAMP

FENDER ASM. TO BODY

VIEW A

VIEW B

INNER FENDER PANEL
TO FENDER

VIEW C

FRT

VIEW D

87950054

Fig. 37 Front fender assembly mounting — all models similar

Convertible Top

TOP REPLACEMENT

1982-94 Vehicles

▶ **See Figures 38, 39, 40, 41, 42, 43, 44, 45, 46 and 47**

1. Install a spacer stick between the No. 3 and No. 4 bow to keep the No. 4 bow in position.

2. Remove the rear belt moldings by removing the attaching screws from rear compartment drain trough. Remove the quarter belt moldings by unfastening the screws and attaching nuts from the rear compartment and underneath the right and left sides of folding top well.

3. Apply a protective cover on the rear deck surface and quarter panel painted areas.

4. Using a sharp grease pencil, mark the location of the complete belt tacking strip (upper edge) on outer surface of top cover.

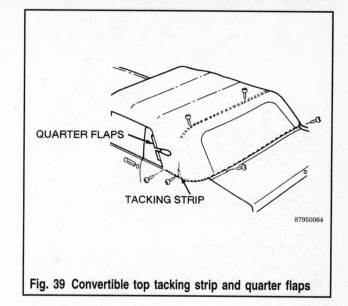

87950064

Fig. 39 Convertible top tacking strip and quarter flaps

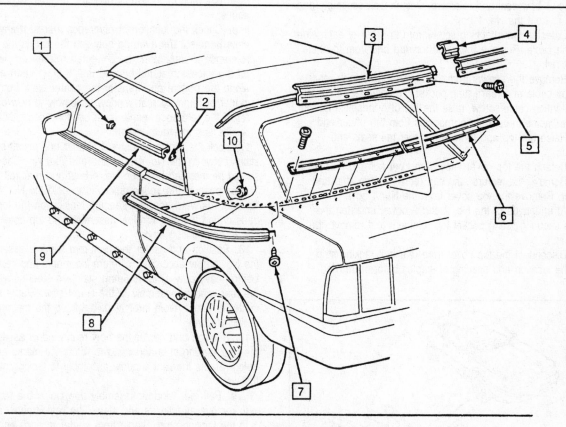

1	QUARTER PANEL BELT MOLDING CAP		6	RETAINER
2	ISOLATOR		7	SCREW
3	MOLDING ASSEMBLY BACK BELT		8	MOLDING QUARTER PANEL BELT
4	BACK BELT MOLDING CAP		9	MOLDING ASSEMBLY QUARTER BELT FRONT
5	SCREW		10	NUT

87950063

Fig. 38 Convertible quarter and back belt moldings

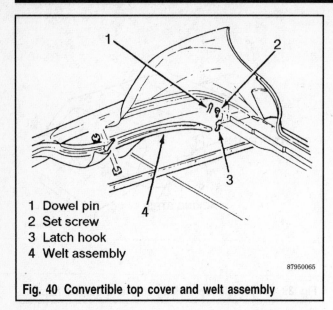

1 Dowel pin
2 Set screw
3 Latch hook
4 Welt assembly

87950065

Fig. 40 Convertible top cover and welt assembly

5. Raise the top to a suitable working height. Remove the front No. 1 bow seal and retainers. Detach welt assembly and top cover from the No. 1 bow.

6. Unfasten the attaching screw from the rear of each side retention cable. Remove the cable forward end from the hole in front rail.

7. Remove the screws from the lower end of each rear retention cable and rear listing pocket. To ease the removal of rear retention cable screw, raise the top off windshield header. Pull the cables through listing pockets from the upper end.

8. Raise the top and remove the rear rail seals and retainers.

9. Detach the top cover flaps from front rail and rear rail.

10. Remove the feature strip cap (end), feature strip and retainer. Remove the top cover from the No. 4 bow.

11. At underside of the No. 2 and 3 bows, unfasten the screws securing listing pocket top retainers and remove the retainers.

12. Disconnect the top cover from rear belt tacking strip. Note the location and spacing of staples before removing them.

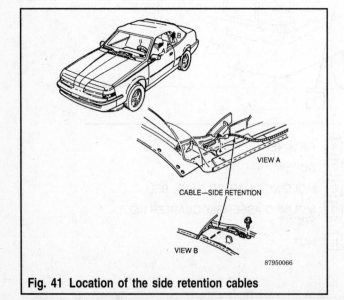

VIEW A

CABLE—SIDE RETENTION

VIEW B

87950066

Fig. 41 Location of the side retention cables

13. Mark the location of rear window outer panels along balance of rear belt tacking strip, and the No. 4 bow (upper and lower edge).

14. Recheck the tack strip location markings on rear window assembly. Remove stay pads and rear window assembly from the rear belt tacking strip and the No. 4 bow. Note the location and spacing of staples before removal.

15. Use a sharp grease pencil and mark the location of all belt molding attaching holes on the lower edge of tacking strip or on quarter panels.

To install:

16. Transfer the reference marks from removed rear window assembly as follows:

   a. Place the new rear window assembly on a clean covered work bench with inner surface down.

   b. Position the removed rear window assembly over new one, carefully align the upper window with the lower one.

   c. While holding both together securely, carefully lay out the trim material of both and transfer the rear window assembly reference marks along bottom portion of tacking strip.

   d. Reverse the rear window assemblies by placing the new rear window assembly over the original as described above.

   e. Check the location of reverence marks. If any difference is noted, the average between the two is the correct reference to use. Mark the corrected references clearly. Trim off the excess material beyond the ½ in. (13mm) allowance along the bottom and transfer the center mark from bottom center of removed rear window assembly to new one. Transfer of the reference marks must be done correctly for best results and minimum rework.

17. Lock the top to windshield header and install spacer sticks between the No. 4 bow and and rear rail. Spacer stick should be installed between No. 4 bow and rear rail back face. The purpose of the spacer sticks is to hold the No. 4 bow in its most rearward position, keeping tension on the top stay pads during the rear window assembly and top cover installation to belt tacking strips.

18. Position and center the new rear window assembly to the No. 4 bow according to reference marks and center notch. Using heavy duty ⅜ in. (9.5mm) stainless steel staples, staple the rear window assembly to the No. 4 bow. Staple from center to ends. Avoid stretching, but keep the material flat during stapling.

19. Position and center the new rear window assembly to the rear tacking strip according to reference marks and center notch. Staple the rear window assembly to tacking strip as follows:

   a. Pull rear window assembly down over the tacking strip to remove all fullness and staple the rear window assembly to the tacking strip. Staple from center to each end of the rear window assembly.

   b. Apply downward tension to the rear window assembly at each point of staple installation.

✴✴WARNING

Excessive heat may cause damage to the rear window. Extreme care should be exercised when following this procedure.

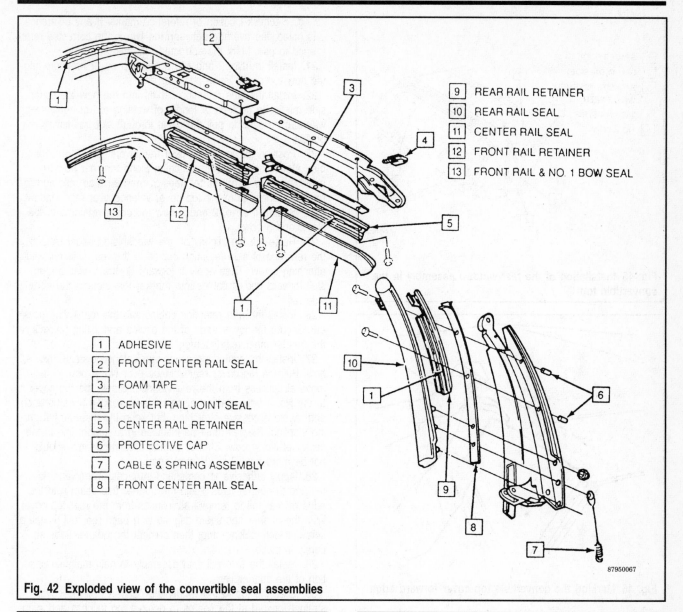

9 REAR RAIL RETAINER
10 REAR RAIL SEAL
11 CENTER RAIL SEAL
12 FRONT RAIL RETAINER
13 FRONT RAIL & NO. 1 BOW SEAL

1 ADHESIVE
2 FRONT CENTER RAIL SEAL
3 FOAM TAPE
4 CENTER RAIL JOINT SEAL
5 CENTER RAIL RETAINER
6 PROTECTIVE CAP
7 CABLE & SPRING ASSEMBLY
8 FRONT CENTER RAIL SEAL

87950067

Fig. 42 Exploded view of the convertible seal assemblies

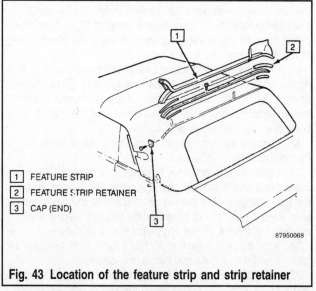

1 FEATURE STRIP
2 FEATURE STRIP RETAINER
3 CAP (END)

87950068

Fig. 43 Location of the feature strip and strip retainer

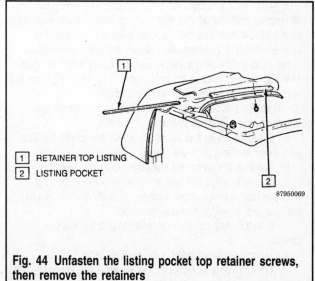

1 RETAINER TOP LISTING
2 LISTING POCKET

87950069

Fig. 44 Unfasten the listing pocket top retainer screws, then remove the retainers

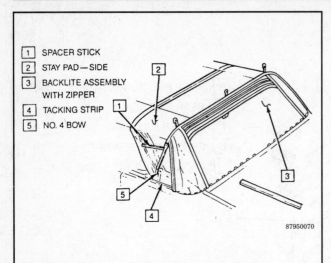

1. SPACER STICK
2. STAY PAD—SIDE
3. BACKLITE ASSEMBLY WITH ZIPPER
4. TACKING STRIP
5. NO. 4 BOW

87950070

Fig. 45 Installation of the rear window assembly in the convertible top

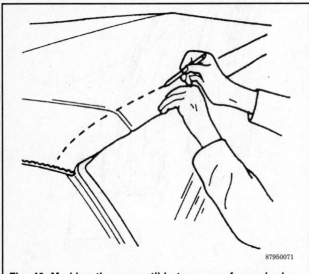

87950071

Fig. 46 Marking the convertible top cover forward edge

c. After rear window has been properly secured, trim off all excess material at the rear tacking strip. Staple stay pads to the No. 4 bow and belt tacking strip and remove the spacer sticks. If wrinkles are present following installation, apply heat to the rear window surface using a hot air gun. The hot air gun should be held about 2 in. (51mm) from the rear window and moved in a circular motion.

20. Transfer the reference marks from the removed top cover to the new one as follows:

a. Place the new top cover on a suitable clean surface, with inner surface of cover down.

b. Position the removed top cover over the new one.

c. Carefully align the rear window opening upper corners and the rear quarter upper corners of both covers. Secure both covers together at these locations.

d. Carefully lay out trim material of quarter area of both covers.

e. Transfer location marks for tacking strip.

f. Then reverse position of the covers by positioning the new cover over the original as described above.

g. Recheck location of reference marks. If any difference is noted, the average between the two is the corrected reference to use. Mark the corrected references clearly.

21. Install the No. 2 and No. 3 bow top cover retainers into the new top cover listing pockets.

22. Install the side retention cables into the new top cover side rail listing pockets. A length of welding rod or equivalent wire can be used to pull the cable through side rail listing pocket.

23. Position the top cover over framework. The top cover may require some lateral stretching along the rear bow to achieve proper fit of quarter flaps to the rear side rails and to remove fullness from the top cover valance over rear window.

24. Secure the No. 2 and 3 bow top cover retainers to the No. 2 and 3 bows.

25. Raise the top slightly off the windshield header. Attach the rear end of side retention cables to the rear side rail with attaching screw. Then apply a forward on the cables and install forward end of cables into the keyhole slots in the front side rail.

26. Install the rear retention cables into the rear listing pockets. Secure the lower ends of the cables and listing pockets to the quarter inner reinforcement with screws.

27. Install the center top cover rear valance over the No. 4 bow. Pull the top cover rear valance over No. 4 bow to remove all fullness from the rear valance. Staple the top cover to the No. 4 bow, starting at center and working towards each end. Avoid excessive stretching, but keep the material flat during stapling. Staples must be installed in a straight line in the center of No. 4 bow. Staples outboard of the seams should not be more than 2 in. (51mm) apart.

28. Apply adhesive to cementing surfaces of the rear side rail and to quarter flaps. Align the quarter flap seam with the edge of rear rail to remove all fullness from the rear top cover. With the quarter flap seam aligned with each rear rail, install a screw at belt tacking strip, then cement the quarter flaps securely in place.

29. Install the side rail seal assembly to help maintain position of the quarter flaps.

30. Lock the top to the windshield header. Pull top cover straight forward at the seams to desired top fullness and align the top cover seams with the notches in No. 1 bow. While maintaining tension on cover over the top of No. 1 bow, make pencil mark on the cover outer surface along the forward edge of top No. 1 bow.

31. Raise the top off header to a suitable working height. Apply adhesive such as 3M 0864 or equivalent, to cementing area of the top No. 1 bow, surface of top cover and to front corner flaps. Pull top cover 1/4 in. (6mm) past the reference point over the No. 1 bow and secure.

32. Trim the excess material to retaining screw holes for front rail and No. 1 bow seal.

33. Lower the top and lock to windshield header. Check appearance of the top trim, top operation and locking action of the top. If additional tension is needed in the top cover, repeat step 30 and pull the top cover farther forward. Staple and recheck the top for proper appearance and operation.

34. Align the welt assembly to No. 1 bow. Fold the vinyl flap back over the welt bulb and staple into position.

35. Apply adhesive to the stapled edge of the welt assembly and fold the vinyl flap over stapled surface of welt assembly.

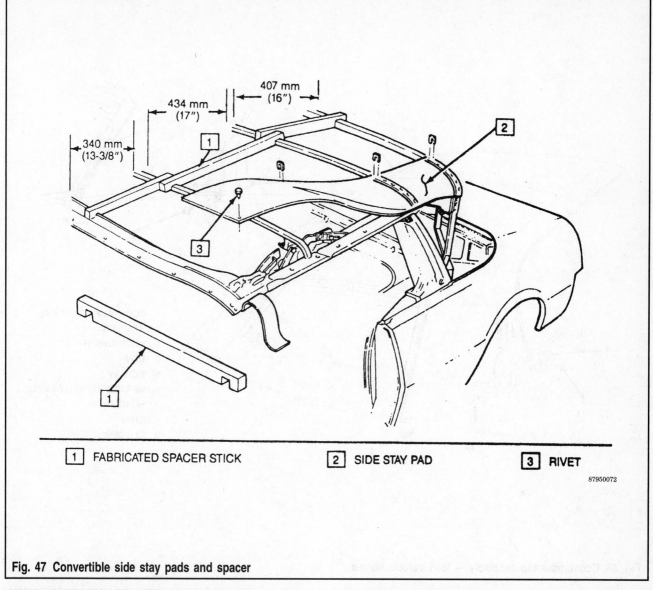

407 mm
(16")

434 mm
(17")

340 mm
(13-3/8")

| 1 | FABRICATED SPACER STICK | 2 | SIDE STAY PAD | 3 | RIVET |

87950072

Fig. 47 Convertible side stay pads and spacer

36. Carefully align the front rail retainers. Secure in position with attaching screws.

37. Apply weatherstrip adhesive to the retainer inner surface. Attach the front rail and No. 1 bow seal assembly to the front rail retainer and across the No. 1 bow. Secure the seal to the No. 1 bow with attaching screws.

38. Lock the top to the windshield header. Staple the top cover to the belt tacking strip starting at the rear rail and working rearward. Apply downward pressure to top cover at each point of staple installation. Avoid excessive stretching, but keep the material flat during stapling.

39. Install a pierce hole in the top material and tacking strip at each out board end of the No. 4 bow for feature strip and cap.

40. Install the rear bow feature strip retainer, feature strip and end caps using a clear silicone sealer.

41. Cut or pierce holes in the top cover and rear window assembly along the tacking strip for belt molding attaching studs and install belt moldings.

42. When complete, the folding top cover should be free from wrinkles and draws. Clean up top material and car as necessary.

1995-96 Vehicles

▶ See Figures 48 and 49

1. Disconnect the negative battery cable.
2. Unlatch the convertible (folding) top.
3. Remove the right and left side quarter trim panels.
4. Unfasten the screws retaining the headliner at the rear rail and quarter inner structure.
5. Remove the screws retaining the headliner to the closeout panel below the backlite.
6. Detach the heated backlite wire leads.
7. Remove the bolt, washer and bushing from the quarter window drive links and spur gears.
8. Carefully grasp and lower the quarter windows.
9. Make sure the note the wire routing, then detach the drive motor wire harness connectors.
10. Remove the retainers and fold the closeout trim panel forward.

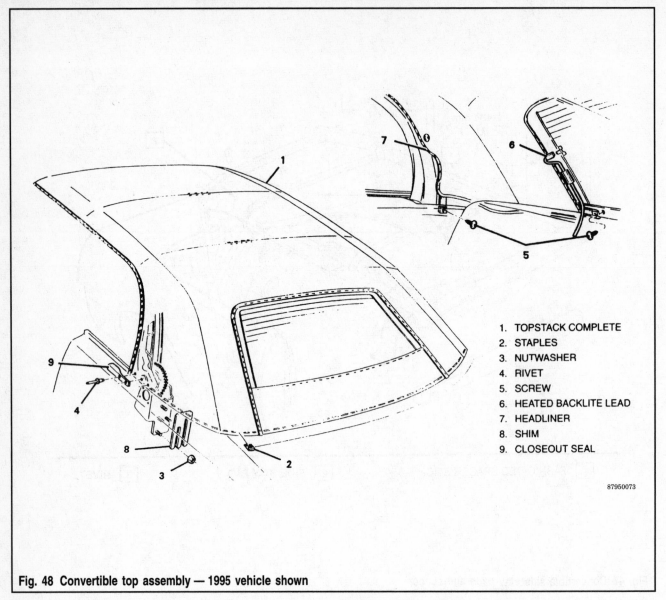

1. TOPSTACK COMPLETE
2. STAPLES
3. NUTWASHER
4. RIVET
5. SCREW
6. HEATED BACKLITE LEAD
7. HEADLINER
8. SHIM
9. CLOSEOUT SEAL

87950073

Fig. 48 Convertible top assembly — 1995 vehicle shown

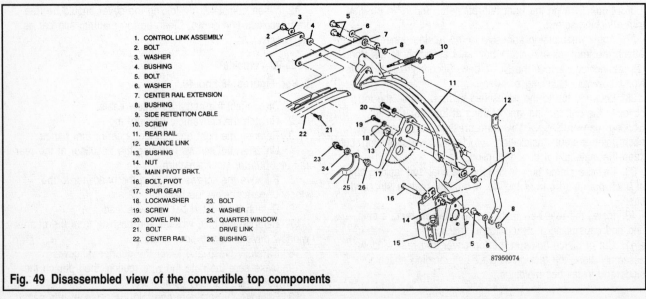

1. CONTROL LINK ASSEMBLY
2. BOLT
3. WASHER
4. BUSHING
5. BOLT
6. WASHER
7. CENTER RAIL EXTENSION
8. BUSHING
9. SIDE RETENTION CABLE
10. SCREW
11. REAR RAIL
12. BALANCE LINK
13. BUSHING
14. NUT
15. MAIN PIVOT BRKT.
16. BOLT, PIVOT
17. SPUR GEAR
18. LOCKWASHER
19. SCREW
20. DOWEL PIN
21. BOLT
22. CENTER RAIL
23. BOLT
24. WASHER
25. QUARTER WINDOW DRIVE LINK
26. BUSHING

87950074

Fig. 49 Disassembled view of the convertible top components

11. Remove the back molding.

12. Remove the right and left side quarter panel belt outer moldings.

13. Unfasten the two staples retaining the convertible cover, backlight and stay pads to the quarter belt tackstrip.

✳✳CAUTION

Protect eye goggles or safety glasses MUST be worn when drilling out the rivets to reduce the chance of personal injury.

14. Use a ⅛ in. (3mm) drill bit to drill out the four rivets retaining the convertible cover to the quarter belt flange.

15. Note the position of any shims used, then unfasten the three nutwashers retaining the main pivot bracket assembly to the mounting bracket.

16. With the help of an assistant, lift the convertible top assembly from the vehicle.

To install:

➡The convertible top assembly should be unfolded or in the UP position during installation to allow access to the main pivot bracket area.

17. As the convertible top is lowered into position, the quarter window drive links must be guided into the main pivot bracket to avoid trapping the links. With the help of an assistant, position the convertible top assembly to the vehicle, aligning the main pivot bracket doll pins with the holes in the mounting brackets.

18. If removed, install shims as noted between the mounting bracket and main pivot brackets.

19. Install the nutwashers retaining main pivot bracket assembly to the mounting bracket. Tighten the nutwashers to 17 ft. lbs. (23 Nm).

20. Attach the drive motor wire harness connectors to the body wire harness, routing the wires as noted during removal.

21. Connect the negative battery cable.

22. Attach the backlite assembly to the tackstrip. Fasten the heated backlite wire harness connectors.

23. Fasten the topcover and rear stay pads to the tackstrip and quarter panel structure flange.

24. Cycle and latch the convertible top to the windshield header and check the top's appearance and function.

25. Install the right and left side quarter panel belt outer moldings, then install the back belt molding.

26. Fasten the closeout trim panel and secure using the retainers.

27. Apply Loctite® 242, or equivalent, to the bolt threads. Carefully raise the quarter window glass and secure the drive links to the spur gears using the bushing, washer and bolt. Tighten the bolts 18 ft. lbs. (25 Nm).

28. Install the screws securing the headliner to the closeout panel below the glass backlite.

29. Fasten the screws securing the headliner to the quarter inner structure and rear rail.

30. Install the right and left side quarter trim panels.

MOTOR REPLACEMENT

If any parts of the motor and pump assembly are found to be inoperable, it is recommended that the entire unit be replaced with a new motor and pump assembly.

1982-94 Vehicles
▶ See Figure 50

1. Make sure the convertible top is in the full up position.

2. Disconnect the negative battery cable.

3. Remove the partition in the rear compartment to expose the motor/pump unit.

4. Disconnect the wiring harness, then remove the ground wire attaching screw and ground wire.

5. Place absorbent rags below hose connections and at the end of the fluid reservoir.

6. Vent the reservoir by removing then installing the filler plug.

7. Disconnect the hydraulic lines and cap open fittings to prevent leakage of fluid. Use a cloth to absorb any leaking fluid. Remove the motor/pump unit.

To install:

8. Fill the reservoir unit with DEXRON IIE® transmission fluid. Position the motor/pump unit in place.

9. Attach the hydraulic hoses, ensuring that each hose assembly has a seal ring in place. Connect the wiring harness, ground wire and attaching screw.

10. Connect the negative battery cable and operate the top through its up and down cycles until all the air has been bled from the hydraulic circuit.

11. Check connections for leaks and recheck the fluid in the reservoir. Level should be even with fill hole, install plug.

1995-96 Vehicles
▶ See Figure 51

TOP UP

1. Disconnect the negative battery cable.

2. Unlatch the convertible top from the windshield header.

3. Remove the quarter trim panel.

4. Unfasten the headliner screws at the rear rail and quarter panel structure. Fold the headliner to access the drive motor assembly.

5. Note the wire routing, then detach the drive motor wire harness connector from the body harness.

6. Unfasten the bolts and lockwashers retaining the motor to the main pivot bracket assembly.

7. Remove the motor assembly by lowering the motor from the bottom of the main pivot bracket.

To install:

8. Position the motor assembly to the main pivot bracket.

9. Apply Loctite® 242, or equivalent, to the bolt threads. Install the bolts and lockwashers retaining the motor to the main pivot bracket. Tighten the bolts to 9 ft. lbs. (12 Nm).

10. Route the motor wire harness over the main pivot bracket and wire harness and attach the wire connector to the body harness.

11. Connect the negative battery cable.

12. Check the convertible top motor operation.

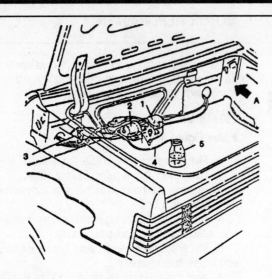

1. MOTOR PUMP ASSEMBLY
2. FILLER PLUG ADAPTER
3. BYPASS VALVE
4. HOSE
5. HYDRAULIC FLUID
   CONTAINER
6. TREE TYPE CLIP

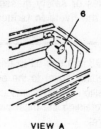

VIEW A

87950075

Fig. 50 Location of the convertible top motor — vehicles through 1994

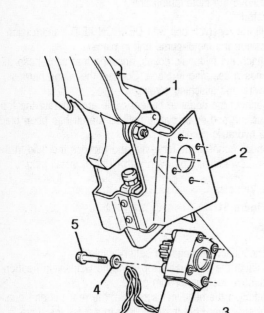

1 Rear rail
2 Main pivot bracket
3 Drive motor
4 Lockwasher
5 Bolt

87950076

Fig. 51 Drive motor assembly mounting — 1995 vehicle shown

13. Fasten the headliner to the rear rail and structure using screws.
14. Install the quarter trim panel.
15. Raise and latch the convertible top.

TOP DOWN

➡If the motor has seized and the convertible top is lowered, place the top bypass switch in the "Emergency Override" position and proceed as follows.

1. Disconnect the negative battery cable.
2. Remove the quarter trim panel.
3. Unfasten the headliner screw from the structure and position the headliner out of the way.
4. Unfasten the No. 4 bow slat-to-main pivot bracket bolt and spacer. Retain the bushing in the slat.
5. Remove the rear rail pivot bolt and nut at the main pivot bracket.
6. Apply Loctite® 242 or equivalent, to the bolt threads, then reinstall the No. 4 bow slat-to-main pivot bracket spacer and bolt. Tighten the bolt to 17 ft. lbs. (23 Nm).
7. Lift the rear rail and the spur gear off the motor gear and, with the help of an assistant, raise the convertible to the closed position. Do not latch the top.
8. Apply Loctite® 242 or equivalent, to the bolt threads, then fasten the bolt to the rear rail with the nut. Tighten the bolt to 17 ft. lbs. (23 Nm).
9. Remove and install the motor assembly, as outlined in the Top Up procedure beginning with Step 4.

Sunroof

The vista vent is a hinged window panel mounted to the roof of the vehicle. The vista vent is opened by moving the latch release handle forward and up to lock it in this position. When open, the rear of the window is raised about 1½ in. (38mm).

The vista vent can also be removed completely. First open the panel as previously described. Then press the latch handle release tab and lift the panel up and back to disengage the front hinges. To reinstall the vista vent, position the forward edge of the opening. Line up the hinge blades with the hinge slots and engage completely. If hinge binds in slot, reposition the panel in opening, DO NOT FORCE! Depress the latch

release tab and engage striker bar into latch recess. Rotate handle down and back to lock in the closed position.

✳✳CAUTION

Never attempt to remove the roof panel while the vehicle is being driven! The panel may either fly off or fall inside which may cause damage or personal injury.

INTERIOR

Instrument Panel

REMOVAL & INSTALLATION

1982-88 Vehicles
▶ **See Figures 52, 53 and 54**

1. Disconnect the negative battery cable.
2. Remove the left side instrument panel hush panel.
3. Remove the lower steering column trim cover and A/C outlet.
4. Remove center A/C duct and right close out panel (2 clips hold the A/C duct in the center). Disconnect the courtesy light.
5. Unfasten three steering column-to-instrument panel bolts and lower the steering column.
6. Remove the glove box door and trunk release switch, if so equipped.
7. Unfasten the two radio-to-instrument panel screws, then detach the electrical connectors and antenna lead from radio.
8. Remove the four cluster to instrument panel screws, disconnect the speedometer cable and remove the screw from the speed sensor.
9. Unfasten the three heater A/C control-to-instrument panel screws. Remove clip and screw securing the bowden cable to heater door.
10. Remove trim plate at right of steering column (spring clip attachment).
11. Detach the lighter connector. Remove headlamp switch knob and the trimplate at the left of the steering column. Unfasten the plastic nut at the headlamp switch, then remove the switch.
12. Remove rear defogger switch, if so equipped. Remove ashtray assembly and ashtray light. Remove hood release cable handle. There is one screw and a plastic nut securing the handle.
13. Remove defroster grilles by carefully prying them up, then unfasten the four screws at defroster outlets.
14. Unfasten the retaining screw, then remove the convenience center, then unfasten the two nuts and screw holding the instrument panel harness and bulk head connector. Remove the brace-to-glove box screw.
15. Remove the nuts at either side of the instrument panel carrier at the lower back of panel, then detach the electrical connectors (The instrument panel duct work must be removed from harness).

16. Remove the carrier and lay on seat. Remove A/C ductwork, screws and clips attaching the wiring harness to carrier.
17. Remove the radio speakers and grilles.
To install:
18. Install the radio speakers and grilles.
19. Install the carrier. Install A/C ductwork, screws and clips attaching the wiring harness to carrier.
20. Fasten the nuts at either side of instrument carrier lower back of panel and attach the electrical connectors.
21. Install the convenience center and secure with the retaining screw, and fasten the instrument panel harness and bulk head connector with the 2 nuts and screw. Install the brace-to-glove box screw.
22. Install the defroster grilles by snapping them into place, and fasten the four screws at defroster outlets.
23. Install rear defogger switch, if so equipped. Install ashtray assembly and ashtray light. Install hood release cable handle and secure with the screw and plastic nut.
24. Attach the lighter connector. Install headlamp switch knob and trimplate at left of steering column. Install the switch, Fasten the plastic nut at headlamp switch.
25. Install the trim plate at right of steering column and secure with the spring clip attachment.
26. Fasten the three heater A/C control-to-I.P. screws. Install clip and screw securing bowden cable to heater door.
27. Connect the speedometer cable and fasten the screw in speed sensor. Fasten the four cluster-to-instrument panel screws.
28. Attach the electrical connectors and antenna lead to radio. Install the 2 radio-to-I.P. screws.
29. Install the glove box door and trunk release switch, if so equipped.
30. Raise steering column, then secure with the three steering column-to-instrument panel bolts.
31. Install center A/C duct and right close out panel (2 clips hold the A/C duct in the center). Connect the courtesy light.
32. Install the lower steering column trim cover and A/C outlet.
33. Fasten the left side instrument panel hush panel.
34. Connect the negative battery cable.

1989-94 Vehicles
▶ **See Figure 55**

1. Disconnect the negative battery cable.
2. Remove the right and left sound insulators, steering column filler and the right and left instrument panel trim plates.
3. Remove the console housing and glove box door.
4. Remove the heater and A/C control head. For details, please refer to the procedure in Section 6 of this manual.

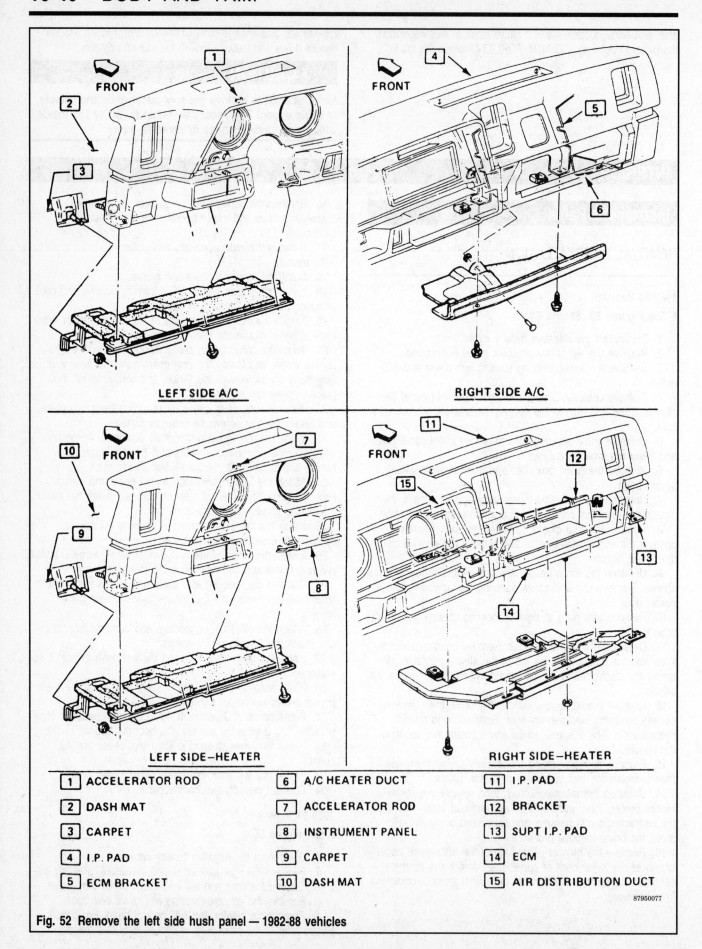

1	ACCELERATOR ROD	6	A/C HEATER DUCT	11	I.P. PAD
2	DASH MAT	7	ACCELERATOR ROD	12	BRACKET
3	CARPET	8	INSTRUMENT PANEL	13	SUPT I.P. PAD
4	I.P. PAD	9	CARPET	14	ECM
5	ECM BRACKET	10	DASH MAT	15	AIR DISTRIBUTION DUCT

Fig. 52 Remove the left side hush panel — 1982-88 vehicles

87950077

1 DASH
PANEL

2 WELD NUTS

3 CENTER REINF

4 PAD ASM.

5 SNAP-IN CLIPS

6 R.H. LOWER
I.P. TRIM PLATE

7 L.H. LOWER
I.P. TRIM PLATE

8 I.P. TRIM PLATE

9 TORX SCREW

10 HUSH PANEL

11 STEERING COLUMN
TRIM COVER

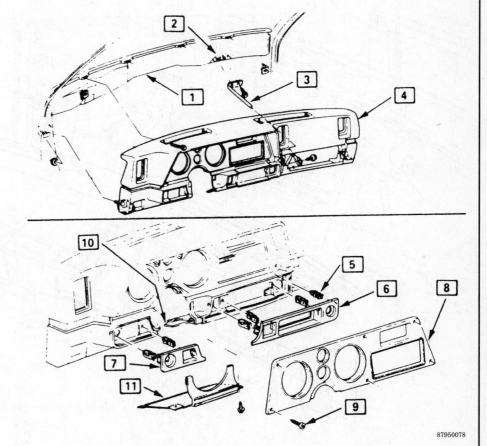

87950078

Fig. 53 Instrument panel and trim plate — 1982-88 vehicles

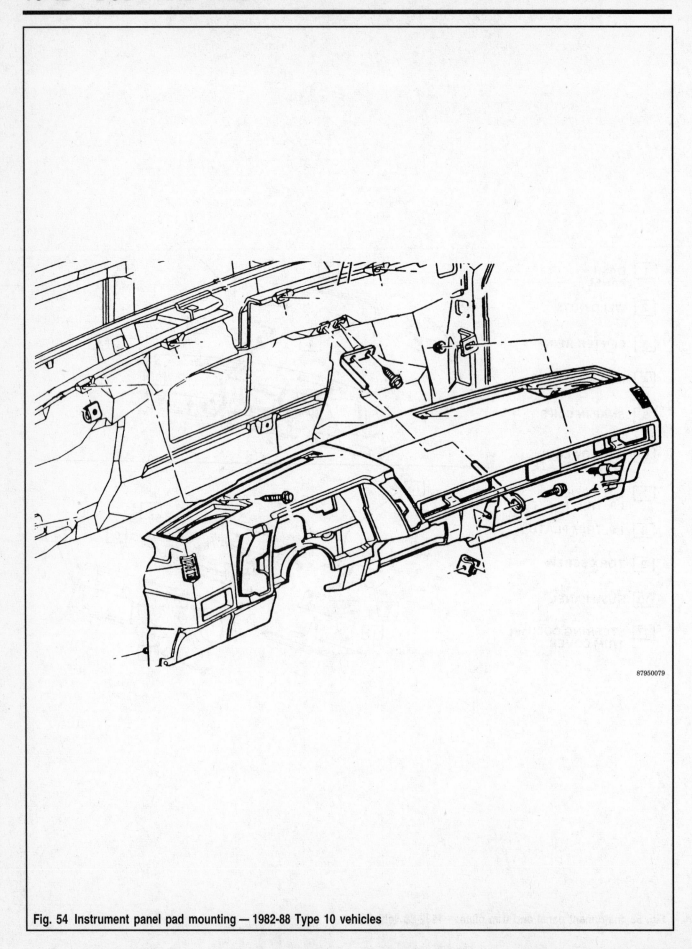

87950079

Fig. 54 Instrument panel pad mounting — 1982-88 Type 10 vehicles

5. Remove the convenience center. Disconnect the forward lamp harness and engine harness from bulkhead.

6. Remove the bulkhead from cowl. Remove the hood release handle (retained by two set screws), and defroster grilles.

7. Unfasten the four upper instrument panel retaining screws located in defroster duct openings. Remove the two lower corner instrument panel retaining nuts.

8. Remove the screw from the instrument panel brace at left side of instrument panel compartment opening.

9. For vehicles equipped with a manual transaxle, unfasten the two nuts securing the wire harness to the neutral start switch.

10. Unfasten the three steering column retaining bolts. There are two at the instrument panel pad and one at the cowl and lower steering column.

11. Pull the instrument panel assembly out far enough to disconnect the ignition switch, headlamp dimmer switch and the turn signal switch. Tag and detach all other electrical wiring connectors, vacuum lines and radio antenna lead to remove the instrument panel assembly.

12. Remove the instrument panel with wiring harness attached.

To install:

13. Position the instrument panel to the cowl and attach all electrical connectors and vacuum hoses.

14. Install the three steering column retaining bolts. Install the screw into instrument panel brace at left side of instrument panel compartment, then tighten to 57 inch lbs. (6 Nm).

15. Fasten the two lower corner instrument panel retaining nuts, then tighten to 12 inch lbs. (2 Nm). Install the four screws through defroster ducts into cowl, then tighten to 12 inch lbs. (2 Nm).

16. For vehicles equipped with a manual transaxle, install the two lower nuts securing the wire harness to neutral start switch.

17. Install defroster grilles, hood release handle, bulkhead and forward lamp and engine harness into bulkhead.

18. Install convenience center, heater A/C control assembly and glove box door.

19. Fasten the console housing, right and left trim plates and the steering column filler.

20. Secure the the left and right sound insulators.

21. Connect the negative battery cable.

1995-96 Vehicles

▶ See Figures 56, 57, 58, 59 and 60

1. If equipped, disable the SIR system, as outlined in Section 6 of this manual.

2. If not done already, disconnect the negative battery cable.

3. Unfasten the defroster grille retaining screw, then remove the grille.

4. To remove the instrument panel end-caps, for Cavalier, use a suitable prytool. Position the tool behind the cover and carefully pry outward. For the Sunfire, unfasten the end-cap retaining screws and remove the cap.

5. For the Cavalier, remove the instrument panel trim pad.

6. Remove the instrument cluster trim plate.

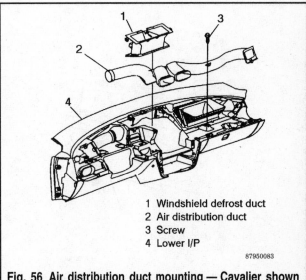

1 Windshield defrost duct
2 Air distribution duct
3 Screw
4 Lower I/P

87950083

Fig. 56 Air distribution duct mounting — Cavalier shown

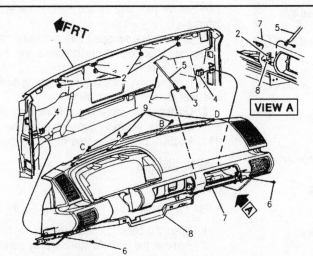

VIEW A

1   DASH PANEL
2   NUT
3   SCREW – 2 N·m (19 LBS. IN.)
4   NUT
5   I/P SUPPORT BRACKET
6   SCREW – 9 N·m (80 LBS. IN.)
7   INSTRUMENT PANEL
8   I/P TIE BAR
9   SCREW – 1.4 N·m (12 LBS. IN.)
A   TIGHTEN 1ST
B   TIGHTEN 2ND
C   TIGHTEN 3RD
D   TIGHTEN 4TH

87950081

Fig. 55 Instrument panel mounting — 1994 Cavalier shown

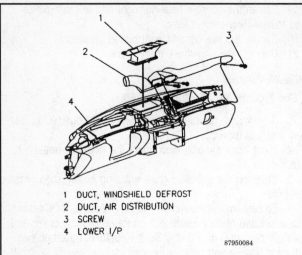

1 DUCT, WINDSHIELD DEFROST
2 DUCT, AIR DISTRIBUTION
3 SCREW
4 LOWER I/P

87950084

Fig. 57 Location of the air distribution duct mounting — Sunfire shown

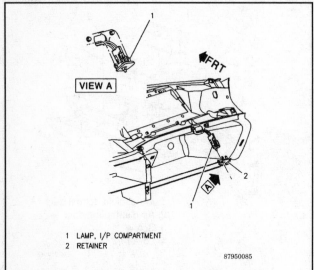

VIEW A

FRT

1 LAMP, I/P COMPARTMENT
2 RETAINER

87950085

Fig. 58 Detach the instrument panel lamp connector

7. As outlined in Section 6 of this manual, remove the heater and A/C control.

8. Remove the radio assembly, as outlined in Section 6 of this manual.

9. Unfasten the air distribution ducts.

10. Detach the instrument panel compartment lamp electrical connector.

11. Unfasten the screws to the tie bar, then remove the instrument panel from the tie bar.

To install:

12. Position the instrument panel to the tie bar, then secure with the retaining screws.

13. Attach the instrument panel compartment lamp connector.

14. Fasten the air distribution ducts.

15. Install the radio and the heater and A/C control.

16. Install the instrument cluster trim plate.

17. For the Cavalier, install the instrument panel trim pad.

18. Install the end caps.

19. Position the defroster grille, then secure with the retaining screw.

20. Enable the SIR system, if equipped. For details, please refer to the procedure located in Section 6 of this manual.

21. Connect the negative battery cable.

Console

REMOVAL & INSTALLATION

1982-94 Vehicles

◆ See Figures 61, 62, 63, 64, 65, 66, 67 and 68

➡Some of these steps may not be applicable for all vehicles.

1. Disconnect the negative battery cable.

2. Block the drive wheels of the vehicles, then place the gear selector/shift lever in the neutral position. Apply the parking brake.

3. Remove the accessory trim plate from the console housing. Remove the console trim plate.

4. Open the front ashtray, then remove the ashtray, and unfasten the screws (some models use Torx® screws) under the ashtray.

5. If necessary for console removal, remove the radio and the A/C and heater control.

6. If necessary, unfasten the console-to-instrument panel retaining screws.

7. For vehicles through 1992, if equipped with an automatic transaxle, gently pry out the emblem in the center of the shift knob, then remove snapring securing knob. Lift trimplate assembly out by pulling front end up first and disconnect wire harness.

8. On vehicles through 1992, equipped with a manual transaxle, remove the shift knob by removing the set screw under the knob or unscrewing the knob, as applicable. If necessary, detach the electrical connector

9. If necessary, unfasten the screws under the trim plate, then remove rear ashtray and remove the screw(s) under the ashtray.

10. On vehicles equipped with a manual transaxle, remove the screw under parking brake handle and 2 screws at sides of console in rear.

11. If necessary, unfasten the retaining screws in the console rear storage compartment.

12. Unfasten any remaining screws, then lift the console up and detach any electrical connectors and out of the vehicle.

13. Installation is the reverse of the removal procedure.

1995-96 Vehicles

CAVALIER

◆ See Figure 69

1. Open the console compartment.

2. Remove the console trim plate by gently prying it upward to disengage the retainers.

3. Unfasten the retaining screws, then remove the console.

4. Installation is the reverse of the removal procedure.

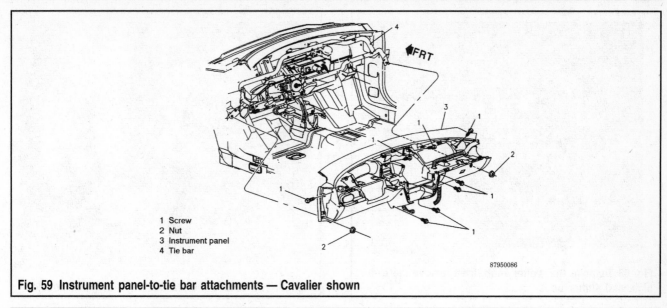

1 Screw
2 Nut
3 Instrument panel
4 Tie bar

87950086

Fig. 59 Instrument panel-to-tie bar attachments — Cavalier shown

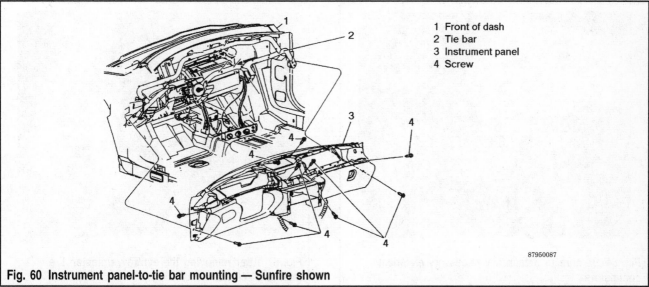

1 Front of dash
2 Tie bar
3 Instrument panel
4 Screw

87950087

Fig. 60 Instrument panel-to-tie bar mounting — Sunfire shown

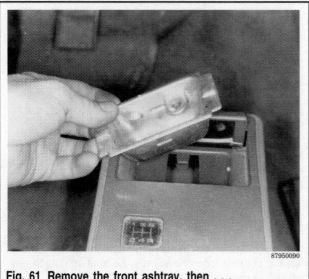

87950090

Fig. 61 Remove the front ashtray, then . . .

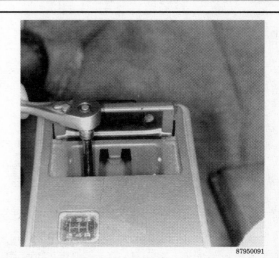

87950091

Fig. 62 . . . unfasten the retaining screws located under the ashtray

Fig. 63 Remove the shifter knob, then remove the trim plate and shifter boot

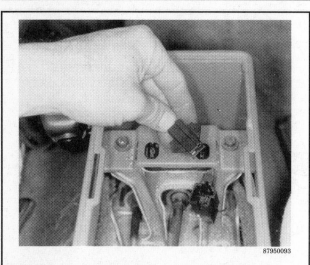

Fig. 64 Be sure to detach any necessary electrical connectors

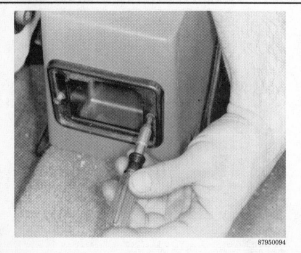

Fig. 65 Unfasten the rear ashtray retaining screws, then . . .

Fig. 66 . . . remove the rear ashtray from the console

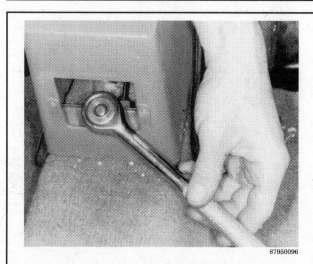

Fig. 67 After removing the ashtray, unfasten the retaining screws

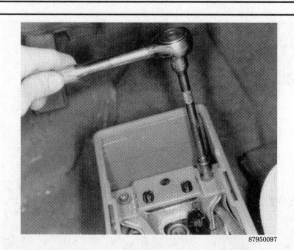

Fig. 68 Unfasten any remaining retaining screws, then lift the console from the vehicle. Be sure to detach any electrical connectors

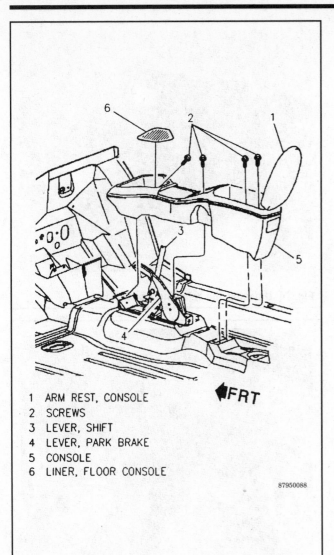

1 ARM REST, CONSOLE
2 SCREWS
3 LEVER, SHIFT
4 LEVER, PARK BRAKE
5 CONSOLE
6 LINER, FLOOR CONSOLE

87950088

Fig. 69 Unfasten the retaining screw, then lift the console from the vehicle — 1995 Cavalier shown

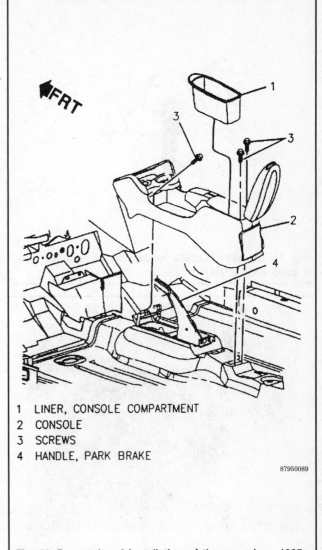

1 LINER, CONSOLE COMPARTMENT
2 CONSOLE
3 SCREWS
4 HANDLE, PARK BRAKE

87950089

Fig. 70 Removal and installation of the console — 1995 Sunfire shown

SUNFIRE

♦ See Figure 70

1. Remove the shift control handle by unfastening the retaining clip and lifting the handle off.
2. Lift off the shift lever boot.
3. Remove the console compartment liner.
4. Unfasten the four retaining screws, then remove the console from the vehicle.
5. Installation is the reverse of the removal procedure.

Door Panel

REMOVAL & INSTALLATION

♦ See Figures 71, 72, 73, 74, 75, 76, 77, 78, 79 and 80

A one piece trim panel is used on styles with standard trim. The custom trim has an upper metal trim panel. The one piece trim hangs over the door inner panel across the top and is secured by clips down the sides and across the bottom. It is retained by screws located in the areas of the top front of the panel assembly.

1. Remove all door inside handles.

→Removing a window crank handle (with a retaining clip inside the handle) without a special tool can be a problem. An alternative method is to take a clean shop towel and wedge it between the window crank handle and the door panel. Move it up, while pulling it from left to right, as in a sawing motion working the clean shop towel until the retaining clip comes free.

2. Remove the door inside locking rod knob.
3. Unfasten the screws inserted through the door armrest and pull the handle assembly into the door inner panel or armrest hanger support bracket.
4. On styles with remote control mirrors assemblies, disengage the end of the mirror control cable from the bezel on the standard trim, or from the upper trim panel on the custom trim. On custom trim, remove the upper trim panel.

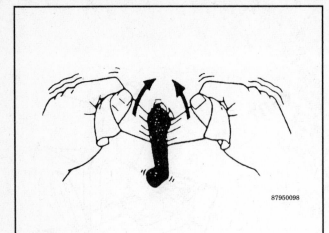

Fig. 71 The window crank handle may be removed with a clean shop towel

Fig. 72 Use a suitable tool to remove the trim "buttons", then . . .

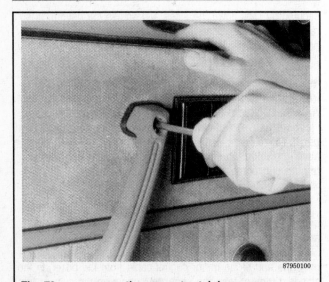

Fig. 73 . . . remove the armrest retaining screws

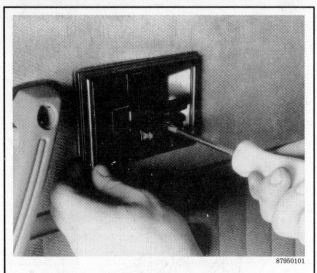

Fig. 74 Unfasten the retaining screw, then . . .

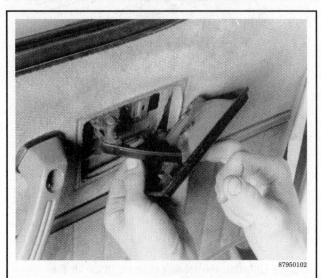

Fig. 75 . . . remove the inside door handle trim piece

5. On styles with power window or door lock controls located in the door trim panel, disconnect the wire harnesses at the switch assemblies. On the four door sedan and the two door hatchback, remove the switch cover by pushing down at the switch area and pulling down at the bottom of the cover. The switch and base may be removed from the trim with the cover removed.

6. Remove the remote control handle bezel screws.

7. Unfasten the screws used to hold the armrest to the inner panel.

8. Remove the screws and plastic retainers from the perimeter of the door trim using tool BT-7323A or equivalent and a screwdriver. To remove the trim panel, push the trim panel upward and outboard to disengage from the door inner panel at the beltline.

9. On styles with an insulator pad fastened to the door inner panel, use tool J-21104 or equivalent to remove the fasteners and the insulator pad.

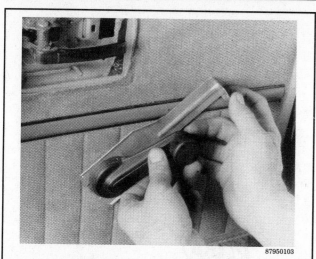

Fig. 76 Use of this special tool is the preferred method to remove the window crank handle

Fig. 77 Remove the window crank handle, then . . .

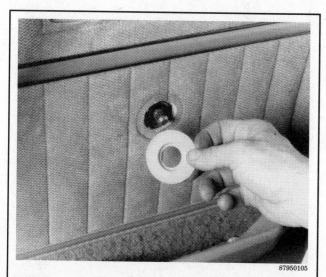

Fig. 78 . . . remove the washer from the door panel

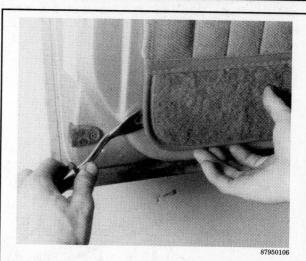

Fig. 79 A trim panel remover tool is very helpful to disengage the retainers when removing the door panel

10. On styles with the water defector held in place by fasteners, use tool BT-7323A or equivalent to remove the fasteners and the water deflector.

11. On styles with the armrest bracket riveted to the inner panel and installed over the water deflector, drill out the armrest bracket rivets using a 3/16 in. (5mm) drill bit.

To install:

12. To install the insulator pad or water deflector, locate the fasteners in the holes in the door inner panel and press in place. Replace all tape which may have been applied to assist in holding insulator pad or water deflector in place. Where necessary, install the armrest support bracket over the water deflector and onto the door inner panel using 3/16 in. x 11/32 in. (5mm x 9mm) rivets.

13. Before installing the door trim panel, check that all trim retainers are securely installed to the assembly and are not damaged. Replace retainers where required.

14. Attach all electrical components.

15. To install the door trim panel, locate the top of the assembly over the upper flange of the door inner panel, inserting the door handle through the handle slot in the panel and press down on the trim panel to engage the upper retaining clips.

16. Position the trim panel to the door inner panel so the trim retainers are align with the attaching holes in the panel and tap the retainers into the holes with the palm of your hand or a clean rubber mallet.

17. Install all previously removed items.

Door Locks

REMOVAL & INSTALLATION

▶ **See Figures 81 and 82**

1. Raise the window to the full up position.
2. Remove the inside door trim panel.
3. Detach the water deflector enough to access the lock actuator.
4. Disconnect the outside handle-to-lock assembly rod.

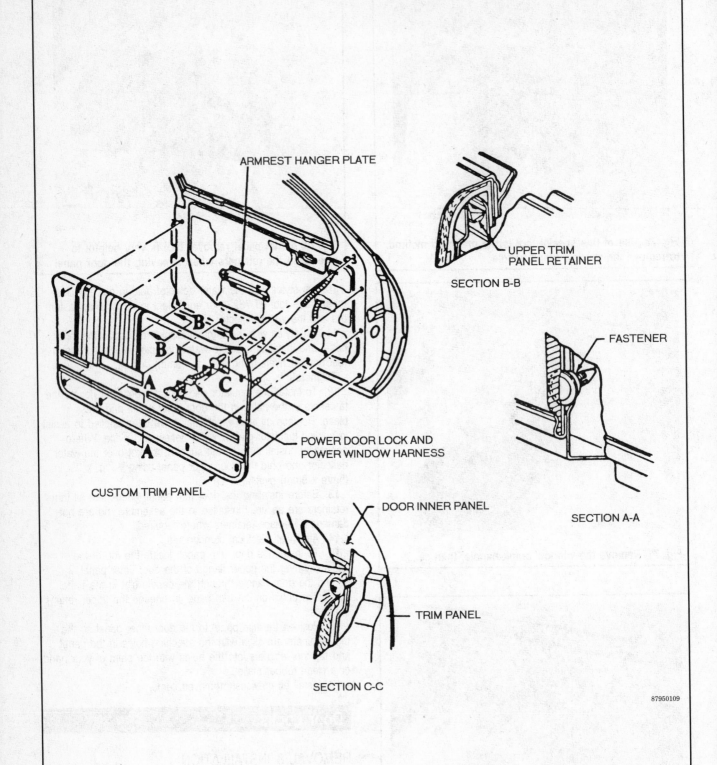

ARMREST HANGER PLATE

UPPER TRIM
PANEL RETAINER

SECTION B-B

FASTENER

SECTION A-A

POWER DOOR LOCK AND
POWER WINDOW HARNESS

CUSTOM TRIM PANEL

DOOR INNER PANEL

TRIM PANEL

SECTION C-C

87950109

Fig. 80 Common front door trim panel retention and fastener locations

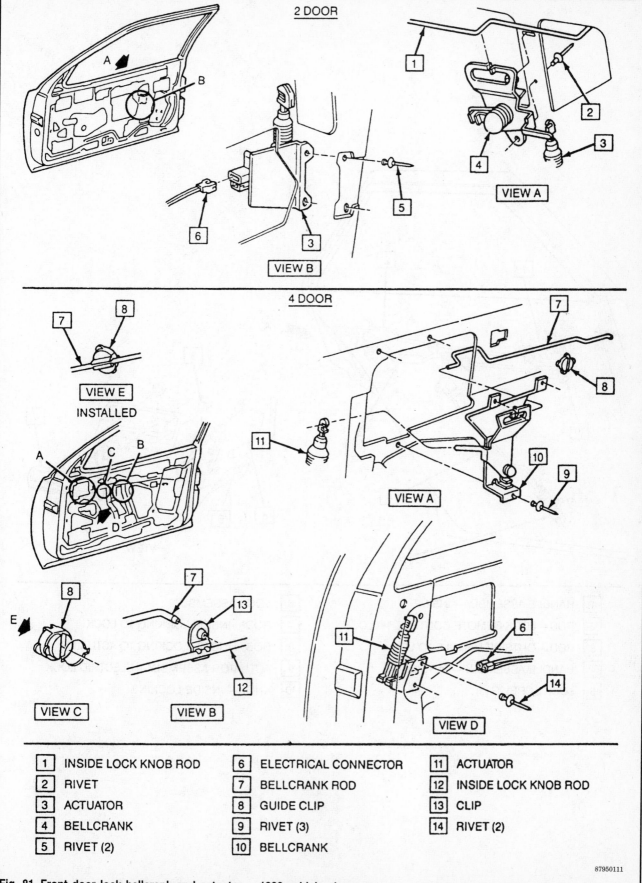

Fig. 81 Front door lock bellcrank and actuator — 1992 vehicle shown

1	INSIDE LOCK KNOB ROD	6	ELECTRICAL CONNECTOR	11	ACTUATOR
2	RIVET	7	BELLCRANK ROD	12	INSIDE LOCK KNOB ROD
3	ACTUATOR	8	GUIDE CLIP	13	CLIP
4	BELLCRANK	9	RIVET (3)	14	RIVET (2)
5	RIVET (2)	10	BELLCRANK		

87950111

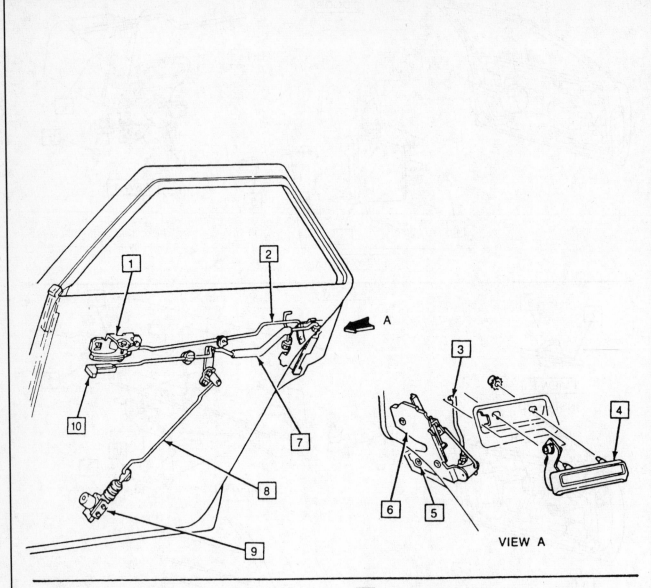

1	HANDLE ASSEMBLY—INSIDE	6	LOCK ASSEMBLY
2	ROD—LOCK REMOTE CONTROL TO LOCK	7	ROD—INSIDE LOCKING TO LOCK
3	ROD—OUTSIDE HANDLE TO LOCK	8	ROD—INSIDE LOCKING TO ACTUATOR
4	HANDLE ASSEMBLY—OUTSIDE	9	ACTUATOR ASSEMBLY—ELECTRIC LOCK
5	LOCK SCREWS (3)	10	KNOB—INSIDE LOCKING

87950113

Fig. 82 Rear door lock system — 1992 vehicle shown

5. Disconnect the lock cylinder-to-lock assembly rod.

6. Disconnect the inside handle-to-lock assembly rod.

7. Unfasten the lock assembly screws/bolts and remove the lock from the door. If equipped, detach the electrical connectors.

To install:

8. Attach the electrical connector (if equipped), position the lock assembly to the door and install the retaining screws/bolts. Tighten the screws/bolts to 62 inch lbs. (7 Nm). Do NOT overtighten.

9. Attach the outside handle to the lock assembly rod.

10. Connect the lock cylinder to the lock assembly rod.

11. Connect the inside handle to the lock rod and inside locking rod.

12. Fasten the water deflector.

13. Install the inside door trim panel.

Front Door Glass

REMOVAL & INSTALLATION

Except Convertible

1. Raise the door window to the full up position and remove the door trim panel and water deflector.

2. Unfasten the bolts holding the front glass retainer to the door inner panel and remove the retainer through the rear access hole. Lower the glass to approximately 3 in. (76mm) above the beltline.

3. Rotate the glass forward to disengage the window regulator roller from the sash channel.

4. Lower the glass into the door to disengage the rear guide (on the glass) from the rear run channel.

5. Using care, raise the glass while tilting forward and remove the glass inboard of the upper frame.

To install:

6. Tilt the front edge of the glass downward to locate the glass in the door.

7. Apply pressure rearward and snap the glass rear guide into the rear run channel.

8. Lower the glass to about 3 in. (76mm) above the beltline and install the widow regulator roller to sash channel.

9. Run the glass to the full up position.

10. Place the front glass retainer in position and install the bolts.

11. Check the window to make sure it operates correctly, then install the remaining trim parts.

Convertible

▶ **See Figure 83**

1. Remove the door trim panel, sound absorber, armrest bracket and water deflector.

2. Position the glass so that the up stop spanner nut on the glass is visible through the access hole.

3. Using tool J-22055 or equivalent, remove the spanner nut, bushing and stop from the glass.

4. Position the glass so the spanner nuts are visible through the access hole.

5. Remove the spanner nuts and bushings.

6. Loosen the upper stabilizers.

7. Disengage the glass from the studs on the sash where the spanner nuts were removed.

8. Lower the regulator to the full-down position.

9. Grasp the glass and pull the glass up, with the front of the glass tilted down and remove the glass.

10. Installation is the reverse of removal. Before installing trim parts, check the window operation for proper alignment and adjust as needed.

Rear Door Glass

REMOVAL & INSTALLATION

▶ **See Figure 84**

➡ **If equipped, the stationary vent assembly must be removed with the rear glass assembly as a unit.**

1. Remove the door trim panel and the water deflector.

2. Lower the glass to the full down position.

3. Remove the screws at the top of the division channel.

4. Unfasten the bolt holding the vent glass support at the belt.

5. Remove the screws at the rear of the door face holding the bottom of the division to the door.

6. Push the stationary vent assembly down and forward to disengage the vent assembly from the run channel. Now that the vent assembly is inboard of the door frame, lift up until the vent assembly is stopped against the door glass.

7. Raise the door glass 6-8 in. (152-203mm) and tilt the whole assembly rearward and disengage the roller from the glass sash channel.

To install:

8. Place the rear door glass in the vent division channel.

9. Load the rear window and vent assembly by lowering the assemblies through the door belt opening. Rotate the glass forward to engage the regulator roller in the glass sash channel. Reposition the vent glass into the door frame.

10. Install the screws at the top of the division channel.

11. Fasten the screws at the rear face of the door holding division and lower support in place.

12. Fasten the bolt securing the division channel support at the belt.

13. Replace all previously removed trim.

Front Window Regulator And Motor

➡ **The following procedure includes both manual and power window regulator removal and installation. Besides the regulators, window motors and rollers including the washer and pin are serviced separately.**

REMOVAL & INSTALLATION

Except Convertible

▶ **See Figure 85**

1. Remove the door trim panel and the water deflector.

2. Raise the glass to the full up position and tape the glass to the door frame using fabric tape.

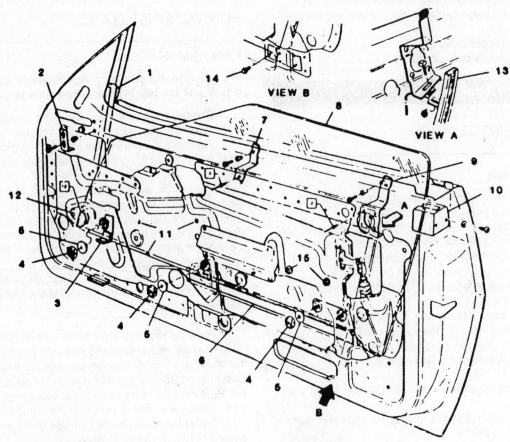

1. Front glass run channel
2. Front up stop
3. Catch—front up stop
4. Glass retainer
5. Bushing
6. Cam assembly door glass
7. Front stabilizer
8. Glass assembly
9. Rear stabilizer
10. Guide block
11. Rivets—regulator
12. Rivets—regulator motor
13. Rear up stop block
14. Rivets—rear cam assembly lower
15. Attaching nuts inner panel cam door reinforcement

87950115

Fig. 83 Front door glass and related hardware — convertible

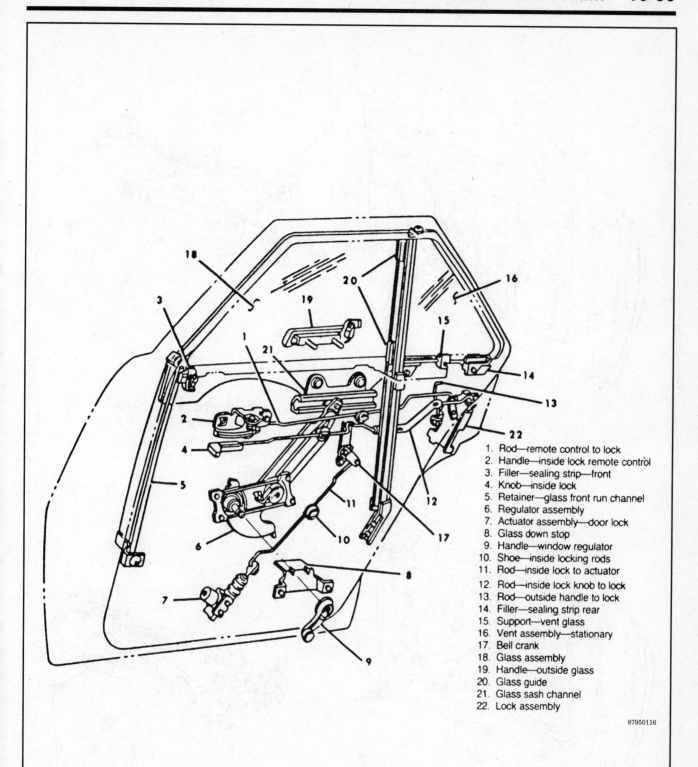

1. Rod—remote control to lock
2. Handle—inside lock remote control
3. Filler—sealing strip—front
4. Knob—inside lock
5. Retainer—glass front run channel
6. Regulator assembly
7. Actuator assembly—door lock
8. Glass down stop
9. Handle—window regulator
10. Shoe—inside locking rods
11. Rod—inside lock to actuator
12. Rod—inside lock knob to lock
13. Rod—outside handle to lock
14. Filler—sealing strip rear
15. Support—vent glass
16. Vent assembly—stationary
17. Bell crank
18. Glass assembly
19. Handle—outside glass
20. Glass guide
21. Glass sash channel
22. Lock assembly

87950116

Fig. 84 Rear door glass and related hardware

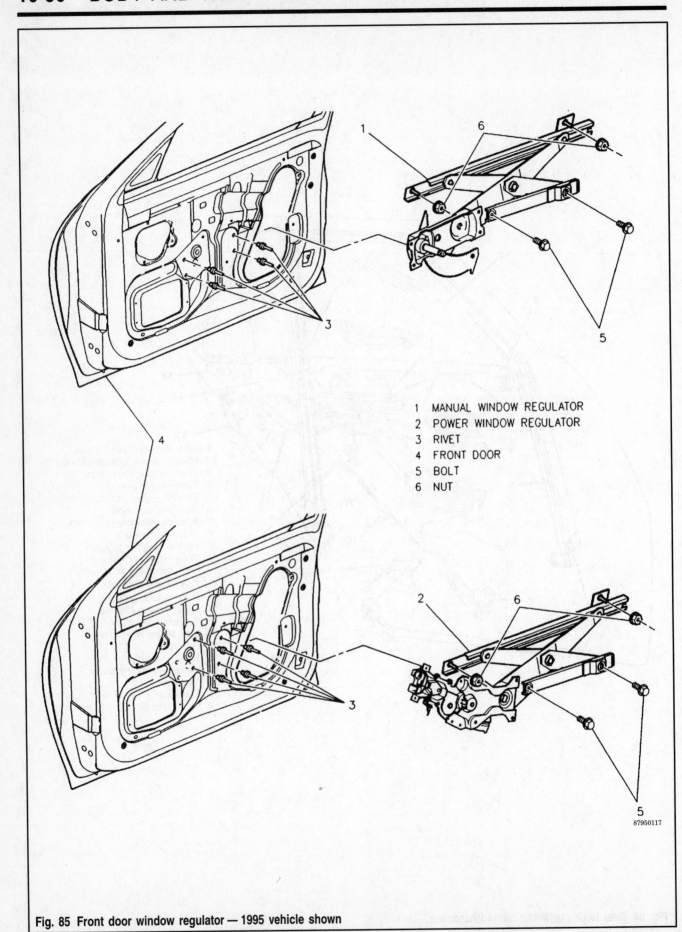

1 MANUAL WINDOW REGULATOR
2 POWER WINDOW REGULATOR
3 RIVET
4 FRONT DOOR
5 BOLT
6 NUT

87950117

Fig. 85 Front door window regulator — 1995 vehicle shown

3. Punch out the center pins of the regulator rivets using a $\frac{1}{4}$ in. (6mm) drill bit. On electric regulators, drill out the rivets supporting the motor to the door inner panel.

4. Move the regulator rearward and disconnect the wiring harness from the motor, if so equipped. Disengage the roller on the regulator lift arm from the glass sash channel.

5. Remove the regulator through the rear access hole.

6. Using a $\frac{3}{16}$ in. (5mm) drill bit, drill out the motor attaching rivets and remove the motor from the regulator, if so equipped.

To install:

7. If so equipped, attach the motor to the regulator using a rivet tool and $\frac{3}{16}$ in. (5mm) rivets or $\frac{3}{16}$ in. (5mm) nuts and bolts.

8. Place the regulator through the rear access hole into the door inner panel. If an electric regulator is being installed, connect the wire connector to the motor prior to installing the regulator in the panel.

9. Locate the lift arm roller into the glass sash channel.

10. Using rivet tool J-29022 or equivalent, rivet the regulator to the inner panel of the door using $\frac{1}{4}$ in. x $\frac{1}{2}$ in. (6mm x 13mm) aluminum peel type rivets (part No. 9436175 or equivalent). If a rivet tool is not available, use the following nut and bolt method:

a. Install U-clips on the regulator and motor (if so equipped), at the attaching locations. Be sure to install clips with clinch nuts on the outboard side of the regulator.

b. Place the regulator through the rear access hole into the door inner panel. If an electric regulator is being installed, connect the wire connector to the motor prior to installing the regulator in the panel.

c. Locate the lift arm roller into the glass sash channel.

d. Align the regulator with the clinch nuts to the holes in the inner panel.

e. Attach the regulator and motor to the door inner panel with $\frac{1}{4}$ in. screws. Tighten the screws to 90-125 inch lbs.

11. If an electrical window regulator is being installed use a rivet mentioned in step 10 to rivet the regulator motor to the door inner panel.

12. Replace all previously removed parts.

Convertible

1. Remove the door trim panel, sound absorber, armrest bracket and water deflector.

2. Using a $\frac{1}{4}$ in. (6mm) drill bit, drill out the rivets supporting the motor to the door inner panel.

3. Disconnect the electrical connector from the regulator motor.

4. Support the door glass in the full-up position, using rubber wedge door stops.

5. Remove the nuts holding the cam assembly door reinforcement to the inner panel and remove the cam assembly.

6. Remove the bolt holding the upper portion of the rear cam assembly to the inner panel.

7. Using a $\frac{3}{16}$ in. (5mm) drill bit, drill out the rivets, holding the lower section of the rear cam assembly to the inner panel.

8. Remove the up stop from the rear cam assembly.

9. Remove the rear cam assembly through the access hole.

10. Disengage the regulator from the glass sash channel and remove the regulator through the access hole.

❋❋CAUTION

When removing the electric motor from the regulator, the sector gear must be locked in position. The regulator lift arm is under tension from the counterbalance spring and could cause personal injury if the sector gear is not locked in position.

11. If equipped with an electric window regulator and you wish to remove the motor from the regulator proceed as follows:

a. Drill a hole through the regulator sector gear and backplate and install a bolt and nut to lock the sector gear in position.

b. Using a $\frac{3}{16}$ in. (5mm) drill bit, drill out the motor attaching rivets and remove the motor from the regulator.

c. To install the motor to the regulator use a rivet tool J-29022 or equivalent and install $\frac{3}{16}$ in. (5mm) rivets or $\frac{3}{16}$ in. (5mm) nuts and bolts. Remove the bolt and nut used to secure the sector gear in position.

To install:

12. Make sure the regulator is in the full up position.

13. Install the regulator arm rollers to the glass sash channel.

14. Install the rear cam assembly using $\frac{3}{16}$ in. (5mm) aluminum peel-type rivets making sure to install the up stop in the cam assembly.

15. Connect the electrical connector to the motor on the regulator.

16. Engage the roller on the regulator lift arm in the cam assembly door reinforcement.

17. Install the cam assembly door reinforcement to the inner panel.

18. Align the attaching holes in the regulator with the holes in the inner panel.

19. Install the regulator to the inner panel, using a rivet gun and $\frac{1}{4}$ in. x $\frac{1}{2}$ in. (6mm x 13mm) aluminum peel type rivets.

Rear Window Regulator

➡The following procedure includes both manual and power window regulator removal and installation. Besides the regulators, window motors and rollers including the washer and pin are serviced separately.

REMOVAL & INSTALLATION

♦ See Figure 86

1. Remove the door trim panel and the water deflector.

2. Raise the glass to the full up position and tape the glass to the door frame using fabric tape.

3. Punch out the center pins of the regulator rivets using a $\frac{1}{4}$ in. (6mm) drill bit. On electric regulators, drill out the rivets supporting the motor to the door inner panel.

4. Disconnect the wiring harness from the motor, if so equipped. Disengage the roller on the regulator lift arm from the glass sash channel.

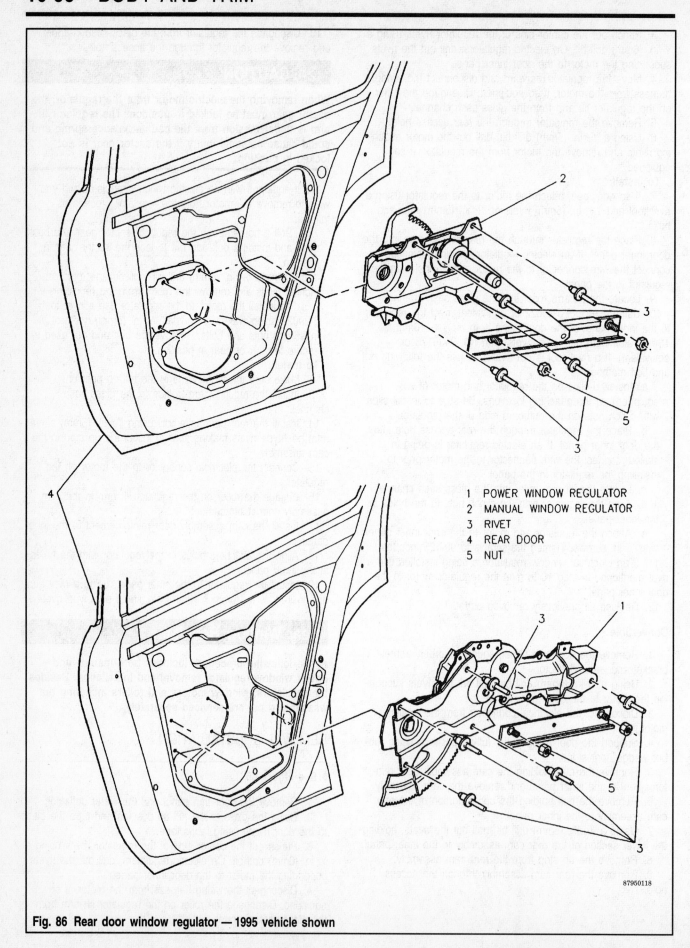

1 POWER WINDOW REGULATOR
2 MANUAL WINDOW REGULATOR
3 RIVET
4 REAR DOOR
5 NUT

87950118

Fig. 86 Rear door window regulator — 1995 vehicle shown

5. Remove the regulator through the rear access hole.

6. Using a ³/₁₆ in. (5mm) drill bit, drill out the motor attaching rivets and remove the motor from the regulator, if so equipped.

To install:

7. If so equipped, attach the motor to the regulator using a rivet tool and ³/₁₆ in. (5mm) rivets or ³/₁₆ in. (5mm) nuts and bolts.

8. Place the regulator through the rear access hole into the door inner panel. If an electric regulator is being installed, connect the wire connector to the motor prior to installing regulator in the panel.

9. Locate the lift arm roller into the glass sash channel.

10. Using rivet tool J-29022 or equivalent, rivet the regulator to the inner panel of the door using ¼ in. x ½ in. (6mm x 13mm) aluminum peel type rivets (part No. 9436175 or equivalent). If a rivet tool is not available, use the following nut and bolt method:

   a. Install U-clips on the regulator and motor (if so equipped), at the attaching locations. Be sure to install clips with clinch nuts on the outboard side of the regulator.

   b. Place the regulator through the rear access hole into the door inner panel. If an electric regulator is being installed, connect the wire connector to the motor prior to installing the regulator in the panel.

   c. Locate the lift arm roller into the glass sash channel.

   d. Align the regulator with the clinch nuts to the holes in the inner panel.

   e. Attach the regulator and motor to the door inner panel with ¼ in. screws. Tighten the screws to 90-125 inch lbs.

11. If an electrical window regulator is being installed use a rivet mentioned in step 10 to rivet the regulator motor to the door inner panel.

12. Replace all previously removed parts.

Windshield Glass

REMOVAL & INSTALLATION

▶ **See Figures 87, 88, 89, 90 and 91**

1. Remove the wiper arms and blades, if applicable.

2. Remove the lower windshield glass support. On 1989-96 models, remove the top vent grille panel if applicable.

3. Remove reveal moldings and/or retainers from around the glass.

4. If rear glass is to be removed, remove the quarter upper trim panels to access rear defogger if so equipped. Disconnect the rear defogger feed wire and ground wire.

5. Mask off area around the window to protect the painted surfaces.

6. Using a cold knife No. J24402-A and /or a power tool with a reciprocating blade, cut around the entire perimeter of the window. The blade of the tool must be kept as close as possible to the window edge during the cutout procedure. Remove the window glass.

To install:

7. If reusing the same window glass, clean all residue from glass completely. Trim the old urethane evenly around the window frame. Touch up all nicks and scratches with the cor-

rect color paint around frame do not let the paint contaminate the urethane.

8. Install the acoustic sealing strip, if replacing the windshield. Peel the protective backing from sealing strip and install onto window glass inboard of bottom edge.

9. Install the reveal molding. Position the window in opening, be sure the window sits flush with the body, if it does not sit flush remove the window glass and trim the urethane around the entire perimeter to bring the window flush with body. Apply tape from window to the body then slit the tape along window edge this will help align the window upon installation, remove the window.

10. Apply the clear primer around the edge of the window (supplied in window installation kit No. 12345633 or equivalent). Apply the black primer to frame edge only if the urethane had to be removed from the body. If black primer was used wait five minutes before apply the necessary urethane.

11. With the aid of a helper lift the windshield into opening. On rear window installations it will be necessary to use suction cups to position the window into opening. With window in opening align the tape marks.

12. Press window firmly to wet out and set adhesive. Use care to avoid excessive squeeze out which would cause an appearance problem. Using a disposable brush or flat blade tool, paddle the material around the edge of window to ensure a water tight seal. If necessary paddle in addition material around the edge to fill voids in seal.

13. Apply tape from top of window glass to roof and also the sides. Water test the vehicle at once with a garden hose; do not spray a hard stream directly onto the urethane sealer. If any leaks are found paddle in extra sealer to stop leak.

14. Install the upper trim panels if removed. Connect the rear defogger connectors, if so equipped.

15. Install the shroud top vent grille panel, if removed. Install the wipers, if removed. Allow 6 hours for the urethane to cure.

Inside Rearview Mirror

REPLACEMENT

The rearview mirror is attached to a support which is secured to the windshield glass. This support is installed by the glass supplier using a plastic-polyvinyl butyl adhesive.

Service replacement windshield glass has the mirror support bonded to the glass assembly.

Service kits are available to replace a detached mirror support or install a new part. Follow the manufacturer's instructions for replacement.

Front Seat

REMOVAL & INSTALLATION

▶ **See Figures 92, 93 and 94**

1. Operate the seat to the full-forward position. If a six way power seat is operable, move the seat to the full-forward and

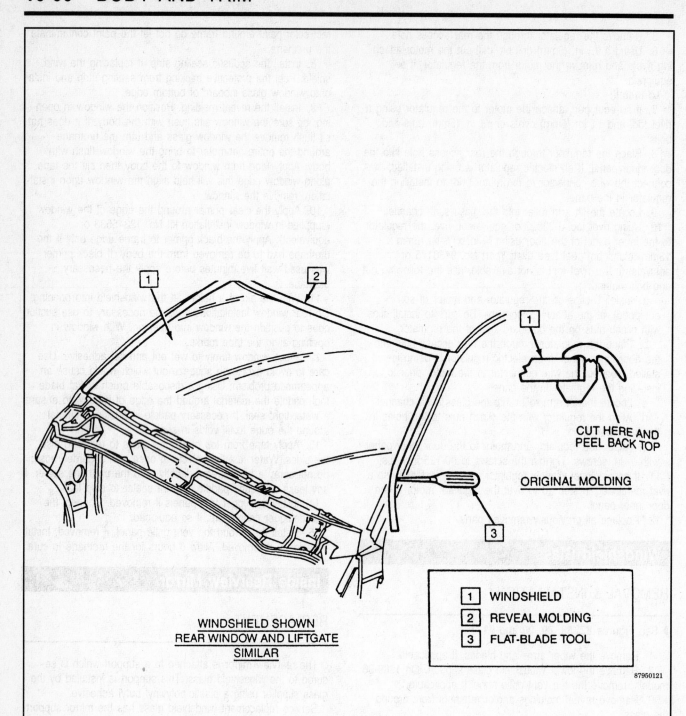

CUT HERE AND PEEL BACK TOP

ORIGINAL MOLDING

WINDSHIELD SHOWN
REAR WINDOW AND LIFTGATE
SIMILAR

1	WINDSHIELD
2	REVEAL MOLDING
3	FLAT-BLADE TOOL

87950121

Fig. 87 Removal of the reveal molding

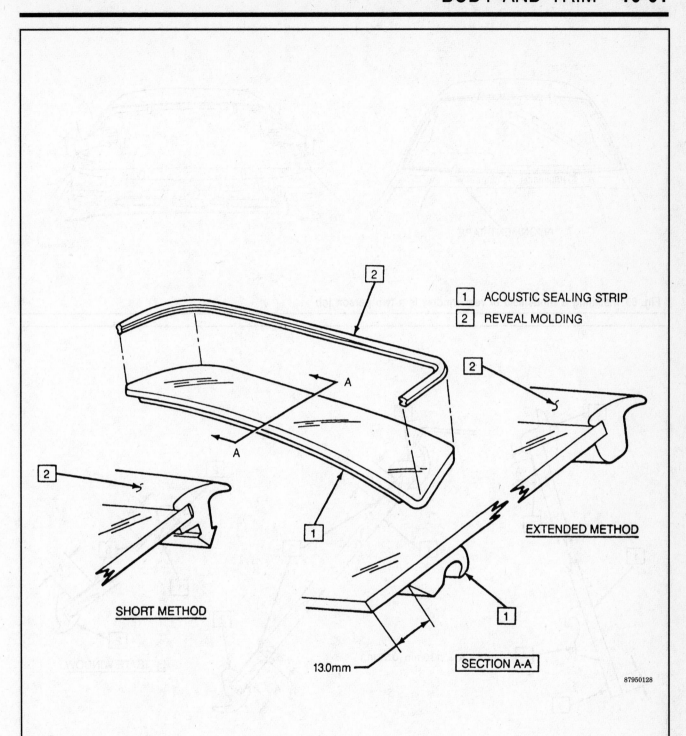

1 ACOUSTIC SEALING STRIP
2 REVEAL MOLDING

A

SHORT METHOD

EXTENDED METHOD

13.0mm

SECTION A-A

87950128

Fig. 88 Installation of the windshield reveal molding

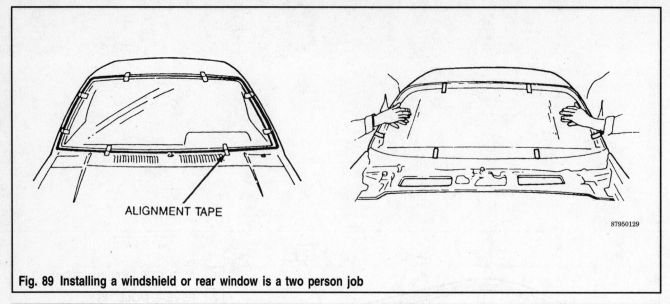

Fig. 89 Installing a windshield or rear window is a two person job

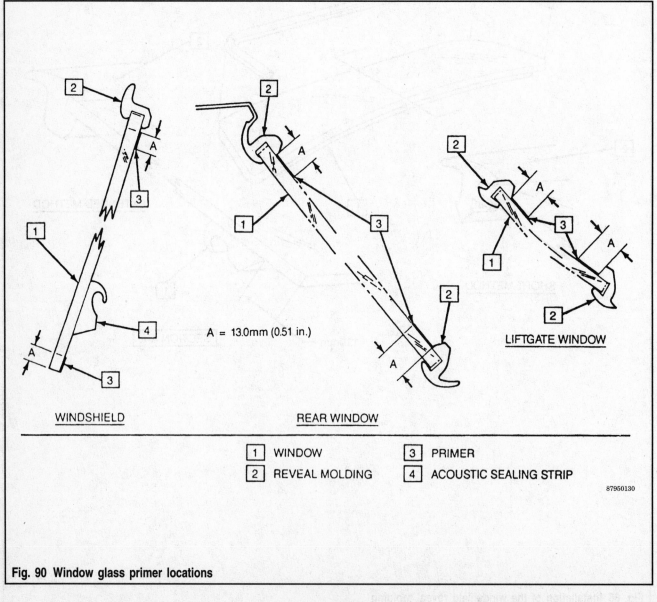

A = 13.0mm (0.51 in.)

WINDSHIELD   REAR WINDOW   LIFTGATE WINDOW

| 1 | WINDOW | 3 | PRIMER |
| 2 | REVEAL MOLDING | 4 | ACOUSTIC SEALING STRIP |

Fig. 90 Window glass primer locations

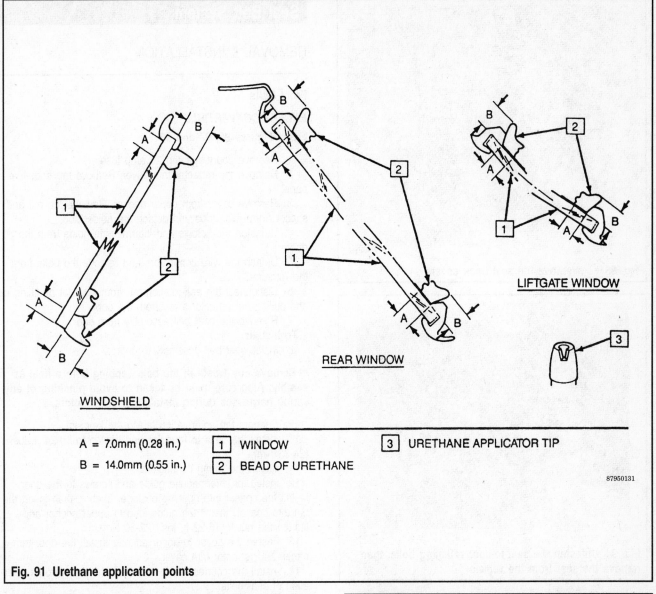

A = 7.0mm (0.28 in.)
B = 14.0mm (0.55 in.)

1   WINDOW
2   BEAD OF URETHANE
3   URETHANE APPLICATOR TIP

87950131

Fig. 91 Urethane application points

up positions. To gain access to the adjuster-to-floor pan retaining nuts, remove the adjuster rear foot covers or carpet retainers.

2. Remove the track covers where necessary, then remove the rear attaching nuts. Remove the front foot covers, then remove the adjuster-to-floor pan front attaching nuts.

3. On seats with power adjusters, tilt the seat rearward and disconnect the feed wire connector.

4. Remove the seat assembly from the car.

5. To install the seat assembly reverse the removal procedure. Tighten the seat adjuster-to-floor pan attaching bolts or nuts to 21 ft. lbs. (28 Nm).

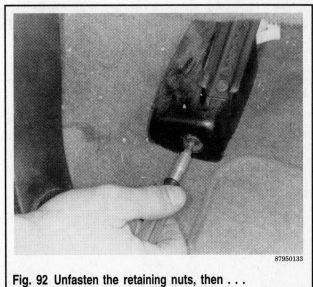

87950133

Fig. 92 Unfasten the retaining nuts, then . . .

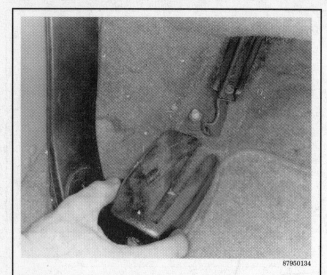

Fig. 93 . . . remove the seat track covers

Fig. 94 Unfasten the seat-to-floor retaining bolts, then remove the seat from the vehicle

Rear Seat Cushion

REMOVAL & INSTALLATION

▶ See Figure 95

1. Remove the rear seat cushion attaching bolts, located at the center of the right and left sections of the rear seat cushion.
2. Lift the cushion upward and remove from the vehicle.
3. To install, reverse the removal procedure. Tighten the seat cushion attaching bolts to 14-20 ft. lbs. (19-27 Nm).

Seat Belt System

REMOVAL & INSTALLATION

Front Belts

EXCEPT CONVERTIBLE

▶ See Figures 96, 97 and 98

1. Remove courtesy lamp 20 amp fuse.
2. Remove the retractor trim cover. Remove the door trim panel.
3. Remove cover from upper anchor. Remove the nut and spacer from guide loop and detach the guide loop.
4. Unfasten the screws and intermediate guide from the door.
5. Detach the wire connectors and remove the bolts from the retractor.
6. Disconnect the anti-rotation tab from key slot by lifting up and pulling out retractor away from the door.
7. Remove the seat belt assembly from door.
   To install:
8. Install seat belt assembly to door.

➡Remove any twists in the belt webbing before final assembly. Also care must be taken to avoid pinching of any wiring harnesses during installation of retractors.

9. Connect the anti-rotation tab to the key slot.
10. Install the bolts to retractor and tighten to 18-24 ft. lbs. (24-33 Nm).
11. Attach the wiring connectors.
12. Install the intermediate guide and screws to the door. Install the spacer into opening of upper anchor, then insert the nut into spacer. Install the guide loop to upper anchor and tighten the nut to 16-22 ft. lbs. (22-30 Nm).
13. Fasten the cover to upper anchor. Install the door trim panel, and retractor trim cover.
14. Install the courtesy lamp fuse and check for proper operation of seat belts.

CONVERTIBLE

▶ See Figures 99 and 100

1. Remove courtesy lamp 20 amp fuse.
2. Unsnap the guide loop cover to gain access to the guide loop retaining bolt. Remove the bolt and spacer.
3. Disconnect the seat belt tower cover. Remove the retractor cover.
4. Remove the armrest and pull handle.
5. Unfasten the bolt and guide loop bracket, nut and screw.
6. Remove the bolt and seat belt tower support.
7. Detach the wire connectors, and shoulder belt retractor from key slot.
8. Unfasten the bolts and remove the lap belt retractor.
   To install:
9. Install the lap belt retractor and bolts, tighten to 22 ft. lbs. (30 Nm).

➡Remove any twists in the belt webbing before final assembly. Also care must be taken to avoid pinching of any wiring harnesses during installation of retractors.

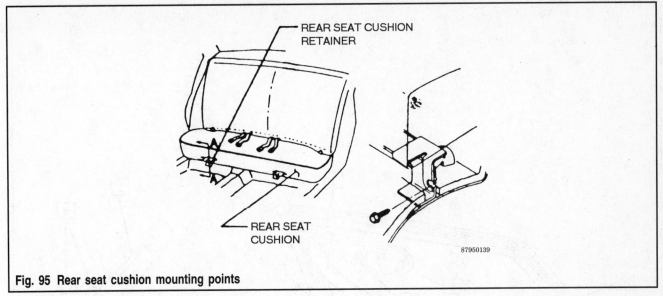

REAR SEAT CUSHION
RETAINER

REAR SEAT
CUSHION

87950139

Fig. 95 Rear seat cushion mounting points

10. Connect the shoulder belt retractor to the key slot. Attach the wire connectors.

11. Install the seat belt tower support and tighten the bolt to 22 ft. lbs. (30 Nm) tighten the screw to 22 ft. lbs. (30 Nm) and the nut to 12 ft. lbs. (16 Nm).

12. Install the guide loop bracket and bolt, tighten to 12 ft. lbs. (16 Nm).

13. Install the armrest and pull handle, and seat belt tower cover.

14. Insert the bolt through the guide loop cover and guide loop, then install the spacer onto bolt. Position the guide loop onto tower cover and thread the bolt into tower support, tighten to 22 ft. lbs. (30 Nm). Close the guide loop cover.

15. Install the courtesy lamp fuse and check for proper operation of seat belts.

Rear Seat Belts

▶ See Figure 101

1. Remove the rear seat cushion, seat back, lower quarter trim panel and anchor bolt.

2. Remove the retractor bolt and escutcheon. On convertible model, lift the escutcheon to expose the guide loop bolt then remove the escutcheon bolt and spacer.

3. Remove the belt anchor end through shelf opening into trunk area. On convertible model, pull the seat belt assembly through the brace, remove the bolt and seat belt assembly from vehicle.

To install:

➡**Remove any twists in the belt webbing before final assembly.**

4. Install the belt anchor end through shelf opening. On convertible models, position the retractor assembly onto brace, install bolt and tighten to 22 ft. lbs. (30 Nm).

5. Install the escutcheon and retractor bolt, tighten to 22 ft. lbs. (30 Nm). Install the anchor bolt and tighten to 26-35 ft. lbs. (35-47 Nm). On convertible models, feed the seat belt assembly through brace, position the spacer, guide loop and escutcheon. Install the bolt and tighten to 22 ft. lbs. (30 Nm).

6. On convertible model, thread seat belt webbing through escutcheon, position anchor end of seat belt install bolt and tighten to 26-35 ft. lbs. (35-47 Nm).

7. Install the lower quarter trim panel, rear seat back and cushion.

Power Seat Motors

REMOVAL & INSTALLATION

1. Remove the front seat assembly and place upside down on a clean surface.

2. Disconnect the motor feed wires from the motor.

3. Remove the nut securing the front of the motor support bracket to the inboard adjuster and withdraw the assembly from the adjuster and the gear nut drives.

4. Disconnect the drive cables from the motor and complete the removal of the support bracket with motors attached.

5. Grind off the peened over ends(s) of the grommet assembly securing the motor to the support and separate the motors from the support, as required.

6. To install, reverse the removal procedure except as noted:

   a. Drill out the top end of the grommet assembly using a $\frac{3}{16}$ in. (5mm) drill.

   b. Install the grommet assembly to the motor support bracket and secure the motor to the grommet using a $\frac{3}{16}$ in. (5mm) rivet.

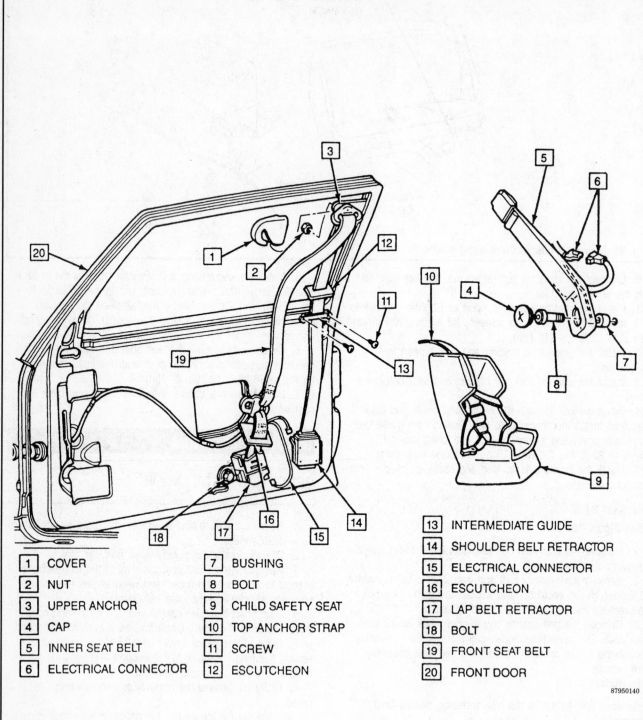

1	COVER	**7**	BUSHING	
2	NUT	**8**	BOLT	
3	UPPER ANCHOR	**9**	CHILD SAFETY SEAT	
4	CAP	**10**	TOP ANCHOR STRAP	
5	INNER SEAT BELT	**11**	SCREW	
6	ELECTRICAL CONNECTOR	**12**	ESCUTCHEON	

13	INTERMEDIATE GUIDE
14	SHOULDER BELT RETRACTOR
15	ELECTRICAL CONNECTOR
16	ESCUTCHEON
17	LAP BELT RETRACTOR
18	BOLT
19	FRONT SEAT BELT
20	FRONT DOOR

87950140

Fig. 96 Front seat belts — except convertible

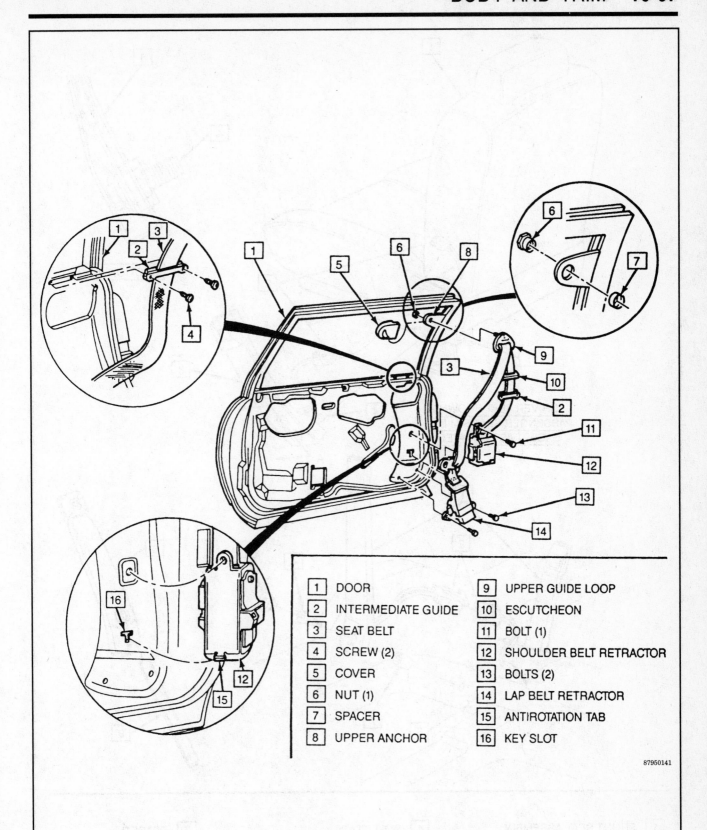

1	DOOR	9	UPPER GUIDE LOOP
2	INTERMEDIATE GUIDE	10	ESCUTCHEON
3	SEAT BELT	11	BOLT (1)
4	SCREW (2)	12	SHOULDER BELT RETRACTOR
5	COVER	13	BOLTS (2)
6	NUT (1)	14	LAP BELT RETRACTOR
7	SPACER	15	ANTIROTATION TAB
8	UPPER ANCHOR	16	KEY SLOT

87950141

Fig. 97 Front outer seat belt — except convertible

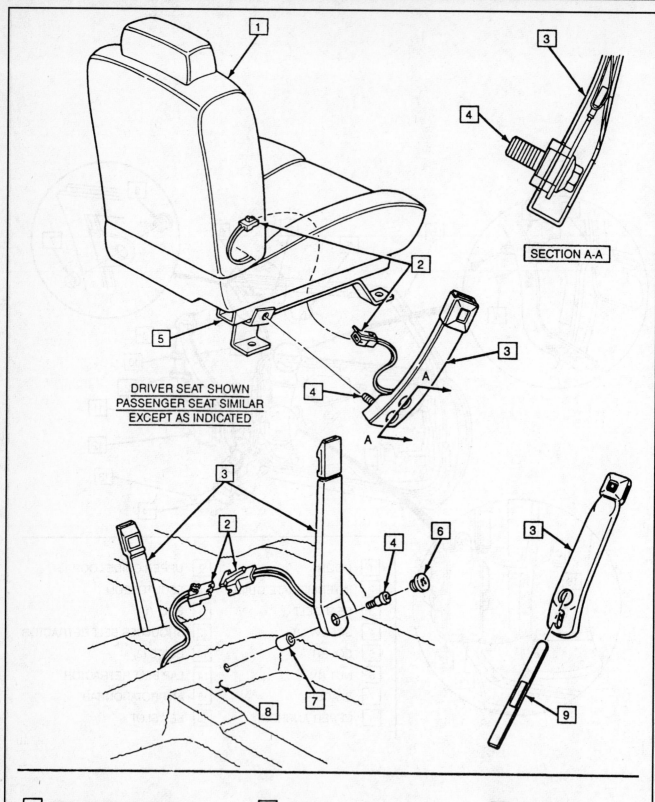

SECTION A-A

DRIVER SEAT SHOWN
PASSENGER SEAT SIMILAR
EXCEPT AS INDICATED

1	FRONT SEAT ASSEMBLY	4	BOLT (2)	7	SPACER
2	ELECTRICAL CONNECTORS (DRIVER'S SEAT ONLY)	5	SEAT ADJUSTER ASSEMBLY	8	FLOOR PAN CARPET
3	FRONT SEAT INNER SEAT BELT	6	BELT SLEEVE PLUG	9	STIFFENER

87950142

Fig. 98 Front seat inner seat belt assembly — except convertible

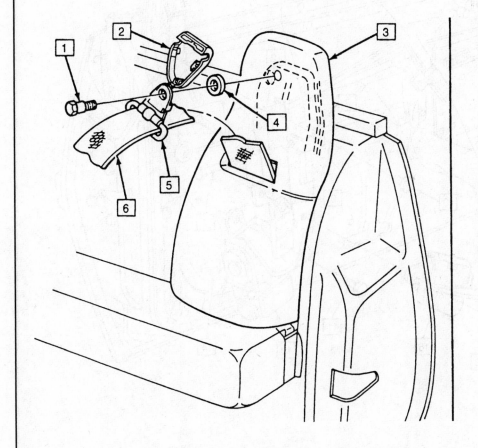

1	BOLT. 30 N·m (22 lbs. ft.)
2	GUIDE LOOP COVER
3	TOWER COVER
4	SPACER
5	GUIDE LOOP
6	SEAT BELT

87950143

Fig. 99 Upper attachment of the front seat belt — convertible

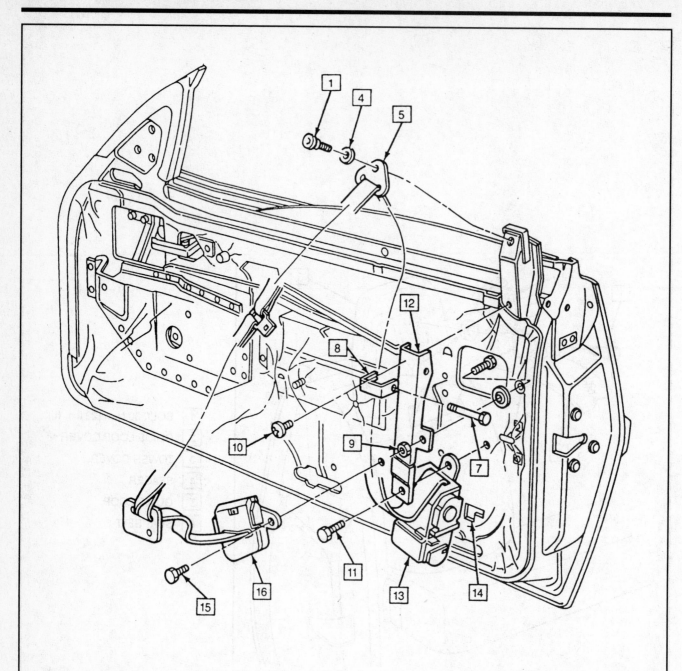

1	BOLT, 30 N·m (22 lbs. ft.)	**9**	NUT, 16 N·m (12 lbs. ft)	**13**	SHOULDER BELT RETRACTOR
4	SPACER	**10**	SCREW, 30 N·m (22 lbs. ft.)	**14**	KEY SLOT
5	GUIDE LOOP	**11**	BOLT, 30 N·m (22 lbs. ft.)	**15**	BOLT, 30 N·m (22 lbs. ft.)
7	BOLT, 16 N·m (12 lbs. ft.)	**12**	SEAT BELT TOWER SUPPORT	**16**	LAP BELT RETRACTOR
8	GUIDE LOOP BRACKET				

87950144

Fig. 100 Seat belt assembly and lower support mounting — convertible

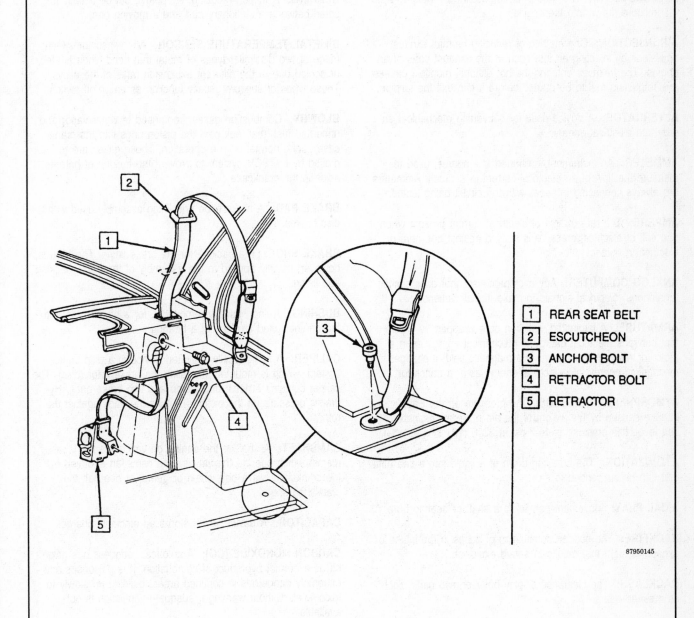

1	REAR SEAT BELT
2	ESCUTCHEON
3	ANCHOR BOLT
4	RETRACTOR BOLT
5	RETRACTOR

87950145

Fig. 101 Rear seat belt removal and installation

GLOSSARY

AIR/FUEL RATIO: The ratio of air-to-gasoline by weight in the fuel mixture drawn into the engine.

AIR INJECTION: One method of reducing harmful exhaust emissions by injecting air into each of the exhaust ports of an engine. The fresh air entering the hot exhaust manifold causes any remaining fuel to be burned before it can exit the tailpipe.

ALTERNATOR: A device used for converting mechanical energy into electrical energy.

AMMETER: An instrument, calibrated in amperes, used to measure the flow of an electrical current in a circuit. Ammeters are always connected in series with the circuit being tested.

AMPERE: The rate of flow of electrical current present when one volt of electrical pressure is applied against one ohm of electrical resistance.

ANALOG COMPUTER: Any microprocessor that uses similar (analogous) electrical signals to make its calculations.

ARMATURE: A laminated, soft iron core wrapped by a wire that converts electrical energy to mechanical energy as in a motor or relay. When rotated in a magnetic field, it changes mechanical energy into electrical energy as in a generator.

ATMOSPHERIC PRESSURE: The pressure on the Earth's surface caused by the weight of the air in the atmosphere. At sea level, this pressure is 14.7 psi at 32°F (101 kPa at 0°C).

ATOMIZATION: The breaking down of a liquid into a fine mist that can be suspended in air.

AXIAL PLAY: Movement parallel to a shaft or bearing bore.

BACKFIRE: The sudden combustion of gases in the intake or exhaust system that results in a loud explosion.

BACKLASH: The clearance or play between two parts, such as meshed gears.

BACKPRESSURE: Restrictions in the exhaust system that slow the exit of exhaust gases from the combustion chamber.

BAKELITE: A heat resistant, plastic insulator material commonly used in printed circuit boards and transistorized components.

BALL BEARING: A bearing made up of hardened inner and outer races between which hardened steel balls roll.

BALLAST RESISTOR: A resistor in the primary ignition circuit that lowers voltage after the engine is started to reduce wear on ignition components.

BEARING: A friction reducing, supportive device usually located between a stationary part and a moving part.

BIMETAL TEMPERATURE SENSOR: Any sensor or switch made of two dissimilar types of metal that bend when heated or cooled due to the different expansion rates of the alloys. These types of sensors usually function as an on/off switch.

BLOWBY: Combustion gases, composed of water vapor and unburned fuel, that leak past the piston rings into the crankcase during normal engine operation. These gases are removed by the PCV system to prevent the buildup of harmful acids in the crankcase.

BRAKE PAD: A brake shoe and lining assembly used with disc brakes.

BRAKE SHOE: The backing for the brake lining. The term is, however, usually applied to the assembly of the brake backing and lining.

BUSHING: A liner, usually removable, for a bearing; an anti-friction liner used in place of a bearing.

CALIPER: A hydraulically activated device in a disc brake system, which is mounted straddling the brake rotor (disc). The caliper contains at least one piston and two brake pads. Hydraulic pressure on the piston(s) forces the pads against the rotor.

CAMSHAFT: A shaft in the engine on which are the lobes (cams) which operate the valves. The camshaft is driven by the crankshaft, via a belt, chain or gears, at one half the crankshaft speed.

CAPACITOR: A device which stores an electrical charge.

CARBON MONOXIDE (CO): A colorless, odorless gas given off as a normal byproduct of combustion. It is poisonous and extremely dangerous in confined areas, building up slowly to toxic levels without warning if adequate ventilation is not available.

CARBURETOR: A device, usually mounted on the intake manifold of an engine, which mixes the air and fuel in the proper proportion to allow even combustion.

CATALYTIC CONVERTER: A device installed in the exhaust system, like a muffler, that converts harmful byproducts of combustion into carbon dioxide and water vapor by means of a heat-producing chemical reaction.

CENTRIFUGAL ADVANCE: A mechanical method of advancing the spark timing by using flyweights in the distributor that react to centrifugal force generated by the distributor shaft rotation.

CHECK VALVE: Any one-way valve installed to permit the flow of air, fuel or vacuum in one direction only.

CHOKE: A device, usually a moveable valve, placed in the intake path of a carburetor to restrict the flow of air.

CIRCUIT: Any unbroken path through which an electrical current can flow. Also used to describe fuel flow in some instances.

CIRCUIT BREAKER: A switch which protects an electrical circuit from overload by opening the circuit when the current flow exceeds a predetermined level. Some circuit breakers must be reset manually, while most reset automatically.

COIL (IGNITION): A transformer in the ignition circuit which steps up the voltage provided to the spark plugs.

COMBINATION MANIFOLD: An assembly which includes both the intake and exhaust manifolds in one casting.

COMBINATION VALVE: A device used in some fuel systems that routes fuel vapors to a charcoal storage canister instead of venting them into the atmosphere. The valve relieves fuel tank pressure and allows fresh air into the tank as the fuel level drops to prevent a vapor lock situation.

COMPRESSION RATIO: The comparison of the total volume of the cylinder and combustion chamber with the piston at BDC and the piston at TDC.

CONDENSER: 1. An electrical device which acts to store an electrical charge, preventing voltage surges. 2. A radiator-like device in the air conditioning system in which refrigerant gas condenses into a liquid, giving off heat.

CONDUCTOR: Any material through which an electrical current can be transmitted easily.

CONTINUITY: Continuous or complete circuit. Can be checked with an ohmmeter.

COUNTERSHAFT: An intermediate shaft which is rotated by a mainshaft and transmits, in turn, that rotation to a working part.

CRANKCASE: The lower part of an engine in which the crankshaft and related parts operate.

CRANKSHAFT: The main driving shaft of an engine which receives reciprocating motion from the pistons and converts it to rotary motion.

CYLINDER: In an engine, the round hole in the engine block in which the piston(s) ride.

CYLINDER BLOCK: The main structural member of an engine in which is found the cylinders, crankshaft and other principal parts.

CYLINDER HEAD: The detachable portion of the engine, usually fastened to the top of the cylinder block and containing all or most of the combustion chambers. On overhead valve engines, it contains the valves and their operating parts. On overhead cam engines, it contains the camshaft as well.

DEAD CENTER: The extreme top or bottom of the piston stroke.

DETONATION: An unwanted explosion of the air/fuel mixture in the combustion chamber caused by excess heat and compression, advanced timing, or an overly lean mixture. Also referred to as "ping".

DIAPHRAGM: A thin, flexible wall separating two cavities, such as in a vacuum advance unit.

DIESELING: A condition in which hot spots in the combustion chamber cause the engine to run on after the key is turned off.

DIFFERENTIAL: A geared assembly which allows the transmission of motion between drive axles, giving one axle the ability to turn faster than the other.

DIODE: An electrical device that will allow current to flow in one direction only.

DISC BRAKE: A hydraulic braking assembly consisting of a brake disc, or rotor, mounted on an axle, and a caliper assembly containing, usually two brake pads which are activated by hydraulic pressure. The pads are forced against the sides of the disc, creating friction which slows the vehicle.

DISTRIBUTOR: A mechanically driven device on an engine which is responsible for electrically firing the spark plug at a predetermined point of the piston stroke.

DOWEL PIN: A pin, inserted in mating holes in two different parts allowing those parts to maintain a fixed relationship.

DRUM BRAKE: A braking system which consists of two brake shoes and one or two wheel cylinders, mounted on a fixed backing plate, and a brake drum, mounted on an axle, which revolves around the assembly.

DWELL: The rate, measured in degrees of shaft rotation, at which an electrical circuit cycles on and off.

ELECTRONIC CONTROL UNIT (ECU): Ignition module, module, amplifier or igniter. See Module for definition.

ELECTRONIC IGNITION: A system in which the timing and firing of the spark plugs is controlled by an electronic control unit, usually called a module. These systems have no points or condenser.

END-PLAY: The measured amount of axial movement in a shaft.

ENGINE: A device that converts heat into mechanical energy.

EXHAUST MANIFOLD: A set of cast passages or pipes which conduct exhaust gases from the engine.

FEELER GAUGE: A blade, usually metal, of precisely predetermined thickness, used to measure the clearance between two parts.

FIRING ORDER: The order in which combustion occurs in the cylinders of an engine. Also the order in which spark is distributed to the plugs by the distributor.

FLOODING: The presence of too much fuel in the intake manifold and combustion chamber which prevents the air/fuel mixture from firing, thereby causing a no-start situation.

FLYWHEEL: A disc shaped part bolted to the rear end of the crankshaft. Around the outer perimeter is affixed the ring gear. The starter drive engages the ring gear, turning the flywheel, which rotates the crankshaft, imparting the initial starting motion to the engine.

FOOT POUND (ft. lbs. or sometimes, ft.lb.): The amount of energy or work needed to raise an item weighing one pound, a distance of one foot.

FUSE: A protective device in a circuit which prevents circuit overload by breaking the circuit when a specific amperage is present. The device is constructed around a strip or wire of a lower amperage rating than the circuit it is designed to protect. When an amperage higher than that stamped on the fuse is present in the circuit, the strip or wire melts, opening the circuit.

GEAR RATIO: The ratio between the number of teeth on meshing gears.

GENERATOR: A device which converts mechanical energy into electrical energy.

HEAT RANGE: The measure of a spark plug's ability to dissipate heat from its firing end. The higher the heat range, the hotter the plug fires.

HUB: The center part of a wheel or gear.

HYDROCARBON (HC): Any chemical compound made up of hydrogen and carbon. A major pollutant formed by the engine as a byproduct of combustion.

HYDROMETER: An instrument used to measure the specific gravity of a solution.

INCH POUND (inch lbs.; sometimes in.lb. or in. lbs.): One twelfth of a foot pound.

INDUCTION: A means of transferring electrical energy in the form of a magnetic field. Principle used in the ignition coil to increase voltage.

INJECTOR: A device which receives metered fuel under relatively low pressure and is activated to inject the fuel into the engine under relatively high pressure at a predetermined time.

INPUT SHAFT: The shaft to which torque is applied, usually carrying the driving gear or gears.

INTAKE MANIFOLD: A casting of passages or pipes used to conduct air or a fuel/air mixture to the cylinders.

JOURNAL: The bearing surface within which a shaft operates.

KEY: A small block usually fitted in a notch between a shaft and a hub to prevent slippage of the two parts.

MANIFOLD: A casting of passages or set of pipes which connect the cylinders to an inlet or outlet source.

MANIFOLD VACUUM: Low pressure in an engine intake manifold formed just below the throttle plates. Manifold vacuum is highest at idle and drops under acceleration.

MASTER CYLINDER: The primary fluid pressurizing device in a hydraulic system. In automotive use, it is found in brake and hydraulic clutch systems and is pedal activated, either directly or, in a power brake system, through the power booster.

MODULE: Electronic control unit, amplifier or igniter of solid state or integrated design which controls the current flow in the ignition primary circuit based on input from the pick-up coil. When the module opens the primary circuit, high secondary voltage is induced in the coil.

NEEDLE BEARING: A bearing which consists of a number (usually a large number) of long, thin rollers.

OHM:(Ω) The unit used to measure the resistance of conductor-to-electrical flow. One ohm is the amount of resistance that limits current flow to one ampere in a circuit with one volt of pressure.

OHMMETER: An instrument used for measuring the resistance, in ohms, in an electrical circuit.

OUTPUT SHAFT: The shaft which transmits torque from a device, such as a transmission.

OVERDRIVE: A gear assembly which produces more shaft revolutions than that transmitted to it.

OVERHEAD CAMSHAFT (OHC): An engine configuration in which the camshaft is mounted on top of the cylinder head and operates the valve either directly or by means of rocker arms.

OVERHEAD VALVE (OHV): An engine configuration in which all of the valves are located in the cylinder head and the camshaft is located in the cylinder block. The camshaft operates the valves via lifters and pushrods.

OXIDES OF NITROGEN (NOx): Chemical compounds of nitrogen produced as a byproduct of combustion. They combine with hydrocarbons to produce smog.

OXYGEN SENSOR: Used with the feedback system to sense the presence of oxygen in the exhaust gas and signal the computer which can reference the voltage signal to an air/fuel ratio.

PINION: The smaller of two meshing gears.

PISTON RING: An open-ended ring which fits into a groove on the outer diameter of the piston. Its chief function is to form a seal between the piston and cylinder wall. Most automotive pistons have three rings: two for compression sealing; one for oil sealing.

PRELOAD: A predetermined load placed on a bearing during assembly or by adjustment.

PRIMARY CIRCUIT: The low voltage side of the ignition system which consists of the ignition switch, ballast resistor or resistance wire, bypass, coil, electronic control unit and pick-up coil as well as the connecting wires and harnesses.

PRESS FIT: The mating of two parts under pressure, due to the inner diameter of one being smaller than the outer diameter of the other, or vice versa; an interference fit.

RACE: The surface on the inner or outer ring of a bearing on which the balls, needles or rollers move.

REGULATOR: A device which maintains the amperage and/or voltage levels of a circuit at predetermined values.

RELAY: A switch which automatically opens and/or closes a circuit.

RESISTANCE: The opposition to the flow of current through a circuit or electrical device, and is measured in ohms. Resistance is equal to the voltage divided by the amperage.

RESISTOR: A device, usually made of wire, which offers a preset amount of resistance in an electrical circuit.

RING GEAR: The name given to a ring-shaped gear attached to a differential case, or affixed to a flywheel or as part of a planetary gear set.

ROLLER BEARING: A bearing made up of hardened inner and outer races between which hardened steel rollers move.

ROTOR: 1. The disc-shaped part of a disc brake assembly, upon which the brake pads bear; also called, brake disc. 2. The device mounted atop the distributor shaft, which passes current to the distributor cap tower contacts.

SECONDARY CIRCUIT: The high voltage side of the ignition system, usually above 20,000 volts. The secondary includes the ignition coil, coil wire, distributor cap and rotor, spark plug wires and spark plugs.

SENDING UNIT: A mechanical, electrical, hydraulic or electromagnetic device which transmits information to a gauge.

SENSOR: Any device designed to measure engine operating conditions or ambient pressures and temperatures. Usually electronic in nature and designed to send a voltage signal to an on-board computer, some sensors may operate as a simple on/off switch or they may provide a variable voltage signal (like a potentiometer) as conditions or measured parameters change.

SHIM: Spacers of precise, predetermined thickness used between parts to establish a proper working relationship.

SLAVE CYLINDER: In automotive use, a device in the hydraulic clutch system which is activated by hydraulic force, disengaging the clutch.

SOLENOID: A coil used to produce a magnetic field, the effect of which is to produce work.

SPARK PLUG: A device screwed into the combustion chamber of a spark ignition engine. The basic construction is a conductive core inside of a ceramic insulator, mounted in an outer conductive base. An electrical charge from the spark plug wire travels along the conductive core and jumps a preset air gap to a grounding point or points at the end of the conductive base. The resultant spark ignites the fuel/air mixture in the combustion chamber.

SPLINES: Ridges machined or cast onto the outer diameter of a shaft or inner diameter of a bore to enable parts to mate without rotation.

TACHOMETER: A device used to measure the rotary speed of an engine, shaft, gear, etc., usually in rotations per minute.

THERMOSTAT: A valve, located in the cooling system of an engine, which is closed when cold and opens gradually in response to engine heating, controlling the temperature of the coolant and rate of coolant flow.

TOP DEAD CENTER (TDC): The point at which the piston reaches the top of its travel on the compression stroke.

TORQUE: The twisting force applied to an object.

TORQUE CONVERTER: A turbine used to transmit power from a driving member to a driven member via hydraulic action, providing changes in drive ratio and torque. In automotive use, it links the driveplate at the rear of the engine to the automatic transmission.

TRANSDUCER: A device used to change a force into an electrical signal.

TRANSISTOR: A semi-conductor component which can be actuated by a small voltage to perform an electrical switching function.

TUNE-UP: A regular maintenance function, usually associated with the replacement and adjustment of parts and components in the electrical and fuel systems of a vehicle for the purpose of attaining optimum performance.

TURBOCHARGER: An exhaust driven pump which compresses intake air and forces it into the combustion chambers at higher than atmospheric pressures. The increased air pressure allows more fuel to be burned and results in increased horsepower being produced.

VACUUM ADVANCE: A device which advances the ignition timing in response to increased engine vacuum.

VACUUM GAUGE: An instrument used to measure the presence of vacuum in a chamber.

VALVE: A device which control the pressure, direction of flow or rate of flow of a liquid or gas.

VALVE CLEARANCE: The measured gap between the end of the valve stem and the rocker arm, cam lobe or follower that activates the valve.

VISCOSITY: The rating of a liquid's internal resistance to flow.

VOLTMETER: An instrument used for measuring electrical force in units called volts. Voltmeters are always connected parallel with the circuit being tested.

WHEEL CYLINDER: Found in the automotive drum brake assembly, it is a device, actuated by hydraulic pressure, which, through internal pistons, pushes the brake shoes outward against the drums.

AIR CONDITIONER
ACCUMULATOR
REMOVAL & INSTALLATION 6-29
AIR CONDITIONING PRESSURE SENSOR
REMOVAL & INSTALLATION 6-33
BLOWER SWITCH
REMOVAL & INSTALLATION 6-27
COMPRESSOR
REMOVAL & INSTALLATION 6-22
CONDENSER
REMOVAL & INSTALLATION 6-24
CONTROL PANEL
REMOVAL & INSTALLATION 6-27
CYCLING CLUTCH SWITCH
REMOVAL & INSTALLATION 6-33
EVAPORATOR CORE
REMOVAL & INSTALLATION 6-25
EXPANSION (ORIFICE) VALVE/TUBE
REMOVAL & INSTALLATION 6-28
REFRIGERANT LINES
DISCONNECT & CONNECT 6-31
TEMPERATURE CONTROL CABLE
ADJUSTMENT 6-33
REMOVAL & INSTALLATION 6-31
AIR POLLUTION
AUTOMOTIVE POLLUTANTS
HEAT TRANSFER 4-3
TEMPERATURE INVERSION 4-2
INDUSTRIAL POLLUTANTS 4-2
NATURAL POLLUTANTS 4-2
ANTI-LOCK BRAKE SYSTEM (ABS)
ABS CONTROL MODULE
REMOVAL & INSTALLATION 9-54
ABS HYDRAULIC MODULATOR ASSEMBLY BLEEDER VALVES
REMOVAL & INSTALLATION 9-50
ABS HYDRAULIC MODULATOR SOLENOID
REMOVAL & INSTALLATION 9-56
ABS HYDRAULIC MODULATOR/MASTER CYLINDER ASSEMBLY
REMOVAL & INSTALLATION 9-52
ABS LAMP DRIVER MODULE
REMOVAL & INSTALLATION 9-50
ABS SERVICE
PRECAUTIONS 9-50
DESCRIPTION AND OPERATION
BASIC KNOWLEDGE REQUIRED 9-32
ENHANCED DIAGNOSTICS 9-32
ONBOARD DIAGNOSTICS 9-32
DIAGNOSTIC PROCEDURES
CLEARING CODES 9-43
DISPLAYING CODES 9-43
INTERMITTENT FAILURES 9-43
INTERMITTENTS AND POOR CONNECTIONS 9-43
ELECTRICAL CONNECTORS 9-50
ENABLE RELAY
REMOVAL & INSTALLATION 9-50
FILLING AND BLEEDING
BLEEDING THE ABS HYDRAULIC SYSTEM 9-57
SYSTEM FILLING 9-56
FLUID LEVEL SENSOR
REMOVAL & INSTALLATION 9-50
SPEED SENSORS
REMOVAL & INSTALLATION 9-54
AUTOMATIC TRANSAXLE
ADJUSTMENTS
SHIFT CONTROL CABLE ADJUSTMENT 7-60
THROTTLE VALVE (TV) CABLE ADJUSTMENT 7-60
FLUID PAN AND FILTER 7-60
HALFSHAFTS 7-68
IDENTIFICATION 7-60
NEUTRAL START/BACK-UP LIGHT SWITCH
REMOVAL & INSTALLATION 7-60

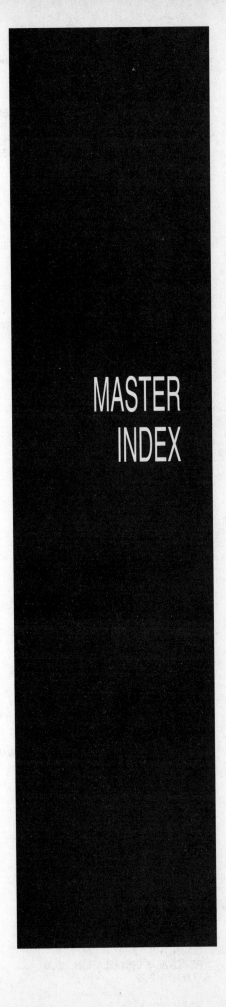

MASTER
INDEX

TRANSAXLE
  REMOVAL & INSTALLATION 7-61
UNDERSTANDING AUTOMATIC TRANSAXLES
  THE HYDRAULIC CONTROL SYSTEM 7-59
  THE PLANETARY GEARBOX 7-59
  THE SERVOS AND ACCUMULATORS 7-59
  THE TORQUE CONVERTER 7-58
AUTOMOTIVE EMISSIONS
CRANKCASE EMISSIONS 4-5
EVAPORATIVE EMISSIONS 4-5
EXHAUST GASES
  CARBON MONOXIDE 4-4
  HYDROCARBONS 4-3
  NITROGEN 4-4
  OXIDES OF SULFUR 4-4
  PARTICULATE MATTER 4-4
BASIC FUEL SYSTEM DIAGNOSIS
PRECAUTIONS 5-2
BOTTOM FEED PORT (BFP) INJECTION SYSTEM
BOTTOM FEED PORT FUEL INJECTORS
  REMOVAL & INSTALLATION 5-27
FUEL PRESSURE REGULATOR
  REMOVAL & INSTALLATION 5-28
FUEL SYSTEM PRESSURE RELIEF
  1992 VEHICLES 5-27
  1993-96 VEHICLES 5-27
SYSTEM DESCRIPTION 5-25
BRAKE OPERATING SYSTEM
ADJUSTMENT
  DISC BRAKES 9-2
  DRUM BRAKES 9-2
BLEEDING THE BRAKE SYSTEM
  MANUAL BLEEDING 9-10
  PRESSURE BLEEDING 9-12
BRAKE HOSES AND PIPES
  BRAKE PIPE FLARING 9-9
  REMOVAL & INSTALLATION 9-9
BRAKE LIGHT SWITCH
  REMOVAL & INSTALLATION 9-3
BRAKE PEDAL
  REMOVAL & INSTALLATION 9-4
CONDITIONS THAT AFFECT BRAKE PERFORMANCE
  TIRES 9-2
  TRAILER TOWING 9-2
  VEHICLE LOADING 9-2
  WHEEL ALIGNMENT 9-2
MASTER CYLINDER
  REMOVAL & INSTALLATION 9-4
POWER BRAKE/VACUUM BOOSTER
  REMOVAL & INSTALLATION 9-4
PROPORTIONING VALVES AND FAILURE WARNING SWITCH
  REMOVAL & INSTALLATION 9-6
CARBURETED FUEL SYSTEM
CARBURETOR
  ADJUSTMENTS 5-4
  MODEL IDENTIFICATION 5-3
  OVERHAUL 5-8
  PRELIMINARY CHECKS 5-3
  REMOVAL & INSTALLATION 5-8
MECHANICAL FUEL PUMP
  REMOVAL & INSTALLATION 5-2
  TESTING 5-3
CHARGING SYSTEM
ALTERNATOR PRECAUTIONS 2-19
ALTERNATOR
  DIAGNOSIS 2-19
  REMOVAL & INSTALLATION 2-20
BATTERY 2-22

DESCRIPTION AND OPERATION 2-17
REGULATOR
  REMOVAL & INSTALLATION 2-22
CIRCUIT PROTECTION
CIRCUIT BREAKERS
  REPLACEMENT 6-69
FLASHERS
  REPLACEMENT 6-70
FUSES BLOCK AND FUSES
  REPLACEMENT 6-68
FUSIBLE LINKS
  REPLACEMENT 6-69
CLUTCH
ACTUATOR (SLAVE) CYLINDER
  HYDRAULIC SYSTEM BLEEDING 7-57
  REMOVAL & INSTALLATION 7-56
ADJUSTMENT 7-47
CLUTCH CABLE
  REMOVAL & INSTALLATION 7-48
CLUTCH HYDRAULIC SYSTEM
  REMOVAL & INSTALLATION 7-51
CLUTCH MASTER CYLINDER
  REMOVAL & INSTALLATION 7-56
CLUTCH PEDAL
  REMOVAL & INSTALLATION 7-47
DRIVEN DISC AND PRESSURE PLATE/CLUTCH COVER AND DISC
  REMOVAL & INSTALLATION 7-49
UNDERSTANDING THE CLUTCH 7-46
COMPONENT LOCATION DIAGRAMS 4-56
CRUISE CONTROL
CONTROL MODULE
  REMOVAL & INSTALLATION 6-34
CONTROL SWITCHES
  REMOVAL & INSTALLATION 6-34
SERVO UNIT
  REMOVAL & INSTALLATION 6-36
VEHICLE SPEED SENSOR (VSS)
  REMOVAL & INSTALLATION 6-34
DIRECT IGNITION SYSTEM (DIS) AND ELECTRONIC IGNITION (EI) SYSTEMS
DIAGNOSIS AND TESTING
  EST PERFORMANCE 2-12
  SYSTEM PERFORMANCE 2-12
GENERAL INFORMATION
  SYSTEM COMPONENTS 2-10
IGNITION COIL ASSEMBLY
  REMOVAL & INSTALLATION 2-12
IGNITION MODULE
  REMOVAL & INSTALLATION 2-14
ELECTRONIC ENGINE CONTROLS
CAMSHAFT POSITION (CMP) SENSOR
  OPERATION 4-37
  REMOVAL & INSTALLATION 4-37
CRANKSHAFT POSITION (CKP) SENSOR
  OPERATION 4-37
  REMOVAL & INSTALLATION 4-37
  TESTING 4-37
ENGINE COOLANT TEMPERATURE (ECT) SENSOR
  OPERATION 4-32
  REMOVAL & INSTALLATION 4-33
  TESTING 4-33
ENGINE/POWERTRAIN CONTROL MODULE (ECM/PCM)
  FUNCTIONAL CHECK 4-30
  OPERATION 4-28
  REMOVAL & INSTALLATION 4-28
GENERAL INFORMATION 4-27

IDLE AIR CONTROL (IAC) VALVE
  OPERATION 4-31
  REMOVAL & INSTALLATION 4-32
KNOCK SENSOR (KS)
  OPERATION 4-40
  REMOVAL & INSTALLATION 4-40
MANIFOLD ABSOLUTE PRESSURE (MAP) SENSOR
  OPERATION 4-35
  REMOVAL & INSTALLATION 4-35
  TESTING 4-35
MANIFOLD AIR TEMPERATURE (MAT)/INTAKE AIR
  TEMPERATURE (IAT) SENSOR
  OPERATION 4-34
  REMOVAL & INSTALLATION 4-34
  TESTING 4-34
OXYGEN (O₂) SENSOR
  OPERATION 4-30
  REMOVAL & INSTALLATION 4-31
  TESTING 4-30
PARK/NEUTRAL SWITCH
  OPERATION 4-38
  REMOVAL & INSTALLATION 4-39
  TESTING 4-38
THROTTLE POSITION (TP) SENSOR
  ADJUSTMENT 4-36
  OPERATION 4-35
  REMOVAL & INSTALLATION 4-36
  TESTING 4-36
VEHICLE SPEED SENSOR (VSS)
  OPERATION 4-39
  REMOVAL & INSTALLATION 4-40
  TESTING 4-39
EMISSION CONTROLS
AIR INJECTION REACTION (AIR) MANAGEMENT SYSTEM
  OPERATION 4-23
  REMOVAL & INSTALLATION 4-23
CATALYTIC CONVERTER
  OPERATION 4-20
  TESTING 4-20
CRANKCASE VENTILATION SYSTEM
  OPERATION 4-6
  REMOVAL & INSTALLATION 4-7
  TESTING 4-7
EARLY FUEL EVAPORATION (EFE) SYSTEM
  OPERATION 4-25
  REMOVAL & INSTALLATION 4-25
  TESTING 4-25
EVAPORATIVE EMISSION CONTROL SYSTEM
  OPERATION 4-7
  REMOVAL & INSTALLATION 4-8
  TESTING 4-8
EXHAUST GAS RECIRCULATION (EGR) SYSTEM
  OPERATION 4-9
  REMOVAL & INSTALLATION 4-19
  TESTING 4-11
THERMOSTATIC AIR CLEANER (THERMAC)
  OPERATION 4-21
  REMOVAL & INSTALLATION 4-22
  TESTING 4-21
ENGINE MECHANICAL
BLOCK HEATER
  REMOVAL & INSTALLATION 3-115
CAMSHAFT CARRIER COVER
  REMOVAL & INSTALLATION 3-32
CAMSHAFT SPROCKET
  REMOVAL & INSTALLATION 3-101
CAMSHAFT
  BEARING REPLACEMENT 3-107

  REMOVAL & INSTALLATION 3-103
CRANKSHAFT AND MAIN BEARINGS
  BEARING REPLACEMENT 3-119
  CHECKING BEARING CLEARANCE 3-120
  REMOVAL & INSTALLATION 3-118
CRANKSHAFT SPROCKET
  REMOVAL & INSTALLATION 3-102
CYLINDER HEAD
  CLEANING & INSPECTION 3-79
  REMOVAL & INSTALLATION 3-68
  RESURFACING 3-80
ELECTRIC COOLING FAN
  REMOVAL & INSTALLATION 3-64
ENGINE CORE PLUGS (FREEZE PLUGS)
  REMOVAL & INSTALLATION 3-114
ENGINE OVERHAUL TIPS
  INSPECTION TECHNIQUES 3-2
  OVERHAUL TIPS 3-2
  REPAIRING DAMAGED THREADS 3-2
  TOOLS 3-2
ENGINE
  REMOVAL & INSTALLATION 3-19
EXHAUST MANIFOLD
  REMOVAL & INSTALLATION 3-53
INTAKE MANIFOLD
  REMOVAL & INSTALLATION 3-44
OIL PAN
  REMOVAL & INSTALLATION 3-83
OIL PUMP
  REMOVAL & INSTALLATION 3-87
PISTONS AND CONNECTING RODS
  CLEANING AND INSPECTION 3-109
  HONING 3-111
  INSTALLATION 3-113
  PISTON PIN REPLACEMENT 3-112
  PISTON RING REPLACEMENT 3-112
  REMOVAL 3-107
RADIATOR
  REMOVAL & INSTALLATION 3-61
REAR MAIN OIL SEAL
  REMOVAL & INSTALLATION 3-115
ROCKER ARM (VALVE) COVER
  REMOVAL & INSTALLATION 3-29
ROCKER ARMS AND PUSHRODS
  REMOVAL & INSTALLATION 3-36
THERMOSTAT
  REMOVAL & INSTALLATION 3-39
TIMING BELT COVER
  REMOVAL & INSTALLATION 3-89
TIMING BELT REAR COVER
  REMOVAL & INSTALLATION 3-103
TIMING BELT
  REMOVAL & INSTALLATION 3-97
TIMING CHAIN AND SPROCKETS
  REMOVAL & INSTALLATION 3-93
TIMING CHAIN COVER OIL SEAL
  REPLACEMENT 3-93
TIMING CHAIN FRONT COVER
  REMOVAL & INSTALLATION 3-90
TURBOCHARGER
  REMOVAL & INSTALLATION 3-60
VALVE LIFTERS
  REMOVAL & INSTALLATION 3-83
VALVE SEATS
  REPLACEMENT 3-82
VALVE STEM OIL SEALS
  REPLACEMENT 3-82

VALVES AND SPRINGS
  INSPECTION 3-81
    REMOVAL & INSTALLATION 3-81
WATER PUMP
  REMOVAL & INSTALLATION 3-65
ENTERTAINMENT SYSTEMS
RADIO RECEIVER/TAPE PLAYER/CD PLAYER
  REMOVAL & INSTALLATION 6-37
SPEAKERS
  REMOVAL & INSTALLATION 6-39
EXHAUST SYSTEM
GENERAL INFORMATION
  COMPONENT REPLACEMENT 3-122
  SPECIAL TOOLS 3-121
EXTERIOR
ANTENNA
  REMOVAL & INSTALLATION 10-28
CONVERTIBLE TOP
  MOTOR REPLACEMENT 10-37
  TOP REPLACEMENT 10-31
DOORS
  ADJUSTMENTS 10-3
  REMOVAL & INSTALLATION 10-2
FENDERS
  REMOVAL & INSTALLATION 10-28
FRONT BUMPERS
  REMOVAL & INSTALLATION 10-7
GRILLE
  REMOVAL & INSTALLATION 10-21
HATCHBACK ASSEMBLY
  ADJUSTMENTS 10-5
  REMOVAL & INSTALLATION 10-5
HOOD
  ALIGNMENT 10-4
  REMOVAL & INSTALLATION 10-4
LIFT GATE (STATION WAGON)
  REMOVAL & INSTALLATION 10-6
MOLDING, EMBLEM AND NAME PLATE
  REPLACEMENT 10-3
OUTSIDE MIRRORS
  REMOVAL & INSTALLATION 10-28
REAR BUMPERS
  REMOVAL & INSTALLATION 10-20
SUNROOF 10-38
TRUNK LID
  ADJUSTMENTS 10-5
  REMOVAL & INSTALLATION 10-5
FIRING ORDERS 2-16
FLUIDS AND LUBRICANTS
AUTOMATIC TRANSAXLE
  DRAIN AND REFILL 1-52
  FLUID RECOMMENDATION 1-51
  LEVEL CHECK 1-51
BODY LUBRICATION
  ACCELERATOR LINKAGE 1-60
  DOOR HINGES 1-60
  HOOD LATCH AND HINGES 1-60
  PARKING BRAKE LINKAGE 1-60
  TRANSAXLE SHIFT LINKAGE 1-60
BRAKE MASTER CYLINDER
  FLUID RECOMMENDATION 1-57
  LEVEL CHECK 1-57
CHASSIS GREASING 1-60
CLUTCH MASTER CYLINDER
  FLUID RECOMMENDATIONS 1-58
  LEVEL CHECK 1-58
COOLING SYSTEM
  COOLING SYSTEM INSPECTION 1-54

DRAIN AND REFILL 1-55
  FLUID RECOMMENDATIONS 1-54
  FLUSHING AND CLEANING THE SYSTEM 1-56
  LEVEL CHECK 1-54
ENGINE
  OIL AND FILTER CHANGE 1-48
  OIL LEVEL CHECK 1-47
FLUID DISPOSAL 1-45
FUEL AND ENGINE OIL RECOMMENDATIONS
  ENGINE OIL 1-46
  FUEL 1-46
MANUAL TRANSAXLE
  DRAIN AND REFILL 1-51
  FLUID RECOMMENDATIONS 1-50
  LEVEL CHECK 1-50
POWER STEERING PUMP
  FLUID RECOMMENDATIONS 1-58
  LEVEL CHECK 1-59
STEERING GEAR 1-59
WHEEL BEARINGS 1-61
WINDSHIELD WASHER PUMP
  FLUID RECOMMENDATIONS AND LEVEL CHECK 1-59
FRONT DISC BRAKES
BRAKE CALIPER
  OVERHAUL 9-17
  REMOVAL & INSTALLATION 9-15
BRAKE DISC (ROTOR)
  INSPECTION 9-18
  REMOVAL & INSTALLATION 9-18
BRAKE PADS
  INSPECTION 9-14
  REMOVAL & INSTALLATION 9-12
FRONT SUSPENSION
CONTROL ARM/SUSPENSION SUPPORT
  CONTROL ARM BUSHING REPLACEMENT 8-16
  REMOVAL & INSTALLATION 8-12
FRONT END ALIGNMENT
  CAMBER 8-19
  CASTER 8-19
  TOE-IN 8-19
FRONT HUB AND BEARING
  REMOVAL & INSTALLATION 8-16
LOWER BALL JOINT
  INSPECTION 8-8
  REMOVAL & INSTALLATION 8-8
MACPHERSON STRUTS
  OVERHAUL 8-6
  REMOVAL & INSTALLATION 8-4
STABILIZER SHAFT (SWAY BAR)
  REMOVAL & INSTALLATION 8-12
STEERING KNUCKLE
  REMOVAL & INSTALLATION 8-16
STRUT CARTRIDGE
  REMOVAL & INSTALLATION 8-8
FUEL LINE FITTINGS
QUICK-CONNECT FITTINGS
  REMOVAL & INSTALLATION 5-2
FUEL TANK
TANK ASSEMBLY
  MODULAR FUEL SENDER ASSEMBLY REPLACEMENT 5-45
  REMOVAL & INSTALLATION 5-43
HEATER
BLOWER MOTOR
  REMOVAL & INSTALLATION 6-15
BLOWER SWITCH
  REMOVAL & INSTALLATION 6-20
CONTROL PANEL
  REMOVAL & INSTALLATION 6-20

HEATER CORE
  REMOVAL & INSTALLATION 6-16
TEMPERATURE CONTROL CABLE
  ADJUSTMENT 6-20
  REMOVAL & INSTALLATION 6-20
HIGH ENERGY IGNITION (HEI) SYSTEM
  DIAGNOSIS & TESTING
    ELECTRONIC SPARK CONTROL (ESC) SYSTEM 2-5
    ELECTRONIC SPARK TIMING (EST) SYSTEM 2-4
    HALL EFFECT SWITCH 2-4
    IGNITION COIL 2-3
    IGNITION MODULE 2-4
    PICK-UP COIL 2-3
    SECONDARY SPARK 2-3
  DISTRIBUTOR
    INSTALLATION IF THE ENGINE WAS DISTURBED 2-9
    REMOVAL & INSTALLATION 2-8
  GENERAL INFORMATION
    HEI SYSTEM PRECAUTIONS 2-2
  HALL EFFECT SWITCH
    REMOVAL & INSTALLATION 2-8
  IGNITION COIL
    REMOVAL & INSTALLATION 2-5
  IGNITION MODULE
    REMOVAL & INSTALLATION 2-7
  PICK-UP COIL
    REMOVAL & INSTALLATION 2-6
HOW TO USE THIS BOOK 1-2
INSTRUMENTS AND SWITCHES
  CLOCK
    REMOVAL & INSTALLATION 6-58
  HEADLIGHT SWITCH
    REMOVAL & INSTALLATION 6-57
  IGNITION SWITCH 6-58
  INSTRUMENT CLUSTER
    REMOVAL & INSTALLATION 6-52
  SPEEDOMETER CABLE
    REMOVAL & INSTALLATION 6-54
  SPEEDOMETER, TACHOMETER AND GAUGES
    REMOVAL & INSTALLATION 6-54
  WINDSHIELD WIPER SWITCH
    REMOVAL & INSTALLATION 6-55
INTERIOR
  CONSOLE
    REMOVAL & INSTALLATION 10-44
  DOOR LOCKS
    REMOVAL & INSTALLATION 10-49
  DOOR PANEL
    REMOVAL & INSTALLATION 10-47
  FRONT DOOR GLASS
    REMOVAL & INSTALLATION 10-53
  FRONT SEAT
    REMOVAL & INSTALLATION 10-59
  FRONT WINDOW REGULATOR AND MOTOR
    REMOVAL & INSTALLATION 10-53
  INSIDE REARVIEW MIRROR
    REPLACEMENT 10-59
  INSTRUMENT PANEL
    REMOVAL & INSTALLATION 10-39
  POWER SEAT MOTORS
    REMOVAL & INSTALLATION 10-65
  REAR DOOR GLASS
    REMOVAL & INSTALLATION 10-53
  REAR SEAT CUSHION
    REMOVAL & INSTALLATION 10-64
  REAR WINDOW REGULATOR
    REMOVAL & INSTALLATION 10-57

SEAT BELT SYSTEM
  REMOVAL & INSTALLATION 10-64
WINDSHIELD GLASS
  REMOVAL & INSTALLATION 10-59
JACKING 1-63
JUMP STARTING A DEAD BATTERY
  JUMP STARTING PRECAUTIONS 1-62
  JUMP STARTING PROCEDURE 1-62
LIGHTING
  FOG LAMPS
    REMOVAL & INSTALLATION 6-67
  HEADLIGHTS
    HEADLIGHT AIMING 6-61
    REMOVAL & INSTALLATION 6-58
  SIGNAL AND MARKER LIGHTS
    REMOVAL & INSTALLATION 6-62
MANUAL TRANSAXLE
  ADJUSTMENTS
    LINKAGE 7-2
  BACK-UP LIGHT SWITCH
    REMOVAL & INSTALLATION 7-4
  CLUTCH SWITCH
    REMOVAL & INSTALLATION 7-3
  DRIVE AXLES (HALFSHAFTS)
    CV-JOINT OVERHAUL 7-20
    REMOVAL & INSTALLATION 7-17
  IDENTIFICATION 7-2
  INTERMEDIATE SHAFT
    REMOVAL & INSTALLATION 7-13
  TRANSAXLE
    REMOVAL & INSTALLATION 7-4
  UNDERSTANDING THE TRANSAXLE 7-2
MODEL 300 AND 500 THROTTLE BODY (TBI) INJECTION SYSTEMS
  FUEL INJECTOR
    REMOVAL & INSTALLATION 5-15
  FUEL METER BODY
    REMOVAL & INSTALLATION 5-18
  FUEL METER COVER
    REMOVAL & INSTALLATION 5-18
  FUEL PRESSURE REGULATOR/COMPENSATOR
    REMOVAL & INSTALLATION 5-17
  FUEL PUMP
    REMOVAL & INSTALLATION 5-15
    TESTING 5-14
  RELIEVING FUEL SYSTEM PRESSURE
    1985-86 2.0L (OHV) 5-14
    EXCEPT 1985-86 2.0L (OHV) ENGINES 5-14
  SYSTEM DESCRIPTION 5-13
  THROTTLE BODY
    REMOVAL & INSTALLATION 5-15
MODEL 700 THROTTLE BODY INJECTION (TBI) SYSTEM
  FUEL INJECTOR
    REMOVAL & INSTALLATION 5-23
  FUEL PRESSURE REGULATOR
    REMOVAL & INSTALLATION 5-24
  FUEL PUMP
    REMOVAL & INSTALLATION 5-20
    TESTING 5-20
  FUEL SYSTEM PRESSURE RELEASE
    2.0L 0HC ENGINE 5-20
    2.0L AND 2.2L OHV ENGINES 5-20
  SYSTEM DESCRIPTION 5-19
  THROTTLE BODY
    REMOVAL & INSTALLATION 5-21
  TUBE MODULE ASSEMBLY
    REMOVAL & INSTALLATION 5-25

**MULTI-PORT (MFI) & SEQUENTIAL (SFI) FUEL INJECTION
  SYSTEMS**
  FUEL INJECTORS
    REMOVAL & INSTALLATION   5-33
  FUEL PRESSURE REGULATOR
    REMOVAL & INSTALLATION   5-35
  FUEL PUMP
    REMOVAL & INSTALLATION   5-31
    TESTING   5-30
  FUEL RAIL ASSEMBLY
    REMOVAL & INSTALLATION   5-37
  GENERAL INFORMATION   5-29
  RELIEVING FUEL SYSTEM PRESSURE
    1.8L AND 2.0L OHC ENGINES   5-30
    1992 2.0L (VIN H) ENGINES   5-30
    2.3L AND 2.4L ENGINES   5-30
    2.8L AND 3.1L ENGINES   5-30
  THROTTLE BODY
    REMOVAL & INSTALLATION   5-31
PARKING BRAKE
  CABLES
    ADJUSTMENT   9-31
    REMOVAL & INSTALLATION   9-25
  PARKING BRAKE LEVER
    REMOVAL & INSTALLATION   9-31
REAR DRUM BRAKES
  BRAKE BACKING PLATE
    REMOVAL & INSTALLATION   9-24
  BRAKE DRUMS
    INSPECTION   9-19
    REMOVAL & INSTALLATION   9-19
  BRAKE SHOES
    INSPECTION   9-19
    REMOVAL & INSTALLATION   9-19
  WHEEL CYLINDERS
    REMOVAL & INSTALLATION   9-23
REAR SUSPENSION
  COIL SPRINGS
    REMOVAL & INSTALLATION   8-22
  COIL-OVER SHOCK ABSORBER
    REMOVAL & INSTALLATION   8-25
  REAR AXLE/CONTROL ARM
    REMOVAL & INSTALLATION   8-25
  REAR END ALIGNMENT   8-26
  REAR HUB AND BEARING
    REMOVAL & INSTALLATION   8-26
  SHOCK ABSORBERS
    REMOVAL & INSTALLATION   8-22
    TESTING   8-22
  STABILIZER BAR
    REMOVAL & INSTALLATION   8-26
ROUTINE MAINTENANCE
  AIR CLEANER
    REMOVAL & INSTALLATION   1-16
  AIR CONDITIONING
    DISCHARGING, EVACUATING AND CHARGING   1-41
    GENERAL SERVICING PROCEDURES   1-39
    SAFETY PRECAUTIONS   1-37
    SYSTEM INSPECTION   1-40
  BATTERY
    GENERAL MAINTENANCE   1-23
    REPLACEMENT   1-25
    TESTING THE MAINTENANCE FREE BATTERY   1-24
  CV-BOOT
    INSPECTION   1-28
  DISTRIBUTOR CAP AND ROTOR
    REMOVAL & INSTALLATION   1-34

EARLY FUEL EVAPORATION (EFE) HEATER
    REMOVAL & INSTALLATION   1-25
  EVAPORATIVE CANISTER
    FUNCTIONAL TEST   1-21
    REMOVAL & INSTALLATION   1-21
  FUEL FILTER
    FUEL PRESSURE RELEASE   1-16
    REMOVAL & INSTALLATION   1-17
  HOSES   1-27
  IDLE SPEED AND MIXTURE ADJUSTMENTS
    CARBURETED ENGINES   1-37
    FUEL INJECTED ENGINES   1-37
  IGNITION TIMING
    GENERAL INFORMATION   1-35
    INSPECTION & ADJUSTMENT   1-36
  PCV VALVE
    FUNCTIONAL CHECK   1-21
    REMOVAL & INSTALLATION   1-19
  SERPENTINE DRIVE BELTS
    INSPECTION AND ADJUSTMENT   1-27
    REPLACEMENT   1-27
  SPARK PLUG WIRES
    REMOVAL & INSTALLATION   1-34
    TESTING   1-33
  SPARK PLUGS
    GENERAL INFORMATION   1-28
    INSPECTION   1-32
    INSTALLATION   1-33
    REMOVAL   1-31
  STANDARD DRIVE BELTS
    INSPECTION AND ADJUSTMENT   1-26
    REPLACEMENT   1-26
  TIMING BELT
    INSPECTION   1-27
  TIRES AND WHEELS
    CARE OF SPECIAL WHEELS   1-45
    TIRE DESIGN   1-43
    TIRE INFLATION   1-45
    TIRE ROTATION   1-43
    TIRE STORAGE   1-45
  WINDSHIELD WIPERS
    BLADE REPLACEMENT   1-41
SENDING UNITS AND SENSORS
  COOLANT TEMPERATURE SENDING UNIT
    REMOVAL & INSTALLATION   2-31
  OIL PRESSURE SWITCH
    REMOVAL & INSTALLATION   2-32
  RADIATOR FAN TEMPERATURE SWITCH
    REMOVAL & INSTALLATION   2-31
SERIAL NUMBER IDENTIFICATION
  BODY   1-8
  ENGINE   1-8
  TRANSAXLE   1-10
  VEHICLE EMISSION CONTROL INFORMATION (VECI)
   LABEL   1-10
  VEHICLE   1-8
SERVICING YOUR VEHICLE SAFELY
  DO'S   1-6
  DON'TS   1-7
SPECIFICATIONS CHARTS
  ALTERNATOR SPECIFICATIONS   2-24
  BRAKE SPECIFICATIONS   9-60
  CAMSHAFT SPECIFICATIONS   3-9
  CAPACITIES   1-64
  CARBURETOR SPECIFICATIONS   5-13
  CRANKSHAFT AND CONNECTING ROD SPECIFICATIONS   3-12
  ENGINE IDENTIFICATION   1-8
  GENERAL ENGINE SPECIFICATIONS   3-4

MAINTENANCE INTERVALS 1-64
PISTON AND RING SPECIFICATIONS 3-15
STARTER SPECIFICATIONS 2-30
TORQUE SPECIFICATIONS 3-18
TUNE-UP SPECIFICATIONS 1-37
VALVE SPECIFICATIONS 3-6
VEHICLE IDENTIFICATION 1-8
WHEEL ALIGNMENT SPECIFICATIONS 8-19
STARTING SYSTEM
DESCRIPTION AND OPERATION 2-24
STARTER
REMOVAL & INSTALLATION 2-25
SOLENOID REPLACEMENT 2-30
TESTING 2-25
STEERING
IGNITION LOCK CYLINDER
REMOVAL & INSTALLATION 8-35
IGNITION SWITCH
REMOVAL & INSTALLATION 8-31
POWER STEERING PUMP
REMOVAL & INSTALLATION 8-41
SYSTEM BLEEDING 8-42
RACK AND PINION UNIT
REMOVAL & INSTALLATION 8-40
STEERING COLUMN HOUSING STEERING SHAFT AND IGNITION
SWITCH HOUSING JACKET BUSHING
DISASSEMBLY 8-36
STEERING COLUMN
REMOVAL & INSTALLATION 8-37
STEERING LINKAGE
REMOVAL & INSTALLATION 8-39
STEERING WHEEL
REMOVAL & INSTALLATION 8-28
TURN SIGNAL (COMBINATION) SWITCH
REMOVAL & INSTALLATION 8-29
WINDSHIELD WIPER SWITCH
REMOVAL & INSTALLATION 8-35
SUPPLEMENTAL INFLATABLE RESTRAINT (SIR) SYSTEM
GENERAL INFORMATION
DISABLING THE SYSTEM 6-13
ENABLING THE SYSTEM 6-13
SERVICE PRECAUTIONS 6-13
SYSTEM COMPONENTS 6-11
SYSTEM OPERATION 6-11
TOOLS AND EQUIPMENT
SPECIAL TOOLS 1-5
TOWING THE VEHICLE 1-62
TRAILER TOWING
COOLING
ENGINE 1-61
TRANSMISSION 1-61

GENERAL RECOMMENDATIONS 1-61
HANDLING A TRAILER 1-62
HITCH WEIGHT 1-61
TRAILER WEIGHT 1-61
TRAILER WIRING 6-68
TROUBLE CODES
CLEARING CODES 4-43
DIAGNOSIS AND TESTING
TROUBLESHOOTING 4-42
GENERAL INFORMATION
DASHBOARD WARNING LAMP 4-41
LEARNING ABILITY 4-41
READING CODES 4-43
TOOLS AND EQUIPMENT
ELECTRICAL TOOLS 4-42
SCAN TOOLS 4-41
**UNDERSTANDING AND TROUBLESHOOTING ELECTRICAL
SYSTEMS**
ADD-ON ELECTRICAL EQUIPMENT 6-10
ELECTRICAL TROUBLESHOOTING
BASIC TROUBLESHOOTING THEORY 6-4
TEST EQUIPMENT 6-4
TESTING 6-6
SAFETY PRECAUTIONS 6-2
UNDERSTANDING BASIC ELECTRICITY
AUTOMOTIVE CIRCUITS 6-3
CIRCUITS 6-3
SHORT CIRCUITS 6-3
THE WATER ANALOGY 6-2
WIRING HARNESSES
WIRING REPAIR 6-9
VACUUM DIAGRAMS 4-67
WHEELS
FRONT AND REAR WHEELS
INSPECTION 8-2
REMOVAL & INSTALLATION 8-2
WHEEL LUG STUDS
REPLACEMENT 8-2
WINDSHIELD WIPERS AND WASHERS
REAR WINDOW WIPER MOTOR
REMOVAL & INSTALLATION 6-48
WINDSHIELD WASHER FLUID RESERVOIR & PUMP
REMOVAL & INSTALLATION 6-49
WINDSHIELD WIPER BLADE AND ARM
ADJUSTMENT 6-45
REMOVAL & INSTALLATION 6-44
WINDSHIELD WIPER MOTOR
REMOVAL & INSTALLATION 6-45
WIPER LINKAGE
REMOVAL & INSTALLATION 6-49
WIRING DIAGRAMS 6-71